مکتبۃ المدینہ
MAKTABA TUL MADINA

فَیضانِ سُنَّت

Faizan-e-Sunnat

Blessings of Sunnah

VOLUME 1

Shaykh-e-Tariqat, Ameer-e-Ahl-e-Sunnat,
Founder of Dawat-e-Islami, 'Allamah Maulana Abu Bilal

Muhammad Ilyas Attar

Qadiri Razavi دَامَتْ بَرَكَاتُهُمُ الْعَالِيَه

Translated into English by

Majlis-e-Tarajim (Dawat-e-Islami)

Maktaba-tul-Madinah

PAKISTAN: Maktaba-tul-Madinah, Alami Madani Markaz, Faizan-e-Madinah, Mahallah Saudagran, Purani Sabzi Mandi - Karachi.
Contact: +92-21-34921390 - 3548292

UK: 80-82 Bordesley Green Road, Birmingham, B9 4TA.
Contact: 07989996380 - 07867860092
Email: uk@dawateislami.net

USA: Faizan-e-Madina, P. O. Box 36216, Houston, Tx 77274.
Contact: +713-459-1581, 832-618-5101

INDIA: 19/20 Muhammad Ali Road, Opposite Mandvi Post Office Mumbai - 400 003.
Contact: +91-022-23454429

BANGLADESH: K.M Bhovan, 1st Floor, 11, Andar Killa Chittagong.

HONG KONG: Faizan-e-Madina, M/F-75, Ho Pui Street, Tsuen Wan N.T.
Contact: +85-98750884 - 31451557

SOUTH AFRICA: 163 – 7th Avenue, Mayfair, Johannesburg, South Africa.
Contact: 0027-82699-1168

KENYA: Kanz-ul-Iman, Near Al-Farooq Hospital, Tonoka Area Mvita, Mombasa.
Contact: +254-721-521916

TORONTO CANADA: 1060 Britannia Road Unit 20, 21 Mississauga ONT Canada.
Contact: +141-664-82261

MOZAMBIQUE: AV Joshina Machel, No 275, Maputo, Mozambique.
Contact: +258848426112

SOUTH KOREA: 574-19 Ship Jeon Dong Bupyeong Gu, Incheon, South Korea.
Contact: +821091696392

AUSTRALIA: Faizan-e-Madinah Community Centre, 64 Karrabah Rd, auburn, Sydney Nsw 2144.
Contact: +61423694117

C-LANKA: Faizan-e-Madinah no. 10 Messenger Street, Colombo no. 12, C-Lanka.
Contact: +94773726622

Blessings of Sunnah

An English translation of 'Faizan-e-Sunnat (Volume 1)'

◆

Edition:	First
Translated by:	Majlis-e-Tarājim (Dawat-e-Islami)
Publisher:	Maktaba-tul-Madinah
1st Publication:	Rabī'-ul-Awwal, 1435 AH (January, 2014)
Quantity:	10000
2nd Publication:	Rajab-ul-Murajjab, 1437 AH (April, 2016)
Quantity:	2000
ISBN:	978-969-579-529-3

SPONSORSHIP

Please feel free to contact us if you wish to sponsor the printing of a religious book or a booklet for the Isal-e-Sawab of your deceased family members.

Maktaba-tul-Madinah

Aalami Madani Markaz, Faizan-e-Madinah Mahallah Saudagran, Purani Sabzi Mandi, Bab-ul-Madinah, Karachi, Pakistan

✉ **E-mail:** maktabaglobal@dawateislami.net – maktaba@dawateislami.net

✆ **Phone:** +92-21-34921389-93

💻 **Web:** www.dawateislami.net

اَلۡحَمۡدُ لِلّٰہِ رَبِّ الۡعٰلَمِیۡنَ وَ الصَّلٰوۃُ وَالسَّلَامُ عَلٰی سَیِّدِ الۡمُرۡسَلِیۡنَ
اَمَّا بَعۡدُ فَاَعُوۡذُ بِاللّٰہِ مِنَ الشَّیۡطٰنِ الرَّجِیۡمِ ؕ بِسۡمِ اللّٰہِ الرَّحۡمٰنِ الرَّحِیۡمِ ؕ

Du'ā for Reading the Book

Read the following Du'ā (supplication) before you study a religious book or an Islamic lesson, you will remember whatever you study, اِنۡ شَآءَاللّٰہ عَزَّوَجَلَّ:

اَللّٰهُمَّ افْتَحْ عَلَيْنَا حِكْمَتَكَ وَانْشُرْ
عَلَيْنَا رَحْمَتَكَ يَا ذَاالْجَلَالِ وَالْاِكْرَام

Translation

Yā Allah عَزَّوَجَلَّ! Open the doors of knowledge and wisdom for us, and have mercy on us! O the One who is the most Honourable and Glorious!

(Al-Mustaṭraf, vol. 1, pp. 40)

Note: Recite Ṣalāt-'Alan-Nabī صَلَّى اللهُ عَلَيْهِ وَالِهٖ وَسَلَّم once before and after the Du'ā.

Contents at a Glance

Faizan-e-Sunnat

اَلۡحَمۡدُ لِلّٰہِ رَبِّ الۡعٰلَمِیۡنَ وَ الصَّلٰوۃُ وَالسَّلَامُ عَلٰی سَیِّدِ الۡمُرۡسَلِیۡنَ

اَمَّا بَعۡدُ فَاَعُوۡذُ بِاللّٰہِ مِنَ الشَّیۡطٰنِ الرَّجِیۡمِ ؕ بِسۡمِ اللّٰہِ الرَّحۡمٰنِ الرَّحِیۡمِ ؕ

A Brief Introduction to the Author

In every era, Allah عَزَّوَجَلَّ sent such holy personalities to the Ummaĥ of His Beloved Prophet صَلَّى اللهُ تَعَالٰی عَلَيْهِ وَاٰلِهٖ وَسَلَّم who excellently fulfilled the obligation of 'اَمْرٌ بِالْمَعْرُوْفِ وَنَهْيٌ عَنِ الْمُنْكَر', i.e. *calling people towards righteousness and preventing them from evils.* These righteous individuals inculcated other Muslims with the mindset: *I must strive to reform myself and the people of the entire world,* اِنْ شَآءَالله عَزَّوَجَلَّ.

One of such spiritual and scholarly personalities is Shaykh-e-Ṭarīqat Amīr-e-Aĥl-e-Sunnat, founder of Dawat-e-Islami 'Allāmaĥ Maulānā Abu Bilal Muhammad Ilyas Attar Qadiri Razavi Ziyaee دَامَتْ بَرَكَاتُهُمُ الْعَالِيَه. He was born on a Wednesday on 26th Ramadan-ul-Mubārak 1369 A.H. (12th July 1950) in Bāb-ul-Madīnaĥ (Karachi), Pakistan. Since his father had passed away when he was an infant, he had to face financial problems but he did not lose courage and earned Ḥalāl sustenance to meet the needs of his family. From an early age, he was fond of going to the Masjid for offering Ṣalāĥ and for reciting and listening to Na'ats. When he became rather mature, he acquired the great treasure of religious knowledge by keeping the company of the scholars of the Aĥl-e-Sunnat and by studying religious books. After some time, he became the Imām of a Masjid and struggled hard to promote 'the call to righteousness.' Impressed by his good manners, humility, sociability and a passion for religious preaching, a large number of people, especially the young became his sincere companions.

In September 1981, he launched the Madanī campaign of Dawat-e-Islami with the help of the devotees of Rasūl. Allah عَزَّوَجَلَّ has blessed him with enthusiasm for the protection of Muslims' faith and reforming of their character. He would travel by bus and train to far-flung and remote areas and cities where he would deliver speeches. When he used to go to any area of Bāb-ul-Madīnaĥ (Karachi) for delivering a speech or for any other religious activity, he would often carry his meal including even salt and drinking water with him so that he would not ask anyone for anything. At times, he was not allowed to deliver speeches in Masājid but he did not get disappointed.

In the earlier days, after delivering speeches he would often return home at night walking 5 to 6 kilometres because the public transport would drop him half way and he did not have enough money to afford taxi or rickshaw fare. Sometimes, someone would give him a lift, covering some distance. He used to be criticized and sometimes even attacked but he did not lose courage and remained committed to his cause in spite of facing severe hardships and hurdles. Under his excellent organizational and spiritual guidance, Dawat-e-Islami soon emerged as a global & non-political movement of the Quran and Sunnaĥ and is currently serving Islam in more than ninety different departments some of which include Jāmi'a-tul-Madīnaĥ, Madrasa-ṭul-Madīnaĥ, Dār-ul-Madīnaĥ, Dār-ul-Iftā Aĥl-e-Sunnat, Al-Madīna-tul-'Ilmiyyaĥ, Maktaba-tul-Madīnaĥ, Majlis-e-Tarājim, Majlis I.T., Majlis Madanī Qāfilaĥ, Majlis Madanī In'āmāt and Madanī channel. By the grace of Allah عَزَّوَجَلَّ, the message of Dawat-e-Islami has so far reached more than 187 countries of the world.

By making individual efforts and by virtue of his Sunnaĥ-Inspiring speeches that he delivered in the Ijtimā'āt of Dawat-e-Islami, he has brought a Madanī revolution in the lives of millions of Muslims, especially among the young Islamic brothers and sisters. Countless sinful youths repented of their sins, adopting Sunnaĥs in their lives. Those previously not offering Ṣalāĥ not only started offering Ṣalāĥ but also many progressed even further becoming the Imāms of Masājid; disobedient and rude offspring began to respect and obey their parents; many of those wandering in the dark valley of Kufr were blessed with the light of Īmān; those dreaming of the sensual beauty of European countries became anxious and desirous of beholding the beauty of the Holy Ka'baĥ and the grand green dome of beloved Madīnaĥ; those who used to get worried and grieved about their worldly matters only, got the Madanī mindset of pondering over their afterlife; those fond of reading romantic novels got attracted to reading the books and booklets of the scholars of the Aĥl-e-Sunnat; those fond of excursions started travelling with Madanī Qāfilaĥs; those who were wicked and impious became practicing Muslims by acting upon Madanī In'āmāt; those women who used to visit shopping malls, entertainment centres, night clubs and cinema theatres immodestly, have adopted Shar'ī veiling; those whose aim was just to accumulate the wealth of the world adopted the Madanī aim, '*I must strive to reform myself and the people of the entire world,* اِنْ شَآءَاللّٰه عَزَّوَجَلَّ.' In short, 'the call to righteousness' was greatly promoted, bringing the blessings of Sunnaĥ everywhere.

The most important thing is that he has revolutionized the mindset of millions of people by virtue of individual and collective efforts within a very short period of time. Inspired by his efforts, thousands of Islamic brothers and sisters are becoming scholars of Islam at Jāmi'a-tul-Madīnaĥ so as to attain success in their worldly life as well as in the afterlife, rather than making their career in any worldly profession. Thousands of children are learning the correct recitation of the Holy Quran and are becoming Ḥuffāẓ. There was a time when hardly one or two elderly persons used to perform I'tikāf in the last ten days of Ramadan but today thousands of Islamic brothers not only perform I'tikāf for the last ten days but also for the whole month of Ramadan. Many of these Mu'takifīn also travel with Madanī Qāfilaĥs on the night and day of Eid immediately after I'tikāf instead of returning home. Thousands of people who were clean-shaven and fond of non-Islamic clothing have adorned their faces with beards and heads with turbans, showing a sign of love for the Sunnaĥs of the Beloved and Blessed Prophet صَلَّى اللّٰه تَعَالٰى عَلَيْهِ وَاٰلِهٖ وَسَلَّم. All this irrefutably shows that Amīr-e-Aĥl-e-Sunnat دَامَتْ بَرَكَاتُهُمُ الْعَالِيَه has caused an Islamic revolution in the hearts of millions of people all over the world, and has revived Islamic values in the 15th century.

It is only by the grace of Allah عَزَّوَجَلَّ that these great successes have been achieved. In addition to his speeches and Madanī Mużākaraĥs, he has also written more than one hundred and twenty five booklets and books, most of which have been translated into various languages and have reached different countries of the world. By the grace of Allah عَزَّوَجَلَّ, he is busy writing further books and booklets because Islamic writings have become a part of his life. Based on the teachings of the Holy Quran, blessed Aḥādīš, sayings of pious predecessors and Taṣawwuf, he has collected countless Madanī pearls in his books. In your hands is the English translation of his masterpiece *Faīzān-e-Sunnat* (vol. 1). It is a Sunnaĥ-Inspiring world-famous book, by reading which, millions of men and women have started treading the path of piety. In order to meet the demand for it from all over the world, its printing process continues almost the whole year. To write books may be something usual but to inspire millions of the devotees of Rasūl to study those books and follow their teachings is, of course, something absolutely unusual.

May Allah عَزَّوَجَلَّ further enhance the enthusiasm of the author for knowledge and righteous deeds. May Almighty Allah عَزَّوَجَلَّ bless him with a long life with good health, and protect him from enemies and from those jealous of him.

اٰمِيْن بِجَاهِ النَّبِيِّ الْاَمِيْن صَلَّى اللهُ تَعَالٰى عَلَيْهِ وَاٰلِهٖ وَسَلَّم

Majlis-e-Tarājim (Dawat-e-Islami)

Ramadan-ul-Mubārak, 1434 AH

July, 2013

Commendations* from Honourable Muftis and Scholars

* These commendations were made in Urdu language. The Translation Majlis has translated them into English.

Commendation

From: An upholder of Dawat-e-Islami, a practising scholar 'Allāmaĥ Maulānā Muhammad Ismā'īl Qādirī Razavī Nūrī مُدَّظِلُّهُ الْعَالِی. *(Shaykh-ul-Ḥadīš and Raīs Dār-ul-Iftā, Dār-ul-'Ulūm Amjadiyyaĥ Bāb-ul-Madīnaĥ Karachi).*

اَلْحَمْدُ لِلّٰهِ رَبِّ الْعٰلَمِيْنَ وَالصَّلٰوةُ وَالسَّلَامُ عَلٰى سَيِّدِ الْمُرْسَلِيْنَ اَمَّا بَعْدُ

I had the privilege of studying the four chapters of '*Faīzān-e-Sunnat*' (volume 1, published in 1427 A.H.) compiled by Amīr-e-Aĥl-e-Sunnat, founder of Dawat-e-Islami, 'Allāmaĥ Maulānā Muhammad Ilyas Attar Qadiri مُدَّظِلُّهُ الْعَالِی. He is globally acknowledged to have rendered great services for Islam. By virtue of his untiring efforts, millions of Muslims, especially the young, have started treading the path of piety and guiding others to the same path. Today, the Madanī Qāfilaĥs of Dawat-e-Islami are seen both within and outside Pakistan. My latest information is that the message of Dawat-e-Islami has so far reached 60 countries of the world.

In this book, he has collected such pearls of knowledge and words of wisdom that one can only attain after he has studied hundreds of books. This book is highly useful for the acquisition of the knowledge of Shar'ī rulings as well as that of Taṣawwuf, اَللّٰهُمَّ زِدْ فَزِدْ. The inclusion of Quranic verses, Aḥādīš, sayings of saints and interesting parables have further enhanced the beauty of this book. The references from source books given with Aḥādīš, narrations and rulings have made this book useful to 'Ulamā. Further, I am very much delighted to see that this book also contains some parables of the scholars and saints of Aĥl-e-Sunnat, showing the compiler's affection for them. One of its advantages is that our future generation will also become aware of the religious services made by saints and scholars of Aĥl-e-Sunnat. May Allah عَزَّوَجَلَّ reward the compiler for this great endeavour, and enable every Muslim to study it and give Dars from it.

اٰمِيْن بِجَاهِ النَّبِيِّ الْاَمِيْن صَلَّى اللهُ تَعَالٰى عَلَيْهِ وَاٰلِهٖ وَسَلَّم

Dār-ul-'Ulūm Amjadiyyaĥ
17 Muharram 1428 / 6-2-2007

Commendation

From: Sharaf-e-Millat, Ustāz-ul-'Ulamā Shaykh 'Allāmaĥ Maulānā Muhammad 'Abdul Ḥakīm Sharaf Qādirī رحمۃ اللہ تعالٰی علیہ

بِسْمِ اللهِ الرَّحْمٰنِ الرَّحِيْم نَحْمَدُهٗ وَنُصَلِّيْ عَلٰى رَسُوْلِهِ الْكَرِيْم

It is stated in a blessed Ḥadīš: مَنْ اَحْيَا سُنَّتِيْ بَعْدَ مَا اُمِيْتَتْ فَلَهٗ اَجْرُ مِئَةِ شَهِيْدٍ '*There is the reward of hundred martyrs for the one who has revived any such Sunnaĥ of mine that had been abandoned.*' In the light of the foregoing Ḥadīš, try to imagine the reward of the huge number of martyrs that will be given to Amīr-e-Dawat-e-Islami 'Allāmaĥ Maulānā Muhammad Ilyas Attar Qadiri دامت برکاتہم العالیہ and Dawat-e-Islami's preachers whose concerted efforts have inspired millions of people to start offering Ṣalāĥ regularly and adopt Sunnaĥs of the Beloved and Blessed Prophet صَلَّى اللهُ تَعَالٰى عَلَيْهِ وَاٰلِهٖ وَسَلَّم. This great success has been achieved by the sincere efforts and services of Amīr-e-Dawat-e-Islami, especially by his speeches and his book '*Faīzān-e-Sunnat.*'

In my opinion, this book is a best-seller in Pakistan. Its language is simple with an advice-giving and preaching style. Here in front of me is the first volume of *Faīzān-e-Sunnat* published in 1427 A.H. This volume contains four chapters.

1. Blessings of بِسْمِ اللّٰه
2. Islamic Manners of Eating
3. Excellence of Hunger
4. Blessings of Ramadan

A commendable feature of this book is that source books references have also been given with Quranic verses, Aḥādīš and Shar'ī rulings further enhancing the importance of this book. Today, when the darkness of non-Islamic beliefs and culture is being spread everywhere in the name of moderation and broadmindedness, the need to spread the teachings and Sunnaĥs of the Holy Prophet صَلَّى اللهُ تَعَالٰى عَلَيْهِ وَاٰلِهٖ وَسَلَّم has also increased many hundred-fold.

6 Żul-Ḥijjaĥ 1428 A.H. / 28-December-2006

Commendation

From: Khayr-ul-Aẓkiyā, Ustāz-ul-'Ulamā-wal-Mashāikh, Jāmi' Ma'qūl-o-Manqūl, Shaykh 'Allāmaĥ Maulānā Khuwājaĥ Muẓaffar Ḥusayn Sahib دَامَتْ بَرَكَاتُهُمُ الْعَالِيَه. *(Shaykh-ul-Ḥadīš Dār-ul-'Ulūm Nūr-ul-Ḥaq, Chara Muhammad Pur, Faizabad – UP, Al-Hind).*

بِسْمِ اللهِ الرَّحْمٰنِ الرَّحِيْمِ ط نَحْمَدُهٗ وَنُصَلِّيْ عَلٰى رَسُوْلِهِ الْكَرِيْم

By the grace of Allah عَزَّوَجَلَّ, the undersigned has got the privilege of making commendations for the precious books of many Aĥl-e-Sunnat scholars particularly including Fakhr-ul-Amāsil, Bahr-ul-'Ulūm Shaykh 'Allāmaĥ Muftī Afzal Ḥusayn Sahib Mongiri (Ex-Dean, Manẓar-e-Islam, Bareilly Sharīf). I have made commendations for almost all such books of his that were published in India. When the Nigrān of Dawat-e-Islami's Majlis for 'Ulamā and Mashāikh presented *Faīzān-e-Sunnat* (published in 1427, volume 1) to me, I was overjoyed, and made this commendation.

The Holy Quran, a complete code of life, has many 'اَمْرٌ وَنَهْيٌ' (i.e. commandments) for guiding people to the straight path. Saying لَقَدْ كَانَ لَكُمْ فِيْ رَسُوْلِ اللهِ اُسْوَةٌ حَسَنَةٌ, Allah عَزَّوَجَلَّ has mentioned a shining example, and has declared it extremely important for man to follow this example. In other words, the Holy Quran is a great and glorious book, and it is as if the sayings and actions of the Holy Prophet صَلَّى اللهُ تَعَالٰى عَلَيْهِ وَاٰلِهٖ وَسَلَّم are its practical exegesis. By following this shining example, dust-created man attains the attributes of angels. These sayings and actions of the Holy Prophet صَلَّى اللهُ تَعَالٰى عَلَيْهِ وَاٰلِهٖ وَسَلَّم were scattered in numerous books of Aḥādīš and other books of Islamic saints and scholars.

May the rain of bounty and mercy be showered on Amīr-e-Aĥl-e-Sunnat, founder of Dawat-e-Islami, a devotee to Madīnaĥ, 'Allāmaĥ Maulānā Muhammad Ilyas Attar Qadiri Razavi Ziyaee دَامَتْ بَرَكَاتُهُمُ الْعَالِيَه who has excellently collected these 'fragrant flowers' and has presented this bouquet in the form of '*Faīzān-e-Sunnat*' to those whose hearts keep thudding in the remembrance of the Noble Prophet صَلَّى اللهُ تَعَالٰى عَلَيْهِ وَاٰلِهٖ وَسَلَّم. When this book came out with the simplicity of its language and smooth flow of its text, people began to go through it tearfully and wholeheartedly.

When its first edition was given to me, I was so impressed by it that I read it repeatedly and tearfully in the state of Wuḍū. Its new edition is even more attractive and useful. References from source books, additions and amendments have further enhanced the beauty and usefulness of this book. Moreover, the inclusion of the faith-refreshing incidents of the Sunnaĥ-Inspiring Madanī Qāfilaĥs of Dawat-e-Islami, a global & non-political movement of the Quran and Sunnaĥ, is a unique feature of this book.

As far as I know, it is a best-seller in Pakistan. It has become famous in many other countries of the world within a very short period of time. I have learnt that there are even such devotees in Dawat-e-Islami who have studied this 1500 pages-containing book '*Faīzān-e-Sunnat*' (Urdu version) within 15 days and some even in just 7 days. This shows the usefulness and heart-capturing writing style of this book.

It is my request to every Muslim to buy and keep this book in their home, and gift it to others. One should also give this book to one's daughter or sister as dowry on the occasion of her marriage. The wealthy, in particular, should purchase this book in bulk and donate it to Masājid, Madāris and shrines. All male and female preachers of Dawat-e-Islami and all ordinary people as well as 'special ones' should give Dars of this book at homes, Masājid, shops, factories, markets and other busy places. It is stated in a Ḥadīš that the one who revives an abandoned Sunnaĥ attains the reward of hundred martyrs. Let's all promise to act upon and revive abandoned Sunnaĥs, and gain the reward of thousands of martyrs by keeping this promise of us.

Khuwājaĥ Muẓaffar Ḥusayn Razavī
26 Muḥarram-ul-Ḥarām 1428 A.H.
Shaykh-ul-Ḥadīš Dār-ul-'Ulūm Nūr-ul-Ḥaq, Chara Muhammad Pur,
Faizabad – UP, Al-Hind

اَلْحَمْدُ لِلّٰهِ رَبِّ الْعٰلَمِيْنَ وَ الصَّلٰوةُ وَالسَّلَامُ عَلٰى سَيِّدِ الْمُرْسَلِيْنَ
اَمَّا بَعْدُ فَاَعُوْذُ بِاللّٰهِ مِنَ الشَّيْطٰنِ الرَّجِيْمِ ؕ بِسْمِ اللّٰهِ الرَّحْمٰنِ الرَّحِيْمِ ؕ

23 Intentions for Reading this Book

The Holy Prophet صَلَّى اللهُ تَعَالٰى عَلَيْهِ وَاٰلِهٖ وَسَلَّم has stated, نِيَّةُ الْمُؤْمِنِ خَيْرٌ مِّنْ عَمَلِهٖ *'The intention of a Muslim is better than his deed.'* *(Mu'jam Kabīr, vol. 6, pp. 185, Ḥadīš 5942)*

Two Madanī pearls

- Without a good intention, no reward is granted for a righteous deed.
- The more righteous intentions one makes, the greater reward he will attain.

Intentions

1-4. Every time I read this book, I will start by reciting Ḥamd[1], Ṣalāt[2], Ta'awwūż[3] and Tasmiyyaĥ[4] (by reading the Arabic lines given at the top of this page you will be acting on all these four intentions).

5. I will read this book from beginning to end for the pleasure of Allah عَزَّوَجَلَّ.

6-7. To the best of my ability, I will try to read it whilst in the state of Wuḍū[6] and facing the Qiblaĥ[7].

8. I will behold the Quranic verses,

9. and the blessed Aḥādīš

10. (Whilst reading the book) Whenever I read the name of Allah, I will say عَزَّوَجَلَّ,

11. and whenever I read the blessed name of the Beloved and Blessed Prophet I will read صَلَّى اللهُ تَعَالٰى عَلَيْهِ وَاٰلِهٖ وَسَلَّم.

12. Acting upon the advice given in the narration: عِنْدَ ذِكْرِالصَّالِحِيْنَ تَنَزَّلُ الرَّحْمَةُ '*Mercy descends at the time of the mentioning of the pious.*' *(Ḥilyat-ul-Auliyā, vol. 7, pp. 335, Ḥadīš 10750)* I will reap the blessings of the mentioning of the pious by relating the parables of pious saints from this book, to others.

13. (On my personal copy) I will underline essential and important things and points to highlight them.

14. I will note down important points whilst studying.

15. I will persuade others to read this book.

16. With the intention of acting upon the Ḥadīš تَهَادَوْا تَحَابُّوْا '*Give gifts to each other, it will enhance affection amongst you,*' *(Muwaṭṭā Imām Mālik, vol. 2, pp. 407, Ḥadīš 1731)* I shall buy this book (one, or as many as I can afford) and will gift it to others. (Gift it to scholars and Imāms, you will gain more reward, اِنْ شَآءَاللّٰہ عَزَّوَجَلَّ).

17. I will donate Šawāb of reading this book to the entire Ummaĥ.

18. If I find any Shar'ī mistake, I will inform the publisher about the mistake in writing (verbal information is usually ineffective).

19. I will routinely give Dars from this book.

20. I will read this book from beginning to end every year.

21. If I am unable to understand any ruling, I will consult scholars for its clarification with the intention of acting upon the verse:

فَسْـَٔلُوْۤا اَهْلَ الذِّكْرِ اِنْ كُنْتُمْ لَا تَعْلَمُوْنَ ﴿۴۳﴾

O people! Ask those who have knowledge if you know not.

[Kanz-ul-Īmān (Translation of Quran)] (Part 14, Sūraĥ An-Naḥl, verse 43)

22. If I find some ruling difficult to understand, I will repeatedly read it.

23. I will convey Islamic teachings to those who don't know.

اَلْحَمْدُ لِلّٰهِ رَبِّ الْعٰلَمِيْنَ وَ الصَّلٰوةُ وَ السَّلَامُ عَلٰى سَيِّدِ الْمُرْسَلِيْنَ
اَمَّا بَعْدُ فَاَعُوْذُ بِاللّٰهِ مِنَ الشَّيْطٰنِ الرَّجِيْمِ ؕ بِسْمِ اللّٰهِ الرَّحْمٰنِ الرَّحِيْمِ ؕ

Foreword

From: Shaykh-e-Ṭarīqat, Amīr-e-Aĥl-e-Sunnat, founder of Dawat-e-Islami, 'Allāmaĥ Maulānā Abū Bilāl Muhammad Ilyas Attar Qadiri Razavi دَامَتْ بَرَكَاتُهُمُ الْعَالِيَه.

The Beloved and Blessed Prophet صَلَّى اللهُ تَعَالٰى عَلَيْهِ وَاٰلِهٖ وَسَلَّم has stated, 'Whoever conveys an Islamic teaching to my Ummaĥ so that Sunnaĥ would be established by it or corrupt beliefs would be removed by it, will enter Heaven.' *(Ḥilyat-ul-Auliyā, vol. 10, pp. 45, Ḥadīš 14466)* It is one of the Madanī activities of Dawat-e-Islami, a global & non-political movement of the Quran and Sunnaĥ, for every Islamic brother to give or listen to two Dars daily (at Masjid, house etc). For the fulfilment of the Madanī activity of Dars, I have got the privilege of presenting the book '*Faīzān-e-Sunnat*' (volume 1) with good intentions. Give Dars (that is, read out passages to Muslims) from this book in abundance. Overwhelmed by hearing the Dars given by you, if anyone starts treading the path of Quran and Sunnaĥs, you will also become successful, اِنْ شَآءَاللّٰه عَزَّوَجَلَّ. The Noble Prophet صَلَّى اللهُ تَعَالٰى عَلَيْهِ وَاٰلِهٖ وَسَلَّم has stated, 'If Allah عَزَّوَجَلَّ blesses even a single person with guidance by you, this is better for you than red camels.' *(Ṣaḥīḥ Muslim, pp. 1311, Ḥadīš 2406)*

'*Faīzān-e-Sunnat*' (volume 1) contains four chapters and nearly 1572 pages (in Urdu version). Along with scholars and the elite, a huge number of ordinary people have also joined the Sunnaĥ-Inspiring movement of Dawat-e-Islami. For the convenience of ordinary people, I have used simple language and maintained an easily understandable writing style. At some places, I have intentionally used difficult words along with their meaning under brackets so that the less educated Islamic brothers and sisters would not face difficulty whilst reading the same words in other Islamic books. We have done our utmost to remove flaws and errors from this book but the possibility of mistakes cannot still be ruled out. Therefore, if you find any Shar'ī mistake in this book, please inform me about it in writing, and get deserving of reward. I will not argue unreasonably in favour of my standpoint but will back down from it with thanks.

I am deeply indebted to the scholars of Al-Madīna-tul-'Ilmiyyaĥ, an important Sunnī scholars comprising department of Dawat-e-Islami, who have checked each and every word of this book and provided references of original books, further enhancing its usefulness for the male and female preachers of Dawat-e-Islami as well as for scholars, orators, authors and compilers. جَزَى اللهُ عَنَّا عُلَمَائَنَا اَحْسَنَ الْجَزَاء That is, *may Allah* عَزَّوَجَلَّ *give a better reward to our scholars.*

Du'ā of Attar

Yā Allah عَزَّوَجَلَّ! Whoever reads complete *Faīzān-e-Sunnat* (volume 1) within 163 days, be blessed with steadfastness in Īmān, beholding the Holy Prophet صَلَّى اللهُ تَعَالٰى عَلَيْهِ وَاٰلِهٖ وَسَلَّم during his death agonies, comfort in his grave and on resurrection, forgiveness without accountability out of Your mercy, and an abode in Jannat-ul-Firdaus in the neighbourhood of Your Beloved Prophet صَلَّى اللهُ تَعَالٰى عَلَيْهِ وَاٰلِهٖ وَسَلَّم. May all these prayers be answered for me, scholars, checkers and all those who cooperated in the completion of this book, including the Nigrān and members of Majlis Maktaba-tul-Madīnaĥ, and the whole staff of Maktaba-tul-Madīnaĥ. Yā Allah عَزَّوَجَلَّ! Forgive the entire Ummaĥ.

اٰمِين بِجَاهِ النَّبِيِّ الْاَمِين صَلَّى اللهُ تَعَالٰى عَلَيْهِ وَاٰلِهٖ وَسَلَّم

11 Ramadan-ul-Mubārak, 1427 A.H.

اَلۡحَمۡدُ لِلّٰہِ رَبِّ الۡعٰلَمِیۡنَ وَ الصَّلٰوۃُ وَ السَّلَامُ عَلٰی سَیِّدِ الۡمُرۡسَلِیۡنَ

اَمَّا بَعۡدُ فَاَعُوۡذُ بِاللّٰہِ مِنَ الشَّیۡطٰنِ الرَّجِیۡمِ ؕ بِسۡمِ اللّٰہِ الرَّحۡمٰنِ الرَّحِیۡمِ ؕ

Gift from Attar

Yā Allah عَزَّوَجَلَّ! Accept (my endeavour of compiling) *Faīzān-e-Sunnat* (volume 1) in Your court and grant its reward, not according to my faulty deed but according to Your infinite mercy. Yā Allah عَزَّوَجَلَّ! Convey its reward from me to Your Beloved Prophet صَلَّى اللّٰهُ تَعَالٰى عَلَيْهِ وَاٰلِهٖ وَسَلَّم. Through Your Beloved Prophet صَلَّى اللّٰهُ تَعَالٰى عَلَيْهِ وَاٰلِهٖ وَسَلَّم, send its reward to all other Prophets عَلَيْهِمُ السَّلَام, Ṣaḥābaĥ and Tābi'īn رَضِىَ اللّٰهُ تَعَالٰى عَنْهُم, Āimma-e-Mujtaĥidīn and all scholars and saints رَحِمَهُمُ اللّٰهُ تَعَالٰى. Yā Allah عَزَّوَجَلَّ! Convey its reward to Āimma-e-Mażāĥib-e-Arba'aĥ and Salāsil-e-Arba'aĥ particularly including Sayyidunā Imām A'ẓam عَلَيْهِ رَحْمَةُ اللّٰهِ الْاَكْرَم, Sayyidunā Ghauš-e-A'ẓam عَلَيْهِ رَحْمَةُ اللّٰهِ الْاَعْظَم, Sayyidunā Mujaddid A'ẓam Imām Aḥmad Razā Khān عَلَيْهِ رَحْمَةُ الرَّحْمٰن, Sayyidī-o-Murshidī Quṭb-e-Madīnaĥ Maulānā Ziyāuddīn Madanī عَلَيْهِ رَحْمَةُ اللّٰهِ الْغَنِى, my honourable parents, Muftī-e-Dawat-e-Islami Al-Ḥāj, Al-Ḥāfiẓ Muhammad Fārūq Al-'Aṭṭārī Al-Madanī عَلَيْهِ رَحْمَةُ اللّٰهِ الْغَنِى, Bulbul-e-Rauza-e-Rasūl Ḥājī Muhammad Mushtāq 'Aṭṭārī عَلَيْهِ رَحْمَةُ الْبَارِى, all those deceased Islamic brothers and sisters who were associated with Dawat-e-Islami and every Muslim jinn and human. Yā Allah عَزَّوَجَلَّ! Particularly convey its reward to every such male and female preacher of Dawat-e-Islami who gets the privilege of giving two Dars from *Faīzān-e-Sunnat* (volume 1) daily for at least 40 days.

اٰمِيْن بِجَاهِ النَّبِيِّ الْاَمِيْن صَلَّى اللّٰهُ تَعَالٰى عَلَيْهِ وَاٰلِهٖ وَسَلَّم

11 Ramadan-ul-Mubārak, 1427 A.H.

اَلۡحَمۡدُ لِلّٰہِ رَبِّ الۡعٰلَمِیۡنَ وَ الصَّلٰوۃُ وَ السَّلَامُ عَلٰی سَیِّدِ الۡمُرۡسَلِیۡنَ

اَمَّا بَعۡدُ فَاَعُوۡذُ بِاللّٰہِ مِنَ الشَّیۡطٰنِ الرَّجِیۡمِ ؕ بِسۡمِ اللّٰہِ الرَّحۡمٰنِ الرَّحِیۡمِ ؕ

Translator's Notes

Dear Islamic brothers! Dawat-e-Islami's Majlis-e-Tarājim, a department responsible for reproducing the books and booklets of Amīr-e-Aĥl-e-Sunnat founder of Dawat-e-Islami 'Allāmaĥ Maulānā Abu Bilal Muhammad Ilyas Attar Qadiri Razavi دَامَتۡ بَرَكَاتُهُمُ الۡعَالِيَه into various languages of the world, is pleased to present the book '*Faīzān-e-Sunnat*' in English under the title of '*Blessings of Sunnaĥ*'

Although any translation is inevitably a form of interpretation, we have tried our level best to convey the thought of the author in its true sense. To facilitate the pronunciation of Arabic letters, a transliteration chart has been added. Terms of Islamic Jurisprudence have not been translated as a caution because in most cases, an English word cannot be a full substitute of an Islamic term. However, a glossary has been given at the end of the book, elaborating Islamic terms. For the convenience of the Islamic brothers and sisters who will be delivering Dars from this book, a brief chapter containing forty Aḥādīš regarding the excellence of Ṣalāt-'Alan-Nabī has also been added. Further, an index and a bibliography have also been given.

This translation has been accomplished by the grace of Almighty Allah عَزَّوَجَلَّ, by the favour of His Noble Prophet صَلَّى اللّٰهُ تَعَالٰى عَلَيْهِ وَاٰلِهٖ وَسَلَّم and the spiritual support of our great Shaykh, the founder of Dawat-e-Islami, 'Allāmaĥ Maulānā Abu Bilal Muhammad Ilyas Attar Qadiri Razavi دَامَتۡ بَرَكَاتُهُمُ الۡعَالِيَه. If there is any shortcoming in this work, it may be a human error on the part of the *Translation Majlis*, not that of the author of the original book. Therefore, if you find any mistake in it, kindly notify us of it in writing at the following postal or email address with the intention of earning reward (Šawāb).

Majlis-e-Tarājim (Translation department)
Alami Madani Markaz, Faizan-e-Madinah Mahallah Saudagran,
Purani Sabzi Mandi, Bab-ul-Madinah, Karachi, Pakistan
Phone: ☎ +92-21-34921389, 90, 91
Email: translation@dawateislami.net

فیضانِ بسم اللہ

Blessings of بسم اللہ

Shaykh-e-Tariqat, Ameer-e-Ahl-e-Sunnat
Founder of Dawat-e-Islami
Allamah Maulana Abu Bilal
MUHAMMAD ILYAS
Attar Qadiri Razavi دامت برکاتہم العالیہ

مکتبۃ المدینہ
MAKTABA TUL MADINAH
MC 1286

اَلْحَمْدُ لِلّٰهِ رَبِّ الْعٰلَمِيْنَ وَ الصَّلٰوةُ وَ السَّلَامُ عَلٰى سَيِّدِ الْمُرْسَلِيْنَ
اَمَّا بَعْدُ فَاَعُوْذُ بِاللّٰهِ مِنَ الشَّيْطٰنِ الرَّجِيْمِ ؕ بِسْمِ اللّٰهِ الرَّحْمٰنِ الرَّحِيْمِ ؕ

Blessings of بِسْمِ اللّٰه

The Prophet of mankind, the Peace of our heart and mind, the most Generous and Kind صَلَّى اللهُ تَعَالٰى عَلَيْهِ وَاٰلِهٖ وَسَلَّم has stated, 'The one who sends Ṣalāt upon me one time, Allah عَزَّوَجَلَّ will shower mercy upon him ten times.' *(Ṣaḥīḥ Muslim, vol. 1, pp. 175, Ḥadīš 408)*

صَلُّوْا عَلَى الْحَبِيْب   صَلَّى اللهُ تَعَالٰى عَلٰى مُحَمَّد

Endeavour remains unfinished

The Prophet of Raḥmaĥ, the Intercessor of Ummaĥ, the Owner of Jannaĥ صَلَّى اللهُ تَعَالٰى عَلَيْهِ وَاٰلِهٖ وَسَلَّم has stated, 'Any important work which is started without (reciting) بِسْمِ اللهِ الرَّحْمٰنِ الرَّحِيْم remains unfinished.' *(Ad-Dur-rul-Manšūr, vol. 1, pp. 26)*

Keep on reciting بِسْمِ اللّٰه

Dear Islamic brothers! Before eating anything, drinking water or any beverage, serving food and water to others, putting things down, picking things up, washing, cooking, reciting, studying, teaching, walking, driving, standing up, sitting down, turning on the light or the fan, laying or removing the dining mat, folding or spreading the bed sheet, opening or closing the shop, locking or unlocking, applying oil or perfume, delivering a speech, reciting a Na'at, adorning one's head with turban, wearing shoes, opening or closing the door, that is to say, before starting any permissible act (when there is no Shar'ī prohibition), it is of great virtue to make a habit of reciting بِسْمِ اللهِ الرَّحْمٰنِ الرَّحِيْم attaining its blessings.

Protection of things from jinns

Sayyīdunā Ṣafwān Bin Sulaym رَحْمَةُ اللهِ تَعَالٰی عَلَيْه has stated, 'Jinns use the things and clothes of human beings. Whenever anyone of you picks up clothes (to put on) or puts them down (after taking them off), he should recite بِسْمِ اللّٰه because the name of Allah عَزَّوَجَلَّ will be a seal for it.' (In other words, by virtue of the recitation of بِسْمِ اللّٰه, jinns will not be able to use the clothes). *(Luqṭ-ul-Marjān, pp. 98)*

Dear Islamic brothers! Similarly, whilst picking up or putting down anything, one should make a habit of reciting بِسْمِ اللهِ الرَّحْمٰنِ الرَّحِيْم he will remain safe from the involvement of wicked jinns, اِنْ شَآءَاللّٰه عَزَّوَجَلَّ.

صَلُّوْا عَلَى الْحَبِيْب   صَلَّى اللهُ تَعَالٰى عَلٰى مُحَمَّد

Recite بِسْمِ اللّٰه correctly

When reciting بِسْمِ اللهِ الرَّحْمٰنِ الرَّحِيْم one must ensure that every letter is pronounced from its correct point of articulation. Furthermore, if there is no noise interference, it is also essential that the voice be loud enough for the reciter to hear it. Some people mispronounce letters due to haste. It is prohibited to do this deliberately. If the meaning becomes distorted [due to mispronunciation] it will be a sin.

Hence those who recite incorrectly due to the habit of reciting hastily should rectify their pronunciation and recitation. If there is no specific reason for reciting complete بِسْمِ اللهِ الرَّحْمٰنِ الرَّحِيْم, one may also recite just بِسْمِ اللّٰه.

Excitement prevailed

Sayyidunā Jābir Bin 'Abdullāĥ رَضِیَ اللهُ تَعَالٰی عَنْهُ has stated, 'When بِسْمِ اللهِ الرَّحْمٰنِ الرَّحِيْم was revealed, the clouds rushed towards the east, the winds became still, the ocean turned turbulent, the quadruped listened attentively, the devils were stoned from the skies, and Allah عَزَّوَجَلَّ said, 'I swear by My Honour and Majesty! I will bless the thing with which بِسْمِ اللهِ الرَّحْمٰنِ الرَّحِيْم is recited.' *(Ad-Dur-rul-Manšūr, vol. 1, pp. 26)*

بِسْمِ اللّٰهِ الرَّحْمٰنِ الرَّحِيْم is a portion of the 30th verse of Sūraĥ An-Naml in the 19th part. It is also a complete Quranic verse revealed for separation between two Sūraĥs [of the Holy Quran]. *(Ḥalbī Kabīr, pp. 307)*

Comprehensiveness of the letter 'ب' in بِسْمِ اللّٰه

Allah عَزَّوَجَلَّ has revealed scriptures and books to some of His Prophets عَلَيْهِمُ السَّلَام. The number of these scriptures and books total 104. Out of these, 50 scriptures were revealed to Sayyidunā Shīš عَلٰى نَبِيِّنَا وَ عَلَيْهِ الصَّلٰوةُ وَالسَّلَام, 30 to Sayyidunā Idrīs عَلٰى نَبِيِّنَا وَ عَلَيْهِ الصَّلٰوةُ وَالسَّلَام and 10 to Sayyidunā Ibrāĥīm عَلٰى نَبِيِّنَا وَ عَلَيْهِ الصَّلٰوةُ وَالسَّلَام. Further, prior to the revelation of the Tawrāt, 10 scriptures were revealed to Sayyidunā Mūsā عَلٰى نَبِيِّنَا وَ عَلَيْهِ الصَّلٰوةُ وَالسَّلَام as well. In addition, four major holy books were also revealed:

1. The holy Tawrāt was revealed to Sayyidunā Mūsā عَلَيْهِ السَّلَام.
2. The holy Zabūr was revealed to Sayyidunā Dāwūd عَلَيْهِ السَّلَام.
3. The holy Injīl was revealed to Sayyidunā 'Īsā عَلَيْهِ السَّلَام.
4. The Holy Quran was revealed to the Most Noble Prophet Muhammad صَلَّى اللهُ تَعَالٰى عَلَيْهِ وَاٰلِهٖ وَسَلَّم.
   (Al-Iḥsān bittartīb Ṣaḥīḥ Ibn Ḥibbān, vol. 1, pp. 288) (Ḥilyat-ul-Auliyā, vol. 1, pp. 222)

The content of all these books and scriptures are included in the Holy Quran and the summary of the entire Quran is present in Sūraĥ Al-Fātiḥaĥ. The summary of Sūraĥ Al-Fātiḥaĥ is contained in بِسْمِ اللّٰهِ الرَّحْمٰنِ الرَّحِيْم while that of بِسْمِ اللّٰهِ الرَّحْمٰنِ الرَّحِيْم is within its letter 'ب'. It implies بِيْ كَانَ مَا كَانَ وَبِيْ يَكُوْنُ مَا يَكُوْنُ '*Whatever there is, is only from Me (i.e. from Allah* عَزَّوَجَلَّ*) and whatever there will be, will be only from Me (i.e. from Allah* عَزَّوَجَلَّ*).*' *(Al-Majālis-us-Saniyyaĥ, pp. 3)*

صَلُّوْا عَلَى الْحَبِيْب صَلَّى اللهُ تَعَالٰى عَلٰى مُحَمَّد

Ism-e-A'ẓam

It is reported by Sayyīdunā 'Abdullāĥ Ibn 'Abbās رَضِیَ اللهُ تَعَالٰی عَنْهُمَا that Amīr-ul-Mūminīn Sayyīđunā 'Ušmān Ibn 'Affān رَضِیَ اللهُ تَعَالٰی عَنْه asked the Holy Prophet صَلَّى اللهُ تَعَالٰى عَلَيْهِ وَاٰلِهٖ وَسَلَّم about (the excellence of) بِسۡمِ اللّٰہِ الرَّحۡمٰنِ الرَّحِیۡمِ. The Holy Prophet صَلَّی اللّٰہُ تَعَالٰی عَلَیْہِ وَاٰلِہٖ وَسَلَّم replied, 'It is one of the names of Allah عَزَّوَجَلَّ and is as close to the Ism-e-A'ẓam of Allah عَزَّوَجَلَّ as the blackness of the eye is to its whiteness.' *(Al-Mustadrak, vol. 1, pp. 738, Ḥadīš 2071)*

Prayer made with Ism-e-A'ẓam is answered

Dear Islamic brothers! There are many virtues of Ism-e-A'ẓam and the Du'ā made with it is accepted. The respected father of A'lā Ḥaḍrat, Raīs-ul-Mutakallimīn, Maulānā Naqī 'Alī Khān عَلَیْہِ رَحْمَۃُ الرَّحْمٰن has stated, 'Some scholars have said that بِسۡمِ اللّٰہِ الرَّحۡمٰنِ الرَّحِیۡمِ is Ism-e-A'ẓam. The honourable Ghauš Shaykh 'Abdul Qādir Jīlānī قُدِّسَ سِرُّہُ الرَّبَّانِی has narrated that بِسۡمِ اللّٰہ (when recited) by the tongue of an 'Ārif[1] is like the word كُنۡ (i.e. be) from divine words.' *(Aḥsan-ul-Wi'ā, pp. 6)*

Dear Islamic brothers! In order to have blessings in our righteous and permissible acts, we should recite بِسۡمِ اللّٰہِ الرَّحۡمٰنِ الرَّحِیۡمِ before we do them. If you aspire to develop the habit of reciting بِسۡمِ اللّٰہِ الرَّحۡمٰنِ الرَّحِیۡمِ prior to every permissible act, travel routinely with the Sunnaĥ-Inspiring Madanī Qāfilaĥs of Dawat-e-Islami in the company of the devotees of Rasūl. اَلْحَمْدُ لِلّٰہ عَزَّوَجَلَّ! There are many instances where the problems of the Islamic brothers travelling with Dawat-e-Islami's Madanī Qāfilaĥs have been solved by virtue of making Du'ā during Madanī Qāfilaĥs.

Crooked nose

Here is a summary of the incident of an Islamic brother. He has stated, 'The bone of my nose was crooked. I also had prolonged headache and eye pain. I had intended to undergo an operation in Nishtar Medical Hospital situated in Madīna-tul-Auliyā, Multan. Fortunately, I was privileged to travel to Pakpattan with a Sunnaĥ-Inspiring Madanī Qāfilaĥ of Dawat-e-Islami in the company of the devotees of Rasūl.

I had already heard that the prayers made during Madanī Qāfilaĥs are answered, so I prayed to Allah عَزَّوَجَلَّ in these words, 'O Allah عَزَّوَجَلَّ! By virtue of Dawat-e-Islami's Madanī Qāfilaĥ, straighten my nose bone!' A few days after the Madanī Qāfilaĥ, I looked in the

[1] An 'Ārif is the one possessing the gnosis of divine attributes.

mirror and was overjoyed to notice that my nose was no longer crooked but had been straightened and was completely normal by the blessing of the Du'ā made during the Madanī Qāfilaĥ in the company of the devotees of Rasūl!'

Sīkĥnay Sunnatayn Qāfilay mayn chalo
Lūtnay raḥmatayn Qāfilay mayn chalo
Laynay ko barakatayn Qāfilay mayn chalo
Pāo gey rāḥatayn Qāfilay mayn chalo

To learn Sunnaĥs, travel with Madanī Qāfilaĥ;
To reap mercies, travel with Madanī Qāfilaĥ
To gain blessings, travel with Madanī Qāfilaĥ,
To get tranquillity, travel with Madanī Qāfilaĥ

صَلُّوْا عَلَى الْحَبِيْب صَلَّى اللّٰهُ تَعَالٰى عَلٰى مُحَمَّد

Dear Islamic brothers! Without doubt, the Du'ā made by travellers is accepted, and the Du'ā made by the traveller of the path of Allah in the company of the devotees of Rasūl is obviously more likely to be accepted.

Describing the factors that may well lead to the acceptance of Du'ā, the honourable father of A'lā Ḥaḍrat, Maulānā Naqī 'Alī Khān عَلَيْهِ رَحْمَةُ الرَّحْمٰن has stated on page 57 of his marvellous book '*Aḥsan-ul-Wi'ā*', 'The gatherings of the Auliyā and 'Ulamā (i.e. the Du'ā made in the gathering or closeness of any Islamic saint or Sunnī scholar is accepted).'

Adding a footnote to this, A'lā Ḥaḍrat رَحْمَةُ اللّٰهِ تَعَالٰى عَلَيْه has stated referring to scholars and saints, 'Allah عَزَّوَجَلَّ says in an authentic Ḥadīš Qudsī, هُمُ الْقَوْمُ لَا يَشْقٰى بِهِمْ جَلِيْسُهُم '*These are those in whose company one is not ill-fated.*'

یک زمانہ صحبتِ با اولیاء بہتر از صد سالہ طاعت بے ریا

(A moment spent in the company of the honourable friends of Allah is better than a hundred years of sincere worship).

Whether a saint is apparently alive or is resting in his blessed shrine, his nearness is a means of the acceptance of Du'ā. The leader of millions of Shāfi'ī brothers, Sayyidunā Imām Shāfi'ī عَلَيْهِ رَحْمَةُ اللّٰهِ الْقَوِى has stated, 'Whenever I am in need of something, I offer 2 Rak'āt Ṣalāĥ, pay a visit to the blessed shrine of Imām A'ẓam Abū Ḥanīfaĥ رَحْمَةُ اللّٰهِ تَعَالٰى عَلَيْه and make Du'ā there. [By virtue of this] Allah عَزَّوَجَلَّ fulfils my need.' *(Al-Khayrāt-ul-Ḥisān, pp. 230)*

Saintly miracle of A'la Hadrat رَحْمَةُ اللهِ عَلَيْه

This shows that at the shrines of saints Du'ās are accepted, pleas are listened to and desires are fulfilled. In his own words, A'lā Ḥaḍrat رَحْمَةُ اللهِ تَعَالٰى عَلَيْه has related his personal incident which took place when he was a young man of 21 years. He رَحْمَةُ اللّٰهِ تَعَالٰى عَلَيْه has stated, 'On 17th Rabī'-ul-Ākhir 1293 A.H., when I was 21 years of age, I was fortunate enough to visit the blessed shrine of the eminent saint Maḥbūb-e-Ilāĥī, Niẓām-ul-Ḥaq Waddīn, Sultan-ul-Auliyā رَحْمَةُ اللهِ تَعَالٰى عَلَيْه along with my honourable father and Shaykh Maulānā Muhammad 'Abdul Qādir Badāyūnī دَامَتْ بَرَكَاتُهُمُ الْعَالِيَه.

Outside, there was offensive and disturbing activity all around the blessed shrine. It was so noisy and deafening that one could hardly hear anything else. Both the dignified saints, with their peaceful hearts, entered the sacred chamber of the shrine where the tomb of Sultan-ul-Auliyā رَحْمَةُ اللّٰهِ تَعَالٰى عَلَيْه was situated and occupied themselves.

I, disturbed by the noise of the evil activities, stood at the blessed doorstep and requested in the court of Sultan-ul-Auliyā رَحْمَةُ اللهِ تَعَالٰى عَلَيْه, 'O my Master! These noises are causing hindrance to what this servant has come here for.' Then, reciting بِسْمِ اللّٰه, I placed my right foot inside the blessed chamber and, by the grace of Almighty Allah عَزَّوَجَلَّ, the noise was no more. I thought that people had perhaps become silent but as I turned around, I saw the same immoral activities go on there. When I placed my foot outside the chamber, there was the same noise again.

Reciting 'بِسْمِ اللّٰه' I placed my right foot inside the blessed chamber again. By the grace of Allah عَزَّوَجَلَّ, the noise was no more again. I then realized that this was a divinely-bestowed saintly miracle of Sultan-ul-Auliyā رَحْمَةُ اللّٰهِ تَعَالٰى عَلَيْه and mercy and assistance for me, a worthless servant.

Expressing gratitude, I entered the blessed chamber and occupied myself. Until I remained there, I did not hear any noise. When I came out, I was disturbed by the same noisy environment, even facing difficulty in getting to my accommodation situated at some distance from the blessed shrine. I have mentioned this incident of mine with some righteous intentions. Firstly, it was a divine favour for me, and Allah عَزَّوَجَلَّ has said regarding His favours:

وَ اَمَّا بِنِعْمَةِ رَبِّكَ فَحَدِّثْ ﴿۱۱﴾

And publicise well the bounty of your Lord.

[Kanz-ul-Īmān (Translation of Quran)] (Part 30, Sūraĥ Aḍ-Ḍuḥā, verse 11)

In addition, this contains glad tidings for the devotees of blessed saints and causes trouble for those who deny. O Allah عَزَّوَجَلَّ! For the sake of Your beloved ones رَحِمَهُمُ اللّٰهُ تَعَالٰی, grant us the unlimited blessings of Your beloved saints رَحِمَهُمُ اللّٰهُ تَعَالٰی in this world, in the Hereafter, in the grave, and on the Day of Judgement.' *(Aḥsan-ul-Wi'ā, pp. 60)*

صَلُّوْا عَلَى الْحَبِيْب صَلَّى اللّٰهُ تَعَالٰى عَلٰى مُحَمَّد

Dear Islamic brothers! This is a parable of Delhi, the city of 22 saints. This incident contains a saintly miracle of Khuwājaĥ Maḥbūb-e-Ilāĥī, Niẓāmuddīn Auliyā رَحْمَةُ اللّٰهِ تَعَالٰی عَلَيْه as well as that of A'lā Ḥaḍrat رَحْمَةُ اللّٰهِ تَعَالٰی عَلَيْه. When A'lā Ḥaḍrat رَحْمَةُ اللّٰهِ تَعَالٰی عَلَيْه stepped into the chamber where the blessed tomb was situated, he would not hear the noise of drum-beating and other musical instruments.

We have also learnt from this parable that even if some ignorant people are committing such acts not allowed by Sharī'aĥ at the shrines of the Auliyā [saints] and we are unable to prevent them, we should not still deprive ourselves of visiting the blessed shrines of Auliyā. However, it is Wājib to abstain from getting involved in these evil acts and to consider them evil in our heart. One should even refrain from looking at such things.

Mysterious old man and black jinn

Once, in the pleasant atmosphere of Masjid-un-Nabawī عَلٰی صَاحِبِهَا الصَّلٰوۃُ وَالسَّلَام Sayyidunā 'Umar Fārūq A'ẓam and some other honourable companions رَضِیَ اللّٰہُ تَعَالٰی عَنْهُم were having a discussion about the excellence of the Holy Quran. During the discussion, Sayyidunā 'Amr Bin Ma'dīkarib رَضِیَ اللّٰہُ تَعَالٰی عَنْهُ politely said, 'O leader of believers! Why don't you talk about the marvels of بِسۡمِ اللّٰہِ الرَّحۡمٰنِ الرَّحِیۡم! I swear by Allah عَزَّوَجَلَّ! بِسۡمِ اللّٰہِ الرَّحۡمٰنِ الرَّحِیۡم is a great marvel.'

Sitting up straight, Sayyidunā 'Umar Fārūq A'ẓam رَضِیَ اللّٰہُ تَعَالٰی عَنْهُ responded, 'O Abū Šaur! (This was the Kunyaĥ[1] of Sayyidunā 'Amr Bin Ma'dīkarib) Please tell us about any such marvel.' Sayyidunā 'Amr Bin Ma'dīkarib رَضِیَ اللّٰہُ تَعَالٰی عَنْهُ said, 'A severe famine once occurred during (the pre-Islamic era) of ignorance. In search of food I passed by a jungle. From some distance, I caught sight of a tent. Near the tent was a horse and some cattle. As I went closer, I saw that inside the tent was a beautiful woman and an elderly man who was sitting leaning against something.

Threatening the old man, I said, 'Give me whatever you have!' He replied, 'O man! If you need any hospitality from us, then please come. If you need help, we will help you.' I said, 'Stop making things up and give me whatever you have.' The old man hardly managed to stand up and, reciting بِسۡمِ اللّٰہِ الرَّحۡمٰنِ الرَّحِیۡم, pounced on me. In no time, he threw me down on the ground, sitting on my chest and then said, 'Now tell me, shall I kill you or leave you?' I replied fearfully, 'Leave me,' Hearing this, he got off my chest.

Rebuking myself, I said inwardly, 'O 'Amr! You are a famous horseman of Arabia. To run away after being overpowered by this weak and old man is a cowardly and unmanly act; it is better to be killed than to be faced with this humiliation.' Thus, I threatened him again, 'Give me whatever you have!' Hearing this, the mysterious old man attacked me again reciting بِسۡمِ اللّٰہِ الرَّحۡمٰنِ الرَّحِیۡم. In an instant, he threw me down on the ground, jumped onto my chest and said, 'Tell me, shall I kill you or release you?' I replied, 'Please forgive me,' so he released me again. But then, I did the same once again threatening him and demanding his possessions.

[1] Kunyaĥ – patronymic appellation

Reciting بِسْمِ اللّٰهِ الرَّحْمٰنِ الرَّحِيْم he once again attacked and overpowered me. I again pleaded, 'Please release me,' but he replied, 'This is for the third time. I will not release you so easily now.' Saying this, he called out, 'O girl! Bring me the sharp sword.' She brought the sword with which he cut hair from the front of my head, and then released me.

It was customary among the Arabs to cut hair from the front of the head of a defeated person, indicating that the person has been defeated in a fight. The defeated person would be ashamed of facing his family until his front hair grew again. Therefore, I had to stay there for an entire year serving the mysterious old man. After the year ended, the old man took me to a valley where he recited بِسْمِ اللّٰهِ الرَّحْمٰنِ الرَّحِيْم aloud. Immediately all birds came out of their nests and flew away. When he recited it again, all beasts came out of their hideouts and went away. As he recited it aloud for the third time, a frightening black jinn in woollen clothes, as tall as a date tree trunk, suddenly appeared. Seeing the jinn, I felt a shiver of fear run through me.

Addressing me, the mysterious old man said, 'O 'Amr! Pluck up the courage. If the jinn overpowers me, just say that my companion will win next time by virtue of بِسْمِ اللّٰهِ الرَّحْمٰنِ الرَّحِيْم!' Thereafter, the mysterious old man and the black jinn wrestled with each other. The old man lost and the black jinn overpowered him. Seeing this, I said, 'Next time my companion will win because of Lāt and 'Uzzā (i.e. the names of two idols of unbelievers).'

Hearing this, the mysterious old man slapped me on the face so hard that I lost my senses for a moment and felt as if my head would be separated from my body. Apologizing to him I assured him of not doing so again. Both of them started fighting again. This time, the mysterious old man held the black jinn down, so I exclaimed, 'My companion has won by the blessings of بِسْمِ اللّٰهِ الرَّحْمٰنِ الرَّحِيْم!'

As soon as I said this, the mysterious old man sank the jinn into the ground like a piece of wood, cut his belly open, pulled out something similar to a lantern and told me, 'O 'Amr! This is his deception and unbelief.' I asked the mysterious old man, 'What is the story about you and the black jinn?' He replied, 'A non-Muslim jinn was my friend. Every year a jinn from his community fights me, and Allah عَزَّوَجَلَّ blesses me with victory by virtue of بِسْمِ اللّٰهِ الرَّحْمٰنِ الرَّحِيْم.'

We then went ahead and reached a place where the mysterious old man fell asleep. Seizing the opportunity, I snatched his sword and struck his legs so hard that they became separated from his body. He screamed out, 'O deceiver! You have brutally deceived me!' I didn't give him a chance to recover and struck him repeatedly, butchering him into pieces. When I returned to the tent, the girl asked, 'O 'Amr, what about the fight with the jinn?' I replied, 'The jinns have killed the old man.' She responded, 'You are a liar! O disloyal person! The jinns haven't killed him but you have killed him!' Having said this, she began to weep desperately and recited 5 Arabic couplets whose translation is as follows:

1. O my eyes! Shed tears for that horseman who was brave and bold.
2. O 'Amr! You should be regretting about your life because your friend has lost his life.
3. And (O 'Amr! After you have killed your friend with your own hands) how can you strut in front of (your tribe) Banī Zubaydaĥ and the unbelievers?
4. I swear by my age! (O 'Amr!) If you were a true warrior (that is, if you had manly fought him without deception) then his sharp sword would have indeed killed you.
5. May the real King (Allah عَزَّوَجَلَّ) give you a disgraceful and ugly return (for your crime) and may you live a disgraceful and appalling life (in the same way as you have treated your friend disgracefully).

Furious, I advanced to kill her, but astonishingly she disappeared from my sight as if the earth had swallowed her! *(Luqṭ-ul-Marjān, pp. 141)*

صَلُّوْا عَلَى الْحَبِيْب صَلَّى اللّٰهُ تَعَالٰى عَلٰى مُحَمَّد

Dear Islamic brothers! Did you see the amazing blessings of بِسْمِ اللّٰهِ الرَّحْمٰنِ الرَّحِيْم? In order to attain these blessings, travel with Dawat-e-Islami's Madanī Qāfilaĥs in the company of the devotees of Rasūl. اِنْ شَآءَاللّٰه عَزَّوَجَلَّ, Your problems will amazingly be solved and you will be helped from Ghayb by the grace and bounties of Allah عَزَّوَجَلَّ.

Virtuous intention leads to destination

A Madanī Qāfilaĥ of the devotees of Rasūl travelled to Kapadvanj (Gujrat, India). During the area visit to call people towards righteousness, the participants of the Qāfilaĥ came across a drinker. Making individual effort, the devotees of Rasūl requested him to accompany them to the Masjid.

Impressed by the polite and humble manners of the Islamic brothers whose heads were adorned with green turbans, he joined them immediately. By the blessings of the company of the devotees of Rasūl, he repented of his sins, grew a beard, adorned his head with the crown of a green turban and developed a mindset of wearing Madanī dress. He travelled with a Madanī Qāfilaĥ for 6 days, and made the intention of travelling for further 92 days, but didn't have the expenses for the travel.

One day, he met a relative of his. The relative was astonished to see that a notorious person of society and a drinker had transformed remarkably, growing a beard and wearing a Madanī dress with a green turban on his head. He was told that travelling with a Madanī Qāfilaĥ had caused this great positive change in his life and he had also made a firm intention of travelling with a 92-day Madanī Qāfilaĥ but could not travel for the time being due to financial constraint. His relative responded, 'Don't worry about money. Not only will I provide the expenses of the 92-day Madanī Qāfilaĥ but will also provide for his family for 92 days.' In this way, the brother travelled with a Madanī Qāfilaĥ for 92 days.

Ghaybī imdād ĥo, gĥar bĥī ābād ĥo
Rizq kay dar kĥulayn, barakatayn bĥī milayn
Chal kay khud daykĥ layn, Qāfilay mayn chalo
Luṭf-e-Ḥaq daykĥ layn, Qāfilay mayn chalo

Help from Ghayb will arrive and home will thrive
Door of sustenance will open and blessings will shower
Experience it in person, travel with Madanī Qāfilaĥ
See divine bounty, travel with Madanī Qāfilaĥ

صَلُّوْا عَلَى الْحَبِيْب   صَلَّى اللّٰهُ تَعَالٰى عَلٰى مُحَمَّد

Five Madanī pearls

Sayyidunā 'Abdullāĥ Bin 'Amr Bin 'Āṣ رَضِیَ اللهُ تَعَالٰی عَنْهُ has stated, 'If a person adopts five habits, he will be privileged in the worldly life as well as in the afterlife:

1. To recite لَآ اِلٰهَ اِلَّا اللهُ مُحَمَّدٌ رَّسُوْلُ اللهِ from time to time.

2. To recite اِنَّا لِلّٰهِ وَ اِنَّآ اِلَيْهِ رٰجِعُوْنَ and لَاحَوْلَ وَلَا قُوَّةَ اِلَّا بِاللهِ الْعَلِيِّ الْعَظِيْمِ in trouble (i.e. illness, suffering a loss or on hearing news of any adversity).

3. To recite اَلْحَمْدُ لِلّٰهِ رَبِّ الْعٰلَمِيْنَ as gratitude on gaining any favour.

4. To recite بِسْمِ اللهِ الرَّحْمٰنِ الرَّحِيْمِ before starting any (permissible) act.

5. To recite اَسْتَغْفِرُ اللهَ الْعَظِيْمَ وَاَتُوْبُ اِلَيْهِ[1] in case of the occurrence of a sin.

(Al-Munabbiĥāt, pp. 58)

Charity analogous to status

A renowned commentator of Ḥadīš and Quran Muftī Aḥmad Yār Khān عَلَيْهِ رَحْمَةُ الْحَنَّان has stated, 'In بِسْمِ اللهِ الرَّحْمٰنِ الرَّحِيْمِ, Allah عَزَّوَجَلَّ has mentioned His 2 attributes of mercy (i.e. رَحْمٰن and رَحِيْم) with His self-name (i.e. Allah) because it (i.e. the name Allah) was awe-inspiring, whereas رَحْمٰن and رَحِيْم have mercy.

When people heard the name 'Allah عَزَّوَجَلَّ' even the pious dared not ask anything but when they heard the names رَحْمٰن and رَحِيْم even the sinners and wrongdoers were encouraged to implore Allah عَزَّوَجَلَّ. It is indeed a fact that no one can utter a single word at the time of His wrath while everyone can rejoice at the time of His mercy. In relation to this, there is a wonderful incident mentioned in *Tafsīr Kabīr*. A beggar once reached the luxuriously decorated door of a very wealthy person's house and begged for something but was given something cheap and insignificant. Taking it, the beggar left.

---

[1] **Translation:** I repent to Allah عَزَّوَجَلَّ the Most Magnificent, seeking forgiveness from Him.

The next day, he came again with a big spade in his hands and started to dig the ground beneath the door. Seeing this, the owner of the house shouted, 'What are you doing?' The beggar replied, 'Either give charity according to the beauty of your door or make your door according to the charity you have given.' That is to say, since you have made such a splendid door, indicating that you are a wealthy person, it is necessary for you to give more charity compared to others. We sinful beggars also implore, 'O Allah عَزَّوَجَلَّ! Bless us with bounties, not according to our worth and value, but according to Your generosity and kindness. Without doubt, we are sinners, but Your attribute of forgiveness is much greater than our sins.' *(Tafsīr-e-Na'īmī, pp. 40, part 1)*

Gunaĥ-e-gadā kā ḥisāb kyā woĥ agarcheĥ lākĥ say ĥayn siwā
Magar ay 'Affū Tayray 'afw kā na ḥisāb ĥay na shumār ĥay

Though there is no measure of the sins of this servant
O the Most Forgiving, Your mercy is beyond measurement

صَلُّوْا عَلَى الْحَبِيْب صَلَّى اللّٰهُ تَعَالٰى عَلٰى مُحَمَّد

Dear Islamic brothers! Allah عَزَّوَجَلَّ is indeed رَحْمٰن and رَحِيْم. The one pinning his hopes on divine mercy expecting good from Allah عَزَّوَجَلَّ can never be deprived of the mercy of Allah عَزَّوَجَلَّ, and will succeed in the worldly life as well as in the afterlife.

Parable of mercy

It is stated on page 38 of the first part of *Tafsīr Na'īmī* that there were two brothers. One of them was pious while the other was a sinner. When the sinful brother was on his deathbed, the pious brother said to him, 'See, I always admonished and advised you but you did not give up sins. Tell me what would happen to you now?' The sinful brother replied, 'If, on the Judgement Day, Allah عَزَّوَجَلَّ allowed my mother to decide my fate, where would she send me, to Paradise or to Hell?' The pious brother replied, 'Mother will, of course, send you to Paradise.' The sinful brother responded, 'My Allah عَزَّوَجَلَّ is more merciful than even my mother.' Saying this, he passed away.

At night, the elder brother had a dream in which he saw his deceased brother in a very peaceful and comfortable state, so he asked the reason of his forgiveness. The deceased brother replied, 'The very words I had uttered at the time of my death brought about the forgiveness of all of my sins.'

May Allah عَزَّوَجَلَّ have mercy on them and forgive us without accountability for their sake!

Ĥum gunāĥgāraun pay Tayrī meĥarbānī chāĥiye
Sab gunāĥ dĥul jāyaīn gayn, raḥmat kā pānī chāĥiye

For us worthless sinners, Your favour is required
All sins will be washed away; rain of mercy is required

صَلُّوْا عَلَى الْحَبِيْب صَلَّى اللّٰهُ تَعَالٰى عَلٰى مُحَمَّد

Dear Islamic brothers! Indeed the mercy of Allah عَزَّوَجَلَّ is immense. Even a single word uttered by a person can lead him to salvation or damnation. As mentioned in the above parable, a single sentence brought about the salvation of a sinner. Likewise, if a person utters explicit words of Kufr [unbelief] and dies without repenting, he will face eternal damnation in Hell.

An excellent way of protecting oneself from damnation and attaining salvation is to travel in the company of the devotees of Rasūl with the Sunnaĥ-Inspiring Madanī Qāfilaĥs of Dawat-e-Islami, a global & non political religious movement of the Quran and Sunnaĥ. Even if the one who has made a firm intention of travelling is unable to travel for some reason, he will still gain its blessings, اِنْ شَآءَاللّٰه عَزَّوَجَلَّ. Listen to the faith-refreshing parable of a fortunate person who had made an intention to travel with a Madanī Qāfilaĥ.

Swing in garden

Impressed by the 'area visit to call people towards righteousness' being carried out in an area of Hyderabad (Sindh, Pakistan), a modern young man attended the Masjid where he listened to a Sunnaĥ-Inspiring speech during which the attendees were encouraged to travel with Madanī Qāfilaĥs. Expressing his willingness to travel with a Madanī Qāfilaĥ, the young man also got his name registered.

A few days before his departure with the Madanī Qāfilaĥ, he passed away. Someone from his family had a dream in which he saw the deceased swing cheerfully in a beautiful lush green garden. The dreaming person asked, 'How did you get here?' He replied, 'I have got here with the Madanī Qāfilaĥ of Dawat-e-Islami! Allah عَزَّوَجَلَّ has blessed me greatly. Please ask my mother not to grieve for me as I am very comfortable here.'

Khuld mayn ĥogā ĥamārā dākhilaĥ is shān say
Yā Rasūlallāĥ صَلَّى اللّٰهُ تَعَالٰى عَلَيْهِ وَاٰلِهٖ وَسَلَّم *kā na'raĥ lagātay jāyaīn gayn*

Whilst entering Paradise with glory, اِنْ شَآءَ اللّٰه عَزَّوَجَلَّ
We will be chanting the slogan 'Yā Rasūlallāĥ صَلَّى اللّٰهُ تَعَالٰى عَلَيْهِ وَاٰلِهٖ وَسَلَّم

صَلُّوْا عَلَى الْحَبِيْب صَلَّى اللّٰهُ تَعَالٰى عَلٰى مُحَمَّد

By Sharī'aĥ, the dream of a non-Prophet is not a proof. We should, therefore, hope for the mercy of Allah عَزَّوَجَلَّ and fear His Hidden Plan as well. All this depends upon the will of Allah عَزَّوَجَلَّ. If He عَزَّوَجَلَّ wills, He can punish a person for even a single sin, and if He عَزَّوَجَلَّ wills, He can bestow His grace on a person by virtue of a single deed of piety or He عَزَّوَجَلَّ may forgive someone solely by virtue of His mercy and grace. The Most Merciful Allah عَزَّوَجَلَّ says in part 24, Sūraĥ Az-Zumar, verse 53:

قُلْ يٰعِبَادِيَ الَّذِيْنَ اَسْرَفُوْا عَلٰۤى اَنْفُسِهِمْ
لَا تَقْنَطُوْا مِنْ رَّحْمَةِ اللّٰهِ ؕ اِنَّ اللّٰهَ يَغْفِرُ الذُّنُوْبَ جَمِيْعًا ؕ اِنَّهٗ هُوَ الْغَفُوْرُ الرَّحِيْمُ ﴿۵۳﴾

You proclaim, 'O My servants who have wronged themselves! Do not give up hope of the mercy of Allah عَزَّوَجَلَّ; indeed Allah عَزَّوَجَلَّ forgives all sins; indeed only He عَزَّوَجَلَّ is the Most Forgiving, the Most Merciful.'

[Kanz-ul-Īmān (Translation of Quran)]

The following incident is reported in Bukhārī, the most authentic book of Aḥādīš:

Murderer of 100 people was forgiven

A person from Banī Isrāīl had murdered 99 people. He approached a Christian monk and asked, 'Is there any way of repentance for me, a grave sinner?' The monk's (response) disappointed him so he murdered the monk as well but he became regretful again and visited different people to find a way of repentance. Eventually, someone suggested that he go to a certain town (where he could seek the help of a Walī of Allah). Therefore, he set off for that town but fell severely ill on the way. When he was close to his death he turned his chest towards that town and then died.

At the time of taking away him (i.e. his soul) a disagreement arose between the angels of mercy and those of punishment. Allah عَزَّوَجَلَّ commanded the part of the earth (i.e. the distance) between the deceased and the town to reduce in length so that (the town) is closer to him. He عَزَّوَجَلَّ also commanded the part of the earth between the place from where he had set off and the place where he had died to lengthen in distance. He عَزَّوَجَلَّ then ordered the measurement (of the two distances).

(After the measurement) The deceased was found to have been one hand span closer to the town, so Allah عَزَّوَجَلَّ forgave him. *(Ṣaḥīḥ Bukhārī, vol. 2, pp. 466, Ḥadīš 3470)*

May Allah عَزَّوَجَلَّ have mercy on him and forgive us without accountability for his sake!

صَلُّوْا عَلَى الْحَبِيْب   صَلَّى اللّٰهُ تَعَالٰى عَلٰى مُحَمَّد

Dear Islamic brothers! As clear from the above parable, it is a very virtuous act to visit the Auliyā of Allah and make their town the Qiblaĥ of one's soul, with reverence. Rejoice at the mercy of Allah who has forgiven the murderer of 100 people merely by virtue of His mercy. If Allah عَزَّوَجَلَّ also showers His mercy on the fortunate young man who had intended to travel with a Sunnaĥ-Inspiring Madanī Qāfilaĥ in the company of the devotees of Rasūl, then this is also His immense mercy. Indeed Allah عَزَّوَجَلَّ is omnipotent.

It is my Madanī suggestion that one should always remain associated with Dawat-e-Islami. اِنْ شَآءَاللّٰه عَزَّوَجَلَّ, One will attain success in the worldly life as well as in the afterlife. Words cannot express the blessings of the Madanī environment of Dawat-e-Islami! Indeed, the company of the devotees of Rasūl bears fruit. Not only does one attain blessings in his life but also at the time of his demise. Sometimes, the devotees of Rasūl meet their death in an enviable way. Here is the account of one such enviable demise:

Enviable demise

Muhammad Wasīm 'Aṭṭārī from North Karachi, Bāb-ul-Madīnaĥ used to visit Sag-e-Madīnaĥ[1]. He suffered from hand cancer that resulted in the amputation of his hand. An Islamic brother from his area has stated, 'Brother Wasīm was in severe agony. I visited him at hospital and said in a consoling tone, 'O devotee! Don't grieve over the amputation of your left hand; اَلۡحَمۡدُ لِلّٰه عَزَّوَجَلَّ, your right hand is safe, and the greatest privilege is that your Īmān (faith) is also safe, اِنۡ شَآءَاللّٰه عَزَّوَجَلَّ.' I found him very patient, اَلۡحَمۡدُ لِلّٰه عَزَّوَجَلَّ. He just kept on smiling. He even rose from his bed and came outside to say me farewell.

Gradually, the pain in his hand was relieved but another ordeal lay in store for him. Fluid accumulated in his lungs, causing him severe pain and agony again. His condition deteriorated as the days passed. Eventually, one day, his pain intensified; he started making Żikr of Allah عَزَّوَجَلَّ. The room remained echoing all day with the sounds of the Żikr of 'Allah, Allah.' He was in a seriously critical condition and was asked to be taken to hospital but he refused. His paternal grandmother embraced him affectionately. He recited Kalimaĥ Ṭayyibaĥ لَآ اِلٰهَ اِلَّا اللّٰهُ مُحَمَّدٌ رَّسُوۡلُ اللّٰهِ and the soul of the 22-year old Muhammad Wasīm 'Aṭṭārī left his body, اِنَّا لِلّٰهِ وَ اِنَّآ اِلَيۡهِ رٰجِعُوۡنَ.

When the deceased was being carried for Ghusl (ritual bathing) the cloth from over his face slid away, exposing his rose-like blooming face. After the Ghusl, his face became even more handsome and radiant. After the burial, the devotees of Rasūl were reciting Na'ats when a pleasant fragrance emanated from his grave, refreshing the senses of those present. A family member of the deceased dreamt that the late Muhammad Wasīm Aṭṭārī was in a room adorned with flowers. The dreaming person asked, 'Where are you living?' Pointing towards the room, he replied, 'This is my home and I am very happy here.' He then reclined on a beautifully decorated bed.

[1] Amīr-e-Aĥl-e-Sunnat دَامَتۡ بَرَکَاتُهُمُ الۡعَالِيَه refers to himself as 'Sag-e-Madīnaĥ' out of humbleness.

[Translator's Note]

The father of the deceased also dreamt that he was present by the grave of Muhammad Wasīm Aṭṭārī. All of a sudden, the grave opened and the deceased emerged from it with a beautiful green turban on his head and a white shroud on his body. A little conversation took place between the two. He then entered the grave which closed again.

May Allah عَزَّوَجَلَّ have mercy on him and forgive us without accountability for his sake!

O Allah عَزَّوَجَلَّ! Forgive me, the deceased and the Ummaĥ of the Beloved and Blessed Prophet صَلَّى اللهُ تَعَالٰى عَلَيْهِ وَاٰلِهٖ وَسَلَّم. Bless us all with steadfastness in the Madanī environment of Dawat-e-Islami and with the privilege of making Żikr and reciting Ṣalāt-'Alan-Nabī ﷺ as well as Kalimaĥ Ṭayyibaĥ at the time of our death.

اٰمِيْن بِجَاهِ النَّبِيِّ الْاَمِيْن صَلَّى اللهُ تَعَالٰى عَلَيْهِ وَاٰلِهٖ وَسَلَّم

'Āṣī ĥūn, maghfirat kī Du'āeyn ĥazār do
Na'at-e-Nabī sunā kay laḥad mayn utār do

Make thousands of supplications for my forgiveness as I am a sinner
Recite Na'at of Beloved Prophet while laying me in grave, O brother

To say 'do بِسْمِ اللّٰه' is prohibited

Some (Urdu-speaking) people say, 'Do بِسْمِ اللّٰه!', 'Let's do بِسْمِ اللّٰه!' or 'I have done بِسْمِ اللّٰه!' When traders sell the first item of the day, some of them call it بِسْمِ اللّٰه. For example, some say, 'My بِسْمِ اللّٰه hasn't yet taken place this morning!' All above phrases are wrong expressions. Similarly, if a person comes whilst another person is eating, the eating person often says to him, 'Come and eat with me.' The common reply on this occasion is, 'بِسْمِ اللّٰه' or 'do بِسْمِ اللّٰه.'

It is stated in *Baĥār-e-Sharī'at*, part 16, page 32, 'Scholars have strictly prohibited saying بِسْمِ اللّٰه on such an occasion.' However, one may say like this, 'Recite بِسْمِ اللّٰه and eat.' It is better to say supplicatory words on such occasions, like بَارَكَ اللهُ لَنَا وَلَكُمْ (*May Allah* عَزَّوَجَلَّ *bless us and you*) or one can also say it in his mother tongue, 'May Allah عَزَّوَجَلَّ bless you.'

When is it Kufr to recite بِسۡمِ اللّٰه?

بِسۡمِ اللّٰه should never ever be recited before a Ḥarām and impermissible act. It is stated in '*Fatāwā 'Ālamgīrī*' that it is Kufr to say بِسۡمِ اللّٰه when consuming alcohol, fornicating or gambling. *(Fatāwā 'Ālamgīrī, vol. 2, pp. 273)*

Angels keep on recording virtues

It is narrated by Sayyidunā Abū Ĥurayraĥ رَضِیَ اللہُ تَعَالٰی عَنۡهُ that the Prophet of Raḥmaĥ, the Intercessor of Ummaĥ, the Owner of Jannaĥ صَلَّى اللهُ تَعَالٰی عَلَيۡهِ وَاٰلِهٖ وَسَلَّم has stated, 'O Abū Ĥurayraĥ (رَضِیَ اللہُ تَعَالٰی عَنۡهُ)! When you make Wuḍū, recite بِسۡمِ اللهِ وَالۡحَمۡدُ لِلّٰه as your angels (i.e. Kirāman and Kātibīn) will continue to record virtues for you for as long as your Wuḍū exists.'
(Ṭabarānī Ṣaghīr, vol. 1, pp. 73, Ḥadīš 186)

Virtue for every step

If a person recites بِسۡمِ اللّٰه and اَلۡحَمۡدُ لِلّٰه when mounting an animal, one virtue will be recorded for him (i.e. the rider) for every step the animal takes. *(Tafsīr-e-Na'īmī, vol. 1, pp. 42)*

Virtues when sailing on ship

If a person recites بِسۡمِ اللّٰه and اَلۡحَمۡدُ لِلّٰه when boarding a ship, virtues will continuously be recorded for him for as long as he is on board. *(Tafsīr-e-Na'īmī, vol. 1, pp. 42)*

Dear Islamic brothers! The virtues of بِسۡمِ اللهِ الرَّحۡمٰنِ الرَّحِيۡم are too many to be mentioned. The one reading or listening to its virtues feels like reciting بِسۡمِ اللهِ الرَّحۡمٰنِ الرَّحِيۡم all the time. However, one can only gain this privilege if graced by Allah عَزَّوَجَلَّ. By the bestowment of Allah عَزَّوَجَلَّ, one of the ways of developing the habit of reciting بِسۡمِ اللهِ الرَّحۡمٰنِ الرَّحِيۡم is to make individual effort on each other remaining associated with the Madanī environment of Dawat-e-Islami. Indeed, individual effort has always played a vital role in Islamic preaching. All the Prophets عَلَيۡهِمُ السَّلَام including our Beloved Prophet Muhammad صَلَّى اللهُ تَعَالٰی عَلَيۡهِ وَاٰلِهٖ وَسَلَّم have made individual effort, calling people towards salvation.

اَلۡحَمۡدُ لِلّٰہ عَزَّوَجَلَّ, The preachers of Dawat-e-Islami are also acting upon the Sunnaĥ of making individual effort, brightening the candle of Prophet's devotion in the hearts of people. Sometimes, these preachers write to me as regards the blessings of their individual effort.

Individual effort inspired driver

Here is a summary of a letter I received from a devotee of Rasūl. In order to attend the weekly Sunnaĥ-Inspiring Ijtimā' of Dawat-e-Islami which is held every Thursday-night, thousands of Islamic brothers come to the Madanī Markaz of Dawat-e-Islami, Faīzān-e-Madīnaĥ, Bāb-ul-Madīnaĥ Karachi, via buses which are parked at a particular place.

While passing the parking area, I noticed that a bus-driver was smoking opium listening to songs in his empty bus. I met the driver politely. اَلۡحَمۡدُ لِلّٰہ عَزَّوَجَلَّ, By the blessing of the meeting, he immediately turned the cassette player off and extinguished the opium-filled cigarette either. With a smile, I gave him a Sunnaĥ-Inspiring speech audio-cassette namely '*The First Night in Grave*' which he played instantly. I also sat with him to listen to the speech as listening to speech with others is a useful way to persuade them. اَلۡحَمۡدُ لِلّٰہ عَزَّوَجَلَّ, Impressed by listening to the speech, he repented of his sins and came to Faīzān-e-Madīnaĥ with me to attend the Ijtimā'.

صَلُّوۡا عَلَی الۡحَبِیۡب صَلَّی اللّٰهُ تَعَالٰی عَلٰی مُحَمَّد

Gift of speech-cassettes

Dear Islamic brothers! Did you realize how effective and useful individual effort is! We should preach to every Muslim individually and persuade them to offer Ṣalāĥ. Whenever you come to attend the Ijtimā' etc. by bus or wagon, you should request the driver as well as the conductor to attend the Ijtimā'. If they do not get prepared, give them a CD/DVD/audio cassette with a request to listen to it. Take the cassette back from them after they have listened and give another cassette.

Make every possible effort to take song CDs/DVDs/cassettes from them and get speeches dubbed into those cassettes and then return them. In this way, at least a few sinful cassettes will be wiped out, اِنْ شَآءَاللّٰه عَزَّوَجَلَّ. One should never give up making individual effort and advising others. Allah عَزَّوَجَلَّ has said in Sūraĥ Aż-Żāriyāt, verse 55 part 27:

وَ ذَكِّرْ فَاِنَّ الذِّكْرٰى تَنْفَعُ الْمُؤْمِنِيْنَ ﴿۵۵﴾

And advise, for advice benefits the Muslims.

[Kanz-ul-Īmān (Translation of Quran)]

Reward is certain even if others do not accept advice

Even if someone does not accept what we preach to him, we will still be rewarded for calling him towards righteousness, اِنْ شَآءَاللّٰه عَزَّوَجَلَّ. Ḥujjat-ul-Islam Sayyidunā Imām Muhammad Ghazālī عَلَيْهِ رَحْمَةُ اللّٰهِ الْوَالِى has stated in '*Mukāshafa-tul-Qulūb*', 'Sayyidunā Mūsā عَلٰى نَبِيِّنَا وَ عَلَيْهِ الصَّلٰوةُ وَالسَّلَام once humbly asked, 'O Allah عَزَّوَجَلَّ! What is the reward for the person who calls his brother, ordering him to do righteous deeds and preventing him from evil?' Allah عَزَّوَجَلَّ said, 'For every sentence he utters, I record (for him) the reward of one year's worship, and I have Ḥayā (shyness) to punish him in Hell.' *(Mukāshafa-tul-Qulūb, pp. 48)*

Better than kingship of entire world

If someone is inspired to offer Ṣalāĥ and adopt Sunnaĥ by virtue of the individual effort made by you, you will also be greatly rewarded. The Holy Prophet صَلَّى اللّٰهُ تَعَالٰى عَلَيْهِ وَاٰلِهٖ وَسَلَّم has stated, '(If) Allah عَزَّوَجَلَّ blesses someone with (true) guidance by you, it is better than the kingship of the entire world for you.' *(Al-Jāmi'-uṣ-Ṣaghīr, pp. 444, Ḥadīš 7219)*

Lethal poison turned harmless

Some fire worshippers once asked Sayyidunā Khālid Bin Walīd رَضِىَ اللّٰهُ تَعَالٰى عَنْهُ to show them any such sign that would make the truthfulness of Islam evident to them. He رَضِىَ اللّٰهُ تَعَالٰى عَنْهُ asked for a deadly poison. After the poison was brought, he recited بِسْمِ اللّٰهِ الرَّحْمٰنِ الرَّحِيْم and consumed it.

By the blessings of بِسْمِ اللّٰه the deadly poison caused him no harm. Seeing this, the fire worshippers spontaneously proclaimed, 'Islam is the truest religion.' *(Tafsīr Kabīr, vol. 1, pp. 155)*

صَلُّوْا عَلَى الْحَبِيْب صَلَّى اللهُ تَعَالٰى عَلٰى مُحَمَّد

Dear Islamic brothers! As the above parable shows, by reciting بِسْمِ اللهِ الرَّحْمٰنِ الرَّحِيْم before eating and drinking anything, one remains safe from the harmful ingredients of the food (if any) besides attaining a great reward in the Hereafter, اِنْ شَآءَاللّٰه عَزَّوَجَلَّ.

This incident of the poison not harming Sayyidunā Khālid Bin Walīd رَضِىَ اللّٰهُ تَعَالٰى عَنْهُ is also found in other books with some slight changes; it is also possible that this saintly miracle may have taken place more than once.

Lethal poison

When Sayyidunā Khālid Bin Walīd رَضِىَ اللّٰهُ تَعَالٰى عَنْهُ along with his army camped in a place called Hīraĥ, his companions said, 'We fear that these 'Ajamīs (non-Arabs) might poison you; so please be cautious.' He رَضِىَ اللّٰهُ تَعَالٰى عَنْهُ responded, 'Let me see how deadly the poison of these 'Ajamīs is! Give the poison to me.' The companions did as were asked. Reciting بِسْمِ اللّٰه, Sayyidunā Khālid Bin Walīd رَضِىَ اللّٰهُ تَعَالٰى عَنْهُ consumed the poison but remained quite unharmed, اَلْحَمْدُلِلّٰه عَزَّوَجَلَّ.

According to the narration reported by 'Kalbī', there was a non-Muslim priest whose name was 'Abdul Masīḥ. He had such a deadly poison that the person drinking it was certain to die within an hour.

When informed about it, Sayyidunā Khālid Bin Walīd رَضِىَ اللّٰهُ تَعَالٰى عَنْهُ asked for that poison. The non-Muslim priest brought the poison which Sayyidunā Khālid Bin Walīd consumed reciting بِسْمِ اللهِ وَ بِاللهِ رَبِّ الْاَرْضِ وَالسَّمَآءِ بِسْمِ اللهِ الَّذِىْ لَايَضُرُّ مَعَ اسْمِهٖ دَاءٌ in the presence of the priest! Upon seeing this, 'Abdul Masīḥ addressed his nation saying, 'O my nation! To my utter astonishment, he is still alive despite taking this lethal poison. It is now better for us to reconcile with them; or else they would certainly overpower us.'

This incident occurred during the caliphate of Sayyidunā Abū Bakr Ṣiddīq رَضِىَ اللهُ تَعَالٰى عَنْهُ *(Ḥujjatullāhi-'alal-'Ālamīn, pp. 617)*

May Allah عَزَّوَجَلَّ have mercy on them and forgive us without accountability for their sake!

صَلُّوْا عَلَى الْحَبِيْب صَلَّى اللّٰهُ تَعَالٰى عَلٰى مُحَمَّد

Dear Islamic brothers! Did you see the special favour of Allah عَزَّوَجَلَّ on Sayyidunā Khālid Bin Walīd رَضِىَ اللهُ تَعَالٰى عَنْهُ. It was indeed a divinely-bestowed saintly miracle of Sayyidunā Khālid Bin Walīd رَضِىَ اللهُ تَعَالٰى عَنْهُ that a deadly poison caused him no harm. There are countless types of saintly miracles one of which is to remain protected against deadly things. There have been several instances when poison and other harmful things did not cause any harm to the Auliyā of Allah عَزَّوَجَلَّ.

Fire or garden?

A heretic king once captured a saint رَحْمَةُ اللهِ تَعَالٰى عَلَيْه along with his companions and said in a threatening tone, 'Show some saintly miracle otherwise I will have you martyred along with all your companions.' Pointing towards some camel dung, the saint رَحْمَةُ اللهِ تَعَالٰى عَلَيْه said, 'Bring it and see what it is.' When the dung was brought, it had turned into the pieces of pure gold.

Then, picking up an empty bowl, he رَحْمَةُ اللهِ تَعَالٰى عَلَيْه spun it round and turned it upside down and then gave it to the king. The bowl was now full of water but despite it being turned upside down, not even a single drop of water fell from it. In spite of witnessing these two saintly miracles, the king said, 'All this is witchcraft and magic!' The king then ordered that fire be burned. When the flames shot high into the air, the saint and his companions jumped into the fire, taking the young prince with them. When the king saw his young son fall into the fire, he became extremely anxious.

After a short while, the prince was placed in the king's lap in such a state that there was an apple in his one hand and a pomegranate in the other. The king asked, 'Where were you, my son?' His son replied, 'I was in a garden.' Upon seeing this, the courtiers of the oppressive and heretic king said, 'All this is unfounded (and magic).' The king then said to the saint رَحْمَةُ اللهِ تَعَالٰى عَلَيْه, 'If you drink this cup of poison I will believe you.' The noble saint رَحْمَةُ اللهِ تَعَالٰى عَلَيْه repeatedly drank the cup of poison but remained unharmed. The poison just caused his clothes to tear each time. *(Ḥujjatullāĥi-'alal-'Ālamīn, pp. 211)*

May Allah عَزَّوَجَلَّ have mercy on them and forgive us without accountability for their sake!

Fānūs ban kay jis kī ḥifāẓat ĥawā karay
Woĥ sham'a kyā bujĥay jisay roshan Khudā karay

How can the candle be extinguished that the Almighty has lit
Even the wind becomes a chandelier of protection for it

صَلُّوْا عَلَى الْحَبِيْب صَلَّى اللهُ تَعَالٰى عَلٰى مُحَمَّد

Dear Islamic brothers! Without doubt, the greatness of Islamic saints and their saintly miracles cannot be expressed in words! Devotion to these saints is a prominent feature of Dawat-e-Islami, a global & non-political religious movement of the Quran and Sunnaĥ. Those associated with Dawat-e-Islami are blessed with such divine grace that one is left amazed.

Astonishing accident

On Sunday 26th Rabī'-un-Nūr 1420 A.H. (11 July, 1999) a preacher of Dawat-e-Islami, Muhammad Munīr Ḥusayn 'Aṭṭārī عَلَيْهِ رَحْمَةُ اللّٰهِ الْبَارِی (a resident of Islampura) was badly crushed beneath a lorry at noon on a busy highway in Lala Musa, a famous city of Punjab, Pakistan.

The accident was so tragic that the upper part of his body was separated from the lower part but still he was astonishingly alive and conscious enough to repeatedly recite اَلصَّلٰوةُ وَالسَّلَامُ عَلَيْكَ يَا رَسُوْلَ الله and لَآ اِلٰهَ اِلَّا اللهُ مُحَمَّدٌ رَّسُوْلُ اللهِ aloud. After the doctors of Lala Musa hospital expressed disappointment over the chances of him remaining alive, he was taken to Aziz Bhatti hospital in Gujrat city.

The Islamic brother taking him to hospital has sworn that اَلْحَمْدُ لِلّٰه عَزَّوَجَلَّ Muhammad Munīr Ḥusayn 'Aṭṭārī عَلَيْهِ رَحْمَةُ اللّٰهِ الْبَارِی kept reciting Ṣalāt-'Alan-Nabī ﷺ and Kalimaĥ Ṭayyibaĥ throughout the way. When the doctors of Aziz Bhatti hospital saw this Madanī scene, they were also amazed how he was still alive and conscious enough to repeatedly recite Kalimaĥ Ṭayyibaĥ and Ṣalāt-'Alan-Nabī & Salām. They remarked, 'We have never seen such a courageous and remarkable man ever before!'

After a short while, Muhammad Munīr Ḥusayn 'Aṭṭārī, a fortunate devotee of Rasūl, desperately offered his heartfelt pleading in the court of the Beloved Prophet صَلَّى اللّٰهُ تَعَالٰى عَلَيْهِ وَاٰلِهٖ وَسَلَّم in these words:

Yā Rasūlallāĥ صَلَّى اللّٰهُ تَعَالٰى عَلَيْهِ وَاٰلِهٖ وَسَلَّم *please come!*
Yā Rasūlallāĥ صَلَّى اللّٰهُ تَعَالٰى عَلَيْهِ وَاٰلِهٖ وَسَلَّم *please help me!*
Yā Rasūlallāĥ صَلَّى اللّٰهُ تَعَالٰى عَلَيْهِ وَاٰلِهٖ وَسَلَّم *please forgive me!*

After this, he recited لَآ اِلٰهَ اِلَّا اللّٰهُ مُحَمَّدٌ رَّسُوْلُ اللّٰهِ and his soul left his body, blessing him with martyrdom. According to Islamic jurisprudence, the Muslim who has passed away in an accident is a martyr.

May Allah عَزَّوَجَلَّ have mercy on him and forgive us without accountability for his sake!

Waking Muslims for Ṣalāt-ul-Fajr is Sunnaĥ

Dear Islamic brothers! This incident was published in many newspapers at that time. اَلْحَمْدُ لِلّٰه عَزَّوَجَلَّ, The martyr of Dawat-e-Islami, Muhammad Munīr Ḥusayn 'Aṭṭārī عَلَيْهِ رَحْمَةُ اللّٰهِ الْبَارِى was a responsible preacher of Dawat-e-Islami and had returned from a Sunnaĥ-Inspiring Madanī Qāfilaĥ of Rasūl's devotees just a day before the accident. The deceased would do Ṣadā-e-Madīnaĥ daily. In the Madanī environment of Dawat-e-Islami, waking Muslims for Ṣalāt-ul-Fajr is referred to as Ṣadā-e-Madīnaĥ. اَلْحَمْدُ لِلّٰه عَزَّوَجَلَّ, Countless fortunate Islamic brothers act upon this Sunnaĥ. Waking Muslims for Ṣalāt-ul-Fajr is also a Sunnaĥ as obvious from the following narration.

Sayyidunā Abū Bakraĥ رَضِىَ اللّٰهُ تَعَالٰى عَنْه (who was a companion from the tribe of Banī Šaqīf) has stated, 'I went for Ṣalāt-ul-Fajr with the Beloved and Blessed Prophet صَلَّى اللّٰهُ تَعَالٰى عَلَيْهِ وَاٰلِهٖ وَسَلَّم. When he صَلَّى اللّٰهُ تَعَالٰى عَلَيْهِ وَاٰلِهٖ وَسَلَّم passed by a sleeping person, he would call him for Ṣalāĥ or wake him up with his blessed foot.' *(Sunan Abī Dāwūd, vol. 2, pp. 33, Ḥadīš 1264)*

Who can wake others with foot?

The fortunate brothers doing Ṣadā-e-Madīnaĥ attain the reward of practicing a Sunnaĥ, اَلْحَمْدُ لِلّٰه عَزَّوَجَلَّ. Remember! Not everyone is permitted to wake up a sleeping person with foot. Only a pious and elderly person can wake up the sleeping person with foot as the sleeping one would not resent it. However, there is no harm in waking up a sleeping person by gently pressing his feet with hands provided there is no Shar'ī prohibition.

Indeed, if our Beloved and Blessed Prophet صَلَّى اللّٰهُ تَعَالٰى عَلَيْهِ وَاٰلِهٖ وَسَلَّم awakens a devotee of his with his blessed foot, the sleeping fortune of that devotee will be awoken. And if he صَلَّى اللّٰهُ تَعَالٰى عَلَيْهِ وَاٰلِهٖ وَسَلَّم places his blessed foot over the head, eyes or chest of a fortunate one, by Allah عَزَّوَجَلَّ, he صَلَّى اللّٰهُ تَعَالٰى عَلَيْهِ وَاٰلِهٖ وَسَلَّم will bless that person with comfort and peace in the worldly life as well as in the afterlife.

Aīk ṫhokar mayn Uḥud kā zalzalaĥ jātā raĥā
Rakĥtī ĥayn kitnā waqār اَللّٰهُ اَكْبَر ayṙiyān

In one kick the tremor of Uḥud died down
How great power the blessed heels own

Yeĥ dil yeĥ jigar ĥay yeĥ ānkĥain yeĥ sar ĥay
Jidĥar chāĥo rakĥo qadam Jān-e-'Ālam صَلَّى اللّٰهُ تَعَالٰى عَلَيْهِ وَاٰلِهٖ وَسَلَّم

Place your foot wherever you wish, O Prophet صَلَّى اللّٰهُ تَعَالٰى عَلَيْهِ وَاٰلِهٖ وَسَلَّم *dear*
My heart, eyes and head are all in wait here

صَلُّوْا عَلَى الْحَبِيْب صَلَّى اللّٰهُ تَعَالٰى عَلٰى مُحَمَّد

Excellence of reciting Kalimaĥ at time of death

اَلْحَمْدُ لِلّٰه عَزَّوَجَلَّ, It seems Muhammad Munīr Ḥusayn Aṭṭārī's services to Dawat-e-Islami have born fruit as he was granted the privilege of reciting Kalimaĥ Ṭayyibaĥ in the last moments of his life. Indeed the one blessed with reciting Kalimaĥ at the time of his death will attain salvation in the afterlife. The Prophet of Raḥmaĥ, the Intercessor of Ummaĥ, the Owner of Jannaĥ صَلَّى اللّٰهُ تَعَالٰى عَلَيْهِ وَاٰلِهٖ وَسَلَّم has stated, 'The one whose last words are لَآ اِلٰهَ اِلَّا اللّٰه will enter Paradise.' *(Sunan Abī Dāwūd, vol. 3, pp. 132, Ḥadīš 3116)*

Fazl-o-karam jis per bĥī ĥuwā
Us nay martay-dam Kalimaĥ
Pařĥ liyā aur Jannat mayn gayā لَآ اِلٰہَ اِلَّا اللہ

At the time of death, whoever recites Kalimaĥ
Will enter Paradise by divine Raḥmaĥ

صَلُّوۡا عَلَى الۡحَبِيۡب صَلَّى اللهُ تَعَالٰى عَلٰى مُحَمَّد

A strong & healthy Satan

Two Satans once met each other. One of them was strong and healthy while the other was weak and feeble. The healthy Satan asked the feeble one, 'Brother! Why are you so weak?' He replied, 'I am (deputed) to be with such a pious person who recites بِسۡمِ اللّٰہ before entering his house, eating and drinking anything; so I have to stay away from him but, my dear, you are very strong and healthy; what is the secret behind it?'

The fat Satan replied, 'I am appointed to be with such a heedless person who does not recite بِسۡمِ اللّٰہ before entering his house and eating & drinking anything, so I take part in all of his activities and I keep riding him as one rides an animal (and this is the only secret of my good health).' *(Asrār-ul-Fātiḥaĥ, pp. 155)*

Names of 9 Satans and their tasks

Dear Islamic brothers! We have learnt from the foregoing narration that if we desire blessings in our acts with protection from satanic involvement in them, we should always recite بِسۡمِ اللّٰہ before commencing every permissible act. Otherwise the accursed Satan will get involved in every act. Satan has a lot of offspring that have particular (satanic) duties.

'Allāmaĥ Ibn Ḥajar 'Asqalānī قُدِّسَ سِرُّہُ الرَّبَّانِی has quoted that Amīr-ul-Mūminīn, Sayyidunā 'Umar Fārūq A'ẓam رَضِیَ اللّٰہُ تَعَالٰی عَنۡہُ has stated that Satan has 9 offspring:

(1) Zalītūn (2) Wašīn (3) Laqūs (4) A'wān (5) Ĥaffāf (6) Murraĥ (7) Musawwiṭ (8) Dāsīm (9) Walĥān

1. **Zalītūn** is appointed at marketplaces where he places his flag.
2. **Wašīn** is appointed to make people suffer unforeseen problems.
3. **Laqūs** is appointed to fire worshippers.
4. **A'wān** is appointed to rulers.
5. **Ĥaffāf** is appointed to alcoholics.
6. **Murraĥ** is appointed to those singing songs and playing musical instruments.
7. **Musawwiṭ** is appointed to spread rumours. It makes people believe and spread rumours, keeping them unaware of the truth.
8. **Dāsīm** is appointed to houses. If a person does not recite بِسْمِ اللّٰه when stepping in his house, nor does he make Salām after he has entered, then this Satan engenders family discords, even causing divorce or Khulā or physical assault.
9. **Walĥān** is appointed to cause satanic deception in one's heart during Wuḍū, Ṣalāĥ and other acts of worship. *(Al-Munabbiĥāt, pp. 91)*

Solution to family discords

A renowned commentator of the Quran, Ḥakīm-ul-Ummat, Muftī Aḥmad Yār Khān عَلَيْهِ رَحْمَةُ الْمَنَّان has stated, 'When entering his house, one should recite بِسْمِ اللّٰهِ الرَّحْمٰنِ الرَّحِيْم and place the right foot first into the house. One should then say Salām to the household. If no one is present in house, one should say اَلسَّلَامُ عَلَيْكَ اَيُّهَا النَّبِيُّ وَرَحْمَةُ اللّٰهِ وَبَرَكَاتُهٗ. Some saints would recite بِسْمِ اللّٰهِ الرَّحْمٰنِ الرَّحِيْم and Sūraĥ Al-Ikhlāṣ as they entered their houses in the beginning of the day. This brings about harmony in the household preventing quarrel, and increases blessing in sustenance.' *(Mirāt-ul-Manājīḥ, vol. 6, pp. 9)*

Yā Ilāĥī عَزَّوَجَلَّ ĥar gĥaṛī Shayṭān say maḥfūẓ rakĥ
Day jagaĥ Firdaus mayn nīrān say maḥfūẓ rakĥ

O Almighty عَزَّوَجَلَّ! Keep us secured from Satan every moment
Give us an abode in Paradise and protect us from punishment

صَلُّوْا عَلَى الْحَبِيْب صَلَّى اللهُ تَعَالٰى عَلٰى مُحَمَّد

Do recite بِسۡمِ اللّٰہ before eating

It is a Sunnaĥ to recite بِسۡمِ اللّٰہ before eating and drinking (any permissible thing). Sayyidunā Ḥużayfaĥ رَضِیَ اللهُ تَعَالٰی عَنۡهُ has narrated that the Noble Rasūl صَلَّی اللهُ تَعَالٰی عَلَیۡهِ وَاٰلِهٖ وَسَلَّم has stated, 'The food on which بِسۡمِ اللّٰہ is not recited becomes Ḥalāl for Satan.' (In other words, Satan also joins in consuming the food before eating which بِسۡمِ اللّٰہ is not recited). *(Ṣaḥīḥ Muslim, vol. 2, pp. 172, Ḥadīš 2017)*

Save food from Satan

The food before eating which بِسۡمِ اللّٰہ is not recited contains no blessings. Sayyidunā Abū Ayyūb Anṣārī رَضِیَ اللهُ تَعَالٰی عَنۡهُ has narrated, 'We were once present in the blessed company of the Prophet of Raḥmaĥ, the Intercessor of Ummaĥ صَلَّی اللهُ تَعَالٰی عَلَیۡهِ وَاٰلِهٖ وَسَلَّم when food was served. In the beginning there was such blessing that we had never seen before, but towards the end, we observed no blessings. We asked the Holy Prophet صَلَّی اللهُ تَعَالٰی عَلَیۡهِ وَاٰلِهٖ وَسَلَّم, 'Yā Rasūlallāĥ صَلَّی اللهُ تَعَالٰی عَلَیۡهِ وَاٰلِهٖ وَسَلَّم, what is the reason for this?' He صَلَّی اللهُ تَعَالٰی عَلَیۡهِ وَاٰلِهٖ وَسَلَّم replied, 'All of us had recited بِسۡمِ اللّٰہ prior to eating, then a person who had not recited بِسۡمِ اللّٰہ sat down to eat, and Satan also ate with him.' *(Sharḥ-us-Sunnaĥ, vol. 6, pp. 62, Ḥadīš 2818)*

If one forgets to recite بِسۡمِ اللّٰہ ...

Umm-ul-Mūminīn, Sayyidatunā 'Āishaĥ Ṣiddīqaĥ رَضِیَ اللهُ تَعَالٰی عَنۡهَا has narrated that the Noble Prophet صَلَّی اللهُ تَعَالٰی عَلَیۡهِ وَاٰلِهٖ وَسَلَّم has stated, 'When a person eats food, he should mention the name of Allah عَزَّوَجَلَّ, i.e. recite بِسۡمِ اللّٰہ. If he forgets to recite بِسۡمِ اللّٰہ in the beginning, he should recite بِسۡمِ اللهِ اَوَّلَهٗ وَاٰخِرَهٗ.' *(Sunan Abī Dāwūd, vol. 3, pp. 356, Ḥadīš 3767)*

Satan threw up!

Sayyidunā Umayyaĥ Bin Makhshī رَضِیَ اللہُ تَعَالٰی عَنْہُ has stated, 'A person was eating food without reciting بِسْمِ اللّٰه in the presence of the Beloved and Blessed Prophet صَلَّی اللہُ تَعَالٰی عَلَیْہِ وَاٰلِہٖ وَسَلَّم. When he was about to eat the last morsel, he recalled and recited بِسْمِ اللهِ اَوَّلَهٗ وَاٰخِرَهٗ. (Seeing this) The Holy Prophet صَلَّی اللہُ تَعَالٰی عَلَیْہِ وَاٰلِہٖ وَسَلَّم said with a smile, 'Satan was also eating with this person. When he mentioned the name of Allah عَزَّوَجَلَّ, Satan spewed up what was in his stomach.' *(Sunan Abī Dāwūd, vol. 3, pp. 356, Ḥadīš 3768)*

صَلُّوْا عَلَى الْحَبِيْب صَلَّى اللهُ تَعَالٰى عَلٰى مُحَمَّد

Nothing is hidden from Blessed Eyes of Mustafa صَلَّی اللہُ تَعَالٰی عَلَیْہِ وَاٰلِہٖ وَسَلَّم

Dear Islamic brothers! One should recite بِسْمِ اللهِ الرَّحْمٰنِ الرَّحِيْم whenever one eats food. If someone eats without reciting بِسْمِ اللّٰه, a Satan named 'Qarīn' joins him in the meal. It is evident from the Ḥadīš narrated by Sayyidunā Umayyaĥ Bin Makhshī رَضِیَ اللہُ تَعَالٰی عَنْہُ that the blessed eyes of the Prophet of mankind, the Peace of our heart and mind, the most Generous and Kind صَلَّی اللہُ تَعَالٰی عَلَیْہِ وَاٰلِہٖ وَسَلَّم saw everything, which is why he صَلَّی اللہُ تَعَالٰی عَلَیْہِ وَاٰلِہٖ وَسَلَّم smiled upon seeing Satan's dismay.

A renowned commentator of the Quran, Ḥakīm-ul-Ummat, Muftī Aḥmad Yār Khān عَلَیْہِ رَحْمَۃُ الْمَنَّان has stated, 'The Holy Prophet صَلَّی اللہُ تَعَالٰی عَلَیْہِ وَاٰلِہٖ وَسَلَّم is able enough to see even hidden creatures. The Ḥadīš is very explicit in its meaning and does not require any elaboration or interpretation. As we do not eat the food in which a fly has fallen (and is still present in it), similarly, Satan cannot digest the food before eating which the name of Allah عَزَّوَجَلَّ is mentioned. Though the food thrown up by Satan is of no use to us, Satan falls sick and has to remain hungry, and the lost blessing of our food is restored. Thus, there is one advantage for us and two disadvantages for Satan.

It is also possible that Satan may not even eat with us in the future for fear that perhaps we would recite بِسْمِ اللّٰه during the meal and he would have to again vomit the food he has eaten. The person mentioned in the Ḥadīš was probably eating alone. Had he been eating in the company of the Beloved and Blessed Prophet صَلَّى اللهُ تَعَالٰى عَلَيْهِ وَاٰلِهٖ وَسَلَّم he would not have forgotten to recite بِسْمِ اللّٰه because the people present there used to recite بِسْمِ اللّٰه aloud and would instruct others to do the same.' *(Mirāt Sharḥ-e-Mishkāt, vol. 6, pp. 30)*

اَلْحَمْدُ لِلّٰه عَزَّوَجَلَّ, In the Madanī Qāfilaĥs of Dawat-e-Islami, Du'ās with بِسْمِ اللّٰه are often recited loudly both before and after the meal. One travelling with Madanī Qāfilaĥs often gets the privilege of learning Du'ās and Sunnaĥs. You should also routinely travel with Madanī Qāfilaĥs. Words cannot express the blessings of Madanī Qāfilaĥs of the devotees of Rasūl! Listen to one of such accounts and rejoice.

Ṣiddīq Akbar رَضِىَ اللهُ عَنْهُ performed Madanī operation

Here is a summary of the account given by a devotee of Rasūl: 'Our Sunnaĥ-Inspiring Madanī Qāfilaĥ travelled to Naka Khari (Baluchistan, Pakistan). One of the participants of the Qāfilaĥ had a migraine[1] because of four small lumps on his head. When the pain occurred, he would writhe in agony, causing the affected part of his face to turn black. One night, he was writhing in agony, so we gave him some painkillers and made him sleep. When he woke up in the morning, he was very happy. He told us, 'By the grace of Allah عَزَّوَجَلَّ, I was blessed with the vision of the Noble Prophet صَلَّى اللهُ تَعَالٰى عَلَيْهِ وَاٰلِهٖ وَسَلَّم and his four closest companions رَضِىَ اللهُ تَعَالٰى عَنْهُم in my dream. Pointing towards me, the Beloved and Blessed Prophet صَلَّى اللهُ تَعَالٰى عَلَيْهِ وَاٰلِهٖ وَسَلَّم said to Ṣiddīq Akbar رَضِىَ اللهُ تَعَالٰى عَنْهُ, 'Remove his headache.'

So the Holy Prophet's companion of the cave and the shrine, Sayyidunā Abū Bakr Ṣiddīq رَضِىَ اللهُ تَعَالٰى عَنْهُ performed a Madanī operation in such a way that he opened up my head, removed four black lumps from my brain and then said, 'Son, nothing will happen to you now.'

That brother was really cured. On his return from the Madanī Qāfilaĥ, when he went for a medical check up, the doctor exclaimed with wonder, 'Brother! This is amazing! All the four lumps have vanished from your brain!' Upon this, he tearfully mentioned his dream and the blessing of travelling with the Madanī Qāfilaĥ.' Highly impressed by listening to this, 12 members of hospital staff including some doctors made the intention of travelling with a 12-day Madanī Qāfilaĥ. Some doctors also intended to adorn their

[1] Migraine is a type of severe headache affecting only one side of the head.

faces with the symbol of devotion to the Beloved and Blessed Prophet صَلَّى اللهُ تَعَالٰى عَلَيْهِ وَاٰلِهٖ وَسَلَّم, i.e. the Sunnaĥ of beard.

Ĥay Nabī ﷺ kī naẓar Qāfilay wālon per
Āo sāray chalayn Qāfilay mayn chalo
Sīkĥnay Sunnatayn Qāfilay mayn chalo
Lūṫnay raḥmatayn Qāfilay mayn chalo

To learn Sunnaĥ and reap blessings, travel with Qāfilaĥ
To be blessed with mercy of Prophet ﷺ, travel with Qāfilaĥ

صَلُّوْا عَلَى الْحَبِيْب صَلَّى اللهُ تَعَالٰى عَلٰى مُحَمَّد

Dear Islamic brothers! This incident of a person being cured in the state of dream is not new. By the bestowment of Allah عَزَّوَجَلَّ, the Prophet of Raḥmaĥ, the Intercessor of Ummaĥ, the Owner of Jannaĥ صَلَّى اللهُ تَعَالٰى عَلَيْهِ وَاٰلِهٖ وَسَلَّم cures illnesses. Refresh your faith by listening to the following five accounts, about people being cured by virtue of dreams, narrated by Sayyidunā Imām Yūsuf Bin Ismā'īl Nabĥānī قُدِّسَ سِرُّهُ الرَّبَّانِي in the second volume of his renowned book entitled حُجَّةُ اللهِ عَلَى الْعٰلَمِيْن فِيْ مُعْجِزَاتِ سَيِّدِ الْمُرْسَلِيْن

1. Prophet ﷺ restored eyesight

Sayyidunā Muhammad Bin Mubārak Ḥarbī عَلَيْهِ رَحْمَةُ اللهِ الْقَوِى has reported, 'Alī Abul Kabīr عَلَيْهِ رَحْمَةُ اللهِ الْقَدِيْر was visually impaired. He once had a dream in which he beheld the Beloved and Blessed Rasūl صَلَّى اللهُ تَعَالٰى عَلَيْهِ وَاٰلِهٖ وَسَلَّم. The Holy Prophet صَلَّى اللهُ تَعَالٰى عَلَيْهِ وَاٰلِهٖ وَسَلَّم passed his cure-providing hand over the eyes of 'Alī Abul Kabīr. When he woke up in the morning, he had gained his eyesight!' *(Ḥujjatullāhi-'alal-'Ālamīn, vol. 2, pp. 526)*

Āńkĥ 'aṭā kī-jiye, us mayn ziyā dī-jiye
Jalwaĥ qarīb ā gayā tum pay karauřon Durūd

Bless me with insight so that I may behold your vision
May blessings be upon you in millions

صَلُّوْا عَلَى الْحَبِيْب صَلَّى اللهُ تَعَالٰى عَلٰى مُحَمَّد

2. Prophet ﷺ cured tumorous lumps

Sayyidunā Taqiyyuddīn Abū Muhammad 'Abdus Salām عَلَيْهِ رَحْمَةُ رَبِّ الْاَنَام has stated, 'My brother Ibrāĥīm had lumps in his throat and was in severe agony. He once had a dream in which he beheld the Holy Prophet صَلَّى اللهُ تَعَالٰى عَلَيْهِ وَاٰلِهٖ وَسَلَّم. (In his dream) He requested, 'O Beloved Prophet صَلَّى اللهُ تَعَالٰى عَلَيْهِ وَاٰلِهٖ وَسَلَّم! I have suffered from acute pain due to this illness.' The Prophet of Raḥmaĥ, the Intercessor of Ummaĥ صَلَّى اللهُ تَعَالٰى عَلَيْهِ وَاٰلِهٖ وَسَلَّم replied, 'Your plea has been listened to.' اَلْحَمْدُ لِلّٰه عَزَّوَجَلَّ, By the blessings of the Noble Prophet صَلَّى اللهُ تَعَالٰى عَلَيْهِ وَاٰلِهٖ وَسَلَّم, my brother was cured.' *(Ḥujjatullāĥi-'alal-'Ālamīn, vol. 2, pp. 526)*

Sar-e-bālīn unĥayn raḥmat kī adā lāyī ĥay
Ḥāl bigřā ĥay to bīmār kī ban āyī ĥay

He has come to his dying devotee
Manifesting his attribute of mercy

صَلُّوا عَلَى الْحَبِيب　　صَلَّى اللهُ تَعَالٰى عَلٰى مُحَمَّد

3. Prophet ﷺ cured asthma

A noble saint رَحْمَةُ اللهِ تَعَالٰى عَلَيْه has stated, 'I was seriously ill and was bedridden in my home. My elderly father رَحْمَةُ اللهِ تَعَالٰى عَلَيْه was also confined to bed with asthma on the upper floor of home. Neither I was able to go upstairs nor could my father come downstairs.

اَلْحَمْدُ لِلّٰه عَزَّوَجَلَّ, One night, I was fortunately blessed with the vision of the Holy Prophet صَلَّى اللهُ تَعَالٰى عَلَيْهِ وَاٰلِهٖ وَسَلَّم in my dream. I presented a pillow to the Holy Prophet صَلَّى اللهُ تَعَالٰى عَلَيْهِ وَاٰلِهٖ وَسَلَّم and he sat down leaning against it. I pleaded with the Noble Prophet صَلَّى اللهُ تَعَالٰى عَلَيْهِ وَاٰلِهٖ وَسَلَّم for the cure of my illness and that of my elderly father. Upon hearing my plea, he صَلَّى اللهُ تَعَالٰى عَلَيْهِ وَاٰلِهٖ وَسَلَّم went upstairs.

At the time of Ṣalāt-ul-Fajr, I heard sounds of someone groaning with pain. In fact, it was my respected father descending from upstairs. He came to me and said, 'Son, I have been blessed tonight with the bounty of the Beloved and Blessed Prophet صَلَّى اللهُ تَعَالٰى عَلَيْهِ وَاٰلِهٖ وَسَلَّم.' I responded, 'O beloved father! The Noble Prophet صَلَّى اللهُ تَعَالٰى عَلَيْهِ وَاٰلِهٖ وَسَلَّم had already blessed this sinner [me] before he صَلَّى اللهُ تَعَالٰى عَلَيْهِ وَاٰلِهٖ وَسَلَّم went upstairs to shower you with bounties.'

اَلْحَمْدُلِلّٰہِ عَلٰی اِحْسَانِہٖ, We both regained health by virtue of the blessings of the Beloved Prophet صَلَّی اللّٰہُ تَعَالٰی عَلَیۡہِ وَاٰلِہٖ وَسَلَّم.' *(Ḥujjatullāĥi-'alal-'Ālamīn, vol. 2, pp. 527)*

Marīẓān-e-jaĥān ko tum shifā daytay ĥo dam bĥar mayn
Khudārā dard kā ĥo mayray darmān Yā Rasūlallāĥ ﷺ

You cure the ill of the world within an instant, Yā Rasūlallāĥ ﷺ
Please remove my worries and troubles for the sake of Allah

صَلُّوْا عَلَى الْحَبِيْب صَلَّى اللّٰهُ تَعَالٰى عَلٰى مُحَمَّد

4. Prophet ﷺ cured leprosy

Sayyidunā Shaykh Abū Isḥāq عَلَیۡہِ رَحۡمَۃُ اللّٰہِ الرَّزَّاق has stated, 'I had a spot of leprosy on my shoulder. اَلْحَمْدُ لِلّٰہ عَزَّوَجَلَّ, In my dream I was blessed with the vision of the Holy Prophet صَلَّی اللّٰہُ تَعَالٰی عَلَیۡہِ وَاٰلِہٖ وَسَلَّم. I mentioned my disease so the Prophet of Raḥmaĥ, the Intercessor of Ummaĥ صَلَّی اللّٰہُ تَعَالٰی عَلَیۡہِ وَاٰلِہٖ وَسَلَّم passed his blessed hand over my shoulder. When I awoke in the morning, I had been cured of leprosy, اَلْحَمْدُ لِلّٰہ عَزَّوَجَلَّ.' *(Ḥujjatullāĥi-'alal-'Ālamīn, vol. 2, pp. 531)*

Marz-e-'iṣyān kī taraqqī say ĥuwā ĥūn jān balab
Mujĥ ko achchā kī-jiye ḥālat mayrī achchī nahīn

To the verge of death the disease of sins has led me
My condition is not good, please cure me

صَلُّوْا عَلَى الْحَبِيْب صَلَّى اللّٰهُ تَعَالٰى عَلٰى مُحَمَّد

5. Prophet ﷺ cured hand blisters

A noble saint رَحۡمَۃُ اللّٰہِ تَعَالٰی عَلَیۡہ has stated that Shaykh Ḥammād رَحۡمَۃُ اللّٰہِ تَعَالٰی عَلَیۡہ got blisters on his hand. The painful blisters had ruptured. The physicians unanimously gave their opinion that the hand should be amputated. Sayyidunā Ḥammād رَحۡمَۃُ اللّٰہِ تَعَالٰی عَلَیۡہ has stated, 'I spent that night in severe pain and restlessness on the roof of my home. I pleaded and made Du'ā in the court of Allah عَزَّوَجَلَّ for cure.

When I slept, my sleeping fortune awoke, blessing me the vision of the Holy Prophet صَلَّى اللهُ تَعَالٰى عَلَيْهِ وَاٰلِهٖ وَسَلَّم in dream. I pleaded, 'Yā Rasūlallāĥ صَلَّى اللهُ تَعَالٰى عَلَيْهِ وَاٰلِهٖ وَسَلَّم! Cure me of my hand blisters!' He صَلَّى اللهُ تَعَالٰى عَلَيْهِ وَاٰلِهٖ وَسَلَّم responded, 'Stretch out your hand.' I did as advised. The Beloved Rasūl صَلَّى اللهُ تَعَالٰى عَلَيْهِ وَاٰلِهٖ وَسَلَّم passed his blessed hand over it and said to me, 'Get up!' As I stood up, اَلْحَمْدُ لِلّٰه عَزَّوَجَلَّ, my hand blisters had been cured by the blessings of the Beloved Prophet صَلَّى اللهُ تَعَالٰى عَلَيْهِ وَاٰلِهٖ وَسَلَّم.' *(Ḥujjatullāĥi-'alal-'Ālamīn, vol. 2, pp. 528)*

Yeĥ marīz mar raĥā ĥay, tayray ĥāth mayn shifā ĥay
Ay Ṭabīb jald ānā, Madanī Madīnay wālay

This patient is dying and the cure is in your hand, O healer!
Come sooner, O sovereign of Madīnaĥ, come sooner

صَلُّوْا عَلَى الْحَبِيْب صَلَّى اللهُ تَعَالٰى عَلٰى مُحَمَّد

Satanic deception

Only Allah عَزَّوَجَلَّ provides cure. By listening to the above parables, one is perplexed by such satanic deception as: Can anyone provide cure besides Allah عَزَّوَجَلَّ?

Cure for satanic deception

Without doubt, by one self, only Allah عَزَّوَجَلَّ provides cure (i.e. the real curer is only Allah عَزَّوَجَلَّ), but by the bestowment of Allah عَزَّوَجَلَّ, His servants can also provide cure. However, if anyone believes that so-and-so person can provide cure to others without the power given by Allah عَزَّوَجَلَّ, then such a person is certainly Kāfir [unbeliever]. Whether it is cure or medicine, no one can give even an iota to others without the power given by Allah عَزَّوَجَلَّ.

Every Muslim has the belief that whatever the Prophets عَلَيْهِمُ السَّلَام and saints رَحِمَهُمُ اللّٰهُ تَعَالٰى give (to others) they give it only by the power given to them by Allah عَزَّوَجَلَّ. Allah عَزَّوَجَلَّ forbid, if anyone has the belief that Allah عَزَّوَجَلَّ has not empowered any Prophet or Islamic saint to cure diseases or to grant anything, then such a person is denying the commandment of the Holy Quran.

Read verse 49 of Sūrah Āl-e-'Imrān in the 3rd part with its translation, اِنْ شَآءَاللّٰه عَزَّوَجَلَّ satanic deception will be eradicated and Satan will be unsuccessful and disappointed. Therefore, mentioning the blessed saying of Sayyidunā 'Īsā عَلَيْهِ السَّلَام, the Noble Quran states:

وَ اُبْرِئُ الْاَكْمَهَ وَ الْاَبْرَصَ وَ اُحْيِ الْمَوْتٰى بِاِذْنِ اللّٰهِ ۚ

And I give cure to the inborn blind and the leper, and I give life to the dead, by the command of Allah.

[Kanz-ul-Īmān (Translation of Quran)] (Part 3, Sūrah Āl-e-'Imrān, verse 49)

Did you notice? Sayyidunā 'Īsā عَلٰى نَبِيِّنَا وَعَلَيْهِ الصَّلٰوةُ وَالسَّلَام is clearly and openly proclaiming that he gives eyesight to the inborn blind, cures the lepers, and even resurrects the dead by virtue of the divinely-bestowed power. Various kinds of powers and authorities have been bestowed upon the Prophets عَلَيْهِمُ السَّلَام by Allah عَزَّوَجَلَّ. Further, by the blessing of the Prophets, powers are also given to the Auliyā, and they can also provide cure and bestow much more.

When Sayyidunā 'Īsā عَلٰى نَبِيِّنَا وَعَلَيْهِ الصَّلٰوةُ وَالسَّلَام possesses such a high status [as mentioned in the Quranic verse], just imagine how phenomenal the status of the Beloved and Blessed Mustafa صَلَّى اللّٰهُ تَعَالٰى عَلَيْهِ وَاٰلِهٖ وَسَلَّم would be, who is the sovereign of all Prophets including even Syyiduna 'Īsā عَلٰى نَبِيِّنَا وَعَلَيْهِ الصَّلٰوةُ وَالسَّلَام!

Remember that the Noble Prophet صَلَّى اللّٰهُ تَعَالٰى عَلَيْهِ وَاٰلِهٖ وَسَلَّم possesses all the virtues of all Prophets and those of the entire creation. In fact, whoever has got any favour has got it by virtue of the Beloved and Blessed Prophet صَلَّى اللّٰهُ تَعَالٰى عَلَيْهِ وَاٰلِهٖ وَسَلَّم

So we have learnt that if Sayyidunā 'Īsā عَلَيْهِ السَّلَام can cure the ill, give eyesight to the blind, and resurrect the dead, the Holy Prophet Muhammad صَلَّى اللّٰهُ تَعَالٰى عَلَيْهِ وَاٰلِهٖ وَسَلَّم can give all these favours (to his devotees) to even a greater degree.

صَلُّوْا عَلَى الْحَبِيْب صَلَّى اللّٰهُ تَعَالٰى عَلٰى مُحَمَّد

76,000 Virtues

It is narrated by Sayyidunā Ibn Mas'ūd رَضِیَ اللّٰہُ تَعَالٰی عَنۡہُ that the Prophet of mankind, the Peace of our heart and mind, the most Generous and Kind صَلَّی اللّٰہُ تَعَالٰی عَلَیۡہِ وَاٰلِہٖ وَسَلَّم has stated, 'One who recites بِسْمِ اللّٰهِ الرَّحْمٰنِ الرَّحِيْم, Allah عَزَّوَجَلَّ will record 4,000 virtues in his book of deeds for very letter, forgive 4,000 of his sins and raise his rank by 4,000 degrees.' *(Firdaus-ul-Akhbār, vol. 4, pp. 26, Ḥadīš 5573)*

Dear Islamic brothers! Rejoice! The immense mercy of Allah عَزَّوَجَلَّ is beyond imagination! Let's compute: بِسْمِ اللّٰهِ الرَّحْمٰنِ الرَّحِيْم consists of 19 letters. Therefore, by reciting بِسْمِ اللّٰهِ الرَّحْمٰنِ الرَّحِيْم once, one will receive 76 thousand virtues, his 76 thousand sins will be forgiven, and his rank will be raised by 76 thousand degrees, وَاللّٰهُ ذُوالْفَضْلِ الْعَظِيْم

Wisdom in not reciting الرَّحْمٰنِ الرَّحِيْم at time of slaughter

Whilst mentioning the infinite mercy of Allah عَزَّوَجَلَّ, Muftī Aḥmad Yār Khān عَلَيْهِ رَحْمَةُ الْمَنَّان has stated, 'Ponder over the fact that بِسْمِ اللّٰهِ الرَّحْمٰنِ الرَّحِيْم is not written in Sūraĥ At-Taubaĥ. Similarly, complete بِسْمِ اللّٰه is not recited at the time of the slaughter of an animal; instead, just 'بِسْمِ اللّٰهِ اَللّٰهُ اَكْبَر' is recited. Have you ever pondered as to what the wisdom behind this is? The wisdom is that the whole Sūraĥ At-Taubaĥ, from start to finish, is about Jihad [war] and killing, which is wrath for the unbelievers. Likewise, the life of the animal is taken at the time of its slaughter, which is also a moment of wrath and coercion. Therefore, one is prevented from mentioning mercy on this occasion.

سُبْحٰنَ اللّٰه عَزَّوَجَلَّ! Hence whoever [makes a habit of reciting] complete بِسْمِ اللّٰه, i.e. بِسْمِ اللّٰهِ الرَّحْمٰنِ الرَّحِيْم will be protected from divine wrath, اِنْ شَآءَاللّٰه عَزَّوَجَلَّ

(Tafsīr-e-Na'īmī, vol. 1, pp. 43)

صَلُّوْا عَلَى الْحَبِيْب صَلَّى اللّٰهُ تَعَالٰى عَلٰى مُحَمَّد

Wisdom in 19 letters of بِسْمِ اللّٰهِ الرَّحْمٰنِ الرَّحِيْم

The number of the letters in بِسْمِ اللّٰهِ الرَّحْمٰنِ الرَّحِيْم is 19 and so is the number of the punishment-inflicting angels in Hell. Thus it is hoped that the punishment from each angel will be averted by the blessing of every letter of بِسْمِ اللّٰهِ الرَّحْمٰنِ الرَّحِيْم.

Another excellence is that day and night consist of 24 hours 5 of which are devoted to the five daily Ṣalāĥ, whereas for the remaining 19 hours, 19 letters of بِسْمِ اللّٰهِ الرَّحْمٰنِ الرَّحِيْم have been granted.

Thus every hour of the one who keeps reciting بِسْمِ اللّٰهِ الرَّحْمٰنِ الرَّحِيْم will be considered to have been spent in worship and the sins of each hour will be forgiven, اِنْ شَآءَاللّٰه عَزَّوَجَلَّ *(Tafsīr Kabīr, vol. 1, pp. 156)*

Relief from torment of grave

Once Sayyidunā 'Īsā عَلٰی نَبِیِّنَا وَ عَلَیْهِ الصَّلٰوۃُ وَالسَّلَام passed by a grave and noticed that the buried person was being punished. After a while, when he passed by it again, he saw that the grave was shining from the inside, and divine mercy was being showered on it.

Astonished, Sayyidunā 'Īsā عَلٰی نَبِیِّنَا وَ عَلَیْهِ الصَّلٰوۃُ وَالسَّلَام requested in the court of Allah عَزَّوَجَلَّ that the secret behind this be told to him. Allah عَزَّوَجَلَّ said, 'O 'Īsā (عَلَیْهِ السَّلَام)! This person was being punished because he was a grave sinner. When he died, he left his wife pregnant who gave birth to a baby boy. Today, his boy was sent to a Madrasaĥ where the teacher made him recite بِسْمِ اللّٰه. I had Ḥayā (shyness) to punish the man under the earth whose son is mentioning My name upon the earth.' *(Tafsīr Kabīr, vol. 1, pp. 155)*

May Allah عَزَّوَجَلَّ have mercy on him and forgive us without accountability for his sake!

Ay Khudā-e-Mustafa mayn tayrī raḥmataun pay qurbān
Ĥo karam say mayrī bakhshish, baṭufail-e-Shāĥ-e-Jīlān رَحْمَةُ اللّٰهِ تَعَالٰی عَلَیْه

Your mercy is infinite, O Rab of Mustafa
Forgive me for the sake of Shāĥ-e-Jīlān رَحْمَةُ اللّٰهِ تَعَالٰی عَلَیْه

سُبْحٰنَ اللّٰه عَزَّوَجَلَّ! We should all teach our children to mention the name of Allah عَزَّوَجَلَّ from their early age instead of teaching them such words as 'Tata' or 'Papa.' Not only will the deceased parents receive the blessings of this, the one teaching and the one learning will also gain its immense blessings.

Therefore, whilst playing with your children, repeatedly say 'Allah' 'Allah' to them with the intention of teaching them. اِنْ شَآءَاللّٰه عَزَّوَجَلَّ, As soon as they are able to speak, they will be uttering the word 'Allah' before they learn to speak any other word.

Madanī upbringing of child

Sayyidunā Saĥl Bin 'Abdullāĥ Tustarī عَلَيْهِ رَحْمَةُ اللّٰهِ الْقَوِى has stated, 'When I was three years old I used to get up at night and see my maternal uncle, Sayyidunā Muhammad Bin Sawār عَلَيْهِ رَحْمَةُ اللّٰهِ الْغَفَّار offer Ṣalāĥ. One day, he asked me, 'Do you not remember Allah عَزَّوَجَلَّ who has created you?' I asked, 'How should I remember Him?' He replied, 'At night, before you go to sleep, imagine as if you are uttering the following sentences thrice in your heart without moving your tongue:

اَللّٰهُ مَعِى، اَللّٰهُ نَاظِرٌ اِلَىَّ، اَللّٰهُ شَاهِدِى

Allah عَزَّوَجَلَّ is with me, Allah عَزَّوَجَلَّ is watching me, Allah عَزَّوَجَلَّ is my witness[1].'

Sayyidunā Saĥl رَحْمَةُ اللّٰهِ تَعَالٰى عَلَيْه goes onto say: I recited these sentences for a few nights and then informed my uncle of this. He asked me to repeat them seven times. I did as was advised and informed him again after a few nights. He then instructed me to recite them eleven times, so I did as was instructed, and this time I felt the pleasure of those words in my heart. After a year passed, my uncle advised, 'Continue to recite what I have taught you until you reach your grave. اِنْ شَآءَاللّٰه عَزَّوَجَلَّ, This will benefit you in the worldly life as well as in the afterlife.'

Sayyidunā Saĥl Bin 'Abdullāĥ Tustarī عَلَيْهِ رَحْمَةُ اللّٰهِ الْقَوِى has further stated, 'Making Żikr in solitude, I continued to recite these words for many years until I felt its great spiritual

[1] If possible, write these sentences on a piece of paper and display it at such a place of the house, shop etc. where it can repeatedly come in your sight.

pleasure in my heart. One day, my uncle asked, 'O Saĥl! Can a person disobey Allah عَزَّوَجَلَّ, whereas Allah عَزَّوَجَلَّ is with him, sees him and is his witness? No, certainly not! Therefore, refrain from sins.'

Then, my respectable uncle got me admitted to a Madrasaĥ. As I did not want my practice of Żikr to be interrupted I persuaded my teacher to let me go home after he teaches me for an hour. اَلْحَمْدُلِلّٰه عَزَّوَجَلَّ, When I was six or seven years old, I had memorized the entire Quran. اَلْحَمْدُلِلّٰه عَزَّوَجَلَّ, I would keep fast every day and eat barley bread [at Saḥarī].

I kept on doing this practice up to the age of 12 years. When I was thirteen, I confronted a religious issue. To find a solution to the issue I took permission from my parents and travelled to Basra (Iraq). I consulted the scholars of Basra about my issue but none of them were able to give me a convincing reply, so I travelled to a place called 'Abbādān. I presented my issue to a renowned scholar of 'Abbādān, Sayyidunā Abū Ḥabīb Ḥamzaĥ Bin Abī 'Abdullāĥ 'Abbādānī قُدِّسَ سِرُّهُ الرَّبَّانِي who provided me with a satisfactory and convincing reply.

I remained in his company for a long time, enhancing my knowledge, gaining spiritual enlightenment and learning manners. I then moved to Tustar. In order to meet my needs, I would purchase one dirham's barley to make bread for me. Every night at the time of Saḥarī, I would eat a piece of bread, made of just 70 grams of saltless barley, without any curry.

This one dirham would be sufficient for me for an entire year. I then intended to eat once every three days. Then I started remaining hungry for 5 days, then for 7 days and then for 25 days (that is, I would eat once every 25 days). I continued to do this practice for 20 years. Later, I travelled and toured for many years. Then I again returned to Tustar where I would perform worship at night for as long as Allah عَزَّوَجَلَّ willed.

Sayyidunā Imām Aḥmad عَلَيْهِ رَحْمَةُ اللّٰهِ الْاَحَد has stated, 'I never saw Sayyidunā Saĥl Bin 'Abdullāĥ Tustarī عَلَيْهِ رَحْمَةُ اللّٰهِ الْقَوِی eat salt throughout his life.' *(Iḥyā-ul-'Ulūm, vol. 3, pp. 91)*

May Allah عَزَّوَجَلَّ have mercy on them and forgive us without accountability for their sake!

صَلُّوْا عَلَى الْحَبِيْب   صَلَّى اللّٰهُ تَعَالٰى عَلٰى مُحَمَّد

Dear Islamic brothers! Fortunate and wise are the parents who are more concerned about the betterment of their children's afterlife than their worldly life. Here is a summary of a faith-refreshing account of a wise mother who made 'individual effort' that finally led to the reform of her son's character. Read and rejoice!

Marvel of Dawat-e-Islami's Tarbiyyatī course

A devotee of Rasūl from Jhang (Pakistan) has related, 'My mother was ill from a long time. She had always longed for me to give up sins and get reformed. Since she very much liked Dawat-e-Islami, she provided me with the expenses and insistently sent me to Faīzān-e-Madīnaĥ, Dawat-e-Islami's global Madanī Markaz situated at Bāb-ul-Madīnaĥ, Karachi. She had also advised me to do Tarbiyyatī course there with the devotees of Rasūl in the merciful atmosphere of Faīzān-e-Madīnaĥ and make Du'ā for her recovery.

اَلْحَمْدُ لِلّٰه عَزَّوَجَلَّ, I came to Bāb-ul-Madīnaĥ, Karachi where I joined the Tarbiyyatī course and travelled with Madanī Qāfilaĥs. I also made Du'ā for my mother's recovery from her disease. When I returned home after the completion of the Tarbiyyatī course, I was overjoyed to see that my severely ill mother had recuperated from her disease by the blessings of the Du'ā made in Faīzān-e-Madīnaĥ during the Tarbiyyatī course.

اَلْحَمْدُ لِلّٰه عَزَّوَجَلَّ, By the blessings of the Tarbiyyatī course, I became steadfast in Ṣalāĥ and joined the Madanī environment of Dawat-e-Islami. I developed an enthusiasm to serve Sunnaĥ and to travel with Madanī Qāfilaĥs. It is my heartfelt desire that every member of my family adopt the Madanī environment of Dawat-e-Islami and that our problems be solved.'

Faīzān-e-Madīnaĥ mayn Allah عَزَّوَجَلَّ *kī raḥmat ĥay*
Ammī ko muyassar ab siḥḥat kī sa'ādat ĥay
Faīzān-e-Madīnaĥ mayn ānay ĥī kī barakat ĥay
Khūb aur bařĥī mujĥ ko Sunnat say maḥabbat ĥay

Mother has been cured and I have become a devotee of Sunnaĥ
By the grace of Allah عَزَّوَجَلَّ *and by the blessings of attending Faīzān-e-Madīnaĥ*

Those who make their children a devotee of the world preventing them from good company, seriously endanger their afterlife. At times, such people have regrets even in this world.

Preventing others from Madanī Qāfilaĥ causes harm

Making individual effort, a devotee of Rasūl (from Madīna-tul-Auliyā Ahmedabad, India) persuaded a young man to travel with a Madanī Qāfilaĥ but the father of the young man prevented him from the travel of religious education for fear of the loss of his worldly education. The young man was unfortunately deprived of the company of the devotees of Rasūl.

As a result, he adopted the company of some wicked friends, turning into an alcoholic. Now, his father realized his grave mistake and requested the same devotee of Rasūl to take his son with a Madanī Qāfilaĥ so that he might give up drinking. The devotee of Rasūl made individual effort again, but the young man had been so addicted to drinking and wicked company that he was no longer prepared to travel with the Madanī Qāfilaĥ. Parents should provide their children with a righteous and Madanī environment from their early age. Otherwise, if children become spoilt as a result of the wicked company, parents will end up regretful.

Once my[1] elder sister told me that an Islamic sister tearfully requested her to make Du'ā for the reform of her son's character. 'Alas, she said, 'I have myself spoiled my son! I enrolled him in the Ḥifẓ [Quranic memorization] class of Madrasa-tul-Madīnaĥ. When he came home after learning Sunnaĥs and etiquettes, he would tell them to us, but we would make fun of him. Disheartened, he eventually gave up going to Madrasa-tul-Madīnaĥ. Now, he has become a loafer due to the company of wicked friends. Coincidentally, I have joined the Madanī environment of Dawat-e-Islami. Now I deeply regret mocking him. Alas! What will become of me!'

صُحبتِ صالِح تُرا صالِح کُنَد   صُحبتِ طالِح تُرا طالِح کُنَد

(The company of the pious will make you pious, whereas that of the wicked will make you wicked).

---

[1] The author, Amīr-e-Aĥl-e-Sunnat دَامَتۡ بَرَکَاتُہُمُ الۡعَالِیَہ

House of beasts

Dear Islamic brothers! Sayyidunā Saĥl Bin 'Abdullāĥ Tustarī عَلَيْهِ رَحْمَةُ اللّٰهِ الْقَوِى was a Ṣiddīq (i.e. a saint from amongst the group of the highest rank). He would refrain from tastes and pleasures. He would not use salt in his food because the use of salt makes the food tasty. Indeed, even if many kinds of spices are added to food, it will remain tasteless unless salt is added to it.

It is also noteworthy that a specified amount of salt is essential for the human body, so this was actually a saintly miracle of Sayyidunā Saĥl Bin 'Abdullāĥ Tustarī عَلَيْهِ رَحْمَةُ اللّٰهِ الْقَوِى that he remained alive without consuming salt for a long time. His blessed house situated in Tustar used to be called 'Bayt-us-Sibā' (i.e. house of beasts) because many beasts (like lions, tigers etc.) would come to his house where he would feed meat to them.

During the ending stage of his life, he رَحْمَةُ اللّٰهِ تَعَالٰى عَلَيْه had become disabled but whenever it was time for Ṣalāĥ his disability would vanish, enabling him to offer his Ṣalāĥ. As soon as he finished Ṣalāĥ, he would become disabled again like before. *(Risāla-tul-Qushayriyyaĥ, pp. 387)*

May Allah عَزَّوَجَلَّ have mercy on him and forgive us without accountability for his sake!

صَلُّوْا عَلَى الْحَبِيْب صَلَّى اللّٰهُ تَعَالٰى عَلٰى مُحَمَّد

Cure for fever

It is narrated that a person once got fever. His respected teacher Shaykh Faqīĥ Walī 'Umar Bin Sa'īd عَلَيْهِ رَحْمَةُ اللّٰهِ الْمَجِيد went to visit him. Giving him a Ta'wīż [amulet], the Shaykh advised him not to unfold and see what the Ta'wīż contained. After the Shaykh left, he wore the Ta'wīż and was instantly cured of fever.

Amazed, he couldn't help seeing what the Ta'wīż contained. As he unfolded it he saw that بِسْمِ اللّٰهِ الرَّحْمٰنِ الرَّحِيْم was written on it. A satanic deception occurred to him that anyone could have written this! As soon as his reverence for his Shaykh diminished, his fever immediately recurred.

Worried, he went to his Shaykh and apologized for his mistake. The Shaykh again prepared a Ta'wīż and fastened it to his arm with his own blessed hands, curing the fever again instantly. Though the Shaykh had not prohibited him this time from unfolding and seeing the inside of the Ta'wīż, he himself refrained from doing so due to his previous experience. Eventually, when he unfolded it after a year, he saw that بِسۡمِ اللّٰہِ الرَّحۡمٰنِ الرَّحِیۡم was written on it.

May Allah عَزَّوَجَلَّ have mercy on him and forgive us without accountability for his sake!

Dear Islamic brothers! Indeed بِسۡمِ اللّٰہِ الرَّحۡمٰنِ الرَّحِیۡم contains immense blessings. It also has cures for diseases. The foregoing parable gives the lesson that if an Islamic saint ever prohibits someone even from any Mubāḥ (permissible) act, he should abstain from it even if he is unable to comprehend the wisdom behind it. Another lesson is that one should not unfold and see the inside of the Ta'wīż as one's reverence may be affected by this. Further, the Ta'wīż is folded in a special way and sometimes particular invocations are also recited whilst it is being folded. Therefore, unfolding and seeing it may reduce its benefits.

5 Madanī cures for fever

لَا یَرَوۡنَ فِیۡهَا شَمۡسًا وَّلَا زَمۡهَرِیۡرًا ﴿۱۳﴾

They will neither see the hot sunshine in it, nor the bitter cold.

[Kanz-ul-Īmān (Translation of Quran)] (Part 29, Sūraĥ Ad-Daĥr, verse 13)

1. Recite this blessed verse 7 times (with Ṣalāt-'Alan-Nabī ﷺ once before and after it) and then make *Dam*[1] (i.e. blow on the patient). اِنۡ شَآءَ اللّٰہ عَزَّوَجَلَّ, The severity of fever will be reduced, and the patient will feel tranquillity. (Note that it is not necessary to recite the translation of the verse).

2. Sayyidunā Imām Ja'far Ṣādiq رَضِیَ اللّٰہُ تَعَالٰی عَنۡہُ has stated, 'Recite Sūraĥ Al-Fātiḥaĥ 40 times (with Ṣalāt-'Alan-Nabī ﷺ once before and after it) and then make *Dam* (i.e. blow on) water and sprinkle some drops of this water on the face of the person suffering from fever. اِنۡ شَآءَ اللّٰہ عَزَّوَجَلَّ, Fever will be cured.'

---

[1] In this book, the word '*Dam*' has been used in the sense of a spiritual remedy with its pronunciation as 'dʌm.' It must not be pronounced as 'dæm.' Note that this word has been italicized in the whole book with its '*D*' capitalized. [Translator's Note]

3. When the Beloved and Blessed Prophet صَلَّى اللهُ تَعَالٰى عَلَيْهِ وَاٰلِهٖ وَسَلَّم had fever, Sayyidunā Jibrāīl عَلَيْهِ السَّلَام recited the following Du'ā and made *Dam*:

بِسْمِ اللّٰهِ اَرْقِيْكَ مِنْ كُلِّ دَآءٍ يُّؤْذِيْكَ
وَمِنْ شَرِّ كُلِّ نَفْسٍ اَوْ عَيْنِ حَاسِدٍ ط اَللّٰهُ يَشْفِيْكَ بِسْمِ اللّٰهِ اَرْقِيْكَ

Translation: With the name of Allah عَزَّوَجَلَّ I make *Dam* on you for every such disease that causes you harm, and (for your protection from) the evil of others and from the evil eye of the jealous. May Allah عَزَّوَجَلَّ cure you. I make *Dam* on you with the name of Allah عَزَّوَجَلَّ.

(Ṣaḥīḥ Muslim, pp. 1202, Ḥadīš 2186)

Recite the Du'ā in Arabic only (with Ṣalāt-'Alan-Nabī ﷺ once before and after it) and then make *Dam* on the patient of fever.

4. The person suffering from fever should frequently recite بِسْمِ اللّٰهِ الْكَبِيْرِ.

5. It is narrated in a blessed Ḥadīš, 'If anyone of you gets fever, sprinkle cold water on him in the morning for 3 days.' *(Al-Mustadrak, vol. 4, pp. 223, Ḥadīš 7438)*

صَلُّوْا عَلَى الْحَبِيْب صَلَّى اللّٰهُ تَعَالٰى عَلٰى مُحَمَّد

اَلْحَمْدُ لِلّٰه عَزَّوَجَلَّ, The Islamic brothers and sisters who are associated with Dawat-e-Islami, a global & non-political religious movement of the Quran and Sunnaĥ, are proud of being the devotees of the Beloved and Blessed Prophet صَلَّى اللهُ تَعَالٰى عَلَيْهِ وَاٰلِهٖ وَسَلَّم. At times, by the blessings of the Du'ā made during the Sunnaĥ-Inspiring Madanī Qāfilaĥs of Dawat-e-Islami in the company of the devotees of Rasūl, even the patients suffering from such diseases declared incurable by doctors get cured, regaining their lost happiness, اَلْحَمْدُ لِلّٰه عَزَّوَجَلَّ.

Eyesight restored

Once a preacher of Dawat-e-Islami from Liaqat colony, Hyderabad (Bāb-ul-Islam Sindh, Pakistan) invited a young man to travel with a Madanī Qāfilaĥ of Dawat-e-Islami. The young man, annoyed and upset, said, 'The operation of my mother's eyes has failed, because of which she has become blind. We are in extreme trouble, and you are asking me to travel with the Madanī Qāfilaĥ!'

Keeping his temper in check and continuing his individual effort, the preacher said in a sympathetic tone making Du'ā for his mother, 'May Allah عَزَّوَجَلَّ bless your mother with cure! What do the doctors say?' He replied, 'The doctors say that she cannot be cured even if taken to America for treatment.' Patting the young man's back sympathetically, the preacher said in a consoling tone, 'Brother! If doctors have disappointed you, why do you give up hope! Doctors cannot cure anyone. It is Allah عَزَّوَجَلَّ who cures everyone. The Du'ā of the traveller is accepted. If you travel with the Madanī Qāfilaĥ in the company of the devotees of Rasūl and make Du'ā for your mother over there, you will get its blessings, اِنْ شَآءَاللّٰه عَزَّوَجَلَّ.'

Impressed and inspired by the sincere individual effort of the preacher, the grieving young man travelled with a Madanī Qāfilaĥ during which he humbly made Du'ā for his mother. When he returned home after the Madanī Qāfilaĥ, he was overjoyed to see that his mother had regained her lost eyesight.

Lūtnay raḥmatayn Qāfilay mayn chalo
Sīkĥnay Sunnatayn Qāfilay mayn chalo
Chashm-e-bīnā milay sukĥ say jīnā milay
Pāo gey rāĥatayn Qāfilay mayn chalo

To reap mercies, travel with the Qāfilaĥ, to learn Sunnaĥs, travel with the Qāfilaĥ
To gain eyesight and peace in life, to find tranquillity, travel with the Qāfilaĥ

Dear Islamic brothers! The Holy Prophet صَلَّى اللّٰهُ تَعَالٰى عَلَيْهِ وَاٰلِهٖ وَسَلَّم has stated, 'Three types of Du'ās are accepted. There is no doubt about their acceptance.

1. The Du'ā made by an oppressed person.
2. The Du'ā made by a traveller.
3. The Du'ā made by a father for his son.' *(Jāmi' Tirmiżī, vol. 5, pp. 280, Ḥadīš 3459)*

If one is travelling with a Madanī Qāfilaĥ in the company of the devotees of Rasūl, his Du'ā is more likely to be accepted. This parable also shows that tolerance is highly needed for individual effort. Even if you are rebuked or beaten, you should still continue to make individual effort without getting disappointed. If you become angry or impolite, then you would cause a great religious loss. Do not give up advising others, as advising will definitely bear fruit. Allah عَزَّوَجَلَّ has declared in verse 55 of Sūraĥ Aż-Żāriyāt in part 27:

وَ ذَكِّرْ فَإِنَّ الذِّكْرٰى تَنْفَعُ الْمُؤْمِنِيْنَ ﴿۵۵﴾

And advise, that the admonition benefits the believers.

[Kanz-ul-Īmān (Translation of Quran)]

Cure for headache

Caesar of Rome once sent a letter to Amīr-ul-Mūminīn Sayyīdunā 'Umar Fārūq A'ẓam رَضِىَ اللّٰهُ تَعَالٰى عَنْهُ. In his letter, he mentioned, 'I have chronic headache; if you have any medicine for this, please send it to me.'

Amīr-ul-Mūminīn Sayyīdunā 'Umar Fārūq A'ẓam رَضِىَ اللّٰهُ تَعَالٰى عَنْهُ sent him a cloth-cap. Whenever Caesar of Rome wore that cap his headache would be relieved, and whenever he removed the cap, his headache would reoccur. Amazed, he eventually unstitched the cap and found a piece of paper on which بِسْمِ اللّٰهِ الرَّحْمٰنِ الرَّحِيْم was written.

(Asrār-ul-Fātiḥaĥ, pp. 163; Tafsīr Kabīr, vol. 1, pp. 155)

Method of treatment by بِسْمِ اللّٰه

Dear Islamic brothers! We have learnt from the foregoing parable that if anyone has a headache, he should write بِسْمِ اللّٰهِ الرَّحْمٰنِ الرَّحِيْم on a piece of paper or have it written, and then fasten it as a Ta'wīż on his head. Write using permanent ink (such as a ball point pen/marker) and leave the circles of ه and all the three م of بِسْمِ اللّٰهِ الرَّحْمٰنِ الرَّحِيْم open.

A principle of Ta'wīż writing is that when writing an Āyaĥ or any particular text, the circle of every circle-containing letter should remain open, e.g. ط ظ ہ ھ ص ض و م ف ق It is not necessary to put diacritical marks.

After you have written it, wrap it in a wax paper or any plastic coating, then encase it in a leather covering or a piece of cloth and fasten it on the head. Those who adorn their heads with the crown of a turban can sew the Ta'wīż inside the cap of their turban. Similarly, Islamic sisters can also sew it on that part of their scarf or veil which rests on the head. If this is done with a firm belief, the headache will be relieved, اِنْ شَآءَاللّٰہ عَزَّوَجَلَّ.

It is not permissible for males to wear a Ta'wīż kept in a gold or silver or any other metallic casing. Likewise, it is also impermissible and a sin for males to wear a chain made of any metal whether or not the chain contains a Ta'wīż.

Further, it is not permissible for males to wear a locket, bracelet or bangle made of gold, silver, steel or any type of metal, whether or not anything is inscribed on it, or even if the blessed name of Allah عَزَّوَجَلَّ or Kalimaĥ Ṭayyibaĥ etc. is inscribed. Women, however, are permitted to wear a Ta'wīż encased in a silver or gold box (i.e. a type of locket).

6 Cures for ache in half-head

1. If somebody has a headache in one half of his head, recite Sūraĥ Al-Ikhlāṣ once (with Ṣalāt-'Alan-Nabī ﷺ once before and after it) and make *Dam* [i.e. blow on him]. If necessary, repeat the *Dam* in this way 3 times, 7 times or 11 times. اِنْ شَآءَاللّٰہ عَزَّوَجَلَّ, The ache will be relieved before the *Dam* is repeated 11 times.

2. Rub a piece of dry ginger[1] in some water, and then rub that rubbed part of the ginger onto the forehead. The ache of half head will be relieved, اِنْ شَآءَاللّٰہ عَزَّوَجَلَّ.

3. Soak some leaves of dry mint and a few raisins in some water for some hours and then drink the water. This will prove to be beneficial, اِنْ شَآءَاللّٰہ عَزَّوَجَلَّ. Ordinary water or water from clay churn should be used.

4. To drink pure ghee-mixed hot milk is also beneficial.

5. To drink coconut water relieves ache of half head and that of entire head.

6. Mix salt in tepid (i.e. lukewarm) water in a large container and keep your feet in it for 12 minutes. This will relieve the ache, اِنْ شَآءَاللّٰہ عَزَّوَجَلَّ. (Duration of this treatment may be changed depending upon the condition of the patient).

[1] Dry ginger can be purchased from a herbalist.

Seven cures for headache

1. لَا يُصَدَّعُوْنَ عَنْهَا وَلَا يُنْزِفُوْنَ ﴿۱۹﴾

With that they will have neither headache nor any (intoxicative) unconsciousness.

[Kanz-ul-Īmān (Translation of Quran)] (Part 27, Sūraĥ Al-Wāqi'aĥ, verse 19)

Recite this verse 3 times, with Ṣalāt-'Alan-Nabī ﷺ once before and after it, and make *Dam* (i.e. blow) on the person who has a headache. He will feel relief, اِنْ شَآءَاللّٰه عَزَّوَجَلَّ.

2. Recite Sūraĥ An-Nās 7 times, with Ṣalāt-'Alan-Nabī ﷺ once before and after it, and make *Dam* on the head of the person suffering from headache. Then ask him whether he still has the ache – if he has, make *Dam* in the same way again. If he still has the pain, repeat this for a third time. No matter how severe the pain of the whole head or half head is, it will be relieved before the *Dam* is made for the third time, اِنْ شَآءَاللّٰه عَزَّوَجَلَّ.

3. Whether it is the pain of the whole head or half head, recite Sūraĥ At-Takāšur once after Ṣalāt-ul-'Aṣr, with Ṣalāt-'Alan-Nabī ﷺ once before and after it, and make *Dam*. The pain will be reduced, اِنْ شَآءَاللّٰه عَزَّوَجَلَّ.

4. Place a pinch of salt onto the tongue and, after 12 minutes, drink a glass of water. No matter what type of headache it is, it will be reduced, اِنْ شَآءَاللّٰه عَزَّوَجَلَّ. (The use of salt is harmful to the patients suffering from high blood pressure).

5. Put one spoon of turmeric into a cup of water and then boil it. After the water has come to the boil, drink it or inhale its steam, headache will be relieved, اِنْ شَآءَاللّٰه عَزَّوَجَلَّ. (Do use turmeric in curries and other foods. The one who consumes a pinch (i.e. about 1 gram) of turmeric every day will be protected from cancer, اِنْ شَآءَاللّٰه عَزَّوَجَلَّ).

6. Before sunrise, eat fresh and warm Jalaybīs (i.e. an Asian sweet) fried in pure ghee. Headache will be relieved, اِنْ شَآءَاللّٰه عَزَّوَجَلَّ.

7. If one ever gets an occasional headache, dissolve 2 painkillers in water and drink it after the meal. The pain will be relieved, اِنْ شَآءَاللّٰه عَزَّوَجَلَّ. (If one has to take any type of

painkiller, one should take it after the meal as it can be harmful if taken on an empty stomach).

Madanī suggestion: If someone's headache is not relieved even after the use of tablets or medicines, he should have his eyesight tested. If the eyesight is weak, he should wear glasses. This will relieve the headache, اِنْ شَآءَاللّٰہ عَزَّوَجَلَّ. If the headache is not still relieved, he should consult a neurologist. Any carelessness in this matter can be extremely detrimental.

Treatment for nosebleed

If anybody's nose bleeds, he should write بِسْمِ اللّٰهِ الرَّحْمٰنِ الرَّحِيْمِ with his index finger starting from his forehead and finishing at the end of the nose. The bleeding will stop, اِنْ شَآءَاللّٰہ عَزَّوَجَلَّ.

Parable about medicine

Muftī Aḥmad Yār Khān عَلَيْهِ رَحْمَةُ الْمَنَّان has stated, 'If a patient recites بِسْمِ اللّٰه before taking medicine, the medicine will be effective, اِنْ شَآءَاللّٰہ عَزَّوَجَلَّ.'

Once Sayyidunā Mūsā عَلٰی نَبِیِّنَا وَ عَلَيْهِ الصَّلٰوةُ وَالسَّلَام got extremely severe stomach pain. He humbly asked Allah عَزَّوَجَلَّ for relief and Allah عَزَّوَجَلَّ ordered him to consume so-and-so herb from a jungle. Therefore, Sayyidunā Mūsā عَلٰی نَبِیِّنَا وَ عَلَيْهِ الصَّلٰوةُ وَالسَّلَام consumed the herb and was immediately cured of the pain.

After some days, the same disease reoccurred so he consumed the same herb again. Contrary to his expectation, his pain became even more severe. He humbly asked the Almighty, 'O Allah عَزَّوَجَلَّ! What is the secret behind this? One medicine has two entirely different effects! When I consumed it first time, it cured me but when I consumed it second time, it intensified my pain!' Allah عَزَّوَجَلَّ said, 'O Mūsā! You used the herb that time with My command but you used it this time of your own accord. O Mūsā! Cure is in My name. Without My name everything of the world is a deadly poison and My name is its cure.' *(Tafsīr-e-Na'īmī, vol.1, pp. 42)*

May Allah عَزَّوَجَلَّ have mercy on him and forgive us without accountability for his sake!

Trust Allah عَزَّوَجَلَّ, not medicine

The foregoing parable shows that one should trust Allah عَزَّوَجَلَّ, not the medicine. If Allah عَزَّوَجَلَّ wills, then the medicine will cure the disease. If He عَزَّوَجَلَّ does not will, then the same medicine will intensify the disease.

It is commonly seen that a particular medicine cures an ill person, but the same medicine, when taken by any other person, triggers negative reaction, causing other serious diseases or physical disability or even death. Whenever one takes any medicine, he should recite either 'بِسْمِ اللهِ الرَّحْمٰنِ الرَّحِيْم' or 'بِسْمِ اللهِ الشَّافِيْ بِسْمِ اللهِ الْكَافِيْ.'

Contentment of soul

Allah عَزَّوَجَلَّ sent a revelation to Sayyidunā Mūsā عَلَيْهِ السَّلَام, 'Every soul is thirsty when leaving the world except for the one that has recited بِسْمِ اللهِ الرَّحْمٰنِ الرَّحِيْم.' *(Asrār-ul-Fātiḥaĥ, pp. 162)*

Virtue of reciting بِسْمِ اللهِ الرَّحْمٰنِ الرَّحِيْم excellently

Sayyidunā 'Alī Murtaḍā كَرَّمَ اللّٰهُ تَعَالٰى وَجْهَهُ الْكَرِيْم has narrated, 'A person recited بِسْمِ اللهِ الرَّحْمٰنِ الرَّحِيْم excellently; so he was forgiven.' *(Shu'ab-ul-Īmān, vol. 2, pp. 546, Ḥadīš 2667)*

Sweetness of divine name leads to salvation

A man once saw a sinful person in a dream and asked 'مَا فَعَلَ اللهُ بِكَ؟ *How has Allah* عَزَّوَجَلَّ *treated you?*' He replied, 'Once, whilst walking past a Madrasaĥ, I heard بِسْمِ اللهِ الرَّحْمٰنِ الرَّحِيْم being recited by somebody. The sweetness of the sweet name of Allah عَزَّوَجَلَّ had a great impact upon my heart. At the very same time, I heard a voice from Ghayb, 'We will not gather two things together (1) Sweetness of the name of Allah عَزَّوَجَلَّ (2) Agonies of death.' *(Anīs-ul-Wā'iẓīn, pp. 4)*

May Allah عَزَّوَجَلَّ have mercy on him and forgive us without accountability for his sake!

Dear Islamic brothers! The foregoing narration shows that the one taking pleasure in the blessed and sacred name of Allah عَزَّوَجَلَّ leaves this world under the shadow of mercy, and death brings for him a message of forgiveness and salvation. The mercy of Allah عَزَّوَجَلَّ is immense and infinite. Even the gravest sinners can be forgiven by virtue of apparently-minor looking deeds.

Raḥmat-e-Ḥaq 'baĥā' na mī juwaīd
Raḥmat-e-Ḥaq 'baĥānaĥ' mī juwaīd

The mercy of Allah عَزَّوَجَلَّ *does not seek a price*
The mercy of Allah عَزَّوَجَلَّ *searches just for an excuse*

Proof on Judgement Day

Muftī Aḥmad Yār Khān عَلَيْهِ رَحْمَةُ الْمَنَّان has stated, 'Describing the excellence and benefits of بِسْمِ اللّٰه the author of *Tafsīr 'Azīzī* has stated that there was a Walī of Allah who made a will on his deathbed that بِسْمِ اللهِ الرَّحْمٰنِ الرَّحِيْم be written on a piece of paper and kept under his shroud. When asked about this, he replied, 'On the Day of Judgement this will be my written proof by which I will beg for divine mercy.' *(Tafsīr-e-Na'īmī, vol. 1, pp. 42)*

May Allah عَزَّوَجَلَّ have mercy on him and forgive us without accountability for his sake!

Milay gā dauno 'ālam kā khazānaĥ parĥ lo بِسْمِ الله
Khudā عَزَّوَجَلَّ *chāĥay to ĥo Jannat ţhikānaĥ parĥ lo* بِسْمِ الله

The treasure of the world and the Hereafter will go to you – recite بِسْمِ الله
If Allah عَزَّوَجَلَّ *wills, your abode will be Paradise – recite* بِسْمِ الله

صَلُّوْا عَلَى الْحَبِيْب صَلَّى اللهُ تَعَالٰى عَلٰى مُحَمَّد
تُوْبُوْا اِلَى الله اَسْتَغْفِرُ الله
صَلُّوْا عَلَى الْحَبِيْب صَلَّى اللهُ تَعَالٰى عَلٰى مُحَمَّد

Protection from torment

It is stated in *Durr-e-Mukhtār*, a renowned book of Ḥanafī Fiqĥ (jurisprudence) that a person made the will that بِسۡمِ اللهِ الرَّحۡمٰنِ الرَّحِيۡم be written on his chest and forehead after his death. When he died, his will was fulfilled.

A few days after his demise, someone saw him in dream and asked as to how he was treated. He replied, 'After I was buried in my grave, the angels of punishment came but when they saw 'بِسۡمِ اللّٰه' written on my forehead, they said, 'You have been saved from punishment!' *(Durr-e-Mukhtār, vol. 3, pp. 156)*

May Allah عَزَّوَجَلَّ have mercy on him and forgive us without accountability for his sake!

How to write on shroud?

Dear Islamic brothers! Whenever a Muslim has passed away, do write بِسۡمِ اللهِ الرَّحۡمٰنِ الرَّحِيۡم and other holy words on his forehead etc. A slight attention of yours can result in forgiveness for the deceased. Further, this virtue of having sympathy for the deceased may also lead to your own forgiveness.

'Allāmaĥ Shāmī رَحْمَةُ اللّٰهِ تَعَالٰى عَلَيْه has stated, 'It could also be done that 'بِسۡمِ اللهِ الرَّحۡمٰنِ الرَّحِيۡم' and 'لَآ اِلٰهَ اِلَّا اللّٰهُ مُحَمَّدٌ رَّسُوْلُ اللّٰهِ' be written on the forehead and the chest of the deceased respectively. Write these with the index finger without using ink, after giving Ghusl to the deceased but before shrouding him/her.' *(Rad-dul-Muḥtār, vol. 3, pp. 157)*

It is not necessary to put diacritical marks. It is permissible to keep Shajaraĥ and 'Aĥd Nāmaĥ in the grave. It is preferable to make a recess-like space in the wall in front of the face of the deceased towards the Qiblaĥ and then keep Shajaraĥ and 'Aĥd Nāmaĥ in it.

It is stated in *Durr-e-Mukhtār* that not only is it permissible to write 'Aĥd Nāmaĥ' on the shroud, there is also a hope of forgiveness for the deceased by virtue of this.

(Baĥār-e-Sharī'at, vol. 4, pp. 108)

Bestowment of forgiveness

On the Day of Judgement, the angels of punishment will capture a person. The angels will be ordered to search his body parts for any virtue. Therefore, they will search all of his body parts but will find no virtue. They will then ask the person to show his tongue so that they would see whether there is any virtue in it. When he takes out his tongue, the angels will see بِسۡمِ اللّٰهِ الرَّحۡمٰنِ الرَّحِيۡم written in white on his tongue. Immediately, it will be announced, 'Go! We have forgiven you!' *(Nuzĥa-tul-Majālis, vol. 1, pp. 25)*

May Allah عَزَّوَجَلَّ have mercy on him and forgive us without accountability for his sake!

Gunāĥgāraun na ĝhabrāo na ĝhabrāo na ĝhabrāo
Naẓar raḥmat pay rakĥo Jannat-ul-Firdaus mayn jāo

O sinners! Do not worry! Do not worry!
Enter Jannat-ul-Firdaus setting your sight on mercy

صَلُّوۡا عَلَى الۡحَبِيۡب　　صَلَّى اللّٰهُ تَعَالٰى عَلٰى مُحَمَّد

Dear Islamic brothers! This is the grace of Allah عَزَّوَجَلَّ that He forgives whoever He wishes. Undoubtedly, that person must have recited 'بِسۡمِ اللّٰهِ الرَّحۡمٰنِ الرَّحِيۡم' with sincerity, which in turn benefited him, as even an apparently minor-looking deed performed with sincerity is very great.

The Prophet of Raḥmaĥ, the Intercessor of Ummaĥ, the Owner of Jannaĥ صَلَّى اللّٰهُ تَعَالٰى عَلَيْهِ وَاٰلِهٖ وَسَلَّم has stated, 'اَخۡلِصۡ دِيۡنَكَ يَكۡفِكَ الۡعَمَلُ الۡقَلِيۡلُ' '*Become sincere in your Dīn [religion]; even little deed will suffice.*' *(Al-Mustadrak, vol. 5, pp. 435, Ḥadīš 7914)*

Ḥujjat-ul-Islam, Imām Muhammad Ghazālī عَلَيْهِ رَحْمَةُ اللّٰهِ الْوَالِى has quoted a saint as saying, 'Sincerity (even) for a moment is a cause of salvation but sincerity is very rarely found.'

(Iḥyā-ul-'Ulūm, vol. 4, pp. 399)

Signs of sincere deed

The companions of Sayyidunā 'Īsā عَلٰی نَبِیِّنَا وَعَلَیۡہِ الصَّلٰوۃُ وَالسَّلَام asked him, 'Whose deed is sincere?' Sayyidunā 'Īsā عَلٰی نَبِیِّنَا وَعَلَیۡہِ الصَّلٰوۃُ وَالسَّلَام replied, 'The deed of only that person will be considered sincere who performs his deed solely for the pleasure of Allah عَزَّوَجَلَّ and dislikes being praised by people for that deed.' *(Iḥyā-ul-'Ulūm, vol. 4, pp. 403)*

May Allah عَزَّوَجَلَّ have mercy on him and forgive us without accountability for his sake!

صَلُّوۡا عَلَی الۡحَبِیۡب　　صَلَّی اللّٰہُ تَعَالٰی عَلٰی مُحَمَّد

O Allah عَزَّوَجَلَّ! For the sake of Your sincere Prophet, Sayyidunā 'Īsā عَلٰی نَبِیِّنَا وَعَلَیۡہِ الصَّلٰوۃُ وَالسَّلَام, forgive us without any reason merely out of Your mercy. Āmīn!

Alas! How sad! We are rapidly falling into the deep abyss of destruction at the hands of our Nafs and Satan! Alas! We are not satisfied unless our deeds and religious actions are admired and praised in the name of encouragement.

Mayrā ĥar 'amal bas Tayray wāsiṭay ĥo
Kar ikhlāṣ aysā 'aṭā Yā Ilāĥī

My every deed be solely for Your pleasure, O Almighty
Bless me with such a treasure of sincerity

Easy invocation for removal of adversities

Sayyidunā 'Alī كَرَّمَ اللّٰہُ تَعَالٰی وَجۡہَہُ الۡکَرِیۡم has narrated that the Holy Prophet صَلَّی اللّٰہُ تَعَالٰی عَلَیۡہِ وَاٰلِہٖ وَسَلَّم has stated, 'O 'Alī (كَرَّمَ اللّٰہُ تَعَالٰی وَجۡہَہُ الۡکَرِیۡم)! Should I not tell you some words to be recited in times of adversity?' Sayyidunā 'Alī كَرَّمَ اللّٰہُ تَعَالٰی وَجۡہَہُ الۡکَرِیۡم replied, 'Of course! Please do tell me. May my life be sacrificed for you! I have indeed learnt all goodness only from you!' He صَلَّی اللّٰہُ تَعَالٰی عَلَیۡہِ وَاٰلِہٖ وَسَلَّم then said, 'Whenever you are in adversity, recite this:

بِسۡمِ اللّٰہِ الرَّحۡمٰنِ الرَّحِیۡمِ وَلَاحَوۡلَ وَلَا قُوَّۃَ اِلَّا بِاللّٰہِ الۡعَلِیِّ الۡعَظِیۡم

Thus, with its blessings, Allah عَزَّوَجَلَّ will remove whichever adversities He wishes.' *('Aml-ul-Yaum wal-Laylaĥ li-Ibn Sunnī, pp. 120)*

Removal of difficulties

Dear Islamic brothers! Whenever you face any adversity such as illness, debt, court case, opposition from enemy, unemployment, unforeseen problem, loss of something, or if you are hurt or beaten by someone, or if you stumble over something or are stuck in a traffic jam or suffer financial or commercial loss or are burgled or your car etc. breaks down - in brief, whether you have a major problem or a minor one, develop a habit of reciting بِسْمِ اللهِ الرَّحْمٰنِ الرَّحِيْمِ وَلَاحَوْلَ وَلَا قُوَّةَ اِلَّا بِاللهِ الْعَلِيِّ الْعَظِيْم. Virtuous intention will lead to destination – that is, if recited with a firm belief, it will benefit you, اِنْ شَآءَالله عَزَّوَجَلَّ.

Another action for the solution to problems is to make Ghusl before Ṣalāt-ul-Jumu'aĥ and put on clean and pure clothes and then recite يَـا اَللهُ 200 times whilst in solitude (with Ṣalāt-'Alan-Nabī ﷺ thrice before and after it). No matter how major the problem is, it will be solved, and whichever type of need one has, it will be fulfilled, اِنْ شَآءَالله عَزَّوَجَلَّ.

اَلْحَمْدُ لِلّٰه عَزَّوَجَلَّ, By the blessings of making Du'ā in the company of the devotees of Rasūl during the Sunnaĥ-Inspiring Madanī Qāfilaĥs of Dawat-e-Islami, the problems of countless Islamic brothers have been solved.

New life

A labourer was hospitalized for the treatment of kidney failure. His wicked nephew came to visit him. Seeing his maternal uncle in an extremely critical condition, he became dejected and tears welled up in his eyes. He had heard that Du'ās made during the Sunnaĥ-Inspiring Madanī Qāfilaĥs of Dawat-e-Islami are accepted. Therefore, he also travelled with a Madanī Qāfilaĥ during which he tearfully made Du'ā for the recovery of his uncle.

When he returned, he was amazed to see that his uncle, who had now recovered from his disease and had come home, was strolling towards the Masjid to offer Ṣalāĥ! Seeing this merciful scene, the young man repented of his sinful life and adopted the beautiful Madanī environment of Dawat-e-Islami!

Marz gambĥīr ĥo, garcheĥ dilgīr ĥo
Ĥaun gī ḥal mushkilayn, Qāfilay mayn chalo
Gham kay bādal ĉhaṫayn aur khushiyān milayn
Dil kī kaliyān kĥilīn Qāfilay mayn chalo

Diseases will be cured, travel with Madanī Qāfilaĥ
Problems will be resolved, travel with Madanī Qāfilaĥ
Clouds of grief will be cleared, travel with Madanī Qāfilaĥ
Rain of happiness will be showered, travel with Madanī Qāfilaĥ

صَلُّوْا عَلَى الْحَبِيْب صَلَّى اللّٰهُ تَعَالٰى عَلٰى مُحَمَّد
تُوْبُوْا اِلَى الله اَسْتَغْفِرُ الله
صَلُّوْا عَلَى الْحَبِيْب صَلَّى اللّٰهُ تَعَالٰى عَلٰى مُحَمَّد

اَلْحَمْدُلِلّٰه عَزَّوَجَلَّ, The Du'ā made from the depths of the heart can never be rejected. Whatever Du'ā is made to Allah عَزَّوَجَلَّ is definitely accepted. Our Merciful Allah عَزَّوَجَلَّ has declared:

وَقَالَ رَبُّكُمُ ادْعُوْنِيْٓ اَسْتَجِبْ لَكُمْ ؕ

And your Rab عَزَّوَجَلَّ has proclaimed, 'Pray to Me, I shall answer your prayer.'

[Kanz-ul-Īmān (Translation of Quran)] (Part 24, Sūraĥ Al-Mūmin, verse 60)

Satanic deception

Undoubtedly, Allah عَزَّوَجَلَّ has declared in the Noble Quran, *pray to Me, I shall answer your prayer*, but often our prayers appear to be unanswered. For example, someone prays that he get a job at a certain firm or organization but his desire isn't fulfilled [and thus it is assumed that the prayer was not answered].

Cure for satanic deception

Misunderstanding about the meaning of the fulfilment of prayer leads to satanic deceptions. There is no doubt about the fulfilment of prayer. However, a prayer may be fulfilled in different ways three of which are mentioned below:

1. (Sometimes) what the praying person asks for is not given to him as it was not good for him, whereas Allah عَزَّوَجَلَّ, the most Merciful, wants what is best for His servants.

وَعَسٰۤى اَنْ تَكْرَهُوْا شَیْــٴًـا وَّ هُوَ خَیْرٌ لَّكُمْۚ

وَعَسٰۤى اَنْ تُحِبُّوْا شَیْــٴًـا وَّ هُوَ شَرٌّ لَّكُمْؕ وَ اللّٰهُ یَعْلَمُ وَ اَنْتُمْ لَا تَعْلَمُوْنَ ﴿۲۱۶﴾

It is likely that you dislike a thing which is better for you; and it is likely that you like a thing which is bad for you; and Allah عَزَّوَجَلَّ knows, and you do not know.

[Kanz-ul-Īmān (Translation of Quran)] (Part 2, Sūraĥ Al-Baqaraĥ, verse 216)

2. (At times) A great adversity or trouble is going to befall the praying person but he is protected from it by Almighty Allah عَزَّوَجَلَّ by virtue of his prayer which apparently seems unfulfilled to him. For example, he was to sustain a fracture to his feet in a motorcycle accident after Ṣalāt-ul-Maghrib on Sunday. After Ṣalāt-ul-'Aṣr on Sunday, he made Du'ā: 'Yā Allah عَزَّوَجَلَّ, so-and-so person owes me 1000 rupees. May he return my money to me!' After offering Ṣalāt-ul-Maghrib, he reached the house of the debtor safe and sound but the debtor did not pay the debt. He thought that his prayer was not answered but, in fact, he is unaware that by the blessing of his apparently unfulfilled looking prayer he has been protected from the trouble of the fracture of feet which was to befall him in an accident whilst he was on his way to the debtor's house.

3. (Sometimes) what the praying person asks for is not given to him but a great deal of reward is given to him in the Hereafter in return. It is mentioned in a blessed Ḥadīš, 'In the Hereafter, when a person sees the rewards of his prayers that were not answered in the world, he will desire, 'If only no prayer of mine had been answered in the world and all had been saved here for (my afterlife).' *(Aḥsan-ul-Wi'ā, pp. 37)*

It is mentioned in another blessed Ḥadīš, 'The doors of Paradise will be opened for the one who is blessed with the ability of making prayer.' *(Aḥsan-ul-Wi'ā, pp. 141)*

A devotee of بِسۡمِ اللّٰہ

A preacher was once describing the excellence of بِسۡمِ اللّٰہ in a congregation. A non-Muslim girl was also present. Impressed by listening to the virtues of بِسۡمِ اللّٰہ, she embraced Islam and developed a habit of reciting بِسۡمِ اللّٰہِ الرَّحۡمٰنِ الرَّحِیۡمِ at the time of sleeping, waking, standing, sitting, walking and doing household chores. In short, she started reciting بِسۡمِ اللّٰہ all the time.

The parents of the girl who were unbelievers were extremely displeased with her. Due to their enmity against Islam they started torturing her and conspired to have her murdered under any false charge. One day, the father of the girl who was a courtier at the royal court gave the King's seal ring to his daughter to keep it in a safe place.

Reciting بِسۡمِ اللّٰہِ الرَّحۡمٰنِ الرَّحِیۡمِ she took the ring and put it into her pocket reciting بِسۡمِ اللّٰہِ الرَّحۡمٰنِ الرَّحِیۡمِ. When night fell and the girl went to sleep, her father secretly took the ring from her pocket and threw it into the river. A fish in the river swallowed the ring.

The next morning, a fisherman cast his fishnet in the river, catching the same fish coincidentally. The fisherman then gifted the fish to the courtier who gave it to his daughter to cook. Reciting بِسۡمِ اللّٰہِ الرَّحۡمٰنِ الرَّحِیۡمِ she took the fish. When she cut open the stomach of the fish whilst reciting بِسۡمِ اللّٰہِ الرَّحۡمٰنِ الرَّحِیۡمِ, she found the same ring. Reciting بِسۡمِ اللّٰہِ الرَّحۡمٰنِ الرَّحِیۡمِ she put the ring into her pocket again and served the cooked fish to her father. After the meal, it was time for her father to go to the royal court, so he asked his daughter for the ring. Reciting بِسۡمِ اللّٰہِ الرَّحۡمٰنِ الرَّحِیۡمِ she took out the ring from her pocket and handed it over to him. Seeing this, he was completely taken aback. In this way, Allah عَزَّوَجَلَّ saved the girl who was a devotee of بِسۡمِ اللّٰہ from being murdered. *(Lam'ān-e-Ṣūfiyā)*

May Allah عَزَّوَجَلَّ have mercy on her and forgive us without accountability for her sake!

Excellence of writing بِسْمِ اللّٰه

Sayyidunā Anas رَضِیَ اللّٰہُ تَعَالٰی عَنْہ has reported that the Prophet of Raḥmaĥ, the Intercessor of Ummaĥ صَلَّی اللّٰہُ تَعَالٰی عَلَیْہِ وَاٰلِہٖ وَسَلَّم has stated, 'The one who has written بِسْمِ اللّٰهِ الرَّحْمٰنِ الرَّحِيْم in a beautiful form for the honour of Allah عَزَّوَجَلَّ, will be forgiven by Allah عَزَّوَجَلَّ.' *(Ad-Dur-rul-Manšūr, vol. 1, pp. 27)*

The honourable father of A'lā Ḥaḍrat, Shaykh Sayyidunā Naqī 'Alī Khān Qādirī عَلَیْہِ رَحْمَۃُ اللّٰہِ الْقَوِی passed away on a Thursday at the time of Ẓuhr in the sacred month of Żul-Qa'da-til-Ḥarām, in 1297 A.H. The last writing of his life was بِسْمِ اللّٰهِ الرَّحْمٰنِ الرَّحِيْم.

Describing the heart-rending moments of his father's demise, A'lā Ḥaḍrat رَحْمَۃُ اللّٰہِ تَعَالٰی عَلَیْہ has stated, 'On the day of his demise, he offered Ṣalāt-ul-Fajr. Before the time of Ẓuĥr started he had passed away. When his soul was going to leave his body, all those present witnessed that he was repeatedly making Salām with his eyes closed (this seems to be an indication that the blessed souls of the Auliyā were gathering to welcome him). During his last breaths, he passed his hands over the parts of his body washed in Wuḍū as though he was making Wuḍū. He even cleaned his nose from the inside. سُبْحٰنَ اللّٰہ عَزَّوَجَلَّ, He acted as if he was offering Ṣalāt-uẓ-Ẓuĥr in the state of unconsciousness.

When his blessed soul was going to leave his body, this Faqīr[1] was present close to his head. By Allah عَزَّوَجَلَّ! A beautiful Nūr (light) was clearly visible to everyone. It arose from his chest and shone on the face like bright lightning, as sunlight reflects in a mirror. This happened for a moment and then disappeared, and his soul also left his body at the very same moment. The last word he uttered was 'Allah عَزَّوَجَلَّ' and the last words he wrote were 'بِسْمِ اللّٰهِ الرَّحْمٰنِ الرَّحِيْم' which he had written on a piece of paper 2 days before his demise.'

After some time, I (i.e. A'lā Ḥaḍrat رَحْمَۃُ اللّٰہِ تَعَالٰی عَلَیْہ) had a dream in which I saw my honourable Murshid رَضِیَ اللّٰہُ تَعَالٰی عَنْہ at the shrine of my honourable father رَحْمَۃُ اللّٰہِ تَعَالٰی عَلَیْہ so I asked, 'Your eminence! You are here?' He replied, 'From today or from now, I will be staying here.' *(Ḥayāt-e-A'lā Ḥaḍrat, vol. 1, pp. 50)*

May Allah عَزَّوَجَلَّ have mercy on them and forgive us without accountability for their sake!

---

[1] A'lā Ḥaḍrat رَحْمَۃُ اللّٰہِ تَعَالٰی عَلَیْہ humbly refers to himself as 'Faqīr' that means a worthless person. [Translator's Note]

Dear Islamic brothers! To attain the great reward of writing بِسْمِ اللهِ الرَّحْمٰنِ الرَّحِيْم, if possible, whilst in the state of Wuḍū, one should occasionally write it on a piece of paper in a beautiful manner. Never write it at such a place where it may be desecrated.

Likewise, do not write verses and sacred words on walls as the paint with sacred writings on them may peel off the wall and fall on the ground. (Take the same care in Masājid as well). As for writing something on the ground or floor, this has been explicitly prohibited by our Beloved Rasūl صَلَّى اللّٰهُ تَعَالٰى عَلَيْهِ وَاٰلِهٖ وَسَلَّم.

Writing on ground

The Prophet of mankind, the Peace of our heart and mind, the most Generous and Kind صَلَّى اللّٰهُ تَعَالٰى عَلَيْهِ وَاٰلِهٖ وَسَلَّم once passed by a place where something was written on the ground. The Holy Prophet صَلَّى اللّٰهُ تَعَالٰى عَلَيْهِ وَاٰلِهٖ وَسَلَّم asked a nearby sitting young man, 'What is written there?' The young man replied, 'بِسْمِ اللّٰه.' The Blessed Rasūl صَلَّى اللّٰهُ تَعَالٰى عَلَيْهِ وَاٰلِهٖ وَسَلَّم said, 'Curse be upon the person who has done this. Keep (the writing of) بِسْمِ اللّٰه at its (proper) place [that is, respect it].' *(Ad-Dur-rul-Manšūr, vol. 1, pp. 29)*

Az-Khudā khawāĥīm taufīq adab
Bay-adab maḥrūm gasht az fazl-e-Rab

(We seek the ability of respecting holy things as the disrespectful are disgraced and deprived of divine bounties)

Respect alphabets of every language

Dear Islamic brothers! One should not write the letters of any language on the ground. Some people are under the impression that there is no need to respect the English language, but this is a grave misunderstanding of theirs. Just ponder! If 'ALLAH' is written in English, will you not respect it? Indeed, you will respect it from the bottom of your heart. If, Allah عَزَّوَجَلَّ forbid, someone places his foot on (the word 'ALLAH' written on a piece of paper etc.) or throws away it with the intention of desecrating it, he will become an unbeliever. Therefore, one should respect the letters of all the languages of the world including English.

It is mentioned on page 396 of the first volume of *Tafsīr Kabīr* that all languages spoken in the world are 'Ilĥāmī' [divinely revealed]. It is obvious that writing the words of any language on the ground is its desecration. These days, some words are painted on the roads by the traffic department for the guidance of drivers, this is wrong. If only they had used signs of different colours (except green) for this purpose. Likewise, doormats with the word 'WELCOME' printed on them should not be placed near doors.

Regretfully, it has become almost impossible these days to respect the letters of languages. Often, the name of the company or manufacturer is printed on rugs, floor sheets, mattresses, duvet covers, bed sheets, bed spreads and bedstead covers etc. Such names are inscribed even on toilets, slippers, shoes and soles. Company name is also printed on the edge of the fabric. Sometimes, the trousers or pyjama gets sewn in such a way that the company name printed on the fabric remains under backside, continuously disrespecting the letters. The most distressing thing is that writing is usually seen even on the bottom of floor tiles. [To avoid disrespect] the writing engraved on floor tiles can be removed by an angle grinder. Those buying these items in bulk can have them prepared without company name by asking the manufacturer to do so at the time of placing their order. But who takes such great pains and develop this Madanī mindset! Well, with the ability granted by Almighty Allah عَزَّوَجَلَّ everything is possible!

Once, in Bāb-ul-Madīnaĥ Karachi, Sag-e-Madīnaĥ[1] was deeply hurt to have seen a red brick with the word 'Umar' inscribed on it. Such red bricks are used in making walls, floors, bathrooms and even toilets. When writing these words, a heart-rending experience of past comes to my mind. Let me share that with you.

Heart-rending recollection of Madīnaĥ

At the eastern side of the sacred Masjid-un-Nabawī, in front of Bāb Jibrāīl, there was an ancient street which led towards Jannat-ul-Baqī'. The devotees used to call it 'Street of Paradise.' Many memorable sites were once located there including the sacred houses of the blessed family of the Holy Prophet صَلَّى اللّٰهُ تَعَالٰى عَلَيْهِ وَاٰلِهٖ وَسَلَّم. Now, that sweet and beautiful Madanī street has been demolished.

[1] The author, Amīr-e-Aĥl-e-Sunnat دَامَتْ بَرَكَاتُهُمُ الْعَالِيَه, refers to himself as 'Sag-e-Madīnaĥ' out of humbleness.

On a delightful evening of 1400 A.H., I (the author) was passing the same 'Street of Paradise' when my eye fell on some Arabic words engraved onto a manhole cover. When I looked closer, I saw that the words 'مَجَارِى الْمَدِيْنَة' were engraved on it. I kissed the words with sentimental reverence and felt inexpressible hatred for those unfortunate people who had engraved the name of my sweet and beloved city Madīnaĥ زَادَهَا اللّٰهُ شَرَفًا وَّتَعْظِيْمًا onto the cover of a manhole. Meanwhile, an old Yemeni who had seen me kiss the blessed words came and told me off. I lowered my head and moved on swiftly. I had only walked a short distance when I heard someone say Salām to me. When I turned around to see who he was, I noticed that he was a person from Pakistan. He met me politely. The odd thing was that he began to apologise to me and said, 'Please don't mind what the old Yemeni has said.'

He further said, 'I am very impressed by your manner of showing respect and reverence at the sacred Masjid-un-Nabawī. I have been consistently following you and taking note of every single movement and action of yours. Please come and stay at my home.' I replied, 'اَلْحَمْدُلِلّٰه عَزَّوَجَلَّ, I have accommodation.' He then said, 'At least eat food with me', I replied, 'I do not need food yet.' Then he said, 'Please accept some money from me as a gift.' Thanking him I explained, 'I am not a needy person; I have enough provisions, اَلْحَمْدُلِلّٰه عَزَّوَجَلَّ.' Anyway, he was someone who possessed correct beliefs and was very affectionate towards me. He was a stranger to me, and I did not meet him again since that casual meeting. May Allah عَزَّوَجَلَّ bless him with great rewards and protect every Muslim from blasphemy and the evil of the blasphemers.

اٰمِيْن بِجَاهِ النَّبِيِّ الْاَمِيْن صَلَّى اللّٰهُ تَعَالٰى عَلَيْهِ وَاٰلِهٖ وَسَلَّم

Maḥfūẓ Khudā rakĥnā sadā bay-adabaun say
Aur mujĥ say bĥī sarzad na kabĥī bay-adabī ĥo

Protect me always from blasphemers, O Almighty
May I never commit any type of blasphemy

Argument of sharp-witted

In Arabic, the word 'Madīnaĥ' means 'a city' so there is nothing wrong with writing the word 'Madīnaĥ' on the cover of a manhole.

Reply by a devotee

In Arabic, the word 'Balad (بَلَد)' is also commonly used for city. Even city council of Madīnaĥ is called 'Baladiyyaĥ' so what prompted them to write the beautiful name of Madīnaĥ on a manhole cover! With the exception of Arabic language, when 'Madīnaĥ' is used in any other language of the world including Urdu, it will mean the holy Madīnaĥ city of the Beloved and Blessed Prophet صَلَّى اللهُ تَعَالٰى عَلَيْهِ وَاٰلِهٖ وَسَلَّم.

Moreover, renowned scholars have included the single word 'Madīnaĥ' in the numerous blessed names of Madīna-tul-Munawwaraĥ زَادَهَا اللّٰهُ شَرَفًا وَّ تَعْظِيْمًا. Further, the books written on the history of Madīna-tul-Munawwaraĥ also affirm the fact that the single word 'Madīnaĥ' refers to the blessed city of the Holy Prophet صَلَّى اللهُ تَعَالٰى عَلَيْهِ وَاٰلِهٖ وَسَلَّم. For example, on page 22 of volume 1 of his book *Wafā-ul-Wafā*, 'Allāmaĥ Nūruddīn 'Alī Bin Aḥmad Assamĥūdī عَلَيْهِ رَحْمَةُ اللّٰهِ الْقَوِى has stated many blessed names of Madīna-tul-Munawwaraĥ one of which is the single word 'Madīnaĥ.'

Anyway, the hearts of devotees can never accept the writing or engraving of the word 'Madīnaĥ' or 'Al-Madīnaĥ' on a manhole cover. What is Al-Madīnaĥ! Only the hearts of true devotees can understand the sanctity of 'Al-Madīnaĥ.' The leader of devotees, Imām of the Aĥl-e-Sunnat, reviver of religion, Maulānā Shāĥ Aḥmad Razā Khān عَلَيْهِ رَحْمَةُ الرَّحْمٰن has explained the significance of Madīnaĥ in his following couplet:

Nām-e-Madīnaĥ lay diyā chalnay lagī nasīm-e-khuld
Sauzish-e-gham ko ĥam nay bĥī kaysī ĥawā batāī kyūn

Mention of Madīnaĥ has made a breeze of Paradise blow
And has caused the grief of our heart to further grow

(Ḥadāiq-e-Bakhshish)

The brother of A'lā Ḥaḍrat رَحْمَةُ اللّٰهِ تَعَالٰى عَلَيْه, Maulānā Ḥasan Razā Khān عَلَيْهِ رَحْمَةُ الْحَنَّان has expressed his devotion to Madīnaĥ in the following couplet:

Raĥayn un kay jalway, basayn un kay jalway
Mayrā dil banay yādgār-e-Madīnaĥ

May holy visions remain in my heart
May thoughts of Madīnaĥ capture my heart

(Żauq-e-Na'at)

Satanic deception

After all, it is very disgusting to kiss the cover of a manhole.

Cure for satanic deception

The cover is on the mouth of the manhole while the waste matter is inside. Therefore, there is no justification in declaring the dry manhole cover unclean which has no apparent signs of uncleanliness upon it. No Muftī of the Islamic world would declare it impermissible to kiss, out of love and devotion, the word 'Al-Madīnaĥ' which has attachment to the holy city Madīna-tul-Munawwaraĥ, even if written or engraved on a dry manhole cover. Indeed, it is only a trait of the devotees of Madīnaĥ كَثَّرَهُمُ اللّٰهُ تَعَالٰی to fervently and delightfully kiss the word 'Al-Madīnaĥ' engraved on a cover placed in a blessed street of the sacred city of the Noble Prophet صَلَّى اللهُ تَعَالٰى عَلَيْهِ وَاٰلِهٖ وَسَلَّم. O the devotees of beloved Madīnaĥ and the Prophet of Madīnaĥ صَلَّى اللهُ تَعَالٰى عَلَيْهِ وَاٰلِهٖ وَسَلَّم! Say delightfully:

Al-Madīnaĥ say ĥamayn to piyār ĥay
اِنْ شَآءَاللّٰه عَزَّوَجَلَّ Apnā bayřā pār ĥay

We have love for Al-Madīnaĥ indeed
اِنْ شَآءَاللّٰه عَزَّوَجَلَّ, We will succeed

صَلُّوْا عَلَى الْحَبِيْب صَلَّى اللهُ تَعَالٰى عَلٰى مُحَمَّد

Drinker forgiven

There were two brothers. One of them was pious, whereas the other was a drinker. The pious person once called his brother and punished him for his habit of drinking alcohol. Whilst returning, the drinker fell into some deep water and drowned. Eventually, he was buried in a grave. At night, the pious person had a dream in which he saw his deceased brother stroll in Paradise. Amazed, he asked, 'You were a drinker and had died in the state of intoxication, how have you entered Paradise?' His deceased brother replied, 'Whilst returning after being beaten by you, I saw on the way a piece of paper with 'بِسْمِ اللهِ الرَّحْمٰنِ الرَّحِيْم' written on it. Picking it up, I swallowed it. I then fell into the deep water and drowned.

After I was buried, Munkar and Nakīr came into my grave and asked questions. I politely said, 'You are questioning me, whereas the pure name of my Beloved Almighty Allah عَزَّوَجَلَّ is in my abdomen!' As I said this, a voice from Ghayb said, صَدَقَ عَبْدِیْ قَدْ غَفَرْتُ لَهٗ *'My servant has spoken the truth. Undoubtedly, I have forgiven him.'* *(Nuzĥa-tul-Majālis, vol. 1, pp. 27)*

May Allah عَزَّوَجَلَّ have mercy on him and forgive us without accountability for his sake!

صَلُّوْا عَلَی الْحَبِیْب صَلَّی اللّٰهُ تَعَالٰی عَلٰی مُحَمَّد
تُوْبُوْا اِلَی اللّٰه اَسْتَغْفِرُ اللّٰه
صَلُّوْا عَلَی الْحَبِیْب صَلَّی اللّٰهُ تَعَالٰی عَلٰی مُحَمَّد

If only every Muslim joins the fold of the Sunnaĥ learning and teaching devotees of Rasūl by associating himself with Dawat-e-Islami, a global & non-political, religious movement of the Quran and Sunnaĥ. If only we all get the privilege of attending every Dars and Sunnaĥ-Inspiring Ijtimā' and wholeheartedly make struggle for these righteous acts.

Reward of forgiveness

An Islamic brother has stated, 'The 3 day Sunnaĥ-Inspiring Ijtimā' of Dawat-e-Islami, a global & non-political, religious movement of the Quran and Sunnaĥ, was going to be held in Bāb-ul-Madīnaĥ Karachi. Large-scale preparations for the Ijtimā' were underway. Special trains from different cities were arranged so that devotees of Rasūl could attend the Ijtimā' from all over the country.

During those days a relative of mine passed away. A few days after his demise, someone from his family saw him in a dream. When asked about his state, the deceased replied, 'I had booked a seat on one of the special trains with the intention of attending Dawat-e-Islami's Sunnaĥ-Inspiring Ijtimā' going to be held in Karachi. Allah عَزَّوَجَلَّ has forgiven me because of that true intention of mine.'

Raḥmat-e-Ḥaq 'baĥā' na mī juwaīd
Raḥmat-e-Ḥaq 'baĥānaĥ' mī juwaīd

The mercy of Allah عَزَّوَجَلَّ does not seek a price
The mercy of Allah عَزَّوَجَلَّ searches just for an excuse

صَلُّوْا عَلَى الْحَبِيْب صَلَّى اللّٰهُ تَعَالٰى عَلٰى مُحَمَّد

Blessings of good intention

Dear Islamic brothers! Did you see how tremendous the virtues of a good intention are? Although that brother could not get the opportunity of attending the Ijtimā', he was fortunately forgiven because of his intention of attending the Ijtimā'. Sayyidunā Ḥasan Baṣrī عَلَيْهِ رَحْمَةُ اللّٰهِ الْقَوِى has stated, 'Man will attain Paradise, not because of a few days' good deeds, but because of good intentions.' *(Kīmiyā-e-Sa'ādat, vol. 2, pp. 861)*

Remember that intention refers to the intention of the heart (i.e. the willingness of heart to do something). If a person (apparently) agrees to do some righteous act but has no intention in his heart, he won't gain the reward of intention. For example, someone is asked to go somewhere tomorrow, and he responds by saying, 'Yes', but he has the intention in his heart that he will not go there. This will be a false promise, and making a false promise is a Ḥarām act leading to Hell.

When the Holy Prophet صَلَّى اللّٰهُ تَعَالٰى عَلَيْهِ وَاٰلِهٖ وَسَلَّم departed for the battle of Tabūk, he صَلَّى اللّٰهُ تَعَالٰى عَلَيْهِ وَاٰلِهٖ وَسَلَّم said, 'In Madīnaĥ Ṭayyibaĥ there are certain people who are with us whenever we cross a valley or invade a place, annoying the unbelievers. Further, when we spend any money or are hungry, they are (also considered) to be with us in all these things despite the fact that they are in Madīna-tul-Munawwaraĥ.' The blessed companions رَضِىَ اللّٰهُ تَعَالٰى عَنْهُم asked, 'Yā Rasūlallāĥ صَلَّى اللّٰهُ تَعَالٰى عَلَيْهِ وَاٰلِهٖ وَسَلَّم, how? They are not with us!' The Beloved and Blessed Rasūl صَلَّى اللّٰهُ تَعَالٰى عَلَيْهِ وَاٰلِهٖ وَسَلَّم said, 'They have been prevented by compulsion.' (In other words, they are deserving of reward because they had a firm intention of participation but could not participate due to some valid compulsion). *(Sunan Kubrā, vol. 9, pp. 24)*

The one using fragrance for the pleasure of Allah عَزَّوَجَلَّ will come on the Day of Judgement in such a manner that his fragrance will be wafting more than that of musk, and the one using fragrance for anyone other than Allah عَزَّوَجَلَّ will come on the Day of Judgement in such a way that his smell will be more foul than that of a carcass. *(Muṣannaf 'Abdur Razzāq, vol. 4, pp. 319, Ḥadīš 7932) (Iḥyā-ul-'Ulūm, vol. 4, pp. 813)*

Quoting a blessed Ḥadīš in his renowned book '*Kīmīyā-e-Sa'ādat*' Ḥujjat-ul-Islam Imām Muhammad Ghazālī عَلَيْهِ رَحْمَةُ اللّٰهِ الْوَالِى has stated that the Beloved and Blessed Prophet صَلَّى اللّٰهُ تَعَالٰى عَلَيْهِ وَاٰلِهٖ وَسَلَّم has said, 'The one borrowing (money etc.) with no intention of returning it is a thief.' *(Attarghīb Wattarĥīb, vol. 2, pp. 602)*

Divine Hidden Plan

Indeed the mercy of Allah عَزَّوَجَلَّ is immense and infinite. He عَزَّوَجَلَّ is independent. No one knows what the Divine Hidden Plan about him is. When the mercy of Allah عَزَّوَجَلَّ dominates, He عَزَّوَجَلَّ blesses a person with the marvellous favours of Paradise by virtue of an apparently minor-looking deed but when He عَزَّوَجَلَّ intends to punish a person, He عَزَّوَجَلَّ punishes him for even any minor sin. Therefore, one should never miss any good deed and should always refrain from every sin. One should always fear the Absolute Independence of Allah عَزَّوَجَلَّ.

A hair-raising parable

'Allāmaĥ 'Abdur Raḥmān Ibn Jauzī عَلَيْهِ رَحْمَةُ اللّٰهِ الْقَوِى has narrated that Sayyidunā Ḥasan Baṣrī عَلَيْهِ رَحْمَةُ اللّٰهِ الْقَوِى was once sitting somewhere along with his friends when some people came dragging the corpse of an executed person. As Sayyidunā Ḥasan Baṣrī عَلَيْهِ رَحْمَةُ اللّٰهِ الْقَوِى glanced at the executed person's face, he instantly fell to the ground unconscious. When he recovered, someone asked him the story. He replied, 'This executed man was once a great worshipper and a pious person.'

More curious, people requested, 'Yā Sayyidī! Please tell us the incident in detail.' The eminent saint then related, 'One day, this worshipper left his house to offer Ṣalāĥ. On the way he caught sight of a non-Muslim girl, and immediately fell in love with her. Unable to resist, he asked her to marry him. The non-Muslim girl asked him to embrace her religion. At first, he prevented himself but eventually gave in to his lust and embraced her religion renouncing Islam.

When he informed the girl that he had embraced her religion, she turned furious and said admonishing him, 'O unfortunate person! You have no good. You are not loyal even to your religion, how could you be loyal to anyone else! O ill-fated person! You have endangered your lifelong worship, piety and even your religion in the craziness of your lust! Listen! You have become an apostate renouncing Islam but I have embraced Islam renouncing that untrue religion, اَلۡحَمۡدُ لِلّٰه عَزَّوَجَلَّ.'

Having said this, she recited Sūraĥ Al-Ikhlāṣ. Someone asked her in astonishment, 'How did you learn this Sūraĥ by heart?' She replied, 'In my dream, I saw that I was about to fall into Hell when a respectable man came there and comforted me saying, 'Don't be afraid. That man has been made atonement for you [i.e. he will enter Hell instead of you].' Then, I saw this unfortunate lover being brought to be thrown into Hell in place of me. Later, the respectable man took me to Paradise where I saw the following words written:

يَمۡحُوا اللّٰهُ مَا يَشَآءُ وَ يُثۡبِتُ ۚۖ وَ عِنۡدَهٗۤ اُمُّ الۡكِتٰبِ ﴿۳۹﴾

Allah عَزَّوَجَلَّ wipes out what He wills and establishes (what He wills) and with Him is the Actual writing.

[Kanz-ul-Īmān (Translation of Quran)] (Part 13, Sūraĥ Ar-Ra'd, verse 39)

Then the respectable man taught me Sūraĥ Al-Ikhlāṣ and when I woke up I had learnt it by heart.'

Sayyidunā Ḥasan Baṣrī عَلَيۡهِ رَحۡمَةُ اللّٰهِ الۡقَوِى then said, 'The fortunate girl became a Muslim but the ill-fated worshipper became an apostate giving in to his lust, and was executed today. نَسۡاَلُ اللّٰهَ الۡعَافِيَة *We beseech Allah عَزَّوَجَلَّ for protection.*' *(Baḥr-ud-Dumū', pp. 76)*

Dear Islamic brothers! Everyone should always fear the Absolute Independence and Hidden Plan of Allah عَزَّوَجَلَّ. None of us knows whether or not we will die with Īmān [faith].

Alas! By Allah عَزَّوَجَلَّ! Because of being born in the world, we are confronted with extremely severe trials and tribulations. In this matter, even animals and insects are better off as they neither have the fear of losing Īmān and suffering the agonies of death nor do they have the fear of facing the horrors of grave, Judgement Day and punishment of Hell.

Kāsh kay mayn dunyā mayn paydā na ĥuwā ĥotā
Qabr-o-ḥashr kā sab gham khatm ĥo gayā ĥotā
Āh! Salb-e-Īmān kā khauf kĥāye jātā ĥay
Kāsh! Mayrī mā nay ĥī mujĥ ko na janā ĥotā
Āĥ! Kaŝrat-e-'iṣyān ĥāye khauf dozakh kā
Kāsh! Is jaĥān kā mayn na bashar banā ĥotā

If only I had never been born in the world
The grief of the grave and resurrection would all have ended
Alas! The fear of losing faith is eating away at me
If only my mother had not given birth to me
Alas! This abundance of sins, and the fear of Hellfire
If only I were not a human in the world

Allah عَزَّوَجَلَّ is Absolutely Independent. We should always fear Him. We should never be heedless of protecting our Īmān. Wicked company is extremely disastrous while pious company and devotion & spiritual link with the pious is very beneficial leading to protection (in the worldly life as well as in the afterlife).

Whoever joins the Madanī environment of Dawat-e-Islami, a global & non-political, religious movement of the Quran and Sunnaĥ, and remains associated with it throughout his life is showered with such mercy that others get astonished!

A pilgrim of Madīnaĥ

Here is a summary of the account given by a preacher of Dawat-e-Islami from Nayaabad area of [Bāb-ul-Madīnaĥ, Karachi]. He has stated: My 70-year-old respectable father, Ḥājī 'Abdur Raḥīm Aṭṭārī (Patnī) spent the early part of his life enjoying the beauties of the world but later he was fortunately blessed with the Madanī environment of Dawat-e-Islami, which caused a Madanī transformation in his life, اَلْحَمْدُلِلّٰہ عَزَّوَجَلَّ.

On the eve of his second Hajj-pilgrimage in 1995, he was extremely delighted and excited. As the moment of his departure approached he got more and more happy. He remained busy the whole night delightedly making preparations for his departure. The house was full of guests gathered to see him off. At last, the moment of his departure had nearly arrived, enhancing his happiness. We were to go to the airport at 4:00 a.m.

At around 3:00 a.m., he placed Iḥrām beside him and lay down in his room to take rest. I also went to my room for some rest. Hardly 15 minutes had passed when I heard a knock on the door of my room. As I opened the door, I saw that my respected mother was standing in a state of anxiety and worry. She told me that my father was having severe pain. I immediately went to his room and saw that he was rubbing his chest in agony. He was rushed to hospital where doctors informed us that he had suffered a heart attack. A deep anxiety prevailed in home. Everyone was extremely saddened by the thought that the time of his departure to Madīnaĥ has arrived and he has been hospitalized.

Alas! The plane left for Madīnaĥ without him. He remained in hospital for 5 days. During his stay in hospital, he suffered four more heart attacks. As long as he remained conscious he did not miss any Ṣalāĥ by the blessings of the Madanī environment of Dawat-e-Islami. As soon as he was told that the time of Ṣalāĥ had started, he would immediately open his eyes. He would then make Tayammum with someone's help, and offer his Ṣalāĥ by gestures due to weakness. He suffered from another attack, falling unconscious.

On hearing the Ażān for Ṣalāt-ul-'Ishā, he blinked slightly, so I said, 'Father, shall I help you make Tayammum for Ṣalāĥ?' He nodded. اَلْحَمْدُلِلّٰه عَزَّوَجَلَّ, I helped him make Tayammum. Folding his hands he uttered 'اَللّٰهُ اَكْبَر' and then fell unconscious again. I anxiously ran out and called out the doctor. He was immediately transferred to the I.C.U. After a few minutes, the doctor came and told me that my father was very fortunate because he recited لَآ اِلٰهَ اِلَّا اللّٰهُ مُحَمَّدٌ رَّسُوْلُ اللّٰهِ aloud and then passed away. اِنَّا لِلّٰهِ وَاِنَّآ اِلَيْهِ رٰجِعُوْنَ ﴿۱۵۶﴾ *(Part 2, Sūraĥ Al-Baqaraĥ, verse 156)*

A Sayyid (descendent of the Prophet) gave Ghusl [ritual bathing] to my respectable father. My father had the habit of counting the number of his invocations (Waẓāif) on his fingers. After he passed away, his fingers were in a position as if he was using his fingers for invocation. Repeated attempts to straighten his fingers failed and they returned to the same state as if he was counting with his fingers. اَلْحَمْدُلِلّٰه عَزَّوَجَلَّ, Many Islamic brothers attended his funeral.

اَلْحَمْدُلِلّٰه عَزَّوَجَلَّ, My elder brother had also arranged to go for Hajj the same year. He was blessed with the privilege of performing Hajj. He (my elder brother) has stated, 'In Madīna-tul-Munawwaraĥ, I made tearful pleas in the court of the Holy Prophet صَلَّى اللّٰهُ تَعَالٰى عَلَيْهِ وَاٰلِهٖ وَسَلَّم that the state of my deceased father be revealed to me. As I went to sleep at night I dreamt that my respected father wearing Iḥrām has come and said, 'I have come here (in Madīnaĥ) to make the intention of 'Umraĥ. You remembered me, so I have come to you. اَلْحَمْدُ لِلّٰه عَزَّوَجَلَّ, I am very happy.'

The next year, my nephew saw, in complete wakefulness, his respected grandfather (i.e. my deceased father Ḥājī 'Abdur Raḥīm 'Aṭṭārī) offer Ṣalāĥ next to him in Masjid-ul-Ḥarām in front of the blessed Ka'baĥ. Having finished Ṣalāĥ, he looked for him a lot but could not find him.

May Allah عَزَّوَجَلَّ have mercy on him and forgive us without accountability for his sake!

Madīnay kā musāfir Sindh say puĥanchā Madīnay mayn
Qadam rakĥnay kī nawbat bĥī na āyī tĥī safīnay mayn

The pilgrim to Madīnaĥ has reached Madīnaĥ from Sindh
Without having the need of travelling by any means

صَلُّوا عَلَى الْحَبِيْب صَلَّى اللهُ تَعَالٰى عَلٰى مُحَمَّد

Allah عَزَّوَجَلَّ is very pleased with those respecting His name. He عَزَّوَجَلَّ showers His grace and bounty on such people. It is also His Hidden Plan that He can become pleased even with an apparently minor-looking deed performed by an extreme sinner and alcoholic and can bless him with the ability of repenting of sins, making him a Walī.

A drinker became a Walī

Before repenting of his sins, Sayyidunā Bishr Ḥāfī عَلَيْهِ رَحْمَةُ اللّٰهِ الْكَافِى was an alcoholic. He رَحْمَةُ اللهِ تَعَالٰى عَلَيْه was once going somewhere in a drunken stupor. On the way, his eye fell on a piece of paper on which 'بِسْمِ اللهِ الرَّحْمٰنِ الرَّحِيْم' was written. He picked it up respectfully. He رَحْمَةُ اللهِ تَعَالٰى عَلَيْه then bought some fragrance which he applied to the paper and then placed it at a high place in reverence.

At night, a saint رَحْمَةُ اللهِ تَعَالٰى عَلَيْه had a dream in which he heard someone say, 'Go and tell Bishr that he made My name fragrant, honoured it and placed it at a high place, We will also purify him.' After the saint woke up, he thought to himself, 'Bishr is an alcoholic; there is perhaps some misunderstanding on my part about the dream.' Then, making Wuḍū and offering Nafl Ṣalāĥ, he went to sleep again but had the same dream for the second and then for the third time with the same instruction, i.e. 'Our message is indeed for Bishr! Go and convey Our message to him!'

Therefore, the saint went out of his house looking for Sayyidunā Bishr رَحْمَةُ اللهِ تَعَالٰى عَلَيْه and learnt that Bishr was in the gathering of alcoholics. Reaching the gathering he called out 'Bishr' but was told by people that Bishr was in a drunken stupor. The saint said to people, 'Go and somehow tell him that a man with a message for him is standing outside.'

Someone went and told him of this. Sayyidunā Bishr Ḥāfī عَلَيْهِ رَحْمَةُ اللّٰهِ الْكَافِى said, 'Ask him as to whose message he has brought.' When asked, the saint replied, 'I have brought the message of Allah عَزَّوَجَلَّ.' When informed of this, Sayyidunā Bishr رَحْمَةُ اللّٰهِ تَعَالٰى عَلَيْه was overwhelmed and immediately came out barefooted. Hearing the divine message, he sincerely repented of his sins and attained such a high spiritual rank that he began to remain barefooted due to the extreme degree of witnessing divine omnipotence. This is why he رَحْمَةُ اللهِ تَعَالٰى عَلَيْه became famously known as Ḥāfī (i.e. the one remaining barefooted). *(Tażkira-tul-Auliyā, pp. 68)*

May Allah عَزَّوَجَلَّ have mercy on them and forgive us without accountability for their sake!

Virtues of showing respect

Dear Islamic brothers! A grave sinner and an alcoholic became a Walī of Allah عَزَّوَجَلَّ merely because of respecting and revering a piece of paper on which the blessed name of Allah عَزَّوَجَلَّ was written. So, why will then we sinners not be blessed with the grace and bounty of Allah عَزَّوَجَلَّ if we also respect those blessed individuals whose hearts, with the name of Allah عَزَّوَجَلَّ engraved on them, remain occupied in divine remembrance. Furthermore, how dear would the respect of Sayyidunā Muhammad صَلَّى اللهُ تَعَالٰى عَلَيْهِ وَاٰلِهٖ وَسَلَّم be to Allah عَزَّوَجَلَّ as he صَلَّى اللهُ تَعَالٰى عَلَيْهِ وَاٰلِهٖ وَسَلَّم is the Sovereign of all Prophets and saints!

Indeed, respecting the name of a holy individual brings about blessings. Sayyidunā Bishr Ḥāfī عَلَيْهِ رَحْمَةُ اللّٰهِ الْكَافِى gained a high spiritual rank by respecting the name of Allah عَزَّوَجَلَّ. If we also respect the name of the Beloved and Blessed Prophet صَلَّى اللّٰهُ تَعَالٰى عَلَيْهِ وَاٰلِهٖ وَسَلَّم why will we not gain respect? On hearing the blessed name, if we kiss our thumbs and touch them to our eyes out of respect, why will we not get its blessings? Sayyidunā Bishr Ḥāfī عَلَيْهِ رَحْمَةُ اللّٰهِ الْكَافِى applied fragrance to the paper on which the name of Allah عَزَّوَجَلَّ was written, so he was purified. If we also sprinkle rose water wherever the Żikr of the Beloved and Blessed Prophet صَلَّى اللّٰهُ تَعَالٰى عَلَيْهِ وَاٰلِهٖ وَسَلَّم is made why would we not be purified?

Even animals pay respect to Walī

Sayyidunā Bishr Ḥāfī عَلَيْهِ رَحْمَةُ اللّٰهِ الْكَافِى would always walk barefooted. As long as he was alive in Baghdad, no animal defecated on the pathways of the city out of respect and reverence so that Sayyidunā Bishr Ḥāfī عَلَيْهِ رَحْمَةُ اللّٰهِ الْكَافِى would not be inconvenienced while walking barefooted.

One day, an animal defecated on a pathway; his owner became worried fearing that Sayyidunā Bishr Ḥāfī عَلَيْهِ رَحْمَةُ اللّٰهِ الْكَافِى has perhaps passed away or else the animal would never defecate on the path. After a short while he heard that the great saint had passed away. *(Aḥsan-ul-Wi'ā, pp. 137)*

May Allah عَزَّوَجَلَّ have mercy on him and forgive us without accountability for his sake!

Forgiveness for the respectful

After the demise of Sayyidunā Bishr Ḥāfī عَلَيْهِ رَحْمَةُ اللّٰهِ الْكَافِى, Qāsim Bin Munabbeĥ saw him in dream and asked, مَا فَعَلَ اللّٰهُ بِكَ؟ '*How has Allah* عَزَّوَجَلَّ *treated you?*' He replied, 'Allah عَزَّوَجَلَّ has forgiven me and told me, 'O Bishr! I have forgiven you as well as all those who attended your funeral Ṣalāĥ.' I then requested, 'O Rab عَزَّوَجَلَّ, forgive even those who love me.' Allah عَزَّوَجَلَّ said, 'I have forgiven all those who would love you till the Day of Judgement.' *(Sharḥ-uṣ-Ṣudūr, pp. 289)*

A'māl na daykĥay yeĥ daykĥā, ĥay mayray Walī kay dar kā gadā
Khāliq عَزَّوَجَلَّ *nay mujĥay yūn bakhsh diyā,* سُبْحٰنَ اللّٰه عَزَّوَجَلَّ سُبْحٰنَ اللّٰه عَزَّوَجَلَّ

My devotion towards a Walī, not my deeds, was acknowledged
My Creator عَزَّوَجَلَّ *has forgiven me for this privilege*

Dear Islamic brothers! By the blessings of respecting بِسۡمِ اللّٰہِ الرَّحۡمٰنِ الرَّحِیۡم, Sayyidunā Bishr Ḥāfī عَلَیۡہِ رَحۡمَۃُ اللّٰہِ الۡکَافِی gained such a great spiritual rank that its blessings are benefitting even us. When he made Du'ā to Allah عَزَّوَجَلَّ, he was given the glad tidings of the forgiveness of those loving him. اِنۡ شَآءَاللّٰہ عَزَّوَجَلَّ, We shall also be successful as we love all Auliyā of Allah عَزَّوَجَلَّ including Sayyidunā Bishr Ḥāfī عَلَیۡہِ رَحۡمَۃُ اللّٰہِ الۡکَافِی

Bishr Ḥāfī say ĥamayn to piyār ĥay
اِنۡ شَآءَاللّٰہ عَزَّوَجَلَّ *Apnā bayřā pār ĥay*

We love Bishr Ḥāfī indeed
اِنۡ شَآءَاللّٰہ عَزَّوَجَلَّ *We will succeed*

Ĥum ko sāray Auliyā say piyār ĥay
اِنۡ شَآءَاللّٰہ عَزَّوَجَلَّ *Apnā bayřā pār ĥay*

We love all Auliyā indeed
اِنۡ شَآءَاللّٰہ عَزَّوَجَلَّ *We will succeed*

صَلُّوۡا عَلَی الۡحَبِیۡب صَلَّی اللّٰهُ تَعَالٰی عَلٰی مُحَمَّد

Excellence of picking up a sacred paper

Sayyidunā 'Alī Murtaḍā كَرَّمَ اللّٰهُ تَعَالٰى وَجۡهَهُ الۡكَرِيۡم has narrated that the Beloved and Blessed Prophet صَلَّی اللّٰہُ تَعَالٰی عَلَیۡہِ وَاٰلِہٖ وَسَلَّم has stated, 'Whoever picks up such a piece of paper, from the ground, on which any name from the names of Allah عَزَّوَجَلَّ is written, Allah عَزَّوَجَلَّ will raise the name of that person in 'Illiyyīn (i.e. the greatest place of souls) and will reduce the punishment of his parents even if they are unbelievers.' *(Majma'-uz-Zawāid, vol. 4, pp. 300)*

Muftī A'ẓam Hind respects papers and alphabet

The beloved son of A'lā Ḥaḍrat, a practising scholar, a Walī of Allah, a devotee of Rasūl, Al-Ḥāj Muhammad Mustafa Razā Khān عَلَیۡہِ رَحۡمَۃُ الۡمَنَّان famously known as 'Muftī A'ẓam Hind' would respect even blank papers and individual letters of the alphabet as these are used in writings of Quran, Aḥādīš and rulings of Sharī'aĥ.

In 1391 A.H., he came to Dār-ul-'Ulūm Rabbāniyyaĥ Banda (India) in order to attend a degree-conferring ceremony. After he got off the vehicle and walked a few steps, his eye fell on a few pieces of tattered papers with some Urdu writings on them. Picking them up instantly, he said, 'One should respect papers and the Arabic alphabet[1] as these are used in the compilation of the Holy Quran, blessed Aḥādīš and exegeses etc.' *(Derived from Muftī A'ẓam kī Istiqāmat-o-Karāmat, pp. 124)*

May Allah عَزَّوَجَلَّ have mercy on him and forgive us without accountability for his sake!

Muftī A'ẓam Hind رَحْمَةُ اللهِ عَلَيْه comforts the troubled

Dear Islamic brothers! Did you notice the enthusiasm of Muftī A'ẓam Hind for respecting Islamic writings etc! The one who respects the letters of the alphabet and even blank papers, how conscious would he be about treating Muslims with respect!

Muftī A'ẓam Hind رَحْمَةُ اللّٰهِ تَعَالٰی عَلَيْه would not miss any opportunity in comforting and sympathizing with the troubled Muslims. He would always avoid breaking the heart of Muslims, and was extremely eager to be of benefit to them. Why wouldn't he be eager to do so as the Holy Prophet صَلَّى اللهُ تَعَالٰی عَلَيْهِ وَاٰلِهٖ وَسَلَّم whose devotee he was has stated: خَيْرُ النَّاسِ اَنْفَعُهُمْ لِلنَّاسِ That is, '*Better person among people is the one who benefits people.*' *(Al-Jāmi'-uṣ-Ṣaghīr, pp. 246, Ḥadīš 4044)* Here is now a unique parable showing a Madanī glimpse of the observance of this Ḥadīš.

Muftī A'ẓam Hind رَحْمَةُ اللّٰهِ تَعَالٰی عَلَيْه was once invited to a special occasion at Madrasaĥ Faīz-ul-'Ulūm (Jamshedpur, Jharkhand India). After the ceremony ended, he got out of the Madrasaĥ to return. He had just got in the rickshaw to go to the railway station when a person came and requested, 'Your highness! Please give me some Ta'wīż for my such-and-such problem.' The head of the Madrasaĥ 'Allāmaĥ Arshad-ul-Qādirī said to that person, 'The train is about to leave, and you have come now to take Ta'wīż!'

Muftī A'ẓam Hind رَحْمَةُ اللّٰهِ تَعَالٰی عَلَيْه forbade 'Allāmaĥ Arshad-ul-Qādirī (زِيْدَ مَجْدُهٗ)[2] from stopping the person. 'Allāmaĥ Arshad-ul-Qādirī requested, 'Your highness! The train will leave!'

---

[1] Apart from a few, most of Urdu language letters of the alphabet are also Arabic.

[2] This account was probably written in the life of 'Allāmaĥ Arshad-ul-Qādirī as the Arabic words زِيْدَ مَجْدُهٗ are commonly used with a living person.

Listening to this, what Muftī A'ẓam Hind رَحْمَةُ اللّٰهِ تَعَالٰی عَلَیْه replied shows his divine fear and his sincere yearning for the comfort of the troubled Ummaĥ and is worthy of being written in gold letters. He said, 'Let the train leave, I'll take another train. If, on the Judgement Day, Allah عَزَّوَجَلَّ asked me as to why I did not help so-and-so servant of Him in his difficulty, what reply will I give?' Saying this, he had his entire luggage unloaded from the rickshaw. *(Muftī A'ẓam kī Istiqāmat-o-Karāmat, pp. 120, 121)*

May Allah عَزَّوَجَلَّ have mercy on him and forgive us without accountability for his sake!

Blessing of sacred paper

The cause for the repentance of Sayyidunā Manṣūr Bin 'Ammār عَلَیْهِ رَحْمَةُ اللّٰهِ الْغَفَّار was that once he found a piece of paper, with بِسْمِ اللّٰهِ الرَّحْمٰنِ الرَّحِیْم written on it, lying on the ground. When he could not find any appropriate place to put the paper, he swallowed it so that it would not be desecrated. The following night he had a dream in which he saw someone say, 'By the blessings of the respect you showed for the sacred piece of paper, Allah عَزَّوَجَلَّ has opened the doors of wisdom for you.' *(Risāla-tul-Qushayriyyaĥ, pp. 48)*

May Allah عَزَّوَجَلَّ have mercy on him and forgive us without accountability for his sake!

صَلُّوْا عَلَى الْحَبِيْب　　صَلَّى اللّٰهُ تَعَالٰى عَلٰى مُحَمَّد

Dear Islamic brothers! Did you see? The one respectfully picking up a piece of paper on which بِسْمِ اللّٰهِ الرَّحْمٰنِ الرَّحِیْم was written was blessed by Allah عَزَّوَجَلَّ with repentance as well as with the rank of Wilāyaĥ and even that of 'Awtād.'

It is stated in *Baĥjat-ul-Asrār* that Sayyidunā Shaykh Abū Bakr Bin Ĥawār عَلَیْهِ رَحْمَةُ اللّٰهِ الْغَفَّار has said, 'There are 7 Awtād of Iraq:

1. Sayyidunā Shaykh Ma'rūf Karkhī
2. Sayyidunā Shaykh Imām Aḥmad Bin Ḥanbal
3. Sayyidunā Shaykh Bishr Ḥāfī

4. Sayyidunā Shaykh Manṣūr Bin ʻAmmār
5. Sayyidunā Shaykh Junayd
6. Sayyidunā Shaykh Saĥl Bin ʻAbdullāĥ Tustarī
7. Sayyidunā Shaykh ʻAbdul Qādir Jīlānī رَحِمَهُمُ اللّٰهُ تَعَالٰی اَجْمَعِیْن.

(Our beloved Ghauš-e-A'ẓam رَحْمَةُ اللهِ تَعَالٰی عَلَيْه was not yet even born when Sayyidunā Shaykh Abū Bakr Bin Ĥawār عَلَيْهِ رَحْمَةُ اللّٰهِ الْغَفَّار said this. Therefore, listening to this news of Ghayb, people asked) 'Who is 'Abdul Qādir Jīlānī?' Sayyidunā Shaykh Abū Bakr Bin Ĥawār عَلَيْهِ رَحْمَةُ اللّٰهِ الْغَفَّار replied, 'He will be an 'Ajamī 'Sharīf' (the Arabs refer to the honourable descendents of the Prophet as 'Sharīf' and 'Ḥabīb', whereas the word 'Sayyid' is used in place of 'Sir.' Therefore, what is meant here is that 'Abdul Qādir Jīlānī will be a non-Arab Sayyid) who will reside in Baghdad. He will be born in the 5th century Ĥijrī and will be from among the Ṣiddīqīn (i.e. the highest ranking category of saints). Awtād are those who are the sovereigns of the world and the Quṭubs of the earth.' *(Baĥjat-ul-Asrār, pp. 385)*

May Allah عَزَّوَجَلَّ have mercy on them and forgive us without accountability for their sake!

A Quṭb is such a Walī of Allah who is in charge of the (spiritual) administration of a part of the world (i.e. a city etc.).

Parable of four Du'ās

By the blessings of respecting the piece of paper on which بِسْمِ اللّٰه was written, Sayyidunā Manṣūr Bin 'Ammār عَلَيْهِ رَحْمَةُ اللّٰهِ الْغَفَّار was raised to the rank of the greatest saints. He would earnestly spread the call to righteousness and countless people would come to listen to his speeches reverentially.

In his congregation, a deserving beggar once asked for four dirhams. Sayyidunā Manṣūr Bin 'Ammār عَلَيْهِ رَحْمَةُ اللّٰهِ الْغَفَّار announced, 'If someone gives this person four dirhams, I will make four Du'ās for him in return.' Coincidentally, a slave was passing there. As he heard the merciful voice of the saint, he instantly came to the congregation and gave four dirhams to the beggar. Sayyidunā Manṣūr رَحْمَةُ اللهِ تَعَالٰی عَلَيْه then asked the slave, 'Which four Du'ās would you like me to make for you?' The slave replied:

1. (Make Du'ā that) I be freed from slavery.
2. I receive recompense for these dirhams.
3. I and my master be blessed with sincere repentance.
4. I, my master, you and all those present be forgiven.

Raising his hands Sayyidunā Manṣūr Bin 'Ammār عَلَيۡهِ رَحۡمَةُ اللّٰهِ الۡغَفَّار made these Du'ās. The slave then left. Since the slave reached home late, his master asked him the reason of being late. The slave related the whole incident to his master. Hearing this, the master asked, 'What was your first Du'ā?' The slave replied, 'I asked for my freedom from slavery.'

On hearing this, his master said spontaneously, 'Go! You are free from slavery.' He then asked, 'What was your second Du'ā?' The slave replied, 'I asked for recompense for the four dirhams I gave.' His master said, 'In return for your four dirhams, I will give you four thousand dirhams.' He then asked, 'What was your third Du'ā?' The slave replied, 'I requested that I and my master be blessed with sincere repentance from sins.'

As soon as the master heard this, he immediately made Istighfār and said, 'I repent of all of my sins in the court of Allah عَزَّوَجَلَّ.' He then asked about the fourth Du'ā. The slave replied, 'I requested that I, my master, the saint and all the participants of the congregation be forgiven.' When the master heard this, he said, 'I have done the three things which were in my authority. The fourth thing, forgiveness for all, is beyond my power.' That night, the master had a dream in which he heard a voice say, 'You have done what was in your power. I am اَرۡحَمُ الرّٰحِمِيۡن[1]; I have forgiven you, your slave, Manṣūr and all those who were present in the congregation.' *(Rauḍ-ur-Riyāḥīn, pp. 222)*

May Allah عَزَّوَجَلَّ have mercy on them and forgive us without accountability for their sake!

Du'ā-e-Walī mayn woĥ tāšīr daykĥī
Badaltī ĥazāraun kī taqdīr daykĥī

By the effect of the supplication of a saint
Destiny of thousands of people is changed

صَلُّوۡا عَلَى الۡحَبِيۡب صَلَّى اللّٰهُ تَعَالٰى عَلٰى مُحَمَّد

[1] The Most Merciful of all those who show mercy.

Broken clay pot

One day, Shaykh Sayyidunā Mujaddid Alf-e-Šānī قُدِّسَ سِرُّهُ الرَّبَّانِي, a great saint of the Naqshbandīyyaĥ order, saw in a public toilet a filth-covered slightly broken large pot, used for the cleaning of the toilet. On looking closer he became anxious to notice that the word 'ALLAH' was engraved on the pot! Leaping forward, he picked up the pot, asked his servant to bring him a jug of water and cleaned it thoroughly with his own blessed hands, making it pure. Then, wrapping it in a white cloth he placed it at a high place out of respect. The great saint would then drink water in that pot.

One day, he رَحْمَةُ اللهِ تَعَالٰی عَلَيْه received an Ilĥām (i.e. a voice) from Allah عَزَّوَجَلَّ, 'As you have respected my name, I will also elevate your name in the world as well as in the Hereafter.' The great saint رَحْمَةُ اللهِ تَعَالٰی عَلَيْه would often say, 'The high rank I have achieved by respecting the name of Allah عَزَّوَجَلَّ, could not have been achieved even by a hundred years of worship and devotion!' *(Derived from Ḥazarat-ul-Quds, Duftar duwum, pp. 13 Mukāshafa number 35)*

Respect of blank paper

A great saint of the Naqshbandīyyaĥ order, Sayyidunā Shaykh Aḥmad Sarĥindī, famously known as Mujaddid Alf-e-Šānī قُدِّسَ سِرُّهُ الرَّبَّانِي, would even respect blank papers. One day, he was resting on his bed when he suddenly came down from it in anxiety and said, 'It seems as though there is some piece of paper beneath the bed.' *(Zubdat-ul-Maqāmāt, pp. 192)*

Do not kick papers whilst walking

Dear Islamic brothers! The foregoing parable shows that one should respect even blank papers as the Holy Quran, Aḥādīš and Islamic rulings are written on them. اَلْحَمْدُ لِلّٰه عَزَّوَجَلَّ! This parable also shows a clear-cut saintly miracle of Sayyidunā Mujaddid Alf-e-Šānī قُدِّسَ سِرُّهُ الرَّبَّانِي. He became aware of the presence of a piece of paper beneath the bed without apparently seeing it and came down from the bed, giving his devotees a lesson of respecting pieces of paper.

It is stated in 'Bahār-e-Sharī'at', 'It is prohibited to make Istinjā[1] with paper even if it is a blank one or even if the word Abū Jaĥl, the name of an unbeliever, is written on it.' *(Maṭbū'aĥ Madīna-tul-Murshid, part 2, pp. 114)*

The Arabic letters of the word 'أَبُو جَهْل (Abū Jaĥl)' include ا, ب, و, ج, ﻫ, ل which are all Quranic. Therefore, the written word أَبُو جَهْل (not the person Abū Jaĥl) will be respected in the sense that it is not allowed to place it at an impure or dirty place or to stamp on it. Those making and using paper-packets from newspapers should take some lesson from this ruling. مَعَاذَاللّٰهِ عَزَّوَجَلَّ! The newspapers used in packet-making are disrespected in several ways. For example, مَعَاذَ اللّٰهِ عَزَّوَجَلَّ, these are first thrown into the waste bin of home, then trampled upon in streets and eventually, covered in filth and dirt, reach the rubbish dump.

Furthermore, مَعَاذَ اللّٰهِ عَزَّوَجَلَّ, it is an inappropriate habit of some people that whilst walking in streets they kick different things which have writings on them such as cardboard boxes, newspapers and other types of papers. In actual fact, the virtuous act is to pick up such papers and cardboards and put them at a proper place where they would not be disrespected, or to dispose of them appropriately [e.g. by putting them into sea].

In any case, it is extremely essential to avoid kicking them and throwing them here and there. Similarly, it is also necessary to avoid cleaning or drying dishes or tables with newspapers or papers which have writing on them, drying one's hands with them, stamping on them, or spreading them on the ground to sit on etc.

Shavings of wooden pen

It is stated in *Bahār-e-Sharī'at*, 'The shavings of an unused wooden pen or pencil can be thrown away but those of a 'used' one should not be disposed of at a place where they may be disrespected. (This shows that even the shavings have to be respected, then why wouldn't the used pen or pencil be respected?) Furthermore, it is Makrūĥ to put anything on a piece of paper on which the blessed name of Allah عَزَّوَجَلَّ is written. However, it is not Makrūĥ to put money into a polythene bag even if divine names are printed on it. To wipe hands with a piece of paper after eating is also Makrūĥ.' *(Bahār-e-Sharī'at, part 16, pp. 119)*

---

[1] For details about Istinjā, see the booklet *'Method of Istinjā'* published by Maktaba-tul-Madīnaĥ.

[Translator's Note]

However, respected scholars have allowed the use of tissue papers for wiping hands. Similarly, it is also allowed to use toilet papers for drying private parts when free clods etc. are not available. This is because the tissue papers and the toilet ones are obviously made for the above-mentioned purposes, not for writing, whereas ordinary paper is made to be used for writing.

صَلُّوْا عَلَى الْحَبِيْب صَلَّى اللّٰهُ تَعَالٰى عَلٰى مُحَمَّد

Respect for even dot of ink

Sayyidunā Muhammad Ĥāshim Kishmī عَلَيْهِ رَحْمَةُ اللّٰهِ الْقَوِى has stated, 'I was once present in the blessed court of Sayyidunā Mujaddid Alf-e-Šānī قُدِّسَ سِرُّہُ الرَّبَّانِي, a great saint of the Naqshbandīyyaĥ order. He was busy with his written work when he needed to go to the toilet. He went but immediately came out and asked for a jug of water. Then, washing the nail of his blessed left hand thumb, he went to the toilet again.

Having relieved himself, he came out and said, 'As soon as I sat down in the toilet, my eye fell on an ink dot on the nail of my left hand thumb which I had put to test the pen (whether or not it was working). As I had put this dot with the pen by which I write Quranic letters I considered it disrespectful to remain there with this ink dot on my thumb. (All letters of Arabic language and most ones of Persian and Urdu are Quranic). Though there was an intense need of urination, the pain of the disrespect for (that dot) was much severer than that of urination. Therefore, I came out instantly and removed the dot.' *(Zubdat-ul-Maqāmāt, pp. 180)*

Do not paste posters on walls

اللّٰه! اللّٰه! A great saint of the Naqshbandīyyaĥ order, Sayyidunā Mujaddid Alf-e-Šānī قُدِّسَ سِرُّہُ الرَّبَّانِي would respect even a dot from the ink of a pen, whereas our state is that if our hand is stained with dots and marks whilst we are writing, we normally wash them off into the drain. When a pen or pencil becomes unusable, we dispose of it in the waste bin from where it is then thrown into the rubbish dump.

Most of those writing on blackboards with chalk wipe off unhesitatingly even sacred writings of Aḥādīš, let alone ordinary ones, not caring about the respect for the particles of chalk dust. Openly ignoring people rights, different words and slogans are chalked on walls; posters with different writings on them including religious ones are put up on others' hoardings as well as on the external walls of peoples' houses and shops etc. without their permission. In case of the resentment of the owners, these acts will be considered Ḥarām leading to Hell.

In addition, everyone is aware that religious posters pasted on walls eventually peel off walls and fall onto the ground in pieces which are then so badly disrespected that even its thought makes one tremble. If only the trend of hanging card pasted posters at appropriate places be developed instead of pasting posters directly on walls. These posters should be removed after the need is over. Similarly, banners should also be removed after their need is over or else they may also fall in pieces scattering on the ground.

Do not sell newspapers as waste

Dear Islamic brothers! These days, newspapers (in Islamic countries) usually contain بِسْمِ اللّٰهِ الرَّحْمٰنِ الرَّحِيْم, sacred Quranic verses, blessed Aḥādīš and Islamic writings, and people sell them off to waste paper collectors just for the sake of some coins. Extremely regretfully! These types of newspapers are even seen in dirty drains and sewers. If only we had respected sacred writings!

O my courageous Islamic brothers! Instead of selling newspapers just for some meagre money, please put them into the deep part of sea. اِنْ شَآءَاللّٰه عَزَّوَجَلَّ, You will get its blessings in the worldly life as well as in the afterlife. O my trading Islamic brothers! You should also avoid making paper packets from newspapers in honour and devotion to Allah عَزَّوَجَلَّ and His Beloved Prophet صَلَّى اللّٰهُ تَعَالٰى عَلَيْهِ وَاٰلِهٖ وَسَلَّم.

Some people separate religious writings containing parts of the newspaper and then use the rest to wrap up bundles and other things, assuming that they are not committing any disrespect. These people are requested to put the entire newspaper into sea because whether it is a news item or a film advertisement, it contains many Islamic names including even the words 'Allah' and 'Muhammad' such as 'Abdullāĥ, 'Abdur Raḥmān, Ghulām Muhammad etc.

Whether it is Urdu or Sindhi, English or Hindi, there is a possibility of the presence of sacred names in every newspaper of the world whichever the language. In fact, the alphabet of every language of the world should be respected as, according to the author of *Tafsīr Ṣāwī*, all languages spoken in the world are Ilĥāmī. *(Tafsīr Ṣāwī, vol. 1, pp. 30)* Therefore, it is better and safer to put them into sea. Allah عَزَّوَجَلَّ will certainly reward you for your act of respecting sacred writings.

Insanity of father

A young man once came to Sag-e-Madīnaĥ[1] and said, 'Please make Du'ā for my father who is insane. He has the crazy habit of picking up newspapers and pieces of written papers from streets, and then putting them into sea. He does not also take the money I offer to him.'

Realising the situation I asked the young man, 'Are you a government employee?' He replied in the affirmative. I then said, 'Convey my Salām to your respectable father with a request to make Du'ā for my forgiveness; you should serve and look after him. The reason why he collects newspapers etc. is that newspapers contain sacred writings, and the reason why he does not take your money is that you are a government employee, and most of government employees receive unlawful salaries because of not fulfilling their duties properly.' Hearing this, he admitted that he did not properly fulfill his working duties.

Dear Islamic brothers! Like the father of the young man كَثَّرَ اللهُ تَعَالٰى اَمْثَالَهُمْ [that is, *may Allah* عَزَّوَجَلَّ *increase the number of such people*], if every Muslim gets 'Madanī insanity' then indeed the light of piety and blessings will prevail everywhere, turning our society into a 'Madanī society.'

صَلُّوْا عَلَى الْحَبِيْب صَلَّى اللهُ تَعَالٰى عَلٰى مُحَمَّد

Dear Islamic brothers! In order to develop a 'Madanī mindset', make it a habit to travel with Madanī Qāfilaĥs with the devotees of Rasūl. Listen to a faith-refreshing incident of the bounties of the Noble Prophet صَلَّى اللهُ تَعَالٰى عَلَيْهِ وَاٰلِهٖ وَسَلَّم on the participants of Dawat-e-Islami's Madanī Qāfilaĥs.

---

[1] The author, Amīr-e-Aĥl-e-Sunnat دَامَتْ بَرَكَاتُهُمُ الْعَالِيَه refers to himself as 'Sag-e-Madīnaĥ' out of humbleness.

Bounty of the Prophet ﷺ for Madanī Qāfilaĥ travellers

Here is a summary of the account given by a devotee of Rasūl. He has stated: Our Sunnaĥ-Inspiring Madanī Qāfilaĥ travelled from Hyderabad (Bāb-ul-Islam, Sindh) to Khyber Pakhtunkhwa. Having spent three days in a Masjid, we left for another area but got lost on the way, ending up in a jungle. Night had fallen and darkness had prevailed everywhere. There were no signs of population far and wide. Every passing moment increased our concern and worry. Then, there was a glimmer of hope as we caught a glimpse of what seemed to be a lamp flickering in the distance. We hurried towards it out of joy, but it suddenly disappeared just after a few moments, leaving us standing in astonishment and anxiety. We were unable to decide what to do and where to go!

We remained in the state of fear for a while. All of a sudden, the light appeared again from the same direction. Mentioning the name of Allah عَزَّوَجَلَّ and plucking up the courage, we headed swiftly towards the light again, hoping to get help from someone. When we approached, we saw a standing person with a lamp in his hand. He met us warmly and took us to his house where we found 12 cups already arranged for 12 participants of the Madanī Qāfilaĥ. Tea had also been prepared in advance! He served us with hot tea. We were astonished at this timely help from Ghayb and the prior arrangement of 12 cups of tea.

When asked, our host who was a stranger to us revealed, 'I was asleep when my sleeping fortune awoke, blessing me with the vision of the Noble Prophet صَلَّى اللهُ تَعَالٰى عَلَيْهِ وَاٰلِهٖ وَسَلَّم in my dream. He صَلَّى اللهُ تَعَالٰى عَلَيْهِ وَاٰلِهٖ وَسَلَّم said, 'The travellers of a Madanī Qāfilaĥ of Dawat-e-Islami have got lost on the way. Stand outside with a lamp in order to help them.' I awoke and stood outside with the lamp. I kept standing in wait for a while but couldn't see anybody. I thought perhaps I misunderstood the dream. I felt very sleepy so I returned home and went to sleep again.

My eyes closed but the door of my heart opened, and I was privileged to see the blessed face of the Prophet of Raḥmaĥ, the Intercessor of Ummaĥ صَلَّى اللهُ تَعَالٰى عَلَيْهِ وَاٰلِهٖ وَسَلَّم once again. His blessed lips moved and the following words were uttered: 'O devotee! There are 12 travellers in the Madanī Qāfilaĥ; arrange tea for them and immediately stand outside with a lamp.' Preparing tea instantly I stood outside with a lamp. Soon the Madanī Qāfilaĥ of the devotees of Rasūl also arrived.'

Meal from Prophet ﷺ

Dear Islamic brothers! This incident has made it clear that the Holy Prophet صَلَّى اللهُ تَعَالٰى عَلَيْهِ وَاٰلِهٖ وَسَلَّم possesses the knowledge of Ghayb and holds Dawat-e-Islami dear, a movement of the rightly-guided Muslims. اَلْحَمْدُ لِلّٰه عَزَّوَجَلَّ, Our Holy Prophet صَلَّى اللهُ تَعَالٰى عَلَيْهِ وَاٰلِهٖ وَسَلَّم always keeps his devotees in his merciful gaze, helps them when in trouble, and feeds them when hungry.

Imām Yūsuf Bin Ismā'īl Nabĥānī قُدِّسَ سِرُّهُ الرَّبَّانِی has narrated that Shaykh Abul 'Abbās Aḥmad Bin Nafīs Tūnisī عَلَيْهِ رَحْمَةُ اللهِ الْقَوِی has stated, 'During my stay in Madīna-tul-Munawwaraĥ, I once experienced extreme hunger. Presenting myself at the blessed tomb of the Holy Prophet صَلَّى اللهُ تَعَالٰى عَلَيْهِ وَاٰلِهٖ وَسَلَّم, I pleaded, 'Yā Rasūlallāĥ صَلَّى اللهُ تَعَالٰى عَلَيْهِ وَاٰلِهٖ وَسَلَّم! I am hungry.' Suddenly, I fell asleep. Meanwhile, someone awoke me and asked me to go with him. I agreed so he took me to his house. Serving me with dates, butter and wheat bread he said, 'Eat until you are satiated because my blessed ancestor Sayyidunā Muhammad صَلَّى اللهُ تَعَالٰى عَلَيْهِ وَاٰلِهٖ وَسَلَّم has commanded me to be hospitable to you. Come to me whenever you feel hunger in future.'

(Ḥujjatullāĥi-'alal-'Ālamīn, vol. 2, pp. 573)

Pītay ĥayn tayray dar kā, kĥātay ĥayn tayray dar kā
Pānī ĥay tayrā pānī dānaĥ ĥay tayrā dānaĥ

What we drink is from your court
What we eat is from your court

(Sāmān-e-Bakhshish)

Respect alphabet of every language

Dear Islamic brothers! Never write 'بِسْمِ اللهِ الرَّحْمٰنِ الرَّحِيْم' or any other sacred names at such things where there is a possibility of them being desecrated. Nothing should be written on the ground in any language, and the alphabet of all languages should be respected. Do not place your foot on such a thing or place where something is written in any language. The doormats with the word 'WELCOME' printed or embroidered on them should not be placed outside the door. If the name of the company is printed on footwear, even if in English, one should remove the name before one uses the footwear.

Often, labels with manufacturer name printed in English, Arabic or Urdu are attached to even prayer-mats. Sadly, these labels are often sewn near the foot of the prayer-mat.

Furthermore, such written labels are also seen on plastic mats, blankets, towels etc. These labels should be removed and disposed of appropriately by being put into sea.

Labels with manufacturer name are often found on bed mattresses. If only these companies would not test us in this way! Carefully consider the jurisprudential clause stated on page 237 of the 16th part of *Baĥār-e-Sharī'at* with reference to *Rad-dul-Muḥtār*, 'If anything is written on bedding or prayer-mat then it is not permissible to use it regardless of whether the words are printed or embroidered or written with ink. The same ruling will apply even if separate letters are written as separate letters are also to be respected.'

The author of *Baĥār-e-Sharī'at* رَحْمَةُ اللهِ تَعَالٰى عَلَيْه has further stated, 'Writing is often seen on dining mats. This sort of dining mat (with company name or couplets printed or written on it) should not be used, nor should food be served on it. (In some parts of the subcontinent) couplets are written on some people's pillows; these should not also be used.'

In any case, whether it is a prayer-mat or a carpet, a floor covering that one has hired[1] or bought for his home, a pillow or a mattress – anything one sits or places his foot on should contain no writing in any language, nor should any printed label be attached to it. The manufacturing company name and address containing sticker is usually pasted underneath carpets and rugs; wet this type of sticker and peel it away after a few minutes.

Arabic writings should particularly be respected as Arabic is the sacred language of our Arab Prophet صَلَّى اللهُ تَعَالٰى عَلَيْهِ وَاٰلِهٖ وَسَلَّم as well as the language of the Holy Quran and that of the Paradise dwellers. Allah عَزَّوَجَلَّ forbid, it is extremely disrespectful and unfortunate to throw away Arabic writings or put them into garbage bins even if printed on food and drink packaging.

Sacred links of numbers

Sometimes, though no word, a number is often printed on footwear. A devotee does not like to place his foot on any number as every number has some sacred link.

[1] It is common in some parts of the subcontinent to hire floor coverings and crockery, especially on the occasion of some gathering. [Translator's Note]

For example, it is stated on page 22 of *Aḥsan-ul-Wi'ā* about the repetition of Du'ā in odd number, 'Allah عَزَّوَجَلَّ is 'Witr' (alone) and likes Witr (i.e. odd numbers such as 1, 3, 5, 7 etc.). 5 is better, and Allah عَزَّوَجَلَّ very much likes the number 7, and the very least is 3. (In other words, whenever one makes Du'ā, he should repeat it seven times or else five times or at least three times).'

Even numbers also have a great deal of sacred links. For example, the sacred link in the number 2 is that the 'Urs of Sayyidunā Ma'rūf Karkhī عَلَيْهِ رَحْمَةُ اللّٰهِ الْقَوِى and that of Ṣadr-ush-Sharī'aĥ رَحْمَةُ اللّٰهِ تَعَالٰى عَلَيْه, the author of *Bahār-e-Sharī'at* is observed on 2 Muḥarram-ul-Harām and 2 Żul-Qa'da-til-Ḥarām respectively.

The number 4 is linked with the 4 nearest and dearest companions of the Prophet. Whoever is a devotee to the 4 dearest companions will succeed in the worldly life as well as in the afterlife, اِنْ شَآءَاللّٰه عَزَّوَجَلَّ! The number 6 is linked with 6 Rajab-ul-Murajjab, the 'Urs-day of Gharīb Nawāz رَحْمَةُاللّٰهِ تَعَالٰى عَلَيْه, whereas the link of the number 8 is that there are 8 Paradises, and the 'Urs of Maulānā Ḥashmat 'Alī Khān عَلَيْهِ رَحْمَةُ الْمَنَّان is also solemnized on 8 Muḥarram-ul-Harām. The link of the number 10 is that it marks the day of 'Āshūrā, the day when Sayyidunā Imām Ḥusayn رَضِىَ اللّٰهُ تَعَالٰى عَنْه was martyred, and it is also connected with Eid-ul-Aḍḥā. The prominence of the sacred links of 11 and 12 is widespread and celebrated amongst all devotees.

Kiyā ghaur jab Giyārĥwīn Bārĥwīn mayn
Mu'ammaĥ yeĥ ĥam per kĥulā Ghauš-e-A'ẓam رَحْمَةُاللّٰهِ تَعَالٰى عَلَيْه
Tumĥayn waṣl bay-faṣl ĥay Shāĥ-e-Dīn say
Diyā Ḥaq nay yeĥ martabaĥ Ghauš-e-A'ẓam رَحْمَةُاللّٰهِ تَعَالٰى عَلَيْه

When I pondered over the '11th' and the '12th'
I realised the actual matter, O Ghauš-e-A'ẓam رَحْمَةُاللّٰهِ تَعَالٰى عَلَيْه
You have unbroken linage with the Prophet صَلَّى اللّٰهُ تَعَالٰى عَلَيْهِ وَاٰلِهٖ وَسَلَّم
This is your grand status, O Ghauš-e-A'ẓam رَحْمَةُاللّٰهِ تَعَالٰى عَلَيْه

Method of putting sacred papers into sea

Enviable are the fortunate Muslims who pick up newspapers, sacred papers and pieces of cardboard etc. from the ground, on seeing them, and put them into the deep part of the sea or river, respecting them. Sacred papers should not be put into the shallow part of the sea as this generally causes them to float to the shore.

The method of putting them into the sea is as follows: Place them in an empty bag or sack with a heavy stone inside the sack and then do make some cuts in the sack so that water would enter it immediately and it would reach the bottom of the sea.

If the sack is put into the sea without any cut in it, the sea-water will not enter the sack which then sometimes floats for many miles, reaching the shore. At times, the uncivilised or unbelievers empty out the sack at the coast in the greed of getting what it contained, leading to such severe acts of desecration that even its thought makes the heart of a devotee tremble. In order to ensure that the sack containing sacred papers reaches the deep part of the sea, one can take help from a Muslim boatman. In any case, cuts must be made in the sack.

صَلُّوْا عَلَى الْحَبِیْب صَلَّى اللّٰهُ تَعَالٰى عَلٰى مُحَمَّد

Method of burying sacred papers

It is also permissible to bury sacred papers. Describing the method of burying sacred papers, Ṣadr-ush-Sharī'aĥ رَحْمَةُ اللهِ تَعَالٰى عَلَيْه has stated on page 121 of the 16th part of *Bahār-e-Sharī'at* with reference to *'Ālamgīrī*: 'If a copy of the Holy Quran has become so old that it can no longer be used for recitation, and there is likelihood that its pages will come off the binding and be lost, it should then be wrapped in a pure cloth and be buried at a safe place. For this, make a Laḥad (by digging the ground and making an opening, in the Qiblaĥ-facing side of the wall, large enough for all sacred papers to be placed in it) so that soil would not fall on sacred papers. Alternatively, (place the papers into the dug ground), cover it with a plank and then cover the plank with soil so that soil would not fall on the papers. If a copy of the Holy Quran has become old, it should not be burned.'

صَلُّوْا عَلَى الْحَبِیْب صَلَّى اللّٰهُ تَعَالٰى عَلٰى مُحَمَّد

29 Madanī pearls of بِسۡمِ اللّٰه

(The first 10 Madanī pearls are extracted from *Tafsīr-e-Na'īmī*, page 44, part 1).

1. بِسۡمِ اللّٰهِ الرَّحۡمٰنِ الرَّحِيۡم is a complete verse of the Holy Quran, not a part of any Sūraĥ. It has been revealed to separate one Sūraĥ from the other. This is why it is recited in low voice during Ṣalāĥ. However, the Ḥāfiẓ completing the recitation of the entire Quran in Ṣalāt-ut-Tarāwīḥ should recite بِسۡمِ اللّٰهِ الرَّحۡمٰنِ الرَّحِيۡم aloud once with any Sūraĥ.

2. One should begin the recitation of every Sūraĥ with بِسۡمِ اللّٰهِ الرَّحۡمٰنِ الرَّحِيۡم except for Sūraĥ At-Taubaĥ. If, however, one is going to start recitation from Sūraĥ At-Taubaĥ, then he should recite بِسۡمِ اللّٰهِ الرَّحۡمٰنِ الرَّحِيۡم for the commencement of recitation.

3. It is stated in the book *Shāmī,* it is better not to recite بِسۡمِ اللّٰه before smoking a Ḥuqqaĥ [water-pipe] or before eating odorous things (e.g. raw onion, garlic etc.).

4. It is prohibited to recite بِسۡمِ اللّٰه in the lavatory.

5. Whilst one is offering Ṣalāĥ, it is Mustaḥab for him to recite بِسۡمِ اللّٰهِ الرَّحۡمٰنِ الرَّحِيۡم in low voice before he begins the recitation of a Sūraĥ.

6. Any respectable piece of work started without the recitation of بِسۡمِ اللّٰه will have no blessings in it.

7. At the time of laying the deceased into the grave, those doing this job should recite بِسۡمِ اللّٰهِ وَعَلٰى مِلَّةِ رَسُوۡلِ اللّٰهِ.

8. The sermon of Jumu'aĥ, Nikāḥ and (both) Eids etc. should be started with 'اَلۡحَمۡدُ لِلّٰه', that is, بِسۡمِ اللّٰه should be recited in low voice (in the beginning). When the Khaṭīb (i.e. the one delivering the sermon) is going to recite a verse of the Holy Quran during the sermon, he should recite بِسۡمِ اللّٰه aloud (before he recites the verse).

9. It is Wājib to recite بِسۡمِ اللّٰه [i.e. to mention the name of Allah عَزَّوَجَلَّ] at the time of slaughtering an animal. If it is missed deliberately (i.e. the name of Allah عَزَّوَجَلَّ is not

mentioned), the slaughter will be unlawful and the animal will not be Ḥalāl to be consumed. However, if one forgets to recite it, the animal will be Ḥalāl.

10. (In case of Żabḥ-e-Iḍṭirārī, i.e. compelled slaughter) If someone, for example, hunts an animal or a bird with a hunting arrow or a spear or something sharp and recites بِسْمِ اللّٰه at the time of shooting the arrow etc. at the animal, the animal will be Ḥalāl (to be consumed) even if it dies before the hunter reaches it.

    If a pet animal runs away from the owner, for example, a cow escapes and falls into a well, or a camel runs away, and someone kills it by an arrow or a spear or a sword after he has recited بِسْمِ اللّٰه, the animal is Ḥalāl, i.e. lawful to be consumed. (However, after reciting بِسْمِ اللّٰه, if someone kills a wild animal or a bird with a stick or a stone or a bullet or a gunshot, the animal or the bird will be Harām because it has died of injury, not because of blood release & flow that is necessary for lawful slaughter. If it was captured whilst injured, it will become Ḥalāl by Żabḥ-e-Shar'ī [Islamic slaughter]. Żabḥ-e-Ikhtiyārī is necessary to render the wild animal or bird Ḥalāl that is in one's captivity, that is, it must be slaughtered as per the stipulated method of Sharī'aĥ with the mention of the name of Allah عَزَّوَجَلَّ).

11. Sayyīdunā Shaykh Abul 'Abbās Aḥmad Bin 'Alī Būnī رَحْمَةُ اللهِ تَعَالٰى عَلَيْه has stated, 'If anyone recites بِسْمِ اللهِ الرَّحْمٰنِ الرَّحِيْم 786 times daily (with Ṣalāt-'Alan-Nabī ﷺ once before and after it) for seven consecutive days, اِنْ شَآءَاللّٰه عَزَّوَجَلَّ his every need will be fulfilled whether it is the need of getting rid of any adversity or attaining any good or that of having prosperity in his business.' *(Shams-ul-Ma'ārif, pp. 73)*

12. Before going to sleep, whoever recites بِسْمِ اللهِ الرَّحْمٰنِ الرَّحِيْم 21 times (with Ṣalāt-'Alan-Nabī ﷺ once before and after it), will be protected that night from Satan, burglary, sudden death and all types of calamities and troubles, اِنْ شَآءَاللّٰه عَزَّوَجَلَّ. *(Shams-ul-Ma'ārif, pp. 73)*

13. Whoever recites بِسْمِ اللهِ الرَّحْمٰنِ الرَّحِيْم 50 times (with Ṣalāt-'Alan-Nabī ﷺ once before and after it) in front of an oppressor, the oppressor will develop fear in his heart for the reciter, and the reciter will remain safe from the mischief of the oppressor. *(Shams-ul-Ma'ārif, pp. 73)*

14. Whoever recites بِسۡمِ اللّٰہِ الرَّحۡمٰنِ الرَّحِیۡم 300 times and Ṣalāt-'Alan-Nabī ﷺ 300 times at the time of sunrise, whilst facing the sun, will be given sustenance by Allah عَزَّوَجَلَّ from such a source that he cannot even imagine. Further (by reciting it daily) he will become wealthy within a year, اِنۡ شَآءَاللّٰہ عَزَّوَجَلَّ. *(Shams-ul-Ma'ārif, pp. 73)*

15. If a person who has a weak memory recites بِسۡمِ اللّٰہِ الرَّحۡمٰنِ الرَّحِیۡم 786 times (with Ṣalāt-'Alan-Nabī ﷺ once before and after it) and makes *Dam* (i.e. blows on) water and then drinks the water, his memory will improve and he will remember whatever he hears, اِنۡ شَآءَاللّٰہ عَزَّوَجَلَّ. *(Shams-ul-Ma'ārif, pp. 73)*

16. If a drought occurs, recite بِسۡمِ اللّٰہِ الرَّحۡمٰنِ الرَّحِیۡم 61 times (with Ṣalāt-'Alan-Nabī ﷺ once before and after it and then make Du'ā), there will be rain (in the drought affected area), اِنۡ شَآءَاللّٰہ عَزَّوَجَلَّ. *(Shams-ul-Ma'ārif, pp. 73)*

17. Write بِسۡمِ اللّٰہِ الرَّحۡمٰنِ الرَّحِیۡم 35 times on a piece of paper (with Ṣalāt-'Alan-Nabī ﷺ once before and after it) and hang it in the house, اِنۡ شَآءَاللّٰہ عَزَّوَجَلَّ Satan will not pass through the house, and there will be a great deal of blessings. If one hangs it in his shop, his business will flourish, اِنۡ شَآءَاللّٰہ عَزَّوَجَلَّ. *(Shams-ul-Ma'ārif, pp. 73)*

18. One who writes بِسۡمِ اللّٰہِ الرَّحۡمٰنِ الرَّحِیۡم 130 times (or gets it written on a piece of paper) on 1st Muḥarram-ul-Ḥarām and keeps it with him (or puts it on as a Ta'wīż after covering it in a plastic coating and getting it sewn in some cloth or leather)[1] - اِنۡ شَآءَاللّٰہ عَزَّوَجَلَّ, he and all of his family members will remain safe from every type of evil throughout their life. *(Shams-ul-Ma'ārif, pp. 74)*

19. If the children of a woman do not survive [i.e. die in infancy] she should write بِسۡمِ اللّٰہِ الرَّحۡمٰنِ الرَّحِیۡم 61 times (or have it written) and keep it with her. اِنۡ شَآءَاللّٰہ عَزَّوَجَلَّ, Her children will remain alive. (By coating it in plastic or sealing it in wax paper and then sewing it in cloth or leather, she may also put it on around her neck or tie it around her arm). *(Shams-ul-Ma'ārif, pp. 74)*

---

[1] Do not wear any type of Ta'wīż in a metal box. Its ruling has already been mentioned on page 48.

20. Write بِسْمِ اللهِ الرَّحْمٰنِ الرَّحِيْم 70 times on a piece of paper and place it inside the shroud of the deceased, the matter pertaining to Munkar and Nakīr[1] will become easier, اِنْ شَآءَاللّٰه عَزَّوَجَلّ. [It is better to make an arch in the wall towards the Qiblaĥ in front of the face of the deceased and place it inside the arch, along with the 'Aĥd Nāmaĥ and Shajaraĥ of the Pīr[2] Sahib of the deceased]. *(Shams-ul-Ma'ārif, pp. 84)*

21. Always recite بِسْمِ اللهِ الرَّحْمٰنِ الرَّحِيْم with correct pronunciation and articulation. Recite بِسۡمِ اللّٰه to a Qārī or an Islamic scholar. If the letters are not pronounced correctly then learn it. Otherwise it is feared that one may suffer loss instead of gaining benefit.

22. It is not necessary to put diacritical marks when writing بِسۡمِ اللّٰه. Whenever you write a verse or text to use it as a Ta'wīż for wearing, drinking or hanging, then ensure that the circles of circle-containing letters are left open. For example, the circle of 'Ĥa (ه)' in الله and that of 'Mīm (م)' in رَحْمٰن (Raḥmān) and رَحِيْم (Raḥīm) should be left open.

23. If one recites بِسۡمِ اللّٰه before one takes off clothes, jinns cannot see his Satr. *('Aml-ul-Yaum wal-Laylaĥ li-Ibn Sunnī, pp. 8)* Whenever you open or close a door, window, cupboard, drawer or whenever you pick up or put down clothes, utensils or any other thing, make it your habit to recite بِسْمِ اللهِ الرَّحْمٰنِ الرَّحِيْم evil jinns will not be able to enter your home, steal or use your belongings, اِنْ شَآءَاللّٰه عَزَّوَجَلّ.

24. If your vehicle skids or jolts, recite بِسۡمِ اللّٰه.

25. Recite بِسْمِ اللهِ الرَّحْمٰنِ الرَّحِيْم before applying oil to hair; otherwise 70 devils will join in.

26. Do recite بِسْمِ اللهِ الرَّحْمٰنِ الرَّحِيْم when closing the door of your house. (By the blessing of this) Satan and wicked jinns will not be able to enter the house, اِنْ شَآءَاللّٰه عَزَّوَجَلّ. *(Ṣaḥīḥ Bukhārī, vol. 6, pp. 312)*

---

[1] The questioning angels of the grave.

[2] Spiritual guide.

27. At night, cover the eating and drinking utensils with something after you have recited بِسۡمِ اللّٰه. If there is nothing to cover with, recite بِسۡمِ اللهِ الرَّحۡمٰنِ الرَّحِیۡم and place a splinter etc. on the edge of the utensil. *(Ṣaḥīḥ Bukhārī, vol. 6, pp. 312)*

    According to a narration of *Ṣaḥīḥ Muslim*, 'During the year there is one such night in which epidemic descends; if the epidemic passes by an uncovered utensil or a water bag with its mouth open, then the epidemic enters it.' *(Ṣaḥīḥ Muslim, pp. 1115, Ḥadīš 2114)*

28. Before sleeping, one should recite بِسۡمِ اللهِ الرَّحۡمٰنِ الرَّحِیۡم and dust off his bedding 3 times, one will remain safe from harmful things, اِنۡ شَآءَاللّٰه عَزَّوَجَلَّ.

29. At the time of lawful trading of your business, whenever you receive something from someone and give something to someone, recite بِسۡمِ اللهِ الرَّحۡمٰنِ الرَّحِیۡم. There will be a great deal of blessings, اِنۡ شَآءَاللّٰه عَزَّوَجَلَّ.

Yā Allah عَزَّوَجَلَّ! Shower us with the blessings of بِسۡمِ اللهِ الرَّحۡمٰنِ الرَّحِیۡم and enable us to recite بِسۡمِ اللهِ الرَّحۡمٰنِ الرَّحِیۡم before we initiate every virtuous and lawful act.

اٰمِین بِجَاہِ النَّبِیِّ الۡاَمِین صَلَّی اللهُ تَعَالٰی عَلَیۡهِ وَاٰلِهٖ وَسَلَّم

صَلُّوۡا عَلَی الۡحَبِیۡب صَلَّی اللهُ تَعَالٰی عَلٰی مُحَمَّد

7 Parables

1. Wood cutter became wealthy

There was a woodcutter who would cut and collect wood and provide for his family by selling them. Since the jungle was situated at the other side of the river he would travel a long distance everyday to reach the jungle crossing the bridge built over the river. This would take a lot of time and was a hindrance to his affluence.

One day, he listened to the excellence of بِسۡمِ اللّٰہِ الرَّحۡمٰنِ الرَّحِیۡم during the speech of a preacher in a Masjid, developing the mindset that even the biggest problem can be solved by the blessing of بِسۡمِ اللّٰه. Therefore, when it was time to go to the jungle, instead of taking the route of the bridge, he started walking on the river water reciting بِسۡمِ اللّٰہِ الرَّحۡمٰنِ الرَّحِیۡم and soon reached the other side easily. After he cut and collected wood, he returned as he had come. By the blessings of بِسۡمِ اللّٰه, he became wealthy within a short period of time. *(Derived from Shams-ul-Wā'iẓīn)*

صَلُّوۡا عَلَی الۡحَبِیۡب صَلَّی اللّٰهُ تَعَالٰی عَلٰی مُحَمَّد

Dear Islamic brothers! All these are the marvels of firm belief. If the belief is not firm, these fruitful results cannot be achieved. As regards 'firm belief' Ḥujjat-ul-Islam Sayyidunā Imām Muhammad Ghazālī عَلَیۡهِ رَحۡمَةُ اللّٰهِ الۡوَالِی has narrated an excellent parable in the exegesis of Sūraĥ Yūsuf.

In Baghdad, a person asked people for a dirham. A renowned Muḥaddiš Sayyidunā Ibn Sammāk رَحۡمَةُ اللّٰهِ تَعَالٰی عَلَیۡه asked him, 'Which Sūraĥ do you know well by heart?' He replied, 'Sūraĥ Al-Fātiḥaĥ.' The eminent scholar said, 'Recite it once and sell its reward to me. I will give you all of my wealth in return.'

The beggar replied, 'Your Eminence! I have come here in compulsion to ask for a dirham, not to sell the Quran!' Saying this, the beggar went to the graveyard. Meanwhile, it rained heavily with hailing. The beggar leapt under a roof for shelter where he came across a rider dressed in green clothes. The rider asked, 'Are you the person who had refused to sell the reward of Sūraĥ Al-Fātiḥaĥ?' The beggar replied in the affirmative. Then, presenting him with a 10,000 dirhams containing bag the rider said, 'Spend this, and when you have spent them all I will give you 10,000 dirhams again, اِنۡ شَآءَاللّٰه عَزَّوَجَلَّ.' The beggar asked, 'But, who are you?' The rider replied, 'I am your firm belief.' The rider then left. *(Derived from Tafsīr Sūraĥ Yūsuf lil-Ghazālī, pp. 17)*

This parable also contains a lesson for those begging money by reciting the Holy Quran as well as for those attending the congregations of Quranic recitation, Na'at and Żikr merely due to their greed for money and food, and also for those reciting the Holy Quran in Tarāwīḥ Ṣalāĥ for money. May Allah عَزَّوَجَلَّ bless us with the imperishable wealth of sincerity and firm belief.

آمِيْن بِجَاهِ النَّبِيِّ الْاَمِيْن صَلَّى اللهُ تَعَالٰى عَلَيْهِ وَاٰلِهٖ وَسَلَّم

Mayrā ĥar 'amal bas Tayray wāsiṭay ĥo
Kar ikhlāṣ aysā 'aṭā Yā Ilāĥī عَزَّوَجَلَّ

My every deed be solely for Your pleasure, O Almighty عَزَّوَجَلَّ
Bless me with such a treasure of sincerity

Dear Islamic brothers! Indeed sincerity is a precious treasure. Whoever finds it becomes successful. Travel with Sunnaĥ-Inspiring Madanī Qāfilaĥs in the company of the devotees of Rasūl, the Madanī mindset of performing deeds with sincerity will be developed, اِنْ شَآءَاللّٰه عَزَّوَجَلَّ. If deeds are sincere, then اِنْ شَآءَاللّٰه عَزَّوَجَلَّ, holy visions will automatically come to their seeker as shown in the following account!

Vision of Prophet ﷺ during cassette Ijtimā'

At the end of the 3-day international Sunnaĥ-Inspiring Ijtimā' of Dawat-e-Islami (held in Ṣaḥrā-e-Madīnaĥ, Madīna-tul-Auliyā Multan) a large number of Madanī Qāfilaĥs of the devotees of Rasūl travel to various villages, towns and cities in order to learn and teach Sunnaĥs. Here is a summary of the account given by a devotee of Rasūl from one of such Madanī Qāfilaĥs.

After the 3-day international Sunnaĥ-Inspiring Ijtimā' (held in 1423 A.H.) ended, a 12-day Sunnaĥ-Inspiring Madanī Qāfilaĥ of the devotees of Rasūl departed from Ṣaḥrā-e-Madīnaĥ, Madīna-tul-Auliyā Multan and reached district Layyah (Punjab, Pakistan).

In accordance with the schedule of the Madanī Qāfilaĥ, when the cassette Ijtimā' was held, a devotee of Rasūl was so greatly moved by the Sunnaĥ-Inspiring speech that he began to cry uncontrollably and eventually passed out.

After he recovered he was very delighted. He exclaimed, 'اَلْحَمْدُ لِلّٰه عَزَّوَجَلَّ I, a sinner, have been blessed with the vision of the Holy Prophet صَلَّى اللهُ تَعَالٰى عَلَيْهِ وَاٰلِهٖ وَسَلَّم!' The next day, when the cassette Ijtimā' was held again, he experienced the same (spiritual) condition and was blessed with the vision of the Beloved and Blessed Prophet صَلَّى اللّٰهُ تَعَالٰى عَلَيْهِ وَاٰلِهٖ وَسَلَّم again. This time he saw that all the participants of the Madanī Qāfilaĥ were also present in the blessed court.

Ānkĥayn jo band ĥaun to muqaddar kĥulayn Ḥasan
Jalway khud āyaīn ṭālib-e-dīdār kī ṭaraf

The eyes close but the fortune awakes, O Ḥasan!
Towards their seeker, advance the holy visions

(Żauq-e-Na'at)

صَلُّوْا عَلَى الْحَبِيْب صَلَّى اللّٰهُ تَعَالٰى عَلٰى مُحَمَّد

Satanic deception

Some people relate their dreams only to impress others, so anyone claiming to have seen the Beloved and Blessed Prophet صَلَّى اللّٰهُ تَعَالٰى عَلَيْهِ وَاٰلِهٖ وَسَلَّم or any other holy individual in his dream should not be believed blindly; he should at least be made to swear to tell the truth.

Cure for satanic deception

The very first Ḥadīš of *Ṣaḥīḥ Bukhārī* says اِنَّمَا الْاَعْمَالُ بِالنِّيَّاتِ, i.e. '*Deeds are dependent upon intentions.*' If someone mentions his dreams to others for show-off, fame and ostentation, he is certainly a sinner, but if someone relates his dreams with good intentions, there is no harm in it. For instance, if a person who has fortunately had a good dream during a Sunnaĥ-Inspiring Madanī Qāfilaĥ of Dawat-e-Islami mentions his dream in this sinful era with the intention of motivating and persuading other people so that they would also travel in the path of Allah and get the satisfaction of heart realizing that Dawat-e-Islami is a Sunnaĥ-Inspiring movement of the rightly-guided Muslims and Rasūl's devotees and so that they would be inspired to join Dawat-e-Islami and protect their faith; so this is a commendable intention, and the one mentioning his dream with this intention will get reward, اِنْ شَآءَ اللّٰه عَزَّوَجَلَّ

Further, mentioning dreams with the intention of expressing gratitude for a divine bounty is also permissible. However, if there's a fear of ostentation, one should not declare one's name as it is safer to do so. Anyway, Allah عَزَّوَجَلَّ knows the intention of the heart. To unreasonably have a bad suspicion about a Muslim is a Ḥarām act leading to Hell. The act of having bad suspicions has been condemned by the Holy Quran and Ḥadīš. Therefore, verse 12, Sūraĥ Al-Ḥujurāt, part 26 says:

يٰۤاَيُّهَا الَّذِيْنَ اٰمَنُوا اجْتَنِبُوْا كَثِيْرًا مِّنَ الظَّنِّ ۫ اِنَّ بَعْضَ الظَّنِّ اِثْمٌ

O those who believe! Avoid more suspicions; verily some suspicion is a sin.

[Kanz-ul-Īmān (Translation of Quran)]

Similarly, it is stated in a Ḥadīš, 'Avoid bad suspicion as bad suspicion is the greatest lie.' *(Ṣaḥīḥ Bukhārī, vol. 6, pp. 166, Ḥadīš 5143)* A'lā Ḥaḍrat Imām Aḥmad Razā Khān عَلَيْهِ رَحْمَةُ الرَّحْمٰن has quoted in *Fatāwā-e-Razawiyyaĥ*, 'Sayyidunā 'Īsā عَلٰى نَبِيِّنَا وَ عَلَيْهِ الصَّلٰوةُ وَالسَّلَام once saw a thief steal something so he عَلَيْهِ السَّلَام said, 'Have you not stolen?' The thief replied, 'By Allah عَزَّوَجَلَّ! I have not stolen anything.' Listening to this, Sayyidunā Īsā عَلٰى نَبِيِّنَا وَ عَلَيْهِ الصَّلٰوةُ وَالسَّلَام said, 'You have not stolen indeed, my eyes have deceived me.'

Dear Islamic brothers! The foregoing parable highlights the importance of respect for a Muslim, giving the lesson that one should hide the faults of a Muslim whilst remaining within the bounds of Sharī'aĥ. It should not happen that one brands a Muslim liar and smooth-talker and unreasonably opens the door of bad suspicions, endangering his own afterlife and, Allah forbid, making himself deserving of Hell.

تُوْبُوْا اِلَى الله　　　اَسْتَغْفِرُ الله

Punishment for relating fabricated dream

Even if someone relates a false and fabricated dream, he is himself responsible for it and is a grave sinner, deserving of the punishment of Hell. The Noble Prophet صَلَّى اللهُ تَعَالٰى عَلَيْهِ وَاٰلِهٖ وَسَلَّم has warned, 'The one relating a false dream will be given the punishment of tying a knot in two grains of barley, on the Judgement Day, and he will never be able to tie the knot.' *(Ṣaḥīḥ Bukhārī, vol. 8, pp. 106, Ḥadīš 7042)*

Speaking without weighing words!

It is stated in another Ḥadīš, 'A person talks and does not ponder over what he talks (whereas his talking contains Ḥarām acts such as lying, backbiting, faultfinding or relating fabricated dreams etc.), so because of this, he falls into (so much depth of) Hell that (the depth) is greater than even the distance between the east and the west.' *(Ṣaḥīḥ Bukhārī, vol. 7, pp. 236, Ḥadīš 6477)* By Sharī'aĥ, it is not Wājib to make the one relating his dream to swear to tell the truth. Further, if he is a liar he might even swear falsely, مَعَاذَاللّٰه عَزَّوَجَلَّ.

Satanic deception

After all, it seems more appropriate to conceal the dream rather than relating it to others.

Cure for satanic deception

The respected and revered Islamic saints knew better than us what appropriate is and what not. Sharī'aĥ has not prohibited relating good dreams so who are we to prevent this! The Holy Quran, Aḥādīš and the books of Islamic saints contain a great deal of dreams. Syyiduna Imām Abul Qāsim Qushayrī رَحْمَةُاللّٰهِ تَعَالٰى عَلَيْه has quoted 66 dreams of Islamic saints on page 368 to 377 in the chapter 'Ruyal Qawm' of his book '*Risālaĥ Qushairiyaĥ.*'

Similarly, Ḥujjat-ul-Islam Sayyidunā Imām Muhammad Ghazālī عَلَيْهِ رَحْمَةُ اللّٰهِ الْوَالِى has also quoted 49 dreams on page 540 to 543 in the chapter '*Manāmāt-ul-Mashāikh*' in the fourth volume of his book '*Iḥyā-ul-Ulūm.*'

Furthermore, 14 dreams of A'lā Ḥaḍrat, Imām-e-Aĥl-e-Sunnat, reviver of Sunnaĥ, eradicator of Bid'aĥ, scholar of Sharī'aĥ, 'Allāmaĥ Maulānā Al-Ḥāj, Al-Qārī, Ash-Shāĥ Imām Aḥmad Razā Khān عَلَيْهِ رَحْمَةُ الرَّحْمٰن have been narrated in his own words on page 424 to 432 of the book '*Ḥayāt-e-A'lā Ḥaḍrat*' (published by Maktaba Nabawiyyaĥ, Ganj Bakhsh road, Lahore). One of these dreams is mentioned below.

Dream of A'la Hadrat رَحْمَةُ اللهِ عَلَيْه

Proving the permissibility of shaking hands with both hands, A'lā Ḥaḍrat رَحْمَةُ اللّٰهِ تَعَالٰى عَلَيْه has written a 40 pages containing booklet entitled 'صَفَايِحُ اللِّجَيْن فِيْ كَوْنِ تَصَافُح بِكَفَّيِ الْيَدَيْن'

(i.e. silver leaves in relation to shaking hands with the palms of both hands). On page 3 of the booklet, A'lā Ḥaḍrat رَحْمَةُ اللهِ تَعَالٰی عَلَيْه has mentioned a detailed account of his dream in which he saw Sayyidunā Imām Qāḍī Khān عَلَيْهِ رَحْمَةُ الْحَنَّان. Further, in order to save Muslims from satanic deceptions and enlighten them, A'lā Ḥaḍrat رَحْمَةُ اللهِ تَعَالٰی عَلَيْه has stated concrete evidences in the booklet proving the permissibility of relating dreams to others.

Prophet ﷺ interprets dream

A'lā Ḥaḍrat رَحْمَةُ اللهِ تَعَالٰی عَلَيْه has stated in the foregoing booklet that authentic Aḥādīš have proven that the Beloved and Blessed Prophet صَلَّى اللهُ تَعَالٰی عَلَيْهِ وَاٰلِهٖ وَسَلَّم would attach great importance to it (i.e. dreams) and consider it highly significant to listen to, ask about, and relate dreams.

Stated here is a Ḥadīš narrated by Samuraĥ Bin Jundab رَضِیَ اللهُ تَعَالٰی عَنْه in *Ṣaḥīḥ Bukhārī* and other books, 'After offering Ṣalāt-ul-Fajr, the Beloved and Blessed Prophet صَلَّى اللهُ تَعَالٰی عَلَيْهِ وَاٰلِهٖ وَسَلَّم would ask the attendees, 'Did anyone have any dream last night?' Whoever had a dream would relate it and the Holy Prophet صَلَّى اللهُ تَعَالٰی عَلَيْهِ وَاٰلِهٖ وَسَلَّم would interpret it.' *(Ṣaḥīḥ Bukhārī, vol. 2, pp. 127, Ḥadīš 1386)*

A'lā Ḥaḍrat رَحْمَةُ اللهِ تَعَالٰی عَلَيْه has further stated, 'Abū Sa'īd Khudrī رَضِیَ اللهُ تَعَالٰی عَنْه has narrated a Ḥadīš reported in *Aḥmad*, *Bukhārī* and *Tirmižī* that the Holy Prophet صَلَّى اللهُ تَعَالٰی عَلَيْهِ وَاٰلِهٖ وَسَلَّم has stated, 'Whenever anyone of you have such a dream that he finds pleasant, it is from Allah عَزَّوَجَلَّ. He should glorify Allah عَزَّوَجَلَّ for this and relate it to other people.' *(Musnad Imām Aḥmad, vol. 2, pp. 502, Ḥadīš 6223)*

Glad tidings will continue

A'lā Ḥaḍrat رَحْمَةُ اللهِ تَعَالٰی عَلَيْه has further stated in the foregoing booklet that the Holy Prophet صَلَّى اللهُ تَعَالٰی عَلَيْهِ وَاٰلِهٖ وَسَلَّم has stated, 'Prophethood has ended. Now, there will be no Prophethood after me, but glad tidings. What are they? (Glad-tidings are) pious dreams which a person has himself or which (others) have about him.' *(Mu'jam Kabīr, vol. 3, pp. 179, Ḥadīš 3051)*

Reward for having favourable dream

A'lā Ḥaḍrat رَحْمَةُ اللهِ تَعَالٰی عَلَيْه has further stated, 'It is also proved by the Sunnaĥ of companions رَضِیَ اللهُ تَعَالٰی عَنْهُم that if any dream favoured their (i.e. companions) verdict they would get delighted by it and enhance the status of the dreaming person.

It is stated in the *Ṣaḥīḥayn*, 'During Hajj Tamattu' Sayyidunā Abū Jamraĥ Ḍab'ī رَضِیَ اللّٰہُ تَعَالٰی عَنْہُ had a dream which favoured the doctrine of Sayyidunā Ibn 'Abbās رَضِیَ اللّٰہُ تَعَالٰی عَنْہُمَا (in terms of jurisprudential rulings). (Hearing that blessed dream) Sayyidunā Ibn 'Abbās رَضِیَ اللّٰہُ تَعَالٰی عَنْہُمَا set a stipend (for him from his own wealth) and began to seat Sayyidunā Abū Jamraĥ Ḍab'ī رَضِیَ اللّٰہُ تَعَالٰی عَنْہُ with him on his own throne since then.' *(Ṣaḥīḥ Bukhārī, vol. 2, pp. 186, Ḥadīš 1567)*

May Allah عَزَّوَجَلَّ have mercy on them and forgive us without accountability for their sake!

Dream of mother of Imām Bukhārī عَلَیْہِ رَحْمَۃُ الْبَارِی

Dear Islamic brothers! You have listened to two narrations, with reference to *Ṣaḥīḥ Bukhārī*, as regards relating dreams to others. The compiler of *Ṣaḥīḥ Bukhārī*, Sayyidunā Shaykh Abū 'Abdullāĥ Muhammad Bin Ismā'īl Bukhārī عَلَیْہِ رَحْمَۃُ اللّٰہِ الْبَارِی compiled blessed Aḥādīš with great care and dedication. He رَحْمَۃُ اللّٰہِ تَعَالٰی عَلَیْہِ has stated, 'اَلْحَمْدُ لِلّٰہ عَزَّوَجَلَّ I have included almost 6000 Aḥādīš in *Ṣaḥīḥ Bukhārī*. I would make Ghusl and offer two Rak'āt Nafl Ṣalāĥ before I wrote any Ḥadīš.'

His respected father Sayyidunā Shaykh Ismā'īl رَحْمَۃُ اللّٰہِ تَعَالٰی عَلَیْہِ was a very pious person and his respected mother was also a very righteous and Mujāba-tud-Du'ā woman (i.e. the one whose prayers are answered). In his childhood, Sayyidunā Imām Bukhārī عَلَیْہِ رَحْمَۃُ اللّٰہِ الْبَارِی lost his eyesight. Saddened by this grief, his respected mother would often weep and tearfully make Du'ā for her son to regain his eyesight.

One night, when she went to sleep, the star of her fortune shone, blessing her in dream with the vision of Sayyidunā Ibrāĥīm Khalīlullāĥ عَلٰی نَبِیِّنَا وَ عَلَیْہِ الصَّلٰوۃُ وَالسَّلَام. He عَلَیْہِ السَّلَام said, 'You have been praying that your son regain his eyesight. Congratulations! Your prayer has been answered, and Allah عَزَّوَجَلَّ has restored your son's eyesight.' In the morning, she saw that Sayyidunā Imām Bukhārī عَلَیْہِ رَحْمَۃُ اللّٰہِ الْبَارِی had regained his lost eyesight. *(Derived from Tafĥīm-ul-Bukhārī, vol. 1, pp. 4)*

May Allah عَزَّوَجَلَّ have mercy on them and forgive us without accountability for their sake!

صَلُّوْا عَلَى الْحَبِیْب صَلَّى اللّٰهُ تَعَالٰى عَلٰى مُحَمَّد

2. Interesting incident of two non-Muslims

A non-Muslim man was madly in love with a non-Muslim woman, and had almost left even eating and drinking in her love. Eventually, he came to the blessed court of Sayyidunā 'Aṭa-ul-Akbar عَلَيْهِ رَحْمَةُ اللّٰهِ الدَّاوَر and told him of the situation. The great saint wrote بِسْمِ اللّٰهِ الرَّحْمٰنِ الرَّحِيْم on a piece of paper and gave it to him saying, 'Swallow this paper hoping that Allah عَزَّوَجَلَّ would bless you with patience in this matter or would make it possible for you to marry her.'

As the non-Muslim man swallowed the paper, (a Madanī transformation took place in his heart and) he said, 'O 'Aṭā رَحْمَةُ اللّٰهِ تَعَالٰى عَلَيْه! I have felt the sweetness of Īmān with Nūr in my heart. I have become free from the love of that woman; please enlighten me about Islam.' Sayyidunā 'Aṭā رَحْمَةُ اللّٰهِ تَعَالٰى عَلَيْه invited him to embrace Islam, and he became a Muslim by the blessings of بِسْمِ اللّٰه.

When that non-Muslim woman heard the news of his acceptance of Islam, she also came to the blessed court of Sayyidunā 'Aṭā-ul-Akbar عَلَيْهِ رَحْمَةُ اللّٰهِ الدَّاوَر and said, 'O leader of Muslims! I am the woman mentioned to you by that newly reverted Muslim. Last night I had a dream in which I saw someone say to me, 'If you wish to see your abode in Paradise then go to the blessed court of Sayyidunā 'Aṭā-ul-Akbar عَلَيْهِ رَحْمَةُ اللّٰهِ الدَّاوَر, he will show you your abode.'

Inspired by what I saw in the dream, I have come to you; please tell me, where is Paradise?' He رَحْمَةُ اللّٰهِ تَعَالٰى عَلَيْه replied, 'If you intend (to go to) Paradise, you will have to open its portal (i.e. door) first, only then you will be able to go towards it.'

She asked, 'How will I be able to open its portal?' He replied, 'Recite بِسْمِ اللّٰهِ الرَّحْمٰنِ الرَّحِيْم.' As soon as she recited بِسْمِ اللّٰه (a Madanī transformation took place in her heart and) she said, 'O 'Aṭā رَحْمَةُ اللّٰهِ تَعَالٰى عَلَيْه! I have found Nūr in my heart and witnessed the divinity of Allah عَزَّوَجَلَّ. Please enlighten me about Islam.' The great saint invited her to embrace Islam, and she also became a Muslim by the blessings of بِسْمِ اللّٰه. She then returned home.

At night, she went to sleep and had a dream in which she found herself to have entered Paradise where she saw palaces and domes. Inscribed on one of the domes of Paradise was بِسْمِ اللّٰهِ الرَّحْمٰنِ الرَّحِيْم لَآ اِلٰهَ اِلَّا اللّٰهُ مُحَمَّدٌ رَّسُوْلُ اللّٰه. As she read the inscription she heard someone say, 'O reciter! Allah عَزَّوَجَلَّ has bestowed upon you (all those heavenly bounties you have seen in dream) by the blessing of what you have recited.'

After she awoke from her dream she pleaded, 'O Allah عَزَّوَجَلَّ! You have turned me out of Paradise after You had made me enter it. O Allah عَزَّوَجَلَّ! For the sake of Your omnipotence, free me from the grief of the world.' When she finished her Du'ā, the roof of her house collapsed on her and she was martyred. So Allah عَزَّوَجَلَّ had mercy on her by the blessings of بِسْمِ اللّٰهِ الرَّحْمٰنِ الرَّحِيْم. *(Qalyūbī Ḥikāyat, pp. 22)*

May Allah عَزَّوَجَلَّ have mercy on them and forgive us without accountability for their sake!

صَلُّوْا عَلَى الْحَبِيْب　　صَلَّى اللّٰهُ تَعَالٰى عَلٰى مُحَمَّد

تُوْبُوْا اِلَى اللّٰه　　اَسْتَغْفِرُ اللّٰه

صَلُّوْا عَلَى الْحَبِيْب　　صَلَّى اللّٰهُ تَعَالٰى عَلٰى مُحَمَّد

بِسْمِ اللّٰه *kī barakat ĥay, kitnī achchĥī qismat ĥay*
Ĥum nay pāyī Jannat ĥay, yeĥ sab Rab عَزَّوَجَلَّ *kī raḥmat ĥay*

By the blessing of بِسْمِ اللّٰه *and the grace of Allah*
We have got a good fortune and will enter heaven soon

Dear Islamic brothers! The mercy of Allah عَزَّوَجَلَّ is immense. By His grace, He guides even the most impious people to the courts of His Auliyā, thereby making them pious and successful.

اَلْحَمْدُلِلّٰه عَزَّوَجَلَّ, Those associated with Dawat-e-Islami, a global & non-political movement of the Quran and Sunnaĥ, are proud to be the devotees of the Auliyā of Allah. When these devotees of saints travel with sincere intentions in Sunnaĥ-Inspiring Madanī Qāfilaĥs, calling people towards righteousness, sometimes, even unbelievers enter the fold of Islam. Here is a marvel of a Madanī Qāfilaĥ.

A non-Muslim embraced Islam

A preacher of Dawat-e-Islami from Khanpur (Punjab, Pakistan) has stated: 'A Sunnaĥ-Inspiring Madanī Qāfilaĥ came to our city from Bāb-ul-Madīnaĥ Karachi. Along with the participants of the Madanī Qāfilaĥ, I was also privileged to take part in the area visit to call people towards righteousness. Gathering people outside a tailor shop we presented the 'call to righteousness.' When the speech ended, a young worker from the shop said, 'I am a non-Muslim. Your 'call to righteousness' has made a profound impact on my heart. Please make me a Muslim.' اَلْحَمْدُلِلّٰه عَزَّوَجَلَّ, he then embraced Islam.

Maqbūl jaĥān bĥar mayn ĥo Dawat-e-Islami
Ṣadaqaĥ tujĥay ay Rab-e-Ghaffār Madīnay kā

May Dawat-e-Islami become glorious throughout the world
For the sake of Madīnaĥ, O the Creator of the world

صَلُّوْا عَلَى الْحَبِيْب صَلَّى اللّٰهُ تَعَالٰى عَلٰى مُحَمَّد

3. Pious elderly wrestler

A non-Muslim robber once entered a grand palace where he found no one except for a pious elderly man and his young daughter. The robber intended to martyr the pious elderly man and capture his daughter along with his wealth. With this evil intention, he attacked the old man, but the weak-looking elderly man turned out to be a strong wrestler! He immediately wrestled the young robber to the ground.

The robber somehow wriggled free and attacked the elderly man but was defeated again. The wrestling continued between them and the pious elderly man defeated the robber every time. Meanwhile, noticing that the old man was reciting something in low voice, the robber asked, 'What are you reciting?' Revealing the secret of his strength, the pious elderly man said with a smile, 'I am a very weak person but I am reciting بِسْمِ اللّٰهِ الرَّحْمٰنِ الرَّحِيْم, so Allah عَزَّوَجَلَّ has enabled me to overpower you.'

As soon as the non-Muslim robber heard this, he was overwhelmed by a Madanī transformation in his heart and remarked, 'How great and glorious would be the religion whose just one invocation of بِسۡمِ اللّٰہِ الرَّحۡمٰنِ الرَّحِیۡم is so marvellous!' Saying this, he embraced Islam by the blessing of hearing the recitation of بِسۡمِ اللّٰہِ الرَّحۡمٰنِ الرَّحِیۡم. A close relationship was then developed between them. When the pious elderly man passed away, the new Muslim was married to the elderly man's daughter and was given all of his wealth along with the grand palace. *(Asrār-ul-Fātiḥaĥ, pp. 165)*

May Allah عَزَّوَجَلَّ have mercy on them and forgive us without accountability for their sake!

Ḥamd ĥay us żāt ko jis nay Musalmān kar diyā
'Ishq-e-Sultan-e-Jaĥān sīnay mayn pinĥān kar diyā

Glory be to the One who has blessed us with Islam
And has filled our heart with devotion to the world's Sultan

Dear Islamic brothers! The pious elderly man was indeed a Walī of Allah. He repeatedly defeated the non-Muslim by the blessings of بِسۡمِ اللّٰہِ الرَّحۡمٰنِ الرَّحِیۡم, which was also a saintly miracle of his. Further, the non-Muslim was also blessed with the gift of Islam by the blessings of بِسۡمِ اللّٰہِ الرَّحۡمٰنِ الرَّحِیۡم. Listen to a faith-refreshing and heart-warming parable of a pious lady who was also a devotee of بِسۡمِ اللّٰه!

صَلُّوْا عَلَى الْحَبِيْب صَلَّى اللّٰهُ تَعَالٰى عَلٰى مُحَمَّد

4. Recovery of pouch from well

There was a pious lady who would often recite بِسۡمِ اللّٰہِ الرَّحۡمٰنِ الرَّحِیۡم. Her husband who was a hypocrite was very annoyed with this habit of her. Furious and jealous, he plotted to disgrace his wife in such a way that she would never forget it. One day, handing over a bag to his wife, he said, 'Keep it in some safe place.' The lady took the bag and kept it in a safe place. A few days later, the husband secretly took the bag and threw it into the well of his house so that his wife would never find it.

After some time, he asked his wife to bring the bag. She came to where she had kept it. As soon as she recited بِسْمِ اللّٰه, Allah عَزَّوَجَلَّ commanded Jibrāīl عَلَيْهِ السَّلَام to go quickly and place the bag where it was. In an instance, Sayyidunā Jibrāīl عَلَيْهِ السَّلَام took the bag out from the well and placed it where it lay. When the pious lady stretched out her hand to take the bag, she found it as she had kept it. Astonished by receiving the bag, her husband sincerely repented to Allah عَزَّوَجَلَّ. *(Qalyūbī Ḥikāyat, pp. 11)*

May Allah عَزَّوَجَلَّ have mercy on them and forgive us without accountability for their sake!

صَلُّوْا عَلَى الْحَبِيْب صَلَّى اللّٰهُ تَعَالٰى عَلٰى مُحَمَّد

Dear Islamic brothers! These are all the marvels of بِسْمِ اللّٰه. The fortunate one who recites بِسْمِ اللّٰهِ الرَّحْمٰنِ الرَّحِيْم before every permissible and respectable act whether it is an important act or a minor one is helped by Ghayb in times of difficulty.

Maḥabbat mayn aysā gumā Yā Ilāĥī
Na pāūn pĥir apnā patā Yā Ilāĥī

May I remain engrossed in Your devotion, O Almighty
May I remain indifferent to the world, O Almighty

5. Palace of Pharaoh

Before claiming divinity, Pharaoh had a palace constructed and had بِسْمِ اللّٰهِ الرَّحْمٰنِ الرَّحِيْم inscribed on its external door. When he claimed divinity, Sayyidunā Mūsā عَلٰى نَبِيِّنَا وَعَلَيْهِ الصَّلٰوةُ وَالسَّلَام asked him to believe in Allah عَزَّوَجَلَّ but he defied. Sayyidunā Mūsā عَلٰى نَبِيِّنَا وَعَلَيْهِ الصَّلٰوةُ وَالسَّلَام humbly said to Allah عَزَّوَجَلَّ, 'O Allah عَزَّوَجَلَّ! I repeatedly call him to You but he does not give up his defiance. I do not see any signs of goodness in him.' Allah عَزَّوَجَلَّ said, 'O Mūsā (عَلٰى نَبِيِّنَا وَعَلَيْهِ الصَّلٰوةُ وَالسَّلَام), you want him to be annihilated as you see his Kufr [unbelief], but I see My name he has had inscribed on his door!' *(Tafsīr Kabīr, vol. 1, pp. 152)*

Protection of home

Dear Islamic brothers! We should write بِسۡمِ اللّٰہِ الرَّحۡمٰنِ الرَّحِیۡم on the external door of our home. اِنۡ شَآءَاللّٰہ عَزَّوَجَلَّ, We will be protected from all types of worldly calamities. Sayyīdunā Imām Fakhruddīn Rāzī رَحۡمَۃُاللّٰہِ تَعَالٰی عَلَیۡہ has stated, 'Whoever writes بِسۡمِ اللّٰہِ الرَّحۡمٰنِ الرَّحِیۡم on the main gate of his house will have no fear of annihilation (in the world only) even if he is an unbeliever; so what would be the extent of protection and blessings for the Muslim on whose heart بِسۡمِ اللّٰہِ الرَّحۡمٰنِ الرَّحِیۡم remains engraved for his entire life!' *(Tafsīr Kabīr, vol. 1, pp. 152)*

صَلُّوۡا عَلَی الۡحَبِیۡب صَلَّی اللّٰہُ تَعَالٰی عَلٰی مُحَمَّد

6. Human or jinn?

It is stated in '*Kitāb-un-Naṣāiḥ*' that the maid of the famous companion Sayyidunā Abū Dardā رَضِیَ اللّٰہُ تَعَالٰی عَنۡہ once asked him, 'Your Eminence! Tell me honestly; are you a human or a jinn?' He رَضِیَ اللّٰہُ تَعَالٰی عَنۡہ replied, 'اَلۡحَمۡدُلِلّٰہ عَزَّوَجَلَّ, I am a human.' The maid said, 'But you do not seem to be a human being to me because I have been poisoning you for the past forty consecutive days but the poison has had no effect on you!' He رَضِیَ اللّٰہُ تَعَالٰی عَنۡہ exclaimed, 'Don't you know that those making the Żikr of Allah عَزَّوَجَلَّ in all types of circumstances cannot be harmed by anything? اَلۡحَمۡدُلِلّٰہ عَزَّوَجَلَّ, I make the Żikr of Allah عَزَّوَجَلَّ with Ism-e-A'ẓam. The maid asked, 'What is the Ism-e-A'ẓam?' He replied (I always recite the following words before I eat or drink anything):

بِسۡمِ اللّٰہِ الَّذِیۡ لَا یَضُرُّ مَعَ اسۡمِہٖ شَیۡءٌ فِی الۡاَرۡضِ وَلَا فِی السَّمَآءِ وَهُوَ السَّمِیۡعُ الۡعَلِیۡم

Translation: I begin with the name of Allah عَزَّوَجَلَّ with the blessings of whose name nothing from the earth and skies can cause any harm. He is the All-Hearing, All-Knowing.

The eminent companion then asked her as to why she poisoned him. She replied that she had done so because she had a grudge against him. Hearing this, he said, 'I free you for the pleasure of Allah عَزَّوَجَلَّ, and forgive you for whatever you have done to me.' *(Ḥayāt-ul-Ḥaywān-ul-Kubrā, vol. 1, pp. 391)*

May Allah عَزَّوَجَلَّ have mercy on him and forgive us without accountability for his sake!

سُبْحٰنَ اللّٰہ عَزَّوَجَلَّ! The virtues and greatness of the blessed companions رَضِیَ اللّٰہُ تَعَالٰی عَنْہُم cannot be expressed in words. The character of these noble individuals truly reflects the exegesis of the divine commandment اِدْفَعْ بِالَّتِیْ ھِیَ اَحْسَنُ (Translation from Kanz-ul-Īmān: '*O listener! Repel the evil with good*'). *(Part 24, Sūraĥ Ḥā-Mīm As-Sajdaĥ, verse 34)*

Instead of having the maid punished who had repeatedly poisoned him, Sayyidunā Abū Dardā رَضِیَ اللّٰہُ تَعَالٰی عَنْہُ freed and forgave her. Listen to one more similar parable.

7. Poisonous food

A maid of Sayyidunā Abū Muslim Khūlanī قُدِّسَ سِرُّہُ الرَّبَّانِی would poison him because of having a grudge against him but the poison had no effect on him. This continued for a long period of time. At last she said, 'I have been poisoning you for a long time, but the poison has had no effect on you!' The eminent saint رَحْمَۃُ اللّٰہِ تَعَالٰی عَلَیْہ asked, 'Why did you do this?' She replied, 'Because you have become very old.' He said, 'اَلْحَمْدُ لِلّٰہ عَزَّوَجَلَّ, I always recite بِسْمِ اللّٰہِ الرَّحْمٰنِ الرَّحِیْم before I eat and drink anything. (By the blessings of this, I have remained protected from the effects of the poison).' Then, he رَحْمَۃُ اللّٰہِ تَعَالٰی عَلَیْہ freed her. *(Qalyūbī Ḥikāyat, pp. 52)*

Bay-nawā muflis-o-muĥtāj gadā kaun? Kay mayn
Sahib-e-Jūd-o-Karam waṣf ĥay kis kā? Tayrā

I am a helpless destitute
And generosity is your attribute

(Żauq-e-Na'at)

صَلُّوْا عَلَی الْحَبِیْب صَلَّی اللّٰہُ تَعَالٰی عَلٰی مُحَمَّد

سُبْحٰنَ اللّٰہ عَزَّوَجَلَّ! How great are the marvels of بِسْمِ اللّٰہ!

Satanic deception

It is evident from above narrations and incidents that even if you eat poison after reciting بِسْمِ اللّٰہ it will not affect you, but who can take such a great risk? We know from experience that if we ever eat spicy food, for example, despite having recited بِسْمِ اللّٰه we get stomach upsets!

Cure for satanic deception

If properly fired from a high-quality gun, a bullet can even kill a lion. In like manner, invocations and Du'ās are like bullets while the tongue of the reciter is like a gun. The Du'ās are the same, but our tongues are not like those of the companions and the noble saints. How can effectiveness be achieved by the tongue committing the sins of lying, backbiting, tale-telling, swearing, hurting and misbehaving others! We also make Du'ā, but when confronted with troubles, we go to pious people and request them to make Du'ā for us. This is simply because everybody has the mindset that the Du'ā uttered by a pure tongue is more effective.

Without doubt, reciting بِسْمِ اللهِ الرَّحْمٰنِ الرَّحِيْم Sayyidunā Khālid Bin Walīd رَضِیَ اللہُ تَعَالٰی عَنْہُ drank poison fearlessly and remained absolutely unharmed from the effect of the poison because his tongue, his heart and his entire body was pure from sins, اَلْحَمْدُلِلّٰه عَزَّوَجَلَّ. This is the blessing of the pure name of Allah عَزَّوَجَلَّ that the poison did not affect him.

Similarly, Sayyidunā Abū Dardā and Sayyidunā Abū Muslim Khūlanī رَضِیَ اللہُ تَعَالٰی عَنْہُمَا would utter the blessed name of Allah عَزَّوَجَلَّ with their pure tongues, and the poison would turn harmless to them. Otherwise, poison is, after all, poison and can cause serious harm to the human body.

How deadly poison is can be further clarified by the following incident extracted from *Kitāb-ul-Ażkiyā'*, 'During the journey, a caravan of Hajj pilgrims reached a water spring and learnt that in the vicinity was a family of expert doctors. The excuse they invented to visit the family was that they scratched the shin of one of their companions with a twig from jungle, leaving it bleeding slightly. Then, taking him to the door of their house, one of them called out, 'Does anyone treat snakebites here?' Hearing this, a little girl came out from the house. After she looked carefully at the wound, she commented, 'No snake has bitten this person; instead, his shin has been scratched by something on which a male poisonous snake had urinated. This person will no longer remain alive and will die when the sun rises tomorrow.' Therefore, what the little girl had predicted happened and that person passed away as soon as the sun rose. *(Ḥayāt-ul-Ḥaywān-ul-Kubrā, vol. 1, pp. 391)*

Yā Allah عَزَّوَجَلَّ! Bless us with the privilege of repeatedly reciting بِسْمِ اللّٰهِ الرَّحْمٰنِ الرَّحِيْم. Forgive us and free us from sins. Yā Allah عَزَّوَجَلَّ! Bless us with martyrdom under the green dome while we are beholding the vision of the Beloved and Blessed Prophet صَلَّى اللهُ تَعَالٰى عَلَيْهِ وَاٰلِهٖ وَسَلَّم, with burial in Jannat-ul-Baqī, and with the neighbourhood of Your Beloved Prophet صَلَّى اللهُ تَعَالٰى عَلَيْهِ وَاٰلِهٖ وَسَلَّم in Jannat-ul-Firdaus! Forgive the entire Ummaĥ of Your Beloved Prophet صَلَّى اللهُ تَعَالٰى عَلَيْهِ وَاٰلِهٖ وَسَلَّم.

اٰمِيْن بِجَاهِ النَّبِيِّ الْاَمِيْن صَلَّى اللهُ تَعَالٰى عَلَيْهِ وَاٰلِهٖ وَسَلَّم

صَلُّوْا عَلَى الْحَبِيْب　　صَلَّى اللّٰهُ تَعَالٰى عَلٰى مُحَمَّد

تُوْبُوْا اِلَى الله　　اَسْتَغْفِرُ الله

صَلُّوْا عَلَى الْحَبِيْب　　صَلَّى اللّٰهُ تَعَالٰى عَلٰى مُحَمَّد

اَلۡحَمۡدُ لِلّٰہِ رَبِّ الۡعٰلَمِیۡنَ وَ الصَّلٰوۃُ وَالسَّلَامُ عَلٰی سَیِّدِ الۡمُرۡسَلِیۡنَ

اَمَّا بَعۡدُ فَاَعُوۡذُ بِاللّٰہِ مِنَ الشَّیۡطٰنِ الرَّجِیۡمِ ؕ بِسۡمِ اللّٰہِ الرَّحۡمٰنِ الرَّحِیۡمِ ؕ

Graciousness of Prophet ﷺ to Maḥmūd Ghaznawī

A person once came to Sultan Maḥmūd Ghaznawī[1] عَلَیۡہِ رَحۡمَۃُ اللّٰہِ الۡقَوِی and said: I had a long-standing desire to see the Beloved and Blessed Prophet صَلَّی اللّٰہُ تَعَالٰی عَلَیۡہِ وَاٰلِہٖ وَسَلَّم. Fortunately, my dearest wish was fulfilled last night, blessing me with the vision of the Holy Prophet صَلَّی اللّٰہُ تَعَالٰی عَلَیۡہِ وَاٰلِہٖ وَسَلَّم. Finding the Beloved and Blessed Prophet صَلَّی اللّٰہُ تَعَالٰی عَلَیۡہِ وَاٰلِہٖ وَسَلَّم in a delightful mood, I pleaded, 'Yā Rasūlallāh صَلَّی اللّٰہُ تَعَالٰی عَلَیۡہِ وَاٰلِہٖ وَسَلَّم, I owe 1000 dirhams and I am not able to pay it. I fear that if I die whilst in debt, the burden of the debt will be on my back.'

The Blessed Prophet صَلَّی اللّٰہُ تَعَالٰی عَلَیۡہِ وَاٰلِہٖ وَسَلَّم said to me, 'Go to Maḥmūd Subuktagīn; he will pay off your debt.' I said, 'I fear he won't believe me. If you tell me some sign to make him believe me, it would be highly gracious of you.' The Noble Rasūl صَلَّی اللّٰہُ تَعَالٰی عَلَیۡہِ وَاٰلِہٖ وَسَلَّم said, 'Go and tell him; O Maḥmūd! You recite Ṣalāt [Durūd] 30,000 times in the first part of the night and, after you wake up from sleep, you recite Ṣalāt further 30,000 times in the latter part of the night. Hearing this sign from you, he will pay off you debt, اِنۡ شَآءَ اللّٰہ عَزَّوَجَلَّ.'

When Sultan Maḥmūd عَلَیۡہِ رَحۡمَۃُ اللّٰہِ الۡوَدُوۡد heard the merciful message from the Holy Prophet صَلَّی اللّٰہُ تَعَالٰی عَلَیۡہِ وَاٰلِہٖ وَسَلَّم, he began to cry. Then, confirming what that debtor had said, he not only paid off his debt but also gave further 1000 dirhams. Astonished, the courtiers said to the king, 'Your Eminence! This person has told something almost impossible and you have still believed it. We remain here in the royal palace with you and have never seen you recite Ṣalāt-'Alan-Nabī ﷺ in such a huge number, nor is it usually possible for a person to recite Ṣalāt-'Alan-Nabī ﷺ 60,000 times within a night.'

Listening to this, Sultan Maḥmūd Ghaznawī عَلَیۡہِ رَحۡمَۃُ اللّٰہِ الۡقَوِی responded, 'You are right but I have heard from Islamic scholars about a particular Ṣalāt-'Alan-Nabī ﷺ. If a person

---

[1] Sultan Maḥmūd Ghaznawī عَلَیۡہِ رَحۡمَۃُ اللّٰہِ الۡقَوِی was an extremely brave king from Ghazni and a great devotee of Rasūl. He lived in the 10th Century AD. His full name was Sultan Nāṣiruddīn Ibn Subuktagīn. He made many conquests, gaining great victories.

recites that Ṣalāt-'Alan-Nabī ﷺ one time, it is as if he has recited Ṣalāt-'Alan-Nabī ﷺ 10,000 times. I recite the same Ṣalāt-'Alan-Nabī ﷺ three times in the first part of the night and three times in the latter part of the night expecting to be given the reward of reciting Ṣalāt-'Alan-Nabī ﷺ 60,000 times every night. When this fortunate devotee of Rasūl brought me the merciful message of the Beloved and Blessed Prophet صَلَّى اللهُ تَعَالٰى عَلَيْهِ وَاٰلِهٖ وَسَلَّم, it confirmed the authenticity of the *Ten Thousand Times Reward Giving Ṣalāt-'Alan-Nabī* ﷺ. I cried in happiness because it proved that the saying of the eminent scholars was absolutely correct, as the Ghayb-knowing Prophet صَلَّى اللهُ تَعَالٰى عَلَيْهِ وَاٰلِهٖ وَسَلَّم testified to it himself.' *(Rūḥ-ul-Bayān, vol. 7, pp. 234)*

May Allah عَزَّوَجَلَّ have mercy on them and forgive us without accountability for their sake!

صَلُّوْا عَلَى الْحَبِيْب   صَلَّى اللهُ تَعَالٰى عَلٰى مُحَمَّد

Ten thousand times reward giving Ṣalāt-'Alan-Nabī ﷺ

اَللّٰهُمَّ صَلِّ عَلٰى سَيِّدِنَا مُحَمَّدٍ مَّا اخْتَلَفَ الْمَلَوَانِ وَتَعَاقَبَ الْعَصْرَانِ وَكَرَّ الْجَدِيْدَانِ وَاسْتَقَلَّ الْفَرْقَدَانِ وَبَلِّغْ رُوْحَهٗ وَاَرْوَاحَ اَهْلِ بَيْتِهٖ مِنَّا التَّحِيَّةَ وَالسَّلَامَ وَبَارِكْ وَسَلِّمْ عَلَيْهِ كَثِيْرًا

O Allah عَزَّوَجَلَّ! Send Ṣalāt upon our sovereign Muhammad صَلَّى اللهُ تَعَالٰى عَلَيْهِ وَاٰلِهٖ وَسَلَّم for as long as days are continuing and morning and evening are coming one by one, and night and day are coming one by one, and for as long as the two stars are high. And (O Allah عَزَّوَجَلَّ) send Salām from us to the soul of the Holy Prophet صَلَّى اللهُ تَعَالٰى عَلَيْهِ وَاٰلِهٖ وَسَلَّم and those of his blessed family. And bless them and send Salām to them a great deal.

آدابِ طعام

ISLAMIC Manners of Eating

Shaykh-e-Tariqat Ameer-e-Ahl-e-Sunnat
the Founder of Dawat-e-Islami
Allamah Maulana Abu Bilal

MUHAMMAD ILYAS
Attar Qadiri Razavi دامت برکاتہم العالیہ

مکتبۃ المدینہ
MAKTABA TUL MADINAH
MC 1286

اَلْحَمْدُ لِلّٰہِ رَبِّ الْعٰلَمِیْنَ وَ الصَّلٰوۃُ وَالسَّلَامُ عَلٰی سَیِّدِ الْمُرْسَلِیْنَ
اَمَّا بَعْدُ فَاَعُوْذُ بِاللّٰہِ مِنَ الشَّیْطٰنِ الرَّجِیْمِ ؕ بِسْمِ اللّٰہِ الرَّحْمٰنِ الرَّحِیْمِ ؕ

Manners of Eating

Although Satan will be using every trick of his trade to prevent you from reading this chapter, go through it from beginning to end. You would perhaps realize that you were unaware of the manners of eating.

Amazing angel

The Prophet of mankind, the Peace of our heart and mind, the most Generous and Kind صَلَّى اللّٰهُ تَعَالٰى عَلَيْهِ وَاٰلِهٖ وَسَلَّم has stated, 'Undoubtedly, Allah عَزَّوَجَلَّ has stationed an angel at my grave who has been granted the power of hearing the voice of every creature. Hence, whosoever, until the Day of Judgement, recites Ṣalāt upon me, he [i.e. the angel] presents that person's name along with his father's name to me. The angel says, 'The so-and-so son of the so-and-so person has recited Ṣalāt upon you.' *(Majma'-uz-Zawāid, vol. 10, pp. 251, Ḥadīš 17291)*

صَلُّوْا عَلَى الْحَبِيْب صَلَّى اللّٰهُ تَعَالٰى عَلٰى مُحَمَّد

سُبْحٰنَ اللّٰہ عَزَّوَجَلَّ! How fortunate indeed is the person who recites Ṣalāt-'Alan-Nabī as his name along with his father's name is presented in the court of the Beloved and Blessed Prophet صَلَّى اللّٰهُ تَعَالٰى عَلَيْهِ وَاٰلِهٖ وَسَلَّم! I would like to draw your attention to a noteworthy and faith-refreshing word of wisdom regarding the foregoing Ḥadīš.

The angel stationed at the glorious grave of the Holy Prophet صَلَّى اللّٰهُ تَعَالٰى عَلَيْهِ وَاٰلِهٖ وَسَلَّم has been granted such enormous hearing power that he can simultaneously hear the low voice of Ṣalāt-recitation of millions of Muslims around the globe and he has also been granted

'Ilm-ul-Ghayb as he is aware of the name of the reciter and that of the reciter's father. If this is the amazing state of the hearing faculty and the 'Ilm-ul-Ghayb of the angel who is just a servant of the court of the Holy Prophet صَلَّى اللهُ تَعَالٰى عَلَيْهِ وَاٰلِهٖ وَسَلَّم; what will be the degree of the powers and 'Ilm-ul-Ghayb of the Noble Prophet صَلَّى اللهُ تَعَالٰى عَلَيْهِ وَاٰلِهٖ وَسَلَّم himself! Why would then he صَلَّى اللهُ تَعَالٰى عَلَيْهِ وَاٰلِهٖ وَسَلَّم not recognize his devotees, listen to their pleas and help them, with the permission of Allah عَزَّوَجَلَّ!

Mayn qurbān is adāye dast gīrī per mayray Āqā صَلَّى اللهُ تَعَالٰى عَلَيْهِ وَاٰلِهٖ وَسَلَّم
Madad ko ā gaye jab bĥī pukārā Yā Rasūlallāĥ صَلَّى اللهُ تَعَالٰى عَلَيْهِ وَاٰلِهٖ وَسَلَّم

Let my life be sacrificed on this mode of assistance
When I invoked, 'Yā Rasūlallāĥ صَلَّى اللهُ تَعَالٰى عَلَيْهِ وَاٰلِهٖ وَسَلَّم*', he arrived for assistance*

صَلُّوْا عَلَى الْحَبِيْب صَلَّى اللهُ تَعَالٰى عَلٰى مُحَمَّد

Eating is worship

Dear Islamic brothers! Food is a great divine favour with many different flavours and tastes for us. It is an act of reward to eat Ḥalāl food with good intentions conforming to Sharī'aĥ and Sunnaĥ.

A renowned exegetist of the Quran, Ḥakīm-ul-Ummat, Shaykh Muftī Aḥmad Yār Khān عَلَيْهِ رَحْمَةُ الْمَنَّان has stated, 'Eating is also a form of worship for a Muslim.' The honourable Muftī has further stated, 'Although Nikāḥ [marriage] is a Sunnaĥ of the Prophets عَلَيْهِمُ السَّلَام, Sayyidunā Yaḥyā and Sayyidunā 'Īsā عَلَيْهِمَا السَّلَام never got married. On the other hand, eating is such a Sunnaĥ which has been practiced by every Prophet عَلَيْهِ السَّلَام from Sayyidunā Ādam Ṣafīyullāĥ عَلَيْهِ السَّلَام to Sayyidunā Muhammad-ur-Rasūlullāĥ صَلَّى اللهُ تَعَالٰى عَلَيْهِ وَاٰلِهٖ وَسَلَّم. If a person dies of hunger, as a result of a hunger strike, he will die a Ḥarām death.' *(Tafsīr Na'īmī, vol. 8, pp. 51)*

Our Holy Prophet صَلَّى اللهُ تَعَالٰى عَلَيْهِ وَاٰلِهٖ وَسَلَّم has stated, 'A grateful eater is like a patient fasting person.' *(Jāmi' Tirmiżī, vol. 4, pp. 219, Ḥadīš 2494)*

Excellence of Ḥalāl morsel

There are many blessings for us in eating according to the Sunnaĥ of Beloved and Blessed Prophet صَلَّى اللّٰهُ تَعَالٰى عَلَيْهِ وَاٰلِهٖ وَسَلَّم. Shaykh Sayyidunā Imām Muhammad Ghazālī عَلَيْهِ رَحْمَةُ اللّٰهِ الْوَالِى has cited the following saying of a saint in the second volume of his world-famous book, *Iḥyā-ul-'Ulūm*: 'When a Muslim eats the first morsel of Ḥalāl food, he is absolved of the sins he committed in the past. [Furthermore,] the one who goes to a place of humiliation in search of Ḥalāl sustenance, his sins fall like the leaves that fall from a tree.' *(Iḥyā-ul-'Ulūm, vol. 2, pp. 116)*

How to make intention for eating?

It is a Sunnaĥ to eat only when one is hungry. One should make the following intention before eating: '*I am eating in order to gain strength to worship Allah* عَزَّوَجَلَّ.' Eating just to relish the taste is not something good. Shaykh Sayyidunā Ibrāĥīm Bin Shaybān عَلَيْهِ رَحْمَةُ الْمَنَّان has stated, 'I have not eaten anything for the mere satisfaction of my Nafs [i.e. carnal desires] for eighty years.' *(Iḥyā-ul-'Ulūm, vol. 2, pp. 5)* One should also make the intention of eating less than one's appetite, as the intention of eating to gain strength for the worship of Allah عَزَّوَجَلَّ will be true only when one eats less than one's appetite because gluttony causes a hindrance in worship. Furthermore, eating less food improves one's health and such a person rarely needs to visit a doctor.

How much food should be consumed?

The Noble Prophet صَلَّى اللّٰهُ تَعَالٰى عَلَيْهِ وَاٰلِهٖ وَسَلَّم has stated, 'Man does not fill a container worse than his stomach. Merely a few morsels are sufficient for him to keep his back straight. If he cannot do so, then he should keep one-third [of his stomach] for food, one third for water and one third for air.' *(Sunan Ibn Mājaĥ, vol. 4, pp. 48, Ḥadīš 3349)*

Significance of intention

The very first Ḥadīš stated in *Bukhārī* is اِنَّمَا الْاَعْمَالُ بِالنِّيَّات (that is, *the reward of deeds depends upon intentions*). *(Ṣaḥīḥ Bukhārī, vol. 1, pp. 5, Ḥadīš 1)*

Remember the fact that reward is given only for the act carried out for the pleasure of Allah عَزَّوَجَلَّ. On the other hand, if an act is carried out for ostentation it will engender sin. If some act is performed without any intention, it will bring about neither reward nor sin, provided that the act is itself Mubāḥ (i.e. permissible). For example, if one makes no intention before consuming something Ḥalāl like ice cream, dessert or bread it will bring about neither reward nor sin. However, on the Day of Judgement, there will be accountability even for Mubāḥ acts as the Prophet of mankind, the Peace of our heart and mind, the most Generous and Kind صَلَّى اللهُ تَعَالٰى عَلَيْهِ وَاٰلِهٖ وَسَلَّم has stated, حَلَالُهَا حِسَابٌ وَّ حَرَامُهَا عَذَابٌ '*There is accountability for its Ḥalāl and torment for its Ḥarām.*' *(Firdaus - bimā Šaur-ul-Khaṭṭāb, vol. 5, pp. 283, Ḥadīš 8192)*

Why was kohl used?

The Noble Prophet صَلَّى اللهُ تَعَالٰى عَلَيْهِ وَاٰلِهٖ وَسَلَّم has stated, 'Without doubt, on the Day of Judgement, one will be questioned about every act even about the use of kohl in his eyes.' *(Ḥilyat-ul-Auliyā, vol. 10, pp. 31, Ḥadīš 14404)* Therefore, it is better and safer to make good intentions before carrying out any Mubāḥ act. A saint has stated that he would like to make a (good) intention before every act including eating, drinking, sleeping and even going to the lavatory. *(Iḥyā-ul-'Ulūm, vol. 4, pp. 126)*

The Noble Prophet صَلَّى اللهُ تَعَالٰى عَلَيْهِ وَاٰلِهٖ وَسَلَّم has stated, 'A Muslim's intention is better than his deeds.' *(Mu'jam Kabīr, vol. 6, pp. 185, Ḥadīš 5942)* Intention implies the willingness of the heart towards an act. It is not necessary to utter the words of the intention. In fact, just verbal utterance without the willingness of the heart will not be valid and reward will not be given.

Here are 43 intentions that can be made at the time of consuming food. One should make as many of them as are conveniently possible for him. It should also be noted that the list of these examples is by no means exhaustive, and those who are familiar with the knowledge of intentions can make many other good intentions using the below-given list as a guide. The more intentions one makes, the more reward one will attain, اِنْ شَآءَاللّٰه عَزَّوَجَلَّ.

43 Intentions of eating

I will

1. make Wuḍū before, and
2. after eating food (i.e. I will wash hands and mouth and rinse it).

I will consume food to gain strength to

3. worship,
4. recite the [Holy Quran],
5. serve my parents,
6. acquire religious knowledge,
7. travel with a Madanī Qāfilaĥ in order to learn Sunnaĥ,
8. partake in the area-visit to call people towards righteousness,
9. ponder over the matters of the Hereafter and
10. earn Ḥalāl sustenance to meet my needs.

(These intentions will be beneficial only when one consumes food less than his appetite. Conversely, excessive eating only engenders laziness in worship, inclination towards sin, stomach ailments and disorders).

[I will]

11. eat sitting on the floor.
12. use a dining-mat[1] according to Sunnaĥ.
13. observe veil within veil[2] (with the kurta or the shawl).
14. sit according to Sunnaĥ.

---

[1] A piece of cloth etc., spread on the ground, on which food, drinks etc. are served.

[2] Veil within veil is the translation of the Urdu term 'Parday mayn Pardaĥ' used in the Madanī environment of Dawat-e-Islami. It refers to the act of wrapping an extra shawl around dress from navel to knees.

[Translator's Note]

15. recite بِسْمِ اللّٰه
16. and other Du'ās prior to consuming food.
17. eat with three fingers.
18. eat small morsels.
19. chew the food properly.
20. recite يَا وَاجِدُ before eating every morsel (or I will recite بِسْمِ اللّٰه and يَا وَاجِدُ prior to consuming every morsel and اَلْحَمْدُلِلّٰه at the end).
21. pick up and eat the grains of food if fall on the dining-mat.
22. break every morsel of the bread above the container of curry (so that every bread crumb falls into the container).
23. lick the bones and spices etc. clean thoroughly.
24. eat less than appetite.
25. wipe the plate clean at the end with the intention of acting upon Sunnaĥ.
26. lick the fingers clean three times.
27. (after cleaning the plate, I will) pour water into it and drink[1] the water to earn the reward of freeing a slave.
28. not get up unnecessarily unless the dining-mat has been removed (as it is also a Sunnaĥ).
29. (after eating, I will) recite Masnūn Du'ās along with Ṣalāt-'Alan-Nabī once before and after the Du'ās.
30. pick my teeth.

---

[1] Pour some water into the plate so that you can easily remove the particles of food that have clung to the plate.

[Translator's Note]

More intentions whilst eating with others

I will

31. not begin eating before an Islamic scholar or a saint, if they are present at the dining-mat,
32. seek the blessings of the company of the Muslims,
33. please others by offering them different items such as water, squash, pieces of meat etc. from the food. (Putting food into someone's plate without his consent is contrary to manners as he may not desire that thing at that time).
34. reap the reward of giving charity by smiling at others,
35. recite the Masnūn Du'ā on seeing someone smiling,

    (The following Du'ā should be recited on seeing a smiling person:

    اَضْحَكَ اللّٰهُ سِنَّكَ

    Translation: 'May Allah عَزَّوَجَلَّ always keep you smiling.')

    (Ṣaḥīḥ Bukhārī, vol. 4, pp. 403, Ḥadīš 3294)

36. tell and persuade others to make the intentions of eating food,
37. tell others of the Sunnaĥs of eating,
38. (if I have the opportunity, I will) make others recite the Du'ās prior to eating,
39. and subsequent to eating,
40. leave the finer items of food such as pieces of meat etc. for others, avoiding greed. (The Holy Prophet صَلَّى اللّٰهُ تَعَالٰى عَلَيْهِ وَاٰلِهٖ وَسَلَّم has stated, 'Whosoever gives others the things that he needs himself is forgiven by Allah عَزَّوَجَلَّ.') *(Itḥāf-us-Sādat-il-Muttaqīn, vol. 9, pp. 779)*
41. gift others floss/toothpick [so that they may pick their teeth],

42. gift others a rubber band to wrap it around the little finger and the ring one so that they would practise eating with three fingers,

43. Recite يَـا وَاجِـدُ aloud before consuming every morsel so that others may also recall and recite it.

Wuḍū of eating protects against destitution

Sayyidunā 'Abdullāĥ Ibn 'Abbās رَضِیَ اللہُ تَعَالٰی عَنۡہُمَا reports the Noble Prophet صَلَّی اللہُ تَعَالٰی عَلَیۡہِ وَاٰلِہٖ وَسَلَّم to have stated, 'Making Wuḍū before and after eating protects against destitution and is one of the Sunnaĥs of the Prophets عَلَیۡہِمُ السَّلَام.' *(Mu'jam Awsaṭ, vol. 5, pp. 231, Ḥadīš 7166)*

Wuḍū of eating increases goodness in home

Sayyidunā Anas رَضِیَ اللہُ تَعَالٰی عَنۡہُ has narrated that the Holy Prophet صَلَّی اللہُ تَعَالٰی عَلَیۡہِ وَاٰلِہٖ وَسَلَّم has stated, 'Anyone who wishes that Allah عَزَّوَجَلَّ increases goodness in his home, should make Wuḍū when food is served as well as when it is removed.' *(Sunan Ibn Mājaĥ, vol. 4, pp. 9, Ḥadīš 3260)*

Excellence of doing Wuḍū of eating

The mother of believers, Sayyidatunā 'Āishaĥ Ṣiddīqaĥ رَضِیَ اللہُ تَعَالٰی عَنۡہَا has narrated that the Holy Prophet صَلَّی اللہُ تَعَالٰی عَلَیۡہِ وَاٰلِہٖ وَسَلَّم has stated, 'To make Wuḍū before eating is one good deed and to make Wuḍū after eating is (equivalent to) two good deeds.' *(Al-Jāmi'-uṣ-Ṣaghīr, pp. 574, Ḥadīš 9682)*

Dear Islamic brothers! One should not be lazy in washing his hands before and after eating. By Allah عَزَّوَجَلَّ! The actual significance of one good deed will be realized on the Day of Judgement when someone would be short of just one good deed and would ask his relatives for it but no one would give him even a single good deed.

Protection from Satan

The Noble Prophet صَلَّى اللّٰہ تَعَالٰی عَلَیْهِ وَاٰلِهٖ وَسَلَّم has stated, 'Making Wuḍū before and after eating (i.e. washing the hands and the mouth) increases one's sustenance and keeps Satan away.' *(Kanz-ul-'Ummāl, vol. 10, pp. 106, Ḥadīš 40755)*

Remedies for protection from illness

Dear Islamic brothers! The Wuḍū of eating is not the same as that of Ṣalāĥ. The Wuḍū for eating includes washing both the hands up to the wrists, washing the mouth and rinsing it. A renowned exegetist of the Quran, Ḥakīm-ul-Ummat Shaykh Muftī Aḥmad Yār Khān عَلَیْهِ رَحْمَةُ الْمَنَّان has stated, 'In the Torah, there was the commandment of washing hands and mouth twice; once before and once after the eating but the Jews erased the former and preserved only the latter. The wisdom in washing hands and rinsing mouth before eating is that these parts of the body may get dirty as the daily activities and chores are done. Similarly, after the food is consumed, hands and mouth are sticky with food. Therefore, hands and mouth should be washed on both occasions. Rinsing the mouth after eating protects against pyorrhoea. Furthermore, a habitual user of Miswāk during Wuḍū remains safe from various teeth and stomach diseases. One should make it a habit to urinate immediately after eating as this protects against kidney and bladder diseases. It is a very tried and trusted remedy.' *(Mirāt-ul-Manājīḥ, vol. 6, pp. 32)*

Mysterious death of truck driver

Dear Islamic brothers! Without doubt, dignity lies in Sunnaĥ. By virtue of acting upon Sunnaĥ, one attains not only great reward but also worldly benefits. Before eating, it is a Sunnaĥ to wash hands up to the wrists. One should wash and rinse the mouth as well. As different chores are carried out with hands that come into contact with many things, the hands are prone to dirt and various kinds of germs. By the blessings of acting upon the Sunnaĥ of washing hands prior to eating, our hands are cleaned from the germs etc. and thus we are protected against many diseases. Remember that one should not wipe hands dry after he has washed them for eating as the germs of the towel may come into contact with hands.

It is reported that a truck driver once ate food at a restaurant and died writhing in pain immediately afterwards. Many other people had also eaten at the same restaurant, but nothing happened to them. After the investigation, it turned out that a poisonous snake was crushed under the tyres of the truck, spreading the poison along the tyres. The truck driver had checked the tyres with bare hands and eaten food afterwards without washing his hands. As a result of eating the meal with unwashed hands with which poison had already come into contact, he died suddenly.

Allah عَزَّوَجَلَّ *kī Raḥmat say Sunnat mayn sharāfat ĥay*
Sarkār صَلَّى اللهُ تَعَالٰى عَلَيْهِ وَاٰلِهٖ وَسَلَّم *kī Sunnat mayn ĥam sab kī ḥifāẓat ĥay*

With the mercy of Allah عَزَّوَجَلَّ*, in Sunnaĥ lies dignity*
With our commitment to it, in it there is safety

Eating in marketplace

Sayyidunā Abū Umāmaĥ رَضِىَ اللهُ تَعَالٰى عَنْهُ has narrated that the Prophet of mankind, the Peace of our heart and mind, the most Generous and Kind صَلَّى اللهُ تَعَالٰى عَلَيْهِ وَاٰلِهٖ وَسَلَّم has stated, 'It is inappropriate to eat in the marketplace.' *(Al-Jāmi'-uṣ-Ṣaghīr, pp. 184, Ḥadīš 3073)*

Ṣadr-ush-Sharī'aĥ, Badr-uṭ-Ṭarīqaĥ, 'Allāmaĥ Maulānā Muftī Muhammad Amjad 'Alī A'ẓamī عَلَيْهِ رَحْمَةُ اللّٰهِ الْقَوِى has stated, 'It is Makrūĥ to eat on the roadside or in the marketplace.' *(Baĥār-e-Sharī'at, part 16, pp. 19)*

Bread from marketplace

Shaykh Sayyidunā Imām Burĥānuddīn Ibrāĥīm Zarnūjī عَلَيْهِ رَحْمَةُ اللّٰهِ الْقَوِى has stated, 'Sayyidunā Imām Muhammad Bin Faḍal رَحْمَةُ اللهِ تَعَالٰى عَلَيْه never ate market-food throughout the period of his Islamic education. Every Friday, his father would bring him food from his village. Once, when his father brought the food he noticed that the bread in his son's room was from the marketplace. Annoyed, he even refused to talk to his son. His son apologetically responded that he had not brought the bread, but his friend had done so without his consent. Hearing this, his father rebuked him and said, 'If you were pious, your friend would never dare to do this.' *(Ta'līm-ul-Muta'allim, pp. 67)*

No blessing in food from marketplace

Dear Islamic brothers! Did you see how ascetic our saints رَحِمَهُمُ اللّٰهُ تَعَالٰی were! They brought up and educated their children so piously that they would not even let them eat food from restaurants and marketplaces. Shaykh Sayyidunā Imām Zarnūjī رَحْمَةُ اللّٰهِ تَعَالٰی عَلَيْه has stated, 'If possible, one should refrain from eating junk food and market-food as it takes one closer to filth and fraud, and distances one from the Żikr of Allah عَزَّوَجَلَّ. One of its reasons is that the poor and the destitute look desperately at the market-food but cannot afford to buy it. They are disheartened, which results in the removal of blessings from this food.' *(Ta'līm-ul-Muta'allim, pp. 88)*

How is it to eat at restaurants?

Those who are in the habit of relishing restaurants' delicious foods should learn some lesson from the foregoing parable. If eating at a marketplace is considered bad, then how inappropriate would it be to eat and drink in restaurants where music is being played and various other irreligious and sinful acts are being committed with shamelessness! Even if music is not being played at a restaurant, its atmosphere generally encourages sinful activities. It is a demeaning environment for the noble and the righteous. Therefore, one should avoid purchasing food from the marketplace unless he is in dire need of food and has no other alternative. Still, he should eat the food at a private place. However, the one who is helpless is excused. Remember that if movies or dramas are being watched or music is being played at a restaurant, one should refrain from going over there, as it is a sin to listen to music deliberately. The following narration should elaborate the point further.

It is Wājib to avoid listening to music

Shaykh Sayyidunā 'Allāmaĥ Shāmī عَلَيْهِ رَحْمَةُ اللّٰهِ الْقَوِی has narrated that dancing (in a wiggling manner), making fun of others, clapping, playing the sitar [a type of Indian guitar], the harp, the violin, the flute and blowing the bugle are all Makrūĥ Taḥrīmī, (i.e. almost Ḥarām) as these are the practices of the unbelievers. To listen to the sound of the flute and that of other such [musical] instruments is also Ḥarām. If one hears suddenly or unintentionally, he is excused. However, it is Wājib for him to make every possible effort to avoid listening to it. *(Rad-dul-Muḥtār, vol. 9, pp. 566)*

Inserting fingers into openings of ears

Dear Islamic brothers! Fortunate are those who listen to the Quran, Na'at and Sunnaĥ-Inspiring speeches, and if the sound of songs or music ever reaches their ears, they make every possible effort not to listen to it and move away from that place inserting their fingers into the openings of their ears due to the fear of Allah عَزَّوَجَلَّ.

Sayyidunā Nāfi' رَضِیَ اللّٰہُ تَعَالٰی عَنْہُ has stated, '(When I was young) I was going somewhere with Sayyidunā 'Abdullāĥ Bin 'Umar رَضِیَ اللّٰہُ تَعَالٰی عَنْہُمَا. On the way, we heard the sound of trumpet-blowing. Ibn 'Umar رَضِیَ اللّٰہُ تَعَالٰی عَنْہُ immediately put his fingers into his ears and moved to the other side of the road. Thereafter, he asked, 'Nāfi' رَضِیَ اللّٰہُ تَعَالٰی عَنْہُ! Can you still hear the sound [of the trumpet]?' I replied, 'No more.' Then, taking his fingers out of the openings of his ears, he said, 'Once, I was going somewhere along with the Holy Prophet صَلَّی اللّٰہُ تَعَالٰی عَلَیْہِ وَاٰلِہٖ وَسَلَّم; he did exactly the same as I have done now.' *(Sunan Abī Dāwūd, vol. 4, pp. 307, Ḥadīš 4924)*

Move away, if sound of music reaches ears

We have learnt from the foregoing narration that if the sound of music ever reaches our ears, we should immediately move away from where the sound is coming inserting fingers into the openings of our ears. If we remained over there sitting or standing, even though we have inserted fingers into the openings of our ears, or if we moved just slightly to a side, then we would not be able to avoid listening to the sound of music. It is Wājib to make every possible effort to avoid listening to music whether or not we insert fingers into our ears.

Woe! Nowadays, it has become extremely difficult to avoid music. Wherever one goes, whether it is vehicle or aeroplane, home or shop, restaurant or marketplace one hears the sound of songs and music. If a devotee of the Rasūl avoids this sin by inserting fingers into his ears, he is ridiculed.

Wo daur āyā kay dīwāna-e-Nabī kay liye
Ĥar aīk ĥātĥ mayn pattĥar dikhāyī daytā ĥay

Devotee of the Rasūl is disdained
Every hand has a stone aimed

Dear Islamic brothers! By the blessings of the Madanī environment of Dawat-e-Islami, immeasurably astounding changes take place in one's life. Many individuals have been reported to have wished that if only they had joined the Madanī environment of Dawat-e-Islami long ago! Here is a glimpse of the blessing of Dawat-e-Islami's Madanī environment.

Blessing of giving Dars at home

An Islamic brother from Akola [a state of Maharashtra, India] has stated: 'Due to the company of those who have corrupt beliefs, my family was briskly falling into the abyss of sins and wrong beliefs. Once, while the entire family was watching TV, my 17-year-old brother, who had begun to attend Dawat-e-Islami's Ijtimā', entered the room with his back towards the television we were watching. Taking something from the wardrobe he left in the same manner as he had entered the room. Infuriated by his strange behaviour, I yelled out, 'What is wrong with you today; you are acting childishly?' Despite hearing my harsh words, he went into the other room silently without responding to me.

Explaining to me, my mother said that he had sworn not to watch television. In anger, I stopped talking to him. He started giving Dars from *Faīzān-e-Sunnat* at home. Initially, I did not attend the Dars, but one day I also sat with the household to listen to what he delivers in the Dars. When I heard the Dars, I was impressed by it and began to attend it regularly. Gradually, the rust of my heart began to be removed, and I started attending the weekly Sunnaĥ-Inspiring Ijtimā' of Dawat-e-Islami.

اَلْحَمْدُ لِلّٰه عَزَّوَجَلَّ I came to my senses, refrained from the company of those who have corrupt beliefs, and began to grow a beard. Further, I started listening to the audio-cassettes of Sunnaĥ-Inspiring speeches released by Maktaba-tul-Madīnaĥ in lieu of the misleading speeches I used to listen to fondly. There were televisions in all four rooms of our home; we threw them away with mutual consent.

Burī suḥbataun say kināraĥ kashī kar
Aur achchaun kay pās ā kay pā Madanī Māḥaul

Tumĥayn luṭf ā jāye gā zindagī kā
Qarīb ā kay daykĥo żarā Madanī Māḥaul

Abstain from bad company; seek company of the good,
Adopt the Madanī environment
You will enjoy your life, come closer and look,
the beauty of the Madanī environment

صَلُّوْا عَلَى الْحَبِيْب   صَلَّى اللهُ تَعَالٰى عَلٰى مُحَمَّد

A means to protect Īmān

Dear Islamic brothers! اَلْحَمْدُ لِلّٰه عَزَّوَجَلَّ Giving Dars at home is an effective way of guarding one's Īmān and reforming one's character. Similarly, there is a Madanī activity of filling out the booklet of Madanī In'āmāt daily practicing Fikr-e-Madīnaĥ, which is a powerful tool for the character-building of Islamic brothers and sisters. The twelfth question in the Madanī In'āmāt booklet is in regard to delivering or listening to two Dars a day, one of which should be delivered at home. All of you are requested to start giving Dars at your home.

'Amal kā ĥo jazbaĥ 'aṭā Yā Ilāĥī عَزَّوَجَلَّ
Gunāĥaun say mujĥ ko bachā Yā Ilāĥī عَزَّوَجَلَّ
Sa'ādat milay Dars-e-Faīzān-e-Sunnat
Ki rozānaĥ dau martabaĥ Yā Ilāĥī عَزَّوَجَلَّ

Grant us a passion to do good deeds, O my Allah عَزَّوَجَلَّ
Protect us from sins and bad deeds, O my Allah عَزَّوَجَلَّ
May we be fortunate to give Dars of Faīzān-e-Sunnat
Twice a day O my Allah عَزَّوَجَلَّ

اٰمِيْن بِجَاهِ النَّبِيِّ الْاَمِيْن صَلَّى اللهُ تَعَالٰى عَلَيْهِ وَاٰلِهٖ وَسَلَّم

صَلُّوْا عَلَى الْحَبِيْب   صَلَّى اللهُ تَعَالٰى عَلٰى مُحَمَّد

Light in grave

Listen to the excellence of delivering Dars and Sunnaĥ-Inspiring speeches. 'Allāmaĥ Jalāluddīn Suyūṭī Shāfi'ī عَلَيْهِ رَحْمَةُ اللّٰهِ الْقَوِى has narrated in '*Sharḥ-uṣ-Ṣudūr*' that Allah عَزَّوَجَلَّ sent a revelation to Sayyidunā Mūsā عَلٰى نَبِيِّنَا وَعَلَيْهِ الصَّلٰوةُ وَالسَّلَام, 'Learn righteous things and teach them to others; I [Allah عَزَّوَجَلَّ] will brighten the graves of those who learn and teach good so that they would not have any fear.' *(Ḥilyat-ul-Auliyā, vol. 6, pp. 5, Ḥadīš 7622)*

Graves will be radiant

The foregoing narration highlights the reward of learning and teaching righteous things. Those who deliver as well as those who listen to Sunnaĥ-Inspiring speeches and Dars will surely be blissful and successful and their graves will be radiant from the inside, اِنْ شَآءَاللّٰه عَزَّوَجَلَّ. Furthermore, they will not have any fear, اِنْ شَآءَاللّٰه عَزَّوَجَلَّ.

Likewise, those who spread righteousness making individual effort, travel with Madanī Qāfilaĥ, inspire others to practice Fikr-e-Madīnaĥ by filling their Madanī In'āmāt booklet, persuade others to attend Sunnaĥ-Inspiring Ijtimā', and those who listen to righteous things by attending Dars, Sunnaĥ-Inspiring speeches etc., the graves of all these people will also be radiant for the sake of the Nūr of the Holy Prophet صَلَّى اللّٰهُ تَعَالٰى عَلَيْهِ وَاٰلِهٖ وَسَلَّم.

Qabr mayn leĥrā-ayn gey tā-ḥashr chasmay Nūr kay
Jalwaĥ farmā ĥogī jab ṭal'at Rasūlullāĥ صَلَّى اللّٰهُ تَعَالٰى عَلَيْهِ وَاٰلِهٖ وَسَلَّم *kī*

In the grave until Qiyāmaĥ, rays of light will flow clear
When the blessed face of the Prophet صَلَّى اللّٰهُ تَعَالٰى عَلَيْهِ وَاٰلِهٖ وَسَلَّم *will appear*

(Ḥadāiq-e-Bakhshish)

صَلُّوْا عَلَى الْحَبِيْب صَلَّى اللّٰهُ تَعَالٰى عَلٰى مُحَمَّد

Reforming one's family is necessary

Dear Islamic brothers! It is imperative that we reform ourselves and our family. Allah عَزَّوَجَلَّ says in the Quran in Sūraĥ At-Taḥrīm, part 28, verse 6:

يَاَيُّهَا الَّذِيْنَ اٰمَنُوْا قُوْۤا اَنْفُسَكُمْ وَ اَهْلِيْكُمْ نَارًا وَّقُوْدُهَا النَّاسُ وَ الْحِجَارَةُ

O those who believe! Save yourselves and your families from the fire whose fuel is men and stones.

[Kanz-ul-Īmān (Translation of Quran)] (Part 28, Sūraĥ At-Taḥrīm, verse 6)

اَلْحَمْدُلِلّٰه عَزَّوَجَلَّ, One of the ways of carrying out the above-mentioned commandment is to give Dars to the household. In addition, it would also be beneficial to read and make others read the various booklets published by Maktaba-tul-Madīnaĥ. Similarly, listening to the audio-cassettes of speeches and Madanī Mużākaraĥ [question and answer sessions] and watching VCDs and Madanī channel will also prove to be very effective in reforming oneself as well as one's family. اَلْحَمْدُلِلّٰه عَزَّوَجَلَّ, Many incidents have been reported about the reform of people by virtue of Sunnaĥ-Inspiring speeches and booklets. Here is one such account.

Blessing of reading Maktaba-tul-Madīnaĥ's booklet

An Islamic brother from Bahawalpur (Punjab) has reported: 'Due to the company of wicked friends at school, I had become addicted to movies. I would even travel to other cities like Lahore, Karachi and Okara just for watching movies. As a result of watching pornographic movies I would follow unveiled college girls. I would shave my beard every day. Even worse, I had the obsession to work in theatres, circuses and the circle of death[1]. My family was extremely worried and concerned.

One day, my father spoke to a responsible Islamic brother of Dawat-e-Islami in our area and made me travel with a Madanī Qāfilaĥ in the company of the devotees of the Rasūl. On the last day, the Amīr of the Qāfilaĥ gave me a booklet entitled '*Black Scorpions*' (published by Maktaba-tul-Madīnaĥ). When I read the booklet, I trembled with fear. I immediately repented and made a firm intention to grow a fist-length beard on my face. Having returned, I attended the weekly Sunnaĥ-Inspiring Ijtimā' and purchased the audio-cassette entitled '*Ḋhal jāye gī yeĥ Jawānī*' [You will not Stay Young] from Maktaba-tul-Madīnaĥ. When I came home and heard the speech, it changed my whole life.

---

[1] Circle of death is a deep well like structure in which a motorbike is ridden on the inside edge. It is extremely dangerous for the rider. [Translator's Note]

اَلْحَمْدُلِلّٰه عَزَّوَجَلَّ, I started offering Ṣalāĥ regularly and taking part in the Madanī activities of Dawat-e-Islami. اَلْحَمْدُلِلّٰه عَزَّوَجَلَّ, I am now making efforts as a responsible for Madanī Qāfilaĥ in my city.'

صَلُّوْا عَلَى الْحَبِيْب صَلَّى اللهُ تَعَالٰى عَلٰى مُحَمَّد

Blessing in eating with others

The second caliph, Amīr-ul-Mūminīn Sayyidunā 'Umar Fārūq A'ẓam رَضِیَ اللهُ تَعَالٰی عَنْهُ has narrated that Beloved Rasūl of Allah صَلَّی اللهُ تَعَالٰی عَلَیْهِ وَاٰلِهٖ وَسَلَّم has stated, 'Eat together. Do not eat separately, as blessing is with the group.' *(Sunan Ibn Mājaĥ, vol. 4, pp. 21, Ḥadīš 3287)*

A way of being satiated

Sayyidunā Waḥshī Bin Ḥarb عَلَیْهِ رَحْمَةُ الرَّب has narrated via his grandfather that the blessed companions رَضِیَ اللّٰهُ تَعَالٰی عَنْهُم once said to the Holy Prophet صَلَّی اللهُ تَعَالٰی عَلَیْهِ وَاٰلِهٖ وَسَلَّم 'Yā Rasūlallāĥ صَلَّی اللهُ تَعَالٰی عَلَیْهِ وَاٰلِهٖ وَسَلَّم! We eat, yet we are not satiated.' The Holy Prophet صَلَّی اللهُ تَعَالٰی عَلَیْهِ وَاٰلِهٖ وَسَلَّم responded, 'You must be eating individually?' They replied, 'Yes.' The Noble Prophet صَلَّی اللهُ تَعَالٰی عَلَیْهِ وَاٰلِهٖ وَسَلَّم then said, 'Eat sitting together and recite بِسْمِ اللّٰه, there will be blessing in your food.' *(Sunan Abī Dāwūd, vol. 3, pp. 486, Ḥadīš 3764)*

Excellence of eating together

There are glad tidings for those who eat sitting together at a dining-mat. Sayyidunā Anas Bin Mālik رَضِیَ اللهُ تَعَالٰی عَنْهُ has narrated: 'When Allah عَزَّوَجَلَّ sees a Muslim eat at a dining-mat sitting along with his wife and children, He عَزَّوَجَلَّ is pleased by this action the most because when they sit together to eat, Allah عَزَّوَجَلَّ sees them with mercy and forgives them before they separate.' *(Tanbīĥ-ul-Ghāfilīn, pp. 343)*

Cure for stomach in eating together

A professor of pathology has discovered that when some people eat sitting together, their bacteria are mixed in the food. These bacteria destroy other pathogenic bacteria that can cause diseases. At times, healthy bacteria are mixed which help cure stomach diseases.

Food for one is sufficient for two

Sayyidunā Jābir رَضِیَ اللهُ تَعَالٰی عَنۡهُ has narrated the Holy Prophet صَلَّی اللهُ تَعَالٰی عَلَیۡهِ وَاٰلِهٖ وَسَلَّم to have stated, 'The food of one is sufficient for two. The food of two is sufficient for four and that of four is sufficient for eight.' *(Ṣaḥīḥ Muslim, pp. 1140, Ḥadīš 2059)* The Holy Prophet صَلَّی اللهُ تَعَالٰی عَلَیۡهِ وَاٰلِهٖ وَسَلَّم has stated, 'The food of two is sufficient for three and that of three is sufficient for four.' *(Ṣaḥīḥ Bukhārī, vol. 6, pp. 346, Ḥadīš 5392)*

Lesson of contentment

Commenting on the foregoing Ḥadīš, a renowned exegetist of the Quran, Shaykh Muftī Aḥmad Yār Khān عَلَیۡهِ رَحۡمَةُ الۡحَنَّان has stated, 'If there are more people and less food, all of them should eat a little less than their appetite. In other words, three should be content with the food of two, and four should be content with the food of three. Although they may not be full, they will not have weakness, and will be able to perform worship properly. This Ḥadīš contains a noteworthy lesson of having contentment and being considerate towards others.' *(Mirāt-ul-Manājīḥ, vol. 6, pp. 16)*

Reduction in stipend

Once, the first caliph of the Prophet Sayyidunā Ṣiddīq Akbar's respectable wife رَضِیَ اللهُ تَعَالٰی عَنۡهَا expressed the desire of eating halvah [i.e. a type of sweet dish]. He said that they did not have enough money to buy halvah. She suggested that she would save a little money from their daily expenditures so that they would buy halvah. He gave his consent to this, therefore, she started saving money. After a few days, she gave the money to him for buying halvah. Instead of buying halvah, he deposited that money in the Bayt-ul-Māl [i.e. the state treasury] and said to the treasurer, 'This money is in excess of our needs'. He then got his monthly stipend reduced in proportion to that deposited money. *(Al-Kāmil fit-Tārīkh, vol. 2, pp. 271)*

Dear Islamic brothers! By reading or listening to the above parable we should also learn some lesson of piety and contentment rather than just expressing accolades and praises. Particularly, government officers, the Imāms of Masājid, the teachers of religious schools, the Muslims who are associated with various religious departments and those in authority should all learn a lesson of contentment and self-respect, avoiding greed and thus making their Hereafter better. If only we would be content with earning little income and long for the accumulation of the immortal treasure of good deeds, instead of arguing for increase in our salary, just on the provocation of our Nafs, comparing it with others' salaries saying such sentences as: '*my salary is less and his is so high.*' Listen to one more parable about Sayyidunā Abū Bakr Ṣiddīq's رضی اللہ تعالٰی عنہ piety and his disinterest in worldly wealth.

Caution regarding endowed things

Sayyidunā Imām Ḥasan Mujtabā رضی اللہ تعالٰی عنہ has narrated that, at the time of his demise, Khalīfa-tur-Rasūl Sayyidunā Abū Bakr Ṣiddīq رضی اللہ تعالٰی عنہ called his daughter, Sayyidatunā 'Āishaĥ Ṣiddīqaĥ رضی اللہ تعالٰی عنہا and said, 'Listen! The she-camel whose milk we drink, the bowl in which we eat, and the shawl I wear, have all been taken from the Bayt-ul-Māl [i.e. the state treasury]. We can only use these things as long as I hold the office of the caliphate [of the Muslims]. When I pass away, give all of these things to Sayyidunā 'Umar Fārūq A'ẓam رضی اللہ تعالٰی عنہ.'

When Sayyidunā Abū Bakr Ṣiddīq رضی اللہ تعالٰی عنہ passed away, as per his will, all of these things were sent to Sayyidunā 'Umar Fārūq A'ẓam رضی اللہ تعالٰی عنہ. [When Sayyidunā 'Umar Fārūq A'ẓam رضی اللہ تعالٰی عنہ came to know about it,] he رضی اللہ تعالٰی عنہ said, 'May Allah عَزَّوَجَلَّ shower mercy upon Abū Bakr (رضی اللہ تعالٰی عنہ); he has set a tough example for his successors.' *(Tārīkh-ul-Khulafā, pp. 60)*

Forgiveness for eater

One should recite بِسْمِ اللّٰه while initiating any righteous act as it is a Sunnaĥ to do so. Similarly, it is also a Sunnaĥ to recite بِسْمِ اللّٰه prior to eating and drinking something as this brings about many blessings. Hence Sayyidunā Anas رضی اللہ تعالٰی عنہ has narrated that the Prophet of mankind, the Peace of our heart and mind, the most Generous and Kind صَلَّی اللّٰہُ تَعَالٰی عَلَیْہِ وَاٰلِہٖ وَسَلَّم has stated, 'A person is served with food and is forgiven before the food is removed. This is because he recites بِسْمِ اللّٰه when served with food and اَلْحَمْدُلِلّٰه when the food is removed.' *(Al-Jāmi'-uṣ-Ṣaghīr, pp. 122, Ḥadīš 1974)*

It is not Sunnaĥ to eat at dining table

Sayyidunā Anas رَضِیَ اللہُ تَعَالٰی عَنْہُ has narrated a Ḥadīš mentioned in *Ṣaḥīḥ Bukhārī* that the Noble Prophet صَلَّى اللهُ تَعَالٰى عَلَيْهِ وَاٰلِهٖ وَسَلَّم would not eat at a dining-table; nor in small bowls. [Furthermore,] thin bread was not prepared for him. When Sayyidunā Qatādaĥ رَضِیَ اللہُ تَعَالٰی عَنْہُ was asked as to what the Holy Prophet صَلَّى اللهُ تَعَالٰى عَلَيْهِ وَاٰلِهٖ وَسَلَّم and his companions رَضِیَ اللّٰہُ تَعَالٰی عَنْھُم would eat food at; he رَضِیَ اللہُ تَعَالٰی عَنْہُ replied that they would eat at a dining-mat. *(Ṣaḥīḥ Bukhārī, vol. 3, pp. 532, Ḥadīš 5415)*

Muftī Muhammad Amjad 'Alī A'ẓamī عَلَيْهِ رَحْمَةُ الْقَوِى states

Dear Islamic brothers! Although it is not a sin to eat at a dining table, it is not a Sunnaĥ to do so. Ṣadr-ush-Sharī'aĥ, Badr-uṭ-Ṭarīqaĥ 'Allāmaĥ Maulānā Muftī Amjad 'Alī A'ẓamī عَلَيْهِ رَحْمَةُ اللّٰهِ الْقَوِى has stated in the 16th part of *Baĥār-e-Sharī'at*, 'Meal is served to the rich at tables so that they would not have to bow while eating. This was a custom of the arrogant. Even today, some people follow the practice of the arrogant by eating at a table. Similarly, eating in small bowls is also a custom of the rich as different foods are served to them in small bowls or plates.' *(Baĥār-e-Sharī'at, part 16, pp. 12)*

Which type of dining-mat is Sunnaĥ?

A renowned exegetist of the Quran, Ḥakīm-ul-Ummat, Shaykh Muftī Aḥmad Yār Khān عَلَيْهِ رَحْمَةُ الْمَنَّان has stated, 'It is a Sunnaĥ to bow a little in front of the food. The dining mat used by the Holy Prophet صَلَّى اللهُ تَعَالٰى عَلَيْهِ وَاٰلِهٖ وَسَلَّم was made of either cloth or leather or palm tree leaves. The dining-mat used to be spread on the floor and the Holy Prophet صَلَّى اللهُ تَعَالٰى عَلَيْهِ وَاٰلِهٖ وَسَلَّم would also sit on the floor for eating.' *(Mirāt-ul-Manājīḥ, vol. 6, pp. 13)*

Dear Islamic brothers! Though it is not a sin to eat at a table, the Sunnaĥ is to eat at a dining-mat laid on the floor. [Remember] dignity lies in following Sunnaĥ. Unfortunately, these days, most of the Muslims seem to have drifted away from this Sunnaĥ. The trend of eating at tables has grown even in religious families. Likewise, in weddings, people are seen eating food standing around the table even without using chairs! Alas, when will Sunnaĥ be revived!

Sunnatayn ‘ām karayn Dīn kā ĥam kām karayn
Nayk ban jāyaīn Musalmān Madīnay wālay

May we serve Islam and propagate Sunnaĥ, O Prophet صَلَّى اللهُ تَعَالٰى عَلَيْهِ وَاٰلِهٖ وَسَلَّم
May we attain righteousness, O Prophet صَلَّى اللهُ تَعَالٰى عَلَيْهِ وَاٰلِهٖ وَسَلَّم

Żikr of Allah عَزَّوَجَلَّ on every morsel

Sayyidunā Anas رَضِىَ اللهُ تَعَالٰى عَنْهُ has narrated, ‘Allah عَزَّوَجَلَّ is pleased with His servant who glorifies Allah عَزَّوَجَلَّ after consuming a morsel of food and drinking water.’ *(Ṣaḥīḥ Muslim, pp. 1463, Ḥadīš 2734)*

Way of doing Żikr on every morsel

سُبْحٰنَ اللّٰه عَزَّوَجَلَّ! How easy way of attaining the pleasure of Allah عَزَّوَجَلَّ it is! By Allah عَزَّوَجَلَّ, no privilege is greater than the attainment of His pleasure. The one with whom Allah عَزَّوَجَلَّ is pleased, will be blessed with beholding Him and entering Paradise. Try to make it your habit to make the Żikr of Allah عَزَّوَجَلَّ before eating every morsel and drinking every sip and to recite اَلْحَمْدُ لِلّٰه after eating the morsel and drinking the sip so that the mealtime is not spent in heedlessness.

If possible, make a habit to recite اَلْحَمْدُ لِلّٰه, يَا وَاجِدُ and بِسْمِ اللّٰه between every two morsels. In this way, every morsel will begin with بِسْمِ اللّٰه and يَا وَاجِدُ and will end with the glorification of Allah عَزَّوَجَلَّ. [By doing this] اِنْ شَآءَ اللّٰه عَزَّوَجَلَّ one will gain a great deal of reward. It is stated in Maktaba-tul-Madīnaĥ’s published pocket-sized booklet entitled ‘*40 Spiritual Cures*[1]’ that whoever recites يَا وَاجِدُ prior to eating every morsel, that food will become Nūr in his stomach, curing diseases اِنْ شَآءَ اللّٰه عَزَّوَجَلَّ.

Kar ulfat mayn apnī fanā Yā Ilāĥī عَزَّوَجَلَّ
‘Aṭā karday Apnī Rizā Yā Ilāĥī عَزَّوَجَلَّ

Grant us utter devotion in Your love O Allah عَزَّوَجَلَّ
Grant us Your pleasure, O Allah عَزَّوَجَلَّ

[1] Get this booklet from Maktaba-tul-Madīnaĥ.

Dear Islamic brothers! Make a habit of travelling with Madanī Qāfilaĥs of Dawat-e-Islami with Rasūl's devotees. اِنْ شَآءَاللّٰه عَزَّوَجَلَّ, You will gain practical learning of Sunnaĥ pertaining to eating food. اِنْ شَآءَاللّٰه عَزَّوَجَلَّ Such a meal would be served some day which will delight you. So let me tell you, in my own way, a Madanī incident of Islamic brothers:

Hospitality of Madanī Qāfilaĥ by Dātā Ganj Bakhsh رَحْمَةُ اللهِ عَلَيْه

An Islamic brother has narrated, 'Our Madanī Qāfilaĥ was staying for three days in the Masjid adjacent to the shrine of Dātā Sahib رَحْمَةُ اللهِ تَعَالٰی عَلَيْه in the city of Markaz-ul-Auliyā, Lahore. According to the schedule, we were busy learning Sunnaĥ when a person arrived and met us very warmly. The person then said, 'اَلْحَمْدُلِلّٰه عَزَّوَجَلَّ! My fortune awoke last night. I had a dream in which I saw Dātā Ganj Bakhsh 'Alī Ĥajwayrī عَلَيْهِ رَحْمَةُ اللهِ الْقَوِی who said to me, 'A Madanī Qāfilaĥ of Dawat-e-Islami is staying in my Masjid for three days, prepare food for them.' Therefore, I have prepared and brought food for the participants of the Madanī Qāfilaĥ. Please accept it.'

Kyā gharaz dar dar pĥirūn mayn bĥīk laynay kay liye
Ĥay salāmat āstānā āp kā Dātā piyā رَحْمَةُ اللهِ تَعَالٰی عَلَيْه
Jĥauliyān bĥar bĥar kay lay jātay ĥayn mangtay rāt din
Ĥo mayrī ummīd kā gulshan ĥarā Dātā piyā رَحْمَةُ اللهِ تَعَالٰی عَلَيْه

Why should I restlessly run around?
When I have your court sound, O Ganj Bakhsh رَحْمَةُ اللهِ تَعَالٰی عَلَيْه
People fill their baskets aplenty, day and night
May my desires also be fulfilled, O Ganj Bakhsh رَحْمَةُ اللهِ تَعَالٰی عَلَيْه

صَلُّوْا عَلَى الْحَبِيْب　　صَلَّى اللهُ تَعَالٰى عَلٰى مُحَمَّد

Saint رَحْمَةُ اللهِ عَلَيْه helped from within tomb

سُبْحٰنَ اللّٰه عَزَّوَجَلَّ! The saints help their visitors from within their blessed tombs. Ḥujjat-ul-Islam Sayyidunā Imām Muhammad Ghazālī عَلَيْهِ رَحْمَةُ اللهِ الْوَالِی has narrated that a Shāfi'ī shrine-caretaker from Makkaĥ Mukarramaĥ stated that there was a poor Egyptian person who had lately become the father of a baby. The destitute contacted a social worker who took the newborn's father to several people for financial assistance, but no one helped. At last, they went to a shrine where the social worker beseeched, 'Yā Sayyidī! May Allah عَزَّوَجَلَّ bless you! In your apparent life, you would give a lot. Today we asked several people for the newborn, yet no one gave anything.' Thereafter, the social worker gave the newborn's father half a dinar[1] as debt and said, 'Whenever you are able to repay this debt, you may repay it.' After that, both of them went their separate ways.

That night the social worker saw the same saint in his dream. The saint said, 'I heard what you said to me but was not allowed to reply at that time. Go to my family and ask them to dig underneath the stove. They would find there 500 dinar in a bag. Give this entire amount to the newborn's father.'

Hence, the social worker went to the saint's family and told them the whole situation. The family dug underneath the stove where they found 500 dinar which they offered to the social worker. That social worker responded, 'What is the credibility of my dream? All this belongs to you.' They responded, 'When our pious predecessor is showing generosity even after leaving this world, why should we not do!' They then insistently handed over the entire amount to the social worker, who gave it to the newborn's father and told him of the entire incident. Taking just one dinar out of 500 ones (half for paying his debt and half for his expenditures) the poor man said, 'This is sufficient for me.' He then gave the rest of the money to the social worker and asked him to distribute it among the poor and the destitute. The narrator of this amazing parable remarked that he was unable to decide as to which one of them was more generous. *(Iḥyā-ul-'Ulūm, vol. 3, pp. 309)*

May Allah عَزَّوَجَلَّ have mercy on them and forgive us without accountability for their sake!

Khālī kabĥī pĥayrā ĥī naĥīn apnay gadā ko
Ay sāilon māngo to żarā ĥātĥ bařhā kar
Khud apnay bĥikārī kī bĥarā kartay ĥayn jĥaulī
Khud keĥtay ĥayn Yā Rab عَزَّوَجَلَّ *mayray mangtā kā bĥalā kar*

[1] Currency used at that time. [Translator's Note]

The saint has never returned the servant empty handed
O servant just ask with your hand stretched
They fill the baskets of the beseecher
and say 'Yā Allah عَزَّوَجَلَّ grant good to the seeker'

صَلُّوْا عَلَى الْحَبِيْب صَلَّى اللّٰهُ تَعَالٰى عَلٰى مُحَمَّد

Saints رَحِمَهُمُ اللّٰهُ تَعَالٰى benefit others even after demise

Dear Islamic brothers! The foregoing parable clearly highlights the belief of the Muslims of past to seek help from saints in hour of need. They were well-aware of the fact that it is Allah عَزَّوَجَلَّ who has empowered the saints to help and assist people. By the grace of Allah عَزَّوَجَلَّ, the saints رَحِمَهُمُ اللّٰهُ تَعَالٰى are alive in their graves; they listen, guide and help the visitors and are aware of the affairs of their families. This is why the saint of the foregoing shrine guided the social worker in his dream and helped the father of the newborn child.

'Allāmaĥ Ibn 'Ābidīn Shāmī عَلَيْهِ رَحْمَةُ اللّٰهِ الْقَوِى has stated, 'The saints are at different ranks (levels) in the court of Allah عَزَّوَجَلَّ and are able to help the visitors according to their gnosis and insight.' *(Rad-dul-Muḥtār, vol. 1, pp. 604)*

Ĥam ko sāray Auliyā رَحِمَهُمُ اللّٰهُ تَعَالٰى say piyār ĥay
اِنْ شَآءَاللّٰه عَزَّوَجَلَّ Apnā bayřā pār ĥay

We love all saints of Allah indeed
اِنْ شَآءَاللّٰه عَزَّوَجَلَّ We will succeed

Which food causes illness?

Sayyidunā 'Uqbaĥ Bin 'Āmir رَضِىَ اللّٰهُ تَعَالٰى عَنْهُ has narrated that the Beloved and Blessed Prophet صَلَّى اللّٰهُ تَعَالٰى عَلَيْهِ وَاٰلِهٖ وَسَلَّم has stated, 'The food on which Allah's name is not mentioned causes illness and contains no blessings. The atonement (for not mentioning Allah's name) is to recite بِسْمِ اللّٰه and then eat something if the dining-mat has not yet been removed. If the dining-mat has been removed, then recite بِسْمِ اللّٰه and lick the fingers clean.' *(Al-Jāmi'-uṣ-Ṣaghīr, pp. 394, Ḥadīš 6327)*

Food becomes Ḥalāl for Satan

Sayyidunā Ḥużayfaĥ رَضِیَ اللهُ تَعَالٰی عَنْهُ has narrated that the Noble Prophet صَلَّی اللهُ تَعَالٰی عَلَیْهِ وَاٰلِهٖ وَسَلَّم has stated, 'The food on which بِسۡمِ اللّٰه is not recited becomes Ḥalāl for Satan.' *(Ṣaḥīḥ Muslim, pp. 1116, Ḥadīš 2017)* (In other words, Satan also joins in consuming such food).

Save food from Satan

The food before eating which بِسۡمِ اللّٰه is not recited has no blessings. Sayyidunā Abū Ayyūb Anṣārī رَضِیَ اللهُ تَعَالٰی عَنْهُ has narrated, 'We were once present in the blessed company of the Prophet of Raḥmaĥ, the Intercessor of Ummaĥ صَلَّی اللهُ تَعَالٰی عَلَیْهِ وَاٰلِهٖ وَسَلَّم when food was served. At the beginning of the meal there was so much blessing that we had never seen such blessing before, but near the end, we observed no blessings. We asked the Beloved and Blessed Prophet صَلَّی اللهُ تَعَالٰی عَلَیْهِ وَاٰلِهٖ وَسَلَّم, 'Yā Rasūlallāĥ صَلَّی اللهُ تَعَالٰی عَلَیْهِ وَاٰلِهٖ وَسَلَّم, what is the reason behind this?' He صَلَّی اللهُ تَعَالٰی عَلَیْهِ وَاٰلِهٖ وَسَلَّم replied, 'All of us had recited بِسۡمِ اللّٰه prior to eating, but then a person who had not recited بِسۡمِ اللّٰه sat down to eat, and Satan also ate with him.' *(Sharḥ-us-Sunnaĥ, vol. 6, pp. 62, Ḥadīš 2818)*

Protection from Satan

Sayyidunā Salmān Fārsī رَضِیَ اللهُ تَعَالٰی عَنْهُ has narrated that the Noble Prophet صَلَّی اللهُ تَعَالٰی عَلَیْهِ وَاٰلِهٖ وَسَلَّم has stated, 'Whoever wishes that Satan neither eats with him, nor takes siesta with him and nor spends night with him, should say Salām while entering his home and recite بِسۡمِ اللّٰه prior to eating.' *(Mu'jam Kabīr, vol. 6, pp. 240, Ḥadīš 6102)*

Solution to family discords

A renowned exegetist of the Quran, Ḥakīm-ul-Ummat, Muftī Aḥmad Yār Khān عَلَیْهِ رَحْمَةُ الْمَنَّان has stated, 'When entering home, one should recite بِسۡمِ اللهِ الرَّحۡمٰنِ الرَّحِيۡم and place the right foot first into home. One should then say Salām to the household. If no one is present in home, one should say اَلسَّلَامُ عَلَيْكَ اَيُّهَا النَّبِيُّ وَرَحۡمَةُ اللهِ وَبَرَكَاتُهٗ.

Some saints have been seen reciting بِسْمِ اللّٰهِ الرَّحْمٰنِ الرَّحِيْم and Sūraĥ Al-Ikhlāṣ as they entered their homes at the beginning of the day. This brings about harmony in the household preventing quarrel and increases blessing in sustenance.' *(Mirāt-ul-Manājīḥ, vol. 6, pp. 9)*

What to do if one forgets to recite بِسْمِ اللّٰه?

The mother of believers, Sayyidatunā 'Āishaĥ Ṣiddīqaĥ رَضِیَ اللہُ تَعَالٰی عَنْہَا has narrated that the Beloved and Blessed Prophet صَلَّی اللہُ تَعَالٰی عَلَیْہِ وَاٰلِہٖ وَسَلَّم has stated, 'When a person eats, he should mention the name of Allah عَزَّوَجَلَّ, i.e. recite بِسْمِ اللّٰه. If he forgets to recite بِسْمِ اللّٰه in the beginning, he should recite بِسْمِ اللّٰهِ اَوَّلَهٗ وَاٰخِرَهٗ.' *(Sunan Abī Dāwūd, vol. 3, pp. 487, Ḥadīš 3767)*

Satan threw up!

Sayyidunā Umayyaĥ Bin Makhshī رَضِیَ اللہُ تَعَالٰی عَنْہُ has stated, 'A person was eating food without reciting بِسْمِ اللّٰه. When he was about to eat the last morsel, he recalled and recited بِسْمِ اللّٰهِ اَوَّلَهٗ وَاٰخِرَهٗ. (Seeing this) The Holy Prophet صَلَّی اللہُ تَعَالٰی عَلَیْہِ وَاٰلِہٖ وَسَلَّم said with a smile, 'Satan was also eating with this person. When he mentioned the name of Allah عَزَّوَجَلَّ, Satan spewed up what was in his stomach.' *(Sunan Abī Dāwūd, vol. 3, pp. 356, Ḥadīš 3768)*

Nothing is hidden from Blessed Eyes of Mustafa صَلَّی اللہُ تَعَالٰی عَلَیْہِ وَاٰلِہٖ وَسَلَّم

Dear Islamic brothers! One should recite بِسْمِ اللّٰهِ الرَّحْمٰنِ الرَّحِيْم whenever one eats food. If someone eats without reciting بِسْمِ اللّٰه, a Satan named 'Qarīn' joins him in the meal. It is evident from the Ḥadīš narrated by Sayyidunā Umayyaĥ Bin Makhshī رَضِیَ اللہُ تَعَالٰی عَنْہُ that the blessed eyes of the Holy Prophet صَلَّی اللہُ تَعَالٰی عَلَیْہِ وَاٰلِہٖ وَسَلَّم saw everything, which is why he صَلَّی اللہُ تَعَالٰی عَلَیْہِ وَاٰلِہٖ وَسَلَّم smiled upon seeing Satan's dismay.

A renowned exegetist of the Quran, Ḥakīm-ul-Ummat, Muftī Aḥmad Yār Khān عَلَیْہِ رَحْمَۃُ الْمَنَّان has stated, 'The Holy Prophet صَلَّی اللہُ تَعَالٰی عَلَیْہِ وَاٰلِہٖ وَسَلَّم is able enough to see even the hidden creatures. The Ḥadīš is very explicit in its meaning and does not require any elaboration or interpretation. As we do not eat the food in which a fly has fallen (and is still present in it), similarly, Satan cannot digest the food before eating which the name of Allah عَزَّوَجَلَّ is mentioned. Though the food thrown up by Satan is of no use to us, Satan falls sick and has to remain hungry, and the lost blessing of our food is restored. Thus, there is one advantage for us and two disadvantages for Satan.

It is also possible that Satan may not even eat with us in the future for fear that perhaps we would recite بِسْمِ اللّٰه and he would have to again vomit the food he has eaten. The person mentioned in the Ḥadīš was probably eating alone. Had he been eating in the company of the Noble Prophet صَلَّى اللّٰهُ تَعَالٰى عَلَيْهِ وَاٰلِهٖ وَسَلَّم he would not have forgotten to recite بِسْمِ اللّٰه because the people present there used to recite بِسْمِ اللّٰه aloud and would instruct others to do the same.' *(Mirāt-ul-Manājīḥ, vol. 6, pp. 30)*

Dear Islamic brothers! اَلْحَمْدُلِلّٰه عَزَّوَجَلَّ! There's plenty of opportunity to learn and recite Du'ā in the Madanī environment of Dawat-e-Islami, especially in its Madanī Qāfilaĥ. Words cannot simply express the blessings of Dawat-e-Islami! Here is an amazing account.

Bedridden mother recovers

An Islamic brother from Bāb-ul-Madīnaĥ, Karachi has stated: My mother was so seriously ill that she was even unable to rise from bed. Even the doctors had disappointed us declaring that she would no longer recover. I had heard that the prayers of those travelling with the devotees of Rasūl in the Madanī Qāfilaĥ of Dawat-e-Islami are answered and illnesses are cured. Therefore, plucking up the courage, I decided to travel with Madanī Qāfilaĥ. I made my way to the Madanī Training Centre in the global Madanī Markaz Faīzān-e-Madīnaĥ where I expressed my intention to travel in a Madanī Qāfilaĥ for 3 days. The Islamic brothers met me very warmly and made arrangements instantly.

In the company of the devotees of the Rasūl our Madanī Qāfilaĥ reached a village near Ṣaḥrā-e-Madīnaĥ of Bāb-ul-Islam Sindh, Pakistan. During the Qāfilaĥ, I informed the Islamic brothers of my ailing mother and her critical condition. They comforted me and made Du'ā for her recovery. Making individual effort, the Amīr of the Qāfilaĥ persuaded me to travel with another Madanī Qāfilaĥ for 30 days. I made my intention for that. During those 3 days, I prayed a lot for my mother, weeping and beseeching for her recovery.

On the third day, I had a dream in which I saw a saint who had a shining face. The saint comforted me saying, 'Do not worry about your mother, اِنْ شَآءَاللّٰه عَزَّوَجَلَّ she will get better.' After I spent 3 days with the Madanī Qāfilaĥ, I returned home. As I knocked, the door opened; I was astonished to see that the mother of mine who was unable even to rise from bed had opened the door herself. I kissed her feet out of joy and told her of the dream. I then left with the devotees of the Rasūl in the Madanī Qāfilaĥ for 30 days after seeking permission from her.

Mā jo bīmār ĥo qarz kā bār ĥo ranj-o-gham mat karayn Qāfilay mayn chalo
Rab عَزَّوَجَلَّ *kay dar per jĥukayn iltijā-ayn karayn bāb-e-raḥmat kĥulayn Qāfilay mayn chalo*
Dil kī kālak dĥulay marz-e-'iṣyān ṭalay āo sab chal pařayn Qāfilay mayn chalo

For recovery of ill mother, for payment of debt from other, for relief from grief and dither, travel with the Qāfilaĥ
Bow down before Allah عَزَّوَجَلَّ*, entreat and beseech to be blessed with His grace, travel with the Qāfilaĥ*
May the filth of heart wash away, and decadent ways go away travel with the Qāfilaĥ

صَلُّوْا عَلَى الْحَبِيْب　　صَلَّى اللّٰهُ تَعَالٰى عَلٰى مُحَمَّد

Dear Islamic brothers! Did you see? By the blessings of making Du'ā during the Madanī Qāfilaĥ, the bed-ridden mother of an Islamic brother recovered from her chronic disease. Words cannot fully express the blessings of Du'ās. Sayyidunā 'Alī رَضِىَ اللّٰهُ تَعَالٰى عَنْهُ has reported the Holy Prophet صَلَّى اللّٰهُ تَعَالٰى عَلَيْهِ وَاٰلِهٖ وَسَلَّم to have stated:

اَلدُّعَآءُ سِلَاحُ الْمُؤْمِنِ، وَعِمَادُ الدِّيْنِ، وَنُوْرُ السَّمٰوَاتِ وَالْاَرْضِ

'Du'ā is a weapon of a Muslim, a pillar of faith and a light from the heavens and the earth.'

(Musnad Abī Ya'lā, vol. 1, pp. 215, Ḥadīš 435)

Now let us briefly look at the Madanī pearls pertaining to Du'ās.

17 Madanī pearls of making Du'ā

(Almost all of these Madanī pearls are extracted from the book titled, 'Aḥsan-ul-Wi'ā-lī-Ādāb-id-Du'ā ma' Sharḥ Żayl-ul-Mudda'ā-lī-Aḥsan-ul-Wi'ā' published by Maktaba-tul-Madīnaĥ)

1. It is Wājib to make Du'ā at least 20 times a day. اَلْحَمْدُلِلّٰه عَزَّوَجَلَّ, Those who offer Ṣalāĥ regularly perform this Wājib by reciting Sūraĥ Al-Fātiḥaĥ as the following two verses of Sūraĥ Al-Fātiḥaĥ are Du'ās.

   a. **All glorification is to Allah عَزَّوَجَلَّ, the Creator of the worlds.** اَلۡحَمۡدُ لِلّٰہِ رَبِّ الۡعٰلَمِیۡنَ ۙ

   b. **Make us walk on the straight path.** اِہۡدِ نَا الصِّرَاطَ الۡمُسۡتَقِیۡمَ ۙ

   (Aḥsan-ul-Wi'ā, pp. 123-124)

2. Do not exceed the limit whilst making Du'ā. For example, do not ask for the status of the Noble Prophets عَلَيْهِمُ السَّلَام or for the ability to climb the skies [Heavens]. It is also forbidden to ask for every good and every excellence of the world and the Hereafter as 'all excellences' also include the ranks of the Noble Prophets عَلَيْهِمُ السَّلَام which are unattainable. *(Aḥsan-ul-Wi'ā, pp. 80-81)*

3. Whilst making Du'ā, do not ask for the thing that is impossible or almost impossible. For instance, making Du'ā to remain always healthy or protected from every trouble amounts to asking for the thing nearly impossible. Similarly, a tall person should not make Du'ā to become shorter, nor should a person with small eyes ask for the big ones as these matters have been (divinely) predetermined. *(Aḥsan-ul-Wi'ā, pp. 81)*

4. Do not make Du'ā for a sin as such a Du'ā is itself a sin. For example, making Du'ā to get others' wealth unlawfully is not permissible. *(Aḥsan-ul-Wi'ā, pp. 82)*

5. Do not make Du'ā to break ties. [In other words, do not make such Du'ā as so-and-so relatives end up in quarrel with each other]. *(Aḥsan-ul-Wi'ā, pp. 82)*

6. Do not ask Allah عَزَّوَجَلَّ for just inferior things as Allah عَزَّوَجَلَّ is omnipotent. Keep all your attention directed towards Allah عَزَّوَجَلَّ and ask Him for everything. *(Aḥsan-ul-Wi'ā, pp. 84)*

7. One should not make Du'ā for his death due to troubles and tribulations. Remember that it is impermissible to desire death to avoid worldly loss but permissible to avoid religious loss. *(Aḥsan-ul-Wi'ā, pp. 85-87)*

8. Without a Shar'ī (lawful) need, do not make Du'ā for the death and ruin of any one. However, if it is sure or likely that a certain unbeliever who is a danger to Islam will never embrace Islam or an oppressor will neither repent nor give up his oppression and his death and ruin would bring about ease and peace for people, it is permissible to curse such a person. *(Aḥsan-ul-Wi'ā, pp. 86-89)*

9. It is not permissible to make such a curse that so-and-so Muslim become an unbeliever as, according to some scholars, making such a curse is itself Kufr [unbelief]. However, the actual verdict is that if the curse is made considering Kufr good or Islam bad, it is undoubtedly Kufr, otherwise it is a grave sin as wishing a Muslim harm is a major sin, and wishing the loss of a Muslim's faith is the worst of all harms. *(Aḥsan-ul-Wi'ā, pp. 90)*

10. Neither curse a Muslim nor call him a 'cursed one' or a 'rejected one.' Further, do not curse any such non-Muslim by name whose death on Kufr is not certain. Similarly, it is also prohibited to curse mosquitoes, wind, animals and non-living things such as stones, iron etc. However, some animals like the scorpion etc. have been cursed in Ḥadīš. *(Aḥsan-ul-Wi'ā, pp. 90)*

11. Do not make such a curse against a Muslim as, '*May the wrath of Allah عَزَّوَجَلَّ be upon you! May you enter Hell!*' as it has been prohibited in Ḥadīš. *(Aḥsan-ul-Wi'ā, pp. 100)*

12. Making Du'ā for the forgiveness of an unbeliever who has died in the state of Kufr is Ḥarām and Kufr. *(Aḥsan-ul-Wi'ā, pp. 101)*

13. It is not permissible to ask Allah عَزَّوَجَلَّ to forgive all sins of all Muslims as it is contrary to various Aḥādīš which declare that certain Muslims will enter Hell. *(Aḥsan-ul-Wi'ā, pp. 106)* However, it is permissible to ask that the entire Ummaĥ of the Holy Prophet صَلَّى اللّٰهُ تَعَالٰى عَلَيْهِ وَاٰلِهٖ وَسَلَّم be forgiven or that all Muslims be forgiven. *(Aḥsan-ul-Wi'ā, pp. 102)*

14. One should not curse oneself, one's family, children, relatives, friends and wealth. If the Du'ā is accepted, he will have to regret. *(Aḥsan-ul-Wi'ā, pp. 107)*

15. One should not make Du'ā for that which he already has. For example, a male should not pray, '*Yā Allah* عَزَّوَجَلَّ, *make me a male*' as it is nothing but mockery. However, it is permissible to make the Du'ā that leads to such benefits as the fulfilment of the commandment of Sharī'aĥ, or that shows humility and servitude, or that inculcates devotion to Allah عَزَّوَجَلَّ and His Prophet صَلَّى اللهُ تَعَالٰى عَلَيْهِ وَاٰلِهٖ وَسَلَّم, or that inspires inclination to Islam or Muslims, or that instils hatred towards unbelief or unbelievers, even if the attainment of what is being asked for, is certain. For example, recitation of Ṣalāt-'Alan-Nabī, making Du'ā of wasīlaĥ (for the Holy Prophet صَلَّى اللهُ تَعَالٰى عَلَيْهِ وَاٰلِهٖ وَسَلَّم) Du'ā for sticking to the righteous path, or for wrath on the enemies of Allah and His Prophet. *(Aḥsan-ul-Wi'ā, pp. 108 & 109)*

16. Avoid narrow-mindedness while making Du'ā. For example, do not make Du'ā in such manners: '*Yā Allah* عَزَّوَجَلَّ, *have mercy only on me*' or '*Yā Allah* عَزَّوَجَلَّ, *have mercy only on me and so-and-so friend of mine.*' *(Aḥsan-ul-Wi'ā, pp. 109)* It is better to include all Muslims in Du'ā. One of its benefits is that even if the seeker of Du'ā is not worthy of the thing he is asking for, he will attain it because of those pious Muslims who were also included in the Du'ā.

17. Ḥujjat-ul-Islam, Shaykh Sayyidunā Imām Muhammad Ghazālī عَلَيْهِ رَحْمَةُ اللّٰهِ الْوَالِى has stated, 'One should make Du'ā with absolute belief and certainty that it would be accepted.' *(Iḥyā-ul-'Ulūm, vol. 4, pp. 770)*

A Sunnaĥ of sitting

One of the Sunnaĥs of sitting while eating is to keep the right knee erect, fold the left leg and sit on it. Another Sunnaĥ of sitting is stated in a Ḥadīš. Therefore, Sayyidunā Anas رَضِىَ اللهُ تَعَالٰى عَنْهُ has stated, 'I once saw the Prophet of Raḥmaĥ, the Intercessor of Ummaĥ صَلَّى اللهُ تَعَالٰى عَلَيْهِ وَاٰلِهٖ وَسَلَّم eat dry dates. The Holy Prophet صَلَّى اللهُ تَعَالٰى عَلَيْهِ وَاٰلِهٖ وَسَلَّم was sitting on the floor in such a manner that both of his blessed knees were in upright position.' *(Ṣaḥīḥ Muslim, pp. 1130, Ḥadīš 2044)*

Benefits of keeping knees upright whilst eating

Dear Islamic brothers! Sitting on the floor with both knees upright and the behind [i.e. buttocks] touching the floor prevents over-eating, giving protection from many illnesses. Sitting with the right knee erect and the left leg folded prevents spleen problems. This also makes the thigh muscles stronger, whereas sitting cross-legged increases obesity and causes the belly to bulge. Sitting cross-legged also increases the risk of colitis. Once a person said, 'I once saw an Englishman who was eating something sitting on the floor with both his knees upright and the behind touching the ground. I curiously asked him as to why he was sitting in that position. Indicating his bulged belly, he replied, 'To flatten it.'

Eating and veil within veil

While eating according to Sunnaĥ, Islamic brothers and sisters should cover the area from the knees to the toes properly with a shawl. If the kurta [shirt] is long enough, then one can use it to cover this area. Not observing veil within veil, sometimes, makes it extremely difficult for other sitting people with you to guard their gaze. Even when alone, one should observe veil within veil as one should adopt modesty for Allah عَزَّوَجَلَّ the most. If you have the intention of adopting modesty for Allah عَزَّوَجَلَّ you will earn great reward, اِنْ شَآءَاللّٰه عَزَّوَجَلَّ.

While sitting with others, by observing veil within veil, one can make the intention of assisting them in guarding their gaze. One should strive to make righteous intentions. The more good intentions one makes, the more reward he will attain. The Beloved and Blessed Prophet صَلَّى اللّٰهُ تَعَالٰى عَلَيْهِ وَاٰلِهٖ وَسَلَّم has stated, 'Intention of a Muslim is better than his deeds.' *(Mu'jam Kabīr, vol. 6, pp. 185, Ḥadīš 5942)*

To eat at table

Imām Aḥmad Razā Khān عَلَيْهِ رَحْمَةُ الرَّحْمٰن has stated, 'If someone eats food with his shoes on just for the reason that he is sitting on bare floor, he will be missing a Sunnat-ul-Mustaḥabbaĥ. It was better for him to take off his shoes. On the other hand, it is a practice of the non-Muslims to serve food on a table and eat while sitting on a chair with shoes on.

Therefore, one should refrain from this action as the Holy Prophet صَلَّى اللهُ تَعَالٰى عَلَيْهِ وَاٰلِهٖ وَسَلَّم has stated, مَنْ تَشَبَّهَ بِقَوْمٍ فَهُوَ مِنْهُمْ that is 'Whoever imitates a community, is from amongst them.' *(Sunan Abī Dāwūd, vol. 4, pp. 62, Ḥadīš 4031)*

Causes of broken marriage

Dear Islamic brothers! Tragically, it has now become a part of our life to imitate the non-Muslims in many ways. Marriage is indeed a very graceful Sunnaĥ but many Sunnaĥs and even Farāiḍ are brutally cast aside during a marriage ceremony these days. Marriage ceremonies now contain indecent activities such as playing music and movies, dancing and drum-beating. مَعَاذَاللّٰه عَزَّوَجَلَّ, Is there any Ḥarām act that is not committed in weddings today! Even before the wedding, the fiancé makes his fiancée wear a ring with his own hand. They go for outings and excursions together. Many other sinful acts are committed openly. Men are called to make videos of women. The food is served on tables. Some people don't even use chairs; they just stand around the table, buffet style, take what they want from it and then eat walking around. All this is contrary to Sunnaĥ.

Just ponder! Does marriage really bring joy and happiness today? More often than not, couples complain of their discords and troubled relationships at home. Perhaps this is the worldly punishment of committing non-Islamic acts on the occasion of marriage. How severe will be the punishment of the Hereafter, if Allah عَزَّوَجَلَّ is displeased? May Allah عَزَّوَجَلَّ protect us from adopting non-Islamic fashions and customs and make us an embodiment of Sunnaĥ.

اٰمِیْن بِجَاہِ النَّبِیِّ الْاَمِیْن صَلَّى اللهُ تَعَالٰى عَلَيْهِ وَاٰلِهٖ وَسَلَّم

Dear Islamic brothers! Join the company of the Madanī environment of Dawat-e-Islami. اِنْ شَآءَاللّٰه عَزَّوَجَلَّ, You will reap many blessings. A preacher of Dawat-e-Islami has narrated the event that inspired him to join Dawat-e-Islami.

How I joined Dawat-e-Islami!

An Islamic brother from Mandangarh, Ratnagiri district in the state of Maharashtra [India] has stated, 'In 2002, I joined a local gang of thugs due to bad company. I would abuse and even beat people. I would deliberately quarrel and scuffle with others. If there was any new fashion, I was the first to adopt it. I would change my clothes several times a day and jeans were the only pants I would wear. I used to hang around with loafers. Going home very late at night and sleeping during the day, was a daily routine of mine. My father had already passed away; whenever my mother tried to advise me, I would answer her back.

Luckily, I once met a bearded and turbaned Islamic brother of Dawat-e-Islami who gifted me a booklet titled '*King of Jinns*' published by Maktaba-tul-Madīnaĥ. I read the booklet and was very impressed by it.

In the month of Ramadan, I had the opportunity to attend a Masjid where I happened to see a calm and collected young man dressed in white clothes with a green turban on his head. I learnt that he was a Mu'takif[1] in the Masjid. When he started Dars from the book '*Faīzān-e-Sunnat*', I also sat down to listen. After he delivered Dars, he explained to me the blessings of the righteous Madanī environment of Dawat-e-Islami, making individual effort. His dress was very simple even with some patches on it. The food that came for him from his house was also very simple.

Highly impressed by his simplicity, I developed a liking for him and began to visit him regularly. He was going to get married after Eid-ul-Fiṭr. Though very poor, he did not give any impression of his difficulty, nor asked anyone for financial assistance. His contentment and self-respect further inspired me. اَلْحَمْدُلِلّٰه عَزَّوَجَلَّ, My admiration for Dawat-e-Islami greatly increased and I travelled with an 8-day Madanī Qāfilaĥ with the devotees of Rasūl.

By the blessing of travelling with the Madanī Qāfilaĥ, a Madanī transformation took place in my life. I sincerely repented of my past sins and joined Dawat-e-Islami. اَلْحَمْدُلِلّٰه عَزَّوَجَلَّ, I am presently serving Dawat-e-Islami as a local Nigrān in my area.

---

[1] The one staying in a Masjid with the intention of I'tikāf. [Translator's Note]

Sādgī chāĥiye, 'ājizī chāĥiye, āp ko gar chalayn, Qāfilay mayn chalo
Khūb khuddāriyān, aur khush akhlāqiyān, āiye sīkĥ layn Qāfilay mayn chalo
Āshiqān-e-Rasūl, lāye Sunnat kay pĥūl, āo laynay chalayn, Qāfilay mayn chalo

To adopt simplicity and modesty, travel with Qāfilaĥ
To learn self-respect and good character, travel with Qāfilaĥ
To attain pearls of Sunnaĥ offered by devotees of the Rasūl, travel with Qāfilaĥ

صَلُّوْا عَلَى الْحَبِيْب صَلَّى اللّٰهُ تَعَالٰى عَلٰى مُحَمَّد

Dear Islamic brothers! To wear trendy clothes and beautiful turbans is not necessary for Islamic preaching. One can excellently preach Islamic teachings even in patched clothes and a simple turban.

Excellence of simple dress

If those who are fashion fanatic and wear clothes of the latest attractive style in imitation of the non-Muslims adopt simplicity, they will be successful in the worldly life and in the afterlife. Hence, read the excellence of wearing simple dress. The Prophet of mankind, the Peace of our heart and mind, the most Generous and Kind صَلَّى اللّٰهُ تَعَالٰى عَلَيْهِ وَاٰلِهٖ وَسَلَّم has stated, 'Despite having the means to wear good clothing, if a person avoids them due to humility, Allah عَزَّوَجَلَّ will make him wear the attire of Karāmaĥ [heavenly dress].' *(Sunan Abī Dāwūd, vol. 4, pp. 326, Ḥadīš 4778)*

Beware! The fashionable!

Dear Islamic brothers! Rejoice! The foregoing Ḥadīš clearly shows that the one wearing simple clothes for the pleasure of Allah عَزَّوَجَلَّ despite having the means to wear elegant ones will be granted a heavenly attire. And, obviously, the one wearing heavenly attire will definitely enter the Heaven. Those who wear attractive, elegant and dazzling dresses to impress others or to show off their wealth just for the satisfaction of their carnal desires, should read the following narration and learn a lesson from it.

Sayyidunā 'Abdullāĥ Ibn 'Umar رَضِیَ اللہُ تَعَالٰی عَنۡہُمَا has narrated that the Beloved and Blessed Prophet صَلَّی اللہُ تَعَالٰی عَلَیۡہِ وَاٰلِہٖ وَسَلَّم has stated, 'The one wearing attire of fame in the world will be made to wear the dress of disgrace by Allah عَزَّوَجَلَّ on the Day of Judgement.' *(Sunan Ibn Mājaĥ, vol. 4, pp. 163, Ḥadīš 3606)*

What is 'attire of fame?'

Commenting on the foregoing Ḥadīš, a renowned scholar of Islam, an exegetist of the Quran, Muftī Aḥmad Yār Khān عَلَیۡہِ رَحۡمَۃُ الۡحَنَّان has stated, 'Attire (of fame) implies such a dress which gives the impression that the one wearing it is a rich or a pious person. In other words, the dress a person wears with the intention of being treated with respect will be considered attire of fame for him.' The compiler of the book '*Mirqāt*' has further stated, 'To wear funny dress which makes people laugh is also considered attire of fame.' *(Mirāt-ul-Manājīḥ, vol. 6, pp. 109)*

Dear Islamic brothers! Undoubtedly, this is a very tough test. It is imperative that we carefully consider our clothing and avoid ostentation. Those who use simple clothing, turbans and shawls to impress others with their simplicity are also ostentatious, and deserve Hell. Thus, we should beg Allah عَزَّوَجَلَّ for sincerity.

Mayrā ĥar 'amal bas Tayray wāsiṭay ĥo; kar Ikhlāṣ aysā, 'aṭā Yā Ilāĥī عَزَّوَجَلَّ
Riyā kāriyaun say, siyāĥ kāriyaun say; bachā Yā Ilāĥī, bachā Yā Ilāĥī عَزَّوَجَلَّ

May my every deed be for You; grant me such sincerity, Yā Allah عَزَّوَجَلَّ*!*
Save me from ostentation and iniquity, Yā Allah عَزَّوَجَلَّ*!*

A matter of concern for the fashionable

Those who only wear fashionably designed clothes and consider it beneath their dignity to wear slightly old or patched clothes should repeatedly read the following narration and get some lesson.

Sayyidunā Abū Umāmaĥ Iyās Bin Ša'labaĥ رَضِیَ اللہُ تَعَالٰی عَنۡہُ has narrated that the Holy Prophet صَلَّی اللہُ تَعَالٰی عَلَیۡہِ وَاٰلِہٖ وَسَلَّم has stated, 'Do you not listen? Do you not listen? It is from (one's) Īmān that (one's) cloth gets old. Undoubtedly, it is from (one's) Īmān that (one's) cloth gets old.' *(Sunan Abī Dāwūd, vol. 4, pp. 102, Ḥadīš 4161)*

Commenting on the foregoing Ḥadīš, Sayyidunā Shāĥ 'Abdul Ḥaq Muḥaddiš Diĥlvī عَلَيْهِ رَحْمَةُ اللّٰهِ الْقَوِى has stated, 'To refrain from adornment is one of the manners of the Muslims.' *(Ashi'at-ul-Lam'āt, vol. 3, pp. 585)*

Excellence of patched up clothes

Sayyidunā 'Amr Bin Qays رَضِىَ اللّٰهُ تَعَالٰى عَنْهُ has narrated that someone once asked Sayyidunā Alī Murtaḍā رَضِىَ اللّٰهُ تَعَالٰى عَنْهُ, 'Why do you patch your kameez (a type of long, loose and full-sleeved shirt)?' He رَضِىَ اللّٰهُ تَعَالٰى عَنْهُ replied, '(I do so) because it keeps the heart soft and a Muslim adopts it (i.e. the heart of a Muslim should be soft).' *(Ḥilyat-ul-Auliyā, vol. 1, pp. 124, Ḥadīš 254)*

How is it to eat whilst standing?

Sayyidunā Anas Bin Mālik رَضِىَ اللّٰهُ تَعَالٰى عَنْهُ has narrated that Rasūlullāĥ صَلَّى اللّٰهُ تَعَالٰى عَلَيْهِ وَاٰلِهٖ وَسَلَّم prohibited eating and drinking whilst one is standing. *(Majma'-uz-Zawāid, vol. 5, pp. 23, Ḥadīš 7921)*

Medical harms of eating whilst standing

A famous Italian dietician has stated, 'Eating while standing causes spleen and heart diseases. It also engenders psychological disorders. Sometimes, it causes such high level of insanity that the affected person fails to recognize even his close relatives.'

Eat and drink with right hand

It is a Sunnaĥ to eat and drink with the right hand. Sayyidunā 'Abdullāĥ Ibn 'Umar رَضِىَ اللّٰهُ تَعَالٰى عَنْهُ has narrated that the Beloved and Blessed Prophet صَلَّى اللّٰهُ تَعَالٰى عَلَيْهِ وَاٰلِهٖ وَسَلَّم has stated, 'Whenever anyone eats, he should eat with his right hand and whenever he drinks, he should drink with his right hand.' *(Ṣaḥīḥ Muslim, pp. 1117, Ḥadīš 2174)*

Satan's practice

Sayyidunā 'Abdullāĥ Ibn 'Umar رَضِىَ اللّٰهُ تَعَالٰى عَنْهُمَا has narrated that the Beloved and Blessed Rasūl صَلَّى اللّٰهُ تَعَالٰى عَلَيْهِ وَاٰلِهٖ وَسَلَّم has stated, 'No one should eat or drink with his left hand as eating and drinking with the left hand is a practice of Satan.' *(Ṣaḥīḥ Muslim, pp. 1117, Ḥadīš 2174)*

Give and take with right hand

Sayyidunā Abū Ĥurayraĥ رَضِیَ اللّٰہُ تَعَالٰی عَنْہ has narrated that the Prophet of mankind, the Peace of our heart and mind, the most Generous and Kind صَلَّی اللّٰہُ تَعَالٰی عَلَیْہِ وَاٰلِہٖ وَسَلَّم has stated, 'All of you should eat and drink with the right hand; and take and give with the right hand because Satan eats, drinks, gives and takes with the left hand.'

(Sunan Ibn Mājaĥ, vol. 4, pp. 12, Ḥadīš 3266)

Use of left hand in everything!

Dear Islamic brothers! Unfortunately, today we are so engrossed in worldly affairs that we do not pay attention to the Sunnaĥ of the Beloved and Blessed Prophet صَلَّی اللّٰہُ تَعَالٰی عَلَیْہِ وَاٰلِہٖ وَسَلَّم. Remember! It is clearly stated in a Ḥadīš that Satan floats with blood in the arteries of man. *(Ṣaḥīḥ Muslim, pp. 1197, Ḥadīš 2174)*

It is obvious that Satan will not let us follow Sunnaĥ. It is often observed that though people eat with the right hand, they peck a few grains with the left one. Another common observation is that since the right hand is stained with food because of eating with it, people drink water with the left hand! When tea is served to people in a cup with its saucer, some people tend to hold the cup in the right hand but sip the tea from the saucer which is in the left hand! It is also commonplace to pass items during a meal with the left hand.

When someone serves water to others, he holds the jug with his right hand and offers the glass of water to others with his left hand! It is stated on page 374 of the book '*Ḥayāt-e-Muḥaddiš-e-A'ẓam*', the grand Muḥaddiš of Pakistan, Maulānā Muhammad Sardār Aḥmad Qādirī Chishtī عَلَیْہِ رَحْمَۃُ اللّٰہِ الْقَوِی has said, 'One should make a habit of giving and taking things with his right hand. This habit should be so deeply embedded that one's right hand spontaneously stretches out to receive one's book of deeds when given to him on the Day of Judgement. This will indeed lead to salvation.'

Dear Islamic brothers! Ponder how strongly the Noble Prophet صَلَّی اللّٰہُ تَعَالٰی عَلَیْہِ وَاٰلِہٖ وَسَلَّم disliked eating and drinking with the left hand.

Right hand never raised

Sayyidunā Salamaĥ Bin Akwa' رَضِیَ اللّٰہُ تَعَالٰی عَنْہُ has narrated: 'A person was eating food with his left hand in the presence of the Beloved and Blessed Prophet صَلَّی اللّٰہُ تَعَالٰی عَلَیْہِ وَاٰلِہٖ وَسَلَّم. The Noble Prophet صَلَّی اللّٰہُ تَعَالٰی عَلَیْہِ وَاٰلِہٖ وَسَلَّم advised him, 'Eat with your right hand.' He replied, 'I cannot eat with my right hand.' (The Holy Prophet صَلَّی اللّٰہُ تَعَالٰی عَلَیْہِ وَاٰلِہٖ وَسَلَّم, with divinely bestowed knowledge of Ghayb, understood that the person had refused merely because of pride and arrogance). Therefore, he صَلَّی اللّٰہُ تَعَالٰی عَلَیْہِ وَاٰلِہٖ وَسَلَّم replied, لَااسْتَطَعْتَ, that is, may you never have the strength to do so (i.e. may you never be able to lift your right hand). As he had refused to eat with his right hand because of arrogance, he could not lift his right hand again towards his mouth since then.' *(Ṣaḥīḥ Muslim, pp. 1118, Ḥadīš 2021)*

Face disfigured

Dear Islamic brothers! The greatness of the blessed tongue of the Beloved and Blessed Prophet صَلَّی اللّٰہُ تَعَالٰی عَلَیْہِ وَاٰلِہٖ وَسَلَّم is that whatever he says, comes to pass! Indeed the status of the Holy Prophet صَلَّی اللّٰہُ تَعَالٰی عَلَیْہِ وَاٰلِہٖ وَسَلَّم is very high. Here is an incident that shows the status of one of his devotees.

It is reported that a woman used to peep at the famous companion, Sayyidunā Sa'd Bin Abī Waqqās رَضِیَ اللّٰہُ تَعَالٰی عَنْہُ. He asked her several times not to do so, but she did not give up her indecent habit. One day when she peeped at him again, he uttered these words in wrath, شَاهَ وَجْهُكِ (*May your face be disfigured*). Immediately, her face turned back, replacing the back of her neck with her face. *(Jāmi' Karāmāt-e-Auliyā, vol. 1, pp. 112)*

Maḥfūẓ Shaĥā صَلَّی اللّٰہُ تَعَالٰی عَلَیْہِ وَاٰلِہٖ وَسَلَّم rakĥnā sadā bay-adabaun say
Aur mujĥ say bĥī sarzad na koī bay-adabī ĥo

O Prophet صَلَّی اللّٰہُ تَعَالٰی عَلَیْہِ وَاٰلِہٖ وَسَلَّم! Protect me from blasphemers
May I also not commit blasphemy ever!

The immediate effect of the words of Sayyidunā Sa'd Bin Abī Waqqās رَضِیَ اللّٰہُ تَعَالٰی عَنْہُ was indeed the fruit of the blessed Du'ā the Beloved and Blessed Prophet صَلَّی اللّٰہُ تَعَالٰی عَلَیْہِ وَاٰلِہٖ وَسَلَّم made for him. It is stated in *Jāmi' Tirmiżī* and other books of Aḥādīš that the Noble

Prophet صَلَّى اللهُ تَعَالٰى عَلَيْهِ وَاٰلِهٖ وَسَلَّم once made Du'ā, اَللّٰھُمَّ اسْتَجِبْ لِسَعْدٍ اِذَا دَعَاكَ (*O Allah* عَزَّوَجَلَّ*! Whenever Sa'd makes Du'ā to You, accept it*). *(Jāmi' Tirmiżī, vol. 5, pp. 418, Ḥadīš 3772)*

The honourable Muḥaddišīn رَحِمَهُمُ اللّٰهُ تَعَالٰی have stated, 'Whenever Sayyidunā Sa'd Bin Abī Waqqās رَضِیَ اللّٰهُ تَعَالٰی عَنْهُ made Du'ā, it was accepted.' *(Jāmi' Karāmāt-e-Auliyā, vol. 1, pp. 113)*

Dear Islamic brothers! Indeed the blessed companions رَضِیَ اللّٰهُ تَعَالٰی عَنْهُم have very high prestige. Even those who are their devotees, the Auliyā رَحِمَهُمُ اللّٰهُ تَعَالٰی, hold very high ranks.

Ṣabāḥī becomes blind

An eminent Muḥaddiš and a great scholar Sayyidunā 'Abdullāĥ Bin Waĥb عَلَيْهِ الرَّحْمَةُ الرَّبّ knew one hundred thousand Aḥādīš by heart. When 'Ubbād Bin Muhammad, the then Egyptian ruler, decided to appoint him as the Qāḍī (i.e. the judge), he رَحْمَةُ اللهِ تَعَالٰی عَلَيْه hid himself to keep from taking up the judicial position. A person named Ṣabāḥī who was jealous of the great Shaykh went to the ruler and lied to him, 'Abdullāĥ Bin Waĥb once told me that he wanted to become the Qāḍī, but he has now purposely hidden himself just to disobey you.' Enraged by listening to this, the ruler had the house of Sayyidunā 'Abdullāĥ Bin Waĥb عَلَيْهِ الرَّحْمَةُ الرَّبّ demolished. When Sayyidunā 'Abdullāĥ Bin Waĥb عَلَيْهِ الرَّحْمَةُ الرَّبّ came to know of this, he cursed Ṣabāḥī in wrath, 'Yā Allah عَزَّوَجَلَّ! Make Ṣabāḥī blind.' As a result, Ṣabāḥī lost his eyesight on the eighth day of the incident.

Sayyidunā 'Abdullāĥ Bin Waĥb عَلَيْهِ الرَّحْمَةُ الرَّبّ always feared Allah عَزَّوَجَلَّ. One day, while listening to the descriptions of the Day of Judgement, he رَحْمَةُ اللهِ تَعَالٰی عَلَيْه was overcome with fear and passed out. After he regained consciousness, he رَحْمَةُ اللهِ تَعَالٰی عَلَيْه lived only for a few more days during which he did not converse with anyone. He passed away in 197 A.H. *(Tażkira-tul-Ḥuffāẓ, vol.1, pp. 223)*

May Allah عَزَّوَجَلَّ have mercy on him and forgive us without accountability for his sake!

Auliyā رَحِمَهُمُ اللّٰهُ تَعَالٰی *kā jo koī ĥo bay-adab*
Nāzil us per ĥotā ĥay qaĥar-o-ghazab

Whoever disrespects the friends of Allah عَزَّوَجَلَّ
Upon him rains the wrath of Allah عَزَّوَجَلَّ

Yā Rab عَزَّوَجَلَّ of the Noble Prophet صَلَّى اللهُ تَعَالٰى عَلَيْهِ وَاٰلِهٖ وَسَلَّم! Bless us with true respect and reverence for Your Beloved Prophet صَلَّى اللهُ تَعَالٰى عَلَيْهِ وَاٰلِهٖ وَسَلَّم, for his noble companions رَضِىَ اللهُ تَعَالٰى عَنْهُم and for Your dignified saints رَحِمَهُمُ اللهُ تَعَالٰى. Yā Allah عَزَّوَجَلَّ! Guard us from the evil of blasphemers and protect us from blasphemy and disrespect for Your beloved ones. Make us the true and sincere devotees of Your Beloved Rasūl صَلَّى اللهُ تَعَالٰى عَلَيْهِ وَاٰلِهٖ وَسَلَّم!

اٰمِيْن بِجَاهِ النَّبِيِّ الْاَمِيْن صَلَّى اللهُ تَعَالٰى عَلَيْهِ وَاٰلِهٖ وَسَلَّم

Yā Rab عَزَّوَجَلَّ mayn Tayray khauf say rautā raĥūn ĥar dam
Dīwānaĥ Shaĥanshāĥ-e-Madīnaĥ صَلَّى اللهُ تَعَالٰى عَلَيْهِ وَاٰلِهٖ وَسَلَّم kā banā day

May I stay weeping with Your fear, O Allah عَزَّوَجَلَّ
Make me a devotee of Your Prophet صَلَّى اللهُ تَعَالٰى عَلَيْهِ وَاٰلِهٖ وَسَلَّم O Allah عَزَّوَجَلَّ

صَلُّوْا عَلَى الْحَبِيْب صَلَّى اللهُ تَعَالٰى عَلٰى مُحَمَّد

Post-demise individual effort from saint رَحْمَةُ اللهِ عَلَيْه

Dear Islamic brothers! اَلْحَمْدُلِلّٰه عَزَّوَجَلَّ, the saints of Islam are highly regarded in the Madanī environment of Dawat-e-Islami. Truly, by the grace of Allah عَزَّوَجَلَّ, Dawat-e-Islami is flourishing by virtue of the blessings of saints رَحِمَهُمُ اللهُ تَعَالٰى.

An Islamic brother has narrated the following faith-refreshing incident about a deceased saint رَحْمَةُ اللهِ تَعَالٰى عَلَيْه who persuaded an Islamic brother to travel with a Madanī Qāfilaĥ, making individual effort from within his blessed grave. Here is a summary of the incident:

اَلْحَمْدُلِلّٰه عَزَّوَجَلَّ, A Madanī Qāfilaĥ of devotees of the Rasūl travelled from Chakwal (Punjab, Pakistan) to Muzaffarabad and surrounding villages to promote the message of Sunnaĥ. During the journey, they stayed for a while in a town called 'Anwār Sharīf' where four other Islamic brothers also joined the Madanī Qāfilaĥ for three days. Amongst them was an Islamic brother who was a descendant of a saint رَحْمَةُ اللهِ تَعَالٰى عَلَيْه whose shrine is situated in 'Anwār Sharīf.'

Spreading the call to righteousness, the Madanī Qāfilaĥ reached a town called 'Garhi Dupatta.' After the brothers from Anwār Sharīf had spent three days with the Madanī Qāfilaĥ, the descendant of that saint remarked, 'I will not return [to Anwār Sharīf], because last night I had a dream in which I saw my ancestor (the saint رَحْمَةُ اللهِ تَعَالٰی عَلَیْه) who told me in dream, 'Son! Do not return home, travel ahead with the Madanī Qāfilaĥ.'

This gave a tremendous boost to the travellers of the Madanī Qāfilaĥ. Everyone's morale was raised, and all four Islamic brothers from Anwār Sharīf travelled further with the Madanī Qāfilaĥ.

Daytay ĥayn fayz-e-'ām, Auliyā kirām رَحِمَهُمُ اللّٰهُ تَعَالٰی
Lūtnay sab chalayn, Qāfilay mayn chalo
Auliyā رَحِمَهُمُ اللّٰهُ تَعَالٰی *kā karam, tum per ĥo lā-jazam*
Mil kar sab chal pařayn, Qāfilay mayn chalo

Saints رَحِمَهُمُ اللّٰهُ تَعَالٰی *shower blessings indiscriminately;*
Let's reap their grace and travel with Qāfilaĥ
Their kindness, we will surely get
Let's all travel together with Qāfilaĥ

صَلُّوْا عَلَی الْحَبِیْب صَلَّی اللّٰهُ تَعَالٰی عَلٰی مُحَمَّد

A mare gifted in dream

Dear Islamic brothers! One should not be astonished by the deceased saint's guiding his descendant in dream. By the bestowment of Allah عَزَّوَجَلَّ, the pious people رَحِمَهُمُ اللّٰهُ تَعَالٰی are capable enough to do many things.

Khuwājaĥ Amīr Khurd Kirmānī قُدِّسَ سِرُّهُ الرَّبَّانِی has stated that Sayyidunā Maḥbūb Ilāĥī Niẓāmuddīn Auliyā رَحْمَةُ اللهِ تَعَالٰی عَلَیْه has narrated, 'Before moving to Gyaspur [India], I used to walk 3 kilometres to a Masjid in Kaylu Khari to offer Ṣalāt-ul-Jumu'aĥ. Once, while I was walking to the Masjid in the state of fast, gusts of hot air were blowing. Dizzy, I sat down near a shop, and thought that if I had some means of transportation, it would be easier. I then recited a couplet of great Shaykh Sa'dī عَلَیْهِ رَحْمَةُ اللّٰهِ الْهَادِی

مَا قَدَم اَز سَر کُنِیم دَر طَلَبِ دُوسْتَاں   رَاہ بَجَائے بُرْد ہَر کِہ بَاَقْدَام رَفْت

To meet our friends, we walk on our heads instead of feet as those walking on their feet on this path do not advance.

Then I repented of wishing an easier means of travel. After three days, caliph Malik Yār Parān brought me a mare and said, 'During the last three nights, I dreamt that my Shaykh instructed me to give the mare to so-and-so person; therefore, please accept this gift.' I replied, 'Your Shaykh may certainly have ordered you but I cannot accept this gift unless my Shaykh asks me to do so.' The very same night, I had a dream in which I saw my Shaykh Sayyidunā Bābā Farīduddīn Ganj Shakar رَحْمَةُ اللهِ تَعَالٰى عَلَيْه who told me, 'Accept the mare to gratify caliph Malik Yār Parān.' The next day when caliph Malik brought the mare, I accepted it, considering it as a divine gift.' *(Siyar-ul-Auliyā, pp. 246)*

صَلُّوا عَلَى الْحَبِيْب   صَلَّى اللهُ تَعَالٰى عَلٰى مُحَمَّد

Eat only from your side

If there is only one type of food in the plate, it is a Sunnaĥ to eat from one's own side. Sayyidunā 'Umar Bin Abī Salamaĥ[1] رَضِىَ اللهُ تَعَالٰى عَنْه has narrated, 'In my childhood, I was brought up in the blessed house of the Holy Prophet صَلَّى اللهُ تَعَالٰى عَلَيْهِ وَاٰلِهٖ وَسَلَّم. While eating, I would stretch my hand all over the plate. The Prophet of Raḥmaĥ, the Intercessor of Ummaĥ, the Owner of Jannaĥ صَلَّى اللهُ تَعَالٰى عَلَيْهِ وَاٰلِهٖ وَسَلَّم would instruct me, 'Recite بِسْمِ اللّٰه and eat with your right hand from the portion of the plate nearest to you.' *(Ṣaḥīḥ Bukhārī, vol. 3, pp. 521, Ḥadīš 5376)*

Don't eat from centre of plate

Sayyidunā 'Abdullāĥ Ibn 'Abbās رَضِىَ اللهُ تَعَالٰى عَنْهُمَا has narrated that the Prophet of mankind, the Peace of our heart and mind, the most Generous and Kind صَلَّى اللهُ تَعَالٰى عَلَيْهِ وَاٰلِهٖ وَسَلَّم has stated,

---

[1] 'Umar Bin Abī Salamaĥ was the son of Sayyidatunā Umm-e-Salamaĥ رَضِىَ اللهُ تَعَالٰى عَنْهَا. He was born from her former husband before she got married with the Holy Prophet صَلَّى اللهُ تَعَالٰى عَلَيْهِ وَاٰلِهٖ وَسَلَّم

'Indeed blessing descends at the centre of the plate, therefore, eat from the sides (of the plate) and not from the middle.' *(Jāmi' Tirmiżī, vol. 3, pp. 316, Ḥadīš 1812)*

Avoid eating from centre of plate

Dear Islamic brothers! All of us should ponder as to whether or not we practise this Sunnaĥ. It is commonly noticed that even most of those appearing to be practising Muslims do not act upon this Sunnaĥ! Virtually everyone begins eating from the centre of the plate. It seems as if Satan holds our hand and takes it to the centre of the plate to deprive us of this great blessing. Undoubtedly, Satan leaves no stone unturned to deprive the Muslims of blessings.

Elaborating on the foregoing Ḥadīš Muftī Aḥmad Yār Khān عَلَيْهِ رَحْمَةُ الْمَنَّان has stated, 'The mercy of Allah عَزَّوَجَلَّ descends at the centre of the plate. To eat from the centre of the plate is a sign of greed and a greedy person is deprived of Allah's mercy. Furthermore, this Ḥadīš also illustrates that the mercy of Allah عَزَّوَجَلَّ descends when Muslims are eating, especially with the intention of abiding by Sunnaĥ.' *(Mirāt-ul-Manājīḥ, vol. 6, pp. 33-34)*

Do not embarrass others

Sayyidunā 'Abdullāĥ Ibn 'Umar رَضِىَ اللّٰهُ تَعَالٰى عَنْهُمَا has narrated that the Prophet of mankind, the Peace of our heart and mind, the most Generous and Kind صَلَّى اللّٰهُ تَعَالٰى عَلَيْهِ وَاٰلِهٖ وَسَلَّم has stated, 'When the dining-mat is laid, each one of you should eat from your own side [when eating in the same platter etc.] and do not eat from the sides of others. Avoid eating from the centre of the plate [because blessings descend over there]. No one should get up unless the dining-mat has been removed. (And) No one should stop eating unless others have also stopped, even if he has been satiated. He should also continue to eat with others because if he stops eating, it will cause embarrassment to others who will (also follow suit and) stop eating even though they may need to eat more.' *(Shu'ab-ul-Īmān, vol. 5, pp. 83, Ḥadīš 5864)*

Explanation of descending of blessings in centre

Muftī Aḥmad Yār Khān عَلَيْهِ رَحْمَةُ الْمَنَّان has stated, 'Eat from the side of the plate near you [when eating together in the same plate]. Don't eat from the centre because blessing descends in the centre of the plate and spreads towards the edges. If you eat from the centre the blessings may perhaps stop descending. In short, the place of the descending of blessings is different from that of reaping them.' *(Mirāt-ul-Manājīḥ, vol. 6, pp. 63)*

Five Sunnaĥs pertaining to eating

Dear Islamic brothers! Five Sunnaĥs of consuming food were described in the above Ḥadīš:

1. To eat from the portion of the plate that is in front of you.
2. Not to eat from the side of the other, when eating with others.
3. Not to eat from the centre of the plate.
4. The dining-mat should be removed before the eating people get up. (Sadly, nowadays, the trend is quite the opposite; people get up first and then the dining-mat is removed).
5. If others are eating with you, do not stop eating until everyone has finished.

Regretfully, today, we hardly find anyone acting upon these Sunnaĥ. In order to learn various Sunnaĥ and remove hesitation in acting upon them, especially in the presence of others, one should travel with Dawat-e-Islami's Sunnaĥ-Inspiring Madanī Qāfilaĥ and practise Sunnaĥ there. اِنْ شَآءَاللّٰه عَزَّوَجَلَّ, By the blessings of travelling with Madanī Qāfilaĥs, it will become very easy to act upon Sunnaĥ.

Defence against nightmares

Words cannot express the blessings of Madanī Qāfilaĥ! Here is a summarized account of an Islamic brother who often used to have nightmares. He said, 'I travelled with a 30-day Sunnaĥ-Inspiring Madanī Qāfilaĥ of Dawat-e-Islami with Rasūl's devotees. اَلْحَمْدُ لِلّٰه عَزَّوَجَلَّ, by the blessing of this Madanī Qāfilaĥ, I no longer have nightmares. Instead, I now dream of the adorable city of Madīnaĥ. Sometimes, I dream of offering Ṣalāĥ or reciting the Holy Quran.'

Dear Islamic brothers! At bedtime, recite يَا مُتَكَبِّرُ 21 times with Ṣalāt-'Alan-Nabī once before and after it. اِنْ شَآءَاللّٰه عَزَّوَجَلَّ, you will not have nightmares.

If a platter contains different types of food such as pilaf, sweet rice, pickle etc., it is allowed to eat from different sides of the platter in this case.

A platter of different dates

Sayyidunā 'Ikrāsh رضی اللہ تعالٰی عنہ has narrated, 'Šarīd[1] was once served to the Beloved and Blessed Prophet صَلَّى اللهُ تَعَالٰى عَلَيْهِ وَاٰلِهٖ وَسَلَّم. We started eating with him. I was stretching my hand all over the plate. Seeing this, the Noble Prophet صَلَّى اللهُ تَعَالٰى عَلَيْهِ وَاٰلِهٖ وَسَلَّم said, 'O 'Ikrāsh رضی اللہ تعالٰی عنہ! Eat from one side because there is only one type of food in this plate.' Afterward we were served with a platter of different varieties of fresh dates. The blessed hand of the Holy Prophet صَلَّى اللهُ تَعَالٰى عَلَيْهِ وَاٰلِهٖ وَسَلَّم stretched towards different varieties of dates and he صَلَّى اللهُ تَعَالٰى عَلَيْهِ وَاٰلِهٖ وَسَلَّم said, 'O 'Ikrāsh رضی اللہ تعالٰی عنہ! Eat from wherever you wish because these [dates] are of different varieties.' *(Sunan Ibn Mājah, vol. 4, pp. 15, Ḥadīš 3274)*

Eating with five fingers is a practice of the uncivilized

Sayyidunā 'Abdullāĥ Ibn 'Abbās رضی اللہ تعالٰی عنہما has narrated that the Beloved and Blessed Rasūl صَلَّى اللهُ تَعَالٰى عَلَيْهِ وَاٰلِهٖ وَسَلَّم once indicated his thumb and the index finger and said, 'Do not eat with these two fingers but eat with three fingers (i.e. the index finger, the middle one and the thumb) as this is Sunnaĥ. Avoid eating with five fingers as this is a practice of the uncivilized.' *(Kanz-ul-'Ummāl, vol. 5, pp. 115, Ḥadīš 40872)*

Satan's manner of eating

Sayyidunā Abū Ĥurayraĥ رضی اللہ تعالٰی عنہ has narrated that the Prophet of mankind, the Peace of our heart and mind, the most Generous and Kind صَلَّى اللهُ تَعَالٰى عَلَيْهِ وَاٰلِهٖ وَسَلَّم has stated, 'Eating with one finger is a practice of Satan, eating with two fingers is a practice of the arrogant and eating with three fingers is a practice of the Holy Prophets عَلَيْهِمُ السَّلَام.' *(Al-Jāmi'-uṣ-Ṣaghīr, pp. 184, Ḥadīš 3074)*

However, the Noble Prophet صَلَّى اللهُ تَعَالٰى عَلَيْهِ وَاٰلِهٖ وَسَلَّم would occasionally eat with four fingers as well. *(Al-Jāmi'-uṣ-Ṣaghīr, pp. 250, Ḥadīš 6942)*

---

[1] Šarīd is a dish made with pieces of bread mixed with stew and gravy sauce. It can also be prepared with vegetables instead of meat.

Proper manner of eating with three fingers

Dear Islamic brothers! Eating with three fingers would allow small morsels which would be chewed easily. Well-chewed morsels will properly get mixed with the digestive enzymes in saliva, helping their digestion. Sayyidunā Mullā 'Alī Qārī عَلَيْهِ رَحْمَةُ الْبَارِى has stated, 'Eating with five fingers is a sign of the greedy.' *(Mirqāt-ul-Mafātīḥ, vol. 8, pp. 9)* It is not difficult to eat bread with three fingers. You just have to pay a little heed, and you would be able to do so easily. However, eating rice with three fingers may be somewhat difficult, but not for those who have a Madanī mindset and a devotion to Sunnaĥ. Surely there is grace in acting on every Sunnaĥ. One should avoid eating with five fingers in the greed of eating big morsels.

In order to make a habit of eating with three fingers, at mealtimes, one may bend the ring finger and the little one and wrap a rubber band around them or whilst eating, one may take a small piece of bread in his palm and hold it with the ring finger and the little one. If one is sincere, these tips will help one get into the habit of eating with three fingers اِنْ شَآءَاللّٰه عَزَّوَجَلَّ. Once this becomes a routine, one will no longer be in the need of using these techniques. If rice grains are well separated and it is impossible to eat rice with three fingers, one may use four or five fingers. However, make sure that neither the palm nor the base of the fingers is stained with food.

Eating with spoon

It is contrary to Sunnaĥ to eat with a knife, fork or spoon. Our pious saints رَحِمَهُمُ اللّٰهُ تَعَالٰی used to refrain from using a spoon because the Beloved and Blessed Rasūl صَلَّى اللّٰهُ تَعَالٰى عَلَيْهِ وَاٰلِهٖ وَسَلَّم would eat with three fingers. Sayyidunā Ibrāĥīm Bājūrī رَحْمَةُ اللّٰهِ تَعَالٰی عَلَيْه has narrated, 'Once food was served to the Abbasid caliph, Māmūn-ur-Rashīd with a spoon. The Qāḍī-ul-Quḍā [chief justice], Sayyidunā Imām Abū Yūsuf رَحْمَةُ اللّٰهِ تَعَالٰی عَلَيْه who was also present over there said, 'Allah عَزَّوَجَلَّ has stated in Sūraĥ Banī Isrāīl,

وَلَقَدْ كَرَّمْنَا بَنِيْٓ اٰدَمَ

And no doubt, We honoured the descendants of Ādam.

[Kanz-ul-Īmān (Translation of Quran)] (Part 15, Sūraĥ Banī Isrāīl, verse 70)

O caliph! In the exegesis of this verse, your grandfather Sayyidunā 'Abdullāĥ Ibn 'Abbās رَضِیَ اللّٰہُ تَعَالٰی عَنْهُمَا has stated, 'We have made fingers for them with which they eat.' Listening to this, Māmūn-ur-Rashīd refrained from using a spoon and ate with his fingers.' *(Mawāĥib-ul-Ladunniyyaĥ, pp. 114)*

When can one eat with spoon?

Dear Islamic brothers! One can use a spoon when food cannot be eaten with fingers or cannot be drunk (e.g. food like yoghurt). Similarly, if one's hand is injured or is dirty and water is not available to wash it, there is no harm in eating with a spoon. Further, it is also permissible to use a knife to cut large pieces of cooked meat etc.

Medical benefits of eating with hand

Dear Islamic brothers! Medical practitioners have agreed that when a person eats with his fingers, certain digestive enzymes are secreted by his fingers and get mixed with food. This inhibits the deficiency of insulin, and is also beneficial to the diabetic patients. By licking the fingers clean after eating, digestive enzymes are properly consumed and swallowed into the stomach, which is very beneficial to the eyes, the brain and the stomach. This is a great cure for various diseases of the stomach, the brain and the heart.

Appendicitis was cured

Dear Islamic brothers! In order to get used to acting upon the Sunnaĥs of eating, accustom yourself to travelling with the Madanī Qāfilaĥ. اَلْحَمْدُ لِلّٰہ عَزَّوَجَلَّ, by the blessing of Madanī Qāfilaĥ, many wicked individuals have adopted a pious and righteous life-style. An Islamic brother from Mathura, India has stated:

'I was a fashionable youngster and would often watch movies. Fortunately, I once listened to a Sunnaĥ-Inspiring speech titled '*The Perils of Television*' released by Maktaba-tul-Madīnaĥ. The speech transformed my life, inspiring me to join the Madanī environment of Dawat-e-Islami. I suffered from appendicitis, and the doctors had advised me to have an operation for its treatment. I was terrified. Meanwhile, as a result of the individual effort of a preacher of Dawat-e-Islami, I travelled with a 3-day Sunnaĥ-Inspiring Madanī Qāfilaĥ with devotees of the Rasūl, for the first time in my life.

اَلْحَمْدُ لِلّٰه عَزَّوَجَلَّ, By the blessings of the Madanī Qāfilaĥ, my disease was cured without any operation. اَلْحَمْدُلِلّٰه عَزَّوَجَلَّ, Highly inspired by this, I now travel with a 3-day Madanī Qāfilaĥ every month. Furthermore, I hand in my Madanī In'āmāt booklet every month and wake up the Muslims for Ṣalāt-ul-Fajr every morning acting upon the Madanī In'ām of Ṣadā-e-Madīnaĥ.'

Bay-'amal, bā-'amal bantay ĥayn sar basar

Tū bĥī ay bĥāī kar Qāfilay mayn safar

Achchī ṣuḥbat say ṫĥandā ĥo tayrā jigar

Kāsh kar lay agar Qāfilay mayn safar

Impious becomes pious in the Madanī Qāfilaĥ
O my brother! Travel in the Madanī Qāfilaĥ
Pious company may bring joy your way,
If only you will travel in the Madanī Qāfilaĥ

صَلُّوْا عَلَى الْحَبِيْب   صَلَّى اللهُ تَعَالٰى عَلٰى مُحَمَّد

Surgery in consciousness

Dear Islamic brothers! Did you see the blessings of travelling with the Madanī Qāfilaĥ? Remember that sickness or trouble usually brings about mercy for a Muslim. You have just heard that the Islamic brother who had appendicitis was cured by the blessing of travelling with a Madanī Qāfilaĥ and, impressed by this amazing blessing, he joined the Madanī environment. Furthermore, the fact that he became steadfast in the Madanī environment, is indeed another great blessing for him.

If you ever face problems and troubles, endure them with patience and earn great reward. The manner in which our saints رَحِمَهُمُ اللّٰهُ تَعَالٰی would manifest patience on facing troubles in the enthusiasm of reaping reward is indeed marvellous and highly inspiring. Here is an account showing the spirit of our saints رَحِمَهُمُ اللّٰهُ تَعَالٰی.

'Allāmaĥ Maulānā Muftī Sharīf-ul-Ḥaq Amjadī عَلَيْهِ رَحْمَةُ اللّٰهِ الْقَوِی has narrated the following account in *Nuzĥa-tul-Qārī Sharḥ Ṣaḥīḥ-ul-Bukhārī*, volume 2, page 213 to 215: 'Sayyidunā 'Urwaĥ رَضِیَ اللّٰهُ تَعَالٰی عَنْهُ was a son of the famous Anṣārī companion, Sayyidunā

Zubayr Bin 'Awām رَضِیَ اللهُ تَعَالٰی عَنْهُ and Sayyidatunā Asmā Bint-e-Abū Bakr رَضِیَ اللهُ تَعَالٰی عَنْهُمَا. He رَضِیَ اللهُ تَعَالٰی عَنْهُ was a nephew of Sayyidatunā 'Āishaĥ Ṣiddīqaĥ رَضِیَ اللهُ تَعَالٰی عَنْهَا and a blood brother of Sayyidunā 'Abdullāĥ Bin Zubayr رَضِیَ اللهُ تَعَالٰی عَنْهُمَا. He رَضِیَ اللهُ تَعَالٰی عَنْهُ was also one of the seven renowned scholars of Madīnaĥ. He رَضِیَ اللهُ تَعَالٰی عَنْهُ was a pious, upright and righteous saint who used to worship devotedly, especially at nights. He رَضِیَ اللهُ تَعَالٰی عَنْهُ would read a quarter of the Holy Quran every day and would recite a quarter every night in Ṣalāt-ut-Taĥajjud. The caliph Walīd Bin 'Abdul Malik used to say that if anyone wished to see a Heaven dweller, they should see Sayyidunā 'Urwaĥ رَضِیَ اللهُ تَعَالٰی عَنْهُ.

Once, he [Sayyidunā 'Urwaĥ] رَضِیَ اللهُ تَعَالٰی عَنْهُ travelled several miles to meet Walīd Bin 'Abdul Malik. During this journey he رَضِیَ اللهُ تَعَالٰی عَنْهُ suffered from a severe infection that rotted his foot. Walīd suggested him to have his foot amputated but he رَضِیَ اللهُ تَعَالٰی عَنْهُ declined. The disease spread to his shin. Walīd, out of concern, told Sayyidunā 'Urwaĥ رَضِیَ اللهُ تَعَالٰی عَنْهُ that if his leg was not amputated, the disease would spread to his entire body. The great saint رَضِیَ اللهُ تَعَالٰی عَنْهُ finally agreed. The surgeon arrived and asked him to drink some alcohol so that he would not feel any pain during the amputation. He رَضِیَ اللهُ تَعَالٰی عَنْهُ replied, 'I do not want relief by the thing declared Ḥarām by Allah عَزَّوَجَلَّ.' The surgeon then recommended that Sayyidunā 'Urwaĥ رَضِیَ اللهُ تَعَالٰی عَنْهُ take some medicine that would put him to sleep. He رَضِیَ اللهُ تَعَالٰی عَنْهُ replied, 'I wish to experience the pain while my leg is being amputated so that I would get an opportunity of having patience and gaining reward.' He رَضِیَ اللهُ تَعَالٰی عَنْهُ was then asked if a few individuals could hold him down but he رَضِیَ اللهُ تَعَالٰی عَنْهُ replied that there was no need for this.

Therefore, the flesh of his foot was first cut with a knife and then his bone was cut with a saw. Amazingly, he رَضِیَ اللهُ تَعَالٰی عَنْهُ did not utter even a single word of complaint. All the while, he رَضِیَ اللهُ تَعَالٰی عَنْهُ continued to do the Żikr of Allah's blessed names. When the open wound was cauterized with a heated iron and olive oil, he رَضِیَ اللهُ تَعَالٰی عَنْهُ fainted due to extreme pain. After he regained consciousness, he رَضِیَ اللهُ تَعَالٰی عَنْهُ wiped perspiration from his face. Then, picking up the severed leg and looking at it, he رَضِیَ اللهُ تَعَالٰی عَنْهُ said, 'By Allah عَزَّوَجَلَّ Who had enabled me to walk by you! I never walked by you towards any sin.' Despite being present in the same hall, the caliph who was busy with conversation remained unaware that the operation was going on. He only became aware of it when the smell of the cauterization process spread after the operation.'

Martyrdom of son

Another test for Sayyidunā 'Urwaĥ رضی اللہ تعالی عنہ on this journey was that his beloved son Sayyidunā Muhammad Bin 'Urwaĥ رضی اللہ تعالی عنہما was martyred by some animal of the royal stable of the caliph. When he رضی اللہ تعالی عنہ returned to Madīnaĥ, he رضی اللہ تعالی عنہ recited the following part of the 62nd verse of Al-Kaĥf:

لَقَدْ لَقِيْنَا مِنْ سَفَرِنَا هٰذَا نَصَبًا ﴿۶۲﴾

We have no doubt faced great hardship in this Journey.

[Kanz-ul-Īmān (Translation of Quran)] (Part 15, Sūraĥ Al-Kaĥf, verse 62)

Generosity of Sayyidunā 'Urwaĥ رَضِیَ اللہُ عَنْہُ

Sayyidunā 'Urwaĥ رضی اللہ تعالی عنہ was very generous. When the fruits harvesting season approached, he would allow people to eat and take fruits with them from his orchard. Whenever he رضی اللہ تعالی عنہ went to his orchard, he would often recite the following part of the 39th verse of Sūraĥ Al-Kaĥf:

وَلَوْلَآ اِذْ دَخَلْتَ جَنَّتَكَ قُلْتَ مَا شَآءَ اللّٰهُ ۙ لَا قُوَّةَ اِلَّا بِاللّٰهِ ۚ

And why it was not so that when you entered your garden then you would have said, as Allah عَزَّوَجَلَّ wills, we have no power but the help from Allah عَزَّوَجَلَّ.

[Kanz-ul-Īmān (Translation of Quran)] (Part 15, Sūraĥ Al-Kaĥf, verse 39)

To eat while resting [one's back] against a support is not Sunnaĥ

The Prophet of mankind, the Peace of our heart and mind, the most Generous and Kind صَلَّی اللہُ تَعَالٰی عَلَیْہِ وَاٰلِہٖ وَسَلَّم has stated, 'I do not eat while resting [my back] against a support.'

(Kanz-ul-'Ummāl, vol. 15, pp. 102, Ḥadīš 40704)

Do not eat while resting against a support

Sayyidunā Abū Dardā رَضِیَ اللّٰہُ تَعَالٰی عَنْہُ has narrated that the Noble Prophet صَلَّی اللّٰہُ تَعَالٰی عَلَیْہِ وَاٰلِہٖ وَسَلَّم has stated, 'You should not eat while resting against a support.' *(Majma'-uz-Zawāid, vol. 5, pp. 22, Ḥadīš 7918)*

Four postures of 'resting against a support'

There are four sitting postures of resting against a support:

1. To sit bending rightwards or leftwards.
2. To sit cross-legged.
3. To sit on the floor resting one hand on it.
4. To sit resting one's back against a support like a wall (or a chair etc.).

It is not recommended to sit in these postures during mealtimes. A good sitting posture at mealtimes is to sit either with the legs folded like sitting in Ṣalāĥ or with both knees raised upwards. These two postures are also medically beneficial to the body. It is inappropriate to eat while standing. *(Mirāt-ul-Manājīḥ, vol. 6, pp. 12)*

Medical harms of resting against a support whilst eating

Dear Islamic brothers! It is a Sunnaĥ not to rest one's back against a support whilst eating. There are also three medical harms in missing this Sunnaĥ.

1. One will not be able to chew the food properly and, because of this, the required quantity of saliva which helps digest starch will not properly get mixed with the food, affecting one's digestive system.

2. As a result of resting one's back against a support while eating in a sitting posture, the stomach expands allowing excessive food to go into the stomach and thus causing indigestion.

3. Resting one's back against a support while eating in a sitting posture also harms liver and intestines.

Ḥujjat-ul-Islam, Sayyidunā Imām Muhammad Ghazālī عَلَيۡهِ رَحۡمَةُ اللّٰهِ الۡوَالِی has stated that it is also harmful to the stomach to drink water while resting against a support. *(Iḥyā-ul-'Ulūm, vol. 2, pp. 5)*

Treat bread with respect

It is Sunnaĥ to pick up and eat a piece of bread that has fallen on the ground. Sayyidatunā 'Āishaĥ Ṣiddīqaĥ رَضِیَ اللّٰهُ تَعَالٰی عَنۡهَا has narrated that Rasūlullāĥ صَلَّى اللّٰهُ تَعَالٰى عَلَيۡهِ وَاٰلِهٖ وَسَلَّم once entered his blessed home and saw a fallen piece of bread. He صَلَّى اللّٰهُ تَعَالٰى عَلَيۡهِ وَاٰلِهٖ وَسَلَّم picked it up, cleaned and ate it. He صَلَّى اللّٰهُ تَعَالٰى عَلَيۡهِ وَاٰلِهٖ وَسَلَّم then said, 'O 'Āishaĥ (رَضِیَ اللّٰهُ تَعَالٰی عَنۡهَا)! Respect that which is good because when this (i.e. the bread) has run away from a nation, then it has never returned.' *(Sunan Ibn Mājaĥ, vol. 4, pp. 50, Ḥadīš 3353)*

Repent of wasting food

Dear Islamic brothers! Today, virtually everyone seems to be complaining of deprivation and lack of blessing in sustenance. Perhaps, disrespect and waste of food may be one of its reasons. Today, you would hardly find a Muslim who does not waste food. Everywhere, whether it is a wedding feast or a Niyāz-meal of a saint, you will see people waste food. Regretfully, a lot of food is also carelessly dropped on the dining-mat during meals. After the food has been consumed, remnants of food and meat still remain on the bones and spices, which are then carelessly thrown away. After eating once, most people do not even think of reusing the food left in plates, bowls and pots and it eventually ends up in the garbage.

Dear Islamic brothers! One should repent of Isrāf he has committed till now and make a firm intention never to waste even a single speck of food and a single drop of soup. By Allah عَزَّوَجَلَّ! On the Day of Judgement, one will surely be held accountable for every speck of food he wasted in the world. Without doubt, no one has the power to bear accountability on the Day of Judgement. Repent sincerely. Recite Ṣalāt-'Alan-Nabī and plead, 'O Allah عَزَّوَجَلَّ! I repent of Isrāf which I have committed till today as well as of all my minor and major sins. With Your grant and assistance I will strive to refrain from all sins in the future. Yā Allah عَزَّوَجَلَّ! Forgive me without holding me accountable.'

اٰمِيۡن بِجَاهِ النَّبِيِّ الۡاَمِيۡن صَلَّى اللّٰهُ تَعَالٰى عَلَيۡهِ وَاٰلِهٖ وَسَلَّم

Ṣadaqaĥ Piyāray صَلَّى اللّٰهُ تَعَالٰى عَلَيْهِ وَاٰلِهٖ وَسَلَّم *kī ḥayā kā kay na lay mujĥ say ḥisāb*
Bakhsh bay-pūĉhay lajāye ko lajānā kyā ĥay

For the sake of Your beloved صَلَّى اللّٰهُ تَعَالٰى عَلَيْهِ وَاٰلِهٖ وَسَلَّم*, do not put me on accountability*
Forgive me without questioning; I am already grieved and guilty

(Ḥadāiq-e-Bakhshish)

In Sūraĥ Al-A'rāf, verse 31, Allah عَزَّوَجَلَّ says,

كُلُوْا وَ اشْرَبُوْا وَلَا تُسْرِفُوْا ۚ اِنَّهٗ لَا يُحِبُّ الْمُسْرِفِيْنَ ﴿۳۱﴾

And eat and drink and do not exceed the limit. Undoubtedly, those exceeding the limit are not liked by Him.

[Kanz-ul-Īmān (Translation of Quran)] (Part 8, Sūraĥ Al-A'rāf, verse 31)

What does Isrāf mean?

A renowned exegetist of the Quran, Muftī Aḥmad Yār Khān عَلَيْهِ رَحْمَةُ الْمَنَّان has stated on page 390 of the 8th volume of *Tafsīr-e-Na'īmī* that there are several exegeses of Isrāf [i.e. waste] some of which include:

1. To consider Ḥalāl things as Ḥarām.
2. To use Ḥarām things.
3. To eat, drink or wear more than one's requirements.
4. To eat, drink and wear whatever one desires.
5. To eat and drink repeatedly during the day and night, engendering illness and damaging the stomach.
6. To eat and drink things harmful to the body.
7. To keep obsessing about clothes and food as to what one will wear or eat next time. *(Rūḥ-ul-Bayān, vol. 3, pp. 154)*
8. To eat to be heedless.

9. To eat with the intention of committing sins.

10. To accustom oneself to high quality foods and fancy dresses to such an extent that one is not able to eat or drink ordinary and simple things.

11. To assume that one has attained high quality food by his personal accomplishments only.

In short, the word 'Isrāf' has a number of exegeses. Sayyidunā 'Umar Fārūq A'ẓam رَضِیَ اللّٰہُ تَعَالٰی عَنْہُ has stated, 'One should avoid stuffing oneself as it causes illness in the body, damages the stomach and engenders indolence in Ṣalāĥ. Adopt moderation in eating and drinking as this is a cure for numerous diseases. Allah عَزَّوَجَلَّ dislikes an obese[1] person.' *(Kashf-ul-Khifā, vol. 1, pp. 221, Ḥadīš 760)* It is also stated that the one letting his desire dominate his religion, will be annihilated. *(Rūḥ-ul-Ma'ānī, vol. 4, pp. 163) (Tafsīr Na'īmī, vol. 8, pp. 390)*

Excellence of slim body

Dear Islamic brothers! In addition to eating less, reduce the intake of super fine flour, sugar and fatty foods as per the advice of your doctor as this improves the digestive system, decreasing the body weight. By virtue of this, the bulged belly returns to its normal state and one looks more handsome[2]. Allah عَزَّوَجَلَّ likes the slim Muslim who eats less. Sayyidunā 'Abdullāĥ Ibn 'Abbās رَضِیَ اللّٰہُ تَعَالٰی عَنْہُمَا has narrated that the Prophet of mankind, the Peace of our heart and mind, the most Generous and Kind صَلَّی اللّٰہُ تَعَالٰی عَلَیْہِ وَاٰلِہٖ وَسَلَّم has stated, 'The dearest to Allah عَزَّوَجَلَّ amongst you is the one who eats less and has a lean body.' *(Al-Jāmi'-uṣ-Ṣaghīr, pp. 20, Ḥadīš 221)*

Dear Islamic brothers! In order to keep up the spirit of performing righteous deeds, it is imperative that one joins a righteous Madanī environment with heart and soul. Although one may attain spirit to perform righteous deeds even without a Madanī environment, it is extremely difficult to attain steadfastness due to the lack of pious company. One should, therefore, make a habit of travelling with Madanī Qāfilaĥ along with the devotees of the Rasūl! اَلْحَمْدُ لِلّٰہ عَزَّوَجَلَّ, Dawat-e-Islami is promoting the message of Sunnaĥ throughout the

[1] To hurt a Muslim by laughing at him because of his obesity is a sin.

[2] To learn how to decrease body weight, read *Faīzān-e-Sunnat's* chapter '*Excellence of Hunger*' from page 457 to 460.

world. Here is a faith-refreshing incident which will enlighten and brighten your heart and mind.

A non-Muslim embraces Islam

An Islamic brother from Tehsil Tanda district Ambyed, Karnagar, U.P. India has stated that he was previously a non-Muslim. Once someone gifted him Maktaba-tul-Madīnaĥ's published booklet entitled '*The Respect of a Muslim*.' Amazed by reading the booklet, he realized that Islam which he had always hated, gives the message of peace and harmony. The words of the booklet captured his heart, making him develop an intense liking for Islam.

One day, while he was travelling in a bus, a group of bearded and turbaned Islamic brothers boarded the same bus. He understood that they were Muslims. As he had already developed a liking for Islam, he began to look at them with admiration. One of the Islamic brothers from amongst them began reciting Na'at, attracting that non-Muslim.

Noticing his interest, an Islamic brother approached him and started conversation. The Islamic brother discerned that the person was a non Muslim and thus urged him to embrace Islam in a very courteous manner. Since he had already been impressed by Islam as a result of reading the booklet '*The Respect of a Muslim*', the humble words of the brother further motivated him, and he embraced Islam. اَلۡحَمۡدُلِلّٰہ عَزَّوَجَلَّ, at the time of the writing of this account, four months have passed since he embraced Islam. He has started offering Ṣalāĥ regularly and has also made the intention of growing a beard. Furthermore, he has also joined the Madanī environment of Dawat-e-Islami and travels with the Madanī Qāfilaĥ.

Kāfiraun ko chalayn, Mushrikon ko chalayn, da'wat-e-Dīn dayn Qāfilay mayn chalo
Dīn pĥaylāiye, sab chalay āiye, mil kay sāray chalayn, Qāfilay mayn chalo

To call infidels and unbelievers to Islam, travel with Qāfilaĥ
To preach and promote Islamic teachings, travel with Qāfilaĥ

صَلُّوۡا عَلَی الۡحَبِیۡب   صَلَّی اللّٰہُ تَعَالٰی عَلٰی مُحَمَّد

Don't forgo Sunnaĥ in shyness

The beloved companions رَضِیَ اللّٰہُ تَعَالٰی عَنۡہُمۡ were indeed the true devotees of the Noble Prophet صَلَّی اللّٰہُ تَعَالٰی عَلَیۡہِ وَاٰلِہٖ وَسَلَّم. Nothing, neither the lure of the fleeting things of this world nor any regard for any one, could prevent them from practising Sunnaĥ.

Sayyidunā Ḥasan Baṣrī رَضِیَ اللّٰہُ تَعَالٰی عَنۡہُ has narrated that Sayyidunā Ma'qil Bin Yasār رَضِیَ اللّٰہُ تَعَالٰی عَنۡہُ (who was the chief of the Muslims of that area) was once eating food when a morsel fell from his hand on the ground. He رَضِیَ اللّٰہُ تَعَالٰی عَنۡہُ picked it up, cleaned and then ate it. Seeing this, some uncivilized people who were present over there gave him a contemptuous look. Someone said to him, 'May Allah عَزَّوَجَلَّ bless our chief! O our leader! These uncivilized people are looking scornfully at you because you have eaten a fallen morsel despite the availability of food.' Listening to this, he رَضِیَ اللّٰہُ تَعَالٰی عَنۡہُ replied, 'I cannot give up what I have learnt from the Holy Prophet صَلَّی اللّٰہُ تَعَالٰی عَلَیۡہِ وَاٰلِہٖ وَسَلَّم merely because of these 'Ajamīs [non-Arabs]. If a morsel of food ever fell down, we would ask each other to pick it up, clean and eat it, and not leave it for Satan [to consume].' *(Sunan Ibn Mājaĥ, vol. 4, pp. 17, Ḥadīš 3278)*

Rūḥ-e-Īmān maghz-e-Quran jān-e-Dīn
Ĥast Ḥubb-e-Raḥmat-ul-lil-'Ālamīn صَلَّی اللّٰہُ تَعَالٰی عَلَیۡہِ وَاٰلِہٖ وَسَلَّم

Soul of faith, heart of Quran, strength of Dīn
Is the love of Raḥmat-ul-lil-'Ālamīn صَلَّی اللّٰہُ تَعَالٰی عَلَیۡہِ وَاٰلِہٖ وَسَلَّم

Make individual effort

Dear Islamic brothers! Did you see how intensely Sayyidunā Ma'qil Bin Yasār رَضِیَ اللّٰہُ تَعَالٰی عَنۡہُ, an eminent companion, loved Sunnaĥ! Paying no heed to the insulting and annoying behaviour of the 'Ajamīs, he رَضِیَ اللّٰہُ تَعَالٰی عَنۡہُ continued to practice upon Sunnaĥ unflinchingly.

Unfortunately, some unwise Muslims these days do not grow their beard assuming it to be a wise act in the modern era. In fact, a true wise act is to grow a beard, wear dress and turban according to Sunnaĥ and carry out one's daily routines like eating, walking etc. conforming to Sunnaĥ completely, no matter how unfavourable the environment is, and how severe the opposition of the opponents and corrupt beliefs possessing people is.

Furthermore, one should also strive to call people towards righteousness. اِنْ شَآءَاللّٰہ عَزَّوَجَلَّ, our mutual efforts will produce fruitful results, the truth will prevail, Satan will be disgraced and the message of Sunnaĥ will spread everywhere. Those who love the fleeting things of this worldly life will become sincere devotees of the Rasūl. The Nūr of the Beloved and Blessed Prophet صَلَّى اللهُ تَعَالٰى عَلَيْهِ وَاٰلِهٖ وَسَلَّم will enlighten every household.

Khāk sūraj say andĥayron kā izālaĥ ĥogā
Āp صَلَّى اللهُ تَعَالٰى عَلَيْهِ وَاٰلِهٖ وَسَلَّم *āyaīn to mayray għar mayn ujālā ĥogā*
Ĥogā sayrāb sar-e-Kawšar-o-Tasnīm woĥī
Jis kay ĥātĥaun mayn Madīnay kā piyālaĥ ĥogā

Will the sun make the darkness disappear?
My household will enlighten when you صَلَّى اللهُ تَعَالٰى عَلَيْهِ وَاٰلِهٖ وَسَلَّم *appear*
Only he will quench his thirst at the fountain of Kawšar
Who will, to the cup of Madīnaĥ in his hands, adhere

صَلُّوْا عَلَى الْحَبِيْب صَلَّى اللهُ تَعَالٰى عَلٰى مُحَمَّد

Here is an incident showing the blessing of making individual effort.

A non-Muslim embraces Islam

A ninety-two day Madanī Qāfilaĥ of Rasūl's devotees reached Colombo from the global Madanī Markaz of Dawat-e-Islami, Faīzān-e-Madīnaĥ, Bāb-ul-Madīnaĥ, Karachi [Pakistan]. The day when the Madanī Qāfilaĥ was to leave for the district of Aero for thirty days, an Islamic brother brought a young non-Muslim to the Amīr of the Qāfilaĥ. Describing some aspects of the great character of the Noble Prophet صَلَّى اللهُ تَعَالٰى عَلَيْهِ وَاٰلِهٖ وَسَلَّم, the Amīr of the Madanī Qāfilaĥ invited the young man to embrace Islam. The young man asked some questions which were answered and he embraced Islam by virtue of individual effort, اَلْحَمْدُ لِلّٰہ عَزَّوَجَلَّ.

صَلُّوْا عَلَى الْحَبِيْب صَلَّى اللهُ تَعَالٰى عَلٰى مُحَمَّد

Protection of offspring from unwisdom

The Prophet of mankind, the Peace of our heart and mind, the most Generous and Kind صَلَّى اللهُ تَعَالٰى عَلَيْهِ وَاٰلِهٖ وَسَلَّم has stated, 'The one who picks up the bits of food that have fallen on the dining-mat and eats them, will live a life of affluence and his offspring and the offspring of his offspring will be protected from unwisdom.' *(Kanz-ul-'Ummāl, vol. 15, pp. 111, Ḥadīš 40815)*

A remedy for destitution

An eminent scholar of Ḥadīš, Sayyidunā Ĥudbaĥ Bin Khālid عَلَيْهِ رَحْمَةُ اللّٰهِ الْمَاجِد was once invited by the caliph of Baghdad, Māmūn-ur-Rashīd. After eating, the great scholar began to pick up and eat the bits of food that had fallen down. Astonished, the caliph asked, 'O Shaykh رَحْمَةُ اللّٰهِ تَعَالٰى عَلَيْه! Are you not full yet?' He رَحْمَةُ اللّٰهِ تَعَالٰى عَلَيْه replied, 'I am certainly full but I have heard a Ḥadīš from Sayyidunā Ḥammād Bin Salamaĥ رَضِیَ اللّٰهُ تَعَالٰی عَنْهُ, 'Whoever picks up and eats fallen grains of food from the dining-mat, will be free from the fear of poverty.' I (the Shaykh) am merely practicing upon this Ḥadīš.'

Highly impressed, the caliph gestured to a servant who brought a thousand dinars [gold coins] wrapped up in a handkerchief and gave it to Sayyidunā Ĥudbaĥ Bin Khālid عَلَيْهِ رَحْمَةُ اللّٰهِ الْمَاجِد as a gift. The eminent scholar said, 'اَلْحَمْدُ لِلّٰه عَزَّوَجَلَّ! The blessing of the Ḥadīš has taken place right away.' *(Šamarāt-ul-Awrāq, vol. 1, pp. 8)*

Don't forgo any Sunnaĥ due to shyness

Dear Islamic brothers! It is evident from the above parable that our pious saints رَحِمَهُمُ اللّٰهُ تَعَالٰى would never forgo a Sunnaĥ under any circumstance. They had no hesitation in acting upon Sunnaĥ in the presence of the rich and even the king. This parable contains ample lesson for those Islamic brothers who forgo the Sunnaĥ of eating, drinking and that of turban and beard merely out of shyness with people.

Undoubtedly, acting upon Sunnaĥ will lead to success in the world as well as in the Hereafter. At times, the blessings of acting upon Sunnaĥ take place instantly in the world, as described in the above parable that Sayyidunā Ĥudbaĥ Bin Khālid عَلَيْهِ رَحْمَةُ اللّٰهِ الْمَاجِد immediately received a thousand dinars and became affluent.

Jo apnay dil kay guldastay mayn Sunnat ko sajātay ĥayn
Woĥ bayshak raḥmatayn dauno jaĥān mayn Ḥaq عَزَّوَجَلَّ say pātay ĥayn

Sunnaĥ in their hearts, who keep
Blessings from Allah عَزَّوَجَلَّ in both worlds, they reap

Dear Islamic brothers! As there are causes of blessing in sustenance, there are also causes of deprivation in it. If we avoid them we will have a lot of blessing, اِنْ شَآءَاللّٰه عَزَّوَجَلَّ. Here are 44 causes of deprivation in sustenance.

44 Causes of deprivation

1. To eat without washing hands.
2. To eat without covering the head.
3. To eat in the dark.
4. To eat and drink sitting at the doorstep.
5. To eat near the deceased.
6. To eat without bathing after sexual intercourse or nocturnal emission.
7. To delay eating after the food has been served.
8. To eat on a bed without laying a dining-mat.
9. To eat on a bed whilst you are sitting by the headboard and the food is served towards the direction where you put your feet, (when you sleep on this bed).
10. To bite off the bread instead of breaking it with the hands (those who eat burgers should also take care).
11. To use broken clay or porcelain plates, cups etc. (It is Makrūĥ to drink water, tea etc. from the side of a cup that is broken. Do not use the plates, cups etc. that are cracked as many harmful germs and bacteria may be embedded in the cracks and may cause deceases).
12. Not to clean used plates, pots etc.

13. To wash hands in the container used for eating.
14. To swallow food-particles stuck in the teeth after removing them by dental floss or toothpick etc.
15. To leave the plates, glasses etc. used for eating uncovered. One should recite بِسْمِ اللّٰه and cover them because if left uncovered, calamities descend into the food and drink and spoil them, causing illness.
16. To throw bread at such places where it would be treated with disrespect and get trampled by people's feet. *(Edited from Sunnī Bahashtī Zaywar, pp. 595-601)*

The following are the causes that Sayyidunā Burhānuddīn Zarnūjī رَحْمَةُ اللهِ تَعَالٰى عَلَيْه has mentioned.

17. To sleep in excess. (This can also cause ignorance).
18. To sleep naked.
19. To urinate shamelessly. (Those that urinate in public on roadsides should pay heed).
20. To be lazy in picking up fallen crumbs or bits of food from the dining-mat.
21. To burn the peel of onion or garlic.
22. To sweep home with clothes.
23. To sweep at night.
24. To leave trash (garbage) inside home.
25. To walk ahead of the Mashāikh (scholars and saints).
26. To call parents by their names.
27. To clean hands with mud or sand.
28. To stand leaning on a side of the door.
29. To make Wuḍū in the lavatory.
30. To sew clothes etc. whilst having them on (wearing them).

31. To wipe one's face with the dress one is wearing.
32. To leave spiders' webs in home.
33. To be lazy in offering Ṣalāĥ.
34. To exit the Masjid early after offering Ṣalāt-ul-Fajr.
35. To go to the market very early in the morning.
36. To come back from the marketplace late.
37. To curse children. (Some women often curse their children. Then they also complain about the lack of blessings in sustenance).
38. To commit sins, specifically lies.
39. To put out an oil lamp by blowing.
40. To use a broken comb.
41. Not to make Du'ā for parents.
42. To wrap the turban around the head whilst sitting.
43. To put on pants or pyjamas whilst standing.
44. To avoid performing good deeds. *(Ta'līm-ul-Muta'allim Ṭarīq-ut-Ta'allum, pp. 73-76)*

صَلُّوْا عَلَى الْحَبِيْب صَلَّى اللّٰهُ تَعَالٰى عَلٰى مُحَمَّد

Excellence of eating fallen pieces of bread

Dear Islamic brothers! The mercy of Allah عَزَّوَجَلَّ is infinite indeed. At times, an act seems to be very minor, but its virtue is very great. Sayyidunā 'Abdullāĥ Bin Umm-e-Ḥarām رَضِیَ اللّٰہُ تَعَالٰی عَنْهُ has narrated that the Prophet of mankind, the Peace of our heart and mind, the most Generous and Kind صَلَّى اللّٰهُ تَعَالٰى عَلَيْهِ وَاٰلِهٖ وَسَلَّم has stated, 'Treat bread with respect as it is from amongst the blessings of the heavens and earth. Whoever eats a fallen piece of bread from the dining-mat will be forgiven.' *(Al-Jāmi'-uṣ-Ṣaghīr, pp. 88, Ḥadīš 1426)*

سُبْحٰنَ اللّٰه عَزَّوَجَلَّ, Dear Islamic brothers! If only we have no hesitation in eating the fallen grains of bread, and get entitled to this great virtue of forgiveness.

Ṭālib-e-maghfirat ĥūn Yā Allah عَزَّوَجَلَّ
Bakhsh day baĥr-e-Mustafa صَلَّى اللّٰهُ تَعَالٰى عَلَيْهِ وَاٰلِهٖ وَسَلَّم *Yā Rab* عَزَّوَجَلَّ

I seek forgiveness for I have erred, Yā Allah عَزَّوَجَلَّ
Pardon me for the sake of Mustafa صَلَّى اللّٰهُ تَعَالٰى عَلَيْهِ وَاٰلِهٖ وَسَلَّم*, Yā Allah* عَزَّوَجَلَّ

صَلُّوْا عَلَى الْحَبِيْب صَلَّى اللّٰهُ تَعَالٰى عَلٰى مُحَمَّد

Parable about piece of bread

One day Sayyidunā 'Abdullāĥ Bin 'Umar رَضِىَ اللّٰهُ تَعَالٰى عَنْهُمَا saw a fallen piece of bread. He رَضِىَ اللّٰهُ تَعَالٰى عَنْهُ instructed his slave to pick it up, clean and keep it. At the time of Ifṭār, he رَضِىَ اللّٰهُ تَعَالٰى عَنْهُ asked his slave for that piece of bread. The slave told him that he had already eaten it. Hearing this, he رَضِىَ اللّٰهُ تَعَالٰى عَنْهُ said to the slave, 'Go! I set you free because I once heard the Beloved and Blessed Prophet صَلَّى اللّٰهُ تَعَالٰى عَلَيْهِ وَاٰلِهٖ وَسَلَّم say, 'Whoever eats a fallen piece of bread, Allah عَزَّوَجَلَّ forgives that person before it reaches his stomach.' So how can I keep the person in servitude who has become entitled to forgiveness?' *(Tanbīĥ-ul-Ghāfilīn, pp. 348, Ḥadīš 514)*

Madanī mindset

سُبْحٰنَ اللّٰه عَزَّوَجَلَّ, What an amazing Madanī mindset our eminent saints رَحِمَهُمُ اللّٰهُ تَعَالٰى had. Since the slave had been entitled to forgiveness because of eating a fallen piece of bread, the master also freed him from slavery.

Yā Allah عَزَّوَجَلَّ! For the sake of Your Beloved Prophet صَلَّى اللّٰهُ تَعَالٰى عَلَيْهِ وَاٰلِهٖ وَسَلَّم, bestow upon us the Madanī mindset as well as the true love and devotion to Sunnaĥ. If we ever see fallen piece of bread, grant us the privilege to pick it up, kiss it (in respect), clean it and eat it. Yā Allah عَزَّوَجَلَّ, may our hesitancy of acting upon Sunnaĥ go away and may we be forgiven!

اٰمِيْن بِجَاهِ النَّبِيِّ الْاَمِيْن صَلَّى اللّٰهُ تَعَالٰى عَلَيْهِ وَاٰلِهٖ وَسَلَّم

Sunnataun say mujĥay maḥabbat day
Mayray Murshid kā wāsiṭaĥ Yā Rab عَزَّوَجَلَّ

Grant me love and devotion to Sunnaĥ
For the sake of my Murshid, Yā Allah عَزَّوَجَلَّ

Extend dining-mat

It has been the practice of the saints رَحِمَهُمُ اللّٰهُ تَعَالٰى that when they finished eating, they never used to say 'remove the dining-mat' but rather 'extend the dining-mat' or 'augment the food.' This would be, in essence, a Du'ā for abundance in food and for blessings, affluence and prosperity. *(Sunnī Baĥashtī Zaywar, pp. 566)*

Blessing of reading booklet 'Dreadful Camel'

Dear Islamic brothers! In order to attain blessings in the worldly life as well as in the afterlife, join the Madanī environment of Dawat-e-Islami. Words cannot express how blessed Dawat-e-Islami is! Here is a summarized account of an Islamic brother from Kolkata (India): 'I was a fashionable young man and was very far from Sunnaĥs. One night as I was returning home, I noticed a group of Islamic brothers who had adorned their heads with green turbans. On asking, I learnt that a Madanī Qāfilaĥ of Dawat-e-Islami's devotees of Rasūl had arrived in our area from Bombay and the Islamic brothers of the Qāfilaĥ were going to attend a Sunnaĥ-Inspiring Ijtimā'. A thought came into my mind that these Islamic brothers had travelled a long distance to come to our city, I should also at least listen to them. Therefore, I joined them and attended the Ijtimā'. After the Ijtimā', they distributed booklets published by Maktaba-tul-Madīnaĥ. I was also fortunate to receive a booklet.

The title of the booklet was '*A Dreadful Camel.*' After I arrived home, I put the booklet on the shelf thinking that I would read it tomorrow. I prepared to go to sleep. Before going to bed, I opened the booklet just to get a glimpse of it. As I turned the page, I saw the first sentence, 'No matter how lazy Satan makes you feel, read this booklet in its entirety, you will feel a Madanī transformation in your heart اِنْ شَآءَاللّٰه عَزَّوَجَلَّ.' Inspired by reading this sentence, I thought that Satan will not certainly let me read this, why delay? I should not delay a good deed. I then started reading the booklet.

By Allah عَزَّوَجَلَّ before Whom everyone will be held accountable for their deeds on the Day of Judgement, tears welled up in my eyes as I read about the heartfelt narratives describing the oppression and hardships faced by the Holy Prophet صَلَّى اللهُ تَعَالٰى عَلَيْهِ وَاٰلِهٖ وَسَلَّم from the unbelievers. The heart-rending accounts took away my sleep and I wept for a long time. That night I made a firm intention to travel with a Madanī Qāfilaĥ the next morning.

The next day I sought permission from my parents, who happily agreed, and I travelled with a Madanī Qāfilaĥ for three days with the devotees of the Rasūl. The Madanī Qāfilaĥ transformed me. اَلْحَمْدُ لِلّٰه عَزَّوَجَلَّ, I started offering Ṣalāĥ, wearing white clothes along with the green turban according to Sunnaĥ. When my mother saw me, now a different person, she was extremely pleased and showered me with many Du'ās. Even my relatives were extremely pleased with me. اَلْحَمْدُ لِلّٰه عَزَّوَجَلَّ, Nowadays I am busy serving Sunnaĥ as a Nigrān of a local district Mushāvirat.'

Āshiqān-e-Rasūl, lāye Jannat kay pĥūl, āo laynay chalayn, Qāfilay mayn chalo
Bĥāgtay ĥayn kaĥān ā bĥī jāyaīn yaĥān pāyaīn gey Jannatayn Qāfilay mayn chalo

Devotees of Rasūl have brought pearls of Heaven, come to gather them, let's travel with Qāfilaĥ
Don't run here and there, just come here, one will be granted Paradise, let's travel with Qāfilaĥ

Distribute booklets

Dear Islamic brothers! Did you see how the Madanī environment of Dawat-e-Islami transformed a fashionable young man? The foregoing account also highlights the importance of distributing booklets published by Maktaba-tul-Madīnaĥ. By reading just a single booklet, the young man was inspired to travel with the Madanī Qāfilaĥ, and adopt Sunnaĥ in his life. Therefore, for the Īṣāl-e-Šawāb of your deceased relatives, purchase Sunnaĥ-Inspiring booklets and various pamphlets of Madanī pearls and distribute them on different occasions such as 'Urs of saints رَحِمَهُمُ اللهُ تَعَالٰى, Sunnaĥ-Inspiring Ijtimā'āt, wedding receptions, funeral processions and Mīlād gatherings etc. One can also gift a booklet along with the wedding invitation envelope. If even a single person starts offering Ṣalāĥ and practicing Sunnaĥ because of reading the booklet given by you, this will indeed bring about blessings for you in the worldly life as well as in the afterlife, اِنْ شَآءَاللّٰه عَزَّوَجَلَّ.

Ĥar maĥīnay jo koī bāraĥ risālay bānṫ day
إن شَآءَالله عَزَّوَجَلَّ Do jaĥān mayn us kā bayřā pār ĥay

Twelve booklets a month; whoever gifts to others
إن شَآءَالله عَزَّوَجَلَّ In both worlds he will prosper

صَلُّوْا عَلَى الْحَبِيْب صَلَّى اللهُ تَعَالٰى عَلٰى مُحَمَّد

Licking fingers clean is Sunnaĥ

Sayyidunā 'Āmir Bin Rabi'aĥ رَضِىَ اللهُ تَعَالٰى عَنْهُ has narrated that the Prophet of mankind, the Peace of our heart and mind, the most Generous and Kind صَلَّى اللهُ تَعَالٰى عَلَيْهِ وَاٰلِهٖ وَسَلَّم would eat food with three fingers and would lick them clean after eating the food. *(Majma'-uz-Zawāid, vol. 5, pp. 23, Ḥadīš 7923)*

We do not know which part of food possesses blessings

Sayyidunā Jābir رَضِىَ اللهُ تَعَالٰى عَنْهُ has narrated that the Beloved and Blessed Rasūl صَلَّى اللهُ تَعَالٰى عَلَيْهِ وَاٰلِهٖ وَسَلَّم ordered (us) to lick the fingers and wipe the used dish clean, and said, 'You do not know as to which part of food has blessings.' *(Ṣaḥīḥ Muslim, pp. 1122, Ḥadīš 2023)*

صَلُّوْا عَلَى الْحَبِيْب صَلَّى اللهُ تَعَالٰى عَلٰى مُحَمَّد

How to reap blessings of food?

Dear Islamic brothers! Extremely regretfully! The eating manners of today's Muslims show that there would be only a few fortunate people who will be reaping the blessings of food by consuming it according to Sunnaĥ. In the above Ḥadīš, it is clearly stated that we are not aware of the part of the food which contains blessings. We should, therefore, try not to waste even a single particle of food. We should consume all the meat and the edible particles of food on the bones so that no remnant goes to waste.

We can also jerk the bone into the plate so that edible particles from inside the bone can come out and be consumed. If possible, we should also consume spices such as cardamom, peppercorn, clove, cinnamon etc. cooked with food, إِنْ شَآءَاللّٰه عَزَّوَجَلَّ, it will also benefit us. However, there is no sin if these items cannot be eaten. Rather than throwing away green chillies used in food, if possible, one should take them out from food before eating and preserve them for reuse. Most people throw away fish skin; one should eat this as well. In short, all harmless edibles in food should be consumed, including the remnants of food on the fingers and those that are in the plate.

Order of licking fingers clean

Sayyidunā Ka'b Bin 'Ujraĥ رَضِیَ اللّٰهُ تَعَالٰی عَنْهُ has narrated, 'I once saw the Prophet of Raḥmaĥ, the Intercessor of Ummaĥ صَلَّى اللّٰهُ تَعَالٰی عَلَيْهِ وَاٰلِهٖ وَسَلَّم eat with his thumb, the index finger and the middle one. Then I saw that he صَلَّى اللّٰهُ تَعَالٰی عَلَيْهِ وَاٰلِهٖ وَسَلَّم licked his fingers clean before wiping them; (he) first licked the middle finger, then the index one, and finally the thumb.' *(Majma'-uz-Zawāid, vol. 5, pp. 29, Ḥadīš 7941)*

Licking fingers clean thrice is Sunnaĥ

Dear Islamic brothers! It is a Sunnaĥ to lick the fingers clean three times. If there are still particles of food on the fingers even after one has licked them thrice, one should lick them a few more times so that no particle of food remains in fingers. It is stated in '*Shamāil-e-Tirmiżī*' that the Holy Prophet صَلَّى اللّٰهُ تَعَالٰی عَلَيْهِ وَاٰلِهٖ وَسَلَّم would lick his fingers clean three times (after eating). *(Shamāil-ut-Tirmiżī, pp. 61, Ḥadīš 138)*

Wiping plate clean is Sunnaĥ

The Prophet of Raḥmaĥ, the Intercessor of Ummaĥ, the Owner of Jannaĥ صَلَّى اللّٰهُ تَعَالٰی عَلَيْهِ وَاٰلِهٖ وَسَلَّم has stated, 'Whoever licks his fingers and [wipes] the plate after eating, Allah عَزَّوَجَلَّ will keep him satiated in the world and the Hereafter.' *(Mu'jam Kabīr, vol. 18, pp. 261, Ḥadīš 653)*

صَلُّوْا عَلَى الْحَبِيْب　　صَلَّى اللّٰهُ تَعَالٰى عَلٰى مُحَمَّد

More blessings at end

The Beloved and Blessed Prophet صَلَّى اللهُ تَعَالٰى عَلَيْهِ وَاٰلِهٖ وَسَلَّم has stated, 'The plate should not be removed unless the eater has wiped it clean himself or has made someone else wipe it clean as there are (more) blessings at the end.' *(Kanz-ul-'Ummāl, vol. 15, pp. 111)*

Plate prays for forgiveness

Sayyidunā Nubayshaĥ رَضِىَ اللهُ تَعَالٰى عَنْهُ has narrated that the Noble Prophet صَلَّى اللهُ تَعَالٰى عَلَيْهِ وَاٰلِهٖ وَسَلَّم has stated, 'Whoever wipes the plate clean after eating, the plate will make Du'ā for his forgiveness.' *(Sunan Ibn Mājaĥ, vol. 4, pp. 14, Ḥadīš 3271)*

In another Ḥadīš it is mentioned that the plate says, 'O Allah عَزَّوَجَلَّ! Free him from Hell as he has freed me from Satan.' *(Kanz-ul-'Ummāl, vol. 15, pp. 111, Ḥadīš 40822)*

A renowned exegetist of the Quran, Muftī Aḥmad Yār Khān عَلَيْهِ رَحْمَةُ الْمَنَّان has stated, 'If the plate etc. used for eating is left without being wiped clean, then Satan licks it.' *(Mirāt-ul-Manājīḥ, vol. 6, pp. 52)*

Wisdom in wiping plate clean

In the same book, Muftī Aḥmad Yār Khān عَلَيْهِ رَحْمَةُ الْمَنَّان has stated, 'Wiping the plate clean after eating shows respect for food and saves it from being wasted. Leaving the plate with particles of food on it causes the flies to settle on it. Furthermore, مَعَاذَ اللّٰه عَزَّوَجَلَّ, the leftover food is usually thrown into garbage, which is disrespect for food. If every person left a little food on his plate every day, it would amount to pounds upon pounds going to waste daily. In short, there are many virtues in wiping the used plate clean.' *(Mirāt-ul-Manājīḥ, vol. 6, pp. 38)*

A faith-refreshing statement

The Noble Prophet صَلَّى اللهُ تَعَالٰى عَلَيْهِ وَاٰلِهٖ وَسَلَّم has stated, 'It is dearer to me to wipe the bowl clean than to give an entire bowl of food in charity.' *(Kanz-ul-'Ummāl, vol. 15, pp. 111, Ḥadīš 40821)* (This is because the act of wiping the bowl clean shows humility, which is more superior in reward than giving food in charity).

Rasūlullāĥ صَلَّى اللّٰهُ تَعَالٰى عَلَيْهِ وَاٰلِهٖ وَسَلَّم has stated, 'Whoever wipes the plate and licks his fingers clean, Allah عَزَّوَجَلَّ will fill his stomach in the world and the Hereafter.' (In other words, he will be saved from destitution and starvation in the world, from hunger on the Day of Judgement and will be granted refuge from Hell because no one's stomach will be full in Hell). *(Mu'jam Kabīr, vol. 18, pp. 261, Ḥadīš 653)*

صَلُّوْا عَلَى الْحَبِيْب　　صَلَّى اللّٰهُ تَعَالٰى عَلٰى مُحَمَّد

Reward of freeing slave

Ḥujjat-ul-Islam Sayyidunā Imām Muhammad Ghazālī عَلَيْهِ رَحْمَةُ اللّٰهِ الْوَالِى has stated, 'The one who wipes the dish clean after eating, pours some water into it and then drinks that water gets the reward of freeing a slave.' *(Iḥyā-ul-'Ulūm, vol. 2, pp. 7)*

Drinking water from plate

Dear Islamic brothers! One should wipe clean not only the plates but also any other container used to cook, eat or store food; like the glasses used to drink liquids (fruit juices, milk shakes, tea etc.) bowls, pots, frying pans, kettles, eating and serving spoons etc. should all be wiped clean. Leftover food in large pots is usually thrown away. Make sure that no particle of food goes to waste. One can also store in fridge the water used to rinse large pots, for later use in cooking. These practices are only possible by divinely-bestowed ability. When no particles of food remain on the plate or cup, only then one can say that it is clean. It is often observed that the plate etc. is not properly cleaned if rinsed just once. Therefore, one can rinse it twice or thrice using one's finger and drink this water[1] so that no particle of food goes to waste and the plate is also properly cleaned.

Leftover drops of water

Even after one has drunk water used for rinsing the plate, some drops of water often remain in the plates and bowls. Therefore, one should use one's fingers to gather those

[1] Note that rinsing the plate or container here refers to the act of pouring some drinking water into it and cleaning it without using any soap. [Translator's Note]

drops of water so that it is easier to drink them. Similarly, upon finishing the drink, a closer look will reveal that there are drops going down the glass or bottle which accumulate at the bottom. One should drink those as well. It is reported in a Ḥadīš that one does not know which particles of food contain blessings. I wish that we rinse the used plate, glass, cup etc. thoroughly so that they are so clean that one cannot distinguish between them and the unused washed ones.

Medical benefits of drinking water used for rinsing dish

اَلۡحَمۡدُ لِلّٰه عَزَّوَجَلَّ! No Sunnaĥ is devoid of wisdom. Modern scientific research has also acknowledged that vitamins, especially vitamin B complex, are mainly found at the bottom of the meal pot rather than its surface. Furthermore, essential minerals are only found at the bottom. Consuming these essential minerals by licking the pot clean or drinking its water protects against diseases.

Kidney stones eliminated

By the blessings of travelling with the Madanī Qāfilaĥs of Dawat-e-Islami, many problems are solved and many diseases are cured. Here is an incident of an Islamic brother in his own words: 'On our way back from Baluchistan, our 12-day Madanī Qāfilaĥ stopped at a railway station. Making individual effort, we started to inspire people towards righteousness. Meanwhile, we came across an Islamic brother who told us of the blessings that he had personally experienced in the Madanī Qāfilaĥ. He explained to us that he had severe kidney pain because of stones in his kidney. Doctors had recommended an operation. He met an Islamic brother who comforted him and tried to persuade him to travel with the Madanī Qāfilaĥ by telling him that the prayer (Du'ā) of a traveller is answered and problems are also solved, اِنۡ شَآءَالله عَزَّوَجَلَّ.

Impressed by the polite manner of the Islamic brother, he made a firm intention to travel with the Madanī Qāfilaĥ for three days. اَلۡحَمۡدُ لِلّٰه عَزَّوَجَلَّ, During the Madanī Qāfilaĥ, the stones in his kidney were eliminated. Doctors were astonished to know about it as there was no remedy for this disease in medical science except for an operation.

Garchay bīmāriyān, tang karayn paťhriyān, pāo gey ṣiḥḥatayn Qāfilay mayn chalo
Gĥar mayn nāchāqiyān, ĥaun yā tangdastiyān, pāyaīn gey barkatayn Qāfilay mayn chalo

If you are sick and have kidney stones,
You'll attain good health, travel with Qāfilaĥ
If you are destitute and have family disputes
You'll obtain blessings, travel with Qāfilaĥ

صَلُّوْا عَلَى الْحَبِيْب   صَلَّى اللّٰهُ تَعَالٰى عَلٰى مُحَمَّد

Avoid eating hot food

Sayyidunā Jābir رَضِیَ اللّٰہُ تَعَالٰی عَنْہُ has reported that the Prophet of Raḥmaĥ, the Intercessor of Ummaĥ, the Owner of Jannaĥ صَلَّی اللّٰہُ تَعَالٰی عَلَیْہِ وَاٰلِہٖ وَسَلَّم has stated, 'Allow hot food to cool before eating, as hot food contains no blessing.' *(Al-Mustadrak, vol. 4, pp. 132, Ḥadīš 7125)*

How much cool should food be?

Sayyidatunā Juvayrīyaĥ رَضِیَ اللّٰہُ تَعَالٰی عَنْہَا has narrated that the Noble Rasūl صَلَّی اللّٰہُ تَعَالٰی عَلَیْہِ وَاٰلِہٖ وَسَلَّم did not like to consume hot food unless steam had stopped rising from it. *(Majma'-uz-Zawāid, vol. 5, pp. 13, Ḥadīš 7883)*

Harms of hot food

Dear Islamic brothers! Food should be cooled before being consumed, but not to the extent of being tasteless. One should allow the steam to stop rising from it. A renowned exegetist of the Quran, Muftī Aḥmad Yār Khān عَلَیْہِ رَحْمَۃُ الْمَنَّان has stated that allowing the food to cool a little and not cooling it by blowing onto it are two means of attaining blessings [of the food]. Furthermore, it is easier to eat that way. *(Mirāt-ul-Manājīḥ, vol. 6, pp. 52)*

To eat extremely hot food or drink steaming tea or coffee increases the risk of gastritis [inflammation of the stomach] and blisters in the mouth and the throat. To drink very cold water, right after a hot beverage or food, harms the gums and the stomach.

If fly falls into food, then...

It is a sin to throw away the food or drink into which a fly has fallen. If it ever happens, submerge the fly completely into the food or drink; then throw the fly away and continue with your meal, without disgust. The Beloved and Blessed Prophet صَلَّى اللهُ تَعَالٰى عَلَيْهِ وَاٰلِهٖ وَسَلَّم has stated, 'If a fly falls into food, submerge it completely, (and then throw it away), as one of its wings has cure while the other has disease. When it falls into food, it first sets the wing of disease (into food), therefore, submerge it completely [so that the wing that contains cure removes the effect of the wing of disease].' *(Sunan Abī Dāwūd, vol. 3, pp. 511, Ḥadīš 3844)*

Science also acknowledges

Dear Islamic brothers! How vast the vision of the Holy Prophet صَلَّى اللهُ تَعَالٰى عَلَيْهِ وَاٰلِهٖ وَسَلَّم is! Science has also now acknowledged what our Noble Prophet صَلَّى اللهُ تَعَالٰى عَلَيْهِ وَاٰلِهٖ وَسَلَّم revealed long before. Scientists have finally reached the conclusion that one of the wings of the fly has a dangerous virus while the other wing has the anti-virus. When a fly falls into food or drink like tea, milk, water etc., it sets the virus wing into food, making the food harmful and causing the risk of disease for the eater. Therefore, submerging the fly completely destroys the virus, making the food harmless.

Bite meat

Sayyidatunā 'Āishaĥ Ṣiddīqaĥ رَضِىَ اللهُ تَعَالٰى عَنْهَا has narrated that the Beloved and Blessed Prophet صَلَّى اللهُ تَعَالٰى عَلَيْهِ وَاٰلِهٖ وَسَلَّم has stated, 'Do not cut meat with a knife (when eating it), as this is a practice of the 'Ajamīs [non-Arabs]. Eat meat by biting it as this is more tasteful and delightful.' *(Sunan Abī Dāwūd, vol. 3, pp. 511, Ḥadīš 3844)* However, one can use a knife to cut large portions of meat [especially when eating roasted meat].

Remove black strands from chicken's leg

According to the research of A'lā Ḥaḍrat Imām Aḥmad Razā Khān عَلَيْهِ رَحْمَةُ الْمَنَّان, there are 22 things in the Żabīḥaĥ[1] which are either Ḥarām or forbidden or Makrūĥ to be eaten.

[1] Żabīḥaĥ is that Ḥalāl animal which has been slaughtered in Islamic way. [Translator's Note]

Amongst them is white strand-like spinal cord which extends from the base of the brain through the length of the backbone. Similarly, tendons and lymph glands [also called lymph nodes] are also Ḥarām to be eaten. Tendons are two bands of dense, tough, inelastic, white, fibrous tissue, on both sides of the neck, which serve to connect the shoulder muscles to the neck; these don't become tender easily.

Moreover, though pure, the blood remaining inside the meat is forbidden to be consumed. [It is not difficult to identify these strands as] they turn black when cooked. Therefore, one should be careful when eating the portions of the meat in which blood normally accumulates. For example, remove black thread like strands from the neck, the wings and the legs of the cooked chicken-meat as these are blood vessels which have turned black after being cooked. One should also avoid eating the tendons and spinal cord of the chicken.

Lost brother found after 12 years

Dear Islamic brothers! Make an ardent effort to routinely travel with the Madanī Qāfilaĥ with the devotees of the Rasūl to learn Sunnaĥ. اِنْ شَآءَاللّٰه عَزَّوَجَلَّ, Your worldly complications and problems will be resolved. Furthermore, you will also gather many pearls of religious knowledge. Here is an account in this regard:

A Madanī Qāfilaĥ travelled to Sabzpur (Haripur, Khyber Pakhtunkhwa, Pakistan). One of the participants of the Qāfilaĥ has reported, 'My elder brother went abroad to make a living. It's twelve years since we last heard from him. His three children and their mother were all under my care and I have to provide for them, facing financial problem. I have travelled with this Madanī Qāfilaĥ along with the devotees of Rasūl with the intention of making Du'ā for the ease of my extreme circumstantial hardship.'

A week after the Qāfilaĥ, the same Islamic brother attended a Madanī Mashwaraĥ[1]. His face was gleaming with happiness and his sentiments were very highly inspiring. He told us with tears of joy running down his cheeks, 'اَلْحَمْدُ لِلّٰه عَزَّوَجَلَّ, By the blessing of travelling with the Madanī Qāfilaĥ, we have finally received a phone call from the elder brother, who went missing nearly 12 years back. He has also sent us 125 thousand rupees.'

---

[1] A Madanī Mashwaraĥ is a meeting to discuss and review the Madanī activities of Dawat-e-Islami. [Translator's Note]

Jo kay mafqūd ĥo woĥ bĥī maujūd ĥo
إِنْ شَاءَ اللهُ عَزَّوَجَلَّ Chalayn Qāfilay mayn chalo
Dūr ĥaun sāray gham ĥogā Rab عَزَّوَجَلَّ kā karam
Gham kay māray sunayn Qāfilay mayn chalo

Those that are lost will find their ways
إِنْ شَاءَ اللهُ عَزَّوَجَلَّ, Do travel with Qāfilaĥ
Allah عَزَّوَجَلَّ will bless and liberate you from difficult days
And remove your grief, do travel with Qāfilaĥ

Wisdom in Du'ā not being accepted

اَلْحَمْدُ لِلّٰه عَزَّوَجَلَّ, There are many individuals whose Du'ās have been accepted in the Madanī Qāfilaĥs of Dawat-e-Islami. However, there may be many others whose desires may not have been fulfilled. If one does not see signs of his Du'ā being accepted, one should still be content with the will of Allah عَزَّوَجَلَّ. What we ask for is often not in our best interest.

The father of A'lā Ḥaḍrat, Shaykh 'Allāmaĥ, Maulānā Naqī 'Alī Khān عَلَيْهِ رَحْمَةُ الرَّحْمٰن has stated in his book '*Aḥsan-ul-Wi'ā*'', 'At times, you ask Allah عَزَّوَجَلَّ for something out of your unwisdom but He عَزَّوَجَلَّ may not fulfil your Du'ā with His infinite wisdom and mercy, because the fulfilment of Du'ā in that matter is not in the best of your interest. For example, you might seek wealth, but its acquisition will put your Īmān in jeopardy or you may seek good health but it is harmful to your Hereafter in the infinite knowledge of Allah عَزَّوَجَلَّ. Hence, it is better that these Du'ās remain unfulfilled. Consider this verse:

عَسٰۤى اَنْ تُحِبُّوْا شَیْــٴًـا وَّ هُوَ شَرٌّ لَّكُمْؕ

It is likely that you like a thing which is bad for you.

[Kanz-ul-Īmān (Translation of Quran)] (Part 2, Sūraĥ Al-Baqaraĥ, verse 216)

Thank Him for not fulfilling those Du'ās which are not in your interest. At times, the reward of Du'ā is stored for you in the Hereafter. You ask for the meagre wealth and the fleeting things of the world, whereas Allah عَزَّوَجَلَّ has stored the treasures of the Hereafter for you. This should be an occasion of expressing gratitude, not complaint.'

Picking one's teeth

It is a Sunnaĥ to pick teeth with a toothpick or a splinter. Some people use one end of the matchstick and throw away its combustible end, wasting the matchstick. They should not do that. It is better to use a toothpick instead.

The importance of picking one's teeth has been described in several Aḥādīš. Thus, it is narrated by Sayyidunā Abū Ĥurayraĥ رَضِیَ اللهُ تَعَالٰی عَنْهُ that the Holy Prophet صَلَّى اللهُ تَعَالٰى عَلَيْهِ وَاٰلِهٖ وَسَلَّم has stated, 'One who eats food and removes [the bits of food if embedded between his teeth] by using a toothpick, should spit it out, and if he removes them using his tongue he should swallow it. One who does this has done well, and if he does not do it; there is no harm.' *(Sunan Abī Dāwūd, vol. 1, pp. 46, Ḥadīš 35)*

Kirāman Kātibīn & those who don't pick their teeth

Sayyidunā Abū Ayyūb Anṣārī رَضِیَ اللهُ تَعَالٰی عَنْهُ has narrated that the Noble Rasūl صَلَّى اللهُ تَعَالٰى عَلَيْهِ وَاٰلِهٖ وَسَلَّم once approached us and said, 'How admirable are the ones who do Khilāl.' The companions رَضِیَ اللهُ تَعَالٰی عَنْهُم asked, Yā Rasūlallāĥ صَلَّى اللهُ تَعَالٰى عَلَيْهِ وَاٰلِهٖ وَسَلَّم, with what those admirable ones do Khilāl?' The Holy Prophet صَلَّى اللهُ تَعَالٰى عَلَيْهِ وَاٰلِهٖ وَسَلَّم replied, 'The ones who do Khilāl during Wuḍū and the ones who do Khilāl after eating. Khilāl in Wuḍū is to rinse the mouth, sniff water into the nostrils and (do Khilāl of) the fingers whereas the Khilāl of eating is [to pick one's teeth] after eating. There is nothing more disturbing to Kirāman Kātibīn[1] than to see a person (to whom they have been assigned) offer his Ṣalāĥ with something stuck between his teeth.' *(Mu'jam Kabīr, vol. 4, pp. 177, Ḥadīš 4061)*

Pān eaters should pay heed

A'lā Ḥaḍrat, Imām-e-Aĥl-e-Sunnat, reviver of Sunnaĥ, eradicator of Bid'aĥ, scholar of Sharī'aĥ, guide of Ṭarīqaĥ, 'Allāmaĥ Maulānā Al-Ḥāj Al-Ḥāfiẓ Al-Qārī Ash-Shāĥ Imām

[1] The two deeds-recording angels.

Aḥmad Razā Khān عَلَيْهِ رَحْمَةُ الرَّحْمٰن has stated, 'Those who are addicted to Pān know from experience that small particles of betel nuts and betel (i.e. Pān) get stuck in all parts of the mouth (especially when there are gaps in teeth) and rinsing the mouth three times or even ten times does not help in cleaning it properly. In fact, even using a toothpick or Miswāk does not suffice. These particles of betel and betel nut can only be removed by rinsing the mouth thoroughly with water multiple times and moving the water around each time. Rinsing the mouth in this way cannot be limited to a fixed number.

Cleaning the mouth properly has been stressed greatly. It is mentioned in numerous Aḥādīš that when a person stands to offer Ṣalāĥ, an angel places his mouth on the mouth of the Ṣalāĥ-offering person and anything the person recites comes out of his mouth and enters the mouth of the angel. If, at that time, there are bits of food stuck between his teeth, the angels feel so much distress by it that nothing else causes so much distress to them.

The Beloved and Blessed Rasūl صَلَّى اللهُ تَعَالٰى عَلَيْهِ وَاٰلِهٖ وَسَلَّم has stated, 'When any one of you stand at night to offer Ṣalāĥ, you should clean your teeth with a Miswāk because when you recite the Quran, an angel places his mouth on yours and anything coming out of your mouth enters the mouth of that angel.' *(Shu'ab-ul-Īmān, vol. 2, pp. 381, Ḥadīš 2117)*

There is a report narrated by Sayyidunā Abū Ayyūb Anṣārī رَضِىَ اللهُ تَعَالٰى عَنْهُ in the book *Kabīr* written by Imām Ṭabarānī رَحْمَةُ اللهِ تَعَالٰى عَلَيْه that there is nothing more troublesome for both angels than to see their companion offer Ṣalāĥ with bits of food stuck between his teeth. *(Mu'jam Kabīr, vol. 4, pp. 177, Ḥadīš 4061, Fatāwā Razawiyyaĥ, vol. 1, pp. 624-625)*

Weakness of teeth

Sayyidunā Ibn 'Umar رَضِىَ اللهُ تَعَالٰى عَنْهُمَا has stated, 'The bits of food which remain stuck between molars weaken the molars.' *(Majma'-uz-Zawāid, vol. 5, pp. 32, Ḥadīš 7952)*

Which toothpick be used?

Dear Islamic brothers! Whenever you eat food or anything else you should pick your teeth after eating. The toothpick should preferably be made of margosa [Neem] tree as its strong bitter taste is good for cleaning the mouth and the gums. The toothpicks available in the market are usually thick and fragile. Several good toothpicks can also be prepared, with the help of a razor, from the veins of coconut palm leaves or a straw from the date palm leaf.

Strands of meat are often embedded between the teeth and in the corners of the mouth, which are extremely difficult to be removed by toothpick etc. One can use a dental floss to remove the stuck food particles. One could also use a dental scaler made of stainless steel [instrument used by dentists] but one has to be highly cautious when using these instruments and also learn their proper use, as their improper use could hurt the gums severely.

Seven intentions for picking one's teeth

It is stated in a Ḥadīš that the Holy Prophet صَلَّى اللّٰهُ تَعَالٰى عَلَيْهِ وَاٰلِهٖ وَسَلَّم has said, 'The intention of a Muslim is better than his actions.' *(Mu'jam Kabīr, vol. 6, pp. 185, Ḥadīš 5942)*

Therefore, one should make the following intentions before picking one's teeth by using a toothpick etc. One could also make these intentions even before starting the meal, gaining a treasure of reward.

1. I will act upon the Sunnaĥ of Khilāl (using a toothpick) after eating.
2. I will recite بِسْمِ اللّٰه before picking my teeth.
3. I will gain help in using Miswāk by picking my teeth. (When food-particles get stuck in the gums, they may rot weakening the gums and causing gum-bleeding, and then it is difficult to use Miswāk).
4. By picking my teeth, I will make it easy for myself to rinse the mouth thoroughly during Wuḍū. (The entire mouth should be thoroughly washed, including the areas around the teeth and the gaps in between them. It is Sunnat-ul-Muakkadaĥ to rinse the mouth three times during Wuḍū in the above way. During Ghusl it is Farḍ to rinse the mouth once and Sunnaĥ to rinse it thrice in the above manner).
5. By picking my teeth, I will protect my mouth from diseases thereby gaining strength to worship. (When the toothpick is used, leftover food particles are removed and this in turn protects the gums against diseases. Thus good health helps perform worship).

6. I will strive to protect myself from bad breath so that I may attend the Masjid. (Obviously, the food particles stuck between teeth eventually rot, which leads to bad breath and when one has bad breath, it is Ḥarām for him to enter the Masjid).

7. I will avoid causing trouble to the angels. (If a person recites the Quran during Ṣalāĥ with bits of food in his mouth, angels are discomforted by it).

How to rinse mouth

The proper manner of rinsing the mouth in Wuḍū is that the water reaches every corner of the mouth including the spaces between the teeth. During Wuḍū it is Sunnaĥ to rinse the mouth thrice in the manner described above. In Ghusl it is Farḍ to rinse the mouth once and Sunnaĥ to do so thrice. During Ghusl, one should also gargle provided that he is not fasting. It is imperative to remove all the particles of food and strands of meat stuck between the teeth. If the strand of meat or piece of betel nut is so firmly embedded that it does not come out despite the repeated rinsing of the mouth one should no longer try to remove it as one's gums may be hurt; the one who is helpless is excused.

Medical benefits of picking teeth

More than 14 centuries ago, our Noble Prophet صَلَّى اللّٰهُ تَعَالٰى عَلَيْهِ وَاٰلِهٖ وَسَلَّم described the importance of picking one's teeth, giving protection against many diseases. Now after many centuries scientists have also realized the importance of doing so. Describing the medical benefits of picking one's teeth, doctors have declared that bits of food get stuck in between one's teeth and gums after one has eaten the food. If they are not removed, these bits rot, forming a film of some special type of plasma on the surface of the teeth, which weakens the teeth and results in the inflammation and degeneration of the gums and teeth-surrounding tissues. Gums detach from the teeth which eventually fall.

Furthermore, one may also suffer from the gum disease called Pyorrhoea, which results in the discharge of pus from the gums. This pus then mixes with the food and enters the stomach unnoticed, increasing the risk of many fatal diseases.

Gum cancer

In addition to decreasing the intake of food, those who habitually consume tea and Pān [betel] should also reduce consuming these items. Let it not be that you reduce the intake of food, but your Nafs begins to deceive you into consuming tea and Pān in excess in the name of removing your hunger. Tea is harmful to the kidneys. It is safer to give up the habit of eating Pān and scented aniseed and betel nut etc. Those who constantly chomp on these items are prone to the cancer of throat, gums and mouth. Due to the excessive use of Pān, the mouth becomes red and, if the gums begin to bleed or ooze pus, then this causes the blood and pus to go into the stomach unnoticed. As these people do not feel any pain for a long time despite the ooze of pus, they will perhaps realise this danger only when, Allah عَزَّوَجَلَّ forbids, they will have suffered from any lethal disease.

Harms of fake Katthā

It is highly likely that Katthā is not produced in Pakistan. The greedy people who do not care about ruining the worldly life of Pān eaters and the afterlife of their own add the colour used in leather-dyeing to sand and sell it as Katthā. As a result, Pān eaters in Pakistan become victims, suffering from various diseases.

Do not consume fake Katthā knowingly. Those selling this fake product as well as those selling the Pān with fake Katthā should repent sincerely. Similarly, those who deliberately eat sand should also desist from it. According to Islamic law, there is no harm in eating a little sand; however, it is Ḥarām to eat sand in the quantity that causes harm. *(Rad-dul-Muḥtār, vol. 1, pp. 364) (Bahār-e-Sharī'at, vol. 2, pp. 63)*

Causes of gum-bleeding

Some people's gums bleed as they use Miswāk, and this blood may also go into the stomach with food. One of its causes is an upset stomach. Such people should have treatments for ailments like constipation. One should refrain from gas and flatulence causing food. In addition, one should eat less than one's appetite and avoid untimely meals. Another cause of it is the build-up of tartar between the teeth, which forms due to one's carelessness in cleaning the teeth. One should visit a dentist. If the dentist is righteous and there is no other hindrance he will scale your teeth in a single visit; otherwise he may call you for multiple sessions in order to obtain extra money from you.

صَلُّوْا عَلَى الْحَبِيْب صَلَّى اللّٰهُ تَعَالٰى عَلٰى مُحَمَّد

Miswāk is best remedy for dental diseases

If one uses Miswāk properly he will never suffer from any dental disease, اِنْ شَآءَاللّٰه عَزَّوَجَلَّ. You might be thinking that you have been using Miswāk for many years, yet both your teeth and stomach are ill. My dear naive Islamic brother! This is not the fault of Miswāk, but rather that of your own. From my experience, I have reached the conclusion that there may be only a few people amongst a million who use Miswāk properly. We use Miswāk in a rush during Wuḍū. In other words we don't use Miswāk but fulfil just its formality.

14 Madanī pearls pertaining to Miswāk

1. Miswāk should be as thick as the little finger.
2. Miswāk should not be longer than one's hand span[1] as Satan sits on the Miswāk longer than this.
3. The strands of Miswāk should be soft; otherwise, they might cause space between teeth and gums.
4. Use a fresh Miswāk, if available. Otherwise, place it in a glass of water to make it soft.
5. Trim the strands of Miswāk every day as they are beneficial so long as they have some bitterness.
6. Brush your teeth horizontally with Miswāk.
7. Always brush your teeth with Miswāk at least thrice.

---

[1] The distance between the tip of the thumb and that of the little finger when the hand is fully extended.

[Translator's Note]

8. And wash it after every use.

9. Hold the Miswāk in the right hand in such a manner that the little finger remains at the bottom, and the middle three fingers remain on it while the thumb remains at the top (near the soft strands that are used to brush the teeth).

10. Brush (with Miswāk) the upper teeth of the right side first and then the left. Thereafter, clean the lower teeth again starting from the right and then the left.

11. To use Miswāk while one is lying on his back can cause the spleen to enlarge.

12. To use Miswāk when held in fist can cause piles.

13. Miswāk is a pre-Wuḍū Sunnaĥ. However, it becomes Sunnat-ul-Muakkadaĥ when foul smell emanates from the mouth. *(Fatāwā Razawiyyaĥ (Jadīd), vol. 1, pp. 223)*

14. Do not throw away a used Miswāk or its strands as it is an instrument used to act upon a Sunnaĥ. Rather, keep it somewhere respectfully, bury it or put it into sea-water.

(For detailed information, go through the 2nd volume of *Baĥār-e-Sharī'at* from page 17 to 18).

4 Madanī pearls pertaining to healthy teeth

1. After one has eaten any food or drunk any beverage, one should thoroughly rinse one's mouth thrice. Rinse every part of the mouth thoroughly each time and let the water remain in the mouth for at least half a minute before spitting it out.

2. Whenever conveniently possible, one should rinse one's mouth daily at different times. Allow the water to remain for a few minutes before spitting it out.

3. The use of salt-mixed tepid (slightly warm) water is much more beneficial. Its regular use will remove the bits of food stuck between the teeth, اِنْ شَآءَاللّٰه عَزَّوَجَلَّ. Moreover, the gums won't bleed either.

4. To rub olive oil on the teeth makes the gums and loose-teeth stronger.

Remedy for bad breath

If a person has bad breath or foul smell emanates from his mouth, he should eat coriander by chewing it properly. Cleaning the teeth with fresh or dry petals of rose is also an effective remedy. The foul odour will go away, اِنْ شَآءَاللّٰه عَزَّوَجَلَّ. However, if the cause of the foul smell is any stomach-disease, then one should eat less than one's appetite. By the blessing of doing so, bad breath and many other diseases including the aches and pains of legs and various other body parts, constipation, heartburn, blisters in the mouth, reoccurring cold and cough, sore throat and gum bleeding etc. will be cured, اِنْ شَآءَاللّٰه عَزَّوَجَلَّ. The cure for 80 percent of diseases lies in eating less. For further elaboration on this, one may refer to a chapter of *Faīzān-e-Sunnat* entitled '*Excellence of Hunger.*' If our carnal desires are overpowered, most of our diseases will automatically be cured.

Spiritual cure for bad breath

One should recite the following Ṣalāt-'Alan-Nabī, whenever possible, 11 times in a single breath. اِنْ شَآءَاللّٰه عَزَّوَجَلَّ, This would cure bad breath.

اَللّٰهُمَّ صَلِّ وَسَلِّمْ عَلَى النَّبِيِّ الطَّاهِرِ

How to recite in a single breath

In order to recite the above Ṣalāt-'Alan-Nabī in one breath, one should close the mouth and breathe in slowly through the nose. Try to fill as much air into the lungs as possible. Now recite the Ṣalāt-'Alan-Nabī. By practicing this a few times, one will be able to recite it 11 times in a single breath, اِنْ شَآءَاللّٰه عَزَّوَجَلَّ.

To hold breath for as long as possible in the foregoing way and then exhale it slowly from the mouth is very beneficial to health. One should do this daily a few times during the day, especially in the open air. A senior Hakim [doctor of herbal medicines] once told me that he could hold his breath for about half an hour, or rather, two hours. During this time, he is able enough to recite his various invocations. He also mentioned that there are certain experts who can hold their breath for a very long time; they inhale in the morning and exhale in the evening!

5 Fragrant mouths

Here is an incident regarding a miracle of the Beloved and Blessed Prophet صَلَّى اللهُ تَعَالٰى عَلَيْهِ وَاٰلِهٖ وَسَلَّم that rendered the mouths of five fortunate Ṣaḥābiyāt رَضِىَ اللّٰه تَعَالٰى عَنْهُنَّ fragrant forever. Therefore, Sayyidaĥ 'Umayraĥ Bint-e-Mas'ūd Anṣāriyyaĥ رَضِىَ اللهُ تَعَالٰى عَنْهَا has narrated that she and four sisters of her once came to the court of the Holy Prophet صَلَّى اللهُ تَعَالٰى عَلَيْهِ وَاٰلِهٖ وَسَلَّم to do Bay'at [i.e. swear allegiance]. At that time, the Noble Prophet صَلَّى اللهُ تَعَالٰى عَلَيْهِ وَاٰلِهٖ وَسَلَّم was eating Qadīd (i.e. a type of dried meat). The Holy Prophet صَلَّى اللهُ تَعَالٰى عَلَيْهِ وَاٰلِهٖ وَسَلَّم chewed a piece of meat making it soft and then gave it to them. They distributed it amongst themselves and ate it. By its blessings, fragrance always emanated from their mouths. *(Al-Khaṣāiṣ-ul-Kubrā, vol. 1, pp. 105)*

Sayyidunā Abū Umāmaĥ رَضِىَ اللهُ تَعَالٰى عَنْهُ has narrated that there lived in Madīnaĥ a rude and indecent woman. Once, she passed by the Holy Prophet صَلَّى اللهُ تَعَالٰى عَلَيْهِ وَاٰلِهٖ وَسَلَّم who was eating meat. She also requested a piece of meat from him. The Holy Prophet صَلَّى اللهُ تَعَالٰى عَلَيْهِ وَاٰلِهٖ وَسَلَّم offered a piece to her. Refusing to take it, she requested that she be given the piece that he صَلَّى اللهُ تَعَالٰى عَلَيْهِ وَاٰلِهٖ وَسَلَّم was chewing. He صَلَّى اللهُ تَعَالٰى عَلَيْهِ وَاٰلِهٖ وَسَلَّم then gave a piece, from his blessed mouth, which she swallowed. Since then she was never heard uttering indecent and foul words. *(Al-Khaṣāiṣ-ul-Kubrā, vol. 1, pp. 105)*

Heavy rain

Dear Islamic brothers! Join the Madanī environment of Dawat-e-Islami and attend its Sunnaĥ-Inspiring Ijtimā' regularly. اِنْ شَآءَالله عَزَّوَجَلَّ, You will reap many blessings in the Hereafter and many of your worldly problems will also be resolved. Furthermore, Du'ās will also be accepted in the company of the devotees of the Rasūl. Amīr-ul-Mūminīn, Sayyidunā 'Alī Murtaḍā كَرَّمَ اللهُ تَعَالٰى وَجْهَهُ الْكَرِيْم has narrated the Beloved and Blessed Prophet صَلَّى اللهُ تَعَالٰى عَلَيْهِ وَاٰلِهٖ وَسَلَّم to have stated:

اَلدُّعَآءُ سِلَاحُ الْمُؤْمِنِ، وَعِمَادُ الدِّيْنِ، وَنُوْرُ السَّمٰوَاتِ وَالْاَرْضِ

'Du'ā is a weapon for a Muslim, a pillar of religion and a Nūr from the heavens and the earth.'

(Musnad Abī Ya'lā, vol. 1, pp. 215, Ḥadīš 435)

Du'ā is not turned down, especially when made during a journey. And if Du'ā is made during the journey of a Madanī Qāfilaĥ with the devotees of Rasūl, how close to acceptance it would be! Here is an incident in this respect.

A Madanī Qāfilaĥ was once on a journey in the district of Nikyal (Kashmir, Pakistan). The locals requested the participants of the Madanī Qāfilaĥ to make Du'ā for rain as it had not rained over there for a very long time. The participants of the Madanī Qāfilaĥ arranged for congregational Du'ā attended by many locals. It was daytime and the sun was also brightly shining. The Islamic brothers of the Madanī Qāfilaĥ made Du'ā with absolute humility and sincerity.

اَلْحَمْدُ لِلّٰه عَزَّوَجَلَّ, In a little while, clouds began to appear in the sky from all directions and it began to rain heavily. The locals, drenched in rain, were overjoyed. They were highly impressed by the devotees of the Rasūl of the Madanī Qāfilaĥ. Observing this divine grace on Dawat-e-Islami, many locals joined the Madanī environment of Dawat-e-Islami, flourishing the Madanī activities of Dawat-e-Islami in Nikyal.

Qāfilay mayn żarā, māngo ā kar Du'ā
Ĥaun gī khūb bārishayn, Qāfilay mayn chalo
'Āshiqān-e-Rasūl lay lo jo kuch bĥī pĥūl
Tum ko Sunnat kay dayn Qāfilay mayn chalo

Travel in the Qāfilaĥ and make your Du'ā,
Heavy rains will pour, travel with Qāfilaĥ
Devotees of the Rasūl have brought pearls of Sunnaĥ
To get those pearls, travel with Qāfilaĥ

صَلُّوْا عَلَى الْحَبِيْب صَلَّى اللهُ تَعَالٰى عَلٰى مُحَمَّد

Food stains on one's hand

Sayyidunā 'Abdullāĥ Ibn 'Abbās رَضِیَ اللهُ تَعَالٰی عَنْهُمَا has narrated that the Beloved and Blessed Prophet صَلَّى اللهُ تَعَالٰى عَلَيْهِ وَاٰلِهٖ وَسَلَّم has stated, 'If a person spends the night in such a state that there are stains of oil (or fat from food) on his hands and, as a result, is afflicted with any trouble, he should not blame anyone for this, but himself.' *(Majma'-uz-Zawāid, vol. 5, pp. 33, Ḥadīš 7954)*

Danger of snake

Dear Islamic brothers! After eating, one should thoroughly wash one's hands with soap etc. and then dry them with a towel so that no stain of oil remains in the hand and the smell also goes away. Otherwise, if one shakes his unwashed hands with others, they will be disgusted by it.

Elaborating on the meaning of the word 'trouble' mentioned in the foregoing Ḥadīš, a renowned exegetist of the Quran, Ḥakīm-ul-Ummat, Muftī Aḥmad Yār Khān عَلَيْهِ رَحْمَةُ الْحَنَّان has stated, 'The trouble stated in the foregoing Ḥadīš refers to the biting of a snake or rat, as both of these animals are attracted by the smell of food; or it could also mean the danger of being afflicted with leukoderma[1], as the body parts touched by the stained hands, with bodily sweat, are prone to this disease.' *(Mirāt-ul-Manājīḥ, vol. 6, pp. 38)*

Shaykh Muftī Muhammad Khalīl Khān Barakātī عَلَيْهِ رَحْمَةُ اللّٰهِ الْوَالِى has stated, 'After having eaten food, if a person goes to sleep without washing his hands, Satan licks his hands. مَعَاذَ اللّٰه عَزَّوَجَلَّ! This can also engender leukoderma.' *(Sunnī Baĥashtī Zaywar, pp. 607)*

How is it to use others' utensils?

If food has come from someone else's house, one should empty the container and return it without delay. If it is not possible to do so for the time being, one should keep the container as an entrustment [Amānat] and return it later on. Remember it is not permissible to use someone else's utensils. *(Sunnī Baĥashtī Zaywar, pp. 569)* If anyone has ever committed this sin, he should immediately ask the owner of the utensils to pardon him in addition to seeking forgiveness from Almighty Allah عَزَّوَجَلَّ.

صَلُّوْا عَلَى الْحَبِيْب　　صَلَّى اللّٰهُ تَعَالٰى عَلٰى مُحَمَّد

25 Sunnaĥs of eating

1. The Noble Prophet صَلَّى اللّٰهُ تَعَالٰى عَلَيْهِ وَاٰلِهٖ وَسَلَّم would not lean against anything while eating. *(Sunan Abī Dāwūd, vol. 3, pp. 488, Ḥadīš 3769)*

---

[1] Partial or total loss of skin pigmentation. [Translator's Note]

2. He صَلَّى اللهُ تَعَالٰى عَلَيْهِ وَاٰلِهٖ وَسَلَّم never ate food at a table. *(Derived from Ṣaḥīḥ Bukhārī, vol. 3, pp. 24, Ḥadīš 55386)*

3. He صَلَّى اللهُ تَعَالٰى عَلَيْهِ وَاٰلِهٖ وَسَلَّم would eat what was served to him. *(Ṣaḥīḥ Muslim, pp. 1134, Ḥadīš 2052)*

4. He صَلَّى اللهُ تَعَالٰى عَلَيْهِ وَاٰلِهٖ وَسَلَّم would neither ask his household for food nor express a wish for any specific food. Instead, he صَلَّى اللهُ تَعَالٰى عَلَيْهِ وَاٰلِهٖ وَسَلَّم would eat and drink what was served to him. *(Itḥāf-us-Sādat-il-Muttaqīn, vol. 8, pp. 248)*

5. At times, he صَلَّى اللهُ تَعَالٰى عَلَيْهِ وَاٰلِهٖ وَسَلَّم would take food and drink himself without asking anyone to serve him. *(Sunan Abī Dāwūd, vol. 5, pp. 4, Ḥadīš 3846)*

6. He صَلَّى اللهُ تَعَالٰى عَلَيْهِ وَاٰلِهٖ وَسَلَّم used to eat from the portion that was in front of him. *(Shu'ab-ul-Īmān, vol. 5, pp. 79, Ḥadīš 5846)*

7. He صَلَّى اللهُ تَعَالٰى عَلَيْهِ وَاٰلِهٖ وَسَلَّم used to eat with three fingers. *(Muṣannaf Ibn Abī Shaybah, vol. 5, pp. 559, Ḥadīš 3)*

8. At times, he صَلَّى اللهُ تَعَالٰى عَلَيْهِ وَاٰلِهٖ وَسَلَّم would eat with four fingers. *(Al-Jāmi'-uṣ-Ṣaghīr, pp. 250, Ḥadīš 6942)* However, he صَلَّى اللهُ تَعَالٰى عَلَيْهِ وَاٰلِهٖ وَسَلَّم did not use to eat with two fingers. He صَلَّى اللهُ تَعَالٰى عَلَيْهِ وَاٰلِهٖ وَسَلَّم has said that eating with two fingers is a practice of Satan. *(Al-Jāmi'-uṣ-Ṣaghīr, vol. 5, pp. 249, Ḥadīš 6940)*

9. He صَلَّى اللهُ تَعَالٰى عَلَيْهِ وَاٰلِهٖ وَسَلَّم would eat bread made from unsifted barley. *(Ṣaḥīḥ Bukhārī, vol. 3, pp. 531, Ḥadīš 5410)*

10. Mostly, his blessed food contained dates and water. *(Ṣaḥīḥ Bukhārī, vol. 3, pp. 523, Ḥadīš 5383)*

11. He صَلَّى اللهُ تَعَالٰى عَلَيْهِ وَاٰلِهٖ وَسَلَّم would consume milk and dates together and would declare that these two are fine meals. *(Musnad Imām Aḥmad, vol. 5, pp. 385, Ḥadīš 15893)*

12. His favourite food was meat. *(Jāmi' Tirmiżī, vol. 5, pp. 533, Ḥadīš 178)*

13. He صَلَّى اللهُ تَعَالٰى عَلَيْهِ وَاٰلِهٖ وَسَلَّم would say that meat improves hearing, and is the chief of all foods in the world and the Hereafter. He صَلَّى اللهُ تَعَالٰى عَلَيْهِ وَاٰلِهٖ وَسَلَّم declared, 'If I had asked Allah عَزَّوَجَلَّ to provide me with meat everyday; He عَزَّوَجَلَّ would have provided it.' *(Itḥāf-us-Sādat-il-Muttaqīn, vol. 8, pp. 238)*

14. He صَلَّى اللهُ تَعَالٰی عَلَيْهِ وَاٰلِهٖ وَسَلَّم would make Šarīd with meat and squash and eat it. (That is, he صَلَّى اللهُ تَعَالٰی عَلَيْهِ وَاٰلِهٖ وَسَلَّم would thoroughly soak the pieces of bread in meat and squash curry and then eat it). *(Itḥāf-us-Sādat-il-Muttaqīn, vol. 8, pp. 239)*

15. While eating meat, the Holy Prophet صَلَّى اللهُ تَعَالٰی عَلَيْهِ وَاٰلِهٖ وَسَلَّم would not lower his head towards it[1] but would always lift his hand to his blessed mouth and then bite the meat. *(Jāmi' Tirmiżī, vol. 3, pp. 329, Ḥadīš 1842)*

16. Rasūlullāĥ صَلَّى اللهُ تَعَالٰی عَلَيْهِ وَاٰلِهٖ وَسَلَّم liked meat from the arm and the shoulder of the goat. *(Jāmi' Tirmiżī, vol. 3, pp. 330, Ḥadīš 1842-1844)*

17. The Holy Prophet صَلَّى اللهُ تَعَالٰی عَلَيْهِ وَاٰلِهٖ وَسَلَّم disliked eating the kidney as it is near the urinary organ. *(Kanz-ul-'Ummāl, vol. 7, pp. 41, Ḥadīš 18212)*

18. Although he صَلَّى اللهُ تَعَالٰی عَلَيْهِ وَاٰلِهٖ وَسَلَّم hated eating the spleen, he صَلَّى اللهُ تَعَالٰی عَلَيْهِ وَاٰلِهٖ وَسَلَّم did not declare it Ḥarām to consume it. *(Itḥāf-us-Sādat-il-Muttaqīn, vol. 8, pp. 243)*

19. The Noble Prophet صَلَّى اللهُ تَعَالٰی عَلَيْهِ وَاٰلِهٖ وَسَلَّم would use his fingers to wipe the plate clean and say, 'There is more blessing at the end.' *(Shu'ab-ul-Īmān, vol. 5, pp. 81, Ḥadīš 5854)*

20. He صَلَّى اللهُ تَعَالٰی عَلَيْهِ وَاٰلِهٖ وَسَلَّم liked fresh melon and grapes. *(Kanz-ul-'Ummāl, vol. 7, pp. 41, Ḥadīš 18200)*

21. He صَلَّى اللهُ تَعَالٰی عَلَيْهِ وَاٰلِهٖ وَسَلَّم would eat melon with sugar and bread. *(Itḥāf-us-Sādat-il-Muttaqīn, vol. 8, pp. 236)*

22. At times, he صَلَّى اللهُ تَعَالٰی عَلَيْهِ وَاٰلِهٖ وَسَلَّم would eat melon with ripe dates. *(Jāmi' Tirmiżī, vol. 3, pp. 332, Ḥadīš 1850)*

23. He صَلَّى اللهُ تَعَالٰی عَلَيْهِ وَاٰلِهٖ وَسَلَّم would use both of his hands whilst eating. Once, he صَلَّى اللهُ تَعَالٰی عَلَيْهِ وَاٰلِهٖ وَسَلَّم was eating ripe dates. The dates were in his right hand and the seeds were in his left. A goat passed by. He صَلَّى اللهُ تَعَالٰی عَلَيْهِ وَاٰلِهٖ وَسَلَّم signalled the goat with his left hand that contained date seeds. The goat approached and began to eat the seeds from his left hand while he صَلَّى اللهُ تَعَالٰی عَلَيْهِ وَاٰلِهٖ وَسَلَّم continued to eat with his right hand. This continued until he صَلَّى اللهُ تَعَالٰی عَلَيْهِ وَاٰلِهٖ وَسَلَّم finished and the goat then also left. *(Itḥāf-us-Sādat-il-Muttaqīn, vol. 8, pp. 237)*

24. The Holy Prophet صَلَّى اللهُ تَعَالٰی عَلَيْهِ وَاٰلِهٖ وَسَلَّم did not use to eat raw [uncooked] onions, raw garlic and leek. *(Tārīkh Baghdad, vol. 2, pp. 262)*

---

[1] (Itḥāf-us-Sādat-il-Muttaqīn, vol. 8, pp. 239)

25. He صَلَّى اللهُ تَعَالٰى عَلَيْهِ وَاٰلِهٖ وَسَلَّم never spoke anything bad about food. If he صَلَّى اللهُ تَعَالٰى عَلَيْهِ وَاٰلِهٖ وَسَلَّم liked it, he صَلَّى اللهُ تَعَالٰى عَلَيْهِ وَاٰلِهٖ وَسَلَّم would eat it and if not, he صَلَّى اللهُ تَعَالٰى عَلَيْهِ وَاٰلِهٖ وَسَلَّم would withdraw his hand. *(Ṣaḥīḥ Muslim, pp. 1141, Ḥadīš 2064)*

صَلُّوْا عَلَى الْحَبِيْب صَلَّى اللهُ تَعَالٰى عَلٰى مُحَمَّد

92 Madanī pearls of eating

Make intentions prior to consuming food

1. Instead of eating for merely enjoying taste or gratifying one's desire, one should eat with the righteous intention of attaining strength and energy to worship Allah عَزَّوَجَلَّ. Bear in mind that the above intention can only be true if one eats less than one's appetite or else this would be a false intention as gluttony causes laziness and is a hindrance in worship.

   Further, one should only eat when hungry as it is a Sunnaĥ to do so. To eat without hunger poses health risks hardening the heart, let alone giving strength. Sayyidunā Shaykh Abū Ṭālib Makkī عَلَيْهِ رَحْمَةُ اللهِ القَوِى has stated, 'According to a narration, eating on a full stomach causes leukoderma.' *(Qūt-ul-Qulūb, vol. 2, pp. 326)*

2. Use such a dining-mat on which alphabets, words, statements, names, couplets and logos of the companies are not inscribed in any language; neither in Urdu and English nor in any other language.

3. It is a Sunnaĥ to wash both hands up to the wrists before and after the meal. One should also rinse the mouth and wash the lips. Furthermore, do not wipe the washed hands before eating. The Noble Prophet صَلَّى اللهُ تَعَالٰى عَلَيْهِ وَاٰلِهٖ وَسَلَّم has stated, 'Making Wuḍū before and after the meal (i.e. washing the hands and the mouth) increases one's sustenance and keeps Satan away.' *(Kanz-ul-'Ummāl, vol. 15, pp. 106, Ḥadīš 40755)*

4. If someone does not wash his mouth before eating, he will not be missing a Sunnaĥ. *(Baĥār-e-Sharī'at, pp. 16-18)*

5. While eating, one can keep the left leg folded on the ground so that the thigh is on the calf and raise the right knee; or one can raise both knees with behind (i.e. buttocks) on the ground or sit with both legs folded [as in Ṣalāĥ i.e. thighs on calves]. Sunnaĥ will be fulfilled if one sits in any of these three manners.

Accustom yourself to veil within veil

6. Whilst eating, everyone including Islamic sisters should observe veil within veil. Otherwise, if someone is wearing skin-tight clothes or his shalwār or pyjama is not properly covered by his kurta or shirt, others may not be able to avoid the sin of misusing their eyes. If it is not possible to observe veil within veil one should sit in a folded legs position [as in Ṣalāĥ, i.e. thighs on calves]. By doing so, not only the Sunnaĥ of sitting while eating will be fulfilled but veil will also be observed. One should make a habit of observing veil within veil whenever he sits.

7. It is not a Sunnaĥ to sit cross-legged while eating. This causes the belly to bulge either.

8. Recite بِسۡمِ اللّٰه, بِسۡمِ اللهِ الرَّحۡمٰنِ and بِسۡمِ اللهِ الرَّحۡمٰنِ الرَّحِیۡمِ prior to the first, the second and the third morsel respectively. *(Iḥyā-ul-'Ulūm, vol. 3, pp. 6)*

9. Recite بِسۡمِ اللّٰه loudly so that others also recall it.

10. Recite the following Du'ā prior to eating. The reciter of this Du'ā will not be harmed even by poisonous food, اِنۡ شَآءَالله عَزَّوَجَلَّ. *(Kanz-ul-'Ummāl, vol. 15, pp. 109, Ḥadīš 40792)*

بِسۡمِ اللهِ وَبِاللهِ الَّذِیۡ لَا یَضُرُّ مَعَ اسۡمِهٖ
شَیۡءٌ فِی الۡاَرۡضِ وَلَا فِی السَّمَآءِ یَاحَیُّ یَا قَیُّوۡم

I begin with Allah's name, with the blessing [Barakaĥ] of whose name nothing of the earth nor the skies can cause detriment, O the one Who is ever-alive.

(Kanz-ul-'Ummāl, vol. 15, pp. 109, Ḥadīš 40792)

11. If one forgets reciting بِسۡمِ اللّٰه at the beginning, one should recite the following during the meal on recalling:

بِسۡمِ اللّٰهِ اَوَّلَهٗ وَاٰخِرَهٗ

Translation: I begin and end my meal with the name of Allah عَزَّوَجَلَّ.

Continue to do Żikr of Allah عَزَّوَجَلَّ while eating

12. If anyone recites يَا وَاجِدُ before eating every morsel, the food will become Nūr [light] in his stomach, curing illness.

13. Recite اَللّٰه or بِسۡمِ اللّٰه before consuming every morsel so that the desire for food would not engender heedlessness from Allah's Żikr. In between every two morsels, recite اَلۡحَمۡدُ لِلّٰه, يَا وَاجِدُ and بِسۡمِ اللّٰه so that one would be able to read بِسۡمِ اللّٰه prior to eating every morsel يَا وَاجِدُ in between and اَلۡحَمۡدُ لِلّٰه at the end.

14. It is preferable to eat in a clay container. 'Angels visit the home where clay utensils are used.' *(Rad-dul-Muḥtār, vol. 9, pp. 495)*

15. Do not place the bowl of curry or that of sauce etc. on the bread. *(Rad-dul-Muḥtār, vol. 9, pp. 495)*

16. Do not wipe the hands or clean knives with bread. *(Rad-dul-Muḥtār, vol. 9, pp. 495)*

17. It is a Sunnaĥ to eat at a dining-mat laid on the floor. Do not eat while leaning against anything or bare-headed or leaning one hand on the ground or with shoes on or when lying down or while sitting cross-legged.

18. If bread is served on the dining-mat before the curry, one should begin eating the bread without waiting for the curry to be served. *(Rad-dul-Muḥtār, vol. 9, pp. 490)*

19. Eat a little salt or something salty both prior to and subsequent to eating the food as this protects against seventy diseases. *(Rad-dul-Muḥtār, vol. 9, pp. 491)*

20. Do not break the bread with one hand as this is a practice of the arrogant.

21. Hold the bread in the left hand and break it with the right one as this is a Sunnaĥ. Make a habit of breaking the bread above the plate or the container so that the crumbs of the bread fall onto the food, otherwise the crumbs, if fall on the dining-mat, will go to waste.

22. Eat with the right hand as eating, drinking, taking and giving with the left hand is a practice of Satan.

Make a habit of eating with three fingers

23. Eat with three fingers; the middle finger, the index one and the thumb as this is a Sunnaĥ of the Prophets عَلَيْهِمُ السَّلَام. In order to make a habit of eating with three fingers you may do the following: Bend the ring finger and wrap a rubber band around it or take a small piece of bread in the palm and hold it with the ring finger and the little one or do both simultaneously. Once you get used to it, you will no longer need to adopt the techniques described above. Sayyidunā Mullā 'Alī Qārī عَلَيْهِ رَحْمَةُ اللّٰهِ الْبَارِی has stated, 'It is a practice of the greedy to eat with five fingers.' *(Mirāt-ul-Manājīḥ, vol. 8, pp. 9)* However, one may use four or five fingers to eat if the grains of rice are separated and it is impossible to eat with three fingers.

Breaking crust of bread

24. It is Isrāf to leave the outer crust [harder part] and only eat the soft part from the centre of the bread. However, if the crust (sides or corners of the bread) is not properly cooked, and is injurious to one's health one can break it off and leave it without eating. Similarly, it is also permissible to leave it when it is likely that others will eat it and it will not go to waste. The same ruling will be applied if one wishes to eat only the fluffier and softer part of the bread leaving the rest. *(Baĥār-e-Sharī'at, pp. 18, 19, part 16)*

Intestines are not a substitute for teeth

25. Eat small morsels chewing properly and avoid chomping. If food is swallowed without being chewed properly, the intestines would be overburdened. Remember intestines are not a substitute for teeth.

26. Stretching out the hand or picking up the next morsel before the previous one has been completely swallowed is a sign of greed.

27. It is highly despicable to bite bread. This is also a cause of deprivation of blessings in sustenance. Moreover, eating whilst standing is a practice of the non-Muslims. *(Sunnī Bahashtī Zaywar, pp. 565)*

Fruits be consumed first

28. Fruits are commonly eaten after the meal, whereas Ḥujjat-ul-Islam Sayyidunā Imām Muhammad Ghazālī عَلَيْهِ رَحْمَةُ اللّٰهِ الْوَالِي has stated, 'If there are fruits at mealtime, they should be served and consumed before food as eating them before food is more beneficial from medical point of view. As fruits digest faster, they should be in the lower part of the stomach. Moreover, fruits have been mentioned first even in the glorious Quran. Therefore, Allah عَزَّوَجَلَّ says in the 20-21 verse of Sūraĥ Al-Wāqi'aĥ:

وَفَاكِهَةٍ مِّمَّا يَتَخَيَّرُوْنَ ﴿۲۰﴾ وَلَحْمِ طَيْرٍ مِّمَّا يَشْتَهُوْنَ ﴿۲۱﴾

And fruits that they may like. And meat of birds that they may wish.

[Kanz-ul-Īmān (Translation of Quran)] (Part 27, Sūraĥ Al-Wāqi'aĥ, verse 20-21)

(Iḥyā-ul-'Ulūm, vol. 2, pp. 21)

Imām Aḥmad Razā Khān عَلَيْهِ رَحْمَةُ الرَّحْمٰن has narrated, 'To eat watermelon before food eradicates diseases from the root and purges the bowels.'

(Fatāwā Razawiyyaĥ (Jadīd), vol. 5, pp. 442)

Do not find fault with food

29. Do not find fault with food by making such comments as, '*It is not tasty*', '*It is still raw*', '*It does not have enough salt*', '*It is too spicy*' etc. If you like it, eat it, if not, leave it. However, if one intends to give some advice to the cook one may do so privately in a polite manner.

Finding fault with fruits is despicable

30. To find fault with natural fruits is more despicable compared to the food cooked by humans as there is more human involvement in the preparation of food while the case is not the same in the growing of fruits.

31. Do not eat from the centre of the container as blessing descends at the centre.

32. Eat from the side of the plate [container] that is closest to you and do not stretch out your hand everywhere in the plate.

33. However, if the plate etc. contains many items, one may eat them by stretching out his hand.

صَلُّوْا عَلَى الْحَبِيْب   صَلَّى اللهُ تَعَالٰى عَلٰى مُحَمَّد

Converse virtuously while eating

34. It is a practice of the fire-worshippers to remain quiet while eating considering it a good deed. However, if one does not feel like talking there is no harm in staying quiet. Furthermore, useless talking is never liked. Therefore, one should talk virtuously and righteously while eating. For example, whenever one is eating at home with his family-members or guests, one should tell the Sunnaĥs of eating food and drinking water. I wish that the photocopies of these Madanī pearls regarding eating be displayed at the dining area in the form of frames or in any other proper way and be read aloud, at meal times.

35. Do not talk about disgusting things during the meal. For instance, avoid talking about vomit, diarrhoea, stool etc.

36. Do not stare at the food others are eating.

Give good pieces of meat to others

37. Some people do inappropriate acts while eating. For instance, taking the good pieces of meat for oneself or eating big morsels hurriedly while eating collectively fearing that one might remain hungry or taking more food to one's side or depriving others in any way. All these are the practices of the inconsiderate and the greedy. If one leaves good things for his family-members or others with the intention of self-sacrifice, one will be greatly rewarded اِنْ شَآءَاللّٰه عَزَّوَجَلَّ.

    The Prophet of Raḥmaĥ, the Intercessor of Ummaĥ صَلَّى اللهُ تَعَالٰى عَلَيْهِ وَاٰلِهٖ وَسَلَّم has stated, 'Whoever desired a thing and then preferred others to have it preventing his desire, will be forgiven by Allah عَزَّوَجَلَّ.' *(Itḥāf-us-Sādat-il-Muttaqīn, vol. 9, pp. 779)*

Virtues of eating fallen grains

38. If grains or morsels of food fall during the meal, pick them up, wipe them clean and eat them as there are glad tidings of forgiveness for the one doing so.

39. It is stated in Ḥadīš that whoever picks up grains of food which have fallen on the dining-mat and eats them will live a life of affluence and his offspring and the offspring of his offspring will be protected from unwisdom. *(Kanz-ul-'Ummāl, vol. 15, pp. 111, Ḥadīš 40815)*

40. Ḥujjat-ul-Islam Sayyidunā Imām Muhammad Ghazālī عَلَيْهِ رَحْمَةُ اللّٰهِ الْوَالِى has narrated, 'Pick up (and eat) the pieces and particles of bread, you will get affluent, اِنْ شَآءَاللّٰه عَزَّوَجَلَّ. The children will be born safe and free from disabilities. Furthermore, the pieces of bread will serve as a dowry of heavenly maidens.' *(Iḥyā-ul-'Ulūm, vol. 2, pp. 7)*

41. It is permissible to pick up and kiss a fallen piece of bread.

42. It is permissible to feed the grains and particles of food fallen on the dining-mat to chickens, birds, cows or goats etc. One can also put them at a place where ants can consume them.

Blowing on food is prohibited

43. One should not blow on hot steamy food or tea etc. to cool it as this causes the blessing to be removed. Do not eat very hot food. Wait a little so that the food can be eaten easily. *(Rad-dul-Muḥtār, vol. 9, pp. 491)*

44. Drink water with the right hand during the meal. As the right hand is usually stained with food during the meal, some people hold the glass in the left hand whilst drinking water and only touch a finger of the right hand to it, assuming that they are drinking water with the right hand. This should be avoided.

Learn how to sip water

45. One should recite بِسۡمِ اللّٰهِ الرَّحۡـمٰنِ الرَّحِیۡم before drinking water or any other permissible beverage. Sip water in small gulps ensuring that no sound is produced. Drinking water or any beverage in big gulps can cause liver disease. After one has finished, one should say اَلۡحَمۡدُ لِلّٰه. Regretfully, there would be hardly anyone who would be practising the Sunnaĥ of drinking water by sipping. Practice and adopt this Sunnaĥ.

46. One should stop eating whilst he is still a little hungry.

Taste remains up to root of tongue only

47. It is not a Sunnaĥ to eat in excess. If one desires to eat excessively he should ponder over the fact that the taste of food lasts just for a few seconds. As soon as the food reaches the throat the taste is no more. Therefore, it is not wise to forgo a Sunnaĥ just for relishing the taste that only lasts for a few moments. Further, gluttony can result in sluggishness, laziness in worship, indigestion, obesity in some people, constipation, gas, diabetes and heart diseases.

48. After eating, one should lick fingers clean thrice. Lick the middle finger first, then the index one and then the thumb thrice each. After eating, the Holy Prophet صَلَّی اللّٰہ تَعَالٰی عَلَیۡہِ وَاٰلِہٖ وَسَلَّم would lick his blessed fingers clean thrice. *(Shamāil-ut-Tirmiżī, pp. 61, Ḥadīš 138)*

Lick plate clean

49. Lick the plate clean. It is stated in a Ḥadīš that whoever licks the plate after eating, the plate makes the following Du'ā for him, 'May Almighty Allah عَزَّوَجَلَّ free you from the fire of Hell as you have freed me from Satan.' *(Kanz-ul-'Ummāl, vol. 15, pp. 111, Ḥadīš 40822)* Another narration says that the utensil seeks forgiveness for him. *(Sunan Ibn Mājaĥ, vol. 4, pp. 14, Ḥadīš 3271)*

50. After one has eaten food and licked fingers and utensils clean, one should pour some water into the container and drink that water [so that remnants of food can be collected and consumed]. By doing so, one will be reaping the reward of emancipating a slave. *(Iḥyā-ul-'Ulūm, vol. 2, pp. 7)*

Method of drinking water from licked plate

51. After one has licked the plate etc. clean and drunk the water that one poured into it, make sure that no bits of food and no drops of soup etc. remains in it. One should pour a little water from the top edge of the plate, and then rinse it using his finger. Repeating this twice or thrice will ensure that no particle of food remains in the plate, اِنْ شَآءَاللّٰه عَزَّوَجَلَّ.

52. Even after drinking the water, one should use the fingers to gather the remaining drops of water and then drink them. Let it not be that just a single particle of spice goes to waste, taking away the blessing of food with it. It is stated in a Ḥadīš, 'You do not know which portion of the food contains blessings.' *(Ṣaḥīḥ Muslim, pp. 11123, Ḥadīš 1023)*

53. In the same way, one should also clean other utensils like food-stained pots, eating & serving spoons, jugs, glasses and cups stained with tea, coffee and fruit juices etc. Clean them so that no particle of food remains on them reaping many blessings.

54. To throw away and waste a Muslim's leftover water despite it being in drinkable state is Isrāf (i.e. waste) which is Ḥarām. *(Sunnī Baĥashtī Zaywar, pp. 567)*

55. At the end, one should say اَلْحَمْدُلِلّٰه. In addition, if one has known by heart supplications stated in the Quran and Aḥādīš, one should also recite them.

56. After eating, one should wash hands with soap so that oil and smell would be properly washed away.

Passing hand over certain parts of body after eating is Sunnaĥ

57. It is stated in a Ḥadīš that after eating, the Beloved and Blessed Prophet صَلَّى اللهُ تَعَالٰى عَلَيْهِ وَاٰلِهٖ وَسَلَّم washed his hands and then passed his wet hands over his wrists, mouth and head. He صَلَّى اللهُ تَعَالٰى عَلَيْهِ وَاٰلِهٖ وَسَلَّم then said to his companion رَضِىَ اللهُ تَعَالٰى عَنْهُ, 'O Ikrāsh! This is how Wuḍū is made after eating the thing touched by fire (i.e. the food cooked on fire).'
(Jāmi' Tirmižī, vol. 3, pp. 335, Ḥadīš 1855)

58. It is a Sunnaĥ to pick one's teeth after eating.

Previous sins are forgiven

59. The Prophet of Raḥmaĥ, the Intercessor of Ummaĥ صَلَّى اللهُ تَعَالٰى عَلَيْهِ وَاٰلِهٖ وَسَلَّم has stated, 'Whoever eats food and recites the following Du'ā afterwards, will be forgiven for all of his previous sins.' The Du'ā is as follows:

اَلْحَمْدُ لِلّٰهِ الَّذِیْ اَطْعَمَنِیْ هٰذَا وَرَزَقَنِیْهِ مِنْ غَیْرِ حَوْلٍ مِّنِّیْ وَلَا قُوَّةٍ

All glorification is for Almighty Allah عَزَّوَجَلَّ Who has fed me and has granted me sustenance without my skill and strength.

(Tirmižī, vol. 5, pp. 284)

60. Recite the following supplication after eating:

اَلْحَمْدُ لِلّٰهِ الَّذِیْ اَطْعَمَنَا وَسَقَانَا وَجَعَلَنَا مُسْلِمِیْنَ

I express gratitude to Almighty Allah عَزَّوَجَلَّ Who made us eat and drink and has made us Muslims.

(Sunan Abī Dāwūd, vol. 3, pp. 513, Ḥadīš 3850)

61. If someone else has provided the food, one should also recite the following supplication:

اَللّٰهُمَّ اَطْعِمْ مَنْ اَطْعَمَنِيْ وَاسْقِ مَنْ سَقَانِيْ

Yā Allah عَزَّوَجَلَّ! Feed the one who has fed me and provide the one with drink who has provided me with drink.

(Ṣaḥīḥ Muslim, pp. 136, Ḥadīš 2055)

62. Also recite the following supplication after eating:

اَللّٰهُمَّ بَارِكْ لَنَا فِيْهِ وَاَطْعِمْنَا خَيْرًا مِّنْهُ

Yā Allah عَزَّوَجَلَّ, grant Barakaĥ [blessing] in this food for us, and feed us better food than this.

(Sunan Abī Dāwūd, vol. 3, pp. 475, Ḥadīš 3730)

63. Recite the following after drinking milk:

اَللّٰهُمَّ بَارِكْ لَنَا فِيْهِ وَزِدْنَا مِنْهُ

Yā Allah عَزَّوَجَلَّ! Grant us Barakaĥ [blessing] in this, and grant us more than this.

(Sunan Abī Dāwūd, vol. 3, pp. 475, Ḥadīš 3730)

64. The Noble Prophet صَلَّى اللّٰهُ تَعَالٰى عَلَيْهِ وَاٰلِهٖ وَسَلَّم very much liked halvah [a type of dessert], honey, vinegar, date, watermelon, cucumber and squash.

65. He صَلَّى اللّٰهُ تَعَالٰى عَلَيْهِ وَاٰلِهٖ وَسَلَّم liked the pieces of mutton from the shoulders, neck and loin areas of the animal.

66. At times, the Beloved and Blessed Prophet صَلَّى اللّٰهُ تَعَالٰى عَلَيْهِ وَاٰلِهٖ وَسَلَّم would eat dates with watermelon or with cucumber or bread.

67. Rasūlullāĥ صَلَّى اللّٰهُ تَعَالٰى عَلَيْهِ وَاٰلِهٖ وَسَلَّم very much liked to eat the food present at the bottom of the cooking pot.

68. The Holy Prophet صَلَّى اللهُ تَعَالٰى عَلَيْهِ وَاٰلِهٖ وَسَلَّم very much liked Šarīd in which pieces of bread are mixed with gravy.

69. Eating with one finger is a practice of Satan and eating with two fingers is that of the arrogant. The practice of the Prophets عَلَيْهِمُ السَّلَام is to eat with three fingers.

How much should one eat?

70. One should divide one's hunger into three parts. One part should be for food, one for water and one for air. For example, if one becomes full after eating three breads, he should consume one bread, drink water in place of the second bread, and leave the rest for air. Although it is Mubāḥ, not a sin, to eat till one is full, many worldly and religious benefits and blessings lie in eating less. Try it and see for yourself. Your stomach will be so much healthier that you will be astonished. May Allah عَزَّوَجَلَّ grant us the assistance to observe Madanī guard on the stomach, which is to guard the stomach from Ḥarām things and gluttony.

اٰمِيْن بِجَاهِ النَّبِيِّ الْاَمِيْن صَلَّى اللهُ تَعَالٰى عَلَيْهِ وَاٰلِهٖ وَسَلَّم

Taking siesta is Sunnaĥ

71. Take a siesta after having lunch. To take a siesta is a Sunnaĥ, especially for those who perform worship at night. It facilitates night worship. It is also beneficial to have a walk after dinner. According to doctors, one should walk at least 150 steps after dinner.

72. Do recite اَلْحَمْدُ لِلّٰه after eating.

73. Do not rise unless the dining-mat has been removed.

74. Wash your hands thoroughly after eating and wipe them dry. One can also use soap.

75. It is prohibited to wipe hands dry with paper.

76. It is permissible to wipe hands clean with a towel but one should not wipe hands with the clothes that one is wearing.

Acts causing deprivation of blessings

77. Khalīl-ul-'Ulamā Shaykh Muftī Muhammad Khalīl Khān Barakātī رَحْمَةُ اللهِ تَعَالٰى عَلَيْه has stated, 'To wash hands in the plate etc. in which he has eaten the food removes blessing from the food. Similarly, wiping washed hands dry with one's shirt, pants [pyjama] or scarf also results in the removal of blessing.' *(Sunnī Bahashtī Zaywar, pp. 578)*

78. One should avoid taking vigorous exercise, lifting or dragging heavy objects and doing physically tough activities right after consuming the food, as this may cause appendicitis, intestinal problems and a bulged belly.

79. Recite اَلْحَمْدُ لِلّٰه aloud only when every one has finished eating, otherwise, recite it in low voice. *(Rad-dul-Muḥtār, vol. 9, pp. 490)* Take the same care whilst reciting the post-eating Du'ās, as the other person (who is still eating) may be embarrassed if you recite Du'ās aloud.

How is it to eat fruit from someone else's tree?

80. If someone enters an orchard and finds fruits lying on the ground he cannot eat them without the permission of the owner of the orchard. There are two types of permissions. One is explicit, whereas the other is implicit. In the first case, the owner grants permission to the visitors to eat the fruits fallen on the ground in clearly stated terms. In the second case, the permission is implied, that is, it's customary for the visitors to eat the fruit that has fallen on the ground and the owner does not stop them from doing so.

    It is not permissible for a visitor or a stranger to pluck the fruit from the tree and eat it. However, it will be permissible to do so provided that the fruits are aplenty and it is quite obvious that the owner will not resent even if someone plucks fruits from his orchard and eat. Still, it is not allowed to take the fruit out of the orchard. *(Fatāwā 'Ālamgīrī, vol. 5, pp. 229)*

    The ruling of eating fruits in all the foregoing cases depends upon norms and customs. If the norms and customs are not known or it is obvious that the owner would resent, it is not permissible to eat even the fallen fruits, let alone plucking and eating.

How is it to eat without permission?

81. If one enters the house of his friend and takes the liberty to eat food without his permission or enters his friend's orchard where he plucks a fruit and eats it, it will be permissible provided he knows that his friend would not resent. However, one must ponder over it thoroughly because at times, one is under the impression that his friend will not resent but, in fact, he resents. *(Fatāwā 'Ālamgīrī, vol. 5, pp. 229)*

82. It is forbidden to eat the spinal cord of the sacrificed animal. One should carefully remove it from the neck, ribs and the back bone before preparing food.

83. As the chicken spinal cord is very thin and is extremely difficult to be removed, there is no harm even if it is cooked with the food. However, it should not be consumed. Similarly, one should not also eat the neck muscle and black strand like blood veins of the chicken.

84. It is also Makrūĥ Taḥrīmī to eat the glands of the sacrificed animal. One should, therefore, remove them before cooking.

Heart of chicken

85. Do not throw away the heart of the chicken. One should cut it open vertically in four pieces or in any other proper way, and then wash away the inside blood thoroughly. It can then be cooked with the food.

Do not eat cooked blood vessels

86. Though the blood remaining in the meat of a sacrificed animal is pure, it is forbidden to consume it. Thoroughly inspect and clean the areas of the meat where blood is likely to remain, for example, the neck, the drumsticks and the leg pieces of the chicken. Remove these blood vessels which turn black when cooked.

Do not say 'do بِسْمِ اللّٰه[1]'

87. Let's suppose, for example, a person is consuming food and another person enters. The eating person offers the other person to join in the meal but he replies saying *Do* بِسْمِ اللّٰه, it is strictly forbidden to give this reply on this occasion. Instead of saying this, one should utter the words of Du'ā such as 'May Allah عَزَّوَجَلَّ give you Barakaĥ [blessing] etc.' *(Baĥār-e-Sharī'at, part 16, pp. 32)*

It is Ḥarām to eat rotten meat

88. It is Ḥarām to eat rotten meat. Similarly, one cannot eat the food that has turned bad (rotten). If the food has turned frothy or foul smell emanates from it or fungus has grown over it; then most likely the food has gone off. Curries made of lentils can rot quickly.

Green chillies

89. If possible, reuse the green and red chillies, cloves, cinnamon and other spices usually cooked with food. If possible, after the cooking, separate and store them instead of throwing them away. One can also grind and reuse them.

What should one do with leftover bread?

90. To throw away the leftover food or bread is Isrāf [wasting]. Feed this to the fowls, sheep and cows. One can also cook these breads with gravy, and it would be a very delicious meal, اِنْ شَآءَاللّٰه عَزَّوَجَلَّ.

How is it to eat crab or small shrimp?

91. Except fish, all other animals found in water are Ḥarām to consume. If a fish died naturally without being hunted and floats upside down, it is Ḥarām to eat it. It is also Ḥarām to eat crabs. As for eating shrimps scholars have different opinion in

[1] It is an expression that is commonly used by Urdu speaking people. [Translator's Note]

this regard. Although permissible, one should still refrain from consuming shrimps as it is better to do so.

92. A dead locust is Ḥalāl. It is Ḥalāl to eat fish and locust; one is not required to slaughter them.

Yā Allah عَزَّوَجَلَّ! Forgive us, grant us the capability of reading this book as many times as we memorize the Sunnaĥs and the manners of eating food. Also grant us the capability to act upon them.

اٰمِيْن بِجَاهِ النَّبِيِّ الْاَمِيْن صَلَّى اللّٰهُ تَعَالٰى عَلَيْهِ وَاٰلِهٖ وَسَلَّم

صَلُّوْا عَلَى الْحَبِيْب صَلَّى اللّٰهُ تَعَالٰى عَلٰى مُحَمَّد

تُوْبُوْا اِلَى اللّٰه اَسْتَغْفِرُ اللّٰه

صَلُّوْا عَلَى الْحَبِيْب صَلَّى اللّٰهُ تَعَالٰى عَلٰى مُحَمَّد

Brain tumour

An Islamic brother from Sukkur (Bāb-ul-Islam, Sindh) has given the following statement under oath: A person from our area had brain tumour and had already undergone two surgeries. He was in a pitiable condition. Even doctors had expressed disappointment. Meanwhile, someone advised him to get Ta'wīżāt-e-Aṭṭāriyyaĥ but his family members did not pay attention to it because of his miserable condition.

One day, his younger brother, worried and grieved, came to the stall of Ta'wīżāt-e-Aṭṭāriyyaĥ and said tearfully, 'The elder brother is in extremely critical condition; it seems tonight is the last night of his life. He no longer recognizes anyone, and is having severe difficulty in breathing; please, give me any Ta'wīż for him.' Comforting him, the Islamic brother of the Majlis said: 'Don't be disappointed; Allah عَزَّوَجَلَّ is the giver of the cure. Take these Ta'wīżāt with you; many patients suffering from such diseases declared incurable by doctors have been cured by the blessings of these Ta'wīżāt.'

The next day, his brother, with a happy look on his face, came to the stall and said, 'Going home, as I tied the Ta'wīż to the head of my ill brother (who seemed to be taking the last breaths of his life), he opened his eyes within a few minutes, leaving all the family-members astonished. He then gestured to the family-members to make him sit. اَلْحَمْدُلِلّٰه عَزَّوَجَلَّ! He has now started taking food as well.'

Two days later, the brain-tumour affected Islamic brother came to the stall of Ta'wīżāt-e-Aṭṭāriyyaĥ on his foot to meet the responsible Islamic brothers of the stall and told them that his condition had improved 75 percent, اَلْحَمْدُلِلّٰه عَزَّوَجَلَّ!

صَلُّوْا عَلَى الْحَبِيْب صَلَّى اللّٰهُ تَعَالٰى عَلٰى مُحَمَّد

Ineffective advice

It is narrated that the advice of the one whose stomach is full has no effect (on others) and when he is given advice, his mind refuses to accept it. *(Nuzĥa-tul-Majālis, vol. 1, pp. 178)*

اَلْحَمْدُ لِلّٰهِ رَبِّ الْعٰلَمِيْنَ وَ الصَّلٰوةُ وَ السَّلَامُ عَلٰى سَيِّدِ الْمُرْسَلِيْنَ
اَمَّا بَعْدُ فَاَعُوْذُ بِاللّٰهِ مِنَ الشَّيْطٰنِ الرَّجِيْمِ ؕ بِسْمِ اللّٰهِ الرَّحْمٰنِ الرَّحِيْمِ ؕ

Foods of Jinns

Excellence of Ṣalāt-'Alan-Nabī ﷺ

The Prophet of Raḥmaĥ, the Intercessor of Ummaĥ, the Owner of Jannaĥ صَلَّى اللّٰهُ تَعَالٰى عَلَيْهِ وَاٰلِهٖ وَسَلَّم has stated, 'Whoever recites Ṣalāt upon me hundred times on the day and night of Friday, Allah عَزَّوَجَلَّ will fulfill his hundred needs out of which seventy will be of the Hereafter and thirty will be of the world.' *(Kanz-ul-'Ummāl, vol. 1, pp. 256, Ḥadīš 2239)*

صَلُّوْا عَلَى الْحَبِيْب صَلَّى اللّٰهُ تَعَالٰى عَلٰى مُحَمَّد

Delegation of jinns visited the Holy Prophet ﷺ

Shaykh Sayyidunā 'Abdullāĥ Bin Mas'ūd رَضِىَ اللّٰهُ تَعَالٰى عَنْهُ has narrated that a delegation of jinns once came to the court of the Holy Prophet صَلَّى اللّٰهُ تَعَالٰى عَلَيْهِ وَاٰلِهٖ وَسَلَّم and requested him to prevent his Ummaĥ from using bones, dung and charcoal for cleaning their private parts after defecation or urination as Allah عَزَّوَجَلَّ has put their [i.e. jinns'] sustenance into bones, dung and coal. Therefore, the Beloved and Blessed Prophet صَلَّى اللّٰهُ تَعَالٰى عَلَيْهِ وَاٰلِهٖ وَسَلَّم prohibited his Ummaĥ (from using the above things for this purpose). *(Sunan Abī Dāwūd, vol. 1, pp. 48, Ḥadīš 39)*

صَلُّوْا عَلَى الْحَبِيْب صَلَّى اللّٰهُ تَعَالٰى عَلٰى مُحَمَّد

Population of jinns

Dear Islamic brothers! Jinns are also a creation of Allah عَزَّوَجَلَّ. They have been created from fire. They eat, drink and even get married. Their population is nine-fold more than that of humans. Sayyidunā 'Amr Bikālī رَضِیَ اللهُ تَعَالٰی عَنْه has stated, 'Whenever a human is born, nine jinns are also born.' *(Jāmi'-ul-Bayān, vol. 9, pp. 85, Ḥadīš 24803)*

Jinns at dining-mat of Muslims

Shaykh Jalāluddīn Suyūṭī Shāfi'ī عَلَیْهِ رَحْمَةُ اللّٰهِ الْقَوِی has quoted from a Tabi'ī saint رَحْمَةُ اللهِ تَعَالٰی عَلَیْه, 'Muslim jinns live on the roofs of the houses of all Muslims. When the dining-mat is laid in the house, and the family-members begin eating in the afternoon and evening, the jinns also come down from the roof and join in the meal. Allah عَزَّوَجَلَّ makes these jinns drive the wicked ones off.' *(Luqṭ-ul-Marjān, pp. 44)*

Snake whispers to the Holy Prophet صَلَّى اللهُ عَلَيْهِ وَاٰلِهٖ وَسَلَّم

Sayyidunā Jābir Bin 'Abdullāĥ رَضِیَ اللهُ تَعَالٰی عَنْه has stated, 'Once I was accompanying the Beloved and Blessed Prophet صَلَّى اللهُ تَعَالٰى عَلَيْهِ وَاٰلِهٖ وَسَلَّم when a snake suddenly came and stood next to him. Then, drawing its mouth closer to the Holy Prophet's blessed ear, it whispered something privately to him. The Noble Prophet صَلَّى اللهُ تَعَالٰى عَلَيْهِ وَاٰلِهٖ وَسَلَّم replied, 'That's all right!' The snake then left. I inquired about the snake, so Rasūlullāĥ صَلَّى اللهُ تَعَالٰى عَلَيْهِ وَاٰلِهٖ وَسَلَّم told me, 'It was a jinn and has urged me to prevent my Ummaĥ from using old bones and dung for cleaning after relieving themselves, as this has been made their [the jinns'] sustenance by Allah عَزَّوَجَلَّ.' *(Luqṭ-ul-Marjān, pp. 46)*

Dear Islamic brothers! These narrations show that even the jinns used to plead and beseech our Noble Prophet صَلَّى اللهُ تَعَالٰى عَلَيْهِ وَاٰلِهٖ وَسَلَّم for the solution to their problems. These accounts also show that bones and dung are the foods of the jinns. It is Makrūĥ to use bones, dung and coal for cleaning [after relieving oneself]. Here is another narration in the same context.

Dark jinns

Sayyidunā 'Abdullāĥ Bin Mas'ūd رَضِیَ اللهُ تَعَالٰی عَنْهُ has narrated, 'Before the Ḥijraĥ [the Prophet's migration to Madīnaĥ] once the Beloved and Blessed Prophet صَلَّى اللهُ تَعَالٰی عَلَيْهِ وَاٰلِهٖ وَسَلَّم and I went to the outskirts of Makkaĥ. Drawing a line for me, the Noble Prophet صَلَّى اللهُ تَعَالٰی عَلَيْهِ وَاٰلِهٖ وَسَلَّم instructed, 'Neither speak to anyone until I return nor get afraid if you see something.' Walking a few steps he then sat down. Suddenly, a group of dark men (who seemed to be Ethiopians) came to him. They came in the appearance as Allah Almighty عَزَّوَجَلَّ has described:

كَادُوْا يَكُوْنُوْنَ عَلَيْهِ لِبَدًا ﴿۱۹﴾

It was impending that those jinn may crowd upon him.

[Kanz-ul-Īmān (Translation of Quran)] (Part 29, Sūraĥ Al-Jinn, verse 19)

Then they began to depart saying, 'Yā Rasūlallāĥ صَلَّى اللهُ تَعَالٰی عَلَيْهِ وَاٰلِهٖ وَسَلَّم, our home is very far from here and we will now leave. Please, grant us some provisions for our journey.' The Holy Prophet صَلَّى اللهُ تَعَالٰی عَلَيْهِ وَاٰلِهٖ وَسَلَّم said, 'Dung is your food. The bones you touch will have meat on them for you, and the dung you go near will transform into dates for you.' When they departed, I asked as to who those people were? The Noble Prophet صَلَّى اللهُ تَعَالٰی عَلَيْهِ وَاٰلِهٖ وَسَلَّم replied, 'They were jinns from the city of Naṣībīn.' *(Luqṭ-ul-Marjān, pp. 47)*

Shaĥanshāĥ-o-gadā jinn-o-bashar aur Auliyā رَحِمَهُمُ اللّٰهُ تَعَالٰی
Ĥay sab kā tayray ṭukřon per guzārā Yā Rasūlallāĥ صَلَّى اللهُ تَعَالٰی عَلَيْهِ وَاٰلِهٖ وَسَلَّم

Rich, poor; jinn, men and Auliyā (رَحِمَهُمُ اللّٰهُ تَعَالٰی)
All live on your endowments, Yā Rasūlallāĥ (صَلَّى اللهُ تَعَالٰی عَلَيْهِ وَاٰلِهٖ وَسَلَّم)

صَلُّوْا عَلَى الْحَبِيْب صَلَّى اللهُ تَعَالٰی عَلٰی مُحَمَّد

Jinns are scared of lemons

It is stated in Qāḍī 'Alī Bin Ḥasan Khal'ī's biography that jinns would often visit him but once they came to meet him after an unusually long period of time. When asked about the reason for their long absence, the jinns explained, 'You had a lemon at your house and we do not enter the house in which there are lemons.' *(Luqṭ-ul-Marjān, pp. 103)*

Jinns fear white rooster

Here are two sayings of the Beloved and Blessed Rasūl صَلَّى اللّٰهُ تَعَالٰى عَلَيْهِ وَاٰلِهٖ وَسَلَّم:

1. Keep a white rooster (in home) as neither Satan nor magicians would come near the home, and near its surrounding ones, where there's a white rooster. *(Mu'jam Awsaṭ, vol. 1, pp. 1201, Ḥadīš 677)*

2. 'Do not speak ill of the white rooster as I am its friend and it is mine. Its enemy is my enemy. It drives jinns off as far as its voice reaches.' *(Luqṭ-ul-Marjān, pp. 165)*

Fodder for animals of jinns

A delegation of jinns once came to the court of the Holy Prophet صَلَّى اللّٰهُ تَعَالٰى عَلَيْهِ وَاٰلِهٖ وَسَلَّم and requested him to provide sustenance for them as well as for their animals. The Noble Prophet صَلَّى اللّٰهُ تَعَالٰى عَلَيْهِ وَاٰلِهٖ وَسَلَّم said, 'For you is the bone upon which the name of Allah عَزَّوَجَلَّ is mentioned, i.e. the bone must be from a Ḥalāl and pure animal. The meatless bone will become full of meat for you [in other words, you will receive the bone with meat on it]. And every dropping is the fodder for your animals.' Then he صَلَّى اللّٰهُ تَعَالٰى عَلَيْهِ وَاٰلِهٖ وَسَلَّم ordered humans, 'Do not use bones and droppings for cleaning [after relieving yourself] as these are the provisions for your brethren (Muslim jinns).' *(Ṣaḥīḥ Muslim, pp. 236, Ḥadīš 450)*

Jinns even kidnap people!

Once an Anṣārī[1] companion رَضِیَ اللّٰهُ تَعَالٰی عَنْهُ was kidnapped by some jinns at night as he left his home for Ṣalāt-ul-'Ishā. He was kept in captivity for several years. Having been released, when he returned to Madīnaĥ, Sayyidunā 'Umar Fārūq A'ẓam رَضِیَ اللّٰهُ تَعَالٰی عَنْهُ asked him what had happened. The Anṣārī companion رَضِیَ اللّٰهُ تَعَالٰی عَنْهُ told his story:

---

[1] The companions, who lived in Madīnaĥ, known for their help to the companions who migrated from Makkaĥ. [Translator's Note]

'[Non-Muslim] jinns abducted me. I remained in captivity for a long time. Thereafter, Muslim jinns made Jihad [and fought] against them. I was one of the many captured [by the Muslim jinns]. Consulting each other the Muslim jinns finally decided not to hold me in captivity as I was a Muslim. Therefore, they gave me the option either to stay with them or to return to my family. I chose to return to my family; so they brought me back to Madīnaĥ.'

Sayyidunā 'Umar Fārūq A'ẓam رَضِیَ اللهُ تَعَالٰی عَنْهُ then inquired about their foods, the Anṣārī companion رَضِیَ اللهُ تَعَالٰی عَنْهُ informed, 'They would eat beans and the foods upon which the name of Allah عَزَّوَجَلَّ is not mentioned.' [i.e. the food consumed by someone without reciting بِسْمِ اللّٰه]. When inquired about their drinks, the Anṣārī companion رَضِیَ اللهُ تَعَالٰی عَنْهُ replied, 'Jadaf.' *(Ḥayāt-ul-Ḥaywān-ul-Kubrā, vol. 1, pp. 295)*

'Jadaf' either refers to a kind of Yemini grass which quenches thirst as it is eaten or it refers to the container of water etc. which is left uncovered.' *(An-Niĥāyaĥ fī Gharīb al-Ḥadīš wal-Ašr, vol. 1, pp. 240)*

Protection from jinns and magic

Dear Islamic brothers! This parable reveals that the non-Muslim jinns eat beans and the foods upon which بِسْمِ اللّٰه is not recited. Further, they also eat and drink from the container left uncovered (with food in it). Furthermore, we have also learnt that jinns can abduct humans. This is indeed alarming [to know] because whole army battalions and weaponry are of no use in safeguarding oneself from them. For this, one requires Madanī weapons. Therefore, four 'Madanī weapons' are presented to safeguard ourselves from the wickedness of jinns. These are quoted from the pocket-sized booklet, '*Forty Spiritual Cures*', published by Maktaba-tul-Madīnaĥ:

1. يَا مُهَيْمِنُ — Anyone who recites يَا مُهَيْمِنُ 29 times daily (at any time during the day) will be guarded from calamities and afflictions, اِنْ شَآءَاللّٰه عَزَّوَجَلَّ

2. يَـا وَكِيْلُ — Anyone who recites يَـا وَكِيْلُ seven times, at the time of 'Aṣr, will be protected from calamities and afflictions, اِنْ شَآءَاللّٰه عَزَّوَجَلَّ.

3. يَـا مُحْيِ، يَـا مُمِيْتُ — Magic will not have any effect upon anyone who recites يَـا مُحْيِ، يَـا مُمِيْتُ seven times daily and blows on himself, اِنْ شَآءَاللّٰه عَزَّوَجَلَّ.

4. يَـا قَادِرُ — Anyone who makes a routine of reciting يَـا قَادِرُ whilst washing every organ during Wuḍū, cannot be abducted by his enemies (from amongst humans and jinns) اِنْ شَآءَاللّٰه عَزَّوَجَلَّ. (In addition to reciting يَـا قَادِرُ recite Ṣalāt-'Alan-Nabī while washing every organ during Wuḍū, as it is Mustaḥab). Recite also the invocations for protection permitted by your Shaykh[1].

Jinns can kill people

At times, Muslim jinns also punish wicked humans, as recorded by Ibn 'Aqīl in his book '*Kitāb-ul-Funūn*:' 'We had a home. Anyone staying there at night would be found dead in the morning. Then, a Muslim [who had come from the western areas] bought the house and slept there at night. To people's utter astonishment, nothing happened to him. He lived in the house comfortably for a long time, and then moved to a different abode.

When asked as to how he remained alive in the house where many others were killed, he replied, 'During the night I would recite the Holy Quran after Ṣalāt-ul-'Ishā. Once, as I was busy reciting the Quran as usual, a strange young man came out from the well [near the home] and greeted me with Salām. I was afraid but he asked me not to be. He then requested me to teach him the Quran. Therefore, I began teaching him. Then I asked him about the house. He revealed, 'We are Muslim jinns; we recite the Holy Quran and offer Ṣalāĥ. Usually, alcoholics and wicked people came to stay here; therefore we strangled

[1] Amīr-e-Aĥl-e-Sunnat دَامَتْ بَرَكَاتُهُمُ الْعَالِيَه has compiled the Shajaraĥ Qādiriyyah Razawiyyaĥ 'Aṭṭāriyyaĥ in Urdu language. It lists several invocations for protection. At the time of the writing of this account, this Shajaraĥ has been translated into many languages including Arabic, Sindhi, Hindi, Gujrati, English and French. Amīr-e-Aĥl-e-Sunnat دَامَتْ بَرَكَاتُهُمُ الْعَالِيَه has given all his Murīds [disciples] and Ṭālibīn permission to read the invocations stated in the Shajaraĥ. This pocket-sized Shajaraĥ may be purchased from any branch of Maktaba-tul Madīnaĥ.

them to death.' I told him that I was somewhat scared of him and requested him to come during the day. He assured me that he would do that. Thereafter, he would come out from the well during the day and I would teach him.

One day while I was teaching him the Holy Quran, an exorcist came to our area announcing that he had invocations for curing snake bites, warding off the evil-eye and exorcising ghost etc.

The jinn asked, 'Who is this man?' I said, 'He is an exorcist (i.e. one who recites invocations and blows on people to relieve them of afflictions).' The jinn said, 'Bring him here.' So I brought him in. Suddenly, the jinn transformed into a serpent (i.e. a snake). The exorcist read something and blew towards the serpent, causing it to writhe and fall down onto the centre of the house. The exorcist then captured and entrapped the serpent in his basket. I tried to stop him but he said, 'This is my prey! I'll take it.' I gave him a gold coin so he left the serpent.

After the exorcist left, the serpent transformed back into jinn but he had become weak and turned pale. I inquired, 'What happened?' He replied, 'The exorcist recited the holy names and blew towards me, causing this condition of mine. I had no hopes of remaining alive. When you hear screams from the well, leave this place.' Ibn 'Aqīl continues that the man said, 'I heard the screams during the night, so I left the house in the morning.' *(Luqṭ-ul-Marjān, pp. 105)*

Dear Islamic brothers! This terrifying narrative illustrates that at times mere joking can turn quite costly. It seems that the jinn transformed into the monstrous snake only to tease the exorcist, but the exorcist turned out to be perfect in his art and made such a powerful blow on the snake reciting the holy names that it put the life of the jinn in jeopardy. Therefore, we should refrain from teasing anyone assuming them to be weak.

This narrative also contains a lesson that one should refrain from every type of sin as the nuisance of sins can result in troubles even in the world, like the alcoholics and sinners were strangled to death by jinns. Those who watch movies, dramas and commit various sinful activities should take lesson from this parable, and fear being harmed by any jinn because of their transgressions.

Another lesson this narrative contains is that the worship and recitation of the Holy Quran avert difficulties. Like the jinn of the mysterious house who would strangle people became a student of the Muslim who offered Ṣalāĥ and recited the Quran. Therefore, keep your homes fragrant with the scent of Ṣalāĥ, Quran recitation and Na'ats. Avoid movies and songs. اِنْ شَآءَاللّٰہ عَزَّوَجَلَّ, You will reap great blessings.

To learn how to refrain from sins and perform worship properly, make it your habit to travel with the Madanī Qāfilaĥ regularly with the devotees of the Rasūl. In this way, you will not only reap countless blessings of the Hereafter but also be guarded from worldly calamities, اِنْ شَآءَاللّٰہ عَزَّوَجَلَّ.

Spinal cord compression got cured

An Islamic brother from Bāb-ul-Madīnaĥ, Karachi [Pakistan] has stated that in 2001 he had spinal cord compression which caused severe pain. He tried several medical treatments but was not cured. Doctors told him that an operation was the only option, but there was no surety about the success of the operation. Luckily, as a result of the individual effort of an Islamic brother, he travelled with a 30-day Madanī Qāfilaĥ. اَلْحَمْدُ لِلّٰہ عَزَّوَجَلَّ, By the blessing of the Madanī Qāfilaĥ, his spinal cord compression was healed without an operation and he was relieved of severe pain.

Gar koī marz ĥay to mayrī 'arz ĥay
Pāo gey rāḥatayn Qāfilay mayn chalo
Dard-e-sar ĥo agar yā ĥo dard-e-kamar
Pāo gey ṣiḥḥatayn Qāfilay mayn chalo

Have any illness, to find easiness; let's travel in the Qāfilaĥ
Have any aches, to find wellness; let's travel in the Qāfilaĥ

صَلُّوْا عَلَى الْحَبِيْب صَلَّى اللّٰهُ تَعَالٰى عَلٰى مُحَمَّد

Dear Islamic brothers! How blessed the Madanī Qāfilaĥ is! Here, I would like to make it clear that although it is expected that one's problems may be solved by the blessing of travelling with Madanī Qāfilaĥs, there is no surety about it as these matters depend upon the divine will. People spend thousands of dollars on medical treatment despite having no surety about the cure. No one gives up medical treatment even if he is not cured.

Some even die despite having best treatments, yet no one opposes those treatments. Therefore, even if the illness does not go away by travelling with a Madanī Qāfilaĥ, one should not be deceived by the satanic whisper [Waswasaĥ]. [Remember!] While travelling with a Madanī Qāfilaĥ, one should also make the intentions of acquiring religious knowledge and gaining reward of the Hereafter in addition to the intention of seeking solution to one's worldly problems.

Keep in mind that cure is a blessing, and illness is also a means of mercy. Therefore, we should be patient in every state. There are several virtues of illness and difficulty. The fortunate Muslims earn multitude of rewards by being patient during these trials. Here is an account that exhibits these virtues.

Staying blind is fine by me

Shaykh Sayyidunā Abū Baṣīr عَلَيْهِ رَحْمَةُ اللّٰهِ الْقَدِيْر was a blind person. He has stated, 'Once I visited Shaykh Sayyidunā Imām Bāqir عَلَيْهِ رَحْمَةُ اللّٰهِ الْقَادِر. He passed his hands over my eyes, restoring my eyesight. Then, he passed his hands over my eyes again, making me blind again.'

He then asked me, 'Which condition would you prefer; being able to see and then facing accountability on the Judgement Day for it as well as for all your other deeds or remaining blind and then entering Paradise without accountability?' Sayyidunā Abū Baṣīr عَلَيْهِ رَحْمَةُ اللّٰهِ الْقَدِيْر replied, 'I prefer an entry into Paradise without being held accountable and I am willing to stay blind.' *(Shawāĥid-un-Nubūwwaĥ, pp. 241)*

صَلُّوْا عَلَى الْحَبِيْب صَلَّى اللّٰهُ تَعَالٰی عَلٰی مُحَمَّد

Dear Islamic brothers! Did you realize the spiritual power of the saints of Allah عَزَّوَجَلَّ! By divinely-bestowed authority, they can give sight to the blind and glad tidings of entry into Paradise. Further, we have also learnt that one attains huge reward by having patience on facing hardship.

A Ḥadīš Qudsī contains glad tidings of entry into Paradise for the one having patience on losing eyesight. Therefore, the Beloved and Blessed Prophet صَلَّى اللّٰهُ تَعَالٰى عَلَيْهِ وَاٰلِهٖ وَسَلَّم has stated that Allah عَزَّوَجَلَّ has said, 'If I take away the eyes (i.e. sight) of My servant and he remains patient I will grant Paradise to him in exchange for his eyes.' *(Ṣaḥīḥ Bukhārī, vol. 4, pp. 6, Ḥadīš 5653)*

Ṫūṫay jo sar pay koĥ-e-balā, ṣabr kar
Ay Musalmān! Na tū ḋagmagā, ṣabr kar
Lab pay ḥarf-e-shikāyat na lā, ṣabr kar
Kay yeĥ Sunnat-e-Shāĥ-e-Abrār ĥay

Calamities though may befall
Waver not, be patient through 'em all
O Muslim, hold the lips from complain
This is the Sunnaĥ, in trials and pain

صَلُّوْا عَلَى الْحَبِيْب　　صَلَّى اللّٰهُ تَعَالٰى عَلٰى مُحَمَّد
تُوْبُوْا اِلَى الله　　اَسْتَغْفِرُ الله
صَلُّوْا عَلَى الْحَبِيْب　　صَلَّى اللّٰهُ تَعَالٰى عَلٰى مُحَمَّد

اَلْحَمْدُ لِلّٰهِ رَبِّ الْعٰلَمِيْنَ وَ الصَّلٰوةُ وَ السَّلَامُ عَلٰى سَيِّدِ الْمُرْسَلِيْنَ

اَمَّا بَعْدُ فَاَعُوْذُ بِاللّٰهِ مِنَ الشَّيْطٰنِ الرَّجِيْمِ ؕ بِسْمِ اللّٰهِ الرَّحْمٰنِ الرَّحِيْمِ ؕ

99 Parables

Excellence of Ṣalāt-'Alan-Nabī ﷺ

The Prophet of mankind, the Peace of our heart and mind, the most Generous and Kind صَلَّى اللهُ تَعَالٰى عَلَيْهِ وَاٰلِهٖ وَسَلَّم has stated, 'When the day of Thursday comes, Allah عَزَّوَجَلَّ sends His angels who have papers made of silver and pens made of gold. They write the names of those who recite Ṣalāt on me in abundance on the day of Thursday and the night of Friday.' *(Kanz-ul-'Ummāl, vol. 1, pp. 250, Ḥadīš 2174)*

صَلُّوْا عَلَى الْحَبِيْب صَلَّى اللهُ تَعَالٰى عَلٰى مُحَمَّد

1. Three birds

Sayyidunā Anas Bin Mālik رَضِىَ اللهُ تَعَالٰى عَنْهُ has narrated, 'Once someone gifted some birds to the Beloved and Blessed Prophet صَلَّى اللهُ تَعَالٰى عَلَيْهِ وَاٰلِهٖ وَسَلَّم. He صَلَّى اللهُ تَعَالٰى عَلَيْهِ وَاٰلِهٖ وَسَلَّم gave one of the birds to his maid for cooking and consuming. The next day, she brought the bird with her. Seeing this, the Holy Prophet صَلَّى اللهُ تَعَالٰى عَلَيْهِ وَاٰلِهٖ وَسَلَّم said, 'Did I not order you not to save anything for tomorrow. Undoubtedly, Allah عَزَّوَجَلَّ grants sustenance every day.' *(Shu'ab-ul-Īmān, vol. 2, pp. 118, Ḥadīš 1347)*

May Allah عَزَّوَجَلَّ have mercy on them and forgive us without accountability for their sake!

صَلُّوْا عَلَى الْحَبِيْب صَلَّى اللهُ تَعَالٰى عَلٰى مُحَمَّد

Saving things for next day

Dear Islamic brothers! The Noble Prophet صَلَّى اللّٰهُ تَعَالٰى عَلَيْهِ وَاٰلِهٖ وَسَلَّم had the greatest level of trust in Allah عَزَّوَجَلَّ. He صَلَّى اللّٰهُ تَعَالٰى عَلَيْهِ وَاٰلِهٖ وَسَلَّم never saved food for himself for the next day. He never gave Zakāĥ because he never accumulated any wealth and Zakāĥ never became Farḍ for him. A renowned exegetist of the Quran, Ḥakīm-ul-Ummat, Muftī Aḥmad Yār Khān عَلَيْهِ رَحْمَةُ الْحَنَّان has stated, '[The Prophet] Sayyidunā Ibrāĥīm Khalīlullāĥ عَلَيْهِ السَّلَام ran a knife over the neck of his son. [The saint Ibrāĥīm Bin] Adĥam عَلَيْهِ رَحْمَةُ اللّٰهِ الْاَكْرَم made Du'ā to Allah عَزَّوَجَلَّ for his son, Ibrāĥīm, 'Yā Allah عَزَّوَجَلَّ! May he die because I became heedless of You for a moment when I kissed him.'

This was the enthusiasm and love of these eminent personalities who believed in sacrificing every such thing that keeps them away from their Creator. Sayyidunā Abū Żar Ghifārī رَضِىَ اللّٰهُ تَعَالٰى عَنْهُ was an ascetic saint of the highest degree. The following couplet is a reflexion of his sentiments.

Kauřī na rakĥ kafan ko, taj ḋāl māl-o-dĥan ko
Jis nay diyā ĥay tan ko, day gā woĥī kafan ko

(**Translation:** Don't save anything even for shroud and stay away from wealth. The One who has granted you sustenance will grant you a shroud as well).

Bear in mind that it is not Ḥarām to accumulate Ḥalāl (i.e. lawfully-earned) wealth. Therefore, the honourable Muftī عَلَيْهِ رَحْمَةُ اللّٰهِ الْقَوِى has further stated that it is Ḥalāl to accumulate wealth and leave it after death provided Zakāĥ, Fiṭraĥ, slaughtering [of animals] and the rights of people were fulfilled from it. *(Mirāt-ul-Manājīḥ, vol. 3, pp. 88-89)*

2. Dead goat rose twitching its ear

Sayyidunā Ka'b Bin Mālik رَضِىَ اللّٰهُ تَعَالٰى عَنْهُ has narrated, 'Sayyidunā Jābir Bin 'Abdullāĥ رَضِىَ اللّٰهُ تَعَالٰى عَنْهُ once came to the court of the Holy Prophet صَلَّى اللّٰهُ تَعَالٰى عَلَيْهِ وَاٰلِهٖ وَسَلَّم. He noticed weakness from his facial expressions. He immediately went home where he told his wife, 'Today I have noticed a change on the blessed face of the Noble Prophet صَلَّى اللّٰهُ تَعَالٰى عَلَيْهِ وَاٰلِهٖ وَسَلَّم, and I think it is because of hunger. Do you have anything?' She replied, 'By Allah عَزَّوَجَلَّ, nothing except for this goat and a little flour.' He رَضِیَ اللہُ تَعَالٰی عَنْہُ immediately slaughtered the goat and ordered his wife to cook the meat and bread. When the food was prepared, he brought it in the court of the Holy Prophet صَلَّی اللہُ تَعَالٰی عَلَیْہِ وَاٰلِہٖ وَسَلَّم and served it in a large bowl.

The Prophet of Raḥmaĥ, the Intercessor of Ummaĥ صَلَّی اللہُ تَعَالٰی عَلَیْہِ وَاٰلِہٖ وَسَلَّم said, 'O Jābir, go and call people.' Sayyidunā Jābir رَضِیَ اللہُ تَعَالٰی عَنْہُ abided by what he was ordered. The Holy Prophet صَلَّی اللہُ تَعَالٰی عَلَیْہِ وَاٰلِہٖ وَسَلَّم then ordered, 'Send them to me in small groups.' They entered and began to eat; when one group finished another would come until all the people ate. The quantity of the food did not reduce even after everyone ate. The Noble Prophet صَلَّی اللہُ تَعَالٰی عَلَیْہِ وَاٰلِہٖ وَسَلَّم would order [the people] to eat but not to break the bones. He صَلَّی اللہُ تَعَالٰی عَلَیْہِ وَاٰلِہٖ وَسَلَّم then gathered all the bones in the centre of the container, placed his blessed hand on it and recited something which I (Sayyidunā Jābir) did not hear. In no time, the goat whose meat we had just eaten rose from the dead, twitching its ear.

The Holy Prophet صَلَّی اللہُ تَعَالٰی عَلَیْہِ وَاٰلِہٖ وَسَلَّم said, 'O Jābir! Take your goat back.' I then returned the goat to my wife. Astonished, she asked, 'What is this!' I replied, 'By Allah عَزَّوَجَلَّ, this is the same goat that we slaughtered. Allah عَزَّوَجَلَّ has resurrected it by the blessing of the Du'ā of the Beloved and Blessed Prophet صَلَّی اللہُ تَعَالٰی عَلَیْہِ وَاٰلِہٖ وَسَلَّم.' The narrator goes on to say that his wife said spontaneously, 'I testify that he صَلَّی اللہُ تَعَالٰی عَلَیْہِ وَاٰلِہٖ وَسَلَّم is indeed the Beloved Prophet of Allah صَلَّی اللہُ تَعَالٰی عَلَیْہِ وَاٰلِہٖ وَسَلَّم.' *(Al-Khaṣāiṣ-ul-Kubrā, vol. 2, pp. 112)*

May Allah عَزَّوَجَلَّ have mercy on them and forgive us without accountability for their sake!

صَلُّوْا عَلَی الْحَبِیْب   صَلَّی اللہُ تَعَالٰی عَلٰی مُحَمَّد

3. Children rose from the dead

A well known devotee and admirer of the Beloved and Blessed Prophet, a great scholar, 'Allāmaĥ 'Abdur Raḥmān Jāmī رَحْمَۃُ اللہِ تَعَالٰی عَلَیْہ has narrated, 'Sayyidunā Jābir رَضِیَ اللہُ تَعَالٰی عَنْہُ had sacrificed the goat in the presence of his children. When he finished and left, his children took a knife and went on to the roof of the house where the elder brother told his younger brother 'Let's imitate our father', I will do with you what our father did with the goat.' The elder brother then tied the younger brother's hands together, ran the knife over his throat and beheaded him, holding the head in his hands. When their mother became aware of what had happened, she ran after the elder son who ran away from his mother in fear, fell down from the roof and died. Despite losing her two sons, she did not weep and wail as she did not want to disturb her honourable guest صَلَّى اللهُ تَعَالَى عَلَيْهِ وَاٰلِهٖ وَسَلَّم. With resoluteness she covered the dead bodies of her sons with a piece of cloth, not telling anyone including even her husband, Sayyidunā Jābir رَضِىَ اللهُ تَعَالَى عَنْه.

Though her heart was shedding tears of blood, she still maintained a bold face; fresh and glimmering. In these trying moments she still managed to prepare food. The Holy Prophet صَلَّى اللهُ تَعَالَى عَلَيْهِ وَاٰلِهٖ وَسَلَّم then arrived and the food was served. The very same moment, angel Jibrāīl عَلَيْهِ السَّلَام came and said, 'Yā Rasūlallāh صَلَّى اللهُ تَعَالَى عَلَيْهِ وَاٰلِهٖ وَسَلَّم! Allah عَزَّوَجَلَّ has commanded you to order Jābir رَضِىَ اللهُ تَعَالَى عَنْه to bring his children so that they may also be privileged to eat food with you.' The Noble Prophet صَلَّى اللهُ تَعَالَى عَلَيْهِ وَاٰلِهٖ وَسَلَّم ordered Sayyidunā Jābir رَضِىَ اللهُ تَعَالَى عَنْه to bring his children. Sayyidunā Jābir رَضِىَ اللهُ تَعَالَى عَنْه immediately went and asked his wife as to where the children were. She asked him to inform the Holy Prophet صَلَّى اللهُ تَعَالَى عَلَيْهِ وَاٰلِهٖ وَسَلَّم that the children were not present.

Rasūlullāh صَلَّى اللهُ تَعَالَى عَلَيْهِ وَاٰلِهٖ وَسَلَّم insisted that the children be immediately brought as it was the command of Allah عَزَّوَجَلَّ. Sayyidunā Jābir's رَضِىَ اللهُ تَعَالَى عَنْه bereaved wife burst into tears informing him that she could no longer bring the children. Sayyidunā Jābir رَضِىَ اللهُ تَعَالَى عَنْه asked, 'What is the matter? Why are you weeping?' Taking him inside, his wife informed him of the calamity that had befallen them lifting the cloth to uncover the dead bodies of their children. Seeing this, Sayyidunā Jābir رَضِىَ اللهُ تَعَالَى عَنْه also began to weep. Hence Sayyidunā Jābir رَضِىَ اللهُ تَعَالَى عَنْه placed both the corpses of his children before the Holy Prophet صَلَّى اللهُ تَعَالَى عَلَيْهِ وَاٰلِهٖ وَسَلَّم. The voice of weeping people began to emanate from the house. Allah عَزَّوَجَلَّ sent angel Jibrāīl عَلَيْهِ السَّلَام stating, 'O Jibrāīl عَلَيْهِ السَّلَام! Inform my beloved [Prophet صَلَّى اللهُ تَعَالَى عَلَيْهِ وَاٰلِهٖ وَسَلَّم] that his Rab عَزَّوَجَلَّ states; O My beloved [Prophet صَلَّى اللهُ تَعَالَى عَلَيْهِ وَاٰلِهٖ وَسَلَّم]! You make Du'ā and I will resurrect them.' Hence the Prophet of mankind, the Peace of our heart and mind, the most Generous and Kind صَلَّى اللهُ تَعَالَى عَلَيْهِ وَاٰلِهٖ وَسَلَّم made Du'ā and both children rose from the dead with the command of Allah عَزَّوَجَلَّ.' *(Shawāhid-un-Nubūwwaĥ, pp. 105) (Madārij-un-Nubūwwaĥ, vol. 1, pp. 199)*

May Allah عَزَّوَجَلَّ have mercy on them and forgive us without accountability for their sake!

Qalb-e-murdaĥ ko mayray ab to jilā do Āqā صَلَّى اللّٰهُ تَعَالٰى عَلَيْهِ وَاٰلِهٖ وَسَلَّم
Jām ulfat kā mujĥay apnī pilā do Āqā صَلَّى اللّٰهُ تَعَالٰى عَلَيْهِ وَاٰلِهٖ وَسَلَّم

Revitalise my dead heart, Yā Rasūlallāĥ صَلَّى اللّٰهُ تَعَالٰى عَلَيْهِ وَاٰلِهٖ وَسَلَّم*!*
And instil your devotion, Yā Rasūlallāĥ صَلَّى اللّٰهُ تَعَالٰى عَلَيْهِ وَاٰلِهٖ وَسَلَّم*!*

صَلُّوْا عَلَى الْحَبِيْب صَلَّى اللّٰهُ تَعَالٰى عَلٰى مُحَمَّد

Dear Islamic brothers! How great and glorious the status of our Beloved and Blessed Rasūl صَلَّى اللّٰهُ تَعَالٰى عَلَيْهِ وَاٰلِهٖ وَسَلَّم is! He fed a large number of people with a little amount of food that did not reduce even after all the people ate. Further, he made the goat rise from the dead twitching its ears by reciting blessed words and resurrected Sayyidunā Jābir's رَضِیَ اللّٰهُ تَعَالٰی عَنْهُ children with the command of Allah عَزَّوَجَلَّ.

Murdaun ko jilātay ĥayn rotaun ko ĥansātay ĥayn
Ālām mitātay ĥayn bigřī ko banātay ĥayn
Sarkār صَلَّى اللّٰهُ تَعَالٰى عَلَيْهِ وَاٰلِهٖ وَسَلَّم *kĥilātay ĥayn Sarkār* صَلَّى اللّٰهُ تَعَالٰى عَلَيْهِ وَاٰلِهٖ وَسَلَّم *pilātay ĥayn*
Sultan-o-gadā sab ko Sarkār صَلَّى اللّٰهُ تَعَالٰى عَلَيْهِ وَاٰلِهٖ وَسَلَّم *nibĥātay ĥayn*

He صَلَّى اللّٰهُ تَعَالٰى عَلَيْهِ وَاٰلِهٖ وَسَلَّم *resurrects the deceased and gratifies the grieved*
He sets the things in order, and causes the stress to be relieved
He quenches our thirst and satisfies our hunger
He accommodates both the king and the beggar

4. Seven dates

Sayyidunā 'Irbāḍ Bin Sāriyaĥ رَضِیَ اللّٰهُ تَعَالٰی عَنْهُ has narrated that during the battle of Tabūk the Prophet of Raḥmaĥ, the Intercessor of Ummaĥ صَلَّى اللّٰهُ تَعَالٰى عَلَيْهِ وَاٰلِهٖ وَسَلَّم once asked Sayyidunā Bilāl رَضِیَ اللّٰهُ تَعَالٰی عَنْهُ, 'O Bilāl رَضِیَ اللّٰهُ تَعَالٰی عَنْهُ! Do you have anything to eat?' Sayyidunā Bilāl رَضِیَ اللّٰهُ تَعَالٰی عَنْهُ replied, 'O Prophet of Allah صَلَّى اللّٰهُ تَعَالٰى عَلَيْهِ وَاٰلِهٖ وَسَلَّم! I swear by Allah عَزَّوَجَلَّ that we have emptied our bags but could not find anything to eat.' The Holy Prophet صَلَّى اللّٰهُ تَعَالٰى عَلَيْهِ وَاٰلِهٖ وَسَلَّم said, 'Look carefully and empty your bags properly, perhaps you find something.' Sayyidunā Bilāl رَضِیَ اللّٰهُ تَعَالٰی عَنْهُ has stated that they were three in number. As they emptied their bags again they found seven dates.

Keeping the dates on a piece of paper, the Holy Prophet صَلَّى اللّٰهُ تَعَالٰى عَلَيْهِ وَاٰلِهٖ وَسَلَّم placed his blessed hand over them. He then said to us, 'Recite بِسْمِ اللّٰه and eat.' We then began to eat, taking the dates from under the blessed hand of the Holy Prophet صَلَّى اللّٰهُ تَعَالٰى عَلَيْهِ وَاٰلِهٖ وَسَلَّم. Sayyidunā Bilāl رَضِىَ اللّٰهُ تَعَالٰى عَنْهُ goes onto say that he kept the seeds in his left hand and when he counted them, there were 54 seeds in his hand alone. The other two companions رَضِىَ اللّٰهُ تَعَالٰى عَنْهُم also ate until they were satiated. Sayyidunā 'Irbāḍ Bin Sāriyaĥ رَضِىَ اللّٰهُ تَعَالٰى عَنْهُ has further stated that the Beloved and Blessed Prophet صَلَّى اللّٰهُ تَعَالٰى عَلَيْهِ وَاٰلِهٖ وَسَلَّم raised his blessed hand from over the dates after they had finished eating. The companions رَضِىَ اللّٰهُ تَعَالٰى عَنْهُم were surprised to see that all the seven dates were still present over the piece of paper. Turning to Sayyidunā Bilāl رَضِىَ اللّٰهُ تَعَالٰى عَنْهُ, the Holy Prophet صَلَّى اللّٰهُ تَعَالٰى عَلَيْهِ وَاٰلِهٖ وَسَلَّم then ordered, 'O Bilāl! Keep them safe and do not allow anyone to eat. These dates will be useful later on.'

Sayyidunā Bilāl رَضِىَ اللّٰهُ تَعَالٰى عَنْهُ goes onto to say that the next day at mealtime, the Holy Prophet صَلَّى اللّٰهُ تَعَالٰى عَلَيْهِ وَاٰلِهٖ وَسَلَّم again asked for the dates and did the same thing; that is, he positioned his blessed hand over the dates and commanded us to eat reciting 'بِسْمِ اللّٰه.' On that day, ten of us ate till we all were satiated. When he صَلَّى اللّٰهُ تَعَالٰى عَلَيْهِ وَاٰلِهٖ وَسَلَّم lifted his blessed hand, the seven dates were still present. He صَلَّى اللّٰهُ تَعَالٰى عَلَيْهِ وَاٰلِهٖ وَسَلَّم then said, 'O Bilāl رَضِىَ اللّٰهُ تَعَالٰى عَنْهُ! If I had not felt Ḥayā [shyness] from my Creator عَزَّوَجَلَّ, we could have eaten from these seven dates by the time of returning to Madīnaĥ.' The Holy Prophet صَلَّى اللّٰهُ تَعَالٰى عَلَيْهِ وَاٰلِهٖ وَسَلَّم then gave those dates to a young boy who ate them and left. *(Al-Khaṣāiṣ-ul-Kubrā, vol. 2, pp. 455)*

May Allah عَزَّوَجَلَّ have mercy on them and forgive us without accountability for their sake!

Dear Islamic brothers! What huge authority Allah عَزَّوَجَلَّ has granted to His Beloved and Blessed Rasūl صَلَّى اللّٰهُ تَعَالٰى عَلَيْهِ وَاٰلِهٖ وَسَلَّم! This was indeed a great blessing that several companions رَضِىَ اللّٰهُ تَعَالٰى عَنْهُم were satiated by eating just from seven dates.

Mālik-e-kaunayn ĥayn go pās kucĥ rakĥtay naĥīn
Do jaĥān kī na'matayn ĥayn un kay kĥālī ĥātĥ mayn

He صَلَّى اللّٰهُ تَعَالٰى عَلَيْهِ وَاٰلِهٖ وَسَلَّم does not keep anything, though he is the chief of the world and Hereafter
In his empty hands, he صَلَّى اللّٰهُ تَعَالٰى عَلَيْهِ وَاٰلِهٖ وَسَلَّم possesses favours of the world and Hereafter

صَلُّوْا عَلَى الْحَبِيْب صَلَّى اللّٰهُ تَعَالٰى عَلٰى مُحَمَّد

5. Two movies everyday!

Dear Islamic brothers! Stay associated with the Madanī environment of Dawat-e-Islami, a global & non-political movement for the preaching of Quran and Sunnaĥ. اَلْحَمْدُلِلّٰه عَزَّوَجَلَّ, Dawat-e-Islami has brought about a Madanī revolution in the lives of millions of people. An Islamic brother from 'Aṭṭārābād (Jacobabad, Bāb-ul-Islam, Sindh Pakistan) has described how he joined the Madanī environment. He has stated: 'I was immersed in sins. I would often watch two movies a day and always had a radio with me. I would sell the old radios and get the latest ones. Even at bedtime, I would play the radio and listen to music till around 2 a.m. My mother would turn off the radio after I had gone to sleep listening to music.

Probably, in 1416 A.H. on a Thursday of the holy month of Ramadan, I went to Hyderabad to meet a friend of mine who took me to Dawat-e-Islami's weekly Sunnaĥ-Inspiring Ijtimā' where we heard Amīr-e-Aĥl-e-Sunnat Maulānā Ilyas Qadiri's speech live relayed by telephone from Bāb-ul-Madīnaĥ Karachi. As I listened to the speech, a Madanī transformation took place in my life. Overcome by divine fear, I tearfully repented of my sins. Since then, I joined the Madanī environment of Dawat-e-Islami for good. اَلْحَمْدُلِلّٰه عَزَّوَجَلَّ, I also adorned my face with a fist-length beard as a result of the individual effort of an Islamic brother of 'Aṭṭārābād.'

Mayn to nādān tĥā dānistāĥ bĥī kyā kyā na kiyā
Lāj rakĥ lī, mayray Lajpāl nay ruswā na kiyā

I was unwise as I voluntarily committed acts of condemnation
My saviour saved me from humiliation

صَلُّوْا عَلَى الْحَبِيْب   صَلَّى اللّٰهُ تَعَالٰى عَلٰى مُحَمَّد

6. Blessing in little food

Sayyidunā Ṣuĥayb رَضِیَ اللّٰهُ تَعَالٰی عَنْهُ has narrated: 'I had a little food prepared for the Beloved and Blessed Prophet صَلَّى اللّٰهُ تَعَالٰى عَلَيْهِ وَاٰلِهٖ وَسَلَّم and went to invite him, but could not do so because of the presence of companions رَضِیَ اللّٰهُ تَعَالٰی عَنْهُم with him. I stood silent over there as the food was not sufficient for all of them. When the Noble Prophet صَلَّى اللهُ تَعَالٰى عَلَيْهِ وَاٰلِهٖ وَسَلَّم looked towards me, I signalled requesting him to come to my home to eat. He صَلَّى اللهُ تَعَالٰى عَلَيْهِ وَاٰلِهٖ وَسَلَّم asked, 'These people as well?' I replied, 'No.' The Holy Prophet صَلَّى اللهُ تَعَالٰى عَلَيْهِ وَاٰلِهٖ وَسَلَّم became quiet as I remained standing over there.

After a while, he صَلَّى اللهُ تَعَالٰى عَلَيْهِ وَاٰلِهٖ وَسَلَّم looked towards me again and I signalled my request again. He صَلَّى اللهُ تَعَالٰى عَلَيْهِ وَاٰلِهٖ وَسَلَّم asked again, 'These people?' I said, 'No.' Thereafter, he صَلَّى اللهُ تَعَالٰى عَلَيْهِ وَاٰلِهٖ وَسَلَّم did the same for the third time, so I replied, 'As you wish' but I also informed him that I had a little food which was cooked only for him. The Prophet of mankind, the Peace of our heart and mind, the most Generous and Kind صَلَّى اللهُ تَعَالٰى عَلَيْهِ وَاٰلِهٖ وَسَلَّم came to my home along with his companions رَضِيَ اللّٰهُ تَعَالٰى عَنْهُم. Everyone ate to their satiation but the food was still left.' *(Al-Khaṣāiṣ-ul-Kubrā, vol. 2, pp. 82)*

May Allah عَزَّوَجَلَّ have mercy on them and forgive us without accountability for their sake!

صَلُّوْا عَلَى الْحَبِيْب صَلَّى اللهُ تَعَالٰى عَلٰى مُحَمَّد

Dear Islamic brothers! Without doubt, the Noble Prophet صَلَّى اللهُ تَعَالٰى عَلَيْهِ وَاٰلِهٖ وَسَلَّم is a fountain of blessings and mercy for us. Since the food was in small quantity, the companion had invited only the Holy Prophet صَلَّى اللهُ تَعَالٰى عَلَيْهِ وَاٰلِهٖ وَسَلَّم but, by the blessing of the Prophet of Raḥmaĥ, the Intercessor of Ummaĥ صَلَّى اللهُ تَعَالٰى عَلَيْهِ وَاٰلِهٖ وَسَلَّم, the little food was not only sufficient for many people but was also left at the end, after they had eaten.

Yeĥ sun kar Sakhī āp kā āstānā, ĥay dāman pasāray ĥuway sab zamānaĥ
Nawāsaun kā ṣadaqaĥ nigāĥ-e-karam ĥo, tayray dar pay tayray gadā ā gaye ĥayn

Having heard of your generosity, the world is at your feet
Bestow your mercy for we are thirsty, for the sake of your grandsons; we seek

Words cannot express the greatness of the Holy Prophet صَلَّى اللهُ تَعَالٰى عَلَيْهِ وَاٰلِهٖ وَسَلَّم and his miracles! Even his devotees show great saintly miracles.

7. Blessing in sweets for Mīlād celebration

In Moradabad, Hind [India], a devotee of the Rasūl would zealously celebrate the blessed birth [of the Holy Prophet صَلَّى اللّٰهُ تَعَالٰى عَلَيْهِ وَاٰلِهٖ وَسَلَّم] every year. He would hold a marvellous Mīlād-gathering attended by a large number of Muslims particularly including Ṣadr-ul-Afāḍil 'Allāmaĥ Maulānā Sayyid Muhammad Na'īmuddīn Murādābādī عَلَيْهِ رَحْمَةُ اللّٰهِ الْهَادِى, a spiritual successor [Khalīfaĥ] of Imām Aḥmad Razā Khān عَلَيْهِ رَحْمَةُ الرَّحْمٰن.

One year, more people than usual came. In the end, like every year, when the traditional Indian laḋḋūs[1] [sweets] were being distributed, it seemed that they would only be enough for half of the people. The worried host informed the Shaykh رَحْمَةُ اللّٰهِ تَعَالٰى عَلَيْه of the situation. Taking out his handkerchief from his pocket and handing it to the host, the Shaykh رَحْمَةُ اللّٰهِ تَعَالٰى عَلَيْه said, 'Put it over the dish of the laḋḋūs and distribute them from under the handkerchief without looking at them.' Therefore, the sweets were distributed as per his instruction (and sufficed for all the attendees). When the handkerchief was removed, the quantity of sweets was the same as was before the distribution. *(Extracted from Tārīkh-e-Islam kī 'Aẓīm Shakhṣiyyat Ṣadr-ul-Afāḍil, pp. 343)*

May Allah عَزَّوَجَلَّ have mercy on them and forgive us without accountability for their sake!

Chāĥayn to ishāraun say apnay kāyā ĥī palaṫ dayn dunyā kī
Yeĥ shān ĥay khidmatgāraun kī Sardār صَلَّى اللّٰهُ تَعَالٰى عَلَيْهِ وَاٰلِهٖ وَسَلَّم kā 'ālam kyā ĥogā

With their signals they can change the course of the world
When the devotees have such greatness how will their Rasūl صَلَّى اللّٰهُ تَعَالٰى عَلَيْهِ وَاٰلِهٖ وَسَلَّم be?

صَلُّوْا عَلَى الْحَبِيْب صَلَّى اللّٰهُ تَعَالٰى عَلٰى مُحَمَّد

8. Father is relieved from torment

Dear Islamic brothers! Those joining the Madanī environment of Dawat-e-Islami with righteous intentions get deserving of good in the worldly life as well as in the afterlife. An Islamic brother has stated: 'I was privileged to travel with the devotees of the Rasūl in

[1] This is a sub-continental sweet. It is prepared with flour, made into balls and dipped into sugar.
[Translator's Note]

the Madanī Qāfilaĥ a day after Eid. During the Madanī Qāfilaĥ, I saw my father in a dream. He had passed away two years back. He was in a blissful state; I asked him as to what happened to him after he passed away. He replied, 'I was punished for my sins for some time, but then the torment was removed. He further said, 'Son, never leave the Madanī environment of Dawat-e-Islami as it was by its blessing that I was relieved of the torment.'

May Allah عَزَّوَجَلَّ have mercy on them and forgive us without accountability for their sake!

صَلُّوْا عَلَى الْحَبِيْب صَلَّى اللّٰهُ تَعَالٰى عَلٰى مُحَمَّد

Dear Islamic brothers! The mercy of Allah عَزَّوَجَلَّ is indeed immense. Pious offspring and their Du'ās are a source of perpetual reward and comfort for the deceased parents. The Madanī environment of Dawat-e-Islami is an excellent way to make your children righteous.

Ĥayn Islāmī bĥāī sabĥī bĥāī bĥāī
Ĥay bayḥad maḥabbat bĥarā Madanī Māḥaul
Yaĥān Sunnatayn sīkĥnay ko milayn gī
Dilāye gā khauf-e-Khudā عَزَّوَجَلَّ Madanī Māḥaul
Nabī صَلَّى اللّٰهُ تَعَالٰى عَلَيْهِ وَاٰلِهٖ وَسَلَّم kī maḥabbat mayn raunay kā andāz
Tum ā jāo sikĥlāye gā Madanī Māḥaul

Islamic brothers are all brothers
Filled with love is the Madanī environment
In it, the Sunnaĥ are learned
Brings fear of Allah عَزَّوَجَلَّ the Madanī environment
To shed tears in love of the Prophet صَلَّى اللّٰهُ تَعَالٰى عَلَيْهِ وَاٰلِهٖ وَسَلَّم
Come! You shall learn in the Madanī environment

9. 300 Men metamorphosed into swine

The companions of Prophet Sayyidunā 'Īsā عَلٰى نَبِيِّنَا وَعَلَيْهِ الصَّلٰوةُ وَالسَّلَام once said to him, 'Would your Creator عَزَّوَجَلَّ bless us with heavenly foods by virtue of your Du'ā?' Sayyidunā 'Īsā

عَلٰی نَبِیِّنَا وَعَلَیْهِ الصَّلٰوۃُ وَالسَّلَام replied, 'Do not ask for such miracles and fear Allah عَزَّوَجَلَّ. Abstain from this if you are believers.' They responded, 'Your honour, we have not made this request because of any doubt in your Prophethood or in the absolute power of Allah عَزَّوَجَلَّ, rather there are four purposes for this.

1. The first is, by eating the heavenly foods we would seek its blessings, enlighten our hearts and get closer to Allah عَزَّوَجَلَّ.

2. The second is, we would have 'Ayn-ul-Yaqīn[1] of the glad tidings you have given to us that our prayers are answered by our Creator عَزَّوَجَلَّ. Further, our hearts would have comfort and we would be satisfied to have perfect faith.

3. The third is, we would have 'Ayn-ul-Yaqīn of your truthfulness.

4. The fourth is, we would see this heavenly miracle, bear witness for others and this parable of ours would be a means of completion of the faith for people till the Day of Judgement. And we would become a witness of (your Prophethood) forever.'

Sayyidunā Salmān Fārsī, 'Abdullāĥ Ibn 'Abbās and most of other exegetists رَضِیَ اللّٰهُ تَعَالٰی عَنْهُم have stated, 'When the companions assured Prophet 'Īsā عَلٰی نَبِیِّنَا وَعَلَیْهِ الصَّلٰوۃُ وَالسَّلَام that they had not made this request of heavenly food for mere pleasure, but rather, they had some righteous intentions, Sayyidunā 'Īsā عَلٰی نَبِیِّنَا وَعَلَیْهِ الصَّلٰوۃُ وَالسَّلَام robed himself in a cloak made of jute and wept as he made Du'ā.

اَللّٰهُمَّ رَبَّنَاۤ اَنْزِلْ عَلَیْنَا مَآىِٕدَةً مِّنَ السَّمَآءِ تَكُوْنُ لَنَا عِیْدًا لِّاَوَّلِنَا وَ اٰخِرِنَا وَ اٰیَةً
مِّنْكَ ۚ وَ ارْزُقْنَا وَ اَنْتَ خَیْرُ الرّٰزِقِیْنَ ﴿۱۱۴﴾

O Allah, our Rab عَزَّوَجَلَّ, send down to us a tray of food from the heavens so that it may be an Eid for us, for the first and the last of us and a sign from You, and provide us with sustenance and You are the best Provider of Sustenance.

[Kanz-ul-Īmān (Translation of Quran)] (Part 7, Sūraĥ Al-Māidaĥ, verse 114)

[1] Belief by having seen something with eyes. [Translator's Note]

Hence a red dining-mat covered with clouds descended. All the people saw it as it was descending. It was then positioned amongst the people. Seeing this, Prophet Sayyidunā 'Īsā عَلٰی نَبِیِّنَا وَعَلَیْهِ الصَّلٰوۃُ وَالسَّلَام wept a lot and made the following Du'ā, 'O my Rab عَزَّوَجَلَّ, make me from amongst the thankful. O my Rab عَزَّوَجَلَّ, let this blessing not be a torment for my companions.'

The companions smelt such a fragrance from it that they had never smelt before. Prophet Sayyidunā 'Īsā عَلٰی نَبِیِّنَا وَعَلَیْهِ الصَّلٰوۃُ وَالسَّلَام and his companions bowed down to perform Sajdaĥ of Shukr [prostration of thanks]. Since the dining-mat was covered with a red cloth, Prophet Sayyidunā 'Īsā عَلٰی نَبِیِّنَا وَعَلَیْهِ الصَّلٰوۃُ وَالسَّلَام asked, 'Who will uncover it?' All of his companions requested that he عَلَیْهِ السَّلَام uncover it. Therefore, he made a fresh Wuḍū, offered Ṣalāĥ, made Du'ā' for a long time and then removed the cover.

There were the following things on the dining-mat: Seven fish along with seven pieces of bread. The fish had neither scales nor bones inside. Oil was dripping from them. Near the heads of the fish was vinegar and by their tails was salt. Along the sides were vegetables lined up. It is stated in some narrations that there were five pieces of bread. One piece of bread had olive (oil) on it, the second had honey, the third had ghee (i.e. a type of butter), the fourth had cheese and the fifth had roasted meat on it.

Sham'ūn, one of the companions, asked, 'O Prophet of Allah! Are these foods from the earth or Heaven?' He عَلَیْهِ السَّلَام replied, 'These foods are neither from the earth nor Heaven, they are simply from nature.'

First, the ill, the poor, the starving and those suffering from leukoderma, leprosy and physical disability were called. He عَلَیْهِ السَّلَام said, 'Say بِسْمِ اللّٰه and eat, this is a blessing for you and a calamity for those who deny. Other people were also given the same instruction. Hence seven thousand three hundred people ate the food on the first day. Then that dining-mat ascended as people watched, it flew up and disappeared. All the ill were cured and the poor became wealthy. This dining-mat descended for forty days consecutively or alternate days and people ate from it.

Prophet 'Īsā عَلٰی نَبِیِّنَا وَعَلَیْهِ الصَّلٰوۃُ وَالسَّلَام then received a revelation with the commandment that the wealthy would no longer eat from it, only the poor would do. When this was announced, the wealthy became displeased and said that all this was nothing but magic. The wealthy people who denied the divine commandment were three hundred in number. When they went to sleep in their homes with their families at night, they were fine and well, but when they woke up in the morning, they had been turned into swine. These swine would run around in the streets and eat filthy faeces.

When the people saw their state, they came running to Prophet 'Īsā عَلٰی نَبِیِّنَا وَعَلَیْهِ الصَّلٰوةُ وَالسَّلَام and wept. These swine also gathered around him crying. Prophet 'Īsā عَلٰی نَبِیِّنَا وَعَلَیْهِ الصَّلٰوةُ وَالسَّلَام would call them by their names and they would move their heads in response but could not speak. They lived in this extremely humiliating condition for three days. On the fourth day, they all perished. There were no women or children among them. All the nations that were metamorphosed perished. Their lineage did not continue as this is the divine law. *(Tafsīr Kabīr, vol. 4, pp. 423)*

It is stated in a Ḥadīš of *Tirmižī* that the Beloved and Blessed Prophet صَلَّى اللهُ تَعَالٰى عَلَيْهِ وَاٰلِهٖ وَسَلَّم has stated, 'The dining-mat with bread and meat was sent down (from the skies). It was commanded that there should neither be any breaching in it nor any saving of food for the next day, but those people not only breached but also saved food for the next day, so they were metamorphosed into monkeys and swine.' *(Jāmi' Tirmižī, vol. 5, pp. 44, Ḥadīš 3072)*

These people were ordered not to hide or save anything for the next day but some did and were turned into swine as a result. Sayyidunā 'Abdullāĥ Bin 'Amr رَضِیَ اللهُ تَعَالٰی عَنْهُ has said, 'On the Day of Judgement there will be severe punishment for those non-Muslims of the dining-mat [incident], the supporters of Pharaoh and the hypocrites.' *(Ad-Dur-rul-Manšūr, vol. 3, pp. 237)*

Does Wuḍū become invalid by uttering the word 'swine?'

Dear Islamic brothers! Did you see the high rank of Prophet 'Īsā عَلٰی نَبِیِّنَا وَعَلَیْهِ الصَّلٰوةُ وَالسَّلَام that Allah عَزَّوَجَلَّ sent a Māidaĥ (dining mat) full of blessings by virtue of his Du'ā. The boon one receives in the world often comes with bane. Grateful are successful whereas the ungrateful are unsuccessful. Those who transgress in spite of enjoying boons in abundance are humiliated as stated in the foregoing Quranic account that 300 transgressors were turned into swine that hopelessly roamed around for three days and perished on the fourth. We ask Allah's refuge from His wrath and displeasure.

Some people have the misconception that uttering the word 'pig' or 'swine' or 'Khinzīr[1]' makes one's tongue impure and Wuḍū invalid. This is not true. The word خِنۡزِیۡر (Khinzīr) is mentioned even in the Holy Quran; so saying it does not make one's tongue impure nor does it invalidate Wuḍū.

10. Where is third piece of bread?

A man once came to Prophet 'Īsā عَلٰی نَبِیِّنَا وَعَلَیْهِ الصَّلٰوۃُ وَالسَّلَام and said, 'I wish to stay in your company so that I may acquire the knowledge of Sharī'aĥ. He عَلَیْهِ السَّلَام permitted the man to stay with him. During a journey, they reached a canal where he عَلَیْهِ السَّلَام said, 'Let's eat.' He عَلَیْهِ السَّلَام had three pieces of bread. After both of them had eaten one piece of bread each, Prophet 'Īsā عَلٰی نَبِیِّنَا وَعَلَیْهِ الصَّلٰوۃُ وَالسَّلَام went to drink water from the canal. In the meantime, the man hid the third piece of bread. Having returned, he عَلَیْهِ السَّلَام asked, 'Where is the third piece of bread?' The man told a lie, 'I do not know.' He عَلَیْهِ السَّلَام did not say anything. After a while, Prophet 'Īsā عَلٰی نَبِیِّنَا وَعَلَیْهِ الصَّلٰوۃُ وَالسَّلَام said, 'Let's go ahead.'

On the way, they saw a deer with its two fawns. He عَلَیْهِ السَّلَام called one of the fawns that came to him. He عَلَیْهِ السَّلَام then slaughtered and roasted it and both of them ate it together. After they finished eating, he عَلَیْهِ السَّلَام collected the bones of the fawn and said, 'قُمۡ بِـاِذۡنِ الله.' (*Rise from the dead by the command of Allah* عَزَّوَجَلَّ). In no time, the dead fawn stood up and returned to its mother running. Thereafter, he عَلَیْهِ السَّلَام said to the man, 'I make you swear to Allah عَزَّوَجَلَّ who has empowered me to show this miracle. Tell the truth, where is that third piece of bread?' The man again replied, 'I do not know.' He عَلَیْهِ السَّلَام said, 'Let's move ahead.'

As they walked further, they reached a river where he عَلَیْهِ السَّلَام held that man's hand and continued to walk on the river water until they crossed the river and reached the other side. Thereafter, he عَلَیْهِ السَّلَام said to the man, 'I make you swear to Allah عَزَّوَجَلَّ who has empowered me to show this miracle. Tell the truth, where is that third piece of bread?' The man again replied, 'I do not know.' He عَلَیْهِ السَّلَام said, 'Let's go ahead.'

As they walked further, they reached a desert where Prophet 'Īsā عَلَیْهِ السَّلَام piled up some sand and addressed it, 'O pile of sand, turn into gold by the command of Allah عَزَّوَجَلَّ.' It

[1] Arabic word for swine. [Translator's Note]

immediately turned into gold which he عَلَيْهِ السَّلَام divided into three parts and said, 'One part is mine, the other is yours and the third one is for the one who has taken the third piece of bread.' Upon hearing this, the man immediately said, 'O Prophet of Allah, it was me who had taken the third piece of bread.' Hearing this he عَلَيْهِ السَّلَام said, 'Take all this gold', and then left the man behind.

Wrapping the gold into a shawl the man moved ahead. On the way, he came across two other men. As the two persons noticed that the man had gold, they intended to kill him but he managed to prevent them from doing so by suggesting that the gold be divided into three parts and distributed among them equally. This seemed to satisfy the other two men. He then said, 'One of us should go to the nearby city with a little gold and buy some food so that we would enjoy a luscious meal and distribute the gold afterwards.' Therefore, one of them went and bought food but, overpowered by his greed, he poisoned the food so that the other two men would die and he would take all the gold.

On the other hand, the other two had already conspired to kill him as soon as he would return so that they would divide the gold between them equally. When he returned with food, they both murdered him brutally. After this, they happily ate the food, which had already been poisoned. As a result, the two men also died writhing and the gold remained lying there.

When Prophet 'Īsā عَلٰی نَبِیِّنَا وَعَلَیْهِ الصَّلٰوۃُ وَالسَّلَام returned along with his companions and came across the dead bodies, he عَلَيْهِ السَّلَام pointed to the gold and the bodies of the three men and said, 'See, this is the reality of the world. It is obligatory for you to stay away from it.'
(Itḥāf-us-Sādat-il-Muttaqīn, vol. 9, pp. 735)

Dear Islamic brothers! Did you see! The love of the world leads human to committing inhuman acts and sins like deceiving, defrauding, robbing and even killing others but still, it is not loyal to anyone. Even those enjoying transient worldly luxuries have to face extreme hardships and troubles in return. Our saints were highly cautious and careful about wealth and world. Here are some saints' sayings in condemnation of worldly wealth.

صَلُّوْا عَلَى الْحَبِيْب صَلَّى اللّٰهُ تَعَالٰى عَلٰى مُحَمَّد

Sayings of saints in condemnation of wealth

Ḥujjat-ul-Islam Sayyidunā Imām Muhammad Ghazālī عَلَيْهِ رَحْمَةُ اللّٰهِ الْوَالِى has quoted:

1. Sayyidunā Ḥasan Baṣrī عَلَيْهِ رَحْمَةُ اللّٰهِ الْقَوِى has stated, 'By Allah عَزَّوَجَلَّ! Whoever respects wealth is disgraced by Allah عَزَّوَجَلَّ.'

2. It is narrated that when the first dinar and dirham [coins of gold and silver] were made, Satan picked them up, put them on his forehead and kissed them. He then said, 'Whoever loves these is my slave.' (We ask Allah's refuge).

3. Sayyidunā Samīṭ Bin 'Ijlān عَلَيْهِ رَحْمَةُ الْمَنَّان has stated, 'Dinar and dirham are the reins of the hypocrites whereby they will be dragged towards Hell.'

4. Sayyidunā Yaḥyā Bin Mu'āż رَضِىَ اللّٰهُ تَعَالٰى عَنْهُ has stated, 'Dirham (or wealth) is a scorpion; if you do not know how to cure its sting you should not catch it. If it bites you, its poison will kill you.' When asked as to what its cure was, he رَضِىَ اللّٰهُ تَعَالٰى عَنْهُ replied, 'To earn money by Ḥalāl means and spend it on what is Wājib [obligatory].'

5. Shaykh Sayyidunā 'Alā Bin Ziyād رَحْمَةُ اللّٰهِ تَعَالٰى عَلَيْه has stated, 'The world came to me in a beautiful and attractive form. I said, 'I ask refuge of Allah عَزَّوَجَلَّ from your evil.' It replied, 'If you want to protect yourself from me, you must hate wealth as it is by wealth that man enjoys all kinds of worldly comforts. One avoiding wealth may be able to stay away from the world.'

Sayyidunā Imām Muhammad Ghazālī عَلَيْهِ رَحْمَةُ اللّٰهِ الْوَالِى has quoted some Arabic couplets whose translation is as follows, '*I have found the secret and you should not also think about anything else. Do not assume that piety is in earning wealth. When you have forgone wealth though you could have taken it, then your piety will be considered the piety of a Muslim. Do not be impressed and deceived by the patches on someone's long shirt or with their pyjama above the ankles or with the mark of prostration on their forehead; instead, see if they love worldly wealth or stay away from it.*' *(Iḥyā-ul-'Ulūm, vol. 3, pp. 288)*

Ḥubb-e-dunyā say Tū bachā Yā Rab عَزَّوَجَلَّ
Apnā shaydā mujĥay banā Yā Rab عَزَّوَجَلَّ

Save me from love of the world, Yā Allah عَزَّوَجَلَّ
Make me Your devotee, Yā Allah عَزَّوَجَلَّ

11. An admirer of the Holy Prophet ﷺ

Dear Islamic brothers! اَلْحَمْدُلِلّٰہ عَزَّوَجَلَّ, Many instances have been observed where thieves and robbers were led to the right path by the blessed Madanī environment of Dawat-e-Islami. In order to properly function around the globe, Dawat-e-Islami has set up many Majālis [committees] all around the world, as part of its organizational structure. One of its many functional committees is 'Majlis-e-Rābiṭaĥ bil 'Ulamā wal Mashāikh[1]' which mostly consists of scholars. One of its members went to a famous religious academy known as Jāmi'aĥ Rāshīdiyaĥ in Pir Jo Goth, Bāb-ul-Islam, in the province of Sindh, Pakistan.

During the conversation with the Shaykh-ul-Ḥadīš, the contribution of Dawat-e-Islami in prisons came up. The honourable Shaykh-ul-Ḥadīš shared one of the splendid stories about Dawat-e-Islami's work in prisons, which he had personally experienced. Therefore, he stated that he knew a robber who was notorious in the suburbs of Pir Jo Goth (a village in the province of Sindh, Pakistan). The police raided so many times to arrest him but he often escaped. He was even apprehended many times but was released on account of his connections with influential people.

Eventually, he was apprehended for a crime in Bāb-ul-Madīnaĥ, Karachi, for which he was convicted and sent to prison. After serving his sentence, the robber came to visit the Shaykh. At first glance, the Shaykh could not recognize him, as he was always bareheaded and beardless. Now, his face was illuminating as he had grown a beard, and his head was gleaming as he was crowned with a green turban; showing extreme devotion and love for the Beloved and Blessed Prophet صَلَّى اللّٰه تَعَالٰى عَلَيْهِ وَاٰلِهٖ وَسَلَّم. Marks of prostration on his forehead were indicating his adherence to Ṣalāĥ.

Putting an end to the Shaykh's surprise, he said that he was blessed with joining Dawat-e-Islami during his imprisonment اَلْحَمْدُلِلّٰہ عَزَّوَجَلَّ. He further stated that with the efforts and help of Islamic brothers he was able to free himself from the shackles of sins, becoming an admirer of the Noble Prophet صَلَّى اللّٰه تَعَالٰى عَلَيْهِ وَاٰلِهٖ وَسَلَّم.

صَلُّوْا عَلَى الْحَبِيْب صَلَّى اللّٰهُ تَعَالٰى عَلٰى مُحَمَّد

---

[1] A public relation committee for creating and upholding ties with Islamic scholars. [Translator's Note]

12. Blisters on hands

Sayyidunā Suwayd Bin Ghaflaĥ رَضِیَ اللّٰہُ تَعَالٰی عَنْہُ has stated: I was once present in the court of Amīr-ul-Mūminīn Sayyidunā 'Alī Murtaḍā كَرَّمَ اللّٰهُ تَعَالٰى وَجْهَهُ الْكَرِيْم in the capital city of Kufa. He رَضِیَ اللّٰہُ تَعَالٰی عَنْہُ was served with barley-bread and a cup of milk. The bread was so dry and hard that he رَضِیَ اللّٰہُ تَعَالٰی عَنْہُ had to break it even by keeping it on his knees. Seeing this, I asked his maid Fiḍḍaĥ رَضِیَ اللّٰہُ تَعَالٰی عَنْہَا, 'Do you have no sympathy for him?' This bread has husk, you should sift the barley and make soft bread for him so that he would have no difficulty in breaking it.' Fiḍḍaĥ رَضِیَ اللّٰہُ تَعَالٰی عَنْہَا replied that Amīr-ul-Mūminīn كَرَّمَ اللّٰهُ تَعَالٰى وَجْهَهُ الْكَرِيْم had made her swear that she would never prepare bread for him with sifted barley.

Meanwhile, turning towards me, Amīr-ul-Mūminīn كَرَّمَ اللّٰهُ تَعَالٰى وَجْهَهُ الْكَرِيْم asked, 'O Ibn Ghaflaĥ! What were you saying to her?' I told him what I said to the maid, and then pleaded to him 'O Amīr-ul-Mūminīn كَرَّمَ اللّٰهُ تَعَالٰى وَجْهَهُ الْكَرِيْم, please have mercy on you and do not put yourself in difficulty.' He رَضِیَ اللّٰہُ تَعَالٰی عَنْہُ replied, 'O Ibn Ghaflaĥ! The Holy Prophet صَلَّى اللّٰهُ تَعَالٰى عَلَيْهِ وَاٰلِهٖ وَسَلَّم and his family neither ate wheat bread with satiation for three continuous days nor was bread ever made with sifted flour for them. Once I was extremely hungry in Madīnaĥ Munawwaraĥ, so I went out to look for some work [so that I could get something to eat]. On the way, I came across a lady who was in search of someone to soak some sand in water. I talked to her and she agreed to pay me a single date per bucket of water used for soaking sand. I poured sixteen buckets of water to soak that pile of sand. As a result of doing this, I got blisters on my hands. I took those dates to the Beloved and Blessed Prophet صَلَّى اللّٰهُ تَعَالٰى عَلَيْهِ وَاٰلِهٖ وَسَلَّم and told him the entire story. The Holy Prophet صَلَّى اللّٰهُ تَعَالٰى عَلَيْهِ وَاٰلِهٖ وَسَلَّم ate some of the dates.' *(Safīna-e-Nūḥ, vol. 1, pp. 99)*

May Allah عَزَّوَجَلَّ have mercy on them and forgive us without accountability for their sake!

صَلُّوْا عَلَى الْحَبِيْب صَلَّى اللّٰهُ تَعَالٰى عَلٰى مُحَمَّد

13. Softening heart

Dear Islamic brothers! Did you see that Amīr-ul-Mūminīn Sayyidunā 'Alī Murtaḍā كَرَّمَ اللّٰهُ تَعَالٰى وَجْهَهُ الْكَرِيْم had adopted a very simple and ascetic way of life. Despite facing hardship he رَضِیَ اللّٰہُ تَعَالٰی عَنْہُ never expressed even a single word of complaint. Like his food, his dress was also very simple. Once he رَضِیَ اللهُ تَعَالٰی عَنْهُ was asked as to why he رَضِیَ اللهُ تَعَالٰی عَنْهُ patched up his dress, he replied, 'يَخْشَعُ الْقَلْبُ وَيَقْتَدِى بِهِ الْمُؤْمِنُ' *this [act] softens the heart and a Muslim adopts it* (In other words, the heart of a Muslim should be soft). *(Ḥilyat-ul-Auliyā, vol. 1, pp. 124)*

14. Mending shoes

Sayyidunā 'Abdullāĥ Ibn 'Abbās رَضِیَ اللهُ تَعَالٰی عَنْهُمَا has narrated, 'Once I came to the court of Sayyidunā 'Alī Murtaḍā كَرَّمَ اللّٰهُ تَعَالٰى وَجْهَهُ الْكَرِيْم and found him mending his shoes. Noticing my amazement, he رَضِیَ اللهُ تَعَالٰی عَنْهُ told me that the Noble Prophet صَلَّى اللهُ تَعَالٰى عَلَيْهِ وَاٰلِهٖ وَسَلَّم would mend his blessed slippers and clothes and would allow another person to sit behind him whilst riding. *(Safīna-e-Nūḥ, vol. 1, pp. 98)*

May Allah عَزَّوَجَلَّ have mercy on them and forgive us without accountability for their sake!

15. Savoury Fālūdaĥ*

Once a savoury Fālūdaĥ was served to Amīr-ul-Mūminīn Sayyidunā 'Alī Murtaḍā كَرَّمَ اللّٰهُ تَعَالٰى وَجْهَهُ الْكَرِيْم. He رَضِیَ اللهُ تَعَالٰی عَنْهُ said, 'How tasty, colourful and fragrant it is! (But) I do not wish to make my Nafs habitual of the thing that it is not used to.' *(Ḥilyat-ul-Auliyā, vol. 1, pp. 123, Ḥadīš 247)*

May Allah عَزَّوَجَلَّ have mercy on them and forgive us without accountability for their sake!

Accountability in proportion to favour

Dear Islamic brothers! Countless accolades on the manner in which Amīr-ul-Mūminīn Sayyidunā 'Alī Murtaḍā كَرَّمَ اللّٰهُ تَعَالٰى وَجْهَهُ الْكَرِيْم subdued his Nafs! If only we also occasionally recall this faith-refreshing parable while eating ice cream or cold Fālūdaĥ or having cold drinks on our Nafs' demand!

Remember! The more one makes his Nafs habitual of luxuries, the more defiant and hedonistic his Nafs will be. When the electric fan was uninvented, people were still able to live without it, whereas now some cannot live without air conditioning in summer.

---

* A sub-continental drink with dry fruits etc. [Translator's Note]

Likewise, many of those accustomed to consuming fancy and luscious food usually turn into a bad mood if ever served with simple food. If the food is not to their liking, they even argue with the wife and the mother committing the major sin of hurting others. If you have ever made this mistake, you should instantly repent of it and sincerely apologize to the one you have hurt so that they forgive you. Otherwise, in case of Allah's displeasure, you may have to regret after death.

Remember! The more luxurious favour one enjoys in the world, the more accountable he will have to be on the Day of Judgement. Further, the accountability will be made on the basis of one's personal likes and dislikes. For example, if a person likes bread more than rice, then bread will be considered a big favour for him – thus [in this case] the accountability of bread will be more severe compared to rice and vice versa. This applies to everything. Allah عَزَّوَجَلَّ says in the Holy Quran:

ثُمَّ لَتُسْـَٔلُنَّ يَوْمَئِذٍ عَنِ النَّعِيْمِ ﴿۸﴾

Then, undoubtedly, you will surely be questioned about favours that day.

[Kanz-ul-Īmān (Translation of Quran)] (Part 30, Sūraĥ At-Takāšur, verse 8)

Favours and questioning on Judgement Day

Commenting on this verse, a renowned exegetist of the Quran, Muftī Aḥmad Yār Khān عَلَيْهِ رَحْمَةُ الْمَنَّان has stated: 'One will be questioned about each and every favour, whether it is a bodily favour or a spiritual one; whether it was obtained for meeting a need or satisfying a desire. Questions will also be asked regarding even cold water, shade of a tree and peaceful sleep. The word نَعِيْم [Na'īm] in the verse refers to the same. Aḥādīš also express the same meaning. [In short] The thing granted to one without him being deserving of it is a favour. Everything granted by Allah عَزَّوَجَلَّ is a favour whether it is bodily or spiritual one.'

He continues: 'There are two types of favours. One is 'Kasbī' and the other is 'Waĥbī.' 'Kasbī' favours are the ones that are obtained by our efforts; for example, wealth, rule etc., while 'Waĥbī' favours are simply granted by Allah عَزَّوَجَلَّ; like our body parts, the moon and the sun etc. Three questions will be asked regarding 'Kasbī' favours. First, how was it obtained? Second, how was it spent? Third, what gratitude was offered for it? The last two questions will be asked regarding 'Waĥbī' favours.' *(Nūr-ul-'Irfān, pp. 956)*

Lāj rakĥ lay gunaĥgāraun kī, nām Raḥmān ĥay Tayrā Yā Rab عَزَّوَجَلَّ
'Ayb mayray na kĥaul maḥshar mayn, nām Sattār ĥay Tayrā Yā Rab عَزَّوَجَلَّ
Bay-sabab bakhsh day na pūcĥ 'amal, nām Ghaffār ĥay Tayrā Yā Rab عَزَّوَجَلَّ

Forgive sinners as Your name is Raḥmān O Rab عَزَّوَجَلَّ,
Conceal my faults on the Day of Judgement as Your name is Sattār O Rab عَزَّوَجَلَّ
Forgive me without questioning as Your name is Ghaffār O Rab عَزَّوَجَلَّ

صَلُّوْا عَلَى الْحَبِيْب صَلَّى اللّٰهُ تَعَالٰی عَلٰی مُحَمَّد

Mubāḥ becomes worship

Dear Islamic brothers! If a righteous intention is made when doing a Mubāḥ act (i.e. the one that entails neither reward nor sin), that act turns into an act of reward. The more righteous intentions one makes the more reward he will reap provided the intention appertains to an act of the Hereafter. The famous book of Fiqĥ entitled '*Al-Ashbāĥ Wan-Naẓāir*' states, 'The case of Mubāḥ acts is based on intentions, if the purpose of carrying out those acts is to gain strength to worship Allah عَزَّوَجَلَّ, then that Mubāḥ act is considered worship.' *(Al-Ashbāĥ wan-Naẓāir, vol. 1, pp. 28)*

Mubāḥ deeds for pleasure

One should make as many righteous intentions as possible when doing Mubāḥ deeds (i.e. the ones that entail neither reward nor sin) or eating a Mubāḥ food so that one may reap many rewards. Though the person doing a Mubāḥ act just for pleasure (without any righteous intention) is not a sinner, Ḥujjat-ul-Islam Sayyidunā Imām Muhammad Ghazālī عَلَيْهِ رَحْمَةُ اللّٰهِ الْوَالِى has stated that such a person will be questioned and the one who would be argued with, in the matter of accountability, would be punished. Though the one enjoying Mubāḥ things in the world, won't be punished on the Judgement Day for doing so, his favours of the Hereafter will be reduced equal to the Mubāḥ things [he enjoyed in the world]. Ponder calmly! Isn't it a big loss to suffer reduction in the eternal favours of the Hereafter as a result of enjoying the fleeting and temporal things of the world! *(Iḥyā-ul-'Ulūm, vol. 5, pp. 98)*

Reduction by 100 parts in Hereafter

There is a matter of great concern for those who consume pizzas, fried foods, kebabs, fried turnovers, ice creams, cold drinks, delicious Fālūdaĥ, sweet beverages and other fancy foods as well as for those who desire to have palaces, spacious and huge houses, fancy and expensive attires and other luxuries of the world. Likewise, the healthy, the wealthy, the business tycoons and those seeking positions of authority should all ponder calmly.

Alas! It is stated in *Tażkira-tul-Auliyā* that Sayyidunā Fuḍayl Bin 'Iyāḍ رَحْمَةُ اللهِ تَعَالٰی عَلَیْه has said, 'When one is granted favour in the world, its 100 parts are reduced in the Hereafter. Its reason is that one would only reap in the Hereafter what he sowed in the world. Therefore, it's up to man whether to decrease or increase his favours in the Hereafter. Do not make a habit of using expensive attires and eating fancy foods in the world, for you will be deprived of these things on the day of resurrection.' *(Tażkira-tul-Auliyā, vol. 1, pp. 175)*

Ṣadaqaĥ Piyāray صَلَّى اللهُ تَعَالٰی عَلَیْهِ وَاٰلِہٖ وَسَلَّم *kī ḥayā kā kay na lay mujĥ say ḥisāb*
Bakhsh bay-pūchay lajāye ko lajānā kyā ĥay

For the sake of Your beloved صَلَّى اللهُ تَعَالٰی عَلَیْهِ وَاٰلِہٖ وَسَلَّم*, do not put me on accountability*
Forgive me without questioning; I am already grieved and guilty

Dear Islamic brothers! All the pleasures of the world will eventually come to an end. If only our greed comes to an end before we meet our death. Alas! The attractions of the treacherous world and the empty lives of its seekers! Let me tell you an admonitory incident. Is there anyone to learn a lesson from it!

16. Dance party was underway when...

It is said that on the 3rd of the holy month of Ramadan 1426 A.H. (October 8, 2005), in the Margalla Towers of Islamabad [Pakistan], some Muslims, who were the admirers of the western culture, were enjoying a drinking and dancing party. Leaving aside the honour of the holy month of Ramadan, they were partying with some non-Muslims. While these people were busy with these disgusting sins, oblivious of their doom, a horrifying earthquake suddenly struck the area, causing unimaginable destruction and putting an end to all their entertainment and merriment.

Yād rakĥo! Maut achānak āye gī
Sārī mastī khāk mayn mil jāye gī

Remember! Death will come unexpectedly
And all merriment will come to an end instantly

Earthquake occurs due to sins

My dear Islamic brothers! A'lā Ḥaḍrat, Imām-e-Aĥl-e-Sunnat, reviver of Sunnaĥ, eradicator of Bid'aĥ, scholar of Sharī'aĥ, guide of Ṭarīqaĥ, 'Allāmaĥ Maulānā Al-Ḥāj Al-Ḥāfiẓ Al-Qārī Ash-Shāĥ Imām Aḥmad Razā Khān عَلَيْهِ رَحْمَةُ الرَّحْمٰن has stated, 'The real cause (of an earthquake) is the sins of people.' *(Fatāwā Razawiyyaĥ (Jadīd), vol. 27, pp. 93)*

Alas! These days there is a severe storm of sins everywhere. People commit sins deliberately and fearlessly. Even worse, it seems as if there remains no place on the earth for those performing good deeds and acting upon Sunnaĥ. Alas! On Saturday Ramadan 3, 1426 A.H., October 8, 2005, several people were reported as committing different sins when a horrifying earthquake occurred devastating the eastern part of our dear country, Pakistan. Here are some stories experienced firsthand by the devotees of Rasūl who were travelling in Madanī Qāfilaĥ. Read and repent.

17. Living baby girl boiled in pressure cooker!

It is said that a person from an area of Kashmir had five daughters and the sixth baby was due. One day he told his wife, 'If you give birth to another baby girl, I will kill you along with the newborn.' On the third night of Ramadan, his wife gave birth to another baby girl. Enraged, the cruel man put his cute little alive newborn into a pressure cooker and turned it on, pushing away his screaming wife. Suddenly, the pressure cooker exploded and the horrifying earthquake occurred! That barbaric man was also buried alive. The injured mother of the girl was rescued, and this horrific incident was also probably disclosed by her.

صَلُّوْا عَلَى الْحَبِيْب صَلَّى اللّٰهُ تَعَالٰى عَلٰى مُحَمَّد
تُوْبُوْا اِلَى الله اَسْتَغْفِرُ الله
صَلُّوْا عَلَى الْحَبِيْب صَلَّى اللّٰهُ تَعَالٰى عَلٰى مُحَمَّد

18. A severed head

In the rubble of the earthquake-stricken Margalla Towers, Islamabad, [Pakistan] a head separated from its body was found but the body could not be discovered. Few people recognized the unfortunate person and revealed that he would turn up the volume of music when the sound of Ażān emanated from the Masjid.

Dear Islamic brothers! Except for a few parts of Punjab, this horrible earthquake caused major devastation in the western portion of Pakistan including Kashmir and Khyber Pakhtunkhwa. Hundreds of thousands of people died and countless were injured. Dawat-e-Islami is a non-political movement of Quran and Sunnaĥ. Several Madanī Qāfilaĥs of Dawat-e-Islami went missing in these earthquake stricken areas. They were all found alive afterwards. Read a delightful incident narrated by one of such Qāfilaĥs.

19. Blessings of writing 'يَا رَسُولَ اللّٰه ﷺ'

Seven Islamic brothers from Landhi area of Bāb-ul-Madīnaĥ, Karachi [Pakistan] travelled with a 30-day Madanī Qāfilaĥ. They have narrated their incident in these words: 'We were staying in Jāmi' Masjid Ghauŝiyyaĥ in Abbaspur in the Tehsil [district] Nakar Bala in Kashmir. On the 3rd of Ramadan 1426 A.H. (October 08, 2005) after offering the Ṣalāĥ of Fajr, Ishrāq and Chāsht, we were resting according to the Qāfilaĥ schedule.

All of a sudden, the Masjid began to rock with an intense tremor. All of us woke up and before we could fully get a grip on the matters, the two walls of the Masjid started to crumble with a loud uproar. May our lives be sacrificed on the slogan 'یَا رَسُوْلَ اللّٰه!' The southern wall of the Masjid, which had the words 'یَا رَسُوْلَ اللّٰه صَلَّى اللهُ تَعَالٰى عَلَيْهِ وَاٰلِهٖ وَسَلَّم' inscribed on it, did not fall. The roof fell and rested at an angle against this wall. اَلْحَمْدُ لِلّٰه عَزَّوَجَلَّ, We were barely saved and managed to come out of the rubble alive.

Houses had been demolished all around. Pleas of the injured echoed in the air. People were trapped under the rubble. Several had passed away, while many others were taking their last breaths. We joined the locals and started the rescue efforts. We were able to rescue a one and a half year old baby girl from under the wreckage. [Even in such circumstances,] we managed to offer funeral prayers of several martyrs and took part in their burial. اَلْحَمْدُ لِلّٰه عَزَّوَجَلَّ, Despite the havoc, the locals' appreciation for Dawat-e-Islami was admirable.

Yā Rasūlallāĥ صَلَّى اللهُ تَعَالٰى عَلَيْهِ وَاٰلِهٖ وَسَلَّم *kay na'ray say ĥam ko piyār ĥay*
Jis nay yeĥ na'raĥ lagāyā us kā bayřā pār ĥay

'Yā Rasūlallāĥ صَلَّى اللهُ تَعَالٰى عَلَيْهِ وَاٰلِهٖ وَسَلَّم*', this slogan we love indeed*
Whoever proclaims this; will succeed

صَلُّوْا عَلَى الْحَبِيْب صَلَّى اللهُ تَعَالٰى عَلٰى مُحَمَّد

20. Difficult valley

Sayyidunā Abū Dardā رَضِیَ اللهُ تَعَالٰى عَنْهُ was once sitting with his friends. His wife came and said, 'You are sitting here with these people', by Allah عَزَّوَجَلَّ, we don't even have a fistful of flour in our home.' He رَضِیَ اللهُ تَعَالٰى عَنْهُ replied, 'Why do you forget that we have to face a difficult valley which can only be passed by those who have light weights.' Hearing this, she gladly went back. *(Rauḍ-ur-Riyāḥīn, pp. 110)*

May Allah عَزَّوَجَلَّ have mercy on them and forgive us without accountability for their sake!

صَلُّوْا عَلَى الْحَبِيْب صَلَّى اللهُ تَعَالٰى عَلٰى مُحَمَّد

We should not complain

Dear Islamic brothers! Did you see! How content Sayyidunā Abū Dardā رَضِیَ اللهُ تَعَالٰی عَنْه was, and how obedient his wife was! Hearing an ascetic reply from her husband, she returned home happily. She did not complain despite having nothing to eat at home. Instead of complaining about poverty and domestic problems, one should always implore Allah عَزَّوَجَلَّ and try to be content with His will.

Zabān per shikwa-e-ranj-o-alam lāyā naĥīn kartay;
Nabī صَلَّى اللهُ تَعَالٰى عَلَيْهِ وَاٰلِهٖ وَسَلَّم *kay nām laywā gham say ĝhabrāyā naĥīn kartay*

Tongues never complain under distress
Prophets' followers don't take stress

صَلُّوْا عَلَى الْحَبِيْب صَلَّى اللهُ تَعَالٰى عَلٰى مُحَمَّد

21. Du'ā of the distressed

A man once requested a saint رَحْمَةُ اللهِ تَعَالٰى عَلَيْه, 'I am extremely worried as I cannot manage to provide for my family. Make Du'ā for me.' The saint رَحْمَةُ اللهِ تَعَالٰى عَلَيْه replied, 'Whenever your family complains that they have no bread and food to eat, pray to Allah عَزَّوَجَلَّ at that time, as the prayer made at that time is more likely to be answered.' *(Rauḍ-ur-Riyāḥīn, pp. 11)*

Dear Islamic brothers! Obviously, those suffering intense destitution will be highly grieved and distressed, and the Du'ā of the distressed is accepted. On page 111 of his book entitled '*Aḥsan-ul-Wi'ā lī Ādāb-id-Du'ā*', Shaykh Maulānā Naqī 'Alī Khān عَلَيْهِ رَحْمَةُ الْمَنَّان has listed the types of people whose Du'ā is accepted. The very first in this list is 'a distressed person' (i.e. one who is sad due to worries). Elaborating on this, Imām Aḥmad Razā Khān عَلَيْهِ رَحْمَةُ الرَّحْمٰن has annotated in footnote on the same page, 'A Quranic verse also states that the Du'ā of the grieved and the helpless is accepted.'

اَمَّنْ يُّجِيْبُ الْمُضْطَرَّ اِذَا دَعَاهُ وَ يَكْشِفُ السُّوْٓءَ

Or He عَزَّوَجَلَّ Who answers the prayer of the helpless when he invokes Him and removes the evil.

[Kanz-ul-Īmān (Translation of Quran)] (Part 20, Sūraĥ An-Naml, verse 62)

22. Welcome! O starvation!

A pious person's family once complained to him, 'We have nothing to eat tonight.' He replied, 'Can even we have such a status in the court of Allah عَزَّوَجَلَّ that He عَزَّوَجَلَّ blesses us with starvation! He عَزَّوَجَلَّ grants this status to His friends [Auliyā رَحِمَهُمُ اللّٰهُ تَعَالٰی].'

The pious person goes onto say, 'Some of our saints were in such a state that when they faced starvation they would say, 'Welcome! O the trait of the pious!' (In other words, they would welcome poverty and starvation as these are the traits of the friends of Allah عَزَّوَجَلَّ).
(Rauḍ-ur-Riyāḥīn, pp. 11)

Woĥ 'ishq-e-ḥaqīqī kī lażżat naĥīn pā saktā
Jo ranj-o-muṣībat say dauchār naĥīn ĥotā

Those who do not encounter tribulations and anxiety
Cannot attain the real pleasure of love of Almighty

Leave unnecessary worries aside

Dear Islamic brothers! The foregoing parable contains considerable lesson for such impatient people who obsess about unnecessary worries of the world. Despite the fact that their daughters are very young they worry and agonize over their weddings. They deprive themselves of performing Hajj despite it being Farḍ on them giving the lame excuse that they would first fulfil the 'Farḍ' of their daughters' marriage! Life has no guarantee. No one knows if they will live to see their daughter's wedding. Further, it is also not certain whether their daughters shall climb up the stairs of youth or will meet their death before getting married.

Alas! Several people depart from this world yearning for the materialistic possessions without making preparations for the betterment of their Hereafter. Muslims should be courageous and have trust [in Allah عَزَّوَجَلَّ]. We are worried about the matters of the world, whereas the Creator of the world is our Sustainer.

Dear Islamic brothers! There have been such patient servants of Allah who willingly adopted afflictions. They possessed such high status in the court of Allah عَزَّوَجَلَّ that they considered it inappropriate even to make Du'ā for the removal of their afflictions.

23. A strange patient

Sayyidunā Yūnus عَلٰی نَبِیِّنَا وَعَلَیْهِ الصَّلٰوةُ وَالسَّلَام once told angel Jibrāīl عَلَیْهِ السَّلَام that he wished to see the greatest worshipper of the world. Angel Jibrāīl عَلَیْهِ السَّلَام took him to a person whose arms and legs had severely decayed and separated from the body because of leprosy. Despite being in such a condition, the man uttered these words, 'Yā Allah عَزَّوَجَلَّ! You benefitted me from these body parts as long as You willed, and took them back when You willed. I pinned all my hopes on Your mercy. O my Creator! The attainment of Your pleasure is the only aim of mine.'

Sayyidunā Yūnus عَلٰی نَبِیِّنَا وَعَلَیْهِ الصَّلٰوةُ وَالسَّلَام said 'O Jibrāīl عَلَیْهِ السَّلَام! I asked you to take me to the person who offers Ṣalāĥ and fasts abundantly.' Angel Jibrāīl عَلَیْهِ السَّلَام replied, 'He was a worshipper of the same attributes before being afflicted with this adversity [and ailment]. Now I have been ordered to take away even his eyes.' Therefore, Jibrāīl عَلَیْهِ السَّلَام pointed a finger at his eyes, causing them to come out of their sockets. But still that man uttered the same words, 'Yā Allah عَزَّوَجَلَّ! You benefitted me from these eyes as long as You willed, and took them back when you willed. O my Creator! I pinned all my hopes on Your mercy. The attainment of Your pleasure is the only aim of mine.'

Sayyidunā Jibrāīl عَلَیْهِ السَّلَام then suggested the worshipper, 'Let's make Du'ā together that Allah عَزَّوَجَلَّ bless you with eyes and limbs so that you worship Allah عَزَّوَجَلَّ like before.' The man replied, 'Not at all!' Jibrāīl عَلَیْهِ السَّلَام asked, 'But why not?' The man responded, 'If my Allah عَزَّوَجَلَّ is pleased with this [state] of mine, then I don't need health.' Sayyidunā Yūnus عَلٰی نَبِیِّنَا وَعَلَیْهِ الصَّلٰوةُ وَالسَّلَام commented, 'Indeed, I have not seen a greater worshipper than this man.' Sayyidunā Jibrāīl عَلَیْهِ السَّلَام remarked, 'There is no path better than this for seeking the pleasure of Allah عَزَّوَجَلَّ.' *(Rauḍ-ur-Riyāḥīn, pp. 155)*

May Allah عَزَّوَجَلَّ have mercy on them and forgive us without accountability for their sake!

Jay Sauĥnā mayray dukĥ vich rāzī
Mayn sukĥ nū chullĥay pāvān

If my Allah عَزَّوَجَلَّ is pleased with my adversity
Then I don't need tranquillity

Blessing of hiding adversity

Dear Islamic brothers! Did you see the high level patience of that saint رَحْمَةُ اللهِ تَعَالٰى عَلَيْه? Despite suffering such intense bodily afflictions, he maintained patience. Even after losing his eyes his patience did not relent at all. He was at a high rank of being 'content with the divine will.' He was not even willing to ask Allah عَزَّوَجَلَّ for a cure. His mindset was that if Allah عَزَّوَجَلَّ has willed to make him ill then he did not want to be cured. سُبْحٰنَ اللّٰه عَزَّوَجَلَّ, This was indeed his unique trait. Such people have asserted نَحْنُ نَفْرَحُ بِالْبَلَآءِ كَمَا يَفْرَحُ اَهْلُ الدُّنْيَا بِالنِّعَمِ, that is, '*We are as pleased with receiving adversities and calamities as the materialistic people are pleased with receiving worldly fortunes.*'

Remember! Sometimes, adversity is mercy for a Muslim as it provides an opportunity for him to be patient and reap great reward with an entry into Paradise without accountability. Hence, Sayyidunā Ibn 'Abbās رَضِىَ اللهُ تَعَالٰى عَنْهُ has narrated that the Prophet of Raḥmaĥ, the Intercessor of Ummaĥ صَلَّى اللهُ تَعَالٰى عَلَيْهِ وَاٰلِهٖ وَسَلَّم has stated, 'The one who suffered a trouble in his wealth or life, and then hid it and did not reveal it to people, Allah عَزَّوَجَلَّ has a right to forgive him.' *(Majma'-uz-Zawāid, vol. 10, pp. 450, Ḥadīš 17872)*

It is narrated in another Ḥadīš, 'Whatever adversity a Muslim faces due to ailment, worry, sadness, harm or grief, even if he is pricked by a thorn, Allah عَزَّوَجَلَّ makes this [adversity] an atonement [Kaffāraĥ] for his sins.' *(Ṣaḥīḥ Bukhārī, vol. 4, pp. 3, Ḥadīš 5641)*

Chup karsīn tān mautī milsan, ṣabr karay tān ĥīray
Pā galān wāngaun raulā pāvyn nā mautī nā ĥīray

If you are silent, gem is what you attain
If you are patient, pearl is what you gain
Like the insane, if you cry and complain
Neither pearls nor gems, you obtain

صَلُّوْا عَلَى الْحَبِيْب صَلَّى اللهُ تَعَالٰى عَلٰى مُحَمَّد

24. Narrative of donating reward to Sayyidatunā 'Āishaĥ رَضِیَ اللہ عَنۡھَا

Imām Rabbānī Shaykh Mujaddid Alf Šānī قُدِّسَ سِرُّہُ الرَّبَّانِی has stated, 'Whenever I cooked food I would make its Īṣāl-e-Šawāb to the blessed souls of the Holy Prophet صَلَّی اللہ تَعَالٰی عَلَیۡہِ وَاٰلِہٖ وَسَلَّم and Amīr-ul-Mūminīn Sayyidunā 'Alī Murtaḍā کَرَّمَ اللّٰہُ تَعَالٰی وَجۡھَہُ الۡکَرِیۡم. Likewise, I would also make Īṣāl-e-Šawāb to Sayyidatunā Fāṭima-tuz-Zaĥrā رَضِیَ اللہ تَعَالٰی عَنۡھَا, Imām Ḥasan and Imām Ḥusayn رَضِیَ اللہ تَعَالٰی عَنۡھُمَا but I did not use to mention the names of Ummuĥa-tul-Mūminīn[1] رَضِیَ اللّٰہُ تَعَالٰی عَنۡھُنَّ.

One night, I had a dream in which I saw the Noble Prophet صَلَّی اللہ تَعَالٰی عَلَیۡہِ وَاٰلِہٖ وَسَلَّم. Approaching him I made Salām to him but he صَلَّی اللہ تَعَالٰی عَلَیۡہِ وَاٰلِہٖ وَسَلَّم did not pay attention to me and turned his blessed face from me. He صَلَّی اللہ تَعَالٰی عَلَیۡہِ وَاٰلِہٖ وَسَلَّم then said to me, 'I eat food at the house of 'Āishaĥ (Ṣiddīqaĥ). Whoever wants to send me food should send it to her house.' I immediately understood that the Holy Prophet صَلَّی اللہ تَعَالٰی عَلَیۡہِ وَاٰلِہٖ وَسَلَّم did not pay attention to me because I do not make Īṣāl-e-Šawāb to Umm-ul-Mūminīn Sayyidatunā 'Āishaĥ Ṣiddīqaĥ رَضِیَ اللہ تَعَالٰی عَنۡھَا. Thereafter, I began to include the name of 'Āishaĥ Ṣiddīqaĥ رَضِیَ اللہ تَعَالٰی عَنۡھَا and those of all other Ummuĥa-tul-Mūminīn رَضِیَ اللّٰہُ تَعَالٰی عَنۡھُنَّ as well as those of all the members of the Prophet's blessed household. I also now make Du'ā to Allah عَزَّوَجَلَّ by their sake.'
(Maktūbāt, vol. 2, pp. 85)

May Allah عَزَّوَجَلَّ have mercy on them and forgive us without accountability for their sake!

One should donate reward to all Muslims

Dear Islamic brothers! The foregoing parable makes it clear that the reward donated to someone actually reaches him. Further, we have also learnt that instead of donating reward to a selected few saints, we should send it to all the Muslims. Everyone we donate the reward to, will get complete reward and our reward will not be reduced either.

Furthermore, we have also learnt that Sayyidatunā 'Āishaĥ Ṣiddīqaĥ رَضِیَ اللہ تَعَالٰی عَنۡھَا is very dear to our Noble Prophet صَلَّی اللہ تَعَالٰی عَلَیۡہِ وَاٰلِہٖ وَسَلَّم. When returning from 'Ghazwaĥ[2] Salāsil', Sayyidunā 'Amr Bin 'Āṣ رَضِیَ اللہ تَعَالٰی عَنۡہُ asked, 'Yā Rasūlallāĥ صَلَّی اللہ تَعَالٰی عَلَیۡہِ وَاٰلِہٖ وَسَلَّم who do you like the most amongst people?' The Holy Prophet صَلَّی اللہ تَعَالٰی عَلَیۡہِ وَاٰلِہٖ وَسَلَّم replied, 'Āishaĥ رَضِیَ اللہ تَعَالٰی عَنۡھَا',

---

[1] The honourable wives of the Holy Prophet صَلَّی اللہ تَعَالٰی عَلَیۡہِ وَاٰلِہٖ وَسَلَّم.

[2] A battle in which Rasūlullāĥ صَلَّی اللہ تَعَالٰی عَلَیۡہِ وَاٰلِہٖ وَسَلَّم was present. [Translator's Notes]

he then asked, 'And amongst men?' The Beloved and Blessed Prophet صَلَّى اللّٰه تَعَالٰى عَلَيْهِ وَاٰلِهٖ وَسَلَّم replied, 'Her father (Sayyidunā Abū Bakr رَضِىَ اللّٰه تَعَالٰى عَنْهُ).' *(Ṣaḥīḥ Bukhārī, vol. 2, pp. 519, Ḥadīš 3662)*

صَلُّوْا عَلَى الْحَبِيْب صَلَّى اللّٰهُ تَعَالٰى عَلٰى مُحَمَّد

25. Old lady's faith-refreshing dream

اَلْحَمْدُ لِلّٰه عَزَّوَجَلَّ, Those associated with Dawat-e-Islami are showered with the rain of Allah's mercy. The area-visit to call people towards righteousness has exceptional blessings. Here is an incident of an Islamic brother from Birmingham (UK). He has reported that once, to call people towards righteousness, they were visiting the area 'Small Heath' called 'Makkī Ḥalqah' in the Madanī environment. This area has an extensive Muslim population.

During their visit, while they were going from house to house, they knocked on a door. An elderly lady answered who was originally from Mirpur (Kashmir) and was unable to understand Urdu and English. Therefore, the Islamic brothers bowed their heads down and presented the call to righteousness in Punjabi, her native language, with a request to send the men of her house to the Masjid. She then asked them to listen to her. The Islamic brothers were pressed for time so they all moved along, except for one brother who stayed back. She said, 'Few days ago, I had a blessed dream in which I saw the Beloved and Blessed Prophet صَلَّى اللّٰه تَعَالٰى عَلَيْهِ وَاٰلِهٖ وَسَلَّم come out of the Masjid-un-Nabawī عَلٰى صَاحِبِهَا الصَّلٰوةُ وَالسَّلَام. He صَلَّى اللّٰه تَعَالٰى عَلَيْهِ وَاٰلِهٖ وَسَلَّم was surrounded by several men who were all wearing green turbans. It is Allah's grace that today men with green turbans have come to my home for the call to righteousness.' She was then invited to attend the Islamic sisters' weekly Sunnaĥ-Inspiring Ijtimā'. Now she regularly attends the Ijtimā' with other ladies of her family.

Ĥayn ghulāmaun kay jĥurmaṫ mayn Badruddujā صَلَّى اللّٰه تَعَالٰى عَلَيْهِ وَاٰلِهٖ وَسَلَّم
Nūr ĥī Nūr ĥar sū Madīnay mayn ĥay

Surrounded by devotees is the Holy Prophet صَلَّى اللّٰه تَعَالٰى عَلَيْهِ وَاٰلِهٖ وَسَلَّم
Nūr has prevailed everywhere in Madīnaĥ

صَلُّوْا عَلَى الْحَبِيْب صَلَّى اللّٰهُ تَعَالٰى عَلٰى مُحَمَّد

Madanī revolution among Islamic sisters

Dear Islamic brothers! Did you see the benevolence of our Noble Prophet صَلَّى اللهُ تَعَالٰى عَلَيْهِ وَاٰلِهٖ وَسَلَّم for those associated with Dawat-e-Islami? اَلْحَمْدُلِلّٰه عَزَّوَجَلَّ, The Madanī work of Dawat-e-Islami has flourished not only among Islamic brothers but also among Islamic sisters.

اَلْحَمْدُلِلّٰه عَزَّوَجَلَّ, Millions of Islamic sisters have accepted the Madanī message of Dawat-e-Islami. Countless women who used to lead their lives according to the latest fashions have not only repented of their sins but have also become the devotees of Ummuĥa-tul-Mūminīn رَضِىَ اللهُ تَعَالٰى عَنْهُنَّ and of the Holy Prophet's daughter, Sayyidatunā Fāṭimaĥ رَضِىَ اللهُ تَعَالٰى عَنْهَا. Those who used to visit shopping malls, entertainment centres, night clubs and cinema theatres immodestly with just a scarf around their necks, have made Madanī Burqa'[1] an inseparable part of their dress, following in the footsteps of the great and modest ladies of the Karbalā incident.

اَلْحَمْدُلِلّٰه عَزَّوَجَلَّ, Several Madāris-ul-Madīnaĥ [for girls] have been established where girls and Islamic sisters are memorizing the Holy Quran and learning its proper recitation free of cost. Likewise, several Jāmi'a-tul-Madīnaĥ[2] have also been established where Islamic sisters are becoming scholars. اَلْحَمْدُ لِلّٰه عَزَّوَجَلَّ, The number of female memorizers of the Quran and Madanī scholars are on the rise, in the environment of Dawat-e-Islami.

Mayrī jis qadar ĥayn beĥnayn, sabĥī Madanī Burqa' peĥnayn;
Inĥayn nayk tum banānā Madanī Madīnay wālay صَلَّى اللهُ تَعَالٰى عَلَيْهِ وَاٰلِهٖ وَسَلَّم

May all my sisters wear the Madanī Burqa'
Make them pious, O the Prophet of Allah

صَلُّوْا عَلَى الْحَبِيْب   صَلَّى اللهُ تَعَالٰى عَلٰى مُحَمَّد

---

[1] Madanī Burqa' is a loose black robe that covers the body from over the head to toe.

[2] An institution for learning Islamic sciences run by Dawat-e-Islami. [Translator's Notes]

26. Amazing handkerchief

Sayyidunā 'Ubbād Bin 'Abduṣ Ṣamad رضی اللہ تعالی عنہ has narrated, 'One day we went to the house of Sayyidunā Anas Bin Mālik رضی اللہ تعالی عنہ. He asked his maid to lay down the dining-mat and bring the handkerchief. The handkerchief she brought needed to be washed. He رضی اللہ تعالی عنہ instructed her to put it into fire. Therefore, she put the handkerchief into fire. After a little while, when it was taken out of fire it was as white as milk.

Amazed, we asked, 'What is the secret in this?' Sayyidunā Anas رضی اللہ تعالی عنہ replied, 'This is the handkerchief that the Prophet of Raḥmaĥ, the Intercessor of Ummaĥ, the Owner of Jannaĥ صَلَّی اللہ تعالی علیہ والہ وسلم would wipe his luminous face with. Whenever we need to wash it, we just put it into fire like this, because anything that touches the blessed faces of the Noble Prophets علیہم السلام cannot be burned by fire.' *(Al-Khaṣāiṣ-ul-Kubrā, vol. 2, pp. 134)*

May Allah عزوجل have mercy on them and forgive us without accountability for their sake!

صَلُّوْا عَلَی الْحَبِیْب صَلَّی اللہُ تَعَالٰی عَلٰی مُحَمَّد

Dear Islamic brothers! As regards this great parable Maulānā Rūm علیہ رحمۃ القیوم has stated in his '*Mašnawī Sharīf*',

Ay dil-e-tar sindaĥ az nār-o-'ażāb
Bā chunā dast-o-lab-e-kun iqtarāb
Chūn jamāway rā chunā tashrīf dād
Jān-e-'āshiq rā chaĥā khawāĥad kashād

O heart, who fears the punishment of Hell, why do you not get near the holy hands?
That made a lifeless handkerchief so great that even the fire could not burn it
So why will Hell touch the one who truly loves him?

Āqā صَلَّی اللہ تعالی علیہ والہ وسلم *kā gadā ĥūn ay jaĥannam! Tū bĥī sun lay*
Woĥ kaysay jalay jo kay ghulām-e-Madanī ĥo

O Hell, know that I am a slave of the Holy Prophet
How can he be burnt who is a slave of the Noble Prophet

27. Abū Ĥurayraĥ's رَضِیَ اللّٰہ عَنۡهُ provisions for journey

Sayyidunā Abū Ĥurayraĥ رَضِیَ اللّٰہُ تَعَالٰی عَنۡهُ has stated, 'During a Ghazwaĥ, the Muslim army had nothing to eat. The Prophet of mankind, the Peace of our heart and mind, the most Generous and Kind صَلَّی اللّٰہُ تَعَالٰی عَلَیۡهِ وَاٰلِهٖ وَسَلَّم asked me, 'Do you have anything?' I said that I had some dates in my bag. He صَلَّی اللّٰہُ تَعَالٰی عَلَیۡهِ وَاٰلِهٖ وَسَلَّم asked me to bring the bag. I brought it. There were 21 dates in the bag. The Noble Prophet صَلَّی اللّٰہُ تَعَالٰی عَلَیۡهِ وَاٰلِهٖ وَسَلَّم put his blessed hand over them and made Du'ā. He صَلَّی اللّٰہُ تَعَالٰی عَلَیۡهِ وَاٰلِهٖ وَسَلَّم then said, 'Call ten people.' I called ten people, they came and ate till they were satiated and left. Again, I was ordered to call ten people, they also ate and left.

In groups of ten, people continued to come and eat to their satiation and then leave until the whole army ate. Thereafter, pointing towards the remaining dates he صَلَّی اللّٰہُ تَعَالٰی عَلَیۡهِ وَاٰلِهٖ وَسَلَّم said, 'O Abū Ĥurayraĥ رَضِیَ اللّٰہُ تَعَالٰی عَنۡهُ, put them in your bag and eat from it whenever you like, but do not empty out the bag.' Sayyidunā Abū Ĥurayraĥ رَضِیَ اللّٰہُ تَعَالٰی عَنۡهُ goes onto say, 'I ate dates from that bag not only in the time of the Holy Prophet صَلَّی اللّٰہُ تَعَالٰی عَلَیۡهِ وَاٰلِهٖ وَسَلَّم but also in the reign of Sayyidunā Abū Bakr Ṣiddīq, Sayyidunā 'Umar Fārūq A'ẓam and Sayyidunā 'Ušmān Ghanī رَضِیَ اللّٰہُ تَعَالٰی عَنۡهُم. In addition to distributing dates among people, I also gave about fifty Wasq of dates in the path of Allah and ate more than two hundred Wasq of dates myself. When Sayyidunā 'Ušmān Ghanī رَضِیَ اللّٰہُ تَعَالٰی عَنۡهُ was martyred that bag was stolen from my home.' *(Al-Khaṣāiṣ-ul-Kubrā, vol. 2, pp. 85)*

May Allah عَزَّوَجَلَّ have mercy on them and forgive us without accountability for their sake!

صَلُّوۡا عَلَی الۡحَبِیۡب   صَلَّی اللّٰہُ تَعَالٰی عَلٰی مُحَمَّد

Dear Islamic brothers! A Wasq is equivalent to sixty Ṣā' and one Ṣā' is equal to 270 Tola[1]. In other words, from those twenty one dates, nearly 40000 kilograms of dates were eaten. This is all Allah's gracious bounty that He عَزَّوَجَلَّ has bestowed upon His Beloved and Blessed Prophet صَلَّی اللّٰہُ تَعَالٰی عَلَیۡهِ وَاٰلِهٖ وَسَلَّم so many powers and great miracles. Indeed our Holy Prophet صَلَّی اللّٰہُ تَعَالٰی عَلَیۡهِ وَاٰلِهٖ وَسَلَّم possesses great and glorious status. By his blessings, his devotees are also given many powers. Hence, here is an incident about a saintly miracle

[1] Tola is a weighing unit used in the sub continent. It is approximately 12 grams. [Translator's Note]

of Ṣadr-ul-Afāḍil Sayyid Muhammad Na'īmuddīn Murādābādī عَلَيْهِ رَحْمَةُ اللّٰهِ الْهَادِى who was the Khalīfaĥ of Imām-e-Aĥl-e-Sunnat, Maulānā Shāĥ Imām Aḥmad Razā Khān عَلَيْهِ رَحْمَةُ الرَّحْمٰن

28. Saintly miracle of Sayyid Muhammad Na'īmuddīn Murādābādī عَلَيْهِ رَحْمَةُ الْهَادِى

Maulānā Manẓūr Aḥmad Ghauswī عَلَيْهِ رَحْمَةُ اللّٰهِ الْقَوِى has narrated that Shaykh Sayyid Muhammad Na'īmuddīn Murādābādī عَلَيْهِ رَحْمَةُ اللّٰهِ الْهَادِى, a renowned exegetist of the Quran, would regularly offer Ṣalāt-ul-Fajr with Jamā'at in a local Masjid. Before he went to the Masjid, a big tea pot would be placed over fire for making tea. The tea would be ready on his return.

A large number of people would come to meet him. Usually, there would be almost 50 to 200 people in the gathering. Occasionally, the room and its adjacent hall would overflow with disciples and devotees. As soon as he entered and sat down in the room he would be served with a cup of tea and a biscuit which he would pass to the first person sitting to his right with his own hands. He would pass almost four to six cups in this manner and would let the servants serve the rest. All the attendees would eat and so would the Shaykh رَحْمَةُ اللّٰهِ تَعَالٰی عَلَيْه. This was the Shaykh's breakfast; a cup of tea and a biscuit. Shaykh Maulānā Sayyid Manẓūr Aḥmad رَحْمَةُ اللّٰهِ تَعَالٰی عَلَيْه has asserted that one pot of tea would be sufficient for all the attendees whether they would be in large number or in small. It never happened that more tea had to be prepared in case of the arrival of more people.

It is evident from this incident that this is indeed one of the many daily saintly miracles of Shaykh Sayyid Muhammad Na'īmuddīn Murādābādī عَلَيْهِ رَحْمَةُ اللّٰهِ الْهَادِى. *(Tārīkh-e-Islam kī 'Aẓīm Shakhṣiyyat Ṣadr-ul-Afāḍil, pp. 333-334)*

May Allah عَزَّوَجَلَّ have mercy on them and forgive us without accountability for their sake!

Ĥamayn ay 'Aṭṭār sunnī 'ālimaun say piyār ĥay
اِنْ شَآءَاللّٰه عَزَّوَجَلَّ *Do jaĥān mayn apnā bayřā pār ĥay*

O 'Aṭṭār! We love Sunnī scholars indeed
اِنْ شَآءَاللّٰه عَزَّوَجَلَّ*, In both worlds, we will succeed*

صَلُّوْا عَلَى الْحَبِيْب صَلَّى اللّٰهُ تَعَالٰى عَلٰى مُحَمَّد

29. The disabled should get share

Ḥakīm Muhammad Ashraf Qādirī Chishtī from Sardārābād (Faisalabad) has stated, 'I had got married long ago but was not yet blessed with children. I consulted many doctors, tried different medicines, recited many invocations and made a lot of supplications, but I was still childless. One day, I requested the honourable grand Muḥaddiš of Pakistan Sayyidunā Maulānā Sardār Aḥmad Khān عَلَيْهِ رَحْمَةُ الرَّحْمٰن to make Du'ā for me.

A few days later, my neighbour Chaudĥrī 'Abdul Ghafūr told me that he had seen an honourable Shaykh رَحْمَةُ اللهِ تَعَالٰى عَلَيْه in his dream during the last three nights. He also saw me stand along with the Shaykh رَحْمَةُ اللهِ تَعَالٰى عَلَيْه with a baby boy in my lap. The Shaykh رَحْمَةُ اللهِ تَعَالٰى عَلَيْه told my neighbour in the state of dream that Ḥakīm should give a goat in Ṣadaqaĥ (charity) from which a share should be given to the disabled. Hence, I mentioned this dream to the honourable Shaykh Sardār Aḥmad Khān عَلَيْهِ رَحْمَةُ الرَّحْمٰن and expressed my intention to sacrifice a goat and give it to the Jāmi'aĥ Razawiyyaĥ (the Islamic university used to be supervised by the honourable Shaykh Sardār Aḥmad Khān عَلَيْهِ رَحْمَةُ الرَّحْمٰن). He رَحْمَةُ اللهِ تَعَالٰى عَلَيْه replied, 'O Mr. Ḥakīm! By the grace of Allah عَزَّوَجَلَّ many sacrificial goats are brought here. It is better that you cook meat and bread at your home on Friday, recite Fātiḥaĥ and distribute the food amongst the poor, after Ṣalāt-ul-Jumu'aĥ. Both you and your wife eat this food and the disabled should also be given a share from it.'

The noteworthy point here is that while informing the honourable Shaykh Sardār Aḥmad Khān عَلَيْهِ رَحْمَةُ الرَّحْمٰن about the dream, I made no mention of the share of the disabled. The honourable Shaykh رَحْمَةُ اللهِ تَعَالٰى عَلَيْه mentioned it himself [out of his own awareness] and this was indeed a saintly miracle of him that he himself informed me of Ghayb! Therefore, I did what Shaykh رَحْمَةُ اللهِ تَعَالٰى عَلَيْه asked me to. Later on, by the grace of Allah عَزَّوَجَلَّ and by the blessing of the Du'ā of the honourable grand Muḥaddiš of Pakistan عَلَيْهِ رَحْمَةُ الْمَنَّان I was blessed with a baby boy.' *(Ḥayāt-e-Muḥaddiš-e-A'ẓam, pp. 260)*

صَلُّوا عَلَى الْحَبِيب صَلَّى اللّٰهُ تَعَالٰى عَلٰى مُحَمَّد

30. Name can also work wonders

Dear Islamic brothers! The teacher of scholars, spiritual guide, spiritual successor of A'lā Ḥaḍrat his Excellency the grand Muḥaddiš of Pakistan Maulānā Sardār Aḥmad Qādirī Chishtī عَلَيْهِ رَحْمَةُ اللّٰهِ الْقَوِى was an erudite scholar. Many renowned scholars graduated under his guidance. Many saintly miracles are reported to have taken place from him.

Hence, Maulānā Karam Dīn (Khaṭīb[1] of Masjid Chuck Number 356 GB) has stated, 'Once I had to travel to Sharaqpur to purchase a bull. On the way, I suffered from migraine (i.e. severe headache confined to one side of the head). I finally reached Sharaqpur where I discovered that both the honourable sons (of the deceased saint of Sharaqpur) had gone for Hajj. While returning, the pain became severe. I was in a state of misery and helplessness. As I was walking along the bank of the river, I came across a piece of paper. Picking it up, I wrote the name of the grand Muḥaddiš of Pakistan Maulānā Sardār Aḥmad Qādirī Chishtī عَلَيْهِ رَحْمَةُ اللّٰهِ الْقَوِى on it. I then tied this Ta'wīż [amulet] to the painful area. اَلْحَمْدُ لِلّٰه عَزَّوَجَلَّ, The pain was immediately relieved, and I became well.' *(Ḥayāt-e-Muḥaddiš-e-A'ẓam, pp. 261)*

31. Tube light obeyed

Dear Islamic brothers! One whose name is so blessed, how blessed would be his words! Here is a heart-warming incident about the blessings of the words uttered by the grand Muḥaddiš of Pakistan Maulānā Sardār Aḥmad Khān عَلَيْهِ رَحْمَةُ الْمَنَّان.

Once he was delivering a speech in a Mīlād-Ijtimā' in Jhang Bazaar Ghanta Ghar. The subject of his speech was the Nūr [refulgence] of the Holy Prophet صَلَّى اللّٰهُ تَعَالٰى عَلَيْهِ وَاٰلِهٖ وَسَلَّم. During his speech, his attention was diverted by a repeatedly flickering tube light. Turning towards the tube light and addressing it, he said, 'O tube light, you are flickering, whereas the whole world is enlightened by the Nūr of the Beloved and Blessed Prophet صَلَّى اللّٰهُ تَعَالٰى عَلَيْهِ وَاٰلِهٖ وَسَلَّم. [Therefore,] why are you being ungrateful? Beware! I warn you not to flicker any more…' The slogan 'يَا رَسُولَ اللّٰه صَلَّى اللّٰهُ تَعَالٰى عَلَيْهِ وَاٰلِهٖ وَسَلَّم' echoed everywhere in the air.

[1] The person who delivers Islamic speeches in Masjid. [Translator's Note]

All the attendees witnessed that the tube light remained on without flickering till the end of the Ijtimā'. *(Ḥayāt-e-Muḥaddiš-e-A'ẓam, pp. 263)*

صَلُّوْا عَلَى الْحَبِيْب صَلَّى اللّٰهُ تَعَالٰى عَلٰى مُحَمَّد

Weevils infestation and headaches are prevented

Dear Islamic brothers! How great the practicing scholars are? We should always seek the blessed company of the scholars of Aĥl-e-Sunnat. Shaykh Sayyidunā Kamāluddīn Addamirī رحمۃ اللہ تعالی علیہ has stated, 'Some scholars have told me that if the names of the seven renowned scholars of Madīnaĥ are written on a piece of paper and placed in flour or wheat, that flour will remain safe from the infestation of weevils. Further, if the piece of paper (with names of scholars written on it) is tied to the painful area of the head or if these names are recited and blown upon the head, then the headache will be relieved, اِنْ شَآءَاللّٰه عَزَّوَجَلَّ. Here are the seven names:

عُبَيْدُاللّٰه عُرْوَة قَاسِمْ سَعِيْد اَبُوْ بَكْر سُلَيْمَان خَارِجَه (رَحِمَهُمُ اللّٰهُ تَعَالٰى)

(Ḥayāt-ul-Ḥaywān-ul-Kubrā, vol. 2, pp. 53)

Dear Islamic brothers! It is evident that great blessings lie in the names of true Islamic scholars and the pious. If their names can bring about blessing, then how blessed and sacred their books, speeches, company, visit to their shrines and the meal of their Niyāz would be!

صَلُّوْا عَلَى الْحَبِيْب صَلَّى اللّٰهُ تَعَالٰى عَلٰى مُحَمَّد

32. Dough was given to beggar

A beggar once knocked on the door of the house of Shaykh Sayyidunā Ḥabīb 'Ajamī عَلَيْهِ رَحْمَةُ اللّٰهِ الْقَوِى. His wife had gone to the neighbour's house to make arrangement to light fire so that she could cook bread; leaving behind the dough she had already prepared. The Shaykh رَحْمَةُ اللّٰهِ تَعَالٰى عَلَيْه gave that dough in charity to the beggar in her absence.

When she came back and did not find the dough she asked about it. The Shaykh رَحْمَةُ اللهِ تَعَالٰی عَلَيْه said that someone had taken it to bake bread. On her insistence he finally revealed that he had given it in charity. She replied, 'سُبْحٰنَ اللّٰه عَزَّوَجَلَّ! This is indeed a very good act, but we also need something to eat.' Immediately a person brought some meat and bread. The Shaykh رَحْمَةُ اللهِ تَعَالٰی عَلَيْه said, 'Look! How quickly it was returned to you, along with prepared meat gravy.' *(Rauḍ-ur-Riyāḥīn, pp. 152)*

May Allah عَزَّوَجَلَّ have mercy on them and forgive us without accountability for their sake!

Ṣadaqaĥ does not decrease wealth

Dear Islamic brothers! The things given in the path of Allah عَزَّوَجَلَّ do not go to waste. Besides being entitled to reap great rewards in the Hereafter, sometimes, one is immediately rewarded with something better in the world. There is no doubt that spending money etc. in the path of Allah does not decrease one's wealth but increases it.

Hence Sayyidunā Abū Ĥurayraĥ رَضِیَ اللهُ تَعَالٰی عَنْه has narrated that the Prophet of Raḥmaĥ, the Intercessor of Ummaĥ صَلَّی اللهُ تَعَالٰی عَلَيْهِ وَاٰلِهٖ وَسَلَّم has stated, 'Ṣadaqaĥ [charity] does not decrease wealth and Allah عَزَّوَجَلَّ increases the status of the one who forgives others. Whoever adopts humility for the pleasure of Allah is granted elevation by Allah عَزَّوَجَلَّ.' *(Ṣaḥīḥ Muslim, pp. 1397, Ḥadīš 2588)*

Well-water increases when drawn

A renowned exegetist of the Quran, Muftī Aḥmad Yār Khān عَلَيْهِ رَحْمَةُ الْمَنَّان has stated that it has been observed that the amount of the Zakāĥ of the person who pays it keeps increasing every year. The farmer who plants seeds into the ground empties his sacks apparently but, in fact, fills them with more seeds [after the season]. On the contrary, the farmer storing grain sacks at home may lose them because of rats and weevils. It may also mean that spending the money from which charity is given multiplies it, اِنْ شَآءَاللّٰه عَزَّوَجَلَّ. As we can see that the well-water increases when drawn. *(Mirāt-ul-Manājīḥ, vol. 3, pp. 93)*

Retribution of not giving Zakāĥ

Dear Islamic brothers! Remember! As there are many rewards for the one who gives Zakāĥ, there are also severe punishments for those who do not. Describing the punishments stated in the Quran and Ḥadīš, A'lā Ḥaḍrat, Imām-e-Aĥl-e-Sunnat, reviver of Sunnaĥ, eradicator of Bid'aĥ, scholar of Sharī'aĥ, guide of Ṭarīqaĥ, 'Allāmaĥ Maulānā Al-Ḥāj Al-Ḥāfiẓ Al-Qārī Ash-Shāĥ Imām Aḥmad Razā Khān عَلَيْهِ رَحْمَةُ الرَّحْمٰن has stated, 'The summary is that the gold and the silver whose Zakāĥ was not paid will be seared (heated) on the Day of Judgement. The foreheads, sides and backs of those not giving Zakāĥ will then be branded with this hot gold and silver. A burning stone from Hell will be placed on his head and breast which will pierce the breast and emerge from the shoulders. When placed on the shoulders, it will pierce through the bones and emerge from the breast. It will then pierce the back and emerge from the side. It will then pierce the back of neck and emerge from the forehead. On the Judgement Day the wealth whose Zakāĥ is not given will transform into a fierce serpent and will run after the person who had not paid Zakāĥ. The person will try to stop the serpent with his hand but the serpent will chew his hand and will then coil around his neck. Then taking that person's mouth into its mouth, the serpent will chew his mouth uttering 'I am your wealth', 'I am your treasure.' It will then chew the whole body.' *(Fatāwā Razawiyyaĥ (Jadīd), vol. 10, pp. 153)*

Admonishing the one not giving Zakāĥ, Shaykh Imām Aḥmad Razā Khān عَلَيْهِ رَحْمَةُ الْمَنَّان has further stated the frightening torment of the Judgement Day in these words, 'O dear! Do you think that these sayings of Allah عَزَّوَجَلَّ and His Prophet صَلَّى اللهُ تَعَالٰى عَلَيْهِ وَاٰلِهٖ وَسَلَّم are of no importance? Do you consider these punishments easy to bear on 50,000 years long Day of Judgement? Sear a coin in the fire of this world and brand your body with it. There is no comparison between the fire (of this world) and the blazing inferno (of Hell); between a small coin and the wealth accumulated during the whole life; between the temporary pain in this world and the thousand years' lasting pain in the Hereafter; between the branding with a small coin and bone piercing punishment. May Allah عَزَّوَجَلَّ guide the Muslims! *(Fatāwā Razawiyyaĥ (Jadīd), vol. 10, pp. 175)*

Dear Islamic brothers! Join the righteous environment of Dawat-e-Islami, اِنْ شَآءَاللّٰه عَزَّوَجَلَّ; you will learn the rulings of Sharī'aĥ regarding Zakāĥ and Ṣadaqaĥ and be inspired to act accordingly. Here is a Madanī incident to enhance one's admiration to Dawat-e-Islami.

33. A Korean comes into fold of Islam

A Madanī Qāfilaĥ of the devotees of Rasūl travelled to a locality in Korea. Approaching the Islamic brothers, a non-Muslim Korean national asked them if they were Muslims. The brothers replied, 'اَلۡحَمۡدُلِلّٰہ عَزَّوَجَلَّ we are Muslims.' He then asked as to what they were wearing on their heads. They politely explained to him that they were wearing turbans, a dignified Sunnaĥ of the Noble Prophet صَلَّی اللّٰہ تَعَالٰی عَلَیۡہِ وَاٰلِہٖ وَسَلَّم. He then inquired about the beard. Again the brothers replied that it was also a dignified Sunnaĥ of the Noble Prophet صَلَّی اللّٰہ تَعَالٰی عَلَیۡہِ وَاٰلِہٖ وَسَلَّم.

Inspired, the Korean national then said, 'I had only read about Islam in books but had not seen anyone practise it. This is for the first time that I have witnessed Islam personified. This has impressed me a lot. Kindly, make me a Muslim.' By the grace of Allah عَزَّوَجَلَّ, the non-Muslim embraced Islam by the blessing of beholding the gleaming turbans and beards of the devotees of Rasūl of the Madanī Qāfilaĥ.

Un kā Dīwānaĥ 'Imāmaĥ aur zulf-o-rīsh mayn
Wāĥ! Daykĥo to saĥī lagtā ĥay kitnā shāndār

How dignified looks the devotee of the Rasūl
With a beard on his face and a turban on his head

Dear Islamic brothers! Muslims today have adopted a wicked lifestyle. It is very sad that Muslims' attire and appearance reflect the filthy culture of the non-Muslims. Do not be deceived by satanic whispers that people will stay away from you if you wear a turban or have a beard. In fact, it is not the turban or beard; it is one's misbehaviour, fast-talking and immoral character that make people stay away from him. You should therefore adhere to the Sunnaĥ and become a reflection of it. Reform your character, keep your tongue in control, and be courteous and polite. By doing this, you will see how people come closer to you.

In the incident above, you have just heard how the Sunnaĥ-Inspiring dress and the politeness of the devotees of Rasūl inspired a non-Muslim to revert to Islam. Here is another incident that further illustrates the blessings [Barakaĥ] of travelling in the Madanī Qāfilaĥ.

34. Glowing faces led to embracing Islam

In 1425 A.H. (January 2005), the Nigrān of Dawat-e-Islami's Markazī Majlis-e-Shūrā and a few members of Majlis Berūn-e-Mulk [committee for foreign countries] travelled with a Madanī Qāfilaĥ to South Africa from Bāb-ul-Madīnaĥ, Karachi [Pakistan]. The Qāfilaĥ went to see a land for the construction of Dawat-e-Islami's Madanī Markaz, Faīzān-e-Madīnaĥ. The brothers already present there at the site welcomed them with open arms. Inspired by seeing the glowing faces of the bearded and turbaned devotees of Rasūl, the owner of that piece of land, a non-Muslim, came forward to the Nigrān of Shūrā and said, 'Please make me Muslim.' He was immediately made to repent of unbelief and embrace Islam. Islamic brothers were overwhelmed with joy, and their chanting 'Allah, Allah' filled the air.

Tū dāřĥī bařĥā lay 'Imāmaĥ sajā lay
Ĥay achchĥā, naĥīn ĥay burā Madanī Māḥaul
Yaqīnan Muqaddar kā woĥ ĥay sikandar
Jisay khayr say mil gayā Madanī Māḥaul

Wear beard and turban as part of your garment
Very great, not bad is the Madanī environment
Indeed fortunate is he who, by divine bestowment
Has joined the Madanī environment

صَلُّوْا عَلَى الْحَبِيْب صَلَّى اللّٰهُ تَعَالٰى عَلٰى مُحَمَّد

35. Judge's dough

Shaykh Ṣāliḥ رَحْمَةُ اللهِ تَعَالٰى عَلَيْه, the son of the Imām of millions of Ḥanābilites, Shaykh Sayyidunā Imām Aḥmad Bin Ḥanbal رَحْمَةُ اللهِ تَعَالٰى عَلَيْه, was the Qāḍī (Judge) of Isfahan, [Iran]. Once, Imām Aḥmad's servant prepared bread with the dough he had taken from the kitchen of his son, Shaykh Ṣāliḥ رَحْمَةُ اللهِ تَعَالٰى عَلَيْه. When the servant served the bread to Imām Aḥmad Bin Ḥanbal رَحْمَةُ اللهِ تَعَالٰى عَلَيْه, the Shaykh asked as to why it was very soft. The servant replied that he had taken dough from the kitchen of his son who is the Qāḍī of Isfahan. The Shaykh said, 'Why did you take dough from his kitchen? Now, I will not consume this bread.' He then asked the servant to give the bread to some beggar and instructed him to inform the beggar that the bread was prepared with the dough taken from a judge's house. Coincidently, forty days passed but no beggar came. As a result, the bread went bad. The servant then fed the bread to the fish of the Tigris river. Since then, Shaykh Sayyidunā Imām Aḥmad Bin Ḥanbal رَحْمَةُ اللهِ تَعَالٰى عَلَيْه never ate any fish from that river. What magnificent level of piety the great Imām possessed! *(Tażkira-tul-Auliyā, pp. 197)*

May Allah عَزَّوَجَلَّ have mercy on him and forgive us without accountability for his sake!

Dear Islamic brothers! How pious and ascetic Shaykh Sayyidunā Imām Aḥmad Bin Ḥanbal رَحْمَةُ اللهِ تَعَالٰى عَلَيْه was! He abstained from consuming the bread that had come from the kitchen of his own son just because his son was a judge. Though the money earned by a judge is not Ḥarām, it is extremely difficult for a judge to uphold justice in an equitable way. Even if he is able to maintain justice equitably, a judge is a government employee who receives his salary from state-treasure that is unlikely to be free from unlawful money as the state-treasure is, sometimes, accumulated by unlawful and oppressive means.

Therefore, Shaykh Imām Aḥmad Bin Ḥanbal رَحْمَةُ اللهِ تَعَالٰى عَلَيْه did not eat the bread made from the dough of a judge. He even abstained from consuming fish from the Tigris river just because of an outside chance that the fish may have fed on that bread. This was indeed an immense level of the asceticism of Imām Aḥmad Bin Ḥanbal رَحْمَةُ اللهِ تَعَالٰى عَلَيْه.

36. Saintly miracle of Imām Aḥmad Bin Ḥanbal رَحْمَةُ اللهِ عَلَيْه

Shaykh Sayyidunā Imām Aḥmad Bin Ḥanbal رَحْمَةُ اللهِ تَعَالٰى عَلَيْه possessed a very high rank. It is stated that a woman's feet were paralyzed. She sent her son to the Shaykh رَحْمَةُ اللهِ تَعَالٰى عَلَيْه with a request to make Du'ā for her. When he heard of her condition, he made Wuḍū and began to offer Ṣalāĥ. The young lad returned home. When he knocked at the door of his home, he was amazed to see that it was his mother who had opened the door, and had recovered from paralysis by virtue of the Shaykh's Du'ā. *(Tażkira-tul-Auliyā, pp. 196)* It is an act of great reward to respect the righteous and pious servants of Allah as stated in the following parable.

37. Reward of respecting the pious

A person saw a deceased man in his dream and asked as to how Allah عَزَّوَجَلَّ treated him. The deceased replied, 'Allah عَزَّوَجَلَّ has forgiven me!' The dreaming person asked, 'Which deed led to your forgiveness?' He replied, 'Once Shaykh Sayyidunā Imām Aḥmad Bin Ḥanbal رَحْمَةُ اللّٰهِ تَعَالٰی عَلَیْه was making Wuḍū at a riverbank where I was also sitting at a high place for making Wuḍū. When I noticed that the great Imām رَحْمَةُ اللّٰهِ تَعَالٰی عَلَیْه was sitting downstream from me, I moved to a lower place out of respect. This deed of 'treating the saint with respect' was the cause for my salvation.'

May Allah عَزَّوَجَلَّ have mercy on them and forgive us without accountability for their sake!

صَلُّوْا عَلَى الْحَبِيْب صَلَّى اللّٰهُ تَعَالٰى عَلٰى مُحَمَّد

38. Gold shoes

A renowned Muḥaddiš Shaykh Sayyidunā Muhammad Bin Khuzaymaĥ رَحْمَةُ اللّٰهِ تَعَالٰی عَلَیْه has stated, 'I was deeply sad when Shaykh Sayyidunā Imām Abū 'Abdullāĥ Aḥmad Bin Ḥanbal رَحْمَةُ اللّٰهِ تَعَالٰی عَلَیْه passed away. One night I had a dream in which I saw him walk in a gracefully dignified manner. I asked him, 'O Abū 'Abdullāĥ! What kind of [walking] style is this?' He replied, 'Servants in Paradise walk like this.' Then I asked him, مَا فَعَلَ اللّٰهُ بِكَ 'How did Allah عَزَّوَجَلَّ treat you?' He replied, 'Allah عَزَّوَجَلَّ has not only forgiven and crowned me but has also given me the shoes of gold. He عَزَّوَجَلَّ then said to me, 'O Aḥmad! You have been blessed with all this because you declared the Quran as My (Allah's) Words. Allah عَزَّوَجَلَّ further said, 'Ask me the same Du'ā as you used to do in the world.' I [Imām Aḥmad رَحْمَةُ اللّٰهِ تَعَالٰی عَلَیْه] then made the Du'ā, 'O my Allah عَزَّوَجَلَّ! Everything ...' When I had only said these words, Allah عَزَّوَجَلَّ said, 'Everything is provided for you.' Upon this I said, 'Everything is because of Your omnipotence.' Allah Almighty عَزَّوَجَلَّ replied, 'You have told the truth.'

Then I requested, 'Yā Allah عَزَّوَجَلَّ! Forgive me without holding me accountable.' Allah عَزَّوَجَلَّ said, 'We have forgiven you!' Then Allah عَزَّوَجَلَّ further said, 'O Aḥmad! This is Paradise. Enter it.' When I entered, I saw that Sayyidunā Sufyān Šaurī عَلَیْهِ رَحْمَةُ اللّٰهِ الْقَوِی had two wings whereby he was flying in Paradise from one date tree to another uttering these words,

'All praise is for Allah عَزَّوَجَلَّ who has made His promise come true and has made us inheritors of Paradise. We abide herein wherever we wish and the reward for the people who perform good deeds is indeed excellent.' I asked him, 'How is Shaykh Sayyidunā 'Abdul Waĥĥāb Warrāq عَلَيْهِ رَحْمَةُ الرَّزَّاق?' He told me, 'I left him at the sea of Nūr.' I then inquired about Shaykh Sayyidunā Bishr Ḥāfī عَلَيْهِ رَحْمَةُ اللّٰهِ الْكَافِى. He informed, 'He is present in the court of Allah عَزَّوَجَلَّ. In front of him is a dining-mat and Allah's special attention is towards him and He عَزَّوَجَلَّ is telling him, 'O the one who avoided foods and drinks in the world! Now eat and enjoy in this world.' *(Sharḥ-uṣ-Ṣudūr, pp. 289)*

May Allah عَزَّوَجَلَّ have mercy on them and forgive us without accountability for their sake!

39. Forgiveness on every lash of whip

Dear Islamic brothers! Did you see? When pious people move from this world to the Hereafter after they had endured hardships for their religion, how graciously they are blessed by Allah عَزَّوَجَلَّ! The leader of thousands of Ḥanābilites[1], Shaykh Sayyidunā Abū 'Abdullāĥ Imām Aḥmad Bin Ḥanbal رَحْمَةُ اللّٰهِ تَعَالٰى عَلَيْه faced up to severe agony and torture, just for upholding the truth.

Once the Abbasid caliph, Mu'taṣim Billaĥ ordered one of his executioners to whip Imām Aḥmad Bin Ḥanbal رَحْمَةُ اللّٰهِ تَعَالٰى عَلَيْه. His back was covered in blood as whips rained down on his bare back. He was beaten so severely that even his skin came off. While being whipped, his pyjama started to slip, so he made Du'ā, 'Yā Allah عَزَّوَجَلَّ! You know I am right (i.e. what I have stuck to is the truth). Save me from the unveiling of my Satr[2].' اَلْحَمْدُ لِلّٰه عَزَّوَجَلَّ! The pyjama did not slip any longer. The Imām then fainted. As long as he remained conscious, he would say on every lash of the whip, 'I forgive Mu'taṣim.'

Later on, when he was asked as to why he forgave Mu'taṣim, he رَحْمَةُ اللّٰهِ تَعَالٰى عَلَيْه replied, 'Mu'taṣim is a descendant of Sayyidunā 'Abbās رَضِىَ اللّٰهُ تَعَالٰى عَنْهُ, an uncle of the Holy

[1] Followers of Ḥanbalī school of Islamic law, founded by Shaykh Sayyidunā Imām Aḥmad Bin Ḥanbal رَحْمَةُ اللّٰهِ تَعَالٰى عَلَيْه

[2] The area from below the navel to and including the knees. [Translator's Notes]

Prophet صَلَّى اللهُ تَعَالٰى عَلَيْهِ وَاٰلِهٖ وَسَلَّم. If it is announced on the Judgement Day that Aḥmad Bin Ḥanbal did not forgive the descendant of the uncle of the Holy Prophet صَلَّى اللهُ تَعَالٰى عَلَيْهِ وَاٰلِهٖ وَسَلَّم, I would feel very ashamed of it.' *(Ma'dan-e-Akhlāq, vol. 3, pp. 37-39)*

Shaykh Sayyidunā Fuḍayl Bin 'Iyāḍ رَحْمَةُ اللهِ تَعَالٰى عَلَيْه has reported that Sayyidunā Aḥmad Bin Ḥanbal رَحْمَةُ اللهِ تَعَالٰى عَلَيْه was kept in captivity for 28 months (over two years). During this period, he used to be lashed every night till he fainted. He was lacerated by swords, and was trampled upon. Despite facing so many severe punishments he remained staunch [on his stance]. His steadfastness is really exemplary. *(Ṭabqāt-ul-Kubrā, vol. 1, pp. 79)*

Shaykh Sayyidunā Ḥāfiẓ Ibn Jauzī عَلَيْهِ رَحْمَةُ اللّٰهِ الْقَوِی has narrated from Muhammad Bin Ismā'īl رَحْمَةُ اللهِ تَعَالٰى عَلَيْه that Imām Aḥmad Bin Ḥanbal رَحْمَةُ اللهِ تَعَالٰى عَلَيْه was lashed 80 such whips that would have made even an elephant scream if it had been lashed, but the patience of the Imām is really marvellous. *(Ma'dan-e-Akhlāq, vol. 3, pp. 106)*

Taṙapnā is ṭaraḥ bulbul, kay bāl-o-per na ĥilayn
Adab ĥay lāzmī shāĥaun kay āstānay kā

O nightingale! Writhe without moving your hair and wings
Abiding by the manners of the courts of kings

صَلُّوْا عَلَى الْحَبِيْب صَلَّى اللهُ تَعَالٰى عَلٰى مُحَمَّد

40. Thief instructed to be patient

During captivity, Allah عَزَّوَجَلَّ helped Imām Aḥmad Bin Ḥanbal رَحْمَةُ اللهِ تَعَالٰى عَلَيْه through a man named, Abul Ĥaysam 'Ayyār. One day when the Imām was brought to be lashed, Abul Ĥaysam 'Ayyār approached him and said, 'O Aḥmad رَحْمَةُ اللهِ تَعَالٰى عَلَيْه! I am so-and-so thief, and I received eighteen thousand lashes so that I would confess to robbery and theft. I knew I was a liar but still I did not admit to my crimes. Your stand is lawful. Don't get scared of these whips.' From that day on, whenever the Imām felt pain because of being whipped he used to recall the words of that thief. Afterwards, the Imām رَحْمَةُ اللهِ تَعَالٰى عَلَيْه would always make Du'ā of mercy for him. *(Ṭabqāt-ul-Kubrā, vol. 1, pp. 78-79)*

Shaykh Sayyidunā Bishr Bin Ḥāriš رَحْمَةُ اللهِ تَعَالٰی عَلَيْه has stated: 'He [i.e. the Imām رَحْمَةُ اللهِ تَعَالٰی عَلَيْه] was put in the furnace (i.e. jail) to be tested, and he came out as shining gold (because of his determination). *(Ṭabqāt-ul-Kubrā, vol. 1, pp. 80)*

Bounties of Allah عَزَّوَجَلَّ on His Auliyā رَحِمَهُمُ اللهُ تَعَالٰی

Dear Islamic brothers! Did you see? Allah's special blessings are showered upon those who endure hardships in His path, with a smiling face. Allah عَزَّوَجَلَّ bestowed his bounties upon Shaykh Sayyidunā Bishr Ḥāfī عَلَيْهِ رَحْمَةُ اللّٰهِ الْكَافِی who adopted hunger and thirst to please Allah عَزَّوَجَلَّ subduing his carnal desires.

Likewise, our Ghauš-e-A'ẓam, Shaykh Sayyidunā 'Abdul Qādir Jīlānī قُدِّسَ سِرُّهُ الرَّبَّانِي also suppressed his carnal desires and was disinterested in foods and drinks. Imām Aḥmad Razā رَحْمَةُ اللّٰهِ تَعَالٰی عَلَيْه, a devotee of Rasūl and a great saint, has written a couplet describing the bounties of Allah عَزَّوَجَلَّ upon Ghauš-e-A'ẓam, Shaykh Sayyidunā 'Abdul Qādir Jīlānī قُدِّسَ سِرُّهُ الرَّبَّانِي.

صَلُّوْا عَلَى الْحَبِيْب صَلَّى اللّٰهُ تَعَالٰی عَلٰی مُحَمَّد

◆◆◆

Dear Islamic brothers! In order to learn the knowledge of Sharī'aĥ and Sunnaĥ, remain associated with the Madanī environment of Dawat-e-Islami. اِنْ شَآءَاللّٰه عَزَّوَجَلَّ, You will reap blessings in the worldly life as well as in the afterlife. Here is a faith-refreshing parable regarding the Madanī marvels of Dawat-e-Islami.

41. Brain tumour cured

A brother from Balbahar in district Chandrapur, Maharashtra India, has explained in his own words how he joined the righteous Madanī environment of Dawat-e-Islami. He has stated, 'When I was 7 years of age, my left eye got injured by a stone. Treatments eased the pain but my eyesight got weaker and weaker. Instead of learning a lesson from this injury, I became more heedless and started listening to music and going to dancing clubs.

As a result of committing these sins I had severe pain in my left eye. I was diagnosed with a brain tumour. We visited several hospitals for treatment but my condition worsened. My neck tilted to one side and it became difficult for me even to have meals. My family was very troubled because of my condition. Meanwhile, a Madanī Qāfilaĥ of Dawat-e-Islami arrived in our village. Delivering the call to righteousness, the Islamic brothers of the Madanī Qāfilaĥ invited all of our family's male members to come and listen to the speech in a nearby Masjid. We all excused telling them our situation. The voice of the speech being delivered by the preacher in the Masjid was reaching our home, and we could all hear it clearly. My family members were very impressed by the speech and decided to attend the upcoming Sunnaĥ-Inspiring Ijtimā' in Durug. In the Ijtimā' the speech was followed by an overwhelming Du'ā session. Having returned from the Ijtimā', I got CT scan done, the CT scan report showed that there was no brain tumour, whereas previous reports had confirmed it. My family was so moved by this incident that they themselves adorned my head with a green turban.'

'Aṭāye Ḥabīb-e-Khudā صَلَّی اللّٰہُ تَعَالٰی عَلَیْہِ وَاٰلِہٖ وَسَلَّم *Madanī Māḥaul;*
Ĥay faīzān Ghauš-o-Razā رَحِمَہُمَا اللّٰہُ تَعَالٰی*, Madanī Māḥaul*
Ay bīmār-e-'iṣyān tū ā jā yaĥān per;
Gunāĥaun kī day gā dawā, Madanī Māḥaul
Sanwar jāye gī ākhirat اِنْ شَآءَاللّٰہ عَزَّوَجَلَّ
Tum apnāye rakĥo sadā, Madanī Māḥaul

Gift of the Beloved Prophet is the Madanī environment
Blessing of Ghauš and Razā is the Madanī environment
If you have the illness of sin,
You will get the treatment, come and join the Madanī environment
You will get salvation, Allah عَزَّوَجَلَّ *willing,*
Keep yourself attached to the Madanī environment

صَلُّوْا عَلَی الْحَبِیْب صَلَّی اللّٰہُ تَعَالٰی عَلٰی مُحَمَّد

42. Awareness of heart feelings

Dātā Ganj Bakhsh Shaykh Sayyidunā ‘Alī Ĥajwayrī رَحْمَةُ اللهِ تَعَالٰی عَلَیْه has stated, ‘I and two other friends of mine were on our way to visit Shaykh Ibn ‘Alā رَحْمَةُ اللهِ تَعَالٰی عَلَیْه, in his village called Ramllaĥ. During the journey, we decided that each one of us would keep a wish in heart. I wished that Shaykh Ibn ‘Alā رَحْمَةُ اللهِ تَعَالٰی عَلَیْه tell me the couplets and Du‘ā of Ḥusayn Bin Manṣūr Ḥallāj رَحْمَةُ اللهِ تَعَالٰی عَلَیْه. My other friend wished that his ill spleen be cured, and the third one wished to eat halvah Ṣābūnī (a dessert).

When we arrived, the Shaykh had already got the couplets and Du‘ā of Ḥusayn Bin Manṣūr Ḥallāj رَحْمَةُ اللهِ تَعَالٰی عَلَیْه written for me. He handed it to me as we walked in and then passed his hand over the abdomen of the other friend, curing his spleen. Then, addressing the third friend, he said, ‘Dessert is a fancy food of the kings but you are wearing the dress of the Sufis! Adopt one of the two.’ *(Kashf-ul-Maḥjūb, pp. 384)*

May Allah عَزَّوَجَلَّ have mercy on them and forgive us without accountability for their sake!

43. Did Ḥusayn Bin Manṣūr say ‘اَنَا الْحَقّ’ [Anal-Ḥaqq]?

Dear Islamic brothers! Did you see! By the grace of Allah عَزَّوَجَلَّ, the pious saints can get aware of the inner feelings of a person as obvious from the above parable that Sayyidunā Shaykh Ibn ‘Alā رَحْمَةُ اللهِ تَعَالٰی عَلَیْه, without being informed by anyone, revealed the wish of Dātā Ganj Bakhsh ‘Alī Ĥajwayrī رَحْمَةُ اللهِ تَعَالٰی عَلَیْه and that of his two other companions. Further, he fulfilled the desires of two while bestowed a Madanī pearl of advice upon the third one.

This parable also portrays Ḥusayn Bin Manṣūr Ḥallāj رَحْمَةُ اللهِ تَعَالٰی عَلَیْه in a positive manner. There is a widespread misconception that he had said اَنَا الْحَقّ [Anal-Ḥaqq] literally translated as ‘*I am Ḥaqq (God).*’ Removing this misconception, A’lā Ḥaḍrat, Imām-e-Aĥl-e-Sunnat, Maulānā Shāĥ Imām Aḥmad Raẓā Khān عَلَیْهِ رَحْمَةُ الرَّحْمٰن has stated: ‘Shaykh Sayyidunā Ḥusayn Bin Manṣūr Ḥallāj رَحْمَةُ اللهِ تَعَالٰی عَلَیْه was popularly known as ‘Manṣūr’ but this is his father’s name. His name is Ḥusayn. He was from amongst the greatest saints. One of his sisters was higher than him, by several ranks, in sainthood and gnosis. She used to go to the jungle in the later part of the night and occupy herself with the remembrance of Allah عَزَّوَجَلَّ.

One night he woke up and did not find her in home. He became suspicious. The next night he pretended to be sleeping and as usual his sister got up in the middle of the night and went on her way. He quietly followed her. He saw that a rubies goblet descended from the sky attached to a gold chain. When it reached close to her lips, she started to drink from it. Ḥusayn Bin Manṣūr Ḥallāj رَحْمَةُ اللهِ تَعَالٰى عَلَيْه was anxious to have some of this heavenly beverage, so he called out spontaneously, 'Sister! By Allah عَزَّوَجَلَّ, leave some for me.' She left a sip for him. As soon as he drank that sip, he started hearing a call from every plant and herb, from every wall and door, 'Who is more deserving of being killed in Our path?' He started replying اَنَـا لَاَحَق (Anā La-Aḥaqq) that is '*Certainly, it is me who is the most deserving.*'

People misheard it as اَنَـا الْحَق 'Anal-Ḥaqq' [*I am Ḥaqq (God)*] and assumed that he had claimed divinity. This phrase (i.e. claiming to be God) is a statement of Kufr and proclamation of such a phrase by a Muslim is apostasy. Punishment for apostasy is death penalty. It is stated in *Ṣaḥīḥ Bukhārī* that the Noble Prophet صَلَّى اللهُ تَعَالٰى عَلَيْهِ وَاٰلِهٖ وَسَلَّم has stated, 'Kill the one who converts from his [Islamic] faith.' *(Fatāwā Razawiyyaĥ (Jadīd), vol. 26, pp. 400)*

اَلْحَمْدُ لِلّٰه عَزَّوَجَلَّ! Associating oneself with the Madanī environment of Dawat-e-Islami and travelling in Madanī Qāfilaĥs is an excellent way to rectify one's beliefs and deeds.

صَلُّوْا عَلَى الْحَبِيْب صَلَّى اللهُ تَعَالٰى عَلٰى مُحَمَّد

44. I was alcoholic and thief

An Islamic brother from Bombay, India has stated: 'I had become addicted to drinking and gambling from a very young age. I used to be considered a master of smuggling diamonds and gold into the country. Some Islamic brothers of Dawat-e-Islami would hold a brief religious speech Ijtimā', every Friday, in our area. My mother would ask me to attend it, but I would turn a deaf ear to her. Once due to the individual effort of my mother I attended the speech during which I liked the preacher's manner of delivering the speech but could not comprehend it. After the speech the preacher approached me and, making individual effort, tried to convince me to attend the Sunnaĥ-Inspiring weekly Ijtimā' in 'Govandi', a suburb of Bombay city; I agreed.

At the night of the Ijtimā' I went to a bar with some of my friends who all ordered wine but I did not feel like drinking that night. So, I just ordered a soft drink. My friends looked at me with surprise. I explained to them that someone had invited me to an Ijtimā' and I have to go over there to attend a sermon. Upon hearing this my friends burst into laughter. [One of them said,] 'My friend, this is not the month of Muḥarram. Sermons are held in Muḥarram. I think someone has played a joke on you.' I was also rather dubious but decided that I would go and if there is no Ijtimā' I would just come back. I came out of the bar, got into a rickshaw and went straight to the Ijtimā'. The overwhelming Du'ā of the Ijtimā' made me burst into tears. I repented of all my sins tearfully. After the Ijtimā', making individual effort, a preacher persuaded me to travel with a Madanī Qāfilaĥ.

اَلْحَمْدُ لِلّٰه عَزَّوَجَلَّ, I had the privilege of travelling with the devotees of Rasūl in a Madanī Qāfilaĥ. During the Madanī Qāfilaĥ, I made intentions to grow a beard on my face and to wear a turban. I quit the company of the drunkards and gamblers and joined the Madanī environment of Dawat-e-Islami. I also had an eye disease, which made me feel as if I had a piece of grit in my eye. Doctors could not treat my disease. اَلْحَمْدُ لِلّٰه عَزَّوَجَلَّ, By the blessings of the Madanī environment I was cured from this ailment as well.'

Ĉhoṙo may-naushiyān, mat bako gāliyān
Āo taubaĥ karayn, Qāfilay mayn chalo
Ay sharābī tū ā, ā jūārī tū ā
Ĉhūṫayn bad 'ādatayn, Qāfilay mayn chalo

Avoid abusing and give up drinking
Let's all repent; travel with Qāfilaĥ
Alcoholics come, gamblers you join too
To rid your bad habits; travel with Qāfilaĥ

صَلُّوْا عَلَى الْحَبِيْب صَلَّى اللهُ تَعَالٰى عَلٰى مُحَمَّد

Keep calling others to travel with Qāfilaĥ

Dear Islamic brothers! By the blessing of a Sunnaĥ-Inspiring speech and the individual effort of a preacher of Dawat-e-Islami, an alcoholic and a gambler repented of his sins and joined the Madanī environment by virtue of travelling with Madanī Qāfilaĥ. You should also keep inviting others to travel with Madanī Qāfilaĥs.

In the parable above you heard about an alcoholic. Regretfully, there are many Muslims who are addicted to drinking. While we are at it, let me describe the religious and worldly perils of drinking [and alcoholism].

Punishment of one sip of alcohol

The Beloved and Blessed Rasūl صَلَّى اللهُ تَعَالٰى عَلَيْهِ وَاٰلِهٖ وَسَلَّم has stated, 'Allah عَزَّوَجَلَّ has sent me as a mercy and guide for all the worlds. I have been sent to wipe out musical instruments and the practices of (pre-Islamic era of) ignorance. My Rab عَزَّوَجَلَّ, Mighty and Majestic, swears by His glory and greatness, '(If) any servant of Mine drinks even a single sip of alcohol, I will make him drink the like of it, from the boiling water of Hell, and (if) any servant of Mine abstains from drinking alcohol out of My fear, I shall give him the drink (of pure wine) in Paradise, in the company of good friends.' *(Mu'jam Kabīr, vol. 8, pp. 197, Ḥadīš 7803 & 7804)*

45. Not being able to recite Kalimaĥ

Dear Islamic brothers! It is feared that those who drink alcohol and play chess might not be able to recite Kalimaĥ at the time of their death. Listen to two parables in this context.

Shaykh 'Allāmaĥ Muhammad Bin Aḥmad Żaĥabī عَلَيْهِ رَحْمَةُ اللّٰهِ الْقَوِى has stated, 'A man used to remain in the company of alcoholics. When he was on his deathbed, someone tried to make him recite the Kalimaĥ by reminding him but he replied, 'You drink and give me some too.' مَعَاذَ اللّٰه عَزَّوَجَلَّ, That person died without reciting Kalimaĥ. [Imagine, this is the terrible consequence of just adopting the company of drinkers, so what would be the doom of those who drink themselves!] *(Mu'jam Kabīr, pp. 103)*

46. Nuisance of chess playing

A chess player who was close to his death was advised to recite Kalimaĥ, but he replied, 'Your king!', and then passed away. *(Mu'jam Kabīr, pp. 103)*

Medical harms of alcohol

Dear Islamic brothers! The prohibition of alcohol by Islam contains countless physical and spiritual benefits. Even non-Muslims are admitting its ill-effects. Therefore, a non-Muslim researcher comments that though the human body is immune to the detrimental effects of alcohol in the beginning and the drinker enjoys it, after some time the immunity system of the body is irreparably damaged, causing the harmful effects of alcohol appear permanently. Alcohol harms the liver the most, causing it to shrink. The kidneys are also badly affected, which eventually leads to their failure. Further, heavy drinking also causes the swelling of the brain and nerves. As a result, the nerves weaken and lose functioning. Alcohol drinking also causes swelling of the stomach and weakens the bones.

Alcohol also causes severe deficiency of vitamins in the body, especially of vitamin B and C. If a drinker is a smoker as well, then the harms of alcohol are even worse, giving rise to the danger of high blood pressure, stroke and heart attack. A heavy drinker constantly suffers from tiredness, headaches, nausea and extreme thirst. If alcohol is drunk in a large quantity, it could cause the heart and the lungs to fail, which causes sudden death.

Gar āye sharābī, miṭay ĥar kharābī
Charĥāye gā aysā nashaĥ, Madanī Māḥaul
Agar chaur ḋakū bĥī ā jāyaīn gey to
Sudĥar jāyaīn gey gar milā, Madanī Māḥaul
Namāzayn jo parĥtay naĥīn, un ko lārayb
Namāzī ĥay daytā banā, Madanī Māḥaul

If drunkards come, even they will get reformed;
Such is the intoxication of the Madanī environment
If bandits, thieves join;
They'll turn good, in the Madanī environment
Those who do not pray;
Certainly convert to Muṣallī, in the Madanī environment

صَلُّوا عَلَى الْحَبِيب صَلَّى اللهُ تَعَالٰى عَلٰى مُحَمَّد

47. A blind drinker

I[1] have distinctly remembered that [in Joria Bazaar, Bāb-ul-Madīnaĥ Karachi] there was a young labourer who was very humorous and funny. He was known for his strong build and fast-talking. Then he got blind and started begging. Afterwards, it turned out that he was an alcoholic and once he drank some spoiled [putrid] alcohol, which resulted in his blindness.

Kar lay taubaĥ aur tū mat pī sharāb
Ĥaun geyn warnaĥ do jaĥān tayray kharāb
Jo juwā kĥaylay, piye nādān sharāb
Qabr-o-ḥashr-o-nār mayn pāye 'ażāb

Repent, and quit drinking;
Or your worlds will be hurting;
Gambling and drinking alcohol;
Lead to torment of Hell for body and soul

صَلُّوْا عَلَى الْحَبِيْب صَلَّى اللهُ تَعَالٰى عَلٰى مُحَمَّد

48. Cloth was woven by itself

Shaykh Sayyidunā Aḥmad Naĥarvānī قُدِّسَ سِرُّهُ الرَّبَّانِي, a disciple of Shaykh Sayyidunā Qāḍī Ḥamīduddīn Nāgorī عَلَيْهِ رَحْمَةُ اللّٰهِ الْقَوِى, was a saint of high spiritual rank. Shaykh Sayyidunā Baĥāuddīn Zakariyyā Multānī قُدِّسَ سِرُّهُ الرَّبَّانِي was seldom impressed by anyone but he has remarked that if the devotional practices of Shaykh Sayyidunā Aḥmad Naĥarvānī قُدِّسَ سِرُّهُ الرَّبَّانِي were weighed, they would be equal to the worships of ten Sufis.

Shaykh Sayyidunā Aḥmad Naĥarvānī قُدِّسَ سِرُّهُ الرَّبَّانِي used to weave clothes for his livelihood. Sayyidunā Shaykh Naṣīruddīn Maḥmūd عَلَيْهِ رَحْمَةُ الْمَعْبُوْد has reported that while weaving cloth at his home, at times, Shaykh Naĥarvānī قُدِّسَ سِرُّهُ الرَّبَّانِي would be overwhelmed by divine-remembrance. Whenever he got into this overwhelming spiritual state, the cloth would continue to weave by itself.

---

[1] [The author, Amīr-e-Aĥl-e-Sunnat دَامَتْ بَرَكَاتُهُمُ الْعَالِيَه]

Once his Murshid Shaykh Sayyidunā Qāḍī Ḥamīduddīn Nāgorī عَلَيْهِ رَحْمَةُ اللّٰهِ الْقَوِى came to meet him. While departing, his Murshid asked, 'Aḥmad! For how long will you continue to do this work [of weaving]?' Saying this, he left. Shaykh Sayyidunā Aḥmad Naĥarvānī قُدِّسَ سِرُّهُ الرَّبَّانِى immediately got up to turn off the weaving machine but his hand got caught in it and broke. After this incident he quit weaving altogether and devoted himself to divine worship. His blessed shrine is a source of blessing and enlightenment in Badaun Sharīf, India.

May Allah عَزَّوَجَلَّ have mercy on them and forgive us without accountability for their sake!

صَلُّوْا عَلَى الْحَبِيْب صَلَّى اللّٰهُ تَعَالٰى عَلٰى مُحَمَّد

49. Watermelon seller

Dear Islamic brothers! Scholars and saints have always been present amongst the Muslims from every race and occupation and this process will continue till the Judgement Day. Divine bounty is not limited to any one nation or race. Allah عَزَّوَجَلَّ blesses whomever He عَزَّوَجَلَّ wills. Several saints are always present on the earth, and the affairs of the world carry on by virtue of their blessings.

Someone once complained to Shaykh Sayyidunā Shāĥ 'Abdul 'Azīz Muḥaddiš Diĥlvī عَلَيْهِ رَحْمَةُ اللّٰهِ الْقَوِى, 'Why are the affairs of Delhi in disorder these days?' He replied, 'These days the Abdāl [i.e. spiritual leader of Delhi] is an easy-going person.' The complainer asked, 'Who is he?' He replied, 'He is so-and-so watermelon seller in such-and-such market.' That person visited the Abdāl who was selling watermelons. He requested the Abdāl to cut a watermelon and give him a slice [as if to taste it before purchasing] but rejected it having tasted. Then he asked for another slice. The man kept on doing so until he wasted so many melons. Despite the loss of several melons, the Abdāl did not utter any word of complaint or resentment.

After some time, the same person noticed that the affairs of Delhi were well-organized. He inquired about the current Abdāl. The Shaykh informed, 'The current Abdāl is a water seller at 'Chāndnī Chowk' and receives a Chaĥdām[1] for every glass he sells.' This man

---

[1] A Chaĥdām is a quarter of a penny. [Translator's Note]

went to the Abdāl with a Chaĥdām and asked for a glass of water. The Abdāl gave him the water but he dropped the glass of water and asked for another. The Abdāl asked, 'Do you have another Chaĥdām?' The man said, 'No!' The Abdāl slapped him on the head and remarked, 'Have you thought that I am also like that watermelon-seller!' *(Sachchī Ḥikāyāt, vol. 3, pp. 97)*

May Allah عَزَّوَجَلَّ have mercy on them and forgive us without accountability for their sake!

صَلُّوْا عَلَى الْحَبِيْب　　صَلَّى اللّٰهُ تَعَالٰى عَلٰى مُحَمَّد

Spiritual rulers

Dear Islamic brothers! Saints رَحِمَهُمُ اللّٰهُ تَعَالٰى are the spiritual rulers who, by the bounties of Allah عَزَّوَجَلَّ, can get aware of the unseen matters [Ghayb]. It is not essential that every saint [Walī] is famous. These people are found in virtually every class of society. Sometimes, a saint is a common labourer, a vegetable or fruit seller, a trader or an employee, watchman or a mason. Not everyone can recognize them. Therefore, we should not look down on any Muslim. Some saints are associated with a 'spiritual system' as stated in the following account.

Three hundred & fifty six saints of Allah

Shaykh Sayyidunā Ibn Mas'ūd رَضِىَ اللّٰهُ تَعَالٰى عَنْه has narrated that the Prophet of mankind, the Peace of our heart and mind, the most Generous and Kind صَلَّى اللّٰهُ تَعَالٰى عَلَيْهِ وَاٰلِهٖ وَسَلَّم has stated, 'On earth there are three hundred such servants of Allah whose hearts (spiritually) stay over the heart of Sayyidunā Adam عَلَيْهِ السَّلَام. Similarly, the hearts of forty such pious servants of Allah are on the heart of Sayyidunā Mūsā عَلَيْهِ السَّلَام. Further, the hearts of seven pious servants of Allah (spiritually) stay on the heart of Sayyidunā Ibrāĥīm عَلَيْهِ السَّلَام. Likewise, the hearts of five are on the heart of Sayyidunā Jibrāīl عَلَيْهِ السَّلَام while the hearts of three are on the heart of Sayyidunā Mīkāīl عَلَيْهِ السَّلَام. The heart of one of such persons is on the heart of Sayyidunā Isrāfīl عَلَيْهِ السَّلَام.

When anyone of them passes away, Allah عَزَّوَجَلَّ replaces the deceased one with anyone from the group of the three. If anyone from the group of the three passes away, Allah عَزَّوَجَلَّ

replaces the deceased one by anyone from the group of the five. If anyone from the group of the five passes away, Allah عَزَّوَجَلَّ appoints anyone from the group of the seven. If anyone from the group of the seven passes away, Allah عَزَّوَجَلَّ appoints any one from the group of the forty and, if anyone from the group of the forty passes away, Allah عَزَّوَجَلَّ replaces the deceased one by anyone from the group of the three hundred. If anyone from the three hundred pious men of Allah عَزَّوَجَلَّ passes away, Allah عَزَّوَجَلَّ appoints anyone from common people in place of the deceased one. Through them, people get life, death and rains. Through their blessing plants grow and disasters are warded off.'

Shaykh Sayyidunā Ibn Mas'ūd رَضِىَ اللهُ تَعَالٰى عَنْهُ was asked, 'How do people get life and death through them?' He رَضِىَ اللهُ تَعَالٰى عَنْهُ replied, 'They make Du'ā for increase in the Ummaĥ so the Ummaĥ increases in numbers. They make Du'ā against the tyrants thus the tyrants' power is broken. They ask for rain, so it rains, and the earth sprouts out vegetation for people. [Through their supplications] different disasters are averted from people.' *(Ḥilyat-ul-Auliyā, vol. 1, pp. 40, Ḥadīš 16)*

May Allah عَزَّوَجَلَّ have mercy on them and forgive us without accountability for their sake!

Abdāl

Shaykh Sayyidunā Imām Muhammad Bin 'Alī Ḥakīm Tirmiżī عَلَيْهِ رَحْمَةُ اللّٰهِ الْقَوِى has narrated from Sayyidunā Abū Dardā رَضِىَ اللهُ تَعَالٰى عَنْهُ, 'Without doubt, the Prophets عَلَيْهِمُ السَّلَام were the 'Awtād' of the earth. After all the Prophets عَلَيْهِمُ السَّلَام departed from the world, Allah عَزَّوَجَلَّ made a group of people from the Ummaĥ of Aḥmad as Prophets' successors who are called 'Abdāl' [رَحِمَهُمُ اللّٰهُ تَعَالٰى]. These people are greater than others not only because of their fasts, Ṣalāĥ, devotional invocations and glorification of their Creator عَزَّوَجَلَّ but also because of their superior character, piety, truthfulness, asceticism, righteous intentions, protection of their hearts from the hatred of Muslims, tolerance for the attainment of divine pleasure, patience, wisdom, humility without helplessness, and because of their goodwill towards all Muslims. Thus they are the successors of the Prophets عَلَيْهِمُ السَّلَام.

Allah عَزَّوَجَلَّ has chosen them for His Being and for granting them knowledge and His pleasure. Those are forty Ṣiddīqīn. Amongst them are 30 such Ṣiddīqīn whose trust in Allah عَزَّوَجَلَّ is similar to the trust of the Prophet Sayyidunā Ibrāĥīm عَلٰى نَبِيِّنَا وَعَلَيْهِ الصَّلٰوةُ وَالسَّلَام in

Allah عَزَّوَجَلَّ. By the blessings of these Abdāls disaster are averted, hardships of people are eased, rains shower, and sustenance is granted. Before anyone of them dies, another is appointed by Allah عَزَّوَجَلَّ. They neither curse anyone, nor do they hurt or beat their subordinates. They don't consider anyone inferior. Further, they are not jealous of those who are higher than them in ranks, nor do they are greedy for worldly things. Furthermore, they do not adopt silence to show off, nor are they arrogant and they do not display their humbleness for ostentation.

They are the nicest people to talk to and are more ascetic when it comes to subduing their Nafs. Generosity is an innate part of their character. They always refrain from all such acts disliked by saints. They are not fickle such that one day they are very pious and the next day they are totally heedless, but rather they are steadfast in their state [of devotion]. These Abdāls have a special [spiritual] connection with Allah عَزَّوَجَلَّ. Neither the windstorm nor the fastest horses can catch up to them. Their hearts rise enthusiastically towards the sky for the pleasure of Allah عَزَّوَجَلَّ.' Sayyidunā Abū Dardā رَضِیَ اللهُ تَعَالٰی عَنْهُ then recited this verse:

أُولَٰٓئِكَ حِزْبُ اللَّهِ ۚ أَلَآ إِنَّ حِزْبَ اللَّهِ هُمُ الْمُفْلِحُونَ ﴿٢٢﴾

This is the fold of Allah. Do you hear? The fold of Allah is successful.

[Kanz-ul-Īmān (Translation of Quran)] (Part 28, Sūraĥ Al-Mujādalaĥ, verse 22)

The narrator asked Abū Dardā رَضِیَ اللهُ تَعَالٰی عَنْهُ, 'Which of the traits you have just described is the hardest for me to adopt? And how would I come to know that I have achieved it?' He رَضِیَ اللهُ تَعَالٰی عَنْهُ explained, 'You will be in the middle ranks when you dislike the worldly things. When you hate the materialistic worldly things, you will feel the love of the Hereafter. The more you distance yourself from worldly matters, the deeper love of the Hereafter will develop in your heart and then you will be able to distinguish between beneficial things and harmful ones.' He رَضِیَ اللهُ تَعَالٰی عَنْهُ further added, 'In divine-knowledge, whoever has a sincere quest is granted correctness in his deeds and speech and is protected by Allah عَزَّوَجَلَّ. This is affirmed in His Book (the Holy Quran).' Then the companion رَضِیَ اللهُ تَعَالٰی عَنْهُ recited this verse:

إِنَّ اللّٰهَ مَعَ الَّذِيْنَ اتَّقَوْا وَّ الَّذِيْنَ هُمْ مُّحْسِنُوْنَ ﴿۱۲۸﴾

Indeed, Allah عَزَّوَجَلَّ is with those who fear and do good.

[Kanz-ul-Īmān (Translation of Quran)] (Part 14, Sūraĥ An-Naḥl, verse 128)

He رَضِیَ اللّٰہُ تَعَالٰی عَنْہ continued, 'When we saw this verse (in the Holy Quran), we realized that there is nothing more delightful than seeking the pleasure of Allah.' *(Nawādir-ul-Uṣūl, pp. 168)*

May Allah عَزَّوَجَلَّ have mercy on them and forgive us without accountability for their sake!

صَلُّوْا عَلَى الْحَبِيْب صَلَّى اللّٰهُ تَعَالٰى عَلٰى مُحَمَّد

50. Pleas of hungry religious students

Famous Muḥaddišīn Shaykh Sayyidunā Imām Ṭabarānī, Shaykh Sayyidunā 'Allāmaĥ Ibn-ul-Maqrī and Sayyidunā Abush-Shaykh رَحِمَهُمُ اللّٰهُ تَعَالٰی used to acquire Islamic knowledge in the holy city of Madīnaĥ زَادَهَا اللّٰهُ شَرَفًا وَّتَعْظِيْمًا. Once, they were faced with severe starvation. They all started fasting, but the pangs of hunger left them weak and exhausted. So finally they went to visit the sacred grave of the Holy Prophet صَلَّى اللّٰهُ تَعَالٰى عَلَيْهِ وَاٰلِهٖ وَسَلَّم and pleaded, 'Yā Rasūlallāĥ صَلَّى اللّٰهُ تَعَالٰى عَلَيْهِ وَاٰلِهٖ وَسَلَّم, 'اَلْجُوْع' [that is, *O Prophet of Allah! Hunger*]! Having said this Sayyidunā Imām Ṭabarānī رَحْمَةُ اللّٰهِ تَعَالٰى عَلَيْه remained seated in the blessed shrine and said, 'I will not get up from here unless I either get food or meet my death at this [sanctified] place.'

Mayn in kay dar per paṙā raĥūn gā
Paṙay ĥī reĥnay say kām ĥogā
Nigāĥ-e-raḥmat zarūr ĥogī
Ṭa'ām kā intiẓām ĥogā

I will keep staying at his court
As staying will remove my difficulty
I will be blessed with merciful sight
And food will be arranged for me

Shaykh Sayyidunā 'Allāmaĥ Ibn-ul-Maqrī and Sayyidunā Abush-Shaykh رَحِمَهُمَا اللّٰهُ تَعَالٰی returned to their house. After a little while, there was a knock on the door. As they answered, there was an 'Alawī saint and his two slaves with food in their hands. Explaining, he said, 'You have complained about your hunger in the court of the Beloved and Blessed Prophet صَلَّى اللهُ تَعَالٰی عَلَيْهِ وَاٰلِهٖ وَسَلَّم. اَلْحَمْدُ لِلّٰه عَزَّوَجَلَّ, The Holy Prophet صَلَّى اللهُ تَعَالٰی عَلَيْهِ وَاٰلِهٖ وَسَلَّم has ordered me in my dream to bring food for you. Therefore, whatever I could arrange right away, I have brought for you. Please accept this.' *(Tażkira-tul-Ḥuffāẓ, vol. 3, pp. 121)*

May Allah عَزَّوَجَلَّ have mercy on them and forgive us without accountability for their sake!

Ĥar ṭaraf Madīnay mayn bĥīṛ ĥay faqīron kī
Aīk daynay wālā ĥay kul jaĥān suwālī ĥay

Beggars come to Madīnaĥ
Everywhere you see them, flocking
There is one distributor
The whole world is lined up, begging

صَلُّوْا عَلَى الْحَبِيْب صَلَّى اللهُ تَعَالٰى عَلٰى مُحَمَّد

Pleas are heard by the Holy Prophet صَلَّى اللهُ عَلَيْهِ وَاٰلِهٖ وَسَلَّم

Dear Islamic brothers! We have just learned that our saints endured immense hardships to acquire religious knowledge. They starved, yet diligently and zealously, compiled their works and writings and left them for us, as a bouquet of flowers. Woe, but sadly today, Muslims are not interested in gaining any benefit from these volumes of works. Our saints were enthusiastic about accumulating the treasure of righteous deeds for their Hereafter but most of today's Muslims are only obsessed about accumulating worldly wealth.

From the above parable we have also learnt that when our saints were confronted with adversities, they would wholeheartedly plead the Holy Prophet صَلَّى اللهُ تَعَالٰی عَلَيْهِ وَاٰلِهٖ وَسَلَّم for help. The pleas emanating from the depth of the heart, are always heard by our Noble Prophet صَلَّى اللهُ تَعَالٰی عَلَيْهِ وَاٰلِهٖ وَسَلَّم. My master and a true devotee of Rasūl, A'lā Ḥaḍrat Imām Aḥmad Razā Khān عَلَيْهِ رَحْمَةُ الرَّحْمٰن writes in *Ḥadāiq-e-Bakhshish*:

Wallāĥ عَزَّوَجَلَّ *woĥ* صَلَّى اللهُ تَعَالٰى عَلَيْهِ وَاٰلِهٖ وَسَلَّم *sūn layn geyn faryād ko poĥanchayn gey*
Itnā bĥī to ĥo koī jo 'Āĥ' karay dil say.

By Allah عَزَّوَجَلَّ*, he* صَلَّى اللهُ تَعَالٰى عَلَيْهِ وَاٰلِهٖ وَسَلَّم *will hear and come to comfort;*
Should someone sigh 'Ah' from his heart

By the grace of Allah عَزَّوَجَلَّ, our Noble Prophet صَلَّى اللّٰهُ تَعَالٰى عَلَيْهِ وَاٰلِهٖ وَسَلَّم heard the pleas of his hungry devotees and immediately aided them by sending food.

Dar-e-Rasūl صَلَّى اللهُ تَعَالٰى عَلَيْهِ وَاٰلِهٖ وَسَلَّم *say ay Rāz kyā naĥīn miltā?*
Koī palat kay na khālī gayā Madīnay say

O Rāz! What is not given by beloved صَلَّى اللهُ تَعَالٰى عَلَيْهِ وَاٰلِهٖ وَسَلَّم*?*
No one left Madīnaĥ empty handed!

Dear Islamic brothers! One of the ways of acquiring religious knowledge is to travel with the devotees of Rasūl in the Madanī Qāfilaĥs of Dawat-e-Islami. In addition to the acquisition of knowledge, one's worldly problems are also often resolved [by such travels].

51. Hepatitis C cured

A man was confined to bed with Hepatitis C. Doctors had declared his disease incurable. His son travelled with the devotees of Rasūl in the Sunnaĥ-Inspiring Madanī Qāfilaĥ of Dawat-e-Islami and made sincere Du'ā for his ailing father. When he returned from the Madanī Qāfilaĥ he was overjoyed to see that his father had recovered from his disease and was strolling happily.

Bāp bīmār ĥo, sakht bayzār ĥo
Pāye gā ṣiḥḥatayn, Qāfilay mayn chalo
Wa ĥo bāb-e-karam, dūr ĥaun sāray gham
Pĥir say khushiyān milayn, Qāfilay mayn chalo

Father is ailing, or upset wearily;
Will recover and heal! Travel with Qāfilaĥ
The door of mercy will open removing worry and tension;
Happiness will be regained, travel with Qāfilaĥ

صَلُّوْا عَلَى الْحَبِيْب   صَلَّى اللهُ تَعَالٰى عَلٰى مُحَمَّد

52. An enlightened baker

Shaykh Sayyidunā Saĥal Bin 'Abdullāĥ Tustarī عَلَيْهِ رَحْمَةُ اللّٰهِ الْقَوِى once told his disciples that a certain baker in Basra was a saint. One of the Shaykh's disciples travelled to Basra to meet that saint. Reaching Basra, he located that baker's shop and when he got there, he found the saint baking bread in a clay oven. To protect his beard from fire, the saint had covered it with a piece of cloth. (Back then, almost all Muslim men grew beards and it was a common practice for bakers to cover their beards for safety). The Shaykh's disciple thought that if the baker were a saint, he would not need to protect his beard from fire. He then approached the baker, made Salām and wished to talk. Replying to his Salām, the baker, who was enlightened with spiritual insight [Kashf], said, 'You looked down on me, so now you cannot benefit from my words.' Saying this, the baker refused to converse with him. *(Ar-Risāla-tul-Qushayriyyaĥ, pp. 363)*

May Allah عَزَّوَجَلَّ have mercy on them and forgive us without accountability for their sake!

صَلُّوْا عَلَى الْحَبِيْب صَلَّى اللهُ تَعَالٰى عَلٰى مُحَمَّد

53. A saint رَحْمَةُ اللهِ عَلَيْه in rags

Dear Islamic brothers! The foregoing parable clearly shows that it is not necessary at all for a saint to be famous, wear unusually attractive clothes and turban and have a large number of disciples & devotees. Allah عَزَّوَجَلَّ favours whomever He عَزَّوَجَلَّ wills. Allah عَزَّوَجَلَّ has concealed His saints amongst His servants. Therefore, we should treat every pious person with respect as we do not know who a saint is!

Once I [the author] was travelling with the devotees of Rasūl in a Madanī Qāfilaĥ of Dawat-e-Islami. A beardless, thin and unattractive boy was sitting near us. Dressed in simple clothes, he was lost in his thoughts.

The train stopped at a station for two minutes. Getting off the train, the boy sat on one of the benches at the station. We all began to offer Ṣalāt-ul-'Aṣr with Jamā'at. We had hardly offered just one Rak'at when we heard the whistle [as the train was about to leave]. People started shouting that the train was leaving. We discontinued our Ṣalāĥ and were about to dash to board the train when this boy got up and strictly signalled to me to continue Ṣalāĥ. We again started our Jamā'at.

Amazingly, the train stood there until we had finished our Ṣalāĥ and boarded back on the train. That boy was still sitting there, gazing around, as our train left the station. I reckoned that perhaps he was from amongst those who remain lost in spiritual meditation. He may have held back the train with his spiritual powers.

May Allah عَزَّوَجَلَّ have mercy on him and forgive us without accountability for his sake!

Three concealed in three

Spiritual successor of A'lā Ḥaḍrat, Sayyidunā Abū Yūsuf Muhammad Sharīf Kotlavī عَلَيْهِ رَحْمَةُ اللّٰهِ الْقَوِی has narrated: 'Allah عَزَّوَجَلَّ has concealed three things in three other things:

1. His pleasure in His obedience.
2. His displeasure in His disobedience.
3. His friends among His servants.'

He رَحْمَةُ اللهِ تَعَالٰی عَلَيْه has further stated, 'Therefore, we should do each and every good deed because we do not know as to which deed would please Him. Similarly, we should avoid each and every sin because we do not know which sin would displease Him, no matter how minor it seems to be. For example, using someone else's toothpick (without permission) or using one's neighbour's soil without permission, don't seem to be the matters of concern, but it is possible that the wrath of Allah عَزَّوَجَلَّ be concealed in them. Therefore, one should take care even in such apparently-minor-looking matters.' *(Akhlāq-uṣ-Ṣāliḥīn, pp. 56)*

Dear Islamic brothers! In order to plant the seeds of devotion to the saints of Allah in your heart, stay associated with the Madanī environment that is full of the blessings of saints. Regularly attend Dawat-e-Islami's weekly Sunnaĥ-Inspiring Ijtimā' held in your city and then see how it effects you. Here is a summary of an incident highlighting the benefits of the Ijtimā' to inspire you to attend it.

54. I got rid of wicked habits

A young man from Bāb-ul Madīnaĥ, Karachi has stated: 'I was arrogant because of my good physique and young age. I used to get my clothes tailored according to the latest fashions and trends. I would ride the bus to college, but would not pay the fare. When the money collector asked me to pay the fare I would quarrel with him. Loafing around all night and gambling away money were some of the wicked habits of mine. Sins had become a part of my character. My parents who often used to advise me had also become disappointed. My mother would weep and supplicate for me [but I did not care].

An Islamic brother would casually invite me to attend the weekly Sunnaĥ-Inspiring Ijtimā', but I would turn a deaf ear. Once, on the night of the Ijtimā', he politely insisted, 'Today you will have to go with me.' I tried to excuse but he was persistent. The next thing I knew, he stopped a rickshaw and requested me to go with him. Finally, I yielded to his perseverance and got in the rickshaw. We went to Jāmi' Masjid Gulzār-e-Ḥabīb, the first Madanī Markaz of Dawat-e-Islami.

When the lights were switched off, for Żikr and Du'ā session, I got up to leave thinking that the Ijtimā' had ended. Little did I know that staying for that session would prove to be a turning point in my life. The Islamic brother, my well-wisher, explained to me the situation and made me stay. During Żikr, the uproar of the rhythmic chanting had a deep impact on me. I swear by Allah عَزَّوَجَلَّ! I had neither heard nor seen such spirituality in my entire life. This was followed by an inspiring Du'ā. All one could hear were the sobbing and weeping sounds of the attendees. Even a hard-hearted person like me burst into tears. I repented of my past sins and joined the Madanī environment of Dawat-e-Islami.'

Tumĥayn luṭf ā jāye gā zindagī kā
Qarīb ā kay daykĥo żarā, Madanī Māḥaul
Tanazzul kay geĥray gaṛĥay mayn tĥay un kī
Taraqqī kā bā'iš banā, Madanī Māḥaul
Yaqīnan muqaddar kā woĥ ĥay sikandar
Jisay khayr say mil gayā, Madanī Māḥaul

Enjoy the real taste of life;
Come close and see, the Madanī environment
Those who were in deep pits;
Were set back on track by the Madanī environment
Indeed fortunate is he who, by divine bestowment
Has joined the Madanī environment

First Madanī Markaz of Dawat-e-Islami

Dear Islamic brothers! The above incident is of the beginning era of Dawat-e-Islami. When we started the Madanī work of Dawat-e-Islami in 1401 A.H., we did not have a suitable place where we could conduct our weekly Ijtimā'. During that time, I[1] would personally visit different scholars and Shaykhs of Aĥl-e-Sunnat, in Bāb-ul-Madīnaĥ, Karachi [Pakistan] and request them for their support and cooperation with Dawat-e-Islami. I had a passion and an obsession to establish a broad network of righteous Madanī working for the protection of the faith of the Muslims and reform of their characters and deeds. My zealous enthusiasm can be best reflected in these words: **'I must strive to reform myself and people of the entire world,** اِنْ شَآءَاللّٰہ عَزَّوَجَلَّ**.'**

Anyway, in this context, I visited the eloquent orator of Pakistan, and a true devotee of Rasūl, 'Allāmaĥ Maulānā Al-Ḥāfiẓ Ash-Shāĥ Muhammad Shafī' Okāřvī عَلَيْهِ رَحْمَةُ اللّٰهِ الْقَوِی at his residence. When I informed him about Dawat-e-Islami, he was extremely delighted and handed me a personally signed letter, advocating the cause of Dawat-e-Islami. His devotion for [the propagation of] Maslak [doctrine] of Aĥl-e-Sunnat is highly commendable! He was gracious enough to offer the Jāmi' Masjid Gulzār-e-Ḥabīb for our weekly Ijtimā' without being asked for it. This Masjid is located in the heart of Karachi and was managed under his supervision. Thus, Jāmi' Masjid Gulzār-e-Ḥabīb became the first Madanī Markaz of Dawat-e-Islami.

For several years, during his life and even after his demise, we conducted our weekly Ijtimā' at this Masjid. The number of the devotees of Rasūl kept growing day by day, overflowing the Masjid with the attendees. Allah عَزَّوَجَلَّ provided the means. With the diligence of Islamic brothers we collected almost 22.5 million Pakistani rupees in donation

---

[1] [The author, Amīr-e-Aĥl-e-Sunnat دَامَتْ بَرَكَاتُهُمُ الْعَالِيَه]

and purchased about 10,000 square yards [over 2 acres] of land, near the old Sabzi Mandi, Bāb-ul-Madīnaĥ Karachi. Then we further collected millions in donation to construct the magnificent global Madanī Markaz of Dawat-e-Islami ['Ālamī Madanī Markaz] which includes a grand splendid Masjid, several offices to run Madanī affairs, and another building for Jāmi'a-tul-Madīnaĥ [an Institution for learning Islamic sciences run by Dawat-e-Islami]. From here thousands of Muslims avail blessings of Madīnaĥ as the mercy of Allah عَزَّوَجَلَّ showers over Faīzān-e-Madīnaĥ.

Sunnat kī baĥār āyī Faīzān-e-Madīnaĥ mayn
Raḥmat kī ghaṭā chāī Faīzān-e-Madīnaĥ mayn

The spring of Sunnaĥ has arrived in Faīzān-e-Madīnaĥ;
The clouds of mercy are all around Faīzān-e-Madīnaĥ

صَلُّوا عَلَى الْحَبِيب صَلَّى اللّٰهُ تَعَالٰى عَلٰى مُحَمَّد

55. Parable of 'the orator of Pakistan'

The orator of Pakistan, Maulānā Muhammad Shafī' Okāřvī عَلَيْهِ رَحْمَةُ اللّٰهِ الْقَوِى was an extraordinary devotee of Rasūl. In 1418 A.H., a resident of Madīnaĥ city, Ḥājī Ghulām Shabbīr told me the following faith-refreshing incident. Once the respectable Shaykh Sayyid Khurshīd Aḥmad Shāĥ told him that the orator of Pakistan Maulānā Muhammad Shafī' Okāřvī عَلَيْهِ رَحْمَةُ اللّٰهِ الْقَوِى once met him in tears, while they were in Madīnaĥ, and requested, 'Will you accompany me to the sacred grave [of the Beloved and Blessed Prophet صَلَّى اللّٰهُ تَعَالٰى عَلَيْهِ وَاٰلِهٖ وَسَلَّم]? I have to ask forgiveness from our Noble Prophet صَلَّى اللّٰهُ تَعَالٰى عَلَيْهِ وَاٰلِهٖ وَسَلَّم!'

When asked about this, he replied, 'Yesterday in the holy Masjid of Rasūlullāĥ صَلَّى اللّٰهُ تَعَالٰى عَلَيْهِ وَاٰلِهٖ وَسَلَّم, a disrespectful speaker blasphemed the Noble Prophet صَلَّى اللّٰهُ تَعَالٰى عَلَيْهِ وَاٰلِهٖ وَسَلَّم so I reprimanded him. Matters got out of hand and his supporters came and treated me harshly. Because of this harshness I was deeply disheartened. At night, the Holy Prophet صَلَّى اللّٰهُ تَعَالٰى عَلَيْهِ وَاٰلِهٖ وَسَلَّم blessed me with his vision in dream and said, 'You could not even bear little harshness for me!' Maulānā Shafī' Okāřvī عَلَيْهِ رَحْمَةُ اللّٰهِ الْقَوِى further explained, 'The thing is, I felt a little pride in my heart and considered my insult beneath my dignity. Therefore, the Holy Prophet صَلَّى اللّٰهُ تَعَالٰى عَلَيْهِ وَاٰلِهٖ وَسَلَّم cautioned me. Now I want to go in the court of the Beloved and Blessed Prophet صَلَّى اللهُ تَعَالٰى عَلَيْهِ وَاٰلِهٖ وَسَلَّم and beg forgiveness for my doubtfulness.'

May Allah عَزَّوَجَلَّ have mercy on them and forgive us without accountability for their sake!

صَلُّوْا عَلَى الْحَبِيْب صَلَّى اللهُ تَعَالٰى عَلٰى مُحَمَّد

56. Help from the Holy Prophet ﷺ

سُبْحٰنَ اللّٰه عَزَّوَجَلَّ! The true devotees are treated with great indulgence! We have learned from the above parable that the Beloved and Blessed Prophet صَلَّى اللهُ تَعَالٰى عَلَيْهِ وَاٰلِهٖ وَسَلَّم is always aware of the thoughts and affairs of his devotees, by the powers vested in him by Allah عَزَّوَجَلَّ and he صَلَّى اللهُ تَعَالٰى عَلَيْهِ وَاٰلِهٖ وَسَلَّم at times visits them in their dreams to assist them and to rectify their shortcomings. Let's hear another enlightening narrative in this context:

Sayyidunā Shaykh Yūsuf Bin Ismā'īl Nabĥānī قُدِّسَ سِرُّهُ الرَّبَّانِي has narrated a parable about a Ḥājī from Khorasan who would travel to Makkaĥ for Hajj [pilgrimage], every year. After performing Hajj he would go to Madīnaĥ where he used to visit an 'Alawī saint, Shaykh Sayyidunā Ṭāĥir Bin Yaḥyā رَحْمَةُ اللهِ تَعَالٰى عَلَيْه and gift him some money. Once, a person who was jealous of Shaykh Ṭāĥir met the Khorasani Ḥājī and told him that he was just wasting his money by giving it to Shaykh Ṭāĥir رَحْمَةُ اللهِ تَعَالٰى عَلَيْه because the Shaykh spends all his gifted money inappropriately. Therefore, for the next two years, the Khorasani Ḥājī did not gift anything to the Shaykh. The third year, as he was making preparations for his pilgrimage, he beheld the Holy Prophet صَلَّى اللهُ تَعَالٰى عَلَيْهِ وَاٰلِهٖ وَسَلَّم in dream. The Prophet of mankind, the Peace of our heart and mind, the most Generous and Kind صَلَّى اللهُ تَعَالٰى عَلَيْهِ وَاٰلِهٖ وَسَلَّم said in admonition, 'Regret on you! You have believed a jealous person and ended your kind behaviour with Ṭāĥir. Now make up for it and avoid cutting ties with him in future.'

That Ḥājī from Khorasan was deeply regretful to have formed a negative opinion against the Shaykh because of hearing just one side of the story. Therefore, when he reached Madīnaĥ زَادَهَا اللهُ شَرَفًا وَّتَعْظِيْمًا, he went straight to visit the 'Alawī Shaykh, Sayyidunā Ṭāĥir Bin Yaḥyā رَحْمَةُ اللهِ تَعَالٰى عَلَيْه. As soon as the Shaykh رَحْمَةُ اللهِ تَعَالٰى عَلَيْه saw that Khorasani Ḥājī, the Shaykh رَحْمَةُ اللهِ تَعَالٰى عَلَيْه said, 'If the Beloved and Blessed Prophet صَلَّى اللهُ تَعَالٰى عَلَيْهِ وَاٰلِهٖ وَسَلَّم had not ordered you to come, you were not prepared to meet me. Listening to only one side of the story from my opponent you formed a negative opinion and discontinued your generosity. You have come here today after the Beloved Rasūl صَلَّى اللهُ تَعَالٰى عَلَيْهِ وَاٰلِهٖ وَسَلَّم admonished you in your dream!'

Overwhelmed by hearing this, the Khorasani Ḥājī asked in utter surprise, 'Your grace! How do you come to know all this?' He replied, 'I have known it from the very first year and when you avoided me the second year as well, I was deeply dejected. Then the Holy Prophet صَلَّى اللهُ تَعَالٰى عَلَيْهِ وَاٰلِهٖ وَسَلَّم blessed me with his vision in my dream and consoled me. He also told me what he had told you in your dream.'

The Khorasani Ḥājī gifted a lot of money to the Shaykh رَحْمَةُ اللهِ تَعَالٰى عَلَيْه and kissed his hand and forehead. He then apologized to the Shaykh رَحْمَةُ اللهِ تَعَالٰى عَلَيْه for hurting him by forming a negative opinion about him as a result of hearing just one side of the story. *(Mulakhkhaṣan Ḥujjatullāĥi-'alal-'Ālamīn, pp. 571)*

May Allah عَزَّوَجَلَّ have mercy on them and forgive us without accountability for their sake!

Avoid deciding until you have heard both sides of the story

Dear Islamic brothers! The foregoing parable shows that our Noble Prophet صَلَّى اللهُ تَعَالٰى عَلَيْهِ وَاٰلِهٖ وَسَلَّم is well aware of the affairs of his followers. Sometimes he صَلَّى اللهُ تَعَالٰى عَلَيْهِ وَاٰلِهٖ وَسَلَّم consoles the depressed, reforms the wrongdoers by blessing them with his vision in their dream, conveys call to righteousness, orders the sinners to repent and brings closer those who have grown apart [because of suspicions]. The Ḥājī from Khorasan indulged in suspicion because of listening to the talebearer and formed a negative opinion of the Shaykh, so the Holy Prophet صَلَّى اللهُ تَعَالٰى عَلَيْهِ وَاٰلِهٖ وَسَلَّم cautioned him in his dream.

We have also learnt the lesson that we should avoid tale-bearing and forming any opinion about others merely by listening to a one-sided story. Best course of action would be to completely avoid listening to anything negative about our fellow Muslims, unless Sharī'aĥ permits us to do so. In this way we can avoid several major sins and Ḥarām acts, leading to Hellfire, like backbiting, tale-telling, suspicion about others, laying false blames on others and hurting others' feelings.

Talebearer will not enter Paradise

The Holy Prophet صَلَّى اللّٰهُ تَعَالٰى عَلَيْهِ وَاٰلِهٖ وَسَلَّم has stated, 'Talebearer will not enter Paradise. *(Ṣaḥīḥ Bukhārī, vol. 4, pp. 115, Ḥadīš 6056)* And in another Ḥadīš it is stated: 'Tale-bearing and malice will certainly take one to Hell.' *(Attarghīb Wattarĥīb, vol. 3, pp. 324, Ḥadīš 5)*

Things that diminish one's prestige

Shaykh Sayyidunā Muhammad Bin Qarẓī عَلَيْهِ رَحْمَةُ اللّٰهِ الْقَوِى was once asked, 'Yā Sayyidī! Which habits diminish one's prestige?' He replied, 'Excessive talking, disclosing secrets and believing everyone's (negative) comments (about others).' *(Itḥāf-us-Sādat-il-Muttaqīn, vol. 9, pp. 352)*

Shaykh Sayyidunā Ḥasan Baṣrī عَلَيْهِ رَحْمَةُ اللّٰهِ الْقَوِى has stated, 'One committing the tale-bearing of others to you will also be committing your tale-bearing to others.' [In other words, one speaking ill of others to you will also be speaking ill of you to others].

Ḥujjat-ul-Islam, Shaykh Sayyidunā Imām Muhammad Ghazālī عَلَيْهِ رَحْمَةُ اللّٰهِ الْوَالِى has stated, 'This shows that the talebearer should neither be appreciated nor be trusted. Nor should he be believed. He should be avoided because he does not give up lying, backbiting, deceiving, breaching, jealousy, hypocrisy and having malice. He does not forgo harming others and is among those who disobey divine commandment by spreading hatred and hostility among people instead of bringing them closer. He rebels on the earth.' *(Iḥyā-ul-'Ulūm, vol. 3, pp. 193)* Allah عَزَّوَجَلَّ says in the Quran:

اِنَّمَا السَّبِيْلُ عَلَى الَّذِيْنَ يَظْلِمُوْنَ النَّاسَ وَ يَبْغُوْنَ فِى الْاَرْضِ بِغَيْرِ الْحَقِّ ؕ

The interrogation is only against those who oppress people and rebel on the earth unjustifiably.

[Kanz-ul-Īmān (Translation of Quran)] (Part 25, Sūraĥ Ash-Shūrā, verse 42)

The foregoing verse also applies to the talebearer. A Ḥadīš also reinforces this as stated below.

Signs of pious person

The Prophet of Raḥmaĥ, the Intercessor of Ummaĥ صَلَّى اللّٰهُ تَعَالٰى عَلَيْهِ وَاٰلِهٖ وَسَلَّم has stated, 'Certainly, bad are those who are avoided by people because of the harm they cause to people.' *(Muwaṭṭā Imām Mālik, vol. 2, pp. 403, Ḥadīš 1719)*

He صَلَّى اللّٰهُ تَعَالٰى عَلَيْهِ وَاٰلِهٖ وَسَلَّم has further stated, 'The pious servants of Allah عَزَّوَجَلَّ are those whose (mere) sight makes one remember Allah عَزَّوَجَلَّ and the impious servants of Allah عَزَّوَجَلَّ are those who are talebearers, who cause separation among friends and find fault with the pious.' *(Musnad Imām Aḥmad, vol. 6, pp. 291, Ḥadīš 18020)*

At another instance he صَلَّى اللّٰهُ تَعَالٰى عَلَيْهِ وَاٰلِهٖ وَسَلَّم has warned, 'Beware! Lying blackens the face and tale-bearing is (a cause of) torment in the grave.' *(Musnad Abī Ya'lā, vol. 6, pp. 272, Ḥadīš 7404)* The Beloved and Blessed Prophet صَلَّى اللّٰهُ تَعَالٰى عَلَيْهِ وَاٰلِهٖ وَسَلَّم has also stated, 'Those committing backbiting, taunting others, tale-bearing and finding fault with the innocent will be raised by Allah عَزَّوَجَلَّ (on the Day of Judgement) in the form of dog.' *(Attarghīb Wattarĥīb, vol. 3, pp. 325)*

Yā Rab-e-Muhammad Tū mujĥay nayk banā day
Amrāz gunāĥaun kay mayray sāray miṭā day
Mayn ghībat-o-chughlī say raĥūn dūr ĥamayshaĥ
Ĥar khaṣlat-e-bad say mayrā pīcĥā Tū cĥuřā day
Mayn fāltū bātaun say raĥūn dūr ĥamayshaĥ
Chup reĥnay kā Allah عَزَّوَجَلَّ salīqaĥ Tū sikĥā day

Yā Rab of Muhammad صَلَّى اللّٰهُ تَعَالٰى عَلَيْهِ وَاٰلِهٖ وَسَلَّم, adorn me with piety
Relieve me from my load of sin and immorality
May I always refrain from backbiting and tale-bearing
Help me to kick off all habits of transgressing
May I always avoid idle talk, gossip and chatting
Teach me the art of silence and sobering

صَلُّوْا عَلَى الْحَبِيْب صَلَّى اللّٰهُ تَعَالٰى عَلٰى مُحَمَّد

57. Shaykh assists from his tomb

Here is an incident that took place over 700 years ago. Sultan of Mashāikh Sayyidunā Maḥbūb-e-Ilāhī Niẓāmuddīn Auliyā رَحْمَةُ اللهِ تَعَالَى عَلَيْه has narrated from Maulānā Kathaylī عَلَيْهِ رَحْمَةُ اللّٰهِ الْوَلِى that a famine once struck Delhi. In the state of extreme hunger he (Maulānā Kathaylī عَلَيْهِ رَحْمَةُ اللّٰهِ الْوَلِى) once got some food from somewhere. In the well-wishing of fellow-Muslims, he thought that he should not eat that food alone; instead, he should share it with any other hungry Muslim.

Soon, a righteous individual, robed in a tattered cloak, walked past him. Maulānā Kathaylī عَلَيْهِ رَحْمَةُ اللّٰهِ الْوَلِى asked that pious person to join. Both of them sat down and began to eat the food. During their conversation, Maulānā Kathaylī عَلَيْهِ رَحْمَةُ اللّٰهِ الْوَلِى mentioned to the pious man that he was in debt of 20 rupees. The person said, 'I will make that available for you.' Maulānā Kathaylī عَلَيْهِ رَحْمَةُ اللّٰهِ الْوَلِى thought that this person appears to be destitute, how will he make 20 rupees available for me! After the meal, the pious person took Maulānā Kathaylī عَلَيْهِ رَحْمَةُ اللّٰهِ الْوَلِى to a nearby Masjid. Adjacent to the Masjid was a shrine where they paid homage. The individual stood beside the shrine and sought help, touched his stick to the grave twice, and pleaded in these words, 'My friend needs 20 rupees. Kindly, help him.' The person then turned towards him and said, 'Brother, you may leave now. إِنْ شَآءَاللّٰه عَزَّوَجَلَّ, You will get 20 rupees.'

Maulānā Kathaylī عَلَيْهِ رَحْمَةُ اللّٰهِ الْوَلِى has stated that he kissed the hand of the individual in respect, and then left for the city. He was still puzzled as to where he would get the 20 rupees from. He had a letter as an entrustment [Amānat] which he was to deliver to someone. He رَحْمَةُ اللهِ تَعَالَى عَلَيْه reached his destination to deliver the letter. A Turkish man was sitting at the balcony of his house. Seeing Maulānā Kathaylī عَلَيْهِ رَحْمَةُ اللّٰهِ الْوَلِى he ordered his servants to bring him inside. The servants respectfully led him to the upper floor of the house. The Turkish man greeted Maulānā Kathaylī عَلَيْهِ رَحْمَةُ اللّٰهِ الْوَلِى very politely and graciously. He repeatedly said, 'Are you not the same fellow who was very nice and gracious to me at such-and-such place?' Maulānā Kathaylī عَلَيْهِ رَحْمَةُ اللّٰهِ الْوَلِى replied that he was unable to recall their meeting. The Turkish man said, 'Why are you denying now? Worry not! I do recognize you.' He then brought 20 rupees and, very courteously, placed them onto the palm of Maulānā Kathaylī عَلَيْهِ رَحْمَةُ اللّٰهِ الْوَلِى.' *(Fawāid-ul-Fuwād, pp. 124)*

May Allah عَزَّوَجَلَّ have mercy on them and forgive us without accountability for their sake!

Who causes death?

Dear Islamic brothers! The foregoing parable narrated by Shaykh Sayyidunā Maḥbūb-e-Ilāĥī Niẓāmuddīn Auliyā رَحْمَةُ اللهِ تَعَالٰی عَلَيْه has vitalized our faith. This parable has made it clear that it is permissible to seek help from the saints of Allah عَزَّوَجَلَّ not only in their apparent life but also after their demise. Likewise, it is also permissible to visit the shrine of a saint for help.

However, it must be remembered that the real and absolute provider of everything is indeed Allah عَزَّوَجَلَّ, and the reference made to the saints is not literal. For example, the real and absolute provider of cure is Allah عَزَّوَجَلَّ, but people normally say, 'O doctor! Make me better.' Similarly the true giver of death is Allah عَزَّوَجَلَّ, but the angel Sayyidunā 'Izrāīl عَلَيْهِ السَّلَام has been empowered by Allah عَزَّوَجَلَّ to give death. This fact is stated in the Quran in 11th verse of Sūraĥ As-Sajdaĥ, part 21:

قُلْ يَتَوَفّٰىكُمْ مَّلَكُ الْمَوْتِ الَّذِيْ وُكِّلَ بِكُمْ

Proclaim, the angel of death, who is appointed over you, causes you to die.

[Kanz-ul-Īmān (Translation of Quran)] (Part 21, Sūraĥ As-Sajdaĥ, verse 11)

Dear Islamic brothers! Even after their demise, the saints of Allah can bless others with their vision in the state of wakefulness and can converse with them, as shown in the following parable.

58. Saints are alive

Shaykh Sayyidunā Shāĥ Walīyullāĥ Muḥaddiš Diĥlvī عَلَيْهِ رَحْمَةُ اللهِ الْقَوِی has narrated from his father Shaykh Sayyidunā Shāĥ 'Abdur Raḥīm عَلَيْهِ رَحْمَةُ اللهِ الْكَرِيْم that he once visited the shrine of Sayyidunā Khuwājaĥ Quṭbuddīn Bakhtiyār Kākī عَلَيْهِ رَحْمَةُ اللهِ الْبَاقِي. Considering himself unable to approach the blessed grave because of his sins, he stood at some distance from it. At that very moment, the Shaykh's soul appeared and instructed him to come forward. As he moved forward a few steps he saw that near the blessed grave was a throne brought by four angels from towards the sky and Shaykh Sayyidunā Khuwājaĥ Baĥāuddīn Naqshband رَحْمَةُ اللهِ تَعَالٰی عَلَيْه was seated on the throne.

Both of the Shaykhs رَحِمَهُمَا اللّٰهُ تَعَالٰی began to converse secretly. [Shaykh 'Abdur Raḥīm عَلَيْهِ رَحْمَةُ اللّٰهِ الْكَرِيْم goes onto say] He could not hear their conversation. The angels then picked up the throne and carried it away. Shaykh Sayyidunā Khuwājaĥ Quṭbuddīn Bakhtiyār Kākī عَلَيْهِ رَحْمَةُ اللّٰهِ الْبَاقِي then turned towards him and said, 'Come forward.' He رَحْمَةُ اللّٰهِ تَعَالٰی عَلَيْه then moved a few steps forward. The Shaykh رَحْمَةُ اللّٰهِ تَعَالٰی عَلَيْه repeatedly asked him to come forward and he complied, until he was very close to the honourable Shaykh رَحْمَةُ اللّٰهِ تَعَالٰی عَلَيْه.

The Shaykh رَحْمَةُ اللّٰهِ تَعَالٰی عَلَيْه then asked him, 'What do you say about couplets?' He replied, 'A couplet is a poetical expression; a good couplet is good and a bad one is bad.' The Shaykh رَحْمَةُ اللّٰهِ تَعَالٰی عَلَيْه said, 'بَارَكَ اللّٰهُ عَزَّوَجَلَّ [*may Allah* عَزَّوَجَلَّ *grant you blessings*],' and then asked again 'What do you say about a pleasant voice?' He replied, 'This is a grace of Allah عَزَّوَجَلَّ granted by Him to whomever He عَزَّوَجَلَّ wills.' The Shaykh رَحْمَةُ اللّٰهِ تَعَالٰی عَلَيْه said, 'بَارَكَ اللّٰهُ عَزَّوَجَلَّ,' and asked once again, 'So then, what do you say about the one blessed with both a good couplet and a pleasant voice?' He said, 'That is superb, Allah عَزَّوَجَلَّ grants this to whomever He عَزَّوَجَلَّ wills.' The Shaykh رَحْمَةُ اللّٰهِ تَعَالٰی عَلَيْه said, 'بَارَكَ اللّٰهُ عَزَّوَجَلَّ! You should also, at times, listen to one or two couplets.' He said, 'Your honour, why did you not instruct me in the presence of his Excellency Shaykh Sayyidunā Baĥāuddīn Naqshband رَحْمَةُ اللّٰهِ تَعَالٰی عَلَيْه?' The Shaykh رَحْمَةُ اللّٰهِ تَعَالٰی عَلَيْه either said that it was due to 'respect' or due to 'prudence.' *(Anfās-ul-'Ārifīn, pp. 44)*

Dar-e-wālā pay aīk maylaĥ lagā ĥay
'Ajab is dar kay ṭukřon mayn mazaĥ ĥay
Yaĥān say kab koī khālī pĥirā ĥay
Sakhī Dātā kī yeĥ dawlat sarā ĥay

There is an influx of people at the honourable court
Where there is a strange pleasure in the bestowments
Has anybody ever returned empty-handed from here?
It is the court of the most generous and dear

صَلُّوْا عَلَى الْحَبِيْب صَلَّى اللّٰهُ تَعَالٰى عَلٰى مُحَمَّد

59. Adherence of Imām Aḥmad Razā رَحْمَةُ اللهِ عَلَيْه to Sunnaĥ

A'lā Ḥaḍrat, Imām-e-Aĥl-e-Sunnat, reviver of Sunnaĥ, eradicator of Bid'aĥ, scholar of Sharī'aĥ, guide of Ṭarīqaĥ, 'Allāmaĥ Maulānā Al-Ḥāj Al-Ḥāfiẓ Al-Qārī Ash-Shāĥ Imām Aḥmad Razā Khān عَلَيْهِ رَحْمَةُ الرَّحْمٰن was once invited for a meal. The food had been served but all people present there were waiting for Imām Aḥmad Razā Khān عَلَيْهِ رَحْمَةُ الرَّحْمٰن to begin eating. Picking up a piece of cucumber he ate it. Then he ate the second and the third. Following suit, the guests also stretched their hands out towards the container of cucumber, but A'lā Ḥaḍrat رَحْمَةُ اللهِ تَعَالٰی عَلَيْه stopped them and asked for the cucumber to be given to him all. Hence, he ate all the cucumber served on the dining-mat.

The Shaykh رَحْمَةُ اللهِ تَعَالٰی عَلَيْه would normally eat very little but had unexpectedly eaten all the pieces of cucumber, leaving the guests astonished. When asked about eating all cucumbers, the honourable Shaykh رَحْمَةُ اللهِ تَعَالٰی عَلَيْه explained, 'The first piece was bitter, and so were the second and the third. Since eating cucumber is a Sunnaĥ of the Beloved and Blessed Prophet صَلَّى اللهُ تَعَالٰی عَلَيْهِ وَاٰلِهٖ وَسَلَّم, and this cucumber was bitter, I did not want anyone to spit out the bitter cucumber.'

May Allah عَزَّوَجَلَّ have mercy on him and forgive us without accountability for his sake!

Mujĥ ko mīṫhay Mustafa صَلَّى اللهُ تَعَالٰی عَلَيْهِ وَاٰلِهٖ وَسَلَّم kī Sunnataun say piyār ĥay
اِنْ شَآءَاللّٰه عَزَّوَجَلَّ Do jaĥān mayn apnā bayřā pār ĥay

I love Sunnaĥs of the Beloved and Blessed Prophet صَلَّى اللهُ تَعَالٰی عَلَيْهِ وَاٰلِهٖ وَسَلَّم indeed
In both worlds اِنْ شَآءَاللّٰه عَزَّوَجَلَّ I will succeed

صَلُّوْا عَلَى الْحَبِيْب صَلَّى اللهُ تَعَالٰى عَلٰى مُحَمَّد

Eating dates and cucumber is Sunnaĥ

Dear Islamic brothers! How sincere and true devotee Imām Aḥmad Razā Khān عَلَيْهِ رَحْمَةُ الْمَنَّان was! Indeed, a devotee likes and reveres from the bottom of his heart every such thing associated with his beloved as Imām Aḥmad Razā Khān عَلَيْهِ رَحْمَةُ الْمَنَّان revered cucumber in such a manner that he ate it despite it being bitter just because the Beloved and Blessed Prophet صَلَّى اللهُ تَعَالٰی عَلَيْهِ وَاٰلِهٖ وَسَلَّم liked it.

Shaykh Sayyidunā ‘Abdullāĥ Ibn Ja’far رَضِیَ اللّٰہُ تَعَالٰی عَنْہُ has narrated, ‘I have seen the Noble Prophet صَلَّی اللّٰہُ تَعَالٰی عَلَیْہِ وَاٰلِہٖ وَسَلَّم eat cucumber with dates.’ *(Ṣaḥīḥ Muslim, pp. 130, Ḥadīš 2043)* A renowned exegetist of the Quran, Shaykh Muftī Aḥmad Yār Khān عَلَیْہِ رَحْمَۃُ الْمَنَّان has stated, ‘Dates have a natural tendency of causing warm effects whereas cucumbers have cold effects. Mixing both of them together makes them more effective. At times, the Beloved and Blessed Prophet صَلَّی اللّٰہُ تَعَالٰی عَلَیْہِ وَاٰلِہٖ وَسَلَّم ate dates and cucumber together (that is he chewed them together), and at times he ate them separately (that is he chewed them separately). Occasionally, the Holy Prophet صَلَّی اللّٰہُ تَعَالٰی عَلَیْہِ وَاٰلِہٖ وَسَلَّم ate watermelon and dates together. Eating the two together is very beneficial to one’s health. Mother of believers, Sayyidatunā ‘Āishaĥ Ṣiddīqaĥ رَضِیَ اللّٰہُ تَعَالٰی عَنْہَا has stated, ‘(Before being given away, I was very weak) My mother would try to make me healthier so that she may give me away to the Holy Prophet صَلَّی اللّٰہُ تَعَالٰی عَلَیْہِ وَاٰلِہٖ وَسَلَّم. At last, she fed me dates and cucumber, which made me healthy within a few days.’ *(Sunan Ibn Mājaĥ, vol. 4, pp. 37, Ḥadīš 3324)*

The Prophet of Raḥmaĥ, the Intercessor of Ummaĥ صَلَّی اللّٰہُ تَعَالٰی عَلَیْہِ وَاٰلِہٖ وَسَلَّم liked both dates and cucumber. Some Shaykhs رَحِمَہُمُ اللّٰہُ تَعَالٰی served dates, watermelon and cucumber, in addition to other foods, when they would hold Ijtimā’āt for the Īṣāl-e-Šawāb of the Holy Prophet صَلَّی اللّٰہُ تَعَالٰی عَلَیْہِ وَاٰلِہٖ وَسَلَّم. The basis for their action is the above Ḥadīš.’ *(Mirāt-ul-Manājīḥ, vol. 6, pp. 20-21)*

صَلُّوْا عَلَی الْحَبِیْب صَلَّی اللّٰہُ تَعَالٰی عَلٰی مُحَمَّد

60. I vow not to eat for fifteen days

Shaykh Sayyidunā Abū ‘Abdullāĥ Bin Khafīf عَلَیْہِ رَحْمَۃُ اللّٰہِ اللَّطِیْف was once invited somewhere for a meal. A starving disciple stretched his hand out towards the food before the Shaykh رَحْمَۃُ اللّٰہِ تَعَالٰی عَلَیْہ. Displeased by this, another disciple placed some food into the plate of the starving disciple in annoyance. The starving disciple immediately realized that he had made the mistake of violating the proper manners of eating by stretching his hand to the food before his Shaykh رَحْمَۃُ اللّٰہِ تَعَالٰی عَلَیْہ. To discipline his Nafs and make up for his mistake, he vowed not to eat for fifteen days despite being extremely hungry. *(Ar-Risāla-tul-Qushayriyyaĥ, pp. 179)*

May Allah عَزَّوَجَلَّ have mercy on them and forgive us without accountability for their sake!

صَلُّوْا عَلَی الْحَبِیْب صَلَّی اللّٰہُ تَعَالٰی عَلٰی مُحَمَّد

Scholars should begin eating first

If some people are present at the dining-mat and, any one of them is a saint, the proper manner is that all others should wait unless the saint begins eating. Remember! It is not a condition for a saint to be an elderly person but rather a practicing scholar of Islam is actually a saint. Therefore, if a young scholar is present even in the presence of many old people, the young scholar should start eating first.

The traits of the righteous are unique. When Shaykh Sayyidunā Abū 'Abdullāĥ Bin Khafif's starving disciple, who was himself a righteous person, realized his involuntary mistake on noticing the annoyance of the other disciple, he pledged himself not to eat anything for 15 days in spite of being extremely hungry. In this way, he punished himself despite the fact that he had just stretched out his hand, not eaten anything. The pious men often devise strange disciplinary actions for themselves, as stated in the following parable.

Atonement for putting on left shoe first

It is stated in *Kīmīyā-e-Sa'ādat* that a Shaykh رَحْمَةُ اللهِ تَعَالٰی عَلَیْه once put on his left shoe first by mistake instead of the right one. Extremely saddened by missing this Sunnaĥ, he gave two sacks of wheat in charity to make up for it.

Dear Islamic brothers! It was indeed a unique manner of those great saints. If only we also be blessed with following in their footsteps! In order to learn Sunnaĥs and manners one should make a routine of travelling with Dawat-e-Islami's Madanī Qāfilaĥ along with the devotees of Rasūl as there are many blessings for it. Here is one such incident.

61. Travel to Madīnaĥ

In order to carry out Madanī activities properly, Dawat-e-Islami has divided areas into districts according to its organizational procedure. A responsible Islamic brother of Madanī In'āmāt from one such district of Sheikhupura city once sent me[1] a letter whose summary is as follows:

---

[1] [The author, Amīr-e-Aĥl-e-Sunnat دَامَتْ بَرَكَاتُهُمُ الْعَالِيَه]

اَلْحَمْدُ لِلّٰه عَزَّوَجَلَّ! In 1424 A.H., I was blessed with performing 'Umraĥ and visiting Madīnaĥ زَادَهَا اللّٰهُ شَرَفًا وَّتَعْظِيْمًا. I met a Qārī who was from Kasur, Pakistan. The Qārī said, 'I participated in Dawat-e-Islami's 3-day International Sunnaĥ-Inspiring Ijtimā' held in 1424 A.H. at Ṣaḥrā-e-Madīnaĥ, Madīna-tul-Auliyā Multan. In the Ijtimā' we were persuaded to travel in Madanī Qāfilaĥs and make Du'ā as the Du'ā made during Madanī Qāfilaĥs is accepted by the grace of Allah عَزَّوَجَلَّ.

Inspired, I travelled with a 3-day Sunnaĥ-Inspiring Madanī Qāfilaĥ and earnestly made Du'ā that I be blessed with a visit to the holy city of Madīnaĥ زَادَهَا اللّٰهُ شَرَفًا وَّتَعْظِيْمًا. After the Madanī Qāfilaĥ ended, I returned home. When I went to teach the Quran to children at someone's house as usual, the father of the children was very nice to me and said, 'If you would let me know any of your desires; I wish to please you as you teach the Holy Quran to our children.'

At first I tried to decline his offer, but eventually gave in due to his insistence. I finally informed him of my desire to visit the holy city of Madīnaĥ. He immediately provided me with the finances needed for the blessed journey and in this way I was fortunate to embark on the glorious journey to the holy city of Madīnaĥ, اَلْحَمْدُ لِلّٰه عَزَّوَجَلَّ. Due to the blessings of the Du'ā made during the Madanī Qāfilaĥ I, a sinful and poor person, was blessed with this honour.'

Mujĥ gunaĥgār sā insān Madīnay mayn raĥay
Ban kay Sarkār صَلَّى اللّٰهُ تَعَالٰى عَلَيْهِ وَاٰلِهٖ وَسَلَّم *kā maĥmān Madīnay mayn raĥay*
Yād ātī ĥay mujĥay Aĥl-e-Madīnaĥ kī woĥ bāt
Zindaĥ reĥnā ĥay to insān Madīnay mayn raĥay
Jān-o-dil cĥoř kar yeĥ keĥ kay chalā ĥūn A'ẓam
Ā raĥā ĥūn Mayrā sāmān Madīnay mayn raĥay

May a sinner like me stay in Madīnaĥ
As a guest of the Holy Prophet صَلَّى اللّٰهُ تَعَالٰى عَلَيْهِ وَاٰلِهٖ وَسَلَّم *in Madīnaĥ*
I remember the word of the people of Madīnaĥ
That, if one wants to be alive, one should stay in Madīnaĥ
O A'ẓam, I leave my life and my heart, proclaiming this
'I am coming back; let my belongings remain in Madīnaĥ'

صَلُّوْا عَلَى الْحَبِيْب   صَلَّى اللّٰهُ تَعَالٰى عَلٰى مُحَمَّد

62. Barley grits

Shaykh Sayyidunā 'Umar Bin 'Abdul 'Azīz رَضِیَ اللهُ تَعَالٰی عَنْهُ was once informed that the daily food expense of the army general was 1000 dirhams. Extremely discomforted by hearing this bad news, he رَضِیَ اللهُ تَعَالٰی عَنْهُ made up his mind to reform the army general making individual effort. Therefore, he رَضِیَ اللهُ تَعَالٰی عَنْهُ invited the general to a meal at his house. He رَضِیَ اللهُ تَعَالٰی عَنْهُ had already instructed his cook to prepare barley-grits in addition to a fancy food.

When the general arrived, Sayyidunā 'Umar Bin 'Abdul 'Azīz رَضِیَ اللهُ تَعَالٰی عَنْهُ purposely delayed the meal to such an extent that the general was extremely hungry. He رَضِیَ اللهُ تَعَالٰی عَنْهُ asked the servants to serve the grits first. As the general was very hungry, he began to eat the grits eagerly. By the time the fancy food was served on the dining-mat the general was already full. Pointing towards the fancy food, the wise caliph رَضِیَ اللهُ تَعَالٰی عَنْهُ said, 'Eat! Your food has just been served.' The general responded that he was already full. Amīr-ul-Mūminīn Sayyidunā 'Umar Bin 'Abdul 'Azīz رَضِیَ اللهُ تَعَالٰی عَنْهُ said, 'سُبْحٰنَ اللّٰہ عَزَّوَجَلَّ! Grits are such a fine food that it fills the stomach in addition to being very cheap; one dirham's grits are sufficient for ten people.'

Continuing his words of wisdom, Amīr-ul-Mūminīn رَضِیَ اللهُ تَعَالٰی عَنْهُ then said, 'When you can satisfy your hunger by eating grits, then why do you spend one thousand dirhams every day on your food? O general! Fear Allah عَزَّوَجَلَّ, and do not be among the spendthrift. Give the extra money that you spend on food to the hungry, the destitute and the needy for the pleasure of Allah عَزَّوَجَلَّ.' Inspired by the individual effort made by the pious caliph, the general vowed to adopt simplicity and austerity in his life avoiding extravagance. *(Mughni-yul-Wā'iẓīn, pp. 491)*

May Allah عَزَّوَجَلَّ have mercy on him and forgive us without accountability for his sake!

صَلُّوْا عَلَی الْحَبِیْب صَلَّی اللهُ تَعَالٰی عَلٰی مُحَمَّد

Extravagance leads to deprivation of blessing

Dear Islamic brothers! The more we make ourselves habitual of eating delicious foods, the more our Nafs will demand for even more delicious foods. These days, a large number of people complain of deprivation in sustenance, lack of blessings and inflation. Virtually every individual complains that they are unable to meet their expenses.

Undoubtedly, one major cause of inflation, deprivation of blessings and destitution is extravagance. If one is extravagant and interested in fancy foods, luxuriously decorated houses, fashionable and expensive dresses, he will obviously need a huge amount of money for this decadent lifestyle. Thus, the constant ravings about being 'unable to meet one's expenses' and the 'lack of blessings' will also continue. Shaykh Sayyidunā Imām Ja'far Ṣādiq رَضِىَ اللهُ تَعَالٰى عَنْهُ has stated, 'When the one who has wasted his wealth extravagantly asks Allah عَزَّوَجَلَّ for more wealth, Allah عَزَّوَجَلَّ says (to that person), 'Did I not order you to have moderation? Had you not heard this [verse of the Quran]?

وَالَّذِيْنَ اِذَآ اَنْفَقُوْا لَمْ يُسْرِفُوْا وَلَمْ يَقْتُرُوْا وَكَانَ بَيْنَ ذٰلِكَ قَوَامًا ﴿۶۷﴾

And those who when expend neither exceed the limit nor act miserly and remain between the two in moderation.

[Kanz-ul-Īmān (Translation of Quran)] (Part 19, Sūraĥ Al-Furqān, verse 67)

(Aḥsan-ul-Wi'ā lī Ādāb-id-Du'ā, pp. 75)

Anyway, if one is content with simple and cheap foods and clothing and necessary housing, avoiding unnecessary decorations and gatherings, then the issue of inflation and destitution will automatically come to an end, but how will one be able to get rid of subservience to one's Nafs!

Prayer of three people not answered

The Prophet of mankind, the Peace of our heart and mind, the most Generous and Kind صَلَّى اللهُ تَعَالٰى عَلَيْهِ وَاٰلِهٖ وَسَلَّم has stated, 'There are three types of people whose Du'ā is not accepted by Allah عَزَّوَجَلَّ. (i) The one who takes shelter in a deserted place. (ii) The traveller who camps on a path (road) used by travellers. (iii) The one who lets his animal loose and then asks Allah عَزَّوَجَلَّ to restrain it.' *(Aḥsan-ul-Wi'ā, pp. 73)*

Elaborating on this Ḥadīš, A'lā Ḥaḍrat, Imām-e-Aĥl-e-Sunnat, reviver of Sunnaĥ, eradicator of Bid'aĥ, scholar of Sharī'aĥ, guide of Ṭarīqaĥ, 'Allāmaĥ Maulānā Al-Ḥāj Al-Ḥāfiẓ Al-Qārī Ash-Shāĥ Imām Aḥmad Razā Khān عَلَيْهِ رَحْمَةُ الرَّحْمٰن has stated, 'اَقُوْلُ وَبِاللهِ التَّوْفِيْق With the assistance of Allah عَزَّوَجَلَّ, I say the obvious meaning here is that the Du'ā of these people will not be accepted only in the above matters. This does not mean that no Du'ā of these people even in other matters will be accepted. The reason as to why one's Du'ā (regarding these specific matters) will not be accepted is that he has brought it all on himself. For example, when a person seeks shelter in a deserted house, he is aware of the possible dangers of doing so. There is a greater risk that his possessions may be stolen or he may be robbed by someone or harmed by jinns. So why is he then making Du'ā for protection from these harms as he has brought this on himself by taking shelter in such a house on his own free will.

Similarly, if one chooses to camp on the road where he may be harmed by a thief or a snake or a draft animal; he has brought this on himself. The Prophet of Raḥmaĥ, the Intercessor of Ummaĥ, the Owner of Jannaĥ صَلَّى اللهُ تَعَالٰى عَلَيْهِ وَاٰلِهٖ وَسَلَّم has stated, 'Do not stay on the road at night, as Allah عَزَّوَجَلَّ grants permission to whomever He عَزَّوَجَلَّ wills from His creation, to walk on the road.' Similarly, letting the animal loose and then making Du'ā for its restraint, is nothing but foolishness. Is such a person going to test Allah عَزَّوَجَلَّ? Or مَعَاذَاللّٰه عَزَّوَجَلَّ he considers Allah عَزَّوَجَلَّ subordinate to him? Someone once said to Sayyidunā 'Īsā عَلَيْهِ السَّلَام, 'If you trust Allah عَزَّوَجَلَّ, jump from this mountain.' Sayyidunā 'Īsā عَلَيْهِ السَّلَام replied, 'I do not test my Creator عَزَّوَجَلَّ.' *(Aḥsan-ul-Wi'ā, pp. 73 - 74)*

No solution to self-infliction

Dear Islamic brothers! There is a Persian saying, '*Khud Kardaĥ rā 'Ilāj-e-Nayst*', that is, there is no solution to self-inflicted problems. For example, if someone keeps banging his head on the wall, and then cries, '*My head is bleeding, please help me.*' Clearly, that foolish person will be asked not to bang his head on the wall so that his head would not bleed. Similarly, many unwise individuals eat virtually everything they get. They eat in excess, suffering from obesity, bulged belly, constipation and indigestion. They spend a lot of money on doctors' fees and medicines for the treatment of their diseases but in vain.

In fact, they themselves have the cure for their problems. If they refrain from gluttony, eat only when hungry, and eat less than hunger as stated in Ḥadīš, they will get the cure for their diseases. They should minimize their intake of junk foods like pizzas, burgers, buttered breads, butter, cake, pastries, kebabs, fried turnovers and other fried, fatty, heavily sweetened foods and superfine flour. Avoid ice creams, soft drinks and keep the intake of tea to a minimum (if necessary, take half a cup of tea twice or thrice a day). Refrain from smoking, chewing tobacco, eating Pān[1] and betel-nut. اِنْ شَآءَاللّٰہ عَزَّوَجَلَّ, One will be slim with a flat stomach and a healthy digestion in addition to getting rid of several diseases without taking medicines.

A cause of obesity

Strictly follow my Madanī recommendations just for forty days. اِنْ شَآءَاللّٰہ عَزَّوَجَلَّ, You will see an amazing improvement in your health. First, have your lipid profile and sugar tests done from a good laboratory and seek advice from a health professional. Then start following recommendations with the righteous intention that, 'By attaining good health, I will attain more strength to worship.'

Take the above precautionary measures and reap benefits. Remember that drinking water after having food engenders obesity and increases weight. Therefore, drink little water after consuming food. One should, however, drink a little water during the meal as it is beneficial. If one is obese due to his habit of gulping water in large amounts right after consuming the food, he should treat his obesity by rectifying this habit of his rather than by taking medicines.

Na-samajĥ bīmār ko amrat bĥī zaĥar āmayz ĥay
Sach yeĥī ĥay so dawā kī aīk dawā parĥayz ĥay

For an unwise sick person, even elixir is toxin
The truth is that abstinence is best medicine

15 Examples of putting oneself in dangerous situations

The Du'ā made for protection from the danger that one has brought on oneself is not accepted. The book '*Aḥsan-ul-Wi'ā lī Ādāb-id-Du'ā*' states many such examples.

1. To go out of home without compulsion at such a time of the night when people usually have gone to sleep and streets have worn a deserted look. An authentic

[1] Leaves of betel. [Translator's Note]

Ḥadīš stated in *Ṣaḥīḥ Bukhārī* prohibits this, as calamities are scattered at that time. (Therefore, if one is robbed or harmed by jinns, he should blame only himself).

2. To leave the door open at night or shut the door without reciting بِسْمِ اللّٰه. Remember that Satan can open the door in these cases. If بِسْمِ اللّٰه is recited, then Satan cannot open the door. Furthermore, when a person recites بِسْمِ اللّٰه and enters his home placing his right foot first, Satan remains outside. (Therefore, if one carelessly forgets to recite بِسْمِ اللّٰه and Satan enters his home with him, he is to blame only himself. How can he expect his Du'ā to be accepted in this case?)

3. To leave the pots, pans and other containers of food and drink uncovered without reciting بِسْمِ اللّٰه. Calamities descend into such pots, causing the food and drink to bring illnesses. (The food-containing pots that are not covered by something are used by wicked jinns. Therefore, the Du'ā of those not taking care in this matter will not be accepted as they had already been informed of an excellent recipe for protection from the harm of wicked jinns and illnesses).

4. To take the child out of home at the time of Maghrib as Satan's progeny is scattered at this time. (If one takes his child outside between the time of Maghrib and 'Ishā and any jinn causes harm to the child, one is to blame. Why did one take his child out at this time?)

5. To sleep after having meal without washing hands as Satan licks unwashed hands, which can engender leprosy.

6. To urinate in the bathing area (bathtub etc.), as this causes Satanic whispers [Wasāwis].

7. To sleep at the edge of the roof (which has no fences) because one may fall down from the roof.

8. To begin consuming food without reciting بِسْمِ اللّٰه. Satan joins in eating the food if بِسْمِ اللّٰه is not recited. As a result, the food that would have been sufficient for a few Muslims, is now insufficient.

9. To urinate into the small holes of the earth as these holes may be inhabited by snakes, jinns etc. that could cause harm.

10. On liking anything, whether one's own or one's friend's, not to recite the Du'ā for protection from the evil eye, as the evil eye is a truth that can put a man into his grave, and a camel on the fire (to be cooked). The Du'ā for protection from the evil eye is as follows:

اَللّٰهُمَّ بَارِكْ عَلَيْهِ وَلَا تَضُرَّهٗ مَاشَآءَاللّٰهُ لَا قُوَّةَ اِلَّا بِاللّٰه

O Allah عَزَّوَجَلَّ, shower blessings upon this and no harm should afflict it. Whatever Allah عَزَّوَجَلَّ wills only that happens. Without the assistance of Allah عَزَّوَجَلَّ, one does not have the power to do good deeds.

If one has not learnt the Du'ā by heart, he can also recite مَاشَآءَاللّٰه or بَـارَكَ الله. Muftī Aḥmad Yār Khān عَلَيْهِ رَحْمَةُ الْمَنَّان has stated that if one recites مَاشَآءَاللّٰه or بَـارَكَ الله upon seeing the thing he likes, the thing will not be afflicted with the evil eye. If one looks at that thing astonishingly or expresses the words of astonishment and does not recite مَاشَآءَاللّٰه or بَـارَكَ الله; then the thing is afflicted with the evil eye. *(Mirāt-ul-Manājīḥ, vol. 6, pp. 244)*

11. To travel alone as wicked people and jinns can cause harm. Furthermore, one may face difficulty in every matter.

12. To drink water while standing as this can engender liver problems. Note that it is Mustaḥab to drink Zamzam water and the leftover water from Wuḍū whilst standing.

13. To enter the lavatory without reciting بِسْمِ الـلّٰـه or Du'ā, as one may be harmed by wicked jinns.

14. To adopt the company of sinners, transgressors and those who have corrupt beliefs. Even if one is not influenced by their company, he will at least achieve notoriety.

15. To urinate at a path as one will be humiliated. *(Aḥsan-ul-Wi'ā, pp. 76 - 77)*

63. Means of food

Shaykh Sayyidunā Bāyazīd Bisṭāmī عَلَيْهِ رَحْمَةُ اللّٰهِ الْغَنِی once entered a Masjid to offer Ṣalāĥ with Jamā'at. Having completed the Ṣalāĥ the Imām asked, 'O Bāyazīd! How do you get your food?' He رَحْمَةُ اللّٰهِ تَعَالٰی عَلَیْه replied, 'Wait a little, let me first repeat the Ṣalāĥ we have just offered. You are in doubt about the Sustainer عَزَّوَجَلَّ of the people, so how can the Ṣalāĥ led by you be valid?' *(Rauḍ-ur-Riyāḥīn, pp. 155)*

May Allah عَزَّوَجَلَّ have mercy on him and forgive us without accountability for his sake!

Dear Islamic brothers! Shaykh Sayyidunā Bāyazīd Bisṭāmī عَلَيْهِ رَحْمَةُ اللّٰهِ الْغَنِی was a great saint. Indeed Allah عَزَّوَجَلَّ is the Creator and the Sustainer. When the Imām asked, 'How do you get your food?' The Shaykh رَحْمَةُ اللّٰهِ تَعَالٰی عَلَیْه considered it the weakness of the Imām's faith and thus repeated his Ṣalāĥ. He did it because of his high level of piety. People generally ask these kinds of questions, there is no sin in doing so by Sharī'aĥ.

صَلُّوْا عَلَى الْحَبِيْب صَلَّى اللّٰهُ تَعَالٰى عَلٰى مُحَمَّد

64. Roasted bird

Abul Ḥusayn 'Alawī has narrated, 'Once I desired to eat the meat of a certain Ḥalāl bird. I asked a family member of mine to roast the bird so that I would eat that on return. I then left to visit Shaykh Sayyidunā Ja'far Khuldī عَلَيْهِ رَحْمَةُ اللّٰهِ الْقَوِی. He رَحْمَةُ اللّٰهِ تَعَالٰی عَلَیْه asked me to stay at his house and spend the night over there but I had a strong desire for the roasted bird, so I made some excuse and came home. When the steaming roasted bird was served on the dining-mat, all of a sudden a dog came in, pounced on the bird and ran away with it. The maid was bringing the leftover gravy sauce when she tripped over her own clothes, spilling all the gravy. Afterwards, in the morning, I visited Shaykh Sayyidunā Ja'far Khuldī عَلَيْهِ رَحْمَةُ اللّٰهِ الْقَوِی. As soon as he saw me he commented, 'Whoever does not respect the wishes of the Shaykhs, a dog is made to hurt him.' *(Ar-Risāla-tul-Qushayriyyaĥ, pp. 362)*

May Allah عَزَّوَجَلَّ have mercy on them and forgive us without accountability for their sake!

Dear Islamic brothers! We may have realized from the foregoing parable that it is better for us to respect the wishes of the saints of Allah رَحِمَهُمُ اللّٰهُ تَعَالٰی and carry out the orders given by them instead of giving them excuses, as our cleverness is futile before them. We have also learnt that saints could have divinely-bestowed knowledge of unseen matters ['Ilm-ul-Ghayb]. When the saints of Allah عَزَّوَجَلَّ have such splendid spiritual status, just imagine the status of the Prophet's companions رَضِیَ اللّٰہُ تَعَالٰی عَنْھُم [who are obviously higher in rank].

After this realization, who can envision the immense endowments granted to the Beloved and Blessed Prophet صَلَّی اللّٰہُ تَعَالٰی عَلَیْہِ وَاٰلِہٖ وَسَلَّم by Allah عَزَّوَجَلَّ! Imām Aḥmad Razā Khān عَلَیْہِ رَحْمَۃُ الْمَنَّان has written an excellent couplet:

Sar-e-'Arsh per ĥay tayrī guzar dil-e-farsh per ĥay tayrī naẓar
Malakūt-o-Mulk mayn koī shay naĥīn woĥ jo tujĥ pay 'iyān naĥīn

(Ḥadāiq-e-Bakhshish)

صَلُّوْا عَلَی الْحَبِیْب صَلَّی اللّٰهُ تَعَالٰی عَلٰی مُحَمَّد

65. Good news for birth of baby-girl

Several authentic books contain such accounts that affirm the fact that the knowledge of unseen matters ['Ilm-ul-Ghayb] has been divinely bestowed upon the Prophet's companions رَضِیَ اللّٰہُ تَعَالٰی عَنْھُم.

The leader of thousands of Malikites[1], Shaykh Sayyidunā Imām Mālik Bin Anas رَحْمَۃُ اللّٰہِ تَعَالٰی عَلَیْہ has stated in his world-famous collection of Aḥādīš entitled, '*Muwaṭṭā Imām Mālik*': 'Shaykh Sayyidunā 'Urwaĥ Bin Zubayr رَضِیَ اللّٰہ تَعَالٰی عَنْھُمَا has narrated that Sayyidatunā 'Āishaĥ Ṣiddīqaĥ رَضِیَ اللّٰہُ تَعَالٰی عَنْھَا has stated that the successor of Rasūl, Sayyidunā Abū Bakr Ṣiddīq رَضِیَ اللّٰہُ تَعَالٰی عَنْہُ made his will to her during his fatal disease in these words, 'My dear daughter! All my belongings are now your inheritance, so you distribute it according to the rules laid down in the Holy Quran, among your two brothers ['Abdur Raḥmān &

[1] Followers of Mālikī school of Islamic law founded by Shaykh Sayyidunā Imām Mālik Bin Anas رَحْمَۃُ اللّٰہِ تَعَالٰی عَلَیْہ

[Translator's Note]

Muhammad رَضِىَ اللّٰهُ تَعَالٰی عَنْهُمَا] and your two sisters.' Upon hearing this she رَضِىَ اللّٰهُ تَعَالٰی عَنْهَا asked, 'I have only one sister, Asmā! Who is my other sister?' He رَضِىَ اللّٰهُ تَعَالٰی عَنْهُ said, 'She is in the womb of (your stepmother) Ḥabībaĥ Bint-e-Khārijaĥ رَضِىَ اللّٰهُ تَعَالٰی عَنْهَا. I think she is a girl.' *(Muwaṭṭā Imām Mālik, vol. 2, pp. 270, Ḥadīš 1503)*

Commenting on the foregoing Ḥadīš Shaykh 'Allāmaĥ Muhammad Bin 'Abdul Bāqī Zurqānī قُدِّسَ سِرُّہُ الزَّبَانِی has stated, 'Hence, this came to pass and a baby-girl was born who was named Umm-e-Kulšūm رَضِىَ اللّٰهُ تَعَالٰی عَنْهَا.' *(Sharḥ-uz-Zurqānī 'Alal Muwaṭṭā, vol. 4, pp. 61)*

May Allah عَزَّوَجَلَّ have mercy on them and forgive us without accountability for their sake!

Two saintly miracles proved

Dear Islamic brothers! Commenting on the above narration, Shaykh Sayyidunā 'Allāmaĥ Tājuddīn Subkī عَلَیْہِ رَحْمَۃُ اللّٰهِ الْقَوِی has stated that this narration has proved two saintly miracles of Sayyidunā Abū Bakr Ṣiddīq رَضِىَ اللّٰهُ تَعَالٰی عَنْهُ:

1. Even before his demise, he رَضِىَ اللّٰهُ تَعَالٰی عَنْهُ had been aware that he would die of that disease as is irrefutably obvious from his words '*all my belongings are now your inheritance.*'

2. The new born would be a girl. *(Ḥujjatullāĥi-'alal-'Ālamīn, pp. 612)*

Abū Bakr Ṣiddīq رَضِىَ اللّٰهُ عَنْهُ had 'Ilm-ul-Ghayb

This narration also shows that by the bestowment of Allah عَزَّوَجَلَّ Sayyidunā Abū Bakr Ṣiddīq رَضِىَ اللّٰهُ تَعَالٰی عَنْهُ knew what was in the mother's womb. To understand this ruling, listen carefully to the following Quranic verse and its exegesis. Allah عَزَّوَجَلَّ says in part 21, last verse of Sūraĥ Luqmān:

$$ وَیَعْلَمُ مَا فِی الْاَرْحَامِ ط $$

And (Allah عَزَّوَجَلَّ) knows what in the wombs of mothers is.

[Kanz-ul-Īmān (Translation of Quran)] (Part 21, Sūraĥ Luqmān, verse 34)

Commenting on this verse, successor of A'lā Ḥaḍrat, Ṣadr-ul-Afāḍil 'Allāmaĥ Maulānā Sayyid Muhammad Na'īmuddīn Murādābādī عَلَيْهِ رَحْمَةُ اللّٰهِ الْهَادِى has stated on page 661 of his Quranic exegesis entitled '*Khazāin-ul-'Irfān*' published in Bombay: 'Knowledge of Ghayb is the sole attribute of Allah عَزَّوَجَلَّ. As for the knowledge of Ghayb which Prophets عَلَيْهِمُ السَّلَام and saints رَحِمَهُمُ اللّٰهُ تَعَالٰى possess, this is, in actual fact, bestowed upon them by Allah عَزَّوَجَلَّ as Prophetic and saintly miracles respectively. This (divinely-bestowed knowledge of Prophets and saints) is not contrary to the particularity of the absolute knowledge of Almighty Allah عَزَّوَجَلَّ. Several Quranic verses and Aḥādīš attest to this fact. Some examples of the knowledge of Ghayb include the time of rain, the sex of the unborn baby, what will one do the next day, and the place of one's death etc.

Numerous Prophets عَلَيْهِمُ السَّلَام and saints رَحِمَهُمُ اللّٰهُ تَعَالٰى have given such news and this fact is affirmed by several verses of the Quran and Aḥādīš. Angels told Prophet Ibrāĥīm Khalīlullāĥ عَلٰى نَبِيِّنَا وَعَلَيْهِ الصَّلٰوةُ وَالسَّلَام about the birth of Sayyidunā Isḥāq عَلٰى نَبِيِّنَا وَعَلَيْهِ الصَّلٰوةُ وَالسَّلَام. Prophet Zakariyyā عَلٰى نَبِيِّنَا وَعَلَيْهِ الصَّلٰوةُ وَالسَّلَام was informed by the angels about the birth of Sayyidunā Yaḥyā عَلٰى نَبِيِّنَا وَعَلَيْهِ الصَّلٰوةُ وَالسَّلَام. Likewise, respectable Maryam رَضِىَ اللّٰهُ تَعَالٰى عَنْهَا was given the news of the birth of Sayyidunā 'Īsā عَلٰى نَبِيِّنَا وَعَلَيْهِ الصَّلٰوةُ وَالسَّلَام. Since these blessed individuals were informed by angels, it proves that angles already knew what was in wombs and these individuals also got to know about it. This is proved by the verses of the Quran. The above verse undoubtedly refers to the fact that no one can get to know about it without being told by Allah عَزَّوَجَلَّ. To draw such meaning from the foregoing verse that no one knows about it even if told by Allah عَزَّوَجَلَّ, is nothing but a fabrication that is in contradiction to several Quranic verses and Aḥādīš.

Dear Islamic brothers! Without doubt, by the bestowment of Allah عَزَّوَجَلَّ, the saints رَحِمَهُمُ اللّٰهُ تَعَالٰى can also give the news of the birth of the unborn baby. *(Khazāin-ul-'Irfān, pp. 661)*

66. Good news of birth of baby boy

Shaykh Shāĥ Walīyullāĥ Muḥaddiš Diĥlvī عَلَيْهِ رَحْمَةُ اللّٰهِ الْقَوِى has narrated from his father, Shaykh Shāĥ 'Abdur Raḥīm عَلَيْهِ رَحْمَةُ اللّٰهِ الْكَرِيْم, 'Once I (i.e. the father of Shāĥ Walīyullāĥ) went to visit the shrine of Shaykh Sayyidunā Khuwājaĥ Bakhtiyār Kākī عَلَيْهِ رَحْمَةُ اللّٰهِ الْكَافِى. His soul appeared and told me, 'You will have a baby boy; name him Quṭbuddīn Aḥmad.' Since my wife was quite old at that time I figured that my son would have a son (i.e. my grandson) and this name was suggested for him. Becoming aware of my inner thought Shaykh Sayyidunā Khuwājaĥ Quṭbuddīn Bakhtiyār Kākī عَلَيْهِ رَحْمَةُ اللّٰهِ الْكَافِى said, 'I did not mean what you have understood; he will be your own son.'

Shāĥ Walīyullāĥ رَحْمَةُ اللّٰهِ تَعَالٰى عَلَيْه further reported, 'Long after it, my father married another woman who gave birth to me, the narrator of this incident. By then he [my father] forgot this incident and named me Walīyullāĥ رَحْمَةُ اللّٰهِ تَعَالٰى عَلَيْه, but later on when he recalled it he named me Quṭbuddīn Aḥmad (respecting the wish of Shaykh Sayyidunā Khuwājaĥ Quṭbuddīn Bakhtiyār Kākī عَلَيْهِ رَحْمَةُ اللّٰهِ الْكَافِى).' *(Anfās-ul-'Ārifīn, pp. 44)*

Dear Islamic brothers! It's a long-standing practice of the pious to visit the shrines of saints رَحِمَهُمُ اللّٰهُ تَعَالٰى for the attainment of blessings. The foregoing parable also shows that the deceased saints رَحِمَهُمُ اللّٰهُ تَعَالٰى can also become aware of people's inward thoughts and give future news, by the bestowment of Allah عَزَّوَجَلَّ, as Shaykh Sayyidunā Khuwājaĥ Quṭbuddīn Bakhtiyār Kākī عَلَيْهِ رَحْمَةُ اللّٰهِ الْكَافِى gave Shaykh Shāĥ 'Abdur Raḥīm عَلَيْهِ رَحْمَةُ اللّٰهِ الْكَرِيْم the news of the birth of a baby-boy.

Yaĥīn pātay ĥayn sāray apnā maṭlab
Ĥar aīk kay wāsiṭay yeĥ dar kĥulā ĥay
Mayn dar dar kyūn pĥirūn, dūr dūr sunū kyūn
Mayray Āqā صَلَّى اللّٰهُ تَعَالٰى عَلَيْهِ وَاٰلِهٖ وَسَلَّم*! Mayrā kyā sar pĥirā ĥay!*

Here everyone gets their wishes, at the open door
O my Beloved Prophet صَلَّى اللّٰهُ تَعَالٰى عَلَيْهِ وَاٰلِهٖ وَسَلَّم*! Why should I go chasing door to door*
And be turned away, I am not crazy seeking another door

صَلُّوْا عَلَى الْحَبِيْب   صَلَّى اللّٰهُ تَعَالٰى عَلٰى مُحَمَّد

67. A delicious drink

Shaykh Sayyidunā Ṣāliḥ Marī عَلَيْهِ رَحْمَةُ اللّٰهِ الْقَوِى has stated, 'Once I sent a delicious barley beverage mixed with honey and clarified butter to Shaykh Sayyidunā 'Aṭā Sulamī عَلَيْهِ رَحْمَةُ اللّٰهِ الْقَوِى for two consecutive days, but he sent it back to me the second day. Displeased, I went to his house and asked him, 'Why did you return my gift?' He replied, 'Please do not mind, I drank the beverage the first day, but as I was about to drink it the second day, the 17 verse of Sūraĥ Ibrāĥīm (part 13) occurred to me:

يَّتَجَرَّعُهٗ وَلَا يَكَادُ يُسِيۡغُهٗ وَيَاۡتِيۡهِ الۡمَوۡتُ مِنۡ كُلِّ مَكَانٍ وَّمَا هُوَ بِمَيِّتٍ ؕ وَمِنۡ وَّرَآئِهٖ عَذَابٌ غَلِيۡظٌ ﴿۱۷﴾

He will take its sip little by little with difficulty and there shall be no hope to swallow it, and death shall come to him from all sides, but he shall not die. And there is a terrible torment behind him.

[Kanz-ul-Īmān (Translation of Quran)] (Part 13, Sūraĥ Ibrāĥīm, verse 17)

Shaykh Sayyidunā Ṣāliḥ Marī عَلَيۡهِ رَحۡمَةُ اللّٰهِ الۡقَوِی goes onto to say that hearing this, I was moved to tears and said to myself that I and you are in two different valleys. [In other words, you are much better than me]. *(Iḥyā-ul-'Ulūm, vol. 3, pp. 116)*

Better than 12 months' worship

Dear Islamic brothers! Our pious saints رَحِمَهُمُ اللّٰهُ تَعَالٰی would refrain from satisfying even the lawful desires of their Nafs. If only we would also follow in their footsteps! When we desire to wear nice clothes or eat delicious foods, we should occasionally avoid fulfilling our desire with the intention of attaining the pleasure of Allah عَزَّوَجَلَّ. For example, when we crave for a cold drink on a hot day or when we desire to eat some delicious food in extreme hunger and we have the means to get it either; if only we would be blessed with the privilege of giving it up for the pleasure of Allah عَزَّوَجَلَّ!

Listen to the tremendous benefit of refraining from satisfying the desire of Nafs. Therefore, Shaykh Sayyidunā Abū Sulaymān عَلَيۡهِ رَحۡمَةُ الۡمَنَّان has stated, 'Leaving a desire of Nafs unfulfilled is more beneficial to the heart than even fasting during days and worshipping at nights for twelve months.' *(Iḥyā-ul-'Ulūm, vol. 3, pp. 118)*

Ḥujjat-ul-Islam, Shaykh Sayyidunā Imām Muhammad Ghazālī عَلَيْهِ رَحْمَةُ اللّٰهِ الْوَالِى has stated, 'We should not give free rein even to the lawful desires of Nafs, nor should we follow it in every matter. The more one follows his Nafs's desires and eats fancy foods, the more he should fear as it will be said to the unbelievers on the Day of Judgement:

اَذْهَبْتُمْ طَيِّبٰتِكُمْ فِيْ حَيَاتِكُمُ الدُّنْيَا وَ اسْتَمْتَعْتُمْ بِهَا ۚ

You have exhausted your pure things in your worldly life and used it (fully).

[Kanz-ul-Īmān (Translation of Quran)] (Part 26, Sūraĥ Al-Aḥqāf, verse 20)

Hunger of Holy Prophet ﷺ

Commenting on the foregoing verse, successor of A'lā Ḥaḍrat, Ṣadr-ul-Afāḍil 'Allāmaĥ Maulānā Sayyid Muhammad Na'īmuddīn Murādābādī عَلَيْهِ رَحْمَةُ الْهَادِى has stated in his Quranic commentary titled '*Khazāin-ul-'Irfān*': 'In this Quranic verse, Allah عَزَّوَجَلَّ has admonished the unbelievers on enjoying worldly pleasures; hence the Beloved Prophet صَلَّى اللّٰهُ تَعَالٰى عَلَيْهِ وَاٰلِهٖ وَسَلَّم and his companions رَضِىَ اللّٰهُ تَعَالٰى عَنْهُم refrained from the joys of the world.

In *Ṣaḥīḥ Bukhārī* and *Ṣaḥīḥ Muslim*, it is stated that until the apparent demise of the Noble Prophet صَلَّى اللّٰهُ تَعَالٰى عَلَيْهِ وَاٰلِهٖ وَسَلَّم, the blessed family never ate bread made from barley for two consecutive days. It is also mentioned in a Ḥadīš that at times the whole month passed, but fire would not burn on the stove (for cooking food). The blessed household would merely survive on water and a few dates.

Sayyidunā 'Umar Fārūq A'ẓam رَضِىَ اللّٰهُ تَعَالٰى عَنْهُ has said, 'O people! If I had wanted, I would have eaten better than you and worn better clothes than you, but I want to reserve my pleasures and comforts for my Hereafter.' *(Khazāin-ul-'Irfān, pp. 802)*

صَلُّوْا عَلَى الْحَبِيْب صَلَّى اللّٰهُ تَعَالٰى عَلٰى مُحَمَّد

68. Reward of giving charity on ʻĀshūrā*

On the day of ʻĀshūrā in the city of "Rey" a man approached the Qāḍī [judge] and requested, 'I am a destitute person with a family to support; for the sake of the day of ʻĀshūrā, please give me 2 kilograms of bread, 5 kilograms of meat and 10 dirhams. May Allah عَزَّوَجَلَّ enhance your prestige!' The Qāḍī asked him to come after Ẓuhr Ṣalāĥ. When he came after Ẓuhr Ṣalāĥ, the Qāḍī told him to come after ʻAṣr Ṣalāĥ. When that poor man came again after ʻAṣr, he was once again turned away empty-handed. This broke his heart.

Dejected and depressed he approached a non-Muslim and pleaded, 'Give me something for the sake of this [blessed] day.' He inquired, 'What day is today?' The destitute person informed the non-Muslim that it was the day of ʻĀshūrā, elaborating some excellence of the day. The non-Muslim said, 'You have requested me for the sake of a great day. Tell me what you need.' The needy man told his requirements. Giving him 10 sacks of wheat, 100 kilograms of meat and 20 dirhams, the non-Muslim said, 'In the honour of this great day, all this (i.e. the money and wheat etc.) is now fixed as a monthly allowance for your family.' That night the Qāḍī had a dream in which he saw someone ask him to look upwards. As he looked up he saw two beautiful palaces one of which was made of silver and gold bricks and the other of red rubies. The Qāḍī inquired about the owner of those two palaces and was told that if he had helped the needy man they would have been granted to him, but since he did not help the destitute person despite his repeated visits, these palaces had now been granted to so-and-so non-Muslim.

When the Qāḍī woke up in the morning he was upset. He went to meet the non-Muslim and asked him, 'What 'deed' did you do yesterday? He asked, 'How do you know?' The Qāḍī told him all about his dream offering him one hundred thousand dirhams in exchange for his 'deed.' The non-Muslim said that he would not 'sell' his deed even if given the wealth of the entire world. He further said, 'The mercy of Allah is immense. Saying this, that non-Muslim embraced Islam reciting اَشْهَدُ اَنْ لَّآ اِلٰهَ اِلَّا اللّٰهُ وَاَشْهَدُ اَنَّ مُحَمَّدًا عَبْدُهٗ وَرَسُوْلُهٗ. That is, *I bear witness that no one is worthy to be worshipped except Allah* عَزَّوَجَلَّ, *and I bear witness that Muhammad* صَلَّى اللّٰهُ تَعَالٰى عَلَيْهِ وَاٰلِهٖ وَسَلَّم *is His [distinguished] bondman and Rasūl.'* *(Rauḍ-ur-Riyāḥīn, pp. 152)*

* Tenth day of Muḥarram-ul-Ḥarām, the first Islamic month. [Translator's Note]

Prominence of 'Āshūrā

Dear Islamic brothers! On the day of 'Āshūrā, i.e. the tenth day of Muḥarram-ul-Ḥarām, the grandson of the Prophet, the beloved son of Sayyidatunā Fāṭimaĥ, Sayyidunā Imām Ḥusayn رَضِیَ اللهُ تَعَالٰی عَنْهُ, along with his relatives and companions, was brutally martyred in the state of extreme thirst and hunger. Besides, several other important events took place on this day. In Islam, the day of 'Āshūrā and the month of Muḥarram-ul-Ḥarām are of great significance. After Ramadan, the fasts of Muḥarram-ul-Ḥarām are the most rewarding.

5 Aḥādīš on significance of Muḥarram

1. The Prophet of mankind, the Peace of our heart and mind, the most Generous and Kind صَلَّى اللهُ تَعَالٰى عَلَيْهِ وَاٰلِهٖ وَسَلَّم has stated, 'After Ramadan, the fast of Muḥarram is preferable, and after the obligatory [Ṣalāĥ] the night Ṣalāĥ (Ṣalāt-ul-Layl) is preferable.' *(Ṣaḥīḥ Muslim, pp. 591, Ḥadīš 1163)*

2. The Prophet of Raḥmaĥ, the Intercessor of Ummaĥ صَلَّى اللهُ تَعَالٰى عَلَيْهِ وَاٰلِهٖ وَسَلَّم has stated, 'Every fast of Muḥarram is equivalent to a whole month of fasts.' *(Mu'jam Ṣaghīr, vol. 2, pp. 71)*

3. The Beloved and Blessed Prophet صَلَّى اللهُ تَعَالٰى عَلَيْهِ وَاٰلِهٖ وَسَلَّم has stated, 'Whoever fasted for three days, Thursday, Friday and Saturday, during the month of Muḥarram, the reward of two years' worship will be recorded for him.' *(Majma'-uz-Zawāid, vol. 3, pp. 438, Ḥadīš 5151)*

4. The Noble Prophet صَلَّى اللهُ تَعَالٰى عَلَيْهِ وَاٰلِهٖ وَسَلَّم has stated, 'Fast on the day of 'Āshūrā and oppose the Jews by fasting a day before or after it.' *(Musnad Imām Aḥmad, vol. 1, pp. 518, Ḥadīš 2154)* Therefore, whoever fasts on the 10th of Muḥarram, should also fast either on the 9th or the 11th.

5. Rasūlullāĥ صَلَّى اللهُ تَعَالٰى عَلَيْهِ وَاٰلِهٖ وَسَلَّم has stated, 'Whoever provides his household with sustenance in abundance on the day of 'Āshūrā, Allah عَزَّوَجَلَّ will increase his sustenance for the whole year.'

Protection from illness entire year

A renowned exegetist of the Quran, Muftī Aḥmad Yār Khān عَلَيْهِ رَحْمَةُ الْمَنَّان has stated, 'If a person fasts on the 9th and 10th of Muḥarram he/she will gain immense reward. If someone cooks delicious foods for his family on the 10th of Muḥarram, اِنْ شَآءَاللّٰه عَزَّوَجَلَّ there will be blessings in his house for the whole year. It is better to cook 'Kĥichřǎ' (a dish prepared by cooking grinded lentils, rice and meat together) and make Fātiḥaĥ for Sayyidunā Imām Ḥusayn رَضِىَ اللّٰهُ تَعَالٰى عَنْهُ. This is very tried and trusted. If someone takes a bath on this date (the 10th of Muḥarram) اِنْ شَآءَاللّٰه عَزَّوَجَلَّ he will be protected from illnesses for the whole year because the water of Zamzam reaches all the waters on this day.' *(Tafsīr Rūḥ-ul-Bayān, vol. 4, pp. 142 - Islāmī Zindagī, pp. 102)* The Holy Prophet صَلَّى اللّٰهُ تَعَالٰى عَلَيْهِ وَاٰلِهٖ وَسَلَّم has stated, 'Whoever applies 'Išmad Surmaĥ' (kohl) to his eyes on the day of 'Āshūrā, his eyes shall never hurt.' *(Shu'ab-ul-Īmān, vol. 3, pp. 367, Ḥadīš 3797)*

صَلُّوْا عَلَى الْحَبِيْب   صَلَّى اللّٰهُ تَعَالٰى عَلٰى مُحَمَّد

Devastating earthquake in Pakistan

Dear Islamic brothers! In the Madanī environment of the global & non-political religious movement, Dawat-e-Islami, the mindset of helping the troubled people is inculcated. Here is an account regarding the earthquake believed to be the most destructive in the history of Pakistan by the time of the writing of this account. On Saturday, Ramadan 3, 1426 A.H. (October 8, 2005), at about 8:45 a.m., the quake struck the eastern parts of Pakistan, causing devastation in major parts of Khyber Pakhtunkhwa, Kashmir and some parts of Punjab province.

According to a report, more than two hundred thousand people perished. However, the truth is that no one knows the exact number of the dead! Whole villages, localities and several cities were obliterated into mere heaps of rubble. Whole mountains were uprooted and collapsed on villages. Allah عَزَّوَجَلَّ knows how many smiling faces were buried alive. How can anyone fathom the lives lost? When intending to commit a sin, if only we develop the mindset of avoiding the sin for fear that an earthquake occurs and obliterates us in the blink of an eye while we are committing the sin. (We seek our well-being from Allah عَزَّوَجَلَّ).

619 Truckloads of provisions

Numerous Islamic brothers of Dawat-e-Islami enthusiastically participated in the relief efforts of the quake-victims. Almost 619 truckloads of basic necessities were distributed among the victims and about 120 million rupees were spent by Dawat-e-Islami in this massive relief effort. Several Madanī Qāfilaĥs of Dawat-e-Islami went missing in these earthquake-stricken areas. They were all found well and alive afterwards. Listen to a Madanī incident of one of such Qāfilaĥs.

69. Narrow escape from death

Nine Islamic brothers from Drig colony and Malir (Bāb-ul-Madīnaĥ, Karachi, Pakistan) were staying in a Masjid in Qadirabad district of Bagh (Kashmir). Devotees of Rasūl told their incident in the following words: During the break for rest, five of us were resting while four of us had gone out of the Masjid. It was the 3rd of Ramadan 1426 A.H. at 8:45 a.m. when all of a sudden we felt severe tremors of quake.

Panicked, we jumped over a 5 foot high Masjid wall and started running towards the road. The sounds of the collapsing houses could be heard from everywhere. When we turned around there was an unbelievable scene in front of our eyes; the mountain had been uprooted and fallen over the entire town. When the clouds of dust cleared there was no Masjid or houses [everything had vanished]. All the beautiful buildings had been turned into rubble. Havoc and devastation was everywhere. I think no one from that locality may have survived. We made our way to a nearby town of Nazrabad. The earthquake had caused devastation there too. When our senses were restored we took part in rescue efforts. We broke our fast [i.e. did Ifṭār] there. Then we offered Maghrib Ṣalāĥ with Jamā'at in a section of a Masjid which was left intact after the devastation.

As we left the Masjid after offering Ṣalāĥ, another quake rocked the area, collapsing even the remaining part of that Masjid. اَلْحَمْدُلِلّٰه عَزَّوَجَلَّ The devotees of Rasūl narrowly escaped being killed for the second time. Narrating this incident, a newspaper named 'Qaumi Akhbar' added, 'This Madanī Qāfilaĥ had travelled with a good intention (to spread the call to righteousness), perhaps this is why Allah عَزَّوَجَلَّ has saved them.'

Zalzalaĥ āye gar, ā kay ĉhā jāye gar
Ṣirf Ḥaq عَزَّوَجَلَّ *say ḋarayn, Qāfilay mayn chalo*
Zalzalaĥ ām tĥā, ĥar sū kuĥrām tĥā
Is say lo 'ibratayn Qāfilay mayn chalo

Even if quakes rock, and causes devastations
Fear Allah عَزَّوَجَلَّ *and travel in Qāfilaĥ*
Earthquake caused, everywhere destruction
Take heed from this, and travel in Qāfilaĥ

صَلُّوْا عَلَى الْحَبِيْب   صَلَّى اللهُ تَعَالٰى عَلٰى مُحَمَّد

70. A piece of dry bread

Once a special representative of the ruler of Aĥwāz, Sulaymān Bin 'Alī, came to the house of Sayyidunā Khalīl Baṣrī عَلَيْهِ رَحْمَةُ اللّٰهِ الْقَوِى, a great scholar of his time, with a message that the King had summoned him to the royal court for the teaching of his two princes. On learning the purpose of the arrival of the representative, Sayyidunā Khalīl Baṣrī عَلَيْهِ رَحْمَةُ اللّٰهِ الْقَوِى replied indicating a dry piece of bread in his hand, 'As long as I have this dry bread, I do not need to be a subservient to the royal court.' *(Rūḥānī Ḥikāyāt, vol. 1, pp. 106)*

May Allah عَزَّوَجَلَّ have mercy on him and forgive us without accountability for his sake!

Justujū mayn kyūn pĥirayn māl kī māray māray
Ĥam to Sarkār صَلَّى اللّٰهُ تَعَالٰى عَلَيْهِ وَاٰلِهٖ وَسَلَّم *kay ṫukřon pay palā kartay ĥayn*

Why should we go here and there to look for wealth
We are comfortable with the endowments of our Holy Prophet صَلَّى اللّٰهُ تَعَالٰى عَلَيْهِ وَاٰلِهٖ وَسَلَّم

Invitation from prime minister

Dear Islamic brothers! You can see how the righteous servants of Allah stay away from those in power. On the contrary, if people like us ever happen to receive any such invitation from the prime minister or the president, we will put on our best attire, and be the first to stand in the long line outside the assembly hall even if we have to postpone all our chores and engagements and travel thousands of kilometres.

Alas! All this is caused by subservience to Nafs! Visiting leaders and ministers without compulsion, for personal interests and show-off, attending their ceremonies and parties, receiving medals and accolades from them, having photographs taken with them, framing these photographs and showing them to others or displaying them at home/office etc. are such acts that may cause harm to one's Hereafter but no benefit. However, if one has to visit them for some important religious cause or for protection from their harm, that's a different matter as the one who is helpless, is exempted.

Very bad is the poor person who goes to the door of the rich.	بِئْسَ الْفَقِيْرُ عَلٰى بَابِ الْاَمِيْرِ
Very good is the rich person who goes to the door of the poor.	نِعْمَ الْاَمِيْرُ عَلٰى بَابِ الْفَقِيْرِ

(Shayṭān kī Ḥikāyāt, pp. 71-72)

صَلُّوْا عَلَى الْحَبِيْب صَلَّى اللّٰهُ تَعَالٰى عَلٰى مُحَمَّد

Success in worldly life and afterlife

The trap of Satan is certainly very dangerous. At times, he leads even a religious person to the feet of rulers by deceiving him into assuming his carnal desires as religious benefits. This is the reason why the righteous and heedful servants of Allah always preferred to stay away from those in power. The one adopting contentment rather than eyeing others' wealth greedily is successful in the worldly life as well as in the afterlife. The following parable will show how strongly the righteous servants of Allah disliked rulers, oppressors and dishonest judges.

71. Imām Suyūṭī رَحْمَةُ اللهِ عَلَيْه beheld the refulgent countenance

Sayyidunā 'Allāmaĥ 'Abdul Waĥĥāb Sha'rānī قُدِّسَ سِرُّهُ الرَّبَّانِي has reported that Sayyidunā 'Alī Khawāṣ رَحْمَةُ اللّٰهِ تَعَالٰی عَلَیْه once came across Shaykh 'Abdul Qādir Shāzlī عَلَيْهِ رَحْمَةُ اللّٰهِ الْقَوِی, a companion of 'Allāmaĥ Jalāluddīn Suyūṭī Shāfi'ī عَلَيْهِ رَحْمَةُ اللّٰهِ الْقَوِی. In the hand of Shaykh 'Abdul Qādir Shāzlī عَلَيْهِ رَحْمَةُ اللّٰهِ الْقَوِی was a letter from 'Allāmaĥ Jalāluddīn Suyūṭī Shāfi'ī عَلَيْهِ رَحْمَةُ اللّٰهِ الْقَوِی. The letter was addressed to a man who had requested 'Allāmaĥ Jalāluddīn Suyūṭī Shāfi'ī عَلَيْهِ رَحْمَةُ اللّٰهِ الْقَوِی to intercede with the king on his behalf.

'Allāmaĥ Jalāluddīn Suyūṭī Shāfi'ī عَلَيْهِ رَحْمَةُ اللهِ الْقَوِى had given the following reply in the letter: 'My brother, اَلْحَمْدُ لِلّٰه عَزَّوَجَلَّ, until now I have been blessed with the company of the Noble Prophet صَلَّى اللهُ تَعَالٰى عَلَيْهِ وَاٰلِهٖ وَسَلَّم 75 times in the state of wakefulness. If I had not feared to be deprived of beholding the Holy Prophet صَلَّى اللهُ تَعَالٰى عَلَيْهِ وَاٰلِهٖ وَسَلَّم because of visiting the king and rulers, I would have surely gone to the fort to intercede with the king on your behalf. I am a humble servant of Ḥadīš. I need to be in attendance in the court of the Beloved and Blessed Prophet صَلَّى اللهُ تَعَالٰى عَلَيْهِ وَاٰلِهٖ وَسَلَّم to enquire about the credibility of those Aḥādīš declared unauthentic by Ḥadīš scholars, and its benefit is far greater than your personal benefit.' *(Mīzān-ush-Sharī'at-ul-Kubrā, pp. 48)*

Dear Islamic brothers! You can see the level of deprivation of spiritual insight which can result from visiting rulers. The next parable shows this even more clearly.

72. Why Na'at reciter was deprived

Sayyidunā 'Allāmaĥ 'Abdul Waĥĥāb Sha'rānī قُدِّسَ سِرُّهُ الرَّبَّانِي has stated: Sayyidunā Muhammad Bin Tarīn was a famous Na'at reciter who used to be blessed with beholding the Holy Prophet صَلَّى اللهُ تَعَالٰى عَلَيْهِ وَاٰلِهٖ وَسَلَّم in the state of wakefulness. Once, when he visited the sacred shrine, the Noble Prophet صَلَّى اللهُ تَعَالٰى عَلَيْهِ وَاٰلِهٖ وَسَلَّم spoke to him from within his sacred grave. The Na'at reciter enjoyed these favours from the Holy Prophet صَلَّى اللهُ تَعَالٰى عَلَيْهِ وَاٰلِهٖ وَسَلَّم. One day a person requested the Na'at reciter to intercede with the ruler on his behalf. He went to the ruler and interceded. That ruler honoured him and made him sit on his own seat. After this incident, he was no longer able to have the vision of the Holy Prophet صَلَّى اللهُ تَعَالٰى عَلَيْهِ وَاٰلِهٖ وَسَلَّم. He would often plead in the court of the Noble Prophet صَلَّى اللهُ تَعَالٰى عَلَيْهِ وَاٰلِهٖ وَسَلَّم but remained deprived of this privilege.

Once he recited a couplet of Na'at and was able to behold Rasūlullāĥ صَلَّى اللهُ تَعَالٰى عَلَيْهِ وَاٰلِهٖ وَسَلَّم from afar. The Prophet of Raḥmaĥ, the Intercessor of Ummaĥ صَلَّى اللهُ تَعَالٰى عَلَيْهِ وَاٰلِهٖ وَسَلَّم said, 'You desire to see me despite sitting at the seat of oppressors, there is no way to it.'

Sayyidunā 'Alī Khawāṣ رَحْمَةُ اللهِ تَعَالٰى عَلَيْه goes onto say, 'We did not come to know whether or not that Na'at reciter had the vision of Holy Prophet صَلَّى اللهُ تَعَالٰى عَلَيْهِ وَاٰلِهٖ وَسَلَّم ever again; then he passed away.' *(Mīzān-ush-Sharī'at-ul-Kubrā, pp. 48)*

May Allah عَزَّوَجَلَّ have mercy on him and forgive us without accountability for his sake!

Dear Islamic brothers! Some people are seen running after leaders and politicians for their personal interests. If such people are ever invited to meet the president or the prime minister, they come running. If they ever receive medals from the president or shake hands with him, they consider it a great honour, display the pictures of such occasions and show them to others. The foregoing parable contains considerable lesson for all of these people.

A word to the wise is enough اَلْعَاقِلُ تَكْفِيْهِ الْاِشَارَةُ

Kis chīz kī kamī ĥay Maulā صَلَّى اللهُ تَعَالٰى عَلَيْهِ وَاٰلِهٖ وَسَلَّم tayrī galī mayn
Dunyā tayrī galī mayn 'uqbā tayrī galī mayn
Takht-e-Sikandarī per woĥ thūktay naĥīn ĥayn
Bistar lagā ĥuwā ĥay jin kā tayrī galī mayn

Yā Rasūlallāĥ صَلَّى اللهُ تَعَالٰى عَلَيْهِ وَاٰلِهٖ وَسَلَّم, there is no shortage in your court
The world and the Hereafter are in your court
They do not even spit at the thrones of kings
Those who are the beggars of your court

صَلُّوْا عَلَى الْحَبِيْب صَلَّى اللهُ تَعَالٰى عَلٰى مُحَمَّد

73. Nuisance of eating at royal dining-mat

Sayyidunā Qāḍī Sharīk رَحْمَةُ اللهِ تَعَالٰى عَلَيْه was a righteous and dignified scholar and Muḥaddiš. He رَحْمَةُ اللهِ تَعَالٰى عَلَيْه would stay away from rulers. Once the caliph of Baghdad, Maĥdī 'Abbāsī invited him and said, 'You have three options; you must take up any one of them: accept the post of the Qāḍī [judge] or teach my sons or eat a meal with me.'

After consideration, he رَحْمَةُ اللهِ تَعَالٰى عَلَيْه responded, 'To eat meal with you seems to be easier than the other two options.' So he رَحْمَةُ اللهِ تَعَالٰى عَلَيْه accepted the invitation of the caliph. The caliph asked the chef to make the most delicious foods. When Sayyidunā Qāḍī Sharīk رَحْمَةُ اللهِ تَعَالٰى عَلَيْه arrived, foods were served and he رَحْمَةُ اللهِ تَعَالٰى عَلَيْه ate with the caliph at the royal dining-mat. After the meal, the chef said to the Shaykh رَحْمَةُ اللهِ تَعَالٰى عَلَيْه, 'Your honour, you have now got into trouble; you have been stuck in the 'royal' trap from which you would not be released.' What the chef had said came to pass, as after eating that one meal with the caliph, he رَحْمَةُ اللهِ تَعَالٰی عَلَیْه began teaching the caliph's sons and accepted the office of the judge as well. *(Tārīkh-ul-Khulafā, pp. 221)*

May Allah عَزَّوَجَلَّ have mercy on them and forgive us without accountability for their sake!

Two third of Dīn goes away

Dear Islamic brothers! It is better to stay away from the ruling and wealthy people. The risks of accepting their invitations and gifts are too grave for one's Hereafter as it is then difficult to abstain from praising them and agreeing with everything they say. It is stated in a Ḥadīš that the one who is humble with a wealthy person because of his wealth, two third of his Dīn [i.e. religion] goes away. *(Kashf-ul-Khifā, vol. 2, pp. 215, Ḥadīš 2442)* Commenting on this Ḥadīš Imām Aḥmad Razā Khān عَلَیْهِ رَحْمَةُ الْمَنَّان has stated that humility for worldly wealth is not for Allah عَزَّوَجَلَّ, and is thus Ḥarām. *(Żayl-ul-Mudda'ā lī Aḥsan-il-Wi'ā, pp. 12)*

Condemnation of flattery

In other words, showing humility to any wealthy person merely because of his wealth without Shar'ī permission, is Ḥarām. Sadly, this sin is extremely common these days. A wealthy person is often a cause of trial for others as people are awed by his wealth, even if he does not give even a single penny. Needlessly impressed, people treat such a person with humility to flatter him. The father of Imām Aḥmad Razā Khān عَلَیْهِ رَحْمَةُ الْمَنَّان, 'Allāmaĥ Maulānā Naqī Khān عَلَیْهِ رَحْمَةُ الرَّحْمٰن has quoted: 'It is stated in a Ḥadīš that a Muslim is not a flatterer.' Exaggerated praise that the praised person does not deserve is even worse as it leads to flattery and lying in addition to causing trial for the praised person as praising a person in his presence has been likened to cutting his throat in a Ḥadīš. It is further stated 'Throw dust into the mouths of the praisers who praise people in their presence.' This is strictly prohibited, especially when the one being praised is a Fāsiq [transgressor] as it is stated in Ḥadīš, 'When a Fāsiq is praised, Allah عَزَّوَجَلَّ becomes displeased and His 'Arsh shakes.' *(Aḥsan-ul-Wi'ā li Ādāb-id-Du'ā, pp.154)*

صَلُّوْا عَلَی الْحَبِیْب   صَلَّی اللهُ تَعَالٰی عَلٰی مُحَمَّد

74. Reward of Mālīdaĥ*

A Shaykh رَحْمَةُ اللهِ تَعَالٰی عَلَیْه has stated that once he saw his deceased paternal aunt in a dream and asked as to how she was; she replied, 'I am well as I received the rewards of all my deeds including the reward of even the Mālīdaĥ [i.e. a sweet bread] which I had one day given to a poor person to eat.' *(Sharḥ-uṣ-Ṣudūr, pp. 278)*

May Allah عَزَّوَجَلَّ have mercy on them and forgive us without accountability for their sake!

صَلُّوْا عَلَى الْحَبِیْب صَلَّى اللهُ تَعَالٰی عَلٰی مُحَمَّد

75. A single grape

Dear Islamic brothers! You can see that Allah عَزَّوَجَلَّ gives reward even for the smallest of deeds. Therefore, one should not hesitate to give even an apparently minor looking thing in the path of Allah.

Umm-ul-Mūminīn Sayyidatunā 'Āishaĥ Ṣiddīqaĥ رَضِیَ اللهُ تَعَالٰی عَنْهَا once gave a grape to a needy person. Someone expressed astonishment to this; she said, 'Many particles can be taken from this (grape) whereas Allah عَزَّوَجَلَّ says in the Quran in the 7th verse of Sūraĥ Az-Zilzāl, part 30.

فَمَنْ یَّعْمَلْ مِثْقَالَ ذَرَّةٍ خَیْرًا یَّرَهٗ ﴿۷﴾

Then whoever does good of a weight of a particle, shall see it.

[Kanz-ul-Īmān (Translation of Quran)] (Part 30, Sūraĥ Az-Zilzāl, verse 7)

To give Mālīdaĥ or any Ḥalāl and pure food to a hungry person for the pleasure of Allah عَزَّوَجَلَّ is indeed very virtuous. The Prophet of Raḥmaĥ, the Intercessor of Ummaĥ, the Owner of Jannaĥ صَلَّى اللهُ تَعَالٰی عَلَیْهِ وَاٰلِهٖ وَسَلَّم has stated, 'Whoever fed a hungry person to his satiation would be given shade by Allah عَزَّوَجَلَّ below the 'Arsh.' *(Makārim-ul-Akhlāq, pp. 272)*

صَلُّوْا عَلَى الْحَبِیْب صَلَّى اللهُ تَعَالٰی عَلٰی مُحَمَّد

---

* A type of sweet bread. [Translator's Note]

76. Blessings of making *Dam* in dream

Dear Islamic brothers! In order to have enthusiasm about feeding the hungry and adopting a Sunnaĥ-complying lifestyle, make a habit of travelling with the Sunnaĥ-Inspiring Madanī Qāfilaĥ of Dawat-e-Islami in the company of Rasūl's devotees. اِنْ شَآءَاللّٰه عَزَّوَجَلَّ, You will gain spiritual blessings as well as physical benefits. An Islamic brother has stated an incident somewhat like this: 'My nephew had severe pain because of stomach ulcer. He consulted many doctors and tried different medicines but there was no improvement in his condition. Luckily, he travelled with the devotees of Rasūl in a Sunnaĥ-Inspiring Madanī Qāfilaĥ. When he returned, his health had deteriorated even further. His pitiable state was very painful for us. He had intended that he would neither ask for special diet nor for extra rest during the Madanī Qāfilaĥ. Thus, he ate what was served.

The Islamic brother further added, 'When my nephew went to sleep that night, he saw an elderly preacher of Dawat-e-Islami in his dream. The preacher said, 'I am very pleased with you.' Then he politely inquired about his health, so my nephew complained about his agonizing pain. The preacher then placed his finger on my nephew's chest and blew over him. When he woke up in the morning, he was completely cured, اَلْحَمْدُلِلّٰه عَزَّوَجَلَّ.

Ĥay shifā ĥī shifā; marḥabā! Marḥabā!
Ā kay khud daykĥ layn; Qāfilay mayn chalo
Lūť layn raḥmatayn; khūb layn barakatayn,
Khuwāb achcĥay dikĥayn; Qāfilay mayn chalo

There is cure for disease, which will make you pleased
Come and experience yourself; let's travel in the Qāfilaĥ
Seek the mercy; seek the blessings
See good dreams; let's travel in the Qāfilaĥ

صَلُّوْا عَلَى الْحَبِيْب صَلَّى اللّٰهُ تَعَالٰى عَلٰى مُحَمَّد

77. Unique princess

When the daughter of Shaykh Sayyidunā Shāĥ Kirmānī قُدِّسَ سِرُّهُ الرَّبَّانِي reached the age of marriage he رَحْمَةُ اللّٰهِ تَعَالٰى عَلَيْه received a marriage proposal for his daughter from the neighbouring country's king but he رَحْمَةُ اللّٰهِ تَعَالٰى عَلَيْه turned it down. Then he visited different Masājid in search of a pious young man.

Finally he saw a young man who offered Ṣalāĥ in a proper manner and then humbly made Du'ā. The Shaykh asked him, 'Are you married?' The young man replied in the negative. The Shaykh then inquired, 'Would you like to marry? The girl recites the Holy Quran, offers Ṣalāĥ punctually, keeps fasts and is well-mannered.' The young man responded, 'Who will marry me [as I am a destitute person?]' The Shaykh رَحْمَةُ اللهِ تَعَالٰى عَلَيْه replied, 'I will marry my daughter to you; take these dirhams. Go and buy some pieces of bread, stew and fragrance from the marketplace.'

In this manner Shaykh Shāĥ Kirmānī قُدِّسَ سِرُّهُ الرَّبَّانِي conducted the Nikāḥ [marriage] ceremony of his righteous daughter. When the bride came to the house of the groom, she saw that there was a piece of bread on the flask of water. She asked, 'Why is this bread here?' The groom replied, 'This is yesterday's leftover stale bread which I had saved for my Ifṭār.' Upon hearing this, she began to leave. Seeing this, the groom said, 'I knew beforehand that Shaykh Shāĥ Kirmānī's daughter would not be able to live with a poor man like me.' The bride replied, 'I am going back not because of your destitution, but because of your apparent lack of faith in Allah عَزَّوَجَلَّ. Otherwise, you would not have saved the bread for the next day. I am surprised as to why my father praised you as pious.'

Embarrassed, the groom responded, 'I apologize for this mistake.' But the bride said, 'Your mistake is for you to rectify. Now, either I will stay in this house or this bread.' The groom immediately gave the bread in charity and thanked Allah عَزَّوَجَلَّ for becoming the husband of such a saintly and matchless princess. *(Rauḍ-ur-Riyāḥīn, pp. 103)*

May Allah عَزَّوَجَلَّ have mercy on them and forgive us without accountability for their sake!

Dear Islamic brothers! Did you see how unique the traits of the Mutawakkilīn[1] are! Despite being a princess, the daughter of Shaykh Shāĥ Kirmānī قُدِّسَ سِرُّهُ الرَّبَّانِي had such firm faith in Allah عَزَّوَجَلَّ that she did not desire to save any food for the next day. This was indeed her staunch belief in the fact that Allah عَزَّوَجَلَّ Who has provided sustenance today, can also provide it tomorrow. He عَزَّوَجَلَّ is omnipotent.

[1] A Mutawakkil is the one who has outright trust in Allah عَزَّوَجَلَّ. [Translator's Note]

Birds and animals also do not save anything to eat next time. It is not in their nature to do that. Look at the chicken's trust in the divine providence. If you give it water to drink, it will drink as much as she needs and then will step on the bowl spilling the remaining water on the floor. It is as if she is a 'silent preacher' that is advising us like this: 'O People! You are not content even after accumulating enormous wealth that is sufficient for many years, whereas I have no worry after drinking water just once, because the One [Allah عَزَّوَجَلَّ] who has given water to me right now, will also provide for me later on.'

78. Imām Bukhārī's رَحْمَةُ اللهِ عَلَيْه teacher

Once the prince of some mountainous terrain along with his servants came to visit Sayyidunā Qubīṣaĥ Bin 'Uqbaĥ رَحْمَةُ اللهِ تَعَالٰی عَلَيْه, the teacher of Imām Bukhārī عَلَيْهِ رَحْمَةُ البَارِی. Sayyidunā Qubīṣaĥ رَحْمَةُ اللهِ تَعَالٰی عَلَيْه was a little late in coming out. One of the servants of the prince shouted, 'Your honour, the prince of the Malak-ul-Jabal (i.e. the king of the mountains) is standing at your doorstep and you are not stepping out to receive him.'

Hearing this, Sayyidunā Qubīṣaĥ رَحْمَةُ اللهِ تَعَالٰی عَلَيْه stepped outside with some slices of dry bread in his hands and said showing the pieces to them, 'The person who is content with this (ascetic lifestyle) in the world has nothing to do with the king of the mountains. By Allah عَزَّوَجَلَّ! I will not even talk to him.' Saying this, he shut the door. *(Tażkira-tul-Ḥuffāẓ, vol. 1, pp. 274)*

May Allah عَزَّوَجَلَّ have mercy on him and forgive us without accountability for his sake!

صَلُّوْا عَلَى الْحَبِيْب صَلَّى اللهُ تَعَالٰى عَلٰى مُحَمَّد

Dignity in contentment

Dear Islamic brothers! Those who adopt austerity and are content with simple clothes and foods do not require wealth, nor do they need to flatter the wealthy, whereas the greedy are never satisfied. Greed for wealth is not good. The greedy are afflicted with a wealth-acquiring mania and constantly seek to accumulate wealth until they meet their death. Sayyidunā 'Alī Murtaḍā رَضِیَ اللهُ تَعَالٰی عَنْه has stated, عَزَّ مَنْ قَنَعَ وَذَلَّ مَنْ طَمَعَ *'The one who is content is dignified and the one who is greedy is disgraced.'* *(Rūḥānī Ḥikāyāt, vol. 1, pp. 106)*

Leave the world

Sayyidunā Abū Ĥurayraĥ رَضِیَ اللّٰہُ تَعَالٰی عَنْہُ has narrated that the Prophet of Raḥmaĥ, the Intercessor of Ummaĥ صَلَّی اللّٰہُ تَعَالٰی عَلَیْہِ وَاٰلِہٖ وَسَلَّم once advised him, 'O Abū Ĥurayraĥ (رَضِیَ اللّٰہُ تَعَالٰی عَنْہُ)! When you are starving, survive on a piece of bread and a bowl of water and say, 'I distance myself from the world and its seekers.' *(Al-Kāmil fī Ḍu'fā-ir-Rijāl, vol. 8, pp. 183)*

Do not rely on wealth of others

Sayyidunā Abū Ayyūb Anṣārī رَضِیَ اللّٰہُ تَعَالٰی عَنْہُ, a companion of the Prophet, has narrated that a villager once approached the Holy Prophet صَلَّی اللّٰہُ تَعَالٰی عَلَیْہِ وَاٰلِہٖ وَسَلَّم and asked him for some advice. The Holy Prophet صَلَّی اللّٰہُ تَعَالٰی عَلَیْہِ وَاٰلِہٖ وَسَلَّم said, 'When you offer Ṣalāĥ, offer it (considering it) the last Ṣalāĥ of your life; and do not say any such thing due to which you would have to make an apology tomorrow; and be disappointed with what people have.' *(Sunan Ibn Mājaĥ, vol. 4, pp. 455, Ḥadīš 4171)*

It is better not to take financial gifts from others

Dear Islamic brothers! Do not depend on others' wealth. Even if the other person likes and admires you and has repeatedly offered financial help to you; don't pin any hope on such assurances as they are, in fact, unreliable and false hopes because the heart and mind of a person keep changing. Remember that the one who 'gives' can never be impressed by the one who 'takes.' However, if someone comes to give you [a financial gift] and you refuse to accept it; the giver will certainly be impressed by you.

Ḥujjat-ul-Islam Sayyidunā Imām Muhammad Ghazālī عَلَیْہِ رَحْمَۃُ اللّٰہِ الْوَالِی has stated, 'The luxuries only last for a short while. Then they come to an end. Things will change in a few days. Be content in your life, and you will remain pleased. Give up your desire, and you will live a free life. Death often comes (at the hands of robbers) who come to rob gold, rubies and pearls.' *(Iḥyā-ul-'Ulūm, vol. 3, pp. 298)*

May Allah عَزَّوَجَلَّ have mercy on him and forgive us without accountability for his sake!

One will not be dependent on others

Sayyidunā Muhammad Bin Wāsi' عَلَيْهِ رَحْمَةُ اللّٰهِ الْقَوِی would soak a piece of dry bread in water, eat it and then say, 'One who is content with this shall never be dependent on anyone.' *(Iḥyā-ul-'Ulūm, vol. 3, pp. 295)*

May Allah عَزَّوَجَلَّ have mercy on him and forgive us without accountability for his sake!

Stomach is small

Sayyidunā Samīṭ Bin 'Ijlān عَلَيْهِ رَحْمَةُ الْمَنَّان has stated, 'O man! Your stomach is very small (only a span[1] long); why should then it lead you to Hell? A wise man was once asked, 'What is your wealth?' He replied, 'To appear in a decent state in public, to have inward moderation, and to be disappointed with what people have.' *(Iḥyā-ul-'Ulūm, vol. 3, pp. 298)*

May Allah عَزَّوَجَلَّ have mercy on them and forgive us without accountability for their sake!

The Prophet of mankind, the Peace of our heart and mind, the most Generous and Kind صَلَّى اللّٰهُ تَعَالٰی عَلَيْهِ وَاٰلِهٖ وَسَلَّم has stated, 'Man grows older (but) two of his traits become younger; (his) greed for wealth and greed for age.' *(Ṣaḥīḥ Muslim, pp. 521, Ḥadīš 1047)*

Only sand of grave fills stomach

The Holy Prophet صَلَّى اللّٰهُ تَعَالٰی عَلَيْهِ وَاٰلِهٖ وَسَلَّم has stated, 'If man had two valleys of wealth, he would still wish for a third one. Only the sand of the grave can fill his stomach and Allah عَزَّوَجَلَّ accepts the repentance of the person who repents.' *(Ṣaḥīḥ Muslim, pp. 522, Ḥadīš 1050)*

Sayṫĥ jī ko fikr tĥī aīk aīk kay das das kī-jiye
Maut ā poĥnchī kay mister jān wāpis kī-jiye

The millionaire was planning to multiply his wealth
'Return your life, sir!' Came his sudden death

صَلُّوْا عَلَى الْحَبِيْب صَلَّى اللّٰهُ تَعَالٰى عَلٰى مُحَمَّد

[1] The distance between the tip of the thumb and the tip of the little finger when the hand is fully extended. [Translator's Note]

79. 100 Pieces of bread

When Ḥāfiẓ-ul-Ḥadīš, Sayyidunā Ḥajjāj Baghdādī عَلَيْهِ رَحْمَةُ اللّٰهِ الْهَادِى was going to embark on his journey for the acquisition of religious knowledge, his mother packed 100 pieces of bread in a clay churn. To acquire knowledge of Ḥadīš, he sought the company of the great scholar of Ḥadīš, Sayyidunā Shabābaĥ رَحْمَةُ اللهِ تَعَالٰی عَلَيْه. His mother had given him breads, but he had to make arrangement for the curry, which he did. He chose the curry that always remains fresh and full of blessings. There was no reduction in it even after the passing of many centuries. What was that special curry? It was water from the river Tigris! Every day he would consume a piece of bread by soaking it in the water from the river and would diligently learn his lessons. When the 100 pieces of breads finished, he had to ask for leave. Thus, he unwillingly sought permission from his teacher to depart. *(Tażkira-tul-Ḥuffāẓ, vol. 2, pp. 100)*

May Allah عَزَّوَجَلَّ have mercy on them and forgive us without accountability for their sake!

Dear Islamic brothers! In past, our scholars made countless sacrifices for the acquisition of religious knowledge but, these days, people are not prepared to learn religion despite the availability of free lodging and dining facilities. Indeed religious learning will benefit us in the worldly life as well as in the afterlife. If one cannot enrol in an Islamic school or university, he should at least enrol and complete the 63-day 'Madanī Tarbiyyatī course' at any Madanī Tarbiyyat Gāĥ of Dawat-e-Islami. This course has tremendous blessings and benefits as the following incident shows:

80. Allergy was cured

An Islamic brother has stated, 'I had allergy. I would feel extreme pain in the cold and in the sun. Whenever it rained, I would writhe in agony like a fish out of water. A devotee of Rasūl suggested me to enrol in the 'Tarbiyyatī course' conducted by Dawat-e-Islami. Therefore, I enrolled in the 63-day course that started on 19th of November, 2004 in Faīzān-e-Madīnaĥ, Bāb-ul-Madīnaĥ Karachi, the global Madanī Markaz of Dawat-e-Islami. I was astonished that the chronic allergy on whose treatment I had spent a lot of money visiting numerous doctors, was cured due to the blessing of the company of the devotees of Rasūl, during the 63-day Tarbiyyatī course.

Dawat-e-Islami kī Qayyūm عَزَّوَجَلَّ, dauno jaĥān mayn mach jāye dĥūm
Is pay fidā ĥo bachchaĥ bachchaĥ, Yā Allah عَزَّوَجَلَّ mayrī jĥaulī bĥar day

May Dawat-e-Islami boom!
Throughout the world, Yā Qayyūm عَزَّوَجَلَّ!
May every child become devoted to it!
Yā Allah عَزَّوَجَلَّ! My supplication be fulfilled!

صَلُّوْا عَلَى الْحَبِيْب صَلَّى اللهُ تَعَالٰى عَلٰى مُحَمَّد

What is Tarbiyyatī course?

اَلْحَمْدُلِلّٰه عَزَّوَجَلَّ! The 63-day Tarbiyyatī course provides an opportunity to adopt the company of the devotees of Rasūl. It is so beneficial for one's Hereafter that every Muslim who desires serving Islam would perhaps yearn to enrol in this 63 day course once he is enlightened about its details and curriculum. اَلْحَمْدُ لِلّٰه عَزَّوَجَلَّ, Besides Bāb-ul-Madīnaĥ, Karachi [Pakistan] this course is offered in several other cities around Pakistan. The curriculum entails many sciences of knowledge some of which are Farḍ on every adult and sane Muslim. There are many virtues of acquiring religious knowledge. Hence, it is narrated that the Noble Prophet صَلَّى اللهُ تَعَالٰى عَلَيْهِ وَاٰلِهٖ وَسَلَّم has stated, 'Whoever acquires the knowledge of Dīn (religion), this becomes atonement for his previous sins.' *(Jāmi' Tirmiżī, vol. 4, pp. 295, Ḥadīš 2657)*

اَلْحَمْدُلِلّٰه عَزَّوَجَلَّ, Wuḍū, Ghusl and a practical demonstration of Ṣalāĥ are taught in this course. The curriculum also includes the learning of the method of giving Ghusl to a deceased, shrouding and burying a dead body, funeral Ṣalāĥ and Eid Ṣalāĥ etc. Furthermore, Quranic recitation with proper manners and correct pronunciation of Arabic alphabet is also taught with the help of Madanī Qāidaĥ. Students memorize the last 20 Sūraĥ of the Holy Quran and practice the recitation of Sūraĥ Al-Mulk. There are many virtues of learning the Quran.

Virtues of teaching Quranic recitation to children

The Prophet of mankind, the Peace of our heart and mind, the most Generous and Kind صَلَّى اللهُ تَعَالٰى عَلَيْهِ وَاٰلِهٖ وَسَلَّم has stated, 'One who teaches Quranic recitation to his son will be forgiven for all of his previous and future sins.' *(Majma'-uz-Zawāid, vol. 7, pp. 344, Ḥadīš 11271)*

In another narration the Holy Prophet صَلَّى اللهُ تَعَالٰى عَلَيْهِ وَاٰلِهٖ وَسَلَّم has stated, 'Whoever learns the Quran in his youth, Quran gets intermixed with his flesh and blood. [Furthermore] there are two rewards for the one who learns the Quran in old age and continues to learn it despite being made to forget it repeatedly.' *(Kanz-ul-'Ummāl, vol. 1, pp. 267, Ḥadīš 2378)*

Character-building in Tarbiyyatī course

During the Tarbiyyatī course, special emphasis is laid on the following traits for the character-building of the attendees:

1. Honesty
2. Gentleness
3. Tolerance
4. Humility
5. Forgiving others
6. Manners of conversation
7. Awareness of the perils of backbiting.
8. Manners of making a Madanī [righteous] environment at one's home.
9. Manners of preparing a Madanī Qāfilaĥ and conducting it according to the [prescribed] schedule.
10. Manners of delivering Dars and Bayān [speeches].
11. Manners of area-visit to call people towards righteousness.
12. Manners of making individual effort, the lifeblood of Dawat-e-Islami's Madanī working, and method of acting upon Madanī In'āmāt etc.

During the course, the participants also travel with three Madanī Qāfilaĥs of three days and one Madanī Qāfilaĥ of twelve days which usually takes place near the end of the course. At the end of the twelve days Madanī Qāfilaĥ, a spare day is given for the preparation of the examination which is held the next day. On the last day, the course ends on Du'ā and Ṣalāt-o-Salām. Numerous other things are also taught in the course. In addition, the participants are blessed with a good company of righteous Islamic brothers. Upon the completion of the course, اَلْحَمْدُ لِلّٰہ عَزَّوَجَلَّ, many individuals who used to lead a wicked life vow to offer Ṣalāĥ regularly and become good Muslims. They become righteous earning respect in society.

Therefore, whoever gets the opportunity should learn religious knowledge by enrolling in this [highly informative] course. The Holy Prophet صَلَّى اللهُ تَعَالٰى عَلَيْهِ وَاٰلِهٖ وَسَلَّم has stated, 'On the Day of Judgement, the person with the most wistfulness will be the one who had the opportunity to acquire religious knowledge in the world but did not acquire it, and another person [with the most wistfulness will be the one] who gained religious knowledge and others were benefited by hearing from him (and by acting accordingly) but he did not gain any benefit from it (because he did not act what he preached).' *(Mu'jam Ṣaghīr, pp. 69, Ḥadīš 1058)* Those who cannot enrol for 63 days should approach the Madanī Markaz as they may be permitted to attend the course for less than 63 days.

صَلُّوْا عَلَى الْحَبِيْب صَلَّى اللهُ تَعَالٰى عَلٰى مُحَمَّد

81. Ten for one

An Abdāl of his time, Sayyidunā Abū Ja'far Bin Khaṭṭāb عَلَيْهِ رَحْمَةُ اللهِ التَّوَّاب has stated, 'Once a beggar came to my doorstep and asked for help. I asked my wife if there was something to give to him. She replied that they only had four eggs. I asked her to give them to the beggar. She complied and the beggar left with the eggs. After a little while a friend of mine sent me a basket full of eggs. I asked my wife as to how many eggs were there in the basket. She replied that there were 30 eggs. I asked, 'You gave four eggs to the beggar, so by which calculation these 30 eggs have been sent to us?' She replied, 'There are 30 unbroken eggs and 10 are broken ones.'

Elaborating on this parable, Sayyidunā Shaykh 'Allāmaĥ Yāfi'ī Yemini عَلَيْهِ رَحْمَةُ اللهِ الْقَوِى has stated, 'Out of the [four] eggs that were given to the beggar, one was broken whereas 3 were unbroken. Allah عَزَّوَجَلَّ gave 10 in return for each of the eggs; broken eggs for the broken one, and unbroken eggs for the unbroken ones.' *(Rauḍ-ur-Riyāḥīn, pp. 151)*

May Allah عَزَّوَجَلَّ have mercy on them and forgive us without accountability for ṭheir sake!

Dear Islamic brothers! How merciful Allah عَزَّوَجَلَّ is! In addition to granting rewards in the Hereafter, at times, He عَزَّوَجَلَّ also showers blessings upon us in the world. Sometimes, He عَزَّوَجَلَّ shows clear signs so that people get inspired and motivated (towards His mercy) as obvious from the above parable that Sayyidunā Abū Ja'far Bin Khaṭṭāb عَلَيْهِ رَحْمَةُ اللّٰهِ التَّوَّاب was immediately given 40 eggs in return for 4 eggs. Allah عَزَّوَجَلَّ says in the Holy Quran, Sūraĥ Al-An'ām, verse 160, part 8:

مَنْ جَآءَ بِالْحَسَنَةِ فَلَهٗ عَشْرُ اَمْثَالِهَا ۚ

For one who brings one good deed, are ten like it.

[Kanz-ul-Īmān (Translation of Quran)] (Part 8, Sūraĥ Al-An'ām, verse 160)

Commenting on this verse, Maulānā Sayyid Muhammad Na'īmuddīn Murādābādī عَلَيْهِ رَحْمَةُ اللّٰهِ الْهَادِى has stated: 'The one doing one good deed will be given the reward of ten deeds. However, the reward is not limited to 10, in fact, it is merely dependent on Allah's will. He عَزَّوَجَلَّ may grant 700 times or even countless rewards [for one deed]. In essence, this matter of reward is dependent on the mercy and bounty of Allah عَزَّوَجَلَّ.' *(Khazāin-ul-'Irfān, pp. 241)*

82. Favour returned

Sayyidunā Shaykh Abū Bakr Shiblī عَلَيْهِ رَحْمَةُ اللّٰهِ الْقَوِى once travelled out of Baghdad city along with his forty disciples. At one place he said, 'O People! Allah عَزَّوَجَلَّ is the provider of sustenance to His servants.' He رَحْمَةُ اللّٰهِ تَعَالٰى عَلَيْه then recited the following part of the second and the third verses of Sūraĥ Aṭ-Ṭalāq part 28:

وَمَنْ يَّتَّقِ اللّٰهَ يَجْعَلْ لَّهٗ مَخْرَجًا ۙ﴿۲﴾

وَّ يَرْزُقْهُ مِنْ حَيْثُ لَا يَحْتَسِبُ ؕ وَمَنْ يَّتَوَكَّلْ عَلَى اللّٰهِ فَهُوَ حَسْبُهٗ ؕ

And whoever fears Allah – Allah will create for him a way of deliverance. And will provide him sustenance from such a place he had never even thought of; and whoever relies on Allah – then He is Sufficient for him. *[Kanz-ul-Īmān (Translation of Quran)] (Part 28, Sūraĥ Aṭ-Ṭalāq, verse 2-3)*

Having recited the verses, he رَحْمَةُ اللهِ تَعَالٰى عَلَيْه went somewhere alone, leaving his disciples behind. All the disciples remained lying there starving for three days. The fourth day the Shaykh رَحْمَةُ اللهِ تَعَالٰى عَلَيْه returned and said, 'O People! Allah عَزَّوَجَلَّ has granted permission to seek sustenance. Hence, Allah عَزَّوَجَلَّ says in the 15th verse of Sūraĥ Al-Mulk part 29:

هُوَ الَّذِیۡ جَعَلَ لَکُمُ الۡاَرۡضَ ذَلُوۡلًا فَامۡشُوۡا فِیۡ مَنَاکِبِہَا وَ کُلُوۡا مِنۡ رِّزۡقِہٖ ؕ

It is He Who subjected the earth for you, therefore tread on its paths and eat from Allah's sustenance.

[Kanz-ul-Īmān (Translation of Quran)] (Part 29, Sūraĥ Al-Mulk, verse 15)

He رَحْمَةُ اللهِ تَعَالٰى عَلَيْه then asked his disciples to send anyone from amongst them so that the person may bring some food. The disciples sent a poor person to Baghdad city. He roamed from street to street but could not find any [source of] sustenance. Exhausted, he eventually sat down to rest near a clinic run by a non-Muslim physician. That physician was an expert and would diagnose the disease accurately just by taking the patient's pulse.

After all of his patients left, the physician called in this poor man assuming him to be a patient. Then he took his pulse and, handing him some bread, curry and dessert, he said, 'This is the cure for your illness.' The poor man replied, 'There are forty other patients like me that are afflicted with the same illness.' The physician ordered his servants to bring food for forty people and gave it to the poor man to take it with him. The physician then followed this poor man secretly.

When the food was presented to Shaykh Abū Bakr Shiblī عَلَيْهِ رَحْمَةُ اللّٰهِ الْقَوِی, he did not touch it, and said that there was a strange secret attached to the food. The poor man who had brought the food told the whole event that had taken place. The great Shaykh رَحْمَةُ اللهِ تَعَالٰى عَلَيْه then said, 'That non-Muslim has been so nice to us, shouldn't we give him something in return for his kindness?' The disciples replied, 'What can we poor people give?' The Shaykh رَحْمَةُ اللهِ تَعَالٰى عَلَيْه said, 'We could at least make Du'ā for him, before eating this food.' Hence, they made Du'ā.

The non-Muslim physician was secretly listening to their conversation. The blessings of Du'ā were immediately manifested, causing a Madanī revolution in his heart. He approached Shaykh Abū Bakr Shiblī عَلَيْهِ رَحْمَةُ اللّٰهِ الْقَوِی, repented of unbelief and embraced Islam reciting Kalimaĥ. He also became a disciple of the Shaykh and was elevated to a high spiritual degree. *(Rauḍ-ur-Riyāḥīn, pp. 81)*

May Allah عَزَّوَجَلَّ have mercy on them and forgive us without accountability for their sake!

صَلُّوْا عَلَى الْحَبِيْب صَلَّى اللّٰهُ تَعَالٰى عَلٰى مُحَمَّد

Serving saint رَحْمَةُ اللهِ عَلَيْه bears fruit

Dear Islamic brothers! How uniquely the saints رَحِمَهُمُ اللّٰهُ تَعَالٰی would call people towards righteousness! One who serves them is never left empty-handed. From this parable we have also learnt that we should make Du'ā for the one who is polite and courteous to us. Even if an unbeliever does us a favour, we should at least make Du'ā in return that he be guided to the right path [Islam]. The effects of the Du'ā of Sayyidunā Shaykh Abū Bakr Shiblī عَلَيْهِ رَحْمَةُ اللّٰهِ الْقَوِی and his disciples were manifested and the non-Muslim physician who had served them was blessed with embracing Islam, اَلْحَمْدُ لِلّٰه عَزَّوَجَلَّ.

Du'ā-e-Walī mayn woĥ tāšīr daykĥī
Badaltī ĥazāraun kī taqdīr daykĥī

By the effect of the supplications of a saint
Destiny of thousands of people is changed

One morsel led three to heaven

The non-Muslim physician gave the food to the disciple considering him a destitute man and was blessed with the gift of Islam. If a Muslim feeds the poor, he is entitled to Paradise. Hence, the Prophet of Raḥmaĥ, the Intercessor of Ummaĥ صَلَّى اللّٰهُ تَعَالٰى عَلَيْهِ وَاٰلِهٖ وَسَلَّم has stated, 'Allah عَزَّوَجَلَّ makes three people enter Paradise (by virtue of) a morsel of bread and a handful of dry dates or their like by which a poor [Miskīn] person is benefited. The first is the man who orders [the food to be prepared]; the second is his wife who prepares it, and the third is their servant who gives it to the poor [Miskīn].' The Noble Prophet صَلَّى اللّٰهُ تَعَالٰى عَلَيْهِ وَاٰلِهٖ وَسَلَّم then said, 'All praise is for Allah عَزَّوَجَلَّ who has not left out even our servants [in giving reward].' *(Mu'jam Awsaṭ, vol. 4, pp. 89, Ḥadīš 5309)*

صَلُّوْا عَلَى الْحَبِيْب صَلَّى اللّٰهُ تَعَالٰى عَلٰى مُحَمَّد

Here are five more Aḥādīš on the virtues of feeding others:

1. The better person from amongst you is the one who feeds (others). *(Musnad Imām Aḥmad, vol. 9, pp. 241, Ḥadīš 23984)*
2. To feed [others] and to make Salām commonplace are among the acts which make forgiveness Wājib. *(Makārim-ul-Akhlāq, pp. 375, Ḥadīš 158)*
3. For as long as one's dining-mat remains spread [on the ground], angels continue to shower blessings on him. *(Shu'ab-ul-Īmān, vol. 7, pp. 99, Ḥadīš 9626)*
4. Whoever satisfies the hunger of his Muslim brother and feeds him until he is satiated, will be forgiven by Allah عَزَّوَجَلَّ. *(Majma'-uz-Zawāid, vol. 3, pp. 319, Ḥadīš 4719)*
5. Whoever feeds a hungry person, will be granted a place by Allah عَزَّوَجَلَّ under the shadow of 'Arsh. *(Makārim-ul-Akhlāq, pp. 373)*

اَلْحَمْدُ لِلّٰه عَزَّوَجَلَّ, In the Madanī environment of Dawat-e-Islami, a global & non-political religious movement of the Quran and Sunnaĥ, one is inspired to learn religious knowledge including the Sunnaĥs of eating food and feeding others. Furthermore, many non-Muslims embrace Islam by the blessings of the devotees of Rasūl. Here is one such incident.

83. Strange traveller of Madanī Qāfilaĥ

An Islamic brother from Bandra, Bombay India has stated, 'I was once walking along a roadside when my eye fell on a group of individuals standing at a side of the road. Upon getting closer I saw that one of them was giving Dars from a book titled '*Faīzān-e-Sunnat*.'

I also listened to the Dars and found it extremely captivating. Upon the conclusion of the Dars, one of the brothers approached me and greeted me very courteously. Making individual effort, he then invited me to travel with a Madanī Qāfilaĥ for 3 days. Delighted by what I listened to during the Dars, I spontaneously agreed to travel with the Madanī Qāfilaĥ for 3 days in the company of the devotees of Rasūl.

During the Madanī Qāfilaĥ I attained such tranquillity that cannot be expressed in words. I could no longer conceal my secret and finally revealed to them that I was not a Muslim. I was lost in the dark valley of unbelief. The Dars, individual efforts, the travel in the Madanī Qāfilaĥ and the superior character of Islamic brothers had all highly inspired me. I requested them to do me another favour and make me a Muslim.

اَلْحَمْدُلِلّٰہ عَزَّوَجَلَّ, I repented of my unbelief, recited the Kalimaĥ and entered the fold of Islam.' The brother from India goes onto say, 'This incident took place in December 2004, and now in March 2005 [at the time of the writing of this statement] I have grown a beard and adorned my head with a green turban. Currently, I am travelling in the 63-day Madanī Qāfilaĥ with the devotees of Rasūl to learn and adopt Sunnaĥ.'

Āo ay 'āshiqīn, mil kay tablīgh-e-Dīn
Kāfiraun ko karayn, Qāfilay mayn chalo
Sunnatayn 'ām ĥaun, ām nayk kām ĥaun
Sab karayn koshishayn, Qāfilay mayn chalo

O devotees! Let's preach Islam to the unbelievers,
To achieve this, let's travel with Qāfilaĥ together
May Sunnaĥ propagate, and the righteous deed prosper,
Let's strive and travel with Qāfilaĥ together

صَلُّوْا عَلَى الْحَبِيْب   صَلَّى اللّٰهُ تَعَالٰى عَلٰى مُحَمَّد

84. Trader of Baghdad

A trader in Baghdad had malice towards saints [Auliyā Allah] رَحِمَهُمُ اللّٰهُ تَعَالٰی. One Friday he saw Shaykh Sayyidunā Bishr Ḥāfī عَلَيْهِ رَحْمَةُ اللّٰهِ الْكَافِى leave the Masjid right after Ṣalāt-ul-Jumu'aĥ. He thought to himself that this person (Bishr Ḥāfī عَلَيْهِ رَحْمَةُ اللّٰهِ الْكَافِى) acts as if he is a saint but he has left the Masjid immediately after the Ṣalāĥ; he has no inclination to stay in the Masjid. Thus he decided to follow the honourable Shaykh to see as to where he goes.

On the way, Sayyidunā Bishr Ḥāfī عَلَیْهِ رَحْمَةُ اللّٰهِ الْكَافِی bought some bread from a bakery. This further annoyed the trader and he thought that this person had left the Masjid just for a piece of bread which he would now eat in the shade of a tree. The trader thought that as soon as the person starts eating the bread, he will ask him if this is how a saint should behave, and leave the Masjid just for a piece of bread. He kept on following the honourable Shaykh until the Shaykh entered a Masjid in a village. In the Masjid, lay a sick person. The Shaykh sat beside him and fed him with his own hands.

The trader was astonished to see all this. He then came out of the Masjid to see the village. As he returned to the Masjid the sick person was still there but the Shaykh had left. He asked the sick person as to where the Shaykh had gone. The sick person replied that he had left for Baghdad. He then asked as to how far Baghdad was from that village. The sick person replied that it was 40 miles from the village.

Confused, the trader thought that he was now in trouble as he did not realize at all how far he had come following the great Shaykh. He then asked, 'When will the Shaykh come here again?' The sick person informed him that the Shaykh would come back next Friday. Hence, he decided to stay there for a week as he had no other option.

The following Friday Shaykh Sayyidunā Bishr Ḥāfī عَلَیْهِ رَحْمَةُ اللّٰهِ الْكَافِی came to visit the sick person again and fed him as usual. Sayyidunā Bishr Ḥāfī عَلَیْهِ رَحْمَةُ اللّٰهِ الْكَافِی asked the trader as to why he had followed him. The trader acknowledged his mistake humbly. The Shaykh ordered him to stand up and follow him again. The trader thus followed the Shaykh and reached Baghdad in a little while. By witnessing this saintly miracle of Sayyidunā Bishr Ḥāfī عَلَیْهِ رَحْمَةُ اللّٰهِ الْكَافِی, the trader repented of having malice towards saints and became a humble and sincere devotee of them. *(Rauḍ-ur-Riyāḥīn, pp. 118)*

May Allah عَزَّوَجَلَّ have mercy on them and forgive us without accountability for their sake!

Bad suspicion from wicked heart

Dear Islamic brothers! It is Ḥarām to have a bad suspicion[1] against a Muslim. Imām Aḥmad Razā Khān عَلَيْهِ رَحْمَةُ الْمَنَّان has stated, 'A bad suspicion arises from a wicked heart.' *(Fatāwā Razawiyyaĥ (Jadīd), vol. 22, pp. 400)*

One should never look down on the righteous people, especially the saints of Allah. These pious individuals are sincere in their deeds and have a sympathetic heart for the creation of Allah. Furthermore, these pious people can travel long distances in a twinkling of an eye. At times, the punishment for a bad suspicion is immediately given in the world.

85. Punishment of bad suspicion

Once, in extremely cold weather, Sayyidunā Shaykh Abul Ḥusayn Nūrī's maid Zaytūnaĥ brought him a piece of bread with some milk. He was gathering up pieces of coal to light them so that he would warm himself up. His hands were still blackened by the coal when he began to eat. The fire suddenly ignited and milk spilled over his hands. Feeling disgust, the maid thought to herself that he is famous as a saint but he does not care about his cleanliness!

After a little while, she went out of home to do some chores. Out of the blue another woman grabbed her and accused her of stealing her bundle of clothes and thus dragged her to the police station. When Sayyidunā Shaykh Nūrī رَحْمَةُ اللهِ تَعَالٰی عَلَيْه came to know of this, he went to the police station to vouch for her. The police officer responded that he could not release her as she was accused of theft.

While this conversation was going on, another maid entered the police station with the stolen bundle of clothes. The bundle was handed over to its owner and Zaytūnaĥ was released. The Shaykh رَحْمَةُ اللهِ تَعَالٰی عَلَيْه asked Zaytūnaĥ, 'Would you have bad suspicion any longer against the saints of Allah? [That they do not care about cleanliness]. Ashamed, Zaytūnaĥ replied that she had learnt her lesson and repented of bad suspicion. *(Rauḍ-ur-Riyāḥīn, pp. 136)*

May Allah عَزَّوَجَلَّ have mercy on him and forgive us without accountability for his sake!

---

[1] Bad suspicion here has been used in the sense of the Arabic word سُوْءُ الظَّن which implies forming a negative opinion regarding a Muslim without an explicit Shar'ī proof. [Translator's Note]

Bad suspicion is Ḥarām

Dear Islamic brothers! Did you see how the woman was immediately punished for having a bad suspicion about a saint رَحْمَةُ اللهِ تَعَالٰى عَلَيْه. One should fear Allah عَزَّوَجَلَّ regardless of whether he is punished in this world or not as it is Ḥarām to have bad suspicion about a Muslim. Imām Aḥmad Razā Khān عَلَيْهِ رَحْمَةُ الرَّحْمٰن has stated, 'A bad suspicion arises from a wicked heart.' *(Fatāwā Razawiyyaĥ (Jadīd), vol. 22, pp. 400)* Allah عَزَّوَجَلَّ says in the 36th verse of Sūraĥ Banī Israīl part 15:

وَلَا تَقْفُ مَا لَيْسَ لَكَ بِهٖ عِلْمٌ ؕ اِنَّ السَّمْعَ وَ الْبَصَرَ وَ الْفُؤَادَ كُلُّ اُولٰٓئِكَ كَانَ عَنْهُ مَسْـُٔوْلًا ﴿۳۶﴾

And go not after that thing of which you know not. No doubt the ear and the eye and the heart are all to be questioned of.

[Kanz-ul-Īmān (Translation of Quran)] (Part 15, Sūraĥ Banī Isrāīl, verse 36)

In another verse in Sūraĥ Al-Ḥujurāt, part 26 Allah عَزَّوَجَلَّ says:

يٰٓاَيُّهَا الَّذِيْنَ اٰمَنُوا اجْتَنِبُوْا كَثِيْرًا مِّنَ الظَّنِّ ۫ اِنَّ بَعْضَ الظَّنِّ اِثْمٌ

O those who believe! Avoid more suspicions; verily some suspicion is a sin.

[Kanz-ul-Īmān (Translation of Quran)] (Part 26, Sūraĥ Al-Ḥujurāt, verse 12)

Once the Noble Prophet صَلَّى اللهُ تَعَالٰى عَلَيْهِ وَاٰلِهٖ وَسَلَّم said, 'Did you split his heart so that you would have come to know?' *(Abī Dāwūd, vol. 3, pp. 63, Ḥadīš 2643)* He صَلَّى اللهُ تَعَالٰى عَلَيْهِ وَاٰلِهٖ وَسَلَّم has further stated 'Refrain from bad suspicions because having a (bad) suspicion is the greatest lie.' *(Ṣaḥīḥ Bukhārī, vol. 3, pp. 446, Ḥadīš 5143)*

86. Cry when you see someone cry

Sayyidunā Makḥūl Dimishqī عَلَيْهِ رَحْمَةُ اللهِ الْقَوِی once said, 'When you see someone weep, you also weep with him. Don't have the bad suspicion that he is weeping ostentatiously.

Once I had a bad suspicion against a crying Muslim, so I could not cry for one year as a punishment.' *(Tanbīĥ-ul-Mughtarīn, pp. 122)*

صَلُّوْا عَلَى الْحَبِيْب صَلَّى اللهُ تَعَالٰى عَلٰى مُحَمَّد

87. Nine unbelievers embraced Islam

اَلْحَمْدُلِلّٰه عَزَّوَجَلَّ! There are great blessings of the Madanī Qāfilaĥs of Dawat-e-Islami, a global & non-political religious movement of the Quran and Sunnaĥ. Not only the sinful Muslims get reformed, but the non-Muslims are also, sometimes, blessed with embracing Islam.

A preacher of Dawat-e-Islami has reported: 'About five years back, I gifted a few audio cassettes and booklets released by Maktaba-tul-Madīnaĥ to a non-Muslim college fellow of mine and his friends. One cassette was of Sūraĥ Yāsīn recitation along with its Urdu translation from *Kanz-ul-Īmān* whereas the remaining were speech-cassettes.

On January 5, 2006 I travelled with a Sunnaĥ-Inspiring Madanī Qāfilaĥ of Dawat-e-Islami. Our Madanī Qāfilaĥ reached 'Sakrand' (Bāb-ul-Islam, Sindh, Pakistan) where I came across the same class fellow. He was with a group of his friends who were 15 in number. I asked him about the cassettes and he told me that when he listened to the recitation of Sūraĥ Yāsīn with its translation, he experienced such [inner] peace which he had never experienced before in his entire life.

He further added that since then he had made it a habit to listen to the Quranic recitation sitting outside the Masjid through the loud-speaker in Ramadan during Tarāwīḥ[1] Ṣalāĥ. He also told me that he had listened to the speeches and read the booklets as well. All this had a profound impact on him.'

The preacher continued: 'I then invited him to embrace Islam. He was already impressed with the teachings of Islam but was not yet prepared to convert. I tried for a long time to persuade him and his friends, making individual effort. Finally, by the grace of Allah عَزَّوَجَلَّ,

---

[1] Tarāwīḥ Ṣalāĥ is offered in Ramadan after Ṣalāt-ul-'Ishā with Jamā'at. It is Sunnaĥ to complete the recitation of the whole Quran during this Ṣalāĥ. [Translator's Note]

the effort bore fruit and nine of them embraced Islam right away and the rest of them said that they would consider about it.'

Āo 'ulamā-e-Dīn, baĥr-e-tablīgh-e-Dīn
Mil kay sāray chalayn, Qāfilay mayn chalo
Dūr tārikiyān Kufr kī ĥaun miyān
Āo koshish karayn Qāfilay mayn chalo

Scholars you also come and spread Islamic teachings
Let's all work together and travel with Madanī Qāfilaĥ
Let's remove the darkness of unbelief
Let's all strive and travel with Madanī Qāfilaĥ

صَلُّوْا عَلَى الْحَبِیْب صَلَّى اللهُ تَعَالٰى عَلٰى مُحَمَّد

88. Šarīd* and delicious stew

Sayyidunā Shaykh 'Allāmaĥ Yāfi'ī Yemeni عَلَيْهِ رَحْمَةُ اللّٰهِ الْقَوِی has stated, 'During a journey our caravan arrived in a village. One of us went out and borrowed a cooking pot from a villager and cooked a dessert in it. All of us ate the dessert, except for one man who was not present. That man had gone out with some flour to find someone to bake him some bread from it but he could not find anyone. While roaming around the village he came across an old blind man whom he gifted the flour with the intention of getting reward from Allah عَزَّوَجَلَّ. (This condition should be taken as a concealed favour that it is as if the divine wisdom addressed him that the flour was the sustenance of that blind old man, whereas his sustenance will be provided by divine bounty).

Allah's mercy is immense! After a little while, a villager approached the caravan and took the very same person, who had given his flour to the blind man, to his house and served him with delicious stew and Šarīd.' *(Rauḍ-ur-Riyāḥīn, pp. 153)*

May Allah عَزَّوَجَلَّ have mercy on them and forgive us without accountability for their sake!

---

* Šarīd is a dish made with pieces of bread mixed with stew and gravy sauce. It can also be prepared with vegetables instead of meat. [Translator's Note]

اَلْحَمْدُلِلّٰہ عَزَّوَجَلَّ, Giving food in charity never goes to waste. Sometimes one is rewarded instantly in the world in addition to be deserving of the reward of the Hereafter.

صَلُّوْا عَلَی الْحَبِیْب صَلَّی اللّٰہُ تَعَالٰی عَلٰی مُحَمَّد

89. Stew and dessert

A saint رَحْمَۃُ اللّٰہِ تَعَالٰی عَلَیْہ has reported that a rich businessman was once sitting in a Masjid where he noticed a beggar who was making Du'ā in the following words with his hands raised, 'Yā Allah عَزَّوَجَلَّ! Feed me meat stew and dessert!' When the businessman heard this he said to himself, 'This beggar is just saying this so that I would hear him. By Allah عَزَّوَجَلَّ! If he had directly asked me I would have fed him, but now I will not.'

After a little while, that beggar went to sleep. Meanwhile, a man entered the Masjid with a tray covered with a piece of cloth. His eyes roamed the Masjid as if he was looking for someone. As his eye fell on the sleeping beggar he put his tray down beside him, woke him up and said with humility, 'Here is meat stew and dessert for you, please eat it.' The beggar ate some from it and returned the rest to him. Astonished, the businessman asked the man about it. The man explained, 'I am a labourer. My family has desired for many days to eat meat stew and dessert, but I could not buy these things because of poverty. Today after a long time I got paid one Mišqāl [4.5 grams] of gold for my work. So we prepared this stew and dessert. I took a nap for a little while. I slept but my sleeping fortune woke up, blessing me with the vision of the Beloved and Blessed Prophet صَلَّى اللّٰهُ تَعَالٰى عَلَيْهِ وَاٰلِهٖ وَسَلَّم. As I was engrossed in beholding the Beloved Rasūl صَلَّى اللّٰهُ تَعَالٰى عَلَيْهِ وَاٰلِهٖ وَسَلَّم, his blessed lips began to move and the following words were uttered: 'There is a Walī (saint) in your Masjid who wishes to eat meat stew and dessert. Feed this stew and dessert to him first. He will eat some and return the rest to you. Allah عَزَّوَجَلَّ will bless the rest food for you. In return for this [deed] I will take you to Paradise.' Therefore [the man continued], I have brought the food here right away.'

The businessman said, 'How much money did you spend on this food?' The man replied, 'One Mišqāl.' The businessman offered, 'Take 10 Mišqāl of gold from me and give me a share of one Qīrāṭ in this deed.' He refused, so the businessman offered 20 Mišqāl of gold which was also turned down. The businessman increased his offer up to 50 Mišqāl of gold. Upon this the man replied, 'I will not make you a partner in the deal I have made with the Beloved and Blessed Prophet صَلَّى اللهُ تَعَالٰى عَلَيْهِ وَاٰلِهٖ وَسَلَّم even if you give me all the treasures of the world. If you were predestined to get this privilege you would beat me to it, but Allah عَزَّوَجَلَّ bestows His mercy on whomever He عَزَّوَجَلَّ wills.' *(Rauḍ-ur-Riyāḥīn, pp. 153)*

May Allah عَزَّوَجَلَّ have mercy on them and forgive us without accountability for their sake!

صَلُّوْا عَلَى الْحَبِيْب　　صَلَّى اللهُ تَعَالٰى عَلٰى مُحَمَّد

Dear Islamic brothers! We have learned from the above parable that the saints رَحِمَهُمُ اللّٰهُ تَعَالٰى follow the commandments of Allah عَزَّوَجَلَّ and Allah عَزَّوَجَلَّ fulfils their pleas. We have also learnt that those looking down on the pious servants of Allah in intoxication of their worldly wealth remain deprived of the mercy of Allah and His Beloved and Blessed Rasūl صَلَّى اللهُ تَعَالٰى عَلَيْهِ وَاٰلِهٖ وَسَلَّم. Furthermore, we have also learnt that the Prophet of Raḥmaĥ, the Intercessor of Ummaĥ صَلَّى اللهُ تَعَالٰى عَلَيْهِ وَاٰلِهٖ وَسَلَّم has the divinely-bestowed knowledge of Ghayb; that is why he صَلَّى اللهُ تَعَالٰى عَلَيْهِ وَاٰلِهٖ وَسَلَّم recognized the beggar and blessed the man in his dream, ordering him to go and feed the beggar.

Dear Islamic brothers! We have also realized that sometimes having a bad suspicion against a Muslim can lead to remorse and regret even in the world. Having a bad suspicion against a Muslim is Ḥarām by Sharī'aĥ.

◆◆◆

90. Disabled boy walks!

A gang of robbers once went on a looting spree. At night, they reached an inn in the guise of Mujāĥidīn (warriors of the path of Allah). The inn-owner who was a pious person not only allowed them to stay at the inn at night but also served them with the intention of attaining the pleasure of Allah عَزَّوَجَلَّ.

In the morning, those robbers went somewhere and returned back in the evening to the same inn, after their robbing venture. The inn-owner's walking-impaired son that they had seen last night was now roaming freely. Amazed and surprised, they asked the inn owner, 'Is he not the same disabled boy we saw yesterday?' He replied respectfully, 'Yes!' They asked, 'How did he get cured?' The inn owner replied, 'All this is the blessings of the divine-path travellers like you. The thing is, I fed your yesterday's leftover food to this son of mine and massaged his body with your leftover water, with the intention of curing him. Allah عَزَّوَجَلَّ has cured my disabled son by the blessing of the leftover food and water of you pious people.'

Overwhelmed by hearing this, the robbers were moved to tears and said, 'All this is the fruit of your positive opinion towards us; we are grave sinners. We are not the travellers of the divine path; we are robbers! The manifestation of divine bounty has entirely changed our lives. We make you witness and repent of all our [past] sins.' They all then adopted righteousness and remained steadfast on it till the end of their lives. *(Kitāb-ul-Qalyūbī, pp. 20)*

May Allah عَزَّوَجَلَّ have mercy on them and forgive us without accountability for their sake!

صَلُّوْا عَلَى الْحَبِيْب صَلَّى اللّٰهُ تَعَالٰى عَلٰى مُحَمَّد

Cure in leftovers of Muslim

Dear Islamic brothers! Did you see! The foregoing parable contains a faith-refreshing account of Allah's graciousness. We have also learnt that having positive opinion about Muslims brings about blessings. Another point worth noting is that there is a cure in the leftover of the Muslims.

One more lesson which can be derived from this parable is that an unwavering belief is needed for the acquisition of blessings. For example, the one who is uncertain about the acquisition of blessings when visiting a saint or a saint's shrine can't gain any benefit. Further, there will be no time limit for the acquisition of blessings; it depends on one's fate. Someone is blessed right away while someone's desire is not satisfied even after many years. Irrespective of whether or not one's desire is fulfilled, one should stick to one door, as the Persian saying goes: '*Yak dar gīr-o-muḥkam gīr*' which means '*Hold onto one door and hold it firmly.*'

Koī āyā pā kay chalā gayā, koī 'umr bĥar bĥī na pā sakā
Mayray Maulā عَزَّوَجَلَّ *Tujĥ say gilaĥ naĥīn, yeĥ to apnā apnā naṣīb ĥay*

Someone came, got and left; others took a lifetime to get
My Allah عَزَّوَجَلَّ *there is no complaint to You, this is just fate*

صَلُّوْا عَلَى الْحَبِيْب صَلَّى اللهُ تَعَالٰى عَلٰى مُحَمَّد

91. Paralysis was cured

اَلْحَمْدُلِلّٰه عَزَّوَجَلَّ! Dawat-e-Islami, a global & non-political religious movement of Quran and Sunnaĥ, holds 30-day and last 10-day Sunnaĥ-Inspiring congregational I'tikāf every year in the blessed month of Ramadan in numerous Masājid around the globe. By the blessings of the religious and moral training provided to the Mu'takifīn during the congregational I'tikāf, thousands of sinners sincerely repent of their sins and turn over a new leaf.

Sometimes, by the grace of Allah عَزَّوَجَلَّ, faith-refreshing events take place during the I'tikāf. During one such I'tikāf held in Ramadan in 1425 A.H., at the global Madanī Markaz of Dawat-e-Islami, Faīzān-e-Madīnaĥ, Bāb-ul-Madīnaĥ, Karachi [Pakistan], about 2,000 Islamic brothers were Mu'takif in the Masjid. Amongst them was a 77 year old Ḥāfiẓ Muhammad Ashraf from the Chakwal district (of Punjab, Pakistan). His hands and tongue were paralyzed and his hearing was almost impaired but his faith was marvellous.

One day during Ifṭār meal, he requested the leftover food from one of the preachers of Dawat-e-Islami and ate it reverentially expecting to be blessed. He also requested the preacher to make *Dam* [i.e. blow on] him. His positive opinion bore fruit. Allah's mercy showered on him, curing him of paralysis, اَلْحَمْدُ لِلّٰه عَزَّوَجَلَّ. He narrated his incident of getting cured on stage in front of thousands of people in Faīzān-e-Madīnaĥ, and the joyous clamour of [Żikr] of Allah, Allah filled the air. Several local newspapers also published this pleasing news in those days.

Dawat-e-Islami kī Qayyūm عَزَّوَجَلَّ, dauno jaĥān mayn mach jāye dĥūm
Is pay fidā ĥo bachchaĥ bachchaĥ, Yā Allah عَزَّوَجَلَّ mayrī jĥaulī bĥar day

May Dawat-e-Islami boom!
Throughout the world, Yā Qayyūm عَزَّوَجَلَّ!
May every child become devoted to it!
Yā Allah عَزَّوَجَلَّ! My supplication be fulfilled!

صَلُّوْا عَلَى الْحَبِيْب صَلَّى اللّٰهُ تَعَالٰى عَلٰى مُحَمَّد

Can one hire Sayyid* as servant?

Dear Islamic brothers! We have learnt from this parable that the company of the devotees of Rasūl is very beneficial and their leftovers are so blessed that it can even cure the sick.

Expressing the greatness of Sayyids (i.e. the descendants of the Holy Prophet) and the blessings of the leftovers of a Muslim, A'lā Ḥaḍrat, Imām-e-Aĥl-e-Sunnat, reviver of Sunnaĥ, eradicator of Bid'aĥ, scholar of Sharī'aĥ, guide of Ṭarīqaĥ, 'Allāmaĥ Maulānā Al-Ḥāj Al-Ḥāfiẓ Al-Qārī Ash-Shāĥ Imām Aḥmad Razā Khān عَلَيْهِ رَحْمَةُ الرَّحْمٰن has stated: 'It is not permissible to make a Sayyid do some degrading chore, nor is it permissible to hire him for such a job. However, one can hire a Sayyid for a job which does not entail any degrading tasks. Teachers should completely refrain from beating a Sayyid student. As for the issue of (a Sayyid's) eating the leftovers of a Muslim, it is not degrading since it is described as cure in a Ḥadīš.' *(Kashf-ul-Khifā, vol. 1, pp. 384, Ḥadīš 1403)*

If a Sayyid asks a person for his leftovers, the person should give it to the Sayyid with the intention (of acting upon the Ḥadīš which says that there is cure in a Muslim's leftovers) not with the intention of giving just his leftovers. *(Fatāwā Razawiyyaĥ (Jadīd), vol. 22, pp. 568)*

92. Who can harm one Allah عَزَّوَجَلَّ protects?

Shaykh Sayyidunā 'Alī Bin Ḥarb عَلَيْهِ رَحْمَةُ الرَّب has narrated: 'I was once sailing in a boat in Mosul [i.e. Tigris river] with some young men. When the boat reached the middle of the river, a fish jumped onto our boat from the water. We decided to roast the fish and eat it,

* A descendent of the Holy Prophet. [Translator's Note]

so we anchored our boat on the river bank. As we started gathering wood in the deserted area to light a fire, we saw a horrifying scene. There were the ruins and remains of some ancient buildings, and a man with his hands tied behind his back was lying down. Beside him was lying another man who had been slain. Nearby we also saw a merchandise laden ass.

We asked the tied man about the incident. That man said, 'I rented this ass from this slain man. He brought me to this desolate place deceitfully. Then, tying up my hands he said that he would kill me. I beseeched him not to commit the grave sin of murder and let me go for Allah's sake. I even offered him to take all my belongings and merchandise and assured him of not telling anyone about what has happened, but he was intent on murdering me. Then, with the intention of killing me, he tried to pull out his well tucked dagger from his waist but it did not come out. When he forcefully pulled on his dagger, it came out with a jerk, striking him on his own throat. With his throat slit, he fell onto the ground and died writhing.'

Hearing his story we freed the man. He took his merchandise and left for his house. We returned to our boat to roast the fish but found no fish as it had jumped back into the river.' *(Rauḍ-ur-Riyāḥīn, pp. 139)*

Dear Islamic brothers! Indeed! No one can hurt the one who Allah عَزَّوَجَلَّ protects. His grace is magnificent! The cruel robber got slain by his own hands, getting his just deserts. The fish jumped onto the boat, leading to the release of the tied up man. The sailors landed at the river bank to roast and eat the fish but they were not predestined to eat it. In fact, they were led to the river bank to attain the reward of helping the oppressed tied up man, witnessing a manifestation of the divine omnipotence.

صَلُّوْا عَلَى الْحَبِيْب صَلَّى اللّٰهُ تَعَالٰى عَلٰى مُحَمَّد

93. Means of sustenance

There was a pious person in Masjid-ul-Ḥarām situated in Makka-tul-Mukarramaĥ. He would worship all night and fast during the day. Every evening a man brought him two pieces of bread. He would break his fast [i.e. do Ifṭār] with those pieces of bread and would get busy with worship again. One day a thought crossed his mind: 'I have relied upon a man for bread instead of relying upon the Sustainer of the creation. It is contrary to trust in Allah عَزَّوَجَلَّ.

That evening when the man brought the bread, the worshipper returned it. Three days passed [in hunger]. When his hunger intensified he pleaded to Allah عَزَّوَجَلَّ. That night he saw in his dream that he was present in the court of Allah عَزَّوَجَلَّ who asked him: 'Why did you not take what I sent to you through that man?' The worshipper humbly said: 'A thought occurred to me that I have relied upon a man instead of relying entirely upon You.' Allah عَزَّوَجَلَّ said, 'Who sent you the bread?' The worshipper said, 'Yā Allah عَزَّوَجَلَّ! You sent it to me.' Then that worshipper was ordered, 'Next time when I send you the bread, do not return it.'

In the same dream he saw that the man [who used to bring the bread] was also present in the divine court and was asked, 'Why did you stop giving bread to this worshipper?' He humbly said, 'Yā Allah عَزَّوَجَلَّ! You know it well.' Then Allah عَزَّوَجَلَّ asked him, 'O servant! To whom did you give those breads?' He said, 'To you (that is, in Your path).' He was then ordered, 'You continue your action. Paradise is your reward in return [for this deed].' *(Rauḍ-ur-Riyāḥīn, pp. 68)*

If you get without asking, then...

Dear Islamic brothers! The traits of the saints of Allah are marvellous! Allah عَزَّوَجَلَّ showers His special favours upon the pious and provides for them from Ghayb. If one is not greedy for wealth and the giver will not also be taunting the taker; instead, the giver is expected to be pleased if his gift is accepted and neither there is the fear of the taker's respect being reduced in the eyes of the giver nor is there any possibility of the taker's disgrace in any way, in case of the acceptance of the gift; in short, if one is offered a gift without asking for it, he should accept it provided there is no Shar'ī prohibition.

Hence, Shaykh Sayyidunā Khālid Bin 'Adī Juĥannī عَلَيْهِ رَحْمَةُ اللّٰهِ الْغَنِى has narrated that he heard the Prophet of mankind, the Peace of our heart and mind, the most Generous and Kind صَلَّى اللّٰهُ تَعَالٰى عَلَيْهِ وَاٰلِهٖ وَسَلَّم say: 'Whoever receives something from his brother without asking for it and without having greed for it, should accept it and should not return it because it is the sustenance Allah عَزَّوَجَلَّ has sent to him (through someone).' *(Musnad Imām Aḥmad, vol. 6, pp. 276, Ḥadīš 17958)*

So, we have learnt that if somebody is offered something without him asking for it, there is no harm in accepting it provided he has no greed for that thing. Even if someone is wealthy he may also accept the thing with the intention of pleasing the giver, and if he does not need it he may gift it to someone else or give it in charity. Shaykh Sayyidunā ʻĀid Bin ʻAmr رَضِیَ اللّٰہُ تَعَالٰی عَنْہُ has narrated that the Prophet of Raḥmaĥ, the Intercessor of Ummaĥ صَلَّی اللّٰہُ تَعَالٰی عَلَیْہِ وَاٰلِہٖ وَسَلَّم has stated: 'Whoever gets sustenance without asking (for it) and without having greed for it, should accept it from the bottom of his heart, and if he is wealthy (then after accepting it) he should send it to someone who is more needy than him.' *(Musnad Imām Aḥmad, vol. 7, pp. 362, Ḥadīš 2673)*

Gift or bribe

Dear Islamic brothers! There is no doubt that accepting gifts is a Sunnaĥ, but one should keep in mind that there are different rulings about giving and accepting gifts, and accepting every gift is certainly not Sunnaĥ. In his world-famous book, '*Ṣaḥīḥ Bukhārī*' Shaykh Sayyidunā Imām Bukhārī عَلَیْہِ رَحْمَةُ اللّٰہِ الْبَارِی has included a whole chapter entitled: '(بَابُ مَنْ لَّمْ یَقْبَلِ الْھَدِیَّةَ لِعِلَّةٍ) *The chapter about one who did not accept a gift due to some reason.*'

In this chapter Shaykh Sayyidunā Imām Bukhārī عَلَیْہِ رَحْمَةُ الْبَارِی has narrated a Ḥadīš, leaving out the names of narrators, that Sayyidunā ʻUmar Bin ʻAbdul ʻAzīz رَضِیَ اللّٰہُ تَعَالٰی عَنْہُ has stated, 'In the apparent life of the Holy Prophet صَلَّی اللّٰہُ تَعَالٰی عَلَیْہِ وَاٰلِہٖ وَسَلَّم a gift was a gift but is a bribe nowadays.' *(Ṣaḥīḥ Bukhārī, vol. 2, pp. 174)*

صَلُّوْا عَلَی الْحَبِیْب   صَلَّی اللّٰہُ تَعَالٰی عَلٰی مُحَمَّد

94. A platter of apples

In the exegesis of the foregoing narration, Shaykh ʻAllāmaĥ Badruddīn ʻAynī Ḥanafī عَلَیْہِ رَحْمَةُ اللّٰہِ الْقَوِی has cited the following incident on the authority of Shaykh Sayyidunā Furāt Bin Muslim رَحْمَةُ اللّٰہِ تَعَالٰی عَلَیْہ. Shaykh Sayyidunā ʻUmar Bin ʻAbdul ʻAzīz رَضِیَ اللّٰہُ تَعَالٰی عَنْہُ once desired to eat apples but had no money to buy them.

Sayyidunā Furāt Bin Muslim رَحْمَةُ اللهِ تَعَالٰى عَلَيْه goes onto say, 'We went out with him; near the village we came across some boys who were holding platters of apples (to give as gifts). Taking a platter Shaykh Sayyidunā 'Umar Bin 'Abdul 'Azīz رَضِىَ اللهُ تَعَالٰى عَنْهُ smelt the apples but then returned it. When I asked as to why he returned it, he replied, 'I do not need this.' I asked, 'Did Sayyidunā Rasūlullāĥ صَلَّى اللهُ تَعَالٰى عَلَيْهِ وَاٰلِهٖ وَسَلَّم, Sayyidunā Abū Bakr رَضِىَ اللهُ تَعَالٰى عَنْهُ and Sayyidunā 'Umar Fārūq A'ẓam رَضِىَ اللهُ تَعَالٰى عَنْهُ not use to accept gifts?' He responded, 'They were indeed gifts for them but are bribes for the succeeding governors (and their representatives).' *('Umda-tul-Qārī, vol. 9, pp. 417)*

From whom one shouldn't take gifts?

Dear Islamic brothers! Did you see? Shaykh Sayyidunā 'Umar Bin 'Abdul 'Azīz رَضِىَ اللهُ تَعَالٰى عَنْهُ did not accept apples as gifts. He knew that he was being offered gifts because of being the caliph of the time. Obviously, if he were not the caliph, why would then anyone offer the gift to him?

Every sensible person knows why people give gifts to ministers, assembly members, other government and elected officials, judges and police etc. and why they arrange special meals for them. It is apparent that people do this so that they can get some personal advantage in return or so that it is easier to get such advantage from them in the future. To give gifts or to arrange special meal-gatherings for them because of these two reasons is a form of bribery and both the giver and taker of bribery are worthy of Hell. On such occasions, one cannot be saved from the sin of bribery by saying such sentences as: *we are giving these things as gifts of Eid, or just as sweets or refreshments, or out of happiness, or out of love etc.*

If officials accept gifts or special meals from their subordinates, even if gifts and invitation to special meal-gatherings are given to them with sincerity and do not fall under bribery in any way, it will still lead them to a place of slander. It is a saying of the Beloved and Blessed Rasūl صَلَّى اللهُ تَعَالٰى عَلَيْهِ وَاٰلِهٖ وَسَلَّم, 'The one who believes in Allah عَزَّوَجَلَّ and the Hereafter should not stand at a place of slander.' *(Kashf-ul-Khifā, vol. 2, pp. 227, Ḥadīš 2499)* Hence it is Wājib to stay away from the place of slander and, therefore, it is impermissible to give and accept gifts etc. in the above cases.

If, however, there was the practice of giving and taking gifts and arranging special meal-gatherings for each other even before the official had taken office there is no harm in this case, but if it was less before and now there is more, then this increase [in gifts etc.] is impermissible. If the giver is now wealthier and is giving more because of increase in his wealth, then there is no problem. Further, if the inviter has increased the number of special meal-gatherings after the invited official has taken office then this is also impermissible. If the one giving is Żawilarḥām, that is, blood relative, then there is no problem in giving and taking. (Parents, brother, sister, paternal & maternal grandparents, son, daughter, brother of father & that of mother, sister of mother & that of father etc. are Maḥram [blood relatives] whereas husband of father's sister, husband of sister, wife of father's brother, wife of mother's brother, wife of brother, paternal & maternal cousins etc. are not Żawilarḥām). For example, if one's son or nephew is a judge and the father or uncle of the judge gave him a gift or arranged a special meal-gathering for him then it is permissible for the judge to accept. However, if the case of the father is going before his own son who is a judge, then it is impermissible because of being in a place of slander.

These rulings are not confined to the government officials only; instead, they apply to the people of all social, political and religious positions. Even all the Nigrān of all the Majālis of Dawat-e-Islami and other responsible brothers cannot accept gifts or special meals from their subordinates. The junior Nigrān can accept from the senior one. For example, a member of the Markazī Majlis-e-Shūrā can accept gifts from the Nigrān of Shūrā, but not from other Islamic brothers of Dawat-e-Islami and the Nigrān of Shūrā cannot accept gifts from any Islamic brother of Dawat-e-Islami under him. Similarly, teachers cannot accept gifts from their students or their guardians without Shar'ī permission. However, after the completion of education, if an ex-student gives a gift or special meal to his ex-teacher, the teacher can accept it. 'Ulamā and Shuyūkh [scholars and saints] accept gifts etc. given to them by people in honour of their knowledge and greatness and people do not blame them for bribery either, it is permissible for such scholars and saints to accept gifts as it is not under the category of being in a place of slander.

Dear Islamic brothers! Here are some important questions and answers regarding the difference between bribery and gift. If possible, try to read or listen to them at least three times.

Question: Is it not a Sunnaĥ to accept gifts?

Answer: It is indeed a Sunnaĥ to accept gifts but there are certain conditions for it. Shaykh 'Allāmaĥ Badruddīn 'Aynī Ḥanafī عَلَيْهِ رَحْمَةُ اللّٰهِ الْقَوِى has stated that the Ḥadīš which says, 'Exchange gifts amongst each other as this will increase love[1]' pertains to those who have no position of authority over Muslims. However, the one who has any position of authority over Muslims like a Qāḍī [judge] or a Wālī [governor] must refrain from accepting gifts as these are bribery and a sort of impurity for them, especially for those who did not use to be given gifts before their official position. *(Bināyaĥ Sharḥ-ul-Ĥidāyaĥ, vol. 8, pp. 244)*

To borrow a motorcycle

Question: Can one who is in authority borrow money, car, motorcycle or bicycle etc. from his subordinate? Also kindly let us know, can he buy something from his subordinate in low price by any pretence?

Answer: The one in authority cannot borrow money and other things from his subordinate even if his subordinate offers it himself. Likewise, he cannot do any dealings (i.e. sale and purchase) with his subordinate in a way contrary to established norms. Hence, Shaykh 'Allāmaĥ Shāmī رَحْمَةُ اللّٰهِ تَعَالٰى عَلَيْه has stated, 'It is also Ḥarām for the one in authority to borrow money or something else from the people from whom to accept gifts is Ḥarām for him.' *(Rad-dul-Muḥtār, vol. 8, pp. 48)*

Question: Has A'lā Ḥaḍrat Imām Aḥmad Razā Khān عَلَيْهِ رَحْمَةُ الرَّحْمٰن also given some guidance on the subject [of taking gifts]?

Answer: A'lā Ḥaḍrat, Imām-e-Aĥl-e-Sunnat, reviver of Sunnaĥ, eradicator of Bid'aĥ, scholar of Sharī'aĥ, guide of Ṭarīqaĥ, 'Allāmaĥ Maulānā Al-Ḥāj Al-Ḥāfiẓ Al-Qārī Ash-Shāĥ Imām Aḥmad Razā Khān عَلَيْهِ رَحْمَةُ الرَّحْمٰن has stated, 'I say that the example of these people (i.e. the ones in authority) is like that of village chiefs and employees-supervisors who have control and power over those under them. People give gifts to these chiefs and supervisors for fear of being harmed by them or as a tradition.' *(Fatāwā Razawiyyaĥ (Jadīd), vol. 19, pp. 446)*

---

[1] (Majma'-uz-Zawāid, vol. 4, pp. 260, Ḥadīš 6716)

It is obvious that the prohibition on the acceptance of gifts is not only for the government officials but also for every such person who can cause benefit or harm to people by his authority or influence.

Two kinds of gatherings

Question: What is a 'special meal-gathering?'

Answer: A special meal-gathering is a gathering which is held for a particular person, that is, the gathering will not take place if that particular person does not come.

Question: Also tell us, what is a 'general gathering?'

Answer: A general gathering is that gathering which is not held for anyone in particular, that is, the gathering will take place even if so-and-so particular person does not come.

Question: If a subordinate holds a special meal-gathering for his superior and makes the intention of marking 'Giyārĥwīn' with it, is it still impermissible?

Answer: Yes, as it is evident in this case that if the one in authority does not accept the invitation then there will be no Niyāz[1] of the Giyārĥwīn. However, if it is predetermined that the Niyāz will be held regardless of whether or not the one in authority comes, holding such a gathering is permissible as this would be considered a 'general gathering.' But it would be impermissible to give better and fancy foods to the one in authority compared to others. For example, if other guests are served with ordinary meal, and the one in authority is served with special meal; then it is impermissible to do so.

Question: Can a subordinate accept gifts from his superiors?

Answer: Yes he can. If you read or listen to the following Fatwā issued by A'lā Ḥaḍrat, Imām-e-Aĥl-e-Sunnat, reviver of Sunnaĥ, eradicator of Bid'aĥ, scholar of Sharī'aĥ, guide of Ṭarīqaĥ, 'Allāmaĥ Maulānā Al-Ḥāj Al-Ḥāfiẓ Al-Qārī Ash-Shāĥ Imām Aḥmad Razā Khān عَلَيْهِ رَحْمَةُ الرَّحْمٰن at least three times attentively, اِنْ شَآءَاللّٰه عَزَّوَجَلَّ you will understand the difference between gift and bribery. It will also become clear as to which people one is allowed to accept gifts from and from which people one cannot.

---

[1] Food or sweets served to the Muslims with the intention of presenting its reward to the Shaykh. [Translator's Note]

A'lā Ḥaḍrat رَحْمَةُ اللهِ تَعَالٰی عَلَيْه has stated: 'The one who has some power over people by the position of authority he holds by himself or on behalf of the ruler, is not allowed to accept gifts and invitations of special meal-gatherings. Even if such a person neither oppresses people himself nor puts any pressure on them; nor is he entitled to give any final or non-final decision - like a police officer, collection officer or landlord for peasants, village registrar and village chiefs (who have the authority of deciding the matters of the villagers) - he is not allowed at all to take any type of gift or accept the invitations of special meal-gatherings except for the following three cases:

1. First, he may accept gifts or special invitations from his superior over whom he has no authority and it would not be suspected that the superior would get some advantage for his personal matters from the subordinate by gift and special meal-gathering.

2. Second, he may accept gifts or special invitations from the one who has been giving gifts or inviting him even before he had taken office provided that the amount (or value of the gift etc.) is the same as was before, otherwise the increase will not be permissible. If, for example, the value of the gift is now higher than before or there is an increase in the number of gifts, or gifts or invitations are now being given frequently; in all these cases the increase in gifts or special meal-gatherings is not permissible. However, if the giver's wealth has increased, indicating that the increase (in gift or special meal-gathering) is not because of the receiver's authority but because of the increase in giver's wealth, it would be permissible in this case.

3. Third, he may accept gifts or invitations from close Maḥārim such as parents, offspring and siblings but not from the sons of [paternal and maternal] uncles and aunts as they are not Maḥārim although they are also commonly called brothers (but in reality they are not).'

A'lā Ḥaḍrat رَحْمَةُ اللهِ تَعَالٰی عَلَيْه has further stated: 'Wherever there is prohibition it is based on just slander and the chance that the receiver will as a result be lenient [in dealing with the matters of the giver] even if leniency in the giver's matters is not found. People deal with their worldly matters on the basis of hopes and expectations. If the official accepts gifts and invitations, then surely the giver will expect that it should have an effect on him as the 'effect' of receiving unearned money is often seen. The giver will expect the effect of the given gift etc. to take place either on the spot or anytime in future. And to say that this gift or invitation of special meal-gathering is given because of affection, and not because of the official's position, the Holy Prophet صَلَّى اللهُ تَعَالٰى عَلَيْهِ وَاٰلِهٖ وَسَلَّم has already rejected it. When a person who was sent for the collection of Zakāĥ returned with the collected Zakāĥ, he separated some wealth for himself. Rasūlullāĥ صَلَّى اللهُ تَعَالٰى عَلَيْهِ وَاٰلِهٖ وَسَلَّم said, 'You should have stayed at your mother's home to see how many gifts you would receive!' That is to say that you have received these gifts just because of your position and authority. If you had stayed at home, who would have come to give you anything? *(Ṣaḥīḥ Muslim, pp. 1019, Ḥadīš 1832) (Fatāwā Razawiyyaĥ (Jadīd), vol. 18, pp. 170-171)*

Question: Can a professor or teacher accept gifts from his students?

Answer: If offered gifts from their students, the teachers of the Quran, Dars-e-Niẓāmī and other sciences should be very careful before accepting gifts because they also have authority over some Muslims [e.g. their students].

Explaining the meaning of 'being in authority' 'Allāmaĥ Shāmī رَحْمَةُ اللهِ تَعَالٰى عَلَيْه has stated, 'Amongst the people in authority are those who have authority in markets and cities, those handling endowments and trusts, and every such person who has authority over the matters of the Muslims.' *(Rad-dul-Muḥtār, vol. 8, pp. 50)*

In the light of this quotation, a teacher is also in authority in the sense that he also has power over many matters of students. For a student to remain enrolled at his educational institute is, sometimes, at the mercy of the teacher. A teacher can suspend a student from the grade as a result of his misbehaviour or, sometimes, can even have the student expelled from the institute or can request for it. Similarly, he can disclose questions of exams to students prior to exams, give good marks or even fail the students.

There are many students who have little aspiration to learn but are very much involved in immoral activities. As they are not able to impress the teacher by their abilities, they present gifts and offer lunch/dinner to their teachers from time to time so that they would not be expelled from the institute and would not be failed. Therefore, teachers should not accept gifts and invitations from such students. If it is clear that the gift or the invitation is being offered to the teacher so that such students can get some undue advantage from him, and the teacher is also capable enough to do what they want, it will be a Ḥarām act leading to Hell to accept the gift or invitation in this case.

It is stated in *Shāmī*, 'If a scholar is given a gift so that he would intercede on behalf the giver of the gift or would save him from oppression, that gift is also a form of bribery. The ruling stated for a teacher also applies to an administrator as an administrator, whether that of a purely religious organization or of a political party, also has authority over many matters of the Muslims in some way, and his written or spoken approval or disapproval in any matter may cause benefit or loss to many people. Therefore, he should also be highly cautious before accepting gifts or invitations of special meal-gathering. *(Rad-dul-Muḥtār, vol. 9, pp. 607)*

Two parables of returning gifts

1. Ḥujjat-ul-Islam, Shaykh Sayyidunā Imām Muhammad Ghazālī عَلَيْهِ رَحْمَةُ اللّٰهِ الْوَالِي has cited that Shaykh Sayyidunā Shafīq Balkhī عَلَيْهِ رَحْمَةُ اللّٰهِ الْقَوِی has stated, 'Once I sent some clothes to Shaykh Sayyidunā Sufyān Šaurī رَحْمَةُ اللّٰهِ تَعَالٰی عَلَيْه as a gift but he returned them. I said, 'Yā Sayyidī, I am not your student!' He replied, 'But your brother has heard Ḥadīš from me. I am afraid that my heart might become softer for your brother than for other students.' *(Ḥilyat-ul-Auliyā, vol. 7, pp. 3, Ḥadīš 9302)*

2. Once, Shaykh Sayyidunā Sufyān Šaurī رَحْمَةُ اللّٰهِ تَعَالٰی عَلَيْه received some money as a gift from the son of his friend. At first, he accepted the money but after a while called his friend's son back and returned the money insistently. He did so because his friendship was for the sake of Allah عَزَّوَجَلَّ and he was afraid that the gift might become the (materialistic) return for the friendship. Sayyidunā Mubārak رَحْمَةُ اللّٰهِ تَعَالٰی عَلَيْه, a son of Shaykh Sayyidunā Sufyān Šaurī رَحْمَةُ اللّٰهِ تَعَالٰی عَلَيْه, asked him, 'O Father!' What has happened to you? When you had accepted it, you should have kept it for us!' He رَحْمَةُ اللّٰهِ تَعَالٰی عَلَيْه replied, 'O Mubārak! You will happily and gleefully spend it but it is I who will be questioned about it on the Day of Judgement.' *(Iḥyā-ul-'Ulūm, vol. 3, pp. 408)*

Question: If a subordinate gives dates from Madīnaĥ or water of Zamzam to his superiors, should they accept it?

Answer: They should accept it as there is no fear of the blame of bribery here. Similarly, there is no problem in accepting booklets, [CDs or] cassettes of speeches and other preaching-material or the cards bearing the print of the Holy Prophet's blessed shoe or an inexpensive rosary or a pen worth a few rupees as these are not the kinds of gifts in which one would face slander. Similarly, there is a tradition of giving gifts on some occasions like return from the pilgrimage of Hajj or Madīnaĥ, one's marriage and birth of a child; those in authority can accept gifts on such occasions from those under them. However, if the gift is more expensive or valuable than what is commonly given, then it is not permissible to accept. For example, if it is common to give 100 rupees as gift and one gives 500 or 1200 rupees as gift or a rupee[1]-garland of the same amount, then it will be impermissible because of being in a place of slander[2].

Dear Islamic brothers! Keep close to the Madanī environment of Dawat-e-Islami, a non-political worldwide movement of Quran and Sunnaĥ and travel with its Madanī Qāfilaĥs with the devotees of Rasūl. اِنْ شَآءَاللّٰہ عَزَّوَجَلَّ You will learn various Islamic laws and principles.

To instill a passion of travelling in the Madanī Qāfilaĥ, read on to see the Madanī marvels of the Madanī Qāfilaĥ…

95. They were buried alive

An Islamic brother has reported, 'A Sunnaĥ-Inspiring Madanī Qāfilaĥ of twelve devotees of Rasūl was staying in the Jāmi' Masjid of Nindrai of the district Bagh of Kashmir. According to the schedule of the Qāfilaĥ, on the morning of 3rd Ramadan 1426 A.H., it was time for the morning 'Madanī Mashwaraĥ' after the small break for rest. Upon the instruction of the Amīr of the Qāfilaĥ, eight Islamic brothers were preparing to attend the 'Madanī Mashwaraĥ' whereas four Islamic brothers including me were still lying down out of laziness in the Madrasaĥ adjacent to the Masjid.

Suddenly, we felt as if we were being jolted on a train. Frightened, we got up and ran. All the walls were shaking. The earth cracked open and we fell on our faces. We had not yet recovered ourselves when all of a sudden the roof and walls fell upon us and darkness fell all around us.

[1] It is common in the sub-continent to give a garland made of rupees.

[2] For detailed information of these rulings listen to the cassettes of Madanī Mużākaraĥ no. 71 to 74.

[Translator's Notes]

Alas! The four of us had been buried alive! We started to recite Kalimaĥ and cried for help. We had almost given up the hope of coming out alive. An Islamic brother somehow managed to kick and push a rock, making an opening for the rays of light to come in. اَلْحَمْدُلِلّٰه عَزَّوَجَلَّ, One by one, we all managed to come out from that opening. By the blessings of immediate obedience to the Amīr of the Qāfilaĥ, the other eight devotees of Rasūl had already come out from the Masjid safely.

Zalzalay say amān, day gā Rab-e-Jaĥān عَزَّوَجَلَّ
Sab Du'āeyn karayn, Qāfilay mayn chalo
Ĥo bapā zalzalay, garchay āndĥī chalay
Ṣabr kartay raĥayn, Qāfilay mayn chalo

Protection from earthquake will be given by Almighty
Let's all make supplications in Qāfilaĥ
If earthquakes or tornadoes occur
How to have patience, learn in Qāfilaĥ

Consequence of disobedience

The foregoing incident shows that by the blessing of following Madanī Qāfilaĥ's schedule, the eight Islamic brothers did not get hurt and got out safely, whereas the other four Islamic brothers who were resting in a room out of laziness were temporarily buried alive together although they also managed to come out safely by the blessing of the Madanī Qāfilaĥ. Allah عَزَّوَجَلَّ shows signs in this way that someone comes out safe and sound even from the cave of death whereas someone is captured by death even if he has hidden himself in the strongest of forts. There is no way to escape from death. Hence, Allah عَزَّوَجَلَّ has said in Sūraĥ Al-Jumu'aĥ in part 28, verse 8:

قُلْ اِنَّ الْمَوْتَ الَّذِیْ تَفِرُّوْنَ مِنْهُ فَاِنَّهٗ مُلٰقِیْكُمْ

You proclaim, you will certainly meet the death which you run away from.

[Kanz-ul-Īmān (Translation of Quran)] (Part 28, Sūraĥ Al-Jumu'aĥ, verse 8)

صَلُّوْا عَلَی الْحَبِیْب صَلَّی اللّٰهُ تَعَالٰی عَلٰی مُحَمَّد

96. Wise king

Aḥmad Bin Ṭūlūn, a wise Egyptian king, was once eating meal with his companions in a deserted place when his eye fell on a beggar wearing tattered clothes. The king sent him a piece of bread, fried chicken, meat and beverage through his servant. The servant returned and informed the king, 'Your highness, he was not happy with the food.' Upon hearing this, the king ordered that the beggar be brought to him. When the beggar came, the king asked him some questions which he answered elegantly and showed no signs of nervousness.

The wise king suddenly said, 'You seem to be a spy.' The king then called the official whipper to punish him. Seeing this, the beggar admitted that he was a spy. Seeing this incident a courtier said, 'Your highness, it's like you have done magic.' The wise king replied, 'This is not magic, I caught him by my acute judgment because the food sent to him was so delicious that even the one who had eaten a full meal would desire this meal upon seeing it but this beggar showed no interest in it even though he seemed needy. Moreover, an ordinary man becomes frightened when in the court of a king, but he talked to me boldly. Observing this, I felt that he was a spy (as spies are often trained to have such confidence).' *(Ḥayāt-ul-Ḥaywān-ul-Kubrā, vol. 1, pp. 359)*

صَلُّوْا عَلَى الْحَبِيْب صَلَّى اللهُ تَعَالٰى عَلٰى مُحَمَّد

97. State of Ibn Ṭūlūn in grave

Dear Islamic brothers! Aḥmad Bin Ṭūlūn was a very wise, just, brave, humble, well-mannered, friend of knowledge, and a generous king. He was a Ḥāfiẓ of the Quran and would recite the Quran with a very pleasant voice. With all of these good qualities he was also an oppressor to the extent that his sword was always ready for bloodshed. It is said that the people that he killed and the ones that died in his prisons were nearly eighteen thousand in number. After his death, a man would recite the Holy Quran daily at his graveside. One day Aḥmad Bin Ṭūlūn appeared in the man's dream and said, 'Do not recite the Quran at my grave!' The man asked, 'Why?' Ibn Ṭūlūn replied, 'Whenever any verse is recited at my graveside, I am hit on the head and asked, 'Did you not hear this verse?' *(Ḥayāt-ul-Ḥaywān-ul-Kubrā, vol. 1, pp. 460)*

Alas! The consequence of oppression is certainly very devastating. Since it is generally very difficult for the rulers to refrain from oppression and injustice, it is wise, especially in the present era, to stay away from the apparently attractive looking offices of the government and ministries. We will have also realized that the Ḥāfiẓ of the Quran should act upon the Quranic teachings. May Allah عَزَّوَجَلَّ forgive us, the sinful Muslims being punished in their graves, and the entire Ummaĥ!

اٰمِین بِجَاہِ النَّبِیِّ الْاَمِین صَلَّی اللّٰہ تَعَالٰی عَلَیْہِ وَاٰلِہٖ وَسَلَّم

صَلُّوْا عَلَی الْحَبِیْب صَلَّی اللّٰہُ تَعَالٰی عَلٰی مُحَمَّد

98. Du'ā of forgiveness led to forgiveness

Dear Islamic brothers! We should make Du'ā of forgiveness for all Muslims. It is also beneficial to us. The more people we make Du'ā of forgiveness for, the more virtues and reward we will earn. The Prophet of Raḥmaĥ, the Intercessor of Ummaĥ, the Owner of Jannaĥ صَلَّی اللّٰہ تَعَالٰی عَلَیْہِ وَاٰلِہٖ وَسَلَّم has stated, 'Whoever asks for the forgiveness of all the Muslim men and women, Allah عَزَّوَجَلَّ will write one virtue for him for every Muslim man and woman.' *(Mu'jam Ṣaghīr, pp. 513, Ḥadīš 7419)*

If we intend others good, we will also be treated with good, اِنْ شَآءَاللّٰہ عَزَّوَجَلَّ. Hence 'Allāmaĥ 'Abdur Raḥmān Ṣaffūrī عَلَیْہِ رَحْمَۃُ اللّٰہِ الْقَوِی has quoted, '(After his demise) a pious man appeared in someone's dream. The dreaming person asked the pious man as to how Allah عَزَّوَجَلَّ treated him. He replied, 'Allah عَزَّوَجَلَّ has forgiven me, blessing me with a palace near the palace of so-and-so person. I would perform more worship than that person but he has surpassed me because of a habit of his that I did not have. He would often make the Du'ā, 'Yā Allah عَزَّوَجَلَّ! Forgive all the Muslims of the past, present and future!' *(Nuzĥa-tul-Majālis, vol. 2, pp. 3)*

Ilāĥī عَزَّوَجَلَّ wāsiṭaĥ Piyāray صَلَّی اللّٰہ تَعَالٰی عَلَیْہِ وَاٰلِہٖ وَسَلَّم kā sab kī maghfirat farmā
'Ażāb-e-Nār say ĥam ko Khudāyā عَزَّوَجَلَّ khauf ātā ĥay

For the sake of Your Beloved Prophet صَلَّی اللّٰہ تَعَالٰی عَلَیْہِ وَاٰلِہٖ وَسَلَّم, forgive all
We fear the punishment of Hell, O our Allah عَزَّوَجَلَّ

صَلُّوْا عَلَی الْحَبِیْب صَلَّی اللّٰہُ تَعَالٰی عَلٰی مُحَمَّد

99. 70 Days old corpse

اَلْحَمْدُلِلّٰه عَزَّوَجَلَّ, Dawat-e-Islami, a global & non-political religious movement for the preaching of Quran and Sunnaĥ, provides an opportunity to sympathize with Muslims and gain blessings in the worldly life as well as in the afterlife. Millions of those drowning in the sea of sins are being rescued by Dawat-e-Islami that is a unique Madanī movement of Aĥl-ul-Ḥaq [rightly-guided people].

Let me tell you a faith-refreshing marvel of the Madanī environment of Dawat-e-Islami: 'There was a massive earthquake in the eastern part of Pakistan on Saturday, Ramadan 3, 1426 A.H. (October 8, 2005). Hundreds of thousands of people perished in this massive earthquake. Among the victims was a nineteen year old martyr, Nasrīn 'Aṭṭāriyyaĥ Bint-e-Ghulām Mursalīn of Mīrātasauliyān in Muzaffarabad (Kashmir). She used to attend the weekly Sunnaĥ-Inspiring Ijtimā' of Dawat-e-Islami. For some unavoidable reasons, her father and other family members had to open her grave at around 10 p.m. on Monday night 8 Żul-Qa'da-til-Ḥarām, 1426 A.H. (December 10, 2005). As the grave was opened, those present there smelt a pleasant fragrance emanating from her grave. Nasrīn 'Aṭṭāriyyaĥ's shroud was in its original state and her body was still fresh even after seventy days of her martyrdom.

May Allah عَزَّوَجَلَّ have mercy on her and forgive us without accountability for her sake!

'Aṭāye Ḥabīb-e-Khudā صَلَّى اللهُ تَعَالٰى عَلَيْهِ وَاٰلِهٖ وَسَلَّم *Madanī Māḥaul*
Ĥay Faīzān-e-Ghauš-o-Razā رَحِمَهُمَا اللّٰهُ تَعَالٰى *Madanī Māḥaul*
Salāmat raĥay Yā Khudā عَزَّوَجَلَّ *Madanī Māḥaul*
Bachay naẓar-e-bad say sadā Madanī Māḥaul
Ay Islāmī beĥnaun! Tumĥāray liye bĥī
Suno! Ĥay baĥut kām kā Madanī Māḥaul
Tumĥayn Sunnataun aur parday kay aḥkām
Yeĥ ta'līm farmāye gā Madanī Māḥaul
Sanvar jāye gī ākhirat اِنْ شَآءَاللّٰه عَزَّوَجَلَّ
Tum apnāye rakĥo sadā Madanī Māḥaul

Divine bestowment is the Madanī environment
Blessings of Ghauš and Razā رَحِمَهُمَا اللّٰهُ تَعَالٰى, is the Madanī environment
Yā Allah عَزَّوَجَلَّ, protect forever the Madanī environment
From the evil eye, protect the Madanī environment
O Islamic sisters, for you as well
Is very beneficial the Madanī environment
The rulings of Sunan and veil
Will teach you, the Madanī environment
Your Hereafter shall be better
Stay associated with the Madanī environment

Yā Allah عَزَّوَجَلَّ! Bless us with the true love of Your Beloved Prophet صَلَّى اللّٰهُ تَعَالٰى عَلَيْهِ وَاٰلِهٖ وَسَلَّم, all other Prophets عَلَيْهِمُ السَّلَام, the blessed companions رَضِىَ اللّٰهُ تَعَالٰى عَنْهُم, the Aĥl-e-Bayt عَلَيْهِمُ الرِّضْوَان [family of the Prophet] and the blessed Auliyā رَحِمَهُمُ اللّٰهُ تَعَالٰى. Make us follow in their footsteps and protect our Īmān by their blessings. Grant us peace in the worldly life and in the afterlife. Forgive us and grant us an abode in Jannat-ul-Firdaus, without accountability, in the neighbourhood of Your Beloved and Blessed Prophet صَلَّى اللّٰهُ تَعَالٰى عَلَيْهِ وَاٰلِهٖ وَسَلَّم!

اٰمِيْن بِجَاهِ النَّبِيِّ الْاَمِيْن صَلَّى اللّٰهُ تَعَالٰى عَلَيْهِ وَاٰلِهٖ وَسَلَّم

صَلُّوْا عَلَى الْحَبِيْب صَلَّى اللّٰهُ تَعَالٰى عَلٰى مُحَمَّد
تُوْبُوْا اِلَى اللّٰه اَسْتَغْفِرُ اللّٰه
صَلُّوْا عَلَى الْحَبِيْب صَلَّى اللّٰهُ تَعَالٰى عَلٰى مُحَمَّد

مَدَنِی مُذاکَرہ

MADANI MUZAKARAH

QUESTIONS-ANSWERS

To gain essential and interesting information and guidelines about eating, read on...

Madani Muzakarah

In this chapter you will read about:

- Mann and Salwā
- Why food began to spoil?
- Reasons for food wastage in Madāris
- Who was Jālīnūs?
- Cautions for meat sellers
- Two Madanī cures for indigestion
- Twelve springs gush forth
- Proper method of freezing food
- Airborne fish

اَلْحَمْدُ لِلّٰهِ رَبِّ الْعٰلَمِيْنَ وَ الصَّلٰوةُ وَ السَّلَامُ عَلٰى سَيِّدِ الْمُرْسَلِيْنَ

اَمَّا بَعْدُ فَاَعُوْذُ بِاللّٰهِ مِنَ الشَّيْطٰنِ الرَّجِيْمِ ؕ بِسْمِ اللّٰهِ الرَّحْمٰنِ الرَّحِيْمِ ؕ

Madani Muzakarah*

The following information is beneficial not only to chefs but also to everyone else. Satan may use every trick of the trade to keep you from reading this chapter. Try to counter his deceptions and make an ardent effort to read this chapter in its entirety. Reap many rewards by giving Dars in the Masjid and at home etc.

Virtues of Ṣalāt-'Alan-Nabī ﷺ

The Prophet of Raḥmaĥ, the Intercessor of Ummaĥ, the Owner of Jannaĥ صَلَّى اللهُ تَعَالٰى عَلَيْهِ وَاٰلِهٖ وَسَلَّم has stated, 'The one who writes Ṣalāt [with my name] in a book, angels will continue to seek forgiveness for him as long as my name remains in it.' *(Mu'jam Awsaṭ, vol. 1, pp. 497, Ḥadīš 1835)*

صَلُّوْا عَلَى الْحَبِيْب　　صَلَّى اللهُ تَعَالٰى عَلٰى مُحَمَّد

A Madanī Mashwaraĥ took place on Friday night, the 19th of Rabī'-un-Nūr 1423 A.H. This meeting was held at Bāb-ul-Madīnaĥ, Karachi for the caretakers and the chefs of Dawat-e-Islami's Madāris and Jāmi'a-tul-Madīnaĥ[1]. Many students also participated. After the traditional recitation of the Quran and Na'at, Amīr-e-Aĥl-e-Sunnat 'Allāmaĥ Maulānā, Abu Bilal Muhammad Ilyas Attar Qadiri Razavi دَامَتْ بَرَكَاتُهُمُ الْعَالِيَه delivered many

* A Madanī Mużākaraĥ is a term used in Dawat-e-Islami. It implies a question and answer session with Amīr-e-Aĥl-e-Sunnat دَامَتْ بَرَكَاتُهُمُ الْعَالِيَه

[1] An institution for learning Islamic sciences run by Dawat-e-Islami. [Translator's Notes]

words of wisdom. He urged the attendees to offer every Ṣalāĥ with Jamā'at in the first row of Masjid with Takbīr-e-Aūlā, partake in the weekly Sunnaĥ-Inspiring Ijtimā' from beginning to end, travel with Madanī Qāfilaĥs for three days every month, and fill and hand in Madanī In'āmāt booklets at the end of every [Islamic] month.

Measure food when dishing out

Question: What's the way to save food from going to waste?

Answer: Measure the ingredients when cooking food and also measure the quantity when distributing it. For example, a chef has to prepare Biryānī for ninety two students. As almost eight persons can be fed with one kilogram of rice, he should prepare Biryānī with twelve kilograms of rice.

Give food in the required quantity so that everyone is satiated and the food is also completely consumed. This will be very convenient and you will be able to minimize the wastage of food, اِنْ شَآءَاللّٰه عَزَّوَجَلَّ. If you do not measure the ingredients while cooking, you might cook either more or less than the required quantity. The taste of the leftover Biryānī reduces when reheated.

Six hundred thousand prisoners

Question: When did food begin to rot first?

Answer: Since the time of Banī Isrāīl [descendants of Isrāīl]. Let me tell you the detailed incident. After Pharaoh perished in the river Nile, Prophet Sayyidunā Mūsā عَلَيْهِ السَّلَام, along with 600000 people from Banī Isrāīl, left for 'Bayt-ul-Muqaddas' with the commandment of Allah عَزَّوَجَلَّ to fight against a nation called 'Amāliqaĥ.' When they approached Bayt-ul-Muqaddas, the Banī Isrāīl backed off and denied to fight, even asking Prophet Sayyidunā Mūsā عَلَيْهِ السَّلَام to fight along with his Creator against this warlike nation. Prophet Sayyidunā Mūsā عَلَيْهِ السَّلَام was extremely disheartened by this.

As a result, these 600000 people were trapped in a plain for forty years. This plain was 30 miles long and 27000 yards wide. They would start walking in the morning but end up at the same place, where they had started from, in the evening. This plain was called 'Tīĥ' which means '*the place where the people who have got lost keep wandering.*' *(Tafsīr Na'īmī, vol. 6, pp. 336-351)*

Mann and Salwā

It is stated in '*Rūḥ-ul-Bayān*', 'While the Prophet Sayyidunā Mūsā Kalīmullāĥ عَلَيْهِ السَّلَام was staying in the plains of Tīĥ along with 600000 people from Banī Isrāīl, Allah عَزَّوَجَلَّ sent down two foods for them from the sky. One was called 'Mann' and the other 'Salwā.' 'Mann' was a white honey-like dessert or white honey which would shower from the sky like rain. 'Salwā' was cooked quails that would descend from the sky with the southern winds.

Why food began to spoil?

Prophet Sayyidunā Mūsā Kalīmullāĥ عَلٰى نَبِيِّنَا وَعَلَيْهِ الصَّلٰوةُ وَالسَّلَام [and his Ummaĥ] was ordered by Allah عَزَّوَجَلَّ not to save this food (i.e. Mann and Salwā) for the next day. Some of the people with weak faith feared that they would starve to death in this barren plain, if someday Mann and Salwā did not descend. Therefore, they began to save and conceal this food for the next day. As a result of the disobedience to the Prophet, all the food saved for the next day began to rot and the food ceased to descend from the sky either. *(Rūḥ-ul-Bayān, vol. 1, pp. 142)*

The Beloved and Blessed Prophet صَلَّى اللّٰهُ تَعَالٰى عَلَيْهِ وَاٰلِهٖ وَسَلَّم has stated, 'If there were no Banī Isrāīl, neither food would spoil nor would meat ever rot.'[1] The rotting of meat dates back to the era of Banī Isrāīl. Before that time, food and meat would not rot.

Twelve springs gush forth

Did you see that the disobedience to their Prophet عَلَيْهِ السَّلَام led the people of Banī Isrāīl to such a grave calamity? All those who were over twenty years at the time of being trapped in the plains of 'Tīĥ', died over there.

Since Prophet Sayyidunā Mūsā عَلٰى نَبِيِّنَا وَعَلَيْهِ الصَّلٰوةُ وَالسَّلَام was staying amongst them, Mann and Salwā descended upon these people by his blessings. He عَلَيْهِ السَّلَام struck a rock with his

---

[1] (Ṣaḥīḥ Muslim, pp. 775, Ḥadīš 1470)

blessed staff and twelve springs of water gushed forth. The Banī Isrāil drank water from these springs and also used it for bathing. The dresses they used to wear during this time did not get dirty; nor did these dresses get old and tattered. Their nails and hair did not grow, which meant that they did not need to remove hair and cut nails. At night a shining pillar would appear which would serve as a light source for them. During the day, a cloud would hover overhead to shelter them from the sun. When a child was born amongst them, he would be covered by a shell-like nail dress which would continue to grow as the child grew. During this imprisonment, all of these bounties were bestowed upon them because of the blessing of Prophet Sayyidunā Mūsā Kalīmullāĥ عَلَيْهِ السَّلَام. *(Rūḥ-ul-Ma'ānī, vol. 6, pp. 383)*

Is it permissible for an employee to offer Nafl Ṣalāĥ?

The foregoing Quranic incident shows that sometimes sins and transgressions result in troubles even in the world. The Islamic brothers who are chefs should strive to complete their work and assigned tasks in a proper manner. Some employees today do not properly complete their duties as they do not have a righteous Madanī mindset. Despite not completing their work deliberately, they receive full wages, polluting their earnings.

Remember! An employee cannot even offer Nafl Ṣalāĥ during his duty hours without the permission of his employer. If he feels weakness and is unable to fulfil his duties properly, he cannot even keep a Nafl fast without the permission of his employer. *(Rad-dul-Muḥtār, vol. 9, pp. 97)* However, the employer can neither prevent his employee from offering Farḍ Ṣalāĥ with Jamā'at nor from fasting during the month of Ramadan. The employee must perform this Farḍ worship even if the employer tries to prevent him.

You are a trustee of every grain

Question: Is the chef a trustee of Jāmi'a-tul-Madīnaĥ's kitchen?

Answer: Yes, if someone deliberately misuses even a single grain, he will be accountable for it on the Day of Judgement. May Allah عَزَّوَجَلَّ enable us to preserve every type of entrustment and refrain from breaching! There is severe punishment for breaching. Ḥujjat-ul-Islam, Sayyidunā Imām Muhammad Ghazālī عَلَيْهِ رَحْمَةُ اللّٰهِ الْوَالِی has recorded the following in '*Mukāshafa-tul-Qulūb*':

Grave torments of breaching

On the Day of Judgement, a person will be brought before the court of Allah عَزَّوَجَلَّ. He will be asked, 'Did you return the entrusted thing [i.e. Amānat] of such and such person?' He will reply in the negative. On being ordered, the angel will take him to Hell. He will see that the entrusted thing is kept in the depth of Hell and he will fall towards it. He will reach it after seventy years; he will then pick that thing up and climb up. As he is close to the edge of Hell, he will slip and thus fall into the depth of Hell again. He will continue to climb and fall until he will be blessed with Allah's mercy through the intercession of the Prophet of Raḥmaĥ, the Intercessor of Ummaĥ صَلَّى اللهُ تَعَالٰى عَلَيْهِ وَاٰلِهٖ وَسَلَّم and the owner of that entrusted thing will be pleased with him. *(Mukāshafa-tul-Qulūb, pp. 44, 45)*

Reasons for food wastage in Madāris

[Amīr-e-Aĥl-e-Sunnat Maulānā Ilyas Qadiri دَامَتْ بَرَكَاتُهُمُ الْعَالِيَه asked the chefs] 'Tell me, is more food wasted in restaurants or in Madāris[1]?' The chefs replied, 'In Madāris!' Amīr-e-Aĥl-e-Sunnat دَامَتْ بَرَكَاتُهُمُ الْعَالِيَه then said, 'Actually, the restaurant owner spends money from his own pocket and also has to make a profit on it, which is why he strictly monitors all the matters of his restaurant, ensuring frugality. As for the religious institutions, they are run by public donations; neither the caretakers nor the chefs have to pay any money from their own pockets. Thus, they are very careless. At times the whole carcass of a slaughtered animal that was donated in Ṣadaqaĥ rots due to carelessness, and is then thrown away.

Alas! How tragic it is that the charity donations given by Muslims are wasted in such a ruthless manner! This can result in punishment in the Hereafter. All caretakers of religious and social institutions should remember that the accountability of every grain is to be made on the Day of Judgement. Allah عَزَّوَجَلَّ says in the glorious Quran, part 30, Sūraĥ Az-Zilzāl, verse 7, 8:

---

[1] Plural of Madrasaĥ. [Translator's Note]

فَمَنْ يَّعْمَلْ مِثْقَالَ ذَرَّةٍ خَيْرًا يَّرَهٗ ۝ وَمَنْ يَّعْمَلْ مِثْقَالَ ذَرَّةٍ شَرًّا يَّرَهٗ ۝

So whoever does a good deed equal to the weight of a particle, will see it. And whoever does an evil deed equal to the weight of a particle, will see it.

[Kanz-ul-Īmān (Translation of Quran)] (Part 30, Sūraĥ Az-Zilzāl, verse 7-8)

Proper method of freezing food

Question: Kindly, share with us some Madanī pearls on how to preserve meat and food?

Answer: Make sure that the freezer is working properly. In summer, the freezing capability of the freezer may be affected due to low voltage, increasing the risk of food rotting. In this situation, the food can be left in open air. If hung in open air without any support of wall etc., meat can remain fresh. When you put some gravy in the freezer, make sure that the container is uncovered so that the food can freeze properly. It is better to keep the food in small containers and plastic bags. Food in large containers can spoil because the food may not freeze properly. Kĥichřā[1] and lentils tend to spoil faster than other types of food. Similarly, cooked food made from tomatoes and other sour ingredients also tend to spoil faster.

Preserve raw meat for several days

Question: Is there any way to preserve raw meat so that it remains edible for many days?

Answer: If raw meat is put in the freezer in a large deep container, the meat in the lower part of the container may remain unfrozen and rot. Therefore, keep in mind the proper way of freezing a large quantity of meat. First put a layer of ice at the bottom of the container, then place meat on it and then put another layer of ice, then another layer of meat and put the container into the freezer. In this way, the meat in all parts of the container will properly freeze and will not rot for many days, اِنْ شَآءَ اللّٰه عَزَّوَجَلَّ

[1] A type of food made of wheat, minced meat, lentils and spices. This dish is cooked on low heat to a paste-like consistency. [Translator's Note]

What to do if food rots?

Question: What are the signs of food spoiling?

Answer: Rotting causes a sour [bad] smell to emanate. One can also see froth develop in foods that have gravy. The softer and sour ingredients of the food begin to rot first. Therefore, if sour smell begins to emanate from meat-food, then take the pieces of meat from it, wash them and reuse them (provided that the meat has not gone bad). Do not purposely throw away the meat if it has not gone bad.

Eating rotten meat is Ḥarām

Questions: What shall we do if the meat rots?

Answer: Throw it away. Ṣadr-ush-Sharī'aĥ Muftī Muhammad Amjad 'Alī A'ẓamī عَلَيْهِ رَحْمَةُ اللّٰهِ الْقَوِی has stated, 'Though Ḥarām to be consumed, the meat that has turned rot and smelly is not impure.' *(Al-Ashbāĥ wan-Naẓāir, vol. 1, pp. 418)*

Use of milk that has turned to curd

Question: How should one use milk that has started to turn into curd?

Answer: It is very easy to use milk that has started to turn into curd. Mix honey or sugar with it and cook it on a stove. Its water will evaporate, leaving a delicious sweet-item to be consumed.

Margarine

Question: Is it permissible to eat margarine [vegetable Għī]?

Answer: It is permissible to eat margarine but it is often injurious to health because of being adulterated. Many people have upset stomach today; one of the reasons for this is the use of unhealthy margarine. If healthy margarine is not available, then use cooking oil. Corn oil is better, olive oil is even better.

For healthy life in old age

Question: Kindly, enlighten us with Madanī pearls so that [the use of] margarine, butter and oil are not injurious to our health?

Answer: It takes longer to digest oil, margarine and their likes. Excessive use of them engenders obesity and diseases. If the one decreasing the use of margarine, oil, superfine flour and sugar from his youth is predestined to reach old age, he will enjoy a healthy life in his old age, اِنْ شَآءَاللّٰه عَزَّوَجَلَّ. I humbly urge you to reduce the intake of oil, salt and spices in your foods by half. You will experience its benefits. However, patients should follow the recommendations of their doctors.

Cooking without oil

Question: Is it possible to cook food without oil?

Answer: Of course, it is. Some foods can be cooked without oil like plain rice, lentils and curd curry. It is not needed to add oil to the Pāyā[1] of a cow or a healthy sheep, because the fat on the bones melts and functions as oil. In fact, all types of food can be cooked without oil. Grind coriander leaves, mint and green chillies etc. in large quantity. You can also blend vegetables with it. Now cook the gravy with this paste, adding water, yogurt, green chillies and other spices like cloves, green, cardamom, cinnamon etc. according to your taste. You will get used to it after cooking it a few times, اِنْ شَآءَاللّٰه عَزَّوَجَلَّ

How to ensure proper working of sewer

Question: Kindly guide us on how to keep the kitchen clean?

Answer: It is imperative that you keep the kitchen clean. Clean stains from the walls and floor of the kitchen. Particles of food remain lying here and there in the kitchen and eventually rot, which then leads to germs and bacteria. It is, therefore, necessary to use germ killing detergents to clean the kitchen. Do not let food, spices, bones and oil go into the drain, otherwise the drainage pipes may clog. Clean the oil and spices clung to the pots and pans before you wash them. This will save the drainage from being clogged.

Grit and weevils

Question: Grit (i.e. small pieces of stone) and weevils sometimes get cooked with rice. If someone eats them unknowingly, what will be the ruling for him?

---

[1] A sub-continental dish like a spicy soup made from the bones of cow or sheep etc. [Translator's Note]

Answer: Separate sand, grit and weevils from the rice and lentils etc. before cooking. Remember that it is Ḥarām to eat sand to the extent that it causes harm. Similarly, it is also Ḥarām and a sin to deliberately eat even a single weevil. If weevils have got cooked with the meal; take them out after the cooking and eat the meal. If one is lazy and deliberately leaves grit etc. in the food causing inconvenience for the eaters then the cook, who was responsible for taking those grit and weevils out, will be a sinner.

Don't add whole kidney to food

Question: What is the Islamic ruling regarding the blood that comes out of the animal being slaughtered? Is it permissible to cook whole kidneys in the food, when preparing it?

Answer: One should take great care when cooking meat. The blood that comes out, when the animal is slaughtered, is impure and is Ḥarām to be consumed. Therefore, wash the meat thoroughly so that the blood is drained off. Do not put whole kidneys into the food; cut them open, wash them and then cook them.

Question: Is it permissible to eat the spleen and the kidney?

Answer: It is permissible but the Holy Prophet صَلَّى اللهُ تَعَالٰى عَلَيْهِ وَاٰلِهٖ وَسَلَّم did not like to consume these organs. Here are two Aḥādīš:

1. The Holy Prophet صَلَّى اللهُ تَعَالٰى عَلَيْهِ وَاٰلِهٖ وَسَلَّم disliked consuming the kidney as it is closer to (the organ of) urine. *(Kanz-ul-'Ummāl, vol. 7, pp. 41, Ḥadīš 18212)*

2. The Beloved and Blessed Prophet صَلَّى اللهُ تَعَالٰى عَلَيْهِ وَاٰلِهٖ وَسَلَّم hated consuming the spleen, but did not declare it Ḥarām. *(Itḥāf-us-Sādat-il-Muttaqīn, vol. 8, pp. 243)*

Question: So, should we refrain from consuming the kidney and the spleen?

Answer: The true love and devotion would indeed expect you not to eat them, but do not criticise those who consume them as it is Ḥalāl to do so. It is narrated on the authority of Sayyidunā 'Abdullāĥ Ibn 'Umar رَضِیَ اللهُ تَعَالٰی عَنْهُ that the Beloved and Blessed Rasūl صَلَّى اللهُ تَعَالٰى عَلَيْهِ وَاٰلِهٖ وَسَلَّم has stated, 'Two dead animals and two bloods have been made Ḥalāl for us. The two dead are fish and locusts and the two bloods are the spleen and the liver.' *(Musnad Imām Aḥmad, vol. 2, pp. 415, Ḥadīš 5727)*

Question: So are all types of fish Ḥalāl?

Answer: If a fish has died naturally without being hunted and floats upside down, it is Ḥarām. However, if one kills a fish and then it begins to float upside down it is not Ḥarām. *(Durr-e-Mukhtār, Rad-dul-Muḥtār, vol. 9, pp. 445)*

Airborne fish

Let me tell you an interesting parable about a fish. إِنْ شَآءَاللّٰه عَزَّوَجَلَّ, You will learn amazing facts from it. Hence, the caliph Ĥārūn-ur-Rashīd once let his falcon loose into the air for hunting. The falcon disappeared. After a while, it returned with a fish in between its claws. Astonished, the caliph asked a great scholar of that time Sayyidunā Muqātil رَحْمَةُ اللهِ تَعَالٰی عَلَيْه (about its edibility). The great Shaykh رَحْمَةُ اللهِ تَعَالٰی عَلَيْه replied, 'Your ancestor Sayyidunā 'Abdullāĥ Bin 'Abbās رَضِیَ اللهُ تَعَالٰی عَنْهُمَا has stated, 'Many different creatures live in the air some of which are white coloured. They give birth to fish like creatures that have arms but no wings.' Sayyidunā Muqātil رَحْمَةُ اللهِ تَعَالٰی عَلَيْه then gave permission to consume that fish. *(Ḥayāt-ul-Ḥaywān-ul-Kubrā, vol. 1, pp. 157)*

Eat little quantity of fish

Imām Baĥāuddīn Ibrāĥīm Zarnūjī عَلَيْهِ رَحْمَةُ اللهِ الْقَوِی has stated, 'There is a saying of Ḥakīm Jālīnūs that there are many benefits in pomegranate and a lot of disadvantages in fish, but eating a little fish is better than eating several pomegranates.' *(Ta'līm-ul-Muta'allim, pp. 42)*

Who was Jālīnūs?

Question: Who was Jālīnūs?

Answer: His real name was 'Claudius Galen.' He lived even before the arrival of the Noble Prophet صَلَّى اللهُ تَعَالٰی عَلَيْهِ وَاٰلِهٖ وَسَلَّم. He was born in the year 131 and died in 201. He was the greatest physician in ancient Greece and surpassed all the physicians of his time, in knowledge. Physicians from Greece were famous throughout the world for their expertise in medical science. He was such a great physician that even today after 1800 years, he is still well known.

22 Parts of slaughtered animal forbidden to be consumed

Question: Which parts of the Żabīḥaĥ [slaughtered animal] should not be eaten?

Answer: In reply to a similar question, A'lā Ḥaḍrat Imām Aḥmad Razā Khān عَلَيْهِ رَحْمَةُ الرَّحْمٰن has stated, 'All the parts of a Ḥalāl animal are Ḥalāl except a few ones which are either Ḥarām or prohibited or Makrūĥ. [They include] (1) veins blood (2) gall bladder (3) bladder (4-5) genitals of male and female [animals] (6) testicles (7) glands (8) spinal cord (9) tendons that stretch from the neck to the shoulders (10) liver-blood (11) spleen-blood (12) meat-blood emanating from meat after the slaughter (13) heart-blood (14) bile or gall (i.e. a yellowish fluid in gall bladder) (15) nasal fluid mostly found in sheep (16) anus (17) guts (18) intestines (19) sperm (20) the sperm that has turned into blood (21) the sperm that has turned into a piece of flesh and (22) the one that has turned into a complete animal and was born dead or born alive but died without being slaughtered. *(Fatāwā Razawiyyaĥ, vol. 20, pp. 240, 241)*

Experienced butchers usually remove some of the parts of the animal that are forbidden to be consumed but even they are unaware of some other forbidden parts or they do not pay heed. Therefore, I am going to mention some of the forbidden parts of the animal that are usually cooked with food because of lack of knowledge.

Blood

The blood that oozes out at the time of Żabḥ [slaughtering] is called 'Dam Masfūḥ.' This blood is impure and is Ḥarām to be consumed. Though the blood that remains after slaughtering in some organs like the cut area of the neck, the inside of heart, spleen, liver, small veins in the meat, is not impure, it is still forbidden to consume it. Therefore, one should thoroughly clean these organs before adding them to the food.

There are some very small blood-veins in the meat. It is extremely difficult to identify them. These small veins turn black when cooked. These veins usually appear in brains and in meat from the chicken leg and wing etc. If you see these black strands while eating, remove them. Do not cook the whole heart of a chicken. Cut it open first vertically in four pieces and clean the inside blood.

Spinal cord

Spinal cord is a white thread like strand which extends from the base of the brain through the length of the backbone [spine]. Experienced butchers take out the spinal cord. However, some spinal cord often remains due to their laziness and is cooked with the food. Therefore, separate the spinal cord from neck, ribs and back when washing the meat before cooking. The spinal cord is also found in the neck and backbone of chicken and other birds. As it is extremely difficult to remove it before cooking, remove it before you eat.

Tendons

Tendons are two bands of yellow fibrous tissue, on both sides of the neck, which serve to connect the shoulder muscles to the neck. It is forbidden to consume these tendons. You can easily spot these tendons in cows and goats but it is difficult to find them in small birds like the chicken. Remove them when you are eating. If you cannot identify them, take help from some experienced person.

Lymph glands

Around the neck, throat and also in fat etc., you can find these reddish lymph glands [also called lymph nodes] which in Arabic are called 'Ghaddaĥ.' Do not eat them. Remove them before cooking and if you spot them in cooked meat remove them then.

Testicles

Testicles are called 'Khuṣyaĥ', 'Fauṭaĥ' or 'Bayḍaĥ.' It is Makrūĥ Taḥrīmī to consume them. The testicles of male animals like bull and goat etc. are easily visible. In rooster they are located behind the intestine and are small egg-like structures, remove them [while cleaning the meat].

Tragically, 'Kaṭā-Kaṭ' is a commonly sold food in some of the restaurants of the subcontinent. Besides the liver and heart, it also contains goat and bull testicles. This is prepared on a large iron griddle pan, and is called 'Kaṭā-Kaṭ' perhaps because it is prepared right before the customer using some utensils that make a sound of 'Kaṭ', 'Kaṭ' when it hits against the iron griddle pan.

Guts

Guts contain body waste of the animal. It is Makrūĥ Taḥrīmī to consume the guts of the animal. Tragically several Muslims eat it.

How to identify forbidden things?

Question: How can one learn more details about forbidden things that you have just identified?

Answer: In order to learn details of forbidden parts of the slaughtered animal, all chefs and Islamic brothers should read from page 234 to 241 of the 20th volume of '*Fatāwā Razawiyyaĥ.*' Consult an Islamic scholar, if you do not understand any part of it. Then ask a butcher to identify those organs. Theoretical knowledge is very important, but observation and experience is even better.

How is it to eat bread made by one not offering Ṣalāĥ?

Question: Some people do not eat breads baked by the one who does not offer Ṣalāĥ. Our chefs are sometimes lazy in offering their Ṣalāĥ, please advise them?

Answer: It is permissible to eat the bread made by the one who does not offer Ṣalāĥ. However, if the righteous and the pious do not eat the breads made by the one not offering Ṣalāĥ as an act of censure, with the intention of reforming him, there is no harm in it. The chefs present here work in Islamic Madāris and Jāmi'āt. Many of these institutions are adjacent to Masājid. These chefs should offer not only Farḍ but also Nafl Ṣalāĥ like Awwabīn[1], Taĥajjud, Ishrāq and Chāsht[2]. You are allowed (in our Madāris) to offer these Nawāfils when on duty.

Remember! Neither the cook nor the bread-baker nor their helper is allowed to miss their Farḍ Ṣalāĥ. As soon as you hear the Ṣalāt-'Alan-Nabī recited before the Aẓān, turn all the stoves off. Prepare to go towards the Masjid to offer Ṣalāĥ with Jamā'at and

---

[1] Awwabīn is Nafl Ṣalāĥ offered after the Maghrib Ṣalāĥ. It usually contains six Rak'āt.

[2] Ishrāq and Chāsht are both Nafl Ṣalāĥ which may be offered any time from about twenty minutes after the sunrise till before Ḍaḥwā Kubrā time. Chāsht is also known as Ṣalāt-ud-Ḍuḥā. [Translator's Notes]

Takbīr-e-Aūlā, in the first Ṣaf [row]. I urge the well wisher[1] Islamic brothers to ask the chefs to come to the Masjid for Ṣalāĥ, as they make their rounds to call the students of the Madrasaĥ to come to the Masjid for Ṣalāĥ.

Serving students is a privilege

Question: Are the chefs not fortunate that they have a privilege to serve seekers of Islamic knowledge?

Answer: Indeed, they are fortunate. My dear chefs! Undoubtedly, you are very fortunate that memorizers of the Quran and seekers of Islamic knowledge, who are showered with blessings, eat the food prepared by you. These students [of Islamic sciences] have indeed a high status. When Sayyidunā Abū Dardā رَضِیَ اللّٰہُ تَعَالٰی عَنْہُ saw an Islamic student, he would say to him: 'Marḥabā [welcome], the Holy Prophet صَلَّی اللّٰہُ تَعَالٰی عَلَیْہِ وَاٰلِہٖ وَسَلَّم has particularly made a will regarding you (to be kind and courteous with you).' *(Sunan Dārimī, vol. 1, pp. 111, Ḥadīš 348)*

Students, especially the young ones, are indeed very fortunate that they are spending the precious moments of their life learning Islamic knowledge rather than playing games. They have devoted their young age to the acquisition of Islamic knowledge.

Du'ā of forgiveness for sake of Islamic students

Question: What are your feelings about the students of Jāmi'a-tul-Madīnaĥ?

Answer: I have a deep affection for the students of Dawat-e-Islami's Jāmi'āt and Madāris. I also make Du'ā for my forgiveness by their sake. Although some of them are mischievous, after all they are children! No matter how mischievous the children are, they are dearer to their parents. The mischief of a few students does not imply at all that all the students are ill-mannered.

اَلْحَمْدُ لِلّٰہ عَزَّوَجَلَّ, Our students offer Nafl Ṣalāĥ in addition to Farḍ Ṣalāĥ. اَلْحَمْدُ لِلّٰہ عَزَّوَجَلَّ Many students offer Ṣalāt-ut-Taubaĥ, Taĥajjud, Ishrāq and Chāsht. Thousands of students also hand in their Madanī In'āmāt booklets and a large number of them travel with Madanī

---

[1] In the Madanī environment of Dawat-e-Islami the brothers assigned to usher and call the students for Ṣalāĥ and persuade people to sit near the preacher during Dars and speech are called 'Khayr Khuwāĥ' [well wishers]. [Translator's Note]

Qāfilaĥs. There are also numerous students who have responsibilities of righteous Madanī work of Dawat-e-Islami in nearby localities of these Jāmi'āt and Madāris. اَلْحَمْدُ لِلّٰه عَزَّوَجَلَّ, They are making their religious services in many Masājid. اَللّٰهُمَّ زِدْ فَزِدْ ثُمَّ زِدْ (*Yā Allah* عَزَّوَجَلَّ, *increase this and increase this and then increase this more*).

How to make complaint

Question: The chef Islamic brothers do not pay any heed to the students' complaints!

Answer: Look! Chefs also have self-respect; if they are repeatedly criticized by everyone, they may be offended. It is also apparent that one or two chefs cannot satisfy all the students of the Jāmi'aĥ.

Dear students! Remember that the one who repeatedly complains loses his own respect and his complain becomes ineffective either. Therefore, complaints must be made but just once and in a courteous and comprehensive manner. Written complaints prove to be more effective compared to the oral ones in these matters. Since many students are still immature they sometimes deteriorate the situation because of their improper manner of making complaints. Therefore, it is advised that no student should make the complaint directly to the chefs. Anyone who has a complaint should write to the responsible brother of the Jāmi'a-tul-Madīnaĥ or Madrasa-tul-Madīnaĥ's kitchen. (The chefs were very pleased with this answer of Amīr-e-Aĥl-e-Sunnat دَامَتْ بَرَكَاتُهُمُ الْعَالِيَه).

Who is responsible for burnt food?

Question: Are the chefs excused if they burn the food?

Answer: No, the chef is being paid for cooking and is responsible to ensure that the food is not burnt. The scholars of Islamic jurisprudence رَحِمَهُمُ اللّٰهُ تَعَالٰى have stated that if the chef spoils the food or burns it or leaves it uncooked, he will have to pay the penalty [from his own pocket for the loss]. *(Durr-e-Mukhtār, vol. 9, pp. 22)*

There is a matter of concern here for the responsible brothers. If the chef did not pay the penalty they cannot turn a blind eye to the waste of public endowments in this matter. If it were your own money, then perhaps you would get every penny back, to make up for the losses. In any case, the penalty for any loss of the endowed money because of the spoiling of the food must be paid. One cannot be relieved of any penalties of the past just by saying '*From now on, I will be mindful of this.*' It is necessary to calculate all previous loss and make up for it.

Oven bread and baking soda

Question: Sometimes, there is excessive baking soda in breads, is this not harmful?

Answer: It is important to do everything in moderation. The bread will not be tasty if there is too much baking soda in it. Excess of baking soda hurts the body in addition to spoiling the taste.

Question: What is the method of boiling chickpeas?

Answer: If you want to boil chickpeas, it is better to soak them in water for about eight hours [before boiling them]. You could also use some baking soda [while boiling] to soften them and cook them faster.

How to tenderize hard meat

Question: What is the proper way of tenderizing an old animal meat?

Answer: An old animal meat or hard meat gets tender quickly if unripe papaya is mixed with it whilst being cooked. Unripe papaya fruit is also used with spices in barbecue. Those who enjoy Niĥārī [an Indo-Pak dish] at hotels are usually served with meat from old camels or cows or buffaloes that no longer give milk or cannot be used in farms. This is the magic of the papaya fruit that the hard meat becomes soft and edible. Sugar, peppermints and betel-nuts are also used for tenderizing meat. Letting it cook on the stove also softens the meat. When you cook stew or rice pilaf, put in small pieces of chicken or meat so that it gets fully tender. If the meat is put in larger pots or pans, it gets tender when the required amount of heat is given.

My Madanī suggestion is that one should put some squash for blessings in the stews [as squash was dearly liked by the Beloved and Blessed Prophet صَلَّى اللّٰهُ تَعَالٰى عَلَيْهِ وَاٰلِهٖ وَسَلَّم]. Another benefit of putting vegetables in the meat is that they remove the negative effects of the meat.

Meat that does not get tender

Question: What to do with the meat that does not tenderize in any way?

Answer: There is no solution to it. A'lā Ḥaḍrat Imām Aḥmad Razā Khān عَلَيْهِ رَحْمَةُ الرَّحْمٰن has stated, 'The meat of the animal which has both male and female genitals, urinates from both places, and has no sign that conclusively makes it a male or a female, does not get tender in any way. If slaughtered according to Sharī'aĥ, it would be Ḥalāl. If anyone wants to eat its meat he will have to eat it untenderized as it does not get tender. Its sacrifice [Qurbānī] is not permissible.' *(Fatāwā Razawiyyaĥ (Jadīd), vol. 20, pp. 255)*

Signs of good meat

Question: What are the signs of good meat?

Answer: Meat of an old animal is red, whereas that of a younger one is brownish and usually has less fat. Brownish meat is better. It may be better to buy the last of the meat to be cooked at one's home because the meat sellers first try to palm the purchasers off with fatty and bony meat and the meat remaining in the end may have more flesh[1]! As for vegetables and fruits, the fresh ones sell quickly and the rotten and old ones are left. Seeing this, the saying is true: 'Buy fruits and vegetables in the beginning and meat in the end.'

Animals abuse

Question: Did any Ṣaḥābī [companion of the Prophet] sell meat?

Answer: Yes, Sayyidunā 'Amr Bin 'Āṣ and Sayyidunā Zubayr رَضِیَ اللهُ تَعَالٰی عَنۡهُمَا would sell meat. May all meat sellers follow in the footsteps of these Prophet's companions رَضِیَ اللّٰهُ تَعَالٰی عَنۡهُم.

These days, many sins are committed in this business. The animals raised for getting meat are cruelly treated right from the beginning. No pity is taken on the miserable animal that cannot express its suffering. Without doubt, it is permissible to slaughter the animal, but these days, the animal is oppressed to such an extent during this permissible act that one feels frightened when sees the helplessness of the oppressed animal.

---

[1] It is common in the subcontinent, where meat is not processed unlike the west. [Translator's Note]

Question: Advise us of the things to be mindful of during the slaughtering of animals so that they feel the least amount of pain.

Answer: Find the direction of the Qiblaĥ before making the cow fall on the ground as, having made it lie down, it is very painful to turn it to the direction of Qiblaĥ by dragging it, especially on the rocky earth. All four veins or at least three of them should be cut during the slaughter. Not more than this should be cut. Some people cut more than four veins such that the knife touches the neck joint, causing unnecessary suffering to the animal. After this, do not cut the legs or take off the skin until the animal has completely stopped trembling. Until the soul has left the body, do not put the knife or even the hand on the slit throat.

Just imagine, how painful would it be if someone put their fingers or hands on your wound! In order to make the cow dead early, some butchers take its neck-skin off, stab into its chest and cut the veins of the heart. Similarly, some butchers break the neck of the goat right after slaughtering it. Animals that cannot express their sufferings should not be abused in these ways. Whoever has the power must prevent those causing pain to animals without any lawful reason.

It is stated on page 259 of *Baĥār-e-Sharī'at* (volume 16), 'Abusing animals is worse than abusing Żimmī unbelievers[1], and abusing Żimmī unbelievers is worse than even abusing Muslims because animals have no one to help them except for Allah عَزَّوَجَلَّ. Who will save these poor animals from this abuse!' *(Baĥār-e-Sharī'at, vol. 16, pp. 259)*

Question: How is it to enjoy watching the animals being slaughtered?

Answer: One should have pity on these animals that cannot express their suffering rather than making their slaughtering a spectacle. Just imagine, if you were being slaughtered in place of the animal, what would your condition be! To have pity on the animal while it is being slaughtered is a virtuous deed as a Prophet's companion رَضِیَ اللهُ تَعَالٰی عَنْهُ once told the Beloved and Blessed Prophet صَلَّى اللهُ تَعَالٰی عَلَيْهِ وَاٰلِهٖ وَسَلَّم, 'Yā Rasūlallāĥ صَلَّى اللهُ تَعَالٰی عَلَيْهِ وَاٰلِهٖ وَسَلَّم I have mercy on the goat while slaughtering it.' He صَلَّى اللهُ تَعَالٰی عَلَيْهِ وَاٰلِهٖ وَسَلَّم said, 'If you have mercy on it, Allah عَزَّوَجَلَّ will have mercy on you.' *(Al-Mustadrak, vol. 5, pp. 327, Ḥadīš 7636)*

---

[1] At this time all unbelievers are Ḥarbī.

This Ḥadīš describes an instance of having mercy on the animal being slaughtered lawfully. If an animal is abused, then how gruesome it would be to make a spectacle out of its abuse! If possible, one should explain to the abuser of his wrongdoings and prevent him from doing so. If one cannot do this, then one should feel resentment in his heart and go away from that place. One should not look needlessly when the animals is being slaughtered. Enjoying the wailing and writhing of the animal being slaughtered, smiling, laughing and making this a spectacle are all signs of heedlessness. We should treat the goat with respect, as it is stated in a Ḥadīš, 'Treat the goat with respect and clean dust from it as it is an animal of Paradise.' *(Al-Jāmi'-uṣ-Ṣaghīr, vol. 1, pp. 88, Ḥadīš 1421)*

How is it to slaughter camel from three places?

Question: Nowadays, the camel is slaughtered from three places. To what extent is this correct?

Answer: It is wrongful to slaughter the camel from three places. To slaughter it from just one place is enough. It is a Sunnaĥ to slaughter a camel by Naḥr which implies stabbing a spear or a knife into the lowest part of the camel's throat, cutting its veins. *(Baĥār-e-Sharī'at, part 15, pp. 115)* After Naḥr there is no need to run the knife on the neck of the camel.

Camel was hit with an iron rod!

May all of us be blessed with the privilege of repeatedly performing Hajj, visiting Madīnaĥ and performing ritual sacrifice in Minā[1]! Alas! Such sad incidents were seen during the Hajj pilgrimage of 1422 A.H. that a kind-hearted person would faint at the sight of it. How the innocent camels were being treated! A tall Negro with a heavy iron rod in his hands would swiftly strike the camel with his rod. The innocent camel, caught by surprise, would collapse on the floor, screaming. Then some butchers would come and slaughter it in three places. In some places, they would slaughter a standing camel by Naḥr and streams of blood would gush forth. The camel would try to run but be hit with heavy iron rods, because of which it would collapse on the floor, in severe pain. Then it would be slaughtered in three places.

---

[1] It is Sunnaĥ to perform the sacrifice of Hajj in Minā but nowadays the designated slaughter areas are located in Muzdalifaĥ.

I have not seen these gruesome incidents in person, the Islamic brothers who had gone to do the Qurbānī (sacrifice) for the members of our 'Chal Madīnaĥ' Hajj Qāfilaĥ in 1422 A.H. told it to us as they returned from the slaughter house.

Cautions for meat sellers

Question: Please describe some Madanī pearls for meat sellers.

Answer: Many meat sellers do various wrongdoings, increasing their sins and polluting their earnings. In brief, to sell the stale meat stored in the freezer as fresh meat; to sell the meat of an old cow or bull declaring it a young cow's meat; to stick small udders of a young cow to the old cow's thigh to give the impression that all the meat is from a young cow; to sell bones and things not eaten as a part of the meat to increase its weight deceivingly; to sell meat weighing it by approximation without using the weighing machine (for example, someone asked for a pound of minced meat and the seller just grabbed a fistful and sold it as one pound without weighing). These are all sinful and Ḥarām acts that could lead to Hell.

Prohibition of selling by weighing with approximation

Question: You have just mentioned the prohibition of weighing the minced meat by approximation. This is a matter of grave difficulty for sellers and buyers as it is a common practice to sell things by weighing them with approximation. Is the buyer also a sinner?

Answer: Yes. If the buyer asks for a thing to be sold to him by proper weighing but then purchases it by weighing it with approximation, he is also a sinner. One of the ways of avoiding this sin is to ask for things mentioning their price rather than mentioning their weight. For instance, the buyer may say to the seller: Give it to me for 5 rupees or 12 rupees. In this way, whatever he gives will be permissible to take and both the seller and buyer will be saved from sin. Some sellers say that they will sell the thing by weighing it properly but tend to sell it by weighing with approximation; the buyer should adopt the above technique on such occasions.

Beef samosay sold in marketplace

Question: Can unwashed mince be eaten?

Answer: Unless one is aware that the unwashed mince is impure, there is no harm in eating it, but it's still better and safer to wash it. Those who eat kebabs and samosas from marketplace and in get-togethers should take note. Most of the people that sell kebabs and samosas often do not wash the mince they use. According to them, the taste of the kebabs and samosas reduces if the mince is washed.

Further, listen to what is, sometimes, put into mince purchased from markets. Some remove the skin from the guts of a cow and mix either spleen or, sometimes, Allah عَزَّوَجَلَّ forbid, congealed blood with guts that is minced so that the white flesh of the guts becomes pink in colour, resembling meat. At times, the sellers have garlic, ginger etc. grinded with the mince which can no longer be washed. Spices are mixed and the same mince is used in kebabs and samosas which are then sold. There is a risk of the same type of unclean mince in hotels and restaurants as well. Therefore, don't buy even pakoras from these people that sell these impure kebabs and samosas as the pakoras are also fried in the same fryer in which the unclean mince is put. However, Allah عَزَّوَجَلَّ forbid, I do not say that all kebab, samosa and meat-sellers do such acts, nor am I saying that each and every kebab and samosa seller uses unclean mince. Definitely, mince of pure and clean meat is also available. My request is that mince, kebabs or samosas should be bought from a trustworthy Muslim, and the Muslims who do such fraudulent acts should repent and seek forgiveness.

Dead chickens

These days, many deceptive practices are prevalent [in society]. It is said that whenever there is an outbreak of an epidemic among the chickens, the wicked minded people deceitfully supply the dead chickens to restaurants and kebab and samosa sellers.

Slaughtering a goat close to its death

Question: If a goat is close to its death, can it be slaughtered?

Answer: Yes, but there are certain things one has to be mindful of. If a sick goat was slaughtered and it only moved its mouth, i.e. it opened its mouth then it is Ḥarām but if it closed the mouth then it is Ḥalāl; if it opened the eyes it is Ḥarām, if it closed the eyes then it is Ḥalāl; if it spread its legs then it is Ḥarām and if it folded the legs then it is Ḥalāl; if its hair did not raise it is Ḥarām and if the hair raised then it is Ḥalāl.

In other words, if one is not sure of the animal being alive then one should rely on these signs and if one is sure of the animal being alive then one must not rely upon these signs and the animal will be considered Ḥalāl. *(Fatāwā 'Ālamgīrī, vol. 5, pp. 286)*

Ruling for forgetting Allah's name at time of slaughter

Question: Is the animal Ḥalāl if a Muslim recites only بِسْمِ اللهِ الرَّحْمٰنِ الرَّحِيْم at the time of slaughtering the animal? And what is the ruling, if one forgets to mention the name of Allah عَزَّوَجَلَّ completely?

Answer: Yes, the animal is Ḥalāl. It is necessary to mention the name of Allah عَزَّوَجَلَّ at the time of slaughtering the animal, but it is better to recite بِسْمِ اللهِ اَللّٰهُ اَكْبَرْ . If one mentions the name of Allah عَزَّوَجَلَّ in any other language apart from Arabic, the slaughtered animal will still be Ḥalāl. *(Fatāwā 'Ālamgīrī, vol. 5, pp. 286)*

If one forgets to mention the name of Allah عَزَّوَجَلَّ whilst slaughtering the animal, the animal would still Ḥalāl to be consumed. However, if one deliberately did not mention it, then the animal would be Ḥarām. (For further information on this topic, read '*Baĥār-e-Sharī'at*' volume 15).

Can we eat bones or not?

Question: Can the bones of the slaughtered animal be eaten?

Answer: Yes. A'lā Ḥaḍrat Imām Aḥmad Razā Khān عَلَيْهِ رَحْمَةُ الرَّحْمٰن has stated: 'The bones of a Ḥalāl animal that has been slaughtered are not prohibited in any way, unless there is harm in consuming them.' *(Fatāwā Razawiyyaĥ (Jadīd), vol. 20, pp. 340)*

The white bones which are elastic like plastic are often soft and tasty. Similarly, rib bones and the white pair of bones near the flat bones of the hands are also soft. The windpipe which is above the lungs should be cut vertically and cleaned. The bone of the breast area, which is white, can also be eaten after being cooked. With it is also a black bone which is crispy and tasty as well.

Nearly all the young animals' black bone is crispy. Chew it well and spit out the dry chewed leftovers. The bones which cannot be eaten and chewed can be sucked from their broken part, for taste and nutrition. So, as long as one is enjoying the taste, take benefit from the favours of Allah عَزَّوَجَلَّ and then place it on the dining mat.

Question: We haven't seen any black bone in uncooked meat before!

Answer: It is the reddish bone which turns black when cooked. In fact, when blood is cooked, it turns black.

Madanī pearls for using bones for cures

Question: Tell us some benefits of bones.

Answer: Bones are also divine favours which contain nutrition. Those who buy boneless meat deprive themselves and their family of a divine favour. Indeed, Allah عَزَّوَجَلَّ has not created anything useless. Besides being sustenance, bones also serve as medicines. Doctors advise some patients to drink bone soup. Many of you may have drunk it but none of you may have drunk only meat soup!

Bones are very important. The liquid extracted from bones is used in injections as well. If the one suffering from fever every fourth day eats food mixed with the crushed horns of a cow, he will be cured, اِنْ شَآءَاللّٰه عَزَّوَجَلَّ. The mixture of water and burnt hair of a cow removes toothache. *(Ḥayāt-ul-Ḥaywān-ul-Kubrā, vol. 1, pp. 219)* If someone applies the burnt bones of a pigeon, a Ḥalāl bird, to his wound, the wound will heal by the grace of Allah عَزَّوَجَلَّ. *('Ajāib-ul-Ḥaywānāt, pp. 147)*

Benefits of chicken meat

Question: Kindly state some benefits of chicken.

Answer: To eat chicken strengthens memory. It is also highly beneficial to stomach-pain. It is better to eat the meat of domesticated chickens. These days it is hard to find a domesticated chicken as some vendors colour the feathers of poultry farms smaller baby-chickens and their eggs and sell them as domesticated ones. The sign of a domesticated chicken is that it is thin with a small stomach, whereas the chickens produced in poultry farms are fatter with much meat on them.

How is it to eat bones of chicken?

Question: Is it permissible to eat the bones of chicken?

Answer: Yes. It's been my habit since my childhood to eat the whitish bones of chicken. It is generally assumed that consuming chicken bones is injurious to health. I once asked a qualified dietician about the harms of chicken bones. The dietician who has authored a book on nutrition replied that eating chicken bones causes no ill effects or damage. وَاللّٰهُ وَرَسُوْلُهٗ اَعْلَم عَزَّوَجَلَّ وَ صَلَّى اللّٰه تَعَالٰى عَلَيْهِ وَاٰلِهٖ وَسَلَّم (Allah عَزَّوَجَلَّ and His Noble Prophet صَلَّى اللّٰه تَعَالٰى عَلَيْهِ وَاٰلِهٖ وَسَلَّم know the best).

Can one eat fish bones?

Question: Can we eat fish bones?

Answer: We can eat these bones as well. However, the bones of fish are normally hard and cannot be eaten easily. The bones of some of the fish are soft. For example, the bones of oceanic pomfret fish etc. are soft and tasty. If one cannot swallow these bones, one may chew them properly and then spit out the chewed leftovers.

How is it to eat fish skin?

Question: Can fish skin be eaten?

Answer: Yes. People normally throw away the skin of fish before or after the cooking. One should not do this. If there are no problems or restrictions, one may also eat the skin of fish. Some fish have very tasty skin.

How is it to eat and sell crab?

Question: How is it to eat crab?

Answer: It is Ḥarām. Except for fish, all other sea animals are Ḥarām to be consumed. It is also impermissible to sell crabs. Islamic scholars have stated: 'Apart from fish, it is not allowed to sell any other sea animal like frog, crab, etc. and insects (such as flies, ants) and mice, musk-rats, lizards, chameleon, bandicoot, snakes and scorpions.' *(Fatḥ-ul-Qadīr, vol. 6, pp. 58)*

What to do if stew is burnt?

Question: What should be done if the stew is burnt?

Answer: First take out spices and meat from the upper part of the container, and then fry some onions in any other container. When the onions turn brown, put the spices and meat into this container and then add half a cup of milk. The milk will remove the smell of burning, اِنْ شَآءَاللّٰه عَزَّوَجَلَّ.

How to improve our digestion?

Question: How can we improve our digestion?

Answer: Be careful in what you eat and drink. To eat in excess spoils one's stomach, ruining one's digestive system. It is not a Sunnaĥ to eat without hunger. Whenever you eat, divide your 'hunger' into three parts; one for food, one for water and one for air. After eating, do not sleep till the next one and a half hour to two hours. Eat less meat and more vegetables and fruits. Walk for one hour or at least half an hour daily. Walk at least 150 steps after eating dinner. اِنْ شَآءَاللّٰه عَزَّوَجَلَّ, The stomach-diseases that do not respond to any medicine will be cured. اِنْ شَآءَاللّٰه عَزَّوَجَلَّ, You will be safe from 80% of diseases including heart attack, paralysis of the face and other parts of the body, brain diseases, pain in body parts, throat and tongue diseases, chest and lung diseases, mouth blisters, heart burn, diabetes, high blood pressure, liver and gall bladder diseases etc.

Two Madanī cures for indigestion

1. The one suffering from indigestion should recite the following Quranic verses, and then blow on his hands, and pass his hands on his abdomen. Likewise, he should recite the same verses and blow on his food before eating. اِنْ شَآءَاللّٰه عَزَّوَجَلَّ, Indigestion will be cured. Allah عَزَّوَجَلَّ says in the 43rd and 44th verses of Sūraĥ Al-Mursalāt (part 29):

كُلُوْا وَاشْرَبُوْا هَنِيْٓـًٔا بِمَا كُنْتُمْ تَعْمَلُوْنَ ﴿۴۳﴾ اِنَّا كَذٰلِكَ نَجْزِى الْمُحْسِنِيْنَ ﴿۴۴﴾

Eat and drink with relish, the reward of your doings. Indeed We recompense the righteous like this. *[Kanz-ul-Īmān (Translation of Quran)] (Part 29, Sūraĥ Al-Mursalāt, verse 43-44)*

2. Imām Kamāluddīn Damīrī رَحْمَةُ اللهِ تَعَالٰی عَلَيْه has narrated from a few eminent scholars, 'If a person has eaten something in excess and is fearful of indigestion, he should recite the following three times while passing his hands over his abdomen.

اَللَّيْلَةُ لَيْلَةُ عِيْدِىْ يَا كَرِشِىْ
وَرَضِىَ اللهُ عَنْ سَيِّدِىْ اَبِىْ عَبْدِ اللهِ الْقَرَشِىْ

O my stomach, tonight is the night of my Eid celebration and may Allah عَزَّوَجَلَّ be well pleased with our master, Shaykh Abū 'Abdullāĥ Qarashī رَحْمَةُ اللهِ تَعَالٰی عَلَيْه[1].'

[If he recites during the day, he should say اَلْيَوْمُ يَوْمُ عِيْدِىْ instead of اَللَّيْلَةُ لَيْلَةُ عِيْدِىْ.]
(Ḥayāt-ul-Ḥaywān-ul-Kubrā, vol. 1, pp. 460)

Medicinal cure for constipation

There are several treatments for constipation.

1. Skip a meal or two. اِنْ شَآءَاللّٰه عَزَّوَجَلَّ, This shall relieve the intestines and the stomach will get some rest as well.

2. Eat a decent amount of papaya.

3. Take 1 or 3 spoons of psyllium husk with water. If this does not improve the condition, increase the quantity of the husk. If constipation is reoccurring, repeat this twice or thrice a week.

4. Add half tea spoon of finely ground green tea to water and drink it before sleeping. If possible, do this daily for at least four months. اِنْ شَآءَاللّٰه عَزَّوَجَلَّ, Besides constipation, you will also be protected from various other illnesses. This is also beneficial to the improvement of memory.

---

[1] Shaykh Abū 'Abdullāĥ Qarashī Ĥāshimī عَلَيْهِ رَحْمَةُ اللّٰهِ الْقَوِی was among the eminent saints of Egypt. During the time of Shaykh 'Abdul Qādir Jīlānī رَحْمَةُ اللهِ تَعَالٰی عَلَيْه he was 17 years old. He passed away on 6 Żul-Ḥijjaĥ, 599 A.H. in Jerusalem. *(Fatāwā Africa, pp. 177)*

How to prevent students from dropping food?

Question: While eating, many students drop several grains of food. Please provide a remedy for this?

Answer: This is not limited to students only. This epidemic is widespread these days. There would hardly be only one fortunate Muslim out of thousands who does not waste grains of food. Students should be careful not to waste any bit of food. The management of the Madrasaĥ should be vigilant that every bit of food is eaten by the students because our Madāris are run by public endowments [Waqf].

During mealtimes, some students should serve as 'well wishers' by walking around[1]. They should tell the eating-students the Sunnaĥs of eating and drinking, good intentions of eating and the Du'ās recited before and after the eating. They should politely make the students pick up and eat the bits and pieces of rice and bread dropped on the dining-mat.

Proper way of breaking bread

Question: Please tell us the [proper] way of breaking the bread?

Answer: To break the bread with the right hand whilst holding it in the left one is a Sunnaĥ. In order to avoid dropping bread crumbs on the dining-mat, one should make a habit of extending his hand to the middle of the plate and then breaking a piece of the bread over it so that all the crumbs fall in the plate. The same care should also be taken when eating samosas, pastries, biscuits, cookies, [cakes] and any other food items which are flaky. It is appropriate to finish all pieces of a slice of bread before breaking the other bread.

How to use leftover bread

Question: What should we do with the leftover pieces of bread?

Answer: The charitable donations collected for Madāris can be used for Madāris only, not for anything else. Without permission from Sharī'aĥ, these leftover pieces of bread cannot be used for any other purpose. Store the leftover bread either in a freezer or spread them

[1] A Majlis has been set up in the Jāmi'āt and Madāris of Dawat-e-Islami for this purpose.

out in an open space to dry them out. After two or three days, cook them with curry. اِنْ شَآءَاللّٰہ عَزَّوَجَلَّ, A delicious meal will be prepared. Distribute its small amount at mealtime among each group of the eating students and they would relish it, اِنْ شَآءَاللّٰہ عَزَّوَجَلَّ.

Fallen food bits on dining-mat

Question: What should we do with the bits of food etc. which fall on the dining-mat?

Answer: Pick them up and eat them. At home, instead of wasting the leftover [or fallen] bits of food, feed them to the cows, goats, sparrows, chickens or cats. In this way, you will be able to refrain from disrespecting and wasting food.

How to make intention for eating?

Question: You have told us of making intentions before eating food; how should we make these intentions?

Answer: A Muslim should make good and pious intentions before performing any Mubāḥ act as he will be rewarded for every righteous intention, اِنْ شَآءَاللّٰہ عَزَّوَجَلَّ. Therefore, while eating, one should make the intention of gaining strength to carry out worship. However, this intention would only be valid if you eat less than your appetite. Overeating causes laziness, let alone gaining strength for worship. (For further elaboration on the intentions of eating, see pages 117 to 120 of this book).

Precautions of making tea

Question: Please tell us some precautions for drinking tea.

Answer: Tea is harmful to the patients of kidney and urine diseases. Its use should be curtailed. There are several prerequisites for making good tea: Milk and tea should be of good quality; the sugar, the tea, the cooking pot and the sieve should all be kept away from the aromas and smoke of the kitchen. If a pot has been used for making tea once and you need to make some more tea in the same pot right away, wash the pot properly before you reuse it. Utensils for making tea should be washed separately. The container used for storing tea should be tightly closed [air-tight], otherwise its original aroma will vanish.

Tea should be drunk shortly after being prepared. Its taste changes if reheated. The film which forms on the tea should be removed. It is said that if the film from 100 cups of tea is fed to a cat, it would die because of its poison [i.e. caffeine content].

صَلُّوْا عَلَى الْحَبِيْب صَلَّى اللهُ تَعَالٰى عَلٰى مُحَمَّد

Art of making tea

Question: Please also tell us how to make tea.

Answer: If you wish to drink milk-tea (without adding water) boil milk adequately with sugar in a pot. Then, add tea such that it turns saffron in colour. Let it come to a boil. Keep stirring with a spoon. Boil it two or three times. Now take it off the stove, sieve and serve. If you wish to have regular tea, then adequately boil water with milk and sugar in a pot. Add tea, and follow the method mentioned above. If you like, you can also add small cardamoms.

Can honey be added to tea?

Question: Can we add honey to tea?

Answer: Sure, you can. In fact, if you can afford, you should use honey instead of sugar. Usually, people add a lot of sugar to their tea and enjoy drinking it. Excessive use of this kind of tea is extremely harmful as this could result in diabetes. Those who relish cold drinks and ice creams usually become patients of diabetes. One cold drink contains about seven teaspoons of sugar and an ice cream is like a 'sugar bomb.' If you cannot add honey to your tea, then just reduce the amount of sugar by half.

Dental hygiene

Question: Teeth are usually stained yellow because of drinking tea. Is there any remedy for it?

Answer: A few minutes after you have drunk tea, pour some water in the cup and stir the water [to clean the cup from the inside]. Then take a sip. Use this sip of water to rinse the inside of your mouth by moving the water around and then drink it. Repeat this twice or thrice, till all the water and tea are finished from the cup. In this way, not a single drop of tea will go to waste; the cup will be rinsed clean and the teeth will also be protected from yellow stains. If you do not feel like drinking the water after rinsing your mouth, you may spit it out. The reason why I have told you to rinse your mouth a few minutes after having tea is that drinking cold water right after having hot tea is harmful to teeth. The quantity of water to be used for cup-rinsing and drinking should be very little. If you are able to do this every time you eat [or drink] any thing, your teeth will remain clean and your gums will also be protected from diseases, اِنْ شَآءَاللّٰہ عَزَّوَجَلَّ.

Gum bleeding is a common problem these days. One of its causes is that food particles get stuck in between the teeth and harden like a piece of stone. To use Miswāk or bite or chew anything in this condition causes gum bleeding. If the mouth is rinsed every time [in the manner explained above] after eating, your teeth will remain clean and you will be protected from gum bleeding and other gum and tooth diseases, اِنْ شَآءَاللّٰہ عَزَّوَجَلَّ. Overeating usually upsets the stomach, and causes several illnesses including gums-bleeding to some people. If you adopt moderation in eating, many chronic diseases and gum bleeding will amazingly be healed, اِنْ شَآءَاللّٰہ عَزَّوَجَلَّ. Otherwise, the experience is that the medicines provide a temporary relief and then the disease keeps recurring.

Cleaning yellow teeth

Question: What should a person do whose teeth are already stained yellow?

Answer: He should properly use Miswāk. Mix salt and baking soda in equal weight and rub this mixture very carefully on the teeth so that it does not come into contact with the gums. اِنْ شَآءَاللّٰہ عَزَّوَجَلَّ, Your teeth will amazingly be clean. Do not do this for several days consecutively. Those whose gums are weak or bleed should not do this.

صَلُّوْا عَلَی الْحَبِیْب صَلَّی اللّٰهُ تَعَالٰی عَلٰی مُحَمَّد

تُوْبُوْا اِلَی اللّٰه اَسْتَغْفِرُ اللّٰه

صَلُّوْا عَلَی الْحَبِیْب صَلَّی اللّٰهُ تَعَالٰی عَلٰی مُحَمَّد

If you wish to stay healthy...

Dear students! I advise you to reduce the use of spices and oil in food, and sugar in tea by half. اِنْ شَآءَاللّٰه عَزَّوَجَلَّ, This would improve your health and assist you in fulfilling your righteous Madanī ambition of gaining Islamic education. The following meal-schedule particularly designed for Jāmi'a-tul-Madīnaĥ can also be applied in houses.

Meal schedule for Dawat-e-Islami's Jāmi'a-tul-Madīnaĥ

Day	Breakfast	Lunch	Dinner
Friday	Tea & Rusk	Lentil-meat curry & bread	lentil-spinach curry, bread & tea
Saturday	Chickpea curry, bread & tea	White rice/Meat Pulāow[1]	Mixed vegetables (like squash, potatoes, turnips, sweet squash) & bread
Sunday	Chickpea curry, bread & tea	Lentil-squash curry & bread	Vegetable curry, bread & tea
Monday	Chickpea curry, bread & tea	Lentil curry & bread	Biryānī & tea
Tuesday	Tea & Rusk/bread & tea	Mixed vegetables & bread	Lentil-squash curry, bread & tea
Wednesday	Chickpea curry, bread & tea	Curry & rice/lentil curry & rice	Squash-potato curry, bread & tea
Thursday	Potato curry and bread	Barley porridge/potato-meat curry	Laubiyā beans, bread & tea

صَلُّوْا عَلَى الْحَبِيْب صَلَّى اللّٰهُ تَعَالٰى عَلٰى مُحَمَّد

[1] Indian pilaf

Fulfilment of desires

For the fulfilment of permissible desires, attainment of success and subjugation of enemies, recite the following invocations.

1. اَللّٰهُ رَبِّیْ لَا شَرِیْكَ لَهٗ[1]

Recite it 874 times with Ṣalāt-'Alan-Nabī ﷺ 11 times before and after the invocation. Recite it daily unless the desire is fulfilled. There is no specified time for it. Recite it in a folded-legs sitting posture facing the Qiblaĥ in the state of Wuḍū. Recite the same invocation in countless numbers whilst sitting, standing and walking whether with or without Wuḍū.

2. حَسْبُنَا اللّٰهُ وَنِعْمَ الْوَكِیْلُ[2]

Recite it 450 times with Ṣalāt-'Alan-Nabī ﷺ 11 times before and after the invocation. Recite it daily unless the desire is fulfilled. There is no specific time for it. At the time of anxiety, recite this invocation in abundance.

3. طُفَیْلِ حَضْرَتِ دَسْتْگِیْرْ دُشْمَنْ ہووے زِیْر[3]

Recite the foregoing invocation 111 times after Ṣalāt-ul-'Ishā with Ṣalāt-'Alan-Nabī ﷺ 11 times before and after the invocation. The foregoing three invocations are not only tried and trusted but also very simple. One should not be heedless of them. Whenever you have a desire, recite each of the three invocations in the exact described number. Neither increase nor decrease the numbers deliberately because a key with increased or decreased teeth will not open the lock. Recite the foregoing three invocations daily in the given order unless the desire is fulfilled. If the desire is not so important, recite the first two invocations 100 times daily with Ṣalāt-'Alan-Nabī ﷺ thrice before and after the invocation.

---

[1] **Translation:** Allah عَزَّوَجَلَّ is my Rab, no one is His partner.

[2] **Translation:** Allah عَزَّوَجَلَّ is All-Sufficient for us, and how excellent Disposer of affairs He is. *(Kanz-ul-Īmān) (Sūraĥ Āl-e-'Imrān, verse 173)*

[3] **Translation:** May the enemy be subjugated for the sake of Ghauš-e-A'ẓam رَضِیَ اللّٰهُ تَعَالٰی عَنْهُ!

Nuisance of not reciting Ṣalāt-'Alan-Nabī ﷺ

It is narrated that someone once had a dream in which he saw a deceased person wear the cap of the fire-worshippers on his head. The dreaming person asked the reason for this. The deceased replied, 'Whenever I heard or mentioned the blessed name of the Beloved Prophet صَلَّى اللّٰهُ تَعَالٰى عَلَيْهِ وَاٰلِهٖ وَسَلَّم, I did not use to recite Ṣalāt. This sin has caused my Īmān and mystical knowledge to be lost.'

(Sab'a Sanābil, pp. 35, Maktabaĥ Nūriyaĥ Razawiyyaĥ, Sukkur)

صَلُّوْا عَلَى الْحَبِيْب صَلَّى اللّٰهُ تَعَالٰى عَلٰى مُحَمَّد

Door of goodness close for six types of persons

1. Those not acting upon their knowledge.
2. Those not thanking Allah عَزَّوَجَلَّ for His favours.
3. Those not following in the footsteps of the pious despite adopting their company.
4. Those not taking any lesson despite taking part in the funeral of the deceased.
5. Those not making preparations for the Hereafter despite having wealth.
6. Those not repenting despite committing sins in abundance.

(Yaḥyā Bin Mu'āż رَضِىَ اللّٰهُ تَعَالٰى عَنْهُ)

Letter from Attar

To his Beloved Son

This letter is a collection of Madanī pearls for a healthy lifestyle. One who follows these suggestions will not be dependent on the doctor, اِنْ شَآءَالله عَزَّوَجَلَّ.

اَلۡحَمۡدُ لِلّٰہِ رَبِّ الۡعٰلَمِیۡنَ وَ الصَّلٰوۃُ وَ السَّلَامُ عَلٰی سَیِّدِ الۡمُرۡسَلِیۡنَ
اَمَّا بَعۡدُ فَاَعُوۡذُ بِاللّٰہِ مِنَ الشَّیۡطٰنِ الرَّجِیۡمِ ؕ بِسۡمِ اللّٰہِ الرَّحۡمٰنِ الرَّحِیۡمِ ؕ

Letter from Attar to his Beloved Son

بِسۡمِ اللّٰہِ الرَّحۡمٰنِ الرَّحِیۡمِ

I, Sag-e-Madīnaĥ, Muhammad Ilyas Attar Qadiri Razavi عُفِیَ عَنۡہُ greet my beloved son, a preacher of Dawat-e-Islami, Al-Ḥāj, Abū Usayd Aḥmad 'Ubayd Razā 'Aṭṭārī Madanī سَلَّمَہُ الۡغَنِی from the bottom of my heart. I present you with a delightful and fragrant Salām that has toured the streets of Karbalā, kissed the dome and minaret of the tomb of Imām Ḥusayn رَضِیَ اللہُ تَعَالٰی عَنۡہُ and is full of the blessings of the month of Muḥarram.

اَلسَّلَامُ عَلَیۡکُمۡ وَرَحۡمَۃُ اللهِ وَبَرَکَاتُہٗ اَلۡحَمۡدُلِلّٰہِ رَبِّ الۡعٰلَمِیۡنَ عَلٰی کُلِّ حَالٍ

It is narrated in a Ḥadīš that Sayyidunā Jarīr Bin 'Abdullāĥ رَضِیَ اللہُ تَعَالٰی عَنۡہُ has stated, 'I made Bay'at to the Holy Prophet صَلَّی اللہُ تَعَالٰی عَلَیۡہِ وَاٰلِہٖ وَسَلَّم to establish Ṣalāĥ, pay Zakāĥ and be a well-wisher of the common Muslims.' *(Ṣaḥīḥ Muslim, pp. 48, Ḥadīš 97)*

اَلۡحَمۡدُلِلّٰہ عَزَّوَجَلَّ, With the righteous intention of serving the Muslims and reaping its rewards, I have presented here some Madanī pearls on how to stay healthy, along with my Du'ā. If you desire a healthy life just for the enjoyment of worldly pleasures, then stop reading this letter. If, however, you intend to have good health so that you could carry out worship and preach Sunnaĥ, then read this letter completely making good intentions for earning reward in the Hereafter. Recite Ṣalāt-'Alan-Nabī and read on with good intentions:

صَلُّوۡا عَلَی الۡحَبِیۡب صَلَّی اللّٰہُ تَعَالٰی عَلٰی مُحَمَّد

May Allah عَزَّوَجَلَّ forgive me, you, our family and the entire Ummaĥ! May He عَزَّوَجَلَّ bless us with health and prosperity so that we may consistently serve Islam staying associated with Dawat-e-Islami! May Allah عَزَّوَجَلَّ remove all our diseases and make us a devotee of Madīnaĥ!

اٰمِین بِجَاہِ النَّبِیِّ الْاَمِین صَلَّى اللّٰهُ تَعَالٰى عَلَيْهِ وَاٰلِهٖ وَسَلَّم

I need you for the Madanī activities of Dawat-e-Islami. Please do not be careless and neglectful of your health because sometimes even a minor cut can turn into a deep wound, causing death. It is often observed that where medicine does not work, mere precaution produces amazing results. If new clothes are washed even once, their original charm and value no longer remain. The body of the person who has been cured by medicines is also like a 'washed cloth.' Therefore, as long as possible, it is wise to take food treatments and dietary precautions instead of medicines. Sometimes, medicines also have their side effects.

Nā Samajĥ bīmār ko amrat bĥī zaĥar āmayz ĥay
Such ĥay sau dawā kī aīk dawā parĥayz ĥay

For the unwise patient, even elixir is toxin
The truth is that abstinence is best medicine

General advice regarding food

While preparing any type of food, reduce the use of oil, chillies, salt and spices by half of the quantity usually used in your house. Reduce these things by half by weighing properly, not by approximation. Increase the use of vegetables. Meat stew should be eaten only twice a week and that too in small quantity. If meat stew is often cooked in your home, then make a habit to eat only one piece of meat. Do not eat until you are hungry. Properly chew food as intestines are not a substitute for teeth. Stop eating before your hunger has been fully satisfied. Give up the habit of eating till you are full. Avoid fruit juices that have artificial sweetness or have sugar mixed in them. Limit the use of foods which contain fat, superfine flour and sugar. Also refrain from ice creams, cold drinks, fried foods, commercially cooked dishes and fast foods. Furthermore, abstain from eating toffees, chocolate candies, Pān, Supari [betel nut pieces mixed with fennel seeds and flavours] and sweetened betel-nut pieces. Also avoid smoking and chewing tobacco.

If you wish to drink tea, drink only half a cup just two or three times a day. Add honey to tea instead of sugar. If you use sugar, cut its quantity by half. While making desserts and sweet dishes, use honey instead of sugar. If you cannot afford honey, then add sugar but only a quarter of the amount normally used. Those who have overly sweet tea, desserts and cold drinks are more prone to diabetes. (The patients of diabetes and blood pressure or other diseases should follow the advice of their doctors).

Walk for an hour everyday. If not possible, then walk for at least half an hour. اِنْ شَآءَاللّٰه عَزَّوَجَلَّ, Your lipid profile and weight will remain within the normal range. Furthermore, your belly will not bulge, your digestive system will improve, you will be protected from several ailments, and the diseases you are presently suffering from, will also get cured, اِنْ شَآءَاللّٰه عَزَّوَجَلَّ. You will find yourself more alert and active in performing righteous Madanī activities and worship, اِنْ شَآءَاللّٰه عَزَّوَجَلَّ. Though burdensome for Nafs, these [recommendations] of mine will prove to be very useful. Further, after you have got accustomed to them, you will find it easy to follow them, اِنْ شَآءَاللّٰه عَزَّوَجَلَّ.

Remember! The taste of food lasts just for a few seconds on the tongue. As soon as the morsel has gone down the throat, one can no longer enjoy its taste whether it is dried barley bread or luscious spicy rice Biryānī. Barley bread will make your life easier and Biryānī might make you visit the doctor's clinic repeatedly.

(When an obese person starts to lose weight, sometimes, he might suffer from increased level of uric acid. However, this gets normal gradually. Still it is recommended to get the uric acid level checked every six weeks. To drink water in abundance also reduces uric acid level).

Eat twice a day

If possible, instead of eating thrice a day, eat only twice a day. With the intention of applying Madanī guard[1] to the stomach, eat only when you are hungry and withdraw your hand from the food while you are still hungry. In between meals, do not eat any food from marketplace. If you feel hunger, eat an apple or some fruits. Even though fruits normally increase body weight, they also have tremendous benefits [for the body]. Those

---

[1] Madanī guard of the stomach is a term used in the Madanī environment of Dawat-e-Islami. It refers to the act of refraining from consuming Ḥarām food, and eating even Ḥalāl food less than one's appetite.

[Translator's Note]

who have diabetes or high level of triglycerides should strictly refrain from sweet fruits, dried fruits and root vegetables (that is, the vegetables growing underground such as carrots, reddish, potatoes, sweet potatoes, beets etc). Follow the advice of your doctor. For the pleasure of Allah عَزَّوَجَلَّ, make a habit of keeping the 'fast of [Prophet] Dāwūd عَلٰی نَبِیِّنَا وَعَلَیْہِ الصَّلٰوۃُ وَالسَّلَام' (that is, fast on alternate days). This would solve many problems caused by overeating.

Get your blood tested

Although the human body requires the following substances to a certain extent, their presence in excess is harmful to the body. Therefore, my advice is that all Islamic brothers and sisters should have the following blood tests done.

1. **Lipid Profile:** (This also contains a cholesterol test and is typically performed after 12 to 14 hours fasting).
2. **Glucose:** (If this reveals increased level when performed on an empty stomach, then also get it tested after a meal).
3. **Uric Acid.**
4. **Serum Creatinine:** (This test is done for the diagnosis of kidney damage and risk of kidney failure, if any. It can help give timely treatment to the patient. This should not be ignored as these days the cases of kidney failure are on the rise).

For the pleasure of Allah عَزَّوَجَلَّ, keep a fast and have these tests done after Ṣalāt-ul-'Aṣr - or eat dinner early in the evening and then have these tests performed before breakfast, the next morning. Show the reports to your doctor. A healthy person should have these tests performed at least once every six months. Those who are ill must get done the tests, without delay, recommended by their physician. They can also have the above tests performed with the consultation of their doctor.

It is not wise to avoid the test for fear that if the test-report reveals any disease, it would cause stress. Keep in mind that ignoring a disease is not its cure. This carelessness can result in severe problems in the future. Remember that some perfectly healthy looking young individuals suffer sudden heart failures, meeting their death. One of its major causes is the high level of their lipid profile [in blood].

Those with high level of cholesterol should refrain from these things

1. All types of fat.
2. Things made from clarified butter and cooking oil.
3. Egg-yolk
4. Salted snacks
5. Most bakery items.
6. Beef
7. Pizzas
8. Bread fried in oil.
9. Fried things such as omelette, kebabs, Samosay, Pakořay etc. [i.e. fried turnovers].
10. Cream
11. Butter
12. Ice creams etc.

(Since increased cholesterol level directly affects the heart, consult a doctor as well). There is no harm in eating chicken and fish, and using little amount of corn oil in cooking. If the doctor allows, there is no harm in eating fatless mutton or lamb-meat. According to a medical research, olive oil is beneficial to the patients with increased level of cholesterol as it removes the bad cholesterol [LDL] from blood. If there is an increase in triglycerides in blood, then refrain from all sweet dishes and shrimps.

Uric acid

If uric acid is above normal level, it can cause damage to the kidneys and the brain besides giving rise to the risk of skin diseases and joint pain. Its high level can also lead to liver cancer, مَعَاذَاللّٰہ عَزَّوَجَلَّ. According to a medical research, uric acid is increased in blood by the intake of the foods which have high concentrations of purine. Alcohol-based medications, diuretic medicines (i.e. the ones causing an increase in the flow of urine) and obesity also increase uric acid.

Uric acid patients should avoid...

One who has high level of uric acid should avoid all such food items which contain purine in excess. Purine is found in high concentrations in all types of meat and meat products, meat soup, fish, shrimps, Masūr Dāl [lentils], beans, green peas, spinach, cauliflower and cabbage etc.

Foods with moderate amount of purine

Milk and milk-containing products, eggs, sugar, wheat and wheat-containing foods, starch, sago, clarified butter, margarine, fruits and their juices, salads, most vegetables (besides a few), tomatoes, cold drinks etc. have all moderate amount of purine. According to some doctors, beef is more harmful to the patients of increased level of uric acid. For him, mutton is less harmful than beef, chicken is less injurious than mutton and fish causes less harm than chicken.

Cure for uric acid by water

Drink 40 glasses of water during a day and night. Do not worry even if the water you have drunk reaches up to the throat and the stomach is full. It will soon be discharged in the form of urine. إن شاء الله عزّوجلّ, You will see its benefit within a day. For example, if the normal range of uric acid is between 3 to 7 and your level is 8. Drink 40 glasses of water in a day and night, and it will come down to 7, إن شاء الله عزّوجلّ. If you continue this treatment for the next one or two days, your uric acid level will decrease by one unit per day, إن شاء الله عزّوجلّ. Although the amount of urine will temporarily be increased because of drinking more water, it causes no side effect. Rather, it would clean the stomach, intestines, urinary bladder and the kidneys etc., removing various impurities from the abdomen, إن شاء الله عزّوجلّ. Though there is no harm in eating on the day this treatment is done, remember that drinking water immediately after eating causes obesity, increasing body weight. Therefore, it is advised to drink water 1 or 2 hours after eating. (Also consult an expert and experienced doctor).

Madanī advice

Please paste this letter in your diary. Read out this letter to your family members and Islamic brothers. Suggest them to get the foregoing tests done. If needed, gift copies of this letter to others and earn reward. All the Islamic brothers and sisters are advised to read *Faīzān-e-Sunnat's* chapter entitled '*Excellence of Hunger*' from page 453 to 480. Even if you have already read it, read it again with good intentions.

وَالسَّلَامُ مَعَ الْاِکْرَام

Seeker of passion for Madīnaĥ, Baqī', forgiveness and neighbourhood of the Beloved and Blessed Prophet صَلَّى اللهُ تَعَالٰى عَلَيۡهِ وَاٰلِهٖ وَسَلَّم in Paradise without facing accountability.

Muhammad Ilyas Qadiri
22 Muḥarram-ul-Ḥarām 1427 A.H.

صَلُّوۡا عَلَى الۡحَبِيۡب صَلَّى اللهُ تَعَالٰى عَلٰى مُحَمَّد

تُوۡبُوۡا اِلَى الله اَسۡتَغۡفِرُ الله

صَلُّوۡا عَلَى الۡحَبِيۡب صَلَّى اللهُ تَعَالٰى عَلٰى مُحَمَّد

اَلْحَمْدُ لِلّٰهِ رَبِّ الْعٰلَمِيْنَ وَ الصَّلٰوةُ وَ السَّلَامُ عَلٰى سَيِّدِ الْمُرْسَلِيْنَ

اَمَّا بَعْدُ فَاَعُوْذُ بِاللّٰهِ مِنَ الشَّيْطٰنِ الرَّجِيْمِ ؕ بِسْمِ اللّٰهِ الرَّحْمٰنِ الرَّحِيْمِ ؕ

Sayyidunā Abul Ḥafṣ-ul-Kabīr عَلَيْهِ رَحْمَةُ اللّٰهِ الْقَدِيْر has stated, 'One who backbites a scholar (will come) on the Judgement Day (in such a state that) it will be written on his face; this person is despairing of the mercy of Allah عَزَّوَجَلَّ.' *(Mukāshafa-tul-Qulūb, fī Bayān Al-Ghībaĥ, pp. 71)*

Sayyidunā Abū Żar Ghifārī رَضِیَ اللّٰہُ تَعَالٰی عَنْہ has narrated, 'A scholar is a sign and evidence of Allah عَزَّوَجَلَّ on the earth; whoever criticizes a scholar will be ruined.' *(Kanz-ul-'Ummāl, vol. 10, pp. 77)*

A'lā Ḥaḍrat Imām Aḥmad Raza Khān عَلَيْهِ رَحْمَةُ الرَّحْمٰن has stated, 'To find fault with an Islamic scholar and object to him is Ḥarām. If, because of this, a person stays away from an Islamic scholar and gives up the acquisition of the knowledge of rulings from him, it is fatal for him.' *(Fatāwā Razawiyyaĥ, vol. 23, pp. 711)*

Fearful should be the unwise people who utter such insulting sentences about Islamic scholars as: 'Be careful from him, brother! He is an 'Allāmaĥ Sahib [scholar]!', 'Scholars are greedy', 'They are jealous of us', 'Because of us, no one cares about them', 'Leave him! He's only a Mawlvī', (مَعَاذَ اللّٰه عَزَّوَجَلَّ some people scornfully refer to scholars as), 'These Mullā people!', 'The scholars have made no endeavours for the cause of the Aĥl-e-Sunnat', (sometimes, dislike for the speech style is expressed like this), 'So and so delivers speech like a Mawlvī' etc.

Describing the different cases of the disrespect for an Islamic scholar with Shar'ī verdicts for each, A'lā Ḥaḍrat رَحْمَةُ اللّٰهِ تَعَالٰی عَلَيْه has stated, 'If someone speaks ill of an (Islamic) scholar for the reason that he is a scholar, then this is sheer Kufr [unbelief]. If he considers it Farḍ to treat the scholar with respect because of his religious knowledge but speaks ill of him or swears at him or looks down on him due to some worldly enmity, then he is a severe Fāsiq and Fājir [transgressor]. If he bears malice (towards the Islamic scholar) without any reason, then he is spiritually ill with a filthy inner self, and is likely to commit Kufr [unbelief].

اَلْحَمْدُ لِلّٰهِ رَبِّ الْعٰلَمِيْنَ وَ الصَّلٰوةُ وَ السَّلَامُ عَلٰى سَيِّدِ الْمُرْسَلِيْنَ

اَمَّا بَعْدُ فَاَعُوْذُ بِاللّٰهِ مِنَ الشَّيْطٰنِ الرَّجِيْمِ ؕ بِسْمِ اللّٰهِ الرَّحْمٰنِ الرَّحِيْمِ ؕ

Haji Mushtaq Attari

Excellence of Ṣalāt-'Alan-Nabī ﷺ

The Prophet of mankind, the Peace of our heart and mind, the most Generous and Kind صَلَّى اللهُ تَعَالٰى عَلَيْهِ وَاٰلِهٖ وَسَلَّم has stated, 'When the one who recites Ṣalāt upon me 100 times on Friday comes on the Judgement Day, he will be accompanied by such Nūr that will be sufficient for all the creation, if distributed.' *(Ḥilyat-ul-Auliyā, vol. 8, pp. 49, Ḥadīš 11341)*

صَلُّوْا عَلَى الْحَبِيْب   صَلَّى اللهُ تَعَالٰى عَلٰى مُحَمَّد

An excellent Na'at-reciter, a preacher of Dawat-e-Islami, Al-Ḥāj Abū 'Ubayd Qārī Muhammad Mushtāq Aḥmad 'Aṭṭārī عَلَيْهِ رَحْمَةُ اللهِ الْبَارِى, son of Maulānā Akhlāq Aḥmad, was born on Sunday, Ramadan 18, 1386 A.H. (January 1, 1967), in Bannu (Khyber Pakhtunkhwa, Pakistan). Before he settled in Bāb-ul-Madīnaĥ Karachi, he had lived in Sardarabad (Faisalabad, Pakistan). He served for many years as the Imām of Madīnaĥ Masjid, Orangi town, Bāb-ul-Madīnaĥ Karachi. Since 1995 until his demise, he also served as the Imām and orator of Jāmi' Masjid Kanz-ul-Īmān (Babri Chowk, Bāb-ul-Madīnaĥ, Karachi). He was a Ḥāfiẓ of the 8 parts of the Holy Quran and was an excellent Qārī.

He had completed four years of Dars-e-Niẓāmī but his religious knowledge was no less than a qualified and erudite Islamic scholar. He worked for many years as a senior auditor in the government accounts department. He taught English language in Jāmi'a-tul-Madīnaĥ (Sabz Market, Bāb-ul-Madīnaĥ, Karachi). اَلْحَمْدُ لِلّٰه عَزَّوَجَلَّ, He was privileged to perform Hajj and visit the Holy city of Madīnaĥ four times.

Agarchay dawlat-e-dunyā mayrī sab ĉhīn lī jāye
Mayray dil say na ĥargiz Yā Nabī صَلَّى اللّٰهُ تَعَالٰى عَلَيْهِ وَاٰلِهٖ وَسَلَّم *tayrī wilā niklay*

No matter all of my worldly wealth is taken away
But Prophet's devotion, from my heart, should never go away

Ḥājī Mushtāq 'Aṭṭārī عَلَيْهِ رَحْمَةُ الْبَارِى joins Madanī environment

اَلْحَمْدُ لِلّٰه عَزَّوَجَلَّ, Ḥājī Mushtāq 'Aṭṭārī was a religious-minded person even before joining Dawat-e-Islami's Madanī environment. He had a beard and was a Na'at reciter with a very pleasant voice. He himself narrated to me[1] as to how he joined Dawat-e-Islami's Madanī environment. He reported, 'When I attended Dawat-e-Islami's Sunnaĥ-Inspiring weekly Ijtimā' for the first time at its first Madanī Markaz, Gulzār-e-Ḥabīb Masjid, I began to leave at the end of the Ijtimā', like other brothers. As I was leaving, a bearded and turbaned Islamic brother approached me and shook hands with me warmly. I was impressed by the courteous and polite manner in which he had greeted me. Making individual effort, he managed to make me meet you (Amīr-e-Aĥl-e-Sunnat). Inspired, I joined the Madanī environment of Dawat-e-Islami, اَلْحَمْدُ لِلّٰه عَزَّوَجَلَّ.'

صَلُّوْا عَلَى الْحَبِيْب صَلَّى اللّٰهُ تَعَالٰى عَلٰى مُحَمَّد

Ḥājī Mushtāq 'Aṭṭārī عَلَيْهِ رَحْمَةُ الْبَارِى became Nigrān of Shūrā

اَلْحَمْدُ لِلّٰه عَزَّوَجَلَّ, Allah عَزَّوَجَلَّ had blessed Ḥājī Mushtāq عَلَيْهِ رَحْمَةُ اللّٰهِ الرَّزَّاق with a very pleasant voice. He would often recite Na'at in large Ijtimā'āt, overwhelming the devotees of Rasūl. He was also an excellent preacher, and had a tremendous enthusiasm for Madanī work. Allah عَزَّوَجَلَّ blessed him with higher ranks and in 2000 he was appointed as the Nigrān of Bāb-ul-Madīnaĥ Karachi, with the approval of all the Nigrāns of Karachi. The very same year, in the month of October, he was appointed as the Nigrān of the Markazī Majlis-e-Shūrā of Dawat-e-Islami.

[1] [The author, Amīr-e-Aĥl-e-Sunnat دَامَتْ بَرَكَاتُهُمُ الْعَالِيَه]

Rizā per Rab عَزَّوَجَلَّ *kī rāzī ĥayn tumĥāray ĥam bĥikārī ĥayn*
Ĥamārī ākhirat beĥtar banā do Yā Rasūlallāĥ صَلَّى اللهُ تَعَالٰى عَلَيْهِ وَاٰلِهٖ وَسَلَّم

We are content with the divine will, and are your devotees
Make our Hereafter better, Yā Rasūlallāĥ صَلَّى اللهُ تَعَالٰى عَلَيْهِ وَاٰلِهٖ وَسَلَّم

صَلُّوْا عَلَى الْحَبِيْب صَلَّى اللهُ تَعَالٰى عَلٰى مُحَمَّد

Holy Prophet ﷺ embraced his devotee Mushtāq

A few months before the demise of Ḥājī Mushtāq 'Aṭṭārī عَلَيْهِ رَحْمَةُ اللّٰهِ الْبَارِى, an Islamic brother sent me[1] a letter, mentioning the following statement under oath: 'I had a dream in which I found myself in front of the golden grilles of the tomb of the Holy Prophet صَلَّى اللهُ تَعَالٰى عَلَيْهِ وَاٰلِهٖ وَسَلَّم. As I peeped through one of the three holes of the golden grilles, I saw a faith-refreshing sight. I saw that the Holy Prophet صَلَّى اللهُ تَعَالٰى عَلَيْهِ وَاٰلِهٖ وَسَلَّم is accompanied by Sayyidunā Abū Bakr and Sayyidunā 'Umar رَضِىَ اللهُ تَعَالٰى عَنْهُمَا. Soon, Ḥājī Mushtāq 'Aṭṭārī عَلَيْهِ رَحْمَةُ اللّٰهِ الْبَارِى also appeared. The Holy Prophet صَلَّى اللهُ تَعَالٰى عَلَيْهِ وَاٰلِهٖ وَسَلَّم embraced him and said something which I didn't remember. I then woke up.'

Āp kay qadmaun say lag kar maut kī Yā Mustafa صَلَّى اللهُ تَعَالٰى عَلَيْهِ وَاٰلِهٖ وَسَلَّم
Ārzū kab āye gī bar baykas-o-majbūr kī

When will the desire of this helpless one to die at your feet
Come to fruition, Yā Mustafa صَلَّى اللهُ تَعَالٰى عَلَيْهِ وَاٰلِهٖ وَسَلَّم*! I plead*

صَلُّوْا عَلَى الْحَبِيْب صَلَّى اللهُ تَعَالٰى عَلٰى مُحَمَّد

Awaiting arrival of Ḥājī Mushtāq 'Aṭṭārī عَلَيْهِ رَحْمَةُ الْبَارِى

Since Ḥājī Mushtāq عَلَيْهِ رَحْمَةُ اللّٰهِ الرَّزَّاق was severely ill in those days, I gave the [above-mentioned] faith-refreshing dream containing letter to him so that he would be heartened. I am positive that the Prophet of mankind, the Peace of our heart and mind, the most

[1] [The author, Amīr-e-Aĥl-e-Sunnat دَامَتْ بَرَكَاتُهُمُ الْعَالِيَه]

Generous and Kind صَلَّى اللهُ تَعَالٰى عَلَيْهِ وَاٰلِهٖ وَسَلَّم was very gracious to him. An Islamic brother sent me a letter [whose summary is as follows]: 'اَلْحَمْدُ لِلّٰه عَزَّوَجَلَّ, On the night between Tuesday and Wednesday, I dreamt that the Noble Prophet صَلَّى اللهُ تَعَالٰى عَلَيْهِ وَاٰلِهٖ وَسَلَّم was seated in Masjid-un-Nabawī. Around him were other Prophets عَلَيْهِمُ السَّلَام, Khulafā-e-Rāshidīn رَضِىَ اللّٰهُ تَعَالٰى عَنْهُم, Imām Ḥasan and Ḥusayn رَضِىَ اللّٰهُ تَعَالٰى عَنْهُمَا and countless saints رَحِمَهُمُ اللّٰهُ تَعَالٰى. The air was silent. Turning to Sayyidunā Abū Bakr رَضِىَ اللهُ تَعَالٰى عَنْهُ, the Beloved and Blessed Prophet صَلَّى اللهُ تَعَالٰى عَلَيْهِ وَاٰلِهٖ وَسَلَّم said, '(O Abū Bakr!) Muhammad Mushtāq 'Aṭṭārī is about to come. I will shake hands with him and so should you. He will come here and recite Na'ats to us.' Then I woke up.' On Sha'bān 29, 1423 A.H. (November 5, 2002), I heard that Ḥājī Mushtāq 'Aṭṭārī عَلَيْهِ رَحْمَةُ اللّٰهِ الْبَارِى passed away between 8:15 to 8:30 a.m.

اِنَّا لِلّٰهِ وَ اِنَّاۤ اِلَيْهِ رٰجِعُوْنَ ۝

◆◆◆

صَلُّوْا عَلَى الْحَبِيْب صَلَّى اللهُ تَعَالٰى عَلٰى مُحَمَّد

Dear Islamic brothers! Listening to the above faith-refreshing dream, one can form the positive opinion that deceased Ḥājī Mushtāq 'Aṭṭārī عَلَيْهِ رَحْمَةُ اللّٰهِ الْبَارِى was an acknowledged Na'at reciter in the court of the Beloved and Blessed Prophet صَلَّى اللهُ تَعَالٰى عَلَيْهِ وَاٰلِهٖ وَسَلَّم, which is why glad tidings of 'awaiting his arrival' and 'hearing of Na'at' were given.

صَلُّوْا عَلَى الْحَبِيْب صَلَّى اللهُ تَعَالٰى عَلٰى مُحَمَّد

Funeral of Ḥājī Mushtāq 'Aṭṭārī عَلَيْهِ رَحْمَةُ الْبَارِى

The funeral Ṣalāĥ of Ḥājī Mushtāq عَلَيْهِ رَحْمَةُ اللّٰهِ الرَّزَّاق was offered in Nishtar park, Bāb-ul-Madīnaĥ Karachi. I (Amīr-e-Aĥl-e-Sunnat) have attended many funeral Ṣalāĥs but have never seen as many people as were in his funeral. Many touching sights were witnessed.

People who dearly loved him were crying bitterly. In the heart-breaking sighs and sobs of the grieved and bereaved people, Ḥājī Mushtāq عَلَيْهِ رَحْمَةُ اللّٰهِ الرَّزَّاق was laid to rest in Ṣaḥrā-e-Madīnaĥ (Bāb-ul- Madīnaĥ, Toll Plaza, Karachi) where grief and sorrow filled the air.

Shaĥā 'Aṭṭār kā piyārā ĥay yeĥ Mushtāq 'Aṭṭārī رَحْمَةُ اللّٰهِ تَعَالٰی عَلَيْه
Yeĥī muxdaĥ isay tum bĥī sunā do Yā Rasūlallāĥ صَلَّى اللّٰهُ تَعَالٰى عَلَيْهِ وَاٰلِهٖ وَسَلَّم

Mushtāq 'Aṭṭārī is very dear to 'Aṭṭār
Give him the same glad tidings, Yā Rasūlallāĥ صَلَّى اللّٰهُ تَعَالٰى عَلَيْهِ وَاٰلِهٖ وَسَلَّم

صَلُّوْا عَلَى الْحَبِيْب صَلَّى اللّٰهُ تَعَالٰى عَلٰى مُحَمَّد

A huge amount of Īṣāl-e-Šawāb

An Īṣāl-e-Šawāb Ijtimā' was held in the global Madanī Markaz, Faīzān-e-Madīnaĥ (Bāb-ul-Madīnaĥ Karachi) on the third day of his demise. A large number of Islamic brothers attended the Ijtimā'. A brief list of some of the Īṣāl-e-Šawāb donated by brothers from different cities is as follows:

Recitation of:

1. Quran; 13919 times.
2. The number of the recited various parts of the Quran, 5613.
3. Sūraĥ Yāsīn; 1038 times.
4. Sūraĥ Al-Mulk; 1140 times.
5. Sūraĥ Ar-Raḥmān; 165 times.
6. Sūraĥ Al-Muzzammil; 10 times.
7. Āyat-ul-Kursī; 33592 times.
8. various Sūraĥs; 93186 times.
9. Ṣalāt-'Alan-Nabī, 13888087 times.

10. Kalimaĥ Ṭayyibaĥ, 348400 times.

11. various Tasbīḥāt, 357200 times.

Ilāĥī عَزَّوَجَلَّ *maut āye Gumbad-e-Khazrā kay sāye mayn*
Madīnay mayn janāzaĥ dhūm say 'Aṭṭār kā niklay

O Almighty عَزَّوَجَلَّ*, grant death under the shadow of the green dome*
May 'Aṭṭār's funeral be held in Madīnaĥ

صَلُّوْا عَلَى الْحَبِيْب　　صَلَّى اللّٰهُ تَعَالٰى عَلٰى مُحَمَّد

Some aspects of character of Ḥājī Mushtāq 'Aṭṭārī عَلَيْهِ رَحْمَةُ الْبَارِى

In the light of his personal observation, an Islamic brother has expressed his views regarding the character of Al-Ḥāj Abū 'Ubayd Qārī Muhammad Mushtāq Aḥmad 'Aṭṭārī عَلَيْهِ رَحْمَةُ اللّٰهِ الْبَارِى. His views are as follows:

1. I lived for six years in Orangi town, Bāb-ul-Madīnaĥ Karachi, where Ḥājī Mushtāq عَلَيْهِ رَحْمَةُ اللّٰهِ الرَّزَّاق used to serve as a local Nigrān of Dawat-e-Islami. I never saw him backbite or rebuke anyone.

2. No matter how controversial or organizational issue (as regards Dawat-e-Islami's Madanī work) we were encountered with, he would always solve it wisely and softly.

3. No matter how hurtful things anyone said, he would remain cool, calm and collected.

4. He was very punctual. He would always keep his appointments.

5. Whenever he used to be invited for recitation of Na'at in an Ijtimā' or for conduction of Nikāḥ[1] with an offer of conveyance by the host, he would decline the offer saying that he would come on his own bike.

6. If the host ever offered him money for travelling expense, he would not accept it.

---

[1] Marriage ceremony. [Translator's Note]

7. My marriage was held on December 19, 1996. On my request, Ḥājī Mushtāq 'Aṭṭārī عَلَيْهِ رَحْمَةُ اللّٰهِ الْبَارِی came to Landhi (which is very far from Orangi town). He conducted my Nikāḥ ceremony in addition to reciting the Saĥrā (couplets of Du'ā for the bride and the groom). At the end, we insisted that he travel back to his house in the groom's car or in a taxi which we offered to arrange, but he declined and travelled by bus.

Ḥaḍrat-e-Mushtāq 'Aṭṭārī رَحْمَةُ اللّٰهِ تَعَالٰی عَلَيْه say ĥam ko piyār ĥay
اِنْ شَآءَاللّٰه عَزَّوَجَلَّ Do jaĥān mayn apnā bayřā pār ĥay

We love Mushtāq 'Aṭṭārī رَحْمَةُ اللّٰهِ تَعَالٰی عَلَيْه, indeed
اِنْ شَآءَاللّٰه عَزَّوَجَلَّ, We will succeed

صَلُّوْا عَلَى الْحَبِيْب صَلَّى اللّٰهُ تَعَالٰى عَلٰى مُحَمَّد

Desires fulfilled at shrine of Ḥājī Mushtāq 'Aṭṭārī عَلَيْهِ رَحْمَةُ الْبَارِی

اَلْحَمْدُ لِلّٰه عَزَّوَجَلَّ, Ḥājī Mushtāq عَلَيْهِ رَحْمَةُ اللّٰهِ الرَّزَّاق rests in Ṣaḥrā-e-Madīnaĥ, Bāb-ul-Madīnaĥ Karachi. Countless Islamic brothers from near and far visit his shrine, reaping blessings. An Islamic brother has narrated his own experience. He has stated: 'My wife was expectant. According to doctors, the unborn baby was a girl. Since I already had a girl, I desired a baby boy this time. I came to the shrine of Ḥājī Mushtāq عَلَيْهِ رَحْمَةُ اللّٰهِ الرَّزَّاق and made Du'ā over there. اَلْحَمْدُ لِلّٰه عَزَّوَجَلَّ, The medical report proved wrong and, by the grace of Allah عَزَّوَجَلَّ, my wife gave birth to a baby boy.

Mustafa صَلَّى اللّٰهُ تَعَالٰی عَلَيْهِ وَاٰلِهٖ وَسَلَّم kā ĥay jo bĥī dīwānaĥ
Us pay raḥmat mudām ĥotī ĥay

Whoever is a devotee of Mustafa صَلَّى اللّٰهُ تَعَالٰی عَلَيْهِ وَاٰلِهٖ وَسَلَّم
Is blessed with perpetual mercy

صَلُّوْا عَلَى الْحَبِيْب صَلَّى اللّٰهُ تَعَالٰى عَلٰى مُحَمَّد

Magic spell was cured

An Islamic brother has reported that he was under a magic spell. He visited the shrine of Ḥājī Mushtāq عَلَیْهِ رَحْمَةُ اللهِ الرَّزَّاق with other brothers and made Du'ā over there. He felt as if something has taken hold of him, but after a while, that feeling vanished and he was cured, اَلْحَمْدُ لِلّٰه عَزَّوَجَلَّ.

Sun lo ĥar aīk nayk shakhṣiyyat
Qābil-e-iḥtirām ĥotī ĥay

Listen! All pious people
Are worthy of respect

Yā Allah عَزَّوَجَلَّ! Forgive me, Ḥājī Muhammad Mushtāq 'Aṭṭārī عَلَیْهِ رَحْمَةُ اللهِ البَارِی, all brothers and sisters of Dawat-e-Islami and all Muslims!

اٰمِيْن بِجَاهِ النَّبِيِّ الْاَمِيْن صَلَّى اللهُ تَعَالٰى عَلَيْهِ وَاٰلِهٖ وَسَلَّم

صَلُّوْا عَلَى الْحَبِيْب صَلَّى اللهُ تَعَالٰى عَلٰى مُحَمَّد
تُوْبُوْا اِلَى الله اَسْتَغْفِرُ الله
صَلُّوْا عَلَى الْحَبِيْب صَلَّى اللهُ تَعَالٰى عَلٰى مُحَمَّد

پیٹ کا قفلِ مدینہ

Excellence of HUNGER

Madani Guard
of the Stomach

Shaykh-e-Tariqat Ameer-e-Ahl-e-Sunnat
the Founder of Dawat-e-Islami
Allamah Maulana Abu Bilal
MUHAMMAD ILYAS
Attar Qadiri Razavi دامت برکاتہم العالیہ

مکتبۃ المدینہ
MAKTABA TUL MADINAH
MC 1286

اَلْحَمْدُ لِلّٰهِ رَبِّ الْعٰلَمِيْنَ وَ الصَّلٰوةُ وَ السَّلَامُ عَلٰى سَيِّدِ الْمُرْسَلِيْنَ

اَمَّا بَعْدُ فَاَعُوْذُ بِاللّٰهِ مِنَ الشَّيْطٰنِ الرَّجِيْمِ ؕ بِسْمِ اللّٰهِ الرَّحْمٰنِ الرَّحِيْمِ ؕ

Excellence of Hunger

Satan will use every trick of his trade to keep you from reading this book, but you should counter his every deception and make an ardent effort to go through this chapter in its entirety. Perhaps you will be amazed to see its blessings.

Excellence of reciting Ṣalāt-'Alan-Nabī ﷺ

The Prophet of mankind, the Peace of our heart and mind, the most Generous and Kind صَلَّى اللهُ تَعَالٰى عَلَيْهِ وَاٰلِهٖ وَسَلَّم has said, 'Without doubt, your names along with your identity are presented before me, therefore, recite Ṣalāt (Durūd) upon me in eloquent words.' *(Muṣannaf 'Abdur Razzāq, vol. 2, pp. 214, Ḥadīš 3111)*

صَلُّوْا عَلَى الْحَبِيْب صَلَّى اللهُ تَعَالٰى عَلٰى مُحَمَّد

What does 'Madanī guard' of stomach mean?

Madanī guard of the stomach is to refrain from consuming Ḥarām food and to eat even Ḥalāl food less than one's appetite. The following health related saying of Ḥujjat-ul-Islam, Sayyidunā Imām Muhammad Ghazālī عَلَيْهِ رَحْمَةُ اللّٰهِ الْوَالِى is considered the most appropriate principle for those who wish to apply a Madanī guard on their stomach. The Imām رَحْمَةُ اللّٰهِ تَعَالٰى عَلَيْه has said, 'Whoever eats only when he is hungry and withdraws (his hand) from the food while still hungry, will never be in need of a doctor. Therefore, food should only be consumed when one is absolutely hungry.' *(Iḥyā-ul-'Ulūm, vol. 2, pp. 5)*

Yā Ilāĥī عَزَّوَجَلَّ! Payṫ kā Qufl-e-Madīnaĥ kar ‘aṭā
Az paey Ghauš-o-Razā رَحِمَهُمَا اللهُ تَعَالٰى kar bĥūk kā gawĥar ‘aṭā

O Almighty عَزَّوَجَلَّ, bless us with the Madanī guard for our stomach
For the sake of Ghauš and Razā رَحِمَهُمَا اللهُ تَعَالٰى grant us the gem of hunger

Intentional hunger

Dear Islamic brothers! Although it is permissible to eat until one is full, countless religious and worldly benefits lie in applying a Madanī guard on the stomach. Abstaining from food in compulsion when it is not available is not something remarkable, but refraining from eating and staying hungry for the pleasure of Allah عَزَّوَجَلَّ when food is available in abundance, is indeed an extraordinary feat. It is stated that the Noble Rasūl صَلَّى اللهُ تَعَالٰى عَلَيْهِ وَاٰلِهٖ وَسَلَّم would intentionally remain hungry. *(Shu’ab-ul-Īmān, vol. 5, pp. 26, Ḥadīš 5640)*

Lūṫ lay raḥmat, lagā Qufl-e-Madīnaĥ payṫ kā
Pāye gā Jannat, lagā Qufl-e-Madīnaĥ payṫ kā

Gain divine grace by applying Madanī guard on the stomach
Attain Paradise by applying Madanī guard on the stomach

صَلُّوْا عَلَى الْحَبِيْب صَلَّى اللهُ تَعَالٰى عَلٰى مُحَمَّد

Neighbourhood of the Holy Prophet صَلَّى اللهُ تَعَالٰى عَلَيْهِ وَاٰلِهٖ وَسَلَّم in Paradise

Indeed, intentional hunger is a great Sunnaĥ of our Beloved Prophet صَلَّى اللهُ تَعَالٰى عَلَيْهِ وَاٰلِهٖ وَسَلَّم and words cannot express the excellence of Sunnaĥ. The Holy Prophet صَلَّى اللهُ تَعَالٰى عَلَيْهِ وَاٰلِهٖ وَسَلَّم has stated, ‘He who loves my Sunnaĥ, loves me, and he who loves me will be with me in Paradise.’ *(Mishkāt-ul-Maṣābīḥ, pp. 30)*

In Sūraĥ Al-Aḥqāf, verse 20, Allah عَزَّوَجَلَّ says:

اَذْهَبْتُمْ طَيِّبٰتِكُمْ فِيْ حَيَاتِكُمُ الدُّنْيَا وَاسْتَمْتَعْتُمْ بِهَا ۚ فَالْيَوْمَ تُجْزَوْنَ عَذَابَ الْهُوْنِ

You have exhausted your pure things in your worldly life and used it (fully), therefore, today you shall be awarded the humiliating punishment.

[Kanz-ul-Īmān (Translation of Quran)] (Part 26, Sūraĥ Al-Aḥqāf, verse 20)

Blessed hunger of the Holy Prophet ﷺ

Commenting on the foregoing verse, the spiritual successor of A'lā Ḥaḍrat Imām Aḥmad Razā Khān عَلَيْهِ رَحْمَةُ الرَّحْمٰن, Ṣadr-ul-Afāḍil Shaykh Na'īmuddīn Murādābādī عَلَيْهِ رَحْمَةُ اللّٰهِ الْهَادِى has stated in his renowned exegesis of the Holy Quran, *Khazāin-ul-'Irfān*: In this verse, Allah عَزَّوَجَلَّ has reprimanded the unbelievers for having worldly pleasures. Therefore, the Holy Prophet صَلَّى اللّٰهُ تَعَالٰى عَلَيْهِ وَاٰلِهٖ وَسَلَّم and his companions abstained from worldly pleasures. In *Ṣaḥīḥ Bukhārī* and *Ṣaḥīḥ Muslim*, it is stated that until the apparent demise of the Holy Prophet صَلَّى اللّٰهُ تَعَالٰى عَلَيْهِ وَاٰلِهٖ وَسَلَّم, the blessed family never ate bread made from barley for two consecutive days. It is also mentioned in a Ḥadīš that at times the whole month passed, but fire would not burn on the stove (for cooking food). The blessed household would merely survive on water and a few dates. Sayyidunā 'Umar Fārūq رَضِىَ اللّٰهُ تَعَالٰى عَنْهُ has quoted that the Holy Prophet صَلَّى اللّٰهُ تَعَالٰى عَلَيْهِ وَاٰلِهٖ وَسَلَّم has stated, 'O people! If I had wanted, I would have eaten better than you and worn better clothes than you, but I want to reserve my pleasures and comforts for my Hereafter.' *(Khazāin-ul-'Irfān, pp. 907)*

صَلُّوْا عَلَى الْحَبِيْب صَلَّى اللّٰهُ تَعَالٰى عَلٰى مُحَمَّد

Hungry for many nights

Sayyidunā 'Abdullāĥ Ibn 'Abbās رَضِىَ اللّٰهُ تَعَالٰى عَنْهُ has narrated that the Prophet of Raḥmaĥ, the Intercessor of Ummaĥ, the Owner of Jannaĥ صَلَّى اللّٰهُ تَعَالٰى عَلَيْهِ وَاٰلِهٖ وَسَلَّم used to remain hungry for many nights in succession. His blessed household often did not have anything to eat at night and whenever they would get something to eat, it was mostly bread made from barley. *(Jāmi' Tirmiżī, vol. 4, pp. 160, Ḥadīš 2367)*

Food of blessed family

Sayyidunā Anas رَضِىَ اللّٰهُ تَعَالٰى عَنْهُ has stated that the Holy Prophet صَلَّى اللّٰهُ تَعَالٰى عَلَيْهِ وَاٰلِهٖ وَسَلَّم pawned his armour for barley. He has further stated that he presented some cooked and melted fat with some barley bread in the respected court of the Holy Prophet صَلَّى اللّٰهُ تَعَالٰى عَلَيْهِ وَاٰلِهٖ وَسَلَّم. He heard the Holy Prophet صَلَّى اللّٰهُ تَعَالٰى عَلَيْهِ وَاٰلِهٖ وَسَلَّم say, 'My entire family has never had one 'Sā' (about two kilos and three quarters) of food in the morning and in the evening.' Keep in mind that the family of the Beloved and Blessed Prophet صَلَّى اللّٰهُ تَعَالٰى عَلَيْهِ وَاٰلِهٖ وَسَلَّم consisted of nine different homes. *(Ṣaḥīḥ Bukhārī, vol. 3, pp. 158, Ḥadīš 2508)*

Dear Islamic brothers! This is the remarkable condition of the Noble Rasūl صَلَّى اللهُ تَعَالٰى عَلَيْهِ وَاٰلِهٖ وَسَلَّم who was given the keys to the treasures of both the worlds. The Prophet of mankind, the Peace of our heart and mind, the most Generous and Kind صَلَّى اللهُ تَعَالٰى عَلَيْهِ وَاٰلِهٖ وَسَلَّم adopted Faqr [poverty] intentionally. Otherwise, by Allah عَزَّوَجَلَّ, whoever gets anything, gets it as the Ṣadaqaĥ of the Noble Prophet صَلَّى اللهُ تَعَالٰى عَلَيْهِ وَاٰلِهٖ وَسَلَّم and his spiritual light reaches everything in the universe.

Spiritual insight

It is said that a saint once picked up a piece of bread to eat. When he looked at it with his spiritual insight, he realized that a ray of light emerged from it. When he focused on the direction of the light going upwards, he saw that the light (Nūr) was actually linked to a ray of light of the Beloved Mustafa صَلَّى اللهُ تَعَالٰى عَلَيْهِ وَاٰلِهٖ وَسَلَّم. On looking closer, he discovered that the Nūr of the Holy Prophet صَلَّى اللهُ تَعَالٰى عَلَيْهِ وَاٰلِهٖ وَسَلَّم reached every worldly favour (Na'mat). *(Al-Abrīz, pp. 229)*

Two stones tied to stomach

Sayyidunā Abū Ṭalḥaĥ رَضِىَ اللهُ تَعَالٰى عَنْهُ has narrated that some of the companions once complained to the Holy Prophet صَلَّى اللهُ تَعَالٰى عَلَيْهِ وَاٰلِهٖ وَسَلَّم about their hunger and showed him the stones they had tied to their stomachs. Seeing this, the Beloved and Blessed Prophet صَلَّى اللهُ تَعَالٰى عَلَيْهِ وَاٰلِهٖ وَسَلَّم raised his blessed clothing - revealing the two stones tied to his blessed stomach. Sayyidunā Imām Tirmiżī رَضِىَ اللهُ تَعَالٰى عَنْهُ has stated that stones were tied on the blessed stomach due to severe hunger and weakness. *(Shamāil-e-Tirmiżī, pp. 169, Ḥadīš 372)*

Āp صَلَّى اللهُ تَعَالٰى عَلَيْهِ وَاٰلِهٖ وَسَلَّم bĥūkay raĥay aur payt pay pattĥar bāndĥay
Ĥam ghulāmaun ko milay khuwān Madīnay wālay صَلَّى اللهُ تَعَالٰى عَلَيْهِ وَاٰلِهٖ وَسَلَّم

The Prophet صَلَّى اللهُ تَعَالٰى عَلَيْهِ وَاٰلِهٖ وَسَلَّم remains hungry with stones tied on his blessed stomach
Yet blesses the servants with delicious cuisines

صَلُّوْا عَلَى الْحَبِيْب صَلَّى اللهُ تَعَالٰى عَلٰى مُحَمَّد

Attainment of respect

Sayyidunā Abū Bujayr رَضِیَ اللهُ تَعَالٰی عَنْهُ has narrated that the Beloved and Blessed Prophet صَلَّى اللهُ تَعَالٰى عَلَيْهِ وَاٰلِهٖ وَسَلَّم once felt extreme hunger. He صَلَّى اللهُ تَعَالٰى عَلَيْهِ وَاٰلِهٖ وَسَلَّم took a stone, tied it to his blessed stomach and said, 'Beware! There are many people who eat delicious food and have a lavish lifestyle in this world but, on the Day of Judgement, they will be hungry and naked. Beware! There are many people who strive to become honourable, yet they are gathering provisions of humiliation. Beware! There are many people who are seen humiliating themselves but this is a means of respect for them.' *(Al-Mawāĥib-ul-Ladunniyyaĥ, vol. 2, pp. 123)*

Affectionate sentiments

Dear Islamic brothers! May our lives be sacrificed on the glory and greatness of the Merciful Prophet صَلَّى اللهُ تَعَالٰى عَلَيْهِ وَاٰلِهٖ وَسَلَّم! He صَلَّى اللهُ تَعَالٰى عَلَيْهِ وَاٰلِهٖ وَسَلَّم had great passion for remaining hungry but we, on the other hand, the so-called devotees, are deprived of this Sunnaĥ. If our meal is ever delayed or it is not to our liking, then we start to argue with our family-members. If only we would also adopt intentional hunger and, when feeling intense hunger, gain the honour of tying a stone around our stomach with the intention of acting upon the Sunnaĥ. I wish, if only I were not a human but a stone of the blessed street of the Holy Prophet صَلَّى اللهُ تَعَالٰى عَلَيْهِ وَاٰلِهٖ وَسَلَّم. Alas! If only I were the stone lying in the path where he صَلَّى اللهُ تَعَالٰى عَلَيْهِ وَاٰلِهٖ وَسَلَّم would pass blessing me with kissing his sacred soles. I dare not have the desire to be the stone tied on his blessed stomach, but at least if only I were the stone lying next to the sacred one picked up by him, and as he would stretch his blessed hand to take that sacred stone, I would have the privilege of kissing his blessed hand!

Hunger of Prophet Mūsā عَلَيْهِ السَّلَام

When Sayyidunā Mūsā Kalīmullāĥ عَلٰى نَبِيِّنَا وَعَلَيْهِ الصَّلٰوةُ وَالسَّلَام arrived at the well of Madyan, he was so weak that the green colour of the vegetable he had last consumed was visible from outside his blessed stomach. *(Shamāil-e-Rasūl, pp. 121)* It is also narrated that he عَلَيْهِ السَّلَام did not eat anything during the forty days when he عَلَيْهِ السَّلَام had the privilege of speaking to Allah عَزَّوَجَلَّ. *(Iḥyā-ul-'Ulūm, vol. 3, pp. 91)*

Hunger of Prophet Dāwūd عَلَيْهِ السَّلَام

Sayyidunā Qāḍī 'Iyāḍ رَضِیَ اللہُ تَعَالٰی عَنْہُ has stated, 'The clothing of Prophet Sayyidunā Dāwūd عَلٰی نَبِیِّنَا وَ عَلَیْہِ الصَّلٰوۃُ وَالسَّلَام was made from wool and his bedding from animal hair. He عَلَیْہِ السَّلَام used to eat barley-bread with salt.' *(Shamāil-e-Rasūl, pp. 121)*

Hunger of Prophet 'Īsā عَلَيْهِ السَّلَام

Sayyidunā 'Īsā عَلٰی نَبِیِّنَا وَ عَلَیْہِ الصَّلٰوۃُ وَالسَّلَام never built a house for living. He عَلَیْہِ السَّلَام would rest wherever he felt sleepy. He عَلَیْہِ السَّلَام used to wear clothing made from animal hair and eat the leaves of trees. *(Shamāil-e-Rasūl, pp. 121)*

Hunger of Prophet Yaḥyā عَلَيْهِ السَّلَام

Sayyidunā Yaḥyā عَلٰی نَبِیِّنَا وَ عَلَیْہِ الصَّلٰوۃُ وَالسَّلَام would consume wet grass as his food. He عَلَیْہِ السَّلَام used to weep so much in the fear of Allah عَزَّوَجَلَّ that the tears had left marks on his blessed cheeks. *(Shamāil-e-Rasūl, pp. 121)*

Fāqa-e-Anbiyā kay ṣadaqay mayn
Lażżat-e-Nafs say bachā Yā Rab عَزَّوَجَلَّ

O Allah عَزَّوَجَلَّ*! For the sake of Prophet's starvation*
Save us from desire's satisfaction

صَلُّوْا عَلَی الْحَبِیْب صَلَّی اللهُ تَعَالٰی عَلٰی مُحَمَّد

Sayyidatunā 'Āishaĥ رَضِیَ اللہُ عَنْهَا would cry

Sayyidunā Masrūq رَضِیَ اللہُ تَعَالٰی عَنْہُ has said that once he went to the house of the Noble mother of the believers, Sayyidatunā 'Āishaĥ رَضِیَ اللہُ تَعَالٰی عَنْہَا. She ordered that food be brought for him. She رَضِیَ اللہُ تَعَالٰی عَنْہَا then said, 'Whenever I eat food to my full stomach, I feel like crying.' 'Why?' He asked. She رَضِیَ اللہُ تَعَالٰی عَنْہَا replied, 'I remember the Holy Prophet صَلَّی اللہُ تَعَالٰی عَلَیْہِ وَاٰلِہٖ وَسَلَّم who left us in such a state that he صَلَّی اللہُ تَعَالٰی عَلَیْہِ وَاٰلِہٖ وَسَلَّم never ate meat or bread twice a day to his full stomach.' *(Jāmi' Tirmiżī, vol. 4, pp. 159, Ḥadīš 2363)*

'Āishaĥ Ṣiddīqaĥ رَضِیَ اللہُ تَعَالٰی عَنْہَا *rawtī ťhīn Nabī* صَلَّی اللہُ تَعَالٰی عَلَیْہِ وَاٰلِہٖ وَسَلَّم *kī bĥūk per*
Ĥāye! Bĥartayn ĥayn ghiżāyaīn ĥam shikam mayn ťhūns kar

'Āishaĥ Ṣiddīqaĥ cried remembering the hunger of the Prophet صَلَّی اللہُ تَعَالٰی عَلَیْہِ وَاٰلِہٖ وَسَلَّم
But alas! We are stuffing ourselves with food and beverage

True devotees should reflect

Dear Islamic brothers! Sayyidatunā 'Āishaĥ رَضِیَ اللہُ تَعَالٰی عَنْہَا would cry if she ever ate food to her full stomach. Her condition showed her intense love for the Beloved and Blessed Prophet صَلَّی اللہُ تَعَالٰی عَلَیْہِ وَاٰلِہٖ وَسَلَّم. On the contrary, we keep eating voraciously until our stomach is full, but our desire is not satisfied. Remember that whenever you read or hear about the righteous saints' eating to a full stomach, it means that they filled only one third of the stomach. This is the difference between our full stomach and theirs.

Our Islamic sisters should also learn a lesson from the devotion of Sayyidatunā 'Āishaĥ رَضِیَ اللہُ تَعَالٰی عَنْہَا. If our Islamic sisters join the Madanī environment, attend their local weekly Sunnaĥ-Inspiring Ijtimā', fill in the booklet of Madanī In'āmāt daily, practicing Fikr-e-Madīnaĥ and submit it to their responsible Islamic sister each month, then اِنْ شَآءَاللہ عَزَّوَجَلَّ they will reap innumerable blessings. Listen to a faith-refreshing account of an Islamic sister of Dawat-e-Islami.

Story of an Islamic sister

An Islamic brother from Sanghar (Bāb-ul-Islam, Sindh, Pakistan) made the following statement under oath: My sister, daughter of 'Abdul Ghaffār 'Aṭṭārī, had cancer. Her condition deteriorated slowly. As per the advice of doctors, we arranged for her surgery. Because of the operation, her condition improved a little but after about a year, she became severely ill once again. She was admitted to Rajputana Hospital (Hyderabad, Sindh Pakistan). After a week, her condition became extremely serious. Suddenly, she began to recite the sacred Kalimaĥ (statement of faith) aloud and, from time to time, she would also say اَلصَّلٰوۃُ وَالسَّلَامُ عَلَیْكَ یَا رَسُوْلَ اللہ وَعَلٰی اٰلِكَ وَاَصْحَابِكَ یَا حَبِیْبَ اللہ. Her reciting of 'لَآ اِلٰهَ اِلَّا اللہُ مُحَمَّدٌ رَّسُوْلُ اللہ' echoed in the entire room. It was a unique faith-refreshing scene. The visitors also began to recite the Kalimaĥ and Ṣalāt-'Alan-Nabī with her instead of asking about her condition. The doctors and staff were amazed because they had normally seen the patients cry in agony but this pious patient was lost in the remembrance of Allah عَزَّوَجَلَّ instead of writhing in pain. She remained in the same condition for about 12 hours, and when the Ażān of Maghrib Ṣalāĥ was about to be uttered, she passed away reciting the sacred Kalimaĥ.

May Allah عَزَّوَجَلَّ have mercy on her and forgive us without accountability for her sake!

آمِين بِجَاهِ النَّبِيِّ الْاَمِين صَلَّى اللهُ تَعَالٰى عَلَيْهِ وَاٰلِهٖ وَسَلَّم

اَلْحَمْدُلِلّٰه عَزَّوَجَلَّ! This Islamic sister attained tremendous blessings from the Madanī environment of Dawat-e-Islami. By Allah عَزَّوَجَلَّ! The one who leaves this world reciting the Kalimaĥ is indeed fortunate, as the Prophet of mankind, the Peace of our heart and mind, the most Generous and Kind صَلَّى اللهُ تَعَالٰى عَلَيْهِ وَاٰلِهٖ وَسَلَّم has stated, 'He whose last words are "لَآ اِلٰهَ اِلَّا اللّٰهُ" will enter Paradise.' *(Sunan Abī Dāwūd, vol. 3, pp. 132, Ḥadīš 3116)*

Eating just once every two days

The hunger of our Holy Prophet صَلَّى اللهُ تَعَالٰى عَلَيْهِ وَاٰلِهٖ وَسَلَّم was intentional. The Beloved and Blessed Rasūl صَلَّى اللهُ تَعَالٰى عَلَيْهِ وَاٰلِهٖ وَسَلَّم has stated, 'My Creator presented me with the option of turning the mountains around Makka-tul-Mukarramaĥ into gold for me but I said, 'O Allah عَزَّوَجَلَّ! I wish that I eat one day and remain hungry the next so that when I am hungry, I plead and remember You, and when I eat, I thank and glorify You.' *(Jāmi' Tirmiżī, vol. 4, pp. 55, Ḥadīš 2354)*

Salām un per shikam bĥar kar kabĥī kĥānā na kĥātay tĥay
Salām un per gham-e-Ummat mayn jo ānsū baĥātay tĥay

Salutations for him who did not eat to his satisfaction
Salutations for him who wept for his nation

صَلُّوْا عَلَى الْحَبِيْب صَلَّى اللهُ تَعَالٰى عَلٰى مُحَمَّد

Eating once a day

It is a Sunnaĥ to eat once a day. Sayyidunā Abū Sa'īd Khudrī رَضِیَ اللهُ تَعَالٰی عَنْهُ has narrated that when the Noble Prophet صَلَّی اللهُ تَعَالٰی عَلَیْهِ وَاٰلِهٖ وَسَلَّم would eat in the morning, he would not eat in the evening and when he ate in the evening, he would not eat in the morning. *(Kanz-ul-'Ummāl, vol. 7, pp. 39, Ḥadīš 18173)*

How is it to eat three times a day?

Dear Islamic brothers! It has become a routine to eat three times a day. Although this is not a sin, it is not a Sunnaĥ either. This habit has developed due to the desire of eating and drinking. Keep in mind that the more one eats, the more accountable he will have to be on the Day of Judgement. To eat only once a day is the habitual Sunnaĥ of our Beloved Prophet صَلَّی اللهُ تَعَالٰی عَلَیْهِ وَاٰلِهٖ وَسَلَّم. By the grace of Allah عَزَّوَجَلَّ, acting upon this Sunnaĥ, many pious saints رَحِمَهُمُ اللّٰهُ تَعَالٰی routinely ate just once a day. If one does not adopt this habit, he is not blameworthy. However, there is a matter of concern for such devotees of Rasūl who yearn to follow and propagate Sunnaĥ. Regretfully, some people consume food four or five times a day. Such people often have stomach ailments. Sayyidatunā 'Āishaĥ Ṣiddīqaĥ رَضِیَ اللهُ تَعَالٰی عَنْهَا has narrated that the first Bid'aĥ (innovation in religion) which took place after the apparent demise of the most Honourable Prophet صَلَّی اللهُ تَعَالٰی عَلَیْهِ وَاٰلِهٖ وَسَلَّم was that people started eating to a full stomach. When people fill their stomachs, their Nafs becomes rebellious towards worldly things. (Bear in mind that here Bid'aĥ refers to Bid'aĥ Mubāḥaĥ, i.e. permissible innovation). *(Qūt-ul-Qulūb, vol. 2, pp. 327)*

Satanic deception: On the one hand it is described as a Sunnaĥ to eat once a day, but on the other, Saḥarī and Ifṭārī which consist of two meals are also considered Sunnaĥ. What is the answer to this?

Cure for satanic deception: There is no doubt that Saḥarī and Ifṭārī are both Sunnaĥ. The literal meaning of Ifṭār is 'to break fast.' Therefore, if one swallows only a chickpea, his Ifṭār is valid. Stuffing oneself with food at Saḥarī and Ifṭārī is not a Sunnaĥ. Instead, one can do Ifṭārī and Saḥarī with a mere date or with a few sips of water. If a person consumes one meal during the day such as a curry with bread and then drinks three cups of tea at different times during the same day or eats a single date three times, he would still be considered to have taken just a single meal that day. Similarly, if a person eats a few dates or drinks some water during Ifṭār and consumes a meal at Saḥarī, he would also be considered to have eaten only once that day. In this manner, one would be able to fulfil not only the Sunnaĥ of eating once a day but also that of doing Saḥarī and Ifṭār. However, if a person eats many fruits and other things at Ifṭār, it will be considered a complete meal. Now, if that person eats in Saḥarī too, then he would be considered to have eaten twice that day. Nowadays, the Jamā'at of Ṣalāt-ul-Maghrib is often delayed in Masājid during the sacred month of Ramadan. Listen to the ascetic manner in which A'lā Ḥaḍrat, Imām Aḥmad Razā Khān عَلَيْهِ رَحْمَةُ الرَّحْمٰن would perform his Saḥarī and Ifṭārī.

Eating once and fasting

The honourable Shaykh Muhammad Ḥusayn Sahib Mīraṫĥī رَحْمَةُ اللهِ تَعَالٰی عَلَيْه has stated, 'I once attended I'tikāf from the 20th of Ramadan. When A'lā Ḥaḍrat رَحْمَةُ اللهِ تَعَالٰی عَلَيْه came to the Masjid, he said, 'I also wish to perform I'tikāf, but I cannot find time (due to my religious responsibilities).' At last, on the 26th of Ramadan, he رَحْمَةُ اللهِ تَعَالٰی عَلَيْه also joined in I'tikāf.' Maulānā Muhammad Ḥusayn Mīraṫĥī goes onto say, 'Although A'lā Ḥaḍrat رَحْمَةُ اللهِ تَعَالٰی عَلَيْه would break his fast with a few dates, he was not seen eating any meal. At Saḥarī, a small bowl of Firnī (a sweet dish) and that of Chaṫnī (a sauce) would be served to him, and he رَحْمَةُ اللهِ تَعَالٰی عَلَيْه would eat them. One day, I asked him, 'Your honour! What is the combination between Firnī and Chaṫnī?' He رَحْمَةُ اللهِ تَعَالٰی عَلَيْه replied, 'It is a Sunnaĥ to begin and end the meal with salt; this is why the Chaṫnī is served.' *(Ḥayāt-e-A'lā Ḥaḍrat, vol. 1, pp. 41)*

سُبْحٰنَ اللّٰـه عَزَّوَجَلَّ! The reviver of Sunnaĥ, Sayyidī A'lā Ḥaḍrat رَحْمَةُ اللهِ تَعَالٰی عَلَيْه used to eat a salty sauce before and after the sweet dish to act upon Sunnaĥ. To eat a little salt or a salty sauce before and after eating food protects against seventy diseases.

Yā Ilāĥī عَزَّوَجَلَّ! Mujĥ ko bĥī kar bĥūk kī na'mat 'aṭā
Az ṭufayl-e-Sayyidī-o-Murshidī Aḥmad Razā رَحْمَةُ اللهِ تَعَالٰی عَلَيْه

For the sake of my spiritual master, Imām Aḥmad Razā رَحْمَةُ اللهِ تَعَالٰی عَلَيْه
Bless me with the favour of hunger, O Allah عَزَّوَجَلَّ!

Fasting with one meal

Sayyidunā Imām Muḥiyyuddīn Abū Zakariyyā Yaḥyā Sharaf-un-Nawavī رَحْمَةُ اللهِ تَعَالٰى عَلَيْه, who compiled the famous book of Ḥadīš entitled '*Riyāḍ-uṣ-Ṣāliḥīn*', would fast continuously and eat only once a day, after Ṣalāt-ul-'Ishā. He would perform Saḥarī with only water and slept for only a few moments at night. *(Riyāḍ-uṣ-Ṣāliḥīn, pp. 12)*

Fast with enthusiasm

Dear Islamic brothers! If there is no obstacle in carrying out religious and important worldly activities, and parents are not displeased as well, then one should keep as many Nafl fasts as possible. Many of our pious saints رَحِمَهُمُ اللهُ تَعَالٰى used to do so. اِنْ شَآءَالله عَزَّوَجَلَّ, Due to fasting, every moment of the day will be spent in worship, and one will be saved from excessive eating. In addition, it would also become easier to apply the Madanī guard on the stomach. To gain these benefits, one must ensure that he eats less during Saḥarī and Iftārī. In order to develop enthusiasm and passion for Nafl fasts, listen to or read the chapter (about Nafl fasts) from '*Blessings of Ramadan*' as acquiring the knowledge of the punishments of sins and that of the excellence of good deeds is very effective in refraining from sins and carrying out good deeds. Here is an excellence of fasting.

Gold equal to earth

The Prophet of Raḥmaĥ, the Intercessor of Ummaĥ صَلَّى اللهُ تَعَالٰى عَلَيْهِ وَاٰلِهٖ وَسَلَّم has stated, 'If a person keeps a Nafl fast, his reward will not be complete even if gold equal to the size of the earth is given to him. His (complete) reward will only be given on the Day of Judgement.' *(Musnad Abī Ya'lā, vol. 5, pp. 253)*

صَلُّوْا عَلَى الْحَبِيْب صَلَّى اللهُ تَعَالٰى عَلٰى مُحَمَّد

A dining cloth made of gold

Sayyidunā Abū Dardā رَضِىَ اللهُ تَعَالٰى عَنْه has stated, 'On the Day of Judgement, dining cloths made of gold will be spread below the Divine 'Arsh for those who used to fast in the world. These dining cloths will be embroidered with pearls and diamonds. There will be heavenly fruits, drinks and other types of delicious foods on them. The fasting Muslims will eat from these dining cloths, gaining immense pleasure, while others will be facing severe accountability.' *(Al-budur-us-Sāfiraĥ fil-Umūr-il-Ākhiraĥ, pp. 260)*

Condemnation of those who eat three times a day

Once, someone asked Sayyidunā Saĥl Bin 'Abdullāĥ Tustarī عَلَیۡہِ رَحۡمَۃُ اللّٰہِ الۡقَوِی about eating once a day. He رَحۡمَۃُ اللّٰہِ تَعَالٰی عَلَیۡہ replied, 'This is the food of the Ṣiddīqīn[1].' He رَحۡمَۃُ اللّٰہِ تَعَالٰی عَلَیۡہ was further asked about eating twice a day. He رَحۡمَۃُ اللّٰہِ تَعَالٰی عَلَیۡہ replied, 'This is the food of the Mūminīn[2].' Then he رَحۡمَۃُ اللّٰہِ تَعَالٰی عَلَیۡہ was asked about those who eat three times a day. He رَحۡمَۃُ اللّٰہِ تَعَالٰی عَلَیۡہ replied, 'The family of such a person should keep him with livestock (so that he could eat like animals the whole day).' *(Risāla-tul-Qushayriyyaĥ, pp. 142)*

Dear Islamic brothers! Sayyidunā Saĥl Bin 'Abdullāĥ Tustarī عَلَیۡہِ رَحۡمَۃُ اللّٰہِ الۡقَوِی was one of the saints from the ranks of the Ṣiddīqīn. He رَحۡمَۃُ اللّٰہِ تَعَالٰی عَلَیۡہ himself would not eat anything for twenty days, but did not object to eating twice a day for common Muslims because working throughout the day with a single meal is not possible for everyone. However, he رَحۡمَۃُ اللّٰہِ تَعَالٰی عَلَیۡہ extremely disliked the habit of eating three times a day.

Mujĥ ko bĥūk-o-piyās saĥnay kī Khudā taufīq day
Gum Tayrī yādawn mayn reĥnay kī sadā taufīq day

Bless me with the strength to bear thirst and hunger
May I always remain engrossed in Your remembrance

صَلُّوۡا عَلَی الۡحَبِیۡب   صَلَّی اللّٰہُ تَعَالٰی عَلٰی مُحَمَّد

Survival on dates and water

Sayyidunā 'Urwaĥ رَضِیَ اللّٰہُ تَعَالٰی عَنۡہُ has narrated that once Sayyidatunā 'Āishaĥ رَضِیَ اللّٰہُ تَعَالٰی عَنۡہَا told him, 'O my nephew! We used to see one moon and then the next. In two months, we used to see three moons (and during all this time), fires would not burn (for cooking food) in the houses of the Beloved Prophet صَلَّی اللّٰہُ تَعَالٰی عَلَیۡہِ وَاٰلِہٖ وَسَلَّم.' Sayyidunā 'Urwaĥ رَضِیَ اللّٰہُ تَعَالٰی عَنۡہُ

[1] The highest level and category in sainthood.

[2] The believers, the Muslims.

then asked, 'O dear aunt! How did you manage in those days?' She رَضِیَ اللّٰہُ تَعَالٰی عَنْہَا replied, 'We would survive on two dark things, dates and water. Besides this, the Holy Prophet صَلَّی اللّٰہُ تَعَالٰی عَلَیْہِ وَاٰلِہٖ وَسَلَّم had some Anṣār[1] neighbours who had specially allocated the milk of some of their she-camels or goats for the Holy Prophet صَلَّی اللّٰہُ تَعَالٰی عَلَیْہِ وَاٰلِہٖ وَسَلَّم. Whenever they sent milk to the Holy Prophet صَلَّی اللّٰہُ تَعَالٰی عَلَیْہِ وَاٰلِہٖ وَسَلَّم, he would give the milk to us to drink.' *(Ṣaḥīḥ Bukhārī, vol. 7, pp. 232, Ḥadīš 6459)*

Better than whole night's worship

Ḥujjat-ul-Islam, Sayyidunā Imām Muhammad Ghazālī عَلَیْہِ رَحْمَۃُ اللّٰہِ الْوَالِی has narrated that Sayyidunā Abū Sulaymān رَضِیَ اللّٰہُ تَعَالٰی عَنْہ has stated, 'To reduce one morsel from my dinner is dearer to me than spending the entire night in worship.' He رَضِیَ اللّٰہُ تَعَالٰی عَنْہ has further stated, 'Hunger is one of the treasures of Allah عَزَّوَجَلَّ and is given only to His chosen servants.' *(Iḥyā-ul-'Ulūm, vol. 3, pp. 90)*

Du'ā ĥay kuchĥ na kuchĥ luqmay Khudā kay wāsiṭay cĥořūn
Rižā-e-Ḥaq kī khāṭir lažžat-e-dunyā say munĥ mořūn

May I leave at least some morsels for the pleasure of Allah!
May I stay away from carnal desires for the pleasure of Allah!

Dear Islamic brothers! If only we would be blessed with the treasure of adopting intentional hunger by eating less and applying a Madanī guard on our stomach. سُبْحٰنَ اللّٰہ عَزَّوَجَلَّ, for the saints, hunger is a treasure of divine mercy that is given only to the pious people. Those who acquire this treasure express gratitude as the following account shows.

Treasure of hunger and gratification for it

In his early life, Sayyidunā Ibrāĥīm Bin Adĥam رَحْمَۃُ اللّٰہِ تَعَالٰی عَلَیْہ was the king of Balkh, but he رَحْمَۃُ اللّٰہِ تَعَالٰی عَلَیْہ gave up kingship and adopted the life of poverty and simplicity. Once, he remained hungry for seven consecutive days as he did not have anything to eat. He offered 400 Rak'āt Nafl Ṣalāĥ each day as gratitude during those seven days. Weakened by extreme

[1] Anṣār were the companions in Madīnaĥ who welcomed and helped the companions who migrated from Makkaĥ.

hunger, he رَحْمَةُ اللهِ تَعَالٰى عَلَيْه pleaded in the court of the Almighty, 'O Allah عَزَّوَجَلَّ! If You bless me with a small amount of food so that I could gain the strength to worship You, I would be extremely grateful.' In no time, a young man approached and invited Sayyidunā Ibrāĥīm Bin Adĥam رَحْمَةُ اللهِ تَعَالٰى عَلَيْه to his house for a meal. He رَحْمَةُ اللهِ تَعَالٰى عَلَيْه accompanied the young man to his house. When the young man looked closely at the great saint, he said spontaneously, 'Your Eminence! I am your escaped slave, whatever I own actually belongs to you.' The great saint replied, 'I free you and grant you whatever you possess.' Then, taking permission from the young man he رَحْمَةُ اللهِ تَعَالٰى عَلَيْه departed. After this, he رَحْمَةُ اللهِ تَعَالٰى عَلَيْه expressed his feelings in the court of Allah عَزَّوَجَلَّ, 'O Allah عَزَّوَجَلَّ! I will never desire anyone but You. I asked You only for a piece of bread but You put a lot of world in front of me!' *(Tażkira-tul-Auliyā, pp. 96)*

Kašrat-e-dawlat kī āfat say bachānā Yā Khudā عَزَّوَجَلَّ
Day mujĥay 'ishq-e-Muhammad صَلَّى اللهُ تَعَالٰى عَلَيْهِ وَاٰلِهٖ وَسَلَّم *kā khazānaĥ Yā Khudā* عَزَّوَجَلَّ

Save me from the nuisance of excessive wealth, O Allah عَزَّوَجَلَّ*!*
Bless me with the treasure of devotion to Muhammad ﷺ*, O Allah* عَزَّوَجَلَّ*!*

Perils of a doubtful morsel

It is extremely dangerous to devour whatever you get without considering its permissibility. Sayyidunā Ma'rūf Karkhī عَلَيْهِ رَحْمَةُ اللّٰهِ الْقَوِى has stated, 'A doubtful morsel can, at times, spoil the condition of one's heart to such a degree that the heart does not accept any guidance for the rest of one's life. Sometimes, a doubtful morsel deprives the eater of performing Ṣalāt-ut-Taĥajjud for an entire year. Furthermore, sometimes looking at any impermissible thing deprives a person of reciting the Holy Quran for a very long time.' *(Minĥāj-ul-'Ābidīn, pp. 157)*

صَلُّوْا عَلَى الْحَبِيْب صَلَّى اللهُ تَعَالٰى عَلٰى مُحَمَّد

Ṣalāĥ rejected for 40 days

Dear Islamic brothers! Those who do not have the privilege of concentration and satisfaction of the heart while reciting the Holy Quran and offering Ṣalāĥ, those who do not have touching emotions when listening to a Na'at or making Du'ā and those who do not succeed in offering Ṣalāt-ut-Taĥajjud despite making ardent efforts should certainly learn a lesson from the wise words of Sayyidunā Ma'rūf Karkhī رَحْمَةُ اللهِ تَعَالٰی عَلَیْه. It is necessary to avoid Ḥarām sustenance, or else, one will face nothing but horrific consequences. The Beloved Rasūl صَلَّی اللهُ تَعَالٰی عَلَیْهِ وَاٰلِهٖ وَسَلَّم has stated, 'Whoever consumes a single morsel of Ḥarām food, his Ṣalāĥ will not be accepted for forty days and his Du'ā will be rejected for forty days.' *(Firdaus-ul-Akhbār, vol. 4, pp. 243, Ḥadīš 6263)*

Punishment for consuming a Ḥarām morsel

It is reported that when a person eats a Ḥarām morsel, every angel of the earth and the skies keeps cursing him until that Ḥarām morsel remains in his stomach. If he dies in the same state, Hell will be his abode. *(Mukāshafa-tul-Qulūb, pp. 10)*

Chest filled with Nūr

The Beloved and Blessed Rasūl صَلَّی اللهُ تَعَالٰی عَلَیْهِ وَاٰلِهٖ وَسَلَّم has stated, 'When a person decreases his consumption of food, his chest is filled with Nūr (spiritual light).' *(Al-Jāmi'-uṣ-Ṣaghīr, pp. 35 Ḥadīš 469)*

Four pearls of wisdom

Sayyidunā Ibrāĥīm Bin Adĥam رَحْمَةُ اللهِ تَعَالٰی عَلَیْه has stated: 'I remained in the company of some saints in a mountain of Lebanon; each of them gave me the following pieces of advice to convey to the people.

1. He who fills his stomach with food will not attain pleasure in worship.
2. He who sleeps a lot will not have blessing in his age.
3. He who desires only the pleasure of people, will be despairing of the pleasure of Allah عَزَّوَجَلَّ.
4. He who often backbites and speaks unnecessarily will not die as a Muslim.'

(Minĥāj-ul-'Ābidīn, pp. 107)

Fear of bad end

Dear Islamic brothers! It is a fact that gluttony increases the burden of the stomach and causes lethargy in the body parts, resulting in laziness. This also brings about a lack of concentration in worship. Many people experience this condition during the Tarāwīḥ Ṣalāĥ in Ramadan. It is the age of the so-called food culture. People fondly stuff various foods into their bellies. Further, samosas, kebabs and pakoras also make their contribution to the deterioration of the stomach, and due to excessive use of cold drinks, milkshakes and sour things, the sounds of coughing, belching and throat-clearing echo in the Masājid these days. Furthermore, if any one coughs, others also follow suit and start to cough probably because of the psychological effect, resulting in the increase of the sounds of coughing in the Masjid.

The fourth point mentioned by Sayyidunā Ibrāĥīm Bin Adĥam رَحْمَةُ اللهِ تَعَالٰی عَلَيْه that the one often backbiting and talking unnecessarily will not die as a Muslim is also very alarming. Alas! These days, you can rarely find a Muslim who refrains from useless speech and backbiting. O Allah عَزَّوَجَلَّ! Please protect our faith!

آمِيْن بِجَاهِ النَّبِيِّ الْاَمِيْن صَلَّى اللهُ تَعَالٰی عَلَيْهِ وَاٰلِهٖ وَسَلَّم

Musalmān ĥay 'Aṭṭār Tayrī 'aṭā say
Ĥo Īmān per khātimaĥ Yā Ilāĥī عَزَّوَجَلَّ

By the grace of Allah عَزَّوَجَلَّ*, 'Aṭṭār is Muslim*
May he leave this world with faith, O Allah عَزَّوَجَلَّ

Cover of religion

A person once sought advice from Sayyidunā Ḥāmid Laffāf عَلَيْهِ رَحْمَةُ اللهِ التَّوَّاب. He replied, 'Make a cover for the protection of religion like the cover of the Holy Quran.' When asked as to what the cover of religion meant, he رَحْمَةُ اللهِ تَعَالٰی عَلَيْه replied, 'Refraining from useless speech, unnecessary company of people and excessive eating.' He رَحْمَةُ اللهِ تَعَالٰی عَلَيْه has further said, 'If you knew how the Holy Prophet صَلَّى اللهُ تَعَالٰی عَلَيْهِ وَاٰلِهٖ وَسَلَّم, his companions and the Muslims would be treated in Paradise (as special guests), you would never eat food to a full stomach in the transient life of this mortal world.' *(Tażkira-tul-Wā'iẓīn, pp. 234)*

Sweetness of worship

Ḥujjat-ul-Islam Sayyidunā Imām Muhammad Ghazālī عَلَيْهِ رَحْمَةُ اللّٰهِ الْوَالِى has stated, 'Eating food to a stomach full causes the sweetness of worship to be lost.' Amīr-ul-Mūminīn Sayyidunā Abū Bakr Ṣiddīq رَضِىَ اللهُ تَعَالٰى عَنْهُ has stated, 'Ever since I have become a Muslim, I have not eaten food to a full stomach so that I can be blessed with the sweetness of worship. Likewise, since I became a Muslim, I have not had a full drink in the desire of having the drink of the Vision of Almighty Allah عَزَّوَجَلَّ.' *(Minĥāj-ul-'Ābidīn, pp. 193)*

Sayyidunā Sufyān Šaurī رَحْمَةُ اللهِ تَعَالٰى عَلَيْه has stated, 'Worship is quite an art which is learnt in solitude, and its tool is hunger.' *(ibid)*

Who will be hungry on Day of Judgement?

Sayyidunā Abū Bujayr رَضِىَ اللّٰهُ تَعَالٰى عَنْهُ has narrated that the Beloved and Blessed Prophet صَلَّى اللهُ تَعَالٰى عَلَيْهِ وَاٰلِهٖ وَسَلَّم has stated, 'Many people eat delicious foods and lead a luxurious life in this world, but they will be hungry and naked on the Day of Judgement.' *(Shu'ab-ul-Īmān, vol. 2, pp. 170, Ḥadīš 1461)*

Sayyidunā 'Abdullāĥ Ibn 'Umar رَضِىَ اللهُ تَعَالٰى عَنْهُمَا has narrated that once the Holy Prophet صَلَّى اللهُ تَعَالٰى عَلَيْهِ وَاٰلِهٖ وَسَلَّم heard someone belching, so he صَلَّى اللهُ تَعَالٰى عَلَيْهِ وَاٰلِهٖ وَسَلَّم said, 'Reduce your belch, because the one who fills his stomach the most in the world will be the most hungry on the Day of Judgement.' *(Jāmi' Tirmižī, vol. 4, pp. 217, Ḥadīš 2486)*

Sayyidunā Abū Ṭālib Al-Makkī رَحْمَةُ اللهِ تَعَالٰى عَلَيْه has narrated that the companion who belched on that day was Sayyidunā Abū Juḥayfaĥ رَضِىَ اللهُ تَعَالٰى عَنْهُ. This companion رَضِىَ اللهُ تَعَالٰى عَنْهُ stated, 'By Allah عَزَّوَجَلَّ, I have not eaten food to a full stomach ever since the day when the Holy Prophet صَلَّى اللهُ تَعَالٰى عَلَيْهِ وَاٰلِهٖ وَسَلَّم admonished me and I hope Allah عَزَّوَجَلَّ will protect me (from filling my stomach with food) in the future as well.' *(Qūt-ul-Qulūb, vol. 2, pp. 325)*

Saint with green skin

Sayyidunā Abū Ṭālib Al-Makkī رَحْمَةُ اللهِ تَعَالٰى عَلَيْه was a great scholar, a renowned teacher of Ḥadīš, a religious thinker, an eminent saint and an illustrious Imām of Taṣawwuf. Even Sayyidunā Imām Muhammad Ghazālī عَلَيْهِ رَحْمَةُ اللّٰهِ الْوَالِى has taken considerable help in Taṣawwuf from his book '*Qūt-ul-Qulūb*.' He رَحْمَةُ اللهِ تَعَالٰى عَلَيْه had risen to such a high degree of asceticism (Taqwā) that he gave up eating food altogether and would live off grass. His consumption of grass had caused his skin to become green.

Distribution of almonds and sugar at a funeral

In the last moments of his life, Sayyidunā Abū Ṭālib Al-Makkī رَحْمَةُ اللهِ تَعَالٰى عَلَيْه was requested to make a will. He رَحْمَةُ اللهِ تَعَالٰى عَلَيْه replied, 'Distribute almonds and sugar during my funeral procession if I pass away with faith.' The person asked as to how he would know about it. He رَحْمَةُ اللهِ تَعَالٰى عَلَيْه replied, 'Keep sitting beside me and give your hand into mine. If I pass away in the state of Īmān, I will press your hand firmly.' Therefore, the person held the hand of Sayyidunā Abū Ṭālib Al-Makkī رَحْمَةُ اللهِ تَعَالٰى عَلَيْه. When he رَحْمَةُ اللهِ تَعَالٰى عَلَيْه was about to depart this life, he pressed that person's hand with force and his soul left his body. When his sacred bier[1] was lifted to be taken to the cemetery, almonds and sugar were distributed among the people. The great saint passed away on the 6th of Jumādal-Ākhiraĥ 386 A.H. His shrine, situated in the Mālikiyyaĥ graveyard of Baghdad city, is the focal point for visitors. *(Al-Muntaẓam fī Tārīkh-ul-Muluk-wal-Umam, vol. 14, pp. 385)*

Key to world

Sayyidunā Abū Sulaymān Dārānī رَحْمَةُ اللهِ تَعَالٰى عَلَيْه has stated, 'The key to the world is to fill the stomach and (the key) to the Hereafter is to remain hungry.' *(Nuzĥa-tul-Majālis, vol. 1, pp. 177)*

Whose stomach will be full on the Judgement Day?

Dear Islamic brothers! There is a lesson for those who keep devouring luscious foods without hunger. By Allah عَزَّوَجَلَّ! No one can bear the hunger of the Day of Judgement. Staying hungry in the world is an excellent deed to attain contentment on the Day of Resurrection. The Holy Prophet صَلَّى اللهُ تَعَالٰى عَلَيْهِ وَاٰلِهٖ وَسَلَّم has stated, 'Those who adopt hunger in this world will be satiated on the Day of Judgement.' *(Itḥāf-us-Sādat-il-Muttaqīn, vol. 9, pp. 17)*

Sayyidunā Abū Ĥurayraĥ رَضِیَ اللهُ تَعَالٰی عَنْهُ has narrated that the Rasūl of mankind, the Peace of our heart and mind, the most Generous and Kind صَلَّى اللهُ تَعَالٰى عَلَيْهِ وَاٰلِهٖ وَسَلَّم has stated, 'The hungry person who is patient with hunger and starvation (in this world) will not face the severity of accountability (on the Day of Judgement).' *(Al-budur-us-Sāfiraĥ fil-Umūr-il-Ākhiraĥ, pp. 212)*

---

[1] A frame on which a dead body is placed. [Translator's Note]

Blazing heat of Day of Judgement

Dear Islamic brothers! Consider the indescribable conditions of the Day of Judgement! Severe hardships await those who stuff themselves for the satisfaction of their carnal desires. Alas! The scorching heat of the sun, the ground made of copper, and being barefoot whilst feeling the intensity of hunger and thirst! May Allah عَزَّوَجَلَّ protect us! The obedience to Nafs may lead to tragic consequences.

His Nafs took him to Hell

Two years after the death of his father, Sayyidunā Abul Ḥasan Rāzī رَحْمَةُ اللهِ تَعَالٰی عَلَیْه had a dream in which he saw his late father wearing clothing made of tar. When he asked his father the reason of wearing the clothing of the people of Hell, his father replied, 'My beloved son! My Nafs took me to Hell. Save yourself from the deception of Nafs.' *(Mukāshafa-tul-Qulūb, pp. 20)*

O Allah عَزَّوَجَلَّ! Save us from the mischief of Nafs! Grant us the ability to apply the Madanī guard to our stomach for Your pleasure! Bless us with the enthusiasm to have patience with hunger and thirst! Protect us from the hunger, thirst and extremely severe conditions of the Day of Judgement. Save us from the insufferable torment of Hell!

آمِيْن بِجَاهِ النَّبِيِّ الْاَمِيْن صَلَّى اللهُ تَعَالٰی عَلَيْهِ وَاٰلِهٖ وَسَلَّم

Ten advantages of hunger

1. Purification of the heart.
2. Softness of the heart.
3. Realization of the starvation faced by the poor.
4. Remembrance of the hunger and thirst of the Hereafter.
5. Less inclination towards sins.
6. Less sleep.
7. Ease in worship.
8. Contentment with a little sustenance.
9. Good health.
10. The passion to give money etc. as Ṣadaqaĥ (charity). *(Iḥyā-ul-'Ulūm, vol. 3, pp. 91-96)*

Ḥujjat-ul-Islam, Imām Muhammad Ghazālī عَلَيْهِ رَحْمَةُ اللّٰهِ الْوَالِی quotes some saints as saying, 'Hunger is our best possession.' This means that they have vastness, peace, worship, sweetness (in worship) and beneficial knowledge by having patience with remaining hungry for the pleasure of Allah عَزَّوَجَلَّ. *(Minhāj-ul-'Ābidīn, pp. 108)*

Banquet on the Day of Judgement

A renowned Tābi'ī[1], Sayyidunā Ka'b-ul-Aḥbār رَضِیَ اللّٰهُ تَعَالٰی عَنْهُ has stated, 'On the Day of Judgement, an announcer will call out, 'O you who remained hungry and thirsty for the pleasure of Allah عَزَّوَجَلَّ! Rise.' Hearing this, those who used to remain hungry will arrive at a dining cloth while others will be facing accountability.' *(Nuzĥa-tul-Majālis, vol. 1, pp. 178)*

Doors of Paradise and Hell

Ḥujjat-ul-Islam, Sayyidunā Imām Muhammad Ghazālī عَلَيْهِ رَحْمَةُ اللّٰهِ الْوَالِی has stated that the stomach and private parts are from the doors of Hell whose foundation is built on gluttony (i.e. eating food to a full stomach). On the other hand, humility and modesty are from the doors of Paradise whose foundation is built on hunger. The one who closes the door of Hell for oneself opens the door of Paradise, which is like the difference between the east and the west. Proximity to one door means distance from the other. (In other words, the one who adopts humility by remaining hungry gets closer to Paradise and far from Hell, while the one who indulges in misusing his stomach and private parts gets closer to Hell and further away from Paradise). *(Iḥyā-ul-'Ulūm, vol. 3, pp. 92)*

Physical fitness

Amīr-ul-Mūminīn, Sayyidunā 'Umar Fārūq A'ẓam رَضِیَ اللّٰهُ تَعَالٰی عَنْهُ has stated, 'Refrain from filling your stomach while eating and drinking as it harms the body, causes disease and brings about laziness in worship. To adopt moderation in eating and drinking is necessary for you, as this improves physical fitness and saves oneself from needless expenses.' *(Kanz-ul-'Ummāl, vol. 15, pp. 183, Ḥadīš 41706)*

---

[1] A Muslim saint who saw and met even a single companion of the Holy Prophet صَلَّى اللّٰهُ تَعَالٰی عَلَيْهِ وَاٰلِهٖ وَسَلَّم and who passed away as a Muslim. [Translator's Note]

Six perils of filling the stomach

Sayyidunā Abū Sulaymān Dārānī رَحْمَةُ اللّٰهِ تَعَالٰی عَلَیْه has stated that there are six perils of filling the stomach:

1. Not being able to make Du'ā to Almighty Allah عَزَّوَجَلَّ.
2. Difficulty in benefiting from knowledge and wisdom.
3. No compassion for others (because those who fill their bellies assume that everyone is like them and hence do not have pity for the poor and needy).
4. Worship seems to be a burden.
5. One is surrounded by desires.
6. While others are going to the Masjid, the one who eats in excess is going to the toilet. *(Iḥyā-ul-'Ulūm, vol. 3, pp. 92)*

Dry bread and salt

Shaykh Sayyidunā Muhammad Bin Wāsi' رَحْمَةُ اللّٰهِ تَعَالٰی عَلَیْه used to eat only dry bread with salt and would say, 'He who is content with this (little amount of food) in the world will never be destitute.' *(Mukāshafa-tul-Qulūb, pp. 122)*

Excessive eating impairs wisdom

Ibn Najīḥ رَحْمَةُ اللّٰهِ تَعَالٰی عَلَیْه has narrated that Imām A'ẓam Abū Ḥanīfaĥ رَضِیَ اللّٰهُ تَعَالٰی عَنْه said to him, 'Whenever you have to carry out any important piece of work in the world, do not eat before performing it because food impairs wisdom.' *(Manāqib-e-Abī Ḥanīfaĥ, pp. 351)*

Reason for hardness of heart

Sayyidunā Sufyān Šaurī رَحْمَةُ اللّٰهِ تَعَالٰی عَلَیْه has stated, 'There are two causes of the hardness of the heart. The first is to eat food to a stomach full and the second is to speak in excess.'

Seven morsels

Amīr-ul-Mūminīn, Sayyidunā 'Umar Fārūq A'ẓam رَضِیَ اللّٰهُ تَعَالٰی عَنْه would not eat more than six or seven morsels. *(Iḥyā-ul-'Ulūm, vol. 3, pp. 97)*

Perils of filling stomach

Elaborating on the perils of eating food to a full stomach, Ḥujjat-ul-Islam, Imām Muhammad Ghazālī عَلَيْهِ رَحْمَةُ اللّٰهِ الْوَالِى has stated, 'The eyes of the person who fills his stomach are filled with sleep. Even if he performs Taĥajjud, he feels no sweetness in it. The bachelor who sleeps having filled his stomach, experiences nocturnal emission and it would be difficult for him to perform Ghusl at night with cold water. If he has delayed his Witr Ṣalāĥ until the time of Taĥajjud, then not only does he miss Taĥajjud but also Witr due to nocturnal emission. These are some of the problems of filling the stomach.' *(Iḥyā-ul-'Ulūm, vol. 3, pp. 94)*

Reason of nocturnal emission

Sayyidunā Abū Sulaymān Dārānī رَحْمَةُ اللّٰهِ تَعَالٰى عَلَيْه has stated that nocturnal emission is troublesome. He mentioned this because one misses many acts of worship due to the untimely need of Ghusl. He has further stated that sleep is the root of all troubles and filling the stomach with food is one of its causes. Its cure, however, lies in remaining hungry. *(ibid)*

Satan circulates in body like blood

A Mursal Ḥadīš states, 'Without doubt, Satan circulates in man's body like blood. Therefore, one should narrow (Satan's) ways by hunger and thirst.' *(Itḥāf-us-Sādat-il-Muttaqīn, vol. 9, pp. 12)*

Dear Islamic brothers! A Mursal Ḥadīš is the one a Tābi'ī narrates directly from the Beloved and Blessed Prophet صَلَّى اللّٰهُ تَعَالٰى عَلَيْهِ وَاٰلِهٖ وَسَلَّم leaving the companion out. *(Nuzĥat-un-Naẓr fī Tauḍīḥ Nakhba-tul-Fikr, pp. 63)*

Two rivers

The pious saints رَحِمَهُمُ اللّٰهُ تَعَالٰى have stated, 'To eat food to a full stomach is a stream in Nafs through which Satan makes his inroads. On the contrary, hunger is a stream of the soul through which angels pass.' *(Sab'a Sanābil, pp. 241)*

Hungry for forty days

Dear Islamic brothers! The pious saints would narrow the path of Satan by bearing hunger and thirst. Sayyidunā Saĥl Bin 'Abdullāĥ Tustarī عَلَيْهِ رَحْمَةُ اللّٰهِ الْقَوِى used to remain hungry for forty consecutive days and then he would eat a little. *(Iḥyā-ul-'Ulūm, vol. 3, pp. 98)* Merely one dirham was sufficient for the expenses of his supply of food for a year. *(Risāla-tul-Qushayriyyaĥ, pp. 401)*

Six Madanī pearls

Listen to the following six pieces of advice given by Sayyidunā Saĥl Bin 'Abdullāĥ Tustarī عَلَيْهِ رَحْمَةُ اللّٰهِ الْقَوِى:

1. On the Day of Judgement, no deed will be more beneficial than (the deed of) refraining from excessive eating because this is the Sunnaĥ of the Holy Prophet صَلَّى اللهُ تَعَالٰى عَلَيْهِ وَاٰلِهٖ وَسَلَّم.
2. The wise consider hunger as an extremely advantageous thing for religious and worldly matters.
3. I do not consider anything more harmful than excessive eating to those who desire salvation in the Hereafter.
4. Knowledge and wisdom have been placed in hunger while sin and ignorance have been placed in filling the stomach.
5. He who keeps his Nafs hungry is not disturbed by satanic deceptions (Wasāwis).
6. When a person undergoes hunger, sickness or tribulation the mercy of Allah عَزَّوَجَلَّ turns towards him at that time. *(Iḥyā-ul-'Ulūm, vol. 3, pp. 91)*

The one who fills his stomach is disgraced

It is stated in *Qūt-ul-Qulūb*, 'Hunger is (like) a king and filling stomach is (like) a slave. The hungry person is respected while the one stuffing oneself is humiliated.' It has also been said that hunger brings about a great respect while filling the stomach causes an intense humiliation. Some saints have stated, 'Hunger is the key to the Hereafter and the door of asceticism, whereas filling the stomach is the key to the world and the door of indulgence in worldly pleasures.' *(Qūt-ul-Qulūb, vol. 2, pp. 332)*

Why emphasis on remaining hungry?

Someone once asked Sayyidunā Bāyazīd Bisṭāmī رَحْمَةُ اللهِ تَعَالٰى عَلَيْه as to why he emphasized on remaining hungry. He رَحْمَةُ اللهِ تَعَالٰى عَلَيْه replied, 'If Pharaoh (Fir'awn) were hungry he would never have claimed divinity. If Qārūn were hungry, he would never have rebelled (against the Almighty عَزَّوَجَلَّ).' (In other words, their wealth led them to defiance and disobedience to their Creator). *(Kashf-ul-Maḥjūb, pp. 647)*

Fearlessness from Hidden Plan of Allah عَزَّوَجَلَّ is grave sin

Dear Islamic brothers! Truly, good health and excessive wealth often lead to indulgence in sins. Therefore, those who possess good health or wealth or have authority should fear the Hidden Plan of Allah. Sayyidunā Ḥasan Baṣrī رَحْمَةُ اللهِ تَعَالٰى عَلَيْه has stated, 'If a person possesses ample sustenance, obedient children, wealth, good health, status, respect, property or position in the government, but he does not fear the Divine Hidden Plan – such a person is heedless of the Hidden Plan of Allah.' *(Tanbīĥ-ul-Mughtarīn, pp. 54)*

Sayyidunā Imām Muhammad Bin Aḥmad Żaĥabī رَحْمَةُ اللهِ تَعَالٰى عَلَيْه has included fearlessness from the Hidden Plan of Allah in the list of major sins in his book '*Kitāb-ul-Kabāir.*' Therefore, the poor, the sick and the troubled should also fear the Hidden Plan of Allah as it is possible that these troubles befall them as a test and incessant complaints, impatience and efforts to get rid of poverty through Ḥarām means lead them to ruin in the Hereafter. Furthermore, it is also Wājib for those who live comfortably to fear the Hidden Plan of Allah lest this wealth and worldly comfort engender pride, decadence and transgression and, thus this body and wealth become the cause of them burning in the fire of Hell. In this regard, listen to a Quranic verse and a Ḥadīš and fear the Hidden Plan of Allah.

Respite from Allah عَزَّوَجَلَّ

Sayyidunā 'Uqbaĥ Bin 'Āmir رَضِىَ اللهُ تَعَالٰى عَنْهُ has narrated that the Prophet of Raḥmaĥ, the Intercessor of Ummaĥ صَلَّى اللهُ تَعَالٰى عَلَيْهِ وَاٰلِهٖ وَسَلَّم has stated, 'If you see a person upon whom Allah عَزَّوَجَلَّ bestows (His favours), (but) the person persists in committing sins; (then) this is a mere respite (from Allah عَزَّوَجَلَّ). The Beloved and Blessed Prophet صَلَّى اللهُ تَعَالٰى عَلَيْهِ وَاٰلِهٖ وَسَلَّم then recited the following verse:

فَلَمَّا نَسُوۡا مَا ذُکِّرُوۡا بِہٖ فَتَحۡنَا عَلَیۡہِمۡ اَبۡوَابَ کُلِّ شَیۡءٍ ؕ

حَتّٰۤی اِذَا فَرِحُوۡا بِمَاۤ اُوۡتُوۡۤا اَخَذۡنٰہُمۡ بَغۡتَۃً فَاِذَا ہُمۡ مُّبۡلِسُوۡنَ ﴿۴۴﴾

Then when they forgot the admonition made to them, We opened to them the gates of all things until when they became delighted at what they were given, then We seized them suddenly, now they were left in despair.'

[Kanz-ul-Īmān (Translation of Quran)] (Musnad Imām Aḥmad, vol. 6, pp. 122, Ḥadīš 17313)

(Part 17, Sūraĥ Al-An'ām, verse 44)

Regarding sin as a good act is Kufr

Commenting on the foregoing verse, Muftī Aḥmad Yār Khān عَلَیْہِ رَحْمَۃُ الْمَنَّان has stated, '(From this) we have learnt that the worst of punishments is the hardness of the heart, (because of which) the teachings of the Holy Prophet صَلَّی اللّٰہ تَعَالٰی عَلَیْہِ وَاٰلِہٖ وَسَلَّم do not have an effect on the person. We have also come to know that getting worldly pleasures, despite persistence in sins, is the wrath and punishment from Allah عَزَّوَجَلَّ as the person becomes heedless and indulges fearlessly in sins due to his luxurious possessions. At times, the person is under the impression that sin is good - otherwise, he would not be receiving such bounties. Remember that such a notion is Kufr. (It is Farḍ to consider a sin as a sin and deliberately considering or declaring a sin as good is Kufr.) We have also come to know that the difficulties faced by the pious are a form of divine mercy whereby their (spiritual) status is raised to higher degrees.' *(Nūr-ul-'Irfān, pp. 210)*

Du'ā of the Holy Prophet صَلَّی اللّٰہ عَلَیْہِ وَاٰلِہٖ وَسَلَّم

The Holy Prophet صَلَّی اللّٰہ تَعَالٰی عَلَیْہِ وَاٰلِہٖ وَسَلَّم would often make the following Du'ā:

یَا مُقَلِّبَ الْقُلُوْبِ ثَبِّتْ قَلْبِیْ عَلٰی دِیْنِکَ

O the One Who turns the hearts! Keep my heart steadfast in Your religion.

(Musnad Imām Aḥmad, vol. 4, pp. 515, Ḥadīš 13697)

Four from forty thousand

Sayyidunā 'Abdullāĥ Ibn Mubārak رَحْمَةُ اللهِ تَعَالٰى عَلَيْه has narrated that a wise man chose the following four pieces of advice from forty thousand.

1. Do not trust every woman in every matter.
2. Never rely on your wealth.
3. Do not overburden your stomach (by overeating).
4. Do not acquire such knowledge that does not benefit you, like (information, news etc.). *(Al-Munabbiĥāt lil-'Asqalānī, pp. 47)*

صَلُّوْا عَلَى الْحَبِيْب صَلَّى اللهُ تَعَالٰى عَلٰى مُحَمَّد

Seven intestines

The Prophet of Raḥmaĥ, the Intercessor of Ummaĥ صَلَّى اللّٰهُ تَعَالٰى عَلَيْهِ وَاٰلِهٖ وَسَلَّم has stated, 'The believer eats in one intestine while the unbeliever and the hypocrite eat in seven intestines.' *(Ṣaḥīḥ Bukhārī, vol. 6, pp. 246, Ḥadīš 5394)*

Meaning of seven intestines

Dear Islamic brothers! The foregoing Ḥadīš does not imply that a Muslim possesses only one intestine while an unbeliever possesses seven. Every person possesses seven intestines. What is meant by this Ḥadīš is that gluttony is the habit of the unbelievers.

Elaborating on this Ḥadīš, Ḥujjat-ul-Islam, Imām Muhammad Ghazālī عَلَيْهِ رَحْمَةُ اللّٰهِ الْوَالِى has stated, 'A hypocrite eats seven times more than a Muslim. It may also mean that the desire of a hypocrite (to eat) is seven times more than that of a Muslim. Here, the word 'intestine' alludes to 'desire or craving' because it is the desire which urges a person to consume food. It does not mean that a hypocrite has more intestines than a Muslim.' *(Iḥyā-ul-'Ulūm, vol. 3, pp. 89)*

Difference between diet of Mūmin and that of hypocrite

Sayyidunā Ḥasan Baṣrī رَضِىَ اللهُ تَعَالٰى عَنْهُ has stated, 'A Muslim is like a little sheep or goat, (as) merely a handful of dates and barley and a single gulp of water is sufficient (for it). As for the hypocrite, he is like a wild animal that chews incessantly and then swallows its food. Its stomach does not shrink for its neighbour and it does not sacrifice anything even for its own brother.' *(Qūt-ul-Qulūb, vol. 2, pp. 324)*

Food of Imām Aḥmad Razā رَحْمَةُ اللهِ عَلَيْه

Imām Aḥmad Razā Khān عَلَيْهِ رَحْمَةُ الْمَنَّان used to consume very little food. Shaykh Sayyid Ayyūb 'Alī Shāĥ رَحْمَةُ اللهِ تَعَالٰى عَلَيْه has narrated, 'The food of A'lā Ḥaḍrat رَحْمَةُ اللهِ تَعَالٰى عَلَيْه contained just a small bowl of goat meat gravy without chilli and one or two biscuits made from Sūjī (granulated wheat flour). This was not everyday, at times he did not use to eat even this little amount of food.' *(Ḥayāt-e-A'lā Ḥaḍrat, vol. 1, pp. 27)*

Seven Madanī pearls

The companion Sayyidunā 'Abdullāĥ Ibn 'Abbās رَضِىَ اللهُ تَعَالٰى عَنْهُ has stated that a wise person should prefer seven things to seven other things:

1. He should prefer poverty to wealth.
2. He should prefer (worldly) disgrace to (worldly) respect.
3. He should prefer humility to self-esteem.
4. He should prefer hunger to eating to a full stomach.
5. He should prefer sadness to happiness.
6. He should prefer the poor pious people to the rich people of the world.
7. He should prefer death to life. *(Al-Munabbiĥāt lil-'Asqalānī, pp. 85)*

صَلُّوْا عَلَى الْحَبِيْب　　صَلَّى اللهُ تَعَالٰى عَلٰى مُحَمَّد

Ritual ablution (Wuḍū) after twelve days

Sayyidunā 'Abdul Waĥĥāb Sha'rānī قُدِّسَ سِرُّهُ الرَّبَّانِي has stated, 'I have seen many Auliyā of Allah عَزَّوَجَلَّ who remained resolute in adopting the virtue of hunger. Some of them went to the toilet just once a week as they would be shy from Allah عَزَّوَجَلَّ in repeatedly undressing themselves in the toilet. Shaykh Tājuddīn Żākir رَحْمَةُ اللهِ تَعَالٰى عَلَيْه had reached such a state that he needed to make Wuḍū only once in twelve days (as it would not become invalid).' *(Tanbīĥ-ul-Mughtarīn, pp. 36)*

صَلُّوْا عَلَى الْحَبِيْب صَلَّى اللهُ تَعَالٰى عَلٰى مُحَمَّد

Traveller of Madanī Qāfilaĥ

Dear Islamic brothers! Those who eat less applying the Madanī guard to their stomach, feel less thirst compared to those who eat in excess. Because of drinking less water, they do not have the need to sleep in excess and such people are more energetic after sleeping for only a few hours.

Once, during the early days of Dawat-e-Islami, our Madanī Qāfilaĥ travelled to Punjab from Bāb-ul-Madīnaĥ (Karachi, Pakistan). In this Qāfilaĥ, there was an old person with a white beard who revealed to me (i.e. the author) during the journey that his Wuḍū had been valid for the past two days. He also revealed that his late Murshid used to remain in the state of Wuḍū for fifteen days. All this is the blessing of applying the Madanī guard to the stomach. By doing this, the need of sleeping and that of going to toilet decrease and one can get a lot of time for worshipping and carrying out religious Madanī activities.

Hungry for three days

Sayyidunā Anas رَضِیَ اللهُ تَعَالٰی عَنْه has narrated that once the Lady of Paradise, Sayyidatunā Fāṭima-tuz-Zaĥrā رَضِیَ اللهُ تَعَالٰی عَنْهَا brought a piece of bread and served it to the Holy Prophet صَلَّى اللهُ تَعَالٰى عَلَيْهِ وَاٰلِهٖ وَسَلَّم. When the Holy Prophet صَلَّى اللهُ تَعَالٰى عَلَيْهِ وَاٰلِهٖ وَسَلَّم asked about the bread, she رَضِیَ اللهُ تَعَالٰی عَنْهَا replied, 'I had prepared some bread which I did not like to eat without you, therefore, I have brought this piece of bread here.' The Prophet of Raḥmaĥ, the Intercessor of Ummaĥ صَلَّى اللهُ تَعَالٰى عَلَيْهِ وَاٰلِهٖ وَسَلَّم has said, 'During the last three days, this is the first food which has entered the mouth of your father.' *(Mu'jam Kabīr, vol. 1, pp. 259, Ḥadīš 750)*

اَللّٰهُ اَكْبَر! The one who possesses the keys to the riches of the universe in his blessed hands has no interest in worldly things. This was indeed the intentional hunger of the Holy Prophet صَلَّى اللّٰهُ تَعَالٰى عَلَيْهِ وَاٰلِهٖ وَسَلَّم. As for his generosity, he صَلَّى اللّٰهُ تَعَالٰى عَلَيْهِ وَاٰلِهٖ وَسَلَّم would bestow a lot upon others.

Bowl of milk and seventy companions رَضِىَ اللّٰهُ عَنْهُم

Sayyidunā Abū Ĥurayraĥ رَضِىَ اللّٰهُ تَعَالٰى عَنْهُ has stated, 'By Allah عَزَّوَجَلَّ, who has no partner! I used to tie a stone to my stomach and place it on the floor owing to extreme hunger. One day, I sat on the pathway where people walk. The Holy Prophet صَلَّى اللّٰهُ تَعَالٰى عَلَيْهِ وَاٰلِهٖ وَسَلَّم passed by me smilingly. Seeing me in this state, he صَلَّى اللّٰهُ تَعَالٰى عَلَيْهِ وَاٰلِهٖ وَسَلَّم immediately realized my condition. Then, he صَلَّى اللّٰهُ تَعَالٰى عَلَيْهِ وَاٰلِهٖ وَسَلَّم said, 'O Abū Ĥurayraĥ رَضِىَ اللّٰهُ تَعَالٰى عَنْهُ!' I replied, 'Labbayk (I am present) Yā Rasūlallāĥ صَلَّى اللّٰهُ تَعَالٰى عَلَيْهِ وَاٰلِهٖ وَسَلَّم!' He صَلَّى اللّٰهُ تَعَالٰى عَلَيْهِ وَاٰلِهٖ وَسَلَّم said, 'Come with me.' I followed him until we arrived at one of his blessed homes. Seeking permission, I entered the blessed house. Seeing a bowl of milk, the Beloved and Blessed Prophet صَلَّى اللّٰهُ تَعَالٰى عَلَيْهِ وَاٰلِهٖ وَسَلَّم asked his family members as to where it had come from. They replied that a companion had sent it as a gift for the Noble Rasūl صَلَّى اللّٰهُ تَعَالٰى عَلَيْهِ وَاٰلِهٖ وَسَلَّم. Looking at me, the Holy Prophet صَلَّى اللّٰهُ تَعَالٰى عَلَيْهِ وَاٰلِهٖ وَسَلَّم said, 'O Abū Ĥurayraĥ رَضِىَ اللّٰهُ تَعَالٰى عَنْهُ!' I replied, 'Labbayk Yā Rasūlallāĥ صَلَّى اللّٰهُ تَعَالٰى عَلَيْهِ وَاٰلِهٖ وَسَلَّم.' He then said, 'Go and call the Aĥl-e-Ṣuffaĥ.'

Sayyidunā Abū Ĥurayraĥ رَضِىَ اللّٰهُ تَعَالٰى عَنْهُ has further stated that the Aĥl-e-Ṣuffaĥ were the guests of Islam. They had no houses and wealth, nor did they take help from anyone. Whenever anything came as Ṣadaqaĥ (i.e. alms) to the Holy Prophet صَلَّى اللّٰهُ تَعَالٰى عَلَيْهِ وَاٰلِهٖ وَسَلَّم he صَلَّى اللّٰهُ تَعَالٰى عَلَيْهِ وَاٰلِهٖ وَسَلَّم used to send it to the Aĥl-e-Ṣuffaĥ without taking anything from it, and whenever the Holy Prophet صَلَّى اللّٰهُ تَعَالٰى عَلَيْهِ وَاٰلِهٖ وَسَلَّم received any gift, he صَلَّى اللّٰهُ تَعَالٰى عَلَيْهِ وَاٰلِهٖ وَسَلَّم used to send a portion of it to the Aĥl-e-Ṣuffaĥ and would eat from it. Sayyidunā Abū Ĥurayraĥ رَضِىَ اللّٰهُ تَعَالٰى عَنْهُ goes on to say that he felt rather distressed due to calling all the Aĥl-e-Ṣuffaĥ because just one bowl of milk could not be sufficient for all of them. He also felt that he was certainly more deserving of the milk because he would gain some strength by drinking it. He also knew that the Holy Prophet صَلَّى اللّٰهُ تَعَالٰى عَلَيْهِ وَاٰلِهٖ وَسَلَّم would instruct him to feed the Aĥl-e-Ṣuffaĥ when they arrived, and it would be unlikely that he would get even a few sips of the milk. But he was also aware that it was mandatory to abide by the commandment of Allah عَزَّوَجَلَّ and His Holy Prophet صَلَّى اللّٰهُ تَعَالٰى عَلَيْهِ وَاٰلِهٖ وَسَلَّم. He goes on to say, 'I then went to the Aĥl-e-Ṣuffaĥ and called them. They came, sought permission, entered the blessed house and sat down.' The Holy Prophet صَلَّى اللهُ تَعَالٰى عَلَيْهِ وَاٰلِهٖ وَسَلَّم then said, 'O Abū Ĥurayraĥ رَضِىَ اللهُ تَعَالٰى عَنْه!' I replied, 'Labbayk Yā Rasūlallāĥ صَلَّى اللهُ تَعَالٰى عَلَيْهِ وَاٰلِهٖ وَسَلَّم.' The Holy Prophet صَلَّى اللهُ تَعَالٰى عَلَيْهِ وَاٰلِهٖ وَسَلَّم said, 'Take the bowl of milk and make them drink.' I then gave the bowl of milk to the first person and after drinking as much as he could he returned the bowl to me. I kept giving the bowl of milk to one after another until all of them drank milk. Then, taking the bowl of milk in his blessed hand, the Holy Prophet صَلَّى اللهُ تَعَالٰى عَلَيْهِ وَاٰلِهٖ وَسَلَّم looked at me smilingly and said, 'O Abū Ĥurayraĥ رَضِىَ اللهُ تَعَالٰى عَنْه!' I responded, 'Labbayk Yā Rasūlallāĥ صَلَّى اللهُ تَعَالٰى عَلَيْهِ وَاٰلِهٖ وَسَلَّم!' He صَلَّى اللهُ تَعَالٰى عَلَيْهِ وَاٰلِهٖ وَسَلَّم said, 'Now only I and you are left.' I said, 'Yā Rasūlallāĥ صَلَّى اللهُ تَعَالٰى عَلَيْهِ وَاٰلِهٖ وَسَلَّم! You have spoken the truth.' He صَلَّى اللهُ تَعَالٰى عَلَيْهِ وَاٰلِهٖ وَسَلَّم then said to me, 'Sit down and drink.' I sat down and began to drink the milk. He صَلَّى اللهُ تَعَالٰى عَلَيْهِ وَاٰلِهٖ وَسَلَّم then said, 'Drink.' He صَلَّى اللهُ تَعَالٰى عَلَيْهِ وَاٰلِهٖ وَسَلَّم kept asking me to drink until I said, 'I swear by the One who has sent you with the truth, I am not able to drink anymore.' He صَلَّى اللهُ تَعَالٰى عَلَيْهِ وَاٰلِهٖ وَسَلَّم ordered me to give him the bowl. I handed over the bowl to him. He صَلَّى اللهُ تَعَالٰى عَلَيْهِ وَاٰلِهٖ وَسَلَّم then glorified Allah عَزَّوَجَلَّ and drank the remaining milk reciting بِسْمِ اللّٰه. *(Ṣaḥīḥ Bukhārī, vol. 7, pp. 230, Ḥadīš 6452)*

سُبْحٰنَ اللّٰه عَزَّوَجَلَّ! This is one of the great miracles of the Holy Prophet صَلَّى اللهُ تَعَالٰى عَلَيْهِ وَاٰلِهٖ وَسَلَّم that all the Aĥl-e-Ṣuffaĥ who were nearly seventy in number could not finish a small bowl of milk. Referring to this very incident, A'lā Ḥaḍrat رَحْمَةُ اللهِ تَعَالٰى عَلَيْه has written the following couplet:

Kyūn janāb Bū Ĥurayraĥ رَضِىَ اللهُ تَعَالٰى عَنْه! Thā woĥ kaysā jām-e-shīr
Jis say sattar Ṣāḥibon kā dūdĥ say munĥ pĥir gayā

O Bū Ĥurayraĥ رَضِىَ اللهُ تَعَالٰى عَنْه! How was the sweet beverage!
That filled the mouth of seventy companions with milk

Independence from people

Sayyidunā Abū Yaḥyā Mālik Bin Dīnār عَلَيْهِ رَحْمَةُ اللهِ الْغَفَّار has stated that he once told Sayyidunā Abū 'Abdullāĥ Muhammad Bin Wāsi' رَحْمَةُ اللهِ تَعَالٰى عَلَيْه, 'O Abū 'Abdullāĥ رَحْمَةُ اللهِ تَعَالٰى عَلَيْه! Fortunate is the person who is content with just a little amount of grain and is indifferent to others.' When he heard this, he said to me, 'O Abū Yaḥyā رَحْمَةُ اللهِ تَعَالٰى عَلَيْه! Glad tidings are for the person who is hungry in the morning and evening and the Almighty عَزَّوَجَلَّ is pleased with him.' *(Iḥyā-ul-'Ulūm, vol. 3, pp. 90)*

Ineffective advice

It is narrated that the advice of the one whose stomach is full has no effect (on others) and when he is given advice, his mind refuses to accept it. *(Nuzĥa-tul-Majālis, vol. 1, pp. 178)*

Smell at time of death

Amīr-ul-Mūminīn, Sayyidunā 'Umar Fārūq A'ẓam رَضِیَ اللّٰہُ تَعَالٰی عَنْہُ has stated, 'Refrain from filling your stomach as it is a burden in life and foul smell at the time of death.' *(Iḥyā-ul-'Ulūm, vol. 3, pp. 90)*

When you eat a lot, you also have to earn a lot

Dear Islamic brothers! Sayyidunā 'Umar Fārūq A'ẓam رَضِیَ اللّٰہُ تَعَالٰی عَنْہُ has spoken an outright truth. Really, not applying the Madanī guard to the stomach and eating excessively causes a heavy burden in life as the more one eats, the more he has to earn. He has to work hard to cook the food; then he has to carry its burden in the stomach. Excessive eating is detrimental to the digestive system. As a result, the one who eats excessively is burdened with excessive gas, constipation and many other problems including the burden of doctors' fee and expenses for medication. As soon as the food goes down the throat, the taste disappears and the stomach has to bear the burden for a long time. This leads to one hardship after another. Abstaining from those few moments of pleasure, if only we would develop the mindset of saving ourselves from all these heavy burdens throughout our life, and from foul smell at the time of our death!

No pleasure in worship

It is narrated that if you are in the habit of filling your stomach with food then you should not hope for the pleasure of worship. How can you have light in your heart if you do not carry out worship? And if this worship is performed without (spiritual) pleasure, then how can Nūr (light) enter your heart? *(Minĥāj-ul-'Ābidīn, pp. 107)*

Unconsciousness due to hunger

Sayyidunā Abū Ĥurayraĥ رَضِیَ اللّٰہُ تَعَالٰی عَنْہُ has narrated, 'I used to become unconscious and fall between the pulpit of the Holy Prophet صَلَّی اللّٰہُ تَعَالٰی عَلَیْہِ وَاٰلِہٖ وَسَلَّم and the blessed house of

Sayyidatunā 'Āishaĥ رَضِیَ اللہُ تَعَالٰی عَنۡہَا due to severe hunger. Someone used to come and place his foot on my neck. He would regard me insane but I was completely sane; extreme hunger caused this state.' *(Ṣaḥīḥ Bukhārī, vol. 8, pp. 193, Ḥadīš 7324)*

Dear Islamic brothers! Sayyidunā Abū Ĥurayraĥ رَضِیَ اللہُ تَعَالٰی عَنۡہُ had such an immense passion to acquire Islamic knowledge that he left everything and remained at the blessed feet of the Holy Prophet صَلَّی اللہُ تَعَالٰی عَلَیۡہِ وَاٰلِہٖ وَسَلَّم. He used to live in the state of hunger and seek Islamic knowledge. He also had the honour of narrating the most number of Ḥadīš from the Holy Prophet صَلَّی اللہُ تَعَالٰی عَلَیۡہِ وَاٰلِہٖ وَسَلَّم. On the other hand, the condition of today's students of Islamic knowledge seems to be quite different. It is quite unlikely that the seeker of Islamic knowledge would be able to attain spiritual blessings while continuing to gluttonize, desiring for fame and self-respect, having greed etc. While seeking Islamic knowledge, you must be sincere so that you can attain the mercy of Almighty Allah عَزَّوَجَلَّ. By the grace of Allah عَزَّوَجَلَّ, an excellent way of gaining religious knowledge with spiritual blessings is to travel with the Madanī Qāfilaĥs of Dawat-e-Islami, a global & non-political movement of the Quran and Sunnaĥ. Here is a blessing of a Madanī Qāfilaĥ.

Mysterious pain

An Islamic brother from Punjab has stated, 'I came to Faīzān-e-Madīnaĥ, Karachi, the global Markaz of Dawat-e-Islami to participate in the 'Tarbiyyatī course.' During the course, on a Thursday at about 4 a.m., I felt pain at my left side. The pain was so severe that seven painkillers were injected into me, after which I felt a little relief. As usual, I attended the weekly Sunnaĥ-Inspiring Ijtimā' on Thursday. On the same night, at about 10 p.m., I felt the pain again but it subsided due to the blessing of Du'ā made in the Ijtimā'. After about an hour, the pain recurred. The doctors injected me with three painkillers, I felt some relief.

My condition was such that as soon as I would consume anything, I would feel the same severe spasm of pain. Three or four injections with drips would be administered everyday. I also had an ultrasound done, but the doctors could not diagnose the cause of the pain. While I was in the hospital, I heard that other Islamic brothers of the Tarbiyyatī course were preparing for a twelve day Sunnaĥ-Inspiring Madanī Qāfilaĥ. The doctors advised me not to travel but I could not help joining the Madanī Qāfilaĥ. During the journey, I experienced a little pain while we were on our way to Dera Bugti, Baluchistan. During the Madanī Qāfilaĥ, we also attended the weekly Sunnaĥ-Inspiring Ijtimā' held at Sui on Thursday, and then returned to Dera Bugti.

اَلْحَمْدُلِلّٰہ عَزَّوَجَلَّ, by the blessing of joining the Madanī Qāfilaĥ, the pain disappeared as if there was no pain at all! اَلْحَمْدُلِلّٰہ عَزَّوَجَلَّ, the pain has not recurred ever since. The greatest blessing I attained during the Madanī Qāfilaĥ was that I was blessed with the vision of the Beloved and Blessed Prophet صَلَّى اللهُ تَعَالٰى عَلَيْهِ وَاٰلِهٖ وَسَلَّم in my dream.'

Lūtnay raḥmatayn Qāfilay mayn chalo
Sīkĥnay Sunnatayn Qāfilay mayn chalo
Dard-e-sar ĥo agar dukĥ raĥī ĥo kamar
Pāo gey ṣiḥḥatayn Qāfilay mayn chalo
Ĥay ṭalab dīd kī, dīd kī Eid kī
Kyā 'ajab woĥ dikĥayn Qāfilay mayn chalo

To gain mercy, travel with Madanī Qāfilaĥ
To learn Sunnaĥ, travel with Madanī Qāfilaĥ
If you have headache or backache
You will recover, travel with Madanī Qāfilaĥ
If you have the desire of seeing the Prophet صَلَّى اللهُ تَعَالٰى عَلَيْهِ وَاٰلِهٖ وَسَلَّم
Your desire could be fulfilled, travel with Madanī Qāfilaĥ

صَلُّوْا عَلَى الْحَبِيْب صَلَّى اللهُ تَعَالٰى عَلٰى مُحَمَّد

If only hunger could be purchased

Sayyidunā Yaḥyā Bin Mu'āż رَحْمَةُ اللهِ تَعَالٰى عَلَيْه has stated, 'If hunger were sold in the marketplace, the seeker of the Hereafter would certainly purchase it.' *(Risāla-tul-Qushayriyyaĥ, pp. 141)*

Food is being purchased everywhere

Glory be to Allah عَزَّوَجَلَّ! What can we say about the Madanī mindset of our great saints? Sayyidunā Yaḥyā Bin Mu'āż رَحْمَةُ اللهِ تَعَالٰى عَلَيْه is talking about purchasing hunger, whereas the unwise are engaged in competing for food, as to who can eat the most! These days, the one who eats the most food is considered as the most courageous! Regretfully, today the marketplaces are full of consumers who purchase various kinds of food, which also happen to come along with various diseases. This is the age of 'food culture.' There is a multitude of restaurants and hotels in every area. Pizzas, fries and burgers are being sold at virtually every corner. Dessert and ice cream shops are occupying virtually every shopping center and mall. Apart from the consumers who purchase food to fulfill their needs, there are many who buy food just to satisfy their Nafs (desire) – hoarding and devouring everything they get. They are not concerned about worldly perils of such unchecked activity nor do they care about the severity of accountability in the Hereafter. Everyone is intent only on eating, eating and more eating.

If only we would remember the hunger of our Beloved and Blessed Prophet صَلَّى اللّٰهُ تَعَالٰى عَلَيْهِ وَاٰلِهٖ وَسَلَّم, the companions, the martyrs of Karbalā رَضِىَ اللّٰهُ تَعَالٰى عَنْهُم and the saints رَحِمَهُمُ اللّٰهُ تَعَالٰى! How unfortunate indeed! We are screaming out 'eat, eat, and eat' and these blessed souls are persuading us to adopt 'hunger.' Although we do not miss any opportunity to eat, there must be something beneficial in eating less, due to which the Prophets عَلَيْهِمُ السَّلَام, the companions رَضِىَ اللّٰهُ تَعَالٰى عَنْهُم and the saints رَحِمَهُمُ اللّٰهُ تَعَالٰى are giving us the lesson of eating less.

To eat in excess is attribute of unbelievers

Dear Islamic brothers! Eating just to satisfy the desire of Nafs is not a dignified practice. Ṣadr-ush-Sharī'aĥ, Badr-uṭ-Ṭarīqaĥ, Shaykh Muftī Muhammad Amjad 'Alī A'ẓamī عَلَيْهِ رَحْمَةُ اللّٰهِ الْقَوِى has stated, 'In the Holy Quran, eating just for pleasure and joy has been described as the attribute of the unbelievers. Similarly, excessive eating has been mentioned as an attribute of the unbelievers in a Ḥadīš as well.' *(Bahār-e-Sharī'at, part 16, pp. 30)*

Strength in hunger

Unlike common people, Sayyidunā Saĥl Bin 'Abdullāĥ رَحْمَةُ اللّٰهِ تَعَالٰى عَلَيْه would remain strong in hunger and, he would become weak whenever he ate anything. *(Risāla-tul-Qushayriyyaĥ, pp. 142)*

A Persian poet has said:

Agar lażżat-e-tark-e-lażżat badānī
Digar lażżat-e-Nafs, lażżat-e-nākhwānī

If you realize the pleasure of giving up pleasures
You will never consider the pleasure of Nafs as pleasure at all

Attainment of Taṣawwuf

Sayyidunā Junayd Baghdādī عَلَيْهِ رَحْمَةُ اللّٰهِ الْهَادِى has stated, 'We have not attained Taṣawwuf just by discussions and argumentation but by adopting hunger, aversion to the world and by abandoning the desires of our Nafs.' *(Sab'a Sanābil, pp. 241)*

I am worst person

Sayyidunā 'Ušmān Ghanī رَضِىَ اللّٰهُ تَعَالٰى عَنْهُ has stated that there are five signs of a pious person.

1. He remains in good company.
2. He protects his tongue and private parts.
3. He considers the pleasures of the world as a nuisance and religious blessings as a divine mercy.
4. He does not fill his stomach even with Ḥalāl food for fear of it containing a little Ḥarām.
5. Besides himself, he considers every Muslim forgiven in the Hereafter while he considers only himself as a sinner and fears punishment. *(Al-Munabbiĥāt, pp. 59)*

Pitiable condition due to hunger

Sayyidunā Faḍālaĥ Bin 'Ubayd رَضِىَ اللّٰهُ تَعَالٰى عَنْهُ has narrated that when the Beloved and Blessed Prophet صَلَّى اللّٰهُ تَعَالٰى عَلَيْهِ وَاٰلِهٖ وَسَلَّم used to lead the Jamā'at of Ṣalāĥ, there were some companions رَضِىَ اللّٰهُ تَعَالٰى عَنْهُم who used to fall during the Ṣalāĥ because of severe hunger. These companions were the Aĥl-e-Ṣuffaĥ. The Bedouins used to consider them as insane. When the Holy Prophet صَلَّى اللّٰهُ تَعَالٰى عَلَيْهِ وَاٰلِهٖ وَسَلَّم would finish the Ṣalāĥ, he صَلَّى اللّٰهُ تَعَالٰى عَلَيْهِ وَاٰلِهٖ وَسَلَّم used to turn towards them and say, 'If you knew what reward is in store for you in the court of Allah عَزَّوَجَلَّ, you would wish that your hunger and poverty would prolong even more.' *(Jāmi' Tirmiżī, vol. 4, pp. 162, Ḥadīš 2375)*

Hungry for many days

Some of the companions رَضِىَ اللّٰهُ تَعَالٰى عَنْهُم and saints رَحِمَهُمُ اللّٰهُ تَعَالٰى would not eat anything for many consecutive days. In this regard, Ḥujjat-ul-Islam, Imām Muhammad Ghazālī عَلَيْهِ رَحْمَةُ اللّٰهِ الْوَالِى

has stated, 'Sayyidunā Abū Bakr Ṣiddīq رَضِیَ اللهُ تَعَالٰی عَنْه would not eat anything for six days. Sayyidunā 'Abdullāĥ Bin Zubayr رَضِیَ اللهُ تَعَالٰی عَنْه did not eat for seven days. The student of Sayyidunā 'Abdullāĥ Ibn 'Abbās رَضِیَ اللهُ تَعَالٰی عَنْه namely Abū Jawzaĥ رَضِیَ اللهُ تَعَالٰی عَنْه did not eat for seven days. Sayyidunā Ibrāĥīm Bin Adĥam رَحْمَةُ اللهِ تَعَالٰی عَلَيْه and Sayyidunā Sufyān Šaurī رَحْمَةُ اللهِ تَعَالٰی عَلَيْه remained hungry for three days. All these blessed saints رَحِمَهُمُ اللّٰهُ تَعَالٰی would gain help in walking on the path of the Hereafter by means of hunger.' *(Iḥyā-ul-'Ulūm, vol. 3, pp. 98)*

Remaining hungry for one year

Dear Islamic brothers! Not everyone is strong enough to remain hungry for many days. This was one of the special qualities and marvels of these blessed people. In fact, they used to receive spiritual sustenance. By the bounty of Allah عَزَّوَجَلَّ, some of them remained hungry for forty days consecutively. Our own spiritual guide Ghauš-e-A'ẓam رَحْمَةُ اللهِ تَعَالٰی عَلَيْه, at times used to remain hungry for an entire year and his sustenance used to come directly from Almighty Allah عَزَّوَجَلَّ. In relation to this, A'lā Ḥaḍrat رَحْمَةُ اللهِ تَعَالٰی عَلَيْه has written the following couplet.

Qasmayn day day kay khĩlātā ĥay pilātā ĥay tujĥay
Piyārā Allah عَزَّوَجَلَّ *tayrā chāĥnay wālā tayrā*

(Ḥadāiq-e-Bakhshish)

صَلُّوْا عَلَى الْحَبِيْب صَلَّى اللهُ تَعَالٰى عَلٰى مُحَمَّد

How long can a person live without eating and drinking?

Maintaining the daily routines of life normally despite remaining hungry and thirsty for a long time, is a special quality of the extraordinary servants of Almighty Allah عَزَّوَجَلَّ. These special servants of Allah عَزَّوَجَلَّ receive spiritual nourishment. Common people cannot withstand such a prolonged period of hunger and thirst. Even if someone starts remaining hungry and thirsty like the saints, he will give up hope after a few days and will not have the courage to do so again.

According to medical research, a person can remain hungry for 18 days or if he is very strong, he can remain hungry for 25 days at the most. Likewise, a person can survive for 3 days without water, and 1 to 5 minutes without oxygen.

How much should common person eat?

If a common person who is accustomed to excessive eating succeeds in gradually applying the Madanī guard to the stomach, reducing his food intake to the extent of filling only one third of his stomach, it will be very appropriate and beneficial to him. اِنْ شَآءَاللّٰه عَزَّوَجَلَّ, By doing so, he will gain the blessings of hunger and will not become weak as well. His health will surprisingly improve and he will almost get rid of the expenses of doctors' fee and medicines. If one is not certain about this, then he is advised to experience this and see the results for himself.

Cure for sick heart

Sayyidunā 'Abdullāĥ Anṭākī عَلَيْهِ رَحْمَةُ اللّٰهِ الْقَوِى has stated that there are five remedies for a sick heart:

1. To remain in the company of the pious.
2. To recite the Holy Quran.
3. To eat less.
4. To perform Taĥajjud regularly.
5. To beseech Allah عَزَّوَجَلَّ during the last part of the night.

(Al-Munabbiĥāt, pp. 60)

The bird that lives thousand years

Dear Islamic brothers! Unfortunately, some people eat so much that even their stomach asks for a break. Laziness overpowers them. They can barely stand let alone walk. Such people can be compared to vultures. When a vulture descends to eat the carrion (i.e. the flesh of a dead animal), all other birds stay away because of fear. The vulture eats so excessively that it cannot even fly. In this state even a child can capture it. Therefore, (it can thus be inferred that) not applying the Madanī guard to the stomach, i.e. too much eating is the habit of the carrion-eater; the vulture. It is said that a vulture normally remains alive for a thousand years and likes disgusting odour. It dislikes fragrance and if it ever smells fragrance, it dies. Sayyidunā Imām Ḥasan رَضِىَ اللّٰهُ تَعَالٰى عَنْهُ has stated that when the vulture speaks, it says, 'O man! Live as long as you wish, one day death will seize you.' *(Ḥayāt-ul-Ḥaywān-ul-Kubrā, vol. 2, pp. 474)*

Mosquito can kill camel

Dear Islamic brothers! The greed for relishing taste is severely detrimental. A mosquito yearns for human blood. It sits on the soft skin just above a blood vessel. With its proboscis, it pierces the skin and the blood vessel and thus sucks the blood. Sometimes, it drinks so much blood that it is unable to fly and sometimes its stomach even explodes, causing its death. Almighty Allah عَزَّوَجَلَّ has given such power to the mosquito that it can kill even a camel. It can kill every quadruped. The beast or bird that eats the animal killed by a mosquito's sting also dies instantly. In ancient times, the kings of Iraq had developed a very excruciating and agonizing method of executing the death sentence. They used to bind the criminal naked and throw him by the drains, infested with mosquitoes, where he would die writhing in pain due to stings. (Namrūd was also killed by a mosquito). *(Ḥayāt-ul-Ḥaywān-ul-Kubrā, vol. 1, pp. 184)*

Fat mosquito

Sayyidunā Rabī' Bin Anas رَضِیَ اللهُ تَعَالٰی عَنْهُ has stated, 'As long as a mosquito is hungry, it remains alive. When it eats and drinks, it becomes fat and when it becomes fat, it dies. The condition of man is also like that of a mosquito. When man enjoys luxuries and pleasures of the world, his heart dies.' *(Tanbīĥ-ul-Mughtarīn, pp. 54)*

Dear Islamic brothers! A mosquito dies and turns to dust as soon as it becomes fat. But alas, when a human becomes strong, at times he faces many problems in this world and, in case of the displeasure of Allah عَزَّوَجَلَّ and His Prophet صَلَّى اللهُ تَعَالٰى عَلَيْهِ وَاٰلِهٖ وَسَلَّم as a result of committing sins, he faces severe punishment at the time of his death, in his grave, on the Day of Judgement and in the Hell.

Perils of large body

Sayyidunā Yaḥyā Mu'āż Rāzī رَحْمَةُ اللهِ تَعَالٰی عَلَیْه has stated, 'The one who is in the habit of filling his stomach, his body becomes fat with flesh and the one who is obese with flesh becomes a victim of desires and the one who becomes a victim of desires, his sins increase and the one whose sins increase, his heart becomes hard and he becomes a victim to the calamities and attractions of the world.' *(Al-Munabbiĥāt, pp. 59)*

Sins attack glutton

Dear Islamic brothers! It is certainly a matter of great concern that eating to the extent of filling the stomach opens the door of many sins. Sayyidunā Imām Muhammad Ghazālī عَلَيْهِ رَحْمَةُ اللّٰهِ الْوَالِي has stated, 'Excessive eating causes rebellion in body parts and creates the desire of committing immodest and violent deeds. When a person eats in excess he becomes arrogant, his eyes desire to see immodest things, his ears desire to hear evil things, his tongue wants to speak about indecent things, his private part demands the satisfaction of lust and his feet are keen to move towards impermissible places. On the contrary, if a person is hungry, all of his body parts remain peaceful and they do not desire any evil.' Abū Ja'far عَلَيْهِ رَحْمَةُ اللّٰهِ الْاَكْبَر has stated, 'When the stomach is hungry, all other body parts are at peace. They desire nothing, and when the stomach is full, other body parts become hungry and take the person to committing evil things.' *(Minĥāj-ul-'Ābidīn, pp. 92)*

Excellence of lean body

Sayyidunā 'Abdullāĥ Ibn 'Abbās رَضِىَ اللّٰهُ تَعَالٰى عَنْهُ has narrated that the Prophet of Raḥmaĥ, the Intercessor of Ummaĥ صَلَّى اللّٰهُ تَعَالٰى عَلَيْهِ وَاٰلِهٖ وَسَلَّم has stated, 'The dearest to Allah عَزَّوَجَلَّ amongst you is the person who eats less and has a lean body.' *(Al-Jāmi'-uṣ-Ṣaghīr, pp. 20, Ḥadīš 221)*

Average weight for man and woman

Excessive eating also causes the problems of obesity and potbelly. These days, many people are suffering from this sickness. There should be a proper balance between the height and weight of a person. The weight of a male who is about 5 and half feet (or 66 inches) tall should be around 150 pounds or 68 kg, while that of a female who is about 5 and a quarter feet (63 inches) tall should be around 130 pounds or 59 kg. Their weight should not exceed this. Everyone can calculate his/her weight and compare it to the above-mentioned criterion.

Weight of Sayyidunā Prophet Yūsuf عَلَيْهِ السَّلَام

A proper balance between the height and weight of a person is necessary. In ancient times, people used to be much taller; hence, their weight would also be much more. A renowned exegetist, Muftī Aḥmad Yār Khān عَلَيْهِ رَحْمَةُ الرَّحْمٰن has stated, 'The governor of Egypt bought

Sayyidunā Yūsuf عَلَيْهِ السَّلَام from an Egyptian market, paying gold, silver, musk, pearls and silk equivalent to the weight of Sayyidunā Yūsuf عَلَيْهِ السَّلَام. At that time, his weight was 400 ratals (one ratal is equivalent to half a kilogram) and his age was only twelve years! *(Nūr-ul-'Irfān, pp. 378)* Sayyidunā Yūsuf عَلٰی نَبِیِّنَا وَ عَلَیْهِ الصَّلٰوۃُ وَالسَّلَام was very handsome and his body was well shaped. He was also tall in relation to his weight.

صَلُّوْا عَلَى الْحَبِيْب صَلَّى اللّٰهُ تَعَالٰى عَلٰى مُحَمَّد

Causes of obesity

Bear in mind that taunting, laughing or hurting an obese person in any way without the justification of the Islamic law is a Ḥarām act which can lead to Hell. Further, it is not necessary that a potbelly is always caused by excessive eating, as many of those who eat excessively remain lean & thin. Studying, writing or doing official work for a long time while sitting, travelling by car or a bike instead of walking, eating food sitting in a cross-legged position, eating food sitting on chair with feet hanging, eating very hot food, often leaning the body weight towards the left side, for example, placing left hand on the floor while sitting or eating - can cause a potbelly and obesity. Further, those who do not apply the Madanī guard to their stomach and greedily devour pizzas, fried foods, cold drinks and ice cream should only blame themselves if they are overweight or have a potbelly.

Perhaps people consider cold drinks harmless. One should remember that there are about 7 spoons of sugar in every 250 ml of cold drink. As for ice-cream, it is like a sugar-bomb. An overweight person should not even look at cold drinks and ice creams as these items are actually a sweet poison for him. There are three things which can increase a person's weight:

1. Superfine flour
2. Oil or fat
3. Sweet foods

The aforementioned items are found in virtually all of our foods. To a certain extent, these things are necessary for the human body. An excess of sugar and deficiency of sugar in blood both indicate illness. The amount of these three ingredients would automatically exceed the normal limit in the body of those who overeat, which can cause an increase in weight in addition to many diseases. Some people remain slim and thin despite excessive eating. It does not mean that eating in excess does not cause any harm to them. They may also suffer from stomach and heart ailments. Although excessive eating normally causes heart ailments, stress can also cause a heart attack and even heart failure. If a person avoids the above-mentioned three items from his young age, and if he stays alive until old age, he is expected to remain safe from many diseases and problems in his old age.

صَلُّوْا عَلَى الْحَبِيْب   صَلَّى اللّٰهُ تَعَالٰى عَلٰى مُحَمَّد

Definition of youth

According to dictionaries, a person remains young from maturity until 30 to 40 years. From 30 to 50 years is the period of middle age while old age starts after 50 years. It is better to take precaution in feeding even a new-born baby. When the child reaches puberty, he should be advised and encouraged to avoid harmful things and excessive eating. If a person eats whatever he desires despite reaching the age of 30 years, he will soon experience its harmful effects on his health. As his age increases, diseases will attack him. If a person eats whatever comes into his hand despite reaching the age of 50 years, it is as if he is inviting diseases. It becomes difficult for such people to remain safe from sugar and cholesterol problems.

After 30 years, blood becomes infected with various sicknesses. Therefore, it is advisable to have different blood tests done every six months. If the test indicates any disease, one should have this test done every 1 ½ month besides taking the proper medication. It is a blunder to avoid the test for fear that if the test-report reveals any disease, it would cause stress. Keep in mind that ignoring a disease is not its cure. This carelessness can result in severe problems in the future. There are many people whose hearts suddenly fail. Paralysis has also become very common. May Allah عَزَّوَجَلَّ protect us from all type of diseases and save us from this trial!

اٰمِيْن بِجَاهِ النَّبِيِّ الْاَمِيْن صَلَّى اللّٰهُ تَعَالٰى عَلَيْهِ وَاٰلِهٖ وَسَلَّم

Dangers of pizza

Pizza and other oily fast foods sold in the marketplace quickly cause fatness and obesity. These items are very dangerous to health. In fast foods, inferior quality ingredients and, at times, very stale ingredients are used. In summer, these cooked stale foods develop fungus and germs, which gives rise to the danger of severe food poisoning or even death. In the United Arab Emirates where the quality of hotel food is considered to be very high, a critical article was published in the newspaper 'Khaleej Times' on 14th August 2004 which severely criticised fast food, especially pizza and other oily foods served in the hotels of the capital Abu Dhabi. According to the article, almost three or four such patients who have food poisoning as a result of eating pizza etc. are being admitted in most of the hospitals and clinics of Abu Dhabi every week. These patients have vomiting, diarrhoea, indigestion, fever, weakness and extreme fatigue. One doctor reports that three such patients who ate pizza visited him last week. One of the patients had to be hospitalised for two days. There are also other doctors who had presented their reports in this specific article and all concluded that, 'Consuming pizzas and other market fast foods is tantamount to inviting diseases.'

Dear Islamic brothers! Use of fast foods, pizzas and other fried foods increases the cholesterol level in blood. High cholesterol levels harden and narrow blood vessels, increasing the risk of heart problems. If a patient is in the habit of smoking and has diabetes, there is a high risk of him suffering from stroke or a heart attack. If one wants to have a healthy body, it is very important to consume fresh and simple food and to maintain a proper body weight as this assists in reducing cholesterol levels and obesity.

Story of consumer of pizza

An Islamic brother has given the following statement: 'I was a very thin and slim person. Before joining Dawat-e-Islami I had some modern friends. We used to compete for eating the most food and, in most cases, I used to win the competition. Despite excessive eating, my body was still thin. Then, due to my friendship with a keen consumer of pizza, I got into the habit of eating pizza and drinking pepsi. When I ate pizza for the first time, my weight was around 60 kg. Initially, I would eat pizza just once a month or once every two months but I gradually became so fond of it that I started eating pizza even twice a week. I would also drink either pepsi or coca-cola and enjoyed eating mayonnaise. Slowly my weight began to increase and I was under the false impression that at last 'Now I am getting healthy.' Little did I realise that I was actually heading for my doom. I did not know that pizza was increasing cholesterol in my blood and slowly affecting my heart. My weight steadily increased till I was about 95 kg. I became obese and my stomach expanded outwards like a drum. The cholesterol level increased in my blood, making me suffer from some diseases permanently.

اَلْحَمْدُ لِلّٰه عَزَّوَجَلَّ! Fortunately, by the blessings of the Sunnaĥ-Inspiring Madanī environment of Dawat-e-Islami, I heard about the excellence of applying the Madanī guard to the stomach in an Ijtimā' and made up my mind to decrease my daily food intake. اَلْحَمْدُ لِلّٰه عَزَّوَجَلَّ! By the blessing of eating less, I lost almost 5 kg of weight within a few days, and I now feel active and trim. As I often have to go on journeys, travelling has also become easy for me due to this reduction in my weight. As the Madanī guard on the stomach improves the stomach and eradicates constipation etc., I have now been able to act upon the Madanī In'ām of remaining in the state of Wuḍū all the time.

اَلْحَمْدُ لِلّٰه عَزَّوَجَلَّ! Barley bread is now prepared at my home. Please make Du'ā for me to attain steadfastness and for every Muslim to realize the importance of Madanī guard of the stomach.

As for pizza and other such foods, I am now of the opinion that getting someone into the habit of eating pizza or consuming drinks such as pepsi cola or coca-cola is, in actual fact, enmity in the disguise of friendship.'

Cure for obesity

Developing the habit of eating less by means of the Madanī guard on the stomach for the pleasure of Allah عَزَّوَجَلَّ can protect you against obesity and many illnesses. How nice it would be if we could just give up excessive eating, following the advice of the Noble Prophet صَلَّى اللهُ تَعَالٰى عَلَيْهِ وَاٰلِهٖ وَسَلَّم before it comes to going to hospitals and avoiding excessive eating on the advice of doctors! In this regard, the Noble Prophet صَلَّى اللهُ تَعَالٰى عَلَيْهِ وَاٰلِهٖ وَسَلَّم has stated, 'Man does not fill any container worse than his stomach. A few morsels of food are sufficient to keep his back straight. If he cannot do so, then he should keep one third of his stomach for food, one third for water and one third for air.' ***(Sunan Ibn Mājaĥ, vol. 4, pp. 48, Ḥadīš 3349)***

Get your blood tested

Those who are overweight are advised to get a lipid profile test done, which is a group of blood tests carried out for the diagnosis of heart diseases. These tests also comprise a test to check cholesterol levels. If the stomach is empty from fourteen hours before this test, the result will be more accurate. Also get diabetes tested. How nice it would be if one fasts for the pleasure of Allah عَزَّوَجَلَّ and gets these tests done before sunset. Then, try to reduce weight as per your doctor's advice. Those who are fit and healthy should also have this test done at least every six months so that one can avoid any illnesses before they appear.

Remedy for obesity

Vegetables (other than the ones causing flatulence like the potato etc.) are very beneficial to the reduction of weight. They should be boiled in water only, or for a single person, prepared with one teaspoon of olive oil. There is no harm in adding chillies, spices and turmeric. Everyone should have one gram of turmeric daily as it will protect against cancer, اِنْ شَآءَاللّٰه عَزَّوَجَلَّ. One should consume at least one whole plate of vegetables everyday, prepared in the manner described above. If one wishes to eat bread or rice etc., then one should eat half of a flatbread or half a cup of rice boiled in water and a small piece of meat. If one wishes to eat a mango, he should eat only half a mango in a day. If one wishes to drink tea, he should drink the one prepared with skim milk without sugar, and if this is not possible, then he may add some artificial sweetener to his cup of tea with the advice of his doctor. If you do not have diabetes, add honey in place of sugar. One should often consume salads and cucumbers etc.

The use of olive oil in every type of food would be very beneficial. (If you do not have olive oil, use a little amount of corn oil). Prior to eating, remove all clarified butter or oil that appears on the top of the food with a spoon in such a way that not a single drop remains in the plate. It is not permissible to throw away this oil or clarified butter without the permission of Sharī'aĥ as it would lead to the sin of wasting. Reuse this clarified butter or oil. You should also refrain from eating rice, cow or goat-meat, every type of butter, egg-yolk, cake-pastries, chocolates, sweets, fried salty items, creamy items, sweet dishes, sweet delicacies, ice creams, cold drinks, pakoras, kebabs, and samosas. Avoid every fatty, oily and sweet food.

By refraining from these items, you would be able to reduce your weight and look fit and healthy, اِنْ شَآءَاللّٰه عَزَّوَجَلَّ. Food-charts are also available at clinics which you may follow to maintain your weight. It is better to first discuss (your condition) with your doctor before you attempt to reduce your weight. If possible, try to consult only one doctor because he would become familiar with your bodily conditions and would be able to treat you properly. If you keep changing doctors then each would treat you according to his knowledge and experience and you would become a medical experiment for each one.

Four cures for constipation

In the 2nd volume of *Qūt-ul-Qulūb* (page 365), it is stated that if defecation (excretion of faeces) takes place within 6 hours of eating or it does not take place even after 24 hours, then this condition indicates an ill stomach. Arthritis (i.e. pain in joints) is caused by preventing the release of gas from the body. If the running water of a canal is restricted, it would certainly damage the canal's banks. Similarly, if urine is not released, it would cause damage to the body. One should try to improve the digestive system or else it would be difficult to overcome obesity. Eat vegetables and fruits in abundance. Four cures for constipation are stated below:

1. Eat four or five ripe guavas with seeds, or
2. Eat a considerable amount of papaya. If Allah عَزَّوَجَلَّ wills, this will clean the stomach.
3. Every 4 days one should eat 3 or 4 spoons of psyllium husk or a spoon of digestive powder with water. If Allah عَزَّوَجَلَّ wills, this will clean the stomach. One should not consume psyllium husk or digestive powder every day as it then becomes ineffective.
4. If your doctor permits, take one tablet of Gramex (metronidazole) 400 mg in the morning and one in the evening for five consecutive days every 2 or 3 months. You will find it to be very effective medicine for constipation, indigestion and other stomach illnesses. Whenever you intend to take this tablet, it is necessary to take it for five consecutive days. You may also take this tablet on an empty stomach. However, the best cure for indigestion is to apply the Madanī guard to the stomach.

صَلُّوْا عَلَى الْحَبِيْب صَلَّى اللّٰهُ تَعَالٰى عَلٰى مُحَمَّد

Medication for narcolepsy*

Add a spoon of honey to water (tepid water is more beneficial) and drink it on an empty stomach every morning regularly. If one is fasting, he should have this drink during Ifṭār. By doing this, اِنْ شَآءَاللّٰہ عَزَّوَجَلَّ, he would be protected from obesity and many other diseases, especially stomach illnesses. In order to make it more beneficial, squeeze a whole or half a lemon onto this drink. If a person feels sleepy while studying or attending an Ijtimā' etc., then the above mentioned medication would prove to be an effective cure for this problem.

Best cure for obesity

The best means to protect oneself from obesity is to follow the remedy prescribed by the Healer of all healers, the Noble Prophet صَلَّى اللّٰهُ تَعَالٰى عَلَيْهِ وَاٰلِهٖ وَسَلَّم who has stated, 'Hunger should be divided into three parts; one part (should be) for food, one for water and one for air.' If one adopts this manner of eating he will never suffer from obesity, gas, flatulence, indigestion and constipation.

Diseases caused by excessive eating

Dear Islamic brothers! Not applying the Madanī guard to the stomach and engaging in excessive eating often result in indigestion and constipation. A very famous proverb goes, 'Constipation is the mother of diseases.' According to doctors, most diseases are caused by an ill stomach. There are twelve types of diseases caused by an upset stomach:

1. Brain diseases.
2. Eye diseases.
3. Throat and tongue diseases.
4. Chest and lung diseases.
5. Paralysis of the face and other parts of the body.
6. Numbness in the lower part of the body.
7. Diabetes.

---

* Narcolepsy is a medical condition in which a person undergoes extreme fatigue and suddenly feels sleepy in the daytime.

8. High blood pressure.
9. Brain haemorrhage.
10. Psychological diseases like insanity etc.
11. Liver and gall bladder diseases.
12. Depression.

Remedy to stay healthy

Sayyidunā Ibn Sālim رَحْمَةُ اللهِ تَعَالٰی عَلَيْه has stated, 'If a person eats dry wheat bread in a proper manner, he will not suffer from any disease except death.' When asked as to what was meant by 'manner', he رَحْمَةُ اللهِ تَعَالٰی عَلَيْه replied, 'One should eat only when hungry and stop eating while still hungry.' *(Iḥyā-ul-'Ulūm, vol. 3, pp. 95)*

Signs of hunger

It is a Sunnaĥ not to eat if you are not hungry. Eating food without hunger at a fixed time or just due to the desire for food is not beneficial at all. Defining hunger, Ḥujjat-ul-Islam, Imām Muhammad Ghazālī عَلَيْهِ رَحْمَةُ اللّٰهِ الْوَالِی has stated, 'The sign of hunger is that if one has a piece of bread in his hand, he should eagerly eat the bread without any accompaniment (gravy etc.). If the Nafs desires to eat only bread or desires gravy with bread, it indicates that one is only a little hungry.' *(Iḥyā-ul-'Ulūm, vol. 3, pp. 97)*

Eating more than one's appetite

To eat more than one's appetite is Ḥarām. Here, 'more' refers to eating to such an extent that would cause indigestion or diarrhoea etc. *(Bahār-e-Sharī'at, vol. 16, pp. 30)*

Not everyone's appetite is same

Looking down on someone who eats excessively or forming an ill opinion about him is not permissible as eating to a full stomach is not a sin. Further, the amount of his (required) daily food intake may be more than others. As the sleep of a person may be different to another, i.e. one person becomes fresh and active by sleeping for only two hours, whereas another person may remain lazy and inactive even after sleeping for ten hours, similarly, one person may become full by eating just one piece of bread while another person may remain hungry even after eating four or five pieces of bread. Therefore, if a person who normally eats five pieces of bread reduces his meal to three pieces of bread, obviously, he will be eating less than his hunger and would be considered to have outdone the person whose stomach becomes full by eating only a single piece of bread.

One should look at his own deeds rather than looking at someone else, as this is certainly better for him in the world and the Hereafter. If we point one finger at someone, three fingers are automatically pointed at us. This indicates that we should reform ourselves instead of finding faults with others.

Hurting feelings of one who eats in excess is Ḥarām

Without the permission of Sharī'aĥ, hurting the feelings of the one who eats in excess is a grave sin and a Ḥarām act that leads to Hell. Sometimes, a person eats excessively because of some compulsion; for instance, the patient suffering from the disease called 'Jū'ul Baqar' (i.e. cow's hunger) remains hungry even after eating a lot of food. Such a patient has to repeatedly eat even unwillingly as his hunger is not satisfied. Likewise, the one who suffers from stomach ulcers has to eat something repeatedly because his pain intensifies on an empty stomach. Anyway, if we see someone eat in excess, we must still have a positive opinion about him because eating less is preferable, but having an ill opinion about a Muslim is Ḥarām.

To drink a lot of water

In extremely hot weather, if a person is very thirsty due to fasting and, at the time of Ifṭār, when cold water and sweet drinks are placed before him, leaving sweet drinks and drinking water in a small quantity so that even the thirst is not completely quenched for the pleasure of Allah عَزَّوَجَلَّ is a good deed and an attribute of the pious. However, it is not a sin if a person drinks enough water so that his thirst is quenched. At times, excessive water is drunk for the cure of some diseases like kidney stones.

Normally, it is extremely hard for Nafs to drink water after the thirst has been quenched. There is, however, a difference when it comes to Zamzam water. To look at this water with the intention of worship is equivalent to attaining the reward of one year's worship. Whoever drinks this blessed water and makes Du'ā, his Du'ā is accepted. *(Al-Maslak-ul-Mutaqassiṭ Al-Ma'rūf Manāsik Al-Mullā 'Alī Qārī, pp. 495)*

We should drink as much Zamzam water as possible with the intention of attaining reward. Ṣadr-ush-Sharī'aĥ, Badr-uṭ-Ṭarīqaĥ, Shaykh Muftī Muhammad Amjad 'Alī A'ẓamī عَلَيْهِ رَحْمَةُ اللّٰهِ الْقَوِی has stated, 'When you drink Zamzam, you should drink it in large amount (so that the stomach is full). It is stated in a Ḥadīš that the difference between us and the hypocrites is that the hypocrites do not fill their stomach with Zamzam.' *(Baĥār-e-Sharī'at, vol. 6, pp. 47) (Al-Mustadrak lil-Ḥākim, vol. 1, pp. 646, Ḥadīš 1738)*

Walk a little

After consulting a physiotherapist, everyone should do some light exercise every day according to his age. Doctors say that one should walk at least 150 steps after having dinner. It is my Madanī suggestion to make a habit of reciting the Ṣalāt (Durūd) (صَلَّى اللّٰهُ تَعَالٰى عَلٰى مُحَمَّد) at least 40 times while walking. اِنْ شَآءَاللّٰه عَزَّوَجَلَّ, you will have walked more than 150 steps by the time you complete the recitation of Ṣalāt 40 times.

Everyone should walk for at least an hour every day. Those who do not have a habit of walking should initially walk for about 12 minutes daily reciting the above-mentioned Ṣalāt 313 times. At the end, they should add وَعَلٰى اٰلِهٖ وَاَصْحَابِهٖ وَبَارِكْ وَسَلِّمْ one time. They would be able to cover a kilometre if they recite the Ṣalāt rather slowly. In this manner, they should develop the habit of walking five kilometres daily within thirty days. Islamic sisters should walk within their homes. Instead of sitting, they should also make it a habit to recite their Waẓāif (i.e. invocations) while walking. Please act upon my suggestion and start walking or else, on the advice of your doctor, you may have to run carrying the burden of stress and depression.

صَلُّوْا عَلَى الْحَبِيْب صَلَّى اللّٰهُ تَعَالٰى عَلٰى مُحَمَّد

Overburden

In the last verse of Sūraĥ Al-Baqaraĥ, part 3, Almighty Allah عَزَّوَجَلَّ says:

لَا يُكَلِّفُ اللّٰهُ نَفْسًا اِلَّا وُسْعَهَا ط

Allah does not burden any soul, but to the extent of his strength.

[Kanz-ul-Īmān (Translation of Quran)] (Part 3, Sūraĥ Al-Baqaraĥ, verse 286)

Dear Islamic brothers! There is absolutely no doubt that Allah عَزَّوَجَلَّ never overburdens anyone. Alas! How sad is the state of the greedy person who eats in excess at meals just for the pleasure of his Nafs and devours many other things during the day and night, overburdening his stomach. Obviously, if the person who can carry just 40 kg weight is overburdened with 100 kg weight, he will collapse. In the same way, there is a limit to the functions of the stomach. If someone overeats without chewing food properly, then how will his stomach be able to digest it? As a result, the entire digestive system will be badly affected. The stomach will become ill and begin to cause diseases in other parts of the body. As our Beloved Rasūl صَلَّى اللهُ تَعَالٰى عَلَيْهِ وَاٰلِهٖ وَسَلَّم has rightly stated, 'The stomach is like a pond in the body and the veins are the streams which proceed towards this pond. If the stomach is healthy, the veins return with health and if the stomach is ill, the veins return with disease.' *(Shu'ab-ul-Īmān, vol. 5, pp. 66, Ḥadīš 5796)*

I eat very little

Some Islamic brothers who are either overweight or have stomach illnesses are heard saying that they eat very little. Some of them lie because of the hardness of their hearts while some say this due to their misconception. If we observe what they call 'little eating' we will come to know that their 'little eating' includes quite a lot of food. During breakfast, they eat eggs, bread, cereal, halvah and Pūrī and then during the day they consume a few cold drinks, ice creams, several cups of tea, biscuits, burgers, pieces of cake, few sweet delicacies etc. In this way, the real cause of their obesity and stomach problems is exposed. If someone's stomach gets full by eating a little, he should also cut down on his food intake so that a little desire for hunger remains. In other words, an ant should cut down according to its weight and an elephant should cut down according to its weight.

Precautions of eating less

1. If your father or mother commands you to eat until the stomach is full, you should obey their command.

2. If you are an employee and eating less causes weakness and makes you less efficient at work, it is necessary to seek permission from your employer for eating less in this case.

3. Similarly, if eating less creates an obstacle in acquiring or imparting Islamic knowledge, you should eat according to your needs.

4. If you are eating with a guest and it seems that he may stop eating (in embarrassment) if you do, then you should continue to eat with him.

5. If your host insists that you eat more and there are no obstacles and you are still a little hungry, you may eat a little as making a Muslim happy is a good deed.

   The Holy Prophet صَلَّى اللهُ تَعَالٰى عَلَيْهِ وَاٰلِهٖ وَسَلَّم has stated, 'He who makes happiness enter a Muslim household, Allah عَزَّوَجَلَّ does not like anything else for that person except Paradise.' *(Ṭabarānī Ṣaghīr, vol. 2, pp. 51)*

صَلُّوْا عَلَى الْحَبِيْب صَلَّى اللهُ تَعَالٰى عَلٰى مُحَمَّد

Eating less is preferable but lying is Ḥarām

If you are a guest somewhere and your host insists that you eat more, but you do not want to eat anymore despite having hunger, so be cautious before replying. You should say, for example, 'May Allah عَزَّوَجَلَّ bless you! May Allah عَزَّوَجَلَّ reward you! جَزَاكَ اللهُ خَيْرًا etc.' Do not tell lies. Despite having hunger, some people tell lies on such occasions. Here are some examples of false statements, 'I have eaten a stomach full', 'My stomach is full', 'No, no, there is no place in my stomach', 'I am telling the truth', 'I am not hungry at all.' etc.

Bear in mind that lying is a major sin and a Ḥarām act that could lead to Hell. We should be extremely cautious while treading on the path of Taqwā (asceticism). We must not be deceived by our Nafs into committing Ḥarām deeds like ostentation, lying, having pride, disobedience to parents, belittling and having an ill opinion about Muslims just for fulfilling the Mustaḥab act of eating less, making us deserving of torment of Hell. Remember that Nafs always induces everyone to do evil. The Holy Quran states:

إِنَّ النَّفْسَ لَأَمَّارَةٌ بِالسُّوْٓءِ

Without doubt, Nafs (sensual appetite) is a big commander of evil.

[Kanz-ul-Īmān (Translation of Quran)] (Part 13, Sūraĥ Yūsuf, verse 53)

We should make every possible effort to overcome our Nafs. Without doubt, there are glad tidings of Paradise for the person who overpowers his Nafs and succeeds in preventing it from evil desires. In this regard, the Holy Quran states:

وَ اَمَّا مَنْ خَافَ مَقَامَ رَبِّهٖ وَنَهَى النَّفْسَ عَنِ الْهَوٰى ﴿۴۰﴾ فَاِنَّ الْجَنَّةَ هِيَ الْمَاْوٰى ﴿۴۱﴾

And he who feared standing in front of his Lord and prohibited his Nafs (self) from lust, without doubt, paradise is (his) destination.

[Kanz-ul-Īmān (Translation of Quran)] (Part 30, Sūraĥ An-Nāzi'āt, verse 40, 41)

What is Nafs?

If you have made up your mind to attain the blessings of hunger by applying the Madanī guard to your stomach for the pleasure of Allah عَزَّوَجَلَّ, then remember that you will be strongly opposed by your Nafs. Controlling the Nafs is not easy. In this regard, Sayyidunā Bāyazīd Bisṭāmī رَحْمَةُ اللهِ تَعَالٰى عَلَيْه has stated, 'Nafs is such an attribute which is not satisfied (with anything) but evil.' (In other words, Nafs is happy only with evil). Sayyidunā Sulaymān Dārānī قُدِّسَ سِرُّهُ الرَّبَّانِي has stated, 'Opposing the Nafs is the most virtuous deed.' *(Kashf-ul-Maḥjūb, pp. 395-396)*

Better than one year's worship

Sayyidunā Sulaymān Dārānī قُدِّسَ سِرُّہُ الرَّبَّانِی has stated, 'Abandoning a desire from the desires of Nafs is more beneficial to the heart than fasting and remaining awake (in worship) for the entire year.' *(Jażb-ul-Qulūb, vol. 2, pp. 336)*

صَلُّوْا عَلَى الْحَبِيْب صَلَّى اللهُ تَعَالٰی عَلٰی مُحَمَّد

Baby fox

Some saints have seen their Nafs in physical form. In this regard, Sayyidunā Muhammad 'Alyān Naswī رَحْمَةُ اللهِ تَعَالٰی عَلَيْه has narrated, 'In the beginning, when I realised the harms of Nafs, I felt an intense hatred towards it. One day, an animal in the shape of a baby fox suddenly came out of my throat. Almighty Allah عَزَّوَجَلَّ made me identify it and I became aware that it was my own Nafs. I immediately chased after it and began to stamp on it with my feet. To my utter amazement, the more I struck, the bigger it got. I said, 'O Nafs! Everything is destroyed by pains and wounds, yet you are growing to the contrary.' It replied, 'I am quite different to others. The things which are harmful to others delight me and the things which delight others are harmful to me.' *(Kashf-ul-Maḥjūb, pp. 407)*

We live to eat

Dear Islamic brothers! Did you see how difficult it is to overpower Nafs? Despite difficulties, we should endeavour to control it. One of the ways of controlling Nafs is to do the opposite of what it desires. For example, if it demands you to eat delicious food or eat until you are full, you should not obey it. Only eat what you need. A great saint, Dātā Ganj Bakhsh رَحْمَةُ اللهِ تَعَالٰی عَلَيْه has stated, 'Hunger is the food of the Ṣiddīqīn and a path of Sulūk for the Murīd (disciple). Previously, people used to eat to survive, yet you live to eat.' *(Kashf-ul-Maḥjūb, pp. 605)*

Patient became doctor

It is narrated that once Sayyidunā Shaykh Khuwājaĥ Maḥbūb-e-Ilāĥī Niẓāmuddīn Auliyā رَحْمَةُ اللهِ تَعَالٰی عَلَيْه fell seriously ill. His disciples told him that there was a pundit in the area who could cure people very quickly by reading some incantations. They asked for permission to take him to the pundit. He رَحْمَةُ اللّٰهِ تَعَالٰی عَلَيْه replied that he would never go to an unbeliever for any treatment. His condition worsened and he fell unconscious. The disciples took him to the same pundit. When the pundit read some incantations and blew on the great Shaykh, he immediately regained consciousness and recovered from illness.

When he found himself well, he asked the pundit, 'How did you attain this expertise?' The pundit replied, 'I have promised my teacher that I would always do the opposite of what my Nafs desires. Therefore, whenever I wish to drink cold water, I drink hot water. When I wish to eat rice, I eat bread. In this way, I have attained expertise by continuously opposing my Nafs.'

The great Shaykh then asked him, 'Tell me, does your Nafs permit you to become a Muslim?' He replied in the negative. The great Shaykh then said, 'If it is prohibiting you from becoming a Muslim, then according to your principle, you should become a Muslim by opposing your Nafs.'

These effective words of the great Shaykh had such an intense impact on the heart of the pundit that he said spontaneously, 'I repent of my unbelief and become a Muslim.' He then recited the Kalimaĥ and became a Muslim.

اَلۡحَمۡدُ لِلّٰه عَزَّوَجَلَّ, the pundit cured Khuwājaĥ Niẓāmuddīn Auliyā رَحْمَةُ اللّٰهِ تَعَالٰی عَلَيْه physically and the Shaykh رَحْمَةُ اللّٰهِ تَعَالٰی عَلَيْه cured him spiritually in return. He cured the body of the great Shaykh and the great Shaykh cured his soul. He cured the external bodily illness of the great Shaykh, and the great Shaykh cured his inner illness of Kufr (unbelief).

صَلُّوۡا عَلَی الۡحَبِيۡب صَلَّی اللّٰهُ تَعَالٰی عَلٰی مُحَمَّد

Cancer of gums

In addition to decreasing the intake of food, those who are habitual consumers of tea and Pān (betel) should also reduce their consumption of the aforementioned items. Let it not be that you reduce the intake of food, but your Nafs begins to deceive you into consuming tea and Pān in excess. Tea is harmful to the kidneys. It is safer to give up the habit of eating Pān, lime and scented aniseed and betel nut. Those who constantly chomp on these items are prone to cancer of throat, gums and mouth. Due to the excessive use of Pān, the mouth becomes red and, if the gums begin to bleed or fill with pus, then this causes the blood and pus to go into the stomach unnoticed. Perhaps, these people will only realise this danger when, Allah عَزَّوَجَلَّ forbids, they suffer from any lethal disease.

Danger of fake Katthā*

It is highly likely that Katthā is not produced in Pakistan. The greedy people who do not care about the detrimental consequences of misdeeds in the world and Hereafter add the colour used in leather-dyeing to sand and sell it as Katthā. As a result, Pān eaters in Pakistan become victims and suffer from various diseases.

Taste on tongue and throat only

The taste of food lasts just for a few seconds whether it is a simple barley bread or a buttered one. As soon as the morsel goes down the throat, the taste of that morsel ends. When a person eats in excess, he feels the taste of food only for a few seconds on his tongue but he may have to face its long lasting religious and worldly harms. If somebody ponders calmly, he will realize that facing prolonged accountability in the Hereafter and embracing chronic and lethal diseases just for a few minutes of pleasure is not a wise act. Therefore, it is safer and better to eat less by applying the Madanī guard to the stomach. Sayyidunā Abū Dardā رَضِیَ اللّٰہُ تَعَالٰی عَنْهُ has said, 'Fulfilment of a desire for a few moments' pleasure causes prolonged grief.'

Reality of delicious food

Ponder for a moment. If the delicious aromatic morsel which makes the mouth water and is eaten with joy and pleasure, suddenly comes out of the stomach due to vomit, will anybody like to even look at it? This is the reality of that delicious morsel. This point can further be elaborated with the help of the following parable.

* A thick brown liquid used in Pān.

Thought-provoking story

Once a public toilet was being cleaned and the human faeces was scattered in some part of that area. People were quickly walking past it placing handkerchiefs on their noses. All of a sudden, the faeces spoke; 'O you who are running away! Do you not recognise who I am? I am the one for which you worked so hard. You prepared me with extreme care and consumed me with immense relish. You also hid me in your bellies. How regretful that your little company has turned me into this disgusting state. Why are you running away from me? I am your delicious Biryānī; I am your oily bread; I am your tasty Qaurmaĥ…'

Facts making us realize our reality

Dear Islamic brothers! There are grave lessons to be learnt from the aforementioned parable. The more delicious the food is, the worse its consequences are. The more flavoursome and oily food man eats, the more smelly and disgusting his waste is. To the contrary, the waste of the animals that merely eat grass is far less filthy than that of a human being. Perhaps, on reading or listening to this text, some people may become infuriated or feel disgusted. I would say to them that their anger is useless. Their anger also has a lesson for them.

Calmly ponder on the fact that in spite of being sinners, we brag and show off without even thinking about our reality. We are so despicable that even the most delicious foods turn into a disgusting and foul smelling waste owing to remaining in our stomach for a short while. Even we resent the mentioning of it.

Seeing someone walk arrogantly, Sayyidunā Ṭāūs رَحْمَةُ اللّٰهِ تَعَالٰی عَلَیْه said to him, 'This should not be the gait (the manner of walking) of the person whose stomach is full of filth.' Sayyidunā Muṭarrif رَحْمَةُ اللّٰهِ تَعَالٰی عَلَیْه once saw Muĥallab, the commander of the army of Ḥajjāj Bin Yūsuf. Muĥallab, dressed in clothes made of silk, was walking arrogantly. Seeing him, Sayyidunā Muṭarrif رَحْمَةُ اللّٰهِ تَعَالٰی عَلَیْه objected. Muĥallab looked at him and asked, 'Do you not know who I am?' The great saint replied, 'I know you very well. In the beginning, you were an unclean droplet (semen) and at the end you will be a rotten corpse and everyone knows that you are walking carrying filth in your belly.' When Muĥallab heard these frank and blunt sentences, he became embarrassed and immediately stopped walking arrogantly. Sayyidunā Muṣ'ab Bin Zubayr رَضِیَ اللهُ تَعَالٰی عَنْهُ has stated, 'It is astonishing that man indulges in vanity whereas he has twice come out of the place of urine.'

صَلُّوْا عَلَى الْحَبِيْب صَلَّى اللهُ تَعَالٰى عَلٰى مُحَمَّد

Do you want to eat less?

If you would like to remain steadfast in applying the Madanī guard to your stomach, i.e. eating less, then act upon my Madanī suggestions which will prove to be very beneficial, اِنْ شَآءَ الله عَزَّوَجَلَّ. Make up your mind according to the advice given by Ḥujjat-ul-Islam, Imām Muhammad Ghazālī عَلَيْهِ رَحْمَةُ اللّٰهِ الْوَالِي. Therefore, he رَحْمَةُ اللهِ تَعَالٰی عَلَيْه has stated, 'Eating food to a full stomach is one of the causes of severity in accountability in the Hereafter and torment at the time of death.' He رَحْمَةُ اللهِ تَعَالٰی عَلَيْه has further stated, 'Eating in abundance causes the rewards to decrease in the Hereafter. Hence the pleasure will decrease in the Hereafter equal to the pleasure you attain in the world.' *(Minĥāj-ul-'Ābidīn, pp. 94)*

Food and drink of people of Hell

Dear Islamic brothers! Ignoring such horrific matters for a few moments of pleasures of the tongue is not a wise act. It is safer to apply the Madanī guard to stomach by reducing the intake of food. If one desires eating delicious cuisine, having cold drinks and thus stuffing himself, he should recall the terrible food and drink of the people of Hell, which has been prepared for the unbelievers.

Describing the food of the dwellers of Hell, Almighty Allah عَزَّوَجَلَّ says in part 25, Sūraĥ Ad-Dukhān, verse 43 to 46:

اِنَّ شَجَرَتَ الزَّقُّوْمِ ﴿۴۳﴾ طَعَامُ الْاَثِيْمِ ﴿۴۴﴾ كَالْمُهْلِ ۚ يَغْلِيْ فِي الْبُطُوْنِ ﴿۴۵﴾ كَغَلْيِ الْحَمِيْمِ ﴿۴۶﴾

Verily, the tree of Zaqqum (cactus) is the food of the sinners. Like molten copper, it boils in the bellies. Like the boiling of scalding water.

[Kanz-ul-Īmān (Translation of Quran)] (Part 25, Sūraĥ Ad-Dukhān, verses 43 to 46)

Pertaining to the drink of the people of Hell, Almighty Allah عَزَّوَجَلَّ says in part 26, Sūraĥ Muhammad, verse 15:

وَ سُقُوۡا مَآءً حَمِیۡمًا فَقَطَّعَ اَمۡعَآءَہُمۡ ﴿۱۵﴾

And they will be made to drink boiling water so that it would cut their intestines into pieces.

[Kanz-ul-Īmān (Translation of Quran)] (Sūraĥ Muhammad, verse 15)

Bowl of poison

Mughīš Bin Samī رَضِیَ اللهُ تَعَالٰی عَنۡهُ has stated that when someone will be brought into Hell, he will be told to wait until he is given a gift. He will then be given a bowl of snake poison. When he brings it close to his face, the flesh and bones of his face will cut into pieces and fall. *(Al-budur-us-Sāfiraĥ fil-Umūr-il-Ākhiraĥ, pp. 442)*

Severe accountability for luxuries

If there is a consensus amongst all the members of the family, then reduce the quantity of spices and oil used in the food by half. There is a possibility that the food will become less tasty – when the flavour is less appealing, one will be less inclined to eat. In this manner, it would become easier to apply the Madanī guard to the stomach and eat less. On the Day of Judgement, there will be no accountability for the simple piece of bread which was consumed to satisfy hunger.

Remember! The more delicious food one will eat, the more severe its accountability will be on the Day of Judgement. For example, accountability of a simple dish like Ǩhichřī[1] would be relatively easier than that of a tasty food like Biryānī[2]. Further, the thing which a person likes more will be considered a big bounty for him. For example, if a person likes Ǩhichřī more than Biryānī, then Ǩhichřī will be considered a bigger bounty for him – thus (in this case) the accountability of Ǩhichřī will be more severe as compared to Biryānī. Likewise, the accountability of cold water in comparison to the ordinary one

---

[1] A very simple food made of rice, lentils, salt and some oil.

[2] A sub-continental cuisine made with rice, oil, meat or chicken and spices.

(not cold), and that of delicious food in comparison with simple one, will be more severe. Similarly, the accountability of hot food will be severe compared to the cold one. As cold food becomes tasteless and our Nafs also does not like it, its accountability will not be severe. We will be asked about every bounty on the Day of Judgement.

صَلُّوْا عَلَى الْحَبِيْب صَلَّى اللهُ تَعَالٰى عَلٰى مُحَمَّد

Three questions about every favour

Sayyidunā Imām Muhammad Ghazālī عَلَيْهِ رَحْمَةُ اللّٰهِ الْوَالِى has stated that three questions would be asked about everything:

1. How did you attain it?
2. Where did you spend it?
3. With what intention did you spend it?

(Minĥāj-ul-ʻĀbidīn, pp. 100)

In the last verse of Sūraĥ At-Takāšur, Allah عَزَّوَجَلَّ says:

ثُمَّ لَتُسْـَٔلُنَّ يَوْمَىِٕذٍ عَنِ النَّعِيْمِ ﴿٨﴾

Then, undoubtedly, you will surely be asked about the favours that day.

[Kanz-ul-Īmān (Translation of Quran)]

Dear Islamic brothers! By Allah عَزَّوَجَلَّ, fortunate are those who follow Sunnaĥ despite facing poverty and adverse conditions compared to those who are lost in their wealth and have worldly authority. In the Hereafter, successful is he who is obedient to Allah عَزَّوَجَلَّ and His Prophet صَلَّى اللهُ تَعَالٰى عَلَيْهِ وَاٰلِهٖ وَسَلَّم in spite of facing destitution, sickness and calamities. Listen to an admonitory narration and learn some lesson.

Dive in Hell

Sayyidunā Anas رَضِىَ اللهُ تَعَالٰى عَنْهُ has narrated that the Holy Prophet صَلَّى اللهُ تَعَالٰى عَلَيْهِ وَاٰلِهٖ وَسَلَّم has stated, 'On the Day of Judgement, an unbeliever who possessed untold bounties in the world will be brought. It will be ordered to submerge him into fire. Therefore, he will be dipped into fire and will then be asked, 'O so and so! Were you ever endowed with bounties?' He will reply, 'No, I was never endowed with any bounty.' After this, the Muslim who faced the most difficulties and trying circumstances in the world will be brought. It will be ordered to submerge him into Paradise. Therefore, he will be submerged into Paradise and will then be asked, 'Did you ever face any trouble and hardship?' He will reply, 'No, I never faced any trouble and hardship.' *(Sunan Ibn Mājaĥ, vol. 4, pp. 530, Ḥadīš 4321)*

The foregoing narration makes it clear that Hell is so terrifying that a mere dip in Hell will make the person forget all the attraction, luxuries and the comforts of the world and he would think that he spent his worldly life in difficulties and troubles. On the other hand, a mere immersion in Paradise is so pleasant and delightful that the person will forget all his troubles and grief of the world and he would think that he never faced any predicament.

صَلُّوا عَلَى الْحَبِيْب   صَلَّى اللهُ تَعَالٰى عَلٰى مُحَمَّد

How to develop habit of eating less?

If the person who is accustomed to excessive eating suddenly starts eating less and applies the Madanī guard to his stomach, he may well become weak and, resultantly, give up hope. What one should do is to reduce the amount of food gradually. For example, if a person who eats 12 breads a day wants to reduce his intake by half, he should break 12 breads into 60 pieces and reduce one piece every day. He will be eating 59 pieces the first day, 58 the next and so on. If he persistently continuous to do so, he will succeed in reducing his intake from 12 breads to six within a month without experiencing any weakness, اِنْ شَآءَاللّٰه عَزَّوَجَلَّ. If someone eats only rice, he can also reduce his food in the same way by diminishing one spoon daily.

Be wary, you should not be deceived by your Nafs when you go to any wedding feast etc. or any delicious food is placed before you. On such occasions, your Nafs will try its best to make you eat in excess suggesting that you can continue eating less the next day. If you yield to your Nafs' demands, it will be difficult for you to remain steadfast. No matter how delicious and tempting the food placed before you is, if you stick to your regimen, you will be successful. However, if you ate a little more on an occasion after you have become steadfast in eating less, then occasionally eating a little more would not prove to be an obstacle in returning to your habit of eating less, اِنْ شَآءَاللّٰه عَزَّوَجَلَّ

Specify portion of your food

One should specify his share of food prior to eating such as half a bread, a quarter plate of rice, seven pieces of squash, one or two small pieces of meat, a small piece of potato and three (table) spoons of gravy. After eating the specified amount of food, one should no longer eat anything no matter how hungry he is. If possible, take your specified amount of food in a separate plate before eating; this is probably the most efficient way of applying the Madanī guard to the stomach. If you have taken more food into your plate due to the desire of your Nafs, put the extra amount of food back in the dish.

Once you have taken your fixed amount of food, then do not take more food no matter how strong your desire is, otherwise, Nafs will demand you to eat more things. Nafs, for instance, will say, '*take one more piece of meat or potato; have one more spoon of rice etc.*' Be cautious on special occasions as well. If the one who has not yet become habitual of applying the Madanī guard to his stomach keeps taking a little amount of food from the dish repeatedly, as is the custom these days, then his Nafs may deceive him into excessive eating by making him forget his specified amount of food.

If many people are eating together in the same platter, and the environment is also appropriate, such as the environment of Dawat-e-Islami's Madanī Qāfilaĥ or that of Jāmi'a-tul-Madīnaĥ - then the Islamic brother or the student of Jāmi'a-tul-Madīnaĥ desiring to apply the Madanī guard to stomach should take his specified amount of food from the platter in his own clay-plate according to Madanī In'āmāt, but should still eat sitting with others. If others resent it, then he should eat with them in their platter.

Therefore, the most appropriate method is to specify the number of morsels. For example, if someone is habitual of eating 12 morsels, he can easily eat his specified 12 morsels while sitting with others counting the number of morsels inwardly.

You can mix your food prior to eating

If there are various varieties of food like bread, gravy, rice, samosas etc., it is also possible to take a little quantity of each item and mix all of them together prior to eating. In this way, the flavour of the food may decrease, which will somewhat help in overcoming Nafs but one should be cautious in mixing food in a public gathering. However, if the gathering has been hosted by an Islamic brother of the Madanī environment and it is obvious that mixing the food will not cause resentment in the heart of the host and there is no fear of ostentation as well, then there is no harm in mixing the food. It is better that an Islamic brother ask the host to allow all the guests to eat as they like. If the host grants permission, the guests can eat in any way they prefer. Someone once told me (the author) that he saw a person who took a small portion of various types of food and mixed all of them prior to eating. People expressed surprise at this; he replied that all the food would eventually mix in his stomach, so he had mixed the food beforehand.

Method of eating less in presence of others

One of the ways of avoiding the insistence of the host and ostentation in the presence of others is to eat small morsels with three fingers chewing them properly. Always try to act upon these Sunnaĥs. In wedding feasts etc., people often eat quickly; they are normally so engrossed in eating that nobody will probably notice you. Even then, if you feel that perhaps you will finish earlier than others, you should suck the bones. In this way, you will hopefully finish with others. If somebody eats less in the presence of others because of ostentation so that people consider him as a pious person, it is a Ḥarām act that may lead him to Hell. It is extremely important to refrain from ostentation. The Holy Prophet صَلَّى اللّٰهُ تَعَالٰى عَلَيْهِ وَاٰلِهٖ وَسَلَّم has said, 'Allah عَزَّوَجَلَّ does not accept the deed in which there is ostentation equal to (the amount of) even a particle.' *(Attarghīb Wattarĥīb, vol. 1, pp. 87)*

There is no harm in revealing a good deed with the righteous intention of inspiring others (to do the same) such as expressing gratitude for a divine bounty. Similarly, if religious leaders, teachers and Shuyūkh reveal their deed in the presence of their followers, students and disciples respectively with the same intention, it is also permissible. However, one should carefully ponder whether the objective is to inspire others and express gratitude or not. If the intention of impressing others with piety exists even in the depths of the heart, it is an act of ostentation that may lead to Hell.

Sincerity is key to acceptance

Eating food to a full stomach throughout life is not a sin, but a single act of ostentation in the whole life is a sin, which can lead to Hell. If a person eats less in the presence of others, giving the impression as if he has applied the Madanī guard to his stomach, but when he reaches his home he devours various types of foods like a hungry lion - such a person is an outright show-off (ostentatious) and is worthy of Hell. Without doubt, wise is he who eats in the company of others in such a way that nobody notices his less eating and maintains the Madanī guard to his stomach at his home and other places. Every deed should be performed just for the pleasure of Allah عَزَّوَجَلَّ as sincerity is the key to acceptance.

Trial for those that eat less

Dear Islamic brothers! It is possible that one will face many trials as a result of applying the Madanī guard to the stomach, i.e. making a habit of eating less. In the beginning, you may become weak and peevish. Some 'well-wishers' may well try to talk you out of it, whereas others may frighten you of the impending weakness; thus psychologically stressing you out. Moreover, hunger and desire for food may further increase because of quick digestion of food due to improvement in the digestive system by the blessing of eating less. Further, the aroma of the food being cooked anywhere will make your mouth water and you may yield to excessive eating. Likewise, you may face a tough trial, especially in the month of Ramadan at the time of Ifṭār due to extreme hunger and thirst, when you will be seeing different types of delicious aromatic foods prepared at your home. Similarly, you will find it very difficult to resist the desire of eating on the occasion of Eid-ul-Aḍḥā when roasted and aromatic meat will be placed before you. But, despite all these trials and tests, you should never lose your courage and determination.

Always remember the following Ḥadīš of the Holy Prophet صَلَّى اللهُ تَعَالٰی عَلَيْهِ وَاٰلِهٖ وَسَلَّم, 'The best worship is the one in which there is more hardship.' *(Kashf-ul-Khifā, vol. 1, pp. 175)*

صَلُّوْا عَلَى الْحَبِيْب صَلَّى اللهُ تَعَالٰى عَلٰى مُحَمَّد

Eat less for forty days consecutively

It is also possible that you will succeed in applying the Madanī guard to your stomach for a few days, but you may begin to eat excessively again. You should not give up hope if it happens. You should continue to persevere with the Madanī guard on your stomach. If your habit of less-eating ever breaks, resume it with new spirit. For example, make the intention of applying the Madanī guard to your stomach for seven days in relation to the seven letters of بِسْمِ اللّٰه. In the same manner, apply the Madanī guard to the stomach for twelve days in relation to 12th Rabī'-ul-Awwal, 15 days in relation to the month of Sha'bān and thirty days in Ramadan.

Make an effort to eat less for forty consecutive days. اِنْ شَآءَاللّٰه عَزَّوَجَلَّ, by doing this, you would be blessed with attaining steadfastness in this deed, as Sayyidunā Waĥb Bin Munabbeĥ رَضِىَ اللّٰهُ تَعَالٰى عَنْهُ has stated, 'If a person makes a habit of doing something for forty days, Allah عَزَّوَجَلَّ makes that habit a part of his nature.' *(Risāla-tul-Qushayriyyaĥ, pp. 243)*

صَلُّوْا عَلَى الْحَبِيْب صَلَّى اللهُ تَعَالٰى عَلٰى مُحَمَّد

Steadfastness in less-eating

At times, offer two Rak'āt Nafl Ṣalāĥ with the intention of Ṣalāt-ul-Ḥājāt and make Du'ā to attain steadfastness in applying the Madanī guard to the stomach and to get rid of the greed for food. Study this chapter of '*Faīzān-e-Sunnat*', '*Excellence of Hunger*' every month or when you have the desire of eating in excess. Also go through the third volume of *Iḥyā-ul-Ulūm* which deals with the troubles of filling the stomach with food. It would be very beneficial. It should also be kept in mind that applying the Madanī guard to the stomach will seem difficult only for the few initial days, especially when food is present on the dining-mat. When the dining-mat is removed, desire for food will also vanish. Once you have persistently applied the Madanī guard to your stomach and have experienced its benefits, you will not like to eat in excess. (Remember) After difficulty, there is ease. Allah عَزَّوَجَلَّ says in Sūrah Alam Nashraḥ, verses 5 and 6:

فَاِنَّ مَعَ الْعُسْرِ یُسْرًا ۙ﴿۵﴾ اِنَّ مَعَ الْعُسْرِ یُسْرًا ؕ﴿۶﴾

So, without doubt, there is ease with hardship. Without doubt, there is ease with hardship.

[Kanz-ul-Īmān (Translation of Quran)] (Part 30, Sūrah Alam Nashraḥ, verse 5, 6)

Bitter advice

Those who have a Madanī mindset will make sincere efforts to apply the Madanī guard to their stomach, اِنْ شَآءَاللّٰه عَزَّوَجَلَّ. If they are determined, they will come up with appropriate and practicable ways to succeed. As for those who suffer from the disease of 'Jū'ul Kalb[1]' or have greed for food, even dozens of books and numerous speeches are insufficient for them. Advice in the form of this written material would skim over their heads; they would turn a deaf ear to it and would not bother to ponder with a calm mind. Further, there is a great possibility that they might even criticize the very idea of applying the Madanī guard of the stomach. For such people, a saint has rightly said, 'When the person whose stomach is full is advised, his mind refuses to accept.' *(Nuzĥa-tul-Majālis, vol. 1, pp. 178)*

Such a person is paving the way for Satan and Nafs to tempt him with new tastes and flavours. Such people purchase books of various recipes to learn how to prepare delicious and extravagant cuisine. They repeatedly munch on food and then have to use the lavatory. They become fat and overweight. Such people also waste a lot of money in doctors' fees and medicine whereas they themselves possess the cure for their illnesses. If they apply the Madanī guard to their stomach they could get rid of illnesses, medications and doctors' fees. However, the unwise people who 'live to eat' instead of 'eating to live' will never be able to live a healthy life.

[1] An Arabic expression used for those who are always hungry and look for things to chomp on. Its literal meaning is 'hungry as a dog'.

O Allah عَزَّوَجَلَّ! For the sake of the blessed stones tied to the blessed stomach of Your Beloved Prophet صَلَّى اللهُ تَعَالٰى عَلَيْهِ وَاٰلِهٖ وَسَلَّم due to extreme hunger, bless us with the gifts of less-eating, less-sleeping and less-speaking. For the sake of the hunger of the companions رَضِىَ اللّٰهُ تَعَالٰى عَنْهُم and the Auliyā رَحِمَهُمُ اللّٰهُ تَعَالٰى, bless all of us with graceful hunger and Madanī guard for our stomach.

Ilāĥī عَزَّوَجَلَّ*! Payi kā Qufl-e-Madīnaĥ kar 'aṭā ĥam ko*
Karam say istiqāmat kā khazīnaĥ kar 'aṭā ĥam ko

Enable us to apply Madanī guard to our stomach, O Allah عَزَّوَجَلَّ*!*
Bless us with the treasure of steadfastness, O Allah عَزَّوَجَلَّ

اٰمِيْن بِجَاهِ النَّبِيِّ الْاَمِيْن صَلَّى اللهُ تَعَالٰى عَلَيْهِ وَاٰلِهٖ وَسَلَّم

صَلُّوْا عَلَى الْحَبِيْب صَلَّى اللهُ تَعَالٰى عَلٰى مُحَمَّد
تُوْبُوْا اِلَى الله اَسْتَغْفِرُ الله
صَلُّوْا عَلَى الْحَبِيْب صَلَّى اللهُ تَعَالٰى عَلٰى مُحَمَّد

اَلْحَمْدُ لِلّٰهِ رَبِّ الْعٰلَمِيْنَ وَ الصَّلٰوةُ وَ السَّلَامُ عَلٰى سَيِّدِ الْمُرْسَلِيْنَ

اَمَّا بَعْدُ فَاَعُوْذُ بِاللّٰهِ مِنَ الشَّيْطٰنِ الرَّجِيْمِ ؕ بِسْمِ اللّٰهِ الرَّحْمٰنِ الرَّحِيْمِ ؕ

52 Parables

1. Feast at home of Sayyidunā Jābir رَضِیَ اللّٰهُ عَنْهُ

Sayyidunā Jābir رَضِیَ اللّٰهُ تَعَالٰی عَنْهُ, one of the renowned companions, has narrated: During the battle of Khandaq, while we were digging the trench, a big boulder was unearthed. The companions approached the Holy Prophet صَلَّى اللّٰهُ تَعَالٰى عَلَيْهِ وَاٰلِهٖ وَسَلَّم and told him that they had encountered a very hard boulder. The Beloved and Blessed Prophet صَلَّى اللّٰهُ تَعَالٰى عَلَيْهِ وَاٰلِهٖ وَسَلَّم replied, I am coming (into the trench). The Holy Prophet صَلَّى اللّٰهُ تَعَالٰى عَلَيْهِ وَاٰلِهٖ وَسَلَّم then rose. He صَلَّى اللّٰهُ تَعَالٰى عَلَيْهِ وَاٰلِهٖ وَسَلَّم had stones bound to his blessed stomach. We also had not eaten anything for three days. The Noble Rasūl صَلَّى اللّٰهُ تَعَالٰى عَلَيْهِ وَاٰلِهٖ وَسَلَّم then took a pickaxe and struck the boulder, breaking it into pieces and turning it into a heap of sand. I said, 'O the Beloved and Blessed Prophet صَلَّى اللّٰهُ تَعَالٰى عَلَيْهِ وَاٰلِهٖ وَسَلَّم! Please give me permission to go home.'

On arriving home, I said to my wife that I could no longer bear to see the Noble Prophet صَلَّى اللّٰهُ تَعَالٰى عَلَيْهِ وَاٰلِهٖ وَسَلَّم in this starving condition. Do you have anything to eat? She replied that there was some barley and a small goat. I slaughtered the little goat, kneaded the barley (into dough) and started cooking the food. When the food and breads were about to be prepared, I approached the Beloved and Blessed Prophet صَلَّى اللّٰهُ تَعَالٰى عَلَيْهِ وَاٰلِهٖ وَسَلَّم and said, 'O the Noble Prophet صَلَّى اللّٰهُ تَعَالٰى عَلَيْهِ وَاٰلِهٖ وَسَلَّم! I have a little food; please come along with a few companions.' He صَلَّى اللّٰهُ تَعَالٰى عَلَيْهِ وَاٰلِهٖ وَسَلَّم asked, 'How much food is there?' I told him the quantity of food. He صَلَّى اللّٰهُ تَعَالٰى عَلَيْهِ وَاٰلِهٖ وَسَلَّم replied, 'The food is delicious and sufficient.' He صَلَّى اللّٰهُ تَعَالٰى عَلَيْهِ وَاٰلِهٖ وَسَلَّم then said, 'Tell (her) neither to open the pot nor to remove the bread from the oven until I arrive.' The Holy Prophet صَلَّى اللّٰهُ تَعَالٰى عَلَيْهِ وَاٰلِهٖ وَسَلَّم ordered the companions رَضِیَ اللّٰهُ تَعَالٰی عَنْهُم to accompany him. I went to my house and told my wife, 'May you be blessed, the Holy Prophet صَلَّى اللّٰهُ تَعَالٰى عَلَيْهِ وَاٰلِهٖ وَسَلَّم is coming to our home with the Muĥājirīn, the Anṣār and some other people.' She asked whether the Holy Prophet صَلَّى اللّٰهُ تَعَالٰى عَلَيْهِ وَاٰلِهٖ وَسَلَّم asked about the quantity of food, I replied, 'yes.'

After a short while, the Noble Prophet صَلَّى اللّٰهُ تَعَالٰى عَلَيْهِ وَاٰلِهٖ وَسَلَّم arrived and ordered the companions to enter the house without causing a crowd. Then, the Holy Prophet صَلَّى اللّٰهُ تَعَالٰى عَلَيْهِ وَاٰلِهٖ وَسَلَّم himself began to break the bread with his own blessed hands and place meat on it. Whenever he صَلَّى اللّٰهُ تَعَالٰى عَلَيْهِ وَاٰلِهٖ وَسَلَّم took any bread or meat, he صَلَّى اللّٰهُ تَعَالٰى عَلَيْهِ وَاٰلِهٖ وَسَلَّم immediately closed the oven and the pot and distributed the food among the companions. He صَلَّى اللّٰهُ تَعَالٰى عَلَيْهِ وَاٰلِهٖ وَسَلَّم continued to take meat from the pot and bread from the oven till every companion ate to full stomach, but the food still remained. He صَلَّى اللّٰهُ تَعَالٰى عَلَيْهِ وَاٰلِهٖ وَسَلَّم then said to me, 'Eat and give people (this food) as a gift because people are hungry.'
(Ṣaḥīḥ Bukhārī, vol. 5, pp. 55, Ḥadīš 4101)

May Allah عَزَّوَجَلَّ have mercy on them and forgive us without accountability for their sake!

صَلُّوْا عَلَى الْحَبِيْب صَلَّى اللّٰهُ تَعَالٰى عَلٰى مُحَمَّد

Dear Islamic brothers! The foregoing parable clearly indicates that the Holy Prophet صَلَّى اللّٰهُ تَعَالٰى عَلَيْهِ وَاٰلِهٖ وَسَلَّم adopted intentional hunger. On one hand, he صَلَّى اللّٰهُ تَعَالٰى عَلَيْهِ وَاٰلِهٖ وَسَلَّم tied stones to his blessed stomach due to hunger and, on the other hand, he صَلَّى اللّٰهُ تَعَالٰى عَلَيْهِ وَاٰلِهٖ وَسَلَّم fed a large number of companions with just a little amount of food.

There are thousands of Madanī pearls in this Prophetic miracle[1]. One of these pearls is that our Holy Prophet صَلَّى اللّٰهُ تَعَالٰى عَلَيْهِ وَاٰلِهٖ وَسَلَّم is not helpless. By the grace of Allah عَزَّوَجَلَّ, he صَلَّى اللّٰهُ تَعَالٰى عَلَيْهِ وَاٰلِهٖ وَسَلَّم possesses the treasures of both worlds and has the authority to distribute them.

The aforementioned Madanī parable also highlights the spirit and passion of the companions for spreading the 'call to righteousness' despite facing severe hardships and starvation even by binding stones on their blessed stomachs. We, on the other hand, are not prepared to bear even a little difficulty in the path of Allah عَزَّوَجَلَّ despite having all conveniences and comforts. Without doubt, no Prophet will come now. It is now the duty of the Muslims to invite others towards righteousness. By Allah عَزَّوَجَلَّ! Today the condition of the Muslims has been very miserable. When a true devotee of Islam sees the empty Masājid, his heart sheds tears of blood. Here is an admonitory parable in this respect.

---

[1] Prophetic miracle means Mu'jizaĥ.

2. Madanī Qāfilaĥ inhabited Masjid

An Islamic brother has stated our Madanī Qāfilaĥ travelled from Bāb-ul-Madīnaĥ (Karachi) to Punjab for twelve days in order to learn and spread Sunnaĥ. When we arrived in the town of Sohawa, we discovered that the Masjid where we were to stay was closed. After obtaining the key and opening the Masjid, we noticed that everything was full of dust. It looked as if the Masjid had been closed for a very long time.

اَلْحَمْدُلِلّٰہ عَزَّوَجَلَّ! We all cleaned the Masjid and then visited the town calling the folks towards righteousness and pleading them to come to the Masjid. Regretfully, no one came to the Masjid because of the lack of our sincerity. We, however, did not give up hope. With our trust in Allah عَزَّوَجَلَّ, we entered a nearby playground where we anxiously gave an invitation to the youngsters who were busy playing. اَلْحَمْدُلِلّٰہ عَزَّوَجَلَّ! Their hearts softened and some of them accompanied us to the Masjid on the spot. They offered Ṣalāĥ and listened to the Sunnaĥ-Inspiring speech. At our request, they also made the intention of coming to the Masjid regularly. Looking at this faith-refreshing scene, an approximately 70-year-old man said, 'I used to advise people to come to the Masjid but they turned a deaf ear. اَلْحَمْدُلِلّٰہ عَزَّوَجَلَّ! Today people have once again started attending the Masjid regularly and offering Ṣalāĥ due to the blessing of the Madanī Qāfilaĥ.'

3. Eighty companions رَضِیَ اللہ عَنْہُم and a little food

Sayyidunā Anas رَضِیَ اللہُ تَعَالٰی عَنْہ has narrated that Sayyidunā Abū Ṭalḥaĥ once came home and told Sayyidatunā Umm-e-Sulaym رَضِیَ اللہ تَعَالٰی عَنْہَا, 'I have heard the low voice of the Holy Prophet صَلَّی اللہُ تَعَالٰی عَلَیْہِ وَاٰلِہٖ وَسَلَّم, which indicates his extreme hunger. Do you have anything to eat?' She replied that she had a few pieces of barley bread. She wrapped them in a part of her scarf and placed it under my (Sayyidunā Anas') clothing and covered me with the other part of the scarf. Then, she sent me to the Holy Prophet صَلَّی اللہُ تَعَالٰی عَلَیْہِ وَاٰلِہٖ وَسَلَّم. When I reached the Masjid, I saw that the Beloved and Blessed Prophet صَلَّی اللہُ تَعَالٰی عَلَیْہِ وَاٰلِہٖ وَسَلَّم was sitting with a large group of people. I also stood over there. Seeing me, the Holy Prophet صَلَّی اللہُ تَعَالٰی عَلَیْہِ وَاٰلِہٖ وَسَلَّم asked (revealing the knowledge of Ghayb), 'Did Abū Ṭalḥaĥ رَضِیَ اللہُ تَعَالٰی عَنْہ send you?' I replied, 'Yes, Yā Rasūlallāĥ صَلَّی اللہ تَعَالٰی عَلَیْہِ وَاٰلِہٖ وَسَلَّم.' 'For food?' He صَلَّی اللہ تَعَالٰی عَلَیْہِ وَاٰلِہٖ وَسَلَّم further asked. I replied, 'Yes! O Beloved Prophet صَلَّی اللہُ تَعَالٰی عَلَیْہِ وَاٰلِہٖ وَسَلَّم.' The Holy Prophet صَلَّی اللہُ تَعَالٰی عَلَیْہِ وَاٰلِہٖ وَسَلَّم then asked his companions to accompany him and I began to walk ahead of them till I reached the house and informed Sayyidunā Abū Ṭalḥaĥ رَضِیَ اللہُ تَعَالٰی عَنْہُ of the situation. Sayyidunā Abū Ṭalḥaĥ رَضِیَ اللہُ تَعَالٰی عَنْہُ said, 'O Umm-e-Sulaym (رَضِیَ اللہُ تَعَالٰی عَنْھَا)! The Noble Prophet صَلَّى اللهُ تَعَالٰى عَلَيْهِ وَاٰلِهٖ وَسَلَّم is coming along with many people. We do not have enough food to serve all of them.' She رَضِیَ اللہُ تَعَالٰی عَنْھَا replied, 'Allah عَزَّوَجَلَّ and His Prophet صَلَّى اللهُ تَعَالٰى عَلَيْهِ وَاٰلِهٖ وَسَلَّم know better.'

Sayyidunā Abū Ṭalḥaĥ رَضِیَ اللہُ تَعَالٰی عَنْہُ went and took the Prophet of Raḥmaĥ, the Intercessor of Ummaĥ صَلَّى اللهُ تَعَالٰى عَلَيْهِ وَاٰلِهٖ وَسَلَّم to his house. The Holy Prophet صَلَّى اللهُ تَعَالٰى عَلَيْهِ وَاٰلِهٖ وَسَلَّم said, 'O Umm-e-Sulaym (رَضِیَ اللہُ تَعَالٰی عَنْھَا)! Bring whatever you have.' She presented the same pieces of bread. On the instruction of the Holy Prophet صَلَّى اللهُ تَعَالٰى عَلَيْهِ وَاٰلِهٖ وَسَلَّم, the breads were broken up. Sayyidatunā Umm-e-Sulaym رَضِیَ اللہُ تَعَالٰی عَنْھَا poured some clarified butter on breads which was used as gravy. The Holy Prophet صَلَّى اللهُ تَعَالٰى عَلَيْهِ وَاٰلِهٖ وَسَلَّم then read what Allah عَزَّوَجَلَّ willed and blew on them. He صَلَّى اللهُ تَعَالٰى عَلَيْهِ وَاٰلِهٖ وَسَلَّم then said, 'Let ten of them enter.' Therefore, ten entered, ate the bread till their stomach became full and then left. He صَلَّى اللهُ تَعَالٰى عَلَيْهِ وَاٰلِهٖ وَسَلَّم ordered again, 'Call another ten.' Another ten came, ate and left. He صَلَّى اللهُ تَعَالٰى عَلَيْهِ وَاٰلِهٖ وَسَلَّم kept calling companions in the group of ten until all of them ate and their hunger was satisfied. There were about seventy or eighty companions. *(Ṣaḥīḥ Muslim, vol. 2, pp. 178, Ḥadīš 2040)*

According to another narration, ten would enter and ten would exit until none of them remained hungry, and all of them ate till they were full. When the Beloved and Blessed Prophet صَلَّى اللهُ تَعَالٰى عَلَيْهِ وَاٰلِهٖ وَسَلَّم finally gathered the food, the amount of food was the same as was in the beginning.

Another narration says, ten companions ate food at a time until all the eighty companions ate. After this, the Holy Prophet صَلَّى اللهُ تَعَالٰى عَلَيْهِ وَاٰلِهٖ وَسَلَّم and the household consumed food but it still remained. In another narration, it is also stated that the remaining food was given to the neighbours. *(Ṣaḥīḥ Muslim, vol. 2, pp. 178, Ḥadīš 2040)*

May Allah عَزَّوَجَلَّ have mercy on them and forgive us without accountability for their sake!

صَلُّوْا عَلَى الْحَبِيْب   صَلَّى اللهُ تَعَالٰى عَلٰى مُحَمَّد

Dear Islamic brothers! This was indeed the miracle of the Holy Prophet صَلَّى اللهُ تَعَالٰى عَلَيْهِ وَاٰلِهٖ وَسَلَّم that no reduction took place in the apparent small amount of food despite 80 companions' eating it. How great is the status of the Holy Prophet صَلَّى اللهُ تَعَالٰى عَلَيْهِ وَاٰلِهٖ وَسَلَّم that he remains hungry himself but makes his devotees eat innumerable foods. There is a faith-refreshing Ḥadīš. Therefore, he صَلَّى اللهُ تَعَالٰى عَلَيْهِ وَاٰلِهٖ وَسَلَّم said, 'Allah عَزَّوَجَلَّ bestows and I distribute.' *(Ṣaḥīḥ Bukhārī, vol. 1, pp. 30, Ḥadīš 71)*

4. Gigantic fish

Sayyidunā Abū 'Abdullāĥ Jābir Bin 'Abdullāĥ رَضِىَ اللهُ تَعَالٰى عَنْهُ has narrated: The Holy Prophet صَلَّى اللهُ تَعَالٰى عَلَيْهِ وَاٰلِهٖ وَسَلَّم once sent us to do Jihad against the Quraysh. There were a total of 300 Muslim Mujāĥidīn whose commander was Sayyidunā Abū 'Ubaydaĥ Bin Jarraĥ رَضِىَ اللهُ تَعَالٰى عَنْهُ. We were given a small sack of dates as our provisions for the journey. Sayyidunā Abū 'Ubaydaĥ رَضِىَ اللهُ تَعَالٰى عَنْهُ used to give each one of us a single date every day.

When he was asked as to how they used to survive on merely a single date every day, he replied that they used to suck the date as a little child does and drink water thereafter. This was sufficient for the entire day and night. He goes onto say, we would make the tree leaves (which the camels eat) fall with our spears, soak them in water and then eat the leaves.

While passing through the seashore, we saw a huge thing from afar like a sand dune. When we approached it, we discovered that it was a dead fish. Sayyidunā Abū 'Ubaydaĥ رَضِىَ اللهُ تَعَالٰى عَنْهُ said, 'This is dead (and we cannot eat it)' but then he added, 'No, we have been sent by the Holy Prophet صَلَّى اللهُ تَعَالٰى عَلَيْهِ وَاٰلِهٖ وَسَلَّم and are travelling in the path of Allah عَزَّوَجَلَّ. You people are also suffering from severe hunger; therefore, you may eat this.' We survived on that fish for a month, we were three hundred and all of us became energetic and active. We would carve large amounts of fat from its eye cavity. We also cut buffalo-sized pieces of flesh from the fish. The eye cavity of the fish was so large that Sayyidunā Abū 'Ubaydaĥ رَضِىَ اللهُ تَعَالٰى عَنْهُ made thirteen of us sit within this cavity (and we all sat in it). We took one of its ribs and made it stand like a bow, then put the saddle on a large camel's back; the rib of the fish was so huge that the camel passed beneath the rib without touching it. We also took some dry meat with us as provisions for the journey (ahead).

When we arrived in the Holy city of Madīnaĥ and came in the blessed court of the Holy Prophet صَلَّى اللهُ تَعَالٰى عَلَيْهِ وَاٰلِهٖ وَسَلَّم, we mentioned this incident. The Holy Prophet صَلَّى اللهُ تَعَالٰى عَلَيْهِ وَاٰلِهٖ وَسَلَّم

said, 'That was sustenance Allah عَزَّوَجَلَّ created for you. Do you have some of that meat? If you have, give to me for eating.' We sent the Holy Prophet صَلَّى اللهُ تَعَالٰى عَلَيْهِ وَاٰلِهٖ وَسَلَّم the meat which he صَلَّى اللهُ تَعَالٰى عَلَيْهِ وَاٰلِهٖ وَسَلَّم consumed. *(Ṣaḥīḥ Muslim, vol. 2, pp. 147, Ḥadīš 1935)*

May Allah عَزَّوَجَلَّ have mercy on them and forgive us without accountability for their sake!

صَلُّوْا عَلَى الْحَبِيْب   صَلَّى اللهُ تَعَالٰى عَلٰى مُحَمَّد

5. Amīn-ul-Ummaĥ

Dear Islamic brothers! May our lives be sacrificed on the spirit and enthusiasm of the companions رَضِىَ اللّٰهُ تَعَالٰى عَنْهُم! The resources were so scarce that they had to survive on leaves of trees and a single date a day! Despite facing such tough circumstances, they would fight the enemies of Islam and sacrifice their lives in the path of Allah عَزَّوَجَلَّ

The campaign mentioned in the foregoing parable is called 'Sayf-ul-Baḥr' or 'Jaysh-ul-'Usraĥ.' Sayyidunā Abū 'Ubaydaĥ Bin Jarraĥ رَضِىَ اللّٰهُ تَعَالٰى عَنْهُ, one of the ten great companions called 'Asharaĥ-e-Mubashsharaĥ', was the commander of the Muslim army. The Holy Prophet صَلَّى اللهُ تَعَالٰى عَلَيْهِ وَاٰلِهٖ وَسَلَّم gave him the great title of 'Amīn-ul-Ummaĥ' (the trustworthy for the Ummaĥ).

He embraced Islam in the early Islamic period as a result of the individual effort made by Sayyidunā Abū Bakr Ṣiddīq رَضِىَ اللّٰهُ تَعَالٰى عَنْهُ. He رَضِىَ اللّٰهُ تَعَالٰى عَنْهُ was extremely brave, courageous, tall and his blessed face was thin. During the battle of Uḥud, when two metal-spikes got embedded in the blessed cheek of the Holy Prophet صَلَّى اللهُ تَعَالٰى عَلَيْهِ وَاٰلِهٖ وَسَلَّم, Sayyidunā Abū 'Ubaydaĥ رَضِىَ اللّٰهُ تَعَالٰى عَنْهُ pulled them out from the blessed face of the Beloved and Blessed Prophet صَلَّى اللهُ تَعَالٰى عَلَيْهِ وَاٰلِهٖ وَسَلَّم with his own teeth. Due to this, two of his own front teeth broke. *(Al-Uṣābaĥ fī Tamīz-iṣ-Ṣaḥābaĥ, vol. 3, pp. 476)*

May Allah عَزَّوَجَلَّ have mercy on them and forgive us without accountability for their sake!

صَلُّوْا عَلَى الْحَبِيْب   صَلَّى اللهُ تَعَالٰى عَلٰى مُحَمَّد

Dear Islamic brothers! Finding the huge fish on the occasion of 'Jaysh-ul-'Usraĥ', the companions' eating it for a month and then bringing its flesh to Madīnaĥ on camels without any change in its taste were all indeed saintly miracles of Sayyidunā Abū 'Ubaydaĥ رَضِیَ اللهُ تَعَالٰی عَنْهُ and other companions رَضِیَ اللّٰہُ تَعَالٰی عَنْہُم.

Allah عَزَّوَجَلَّ showers His mercy upon those who tread on His path. He عَزَّوَجَلَّ bestows greatness upon them even in times of trouble. Paying homage to the sacrifices of the companions, every Muslim should always be ready to serve Islam.

اَلْحَمْدُلِلّٰہ عَزَّوَجَلَّ! All the Islamic brothers and sisters of Dawat-e-Islami have a Madanī ambition, that is, 'I must strive to reform myself and the people of the entire world اِنْ شَآءَاللّٰہ عَزَّوَجَلَّ.' In order to accomplish this Madanī ambition, numerous Madanī Qāfilaĥs of Dawat-e-Islami travel from town to town and city to city. Every Muslim should travel with these Madanī Qāfilaĥs and reap the blessings. (In this regard) you have just listened to how amazingly those glorious individuals, treading on the path of Allah عَزَّوَجَلَّ, were blessed with divine help in the form of a gigantic fish. اَلْحَمْدُلِلّٰہ عَزَّوَجَلَّ, even today, those who sincerely endeavour to take the step on the path of Allah عَزَّوَجَلَّ, with the intention of serving Islam, are blessed and graced by the Almighty عَزَّوَجَلَّ. Here is a blessing of Dawat-e-Islami's Madanī Qāfilaĥ.

6. Heart patient was cured

A person from Bāb-ul-Madīnaĥ, Karachi, had a heart disease. Doctors told him that the two arteries of his heart were blocked and suggested angiography to him as the cure. This poor person became extremely worried, as he was unable to afford the expenses of the surgery. Meanwhile, making individual effort, an Islamic brother persuaded him to travel with a Sunnaĥ-Inspiring Madanī Qāfilaĥ of Dawat-e-Islami and make Du'ā. Therefore, he travelled with a 3-days Madanī Qāfilaĥ.

On his return from the Madanī Qāfilaĥ, he felt much better. When he had his tests done, the reports showed no heart disease at all. The doctor asked him astonishingly, 'Two of your heart's arteries were blocked, but now they have opened; how did it happen!' He replied that he had been cured from the lethal heart disease due to the blessing of travelling with Dawat-e-Islami's Madanī Qāfilaĥ.

Lūtnay raḥmatayn Qāfilay mayn chalo
Sīkĥnay Sunnatayn Qāfilay mayn chalo
Dil mayn gar dard ĥo ḍar say rukh zard ĥo
Pāo gey rāḥatayn Qāfilay mayn chalo

To gain mercy, travel with Madanī Qāfilaĥ
To learn Sunnaĥ, travel with Madanī Qāfilaĥ
If you have heart problem and are frightened of it
You will be cured, travel with Madanī Qāfilaĥ

صَلُّوْا عَلَى الْحَبِيْب   صَلَّى اللّٰهُ تَعَالٰى عَلٰى مُحَمَّد

7. Prophet Yaḥyā عَلَيْهِ السَّلَام and Satan

It is narrated that Prophet Yaḥyā عَلٰی نَبِیِّنَا وَعَلَیْهِ الصَّلٰوةُ وَالسَّلَام once saw Satan with many traps (for people) and asked him about them. He replied that those were the traps of sensual desires by which he entraps people. Sayyidunā Yaḥyā عَلٰی نَبِیِّنَا وَعَلَیْهِ الصَّلٰوةُ وَالسَّلَام asked him, 'Do you have any trap for me?' Satan replied, 'No, however, one night you ate food till you were full, so I made it difficult for you to offer your Ṣalāĥ that night.' Upon hearing this, Sayyidunā Yaḥyā عَلَيْهِ السَّلَام said, 'By Allah عَزَّوَجَلَّ! I will never eat food to a full stomach in the future.' Satan responded, 'I will also no longer tell anyone such useful things.' *(Minĥāj-ul-'Ābidīn, pp. 93)*

May Allah عَزَّوَجَلَّ have mercy on him and forgive us without accountability for his sake!

صَلُّوْا عَلَى الْحَبِيْب   صَلَّى اللّٰهُ تَعَالٰى عَلٰى مُحَمَّد

Pleasure in worship

Dear Islamic brothers! Commenting on the foregoing parable, Ḥujjat-ul-Islam, Sayyidunā Muhammad Ghazālī عَلَيْهِ رَحْمَةُ اللّٰهِ الْوَالِی has stated: This is the state of such a noble individual عَلٰی نَبِیِّنَا وَعَلَیْهِ الصَّلٰوةُ وَالسَّلَام who ate food to a full stomach just once in his whole life. What will be the condition of the person remaining hungry just once in his entire life? Can such a person hope to have pleasure in his worship? Eating to a full stomach causes a reduction in worship because when a person eats to a full stomach his body becomes heavy, he feels sleepy and his body parts become lazy. He cannot carry out any work despite making efforts. He lies on the ground all the time like a dead body. It is rightly said that when you become a glutton, then consider yourself like the person in chains. Sayyidunā Abū Sulaymān Dārānī رَحْمَةُ اللهِ تَعَالٰی عَلَيْه has stated, 'I feel the most pleasure in worship when my back touches my stomach due to hunger.' *(Minĥāj-ul-'Ābidīn, pp. 93)*

May Allah عَزَّوَجَلَّ have mercy on them and forgive us without accountability for their sake!

صَلُّوْا عَلَى الْحَبِيْب صَلَّى اللهُ تَعَالٰى عَلٰى مُحَمَّد

8. He spewed milk

Once, a slave of Sayyidunā Abū Bakr Ṣiddīq رَضِیَ اللهُ تَعَالٰی عَنْهُ presented some milk to him. He رَضِیَ اللهُ تَعَالٰی عَنْهُ drank the milk. His slave asked, 'Previously, whenever I presented anything to you, you used to ask about it, but you did not ask about this milk.' Upon hearing this, he رَضِیَ اللهُ تَعَالٰی عَنْهُ asked his slave as to where he had brought the milk from. The slave replied that during the (pre-Islamic) era of ignorance, he had treated a sick person by reciting some incantations and the milk was given to him as the payment of reciting those incantations. Listening to this, Sayyidunā Abū Bakr Ṣiddīq رَضِیَ اللهُ تَعَالٰی عَنْهُ immediately placed his fingers into his throat and spewed out whatever milk he had swallowed. After doing this, he رَضِیَ اللهُ تَعَالٰی عَنْهُ prayed to the Almighty with extreme humility, 'O Allah عَزَّوَجَلَّ! I have done whatever I could do; forgive some of the milk left in the veins.' *(Minĥāj-ul-'Ābidīn, pp. 97)*

May Allah عَزَّوَجَلَّ have mercy on him and forgive us without accountability for his sake!

صَلُّوْا عَلَى الْحَبِيْب صَلَّى اللهُ تَعَالٰى عَلٰى مُحَمَّد

Dear Islamic brothers! How pious and virtuous Sayyidunā Abū Bakr Ṣiddīq رَضِیَ اللهُ تَعَالٰی عَنْهُ was! The unbelievers often used to recite blasphemous incantations to exorcise patients. This practice dates back to the pre Islamic era of ignorance. As the slave had read incantations during the days of ignorance, Sayyidunā Abū Bakr Ṣiddīq رَضِیَ اللهُ تَعَالٰی عَنْهُ spewed out the milk he had swallowed for fear that the slave may have spoken words of Kufr (blasphemy).

9. Roasted meat

Once, Sayyidunā Abū Ĥurayraĥ رَضِیَ اللّٰہُ تَعَالٰی عَنْہُ passed by some people who were eating roasted meat. Seeing him, they offered him to join them but he رَضِیَ اللّٰہُ تَعَالٰی عَنْہُ refused saying that the Holy Prophet صَلَّی اللّٰہُ تَعَالٰی عَلَیْہِ وَاٰلِہٖ وَسَلَّم left the world in such a state that he صَلَّی اللّٰہُ تَعَالٰی عَلَیْہِ وَاٰلِہٖ وَسَلَّم never ate even barley bread to his full stomach. *(Ṣaḥīḥ Bukhārī, vol. 6, pp. 252, Ḥadīš 5414)*

May Allah عَزَّوَجَلَّ have mercy on them and forgive us without accountability for their sake!

Roasted thigh

Dear Islamic brothers! On one hand, Sayyidunā Abū Ĥurayraĥ رَضِیَ اللّٰہُ تَعَالٰی عَنْہُ refused to eat the roasted meat because the memories of the hunger of the Holy Prophet صَلَّی اللّٰہُ تَعَالٰی عَلَیْہِ وَاٰلِہٖ وَسَلَّم brought about grief in him. On the other, there are the so-called devotees like us who pound upon the roasted meat, when placed before us, like a starving lion forgetting all love and grief and devour it so voraciously that we even miss the Jamā'at of Ṣalāĥ.

Alas! The above misdeed is often committed in dinner feasts. Even on the occasions of the Niyāz of Auliyā, which is a Nafl act, many people miss their Jamā'at just because of greed for food. It is my Madanī appeal that whenever you organize any gathering, please ensure that the time of any Ṣalāĥ does not fall during the ceremony. If the time of Ṣalāĥ happens to fall, the host and guests should all immediately proceed to the Masjid forgoing all activity. If you do not have a valid exemption justified by the Sharī'aĥ, it is Wājib (compulsory) to join the first Jamā'at in the Masjid. Even if you offer Ṣalāĥ with Jamā'at at home, you will still be considered a sinner for missing the Wājib Jamā'at. According to some Islamic jurists, the person who does not come to the Masjid before the Iqāmaĥ, is a sinner.

Fear of losing faith at time of death

It is not allowed at all to miss the first Jamā'at of Farḍ Ṣalāĥ held in Masjid on account of attending Ifṭār-dinner, ceremonies, Niyāz (meal served to send reward to Auliyā) and Na'at-reciting etc. In case of holding the Jamā'at of Tarāwīḥ at home or in a hall or a bungalow, it is Wājib to offer the Farḍ-Rak'at (of 'Ishā Ṣalāĥ) with the primary Jamā'at in the Masjid first if there is a Masjid in the vicinity. Those not offering Farḍ Ṣalāĥ with the primary Jamā'at held in Masjid without a valid exemption, despite having capability, should fear.

Sayyidunā 'Abdullāĥ Bin Mas'ūd رضی اللہ تعالٰی عنہ has said, 'The one liking to meet Allah عَزَّوَجَلَّ as a Muslim tomorrow (the Judgement Day) should regularly offer these five Ṣalāĥ with Jamā'at at the place where Ażān is uttered, for Allah عَزَّوَجَلَّ has rendered Sunan-e-Ĥudā (Sunnaĥ of guidance) as Mashrū' for your Prophet صَلَّى اللهُ تَعَالٰى عَلَيْهِ وَاٰلِهٖ وَسَلَّم and Ṣalāĥ with Jamā'at is also one of the Sunan-e-Ĥudā. If you offered Ṣalāĥ at your homes like the one who stays behind and offers in his house, you would leave the Sunnaĥ of your Holy Prophet صَلَّى اللهُ تَعَالٰى عَلَيْهِ وَاٰلِهٖ وَسَلَّم and if you left the Sunnaĥ of your Holy Prophet صَلَّى اللهُ تَعَالٰى عَلَيْهِ وَاٰلِهٖ وَسَلَّم, you would go astray. *(Ṣaḥīḥ Muslim, vol. 1, pp. 232, Ḥadīš 257)*

The foregoing Ḥadīš implies that the one who offers Ṣalāĥ with Jamā'at will die with faith, whereas the one who misses the first Jamā'at of Masjid without the permission of Sharī'aĥ is in the danger of losing his faith at the time of death.

O Allah عَزَّوَجَلَّ! Bless us with offering the daily five Ṣalāĥ with Jamā'at with the first Takbīr (i.e. Takbīr-e-Aūlā) in the first row of the Masjid!

آمِیْن بِجَاہِ النَّبِیِّ الْاَمِیْن صَلَّى اللهُ تَعَالٰى عَلَيْهِ وَاٰلِهٖ وَسَلَّم

◆◆◆

A'lā Ḥaḍrat رَحْمَةُ اللهِ تَعَالٰى عَلَيْه has stated, 'Several Aḥādīš state that when a man stands to offer Ṣalāĥ, an angel places its mouth onto his mouth and whatever he recites, comes out of his mouth and enters the angel's mouth. If anything is stuck between his teeth, the angels are so distressed by it that nothing else distresses them to such an extent.

Mayn pānchon namāzayn pařĥūn bā-Jamā'at
Ĥo taufīq aysī 'aṭā Yā Ilāĥī عَزَّوَجَلَّ

May I offer five Ṣalāĥ with Jamā'at, O Almighty!
Please, bestow upon me this ability!

صَلُّوا عَلَى الْحَبِيب صَلَّى اللهُ تَعَالٰى عَلٰى مُحَمَّد

10. Thought-provoking sermon

Sayyidunā Khālid Bin 'Umayr 'Adawī رَضِیَ اللهُ تَعَالٰی عَنْهُ has narrated that the governor of Basra, Sayyidunā 'Utbaĥ Bin Ghazwān رَضِیَ اللهُ تَعَالٰی عَنْهُ once delivered a sermon. After glorifying Almighty Allah عَزَّوَجَلَّ, he said: Without doubt, the world has declared its end and it is departing with utmost speed. At the moment, only as much part of the world remains as the small amount (of food) is left at the bottom of the pot and the owner of the pot is benefiting from it. You are about to be transferred from this mortal world to an eternal abode. Therefore, take the best of things from the world and depart towards that abode (of Hereafter). We have been told that a stone will be thrown into Hell from its corner that will continue to fall for seventy years, but it will not reach the bottom (despite the seventy year travel). By Allah عَزَّوَجَلَّ! This Hell will certainly be filled. Are you surprised at this? We have also been told that the distance between the two doors of Paradise is of forty years and it will be filled because of the crowd. I was one of the seven people who were with the Holy Prophet صَلَّى اللهُ تَعَالٰی عَلَيْهِ وَاٰلِهٖ وَسَلَّم. Except the leaves of trees, we had nothing to eat and our lip corners had sores (because of eating the leaves). Once I found a piece of cloth which I tore in half sharing the other half with Sa'd Bin Mālik رَضِیَ اللهُ تَعَالٰی عَنْهُ. We both used it as Taĥband (i.e. a piece of cloth used to cover the lower part of the body). (In those days, we suffered such intense hardships and poverty) and today, every one of us is the ruler of a city. I take refuge of Allah عَزَّوَجَلَّ from considering myself dignified but being regarded as despicable by Allah عَزَّوَجَلَّ. *(Ṣaḥīḥ Muslim, vol. 2, pp. 408, Ḥadīš 2967)*

May Allah عَزَّوَجَلَّ have mercy on them and forgive us without accountability for their sake!

Dear Islamic brothers! Did you see that the companions endured starvation in order to promote the 'call to righteousness', (at times) relying only on leaves! They endured extreme hardships but (still managed to) nurture the tree of Islam. In those times, there were severe difficulties as mentioned in the following narration.

11. The first to shoot an arrow in path of Allah

A companion from amongst the 'Asharaĥ-e-Mubashsharaĥ[1] Sayyidunā Sa'd Bin Abī Waqqās رَضِیَ اللّٰہُ تَعَالٰی عَنْہُ has narrated, 'I am the first Arab who shot an arrow in the path of Allah عَزَّوَجَلَّ. We used to fight in battles in the company of the Holy Prophet صَلَّی اللّٰہُ تَعَالٰی عَلَیْہِ وَاٰلِہٖ وَسَلَّم and we had nothing to eat except for the leaves of acacia tree. Our faeces would be like the excrement of the sheep, which has no sign whatsoever of any sticky substances.' *(Ṣaḥīḥ Bukhārī, vol. 7, pp. 231, Ḥadīš 6453)*

May Allah عَزَّوَجَلَّ have mercy on him and forgive us without accountability for his sake!

Dear Islamic brothers! Even after having conveniences, the spirit of these companions did not even relent, let alone end. Rather, they became more fearful lest they consider themselves dignified whereas Allah عَزَّوَجَلَّ is displeased with them. May Almighty Allah عَزَّوَجَلَّ grant us the fervour to spread the 'call to righteousness' for the sake of the companions' spirit of making sacrifices for Islam. Āmīn!

Every Islamic brother should make up his mind that 'I must strive to reform myself and the people of the entire world.' In order to pay homage to the great sacrifices made by companions in the path of Allah عَزَّوَجَلَّ, all of us should travel with the Madanī Qāfilaĥs of Dawat-e-Islami to attain religious and worldly benefits. Here is an account of the blessings of a Madanī Qāfilaĥ.

12. Warts on hand

The following is a report from one of the Islamic brothers from Tando Adam (Sindh, Pakistan). He has said, 'I was very worried for about two years due to warts on my arm. I spent a lot of money on medication and even had an operation performed, but no medicine proved to be effective. Instead, the warts increased in number. I feared that these warts would turn into cancer and my arm would be amputated on that account. May Almighty Allah عَزَّوَجَلَّ keep Dawat-e-Islami's provincial Majlis of Baluchistan happy! They held an Ijtimā' at provincial level in Quetta for two days (27th and 28th of Jumādal Aūlā 1425 A.H.).

[1] The 10 companions who were given the glad tidings from the Holy Prophet صَلَّی اللّٰہُ تَعَالٰی عَلَیْہِ وَاٰلِہٖ وَسَلَّم of entering the Heaven.

Luckily, I also attended this two day Sunnaĥ-Inspiring Ijtimā'. Innumerable Madanī Qāfilaĥ of Dawat-e-Islami travel throughout the world to spread Sunnaĥ. I had already heard that the prayers of the travellers of Madanī Qāfilaĥ are answered. So, plucking up the courage, I also travelled with Dawat-e-Islami's Sunnaĥ-Inspiring Madanī Qāfilaĥ for 12 days from Quetta. I prayed to Allah عَزَّوَجَلَّ with intense humility with the Wasīlaĥ of the Holy Prophet صَلَّى اللهُ تَعَالٰی عَلَیْهِ وَاٰلِهٖ وَسَلَّم. This sinner was blessed and all the warts of my hand disappeared, اَلْحَمْدُ لِلّٰه عَزَّوَجَلَّ. The most amazing thing is that the warts removed by the operation had left their marks on my arm but even the marks of the warts healed during the twelve days Madanī Qāfilaĥ disappeared.'

Lūtnay raḥmatayn Qāfilay mayn chalo
Sīkĥnay Sunnatayn Qāfilay mayn chalo

To gain mercy, travel with Madanī Qāfilaĥ
To learn Sunnaĥ, travel with Madanī Qāfilaĥ

Dear Islamic brothers! The (spiritual) king of Baghdad, Ghauš-e-A'ẓam رَضِیَ اللّٰهُ تَعَالٰی عَنْهُ endeavoured for many years to get rid of the traps of Satan and Nafs. He spent 25 years consecutively in the jungles of Iraq worshipping alone for attaining the pleasure of Allah عَزَّوَجَلَّ.

13. Ghusl for forty times in one night

It is stated in *Baĥjat-ul-Asrār* that Shaykh 'Abdul Qādir Jīlānī رَحْمَةُ اللهِ تَعَالٰی عَلَیْه has stated, 'اَلْحَمْدُ لِلّٰه عَزَّوَجَلَّ, I spent many years in the jungles of Karkh. I used to survive on tree leaves and herbs. Every year, a person used to come and give me a wool gown to wear. In order to get rid of the love of the world, I endured many hardships. I remained anonymous; people would consider me as dumb and insane due to my silence. I used to walk on thorns, enter dangerous caves and horrific valleys without any fear. The world used to appear to me in a beautiful form, but I never turned my attention towards it, اَلْحَمْدُ لِلّٰه عَزَّوَجَلَّ. My Nafs used to plead to me that it would obey whatever I liked and sometimes it used to argue with me. Allah عَزَّوَجَلَّ gave me victory over it. For a long time, I stayed on the plains of Madyan and kept battling against my Nafs. For one year, I consumed the things lying on the ground and did not drink water. For the other year, I drank only water and did not eat anything. Then for one year, I neither ate nor drank anything. I would encounter extreme hardships. One night, I was tested in extreme cold weather. I would repeatedly fall asleep and Ghusl became obligatory for me due to nocturnal emission. I would immediately go to the river and make Ghusl over there. On that night alone, I had to make Ghusl forty times (in icy cold water). *(Baĥjat-ul-Asrār, pp. 164-165)*

May Allah عَزَّوَجَلَّ have mercy on him and forgive us without accountability for his sake!

صَلُّوْا عَلَى الْحَبِيْب صَلَّى اللهُ تَعَالٰى عَلٰى مُحَمَّد

14. Picking bits of food from floor and eating them

The king of Baghdad, Shaykh 'Abdul Qādir Jīlānī رَحْمَةُ اللهِ تَعَالٰى عَلَيْه has stated: I would intend to pick up the fallen things, leaves and grass to eat, but I would leave them making self-sacrifice for others who would also be in search of those things. I would remain hungry. When I became extremely weak and was close to death, I found something lying on the floor near the flower market and picked it up. I sat at a corner to eat it. Suddenly, I saw a non-Arab youngster who had fresh bread and roasted meat, he sat and began to eat. When I saw him eat, my desire for food intensified. When he would take the morsel in his hand to eat, I would spontaneously open my mouth so that he may put the morsel into my mouth. However, I rebuked my Nafs and asked it to be patient as Allah عَزَّوَجَلَّ is with me. I clarified to my Nafs that I would never ask the young man for anything to eat.

All of a sudden, turning towards me, the youngster said, 'Brother! Please come and join me in this meal.' I refused but he insisted. My Nafs also insisted that I eat but I kept advising it to have patience. However, I ate a little due to the insistence of the young man. He then asked me, 'Where are you from?' I told him that I was from Jīlān. He replied that he was also from Jīlān. He asked me if I knew (Shaykh) 'Abdul Qādir رَضِيَ اللهُ تَعَالٰى عَنْهُ, the grandson of the famous ascetic Walī of Allah عَزَّوَجَلَّ, Sayyid 'Abdullāĥ Sawma'ī رَضِيَ اللهُ تَعَالٰى عَنْهُ. I replied that I was the same person. Listening to this, he became a little anxious and said, 'When I was leaving for Baghdad, your mother gave me eight gold coins to give to you. Having reached Baghdad, I kept looking for you but no one gave me your whereabouts until all my money was spent. I have been hungry for three days. When I became helpless due to extreme hunger, I bought some bread and this roasted meat with some of your money.' He then said, 'Your honour! Please eat this food without hesitation because you are its owner. Previously, you were my guest, now I am your guest.' Giving me the remaining money he said, 'I seek your forgiveness, I bought this food in the state of helplessness due to extreme hunger.' (Shaykh said) I became very happy when I heard this. I then gave him the remaining food and money; he accepted and left. *(Ṭabqāt-e-Ḥanābilaĥ, vol. 3, pp. 250)*

May Allah عَزَّوَجَلَّ have mercy on him and forgive us without accountability for his sake!

صَلُّوْا عَلَى الْحَبِيْب صَلَّى اللهُ تَعَالٰى عَلٰى مُحَمَّد

Dear Islamic brothers! To give one's own money to someone else despite facing extreme hunger and helplessness is a very ascetic deed. This is certainly the unique quality of Auliyā. Countless accolades to the hunger and self-sacrifice of Shaykh 'Abdul Qādir Jīlānī رَحْمَةُ اللهِ تَعَالٰى عَلَيْه! If only we would also develop the same passion of self-sacrifice within ourselves. Alas! We are not generous enough to give the remaining food to others even after eating fully and satisfying our appetite; instead, we store the remaining food in the fridge. If only we would develop the mindset of attaining the huge reward of self-sacrifice.

15. After difficulty, there is ease

Quoting Shaykh 'Abdul Qādir Jīlānī رَحْمَةُ اللهِ تَعَالٰى عَلَيْه, 'Allāmaĥ Imām Sha'rānī قُدِّسَ سِرُّهُ الرَّبَّانِي writes in the book *Ṭabqāt-ul-Kubrā*, 'At the beginning, I faced many hardships; when these hardships reached their peak, I lay on the ground and kept reciting verses 5 and 6 of Sūraĥ Alam Nashraḥ which are as follows:

فَاِنَّ مَعَ الْعُسْرِ يُسْرًا ۙ﴿۵﴾ اِنَّ مَعَ الْعُسْرِ يُسْرًا ؕ﴿۶﴾

So, without doubt, there is ease with hardship. Without doubt, there is ease with hardship.

[Kanz-ul-Īmān (Translation of Quran)] (Part 30, Sūraĥ Alam Nashraḥ, verse 5, 6)

By the blessing of these verses of the Holy Quran, all those difficulties were removed.'

May Allah عَزَّوَجَلَّ have mercy on him and forgive us without accountability for his sake!

Dear Islamic brothers! Surely, one has to make sacrifices to achieve something. Our own Shaykh 'Abdul Qādir Jīlānī رَحْمَةُ اللهِ تَعَالٰى عَلَيْه also made many sacrifices and struggled hard in order to attain the closeness of Allah عَزَّوَجَلَّ and pleasure of His Prophet صَلَّى اللهُ تَعَالٰى عَلَيْهِ وَاٰلِهٖ وَسَلَّم, overcome his Nafs and Satan, remain safe from sins and distant from the love of the world, promote the 'call to righteousness' and gain many rewards by preaching and thus bringing countless unbelievers into the fold of Islam. Although we cannot bear as many hardships as our Ghauš-e-A'ẓam رَحْمَةُ اللهِ تَعَالٰى عَلَيْه did, we can at least make a little effort without giving up hope.

O those who have utmost devotion to Shaykh 'Abdul Qādir Jīlānī رَحْمَةُ اللهِ تَعَالٰى عَلَيْه! He spent twenty-five years in the jungles of Iraq enduring extreme hunger and thirst to gain the pleasure of Allah عَزَّوَجَلَّ. If only we also travel with the Madanī Qāfilaĥs of Dawat-e-Islami to propagate Islamic teachings and Sunnaĥ of the Holy Prophet صَلَّى اللهُ تَعَالٰى عَلَيْهِ وَاٰلِهٖ وَسَلَّم throughout the world!

صَلُّوْا عَلَى الْحَبِيْب صَلَّى اللهُ تَعَالٰى عَلٰى مُحَمَّد

16. Eating only ten raisins a day

Abū Aḥmad Ṣaghīr عَلَيْهِ رَحْمَةُ اللهِ الْكَبِيْر has narrated: Sayyidunā Abū 'Abdullāĥ Bin Khafīf رَحْمَةُ اللهِ تَعَالٰى عَلَيْه instructed me to bring only ten raisins for him at the time of Ifṭār. One evening, having sympathy for him, I gave him fifteen raisins. Looking at me, he asked, 'Who asked you to bring fifteen raisins?' He then ate only ten and left the other five. *(Risāla-tul-Qushayriyyaĥ, pp. 143)*

May Allah عَزَّوَجَلَّ have mercy on them and forgive us without accountability for their sake!

Amazing benefits of raisins

Dear Islamic brothers! Did you see? Sayyidunā Abū 'Abdullāĥ رَحْمَةُ اللهِ تَعَالٰى عَلَيْه used to eat only ten raisins a day. Countless accolades on the manner in which the saints used to subdue their Nafs! His choice of eating large raisins was fabulous. The Noble Rasūl صَلَّى اللهُ تَعَالٰى عَلَيْهِ وَاٰلِهٖ وَسَلَّم has stated, 'Eat this (large raisin) because it is a good food. It strengthens the blood vessels and muscles, alleviates weakness and anger, removes phlegm, makes the face attractive and the mouth fragrant.' *(Kashf-ul-Khifā, vol. 2, pp. 431, Ḥadīš 284)*

In the Ḥadīš narrated by Sayyidunā 'Alī كَرَّمَ اللّٰهُ تَعَالٰى وَجْهَهُ الْكَرِيْم, it is also mentioned that the raisin reduces weakness, improves temperament, makes the breath fragrant and eases grief. *(Kanz-ul-'Ummāl, vol. 10, pp. 18, Ḥadīš 28261)*

To drink currant-soaked water is Sunnaĥ

Currants used to be soaked in water for the Noble Prophet صَلَّى اللّٰهُ تَعَالٰى عَلَيْهِ وَاٰلِهٖ وَسَلَّم. Thereafter, he صَلَّى اللّٰهُ تَعَالٰى عَلَيْهِ وَاٰلِهٖ وَسَلَّم would drink the water during the next two days and sometimes till the evening of the third. After this, the servants would either drink the remaining water or pour it somewhere (because their taste would change). *(Sunan Abī Dāwūd, vol. 3, pp. 337, Ḥadīš 3713)*

Raisin is a food as well as a medicine. One can eat it with or without its skin. A famous Muḥaddiš, Sayyidunā Imām Zuĥrī رَحْمَةُ اللّٰهِ تَعَالٰى عَلَيْه has stated, 'He who desires to memorise Ḥadīš should consume (an appropriate quantity of) raisins.' One can also consume raisins with its seed. Imām Zuĥrī رَحْمَةُ اللّٰهِ تَعَالٰى عَلَيْه has stated that the seeds of large raisins are beneficial to stomach. Soak large raisins in water for a few hours, remove the skin, and eat the pulp. The pulp of the raisin is an effective remedy for lung problems and chronic cough. It relieves the pain of the kidney and bladder. It gives strength to the spleen and liver. It softens and strengthens the stomach and assists in the digestion of food.

Cure for cough

Take 40 small raisins (or one can take up to 80, if there is no side effect) and three almonds, recite Ṣalāt-'Alan-Nabī 11 times and blow on them and then eat them daily. اِنْ شَآءَاللّٰه عَزَّوَجَلَّ, this will greatly assist in mitigating one's cough. It will prove to be an effective medicine for phlegm. The amount of small raisins can be increased, if necessary, but give children lesser amounts. Continue to take this medicine until the cough is cured.

Red raisins

Sayyidunā 'Alī كَرَّمَ اللّٰهُ تَعَالٰى وَجْهَهُ الْكَرِيْم has stated that the person who eats 21 red raisins daily will be safe from all those ailments which he is afraid of. *(Abū Nu'aym)*

17. Desire to eat egg plant

Sayyidunā Abū Naṣr Tamār رَحْمَةُ اللهِ تَعَالٰى عَلَيْه has narrated: اَلْحَمْدُ لِلّٰه عَزَّوَجَلَّ, Once Sayyidunā Bishr Ḥāfī رَحْمَةُ اللهِ تَعَالٰى عَلَيْه came to my house at night. I thanked the Almighty عَزَّوَجَلَّ for the arrival of such a great saint in my house. I then said to him, 'Yā Sayyidī (O my master), we bought some meat by selling the yarn that my daughter made from the cotton that came from Khorasan city. It would be a great honour, if you would kindly join us for Ifṭār.' He رَحْمَةُ اللهِ تَعَالٰى عَلَيْه replied, 'If I intended to eat anywhere, I would eat at your house اِنْ شَآءَاللّٰه عَزَّوَجَلَّ.' He رَحْمَةُ اللهِ تَعَالٰى عَلَيْه then continued, 'I have the desire to eat eggplant from many years, but I have not been able to.' I (the narrator) said, 'Yā Sayyidī! What a pleasant coincidence that we have cooked meat with eggplant purchased with Ḥalāl income.' He رَحْمَةُ اللهِ تَعَالٰى عَلَيْه replied, 'I will eat eggplant only when its love is removed from my heart.' *(Risāla-tul-Qushayriyyaĥ, pp. 143)*

May Allah عَزَّوَجَلَّ have mercy on him and forgive us without accountability for his sake!

صَلُّوْا عَلَى الْحَبِيْب صَلَّى اللهُ تَعَالٰى عَلٰى مُحَمَّد

Dear Islamic brothers! Did you see how strictly our pious saints would refrain from following the desires of their Nafs? Sayyidunā Bishr Ḥāfī عَلَيْهِ رَحْمَةُ اللّٰهِ الْكَافِى did not consume eggplant for many years opposing his Nafs. What marvellous Madanī mindset these people had! If their Nafs demanded them to eat, they would not eat; if it insisted them not to eat, they would. In short, they would always go against the desires of their Nafs.

18. Eat and drink

It is reported that the Nafs of Sayyidunā Bishr Ḥāfī عَلَيْهِ رَحْمَةُ اللّٰهِ الْكَافِى desired to eat Bāqilā (vegetables such as peas and beans) but he did not consume it for many years, defying his Nafs. After his demise, someone saw him in a dream and asked how Allah عَزَّوَجَلَّ treated him. He رَحْمَةُ اللهِ تَعَالٰى عَلَيْه replied, 'Giving me the glad-tidings of forgiveness, Allah عَزَّوَجَلَّ said, 'O you who did not eat and drink anything in the world, now eat and drink a lot!' *(Risāla-tul-Qushayriyyaĥ, pp. 406)*

May Allah عَزَّوَجَلَّ have mercy on him and forgive us without accountability for his sake!

صَلُّوْا عَلَى الْحَبِيْب صَلَّى اللهُ تَعَالٰى عَلٰى مُحَمَّد

19. Purpose of eating

Sayyidunā Abū Sa'īd Khazzār عَلَيْهِ رَحْمَةُ اللّٰهِ الْغَفَّار has narrated, 'It was my routine to eat every three days. Once while travelling through a jungle, I became extremely hungry and weak. Thus, I sat at a side. Suddenly, a voice from Ghayb echoed, 'Abū Sa'īd! Are you desirous of eating food to please your Nafs or do you wish to diminish your weakness without food?' I replied, 'O Allah عَزَّوَجَلَّ! I only desire strength.' He رَحْمَةُ اللّٰهِ تَعَالٰی عَلَيْه said that he رَحْمَةُ اللّٰهِ تَعَالٰی عَلَيْه immediately became so energetic and active that he travelled for 12 Manzils without eating and drinking anything.' *(Kashf-ul-Maḥjūb, pp. 453)*

May Allah عَزَّوَجَلَّ have mercy on him and forgive us without accountability for his sake!

صَلُّوْا عَلَى الْحَبِيْب صَلَّى اللّٰهُ تَعَالٰى عَلٰى مُحَمَّد

Dear Islamic brothers! Did you see that the Auliyā of Allah عَزَّوَجَلَّ do not eat for pleasure? Instead, they eat to gain strength so that they could perform worship. They are blessed with spiritual strength without eating and drinking by the special mercy of Allah عَزَّوَجَلَّ. Sayyidunā Abū Sa'īd Khazzār عَلَيْهِ رَحْمَةُ اللّٰهِ الْغَفَّار travelled for 12 Manzils without eating and drinking (by the spiritual strength bestowed upon him by Allah عَزَّوَجَلَّ!) The distance covered in one day is called a Manzil, which implied that he travelled for 12 days without eating and drinking anything.

20. Hiding to avoid eating

Sayyidunā Abū Sa'īd Khazzār عَلَيْهِ رَحْمَةُ اللّٰهِ الْغَفَّار has stated: Once I was travelling with a caravan in the state of extreme hunger. During the journey, a garden of date-palms appeared. My Nafs desired to eat dates but I refused to fulfil its desire. The caravan stayed and camped by the same garden but I went to the jungle where I hid into sand so that my Nafs would not repeatedly demand me to eat dates. After a little while, one of my travelling companions came to where I was hiding. He took me to the camp. I asked him as to how he got to know that I was there. He replied that he heard a voice from Ghayb saying, 'One of my friends is hiding in the sand, go and bring him with you.' *(Tażkira-tul-Auliyā, vol. 2, pp. 36)*

May Allah عَزَّوَجَلَّ have mercy on them and forgive us without accountability for their sake!

صَلُّوْا عَلَى الْحَبِيْب صَلَّى اللّٰهُ تَعَالٰى عَلٰى مُحَمَّد

اَلۡحَمۡدُ لِلّٰہ عَزَّوَجَلَّ! Dawat-e-Islami, a global & non-political movement of Quran and Sunnaĥ, is effectively spreading the message of Sunnaĥ throughout the world. Every Muslim should join this movement for the betterment of his world and the Hereafter and make up his mind that, 'I must strive to reform myself and the people of the entire world.' اِنۡ شَآءَاللّٰہ عَزَّوَجَلَّ

21. Blessing of a saint's company

Sayyidunā Ibrāĥīm Khawāṣ رَحۡمَةُاللّٰہِ تَعَالٰی عَلَیۡہ was once travelling in a jungle; a person approached him and said, 'I wish to accompany you.' When he رَحۡمَةُاللّٰہِ تَعَالٰی عَلَیۡہ looked at the person with spiritual insight, he رَحۡمَةُاللّٰہِ تَعَالٰی عَلَیۡہ felt a sense of resentment towards him. After a little while, the person disclosed, 'I am a non-Muslim monk and I have come from Rome to join your company.' The reason for the resentment was now obvious – it was the Kufr of the monk. He رَحۡمَةُاللّٰہِ تَعَالٰی عَلَیۡہ told the monk, 'I do not have anything to eat and drink, you may get into trouble.' The monk replied, 'Yā Sayyidī! You are renowned throughout the world for your Taqwā (asceticism), but you are still worried about food and drink!'

Surprised at this reply, Sayyidunā Ibrāĥīm Khawāṣ رَحۡمَةُاللّٰہِ تَعَالٰی عَلَیۡہ permitted the monk to accompany him on his journey. They travelled for seven days without eating and drinking anything. The monk, hungry and thirsty, pleaded, 'Yā Sayyidī! I can no longer bear, please arrange for some food and drink.' Sayyidunā Ibrāĥīm Khawāṣ رَحۡمَةُاللّٰہِ تَعَالٰی عَلَیۡہ prostrated and pleaded, 'O Allah عَزَّوَجَلَّ! This unbeliever has pinned his hopes on me. My honour is in Your Power. Do not disgrace me in the eyes of this unbeliever.' As soon as he raised his head from prostration, he saw that there was a tray containing two pieces of bread and two glasses of water. They ate the food, drank water and resumed their journey.

After travelling for another seven days without food, they stopped somewhere. The monk prostrated and made Du'ā. Suddenly, a tray appeared on which there were four pieces of bread and four glasses of water. Sayyidunā Ibrāĥīm Khawāṣ رَحۡمَةُاللّٰہِ تَعَالٰی عَلَیۡہ became astonished and intended not to eat that food as it was apparently sent for an unbeliever. The monk said: Yā Sayyidī! Please eat and listen to two glad tidings. The first is that I embrace Islam, he then recited the Kalimaĥ. Secondly, you hold a very high status in the court of Allah عَزَّوَجَلَّ. When I was in prostration, I made the following Du'ā, 'O Allah عَزَّوَجَلَّ! If Muhammad صَلَّى اللّٰہُ تَعَالٰی عَلَیۡہِ وَاٰلِہٖ وَسَلَّم is Your true Prophet, bestow upon me two pieces of bread and two glasses of water and if Sayyidunā Ibrāĥīm Khawāṣ رَحۡمَةُاللّٰہِ تَعَالٰی عَلَیۡہ is Your friend, please bestow two more pieces of bread and two glasses of water.' Having finished the Du'ā, when I arose from the prostration, I found this tray of food and drink here. Listening to this, Sayyidunā Ibrāĥīm Khawāṣ رَحْمَةُ اللهِ تَعَالٰى عَلَيْه ate the food. اَلْحَمْدُ لِلّٰه عَزَّوَجَلَّ the new Muslim also gained a high status among the Auliyā. *(Kashf-ul-Maḥjūb, pp. 433 to 435)*

May Allah عَزَّوَجَلَّ have mercy on them and forgive us without accountability for their sake!

صَلُّوْا عَلَى الْحَبِيْب صَلَّى اللهُ تَعَالٰى عَلٰى مُحَمَّد

Dear Islamic brothers! Auliyā (often) bear hunger for many days. They are blessed with divine help and food is sent for them from Ghayb. By the mercy of Allah عَزَّوَجَلَّ and the blessing of the company of Sayyidunā Ibrāĥīm Khawāṣ رَحْمَةُ اللهِ تَعَالٰى عَلَيْه even an unbeliever not only embraced Islam but also attained sainthood. Everyone should endeavour to join the company of the pious and refrain from evil company. A Ḥadīš states, 'A good companion is the one whose sight reminds you of Allah عَزَّوَجَلَّ, whose speech increases your (good) deed and whose deed reminds you of the Hereafter.' *(Al-Jāmi'-uṣ-Ṣaghīr, vol. 2, pp. 247, Ḥadīš 4063)*

صَلُّوْا عَلَى الْحَبِيْب صَلَّى اللهُ تَعَالٰى عَلٰى مُحَمَّد

22. Good company, faithful death

Man is influenced by the company that surrounds him. If a sesame seed is placed in the petals of a rose, it acquires the rosy colour and fragrance. Similarly, by the blessings of the Madanī environment of Dawat-e-Islami and the company of the devotees of Rasūl, even a worthless stone turns into a precious sparkling diamond by the mercy of Allah عَزَّوَجَلَّ and His Noble Prophet صَلَّى اللهُ تَعَالٰى عَلَيْهِ وَاٰلِهٖ وَسَلَّم and departs from this world in such a glorious way that others develop a desire to emulate and aspire for a similar death instead of remaining alive. Hence, a person from Tando Allah Yar (Sindh, Pakistan) joined Dawat-e-Islami and began to offer Ṣalāĥ five times a day with the blessing of the company of devotees of Rasūl. In Ramadan, he attended the 10-day Sunnaĥ Inspiring I'tikāf organized by Dawat-e-Islami and memorized some Quranic Sūraĥs, Du'ās and Sunnaĥs.

He also made the intention of growing a fist-length beard, wearing a green turban, attending the weekly Sunnaĥ-Inspiring Ijtimā' and travelling with Madanī Qāfilaĥs. In short, a Madanī transformation took place in his life. He sincerely repented of his past sins and strived to live according to Sunnaĥ.

One day, unfortunately his clothes caught fire, burning almost eighty percent of his body. Even in this critical condition, he was constantly reciting Ṣalāt-'Alan-Nabī and making Żikr instead of complaining. He was also reciting the Du'ās and Sūraĥs he had memorised during the I'tikāf in the company of the devotees of Rasūl. He kept reciting Du'ās and Quranic Sūraĥs for almost 48 hours and, at dawn, during the Ażān of Fajr Ṣalāĥ, he passed away reciting the Kalimaĥ لَآ اِلٰهَ اِلَّا اللهُ مُحَمَّدٌ رَّسُوْلُ اللهِ.

May Allah عَزَّوَجَلَّ have mercy on him and forgive us without accountability for his sake!

صَلُّوْا عَلَى الْحَبِيْب　　صَلَّى اللهُ تَعَالٰى عَلٰى مُحَمَّد

23. Bad company, bad death

Dear Islamic brothers! I presume that the deceased has succeeded. Now listen to a parable of a horrific and frightening doom that highlights the consequences of the prevalent wicked company, non-Islamic environment in homes, watching and listening to movies and songs through T.V, internet, mobiles etc.

The same doctors who treated the fortunate young deceased person remarked, 'Surprisingly, a few days ago a young burnt girl was also brought for treatment in the same ward where the fortunate Islamic brother of Dawat-e-Islami passed away reciting Kalimaĥ. At the time of her death, Allah عَزَّوَجَلَّ forbid, the girl said, 'Let me listen to a song, let me listen to a song, let me watch scenes of dancing, let me watch scenes of dancing.' The unfortunate girl died repeating the same words again and again.' If she was a Muslim, may Almighty Allah عَزَّوَجَلَّ forgive her!

اٰمِيْن بِجَاهِ النَّبِيِّ الْاَمِيْن صَلَّى اللهُ تَعَالٰى عَلَيْهِ وَاٰلِهٖ وَسَلَّم

تُوْبُوْا اِلَى الله　　اَسْتَغْفِرُ الله

Dear Islamic brothers! There is no doubt that everyone will die one day. Would that we also pass away reciting the Kalimaĥ and Ṣalāt-'Alan-Nabī and beholding the Holy Prophet صَلَّى اللّٰهُ تَعَالٰى عَلَيْهِ وَاٰلِهٖ وَسَلَّم! اَلْحَمْدُ لِلّٰه عَزَّوَجَلَّ Dawat-e-Islami, a global & non-political movement for the preaching of Quran and Sunnaĥ, is spreading the message of Sunnaĥ throughout the world. For the betterment in the world and the Hereafter, every one should join the Madanī environment of Dawat-e-Islami and make up his mind that **'I must strive to reform myself and the people of the entire world.'** اِنْ شَآءَ اللّٰه عَزَّوَجَلَّ

24. Hungry lion

Sayyidunā Dātā Ganj Bakhsh رَحْمَةُ اللّٰهِ تَعَالٰى عَلَيْه has narrated that he رَحْمَةُ اللّٰهِ تَعَالٰى عَلَيْه once asked Sayyidunā Shaykh Aḥmad Ḥammādī Sarkhasī رَحْمَةُ اللّٰهِ تَعَالٰى عَلَيْه the reason of his repentance. He replied, 'Once I went on a journey from Sarkhas with my camels. During the journey, while I was passing through a jungle, a hungry lion attacked a camel of mine and injured it severely. The camel fell on to the ground, the lion climbed up a high cliff and began to roar. Listening to its roar, many animals gathered. The lion came down from the cliff and tore the injured camel into pieces but did not eat itself and went back on the cliff again. The gathered animals ate the meat and left. Then, the lion approached the remaining carcass to eat, but a lame fox appeared at a distance. The lion immediately left the carcass and went back on the cliff so that the fox could eat. After the fox ate and went, the lion approached and ate a little of the remaining carcass. (Sayyidunā Shaykh Aḥmad رَحْمَةُ اللّٰهِ تَعَالٰى عَلَيْه said) I was watching from a distance what the lion did. Suddenly, the lion turned its face towards me and said clearly, 'Aḥmad! To sacrifice a morsel is the attribute of dogs, the men walking on the path of truth sacrifice even their lives.' Impressed by this strange event, I repented of my sins, distanced myself from the world and devoted myself to the remembrance of my Creator عَزَّوَجَلَّ.' *(Kashf-ul-Maḥjūb, pp. 383)*

May Allah عَزَّوَجَلَّ have mercy on him and forgive us without accountability for his sake!

Trust of chicken

Dear Islamic brothers! Did you see how the hungry lion set an excellent example of bearing hunger by sacrificing its own prey for other animals and gave profound advice that a morsel's sacrifice is the attribute of dogs, man should sacrifice his life. Yet sadly, the lazy Muslims like us are not expected to sacrifice even one morsel, they seem prepared to snatch food from other's mouth despite stuffing themselves. At times, people fight and even kill each other just for a morsel of food. Despite having a lot of food, some people cause violence just for a piece of bread. It is said that there are only three such creatures that store food; human beings, ants and rats. Apart from these three, no one else stores food. You may have observed the trust of the chicken. After drinking water, it turns the bowl of water upside down by placing its foot at the corner of the bowl. It believes that Allah عَزَّوَجَلَّ who has given water now will give water next time as well.

The pious men of Allah عَزَّوَجَلَّ possess matchless trust. Trust has also been defined in the following words: 'To have trust in only what Allah عَزَّوَجَلَّ gives and become indifferent to what people have.' Those having perfect trust in Allah عَزَّوَجَلَّ possess high status in the court of Allah عَزَّوَجَلَّ. *(Risāla-tul-Qushayriyyaĥ, pp. 169)*

25. Trusting young man

Sayyidunā Ibrāĥīm Khawāṣ رَحْمَةُ اللهِ تَعَالٰى عَلَيْه has narrated: Once, on my way to Syria, I came across a pious young man who requested me to let him stay in my company. I told him that I remain hungry. He said that he would also manage to remain hungry, اِنْ شَآءَاللّٰه عَزَّوَجَلَّ. Four consecutive days passed without eating. Thereafter, someone sent us some food which I presented to him for eating. Seeing this, he said that he had sworn not to eat anything that came through someone. Pleased with his reply, I said that he had indeed revealed a very great point. When he heard this, he responded, 'O Ibrāĥīm رَحْمَةُ اللهِ تَعَالٰى عَلَيْه! Do not falsely praise me because Allah عَزَّوَجَلَّ is fully aware of your trust in Him and your condition.' He further said, 'The least level of trust in Allah عَزَّوَجَلَّ is that your heart should not think of anyone except Allah عَزَّوَجَلَّ in spite of suffering from prolonged starvation.' *(Risāla-tul-Qushayriyyaĥ, pp. 168)*

May Allah عَزَّوَجَلَّ have mercy on them and forgive us without accountability for their sake!

O Allah عَزَّوَجَلَّ! Save us from the mischief of our Nafs and Satan, and bless us with the gift of hunger and make us Your patient and thankful servants. Amīn!

اٰمِين بِجَاهِ النَّبِيِّ الْاَمِين صَلَّى اللهُ تَعَالٰى عَلَيْهِ وَاٰلِهٖ وَسَلَّم

صَلُّوْا عَلَى الْحَبِيْب صَلَّى اللهُ تَعَالٰى عَلٰى مُحَمَّد

26. Sustenance searches

Sayyidunā Abū Ya'qūb Aqṭa' Baṣrī رَحْمَةُ اللهِ تَعَالٰى عَلَيْه has narrated: Once I remained hungry for ten days in Makkaĥ. Weakened by hunger, I went towards the jungle in search of something to eat. On the way, I found an old turnip. I heard as if a voice was saying, 'You remained hungry for ten days and this is what is left for you, an old turnip?' I immediately left it back on the ground and returned to the Masjid-ul-Ḥarām. Meanwhile, a non-Arab approached me and gave me a box saying, 'This box is yours.' I asked him astonishingly as to how the box became mine. He replied, 'We had been travelling by sea for the last ten days; suddenly a huge storm occurred during the voyage, endangering our boat to drown. All of us made the intentions that if Allah عَزَّوَجَلَّ saves us from the storm, we will give Ṣadaqaĥ (alms). I also made the intention of giving this box to the person I would first see in Masjid-ul-Ḥarām, and you are the person I have met first.'

(Sayyidunā Abū Ya'qūb رَحْمَةُ اللهِ تَعَالٰى عَلَيْه goes onto say) When I opened the box, there were some pieces of cake, peeled almonds and sweets in it. I said to myself inwardly, 'My sustenance was coming to me for ten days and I went towards the jungle in its search.' Then, taking a little from the box for myself and returning the rest to the person, I said, 'I have accepted this (gift), now please take the remaining food and give it to your children as a gift from me.' *(Risāla-tul-Qushayriyyaĥ, pp. 169-170)*

May Allah عَزَّوَجَلَّ have mercy on him and forgive us without accountability for his sake!

Dear Islamic brothers! How firm is the trust of the pious in Allah عَزَّوَجَلَّ! Despite remaining hungry for ten days, when he finally got something to eat, he took a little and returned the remainder instead of storing it for the next time. After eating a little food, they did not have any concern or worry about the next meal. They firmly believed that Allah عَزَّوَجَلَّ would provide sustenance to them for as long as they are alive. This fact has clearly been mentioned in the Holy Quran (Sūraĥ Ĥūd, verse 6).

وَمَا مِنْ دَآبَّةٍ فِي الْاَرْضِ اِلَّا عَلَى اللّٰهِ رِزْقُهَا

And there is none walking on earth, but the sustenance of that is on Allah's bounty.

[Kanz-ul-Īmān (Translation of Quran)] (Part 12, Sūraĥ Ĥūd, verse 6)

Dear Islamic brothers! It is also noteworthy that Allah عَزَّوَجَلَّ has certainly taken up the responsibility for providing sustenance to everyone but He عَزَّوَجَلَّ has not taken up the responsibility for forgiving everyone. Therefore, how unwise is the Muslim who strives day and night for his sustenance (which has already been promised), but does not make any effort for his forgiveness!

اَلْحَمْدُلِلّٰہ عَزَّوَجَلَّ! The mindset of asking for forgiveness and success in the Hereafter is developed in the Sunnaĥ-Inspiring Madanī Qāfilaĥs of Dawat-e-Islami.

27. An enthusiastic preacher

It is reported that once a 12-day Sunnaĥ-Inspiring Madanī Qāfilaĥ arrived at Jhelum, Punjab Pakistan. One of the devotees of Rasūl persuaded a young man living in the house opposite the Masjid in which the Madanī Qāfilaĥ stayed to travel with the Madanī Qāfilaĥ. The young man expressed his willingness to join them just for two days and thus he stayed with the Madanī Qāfilaĥ and learnt Sunnaĥ. Due to the blessings of spending two days with the Madanī Qāfilaĥ, he persuaded his entire family to offer Ṣalāĥ regularly. As he was an influential member of his family, almost everyone started offering Ṣalāĥ. He also went to the house of his uncle and invited him towards righteousness. He also encouraged his family to throw the T.V. away from the house due to its evils. اَلْحَمْدُلِلّٰہ عَزَّوَجَلَّ The T.V. was thrown out with mutual consent of his family. The next day, while ironing his clothes, he got an electric shock, which resulted in his sudden demise. His family members remarked that they clearly heard him recite the Kalimaĥ لَآ اِلٰهَ اِلَّا اللّٰهُ مُحَمَّدٌ رَّسُوْلُ اللّٰهِ at the time of his death.

28. Eggs and bread

Sayyidunā Abū Turāb Nakhshabī رَحْمَةُ اللّٰهِ تَعَالٰى عَلَيْه has stated: Once, my Nafs desired to eat eggs with bread during a journey. I reached a village where a person suddenly grabbed hold of me and started saying loudly. 'This person is also one of the thieves.' A crowd gathered around me and hit me seventy lashes assuming that I was an accomplice of the thieves. Then, a person from among the crowd recognised me and shouted, 'This person cannot be a thief, he is Abū Turāb Nakhshabī رَحْمَةُ اللّٰهِ تَعَالٰى عَلَيْه.' Seeing this, people apologized to me and one of them took me to his house where he served me with eggs and bread. I said to my Nafs, 'After receiving seventy lashes, your desire has been fulfilled, now eat eggs and bread.' *(Risāla-tul-Qushayriyyaĥ, pp. 144)*

May Allah عَزَّوَجَلَّ have mercy on him and forgive us without accountability for his sake!

صَلُّوْا عَلَى الْحَبِيْب صَلَّى اللهُ تَعَالٰى عَلٰى مُحَمَّد

29. White cup

Dear Islamic brothers! The Auliyā of Allah عَزَّوَجَلَّ have their own unique ways. They are saved from subservience to their Nafs. The aforementioned saint Sayyidunā Abū Turāb رَحْمَةُ اللهِ تَعَالٰى عَلَيْه was indeed a saint who possesses saintly miracle[1]. Once while he رَحْمَةُ اللهِ تَعَالٰى عَلَيْه was on his way to Madīnaĥ, a disciple complained of thirst in a very desolate and barren area during the journey. He رَحْمَةُ اللهِ تَعَالٰى عَلَيْه immediately struck the ground with his foot and a spring gushed forth with sweet water. Seeing this saintly miracle, another disciple expressed his desire to drink water with a cup. He رَحْمَةُ اللهِ تَعَالٰى عَلَيْه again struck the ground with his hand and a white cup appeared. Shaykh Abul 'Abbās رَحْمَةُ اللهِ تَعَالٰى عَلَيْه, the narrator of this amazing incident, has stated that this miraculous cup remained in their possession during the entire journey till they reached Makkaĥ. *(Tażkira-tul-Auliyā, vol. 1, pp. 264)*

May Allah عَزَّوَجَلَّ have mercy on them and forgive us without accountability for their sake!

Satanic deception: Why was this saint given such a major punishment on desiring to eat eggs and bread, whereas it is not a sin to eat them?

Cure for Satanic deception: Actually, in this manner, the Auliyā of Allah عَزَّوَجَلَّ are not only trained and tested, but their status is also enhanced. Common Muslims are also sometimes tested with tribulations and sicknesses despite apparently not doing anything wrong. In this manner, their sins are erased and their spiritual status is raised. The great Prophets عَلَيْهِمُ السَّلَام were also tested. Who can forget the grave test that befell the martyrs of Karbalā? The Holy Prophet صَلَّى اللهُ تَعَالٰى عَلَيْهِ وَاٰلِهٖ وَسَلَّم himself also faced trials and tribulations.

---

[1] Saintly miracle means Karāmaĥ.

Trials equivalent to status

Sayyidunā Sa'd رضی اللہ تعالیٰ عنہ has narrated that the Holy Prophet صَلَّى اللهُ تَعَالٰى عَلَيْهِ وَاٰلِهٖ وَسَلَّم was once asked about the people who are afflicted with the most difficult trials and tests. The Holy Prophet صَلَّى اللهُ تَعَالٰى عَلَيْهِ وَاٰلِهٖ وَسَلَّم replied, 'The first among them are the Prophets, then those who have high status after them, then those who have high status after them.' In other words, a person faces trial and tribulation according to the level of his Īmān (faith). If he is steadfast in religion, he faces severe trial and tribulation. If he is weak in religion, he is treated with ease. This process continues until he walks on earth (in such a state) that all of his sins are forgiven. *(Jāmi' Tirmiżī, vol. 4, pp. 170, Ḥadīš 2406)*

Anyway, all this depends upon the will of Allah عَزَّوَجَلَّ. The pious remain pleased with Allah's will and if difficulties ever befall them, they gain reward by having patience. Listen to another faith-refreshing parable with regard to remaining happy at the time of troubles and illnesses.

30. Happiness in fever

One day, the Holy Prophet صَلَّى اللهُ تَعَالٰى عَلَيْهِ وَاٰلِهٖ وَسَلَّم said, 'Allah عَزَّوَجَلَّ erases the sins of a Muslim due to the trouble which befalls his body.' Hearing this, Sayyidunā Ubay Bin Ka'b رضی اللہ تعالیٰ عنہ made the following Du'ā, 'O Allah عَزَّوَجَلَّ! Until my death, I ask You for such fever which does not prevent me from offering Ṣalāĥ, fasting, Hajj, 'Umraĥ and fighting in Your cause.' His Du'ā was accepted. The narrator stated that Sayyidunā Ubay Bin Ka'b رضی اللہ تعالیٰ عنہ had fever all the time until he passed away. Even in this feverish state, he used to come to the Masjid, fast, perform Hajj and 'Umraĥ and take part in battles. *(Kanz-ul-'Ummāl, vol. 3, pp. 299, Ḥadīš 8633)*

May Allah عَزَّوَجَلَّ have mercy on him and forgive us without accountability for his sake!

صَلُّوْا عَلَى الْحَبِيْب صَلَّى اللهُ تَعَالٰى عَلٰى مُحَمَّد

Excellence of fever

Dear Islamic brothers! How can the excellence of fever be expressed in words! Sayyidunā Abū Ĥurayraĥ رضی اللہ تعالیٰ عنہ has narrated that once while talking about fever in the presence of the Holy Prophet صَلَّى اللهُ تَعَالٰى عَلَيْهِ وَاٰلِهٖ وَسَلَّم, someone spoke ill of it. The Holy Prophet صَلَّى اللهُ تَعَالٰى عَلَيْهِ وَاٰلِهٖ وَسَلَّم said, 'Do not speak ill of fever because it cleanses the Muslim of sins as fire removes rust from iron.' *(Sunan Ibn Mājaĥ, vol. 4, pp. 104, Ḥadīš 3469)*

31. Fine of eating lentils

Sayyidunā Ibrāĥīm Bin Shaybān عَلَيْهِ رَحْمَةُ الْحَنَّان has narrated: I have not spent any night for rest under a roof for forty years. I had a strong desire to eat lentils to my full stomach. Once, in Syria, someone gave me a plate of cooked lentils which I ate. Having eaten it, I passed by a shop where I saw some bottles hanging on a rack. Assuming that the bottles contained vinegar, I looked at them closely. Someone told me that there was wine in the bottles. Pointing towards some jars, he further said that there was wine in those jars as well. Infuriated, I brought out the wine jars from the shop and began to overturn them on the street. The shop owner thought that I was an officer of the government, thus he was afraid. He stood and watched silently. When he got to know about me, he took me to the governor of Egypt and Syria, Ibn-e-Ṭūlūn. I was hit 200 lashes and was jailed for a long time. Luckily, my respected teacher and spiritual guide, Sayyidunā Abū 'Abdullāĥ Maghribī رَحْمَةُ اللهِ تَعَالٰى عَلَيْه arrived in the town. He asked me, 'What crime did you commit?' I replied that I had eaten a plate of lentils and, as a fine, I was hit 200 lashes in addition to imprisonment. Hearing this, my respected teacher replied, 'You were punished only slightly.' I also told him about the incident of wine-jars. He interceded and got me released. *(Risāla-tul-Qushayriyyaĥ, pp. 153)*

May Allah عَزَّوَجَلَّ have mercy on them and forgive us without accountability for their sake!

صَلُّوْا عَلَى الْحَبِيْب صَلَّى اللهُ تَعَالٰى عَلٰى مُحَمَّد

Dear Islamic brothers! The Auliyā of Allah عَزَّوَجَلَّ always refrain from following their Nafs. If they ever fulfil the demand of their Nafs, they face severe hardships, and in this way, their spiritual status is enhanced. These are private matters between them and their Creator.

32. Fish bone

Sayyidunā Abul Khayr 'Asqalānī قُدِّسَ سِرُّهُ الرَّبَّانِي had the desire to eat fish from many years. Finally, he managed to have fish with Ḥalāl means. As soon as he stretched out his hand to begin eating, a piece of fish bone pricked his finger. The wound went severely septic and his hand had to be amputated. He then beseeched in the court of Allah عَزَّوَجَلَّ, 'O Allah عَزَّوَجَلَّ! This is the state of the person who desired to consume a Ḥalāl thing and stretched out his hand towards it. What will be the condition of the person who desires a Ḥarām thing and stretches out his hand towards it?' *(Risāla-tul-Qushayriyyaĥ, pp. 142)*

May Allah عَزَّوَجَلَّ have mercy on him and forgive us without accountability for his sake!

Dear Islamic brothers! The Madanī mindset of the saints is extraordinary. Even after going through pain and trials, they still manage to pick the positives and adopt humility in the court of their Creator. It is our positive opinion that the pricking of fish bone was a means of further increasing (the spiritual) rank of Sayyidunā Abul Khayr 'Asqalānī قُدِّسَ سِرُّهُ الرَّبَّانِي. Sometimes, the bone pricks people in the throat while eating fish. If this happens, one should have patience because when a Muslim experiences difficulty, either his sins are removed or his spiritual status is enhanced.

Reward of thorn-pricking

Sayyidunā Abū Sa'īd Khudrī and Sayyidunā Abū Ĥurayraĥ رَضِیَ اللّٰہُ تَعَالٰی عَنْہُمَا have narrated that the Holy Prophet صَلَّى اللهُ تَعَالٰى عَلَيْهِ وَاٰلِهٖ وَسَلَّم has stated, 'No sadness, difficulty, anxiety, pain, injury, sorrow or even the pricking of a thorn reaches a Muslim, but Allah عَزَّوَجَلَّ erases the sin of that Muslim (due to these difficulties).' *(Ṣaḥīḥ Bukhārī, vol. 7, pp. 3, Ḥadīš 5641-5642)*

Wisdom of difficulties

The Holy Prophet صَلَّى اللهُ تَعَالٰى عَلَيْهِ وَاٰلِهٖ وَسَلَّم has stated, 'If a high status is predestined for a person in the knowledge of Allah عَزَّوَجَلَّ, but the person is unable to acquire that status by his deeds, so Allah عَزَّوَجَلَّ makes that person suffer financial, physical or family difficulty. He عَزَّوَجَلَّ then blesses that person with patience and makes him reach that high status which was predestined for him in the divine knowledge.' *(Sunan Abī Dāwūd, pp. 123, Ḥadīš 3090)*

Woĥ 'ishq-e-ḥaqīqī kī lażżāt naĥīn pā saktā
Jo ranj-o-muṣībat say dauchār naĥīn ĥotā

He cannot taste the true love and devotion
Who does not face adversity and harsh condition

33. Carrot and honey

Our saints رَحِمَهُمُ اللّٰهُ تَعَالٰی used to oppose their Nafs strongly. Sayyidunā Sarī Saqaṭī رَحْمَةُ اللّٰهِ تَعَالٰی عَلَيْه has stated, 'My Nafs has been urging me that I eat a single carrot dipped in honey (if not more) for the past 30 or 40 years, but I have not fulfilled its desire, اَلْحَمْدُ لِلّٰه عَزَّوَجَلَّ.' *(Risāla-tul-Qushayriyyaĥ, pp. 153)*

May Allah عَزَّوَجَلَّ have mercy on him and forgive us without accountability for his sake!

34. He spat out fig

Sayyidunā Ja'far Bin Naṣīr عَلَيْهِ رَحْمَةُ اللّٰهِ الْقَدِيْر has narrated: Once Sayyidunā Shaykh Junayd Baghdādī عَلَيْهِ رَحْمَةُ اللّٰهِ الْهَادِی gave me a dinar to purchase some figs. I brought some figs from the market. At the time of Ifṭār, he placed a fig in his mouth but then immediately spat it out. He then began to weep and instructed that the figs be taken away. When he was asked as to why he did so, he replied, 'A voice came from my conscience, 'Are you not ashamed of fulfilling the desire you had already forgone for the pleasure of Allah عَزَّوَجَلَّ.' *(Risāla-tul-Qushayriyyaĥ, pp. 154)*

May Allah عَزَّوَجَلَّ have mercy on him and forgive us without accountability for his sake!

A wise man has rightly said, 'One should not give his rein of control to his desire because it will lead him to darkness.' *(ibid, pp. 154)*

35. Confectioner fed them

Shaykh-ul-Muḥaqqiqīn, Khātim-ul-Muḥaddišīn, Shaykh 'Abdul Ḥaq Muḥaddiš Diĥlvī عَلَيْهِ رَحْمَةُ اللّٰهِ الْقَوِی has narrated, 'My spiritual master and guide, Shaykh 'Abdul Waĥĥāb Muttaqī عَلَيْهِ رَحْمَةُ اللّٰهِ الْقَوِی once stayed in a Masjid along with one of his friends for worship during the period of famine. They had already decided not to speak to each other. They also decided neither to ask anyone for food nor eat anything with their own hands. Twenty days passed without eating. On the twenty first day, a confectioner entered the Masjid and placed some food in between both of them and left. As they had already decided not to eat anything with their own hands, they did not eat at all. On the twenty-second day, the confectioner did the same and left. Again, both the saints did not even touch the food. On the twenty-third day, the confectioner brought food and fed them with his own hands.' *(Al-Akhbār-ul-Akhyār ma' Maktūbāt, pp. 278)*

May Allah عَزَّوَجَلَّ have mercy on them and forgive us without accountability for their sake!

صَلُّوا عَلَى الْحَبِيب صَلَّى اللهُ تَعَالٰى عَلٰى مُحَمَّد

36. Leftover bones

Dear Islamic brothers! Sayyidunā Shaykh 'Abdul Waĥĥāb Muttaqī Qādirī Shāżlī عَلَيْهِ رَحْمَةُ اللهِ الْوَلِی was a great saint. He رَحْمَةُ اللهِ تَعَالٰى عَلَيْه would often remain hungry. Once, while discussing the wisdom of hunger, asceticism and avoidance of asking anyone for anything, he stated, 'There was a time when I used to pick up the left over bones thrown from the shops of butchers and the dry stalk of barley which people threw away on the farms. I would wash and boil them in a cauldron and survive on a bowl of this soup. When people came to know of this state of mine, they started bringing different types of (delicious) foods for me. In order to avoid such gifts, I decided to leave that place and never stayed anywhere for more than three days.' *(Al-Akhbār-ul-Akhyār ma' Maktūbāt, pp. 277)*

May Allah عَزَّوَجَلَّ have mercy on him and forgive us without accountability for his sake!

صَلُّوا عَلَى الْحَبِيب صَلَّى اللهُ تَعَالٰى عَلٰى مُحَمَّد

37. Fear before eating

Sayyidunā Waĥb Bin Ward رَحْمَةُ اللهِ تَعَالٰى عَلَيْه used to eat only one flatbread after remaining hungry for two or three consecutive days. Before eating, he used to supplicate to Almighty Allah عَزَّوَجَلَّ in the following manner, 'O Allah عَزَّوَجَلَّ! You are aware that I am not strong enough to worship You without eating; I am fearful of weakness and grief. O Allah عَزَّوَجَلَّ! If there is something unlawful or Ḥarām in this bread, do not punish me if it enters my stomach unknowingly.' After making this Du'ā, he would soak the bread in water and then eat it. *(Minĥāj-ul-'Ābidīn, pp. 98)*

May Allah عَزَّوَجَلَّ have mercy on him and forgive us without accountability for his sake!

We should weep after eating

Dear Islamic brothers! We should be alarmed that we eat virtually anything that comes to our hand without considering (its permissibility). We should fear the accountability of the Hereafter.

Sayyidunā Imām Muhammad Ghazālī عَلَيْهِ رَحْمَةُ اللّٰهِ الْوَالِى has stated in *Iḥyā-ul-'Ulūm*, 'The one who weeps after eating and the one who plays and enjoys after eating cannot be equal.' *(Iḥyā-ul-'Ulūm, vol. 2, pp. 8)* He رَحْمَةُ اللّٰهِ تَعَالٰى عَلَيْه has further stated, 'One should repent and express sadness in case of eating doubtful food so that his tears and sadness can put off the fire of Hell which he might face due to eating the doubtful food.' The Holy Prophet صَلَّى اللّٰهُ تَعَالٰى عَلَيْهِ وَاٰلِهٖ وَسَلَّم has also stated, 'The meat nurtured with Ḥarām, fire (of Hell) is more entitled to it.' *(Shu'ab-ul-Īmān, vol. 5, pp. 56, Ḥadīš 5761)*

صَلُّوْا عَلَى الْحَبِيْب صَلَّى اللّٰهُ تَعَالٰى عَلٰى مُحَمَّد

38. Piece of dry bread

Sayyidunā Junayd Baghdādī عَلَيْهِ رَحْمَةُ اللّٰهِ الْهَادِى has narrated: Sayyidunā Ḥāriš Bin Asad Muḥāsibī رَحْمَةُ اللّٰهِ تَعَالٰى عَلَيْه walked past my house. He رَحْمَةُ اللّٰهِ تَعَالٰى عَلَيْه appeared to be hungry so I requested, 'My dear uncle, please come and eat something.' He رَحْمَةُ اللّٰهِ تَعَالٰى عَلَيْه came to our house but there was nothing for eating except some wedding food, which our neighbours had sent. I offered the same food to him. He رَحْمَةُ اللّٰهِ تَعَالٰى عَلَيْه took a morsel, placed it into his mouth and kept moving it in his mouth without swallowing. Instead of eating the morsel, he رَحْمَةُ اللّٰهِ تَعَالٰى عَلَيْه went to the porch and spat it out. Then, he رَحْمَةُ اللّٰهِ تَعَالٰى عَلَيْه left. When I came across him after some days, I asked him about the food I gave him. He رَحْمَةُ اللّٰهِ تَعَالٰى عَلَيْه replied, 'I was certainly hungry and wanted to eat the food you offered so that I could please you, but there is a promise between me and Allah عَزَّوَجَلَّ that no doubtful food would go down my throat and it is the reason why I could not swallow it.' I told him that the food had come from my neighbour's house on a wedding occasion. I then asked him to come to my house so that I could serve him again. When he رَحْمَةُ اللّٰهِ تَعَالٰى عَلَيْه entered, I served a piece of dry bread which he consumed. He رَحْمَةُ اللّٰهِ تَعَالٰى عَلَيْه then said, 'You should present this type of food to the mystic saints.' *(Risāla-tul-Qushayriyyaĥ, pp. 429-430)*

May Allah عَزَّوَجَلَّ have mercy on him and forgive us without accountability for his sake!

39. His vein would pulsate

Dear Islamic brothers! Did you see that our saints would never consume any doubtful food despite experiencing extreme hunger? Allah عَزَّوَجَلَّ had especial mercy on Sayyidunā Ḥāriš Muḥāsibī رَحْمَةُ اللهِ تَعَالٰى عَلَيْه, as Sayyidunā Abū 'Alī Daqāq عَلَيْهِ رَحْمَةُ اللّٰهِ الرَّزَّاق has narrated that whenever Sayyidunā Ḥāriš Muḥāsibī رَحْمَةُ اللهِ تَعَالٰى عَلَيْه used to stretch out his hand towards any doubtful food, a vein in his finger would start to pulsate. He would immediately refrain from eating that food. *(ibid, pp. 429)*

Similarly, many other saints are also reported to have the saintly miracle of becoming aware of doubtful and Ḥarām food in advance.

May Allah عَزَّوَجَلَّ have mercy on them and forgive us without accountability for their sake!

صَلُّوْا عَلَى الْحَبِيْب   صَلَّى اللهُ تَعَالٰى عَلٰى مُحَمَّد

40. Worshipper and pomegranate

It is reported that a worshipper used to live on a mountain. In the vicinity was a pomegranate tree on which three pomegranates grew every day. He would eat them and continue his worship. Allah عَزَّوَجَلَّ willed to test the worshipper. One day, the pomegranates did not grow but the worshipper remained patient. The same thing happened the next two days. Worried and weakened by hunger, he descended down from the mountain. A house of a non-Muslim lied beside the mountain. The worshipper approached the non-Muslim and begged him for some food. The non-Muslim gave him 4 pieces of bread. (As the worshipper left), the dog of the non-Muslim began to bark at him. The worshipper gave one piece to the dog. After eating it, the dog pursued and barked again. He gave another piece of bread but the dog was still barking. Eventually, he gave all four pieces of bread but the dog did not become silent. Enraged, he said to the dog, 'O despicable and greedy dog! You have no shame, I have begged your master for food which I have given to you but you still do not leave me.' The dog replied, 'I am not more shameless than you! Allah عَزَّوَجَلَّ bestowed upon you a nice sustenance for many years without any struggle, when He عَزَّوَجَلَّ tested you a little you became so worried that you went to His enemy's house to beg.' *(Aḥsan-ul-Wi'ā, pp. 144)*

Dear Islamic brothers! We have learnt from the foregoing parable that if Allah عَزَّوَجَلَّ, who bestows upon us innumerable bounties, ever tests us, we should be patient instead of complaining. The following parable would further clarify this point.

41. Maḥmūd, Ayāz and slice of cucumber

It is reported that once a person gifted a cucumber to Sultan Maḥmūd Ghaznawī عَلَيْهِ رَحْمَةُ اللّٰهِ الْقَوِى, a renowned devotee of Rasūl. The sultan accepted the gift and gave the person a reward. He then cut off a slice and handed it to his beloved slave Ayāz who consumed the slice relishing its taste. Then, Sultan Maḥmūd cut another slice, this time for himself. As soon as he put it into his own mouth, he spat it out instantly, as it was too bitter. Astonished at Ayāz, he asked, 'Ayāz! How did you eat such a bitter thing? Even your facial expression did not reveal any sign of displeasure.' Ayāz replied, 'Respected Sultan! There is no doubt that the piece of cucumber was extremely bitter. When I placed it in my mouth, my wisdom asked me to spit it out but my love told me, 'O Ayāz, beware! This is the same hand which gives you sweet things to eat every day. If it gives you something bitter to eat only one day, it does not matter. To spit it out is contrary to the etiquette of love. Therefore, following the command of love, I consumed the bitter slice of cucumber.' *(Raĥbar-e-Zindagī, pp. 167)*

May Allah عَزَّوَجَلَّ have mercy on them and forgive us without accountability for their sake!

Dear Islamic brothers! Being a Muslim, we all should have the same frame of mind. If Allah عَزَّوَجَلَّ, who has bestowed upon us countless favours, ever tests us with troubles and trials, we should accept them happily. The great is not the one who is loyal only when his object of devotion shows affection for him, but the one who is loyal even when he is ignored by the one he has affection for.

Woĥ 'ishq-e-ḥaqīqī kī lażżāt naĥīn pā saktā
Jo ranj-o-muṣībat say dauchār naĥīn ĥotā

He cannot taste the true love and devotion
Who does not face adversity and harsh condition

صَلُّوْا عَلَى الْحَبِيْب صَلَّى اللّٰهُ تَعَالٰى عَلٰى مُحَمَّد

42. Non-Muslim monk embraces Islam

Making individual effort, a saint once presented Islam to a non-Muslim monk. After a lengthy debate and argument, the monk replied, 'It was a miracle of Sayyidunā Prophet 'Īsā عَلَيْهِ السَّلَام that he would not eat anything for forty consecutive days. This act can only be performed by a Prophet and a Ṣiddīq.' The saint رَحْمَةُ الله تَعَالٰى عَلَيْه replied, 'If I remain hungry for fifty consecutive days, would you embrace Islam giving up your religion and realize that Islam is the true religion and that you are following falsehood?' The non-Muslim replied 'Yes.' Therefore, the saint رَحْمَةُ الله تَعَالٰى عَلَيْه stayed with him for fifty consecutive days without consuming anything. He رَحْمَةُ الله تَعَالٰى عَلَيْه then stayed hungry for another ten days. Having seen this saintly miracle, the monk embraced Islam forthwith. *(Iḥyā-ul-'Ulūm, vol. 3, pp. 98)*

Dear Islamic brothers! No one should misunderstand this parable. It must not be assumed that the saint surpassed Sayyidunā Prophet 'Īsā عَلٰى نَبِيِّنَا وَ عَلَيْهِ الصَّلٰوةُ وَالسَّلَام in status. It is a fundamental Islamic belief that no saint can ever surpass the status of a Prophet عَلَيْهِ السَّلَام. The one believing that a saint is greater than a Holy Prophet عَلَيْهِ السَّلَام immediately becomes a Kāfir (unbeliever). The monk was under the impression that after Sayyidunā Prophet 'Īsā عَلٰى نَبِيِّنَا وَ عَلَيْهِ الصَّلٰوةُ وَالسَّلَام, no devotee of Prophet Muhammad صَلَّى الله تَعَالٰى عَلَيْهِ وَاٰلِهٖ وَسَلَّم could stay hungry for forty days. The saint cleared the misconception of the monk by showing the saintly miracle of staying hungry for 40 days, making it clear that staying hungry for 40 days is not the unique attribute of Sayyidunā Prophet 'Īsā عَلَيْهِ السَّلَام, and the devotees of the Holy Prophet صَلَّى الله تَعَالٰى عَلَيْهِ وَاٰلِهٖ وَسَلَّم can remain alive despite staying hungry for 60 days.

43. Rice and fish

It is reported that a saint رَحْمَةُ الله تَعَالٰى عَلَيْه from Basra refrained from eating fish, rice and bread for 20 years despite the strong desire of his Nafs. After his death, someone saw him in a dream and asked as to how Allah عَزَّوَجَلَّ treated him. He replied, 'Words cannot express the bounties Allah عَزَّوَجَلَّ has bestowed upon me. First, I was given fish, rice and bread and was told to eat as much as I wished.' *(Iḥyā-ul-'Ulūm, vol. 3, pp. 103)*

May Allah عَزَّوَجَلَّ have mercy on him and forgive us without accountability for his sake!

Dear Islamic brothers! Did you see how great the status of those who do not follow their Nafs is? Congratulations to those fortunate people who succeed in bearing hunger, avoiding worldly joys and thus opposing their Nafs just for the pleasure of Allah عَزَّوَجَلَّ! After death, they will be blessed with superb bounties in Paradise. Allah عَزَّوَجَلَّ says in Sūraĥ Al-Ḥāqqaĥ, verse 24:

كُلُوْا وَاشْرَبُوْا هَنِيْٓـًٔا بِمَآ اَسْلَفْتُمْ فِي الْاَيَّامِ الْخَالِيَةِ ﴿۲۴﴾

Eat and drink with relish, recompense for that you sent forth in the days gone by.

[Kanz-ul-Īmān (Translation of Quran)] (Part 29, Sūraĥ Al-Ḥāqqaĥ, verse 24)

44. Beneficial to one's heart

Sayyidunā Shaykh Abū Ṣulaymān Dārānī قُدِّسَ سِرُّهُ النُّوْرَانِي has said, 'To refrain from any desire of Nafs is more beneficial to the heart than a year's fasting and staying up at night (in worship).' *(Iḥyā-ul-'Ulūm, vol. 3, pp. 103)*

May Allah عَزَّوَجَلَّ have mercy on him and forgive us without accountability for his sake!

صَلُّوْا عَلَى الْحَبِيْب　　　صَلَّى اللهُ تَعَالٰى عَلٰى مُحَمَّد

45. Valīmaĥ in Paradise

Ḥujjat-ul-Islam, Sayyidunā Imām Muhammad Ghazālī عَلَيْهِ رَحْمَةُ اللّٰهِ الْوَالِي has stated, 'The saints walking on the path of the Hereafter would avoid the fulfilment of their desires because if a person eats different delicious things to satisfy his desires, his Nafs becomes arrogant and his heart becomes hard. Further, he becomes so interested in the delicious worldly things that the love of worldly joys permanently stays in his heart and he forgets that he will have to stand before his Creator, Allah عَزَّوَجَلَّ. The world is like Paradise and death is like a prison for such a person. On the contrary, the one who treats his Nafs strictly and deprives it of worldly pleasures; the world becomes like a prison for him, he feels uncomfortable in the world and his Nafs likes to get free from the imprisonment of life by leaving the world through death.' Referring to the same point, Sayyidunā Yaḥyā Mu'āż Rāzī رَحْمَةُ اللّٰهِ تَعَالٰى عَلَيْه has stated, 'O the Ṣiddīqin! In order to eat Valīmaĥ (wedding-feast) in Paradise, keep yourself hungry because the desire for food intensifies as much as the Nafs remains hungry.

In other words, when a person is extremely hungry, he really feels the joy of eating. This is the same thing experienced by every fasting person. Therefore, remain as hungry as possible in the world so that you can enjoy the delicious food of Paradise. *(ibid, pp. 99)*

May Allah عَزَّوَجَلَّ have mercy on him and forgive us without accountability for his sake!

صَلُّوْا عَلَى الْحَبِيْب ۝ صَلَّى اللّٰهُ تَعَالٰى عَلٰى مُحَمَّد

46. Dough that dried in sunlight

Sayyidunā 'Utba-tul-Ghulām عَلَيْهِ رَحْمَةُ رَبِّ الْاَنَام used to knead dough and let it dry in the sunlight. After this, he رَحْمَةُ اللّٰهِ تَعَالٰى عَلَيْه would eat it. He رَحْمَةُ اللّٰهِ تَعَالٰى عَلَيْه then used to say, 'One should survive on a mere piece of bread and a little salt so that he could enjoy fried roasted meat and delicious food on the Day of Judgement.' *(Iḥyā-ul-'Ulūm, vol. 3, pp. 100)*

May Allah عَزَّوَجَلَّ have mercy on him and forgive us without accountability for his sake!

47. He did not drink milk for forty years

Sayyidunā Mālik Bin Dīnār عَلَيْهِ رَحْمَةُ اللّٰهِ الْغَفَّار did not drink milk for forty years despite the desire of his Nafs. Once, someone gave him dates as a gift which he immediately gave to his students and said, 'You people eat, I have not even tasted dates for forty years.' *(ibid, pp. 101)*

May Allah عَزَّوَجَلَّ have mercy on him and forgive us without accountability for his sake!

48. Meat and bread

Sayyidunā 'Utba-tul-Ghulām عَلَيْهِ رَحْمَةُ رَبِّ الْاَنَام refrained from eating meat for 7 years. One day, he purchased some bread and meat. After roasting the meat, he رَحْمَةُ اللّٰهِ تَعَالٰى عَلَيْه placed it on the bread. Meanwhile, an orphan came. He رَحْمَةُ اللّٰهِ تَعَالٰى عَلَيْه gave the bread and meat to the orphan and began to weep reciting the eighth verse of Sūrah Ad-Daĥr:

وَيُطْعِمُوْنَ الطَّعَامَ عَلٰى حُبِّهٖ مِسْكِيْنًا وَّيَتِيْمًا وَّاَسِيْرًا ۝

And they feed, for love of Him, the indigent, the orphan and the prisoner.

[Kanz-ul-Īmān (Translation of Quran)] (Part 29, Sūrah Ad-Daĥr, verse 8)

Since then, Sayyidunā 'Utba-tul-Ghulām عَلَیْهِ رَحْمَةُ رَبِّ الْاَنَام did not even taste roasted meat and bread. *(ibid, pp. 211)*

May Allah عَزَّوَجَلَّ have mercy on him and forgive us without accountability for his sake!

صَلُّوْا عَلَى الْحَبِيْب صَلَّى اللهُ تَعَالٰى عَلٰى مُحَمَّد

49. Frightening thunderstorm

Sayyidunā 'Utba-tul-Ghulām عَلَیْهِ رَحْمَةُ رَبِّ الْاَنَام has stated: My Nafs had the desire of consuming dates from many years. One day, I purchased some dates for Ifṭār. Suddenly, a severe thunderstorm occurred, darkening the sky and frightening the people. Looking at this, I said to myself, 'This is your fault because you have obeyed your Nafs purchasing these dates and people are facing this storm because of your sins.' I then made the promise that I would not even taste these dates.' *(ibid, pp. 210)*

May Allah عَزَّوَجَلَّ have mercy on him and forgive us without accountability for his sake!

صَلُّوْا عَلَى الْحَبِيْب صَلَّى اللهُ تَعَالٰى عَلٰى مُحَمَّد

Dear Islamic brothers! It was the humility of this great saint that he considered himself responsible for the horrific thunderstorm. In essence, troubles do not befall due to saints, instead, they are removed due to their blessings. May be an earthquake was about to occur and it may have changed into a mere thunderstorm because of his presence. It is stated that mercy descends at the time of the mentioning of the pious. *(Kashf-ul-Khifā, vol. 2, pp. 91, Ḥadīš 1772)* When divine grace descends at the mentioning of the pious, then what will be the magnitude of divine grace on the place where they are physically present!

50. Green bowl

Sayyidunā Shafīq Bin Ibrāĥīm رَحْمَةُ اللهِ تَعَالٰى عَلَيْه has narrated: I once met Sayyidunā Ibrāĥīm Bin Adĥam رَحْمَةُ اللهِ تَعَالٰى عَلَيْه in Makkaĥ near the birth place of the Beloved and Blessed Prophet صَلَّى اللهُ تَعَالٰى عَلَيْهِ وَاٰلِهٖ وَسَلَّم. He was weeping while sitting on the roadside. I sat next to him and then asked, 'O Abū Isḥāq رَضِىَ اللهُ تَعَالٰى عَنْهُ! (This was his Kunyaĥ), why are you weeping?'

At first, he did not tell me the reason, but when I insisted, he replied, 'O Shafīq! Please keep my secret.' I assured him that I would not disclose his secret, so he رَحْمَةُ اللهِ تَعَالٰی عَلَيْه said, 'My Nafs had a strong desire for Sikbāj (meat with vinegar and fragrant spices) for thirty years but I kept preventing my Nafs from consuming it. Last night, I had a dream in which I saw a young man who had a green bowl of aromatic Sikbāj. Plucking up the courage, I moved away from him but he forwarded the bowl towards me and said, 'O Ibrāhīm, eat.' I replied, 'I will not eat because I have already left it for the pleasure of Allah عَزَّوَجَلَّ.' He said, 'It is Allah عَزَّوَجَلَّ who has granted you this gift, please eat.' I had no answer and began to weep. He insisted, 'May Allah عَزَّوَجَلَّ shower mercy upon you, (eat).' I then told him, 'We have been instructed not to put anything into our stomach until we are absolutely sure that the thing is Ḥalāl.'

The young man said, 'Eat, may Allah عَزَّوَجَلَّ grant you peace! I was given this food and told 'O Khiḍr! Take this food to Ibrāĥīm Bin Adĥam رَحْمَةُ اللهِ تَعَالٰی عَلَيْه and feed him. Allah عَزَّوَجَلَّ had mercy on him for having persistent patience by preventing his Nafs from Sikbāj.' O Ibrāĥīm رَحْمَةُ اللهِ تَعَالٰی عَلَيْه, I have heard the angels say, 'If a person does not accept the thing offered to him, he will not be given that thing even when he asks for it.' I (Ibrāĥīm Bin Adĥam رَحْمَةُ اللهِ تَعَالٰی عَلَيْه) said, 'If it is so, I am prepared for it due to my promise with Allah عَزَّوَجَلَّ.' (I will not eat it). I turned back to return. Meanwhile, giving him something, another young man said, 'O Khiḍr! Feed him with your own hand.' Therefore, Khiḍr began to feed me and then my eyes opened. When I woke up, the taste of the food was still in my mouth. Sayyidunā Shafīq رَحْمَةُ اللهِ تَعَالٰی عَلَيْه has narrated, 'Having heard about this dream, I kissed his hand with love and respect.' *(Iḥyā-ul-'Ulūm, vol. 3, pp. 100-101)*

May Allah عَزَّوَجَلَّ have mercy on them and forgive us without accountability for their sake!

صَلُّوْا عَلَى الْحَبِيْب صَلَّى اللّٰهُ تَعَالٰى عَلٰى مُحَمَّد

Leaving this world with Īmān!

Dear Islamic brothers! Did you see how Sayyidunā Ibrāĥīm Bin Adĥam رَحْمَةُ اللهِ تَعَالٰی عَلَيْه used to oppose his Nafs. He رَحْمَةُ اللهِ تَعَالٰی عَلَيْه refrained from eating Sikbāj for thirty years. By the grace of Allah عَزَّوَجَلَّ, Sayyidunā Khiḍr عَلَيْهِ السَّلَام came to feed him with his own hands. Sayyidunā Khiḍr عَلَيْهِ السَّلَام is a Holy Prophet who is still physically alive in the world.

Here is a Madanī pearl about the blessings of Sayyidunā Khiḍr عَلَيْهِ السَّلَام. In *Tafsīr Ṣāwī*, it is stated that whoever remembers the full name of Sayyidunā Khiḍr عَلٰی نَبِیِّنَا وَ عَلَیْهِ الصَّلٰوۃُ وَالسَّلَام along with his father-name, title and Kunyaĥ, he will leave this world in the state of Īmān. His full name along with father-name, title and Kunyaĥ is '*Abul 'Abbās Balyā Bin Malkān Al-Khiḍr* (اَبُوالْعَبَّاس بَلْیَا بِنْ مَلْکَان اَلْخِضْر).' *(Tafsīr Ṣāwī, vol. 2, pp. 1207)*

May Allah عَزَّوَجَلَّ have mercy on them and forgive us without accountability for their sake!

صَلُّوْا عَلَی الْحَبِیْب صَلَّی اللّٰهُ تَعَالٰی عَلٰی مُحَمَّد

51. He used to speak to his Nafs

The blessed son of Imām A'ẓam Abū Ḥanīfah رَحْمَةُ اللهِ تَعَالٰی عَلَیْه, Sayyidunā Ḥammād رَحْمَةُ اللهِ تَعَالٰی عَلَیْه has narrated: I once went to the house of Sayyidunā Dāwūd Ṭāī رَحْمَةُ اللهِ تَعَالٰی عَلَیْه, I heard a voice from inside the house, 'O Nafs! You desired carrot, I fed it to you. Now you desire for dates. By Allah عَزَّوَجَلَّ! I will never feed you dates.' Saying Salām when I entered, I saw him alone. (In other words, the great Shaykh was addressing his Nafs). *(ibid, pp. 101)*

May Allah عَزَّوَجَلَّ have mercy on them and forgive us without accountability for their sake!

صَلُّوْا عَلَی الْحَبِیْب صَلَّی اللّٰهُ تَعَالٰی عَلٰی مُحَمَّد

52. He vowed not to eat vegetable

Sayyidunā Mālik Bin Ḍaygham عَلَیْهِ رَحْمَةُ اللهِ الْاَکْرَم has stated, 'Once I saw a vegetable while passing through a market in Basra. My Nafs demanded me to eat the vegetable that night. I swore not to eat that vegetable for forty nights.' *(ibid, pp. 101)*

May Allah عَزَّوَجَلَّ have mercy on him and forgive us without accountability for his sake!

صَلُّوْا عَلَی الْحَبِیْب صَلَّی اللّٰهُ تَعَالٰی عَلٰی مُحَمَّد

فیضانِ رمضان

Blessings of RAMADAN

Shaykh-e-Tariqat Amir-e-Ahl-e-Sunnat
the Founder of Dawat-e-Islami
Allamah Maulana Abu Bilal
MUHAMMAD ILYAS
Attar Qadiri Razavi دامت برکاتہم العالیہ

مکتبۃ المدینہ
MAKTABA TUL MADINAH
MC 1286

اَلْحَمْدُ لِلّٰهِ رَبِّ الْعٰلَمِيْنَ وَ الصَّلٰوةُ وَ السَّلَامُ عَلٰى سَيِّدِ الْمُرْسَلِيْنَ

اَمَّا بَعْدُ فَاَعُوْذُ بِاللّٰهِ مِنَ الشَّيْطٰنِ الرَّجِيْمِ ؕ بِسْمِ اللّٰهِ الرَّحْمٰنِ الرَّحِيْمِ ؕ

Excellence of Ramadan

No matter how lazy Satan tries to make you feel, please read this chapter (every year) from beginning to end. اِنْ شَآءَ اللّٰه عَزَّوَجَلَّ, You will see its blessings for yourself.

Excellence of Ṣalāt-'Alan-Nabī صَلَّى اللّٰه عَلَيْهِ وَاٰلِهٖ وَسَلَّم

The Prophet of mankind, the Peace of our heart and mind, the most Generous and Kind صَلَّى اللّٰهُ تَعَالٰى عَلَيْهِ وَاٰلِهٖ وَسَلَّم has said, 'Indeed, he who recites Ṣalāt (Durūd) upon me the most, will be the closest to me on the Day of Judgement.' *(Jāmi' Tirmiżī, vol. 2, pp. 27, Ḥadīš 484)*

صَلُّوْا عَلَى الْحَبِيْب صَلَّى اللّٰهُ تَعَالٰى عَلٰى مُحَمَّد

Dear Islamic brothers! It is a great bounty of Allah عَزَّوَجَلَّ that He عَزَّوَجَلَّ has granted us a tremendous gift in the form of Ramadan, whose every moment is full of mercy. The reward of good deeds is multiplied many times in this month. The reward of a Nafl act is equivalent to that of a Farḍ one, while the reward of a Farḍ act is multiplied 70 times. In this month, even the sleep of a fasting person is considered an act of worship. The divine 'Arsh-holding angels say 'Āmīn' for the Du'ā of the fasting people. According to a Ḥadīš, the fish in the seas ask for forgiveness until Ifṭār for the one who fasts in Ramadan. *(Attarghīb Wattarĥīb, vol. 2, pp. 55, Ḥadīš 6)*

Door of worship

Fast is a hidden form of worship; no one can come to know about your fast until you tell it to others. Allah عَزَّوَجَلَّ likes hidden worship more. A blessed Ḥadīš says, 'Fasting is the door of worship.' *(Al-Jāmi'-uṣ-Ṣaghīr, pp. 146, Ḥadīš 2415)*

Revelation of the Quran

Ramadan is a blessed and sacred month in which Allah عَزَّوَجَلَّ revealed the Holy Quran. He عَزَّوَجَلَّ mentions the revelation of the Holy Quran and Ramadan in these words:

شَهۡرُ رَمَضَانَ الَّذِیۡۤ اُنۡزِلَ فِیۡهِ الۡقُرۡاٰنُ هُدًی لِّلنَّاسِ وَ بَیِّنٰتٍ مِّنَ الۡهُدٰی وَ الۡفُرۡقَانِ ۚ فَمَنۡ شَهِدَ مِنۡکُمُ الشَّهۡرَ فَلۡیَصُمۡهُ ؕ وَ مَنۡ کَانَ مَرِیۡضًا اَوۡ عَلٰی سَفَرٍ فَعِدَّۃٌ مِّنۡ اَیَّامٍ اُخَرَ ؕ یُرِیۡدُ اللّٰهُ بِکُمُ الۡیُسۡرَ وَ لَا یُرِیۡدُ بِکُمُ الۡعُسۡرَ ۫ وَ لِتُکۡمِلُوا الۡعِدَّۃَ وَ لِتُکَبِّرُوا اللّٰهَ عَلٰی مَا هَدٰىکُمۡ وَ لَعَلَّکُمۡ تَشۡکُرُوۡنَ ﴿۱۸۵﴾

The month of Ramadan in which was sent down the Quran - the guidance for mankind, the direction and the clear criteria (to judge between right and wrong). So whoever among you finds this month, must fast for the (whole) month; and whoever is sick or on a journey, may fast the same number in other days. Allah عَزَّوَجَلَّ desires ease for you and does not desire hardship for you so that you complete the count (of fasts), and glorify Allah's greatness for having guided you, and so that you may be grateful.

[Kanz-ul-Īmān (Translation of Quran)] (Part 2, Sūraĥ Al-Baqaraĥ, verse 185)

Definition of Ramadan

Regarding the first part of this verse (شَهۡرُ رَمَضَانَ الَّذِیۡۤ), a renowned exegetist of the Quran, Muftī Aḥmad Yār Khān عَلَيْهِ رَحْمَةُ الْمَنَّان has stated in '*Tafsīr-e-Na'īmī*', 'Like 'رَحْمٰن' (Raḥmān), Ramadan is probably one of the names of Allah عَزَّوَجَلَّ because He عَزَّوَجَلَّ is worshipped the whole day and night in this month. Therefore, it is called Ramadan i.e., 'The Month of Allah عَزَّوَجَلَّ.' As a Masjid or the Holy Ka'baĥ is referred to the house of Allah عَزَّوَجَلَّ because it is the place where Allah عَزَّوَجَلَّ is worshipped, similarly, Ramadan is the month of Allah عَزَّوَجَلَّ because everyone is occupied with fulfilling the commandments of Allah عَزَّوَجَلَّ in this month. Obviously, the fast and the Tarāwīḥ Ṣalāĥ are forms of worship but when a Muslim fasts, his Ḥalāl job or business is also considered worship. The word رَمَضَان (Ramadan) is derived either from the word 'رَمْضَاءٌ' (Ramḍāun) or from the word رَمْض (Ramḍ). The word رَمْضَاءٌ implies the autumn rain which washes the earth and produces a good spring harvest. Since this month also washes the dirt and dust of sins from the heart, making the crops of virtuous deeds blossoming, it is called Ramadan for this reason.

For a good harvest, rain is needed everyday in the first month of the rainy season, four times in the second month and once in the last month. The last rain prepares the crops for harvest. In the like manner, a Muslim does virtuous acts for eleven months and then the fasts of Ramadan prepare the crops of virtues. The word 'رَمْض' (Ramḍ) implies heat or burning. As the Muslims endure the burning of thirst and hunger in Ramadan or as this month burns their sins, it is called Ramadan. (In *Kanz-ul-'Ummāl*, page 217, volume 8 there is a narration reported by Sayyidunā Anas رَضِیَ اللّٰہُ تَعَالٰی عَنْہ that the Beloved and Blessed Prophet صَلَّی اللّٰہُ تَعَالٰی عَلَیْہِ وَاٰلِہٖ وَسَلَّم has said, 'This month is called Ramadan because it burns sins).'

Reasons for names of months

Muftī Aḥmad Yār Khān عَلَیْہِ رَحْمَۃُ الْمَنَّان has stated, 'Some exegetists رَحِمَہُمُ اللّٰہُ تَعَالٰی have said that different names were given to different months in relation to their seasons. (For instance) the month that fell in summer was called Ramadan, the one in spring was called Rabī'-ul-Awwal and the one that fell in water-freezing winter was called Jumādal Aūlā.

In Islam there is always a wonderful reason for a name, and the name is given in relation to the attributes of the thing. This is not found in other terms. We see an ignorant person named 'Muhammad Fāzil' (learned) and a coward is called 'Shayr Baĥādur' (a brave lion) and an ugly man is called 'Yūsuf Khān' but there is no such defect in Islam. Ramadan is a combination of virtues and excellence, which is why it is called Ramadan.'

(Tafsīr-e-Na'īmī, vol. 2, pp. 205)

صَلُّوْا عَلَی الْحَبِیْب صَلَّی اللّٰہُ تَعَالٰی عَلٰی مُحَمَّد

Palace with portal of gold

Sayyidunā Abū Sa'īd Khudrī رَضِیَ اللّٰہُ تَعَالٰی عَنْہ has narrated that the Holy Prophet صَلَّی اللّٰہُ تَعَالٰی عَلَیْہِ وَاٰلِہٖ وَسَلَّم has said, 'On the first night of Ramadan, the portals of the skies and Paradise are opened which remain open until the last night (of the month). So if anyone offers Ṣalāĥ in any night of this month, Allah عَزَّوَجَلَّ will reward him with 1,500 virtues for every Sajdaĥ (prostration) and make a palace of red rubies for him that will have 60,000 gates. The gates will have hinges of gold that will be embroidered with red rubies. Thus, the one who fasts on the first day of Ramadan will be forgiven for his sins until the last day of the month and 70,000 angels will ask for his forgiveness from morning till evening. Each time he prostrates during the day or at night, he will be granted a tree in Heaven and each tree is so huge that a horse rider can ride under its shadow for 500 years.' *(Shu'ab-ul-Īmān, vol. 3, pp. 314, Ḥadīš 3635)*

سُبْحٰنَ اللّٰہ عَزَّوَجَلَّ! Dear Islamic brothers! What an enormous favour our Ḥannān and Mannān Allah عَزَّوَجَلَّ has bestowed upon us by granting us this blessed month for the sake of His Beloved Rasūl صَلَّى اللّٰہ تَعَالٰی عَلَیْهِ وَاٰلِہٖ وَسَلَّم! It is the month in which all the portals of Heaven are opened and the reward for good deeds is greatly increased. According to the foregoing Ḥadīš, the one who offers Ṣalāĥ in any of the nights of Ramadan will be granted the reward of 1,500 good deeds for every Sajdaĥ he performs. Further, there will be a magnificent Heavenly palace as well. This blessed Ḥadīš also contains glad tidings that 70,000 angels make Du'ā for the forgiveness of the fasting Muslims from morning till evening.

صَلُّوا عَلَى الْحَبِيْب صَلَّى اللّٰهُ تَعَالٰى عَلٰى مُحَمَّد

Dear Islamic brothers! اَلْحَمْدُ لِلّٰہ عَزَّوَجَلَّ The mindset of attaining the blessings of Ramadan is developed by adopting the company of devotees of Rasūl who are associated with Dawat-e-Islami, a global & non-political religious movement of the Quran and Sunnaĥ. Otherwise, bad company leads many people to committing sins even in this auspicious month. Let me tell you about a singer who was at one time drowning in the ocean of sins but was rescued by the Madanī environment of Dawat-e-Islami.

I was a singer

An Islamic brother of Orangi Town (Bāb-ul-Madīnaĥ, Karachi) has stated: Unfortunately, I was a singer. I was ruining my life in musical concerts. I was so heedless that I neither offered Ṣalāĥ nor felt guilty about my sins.

Fortunately, making individual effort, a responsible Islamic brother convinced me to attend the 3 day Sunnaĥ-Inspiring Ijtimā' held in 1424 A.H., 2003 in Ṣaḥrā-e-Madīnaĥ near the Toll Plaza, Super Highway, Bāb-ul-Madīnaĥ, Karachi. On the last day, we all attended a very passionate and heart-rending Du'ā that made me feel guilty about my evil deeds. I could not control my emotions and burst into tears, which softened my heart.

اَلْحَمْدُ لِلّٰه عَزَّوَجَلَّ! I joined Dawat-e-Islami, repented of attending musical concerts and began to travel with Madanī Qāfilaĥs. On 25th December 2004, as I was about to leave home to travel with a Madanī Qāfilaĥ, I received a phone call from my younger sister who was very sad. She gave me the news of her new born blind baby girl and told me that doctors remarked that her baby would never be able to see. As she was talking, she could not hold herself back and began to cry. I encouraged her by saying that I would pray for her baby in the Madanī Qāfilaĥ, اِنْ شَآءَاللّٰه عَزَّوَجَلَّ.

During the Madanī Qāfilaĥ, I made supplications myself and asked Rasūl's devotees of the Madanī Qāfilaĥ to pray as well. It was my second day back from the Madanī Qāfilaĥ, I received another phone call from my sister but this time she sounded extremely happy. She told me that her baby Maĥak had got her eyesight, اَلْحَمْدُ لِلّٰه عَزَّوَجَلَّ! Amazed, the doctors remarked they don't know as to how it happened because they didn't have any cure for it. اَلْحَمْدُ لِلّٰه عَزَّوَجَلَّ! At present, I am blessed with the opportunity to carry out the Madanī activities of Dawat-e-Islami as a member of the 'Alāqāi Mushāwarat in Bāb-ul-Madīnaĥ, Karachi.

Āfataun say na ḋar, rakĥ karam per naẓar
Rawshan ānkĥayn milayn, Qāfilay mayn chalo
Āp ko doctor, nay gaw māyūs kar
Bĥī diyā mat ḋarayn, Qāfilay mayn chalo

Don't be scared of adversity, keep gaze on divine bounty
Eyesight will be regained, travel with Madanī Qāfilaĥ
Even if the doctor has disappointed you
Don't give up hope, travel with Madanī Qāfilaĥ

صَلُّوْا عَلَى الْحَبِيْب   صَلَّى اللهُ تَعَالٰى عَلٰى مُحَمَّد

Dear Islamic brothers! Did you see how great the Madanī environment of Dawat-e-Islami is? Many people who were previously wicked and impious are now leading their lives following the Sunnaĥ of Beloved Rasūl صَلَّى اللهُ تَعَالٰى عَلَيْهِ وَاٰلِهٖ وَسَلَّم owing to the blessing of joining the Madanī environment of Dawat-e-Islami. The aforementioned incident also highlights the significance of travelling with Madanī Qāfilaĥs. As the troubles and problems of some people are solved due to travelling in Madanī Qāfilaĥs, the troubles and difficulties of the afterlife will also be relieved due to the intercession of the Beloved and Blessed Prophet صَلَّى اللهُ تَعَالٰى عَلَيْهِ وَاٰلِهٖ وَسَلَّم اِنْ شَآءَ اللّٰه عَزَّوَجَلَّ

Five special blessings

Sayyidunā Jābir Bin 'Abdullāĥ رَضِىَ اللّٰهُ تَعَالٰى عَنْهُ has narrated that the Beloved and Blessed Prophet صَلَّى اللهُ تَعَالٰى عَلَيْهِ وَاٰلِهٖ وَسَلَّم has stated, 'In Ramadan, my Ummaĥ has been gifted five such things which were not given to any other Prophet عَلَيْهِ السَّلَام before me:

1. On the first night of Ramadan, Allah عَزَّوَجَلَّ showers special mercy upon them and the one upon whom Allah عَزَّوَجَلَّ showers special mercy will never be punished.

2. In the evening, Allah عَزَّوَجَلَّ likes the smell emanating from their mouths (due to hunger) more than even musk.

3. Angels pray for their forgiveness every night and day.

4. Allah عَزَّوَجَلَّ orders Heaven to be adorned for His (righteous) people and says, 'Soon they will get rid of the grief of the world and find solace in My house and My bounties.'

5. On the last night of Ramadan, Allah عَزَّوَجَلَّ forgives them all.'

Standing up, a person asked, 'Yā Rasūlallāĥ صَلَّى اللهُ تَعَالٰى عَلَيْهِ وَاٰلِهٖ وَسَلَّم! Is that Layla-tul-Qadr?' He صَلَّى اللهُ تَعَالٰى عَلَيْهِ وَاٰلِهٖ وَسَلَّم replied, 'No. Do you not see that a labourer is given his wage when he finishes his job?' *(Attarghīb Wattarĥīb, vol. 2, pp. 56, Ḥadīš 7)*

Compensation for minor sins

Sayyidunā Abū Ĥurayraĥ رَضِیَ اللّٰہُ تَعَالٰی عَنْهُ has narrated that the Prophet of Raḥmaĥ, the Intercessor of Ummaĥ صَلَّی اللّٰہُ تَعَالٰی عَلَیۡهِ وَاٰلِهٖ وَسَلَّم has stated, 'The five daily Ṣalāĥ and Ṣalāt-ul-Jumu'aĥ compensate for sins till the next Friday, and Ramadan compensates for sins until the next Ramadan, provided that the major sins are avoided.' *(Ṣaḥīḥ Muslim, pp. 144, Ḥadīš 233)*

صَلُّوْا عَلَى الْحَبِيْب صَلَّى اللّٰهُ تَعَالٰى عَلٰى مُحَمَّد

Method of repentance

سُبۡحٰنَ اللّٰہ عَزَّوَجَلَّ! Ramadan is such a blessed month in which rain of mercy showers upon us and it is a means of our minor sins being forgiven. Major sins are forgiven by repentance. The way to repent is to mention the sin one has committed and then feel resentment for it in one's heart and firmly vow not to commit it again. Let us say, for instance, that someone lied. He should say, 'Yā Allah عَزَّوَجَلَّ! I repent of the lie I have told and I will not tell lies again.' Whilst repenting, he must despise the act of lying and be sincere when he says the words 'I will not tell lies again' otherwise his repentance will not be valid. If the right of another person was violated, then it is necessary to seek forgiveness from him in addition to repentance.

صَلُّوْا عَلَى الْحَبِيْب صَلَّى اللّٰهُ تَعَالٰى عَلٰى مُحَمَّد

تُوْبُوْا اِلَى اللّٰه اَسْتَغْفِرُ اللّٰه

صَلُّوْا عَلَى الْحَبِيْب صَلَّى اللّٰهُ تَعَالٰى عَلٰى مُحَمَّد

Dear Islamic brothers! Books of Aḥādīš are full of the virtues of Ramadan. There are so many bounties and blessings in Ramadan that our Holy Prophet صَلَّی اللّٰہُ تَعَالٰی عَلَیۡهِ وَاٰلِهٖ وَسَلَّم even said, 'If my Ummaĥ had known what Ramadan is, they would wish if only Ramadan had remained the whole year.' *(Ṣaḥīḥ Ibn Khuzaymaĥ, vol. 3, pp. 190, Ḥadīš 1886)*

Heart-warming saying of the Holy Prophet ﷺ

Sayyidunā Salmān Fārsī رَضِیَ اللّٰہُ تَعَالٰی عَنْہُ has narrated that on the last day of Sha'bān, the Prophet of Raḥmaĥ, the Intercessor of Ummaĥ, the Owner of Jannaĥ صَلَّى اللهُ تَعَالٰى عَلَيْهِ وَاٰلِهٖ وَسَلَّم said, 'O people! An auspicious and blessed month has approached you. In this month, there is a night that is better than a thousand months. Allah عَزَّوَجَلَّ has made it Farḍ to fast in this sacred month. To offer (Tarāwīḥ Ṣalāĥ) in its nights is Sunnaĥ. If you do a good deed in this month, it will be equivalent to carrying out a Farḍ act in any other month and if you perform a Farḍ act in this month, it will be equivalent to carrying out 70 Farḍ acts in any other month. This is the month of patience whose reward is Heaven. This is the month of sympathy, and the believer's sustenance is increased in this month.

In this month, the one who serves a fasting person with something to do Ifṭār, will be forgiven for his sins and his neck will be freed from the fire of Hell, and he will be rewarded the same as the one who fasted, without any reduction in the reward of the fasting person.' The companions asked humbly, 'Yā Rasūlallāĥ صَلَّى اللهُ تَعَالٰى عَلَيْهِ وَاٰلِهٖ وَسَلَّم! Not all of us possess enough money (to present a meal to the fasting person) for Ifṭār.' He صَلَّى اللهُ تَعَالٰى عَلَيْهِ وَاٰلِهٖ وَسَلَّم replied, 'Allah عَزَّوَجَلَّ will give this reward to the one who offers a sip of milk, a date or a sip of water to the fasting person, and the one who serves the fasting person with a meal so that his stomach is full will be given water from my pond (Kawšar) such that he will never feel thirsty and will enter Heaven.

The first ten days of this month are mercy, the middle ten days are forgiveness and its last ten days are freedom from the fire of Hell. One who treats his slave leniently in this month (by not burdening him with heavy duties) will be forgiven and freed from the fire of Hell. In this month, there are four things which you should do in abundance, two of them will earn the pleasure of Allah عَزَّوَجَلَّ for you, and you cannot do without the other two. The two which will earn you the pleasure of Allah عَزَّوَجَلَّ are:

1. To testify that there is none worthy of worship other than Allah.
2. To ask for forgiveness.

The two which you cannot do without are:

1. To ask Allah عَزَّوَجَلَّ for Heaven.
2. To seek refuge of Allah عَزَّوَجَلَّ from Hell.' *(Ṣaḥīḥ Ibn Khuzaymaĥ, vol. 3, pp. 1887)*

Dear Islamic brothers! This Ḥadīš describes the mercy, blessings and glory of Ramadan in great detail. In this month, we must make special efforts to please Allah عَزَّوَجَلَّ by reciting the blessed Kalimaĥ as many times as possible and by repenting in abundance. We must not neglect asking Allah عَزَّوَجَلَّ for entrance into Heaven and protection from Hell. These are the two things we must persistently ask for.

Four names of Ramadan

اَللهُ اَكْبَر! How blessed Ramadan is! A renowned exegetist of the Quran, Muftī Aḥmad Yār Khān عَلَيْهِ رَحْمَةُ الْمَنَّان has stated in the exegesis of the Quran *Tafsīr-e-Na'īmī*, 'There are four names of this sacred month:

1. Ramadan
2. The month of patience
3. The month of sympathy
4. The month of increased sustenance.'

Elaborating the foregoing names, he رَحْمَةُ اللهِ تَعَالٰی عَلَيْه has further stated, 'Fast is patience whose reward is Allah عَزَّوَجَلَّ. As fasts are observed in this month it is called the month of patience. Sympathy means 'treating others well.' This month is called the month of sympathy because the reward for behaving well (and sympathising) with the Muslims, especially relatives, is increased. In this month sustenance is increased and even the poor enjoy the bounties of Allah عَزَّوَجَلَّ; therefore, it is called the month of increased sustenance.'

(Tafsīr-e-Na'īmī, vol. 2, pp. 208)

صَلُّوْا عَلَی الْحَبِيْب صَلَّی اللهُ تَعَالٰی عَلٰی مُحَمَّد

Thirteen Madanī pearls

(These Madanī pearls are extracted from *Tafsīr-e-Na'īmī*, volume 2).

1. The blessed Ka'baĥ calls the Muslims towards it and distributes its bounties but this month comes to us and distributes blessings. It is as if the Ka'baĥ is a well and Ramadan is a river or the former is a river and the latter is rain.

2. In every month there are specific dates and timings for worship. For example, Hajj is performed in some particular days of Eid-ul-Aḍḥā. Similarly, the 10th date of Muḥarram is the greatest in the whole month; but in Ramadan, specific worships are carried out in every moment of every day. Fasting, doing Ifṭār, waiting for Tarāwīḥ Ṣalāĥ, offering Tarāwīḥ Ṣalāĥ, sleeping or resting so that one can get up for Saḥarī and eating Saḥarī are all worships. In other words, every moment manifests the glory of Allah عَزَّوَجَلَّ.

3. Ramadan is (like) a furnace. As a furnace polishes dirty iron and shapes the polished iron into a device that can be fitted into a machine and as a furnace shapes gold into jewellery and makes it fit to wear, similarly, Ramadan purifies sinners and elevates the ranks of virtuous people.

4. In Ramadan, the reward of a Nafl deed is equivalent to a Farḍ one and the reward of Farḍ deed is increased seventy times.

5. Some scholars have said that if someone dies in the month of Ramadan, he will not be questioned in his grave.

6. Layla-tul-Qadr is also in this blessed month. The verse mentioned earlier says that the Holy Quran was revealed in Ramadan and in another verse Allah عَزَّوَجَلَّ says:

إِنَّآ أَنزَلْنَٰهُ فِى لَيْلَةِ ٱلْقَدْرِ ۝١

Undoubtedly, We sent it down in Layla-tul-Qadr (the blessed and valuable night).

[Kanz-ul-Īmān (Translation of Quran)]

It becomes clear by the combination of both the verses that Layla-tul-Qadr is in Ramadan and it is most probably the 27th night, because there are nine letters in the Arabic words لَيْلَةُ الْقَدْر (Layla-tul-Qadr) and these words appear three times in this Sūraĥ (nine multiplied by three is twenty seven), therefore it may well be the 27th night.

7. In Ramadan, Satan is held in captivity and the gates of Hell are closed. Heaven is adorned and its gates are opened. This is why fewer sins are committed and more

virtuous acts are carried out in these days. Even those who commit sins in this month, do so due to their Nafs or the evil temptations from their accompanying devils.

8. There will be no accountability of what is eaten or drunk in Ramadan.

9. On the Day of Judgement, Ramadan and the Holy Quran will intercede for the fasting person. Ramadan will say, 'Yā Allah عَزَّوَجَلَّ! I prevented him from eating and drinking during the day' and the Holy Quran will say, 'Yā Allah عَزَّوَجَلَّ! I prevented him from sleeping at night by making him recite me and offer his Tarāwīḥ Ṣalāĥ.'

10. In Ramadan, the Prophet of Raḥmaĥ, the Intercessor of Ummaĥ, the Owner of Jannaĥ صَلَّى اللهُ تَعَالٰى عَلَيْهِ وَاٰلِهٖ وَسَلَّم would free every slave and give charity in abundance. In Ramadan, Allah عَزَّوَجَلَّ also frees people from the fire of Hell. Therefore, we should strive to perform virtuous deeds and avoid sins in Ramadan.

11. Ramadan is the only month whose excellence is mentioned in the Holy Quran by name. No other month is mentioned in the Quran by name, nor such virtues of any other month were described. Sayyidatunā Maryam رَضِىَ اللهُ تَعَالٰى عَنْهَا is the only woman whose name is mentioned in the Quran, and Sayyidunā Zayd Ibn Ḥārišaĥ رَضِىَ اللهُ تَعَالٰى عَنْهُ is the only companion whose name is mentioned in the Quran. This proves the greatness of the three.

12. In Ramadan, prayers are answered at the time of Ifṭār and Saḥarī. This privilege has not been given to any other month.

13. There are five letters in the Arabic word رَمَضَان (Ramadan) ر, م, ض, ا and ن. The ر in رَمَضَان refers to the Raḥmat (mercy) of Allah عَزَّوَجَلَّ, م refers to the Maḥabbat (love) of Allah عَزَّوَجَلَّ, ض refers to the Ḍamān (guarantee) from Allah عَزَّوَجَلَّ, ا refers to the Amān (protection) granted by Allah عَزَّوَجَلَّ and ن refers to the Nūr of Allah عَزَّوَجَلَّ.

There are five special worships in Ramadan. Fasting, Tarāwīḥ, recitation of the Holy Quran, I'tikāf, and worship at Layla-tul-Qadr. So anyone who sincerely performs these five forms of worship will deserve the aforementioned five favours.

(Tafsīr-e-Na'īmī, vol. 2, pp. 208)

Heaven is adorned

Dear Islamic brothers! Heaven is adorned the whole year to welcome the month of Ramadan. Sayyidunā 'Abdullāĥ Ibn 'Umar رَضِیَ اللّٰہُ تَعَالٰی عَنۡہُمَا has narrated that the Prophet of mankind, the Peace of our heart and mind, the most Generous and Kind صَلَّی اللّٰہُ تَعَالٰی عَلَیۡہِ وَاٰلِہٖ وَسَلَّم has stated, 'Indeed, Heaven is adorned for Ramadan from the beginning of the year to the end.' He صَلَّی اللّٰہُ تَعَالٰی عَلَیۡہِ وَاٰلِہٖ وَسَلَّم has further stated, 'On the first day of Ramadan, a breeze blows beneath heavenly trees, delighting the big eyed maidens of Heaven. The maidens say, 'Yā Allah عَزَّوَجَلَّ make such servants of Yours our husbands who would feast their eyes on us, and we would feast our eyes on them.' *(Shu'ab-ul-Īmān, vol. 3, pp. 312, Ḥadīš 3633)*

صَلُّوۡا عَلَی الۡحَبِیۡب   صَلَّی اللّٰہُ تَعَالٰی عَلٰی مُحَمَّد

اَلۡحَمۡدُ لِلّٰہ عَزَّوَجَلَّ! Words cannot express the glory of Heaven! May Allah عَزَّوَجَلَّ forgive us without holding us accountable and make us neighbours of His Beloved Rasūl صَلَّی اللّٰہُ تَعَالٰی عَلَیۡہِ وَاٰلِہٖ وَسَلَّم in Jannat-ul-Firdaus!

اَلۡحَمۡدُ لِلّٰہ عَزَّوَجَلَّ! Dawat-e-Islami is a global & non-political religious movement of the Muslims possessing correct Islamic beliefs. Here is a Madanī glimpse of the blessings bestowed upon those associated with this movement:

Neighbourhood of the Beloved Prophet صَلَّی اللّٰہُ تَعَالٰی عَلَیۡہِ وَاٰلِہٖ وَسَلَّم

اَلۡحَمۡدُ لِلّٰہ عَزَّوَجَلَّ! Numerous Jāmi'āt (Islamic universities) under the name of Jāmi'a-tul-Madīnaĥ have been established by Dawat-e-Islami to teach Dars-e-Niẓāmī free of cost to Islamic brothers as well as Islamic sisters.

اَلۡحَمۡدُ لِلّٰہ عَزَّوَجَلَّ! In 1427 A.H., about 160 students from these Jāmi'āt travelled in the path of Allah عَزَّوَجَلَّ for 12 months. Initially they enrolled in the Madanī Qāfilaĥ Course, during which their morale was boosted, and 77 students presented themselves for Madanī Qāfilaĥs for the rest of their lives. Further, the zeal of the students received another tremendous boost when a devotee of Rasūl was blessed with the vision of the Beloved Prophet صَلَّی اللّٰہُ تَعَالٰی عَلَیۡہِ وَاٰلِہٖ وَسَلَّم in a dream. The petal-like lips of the Holy Prophet صَلَّی اللّٰہُ تَعَالٰی عَلَیۡہِ وَاٰلِہٖ وَسَلَّم began to move, and the following words were uttered, 'All those who have presented themselves for the Madanī Qāfilaĥs for their entire lives will be with me in Heaven.’ The devotee who dreamt regretted not to have attained this privilege. The Prophet of Raḥmaĥ, the Intercessor of Ummaĥ, the Owner of Jannaĥ صَلَّى اللهُ تَعَالٰى عَلَيْهِ وَاٰلِهٖ وَسَلَّم became aware of that devotee’s inner feelings and said, ‘If you also want to be amongst them, present yourself (for Madanī Qāfilaĥ) for your whole life.’

Congratulations to devotees of Rasūl on receiving this tremendous news! There is a very strong hope that those fortunate people for whom the news was given will die in the state of Īmān اِنْ شَآءَاللّٰه عَزَّوَجَلَّ, and for the sake of the Noble Rasūl صَلَّى اللهُ تَعَالٰى عَلَيْهِ وَاٰلِهٖ وَسَلَّم they will be blessed with his neighbourhood in Jannat-ul-Firdaus.

However, remember that the dream of an ordinary person is not a proof by Sharī’aĥ, so we cannot declare with certainty that a certain individual will enter Heaven simply on the basis of a dream.

Iżn say Tayray sar-e-Ḥashr kaĥayn kāsh! Ḥuḍūr
Sāth ‘Aṭṭār ko Jannat mayn rakĥūn gā Yā Rab

If only the Prophet صَلَّى اللهُ تَعَالٰى عَلَيْهِ وَاٰلِهٖ وَسَلَّم *would say on Day of Judgement*
I’ll keep ‘Aṭṭār with me in Paradise with Divine Commandment

Sixty thousand forgiven every night

Sayyidunā ‘Abdullāĥ Ibn Masūd رَضِىَ اللّٰهُ تَعَالٰى عَنْهُ has narrated that the Beloved and Blessed Prophet صَلَّى اللهُ تَعَالٰى عَلَيْهِ وَاٰلِهٖ وَسَلَّم has stated, ‘At every night of Ramadan, an announcement is made in the skies till dawn, ‘O seeker of goodness! Complete (i.e. keep worshipping Allah عَزَّوَجَلَّ) and rejoice, and O evil one! Give up your evil and take some lesson. Is there any seeker of forgiveness, his desire will be fulfilled? Is there anyone repenting, his repentance will be accepted? Is there anyone making Du’ā, his Du’ā will be accepted? Is there anyone who seeks anything, he will be given what he wishes for?’ Allah عَزَّوَجَلَّ frees sixty thousand sinners from Hell each evening of Ramadan at the time of sunset, and on the day of Eid He عَزَّوَجَلَّ forgives as many people as the total number of those freed throughout the month.’ *(Ad-Dur-rul-Manšūr, vol. 1, pp. 146)*

O lovers of Madīnaĥ! The arrival of Ramadan is an enormous favour bestowed upon us. The doors of mercy are opened by the grace of Allah عَزَّوَجَلَّ and innumerable people are forgiven. If only we sinners be given the letter of our salvation from Hell by the hands of the Holy Prophet صَلَّى اللّٰهُ تَعَالٰى عَلَيْهِ وَاٰلِهٖ وَسَلَّم for the sake of Ramadan! Imām-e-Aĥl-e-Sunnat رَحْمَةُ اللّٰهِ تَعَالٰى عَلَيْه has made the following plea in the court of the Holy Prophet صَلَّى اللّٰهُ تَعَالٰى عَلَيْهِ وَاٰلِهٖ وَسَلَّم.

Tamannā ĥay farmāiye rawz-e-Maḥshar
Yeĥ tayrī riĥāī kī chitiĥī milī ĥay

I desire being told by the Prophet صَلَّى اللّٰهُ تَعَالٰى عَلَيْهِ وَاٰلِهٖ وَسَلَّم *on resurrection*
Here is the letter of your salvation

One million sinners freed from Hell every day

Whilst mentioning the favours, bounties, mercy and forgiveness from Allah عَزَّوَجَلَّ, one day the Beloved and Blessed Prophet صَلَّى اللّٰهُ تَعَالٰى عَلَيْهِ وَاٰلِهٖ وَسَلَّم said, 'On the first night of Ramadan, Allah عَزَّوَجَلَّ sees His creation with mercy, and if Allah عَزَّوَجَلَّ sees any of His servants with mercy He عَزَّوَجَلَّ will not punish that servant. He عَزَّوَجَلَّ frees one million (sinners) from Hell every day, and on the 29th night He عَزَّوَجَلَّ sets free as many as were freed throughout the month. On the night of Eid-ul-Fiṭr, the angels rejoice and Allah عَزَّوَجَلَّ reveals the specific attribute of His Nūr and says to them, 'O group of angels! What is the reward for a labourer that has completed his work?' They reply that he be given his complete recompense. Allah عَزَّوَجَلَّ then says, 'Be witness that I have forgiven each one of them.' *(Kanz-ul-'Ummāl, vol. 8, pp. 219, Ḥadīš 23702)*

Forgiveness of one million in every moment of Friday

Sayyidunā 'Abdullāĥ Ibn 'Abbās رَضِىَ اللّٰهُ تَعَالٰى عَنْهُمَا has narrated that the Beloved and Blessed Prophet صَلَّى اللّٰهُ تَعَالٰى عَلَيْهِ وَاٰلِهٖ وَسَلَّم has stated, 'In Ramadan, every day at the time of sunset, Allah عَزَّوَجَلَّ frees one million such sinners from Hell for whom Hell had become Wājib due to their sins, and in every moment of Friday (in Ramadan), He عَزَّوَجَلَّ frees one million such sinners from Hell who had deserved damnation.' *(Kanz-ul-'Ummāl, vol. 8, pp. 223, Ḥadīš 23716)*

Dear Islamic brothers! The foregoing Ḥadīš contains a blessed account of great bounties and rewards from Allah عَزَّوَجَلَّ. سُبْحٰنَ اللّٰه عَزَّوَجَلَّ! Every day in Ramadan one million sinners that had deserved Hell are forgiven, and one million sinners are set free from the punishment of Hell in every single moment of Friday, and then on the last night of

Ramadan alone, sinners are freed equal to the total number of the people freed from the punishment of fire throughout the month.

May Allah عَزَّوَجَلَّ also include us in those fortunate forgiven ones!

آمِيْن بِجَاهِ النَّبِيِّ الْاَمِيْن صَلَّى اللّٰهُ تَعَالٰى عَلَيْهِ وَاٰلِهٖ وَسَلَّم

صَلُّوْا عَلَى الْحَبِيْب صَلَّى اللّٰهُ تَعَالٰى عَلٰى مُحَمَّد

Immense goodness

Amīr-ul-Mūminīn, Sayyidunā 'Umar Fārūq رَضِیَ اللّٰہُ تَعَالٰی عَنْهُ would say, 'We welcome the month that purifies us. The whole Ramadan contains goodness; whether it is the fasting of the day or Ṣalāĥ of the night. Spending (money etc.) in this month is like spending in Jihad.' *(Tanbīĥ-ul-Ghāfilīn, pp. 176)*

Spend more

Sayyidunā Ḍamuraĥ رَضِیَ اللّٰہُ تَعَالٰی عَنْهُ has narrated that the Prophet of Raḥmaĥ, the Intercessor of Ummaĥ صَلَّى اللّٰهُ تَعَالٰى عَلَيْهِ وَاٰلِهٖ وَسَلَّم has stated, 'Spend more (money etc.) on your family in Ramadan because spending in Ramadan is like spending in the path of Allah عَزَّوَجَلَّ.' *(Al-Jāmi'-uṣ-Ṣaghīr, pp. 162, Ḥadīš 2716)*

Big eyed maidens

Sayyidunā 'Abdullāĥ Ibn 'Abbās رَضِیَ اللّٰہُ تَعَالٰی عَنْهُمَا has narrated that the Beloved and Blessed Prophet صَلَّى اللّٰهُ تَعَالٰى عَلَيْهِ وَاٰلِهٖ وَسَلَّم has stated, 'On the first day of Ramadan a breeze called Mašīraĥ blows beneath the divine 'Arsh, swaying the leaves of heavenly trees and making such an extremely pleasant sound that no one had heard before. On hearing this sound, big eyed maidens appear, they stand on top of the high heavenly palaces and say, 'Is there anyone to ask for our hand in marriage?' Then they ask (Sayyidunā) Riḍwān عَلَيْهِ السَّلَام, 'What night is this?' (Sayyidunā) Riḍwān عَلَيْهِ السَّلَام recites Talbiyaĥ (i.e. Labbayk) and says, 'It is the first night of Ramadan, the portals of Heaven have been opened for the fasting (Muslims) of the Ummaĥ of Muhammad صَلَّى اللّٰهُ تَعَالٰى عَلَيْهِ وَاٰلِهٖ وَسَلَّم.' *(Attarghīb Wattarĥīb, vol. 2, pp. 60, Ḥadīš 23)*

Two types of darkness removed

It is narrated that Allah عَزَّوَجَلَّ said to Sayyidunā Mūsā Kalīmullāĥ (عَلٰی نَبِیِّنَا وَعَلَیْہِ الصَّلٰوۃُ وَالسَّلَام), 'I have bestowed two types of Nūr upon the Ummaĥ of Muhammad صَلَّی اللّٰہ تَعَالٰی عَلَیْہِ وَاٰلِہٖ وَسَلَّم to protect them from two types of darkness.'

Sayyidunā Mūsā Kalīmullāĥ عَلٰی نَبِیِّنَا وَعَلَیْہِ الصَّلٰوۃُ وَالسَّلَام humbly asked, 'Yā Allah عَزَّوَجَلَّ! What are those two types of Nūr?' Allah عَزَّوَجَلَّ said, 'The Nūr of Ramadan and that of the Quran.' Sayyidunā Mūsā Kalīmullāĥ عَلَیْہِ السَّلَام further asked, 'What are two types of darkness?' Allah عَزَّوَجَلَّ said, 'The darkness of grave and that of the Judgement Day.' *(Durra-tun-Nāṣiḥīn, pp. 9)*

Dear Islamic brothers! Did you see how Allah عَزَّوَجَلَّ is merciful to those who spend Ramadan worshipping wholeheartedly. There is a description of huge mercy and blessings of Ramadan in the previous two narrations. One can earn the pleasure of Allah عَزَّوَجَلَّ and the eternal rewards of Heaven by fasting in Ramadan.

Further, the second narration describes two types of Nūr and darkness. The existence of light is essential for the removal of darkness. What a great favour our Allah عَزَّوَجَلَّ has bestowed upon us by giving us the light of Ramadan and the Quran to remove the darkness of grave and the Judgement Day.

صَلُّوْا عَلَی الْحَبِیْب صَلَّی اللّٰہُ تَعَالٰی عَلٰی مُحَمَّد

Fast and the Holy Quran will intercede

Fasts and the Holy Quran will intercede for the Muslims on the Day of Judgement. The Prophet of mankind, the Peace of our heart and mind, the most Generous and Kind صَلَّی اللّٰہ تَعَالٰی عَلَیْہِ وَاٰلِہٖ وَسَلَّم has stated, 'The fast and the Holy Quran will intercede for people on the Day of Judgement. The fast will say, 'O Merciful Allah عَزَّوَجَلَّ! I prevented him from eating and satisfying his desires during the day, accept my intercession in his favour.' The Holy Quran will say, 'I prevented him from sleeping at night, accept my intercession for him.' Their intercessions will be accepted.' *(Musnad Imām Aḥmad, vol. 2, pp. 586, Ḥadīš 6637)*

Reason for forgiveness

Amīr-ul-Mūminīn, Sayyidunā 'Alī كَرَّمَ اللّٰهُ تَعَالٰى وَجْهَهُ الْكَرِيْم has said, 'If Allah عَزَّوَجَلَّ had intended to punish the Ummaĥ of Muhammad صَلَّى اللهُ تَعَالٰى عَلَيْهِ وَاٰلِهٖ وَسَلَّم He عَزَّوَجَلَّ would never have bestowed upon them Ramadan and Sūraĥ Al-Ikhlāṣ.' *(Nuzĥa-tul-Majālis, vol. 1, pp. 216)*

Reward of hundred thousand Ramadan

Sayyidunā 'Abdullāĥ Ibn 'Abbās رَضِىَ اللّٰهُ تَعَالٰى عَنْهُمَا has narrated that the Prophet of Raḥmaĥ, the Intercessor of Ummaĥ صَلَّى اللهُ تَعَالٰى عَلَيْهِ وَاٰلِهٖ وَسَلَّم has stated, 'The one who spends Ramadan in Makka-tul-Mukarramaĥ, keeps fasts and offers Ṣalāĥ at night as much as possible, Allah عَزَّوَجَلَّ will reward him equivalent to one hundred thousand Ramadan spent elsewhere. He عَزَّوَجَلَّ will give him the reward of freeing a slave every day and every night each as well as the reward of providing a horse for Jihad every day. He عَزَّوَجَلَّ will also give him the reward of a good deed each day and each night.' *(Sunan Ibn Mājaĥ, vol. 3, pp. 523, Ḥadīš 3117)*

Eid in Madīnaĥ!

Dear Islamic brothers! Makka-tul-Mukarramaĥ is the sacred city where the Beloved and Blessed Rasūl صَلَّى اللهُ تَعَالٰى عَلَيْهِ وَاٰلِهٖ وَسَلَّم was born. Allaḥ عَزَّوَجَلَّ has showered great blessings for the sake of His Beloved Prophet صَلَّى اللهُ تَعَالٰى عَلَيْهِ وَاٰلِهٖ وَسَلَّم. If a devotee of Rasūl spends Ramadan in Makka-tul-Mukarramaĥ, keeps fasts over there and offers as many Nawāfil Ṣalāĥ as possible, he will be rewarded equivalent to one hundred thousand Ramadan spent elsewhere, in addition to the reward of setting a slave free every day and every night and that of a good deed each day and night.

May Allah عَزَّوَجَلَّ bless us all with the privilege of spending the blessed month of Ramadan in Makka-tul-Mukarramaĥ and worshipping as much as possible, and then, as soon as Ramadan ends, may we get to the sacred tomb of the Noble Prophet صَلَّى اللهُ تَعَالٰى عَلَيْهِ وَاٰلِهٖ وَسَلَّم to celebrate Eid, crying and begging him for our 'Eid presents' and may we receive our Eid presents from his blessed hands! All this is possible by the mercy of the Blessed Rasūl صَلَّى اللهُ تَعَالٰى عَلَيْهِ وَاٰلِهٖ وَسَلَّم

The Holy Prophet ﷺ would worship devotedly

Dear Islamic brothers! We should worship Allah عَزَّوَجَلَّ abundantly in Ramadan and do every such act that earns us the pleasure of Allah عَزَّوَجَلَّ and His Beloved Prophet صَلَّى اللهُ تَعَالٰى عَلَيْهِ وَاٰلِهٖ وَسَلَّم. If anyone is not forgiven even in this merciful month, when will he be forgiven then? The Beloved and Blessed Prophet صَلَّى اللهُ تَعَالٰى عَلَيْهِ وَاٰلِهٖ وَسَلَّم would devote himself to worship as soon as Ramadan arrived.

Sayyidatunā 'Āishaĥ Ṣiddīqaĥ رَضِىَ اللهُ تَعَالٰى عَنْهَا has said, 'In Ramadan, the Prophet of Raḥmaĥ, the Intercessor of Ummaĥ, the Owner of Jannaĥ صَلَّى اللهُ تَعَالٰى عَلَيْهِ وَاٰلِهٖ وَسَلَّم would devote himself to the worship of Allah عَزَّوَجَلَّ and did not use to come to his blessed bed the whole month.' *(Ad-Dur-rul-Manšūr, vol. 1, pp. 449)*

The Holy Prophet ﷺ would make Du'ā abundantly

She رَضِىَ اللهُ تَعَالٰى عَنْهَا has further said, 'In Ramadan, the colour of the blessed face of the Holy Prophet صَلَّى اللهُ تَعَالٰى عَلَيْهِ وَاٰلِهٖ وَسَلَّم would change. He صَلَّى اللهُ تَعَالٰى عَلَيْهِ وَاٰلِهٖ وَسَلَّم would offer Ṣalāĥ abundantly, make Du'ā in an extremely humble manner and remain overtaken by divine fear.' *(Shu'ab-ul-Īmān, vol. 3, pp. 310, Ḥadīš 3625)*

The Holy Prophet ﷺ would donate abundantly

Dear Islamic brothers! In this month, donating money abundantly is also a Sunnaĥ. Sayyidunā 'Abdullāĥ Ibn 'Abbās رَضِىَ اللهُ تَعَالٰى عَنْهُمَا has said, 'In Ramadan the Prophet of mankind, the Peace of our heart and mind, the most Generous and Kind صَلَّى اللهُ تَعَالٰى عَلَيْهِ وَاٰلِهٖ وَسَلَّم would set free every prisoner and give something to every such person who asked for.' *(Ad-Dur-rul-Manšūr, vol. 1, pp. 449)*

صَلُّوْا عَلَى الْحَبِيْب صَلَّى اللهُ تَعَالٰى عَلٰى مُحَمَّد

Most generous

Sayyidunā 'Abdullāĥ Ibn 'Abbās رَضِىَ اللهُ تَعَالٰى عَنْهُمَا has stated, 'The Holy Prophet صَلَّى اللهُ تَعَالٰى عَلَيْهِ وَاٰلِهٖ وَسَلَّم is the most generous of all people and his ocean of generosity would turn turbulent the most in the moments of Ramadan when the honourable Jibrāīl عَلَيْهِ السَّلَام visited him.

Jibrāīl عَلَيْهِ السَّلَام would come every night and they both would recite the Holy Quran. Rasūlullāĥ صَلَّى اللّٰهُ تَعَالٰى عَلَيْهِ وَاٰلِهٖ وَسَلَّم would demonstrate more generosity than even a fast blowing wind.' *(Ṣaḥīḥ Bukhārī, vol. 1, pp. 9, Ḥadīš 6)*

صَلُّوْا عَلَى الْحَبِيْب صَلَّى اللّٰهُ تَعَالٰى عَلٰى مُحَمَّد

Thousand times more reward

Dear Islamic brothers! The reward of good deeds is multiplied several times in Ramadan, so one should perform as many virtuous deeds as possible. Sayyidunā Ibrāĥīm Nakh'ī رَحْمَةُ اللّٰهِ تَعَالٰى عَلَيْه has stated, 'One day's fast in Ramadan is greater than a thousand fasts (in any other month), making Tasbīḥ (i.e. saying سُبْحٰنَ الله) once in Ramadan is better than saying it a thousand times in any other month and offering one Rak'at of Ṣalāĥ in Ramadan is greater than offering a thousand Rak'āt in any other month.' *(Ad-Dur-rul-Manšūr, vol. 1, pp. 454)*

Excellence of Żikr in Ramadan

Amīr-ul-Mūminīn, Sayyidunā 'Umar Fārūq رَضِىَ اللّٰهُ تَعَالٰى عَنْهُ has narrated that the Prophet of mankind, the Peace of our heart and mind, the most Generous and Kind صَلَّى اللّٰهُ تَعَالٰى عَلَيْهِ وَاٰلِهٖ وَسَلَّم has stated, 'The one who remembers Allah عَزَّوَجَلَّ in Ramadan will be forgiven, and the one who asks Allah عَزَّوَجَلَّ for anything in this month will not be deprived.' *(Shu'ab-ul-Īmān, vol. 3, pp. 311, Ḥadīš 3627)*

Sunnaĥ-Inspiring Ijtimā' and Żikr of Allah عَزَّوَجَلَّ

Dear Islamic brothers! How fortunate are the people who attend Sunnaĥ-Inspiring Ijtimā'āt and ask Allah عَزَّوَجَلَّ for success in the world as well as in the Hereafter. اَلْحَمْدُ لِلّٰه عَزَّوَجَلَّ! The Sunnaĥ-Inspiring Ijtimā' of Dawat-e-Islami, a global & non-political movement for the propagation of the Quran and Sunnaĥ, consists of Żikr from beginning to end because Tilāwaĥ, Na'at, Sunnaĥ-Inspiring speech, Du'ā and Ṣalāt-o-Salām are all different forms of Żikr of Allah عَزَّوَجَلَّ. Here is a blessing of an Ijtimā' of Dawat-e-Islami.

Birth of son after six daughters

An Islamic brother of Markaz-ul-Auliyā (Lahore) gave the following account: Probably, in 2003, an Islamic brother invited me to attend Dawat-e-Islami's 3-day Sunnaĥ-Inspiring global Ijtimā' held in (Ṣaḥrā-e-Madīnaĥ, Madīna-tul-Auliyā, Multan, Pakistan). I told him that I was the father of six girls and that my wife was expecting another baby, I asked him to make Du'ā for a baby boy this time.

Adopting an extraordinary manner of individual effort, the Islamic brother said, 'سُبْحٰنَ اللّٰه عَزَّوَجَلَّ! Then you definitely need to attend the 3-day Sunnaĥ-Inspiring Ijtimā'. In terms of the number of attendees, this is the biggest Ijtimā' of the devotees of Rasūl after Hajj. Attend it and make Du'ā, innumerable pious Islamic brothers attend the Ijtimā', your Du'ā may be accepted due to the blessing of their presence.' His words touched my heart and I decided to attend the Sunnaĥ-Inspiring Ijtimā'. Words cannot express the faith-refreshing atmosphere I felt there. I felt such spiritual peace for the first time in my life.

اَلْحَمْدُلِلّٰه عَزَّوَجَلَّ! A few days later, Allah عَزَّوَجَلَّ blessed me with a baby boy, as beautiful as the moon. My family members were also overjoyed. اَلْحَمْدُلِلّٰه عَزَّوَجَلَّ! I joined the Madanī movement of Dawat-e-Islami. Allah عَزَّوَجَلَّ granted me another baby boy. اَلْحَمْدُلِلّٰه عَزَّوَجَلَّ! At present, I am making efforts as the responsible for Madanī Qāfilaĥ of Dawat-e-Islami in my locality.

Dear Islamic brothers! It is not surprising that mercy is showered on the Madanī environment of Dawat-e-Islami and other Sunnaĥ-Inspiring gatherings because there are probably numerous Auliyā رَحِمَهُمُ اللّٰهُ تَعَالٰى amongst these devotees of Rasūl.

A'lā Ḥaḍrat رَحْمَةُ اللّٰهِ تَعَالٰى عَلَيْه has said, 'There are great blessings in congregations and the Du'ā made in the gathering of Muslims is more likely to be accepted. Scholars have said, 'Wherever forty pious Muslims gather, there will certainly be one Walī of Allah عَزَّوَجَلَّ amongst them.' *(Fatāwā Razawiyyaĥ (Jadīd), vol. 24, pp. 184) (Taysīr Sharḥ Jāmi' Ṣaghīr, vol. 1, pp. 312, Ḥadīš 714)*

Even if your Du'ā is not accepted apparently, you must still avoid uttering words of complaint. Indeed, Allah عَزَّوَجَلَّ knows what is best for us. We must be grateful to Allah عَزَّوَجَلَّ at all times. If He عَزَّوَجَلَّ gives you a boy, thank Him, if He عَزَّوَجَلَّ gives you a girl, thank Him, if He عَزَّوَجَلَّ gives you both, thank Him, and if He عَزَّوَجَلَّ doesn't give you either, still thank Him in all circumstances and situations. Allah عَزَّوَجَلَّ says in verses 49 and 50 of part 25:

لِلّٰهِ مُلْكُ السَّمٰوٰتِ وَالْاَرْضِ ؕ يَخْلُقُ مَا يَشَآءُ ؕ يَهَبُ لِمَنْ يَّشَآءُ اِنَاثًا وَّيَهَبُ لِمَنْ يَّشَآءُ الذُّكُوْرَ ﴿۴۹﴾
اَوْ يُزَوِّجُهُمْ ذُكْرَانًا وَّاِنَاثًا ۚ وَيَجْعَلُ مَنْ يَّشَآءُ عَقِيْمًا ؕ اِنَّهٗ عَلِيْمٌ قَدِيْرٌ ﴿۵۰﴾

For Allah عَزَّوَجَلَّ is the Kingdom of the heavens and the earth, He عَزَّوَجَلَّ creates whatever He عَزَّوَجَلَّ likes. He عَزَّوَجَلَّ bestows daughters on whoever He عَزَّوَجَلَّ likes and He عَزَّوَجَلَّ bestows sons on whoever He عَزَّوَجَلَّ likes. Or He عَزَّوَجَلَّ couples both, the sons and the daughters, and He عَزَّوَجَلَّ makes whoever He عَزَّوَجَلَّ likes barren. Undoubtedly, He عَزَّوَجَلَّ is all knowing, the omnipotent.

[Kanz-ul-Īmān (Translation of Quran)] (Part 25, Ash-Shūrā, verses 49, 50)

'Allāmaĥ Maulānā Sayyid Muhammad Na'īmuddīn Murādābādī عَلَيْهِ رَحْمَةُ اللّٰهِ الْهَادِى has stated, 'Allah عَزَّوَجَلَّ is omnipotent and He عَزَّوَجَلَّ distributes His bounties as He عَزَّوَجَلَّ likes. This was the case with the honourable Prophets عَلَيْهِمُ السَّلَام as well. Sayyidunā Lūṭ عَلَيْهِ السَّلَام and Sayyidunā Shu'ayb عَلَيْهِ السَّلَام had only daughters, no sons. Sayyidunā Ibrāĥīm عَلَيْهِ السَّلَام had only sons and no daughters, and the Noble Prophet Muhammad صَلَّى اللّٰهُ تَعَالٰى عَلَيْهِ وَاٰلِهٖ وَسَلَّم had four sons and four daughters while Sayyidunā Yaḥyā عَلَيْهِ السَّلَام and Sayyidunā 'Īsā عَلَيْهِ السَّلَام did not have any children.' *(Khazāin-ul-'Irfān, pp. 777)*

Devotee of Ramadan

There was a man whose name was Muhammad. He would not offer his Ṣalāĥ all year round, but in the blessed month of Ramadan he used to wear clean and pure clothes and offer all five daily Ṣalāĥ. He would also make up for his missed Ṣalāĥ. People asked him as to why he does so, he replied, 'This is a month of mercy, blessings, repentance and forgiveness, maybe because of this, Allah عَزَّوَجَلَّ forgives me.' After his demise, someone saw him in a dream and asked: مَا فَعَلَ اللّٰهُ بِكَ؟ '*How has Allah عَزَّوَجَلَّ treated you?*' He replied, 'Allah عَزَّوَجَلَّ has forgiven me for honouring the blessed month of Ramadan.' *(Durra-tun-Nāṣiḥīn, pp. 8)*

May Allah عَزَّوَجَلَّ have mercy on him and forgive us without accountability for his sake!

صَلُّوْا عَلَى الْحَبِيْب صَلَّى اللّٰهُ تَعَالٰى عَلٰى مُحَمَّد

Allah عَزَّوَجَلَّ is Absolutely Independent

Dear Islamic brothers! Did you see how immensely Allah عَزَّوَجَلَّ is merciful to those who honour the month of Ramadan (by worshipping and avoiding sins), and how He عَزَّوَجَلَّ forgave the man who disobeyed Him throughout the year but worshipped Him only in Ramadan. It is important that no one should misunderstand this parable. No one should be under the impression that (Allah عَزَّوَجَلَّ forbid) it is now allowed to miss Ṣalāĥ throughout the year, and keep fast and offer Ṣalāĥ only in Ramadan and then walk straight into the Heaven.

Dear Islamic brothers! Forgiveness and punishment all depend upon the will of Allah عَزَّوَجَلَّ. He is Absolutely Independent. If He عَزَّوَجَلَّ wants He عَزَّوَجَلَّ can be pleased with a Muslim for the smallest of virtues due to His mercy; and if He عَزَّوَجَلَّ wants He عَزَّوَجَلَّ can punish anyone despite great virtuous deeds, for the smallest of sins, due to His justice. It is stated in Sūraĥ Al-Baqaraĥ, verse 284:

فَيَغْفِرُ لِمَنْ يَّشَآءُ وَيُعَذِّبُ مَنْ يَّشَآءُ ؕ

He عَزَّوَجَلَّ forgives whoever He عَزَّوَجَلَّ wants and punishes whoever He عَزَّوَجَلَّ wants.

[Kanz-ul-Īmān (Translation of Quran)] (Part 3, Sūraĥ Al-Baqaraĥ, verse 284)

Tū bay-ḥisāb bakhsh kay ĥayn bay-shumār jurm
Daytā ĥūn wāsiṭaĥ Tujĥay Shāĥ-e-Ḥijāz kā

Forgive me without accountability as I have countless sins
For the sake of Your Beloved Prophet صَلَّى اللهُ تَعَالٰى عَلَيْهِ وَاٰلِهٖ وَسَلَّم who is Ḥijāz king

Three are concealed in three

Dear Islamic brothers! We should neither miss any virtuous deed nor commit any sin no matter how minor it seems to be because we don't know which deed will please Allah عَزَّوَجَلَّ and which sin will bring about His displeasure. The caliph of A'lā Ḥaḍrat, Sayyidunā Abū Yūsuf Muhammad Sharīf Muḥaddiš Kotlavī رَحْمَةُ اللهِ تَعَالٰى عَلَيْه has narrated: 'Allah عَزَّوَجَلَّ has concealed three things in three other things:

1. His pleasure in His obedience
2. His displeasure in His disobedience
3. His Auliyā among His servants.'

He رَحْمَةُ اللهِ تَعَالٰى عَلَيْه has further stated, 'Therefore, we should do each and every good deed because we do not know which deed would please Him. Similarly, we should avoid each and every sin because we do not know which sin would displease Him, no matter how minor it seems to be. For example, using someone else's toothpick (without permission) or using one's neighbour's soil without permission, don't seem to be the matters of concern, but it is possible that the wrath of Allah عَزَّوَجَلَّ be concealed in them. Therefore, one should take care even in such minor matters.' *(Akhlāq-uṣ-Ṣāliḥīn, pp. 56)*

Forgiveness for giving water to dog

O seekers of mercy! If Allah عَزَّوَجَلَّ wants to forgive, He عَزَّوَجَلَّ does so even for the smallest of virtuous deeds. There are many narrations in this regard. For example, 'A woman was forgiven just because she gave water to a thirsty dog.' *(Ṣaḥīḥ Bukhārī, vol. 2, pp. 409, Ḥadīš 3321)*

Another Ḥadīš of the Beloved Rasūl صَلَّى اللهُ تَعَالٰى عَلَيْهِ وَاٰلِهٖ وَسَلَّم says that a man removed a tree from the path so that it would not cause difficulty to pedestrians. Allah عَزَّوَجَلَّ became pleased with him and forgave him. *(Ṣaḥīḥ Muslim, pp. 1410, Ḥadīš 1914)*

Another Ḥadīš says a man got salvation for being lenient in demanding debt from a debtor. *(Ṣaḥīḥ Bukhārī, vol. 2, pp. 12, Ḥadīš 2078)* The stories of the mercy of Allah عَزَّوَجَلَّ are too many to be counted.

صَلُّوْا عَلَى الْحَبِيْب صَلَّى اللهُ تَعَالٰى عَلٰى مُحَمَّد

Deeds leading to relief from torment

Dear Islamic brothers! When Allah عَزَّوَجَلَّ showers His mercy on someone, He عَزَّوَجَلَّ accepts even a minor deed and forgives him.

A Ḥadīš mentions several different people who were blessed by Allah عَزَّوَجَلَّ and were saved from torment due to certain deeds.

Sayyidunā 'Abdur Raḥmān Bin Samuraĥ رَضِىَ اللهُ تَعَالٰى عَنْه has narrated that once the Prophet of mankind, the Peace of our heart and mind, the most Generous and Kind صَلَّى اللهُ تَعَالٰى عَلَيْهِ وَاٰلِهٖ وَسَلَّم came (to us) and said, 'Last night I had a dream in which I saw that:

1. The angel of death عَلَيْهِ السَّلَام came to seize a person's soul but his obedience to his parents appeared in front of him and saved him.

2. A man was being punished in his grave but his virtue of performing Wuḍū saved him.

3. A man was surrounded by devils but his act of making the Żikr of Allah عَزَّوَجَلَّ saved him.

4. A man was surrounded by the angels of retribution but his Ṣalāĥ saved him.

5. A man's tongue was hanging due to thirst, he would approach a pond to drink water but was not permitted to drink, then his fasts arrived and quenched his thirst.

6. A man was trying to get closer to the Prophets عَلَيْهِمُ السَّلَام but was not permitted, his Ghusl (ritual bath) arrived and sat him beside me (i.e. next to the Holy Prophet صَلَّى اللّٰهُ تَعَالٰى عَلَيْهِ وَاٰلِهٖ وَسَلَّم).

7. A man was frightened due to be surrounded by intense darkness, but his Hajj and 'Umraĥ came and brought him out of darkness and took him to light.

8. A man wanted to talk to the Muslims but they did not pay him any attention, then his virtue of behaving relatives well asked the Muslims to speak to him, so they began to converse with him.

9. Fire was approaching the face and body of a man who was trying to protect himself by using his arms, but then his charity arrived and served as a shield for him.

10. A man was surrounded by the angels of retribution but his virtue of calling people towards righteousness and preventing them from evil saved him and took him to the angels of mercy.

11. A man was sitting on his knees but there was a veil between him and Allah عَزَّوَجَلَّ, then his good character arrived and made him meet Allah عَزَّوَجَلَّ.

12. The book of the deeds of a man was about to be given to his left hand, but then his fear of Allah عَزَّوَجَلَّ arrived and he was given his book of deeds in his right hand.

13. The weight of a person's good deeds was less (than that of his bad deeds) but his generosity arrived, increasing the weight of his good deeds.

14. A man was standing at the edge of Hell but his fear of Allah عَزَّوَجَلَّ arrived and saved him.

15. A man fell into Hell but the tears he had shed out of the fear of Allah عَزَّوَجَلَّ came and saved him.

16. A man was standing on the bridge of Ṣirāṭ and was shaking like a branch but then his hope that Allah عَزَّوَجَلَّ will have mercy arrived and saved him, and he passed the bridge.

17. A man was crawling across the bridge of Ṣirāṭ, but then his recitation of Ṣalāt upon me stood him up and helped him pass it.

18. One of my followers reached the portals of Heaven but they were closed, then his witness '*There is none worthy to be worshipped except Allah* عَزَّوَجَلَّ' came and the portals opened, allowing him to enter.

Excruciating punishment for telling tales

19. The lips of some people were being cut; I asked Jibrāīl عَلَيْهِ السَّلَام, 'Who are these people?' He replied, 'They used to tell tales.'

Horrific punishment for accusing others of sins

20. Some people were hanging by their tongues, I asked Jibrāīl عَلَيْهِ السَّلَام as to who they were, he replied, 'They used to falsely accuse others of committing sins.' *(Sharḥ-uṣ-Ṣudūr, pp. 182)*

Don't miss any good deed

Dear Islamic brothers! Did you see! Allah عَزَّوَجَلَّ blessed the people who were being punished and set them free by virtue of different deeds such as obedience to parents, Wuḍū, Ṣalāĥ, fasting, Żikr of Allah عَزَّوَجَلَّ, Hajj, 'Umraĥ, behaving relatives well, call to righteousness and prevention from evil, charity, good character, generosity, crying due to fear of Allah عَزَّوَجَلَّ, having hope in Allah عَزَّوَجَلَّ etc.

Remember! All these matters depend upon the will of Allah عَزَّوَجَلَّ. He عَزَّوَجَلَّ is omnipotent, He عَزَّوَجَلَّ forgives or punishes whoever He عَزَّوَجَلَّ wants, and this is His justice. If He عَزَّوَجَلَّ wants, He عَزَّوَجَلَّ forgives by virtue of one (little) deed, but if He عَزَّوَجَلَّ wants, He عَزَّوَجَلَّ punishes for one (little) sin, and His punishment is very severe.

You have heard about the last two men mentioned in the foregoing Ḥadīš. The Holy Prophet صَلَّى اللّٰهُ تَعَالٰى عَلَيْهِ وَاٰلِهٖ وَسَلَّم saw the retribution being given to those who tell tales and falsely accuse people of sins. Therefore, a wise person should not miss even an apparently minor-looking good deed because that good deed might lead to salvation, and he should avoid every type of sin, no matter how minor it seems to be as that sin might lead to punishment.

4 Stories about sinners

1. Fire blazed up in grave

Sayyidunā 'Amr Bin Shuraḥbīl رَضِىَ اللّٰهُ تَعَالٰى عَنْهُ has stated, 'Once a person who was considered very pious passed away. After his burial, the angels of punishment entered his grave and said, 'We will hit you 100 whips as punishment.' Frightened, he asked 'Why will you punish me, I was a righteous person?' They replied, 'We will hit you 50 whips' but he continued to argue with them. At last they decided to hit him only one whip. So they hit him one whip, which filled the entire grave with blazes of fire and burnt him to ashes. When he was revived, he asked shivering with pain, 'Why was I hit this whip?' They answered, 'Once you offered Ṣalāĥ without Wuḍū, and once an oppressed man came to you for help but you did not help him.' *(Sharḥ-uṣ-Ṣudūr, pp. 165)*

Dear Islamic brothers! Did you see even a pious and righteous person was punished in his grave in case of the displeasure of Allah عَزَّوَجَلَّ? May Allah عَزَّوَجَلَّ have mercy on us and forgive us without holding us accountable!

اٰمِيْن بِجَاهِ النَّبِىِّ الْاَمِيْن صَلَّى اللّٰهُ تَعَالٰى عَلَيْهِ وَاٰلِهٖ وَسَلَّم

2. Unjust weighing led to divine wrath

Sayyidunā Ḥāriš Muḥāsibī عَلَيْهِ رَحْمَةُ اللّٰهِ الْقَوِى has stated that there was a person who used to do the work of measuring grain. He left his job and occupied himself with worshipping Allah عَزَّوَجَلَّ.

When he died some of his close relatives saw him in a dream and asked, 'مَا فَعَلَ اللّٰهُ بِكَ؟' (*How has Allah* عَزَّوَجَلَّ *treated you?*) He replied, 'Due to my carelessness, dust had stuck onto the scale I used to use for weighing grain. I did not use to clean it because of which the amount of grain equal to the weight of the dust would reduce at the time of weighing. I am now being punished for that.' *(Akhlāq-uṣ-Ṣāliḥīn, pp. 56)*

3. Screams from grave

Similarly, another man who used to weigh food and sell without cleaning his scales was also punished in his grave after his death, and people even heard him screaming from inside his grave. Some pious people رَحِمَهُمُ اللّٰهُ تَعَالٰی pitied him and prayed for his forgiveness, and by the blessing of their prayers he was relieved from his punishment. *(ibid)*

Where do Ḥarām earnings end up?

There is a lesson in these two admonitory narrations especially for those who weigh things dishonestly. O Muslims! Although, sometimes, an apparent increase takes place in the wealth due to weighing unjustly, no goodness lies in this wealth. At times, these unlawful earnings prove to be a nuisance even in this world. This income may be lost in the form of huge medical fees, expensive medicines, robbery, bribery or theft, and above all, it may well bring about punishment in the Hereafter.

Karlay taubaĥ Rab kī raḥmat ĥay bařī
Qabr mayn warnaĥ sazā ĥogī kařī

Repent as the mercy of Allah is immense
Or else punishment in grave will be intense

صَلُّوْا عَلَى الْحَبِيْب صَلَّى اللّٰهُ تَعَالٰى عَلٰى مُحَمَّد

تُوْبُوْا اِلَى اللّٰه اَسْتَغْفِرُ اللّٰه

صَلُّوْا عَلَى الْحَبِيْب صَلَّى اللّٰهُ تَعَالٰى عَلٰى مُحَمَّد

Two mountains of fire

It is stated in *Rūḥ-ul-Bayān*, 'The one weighing unjustly will be thrown into the depths of Hell on the Day of Judgement, and having been made to sit between two mountains of fire, will be commanded to weigh them. When he approaches the mountains, the fire will burn him.' *(Rūḥ-ul-Bayān, vol. 10, pp. 364)*

Dear Islamic brothers! Ponder for a moment! The foregoing narration contains the admonition of extremely severe punishment for weighing unjustly for the sake of a few despicable coins in this short-lived life. Today, one cannot bear the heat of the world, how can one bear the scorching heat of two mountains in Hell? For the sake of Allah عَزَّوَجَلَّ! Avoid greed for wealth, or else unlawful earnings will lead to ruin in the world as well as in the Hereafter.

4. Burden of a toothpick

Sayyidunā Waĥb Bin Munabbeĥ رَضِیَ اللهُ تَعَالٰی عَنْهُ has stated, 'There was a young Israelite who repented of all previous sins, and spent seventy years worshipping consistently. He would fast during the day and worship at night. He was so pious that he would refrain from resting in any sort of shade and from eating delicious foods.

When he died, some of his close relatives saw him in a dream and asked, 'مَا فَعَلَ اللّٰهُ بِكَ؟' (*How has Allah عَزَّوَجَلَّ treated you?*) He replied, 'Allah عَزَّوَجَلَّ held me accountable, and forgave all of my sins, but unfortunately I am still not allowed to enter Heaven because of using a toothpick without its owner's permission. I had not apologised to its owner.' *(Tanbīĥ-ul-Mughtarīn, pp. 51)*

صَلُّوْا عَلَى الْحَبِيْب صَلَّى اللّٰهُ تَعَالٰى عَلٰى مُحَمَّد

After all a sin is a sin

Dear Islamic brothers! Tremble with fear! When the wrath of Allah عَزَّوَجَلَّ intensifies, one can be punished even for such a sin he considers very minor, as mentioned in the previous narration that a righteous man was prevented from entering Heaven simply because he used a splinter as a toothpick without its owner's permission and died without seeking forgiveness from the owner. Ponder for a moment! What is the worth of a splinter? These days, people defraud others of millions of dollars and feel no remorse at it.

تُوْبُوْا اِلَى الله　　　اَسْتَغْفِرُ الله

Delay in paying debt without respite is sin

O Muslims! Tremble with fear! The matter of fulfilling the rights of other people is very crucial. Violating someone's right, abusing him, frightening him by staring at him aggressively, threatening him, hurting his feelings by telling him off or in any other way, not paying his due debt or delaying the payment of his debt without a Shar'ī exemption; these are all examples of depriving people of their rights.

Remember! If one owes someone money and is not in a position to pay it in cash but can pay it even by selling his household furniture, he must do so. If one does not pay debt without debtor's permission despite having the means to do so, he will remain a sinner unless he pays the debt. Whether he is awake or asleep, a sin will be recorded (in his book of deeds) for each and every moment. In other words, his meter of sins will continue to tick away. It is the consequence of delaying the payment of debt, what will be the severity of the sin of not paying it at all.

Burden of three paisas

A'lā Ḥaḍrat, Imām-e-Aĥl-e-Sunnat, Maulānā Shāĥ Imām Aḥmad Razā Khān عَلَيْهِ رَحْمَةُ الرَّحْمٰن was asked a question about a (supposed) man called Zayd who delayed in paying a debt and made lame excuses without any valid reason. A'lā Ḥaḍrat Imām Aḥmad Razā Khān عَلَيْهِ رَحْمَةُ الرَّحْمٰن answered: 'Zayd is a sinner, corrupt, an oppressor, a liar and liable for punishment, what else does he want to be called! If he dies without paying the debt he will have to give the creditors his good deeds. He will have to give 700 Ṣalāĥ with Jamā'at for approximately 3 paisas (that he owes). If he runs out of good deeds he will have to carry the burden of their (the creditors) sins and will be thrown into Hell.' *(Fatāwā Razawiyyaĥ (Jadīd), vol. 25, pp. 69)*

Dear Islamic brothers! It is impossible for the oppressor to attain salvation without ṣatisfying the oppressed one. However, if Allah عَزَّوَجَلَّ wants He عَزَّوَجَلَّ will reconcile between the oppressed and the oppressor on the Day of Judgement; otherwise, the oppressed will be given the good deeds of the oppressor. If this does not settle the case either, the sins of the oppressed will be given to the oppressor, and though this oppressor may have left the world as a pious man with heaps of good deeds, on Judgement Day he will be left empty-handed and be thrown into Hell. We seek Allah's refuge.

Who will be destitute on Judgement Day?

The Holy Prophet صَلَّى اللّٰهُ تَعَالٰى عَلَيْهِ وَاٰلِهٖ وَسَلَّم once asked his companions رَضِىَ اللّٰهُ تَعَالٰى عَنْهُم, 'Do you know as to who a destitute person is?' They replied, 'Yā Rasūlallāĥ صَلَّى اللّٰهُ تَعَالٰى عَلَيْهِ وَاٰلِهٖ وَسَلَّم the one who does not have wealth is a destitute.' He صَلَّى اللّٰهُ تَعَالٰى عَلَيْهِ وَاٰلِهٖ وَسَلَّم said, 'The destitute in my Ummaĥ is the one who will be brought on the Judgement Day with Ṣalāĥ, fasts and charity (in his book of deeds) but would have abused and accused someone, he would have taken wealth unlawfully and shed blood (or) beaten someone and as a result of these sins, his good deeds will be taken from him. If he runs out of good deeds and there are still claimants (against him), he would have to take the sins of the oppressed (people) and would resultantly be thrown into Hell.' *(Ṣaḥīḥ Muslim, pp. 1394, Ḥadīš 2581)*

صَلُّوْا عَلَى الْحَبِيْب صَلَّى اللّٰهُ تَعَالٰى عَلٰى مُحَمَّد

Who is an oppressor?

Remember! It is not only the murderers, robbers and gangsters that are oppressors; in fact, anyone who violates even a minor right of the other person is an oppressor (and the other is the oppressed). For example, unlawfully taking even a single rupee of the other person, unlawfully scolding someone, staring aggressively at someone, teasing him etc. are all the acts of oppression.

If the oppressed also violated the rights of the oppressor, both of them would be oppressors and the oppressed in this case. There will be many such people who will be the 'oppressed' in one case and the 'oppressor' in the other.

Sayyidunā 'Abdullāĥ Anīs رَحْمَةُ اللهِ تَعَالٰى عَلَيْه has stated that on the Day of Judgement, Allah عَزَّوَجَلَّ will say, 'No one shall enter Hell or Heaven until he/she is held accountable for the rights of people.' So if anyone has violated the rights of others he will not enter Hell or Heaven until he compensates for it. *(Akhlāq-uṣ-Ṣāliḥīn, pp. 55)*

In order to get detailed information about people's rights, please read the booklet '*Aftermath of Cruelty*' published by Maktaba-tul-Madīnaĥ. Yā Allah عَزَّوَجَلَّ protect Muslims from violating each others' rights and enable us to apologize and forgive each other for all previous mistakes in this matter!

اٰمِيْن بِجَاهِ النَّبِيِّ الْاَمِيْن صَلَّى اللهُ تَعَالٰى عَلَيْهِ وَاٰلِهٖ وَسَلَّم

صَلُّوْا عَلَى الْحَبِيْب صَلَّى اللهُ تَعَالٰى عَلٰى مُحَمَّد

Excellence of dying in Ramadan

The fortunate Muslims who die in the blessed month of Ramadan not only remain safe from being questioned and punished in their graves, but also deserve Heaven. The honourable scholars رَحِمَهُمُ اللهُ تَعَالٰى have said, 'The Muslim who dies in this month will go straight into Paradise; as if the gate of Hell is closed for him.' *(Anīs-ul-Wā'iẓīn, pp. 25)*

Glad tidings of Heaven for three people

Sayyidunā 'Abdullāĥ Ibn Mas'ūd رَضِىَ اللهُ تَعَالٰى عَنْهُ has narrated that the Beloved and Blessed Prophet صَلَّى اللهُ تَعَالٰى عَلَيْهِ وَاٰلِهٖ وَسَلَّم has stated, 'If anyone dies at the end of Ramadan he will enter Heaven; if anyone dies at the end of the day of 'Arafaĥ (9th Żul-Ḥijjaĥ) he will enter Heaven too, if anyone dies whilst donating (in the path of Allah عَزَّوَجَلَّ) he will also enter Heaven.' *(Ḥilyat-ul-Auliyā, vol. 5, pp. 26, Ḥadīš 6187)*

Reward for fasting until Judgement Day

Mother of the believers, Sayyidatunā 'Āishaĥ Ṣiddīqaĥ رَضِىَ اللهُ تَعَالٰى عَنْهَا has narrated that the Noble Prophet صَلَّى اللهُ تَعَالٰى عَلَيْهِ وَاٰلِهٖ وَسَلَّم has said, 'If anyone dies in the state of fast, Allah عَزَّوَجَلَّ will bless him with the reward of fasting until the Day of Judgement.' *(Firdaus - bimā Šaur-ul-Khaṭṭāb, vol. 3, pp. 504, Ḥadīš 5557)*

سُبۡحٰنَ اللّٰہ عَزَّوَجَلَّ! How fortunate the fasting person is! If he dies in the state of fast, he will be granted the reward of fasting till the Day of Judgement. Sayyidunā Anas Bin Mālik رَضِیَ اللّٰہ تَعَالٰی عَنۡہُ has said that he heard Rasūlullāĥ صَلَّی اللّٰہ تَعَالٰی عَلَیۡہِ وَاٰلِہٖ وَسَلَّم say, 'Ramadan has come to you, the gates of Heaven are opened and those of Hell are closed, and the devils are held in captivity. The person who finds Ramadan but is not forgiven is a deprived one, because if he is not forgiven even in Ramadan, when will he be forgiven then?' *(Majma'-uz-Zawāid, vol. 3, pp. 345, Ḥadīš 4788)*

Portals of Heaven are opened

Dear Islamic brothers! In Ramadan the gates of mercy and Heaven are opened, those of Hell are closed and the devils are chained. Sayyidunā Abū Ĥurayraĥ رَضِیَ اللّٰہ تَعَالٰی عَنۡہُ has narrated that the Prophet of Raḥmaĥ, the Intercessor of Ummaĥ صَلَّی اللّٰہ تَعَالٰی عَلَیۡہِ وَاٰلِہٖ وَسَلَّم would say to his companions رَضِیَ اللّٰہُ تَعَالٰی عَنۡہُم, 'The month of Ramadan has arrived; it is a very blessed month. Allah عَزَّوَجَلَّ has commanded you to fast in it. In this month, the gates of the skies are opened and those of Hell are closed. Satans are kept in chains. In this month there is a blessed night called Layla-tul-Qadr which is greater than a thousand months. The person who is deprived of its blessings is (completely) deprived.' *(Sunan Nasāī, vol. 4, pp. 129)*

Devils tied in chains

Sayyidunā Abū Ĥurayraĥ رَضِیَ اللّٰہ تَعَالٰی عَنۡہُ has narrated that the Prophet of Raḥmaĥ, the Intercessor of Ummaĥ صَلَّی اللّٰہ تَعَالٰی عَلَیۡہِ وَاٰلِہٖ وَسَلَّم has stated, 'In Ramadan the gates of the skies are opened.' *(Ṣaḥīḥ Bukhārī, vol. 1, pp. 626, Ḥadīš 1899)*

Another narration says that the gates of Paradise are opened and those of Hell are closed (and) the devils are kept in chains. Another narration says that the gates of mercy are opened. *(Ṣaḥīḥ Muslim, pp. 543, Ḥadīš 1079)*

Why are sins committed despite Satan being in chains?

A renowned exegetist of the Quran Shaykh Muftī Aḥmad Yār Khān عَلَیۡہِ رَحۡمَۃُ الۡحَنَّان has stated, 'In Ramadan, the gates of the skies are opened, through which special bounties of Allah عَزَّوَجَلَّ descend upon the earth. The gates of the Heaven are also opened by which the maidens of Heaven become aware that Ramadan has arrived in the world, and so they pray for the people of the world.

Further, it is also said that no one is punished in his grave in Ramadan. It implies that the gates of Hell are closed in Ramadan, due to which the heat of Hell does not reach the graves of sinners and even unbelievers. Satan, along with his offspring, is chained. If anyone commits sins in this month he does so due to the evil of his Nafs, not because of Satan.' *(Mirāt-ul-Manājīḥ, vol. 3, pp. 133)*

Sins are reduced to some extent

Dear Islamic brothers! It is generally observed that the Muslims get more interested in worship in Ramadan compared to other months. It becomes easier to perform righteous deeds and a reduction in sins takes place, though to some extent.

As soon as Satan is released

As soon as Ramadan ends and Satan is released, it seems as if a storm of sins has occurred. Too many sins are committed on Eid day that even the cinemas that are not filled the whole year round become full on Eid day. Fairs that are not seen all year round are held on Eid. It seems Satan is extremely annoyed as a result of being held in captivity a whole month and wants to take revenge within the day of Eid. All amusement parks fill with men and immodest women, theatres are always packed out on Eid, new films and dramas are released just for Eid, and hence countless Muslims become toys in the hands of Satan. However, there are some fortunate Muslims who are not heedless of Allah عَزَّوَجَلَّ and turn down the misleading invitation of Satan.

Mercy on fire worshipper

There was a fire worshipper who lived in Bukhara. One day he was walking through a Muslim marketplace along with his son. His son began to eat something publicly. Seeing his son eating, he slapped him and scolded him saying, 'Aren't you ashamed of eating in the Muslims' market in Ramadan?' His son replied, '(But) Father, you also eat in Ramadan, don't you?' The father replied, 'I don't eat in front of the Muslims, I eat at home where they can't see me, I don't desecrate this holy month.'

After some time, this fire worshipper died. Someone had a dream in which he saw the deceased stroll in Heaven. Amazed, the dreaming person asked, 'You were a fire worshipper; how did you get into Heaven?' He replied, 'You are right; I was a fire worshipper but at the time of death, Allah عَزَّوَجَلَّ blessed me with faith for honouring Ramadan and granted me Heaven after death.' *(Nuzĥa-tul-Majālis, vol. 1, pp. 217)*

Penalty for eating publicly in Ramadan

Dear Islamic brothers! Did you see? Allah عَزَّوَجَلَّ not only blessed a fire worshipper with faith for honouring Ramadan but also granted him the eternal blessings of Heaven. All those heedless brothers who don't honour Ramadan at all despite being Muslims should learn some lesson from this parable. They do not fast, dare to smoke cigarettes and chew Pān (betel) in front of fasting Muslims and some are so shameless that they even eat and drink publicly.

Remember! The honourable scholars of Islam رَحِمَهُمُ اللّٰهُ تَعَالٰی have stated, 'If anyone eats or drinks deliberately in public during the day in Ramadan without a Shar'ī exemption, his punishment is that he will be killed (by the Islamic ruler).'

(Durr-e-Mukhtār ma' Rad-dul-Muḥtār, vol. 3, pp. 392)

Are you not going to die?

Dear Islamic brothers! Please ponder! This is the punishment in this world for those who do not fast (this punishment can only be imposed by an Islamic ruler) then how horrific and severe the punishment of the hereafter will be!

O Muslims! Wake up from the sleep of heedlessness! How long will you make merry in this world? When would you realize the great loss of wasting the previous moments of your life in heedlessness? Are you not going to die?

Remember! A day will certainly come when you will be leaving this world. Death will put an end to all of your luxuries and pleasures. It will make you rest on soil in lieu of your comfortable and cosy mattress. It will take you out of your beautifully decorated rooms full of entertainment devices and lead you to your dark grave, and then, it will be futile to regret. You have a chance now; repent sincerely of your sins and become punctual in your Ṣalāĥ and fasts.

Karlay taubaĥ Rab kī raḥmat ĥay bařī
Qabr mayn warnaĥ sazā hogī kařī

Repent as the mercy of Allah is immense
Or else punishment in grave will be intense

Dear Islamic brothers! In order to get rid of sinful life, join the Madanī environment of Dawat-e-Islami, a global & non-political movement for the propagation of the Quran and Sunnaĥ. اِنْ شَآءَاللّٰه عَزَّوَجَلَّ You will succeed in the worldly life as well as in the afterlife. Here is a blessing of Dawat-e-Islami.

Blessings of Sunnaĥ-Inspiring speeches

The following is a summary of the statement a Pakistani Islamic brother made under oath: From 1987 to 1990 I was affiliated with a political movement. Due to escalating corruption and political unrest in Pakistan, my family talked me into leaving the country, so I ended up travelling to Oman. On November 3, 1990 I joined a garment factory in Muscat.

In 1992 an Islamic brother of Dawat-e-Islami joined our factory as a labourer. As a result of his individual effort, I began to offer Ṣalāĥ اَلْحَمْدُلِلّٰه عَزَّوَجَلَّ. The environment in the factory wasn't good at all. In our department, there were about 8 or 9 cassette players, and songs used to be played all the time in several different languages including Urdu, Punjabi, Pashtu, Hindi, Bengali etc, with the volume always turned up. اَلْحَمْدُلِلّٰه عَزَّوَجَلَّ, due to the blessings of the company of this devotee of Rasūl, I began to hate music, so we both decided to buy the cassettes of Sunnaĥ-Inspiring speeches released by Maktaba-tul-Madīnaĥ and play them in the factory.

In the beginning we faced objections and criticism, but we didn't give up courage. اَلْحَمْدُلِلّٰه عَزَّوَجَلَّ, These Sunnaĥ-Inspiring speeches had a strong positive effect on me. The speeches that inspired me the most included, '*The First Night in Grave*', '*Reality of the World*', '*Unfortunate Groom*', '*The Talking Grave*' and '*Three Graves*' (all in Urdu[1]).

[1] You can buy these recorded speeches from Maktaba-tul-Madīnaĥ in your own country.

I developed a mindset of hating sins and pondering over my Hereafter. The speeches also inspired a few others who began to support us. The devotee of Rasūl, who created this Madanī transformation in my heart, left his job and returned to Pakistan. We managed to get 90 more cassettes of Sunnaĥ-Inspiring speeches from Pakistan.

At first, there were only 50 or 60 men in the factory who would offer Ṣalāĥ but as a result of listening to these speeches this number increased up to 250 اَلْحَمْدُلِلّٰه عَزَّوَجَلَّ. We contributed and bought an expensive 400 watt speaker that was installed to the wall so that we could listen to the speeches easily. We made a schedule of listening to the recitation of Quran from 7:00 to 8:00 in the morning, Na'ats of our Beloved and Blessed Rasūl صَلَّى اللّٰهُ تَعَالٰى عَلَيْهِ وَاٰلِهٖ وَسَلَّم from 8:00 to 9:00 and then a Sunnaĥ-Inspiring speech from 9:00 to 10:00.

Gradually, we collected 500 cassettes. Along with me, five other Islamic brothers also joined Dawat-e-Islami. اَلْحَمْدُ لِلّٰه عَزَّوَجَلَّ we began Masjid Dars and gradually started a Sunnaĥ-Inspiring weekly Ijtimā' in our factory which would be attended by more or less 250 Islamic brothers. Then we started a Madrasa-tul-Madīnaĥ (for adults). Islamic brothers (of the factory) began to act upon Sunnaĥ; several of them adopted the blessed Sunnaĥ of growing a beard, a symbol of devotion to our Beloved and Blessed Prophet صَلَّى اللّٰهُ تَعَالٰى عَلَيْهِ وَاٰلِهٖ وَسَلَّم and 20 to 25 Islamic brothers began to wear the blessed turban.

At first, our manager used to object to us for listening to the cassettes, but the sound of the speeches eventually changed his frame of mind. اَلْحَمْدُلِلّٰه عَزَّوَجَلَّ, impressed and inspired by listening to the Sunnaĥ-Inspiring speeches, he also began to offer Ṣalāĥ and grew a fist-length beard.

The Islamic brother further said: I have returned to Pakistan where I am currently trying to spread Sunnaĥ as a Nigrān (responsible person) of the Mushāwarat of a division in Karachi. As Sunnaĥ-Inspiring cassettes released by Maktaba-tul-Madīnaĥ caused an enormous change in my life I wish every Islamic brother and sister listen to at least one Sunnaĥ-Inspiring speech or Madanī Muẓākaraĥ (i.e. question-answer session) daily, اِنْ شَآءَاللّٰه عَزَّوَجَلَّ this will bring about huge blessings in the world as well as the Hereafter.

Dear Islamic brothers! Did you see the blessings of the cassettes of Sunnaĥ-Inspiring speech released by Maktaba-tul-Madīnaĥ! This brother was very fortunate; there are many other people who have been attending the weekly Ijtimā' for years yet they do not seem to have changed their lives positively to a great extent. This might be because they do not listen to the speeches attentively. How will someone be able to gain the blessings of religious speeches by listening to them inattentively, looking around or talking during the speech? Listening to advice inattentively is a trait of the unbelievers and therefore Muslims must avoid it. Allah عَزَّوَجَلَّ says in verses 2 and 3 of Sūraĥ Al-Anbiyā (part 17):

مَا يَأْتِيْهِمْ مِّنْ ذِكْرٍ مِّنْ رَّبِّهِمْ مُّحْدَثٍ اِلَّا اسْتَمَعُوْهُ وَهُمْ يَلْعَبُوْنَ ﴿۲﴾ لَاهِيَةً قُلُوْبُهُمْ

When any new advice comes to them from their Creator they do not listen to it but inattentively, their hearts are in heedlessness.

[Kanz-ul-Īmān (Translation of Quran)] (Part 17, Sūraĥ Al-Anbiyā, verse 2)

So please make a habit of listening to Sunnaĥ-Inspiring speeches. اِنْ شَآءَاللّٰه عَزَّوَجَلَّ You will be surprised to see the blessings[1].

Whole year's deeds ruined

Sayyidunā 'Abdullāĥ Ibn 'Abbās رَضِیَ اللّٰهُ تَعَالٰی عَنْهُمَا has narrated that the Prophet of mankind, the Peace of our heart and mind, the most Generous and Kind صَلَّى اللهُ تَعَالٰى عَلَيْهِ وَاٰلِهٖ وَسَلَّم has stated, 'Verily, Heaven is adorned for the month of Ramadan from one year to the next. When Ramadan comes, Heaven says, 'Yā Allah عَزَّوَجَلَّ! In this month, give me the people from amongst Your servants who will live in me.' The Heavenly maidens say, 'Yā Allah عَزَّوَجَلَّ in this month, give us our husbands from amongst Your servants.' Then the Holy Prophet صَلَّى اللهُ تَعَالٰى عَلَيْهِ وَاٰلِهٖ وَسَلَّم said, 'In this month, if anyone protects his Nafs avoiding intoxicant, refraining from laying a false blame on a Muslim and all type of sins, Allah عَزَّوَجَلَّ will marry him to 100 heavenly maidens every night, and He عَزَّوَجَلَّ will make for him a palace of gold, silver, rubies and emeralds in Heaven. This palace will be so enormous that even if the whole world is placed into it, the world would take up only as much amount of space as a herd of sheep takes up in the world. If anyone drinks an intoxicant or falsely accuses a Muslim or commits a sin, Allah عَزَّوَجَلَّ will ruin his one year's (good) deeds.

[1] For more accounts of the blessings of Sunnaĥ-Inspiring speeches please buy the booklet '*The Blessings of Sunnaĥ-Inspiring Speeches* (Urdu)' from Maktaba-tul-Madīnaĥ.

Therefore, refrain from heedlessness in Ramadan because it is the month of Allah عَزَّوَجَلَّ. Allah عَزَّوَجَلَّ has given you eleven months to take advantage of His bounties and enjoy them, and He عَزَّوَجَلَّ has specified one month for Himself, so fear (Allah عَزَّوَجَلَّ) concerning Ramadan.' *(Mu'jam Awsaṭ, vol. 2, pp. 414, Ḥadīš 3688)*

Dear Islamic brothers! We have learnt that as there are glad tidings of reward and mercy for those who honour Ramadan, there are warnings as well for those who disrespect it by indulging in sins.

The foregoing Ḥadīš specifically mentions drinking intoxicant and laying a false blame on a Muslim. Remember! Alcohol is the mother of all evils, drinking it is Ḥarām and will lead to Hell. Sayyidunā Jābir رَضِیَ اللہُ تَعَالٰی عَنْهُ has narrated that the Holy Prophet صَلَّی اللہُ تَعَالٰی عَلَیْهِ وَاٰلِهٖ وَسَلَّم has stated, 'It is Ḥarām to consume even a small amount of the thing that intoxicates in large amount.' *(Sunan Abī Dāwūd, vol. 3, pp. 459, Ḥadīš 3681)*

Blood and pus of Hell-dwellers

Laying a false blame on a Muslim is also Ḥarām and leads to Hell. A Ḥadīš states, 'If anyone lays a false blame on a Muslim, Allah عَزَّوَجَلَّ will keep him in *Radgha-tul-Khabāl* until he is relieved of (the harm of) what he said.' *(Sunan Abī Dāwūd, vol. 3, pp. 427, Ḥadīš 3597)*

Radgha-tul-Khabāl is the part of Hell where the blood and pus of Hell-dwellers accumulate. *(Mirāt-ul-Manājīḥ, vol. 5, pp. 313)* Commenting on the part of the Ḥadīš '*Until he is relieved of (the harm of) what he said*' Shāĥ 'Abdul Ḥaq Muḥaddiš Diĥlvī رَحْمَةُ اللہِ تَعَالٰی عَلَیْه has stated, 'It implies that he will be cleansed of this sin either by repenting of it or by suffering its punishment.' *(Ashi'at-ul-Lam'āt, vol. 3, pp. 290)*

Sins in Ramadan!

Sayyidatunā Umm-e-Ĥānī رَضِیَ اللہُ تَعَالٰی عَنْهَا has narrated that the Beloved and Blessed Rasūl صَلَّی اللہُ تَعَالٰی عَلَیْهِ وَاٰلِهٖ وَسَلَّم warned, 'My Ummaĥ will not be disgraced as long as it fulfils the rights of Ramadan.' He صَلَّی اللہُ تَعَالٰی عَلَیْهِ وَاٰلِهٖ وَسَلَّم was asked as to what was meant by the disgrace of Ummaĥ in this matter, he صَلَّی اللہُ تَعَالٰی عَلَیْهِ وَاٰلِهٖ وَسَلَّم replied, 'Committing sins in this month.'

He صَلَّى اللّٰهُ تَعَالٰى عَلَيْهِ وَاٰلِهٖ وَسَلَّم has further stated, 'If anyone fornicates or drinks alcohol in this month Allah عَزَّوَجَلَّ and all His angels curse him, if he dies before the next Ramadan he will not have a single virtue to save him from the fire of Hell. So fear (Allah عَزَّوَجَلَّ) concerning Ramadan. As the reward of good deeds is increased in this month compared to other months, the severity of sins also increases.' *(Mu'jam Ṣaghīr, vol. 9, pp. 60, Ḥadīš 1488)*

تُوْبُوْا اِلَی اللّٰه　　　اَسْتَغْفِرُ اللّٰه

صَلُّوْا عَلَی الْحَبِیْب　　　صَلَّی اللّٰهُ تَعَالٰی عَلٰی مُحَمَّد

Beware, ungrateful ones!

Dear Islamic brothers! Tremble with fear! Don't waste the blessed moments of Ramadan in sinful activities. As rewards for virtuous actions are increased in this month the nuisance of sins is also increased. One who fornicates or drinks alcohol in Ramadan is so unfortunate that if he dies before the next Ramadan he will not have a single virtue to save him from the fire of Hell.

Remember! The fornication of the eyes is to misuse them (by looking at Nā-Maḥram women etc.) and that of the hands is to touch a woman (or an attractive young boy with lust), so beware! In Ramadan, do your best to avoid misusing your eyes in any way. Do not look at women and attractive boys. Apply Madanī guard to your eyes as long as possible (make every possible effort to keep your eyes lowered). Alas! Sometimes even the Muslims who offer Ṣalāĥ and fast face the wrath of Allah عَزَّوَجَلَّ and the punishment of fire as a result of desecrating Ramadan.

Black spot on heart

A Ḥadīš states, 'When a person commits a sin, a black spot is marked on his heart. If he commits another sin another black spot is marked on his heart (and this carries on) until his (whole) heart becomes black. Then advice has no effect on his heart.' *(Ad-Dur-rul-Manšūr, vol. 8, pp. 446)*

It's obvious that if someone's heart is rusty and black then how can words of piety and advice affect him? It becomes extremely difficult for such a person to avoid sins in Ramadan as well as in other months, and he finds it hard to perform good deeds. If somehow he does manage to occupy himself in acts of piety he does not enjoy himself carrying them out and tries to find the ways to avoid the Sunnaĥ-Inspiring Madanī environment. His Nafs makes him have long hopes and he becomes heedless and eventually dissociates himself from the Madanī environment. Such a person wastes the blessed moments of Ramadan, playing and listening to music, playing cards and chess, gossiping, chatting etc. and thereby ruins these sacred and blessed moments.

Cure for blackness of heart

It is absolutely vital to treat this blackness of heart. An extremely effective treatment is to become the disciple of a perfect Murshid. In other words, one should become the disciple of a pious and righteous man who abides by Sunnaĥ, whose vision makes his disciples remember Allah عَزَّوَجَلَّ and His Beloved Rasūl صَلَّى اللهُ تَعَالٰى عَلَيْهِ وَاٰلِهٖ وَسَلَّم, whose speech motivates his followers to offer Ṣalāĥ and act upon the blessed Sunnaĥ and whose company inspires others to prepare for death and the afterlife. If one is fortunate enough to find such a competent Murshid then this blackness of heart will certainly be cured, اِنْ شَآءَ اللّٰه عَزَّوَجَلَّ.

Remember! We are not allowed to pass such comments about any particular Muslim sinner as his heart is black or it has been sealed, due to which he does not accept my call to righteousness. Allah عَزَّوَجَلَّ has the power to make him repent and come onto the straight path. May Allah عَزَّوَجَلَّ remove the blackness of our hearts!

اٰمِيْن بِجَاهِ النَّبِيِّ الْاَمِيْن صَلَّى اللهُ تَعَالٰى عَلَيْهِ وَاٰلِهٖ وَسَلَّم

Here is an admonitory parable, please read it and tremble with fear of Allah عَزَّوَجَلَّ! Those who play cards, chess, video games, watch films and dramas, listen to music etc. despite fasting should particularly listen to it attentively.

Horrific scene of grave!

Once Amīr-ul-Mūminīn, Sayyidunā 'Alī كَرَّمَ اللّٰهُ تَعَالٰى وَجْهَهُ الْكَرِيْم went to a cemetery in Kufa to visit graves. Seeing a newly-prepared grave, he رَضِىَ اللّٰهُ تَعَالٰى عَنْهُ desired to get to know of its internal state, so he رَضِىَ اللّٰهُ تَعَالٰى عَنْهُ implored Allah عَزَّوَجَلَّ humbly, 'Yā Allah عَزَّوَجَلَّ reveal to me the condition of the deceased buried in this grave.' Immediately, all the veils between him and the deceased were lifted. What he saw was a horrific scene; the deceased was being burnt in fire and screaming out for help from Sayyidunā 'Alī رَضِىَ اللّٰهُ تَعَالٰى عَنْهُ:

يَاعَلِيُّ! اَنَاغَرِيْقٌ فِى النَّارِ وَحَرِيْقٌ فِى النَّارِ

O 'Alī كَرَّمَ اللّٰهُ تَعَالٰى وَجْهَهُ الْكَرِيْم! I am drowned in fire and I am burning in fire.

The dreadful scene of the grave and the screams of the deceased person saddened Sayyidunā 'Alī كَرَّمَ اللّٰهُ تَعَالٰى وَجْهَهُ الْكَرِيْم. He lifted his hands in the court of his Merciful Allah عَزَّوَجَلَّ and began to pray with utmost humility for the forgiveness of the deceased. A voice from Ghayb echoed, 'O 'Alī (كَرَّمَ اللّٰهُ تَعَالٰى وَجْهَهُ الْكَرِيْم)! Do not intercede for him as he used to disrespect Ramadan in spite of fasting, he did not refrain from committing sins even in Ramadan, he used to fast during the day but would indulge in sins at night.'

Listening to this voice, Sayyidunā 'Alī كَرَّمَ اللّٰهُ تَعَالٰى وَجْهَهُ الْكَرِيْم became even more sad; he رَضِىَ اللّٰهُ تَعَالٰى عَنْهُ prostrated and began to cry. (With tears in his eyes) he said, 'Yā Allah عَزَّوَجَلَّ! Please accept my supplication, this man has called out to me for help with high hopes, O Creator عَزَّوَجَلَّ do not disappoint me in front of him, have mercy on him and forgive this helpless man.' Sayyidunā 'Alī كَرَّمَ اللّٰهُ تَعَالٰى وَجْهَهُ الْكَرِيْم continued to pray in the court of Allah عَزَّوَجَلَّ. He then heard a voice say, 'O 'Alī (رَضِىَ اللّٰهُ تَعَالٰى عَنْهُ)! We have forgiven him for the sake of your grieved heart.' The man was then relieved of punishment. *(Anīs-ul-Wā'iẓīn, pp. 25)*

Conversation with the deceased

Dear Islamic brothers! Amīr-ul-Mūminīn Sayyidunā 'Alī رَضِىَ اللّٰهُ تَعَالٰى عَنْهُ was blessed with a high spiritual status. By the grace of Allah عَزَّوَجَلَّ he رَضِىَ اللّٰهُ تَعَالٰى عَنْهُ was able to talk with the dead.

Here is another parable: 'Allāmaĥ Jalāluddīn Suyūṭī Shāfi'ī رَحْمَةُ اللهِ تَعَالٰی عَلَيْه has narrated that Sayyidunā Sa'īd Bin Musayyab رَضِیَ اللهُ تَعَالٰی عَنْهُ has said, 'We passed by a cemetery in the company of Amīr-ul-Mūminīn, Sayyidunā 'Alī كَرَّمَ اللّٰهُ تَعَالٰی وَجْهَهُ الْكَرِيْم. He رَضِیَ اللهُ تَعَالٰی عَنْهُ said, 'اَلسَّلَامُ عَلَيْكُمْ يَا اَهْلَ الْقُبُوْرِ وَرَحْمَةُ اللهِ وَبَرَكَاتُهٗ. Will you tell us about your state or shall we tell you about ours?' The narrator said, 'We heard a voice from inside one of the graves, وَعَلَيْكُمُ السَّلَامُ وَرَحْمَةُ اللهِ وَبَرَكَاتُهٗ O Amīr-ul-Mūminīn رَضِیَ اللهُ تَعَالٰی عَنْهُ! Please, tell us what happened in the world after we left.' He رَضِیَ اللهُ تَعَالٰی عَنْهُ replied, 'Your wives have remarried, your wealth has been distributed, your children have become orphans and your enemies are now living in the strong houses you built. Now tell us about your state.'

A voice from within one of the graves said, 'Our shrouds are torn, our hair is messy, our flesh has torn to pieces, our eyes have fallen out onto our cheeks, our nostrils are full of pus, we reaped what we sowed, we suffered loss in what we left behind, and now we are with our deeds. (In other words, the one with righteous deeds will find peace in Heaven, and the evil doer will suffer the consequences of his deeds).' *(Sharḥ-uṣ-Ṣudūr, pp. 209)*

Amusement in nights of Ramadan

Dear Islamic brothers! These two parables should serve as an eye-opener for us. Man makes merry so long as he is alive, but when he dies, his eyes do not close, in actual fact, they open. Righteous deeds and the wealth spent in the path of Allah عَزَّوَجَلَّ benefit the deceased, but it is unlikely that the wealth the deceased leaves behind will be spent wisely. There is just a little hope that the heirs of the deceased will spend his wealth in the path of Allah عَزَّوَجَلَّ for the betterment of his afterlife. If the deceased left unlawful (Ḥarām) wealth and instruments of sins such as musical instruments, a game shop, a music centre, a cinema, a pub, a casino, an illegal business etc. he would face severe and unimaginable suffering in his grave.

In the parable '*Horrific Scene of Grave*' we can imagine the horrible punishment given to the deceased who disrespects Ramadan. All of us should take some lesson from it. Unfortunately, during the sacred nights of Ramadan many youngsters play cricket, football etc. in streets. They not only waste these precious moments by depriving themselves of worshipping but disturb other people as well. They neither worship themselves nor let others do. These amusements make a Muslim heedless of Allah عَزَّوَجَلَّ, therefore righteous Muslims always stay away from them. Let alone playing, the pious Muslims avoid even watching and listening to commentaries of such useless activities. Therefore, we must avoid these things, especially in the sacred moments of Ramadan.

'Passing time' whilst fasting

There are many such unwise people who fast but then put the honour of Ramadan aside and indulge in unlawful activities such as playing chess, cards and listening to music in the name of 'passing time'.

Remember! Playing chess and cards is prohibited even if no money or bet is involved. A'lā Ḥaḍrat رَحْمَةُ اللهِ تَعَالٰی عَلَيْه has declared it Ḥarām to play cards because they have images of living beings printed on them. He رَحْمَةُ اللهِ تَعَالٰی عَلَيْه said, 'Ganjifaĥ (a card game) is prohibited because it shows honour to images in addition to being a useless activity.' *(Fatāwā Razawiyyaĥ (Jadīd), vol. 24, pp. 141)*

What is best form of worship?

O fasting Islamic brothers! O seekers of Heaven! Never waste the precious moments of Ramadan in useless and idle activities! Life is very short, so take advantage of its precious moments. Instead of wasting your time by playing cards and listening to songs in the name of 'passing time' try to utilize it reciting the Holy Quran and Ṣalāt-'Alan-Nabī and remembering Allah عَزَّوَجَلَّ. The more thirst and hunger you endure the more you will be rewarded. It is narrated, 'اَفْضَلُ الْعِبَادَاتِ اَحْمَزُهَا (*The best worship is the one that involves more hardship*).' *(Kashf-ul-Khifā-wa-Muzīl-ul-Ilbās, vol. 1, pp. 141, Ḥadīš 459)*

Imām Sharafuddīn Nawavī رَحْمَةُ اللهِ تَعَالٰی عَلَيْه has said, 'The reward and excellence of worship augments when it involves more hardships and expenses.' *(Sharḥ Ṣaḥīḥ Muslim lin-Nawavī, vol. 1, pp. 390)*

Sayyidunā Ibrāĥīm Bin Adĥam رَحْمَةُ اللهِ تَعَالٰی عَلَيْه has said, 'The harder a deed is in the world the heavier it will be on the scales on the Judgement Day.' *(Tażkira-tul-Auliyā, pp. 95)*

These narrations make it clear that the harder we find it to fast and the more our Nafs resent fasting the heavier our fasts will be on the scale on the Day of Judgement, إِنْ شَآءَ اللّٰه عَزَّوَجَلَّ

Oversleeping in fast

Ḥujjat-ul-Islam Sayyidunā Imām Muhammad Ghazālī عَلَيْهِ رَحْمَةُ اللّٰهِ الْوَالِي has stated in *Kīmīyā-e-Sa'ādat*, 'It is a Sunnaĥ for a fasting person to avoid sleeping in excess during the day, he should remain awake so that he feels hunger and weakness.' *(Kīmiyā-e-Sa'ādat, pp. 185)* (Although it is preferable to sleep a little, if somebody passes his time sleeping he will not be a sinner, provided that he fulfils compulsory worships).

Dear Islamic brothers! It is obvious that if someone spent the whole day whilst sleeping, he would not feel any hardship in fasting. Imagine Ḥujjat-ul-Islam Sayyidunā Imām Muhammad Ghazālī عَلَيْهِ رَحْمَةُ اللّٰهِ الْوَالِي advises us to avoid even oversleeping because our time would waste, so what about the people who misuse their time playing games and committing Ḥarām acts. Are they not unfortunate and deprived ones? Please try to realise the significance of this month, keep fasts wholeheartedly and earn the pleasure of Allah عَزَّوَجَلَّ.

Yā Allah عَزَّوَجَلَّ! Grant every Muslim the blessings of Ramadan! Enable us to make the most of this month positively and save us from disrespecting it!

آمِيْن بِجَاهِ النَّبِيِّ الْاَمِيْن صَلَّى اللّٰهُ تَعَالٰى عَلَيْهِ وَاٰلِهٖ وَسَلَّم

Dear Islamic brothers! In order to develop the motivation of respecting Ramadan, acquiring its blessings, earning virtues and saving yourselves from sins, please join the Madanī environment of Dawat-e-Islami and accompany the devotees of Rasūl in Madanī Qāfilaĥ to acquire knowledge of Sunnaĥ. إِنْ شَآءَ اللّٰه عَزَّوَجَلَّ, You will be amazed to see the results.

Reward of performing Fikr-e-Madīnaĥ daily

Here is a summary of the account given by an Islamic brother. اَلْحَمْدُ لِلّٰه عَزَّوَجَلَّ! I love Madanī In'āmāt and I do Fikr-e-Madīnaĥ every day. Once I travelled with devotees of Rasūl in a Sunnaĥ-Inspiring Madanī Qāfilaĥ of Dawat-e-Islami, a global & non-political movement of the Quran and Sunnaĥ.

Our Qāfilaĥ reached Baluchistan (Pakistan). It was in this Qāfilaĥ that Allah عَزَّوَجَلَّ opened the door of mercy for this sinner. When I slept at night, I saw the Beloved and Blessed Prophet صَلَّى اللهُ تَعَالٰى عَلَيْهِ وَاٰلِهٖ وَسَلَّم in dream. His blessed lips began to move, and these words were uttered, 'I will take with me into Heaven all those who carry out Fikr-e-Madīnaĥ everyday in the Madanī Qāfilaĥ.'

Shukriyaĥ kyūn kar adā ĥo āp kā Yā Mustafa صَلَّى اللهُ تَعَالٰى عَلَيْهِ وَاٰلِهٖ وَسَلَّم
Kay pařawsī khuld mayn apnā banāyā shukriyaĥ

Yā Mustafa صَلَّى اللهُ تَعَالٰى عَلَيْهِ وَاٰلِهٖ وَسَلَّم*! I'll always remain extremely grateful to you*
As you have made me your neighbour in Paradise, I thank you

صَلُّوْا عَلَى الْحَبِيْب صَلَّى اللهُ تَعَالٰى عَلٰى مُحَمَّد

What is Fikr-e-Madīnaĥ?

Dear Islamic brothers! For the betterment of the Muslims in the world as well as in the Hereafter, **72** Madanī In'āmāt for Islamic brothers, **63** for Islamic sisters, **92** for male Islamic students, **83** for female Islamic students and **40** for children have been given in the form of a questionnaire. These Madanī In'āmāt booklets can be bought from Maktaba-tul-Madīnaĥ. These booklets should be filled in everyday and handed in to the relevant responsible person of Dawat-e-Islami within the first ten days of every Madanī (Islamic) month.

Fikr-e-Madīnaĥ is a term used in Dawat-e-Islami which refers to the act of holding oneself accountable for sins, pondering over grave and resurrection, and filling in Madanī In'āmāt booklet whilst reflecting upon virtuous and evil deeds.

Please buy a booklet of Madanī In'āmāt. If you do not want to fill it in for the time being, it does not matter, but at least look at it for 25 seconds every day (in connection with the 25th date of the 'Urs of Imām Aḥmad Razā Khān عَلَيْهِ رَحْمَةُ الرَّحْمٰن). اِنْ شَآءَاللّٰه عَزَّوَجَلَّ Looking at it daily will lead you to reading it, which will eventually lead you to doing Fikr-e-Madīnaĥ and filling it in, and if you begin to fill it in, then you will see its blessings for yourself, اِنْ شَآءَاللّٰه عَزَّوَجَلَّ.

Madanī In'āmāt per kartā ĥay jo koī 'amal
Maghfirat kar bay-ḥisāb us kī Khudā-e-Lam-Yazal

One acting upon Madanī In'āmāt be forgiven, O Almighty
And be blessed with Paradise, without accountability

آمِين بِجَاهِ النَّبِيِّ الْاَمِين صَلَّى اللهُ تَعَالٰى عَلَيْهِ وَاٰلِهٖ وَسَلَّم

صَلُّوْا عَلَى الْحَبِيْب صَلَّى اللهُ تَعَالٰى عَلٰى مُحَمَّد

Five before five

Certainly, life is very short. The time we have once spent will never come back, and any hope of having time in future is deception as we do not know what would happen to us in future. Perhaps we may die the next moment. The Beloved and Blessed Prophet صَلَّى اللّٰهُ تَعَالٰى عَلَيْهِ وَاٰلِهٖ وَسَلَّم has stated, 'Value five things before five things: (1) Youth before old age (2) Health before illness (3) Wealth before deprivation (4) Leisure before busyness [i.e. being busy]. (5) Life before death.'

(Al-Mustadrak, vol. 5, pp. 435, Ḥadīš 7912)

اَلۡحَمۡدُ لِلّٰهِ رَبِّ الۡعٰلَمِيۡنَ وَ الصَّلٰوةُ وَ السَّلَامُ عَلٰى سَيِّدِ الۡمُرۡسَلِيۡنَ

اَمَّا بَعۡدُ فَاَعُوۡذُ بِاللّٰهِ مِنَ الشَّيۡطٰنِ الرَّجِيۡمِ ؕ بِسۡمِ اللّٰهِ الرَّحۡمٰنِ الرَّحِيۡمِ ؕ

Rules of Fasting (Hanafi)*

Excellence of Ṣalāt-'Alan-Nabī صَلَّى اللهُ عَلَيْهِ وَآلِهٖ وَسَلَّم

After the demise of Sayyidunā Shaykh Aḥmad Bin Manṣūr رَحْمَةُ الله تَعَالٰى عَلَيْه, someone from Shiraz had a dream in which he saw Sayyidunā Shaykh Aḥmad Bin Manṣūr رَحْمَةُ الله تَعَالٰى عَلَيْه, dressed in a heavenly garment with a crown of pearls on his head, standing in the Miḥrāb (arch) of the main Masjid of Shiraz. The dreaming person asked as to how Allah عَزَّوَجَلَّ treated him, he رَحْمَةُ الله تَعَالٰى عَلَيْه replied, 'Allah عَزَّوَجَلَّ not only forgave me and bestowed upon me (this) crown but also made me enter the Heaven.' When the dreaming person asked the reason of this great privilege, Sayyidunā Shaykh Aḥmad Bin Manṣūr رَحْمَةُ الله تَعَالٰى عَلَيْه replied, 'I used to recite Ṣalāt upon the Prophet of mankind, the Peace of our heart and mind, the most Generous and Kind صَلَّى اللهُ تَعَالٰى عَلَيْهِ وَاٰلِهٖ وَسَلَّم abundantly and this act of mine brought about my success.' اَلْحَمْدُ لِلّٰهِ رَبِّ الْعٰلَمِيْن *(Al-Qaul-ul-Badī', pp. 254)*

صَلُّوْا عَلَى الْحَبِيْب صَلَّى اللهُ تَعَالٰى عَلٰى مُحَمَّد

Dear Islamic brothers! Allah عَزَّوَجَلَّ has bestowed upon us His great favour in the form of the fasts of Ramadan so that we could attain piety and divine pleasure, as Allah عَزَّوَجَلَّ says in Sūraĥ Al-Baqaraĥ (part 2 verses 183-184):

---

* The rulings mentioned in this chapter are all according to the Ḥanafī school of thought. Therefore, Ḥanbalī, Shāfi'ī and Mālikī Islamic brothers and sisters should refer to the scholars of their respective schools of thought.

يٰۤاَيُّهَا الَّذِيْنَ اٰمَنُوْا كُتِبَ عَلَيْكُمُ الصِّيَامُ كَمَا كُتِبَ عَلَى الَّذِيْنَ مِنْ قَبْلِكُمْ لَعَلَّكُمْ تَتَّقُوْنَ ﴿۱۸۳﴾
اَيَّامًا مَّعْدُوْدٰتٍ ؕ فَمَنْ كَانَ مِنْكُمْ مَّرِيْضًا اَوْ عَلٰى سَفَرٍ فَعِدَّةٌ مِّنْ اَيَّامٍ اُخَرَ ؕ وَعَلَى الَّذِيْنَ يُطِيْقُوْنَهٗ فِدْيَةٌ طَعَامُ
مِسْكِيْنٍ ؕ فَمَنْ تَطَوَّعَ خَيْرًا فَهُوَ خَيْرٌ لَّهٗ ؕ وَاَنْ تَصُوْمُوْا خَيْرٌ لَّكُمْ اِنْ كُنْتُمْ تَعْلَمُوْنَ ﴿۱۸۴﴾

O those who believe! Fasting has been made obligatory upon you as were made obligatory upon those before you, so that you may become pious. The days are counted. Then whosoever among you is ill or on a journey then same number of fasting in other days, and those who have no strength, should give in fine meal to a needy: then whosoever does more good, then that is better for him, and fasting is better for you if you know.

[Kanz-ul-Īmān (Translation of Quran)] (Part 2, Sūraĥ Al-Baqaraĥ, verses 183-184)

For whom fast is Farḍ?

Like Ṣalāĥ, the fasts of Ramadan are also Farḍ for every such (male and female) Muslim who is sane and has reached puberty. It is stated in *Durr-e-Mukhtār* that fasts were declared Farḍ on 10th Sha'bān two years after Ĥijraĥ. *(Durr-e-Mukhtār ma' Rad-dul-Muḥtār, vol. 3, pp. 330)*

Reason of fasts becoming Farḍ

Most of the acts in Islam remind us of faith-refreshing Islamic and historical events. Running between Ṣafā and Marwaĥ reminds us of Sayyidatunā Ĥājiraĥ's رَضِیَ اللہُ تَعَالٰی عَنْہَا walking and running between these two mountains seven times in search of water for her son Sayyidunā Ismā'īl عَلَیْہِ السَّلَام. Allah عَزَّوَجَلَّ liked this act and declared it Wājib for all those who perform Hajj and 'Umraĥ to imitate her in order to keep this act alive.

Likewise, the Holy Prophet صَلَّی اللہُ تَعَالٰی عَلَیْہِ وَاٰلِہٖ وَسَلَّم spent some days of Ramadan in seclusion in the cave of Ḥirā where he صَلَّی اللہُ تَعَالٰی عَلَیْہِ وَاٰلِہٖ وَسَلَّم used to refrain from eating during the day and worship Allah عَزَّوَجَلَّ at night. In order to keep the memory of this blessed act of His Beloved and Blessed Rasūl صَلَّی اللہُ تَعَالٰی عَلَیْہِ وَاٰلِہٖ وَسَلَّم alive Allah عَزَّوَجَلَّ made it Farḍ for us to fast in Ramadan.

Fasts of the Prophets عَلَيۡهِمُ السَّلَام

The people of the previous Ummaĥs also fasted but their manner of fasting was different from ours.

According to narrations, Sayyidunā Ādam عَلٰى نَبِيِّنَا وَ عَلَيۡهِ الصَّلٰوةُ وَالسَّلَام would fast on the 13th, 14th and 15th dates. *(Kanz-ul-'Ummāl, vol. 8, pp. 257, Ḥadīš 24188)*

Sayyidunā Nūḥ عَلٰى نَبِيِّنَا وَ عَلَيۡهِ الصَّلٰوةُ وَالسَّلَام used to fast every day. *(Sunan Ibn Mājaĥ, vol. 2, pp. 333, Ḥadīš 1714)*

Sayyidunā 'Īsā عَلٰى نَبِيِّنَا وَ عَلَيۡهِ الصَّلٰوةُ وَالسَّلَام would fast every day and would never miss even a single fast. *(Kanz-ul-'Ummāl, vol. 8, pp. 304, Ḥadīš 24624)*

Sayyidunā Dāwūd عَلٰى نَبِيِّنَا وَ عَلَيۡهِ الصَّلٰوةُ وَالسَّلَام used to fast on alternate days. *(Ṣaḥīḥ Muslim, pp. 584, Ḥadīš 1189)*

Sayyidunā Sulaymān عَلٰى نَبِيِّنَا وَ عَلَيۡهِ الصَّلٰوةُ وَالسَّلَام used to fast on the first three, the middle three and the last three days of every month. *(Kanz-ul-'Ummāl, vol. 8, pp. 304, Ḥadīš 24624)*

صَلُّوۡا عَلَى الۡحَبِيۡب صَلَّى اللّٰهُ تَعَالٰى عَلٰى مُحَمَّد

Fasting person possesses strong faith

Dear Islamic brothers! (Imagine) It is extremely hot, the throat and lips of the fasting Muslim have been dry due to thirst, he has water and food as well, but he does not even look at them despite extreme thirst and hunger due to his steadfast belief in Allah عَزَّوَجَلَّ. He knows that although no one watches him apparently, in fact, none of his actions is concealed from Allah عَزَّوَجَلَّ. This firm faith of the fasting Muslim is the practical outcome of fast. Other forms of worship involve physical movements and are visible to others but fast is such a form of worship which no one can come to know, only Allah عَزَّوَجَلَّ knows. Even if a person eats secretly, people will still regard him a fasting person, but he refrains from eating for the pleasure of Allah عَزَّوَجَلَّ only.

Dear Islamic brothers! If possible, make your children fast from their early age so that they won't face any difficulty in fasting after they reach the age of puberty. The respected scholars رَحِمَهُمُ اللّٰهُ تَعَالٰی have said, 'When children reach the age of ten and are healthy enough to fast they should be made to fast in Ramadan. If they do not fast despite being healthy enough to do so, they should be strictly made to fast even by beating. If they break it, they will not be ordered to make up for it (do Qaḍā), but if they break their Ṣalāĥ, they will be ordered to offer it again.' *(Rad-dul-Muḥtār, vol. 3, pp. 385)*

Does man fall ill due to fast?

There is a general misconception that a person falls ill as a result of fasting but this has nothing to do with reality. A'lā Ḥaḍrat رَحْمَةُ اللهِ تَعَالٰی عَلَيْه has stated in *Al-Malfūẓ* (part 2, page 143), 'Once I saw my respected father Sayyidunā Maulānā Naqī 'Alī Khān رَحْمَةُ اللهِ تَعَالٰی عَلَيْه in my dream a few weeks before Ramadan; he said, 'Son, you will fall severely ill in the following Ramadan, but be careful, you should not miss even a single fast.' As my father predicted, I did fall severely ill in Ramadan but I did not miss even a single fast. اَلْحَمْدُ لِلّٰه عَزَّوَجَلَّ, Allah عَزَّوَجَلَّ granted me good health by the blessing of fasts. The Noble Prophet صَلَّى اللهُ تَعَالٰی عَلَيْهِ وَاٰلِهٖ وَسَلَّم has said, 'صُوْمُوْا تَصِحُّوْا' (*Fast; you will get healthy*).' *(Ad-Dur-rul-Manšūr, vol. 1, pp. 440)*

Fast improves health

Sayyidunā 'Alī كَرَّمَ اللّٰهُ تَعَالٰی وَجْهَهُ الْكَرِيْم has narrated that the Prophet of Raḥmaĥ, the Intercessor of Ummaĥ صَلَّى اللهُ تَعَالٰی عَلَيْهِ وَاٰلِهٖ وَسَلَّم has said, 'Allah عَزَّوَجَلَّ sent a revelation to one of the Prophets of Banī Isrāīl commanding him to inform his Ummaĥ that if anyone fasts a day for My pleasure, I will grant him good health and reward him greatly.' *(Shu'ab-ul-Īmān, vol. 3, pp. 412, Ḥadīš 3923)*

صَلُّوْا عَلَى الْحَبِيْب صَلَّى اللهُ تَعَالٰی عَلٰی مُحَمَّد

Swollen stomach

Dear Islamic brothers! اَلْحَمْدُ لِلّٰه عَزَّوَجَلَّ, the foregoing Ḥadīš makes it clear that fast not only improves our health but also provides us with an opportunity to get great reward. The scientists of the present age have also accepted this fact.

Therefore, professor Moore Palid of Oxford University has stated, 'While studying Islamic books, I was astonished to know that Islam has given a great gift to its followers in the form of fasts! I also felt like fasting, so I began to fast in conformity with Islamic method. My stomach was swollen for quite a while; surprisingly, I felt an obvious reduction in pain as a result of fasting for just a few days. Therefore, I kept on fasting and recovered from my illness within a month.'

صَلُّوْا عَلَى الْحَبِيْب صَلَّى اللّٰهُ تَعَالٰى عَلٰى مُحَمَّد

Astonishing discoveries

A priest from Holland, Alf Gaal, has stated, 'I made several patients suffering from diabetics, heart and stomach diseases fast continuously for thirty days. Resultantly, the diabetes of the diabetics came under control, the heart patients felt a decrease in their fear and breathing problems, and the condition of the stomach patients improved the most.' Sigmund Freud, a psychologist, has also accepted the fact that fast is an excellent cure for physical stress, depression and mental disorders.

Team of researchers

According to a newspaper report, a team of researchers and doctors from Germany, England and America came to Pakistan in Ramadan. They chose Bāb-ul-Madīnaĥ Karachi, Markaz-ul-Auliyā Lahore, and the city of Muḥaddiš-e-A'ẓam رَحْمَةُ اللّٰهِ تَعَالٰى عَلَيْه Sardarabad (Faisalabad) for their research. The report issued by the researchers after the surveys concluded that the Muslims suffer relatively less ear, nose and throat (E.N.T.) illnesses as a result of ablution (Wuḍū) they make prior to their daily Ṣalāĥ they offer in abundance in the month of Ramadan. The Muslims also get less stomach, liver, heart and nerve problems as they eat less due to fast.

Excessive eating causes illnesses

Dear Islamic brothers! Fast does not cause any illness at all, in fact, people fall ill in Ramadan in consequence of eating oily and fried things at the time of Saḥarī and Ifṭār.

Further, many people eat and drink different things every now and then at night. Therefore, one should avoid excessive eating in Ramadan. At Saḥarī, one should not eat so much food that he ends up burping all day and does not feel any hunger and thirst at all.

In fact, the enjoyment of fast lies in bearing thirst and hunger. Extremely hot weather, dry lips and extreme hunger! If only this condition would remind us of the sweet heat and cool sunshine of Madīna-tul-Munawwaraĥ! And, if only it would remind us of the extremely heart-rending incident of Karbalā where the flowers of Prophet's garden were brutally trampled under feet on the scorching desert. Imām Ḥusayn رَضِیَ اللهُ تَعَالٰی عَنْهُ and his companions sacrificed their lives for Islam in the state of extreme thirst, hunger and helplessness. When we feel even more hunger, if only the thought of the blessed stone our Beloved Rasūl صَلَّى اللّٰهُ تَعَالٰی عَلَيْهِ وَاٰلِهٖ وَسَلَّم tied to his blessed stomach would remind us of his hunger.

Dear Islamic brothers! We should fast in such a way that evokes the memories of our Beloved and Blessed Prophet صَلَّى اللّٰهُ تَعَالٰی عَلَيْهِ وَاٰلِهٖ وَسَلَّم, his companions رَضِیَ اللّٰهُ تَعَالٰی عَنْهُم and other saints رَحِمَهُمُ اللّٰهُ تَعَالٰی.

Delivery without operation

Dear Islamic brothers! Join Dawat-e-Islami, a global & non-political religious movement of the Quran and Sunnaĥ in order to get the spiritual benefits of fast and develop the Madanī mindset. Travel with its Madanī Qāfilaĥs in the company of Rasūl's devotees to learn the Sunnaĥs of the Holy Prophet صَلَّى اللّٰهُ تَعَالٰی عَلَيْهِ وَاٰلِهٖ وَسَلَّم.

سُبْحٰنَ اللّٰه عَزَّوَجَلَّ! There are great blessings of the Sunnaĥ-Inspiring Ijtimā'āt and Madanī Qāfilaĥs of this Madanī movement. Here is a summary of the account given by an Islamic brother of Hyderabad (Bāb-ul-Islam, Sindh) in his own words: In 1998, my wife was expectant; I was in a difficult situation as the doctor had declared that she may have to undergo a caesarean (operation). Meanwhile, the 3-day Sunnaĥ-Inspiring global Ijtimā' of Dawat-e-Islami had also approached. I intended to travel for thirty days with a Madanī Qāfilaĥ in the company of Rasūl's devotees after the Ijtimā'. Prior to leaving for Multan to attend the Ijtimā', I took my bag with me to the hospital where my family members and other relatives assured their co-operation. My wife said her farewell with tears in her eyes.

I pinned all my hopes on the Ijtimā' and Madanī Qāfilaĥ for the solution to the problem as I was too poor to afford the expenses of the operation. I prayed a lot during the Ijtimā'. Having attended the concluding heart-rending supplication of the Ijtimā', when I phoned home, my mother informed me happily: 'Congratulations! Allah عَزَّوَجَلَّ has blessed you with a baby girl last night without an operation.' Delighted and excited by the good news, I asked my mother whether to come home or travel for thirty days. She ordered me to travel with the Madanī Qāfilaĥ saying, 'Son, don't worry, travel for thirty days without any tension.'

Despite having a strong desire to see my new born baby girl, I travelled with the Madanī Qāfilaĥ for thirty days. اَلْحَمْدُلِلّٰه عَزَّوَجَلَّ! My problem was solved due to the blessing of Ijtimā' and Madanī Qāfilaĥ. My family also got very impressed by the blessing of Madanī Qāfilaĥ. Even my wife remarked, 'I feel safe, when you are with a Madanī Qāfilaĥ.'

Operation nā ĥo, koī uljĥan nā ĥo
Gham kay sā-ay ḋĥalayn, Qāfilay mayn chalo
Bīwī bachchay sabĥī, khūb pā-ayn khūshī
Khayriyat say raĥayn, Qāfilay mayn chalo

To avoid operation and to remove tension, travel with Madanī Qāfilaĥ
If you desire protection for your wife and children, travel with Madanī Qāfilaĥ

صَلُّوْا عَلَى الْحَبِيْب صَلَّى اللهُ تَعَالٰى عَلٰى مُحَمَّد

Compensation for previous sins

Sayyidunā Abū Sa'īd Khudrī رَضِىَ اللّٰهُ تَعَالٰى عَنْهُ has narrated that the Beloved and Blessed Prophet صَلَّى اللّٰهُ تَعَالٰى عَلَيْهِ وَاٰلِهٖ وَسَلَّم has said: 'If anyone fasts in Ramadan realising its limits and avoiding what should be avoided, this will compensate for all his previous sins.' *(Al-Iḥsān bittartīb Ṣaḥīḥ Ibn Ḥibbān, vol. 5, pp. 183, Ḥadīš 3424)*

صَلُّوْا عَلَى الْحَبِيْب صَلَّى اللهُ تَعَالٰى عَلٰى مُحَمَّد

Reward for fast

Sayyidunā Abū Ĥurayraĥ رَضِیَ اللهُ تَعَالٰی عَنْهُ has narrated that the Beloved and Blessed Prophet صَلَّی اللهُ تَعَالٰی عَلَیْهِ وَاٰلِهٖ وَسَلَّم has said: 'For every act of piety, man is rewarded ten to seven hundred times more. Allah عَزَّوَجَلَّ said اِلَّا الصَّوْمَ فَاِنَّهٗ لِیْ وَ اَنَا اَجْزِیْ بِهٖ (*except fasting, because fasting is for Me and I will give its reward Myself*).

Allah عَزَّوَجَلَّ also says, 'Man refrains from satisfying his desires and eating food for My pleasure. There are two glad tidings for the man who fasts; one at the time of sunset and the other when he meets his Rab عَزَّوَجَلَّ. Allah عَزَّوَجَلَّ likes the smell emanating from a fasting person's mouth more than the fragrance of musk.' *(Ṣaḥīḥ Muslim, pp. 580, Ḥadīš 1151)*

There is another saying, 'Fasting is a shield; when any of you fast, he should neither utter words of indecency nor shout. If any one else abuses him or wants to fight him, he should say 'I am fasting.' *(Ṣaḥīḥ Bukhārī, vol. 1, pp. 624, Ḥadīš 1894)*

Special reward for fasting

Dear Islamic brothers! The foregoing blessed Aḥādīš mention several virtues of fasting. There is a great reward for the one who fasts abiding by Sharī'aĥ and Sunnaĥ, which involves avoidance not only from eating, drinking and intercourse but also from all the sins. By the grace of Allah عَزَّوَجَلَّ such a fast will compensate for all the previous sins. Especially the Ḥadīš which mentions the words فَاِنَّهٗ لِیْ وَاَنَا اَجْزِیْ بِهٖ (*the fast is for Me and I will give its reward Myself*) is very noteworthy.

According to *Tafsīr-e-Na'īmī*, 'Some Muḥaddišīn[1] have read this Ḥadīš in the following manner اَنَا اُجْزٰی بِهٖ which will then mean '*I am its reward.*' سُبْحٰنَ اللهِ عَزَّوَجَلَّ! So, the fasting person finds even Allah عَزَّوَجَلَّ by fasting.

Reward for virtuous deeds is Paradise

Dear Islamic brothers! Several verses of the glorious Quran mention that the reward for virtuous deeds is Heaven. Allah عَزَّوَجَلَّ says in Sūraĥ Al-Bayyinaĥ (part 30, verses 7 & 8):

---

[1] Highly knowledgeable scholars of Aḥādīš.

إِنَّ الَّذِيْنَ اٰمَنُوْا وَعَمِلُوا الصّٰلِحٰتِ ۙ اُولٰٓئِكَ هُمْ خَيْرُ الْبَرِيَّةِ ۝ جَزَآؤُهُمْ عِنْدَ رَبِّهِمْ جَنّٰتُ عَدْنٍ تَجْرِيْ
مِنْ تَحْتِهَا الْاَنْهٰرُ خٰلِدِيْنَ فِيْهَآ اَبَدًا ۗ رَضِيَ اللّٰهُ عَنْهُمْ وَرَضُوْا عَنْهُ ۗ ذٰلِكَ لِمَنْ خَشِيَ رَبَّهٗ ۝

Undoubtedly, those who believed and did good deeds, are the best of creatures. Their recompense is with their Rab عَزَّوَجَلَّ, gardens of habitation, beneath which flow streams. (They would) abide therein forever, Allah عَزَّوَجَلَّ is well pleased with them and they are pleased with Allah عَزَّوَجَلَّ, this is for him who fears his Rab.

[Kanz-ul-Īmān (Translation of Quran)] (Part 30, Sūraĥ Al-Bayyinaĥ, verses 7, 8)

Saying 'رَضِيَ اللهُ تَعَالٰی عَنْهُ' with name of non-Ṣaḥābī

Dear Islamic brothers! Some people have the misconception that the phrase 'رَضِيَ اللهُ تَعَالٰی عَنْهُ' can only be used with the name of a Ṣaḥābī (companion of the Holy Prophet صَلَّى اللهُ تَعَالٰى عَلَيْهِ وَاٰلِهٖ وَسَلَّم). The last part of the verse, 'رَضِيَ اللّٰهُ عَنْهُمْ وَرَضُوْا عَنْهُ ۗ ذٰلِكَ لِمَنْ خَشِيَ رَبَّهٗ' has refuted this misconception, making it as clear as day that رَضِيَ اللهُ تَعَالٰی عَنْهُ can be written with the name of any such Muslim who fears Allah عَزَّوَجَلَّ. There is no specification of companions or non-companions in this regard. It should remain clear that writing and saying رَضِيَ اللهُ تَعَالٰی عَنْهُ for every Ṣaḥābī and Walī is quite permissible.

A Ṣaḥābī is the one who was blessed either with the company of the Beloved and Blessed Prophet صَلَّى اللهُ تَعَالٰى عَلَيْهِ وَاٰلِهٖ وَسَلَّم or who saw him in his visible life even for a moment in the state of faith, and who passed away in the state of faith either. A Walī, no matter how great he may be, cannot reach the rank of a Ṣaḥābī. Every Ṣaḥābī is just ('Ādil) and is destined to enter Heaven.

Anyhow, returning to the topic of fasting, virtues such as Ṣalāĥ, Hajj, Zakāĥ, helping the poor, visiting the sick, caring for beggars etc. all lead to Heaven but fasting leads to the Creator of Heaven عَزَّوَجَلَّ.

I want owner of pearls

One day, throwing some precious pearls in front of his officers, Maḥmūd Ghaznawī عَلَيْهِ رَحْمَةُ اللّٰهِ الْقَوِی said, 'Take them.' He then left them behind. A few moments later, as he turned back he saw Ayāz follow him on his horse. He asked, 'Ayāz, don't you want any pearls?' He replied, 'Your honour, those who wanted pearls are busy collecting them, it is not the pearls but the owner of the pearls that I seek.'

We belong to Rasūlullāĥ, Heaven belongs to Rasūlullāĥ ﷺ

There is a Ḥadīš in this regard. Sayyidunā Rabī'aĥ Bin Ka'b Aslamī رَضِیَ اللهُ تَعَالٰی عَنْهُ said, 'One day I helped the Holy Prophet صَلَّى اللهُ تَعَالٰى عَلَيْهِ وَاٰلِهٖ وَسَلَّم make Wuḍū. Pleased, Beloved and Blessed Prophet صَلَّى اللهُ تَعَالٰى عَلَيْهِ وَاٰلِهٖ وَسَلَّم said to me, 'سَلْ رَبِيْعَةُ!' [*Rabī'aĥ ask* (you will be given what you ask for)]. I replied, 'اَسْئَلُكَ مُرَافَقَتَكَ فِى الْجَنَّةِ' (*I ask you to keep me in your company in Heaven*).

Tujĥ say tujĥī ko māng lūn to sab kucĥ mil jāye
Saw suwālawn say yeĥī aīk suwāl acĥchā ĥay

To ask you for your closeness is to get everything
This plea is better than hundreds of other pleadings

Rasūlullāĥ صَلَّى اللهُ تَعَالٰى عَلَيْهِ وَاٰلِهٖ وَسَلَّم further asked, 'اَوْ غَيْرَ ذٰلِكَ؟' (*Anything else?*), I replied, 'Just this.' (In other words, Yā Rasūlallāĥ صَلَّى اللهُ تَعَالٰى عَلَيْهِ وَاٰلِهٖ وَسَلَّم! After seeking your closeness in Jannat-ul-Firdaus, what is left in the world and the Hereafter for me to ask for!)

Tujĥ say tujĥī ko māng kar māng lī sārī kāināt
Mujĥ sā koī gadā naĥīn, tujĥ sā koī sakhī naĥīn

By asking you for your closeness I have asked for whole universe
Like me no one is destitute, and like you no one is generous

After Sayyidunā Rabī'aĥ رَضِیَ اللهُ تَعَالٰی عَنْهُ asked for the closeness of the Beloved and Blessed Prophet صَلَّى اللهُ تَعَالٰى عَلَيْهِ وَاٰلِهٖ وَسَلَّم in Jannat-ul-Firdaus and declined to ask for anything else, the Prophet of Raḥmaĥ, the Intercessor of Ummaĥ, the Owner of Jannaĥ صَلَّى اللهُ تَعَالٰى عَلَيْهِ وَاٰلِهٖ وَسَلَّم said: 'فَاَعِنِّىْ عَلٰى نَفْسِكَ بِكَثْرَةِ السُّجُوْدِ' [*Then help me by prostrating abundantly*]. (*Ṣaḥīḥ Muslim, pp. 253, Ḥadīš 489*) (In other words, we have granted you Heaven, now keep offering Nafl Ṣalāĥ abundantly as gratitude).

Ask for anything you want!

سُبْحٰنَ اللّٰه عَزَّوَجَلَّ! This blessed Ḥadīš has refreshed our faith. Sayyidunā Shaykh 'Abdul Ḥaq Muḥaddiš Diĥlvī رَحْمَةُ اللهِ تَعَالٰى عَلَيْه has said, 'The word '*ask*' uttered by the blessed tongue of the Holy Prophet صَلَّى اللّٰهُ تَعَالٰى عَلَيْهِ وَاٰلِهٖ وَسَلَّم without any restriction and limitation shows that he صَلَّى اللّٰهُ تَعَالٰى عَلَيْهِ وَاٰلِهٖ وَسَلَّم has complete authority given to him by Allah عَزَّوَجَلَّ. He صَلَّى اللّٰهُ تَعَالٰى عَلَيْهِ وَاٰلِهٖ وَسَلَّم can give whatever and to whomever he صَلَّى اللّٰهُ تَعَالٰى عَلَيْهِ وَاٰلِهٖ وَسَلَّم wants.' 'Allāmaĥ Būṣirī رَحْمَةُ اللهِ تَعَالٰى عَلَيْه has written the following couplet in his famous Qaṣīdaĥ Burdaĥ Sharīf:

فَاِنَّ مِنْ جُوْدِكَ الدُّنْيَا وَضَرَّتَهَا   وَمِنْ عُلُوْمِكَ عِلْمَ اللَّوْحِ وَالْقَلَمِ

Yā Rasūlallāĥ صَلَّى اللّٰهُ تَعَالٰى عَلَيْهِ وَاٰلِهٖ وَسَلَّم! Both the world as well as the Hereafter are (only) a portion of your generosity. The knowledge of the Lauḥ-e-Maḥfūẓ and the Pen is simply a part of your knowledge.

Agar khayriyat dunyā-o-'uqbā ārzū dārī
Badargāĥash bāyād-e-ĥarcheĥ man khawāĥī tamannā kun

If you want the goodness of the world and the Hereafter
then come to this court and ask for whatever you want

(Ashi'at-ul-Lam'āt, vol. 1, pp. 424-425)

Khāliq-e-Kul nay āp ko Mālik-e-Kul banā diyā
Dauno jaĥān day diye qabza-o-ikhtiyār mayn

The Creator has made you the owner
And has given both worlds in your power

Heavenly portal

Sayyidunā Saĥl Bin 'Abdullāĥ رَضِىَ اللّٰهُ تَعَالٰى عَنْهُ has narrated that the Beloved and Blessed Rasūl صَلَّى اللّٰه تَعَالٰى عَلَيْهِ وَاٰلِهٖ وَسَلَّم has said: 'There is a portal in Heaven called Rayyān. On the Day of Judgement, this portal will be opened for those who fast (in the world); no one else will be allowed to enter through this portal. It will be announced, 'Where are the people who used to fast?' They will stand up and no one else will be allowed to enter through this portal. It will be closed after they enter the Heaven.' *(Ṣaḥīḥ Bukhārī, vol. 1, pp. 625, Ḥadīš 1896)*

Dear Islamic brothers! سُبْحٰنَ اللّٰه عَزَّوَجَلَّ! How fortunate the fasting Muslims are! They will be given great honour on the Day of Judgement. There will also be other fortunate Muslims walking into Heaven, but these Muslims will be given the privilege of entering through the portal called 'Rayyān.'

Excellence of one day's fast

Sayyidunā Salamaĥ Bin Qaiṣar رَضِیَ اللّٰہ تَعَالٰی عَنْہُ has narrated that the Beloved and Blessed Prophet صَلَّى اللّٰهُ تَعَالٰی عَلَيْهِ وَاٰلِهٖ وَسَلَّم has said: 'Anyone who fasts a day for Allah's pleasure, Allah عَزَّوَجَلَّ will move him as far away from Hell as is the distance a baby-crow covers flying continuously until it grows old and dies.' *(Musnad Abī Ya'lā, vol. 1, pp. 383, Ḥadīš 917)*

Age of crow

Dear Islamic brothers! Crows remain alive for a long time. *Ghunya-tuṭ-Ṭālibīn* states: 'A crow can live up to five hundred years.'

Red rubies palace

Amīr-ul-Mūminīn Sayyidunā 'Umar Fārūq A'ẓam رَضِیَ اللّٰہ تَعَالٰی عَنْہُ has narrated that the Beloved and Blessed Prophet صَلَّى اللّٰهُ تَعَالٰی عَلَيْهِ وَاٰلِهٖ وَسَلَّم has said: 'If anyone keeps even a single fast with silence and peace in Ramadan, Allah عَزَّوَجَلَّ will make for him a palace of red rubies or green emeralds.' *(Majma'-uz-Zawāid, vol. 3, pp. 346, Ḥadīš 4792)*

Zakāĥ of body

Sayyidunā Abū Ĥurayraĥ رَضِیَ اللّٰہ تَعَالٰی عَنْہُ has narrated that the Holy Prophet صَلَّى اللّٰهُ تَعَالٰی عَلَيْهِ وَاٰلِهٖ وَسَلَّم has said: 'There is Zakāĥ (charity) for everything, and the Zakāĥ of your body is fasting, and fasting is half of patience.' *(Sunan Ibn Mājaĥ, vol. 2, pp. 347, Ḥadīš 1745)*

Even sleeping is worship

Sayyidunā 'Abdullāĥ Bin Abī Aufā رَضِیَ اللّٰہ تَعَالٰی عَنْہُ has narrated that the Beloved and Blessed Prophet صَلَّى اللّٰهُ تَعَالٰی عَلَيْهِ وَاٰلِهٖ وَسَلَّم has said: 'The sleeping of a fasting person is worship, his silence is Tasbīḥ, his prayers are answered and his deeds are accepted.' *(Shu'ab-ul-Īmān, vol. 3, pp. 415, Ḥadīš 3938)*

سُبۡحٰنَ اللّٰه عَزَّوَجَلَّ! Did you see how fortunate a fasting person is? His sleeping is worship, his silence is Tasbīḥ and his supplications and deeds are accepted by Allah عَزَّوَجَلَّ.

Tayray karam say ay Karīm!
Kaun sī shay milī naĥīn
Jĥawlī ĥamārī tang ĥay,
Tayray yaĥān kamī naĥīn

By Your grace, O Gracious, what haven't we got!
Our begging bowl is small; nothing is short in Your court

Tasbīḥ of body parts

Mother of believers Sayyidatunā 'Āishaĥ Ṣiddīqaĥ رَضِیَ اللّٰهُ تَعَالٰی عَنۡهَا has narrated that the Prophet of Raḥmaĥ, the Intercessor of Ummaĥ صَلَّی اللّٰهُ تَعَالٰی عَلَیۡهِ وَاٰلِهٖ وَسَلَّم has said: 'If anyone is in the state of fast on the morning, the gates of the sky are opened for him, his body parts make Tasbīḥ and the angels in the first sky pray for his forgiveness until sunset. If he offers one or two Rak'āt Ṣalāĥ they become Nūr for him in the skies. The Heavenly maidens who will be his wives say, 'Yā Allah عَزَّوَجَلَّ send him to us, we are anxious to see him.' If he recites لَآ اِلٰهَ اِلَّا اللّٰه or سُبۡحٰنَ اللّٰه or اَللّٰهُ اَكۡبَر, seventy thousand angels will write reward for him until sunset.' *(Shu'ab-ul-Īmān, vol. 3, pp. 299, Ḥadīš 3591)*

سُبۡحٰنَ اللّٰه عَزَّوَجَلَّ! Look! How fortunate a fasting person is! The gates of the sky are opened for him and the angels of the first sky pray for his forgiveness until sunset. If he offers Ṣalāĥ it will be light for him in the sky and the maidens of Heaven will be waiting for him anxiously. Further, if he says لَآ اِلٰهَ اِلَّا اللّٰه or سُبۡحٰنَ اللّٰه or اَللّٰهُ اَكۡبَر, seventy thousand angels will write reward for him until sunset.

Heavenly fruits

Sayyidunā 'Alī كَرَّمَ اللّٰهُ تَعَالٰی وَجۡهَهُ الۡكَرِيۡم has narrated that the Noble Prophet صَلَّی اللّٰهُ تَعَالٰی عَلَیۡهِ وَاٰلِهٖ وَسَلَّم has said: 'The one whom his fast prevents from eating or drinking what he desires, Allah عَزَّوَجَلَّ will make him eat heavenly fruits and have heavenly drinks.' *(Shu'ab-ul-Īmān, vol. 3, pp. 410, Ḥadīš 3917)*

Dining mat of gold

Sayyidunā ‘Abdullāĥ Ibn ‘Abbās رَضِیَ اللّٰہُ تَعَالٰی عَنۡہُمَا has narrated that the Beloved and Blessed Prophet صَلَّی اللّٰہُ تَعَالٰی عَلَیۡہِ وَاٰلِہٖ وَسَلَّم has said: ‘On the Day of Judgement, a dining-mat made of gold will be laid for fasting people whilst other people will be waiting for their accountability.’ *(Kanz-ul-‘Ummāl, vol. 8, pp. 214, Ḥadīš 23640)*

Seven types of deeds

Sayyidunā ‘Abdullāĥ Ibn ‘Umar رَضِیَ اللّٰہُ تَعَالٰی عَنۡہُمَا has narrated that Rasūlullāĥ صَلَّی اللّٰہُ تَعَالٰی عَلَیۡہِ وَاٰلِہٖ وَسَلَّم has said: There are seven types of deeds in the court of Allah عَزَّوَجَلَّ. Two are those that necessitate (two other things) while two are such that their reward is the same; one is such that its reward is ten times; one is such that its reward is seven hundred times and the last is such that no one except Allah عَزَّوَجَلَّ knows its exact reward. The two that necessitate two other things include:

1. If any one meets Allah عَزَّوَجَلَّ having worshipped Him sincerely without associating a partner with Him, Heaven will become Wājib for him.

2. If anyone meets Allah عَزَّوَجَلَّ having associated a partner with Him Hell will become Wājib for him. If anyone commits a sin he will suffer the consequences of only one sin. If anyone intends to perform a good deed he will be given the reward of one deed. If any one carries out a good deed, he will be rewarded ten times. If any one spends (money) in the path of Allah عَزَّوَجَلَّ every dirham he spends will be equivalent to seven hundred dirhams and every dinar will be equivalent to seven hundred dinars; and fasting is for Allah عَزَّوَجَلَّ, no one except Him knows its reward. *(Kanz-ul-‘Ummāl, vol. 8, pp. 211, Ḥadīš 23616)*

Dear Islamic brothers! Anyone who dies with faith will enter Heaven by the grace of Allah عَزَّوَجَلَّ either without being held accountable or (Allah عَزَّوَجَلَّ forbid) after suffering the punishment for his sins. Anyone who dies in the state of unbelief will remain in Hell for eternity. If any one commits a sin he will be punished for only one sin.

Just look at the mercy of Allah عَزَّوَجَلَّ! One will be given the reward for doing a good deed for simply making the intention, and if he carries it out he will be rewarded ten times.

Spending in the path of Allah عَزَّوَجَلَّ will earn him seven hundred times more reward. As for the fasting person, words cannot express his reward as only Allah عَزَّوَجَلَّ knows his reward.

Immeasurable reward

Sayyidunā Ka'b-ul-Aḥbār رَضِىَ اللهُ تَعَالٰى عَنْهُ has said: 'On the Day of Judgement an announcement will be made, 'Every man will reap what he sowed (he will be rewarded equal to his deeds) except the people of the Quran (scholars of the Quran) and those who fasted; they will be given immeasurable reward.' *(Shu'ab-ul-Īmān, vol. 3, pp. 413, Ḥadīš 3928)*

Dear Islamic brothers! In the Hereafter, we will reap whatever we are sowing in the world. Scholars and fasting people are very fortunate as they will be granted immeasurable reward on the Day of Judgement.

Recovery from jaundice

In order to obtain the blessings of fasting and acquire knowledge of Sharī'aĥ, please join the Madanī environment of Dawat-e-Islami, a global & non-political religious movement of the Quran and Sunnaĥ.

So as to improve your character, please buy a Madanī In'āmāt booklet from Maktaba-tul-Madīnaĥ, fill it in daily and hand it in to the relevant responsible Islamic brother of Dawat-e-Islami in your area. Travel with Madanī Qāfilaĥs as well in the company of devotees of Rasūl to learn Sunnaĥ of the Holy Prophet صَلَّى اللهُ تَعَالٰى عَلَيْهِ وَاٰلِهٖ وَسَلَّم.

There are great blessings of travelling with Madanī Qāfilaĥs. An Islamic brother of Hyderabad (Bāb-ul-Islam, Sindh) gave the following statement: (Probably) In 1994, my wife suffered from jaundice. She was in serious condition and was under medical treatment in her parental house in Bāb-ul-Madīnaĥ, Karachi.

As I was already aware of the blessings of Madanī Qāfilaĥs, I travelled with a Madanī Qāfilaĥ for sixty three days. During the Madanī Qāfilaĥ, I visited Bāb-ul-Madīnaĥ, Karachi. Upon phoning, I was informed that she was still in serious condition and her bilirubin had increased to an alarming level. There was no improvement in her condition in spite of 25 glucose drips being administered to her. I tried to comfort her saying that she would recover due to the blessings of the Madanī Qāfilaĥ, اِنْ شَآءَاللّٰه عَزَّوَجَلَّ. I remained in contact with her (during the Madanī Qāfilaĥ).

اَلْحَمْدُ لِلّٰه عَزَّوَجَلَّ! Her condition began to improve day by day. I was to travel out of Bāb-ul-Madīnaĥ after five days. When I phoned to ask about her health I was given the good news that the bilirubin report had been normal and the doctor also expressed satisfaction, اَلْحَمْدُ لِلّٰه عَزَّوَجَلَّ. I glorified Allah عَزَّوَجَلَّ and happily travelled further with the Madanī Qāfilaĥ in the company of devotees of Rasūl.

Far from Hell

Sayyidunā Abū Sa'īd Khudrī رَضِیَ اللّٰهُ تَعَالٰی عَنْهُ has narrated that the Noble Rasūl صَلَّى اللّٰهُ تَعَالٰى عَلَيْهِ وَاٰلِهٖ وَسَلَّم has said: 'If any one fasts for a day in Allah's way, Allah عَزَّوَجَلَّ will move his face as far away from Hell as is the distance of seventy years.' *(Ṣaḥīḥ Bukhārī, vol. 2, pp. 265, Ḥadīš 2840)*

Dear Islamic brothers! As there are countless blessings and benefits of fasting, there are also severe warnings for missing a single fast of Ramadan without a valid exemption of Sharī'aĥ. If anyone misses a single fast in Ramadan deliberately without a valid exemption he will not be able to make up for it even if he fasts for the rest of his life.

Loss of missing one fast

Sayyidunā Abū Ĥurayraĥ رَضِیَ اللّٰهُ تَعَالٰی عَنْهُ has narrated that the Holy Prophet صَلَّى اللّٰهُ تَعَالٰى عَلَيْهِ وَاٰلِهٖ وَسَلَّم has said: 'Anyone who misses one fast in Ramadan without a valid reason or without illness cannot make up for it even if he fasts for the rest of his life.' *(Ṣaḥīḥ Bukhārī, vol. 1, pp. 638, Ḥadīš 1934)*

This means that he can never earn the blessings that lie in the fasts of Ramadan. So therefore we must not deprive ourselves of this huge blessing due to heedlessness. People who fast and then break it without a valid exemption must fear the wrath of Allah عَزَّوَجَلَّ.

People hanging upside down

Sayyidunā Abū Umāmaĥ Bāĥilī رَضِیَ اللّٰهُ تَعَالٰی عَنْهُ has narrated that he heard the Beloved and Blessed Prophet صَلَّى اللّٰهُ تَعَالٰى عَلَيْهِ وَاٰلِهٖ وَسَلَّم say: 'Whilst I was asleep two persons came to me and took me to a mountain. When I got to the middle of the mountain, I heard terrifying sounds. Upon asking about the sounds, I was told, 'These are the voices of the people in Hell.' I proceeded further and saw people who were tied upside down with the veins of their own ankles; their jaws had been torn apart and were bleeding. I asked as to who they were and I was told, 'They used to break their fast before its due time.' *(Al-Iḥsān bittartīb Ṣaḥīḥ Ibn Ḥibbān, vol. 9, pp. 286, Ḥadīš 7448)*

Dear Islamic brothers! Breaking a fast in Ramadan without a valid exemption is a major sin. This Ḥadīš refers to the punishment of the people who fast but then break their fast deliberately before sunset without a valid exemption. Likewise, there is severe punishment of Hell for those who do not fast at all in Ramadan without valid exemption.

May Allah عَزَّوَجَلَّ protect us from His wrath for the sake of His Beloved Rasūl صَلَّى اللّٰهُ تَعَالٰى عَلَيْهِ وَاٰلِهٖ وَسَلَّم!

اٰمِيْن بِجَاهِ النَّبِيِّ الْاَمِيْن صَلَّى اللّٰهُ تَعَالٰى عَلَيْهِ وَاٰلِهٖ وَسَلَّم

صَلُّوْا عَلَى الْحَبِيْب صَلَّى اللّٰهُ تَعَالٰى عَلٰى مُحَمَّد

Three unfortunate people

Sayyidunā Jābir Bin 'Abdullāĥ رَضِىَ اللّٰهُ تَعَالٰى عَنْهُمَا has narrated that the Prophet of mankind, the Peace of our heart and mind, the most Generous and Kind صَلَّى اللّٰهُ تَعَالٰى عَلَيْهِ وَاٰلِهٖ وَسَلَّم has said: 'The one who finds Ramadan but does not fast is unfortunate; the one who has both of his parents or any one of them but does not treat them well is unfortunate; the one who hears me being mentioned but does not recite Ṣalāt is unfortunate.' *(Majma'-uz-Zawāid, vol. 3, pp. 340, Ḥadīš 4773)*

Disgrace

Sayyidunā Abū Ĥurayraĥ رَضِىَ اللّٰهُ تَعَالٰى عَنْهُ has narrated that Rasūlullāĥ صَلَّى اللّٰهُ تَعَالٰى عَلَيْهِ وَاٰلِهٖ وَسَلَّم has said: 'May the person who hears me being mentioned but does not recite Ṣalāt upon me be disgraced! May the person who finds Ramadan but is not forgiven before it departs be disgraced! May the person who has old parents but does not enter Heaven by (respecting and serving) them be disgraced!' *(Musnad Imām Aḥmad, vol. 3, pp. 61, Ḥadīš 7455)*

Three levels of fasting

Dear Islamic brothers! Though the apparent precondition of fast is to abstain from deliberately eating, drinking and intercourse, there are also some manners of fasting which we must get to know so that we can succeed in acquiring all the blessings of fasting. There are three degrees of fasting:

1. The fast of common people.
2. The fast of the pious.
3. The fast of the ascetic.

1. Fast of common people

The literal meaning of fast is 'to abstain' while by Sharī'aĥ, it implies to abstain from deliberately eating, drinking and intercourse from dawn (Ṣubḥ-e-Ṣādiq) to sunset. This is called the fast of the common people.

2. Fast of the pious

In addition to abstaining from eating, drinking and intercourse avoiding all types of evils is the fast of the pious people.

3. Fast of the ascetic

To refrain from all the worldly activities and devote oneself completely to the worship of Allah عَزَّوَجَلَّ is the fast of the ascetic.

Dear Islamic brothers! In addition to abstaining from eating and drinking, we must also prevent all of our body parts from sins.

Saying of Dātā Sahib رَحْمَةُ اللهِ عَلَيْه

Sayyidunā Dātā Ganj Bakhsh 'Alī Ĥajwayrī رَحْمَةُ اللهِ تَعَالٰى عَلَيْه has said: In actual fact, fast implies 'abstinence' which has many conditions such as preventing the stomach from eating and drinking; preventing eyes from seeing someone lustfully; preventing ears from listening to backbiting; preventing the tongue from useless and inflammatory talking; preventing the body from disobeying Allah عَزَّوَجَلَّ in any way and so on. One can be called a true fasting person only when he fulfils all the aforementioned conditions. *(Kashf-ul-Maḥjūb, pp. 353-354)*

Unfortunately! Most of our Islamic brothers and sisters do not follow the manners of fasting at all, they feel proud of remaining thirsty and hungry. Despite fasting, they commit a lot of such acts forbidden by Sharī'aĥ. Even though such a fast will be considered valid but one will not be able to derive spiritual peace and pleasure from such a fast.

صَلُّوْا عَلَى الْحَبِيْب　　صَلَّى اللهُ تَعَالٰى عَلٰى مُحَمَّد

Sin even in fast!

Dear Islamic brothers! Please have pity on yourselves and ponder carefully! In Ramadan, the fasting person avoids eating and drinking during the day, which was absolutely permissible even during the day in other months. Now ponder! Even the acts, such as eating and drinking, which were Ḥalāl (lawful) before Ramadan are forbidden in this sacred month, so the acts which were already Ḥarām such as backbiting, lying, telling tales, suspicion, abusing, watching films, dramas and Nā-Maḥram women etc., shaving the beard or trimming it less than a fist-length, misbehaving parents, hurting others without the permission of Sharī'aĥ will automatically become even more severely Ḥarām.

When a fasting person refrains from eating and drinking pure and clean foods in Ramadan why he does not refrain from unlawful (Ḥarām) acts. So if a person avoids eating and drinking in Ramadan but does not avoid unlawful acts leading to Hell, what type of fasting person he is?

Allah عَزَّوَجَلَّ does not need anything

Remember! The Holy Prophet صَلَّى اللهُ تَعَالٰى عَلَيْهِ وَاٰلِهٖ وَسَلَّم has warned, 'If anyone does not refrain from indecent talking and evil acts (remember) Allah عَزَّوَجَلَّ does not need his remaining hungry and thirsty.' *(Ṣaḥīḥ Bukhārī, vol. 1, pp. 628, Ḥadīš 1903)*

He صَلَّى اللهُ تَعَالٰى عَلَيْهِ وَاٰلِهٖ وَسَلَّم has also said, 'Fasting implies abstaining not only from eating and drinking but also from useless and indecent talking.' *(Al-Mustadrak, vol. 2, pp. 67, Ḥadīš 1611)*

I am fasting

Therefore, as a fasting person refrains from eating and drinking he should also abstain from sins such as lying, backbiting, suspicion, laying a false blame, misusing his tongue etc. The Prophet of Raḥmaĥ, the Intercessor of Ummaĥ صَلَّى اللهُ تَعَالٰى عَلَيْهِ وَاٰلِهٖ وَسَلَّم has also said: If someone fights you or abuses you, you should say to him 'I am fasting.' *(Attarghīb Wattarĥīb, vol. 1, pp. 87, Ḥadīš 1)*

I will eat you

Dear Islamic brothers! These days if a person begins to fight another, he replies, 'Shut up or else I will break my fast by eating you' (Allah عَزَّوَجَلَّ forbid). We must never utter such words and should always remain humble. We can avoid such matters only when we make all of our body parts have fast (by preventing them from committing sins).

Meaning of fasting of body parts

The fast of body parts (e.g. preventing all the body parts from committing sins) is necessary not only in the state of fast, but also throughout the life. This is possible only when we have fear of Allah عَزَّوَجَلَّ in our hearts.

Ponder over the terrifying situation of the Judgement Day! Everyone will be worried about himself; the sun will be showering fire (scorching heat), tongues will be hanging out of mouths due to extreme thirst. Wife, mother and father will be avoiding husband, son and children. Sinners will be caught, their mouths will be sealed and their body parts will testify to their sins. It is mentioned in Sūraĥ Yāsīn:

اَلْيَوْمَ نَخْتِمُ عَلٰٓى اَفْوَاهِهِمْ وَتُكَلِّمُنَآ اَيْدِيْهِمْ وَتَشْهَدُ اَرْجُلُهُمْ بِمَا كَانُوْا يَكْسِبُوْنَ ﴿۶۵﴾

Today, We shall set seal on their mouths and their hands will talk to us and their feet will bear witness of their doings.

[Kanz-ul-Īmān (Translation of Quran)] (Part 23, Sūraĥ Yāsīn, verse 65)

O weak and feeble Islamic brothers! Fear from the troubles and tribulations of the Day of Judgement and make ardent efforts to prevent your body parts from indulging in sins. Here are details of the fasting of the body:

Fasting of eyes

Dear Islamic brothers! We should make our eyes fast by looking at only permissible things such as Masājid, the Holy Quran, the tombs of Auliyā رَحِمَهُمُ اللّٰهُ تَعَالٰی, scholars and pious people. If possible, we should see the Holy Ka'bah, the sacred streets, valleys and mountains of Makka-tul-Mukarramaĥ زَادَهَا اللّٰهُ شَرَفًا وَّ تَعْظِيْمًا, the walls and houses of Madīna-tul-Munawwaraĥ زَادَهَا اللّٰهُ شَرَفًا وَّ تَعْظِيْمًا, the green dome, minarets, deserts, gardens and the blessed Masjid of Madīnaĥ.

Dear Islamic brothers! Please do make your eyes fast. Everyone should make his eyes fast constantly. Never misuse this gift of Allah عَزَّوَجَلَّ in watching what has been prohibited by Sharī'aĥ such as films, dramas, Nā-Maḥram women, attractive boys with lust or any one's private parts and even one's own private parts unnecessarily. Similarly, do not watch games or amusements that make you heedless of divine remembrance like the dance of monkeys and bears on streets (making monkey and bears dance and watching their dance are both impermissible).

Further, avoid watching cricket, wrestling, football, hockey, cards, chess, video games, table football, etc. (both watching and playing them is impermissible. The games that involve exposing one's knees or thighs because of wearing shorts are even worse. Remember, exposing the body from navel to and including knees is not permissible and, any other person's looking at these parts of body is also impermissible). Do not peep into another person's house without his permission, nor look at someone else's letter or notebook without his permission. Remember! A Ḥadīš states, 'Anyone who looks at his brother's letter without his permission looks in fire.' *(Al-Mustadrak, vol. 5, pp. 384, Ḥadīš 7779)*

Uťhay na ānkĥ kabĥī bĥī gunāĥ kī jānib
'Aṭā karam say ĥo aysī ĥamayn ḥayā Yā Rab
Kisī kī khāmiyān daykĥayn na mayrī ānkĥayn aur

Sunayn na kān bĥī 'aybawn kā tażkiraĥ Yā Rab
Dikĥā day aīk jĥalak sabz sabz gumbad kī
Bas un kay jalwaun mayn ā jāye pĥir qażā Yā Rab

May I never look at anything sinful
Bless me with such modesty, Yā Rab
May I do not look at anyone's faults
Nor do my ears hear anyone's faults, Yā Rab
Bless me with a glimpse of green dome
And with death in holy visions, Yā Rab

Fasting of ears

Fast of ears implies listening to only permissible voices and sounds such as recitation of the Holy Quran, Sunnaĥ-Inspiring speeches, useful talking, the Ażān and the Iqāmaĥ, reply to the Ażān and the Iqāmaĥ etc. Never listen to drum-beating, music, songs, useless and indecent jokes, backbiting, telling tales and faults of other people etc. Do not eavesdrop anyone's private conversation.

The Prophet of Raḥmaĥ, the Intercessor of Ummaĥ صَلَّى اللهُ تَعَالٰى عَلَيْهِ وَاٰلِهٖ وَسَلَّم has said: If anyone listens secretly to the conversation of other people who resent it, on the Day of Judgement, molten lead will be poured into his ears. *(Mu'jam Kabīr, vol. 11, pp. 198)*

Sunayn na fuḥsh kalāmī na ghībat-o-chughlī
Tayrī pasand kī bātayn faqaṭ sunā Yā Rab
Andĥayrī qabr kā dil say naĥīn nikaltā ḍar
Karūn gā kyā jo Tu nārāż ĥo gayā Yā Rab
Rasūl-e-Pāk صَلَّى اللهُ تَعَالٰى عَلَيْهِ وَاٰلِهٖ وَسَلَّم *agar muskurātay ā jāyaīn*
To gawr-e-tīraĥ mayn ĥo jāye chāndnā Yā Rab

May I never hear indecent talk, backbiting and tale-telling
May I only hear what You like, Yā Rab
The fear of the dark grave has engulfed me
What will I do if You become displeased, Yā Rab
If the smiling Prophet صَلَّى اللهُ تَعَالٰى عَلَيْهِ وَاٰلِهٖ وَسَلَّم *comes to the grave*
It will become bright, Yā Rab

Fast of tongue

Fast of the tongue implies uttering only permissible and good words such as recitation of the Holy Quran, Żikr, Ṣalāt-'Alan-Nabī, Na'at, Dars, Sunnaĥ-Inspiring speeches, call to righteousness, useful and helpful religious speech etc. Avoid useless talking. Beware! Never misuse your tongue in committing sins such as abusing, lying, telling tales etc. If a spoon becomes impure, it can be washed by pouring one or two glasses of water on it but if the tongue becomes impure due to indecent speech then the water of seven oceans will not be able to purify it.

Ill effects of tongue's misuse

Sayyidunā Anas رَضِیَ اللہُ تَعَالٰی عَنْہُ has narrated a Ḥadīš that one day the Beloved and Blessed Prophet صَلَّی اللہُ تَعَالٰی عَلَیْہِ وَاٰلِہٖ وَسَلَّم ordered his companions رَضِیَ اللہُ تَعَالٰی عَنْہُم to fast and then said: 'None of you is to do Ifṭār until I permit you.' So the people fasted. In the evening, the companions came individually to the Noble Prophet صَلَّی اللہُ تَعَالٰی عَلَیْہِ وَاٰلِہٖ وَسَلَّم and said, 'Yā Rasūlallāĥ صَلَّی اللہُ تَعَالٰی عَلَیْہِ وَاٰلِہٖ وَسَلَّم! I have fasted today, please give me permission to do Ifṭār', the Noble Prophet صَلَّی اللہُ تَعَالٰی عَلَیْہِ وَاٰلِہٖ وَسَلَّم would allow them to do Ifṭār. One of the companions رَضِیَ اللہُ تَعَالٰی عَنْہُ came and said: 'Yā Rasūlallāĥ صَلَّی اللہُ تَعَالٰی عَلَیْہِ وَاٰلِہٖ وَسَلَّم! In my house, there are two girls who have also fasted today, they feel shyness in coming here, please allow them to do Ifṭār.' The Holy Prophet صَلَّی اللہُ تَعَالٰی عَلَیْہِ وَاٰلِہٖ وَسَلَّم turned his face away from him; he asked for the second time, but the Blessed Rasūl صَلَّی اللہُ تَعَالٰی عَلَیْہِ وَاٰلِہٖ وَسَلَّم turned his head away from him again. When he asked for the third time the Holy Prophet صَلَّی اللہُ تَعَالٰی عَلَیْہِ وَاٰلِہٖ وَسَلَّم said, revealing the news of Ghayb, 'Those two girls have not fasted, how (can they say) they have fasted? They have been eating the flesh of people all day long, go and tell them to vomit, if they have fasted.'

The companion رَضِیَ اللہُ تَعَالٰی عَنْہُ went home and told them what the Noble Rasūl صَلَّی اللہُ تَعَالٰی عَلَیْہِ وَاٰلِہٖ وَسَلَّم said. When they vomited, blood and pieces of flesh came out of their mouths. The companion رَضِیَ اللہُ تَعَالٰی عَنْہُ returned to the Holy Prophet صَلَّی اللہُ تَعَالٰی عَلَیْہِ وَاٰلِہٖ وَسَلَّم and told him about the girls' condition. He صَلَّی اللہُ تَعَالٰی عَلَیْہِ وَاٰلِہٖ وَسَلَّم said, 'I swear by the One in whose omnipotence my life is! If it had remained in their stomachs, fire would eat them. (Because they both backbit others).' *(Attarghīb Wattarĥīb, vol. 3, pp. 328, Ḥadīš 15)*

According to another Ḥadīš: When our Beloved and Blessed Prophet صَلَّی اللہُ تَعَالٰی عَلَیْہِ وَاٰلِہٖ وَسَلَّم turned his face away from the companion رَضِیَ اللہُ تَعَالٰی عَنْہُ he رَضِیَ اللہُ تَعَالٰی عَنْہُ came in front of the

Noble Prophet صَلَّى اللّٰهُ تَعَالٰى عَلَيْهِ وَاٰلِهٖ وَسَلَّم and said, 'Yā Rasūlallāĥ صَلَّى اللّٰهُ تَعَالٰى عَلَيْهِ وَاٰلِهٖ وَسَلَّم they both have died' or 'they are about to die.' The Prophet of Raḥmaĥ, the Intercessor of Ummaĥ, the Owner of Jannaĥ صَلَّى اللّٰهُ تَعَالٰى عَلَيْهِ وَاٰلِهٖ وَسَلَّم commanded him to bring the girls to him. When they came he had a pot brought and ordered one of them to vomit in it. She vomited until the pot was full of blood and pieces of flesh. He صَلَّى اللّٰهُ تَعَالٰى عَلَيْهِ وَاٰلِهٖ وَسَلَّم then ordered the other one to vomit; she also vomited as much. The Noble Prophet صَلَّى اللّٰهُ تَعَالٰى عَلَيْهِ وَاٰلِهٖ وَسَلَّم said, 'They fasted from the things that Allah عَزَّوَجَلَّ declared Ḥalāl (i.e. eating, drinking etc.) but broke their fast with the things that Allah عَزَّوَجَلَّ declared Ḥarām. The thing is, they sat together and began to eat the flesh of people (by backbiting[1]).' *(Attarghīb Wattarĥīb, vol. 2, pp. 95, Ḥadīš 8)*

Knowledge of Ghayb of the Holy Prophet صَلَّى اللّٰهُ عَلَيْهِ وَسَلَّم

Dear Islamic brothers! This narration clearly proves that Allah عَزَّوَجَلَّ has given the knowledge of Ghayb to His Beloved Prophet صَلَّى اللّٰهُ تَعَالٰى عَلَيْهِ وَاٰلِهٖ وَسَلَّم who is aware of his Ummaĥ's circumstances, which is why he صَلَّى اللّٰهُ تَعَالٰى عَلَيْهِ وَاٰلِهٖ وَسَلَّم gave the news of Ghayb about those two girls sitting in the Masjid. Further, we have also learnt that committing sins such as backbiting can directly affect fast and can make fasting unbearably painful. Anyhow, whether one is in the state of fast or not, he must control his speech or else it could lead to tragic consequences. If we adopt the following three principles, we would avoid many troubles:

1. Evil-talking is always bad.
2. Silence is better than useless talking.
3. Righteous talking is better than silence.

Mayrī zabān pay Qufl-e-Madīnaĥ lag jāye
Fuzūl gawyī say bachtā raĥūn sadā Yā Rab
Karayn na tang khayālāt-e-bad kabĥī karday
Shu'ūr-o-fikr ko pākīzgī 'aṭā Yā Rab
Bawaqt-e-naz'a salāmat raĥay mayrā Īmān
Mujĥay naṣīb ĥo Kalimaĥ ĥay iltijā Yā Rab

[1] Please read Amīr-e-Aĥl-e-Sunnat's book '*Backbiting – A Cancer in our Society*' published by Maktaba-tul-Madīnaĥ اِنْ شَآءَاللّٰه عَزَّوَجَلَّ it will help you avoid the major sin of backbiting.

May Madanī guard be applied to my tongue
May I always avoid useless talking, Yā Rab
May I never have evil thoughts
Bless my heart and mind with purity, Yā Rab
May my Īmān remain protected while I am dying
'May I recite Kalimaĥ' is my plea, Yā Rab

Fast of hands

Fast of hands is that they only be used for virtuous acts such as touching the Holy Quran in a state of purity and shaking hands with pious people. The Noble Rasūl صَلَّى اللهُ تَعَالٰى عَلَيْهِ وَاٰلِهٖ وَسَلَّم has said, 'When two persons who love each other for Allah عَزَّوَجَلَّ shake hands and recite Ṣalāt on Rasūl their previous sins are forgiven before they leave.' *(Musnad Abī Ya'lā, vol. 3, pp. 95, Ḥadīš 2951)*

If possible, stroke the head of an orphan affectionately as one will be rewarded for every single hair he strokes (boys and girls are considered orphans as long as they are minors. As soon as they reach puberty, they will no longer remain minors. A boy may reach puberty between the age of 12 and 15 while a girl between the age of 9 and 15).

Beware! Never misuse your hand in oppressing someone, taking bribery, stealing, playing cards, flying kites and shaking hands with women (one should avoid shaking hands even with a young attractive beardless boy in case of lust, but do not hurt him, evade him with proper strategy).

Ĥamayshaĥ ĥāth bĥalāyī kay wāsiṭay uṫĥayn
Bachānā ẓulm-o-sitam say mujĥay sadā Yā Rab!
Kaĥīn kā mujĥ ko gunāĥaun nay ab naĥīn cĥauřā
'Ażāb-e-nār say baĥr-e-Nabī bachā Yā Rab!
Ilāĥī aīk bĥī naykī naĥīn ĥay nāmay mayn
Faqaṭ ĥay Tayrī ĥī raḥmat kā āsrā Yā Rab

May my hands always stretch out towards good
Save me from cruelty and oppression, Yā Rab
My sins have ruined me, bringing trouble for me
Save me from Hellfire for Prophet's sake, Yā Rab
Not a single virtue is in my book of deeds, Almighty!
I have pinned all my hopes on Your mercy, Yā Rab

Fast of feet

Fast of feet implies using feet for permissible and good acts such as walking to Masjid or the shrines of saints رَحِمَهُمُ اللّٰهُ تَعَالٰی, visiting scholars and pious people, attending Sunnaĥ-Inspiring Ijtimā', calling people to righteousness, travelling with Madanī Qāfilaĥs in the company of righteous people and helping the needy. If only we would ever walk towards Makka-tul-Mukarramaĥ زَادَهَا اللّٰهُ شَرَفًا وَّ تَعْظِيْمًا and Madīna-tul-Munawwaraĥ زَادَهَا اللّٰهُ شَرَفًا وَّ تَعْظِيْمًا, Minā, 'Arafāt, Muzdalifaĥ and perform Ṭawāf and Sa'ī. Never misuse feet in walking towards cinemas, bad company, playing or watching chess, ludo, cards, cricket, football, videogames, table football etc. If only we would walk towards Madīnaĥ uttering the word 'Madīnaĥ.'

Raĥayn bĥalāyī kī rāĥawn mayn gāmzan ĥar dam
Karayn na rukh mayray pāūn gunāĥ kā Yā Rab!
Madīnay jāyaīn pĥir āyaīn dobāraĥ pĥir jāyaīn
Isī mayn 'umr guzar jāye Yā Khudā Yā Rab!
Baqī'-e-Pāk mayn madfan naṣīb ĥo jāye
Barāye Ghauš-o-Razā Murshidī Ziyā Yā Rab!

May I always tread the path of good
May my feet never turn towards sins, Yā Rab
May I go to Madīnaĥ again and again
And meet my death in Madīnaĥ, Yā Rab
May I be laid to rest in Baqī' Pāk
For the sake of Ghauš, Razā and Ziyā, Yā Rab

Dear Islamic brothers! In fact, we can attain the real blessings of fast when we make all of our body-parts fast, otherwise we will not gain anything apart from thirst and hunger as Sayyidunā Abū Ĥurayraĥ رَضِیَ اللّٰهُ تَعَالٰی عَنْهُ has narrated that our Beloved Rasūl صَلَّى اللّٰهُ تَعَالٰى عَلَيْهِ وَاٰلِهٖ وَسَلَّم has said, 'There are many people who attain nothing but thirst and hunger from their fasts and there are many people who acquire nothing from their Ṣalāĥ except staying awake.' *(Sunan Ibn Mājaĥ, vol. 2, pp. 320, Ḥadīš 1690)*

Therefore, those who do not prevent their body parts from committing sins despite fasting, fail to acquire the real spirituality of fast and those who stay awake till late night gossiping, chatting or playing different games, get nothing but the loss of their health and time in addition to causing difficulty for their Hereafter.

Job in Karachi Electric Supply Company

Dear Islamic brothers! If you want to acquire the real spiritual pleasure of fast and develop a Madanī mindset, please join the Madanī environment of Dawat-e-Islami, a global & non-political religious movement of the Quran and Sunnaĥ and travel with Madanī Qāfilaĥs in the company of the devotees of Rasūl in order to gain knowledge of Sunnaĥ.

سُبْحٰنَ اللّٰه عَزَّوَجَلَّ! There are great blessings of Sunnaĥ-Inspiring Ijtimā' and Madanī Qāfilaĥs. A responsible Islamic brother of Orangi Town Bāb-ul-Madīnaĥ, Karachi gave an account in which he mentioned how he joined the Madanī environment and how he found a job due to the blessing of Dawat-e-Islami. He has stated: 'I began to attend the weekly Ijtimā' of Dawat-e-Islami as a result of the invitation of an Islamic brother in 2003 but I was not regular. I was upset due to unemployment. An Islamic brother persuaded me to join the Madanī Qāfilaĥ course in Faīzān-e-Madīnaĥ, the global Madanī Markaz of Dawat-e-Islami, situated in Bāb-ul-Madīnaĥ, Karachi.

اَلْحَمْدُ لِلّٰه عَزَّوَجَلَّ! The company of the devotees of Rasūl greatly influenced me, enabling me to realize the aim of my life. After the completion of the Madanī Qāfilaĥ course, some of my friends informed me about the vacancies announced by K.E.S.C. (Karachi Electric Supply Company). They all had already applied and suggested that I also do so. Even though I was not so hopeful to get a government job due to corruption, nepotism and bribery in our departments, but I also applied for job owing to their insistence. I took a written test, gave an interview and then underwent a medical test.

Surprisingly, I was the only one who succeeded at every stage despite the fact that there were a lot of influential candidates. On the occasion of the final interview, my family insisted that I wear a shirt and trousers but I had given up wearing those types of clothes due to the blessings of the Madanī Qāfilaĥ course so I went in a white Shalwār and Kameez.

When the officer observed my religious appearance he asked me a few religious questions that I answered quite easily because I had learnt them in the Madanī Qāfilaĥ course. اَلْحَمْدُ لِلّٰه عَزَّوَجَلَّ! I got the job without bribery and any one's intercession. My family was astonished to see the blessings of the Madanī Qāfilaĥ course and the Madanī environment and they developed a liking for Dawat-e-Islami, اَلْحَمْدُ لِلّٰه عَزَّوَجَلَّ.

At present, اَلْحَمْدُلِلّٰہ عَزَّوَجَلَّ I am serving Sunnaĥ as a Nigrān in my area, inspiring people to travel with Madanī Qāfilaĥs and practice Madanī In'āmāt.'

Nawkrī chāĥiye, āyiye āyiye
Qāfilay mayn chalayn, Qāfilay mayn chalo
Tangdastī miṭay, dūr āfat ĥaṭay
Laynay ko barakatayn, Qāfilay mayn chalo

If you need a job brother, do not aimlessly wander
Come and don't bother, travel with Madanī Qāfilaĥ
To avert deprivation and remove tribulation
To gain benediction, travel with Madanī Qāfilaĥ

صَلُّوْا عَلَى الْحَبِيْب صَلَّى اللهُ تَعَالٰى عَلٰى مُحَمَّد

Intention of fast

Dear Islamic brothers! As intention is a precondition for offering Ṣalāĥ and paying Zakāĥ etc., it is necessary for fast as well. Even if an Islamic brother or sister remains hungry and thirsty from dawn to sunset without the intention of fast, his/her fast will not be valid. *(Rad-dul-Muḥtār, vol. 3, pp. 331)*

The time of making the intention for Ramadan fasts, Nafl fasts and fasts of specified vows (Nażr-e-Mu'ayyan) starts after the sun has set and remains until the time of Shar'ī midday (Ḍaḥwā Kubrā) begins.

A fast of specified vow is the one that is kept on a particular day for the pleasure of Allah عَزَّوَجَلَّ to fulfil a vow. For example, if someone says, 'I will fast on every Monday of this year's Rabī'-un-Nūr for the pleasure of Allah عَزَّوَجَلَّ' (it is necessary that the words of vow be uttered loud enough to be heard), it will then become Wājib to fast on that particular day. The intention of these three types of fast can be made within the timings described above, the fast will be valid. *(Rad-dul-Muḥtār, vol. 3, pp. 332)*

How to ascertain midday time (Ḍaḥwā Kubrā)

You might be thinking as to what the time of midday is! An easy way of obtaining the time of Midday (Ḍaḥwā Kubrā) is to find out the duration between dawn and sunset first and then divide it by two; the time of Midday will start as soon as the first half ends.

For example, if some day's time of dawn is 5 a.m. and that of sunset is exactly 6 p.m. then there will be the duration of 13 hours between the dawn and the sunset. Upon dividing the number 13 by two, there will be two halves of 6½ hours, and if we add 6½ hours to 5 a.m. it will become 11:30 a.m. which is the initial time of midday. The intention of these three types of fast cannot be made as soon as the time of midday starts. *(Rad-dul-Muḥtār, vol. 3, pp. 341, Mulakhkhaṣan)*

Except the above-mentioned three types of fasts, it is necessary to make the intention of all other types of fasts within the duration from sunset to dawn (Ṣubḥ-e-Ṣādiq). If somebody makes the intention after dawn (Ṣubḥ-e-Ṣādiq) his intention and fast will not be valid. The fasts whose intention must be made within the night include:

1. The fast for making up for the missed fast of Ramadan.

2. The fast for expiation (Kaffāraĥ).

3. The fast for making up for a Nafl fast. (A Nafl fast becomes Wājib if somebody begins it, and it is a sin to break it without a valid exemption of Sharī'aĥ. In case of breaking a Nafl fast whether due to a Shar'ī exemption or without a Shar'ī exemption, it is Wājib to make up for it).

4. The fast for fulfilling an unspecified vow, (Nażr-e-Ghayr Mu'ayyan) that implies vowing to fast for the pleasure of Allah عَزَّوَجَلَّ without specifying a particular day. Fulfilling such a vow and any other Shar'ī vow made for the pleasure of Allah عَزَّوَجَلَّ is Wājib provided the vow is made loud enough for oneself to hear. For instance, saying 'I will fast for the pleasure of Allah عَزَّوَجَلَّ.' This kind of vow does not mention a particular day, therefore whenever one fasts with the intention of fulfilling this vow, it will be fulfilled.

   It is a condition that the words of the vow be uttered loud enough to be heard by the one who is uttering them. However, if someone utters his vow loud enough for himself to hear but could not hear because of deafness or any noise then his vow is still valid. It is necessary to make the intention of these fasts within the night. *(Derived from Rad-dul-Muḥtār, vol. 3, pp. 344)*

Twenty Madanī pearls regarding intention of fast

1. The time of making the intention for Ramadan fasts, Nafl fasts and fasts of specified vows (Nażr-e-Mu'ayyan) starts after the sun has set and remains until the time of Shar'ī midday (Ḍaḥwā Kubrā) begins. Therefore, if one makes intention anytime during this span, these fasts will be valid. *(Rad-dul-Muḥtār, vol. 3, pp. 332)*

2. The intention of heart (willingness in heart) is, in fact, a valid intention. To utter it verbally is not a condition but is preferable. If one makes the intention for a Ramadan fast at night, he should say:

نَوَيْتُ اَنْ اَصُوْمَ غَدًا لِلّٰهِ تَعَالٰى مِنْ فَرْضِ رَمَضَان

Translation: I have intended to fast tomorrow as a Farḍ fast of Ramadan for Allah عَزَّوَجَلَّ.

3. If one makes the intention in the morning (before midday) he should say:

نَوَيْتُ اَنْ اَصُوْمَ هٰذَا الْيَوْمَ لِلّٰهِ تَعَالٰى مِنْ فَرْضِ رَمَضَان

Translation: I have intended to fast today as a Farḍ fast of Ramadan for Allah عَزَّوَجَلَّ.

(Rad-dul-Muḥtār, vol. 3, pp. 332)

4. To utter the words of intention in Arabic will be valid only when one understands its meaning. Further, making the intention verbally whether in Arabic or in any other language will be valid if the intention is present in the heart as well. *(ibid)*

5. One can also utter the words of intention in his mother tongue provided the intention is present in heart at the time of utterance whether he utters it in Arabic or in any other language. Otherwise, simply uttering the words in a state of inattention will not be valid. However, if someone utters the intention without having it present in heart but later on he makes the intention in heart as well within the stipulated time, it will be valid. *(Rad-dul-Muḥtār, vol. 3, pp. 332)*

6. If one makes intention during the day (but before Shar'ī midday) it is necessary to make the intention of fast from the time of dawn (Ṣubḥ-e-Ṣādiq). If he says 'I am fasting from now onwards (and not since dawn)' his fast will not be valid. *(Al-Jauĥara-tun-Nayyaraĥ, vol. 1, pp. 175)*

7. The intention made between dawn (Ṣubḥ-e-Ṣādiq) and Shar'ī midday will be valid provided one has not done any act that invalidates the fast, from dawn to the time of making the intention. However, if one eats or drinks or engages in intercourse forgetfully after dawn, the intention will still be valid as eating or drinking forgetfully even if one is full will not invalidate the fast. *(Derived from Rad-dul-Muḥtār, vol. 3, pp. 367)*

8. Making such an intention as 'If I'm invited to a meal tomorrow then I won't fast but if I'm not invited then I will fast' is not valid; fast will not be valid in case of making such an ambiguous intention. *(Fatāwā 'Ālamgīrī, vol. 1, pp. 195)*

9. During the day of Ramadan, if somebody neither intended to fast nor intended to miss it, despite knowing that it is the holy month of Ramadan, his fast will not be valid. *(Fatāwā 'Ālamgīrī, vol. 1, pp. 195)*

10. If someone made the intention any time at night after the sunset, then he ate something within the night, his intention will still remain valid. There is no need to make a new one. *(Al-Jauĥara-tun-Nayyaraĥ, vol. 1, pp. 175)*

11. During the night, if someone made the intention to fast but afterwards firmly decided not to fast within the same night, this will invalidate the first intention. If the intention [for fast] is not renewed, his fast will not be valid even if he spends the whole day without eating or drinking like a fasting person. *(Durr-e-Mukhtār ma' Rad-dul-Muḥtār, vol. 3, pp. 345)*

12. As the mere intention of talking during Ṣalāĥ does not invalidate the Ṣalāĥ unless one talks, likewise, only intending to break fast during fasting will not invalidate it. The fast will only become invalid when one physically does the act that invalidates it. *(Al-Jauĥara-tun-Nayyaraĥ, vol. 1, pp. 175)* In other words, even if a person intends to break his fast, it will not become invalid unless he eats, drinks or does any other such act that invalidates it.

13. Eating Saḥarī is equivalent to making the intention regardless of whether it is the fast of Ramadan or any other fast. However, if one intends not to fast that day whilst eating Saḥarī, this Saḥarī will not be considered his intention. *(Al-Jauĥara-tun-Nayyaraĥ, vol. 1, pp. 176)*

14. It is necessary to make a new intention every day for each fast of Ramadan. If one makes the intention for the whole of Ramadan just once on the first day of the month or any other day, it will be regarded as the intention for that (one) day only, not for the rest of the days. *(ibid, pp. 167)*

15. Except for the fast of Ramadan, that of specified vow (Nażr-e-Mu'ayyan) and Nafl fasts, the intention for all other fasts must be made during the night or at the precise time of dawn. Such fasts include Qaḍā fasts of Ramadan, fasts for unspecified vow (Nażr-e-Ghayr Mu'ayyan), Qaḍā of Nafl fasts (i.e. the Qaḍā of the Nafl fast that was broken), Qaḍā of fasts for specified vow, fasts for expiation and Hajj-e-Tamattu'[1]. It is also necessary to specify the type of fast when making the intention. If one makes the intention for any of these fasts on the morning (from dawn till before the midday beings) it will turn into a Nafl fast (and not the one intended), but this Nafl fast must still be completed. If he breaks it, making up for it (by fasting another day) will be Wājib even if he is aware that this is not the fast he had intended but a Nafl one. *(Durr-e-Mukhtār ma' Rad-dul-Muḥtār, vol. 3, pp. 344)*

16. Somebody fasts assuming that he has to make up for a missed fast but then he realises that his assumption was wrong. If he breaks his fast instantly in this case, though there is no harm, it is still preferable to complete it. If he does not break the fast immediately, he will have to complete it, breaking it now will not be permissible. If he breaks this fast, making up for it will be Wājib. *(Rad-dul-Muḥtār, vol. 3, pp. 346)*

---

[1] There are three types of Hajj: 1. Qirān 2. Tamattu' 3. Ifrād. It is Wājib for the one performing Qirān or Tamattu' Hajj to make the ritual sacrifice of the animal after performing Hajj as gratification. As for those who perform Ifrād Hajj it is Mustaḥab. If those performing either of the first two types of Hajj (Qirān or Tamattu') are extremely Miskīn and destitute and cannot afford to sacrifice an animal even by selling their possessions nor do they have money to fulfill this rite, fast for ten days will be Wājib for them as a substitute for the animal sacrifice. Three fasts in the months of Hajj anytime in between 1st Shawwāl-ul-Mukarram to 9th Żul-Ḥijjaĥ after wearing the Iḥrām, preferably on the 7th, 8th and 9th of Żul-Ḥijjaĥ. It is not necessary to observe these fasts consecutively, and the other 7 fasts can be observed any time after 13th Żul-Ḥijjaĥ, preferably after reaching home.

17. After the dawn, the intention for a Qaḍā fast made during the night cannot be changed into the intention of a Nafl fast. *(ibid, pp. 345)*

18. Making the intention of fast whilst offering Ṣalāĥ is also valid. *(Durr-e-Mukhtār ma' Rad-dul-Muḥtār, vol. 3, pp. 345)*

19. If one has missed several fasts, the intention to make up for them should include the words: '*The first fast of Ramadan I missed*' – '*The second fast of Ramadan I missed*' and so on. If he has missed some in the present year and some in the previous year then he should intend in these words: '*The Qaḍā of this Ramadan*' – '*The Qaḍā of that Ramadan.*' Even if he does not specify the day he missed, the fast will still be valid. *(Fatāwā 'Ālamgīrī, vol. 1, pp. 196)*

20. Allah عَزَّوَجَلَّ forbid if one breaks a fast of Ramadan deliberately, it will become Farḍ not only to keep a fast as its Qaḍā but also to fast for 60 days as expiation (provided the conditions of expiation are met). If he fasts for 61 days without specifying the day of Qaḍā fast, then both the Qaḍā and expiation fasts will be valid. *(Fatāwā 'Ālamgīrī, vol. 1, pp. 196)*

Girl with beard

If you want to have a passion for learning the intentions for fasting and other deeds, please travel with the devotees of Rasūl in the Madanī Qāfilaĥs of Dawat-e-Islami, a global & non-political religious movement of the Quran and Sunnaĥ and earn the blessings in the world as well as in the Hereafter. In order to persuade you, I present a blessing which took place in a Madanī Qāfilaĥ. An Islamic brother of Ranchor Line Bāb-ul-Madīnaĥ (Karachi) gave the following account: In our three day Madanī Qāfilaĥ, there was a 26 year old Islamic brother who made a lot of supplications with great humility. When asked about it, he replied that he had a daughter whose face hair was growing like a beard, which was the reason of his anxiety.

He further said that the cause of the problem could not be diagnosed despite X-Rays and test and no medicine proved effective as yet. The participants of the Qāfilaĥ supplicated for his daughter on his request. Two days after the Madanī Qāfilaĥ, when I met the same dejected Islamic brother, he happily informed me that the hair of his daughter's face had disappeared altogether as if there was no hair at all due to the blessing of the Madanī Qāfilaĥ, اَلْحَمْدُلِلّٰه عَزَّوَجَلَّ.

Sixteen Madanī pearls for babies

Dear Islamic brothers! Did you see the blessings of Madanī Qāfilaĥs! In order to protect children from diseases, precautions during the period of their babyhood can prove to be very beneficial. Therefore, here are 16 Madanī pearls of such precautions:

1. Reciting يَا بَرُّ seven times (with Ṣalāt-'Alan-Nabī once before and after it) and blowing on a new born baby (instantly after birth) will protect the baby from afflictions until puberty, اِنْ شَآءَاللّٰہ عَزَّوَجَلَّ.
2. Bathing a new born baby firstly with tepid water mixed with salt and then with ordinary water (not hot) will protect it from spots and boils, اِنْ شَآءَاللّٰہ عَزَّوَجَلَّ.
3. Bathing children for some days with salt-mixed water is very beneficial to their health.
4. Massaging babies with mustard oil after bathing them will be very effective for their health, اِنْ شَآءَاللّٰہ عَزَّوَجَلَّ.
5. Making babies swallow a little honey two or three times a day before feeding them milk is quite beneficial.
6. Keep the baby's head raised at all times even when rocking it in your arms and laying it to sleep; lowering the baby's head and raising its feet is harmful.
7. Extremely bright light will weaken the eyesight of a new born baby.
8. When the baby's gums become strong and it cuts teeth, rub the baby's gums with chicken fat.
9. Rub honey onto the babies gums once or twice a day. Rubbing oil onto its head and neck is beneficial.
10. When the period of suckling the baby is going to end and the child begins to eat, take extra care to make sure that you do not let him/her chew hard foods, instead give the child soft and easily digestible foods.
11. Feed the child cow's or goat's milk as well.

12. If possible, feed the child healthy foods because the energy he gains at this age will help him throughout his life, اِنْ شَآءَالله عَزَّوَجَلَّ
13. Children should not be fed again and again; do not give next food before the digestion of the food given earlier.
14. It is absolutely vital to stop children from eating sweets and Miṫhāī (Asian sweets) as these are very harmful to their health.
15. Dried and fresh fruits are very beneficial to children.
16. The earlier you get your baby boys circumcised the better it is because they will feel less pain and the wound will heal much quicker as well.

Spiritual remedy for protection of mother and baby

If a pregnant woman writes لَآ اِلٰهَ اِلَّا الله or gets it written 55 times on a piece of paper and ties it around her neck or arm in the form of an amulet (Ta'wīż) after wrapping it in plastic and then sewing into a piece of cloth or leather, اِنْ شَآءَالله عَزَّوَجَلَّ her pregnancy will remain safe and the baby will also be protected from afflictions (after the birth).

Moreover, if لَآ اِلٰهَ اِلَّا الله is recited 55 times (with Ṣalāt-'Alan-Nabī once before and after it) and blown onto some water and if that water is used to wet the mouth of the baby as soon as it is born the baby will be intelligent and safe from illnesses, اِنْ شَآءَالله عَزَّوَجَلَّ. Reciting and blowing the same words onto olive oil and then softly massaging the baby's body with it is very beneficial; اِنْ شَآءَالله عَزَّوَجَلَّ this will protect the baby from insects, spiders and harmful animals. Massaging the body of adults with this oil (after reciting the same words) is also beneficial to relieving pain.

Eating Saḥarī is Sunnah

Millions of thanks to Allah عَزَّوَجَلَّ who has granted us a magnificent blessing in the form of fast one of whose important parts is Saḥarī whereby we can attain not only energy but also a lot of reward by divine mercy. Even though unlike us, our Noble Prophet صَلَّى اللهُ تَعَالٰى عَلَيْهِ وَاٰلِهٖ وَسَلَّم did not need to eat and drink, but he صَلَّى اللهُ تَعَالٰى عَلَيْهِ وَاٰلِهٖ وَسَلَّم also used to eat Saḥarī for our ease so that his devotees would also eat considering it a Sunnaĥ of their

Beloved Prophet صَلَّى اللهُ تَعَالٰى عَلَيْهِ وَاٰلِهٖ وَسَلَّم and, in this way, they would get energy during the day as well as the reward for practising a blessed Sunnaĥ.

Some Islamic brothers boast if they ever happen to fast without consuming Saḥarī meal. O devotees of Rasūl! There is nothing extraordinary in fasting without Saḥarī meal. In fact, one should regret and feel remorse to have missed a great Sunnaĥ of Beloved and Blessed Rasūl صَلَّى اللهُ تَعَالٰى عَلَيْهِ وَاٰلِهٖ وَسَلَّم.

Better than a thousand years' worship

Sayyidunā Shaykh Sharafuddīn (known as Bābā Bulbul Shāĥ) رَحْمَةُ اللّٰهِ تَعَالٰى عَلَيْه has said, 'Allah عَزَّوَجَلَّ has blessed me with so much strength that I can spend my whole life without eating, drinking and without fulfilling other needs of mine but I avoid doing so because it isn't the Sunnaĥ of the Holy Prophet صَلَّى اللهُ تَعَالٰى عَلَيْهِ وَاٰلِهٖ وَسَلَّم. To me, abiding by Sunnaĥ is better than a thousand years worship.' Anyhow, the beauty of all deeds lies in following the Sunnaĥ of the Beloved and Blessed Prophet صَلَّى اللهُ تَعَالٰى عَلَيْهِ وَاٰلِهٖ وَسَلَّم

Saḥarī after sleeping was not allowed

In the beginning, it was not allowed to eat and drink after waking from sleep at night. After the sunset, a fasting person could eat and drink only before going to sleep. Once he went to sleep he wasn't allowed to eat after waking up. However, Allah عَزَّوَجَلَّ had mercy upon His servants and gave them permission to eat at Saḥarī. Therefore, mentioning the reason of permission to eat and drink after waking from sleep, 'Allāmaĥ Maulānā Sayyid Muhammad Na'īmuddīn Murādābādī عَلَيْهِ رَحْمَةُ اللّٰهِ الْهَادِى has quoted the following account in his Quranic exegesis *Khazāin-ul-'Irfān*:

Permission of Saḥarī

Sayyidunā Ṣarmaĥ Bin Qays رَضِىَ اللّٰهُ تَعَالٰى عَنْهُمَا was a very hard working man. One evening he رَضِىَ اللهُ تَعَالٰى عَنْه returned home having worked all day long on the fields in the state of fast. He رَضِىَ اللهُ تَعَالٰى عَنْه asked his wife for food, she began to prepare it. As he رَضِىَ اللهُ تَعَالٰى عَنْه was very tired, he fell asleep. When the food was cooked, his wife woke him up but he رَضِىَ اللهُ تَعَالٰى عَنْه refused to eat because in those days eating food after waking up from sleep at night was not allowed. Therefore, he رَضِىَ اللهُ تَعَالٰى عَنْه fasted the next day without eating anything and resultantly, he رَضِیَ اللّٰہُ تَعَالٰی عَنْہُ became so weak that he رَضِیَ اللّٰہُ تَعَالٰی عَنْہُ passed out. *(Tafsīr Khāzin, vol. 1, pp. 126)* So the following verse was revealed regarding him:

وَكُلُوْا وَاشْرَبُوْا حَتّٰى يَتَبَيَّنَ لَكُمُ الْخَيْطُ

الْاَبْيَضُ مِنَ الْخَيْطِ الْاَسْوَدِ مِنَ الْفَجْرِ ۪ ثُمَّ اَتِمُّوا الصِّيَامَ اِلَى الَّيْلِ ۚ

And eat and drink until the white thread becomes distinct to you from the black thread at dawn; then complete the fasts till the coming of night.

[Kanz-ul-Īmān (Translation of Quran)] (Part 2, Sūraĥ Al-Baqaraĥ, verse 187)

This blessed verse refers to night as a 'black thread' and dawn as a white thread. This shows that eating during the nights in Ramadan is permissible.

Dear Islamic brothers! We have also learnt that fast has nothing to do with the Fajr Ażān. It is not permitted to continue eating during the Fajr Ażān. You must stop eating and drinking altogether as soon as the dawn (Ṣubḥ-e-Ṣādiq) breaks whether the Ażān has been uttered or not, and whether you can hear the Ażān or not.

صَلُّوْا عَلَى الْحَبِيْب　　صَلَّى اللّٰهُ تَعَالٰى عَلٰى مُحَمَّد

Nine sayings of Rasūlullāĥ صَلَّی اللّٰہُ تَعَالٰی عَلَیْہِ وَاٰلِہٖ وَسَلَّم

1. Eat Saḥarī because it is a blessed (food). *(Ṣaḥīḥ Bukhārī, vol. 1, pp. 633, Ḥadīš 1923)*

2. The distinguishing factor between us and the people of the book (Aĥl al-Kitāb) lies in eating Saḥarī. *(Ṣaḥīḥ Muslim, pp. 552, Ḥadīš 1096)*

3. Allah عَزَّوَجَلَّ and His angels send mercy upon the people who eat Saḥarī. *(Al-Iḥsān bittartīb Ṣaḥīḥ Ibn Ḥibbān, vol. 5, pp. 194, Ḥadīš 3458)*

4. When Beloved and Blessed Rasūl صَلَّی اللّٰہُ تَعَالٰی عَلَیْہِ وَاٰلِہٖ وَسَلَّم used to call one of his companions to eat Saḥarī with him he would say, 'Come (and) eat the blessed food.' *(Sunan Abī Dāwūd, vol. 2, pp. 442, Ḥadīš 2344)*

5. Eat Saḥarī to gain strength for fast and take rest (siesta) in the afternoon to gain strength for worshipping at night. *(Sunan Ibn Mājaĥ, vol. 2, pp. 321, Ḥadīš 1693)*

6. Saḥarī is a blessing Allah عَزَّوَجَلَّ has granted you (therefore) do not miss it. *(Sunan Kubrā, Nasāī, vol. 2, pp. 79, Ḥadīš 2472)*

7. There are three people who will not be held accountable no matter how much they eat اِنْ شَآءَاللّٰه عَزَّوَجَلَّ, provided the food is Ḥalāl: (a) A fasting person at the time of Ifṭār. (b) The one who eats at Saḥarī and (c) A warrior that protects the Islamic border in the path of Allah عَزَّوَجَلَّ. *(Attarghīb Wattarĥīb, vol. 2, pp. 90, Ḥadīš 9)*

8. Saḥarī is full of blessings, so do not miss it even if you drink just a sip of water. Allah عَزَّوَجَلَّ and His angels send mercy upon the people who consume Saḥarī. *(Musnad Imām Aḥmad, vol. 4, pp. 88, Ḥadīš 11396)*

   Dear Islamic brothers! These sayings of the Noble Prophet صَلَّى اللهُ تَعَالٰى عَلَيْهِ وَاٰلِهٖ وَسَلَّم teach us that Saḥarī is Allah's great bounty which has numerous physical and spiritual benefits for us. This is why the Holy Prophet صَلَّى اللهُ تَعَالٰى عَلَيْهِ وَاٰلِهٖ وَسَلَّم called it a 'blessed breakfast.'

9. Sayyidunā 'Irbāḍ Bin Sāriyaĥ رَضِىَ اللهُ تَعَالٰى عَنْهُ has narrated that once the Beloved and Blessed Prophet صَلَّى اللهُ تَعَالٰى عَلَيْهِ وَاٰلِهٖ وَسَلَّم called him to eat Saḥarī with him during the month of Ramadan and said: 'Come for a blessed breakfast.' *(Sunan Abī Dāwūd, vol. 2, pp. 442, Ḥadīš 2344)*

Is Saḥarī a condition for fast?

No one should have the misconception that Saḥarī is a condition for fast. A fast can be valid even without Saḥarī, but it is not appropriate to miss Saḥarī deliberately as eating Saḥarī is a great Sunnaĥ. It should also be remembered that it is not necessary to eat until you're full at Saḥarī. A few dates and a little water are also sufficient for Saḥarī and eating Saḥarī with dates and water is a blessed Sunnaĥ as well.

Eating Saḥarī with dates and water is Sunnaĥ

Sayyidunā Anas Bin Mālik رَضِىَ اللهُ تَعَالٰى عَنْهُ has said that the Holy Prophet صَلَّى اللهُ تَعَالٰى عَلَيْهِ وَاٰلِهٖ وَسَلَّم used to say to me at the time of Saḥarī, 'I intend to fast, give me something to eat', so I used to give him some dates and water in a cup. *(Sunan Kubrā lin-Nasāī, vol. 2, pp. 80, Ḥadīš 2477)*

Dates, an excellent Saḥarī

Dear Islamic brothers! We have learnt that eating Saḥarī is a Sunnaĥ and eating dates and drinking water at Saḥarī is another Sunnaĥ. Our Noble Prophet صَلَّى اللّٰه تَعَالٰى عَلَيْهِ وَاٰلِهٖ وَسَلَّم has also encouraged us to eat dates at Saḥarī. Sayyidunā Sāib Bin Yazīd رَضِىَ اللّٰه تَعَالٰى عَنْهُ has narrated that the Noble Prophet صَلَّى اللّٰه تَعَالٰى عَلَيْهِ وَاٰلِهٖ وَسَلَّم has said:

Dates are an excellent Saḥarī. نِعْمَ السَّحُوْرُ التَّمْرُ

(Attarghīb Wattarĥīb, vol. 2, pp. 90, Ḥadīš 12)

He صَلَّى اللّٰه تَعَالٰى عَلَيْهِ وَاٰلِهٖ وَسَلَّم has also said:

For a believer dates are an excellent Saḥarī. نِعْمَ سَحُوْرُ الْمُوْمِنِ التَّمْرُ

(Sunan Abī Dāwūd, vol. 2, pp. 443, Ḥadīš 2345)

Dear Islamic brothers! Eating dates and drinking water together isn't a condition for Saḥarī. If one drinks a little bit of water with the intention of Saḥarī the Sunnaĥ will be fulfilled.

Time for Saḥarī

The famous Arabic dictionary '*Qāmūs*' says that 'Saḥarī is the food that is eaten in the morning.' A great Ḥanafī scholar 'Allāmaĥ Maulānā 'Alī Bin Sultan Muhammad Al-Ma'rūf Mullā 'Alī Qārī عَلَيْهِ رَحْمَةُ اللّٰهِ الْبَارِى has said, 'Some (scholars) have said that the time for Saḥarī begins at midnight.' *(Mirqāt-ul-Mafātīḥ, vol. 4, pp. 477)*

Delay in Saḥarī is Mustaḥab as it is mentioned in Ḥadīš that Sayyidunā Ya'lā Bin Murraĥ رَضِىَ اللّٰه تَعَالٰى عَنْهُ has narrated that the Beloved and Blessed Prophet صَلَّى اللّٰه تَعَالٰى عَلَيْهِ وَاٰلِهٖ وَسَلَّم has said: 'There are three things that Allah عَزَّوَجَلَّ likes:

1. To eat Ifṭār without delay after sunset.
2. To delay Saḥarī and
3. To place one hand over the other (while standing) in Ṣalāĥ.'

(Attarghīb Wattarĥīb, vol. 2, pp. 91, Ḥadīš 4)

What is meant by 'delaying Saḥarī?'

Dear Islamic brothers! To delay Saḥarī is Mustaḥab and also earns us more reward but it shouldn't be delayed to the extent that the time of dawn seems to be starting. Here, a question arises as to what is meant by the delay in Saḥarī.

Commenting on the delay in Saḥarī, a renowned exegetist of the Quran, Muftī Aḥmad Yār Khān عَلَيْهِ رَحْمَةُ الْحَنَّان has stated in *Tafsīr-e-Na'īmī*, 'This delay refers to the 'sixth part' of the night.' 'Again, a question arises as to what the sixth part of the night is.' The answer to this question is that by Islamic jurisprudence, the duration from sunset to dawn (Ṣubḥ-e-Ṣādiq) is called 'night.' Let's say for example that the sun sets at 7 p.m. and dawn occurs at 4 a.m., the total duration of night will be 9 hours. If we divide 9 hours into 6 equal parts; the duration of each part will be 1½ hours. Now, eating Saḥarī within the last 1½ hours before dawn (i.e. 2:30 a.m. to 4 a.m.) will be regarded as eating Saḥarī with the delay mentioned in the Ḥadīš. The times for Saḥarī and Ifṭār change every day. The above mentioned method can be used to ascertain the sixth part of any night. If one eats Saḥarī during any part of the night and makes the intention to fast he can still eat at any time during the rest of the night, a new intention is not needed.

Fajr Ażān is for Ṣalāĥ, not for fast

Saḥarī must not be delayed to the extent that the time of dawn (Ṣubḥ-e-Ṣādiq) seems to be starting. Some people keep eating even after dawn during the Ażān saying: *Listen! The sound of that Masjid's Ażān is still coming*, and if they do not eat they at least drink water to 'close their fasts' (despite the Ażān having begun). This doesn't 'close' the fast, in fact it leaves the fast 'completely open' and makes it invalid. Such people will gain nothing except bearing thirst and hunger the whole day. 'Closing the fast' has nothing to do with the Fajr Ażān. It is absolutely vital that one stop eating before the break of dawn (as the previous verse stated).

May Allah عَزَّوَجَلَّ grant every Muslim proper sense and the ability to carry out worships such as Ṣalāĥ and fasting according to their stipulated times!

آمِین بِجَاہِ النَّبِیِّ الْاَمِین صَلَّی اللّٰہُ تَعَالٰی عَلَیْہِ وَاٰلِہٖ وَسَلَّم

صَلُّوْا عَلَی الْحَبِیْب   صَلَّی اللّٰهُ تَعَالٰی عَلٰی مُحَمَّد

Stop eating and drinking

It is observed that people generally rely on the Ażān and sirens to stop eating due to ignorance. Many continue to eat even during the Fajr Ażān. In order to solve this problem it will be very useful to make the following announcement every day in a loud voice in Ramadan in every Masjid, three minutes before dawn:

First say,

صَلُّوْا عَلَى الْحَبِيْب صَلَّى اللهُ تَعَالٰى عَلٰى مُحَمَّد

Then say the following three times: '*O fasting people! The ending time of Saḥarī is (for example) 4:12 a.m. today. The time is about to end. Stop eating and drinking instantly. Do not wait for the Ażān. The Ażān is uttered for the Fajr Ṣalāĥ after the Saḥarī time ends.*' Everyone must keep it mind that the Fajr Ażān is uttered after the Saḥarī time has ended and it is not uttered for closing fast but for the Fajr Ṣalāĥ.

صَلُّوْا عَلَى الْحَبِيْب صَلَّى اللهُ تَعَالٰى عَلٰى مُحَمَّد

Intention to travel with Madanī Qāfilaĥ eased difficulty

Dear Islamic brothers! Please travel in the company of devotees of Rasūl with the Madanī Qāfilaĥs of Dawat-e-Islami, a global & non-political religious movement of the Quran and Sunnaĥ. اِنْ شَآءَاللّٰه عَزَّوَجَلَّ This will bring you great blessings in the world as well as in the Hereafter.

Here is a faith-refreshing statement of an Islamic brother from Landhi (Bāb-ul-Madīnaĥ, Karachi) about the blessing of a Madanī Qāfilaĥ. He has stated: The marriage of my older brother had approached but we were worried as we did not have enough money to afford the expenses of the marriage. I didn't want to borrow money as it could damage the prestige of my beloved Madanī movement Dawat-e-Islami (in case of delay in paying the debt).

One day, I was in extreme anguish. Having offered Ẓuĥr Ṣalāĥ I made the intention that 'If the problem of the shortage of money is solved I'll travel with a Madanī Qāfilaĥ.' After finishing my Ṣalāĥ I met people in the Masjid. While I was busy with making individual effort, the Imām, who was also my uncle and was aware of my difficulty, called me and promised to provide money for the expenses of the marriage, اَلْحَمْدُلِلّٰه عَزَّوَجَلَّ.

I travelled with a Madanī Qāfilaĥ on the very next day. اَلْحَمْدُلِلّٰه عَزَّوَجَلَّ I was relieved of my worries just for making the intention to travel with a Madanī Qāfilaĥ. When the date of the wedding was set we were in debt but now we have not only got rid of the burden of debt, but my brother's marriage has also taken place properly, اَلْحَمْدُلِلّٰه عَزَّوَجَلَّ

صَلُّوْا عَلَى الْحَبِيْب صَلَّى اللهُ تَعَالٰى عَلٰى مُحَمَّد

Dear Islamic brothers! Did you see! The problem of the shortage of money was solved, debt was paid and marriage also took place due to the blessings of a younger brother's intention to travel with a Madanī Qāfilaĥ.

Relief from debts

After every Ṣalāĥ, recite Sūraĥ Quraysh seven times (with Ṣalāt-'Alan-Nabī once before and after it) and make supplication, even huge debt will get paid, اِنْ شَآءَالله عَزَّوَجَلَّ. Continue to recite it until the debt is paid.

Invocation for relief from debts

اَللّٰهُمَّ اكْفِنِيْ بِحَلَالِكَ عَنْ حَرَامِكَ وَاَغْنِنِيْ بِفَضْلِكَ عَمَّنْ سِوَاكَ

Translation: Yā Allah عَزَّوَجَلَّ grant me lawful sustenance and save me from that which is unlawful and make me independent of everyone apart from You, with Your grace.

(With Ṣalāt-'Alan-Nabī once before and after it) Recite it eleven times after every Ṣalāĥ and hundred times every morning and evening until the debt is paid.

According to a narration, once a Mukātab[1] said to Sayyidunā 'Alī كَرَّمَ اللهُ تَعَالٰى وَجْهَهُ الْكَرِيْم 'Please help me, I cannot pay for my release.' He رَضِىَ اللهُ تَعَالٰى عَنْهُ replied: 'Shall I not teach you

[1] A slave who has signed a contract with his owner to be set free in exchange for a payment.

(Al-Mukhtaṣar-ul-Qudūrī, Kitāb-ul-Makātib, pp. 386)

a few words the Beloved Rasūl صَلَّى اللهُ تَعَالٰى عَلَيْهِ وَاٰلِهٖ وَسَلَّم taught me? Even if you owe as much money as mount Ṣīr[1] Allah عَزَّوَجَلَّ will pay (your debt) for you.' The words are as follows:

اَللّٰهُمَّ اكْفِنِيْ بِحَلَالِكَ عَنْ حَرَامِكَ وَاَغْنِنِيْ بِفَضْلِكَ عَمَّنْ سِوَاكَ

Translation: Yā Allah عَزَّوَجَلَّ grant me lawful sustenance and save me from that which is unlawful and make me independent of everyone apart from You, with Your grace.

(Jāmi' Tirmiżī, vol. 5, pp. 329, Ḥadīš 3574)

A Madanī request: Before starting this invocation, distribute at least eleven rupees Niyāz for the Īṣāl-e-Šawāb[2] of Ghauš-e-A'ẓam رَضِیَ اللهُ تَعَالٰی عَنْهُ and at least twenty five rupees Niyāz for the Īṣāl-e-Šawāb of Imām Aḥmad Razā Khān عَلَيْهِ رَحْمَةُ الرَّحْمٰن in case of the fulfilment of your desire (religious booklets etc. can also be distributed).

Definitions of morning and evening: The duration from midnight to the glimmering of the first ray of the sun is called 'morning.' From the starting of Ẓuĥr time up to the sunset is called 'evening.'

Madanī suggestion: The troubled Islamic brothers should travel with Madanī Qāfilaĥs of Dawat-e-Islami in the company of the devotees of Rasūl and make supplication. If someone cannot travel, (for instance, Islamic sisters) they should make any male member of their family travel on behalf of them.

Ifṭār

One should not delay in Ifṭār when it is certain that the sun has set. Do not wait for any siren or Ażān. Eat or drink something instantly but eating fresh or dried dates or drinking water is Sunnaĥ. After eating the date or drinking water recite this Du'ā[3]:

---

[1] The name of a mountain. *(An-Niĥāyaĥ, vol. 3, pp. 61)*

[2] Īṣāl-e-Šawāb refers to the act of spiritually sending the reward of virtuous deeds to the deceased. See its details in the booklet '*Method of Fātiḥaĥ*.'

[3] This Du'ā is usually recited before doing Ifṭār but A'lā Ḥaḍrat Imām-e-Aĥl-e-Sunnat Maulānā Shāĥ Aḥmad Razā Khān عَلَيْهِ رَحْمَةُ الرَّحْمٰن has stated in '*Fatāwā Razawiyyaĥ*, vol. 10, pp. 631' it should be recited after the Ifṭār.

Du'ā for Ifṭār

اَللّٰهُمَّ اِنِّیْ لَكَ صُمْتُ وَبِكَ اٰمَنْتُ وَعَلَيْكَ تَوَكَّلْتُ وَعَلٰى رِزْقِكَ اَفْطَرْتُ

Translation: Yā Allah عَزَّوَجَلَّ I fasted for You and I have faith in You and I put my trust in You and I do Ifṭār with the sustenance given by You.

(Fatāwā 'Ālamgīrī, vol. 1, pp. 200)

Ażān is not condition for Ifṭār

Remember! The Ażān is not a condition for Ifṭār at all. Imagine, how would the people living in far flung areas where there is no Masājid or where the sound of Ażān does not reach, be able to do Ifṭār in this situation. The Maghrib Ażān is uttered for the Maghrib Ṣalāĥ, not for Ifṭār. It will be very appropriate if the following announcement is made thrice immediately after the sunset.

Say it loudly only one time:

صَلُّوْا عَلَى الْحَبِيْب صَلَّى اللّٰهُ تَعَالٰى عَلٰى مُحَمَّد

Then say the following three times:

'O fasting people! Do Ifṭār.'

Eleven virtues of Ifṭār

1. Sayyidunā Saĥl Bin Sa'd رَضِیَ اللّٰہُ تَعَالٰی عَنْہُ has narrated that the Beloved and Blessed Prophet صَلَّی اللّٰہُ تَعَالٰی عَلَیْہِ وَاٰلِہٖ وَسَلَّم has said, 'People will always remain well as long as they hasten to do Ifṭār.' *(Ṣaḥīḥ Bukhārī, vol. 1, pp. 645, Ḥadīš 1957)*

   Dear Islamic brothers! As soon as it is certain that the sun has set, one should instantly do Ifṭār by eating a date or drinking water etc. and recite the Du'ā afterwards so that Ifṭār is not delayed.

2. The Prophet of mankind, the Peace of our heart and mind, the most Generous and Kind صَلَّی اللّٰہُ تَعَالٰی عَلَیْہِ وَاٰلِہٖ وَسَلَّم has said, 'My Ummaĥ will remain steadfast in my Sunnaĥ as

long as they do not wait for the stars to appear for Ifṭār.' *(Al-Iḥsān bittartīb Ṣaḥīḥ Ibn Ḥibbān, vol. 5, pp. 209, Ḥadīš 3501)*

3. Sayyidunā Abū Ĥurayraĥ رَضِیَ اللهُ تَعَالٰی عَنْهُ has narrated that the Prophet of Raḥmaĥ, the Intercessor of Ummaĥ صَلَّى اللهُ تَعَالٰى عَلَيْهِ وَالِهٖ وَسَلَّم has said that Allah عَزَّوَجَلَّ has said, 'Amongst My servants, the one hastening to do Ifṭār is dearer to me.' *(Jāmi' Tirmiżī, vol. 2, pp. 164, Ḥadīš 700)*

سُبْحٰنَ اللّٰه عَزَّوَجَلَّ! If you want to be dear to Allah عَزَّوَجَلَّ, do not engage yourselves in any activity at the time of Ifṭār and do Ifṭār instantly.

4. Sayyidunā Anas Bin Mālik رَضِیَ اللهُ تَعَالٰی عَنْهُ has said, 'I never saw the Beloved and Blessed Prophet صَلَّى اللهُ تَعَالٰى عَلَيْهِ وَالِهٖ وَسَلَّم offer the Maghrib Ṣalāĥ before eating Ifṭār, he would first do Ifṭār even though with a sip of water.' *(Attarghīb Wattarĥīb, vol. 2, pp. 91, Ḥadīš 91)*

5. Sayyidunā Abū Ĥurayraĥ رَضِیَ اللهُ تَعَالٰی عَنْهُ has narrated that the Noble Rasūl صَلَّى اللهُ تَعَالٰى عَلَيْهِ وَالِهٖ وَسَلَّم warned: 'This religion will always remain dominant as long as people hasten to do Ifṭār because the Jews and Christians delay their Ifṭār.' *(Sunan Abī Dāwūd, vol. 2, pp. 446, Ḥadīš 2353)*

Dear Islamic brothers! This Ḥadīš shows that one should do Ifṭār without any delay. Delaying Ifṭār is a practice of the Jews and Christians and we have been prohibited to follow them.

6. Sayyidunā Zayd Bin Khālid Juhanī رَضِیَ اللهُ تَعَالٰی عَنْهُ has narrated that the Prophet of Raḥmaĥ, the Intercessor of Ummaĥ, the Owner of Jannaĥ صَلَّى اللهُ تَعَالٰى عَلَيْهِ وَالِهٖ وَسَلَّم has said:

مَنْ جَهَّزَ غَازِيًا اَوْ حَاجًّا اَوْ خَلَفَهُ فِيْ اَهْلِهٖ اَوْ فَطَّرَ
صَائِمًا كَانَ لَهٗ مِثْلُ اَجْرِهٖ مِنْ غَيْرِ اَنْ يَّنْقُصَ مِنْ اُجُوْرِهِمْ شَيْءٌ

Translation: Anyone who gives provisions to a Ghāzī or a Hajj pilgrim or looks after his family in his absence or serves a fasting person with Ifṭār, will be rewarded the same as him without any reduction in their reward.

(Sunan Kubrā lin-Nasāī, vol. 2, pp. 256, Ḥadīš 3330)

سُبْحٰنَ اللّٰه عَزَّوَجَلَّ! What glad tidings! Whoever furnishes a Ghāzī with provisions will be rewarded the same as him, whoever financially assists a Hajj pilgrim will be rewarded the same as him, and whoever serves a fasting person with Ifṭār will be rewarded the same as him; and there will be no reduction in their rewards. ذَالِكَ فَضْلُ الله

However, it must be remembered that asking people for money in order to perform Hajj or 'Umraĥ is Ḥarām and it is also a sin to give anything to such a person.

Excellent reward for serving someone with Ifṭār

7. Sayyidunā Salmān Fārsī رَضِیَ اللهُ تَعَالٰی عَنْهُ has narrated that the Beloved and Blessed Rasūl صَلَّی اللهُ تَعَالٰی عَلَیْهِ وَاٰلِهٖ وَسَلَّم has said, 'If anyone serves a fasting Muslim with Ifṭār, angels will pray for his forgiveness in Ramadan, and Jibrāīl عَلَیْهِ السَّلَام will pray for his forgiveness at Layla-tul-Qadr.' *(Mu'jam Kabīr, vol. 6, pp. 262, Ḥadīš 6162)*

سُبْحٰنَ اللّٰه عَزَّوَجَلَّ! Look how great and magnificent the blessings and bounties of Allah عَزَّوَجَلَّ are! If a Muslim provides someone with a date or a sip of water for Ifṭār in the month of Ramadan, the angels of Allah عَزَّوَجَلَّ pray for his forgiveness in Ramadan and Sayyidunā Jibrāīl عَلَیْهِ السَّلَام, the chief of all the angels, also prays for his forgiveness at Layla-tul-Qadr. اَلْحَمْدُ لِلّٰهِ عَلٰی اِحسَانِهٖ

Jibrāīl عَلَیْهِ السَّلَام shakes hand with one serving Ifṭār

8. According to a narration, 'If anyone serves a person with Ifṭār in Ramadan with Ḥalāl earnings, the angels will send Durūd upon him at every night of Ramadan, and Jibrāīl عَلَیْهِ السَّلَام will shake his hands with such a person at Layla-tul-Qadr. If Jibrāīl عَلَیْهِ السَّلَام shakes hands with a person, his eyes will shed tears (due to the fear of Allah عَزَّوَجَلَّ) and his heart will become soft.' *(Kanz-ul-'Ummāl, vol. 8, pp. 215, Ḥadīš 23653)*

Excellence of serving fasting Muslim with water

9. Another Ḥadīš states, 'If anyone serves a fasting Muslim with water, Allah عَزَّوَجَلَّ will make him drink water from my pond (Ḥawḍ) and he will not feel thirst till he enters Heaven.' *(Ṣaḥīḥ Ibn Khuzaymaĥ, vol. 3, pp. 192, Ḥadīš 1887)*

10. Sayyidunā Salmān Bin 'Āmir رَضِیَ اللّٰہُ تَعَالٰی عَنۡہُ has narrated that the Prophet of mankind, the Peace of our heart and mind, the most Generous and Kind صَلَّی اللّٰہُ تَعَالٰی عَلَیۡہِ وَاٰلِہٖ وَسَلَّم has said, 'When you do Ifṭār, do it with a fresh or dry date because it is blessed and if you have neither, then do Ifṭār with water because it is a purifier.' *(Jāmi' Tirmiżī, vol. 2, pp. 162, Ḥadīš 695)*

This blessed Ḥadīš encourages us to do Ifṭār with fresh or dried dates because it is Sunnaĥ to do so, but if you have neither of them, use water because it is a purifier.

11. Sayyidunā Anas رَضِیَ اللّٰہُ تَعَالٰی عَنۡہُ has narrated that the Holy Prophet صَلَّی اللّٰہُ تَعَالٰی عَلَیۡہِ وَاٰلِہٖ وَسَلَّم used to do Ifṭār with fresh dates before the (Maghrib) Ṣalāĥ. If the fresh dates were not available he صَلَّی اللّٰہُ تَعَالٰی عَلَیۡہِ وَاٰلِہٖ وَسَلَّم would eat a few dry dates instead and if they were not available either, he would drink a few handfuls of water. *(Sunan Abī Dāwūd, vol. 2, pp. 447, Ḥadīš 2356)*

The foregoing blessed Ḥadīš describes that the Holy Prophet صَلَّی اللّٰہُ تَعَالٰی عَلَیۡہِ وَاٰلِہٖ وَسَلَّم would initially prefer fresh dates for Ifṭār, if they weren't available then dry dates and if they weren't available either, then he صَلَّی اللّٰہُ تَعَالٰی عَلَیۡہِ وَاٰلِہٖ وَسَلَّم would drink water. Therefore, we should first attempt to do Ifṭār with sweet fresh dates, which is a sweet Sunnaĥ of the Noble Prophet صَلَّی اللّٰہُ تَعَالٰی عَلَیۡہِ وَاٰلِہٖ وَسَلَّم. If they aren't available, then dry dates and if they aren't available either, then water.

Dear Islamic brothers! Many blessed Aḥādīš encourage us to use dates at Saḥarī and Ifṭār. Eating dates, drinking dates-soaked water and using dates as a cure are all Sunnaĥs. Dates contain innumerable blessings and cures for numerous illnesses.

Madanī pearls regarding dates

1. The Prophet of Raḥmaĥ, the Intercessor of Ummaĥ صَلَّی اللّٰہُ تَعَالٰی عَلَیۡہِ وَاٰلِہٖ وَسَلَّم has said, 'The 'Ajwaĥ (the best type of date) of 'Āliyaĥ (the name of a place in Madīnaĥ Munawwaraĥ towards Masjid-e-Qubā) is a cure for all illnesses.' According to a narration, 'To eat seven 'Ajwaĥ dates daily for seven days protects against leprosy.' *('Umda-tul-Qārī, vol. 14, pp. 446, Ḥadīš 5768)*

2. The Beloved and Blessed Prophet صَلَّى اللهُ تَعَالٰى عَلَيْهِ وَاٰلِهٖ وَسَلَّم has said, 'The 'Ajwaĥ date is from Heaven; it is a cure for poison.' *(Jāmi' Tirmiżī, vol. 4, pp. 17, Ḥadīš 2073)* A Ḥadīš in *Bukhārī* states, if anyone eats seven 'Ajwaĥ dates in the morning (before eating anything else) he will remain safe from magic and poison that day. *(Ṣaḥīḥ Bukhārī, vol. 3, pp. 540, Ḥadīš 5445)*

3. Sayyidunā Abū Ĥurayraĥ رَضِىَ اللهُ تَعَالٰى عَنْهُ has said, 'Dates protect against appendicitis.' *(Kanz-ul-'Ummāl, vol. 10, pp. 12, Ḥadīš 24191)*

4. The Beloved and Blessed Rasūl صَلَّى اللهُ تَعَالٰى عَلَيْهِ وَاٰلِهٖ وَسَلَّم has said, 'Eating dates in the morning before eating anything else kills stomach worms.' *(Al-Jāmi'-uṣ-Ṣaghīr, pp. 398, Ḥadīš 6394)*

5. Sayyidunā Rabī' Bin Khašīm رَضِىَ اللهُ تَعَالٰى عَنْهُ has said, 'To me, dates and honey are the best cures for a pregnant woman and a sick man respectively.' *(Ad-Dur-rul-Manšūr, vol. 5, pp. 505)*

6. Sayyidī Muhammad Aḥmad Żaĥabī رَحْمَةُ اللهِ تَعَالٰى عَلَيْه has said, 'If a pregnant woman eats dates she will give birth to a baby-boy who will be handsome, tolerant and polite, اِنْ شَآءَ اللّٰه عَزَّوَجَلَّ.'

7. Dates are very beneficial to the one who has become weak due to hunger because they are full of vitamins and revive energy quickly. This is the wisdom of doing Ifṭār with dates.

8. Doing Ifṭār with very cold water may cause stomach problems and the swelling of the liver. Eating dates before drinking cold water reduces this risk but remember that drinking extremely cold water is always harmful.

9. Eating dates with melon or cucumber or dates with watermelon is a Sunnaĥ. Eating dates in this way is very beneficial from medical point of view. According to doctors it overcomes physical and sexual weakness and thinness. However, its greatest benefit is that it is a Sunnaĥ. A Ḥadīš states that eating butter with dates is also Sunnaĥ. *(Sunan Ibn Mājaĥ, vol. 4, pp. 41, Ḥadīš 3334)*

   Eating fresh and dry (old) dates together is also a Sunnaĥ. *Ibn Mājaĥ* mentions, 'When the devil sees someone eat fresh and dry (old) dates together, he regrets that man has become strong by eating fresh dates with dried ones.' *(Sunan Ibn Mājaĥ, vol. 4, pp. 40, Ḥadīš 3330)*

10. Dates are a cure for chronic constipation.

11. Dates are useful for asthma and other diseases related to heart, kidney, gall bladder, bladder and intestine. They treat phlegm and dried skin, strengthen a man's virility (sexual power), and help the flow of urine.

12. Eating grinded dates with their seeds is beneficial to heart problems and cataract (eye disease).

13. Drinking dates-soaked water cures liver problems. This water is also effective for treating diarrhoea. (Leave the date to soak in water at night and then drink it in the morning before eating anything else but don't store it in a freezer).

14. Dates-boiled milk is a very powerful nutrient. It is very useful to overcome the weakness caused by an illness.

15. Wounds heal quickly by eating dates.

16. Date is an effective medicine for jaundice.

17. Fresh and fully ripe dates cure bile problems and acidity.

18. Using the burnt dates-seeds as a tooth powder makes the teeth shiny and removes mouth bad odours.

19. Applying the powder of burnt dates-seeds onto wounds stops bleeding and helps the wounds heal.

20. Burning date seeds in fire and inhaling its smoke dry the warts of piles.

21. Using burnt date tree roots or leaves as a tooth powder is beneficial to treating toothache. Boiling the roots or leaves in water and rinsing mouth with it is also effective for treating toothache.

22. If eating dates causes any side effect to someone, he should eat them with pomegranate juice, poppy seeds or black pepper seeds.

23. Eating half ripe and old dates together is harmful. Similarly, eating dates with grapes, currants, raisins or figs, eating a large quantity of dates immediately after recovering from an illness in weakness and eating dates whilst suffering from an eye infection are all harmful.

24. Not more than approximately 60 grams of dates should be eaten at a time. When eating old dates one should open them up and check them for small red insects and clean them. It is Makrūĥ to eat such dates, without cleaning them, which are suspected to have insects inside them. *('Ūnul Ma'būd, vol. 10, pp. 246)*

    Sellers often rub mustard oil on dates to make them look shiny, so it is better to soak them in water for a few minutes to remove any fly droppings and dirt and then wash them before eating. Fresh ripe tree dates are the most beneficial.

25. Do not throw away the seeds of dates brought from Madīna-tul-Munawwaraĥ زَادَهَا اللّٰهُ شَرَفًا وَّ تَعْظِيْمًا. Instead, keep them in a respectful place or put them into a river. Further, one can gain their blessings by cutting them into tiny pieces which can be kept in a small tin and eaten like nuts. No matter which part of the world any thing comes from, when it enters the atmosphere of Madīna-tul-Munawwaraĥ زَادَهَا اللّٰهُ شَرَفًا وَّ تَعْظِيْمًا it belongs to Madīnaĥ and therefore it becomes an object of respect for devotees.

Du'ā is accepted at time of Ifṭār

Dear Islamic brothers! A fasting Muslim is very fortunate because he continuously earns the pleasure of Allah عَزَّوَجَلَّ. When he makes Du'ā at the time of Ifṭār Allah عَزَّوَجَلَّ accepts his Du'ā due to His grace and mercy. Sayyidunā 'Abdullāĥ Bin 'Amr Bin 'Āṣ رَضِیَ اللّٰہُ تَعَالٰی عَنْہُ has narrated that the Beloved and Blessed Prophet صَلَّی اللّٰہُ تَعَالٰی عَلَیْہِ وَاٰلِہٖ وَسَلَّم has said:

اِنَّ لِلصَّائِمِ عِنْدَ فِطْرِهٖ لَدَعْوَةً مَّا تُرَدُّ

Translation: At the time of Ifṭār, for the fasting person, there is a Du'ā which is not rejected.

(Attarghīb Wattarĥīb, vol. 2, pp. 53, Ḥadīš 29)

Sayyidunā Abū Ĥurayraĥ رَضِیَ اللّٰہُ تَعَالٰی عَنْہُ has narrated that the Holy Prophet صَلَّی اللّٰہُ تَعَالٰی عَلَیْہِ وَاٰلِہٖ وَسَلَّم has said, 'There are three types of Du'ās that are not rejected:

1. The Du'ā of a fasting person at the time of Ifṭār.
2. The Du'ā of a just ruler.

3. The Du'ā of the oppressed. The Du'ā of these three persons are lifted above the clouds by Allah عَزَّوَجَلَّ and the gates of the sky are opened for them and Allah عَزَّوَجَلَّ says, 'I swear by My glory! I will definitely help you, though with a little delay.' *(Sunan Ibn Mājaĥ, vol. 2, pp. 349, Ḥadīš 1752)*

صَلُّوْا عَلَى الْحَبِيْب صَلَّى اللّٰهُ تَعَالٰى عَلٰى مُحَمَّد

All we worry about is eating!

Dear fasting Muslims! Congratulations to you all! There's glad-tidings that your every prayer will be answered at the time of Ifṭār, but unfortunately, our present condition is very sad. At the time of Ifṭār we face a very tough trial as we usually have a great variety of fruits, fried items and drinks in front of us. As we are extremely hungry and thirsty we start to devour the food as soon as the sun sets getting heedless of Du'ā. Many of us miss Rak'āt of the Maghrib Jamā'at due to excessive eating, and some are so lazy that, Allah عَزَّوَجَلَّ forbid, they even miss the whole Jamā'at and offer Maghrib Ṣalāĥ at home!

O seekers of Heaven! Do not be so heedless! Offering Ṣalāĥ with Jamā'at has been greatly stressed by Sharī'aĥ. Always remember! It is a sin to miss the Jamā'at of Ṣalāĥ without a Shar'ī exemption.

Ifṭār precautions

It is better to do Ifṭār with one or a half date then clean mouth properly and offer Ṣalāĥ with complete Jamā'at. These days people eat fruits, fried things etc. in the Masjid and join Jamā'at without cleaning their mouths properly, whereas there shouldn't be a single bit of food or taste in the mouth (when offering Ṣalāĥ).

The Prophet of Raḥmaĥ, the Intercessor of Ummaĥ صَلَّى اللّٰهُ تَعَالٰى عَلَيْهِ وَاٰلِهٖ وَسَلَّم has said, 'Nothing is more troublesome for Kirāman Kātibīn (the two angels that record deeds) than seeing their companion offer Ṣalāĥ in such a condition that something is stuck between his teeth.' *(Mu'jam Kabīr, vol. 4, pp. 177, Ḥadīš 4061)*

A'lā Ḥaḍrat رَحْمَةُ اللهِ تَعَالٰی عَلَيْه has stated, 'Several Aḥādīš state that when a man stands to offer Ṣalāĥ, an angel places its mouth onto his mouth and whatever he recites, comes out of his mouth and enters the angel's mouth. If anything is stuck between his teeth, the angels are so distressed by it that nothing else distresses them to such an extent. The Prophet of mankind, the Peace of our heart and mind, the most Generous and Kind صَلَّى اللهُ تَعَالٰی عَلَيْهِ وَاٰلِهٖ وَسَلَّم has said, 'When any of you stands to offer Ṣalāĥ at night, he should clean his teeth using a Miswāk because when he recites the Holy Quran an angel places its mouth on his mouth and whatever comes out of his mouth, enters the angel's mouth.' *(Kanz-ul-'Ummāl, vol. 9, pp. 319)*

In his '*Kabīr*' Imām Ṭabarānī has quoted Sayyidunā Abū Ayyūb Anṣārī رَضِیَ اللهُ تَعَالٰی عَنْهُ as saying, 'There is nothing more troublesome for the two angels than seeing their companion offer Ṣalāĥ with bits of food stuck between his teeth.' *(Fatāwā Razawiyyaĥ (Jadīd), vol. 1, pp. 624-625)*

It is usually hard for people who do Ifṭār in the Masjid to clean their mouths properly because if they try to do so they may well lose Jamā'at or at least some Rak'āt. It is, therefore, suggested to do Ifṭār with just a date or two and some water and move the water properly inside the mouth so that the sweetness and bits of the date are washed away into the stomach. If necessary, use a tooth pick. If there's no time to clean mouth properly, then it's safer to do Ifṭār with water only.

I appreciate those fasting Muslims who sit in the first row of the Masjid before sunset with a date and some water taking no interest in delicious food. In this way, they will not only be able to clean their mouth easily but also succeed in offering Ṣalāĥ at the first row of the Masjid without missing the first Takbīr.

Du'ā at Ifṭār

Do Ifṭār with one or two dates and then make a Du'ā; at least recite one Māšūr Du'ā (the supplications that have been mentioned in the Quran and Aḥādīš are called 'Māšūr'). Learn at least one of the supplications that were made by Beloved and Blessed Prophet صَلَّى اللهُ تَعَالٰی عَلَيْهِ وَاٰلِهٖ وَسَلَّم at various occasions. One well known Du'ā to be recited after Ifṭār has already been mentioned, here is another one:

The narration mentioned in '*Abī Dāwūd*' states that the Beloved and Blessed Prophet صَلَّى اللهُ تَعَالٰى عَلَيْهِ وَاٰلِهٖ وَسَلَّم used to make the following supplication at the time of Ifṭār:

اَللّٰهُمَّ لَكَ صُمْتُ وَعَلٰى رِزْقِكَ اَفْطَرْتُ

Translation: Yā Allah عَزَّوَجَلَّ! I fasted for You and did Ifṭār with sustenance given by You.

(Sunan Abī Dāwūd, vol. 2, pp. 447, Ḥadīš 2358)

Dear Islamic brothers! The Ḥadīš mentioned earlier states that '*supplications made at the time of Ifṭār are not rejected.*' Sometimes, a question arises as to why the effect of our prayers being answered has not yet taken place whereas many Aḥādīš affirm it.

Dear Islamic brothers! Don't worry in case of apparent delays. The respected father of Sayyidī A'lā Ḥaḍrat Sayyidunā Naqī 'Alī Khān رَحْمَةُ اللهِ تَعَالٰى عَلَيْه has stated on page 7 of '*Aḥsan-ul-Wi'ā li Ādāb-id-Du'ā*':

Three advantages of Du'ā

The Noble Prophet صَلَّى اللهُ تَعَالٰى عَلَيْهِ وَاٰلِهٖ وَسَلَّم has said that every Du'ā contains at least one of the following three advantages:

1. Either his (the one who makes supplication) sin is forgiven or
2. He gets benefit or
3. He will get its reward in the afterlife. In the afterlife when man sees the reward of his prayers that were not answered in the world, he will wish that none of his prayers would be answered in the world and all would be stored for the afterlife. *(Attarghīb Wattarĥīb, vol. 2, pp. 315)*

Five blessings in Du'ā

Dear Islamic brothers! Did you see! Supplications are always beneficial. Therefore, one should not be lazy in making supplication even if its effect does not appear in the world as its reward will surely be given in the Hereafter.

Five Madanī pearls

1. By making Du'ā one fulfills a commandment of Allah عَزَّوَجَلَّ as He عَزَّوَجَلَّ has commanded us to make Du'ā. Therefore, the Holy Quran says:

اُدْعُوْنِیْۤ اَسْتَجِبْ لَكُمْ ؕ

Pray to Me, I shall answer your prayer.

[Kanz-ul-Īmān (Translation of Quran)] (Part 24, Sūraĥ Al-Mūmin, verse 60)

2. Making Du'ā is a Sunnaĥ because the Prophet of Raḥmaĥ, the Intercessor of Ummaĥ, the Owner of Jannaĥ صَلَّى اللهُ تَعَالٰى عَلَيْهِ وَاٰلِهٖ وَسَلَّم often used to make Du'ā. Therefore, making Du'ā leads us to practicing a Sunnaĥ.

3. Making Du'ā is obedience to Rasūlullāĥ صَلَّى اللّٰهُ تَعَالٰى عَلَيْهِ وَاٰلِهٖ وَسَلَّم as well because he صَلَّى اللهُ تَعَالٰى عَلَيْهِ وَاٰلِهٖ وَسَلَّم would advise his devotees to make Du'ā.

4. By making Du'ā, one enters the fold of worshippers because Du'ā is a form of worship, it has even been regarded as the essence of worship. The Prophet of Raḥmaĥ, the Intercessor of Ummaĥ, the Owner of Jannaĥ صَلَّى اللهُ تَعَالٰى عَلَيْهِ وَاٰلِهٖ وَسَلَّم has said:

اَلدُّعَآءُ مُخُّ الْعِبَادَةِ

Translation: 'Du'ā (supplication) is the very essence of worship.'

(Jāmi' Tirmiżī, vol. 5, pp. 243, Ḥadīš 3382)

5. Du'ā entitles one either to the forgiveness of his sins or ease of difficulty in the world or acquisition of reward in the Hereafter.

What sin have I committed?

Dear Islamic brothers! Did you see! By making Du'ā one not only obeys Allah عَزَّوَجَلَّ and His Beloved Rasūl صَلَّى اللهُ تَعَالٰى عَلَيْهِ وَاٰلِهٖ وَسَلَّم but also acts upon a Sunnaĥ, earns the reward of worshipping, and gains numerous other benefits in the world as well as the Hereafter.

Some people are very impatient if there is some delay in the fulfilment of their supplications. They are observed saying even such inappropriate sentences as 'I've been making Du'ā for so long, I've had even pious people make Du'ā for me, there's not a single Pīr I haven't been to, I recite a lot of invocations, I've been to the tombs of saints but Allah عَزَّوَجَلَّ still doesn't fulfil my supplication.' Some even dare to say: 'What sin have I committed, which has resulted in this punishment?'

Is missing Ṣalāĥ not sin!

If such an emotional person is asked if he offers Ṣalāĥ, he will perhaps reply in the negative. Did you see! The words of complaint that 'What sin have I committed, which has resulted in this punishment?' are being expressed openly despite committing the major sin of missing Ṣalāĥ. In other words, it seems, (Allah عَزَّوَجَلَّ forbid) missing Ṣalāĥ isn't a sin at all! If such people just have a look at themselves, they can realize that let alone any misdeed, they are, in fact, committing many misdeeds such as non-Islamic haircut, bare head like the Western people, non-Islamic dress, face like fire worshippers who are the enemies of the Beloved Rasūl صَلَّى اللهُ تَعَالٰى عَلَيْهِ وَاٰلِهٖ وَسَلَّم i.e. without a beard which is a blessed Sunnaĥ of the Holy Prophet صَلَّى اللهُ تَعَالٰى عَلَيْهِ وَاٰلِهٖ وَسَلَّم; following the cultures and traditions of the enemies of Islam and missing even Ṣalāĥ.

Missing Ṣalāĥ is a major sin, shaving the beard is prohibited (Ḥarām), lying, backbiting, telling tales, breaking promises, suspicion, misusing eyes, disobeying parents, abusing, watching films and dramas, listening to music etc. are all sins, but these sins seem invisible to such people and they complain openly 'What misdeed have I done, which has resulted in this punishment?'

If we don't listen to our friend...

Just ponder! If your best friend repeatedly asks you to do something but you don't do it and if you ever need his help, so at first, you will obviously hesitate to ask him because you didn't help him when he needed you. Plucking up the courage, even if you dare to ask him and he doesn't listen then you will not be justified in complaining because you also did not help him.

Now just ponder calmly, there are many things that Allah عَزَّوَجَلَّ has ordered us to do, but how many of them do we actually carry out? To put it bluntly, we are heedless of many of His commandments. I hope you may have understood that Allah's commands are disobeyed and if He عَزَّوَجَلَّ does not manifest the effect of Du'ā then complaints are made. Is it fair?

Please! Try to realize! If you keep on ignoring what your best friend says he might even break ties with you, but look how merciful Allah عَزَّوَجَلَّ is towards His servants. They disobey Him thousands of times but He عَزَّوَجَلَّ still does not exclude them from of the list of His servants, He عَزَّوَجَلَّ continues to shower His grace and mercy upon them.

Ponder! What will happen if He عَزَّوَجَلَّ ceases His bounties as a punishment? We can't even lift a single step without His mercy. If He عَزَّوَجَلَّ stops the free gift of air for just a few minutes the whole world will turn into a gigantic graveyard.

A reason of delay in fulfilment of Du'ā

Dear Islamic brothers! Sometimes, delay in the fulfilment of Du'ā takes place due to such reasons which are beyond our comprehension. Therefore, the Prophet of mankind, the Peace of our heart and mind, the most Generous and Kind صَلَّى اللهُ تَعَالٰى عَلَيْهِ وَاٰلِهٖ وَسَلَّم has said: When a beloved of Allah makes supplication Allah عَزَّوَجَلَّ says to Jibrāīl عَلَيْهِ السَّلَام, 'Wait! Don't give him (anything) so that he asks again because I like his voice' (but) when an unbeliever or a sinner makes supplication He عَزَّوَجَلَّ says, 'O Jibrāīl عَلَيْهِ السَّلَام give him without delay what he wants so that he does not ask again because I don't like his voice.' *(Kanz-ul-'Ummāl, vol. 2, pp. 39, Ḥadīš 3261)*

Parable

Sayyidunā Yaḥyā Bin Sa'īd Bin Qaṭṭān رَضِىَ اللهُ تَعَالٰى عَنْهُ saw Allah عَزَّوَجَلَّ in a dream and asked, 'Yā Allah عَزَّوَجَلَّ! I make supplication abundantly (but) You don't fulfill my supplication?' Allah عَزَّوَجَلَّ replied, 'O Yaḥyā! I like your voice, which is why I delay in fulfilling your supplications.' *(Aḥsan-ul-Wi'ā, pp. 35)*

صَلُّوْا عَلَى الْحَبِيْب صَلَّى اللهُ تَعَالٰى عَلٰى مُحَمَّد

Dear Islamic brothers! The foregoing parable as well as blessed Ḥadīš clarify that Allah عَزَّوَجَلَّ likes the humility of His pious people, which is one of the reasons for the delay in the fulfilment of their supplications. We cannot comprehend these divine strategies. Anyhow, we must not be impatient. Maulānā Naqī 'Alī Khān رَحْمَةُاللهِتَعَالٰی عَلَيْه has stated on page 33 of his book *Aḥsan-ul-Wi'ā* whilst mentioning the manners of making supplication:

Prayers of impatient people are not answered

One of the manners of supplications is to avoid impatience regarding the fulfilment of supplication. A Ḥadīš says: There are three types of people whose prayers are not answered by Allah عَزَّوَجَلَّ. (1) Those who pray for a sin. (2) Those who pray for breaking ties. (3) Those who want their prayers to be answered immediately and say 'My prayer hasn't been answered yet.' *(Attarghīb Wattarĥīb, vol. 2, pp. 314, Ḥadīš 9)*

This Ḥadīš makes it clear that one should not pray for unlawful things because such a prayer will not be answered. Similarly, the prayer that involves the violation of the rights of a relative is also prohibited. Further, one should not grow impatient with apparent delays in the fulfilment of his prayers as such prayers are not answered.

A'lā Ḥaḍrat, Imām-e-Aĥl-e-Sunnat Maulānā Shāĥ Aḥmad Razā Khān عَلَيْهِ رَحْمَةُ الرَّحْمٰن has added a footnote to *Aḥsan-ul-Wi'ā li Ādāb-id-Du'ā* titled *Żail-ul-Mudda'ā li Aḥsan-il-Wi'ā*. In this footnote, he (in his own particular and unique manner) has given the following advice to people who are impatient regarding the fulfilment of their supplications.

Visiting officers again and again but...

Those who have to get any personal advantage from worldly officers are seen waiting for years hoping to be helped by them and wandering around their doorsteps morning and night. As for the officers, they don't even look at them, don't answer them, scold them and express resentment. In fact, it is nothing but the waste of time and money. Even after spending years wandering around the officers, they do not give up hope, and it looks as if it is still the first day.

And when it comes to making supplication in the court of Almighty Allah عَزَّوَجَلَّ, one rarely goes to Him, and even if somebody goes, he looks tired and worried, wants everything instantly; he spends a week reciting something and then starts complaining,

'I recited this, but nothing happened.' Such unwise people close the door of fulfilment themselves. The Prophet of Raḥmaĥ, the Intercessor of Ummaĥ صَلَّى اللهُ تَعَالٰى عَلَيْهِ وَاٰلِهٖ وَسَلَّم has said:

يُسْتَجَابُ لِاَحَدِكُمْ مَا لَمْ يُعَجِّلْ يَقُوْلُ دَعَوْتُ فَلَمْ يَسْتَجِبْ لِيْ

Translation: Your prayers are answered as long as you don't hurry, don't say I prayed (but) my prayer wasn't answered.

(Ṣaḥīḥ Bukhārī, vol. 4, pp. 200, Ḥadīš 6340)

Some even dare to deny the effect of supplications and invocations. In fact, they lose trust in the promises of bounties Allah عَزَّوَجَلَّ has made – وَالْعِيَاذُ بِاللّٰهِ الْكَرِيْمِ الْجَوَّاد

These people should be told 'O the shameless! O the undignified! Ponder calmly. If your friend asks you a thousand times to do something for him but you don't, then you'll hesitate to ask him to do something for you and say to yourself 'I didn't listen to him, how can I ask him for something' but if you dare to ask him and he doesn't do it, then you won't complain and you'll say to yourself 'well, I also didn't do what he asked.' Now compare; how many of the commandments of Allah عَزَّوَجَلَّ do you obey? How shameful is it for you to disobey Him and then want Him to do what you ask?

O unwise person! Just look carefully at yourself from head to toe. There are millions of bounties in your body. When you sleep His innocent servants (angels) protect you. Despite committing sins you are blessed with safety and good health from head to toe, protection from calamities, easy digestion of food, discharge of excrement without difficulty, easy circulation of blood in your body, physical strength, eyesight, numerous bounties descend upon you constantly without having to ask or pray (for them). Then how can you dare to complain if some of your desires are not fulfilled? You don't know what is beneficial to you? You don't know that you were perhaps going to suffer a major calamity but it's your (apparently unfulfilled) supplication that warded it off.

What do you know what reward is being stored for you. His promise is true, prayers are answered in three ways and every former one is better than the latter. If you lose faith then surely you will be doomed and the devil would take you to his side - وَالْعِيَاذُ بِاللّٰهِ سُبْحٰنَهٗ وَتَعَالٰی (*We seek Allah's protection, He* عَزَّوَجَلَّ *is the Glorious*).

O feeble soil! O impure water! Look at yourself and then look at the great privilege you have been granted. He عَزَّوَجَلَّ has permitted you to be present in His court, mention His Glorious name and beg Him. Millions of desires should be sacrificed on this enormous grace.

O impatient! Learn how to beg! Cling to His Glorious court, stay there and keep supplicating in the hope of being blessed. Engross yourself in the pleasure of begging and asking Him so much that you forget even your desires and wishes. Have a firm belief that you will not return from His court empty handed because مَنْ دَقَّ بَابَ الْكَرِيْمِ اِنْفَتَحْ (*When anyone knocks at the door of a generous person it opens for him*) وَبِاللّٰهِ التَّوْفِيْق (*And ability is granted by Allah* عَزَّوَجَلَّ). *(Żaīl-ul-Mudda'ā li Aḥsan-il-Wi'ā, pp. 34-37)*

Delay in fulfilment of Du'ā is blessing

Sayyidunā Maulānā Naqī 'Alī Khān رَحْمَةُ اللّٰهِ تَعَالٰی عَلَیْه has said, 'My dear! Your Allah عَزَّوَجَلَّ says:

I answer the prayer of the praying one when he prays to Me. اُجِيْبُ دَعْوَةَ الدَّاعِ اِذَا دَعَانِ

[Kanz-ul-Īmān (Translation of Quran)] (Part 2, Sūraĥ Al-Baqaraĥ, verse 186)

And how excellent fulfiller (of supplication) We are. فَلَنِعْمَ الْمُجِيْبُوْنَ ﴿۷۵﴾

[Kanz-ul-Īmān (Translation of Quran)] (Part 23, Sūraĥ Aṣ-Ṣāffāt, verse 75)

Pray to Me, I shall answer your prayer. اُدْعُوْنِيْٓ اَسْتَجِبْ لَكُمْ ؕ

[Kanz-ul-Īmān (Translation of Quran)] (Part 24, Sūraĥ Al-Mūmin, verse 60)

So believe that He عَزَّوَجَلَّ will not return you empty handed from His court and He عَزَّوَجَلَّ will fulfil His promise. He عَزَّوَجَلَّ says to His Beloved and Blessed Prophet صَلَّى اللّٰهُ تَعَالٰى عَلَيْهِ وَاٰلِهٖ وَسَلَّم:

And chide not the beggar. وَ اَمَّا السَّآئِلَ فَلَا تَنْهَرْ ﴿۱۰﴾

[Kanz-ul-Īmān (Translation of Quran)] (Part 30, Sūraĥ Aḍ-Ḍuḥā, verse 10)

(So then) how will He عَزَّوَجَلَّ (himself) reject you? In fact, He عَزَّوَجَلَّ blesses you, which is why He عَزَّوَجَلَّ delays in fulfilling your supplications.' اَلْحَمْدُ لِلّٰهِ عَلٰى كُلِّ حَالٍ *(Aḥsan-ul-Wi'ā, pp. 33)*

Relief from sciatica pain

Dear Islamic brothers! اَلْحَمْدُ لِلّٰه عَزَّوَجَلَّ There are a number of instances of prayers being answered in the company of devotees of Rasūl by the blessing of travelling with the Madanī Qāfilaĥs of Dawat-e-Islami, a global & non-political religious movement of the Quran and Sunnaĥ. Here is an account of an Islamic brother in this regard: Our Madanī Qāfilaĥ went to Thatta city. One of the participants had severe sciatica pain. He used to writhe in pain like a fish out of water. One night he couldn't sleep due to severe pain. On the last day the Amīr of Qāfilaĥ said: 'Let's all pray for him together', so we began to pray.

The Islamic brother said that he felt reduction in pain even during the prayer and surprisingly the sciatica pain completely vanished after a short while, اَلْحَمْدُ لِلّٰه عَزَّوَجَلَّ. Many years have passed, he has not felt the same pain again ever since he was relieved of it during the Madanī Qāfilaĥ. اَلْحَمْدُ لِلّٰه عَزَّوَجَلَّ At present, he is responsible for Madanī Qāfilaĥs in his area.

Gar ĥo 'irqun-nisā, yā 'ārizaĥ koī sā
Pāo gey ṣiḥḥatayn, Qāfilay mayn chalo
Dūr bīmāriyān, aur parayshāniyān
Ĥaun gī bas chal pařayn, Qāfilay mayn chalo

If you have sciatica severe, or have illness any other
You will get cured brother, travel with Madanī Qāfilaĥ
Illnesses will be cured and adversities will be removed
Come and see for yourself, travel with Madanī Qāfilaĥ

صَلُّوْا عَلَى الْحَبِيْب　　صَلَّى اللّٰهُ تَعَالٰى عَلٰى مُحَمَّد

Dear Islamic brothers! Did you see! An Islamic brother was relieved of the lethal illness of sciatica by the blessing of a Madanī Qāfilaĥ. Sciatica is an illness that causes extreme pain extending from the hip joint down to the ankle and it continues for years.

Two spiritual remedies for sciatica

1. Place your hand on the painful area, recite Sūraĥ Al-Fātiḥaĥ once and the following phrase اَللّٰهُمَّ اَذْهِبْ عَنِّیْ سُوْءَ مَا اَجِدُ (*Yā Allah* عَزَّوَجَلَّ *relieve me of this illness*) three times (with Ṣalāt-'Alan-Nabī once before and after it) and then blow on the area of the pain. If you want to do it for someone else, then say عَنْهُ (him) instead of عَنِّیْ (me). This is to be done until the illness is cured.

2. Reciting یَا مُحْیِیْ seven times and blowing on oneself will cure wind problems, back and stomach pains, sciatica or any other pain اِنْ شَآءَاللّٰه عَزَّوَجَلَّ. (This is to be done until the pain is cured).

Fourteen points regarding acts that invalidate fast

1. Eating, drinking or having intercourse will result in the invalidation of the fast provided one was aware that he was fasting. *(Rad-dul-Muḥtār, vol. 3, pp. 365)*

2. Smoking a Ḥuqqaĥ, cigar, cigarette or cheroot etc. will also invalidate the fast even if one assumes that the smoke has not reached the throat. *(Baĥār-e-Sharī'at, part 5, pp. 117)*

3. Chewing Pān (betel) or tobacco will also invalidate the fast even if one spits constantly because its tiny particles will definitely reach the throat. *(ibid)*

4. If a fasting person puts something soluble like sugar etc. in his mouth and then swallows his saliva, his fast will become invalid. *(ibid)*

5. If something equal to the size of a chick-pea or larger was stuck between the teeth of a fasting person and he swallowed it, or if it was smaller than a chick-pea but he took it out from the mouth and then put it back in and swallowed it, his fast will become invalid in both the cases. *(Durr-e-Mukhtār, vol. 3, pp. 394)*

6. If gums bleed and blood goes down the throat and its taste is also felt (regardless of whether or not the amount of blood is equal to, more than or less than the saliva) the fast will become invalid in this case, but if the amount of blood is less than saliva and the taste of blood is not felt either, the fast will not become invalid. *(Durr-e-Mukhtār, Rad-dul-Muḥtār, vol. 3, pp. 368)*

7. Despite being aware that he was fasting, if a fasting person inserts a laxative (a medicine) into the anal orifice or inhales medicine through nostrils, his fast will become invalid. *(Fatāwā 'Ālamgīrī, vol. 1, pp. 204)*

8. If water went down the throat unintentionally whilst rinsing the mouth, or if one sniffed water through nose and it reached the brain then the fast will become invalid. However, if it happens in forgetfulness (when one was unaware that he was fasting) fast will not be invalid even if he does it deliberately. Likewise, if someone throws something towards the fasting person and it goes down the throat, his fast will become invalid. *(Al-Jauĥara-tun-Nayyaraĥ, vol. 1, pp. 178)*

9. Drinking or eating something whilst asleep will result in the invalidation of the fast. Similarly, if the mouth of a fasting person was open and a drop of water or a flake of snow goes down his throat his fast will become invalid. *(Al-Jauĥara-tun-Nayyaraĥ, vol. 1, pp. 178)*

10. Swallowing another person's saliva or putting one's own saliva onto one's palm and then swallowing it will invalidate the fast. *(Fatāwā 'Ālamgīrī, vol. 1, pp. 203)*

11. Swallowing the saliva or phlegm that is already in the mouth does not invalidate the fast, spitting the saliva every now and then is not necessary.

12. If one put a coloured string into his mouth, which changes the colour of the saliva and then he swallowed that coloured saliva, his fast would become invalid. *(Fatāwā 'Ālamgīrī, vol. 1, pp. 203)*

13. Swallowing one or two drops of tear will not invalidate the fast, but swallowing many drops whose saltiness is felt in the whole mouth will result in the invalidation of the fast. The same ruling applies to sweat. *(Fatāwā 'Ālamgīrī, vol. 1, pp. 203)*

14. During defecation (i.e. relieving oneself), if the anal orifice appears out, one must dry it properly with a piece of cloth etc. before standing up so that there remains no wetness. If he stands up with drops of water on the anus, causing the water to be absorbed into the body, the fast will become invalid. This is the reason why the respected Islamic jurists رَحِمَهُمُ اللّٰه تَعَالٰی have advised the fasting persons to avoid breathing whilst washing the anus [after defecation]. *(Fatāwā 'Ālamgīrī, vol. 1, pp. 204)*

Vomiting whilst fasting

Some people become worried in case of vomiting in the state of fast. Some are under the impression that vomiting even involuntarily also breaks the fast. This isn't correct. Sayyidunā Abū Ĥurayraĥ رَضِىَ اللّٰهُ تَعَالٰى عَنْهُ has narrated that the Noble Prophet صَلَّى اللّٰهُ تَعَالٰى عَلَيْهِ وَاٰلِهٖ وَسَلَّم has said, 'The fast of a person who vomits involuntarily in Ramadan will not break but if a person vomits deliberately it will break.' *(Kanz-ul-'Ummāl, vol. 8, pp. 230, Ḥadīš 23814)*

He صَلَّى اللّٰهُ تَعَالٰى عَلَيْهِ وَاٰلِهٖ وَسَلَّم has also said, 'The one who vomits involuntarily does not have to do Qaḍā (repetition) for his fast but the one who vomits deliberately must do Qaḍā.' *(Jāmi' Tirmiżī, vol. 2, pp. 173, Ḥadīš 720)*

Seven rulings regarding vomiting

1. In the state of fast, vomiting involuntarily will not invalidate the fast, no matter how much it is (even if a whole bucket fills with vomit). *(Durr-e-Mukhtār, vol. 3, pp. 392)*

2. Deliberate mouthful vomiting will invalidate the fast provided one was aware that he was fasting. *(Durr-e-Mukhtār, vol. 3, pp. 392)*

3. Even deliberate mouthful vomiting will invalidate the fast only when the vomit contains food or water or bile or blood. *(ibid)*

4. Vomiting only phlegm will not invalidate the fast. *(ibid, pp. 394)*

5. Vomiting only a bit (not a mouthful) deliberately will not invalidate the fast. *(Durr-e-Mukhtār, vol. 3, pp. 393)*

6. In case of vomiting less than a mouthful and then swallowing it whilst it is still in the mouth (regardless of whether it is swallowed deliberately or unintentionally) the fast will not become invalid. *(ibid)*

7. Though involuntary mouthful vomiting will not invalidate the fast if one swallows even a chick-pea amount of it, the fast will become invalid. However, if the swallowed amount is less than the size of a chick-pea, the fast will not become invalid. *(Durr-e-Mukhtār, vol. 3, pp. 392)*

Definition of mouthful vomit

The vomit that cannot be prevented without bother is 'mouthful vomit.'

(Fatāwā 'Ālamgīrī, vol. 1, pp. 204)

Five rulings regarding vomiting in state of Wuḍū

1. In the state of Wuḍū, mouthful vomiting that contains food, water or bile will invalidate the Wuḍū (regardless of whether it is deliberate or involuntary). *(Bahār-e-Sharī'at, pp. 26, part 2)*

2. Mouthful vomiting of phlegm will not invalidate the Wuḍū. *(ibid)*

3. Vomiting of flowing blood will invalidate the Wuḍū.

4. Vomiting of flowing blood will invalidate the Wuḍū only when the blood dominates the saliva. *(Rad-dul-Muḥtār, vol. 1, pp. 267)* In other words, if the blood turns the saliva red then it is dominant and therefore Wuḍū will be invalid but if there is more saliva than blood then Wuḍū will not be invalid. The sign of the blood being in less amount is that the vomit (of saliva) will be yellow in colour.

5. If the vomit contains congealed blood that is less than a mouthful, Wuḍū will not be invalid. *(Derived from Bahār-e-Sharī'at, pp. 26, part 2)*

Important advice

Mouthful vomit (excluding phlegm) is impure. Ensure that not even a single drop of it stains your clothes or body. Today people are not aware of it and do not care about drops of vomit, staining their clothes. They even wipe the impure vomit from their mouths etc. with their own clothes. May Allah عَزَّوَجَلَّ enable us to protect ourselves from impurities!

اٰمِيْن بِجَاهِ النَّبِيِّ الْاَمِيْن صَلَّى اللّٰه تَعَالٰى عَلَيْهِ وَاٰلِهٖ وَسَلَّم

صَلُّوْا عَلَى الْحَبِيْب صَلَّى اللّٰهُ تَعَالٰى عَلٰى مُحَمَّد

Eating or drinking forgetfully will not invalidate fast

Sayyidunā Abū Ĥurayrah رَضِىَ اللّٰهُ تَعَالٰى عَنْهُ has narrated that the Prophet of mankind, the Peace of our heart and mind, the most Generous and Kind صَلَّى اللّٰهُ تَعَالٰى عَلَيْهِ وَاٰلِهٖ وَسَلَّم has said, 'The fasting person who eats or drinks forgetfully has to complete his fast because Allah عَزَّوَجَلَّ has fed him.' *(Ṣaḥīḥ Bukhārī, vol. 1, pp. 636, Ḥadīš 1933)*

Twenty one points about acts that do not invalidate fast

1. Eating, drinking or having intercourse forgetfully will not invalidate the fast whether it is a Farḍ fast or a Nafl one. *(Durr-e-Mukhtār, Rad-dul-Muḥtār, vol. 3, pp. 365)*

2. If someone sees a fasting person do any of such acts, it is Wājib for him to remind the fasting person of his fast. If he did not remind, he will be sinner.

   However, if the person is too weak and is unlikely to complete his fast properly in case of not eating the food because of being reminded and, on the other hand, if he eats food, he will not only be able to complete his fast properly but also carry out other worship (and as he is eating forgetfully, his fast will be valid) then it is better not to remind him.

   Some respected scholars رَحِمَهُمُ اللّٰهُ تَعَالٰى have said, 'If the fasting person is young one should remind him but if he's old then there's no harm in not reminding him', but this rule is based on the fact that the young are generally strong (and healthy) and the old are generally weak. In fact, this ruling has nothing to do with old-age and young-age, instead, it applies on the basis of strength and weakness. In other words, if a young man is too weak to complete his fast, it is better not to remind him, and if an old man is strong enough to complete his fast properly, it is Wājib to remind him. *(Rad-dul-Muḥtār, vol. 3, pp. 365)*

3. If a fly or dust or smoke goes down the throat, the fast will not become invalid even if one was aware that he was fasting. Whether it is the flour blowing up whilst being grinded in the grindstone or sieved or it is the dust of grain or dust that is blown by the wind or the hoofs of animals, the fast will not become invalid if the dust goes down the throat in the aforementioned cases. *(Durr-e-Mukhtār, Rad-dul-Muḥtār, vol. 3, pp. 366)*

4. Similarly, if the car or bus smoke or the blowing dust reaches the throat, it will not invalidate the fast even if one was aware that he was fasting.

5. If the smoke of a burning incense stick enters the nose, fast will not be invalid. However, if one takes his nose closer to a burning incense or frankincense and (deliberately) inhales the smoke despite being aware that he was fasting, his fast will become invalid. *(Rad-dul-Muḥtār, vol. 3, pp. 366)*

6. Treating the heat of the body by placing a pierced horn over the area of pain, massaging oil or applying kohl (into eyes) will not invalidate the fast; even if one feels the taste of oil or kohl in throat or even if the colour of the 'kohl' appears in saliva. *(Al-Jauĥara-tun-Nayyaraĥ, vol. 1, pp. 179)*

7. Fast will not be invalid in case of feeling the coolness of the water inside the body after taking bath. *(Fatāwā 'Ālamgīrī, vol. 1, pp. 230)*

8. If one rinses the mouth with water and spits the water out completely, just a little wetness has remained inside the mouth; swallowing this wetness with saliva will not invalidate the fast. *(Rad-dul-Muḥtār, vol. 3, pp. 367)*

9. The fast will not be invalid even if the taste of the medicine being crushed is felt in the throat. *(ibid)*

10. The fast will not be invalid if water enters the ear or even if one pours it deliberately. *(Durr-e-Mukhtār, vol. 3, pp. 367)*

11. Inserting a splinter into the ear to itch it does not invalidate the fast. Even if the splinter comes into contact with ear-dirt and this act is repeatedly done, the fast will not become invalid. *(ibid)*

12. If a tiny particle was in the mouth or was stuck between the teeth and it goes down the throat with saliva, the fast will not become invalid. *(ibid)*

13. If the gums bleed and the blood reaches the throat but does not go down the throat, fast will not be invalid in this case. *(Fatḥ-ul-Qadīr, vol. 2, pp. 258)*

14. Swallowing a fly unintentionally will not invalidate the fast but swallowing it deliberately will invalidate the fast. *(Fatāwā 'Ālamgīrī, vol. 1, pp. 203)*

15. If somebody eats food or drinks water forgetfully, but he spits out the food or water from mouth as soon as he recalls the fast, then his fast will not become invalid, but if he swallows the morsel of food or water that was in his mouth despite recalling the fast, the fast will become invalid. *(ibid)*

16. If a person who was eating before dawn spits out everything in his mouth as soon as the time for Saḥarī ends, his fast will not be invalid but if he swallows the food etc. that was in his mouth, his fast will be invalid. *(Fatāwā 'Ālamgīrī, vol. 1, pp. 203)*

17. Backbiting does not invalidate the fast. *(Durr-e-Mukhtār, vol. 3, pp. 362)* However, backbiting is a major sin. The Holy Quran refers to backbiting as 'eating one's dead brother's flesh' and a Ḥadīš states that 'backbiting is worse than even fornication.' *(Attarghīb Wattarĥīb, vol. 3, pp. 331, Ḥadīš 24)* Backbiting removes the blessings of the fast. *(Baĥār-e-Sharī'at, part 5, pp. 611)*

18. Being in the state of major impurity (when taking ritual bath is obligatory) or even spending the whole day in this impure state will not invalidate the fast. *(Durr-e-Mukhtār, vol. 3, pp. 372)* However, remaining in this state deliberately and missing Ṣalāĥ is a sin and Ḥarām. A Ḥadīš states that the angels of mercy do not enter the house in which there is a 'Junub' (the one who is in the state of major impurity). *(Baĥār-e-Sharī'at, part 5, pp. 116)*

19. If one chews a sesame seed or a tiny particle equal to a sesame seed in size which then goes down the throat with saliva, his fast will not be invalid, however, the fast will be invalid if its taste is felt in the throat. *(Fatḥ-ul-Qadīr, vol. 2, pp. 259)*

20. Swallowing saliva or phlegm of the mouth will not invalidate the fast. *(Rad-dul-Muḥtār, vol. 3, pp. 373)*

21. Swallowing the dried mucus of the nose by inhaling will not invalidate the fast. *(ibid)*

Makrūĥ acts in fasting

Let's have a look at the Makrūĥ acts of fast. Though the fast does not become invalid in case of committing these unpleasant acts, they affect the spirituality of the fast. Here are three blessed Aḥādīš in this regard.

1. Sayyidunā Abū Ĥurayraĥ رَضِیَ اللّٰہُ تَعَالٰی عَنْہُ has narrated that the Beloved and Blessed Prophet صَلَّی اللّٰہُ تَعَالٰی عَلَیْہِ وَاٰلِہٖ وَسَلَّم has said, 'If someone doesn't avoid indecent speech and acts, Allah عَزَّوَجَلَّ doesn't need such a person as he has just left eating and drinking.' *(Ṣaḥīḥ Bukhārī, vol. 1, pp. 628, Ḥadīš 1903)*

2. Sayyidunā Abū Ĥurayraĥ رَضِیَ اللّٰہُ تَعَالٰی عَنْہُ has reported that the Prophet of Raḥmaĥ, the Intercessor of Ummaĥ صَلَّی اللّٰہُ تَعَالٰی عَلَیْہِ وَاٰلِہٖ وَسَلَّم has said, 'The fast is like a shield unless it is torn.' He صَلَّی اللّٰہُ تَعَالٰی عَلَیْہِ وَاٰلِہٖ وَسَلَّم was asked as to how the shield is torn, he صَلَّی اللّٰہُ تَعَالٰی عَلَیْہِ وَاٰلِہٖ وَسَلَّم replied 'By lying or backbiting.' *(Attarghīb Wattarĥīb, vol. 2, pp. 94, Ḥadīš 3)*

3. Sayyidunā 'Āmir Bin Rabī'aĥ رَضِیَ اللّٰہُ تَعَالٰی عَنْہُمَا has said, 'I have repeatedly seen the Holy Prophet صَلَّی اللّٰہُ تَعَالٰی عَلَیْہِ وَاٰلِہٖ وَسَلَّم use a Miswāk in the state of fast.' *(Jāmi' Tirmiżī, vol. 2, pp. 176, Ḥadīš 725)*

Twelve points about Makrūĥ acts in fasts

1. Lying, telling tales, backbiting, unlawful use of eyes, abusing, hurting someone without the permission of Sharī'aĥ, shaving beard etc. all are already prohibited and Ḥarām acts and committing them in the state of fast is even more severely Ḥarām. These sins remove the spirituality of the fast.

2. It is Makrūĥ for a fasting person to unnecessarily taste or chew any thing.

   Tasting food to make sure that salt has been mixed into food in required quantity is a valid exemption for a wife whose ill tempered husband gets annoyed if the food is not to his liking. There is no harm for her in tasting food in this case. Chewing food to make it soft (and edible) for her child is a valid exemption for a mother whose child cannot eat bread and she doesn't have any other soft food to feed the child. She can chew food in this case provided there's no such woman who is experiencing her menses or post natal bleeding[1] or anyone else who can chew the food for the child. Therefore, chewing food to make it soft for a child is not Makrūĥ for her. *(Durr-e-Mukhtār, vol. 3, pp. 395)* However, one must be extremely careful when tasting or chewing food (even for valid reasons) because if one swallows even a small amount, the fast will become invalid.

What is meant by 'tasting?'

Tasting does not imply what people today regard as 'tasting' i.e. 'eating a bit to know the flavour of the food.' This isn't 'tasting' instead, it's 'eating' that will invalidate fast, and if the conditions of expiation are met one will have to give the expiation for it either. Tasting simply means placing a little amount of food onto the tongue to taste its flavour and then spitting it out. It must not be swallowed even in the least amount.

3. There is no harm in tasting the food etc. that one intends to buy in order to avoid the loss of money. However, if there is no such risk, it is Makrūĥ. *(Durr-e-Mukhtār, vol. 3, pp. 395)*

4. Kissing the wife, hugging her or touching her body is not Makrūĥ. However, if one fears that it will lead to ejaculation or intercourse (then it is Makrūĥ). Sucking her lips or tongue during fast is absolutely Makrūĥ. Making sex organs touch each other is also Makrūĥ during fast[2]. *(Rad-dul-Muḥtār, vol. 3, pp. 396)*

5. Smelling a rose, musk etc., applying oil into beard or moustache, and applying kohl into eyes are not Makrūĥ for a fasting person. *(Durr-e-Mukhtār, vol. 3, pp. 397)*

6. There is no harm in smelling or applying any type of 'Iṭr (perfume) onto clothes in the state of fast. *(Rad-dul-Muḥtār, vol. 3, pp. 397)*

7. Using a Miswāk in the state of fast is not Makrūĥ. As it is a Sunnaĥ in other days, it is a Sunnaĥ in fast as well whether it is dry or wet, and whether it is used before the Shar'ī midday or after that, it isn't Makrūĥ any time. *(Rad-dul-Muḥtār, vol. 3, pp. 399)*

---

[1] In the state of menses or post-natal bleeding, it is impermissible and sin for women to fast, offer Ṣalāĥ and recite the Holy Quran. After attaining purity they do not need to make Qaḍā for their Ṣalāĥ but they will have to make Qaḍā for their fasts.

[2] In order to acquire the knowledge of intentions etc., the married men and women should go through point numbers 41, 42 given on the page 385 and 386 of *Fatāwā Razawiyyaĥ*, vol. 23.

8. Most people are under the impression that it is Makrūĥ for a fasting person to use a Miswāk after noon. This is contrary to our Ḥanafī school of thought. *(ibid)*

9. A fasting person should not use such a Miswāk whose strands break off (into mouth) or whose taste is felt in the mouth. *(Fatāwā Razawiyyaĥ referenced, vol. 10, pp. 511)* If a strand of Miswāk or its fragment goes down the throat the fast will become invalid (provided one was aware that he was fasting).

10. It is not Makrūĥ to rinse the mouth or sniff water into the nose or have a bath (apart from performing Wuḍū or obligatory Ghusl) or moisten the body with a wet cloth in order to cool oneself down. However, it is Makrūĥ to wrap a wet cloth around the body showing worry because showing disinterest in worshipping is not good. *(Rad-dul-Muḥtār, vol. 3, pp. 399)*

11. Some fasting Islamic brothers spit repeatedly. They are perhaps under the impression that one shouldn't swallow even his own saliva in fast, whereas it is not correct. However, (deliberately) accumulating saliva in the mouth and then swallowing it is Makrūĥ (it is very unpleasant to do this even when one is not fasting). *(Bahār-e-Sharī'at, pp. 129, part 5)*

12. In the month of Ramadan, it is not permissible to do such a laborious and hard work that causes such intense weakness that makes it probable to break the fast. Therefore, a chapatti (bread) maker should bake chapattis till the afternoon and then take rest for the rest of the day. *(Durr-e-Mukhtār, vol. 3, pp. 400)* The same applies to labourers, builders, masons and the people doing other laborious work. If such people fear that work will cause intense weakness, they should reduce the amount of work so that they can complete their fast (properly).

Piece of paper fell from sky

Dear Islamic brothers! In order to develop enthusiasm to learn the legal rulings of Sharī'aĥ, please travel with devotees of Rasūl of Dawat-e-Islami, a global & non-political religious movement of the Quran and Sunnaĥ. Please travel at least once, اِنْ شَآءَاللّٰه عَزَّوَجَلَّ you will experience such religious benefits that you will be surprised.

The blessing of a Madanī Qāfilaĥ is now presented for your persuasion. Therefore, an Islamic brother of Qasba colony (Bāb-ul-Madīnaĥ, Karachi) has stated: We had many daughters in our family; my uncle had seven daughters while my elder brother had nine daughters and when I got married my wife also gave birth to a baby girl. Like many other people, my family also got worried and suspected as to whether somebody had cast a magic spell preventing the birth of baby boys. I vowed to travel for 30 days in a Madanī Qāfilaĥ, if a baby boy is born.

After a few days, my wife had a dream in which she saw a piece of paper that fell from the sky, the name Bilāl was written on the piece of paper. اَلْحَمْدُ لِلّٰه عَزَّوَجَلَّ! Allah عَزَّوَجَلَّ blessed us with a baby boy due to the blessings of the 30 day Madanī Qāfilaĥ. We were blessed with two more baby boys later on.

By the grace of Allah عَزَّوَجَلَّ! The blessings of the 30 day Madanī Qāfilaĥ did not remain confined to me, but every one in our family who did not have a son was blessed with baby boys. اَلْحَمْدُ لِلّٰه عَزَّوَجَلَّ At present, I am serving Dawat-e-Islami as the responsible of Madanī Qāfilaĥs in my area.

Ā kay tum bā-adab, daykĥ lo faḍal-e-Rab
Madanī munnay milayn, Qāfilay mayn chalo

Come reverentially and see Divine mercy
You'll have boy baby, travel with Madanī Qāfilaĥ

صَلُّوْا عَلَى الْحَبِيْب صَلَّى اللهُ تَعَالٰى عَلٰى مُحَمَّد

Desire not being fulfilled is also reward

Dear Islamic brothers! Did you see how wishes and hopes are fulfilled, grief turns into happiness and difficulty into ease due to the blessings of Madanī Qāfilaĥs. However, it is not necessary that each and every desire will be fulfilled. Sometimes man desires things that aren't beneficial to him and thus his wishes are not satisfied. In such cases, not being granted what one desires is actually a blessing. For instance, a man might ask for a son but the birth of a daughter might actually be better for him. Our Allah عَزَّوَجَلَّ says in the 216th verse of Sūraĥ Al-Baqaraĥ (part 2):

عَسٰۤى اَنْ تُحِبُّوْا شَیْـًٔا وَّ هُوَ شَرٌّ لَّكُمْ ؕ

It may happen that anything may be liked by you and that may not be in your favour.

[Kanz-ul-Īmān (Translation of Quran)] (Part 2, Sūraĥ Al-Baqaraĥ, verse 216)

Excellence of daughter

Remember! The birth of a daughter is a great blessing. Here are 3 Sayings of the Holy Prophet صَلَّى اللهُ تَعَالٰى عَلَيْهِ وَاٰلِهٖ وَسَلَّم in this regard:

1. The man who brings up three daughters will enter Heaven and will be rewarded the same as a warrior who fights (in the way of Allah عَزَّوَجَلَّ) in the state of fast and offers Ṣalāĥ. *(Attarghīb Wattarĥīb, vol. 3, pp. 46, Ḥadīš 26)*

2. Whoever has three daughters or three sisters and treats them well will enter Heaven. *(Jāmi' Tirmižī, vol. 3, pp. 366, Ḥadīš 1919)*

3. If someone brings up three daughters or sisters by teaching them manners and treating them well until they become independent (by either reaching puberty or getting married or getting wealth) Allah عَزَّوَجَلَّ will make him enter paradise. *(Ashi'at-ul-Lam'āt, vol. 4, pp. 132)* When the honourable companions رَضِیَ اللّٰہُ تَعَالٰی عَنْھُم heard this saying they enquired, 'If he brings up two girls?' He صَلَّى اللهُ تَعَالٰى عَلَيْهِ وَاٰلِهٖ وَسَلَّم replied, 'He will gain the same reward.' And if people had asked about (bringing up) one (girl) he صَلَّى اللهُ تَعَالٰى عَلَيْهِ وَاٰلِهٖ وَسَلَّم would have replied the same. *(Sharḥ-us-Sunnaĥ, vol. 6, pp. 452, Ḥadīš 3351)*

Mother of the believers, Sayyidatunā 'Āishaĥ Ṣiddīqaĥ رَضِیَ اللهُ تَعَالٰی عَنْھَا has said, 'A woman came to me along with her two daughters and began to beg[1]. I had nothing but a date which I gave to her. She split the date between her two daughters and left without eating any of it herself. Later, when Beloved Rasūl صَلَّى اللهُ تَعَالٰى عَلَيْهِ وَاٰلِهٖ وَسَلَّم came I told him of this incident. He صَلَّى اللهُ تَعَالٰى عَلَيْهِ وَاٰلِهٖ وَسَلَّم said: [If] the one made responsible for these girls, treats them well, they will become a shield for him against fire (Hell).' *(Ṣaḥīḥ Muslim, pp. 414, Ḥadīš 2629)*

---

[1] Begging is permissible in some cases; the lady رَضِیَ اللهُ تَعَالٰی عَنْھَا must have been in such a helpless state that it was permissible for her to beg. *(Mirāt-ul-Manājīḥ, vol. 6, pp. 545)*

Dear Islamic brothers! Why will mercy not be showered upon the Madanī environment and Sunnaĥ-Inspiring Ijtimā'āt of Dawat-e-Islami as many Auliyā رَحِمَهُمُ اللّٰهُ تَعَالٰی might be present amongst all these devotees of Rasūl.

A'lā Ḥaḍrat رَحْمَةُ اللّٰهِ تَعَالٰی عَلَيْه has said: There are blessings in congregations. The supplications made in congregations of Muslims are more likely to be fulfilled. Scholars have said wherever 40 pious Muslims gather there will definitely be a Walī of Allah عَزَّوَجَلَّ amongst them. *(Fatāwā Razawiyyaĥ referenced, vol. 24, pp. 184 – Taysīr Sharḥ Jāmi'-uṣ-Ṣaghīr, vol. 1, pp. 312, Ḥadīš 714)*

Even if your prayer appears to be unanswered you must avoid uttering words of complaint. Allah عَزَّوَجَلَّ knows what is better for us. We must be grateful to Allah عَزَّوَجَلَّ at all times, if He عَزَّوَجَلَّ gives you a boy thank him, if He عَزَّوَجَلَّ gives you a girl thank him, if He عَزَّوَجَلَّ gives you both thank him, and if He عَزَّوَجَلَّ doesn't give you either still thank him in all states and circumstances. Allah عَزَّوَجَلَّ says in verses 49 and 50 of Sūraĥ Ash-Shūrā:

لِلّٰهِ مُلْكُ السَّمٰوٰتِ وَالْاَرْضِ ؕ يَخْلُقُ مَا يَشَآءُ ؕ يَهَبُ لِمَنْ يَّشَآءُ اِنَاثًا وَّيَهَبُ لِمَنْ يَّشَآءُ الذُّكُوْرَ ﴿۴۹﴾

اَوْ يُزَوِّجُهُمْ ذُكْرَانًا وَّاِنَاثًا ۚ وَيَجْعَلُ مَنْ يَّشَآءُ عَقِيْمًا ؕ اِنَّهٗ عَلِيْمٌ قَدِيْرٌ ﴿۵۰﴾

For Allah عَزَّوَجَلَّ is the Kingdom of the heavens and the earth, He عَزَّوَجَلَّ creates whatever He عَزَّوَجَلَّ likes. He عَزَّوَجَلَّ bestows daughters on whoever He عَزَّوَجَلَّ likes and He عَزَّوَجَلَّ bestows sons on whoever He عَزَّوَجَلَّ likes. Or He عَزَّوَجَلَّ couples both, the sons and the daughters, and He عَزَّوَجَلَّ makes whoever He عَزَّوَجَلَّ likes barren. Undoubtedly, He عَزَّوَجَلَّ is all-knowing, the omnipotent.

[Kanz-ul-Īmān (Translation of Quran)] (Part 25, Sūraĥ Ash-Shūrā, verses 49, 50)

'Allāmaĥ Maulānā Sayyid Muhammad Na'īmuddīn Murādābādī عَلَيْهِ رَحْمَةُ اللّٰهِ الْهَادِی has stated, 'He عَزَّوَجَلَّ is the Creator and Owner of every thing, He عَزَّوَجَلَّ distributes His bounties as He عَزَّوَجَلَّ wants. This was also the case with the honourable Prophets عَلَيْهِمُ السَّلَام. Sayyidunā Lūṭ عَلَيْهِ السَّلَام and Sayyidunā Shu'ayb عَلَيْهِ السَّلَام had only daughters, no sons, while Sayyidunā Ibrāĥīm عَلَيْهِ السَّلَام had only sons, no daughters and the Beloved and Blessed Prophet صَلَّى اللّٰهُ تَعَالٰی عَلَيْهِ وَاٰلِهٖ وَسَلَّم had four sons and four daughters. Sayyidunā Yaḥyā عَلَيْهِ السَّلَام and Sayyidunā 'Īsā عَلَيْهِ السَّلَام did not have any children.' *(Khazāin-ul-'Irfān, pp. 777)*

Valid exemptions for not observing fast

Dear Islamic brothers! Although there are certain conditions and compulsions in which a person is allowed to miss his/her fast, the missed fasts are not forgiven due to compulsions. It is Farḍ to make up for them (do Qaḍā) after being relieved of the compulsion. Even so, there will be no sin in case of missing the fast due to any valid (Shar'ī) compulsion, as clearly stated in '*Bahār-e-Sharī'at*' with the reference of '*Durr-e-Mukhtār.*'

The valid Shar'ī compulsions of missing a fast include travelling, pregnancy, breast feeding, sickness, old age, fear of being killed and Ikrāĥ (i.e. threat of being killed or beaten severely or any body part being cut. If somebody forces the fasting person to break his fast, and if the fasting person knows for sure that threatener would do what he threatens, so he can break his fast in this situation) loss of wisdom and Jihad. If somebody does not fast on account of the aforementioned reasons, he will not be regarded a sinner. *(Durr-e-Mukhtār – Rad-dul-Muḥtār, vol. 3, pp. 402)*

Definition of travelling

It is also permissible to miss a fast whilst one is travelling. Keep the distance of journey in mind. According to the research of Imām-e-Aĥl-e-Sunnat A'lā Ḥaḍrat Maulānā Shāĥ Aḥmad Razā Khān عَلَيْهِ رَحْمَةُ الرَّحْمٰن 'By Sharī'aĥ, the distance of a journey is 57½ miles (almost 92km). Therefore, whoever leaves the vicinity of his city or village with the intention of travelling for the above mentioned distance will be regarded a traveller. By Sharī'aĥ, he can miss fast and make up for it later and he has to offer Ṣalāĥ (with 'Qaṣr'). A traveller can fast, but he will have to reduce his four Rak'āt Ṣalāĥ to two Rak'āt (it is Wājib for him to do so), not doing this is a sin. If someone is unaware of this ruling and offers four Rak'āt, it is Wājib for him to offer two Rak'āt with the intention of Qaṣr. *(Derived from Fatāwā Razawiyyaĥ referenced, vol. 8, pp. 270)*

Therefore, all such four Rak'āt-Ṣalāĥ offered without Qaṣr (reduction) during the journey due to ignorance will have to be repeated with two Rak'āt with the intention of 'Qaṣr' (calculate all such Ṣalāĥ and offer them). However, a traveller will have to offer four Rak'āt if he offers his Ṣalāĥ following a resident (non traveller) Imām. There is no need to repeat Sunan and Witr. The ruling of 'Qaṣr' only applies to the Farḍ Rak'āt of Ẓuĥr, 'Aṣr and 'Ishā: two Rak'āt will be offered instead of four. The Sunan and Witr Ṣalāĥ will be offered as usual without any reduction.

After reaching the destination, if there is the intention to stay over there for a period of less than 15 days he will remain a traveller and the ruling that applies to a traveller will apply to him. However, if he intends to stay there for 15 days or more than 15 days the ruling of a traveller will no longer apply to him and he will be regarded a resident ('Muqīm') therefore he will have to fast and offer Ṣalāĥ completely.

To learn the detailed rulings regarding 'travelling' please refer to *Baĥār-e-Sharī'at*, part 4: Chapter of a Traveller.

Slight illness is not a valid exemption

If someone is severely ill and there is a high probability that his illness will prolong or recovery will be delayed as a result of fasting, he is allowed to miss his fast in this case (further details to follow).

Unfortunately, it is observed these days that people miss fasts or, Allah عَزَّوَجَلَّ forbid, even break fasts having started them due to minor cold, fever and headaches. One should never do so. If someone misses a single fast without a valid exemption he will not be able to regain its blessings even if he spends the rest of his life fasting.

Dear Islamic brothers! Three blessed Aḥādīš are presented before we look at the detailed rulings about the exemptions for missing fasts.

One has a choice to fast or not in journey

1. Mother of the believers, Sayyidatunā 'Āishaĥ Ṣiddīqaĥ رَضِیَ اللہ تَعَالٰی عَنْہَا has said that Sayyidunā Ḥamzaĥ Bin 'Amr Aslamī رَضِیَ اللہ تَعَالٰی عَنْہُ used to fast in abundance. He رَضِیَ اللہ تَعَالٰی عَنْہُ asked the Beloved and Blessed Prophet صَلَّی اللہ تَعَالٰی عَلَیْہِ وَاٰلِہٖ وَسَلَّم 'Shall I fast during journey?' He صَلَّی اللہ تَعَالٰی عَلَیْہِ وَاٰلِہٖ وَسَلَّم replied, 'You have the choice whether to fast or not.' *(Ṣaḥīḥ Bukhārī, vol. 1, pp. 640, Ḥadīš 1943)*

2. Sayyidunā Abū Sa'īd Khudrī رَضِیَ اللہ تَعَالٰی عَنْہُ has said, 'We set out for Jihad with the Holy Prophet صَلَّی اللہ تَعَالٰی عَلَیْہِ وَاٰلِہٖ وَسَلَّم on the 16th of Ramadan; some of us fasted whereas some didn't. Those who fasted didn't object to those who didn't fast and vice versa.' *(Ṣaḥīḥ Muslim, pp. 564, Ḥadīš 1116)*

3. Sayyidunā Anas Bin Mālik Ka'bī رَضِیَ اللہُ تَعَالٰی عَنْہُ has narrated that the Beloved and Blessed Prophet صَلَّی اللہُ تَعَالٰی عَلَیْہِ وَاٰلِہٖ وَسَلَّم has said, 'Allah عَزَّوَجَلَّ has reduced the Ṣalāĥ of a traveller by half (the 4 Rak'āt Ṣalāĥ will be offered as 2 Rak'āt) and exempted travellers and breast feeding and pregnant women from fasting (they are allowed to miss their fasts and make up for them later).' *(Jāmi' Tirmiżī, vol. 2, pp. 170, Ḥadīš 715)*

33 Points about exemptions for not having fast

[Remember that one will have to keep Qaḍā fast for every missed fast after relief from the compulsion].

1. A traveller has the choice whether to fast or not. *(Rad-dul-Muḥtār, vol. 3, pp. 403)*

2. If a traveller and his companion do not suffer any harm in case of fasting, it is preferable to fast during the journey, but if either of them or both will be suffering harm then it is better not to fast. *(Durr-e-Mukhtār, vol. 3, pp. 405)*

3. If a traveller becomes a resident (as per the Shar'ī definition of resident) before Ḍaḥwā Kubrā[1] (Shar'ī midday) and he hasn't yet eaten or drunk anything, it is Wājib for him to make the intention of fast. *(Al-Jauĥara-tun-Nayyaraĥ, vol. 1, pp. 186)* Let's say, for instance, that someone lives in the famous Pakistani city Hyderabad, he leaves Bāb-ul-Madīnaĥ Karachi to head for Hyderabad and arrives there at 10 a.m. If he has not eaten anything since dawn during the journey, it is Wājib for him to make the intention of fast.

4. If somebody sets out a journey at daytime, he cannot break that day's fast because of that journey. However, if he broke the fast during the journey he would not be required to pay expiation for it but doing so is a sin. *(Rad-dul-Muḥtār, vol. 3, pp. 416)* It is Farḍ to make up for this fast.

5. If somebody breaks fast before he sets out his journey and then he begins his journey, expiation will be mandatory for him (provided that the conditions for expiation are met). *(ibid)*

[1] The definition of Ḍaḥwā Kubrā (Shar'ī Midday) has already been mentioned in the section of intention of fast.

6. If somebody begins journey during the daytime (and did not break fast during the journey) but then returned home to take something which he had left at home forgetfully and broke fast, expiation will be Wājib (provided that the conditions of expiation are met). If he had broken it during the journey, only making up for it by fasting another day would have been Farḍ as stated in point number 4. *(Fatāwā 'Ālamgīrī, vol. 1, pp. 207)*

7. If somebody is forced to break fast he can do so, but he will be rewarded if he takes patience. (The definition of 'Ikrāĥ (being forced)' has already been explained on page 642). *(Rad-dul-Muḥtār, vol. 3, pp. 402)*

8. If the life of a fasting person is in danger as a result of being stung by a snake, he should break the fast. *(Rad-dul-Muḥtār, vol. 3, pp. 402)*

9. If anyone breaks his fast due to any of the aforementioned reasons, it is Farḍ for him to make up for it by fasting another day. Maintaining the order in these missed fasts is not Farḍ. Therefore, if he kept Nafl fasts before keeping his Qaḍā fasts, the Nafl fasts will still be valid.

   However, once he is relieved of the compulsion for missing fasts, the ruling is that he must keep his Qaḍā fasts before the arrival of the next Ramadan. A Ḥadīš states, 'If any one has to keep previous Ramadan's fasts as Qaḍā, but he doesn't do, his fasts of the current Ramadan will not be accepted.' *(Majma'-uz-Zawāid, vol. 3, pp. 415)*

   If the next Ramadan arrives and one hasn't yet kept the Qaḍā fasts for the previous Ramadan, he has to keep fast for the present Ramadan first instead of keeping the Qaḍā fast for the previous Ramadan. He has to keep Qaḍā fasts later on. If the one who is neither ill nor traveller, fasts in Ramadan with the intention of making up for the missed fasts of the previous Ramadan, these fasts will not be considered Qaḍā, these are the fasts of the present Ramadan. *(Durr-e-Mukhtār, vol. 3, pp. 405)*

10. If a pregnant or breast feeding woman has credible fear of losing her life or the life of the baby (if she fasts) she is allowed to miss the fast that day, whether she is the baby's mother or the wet nurse, and even if she is being paid to suckle the baby in Ramadan (there is the same ruling for her). *(Durr-e-Mukhtār, Rad-dul-Muḥtār, vol. 3, pp. 403)*

11. Don't fast in the state of such extreme hunger or thirst that brings about the credible risk of death or loss of intellect. *(Durr-e-Mukhtār, Rad-dul-Muḥtār, vol. 3, pp. 402)*

12. If it is highly likely that the illness of a patient will intensify due to fast or the process of recovery will be delayed or if a healthy person is almost sure that he will fall ill, then he is allowed to miss his fast that day (and make up for it later). *(Durr-e-Mukhtār, vol. 3, pp. 403)*

13. As to the aforewritten cases 'high likelihood' is a condition. Just suspicions are not sufficient. There are three ways to determine a 'high likelihood': (1) Visible symptoms (2) Personal experience (3) Advice of a pious Muslim doctor who is qualified (experienced and expert in his particular field).

    If a person broke his fast without any symptom, any previous personal experience or without the advice of a pious Muslim doctor or if he did so just on the advice of a non-Muslim or an impious doctor (for example, a clean-shaven doctor), it will be mandatory for him not only to make Qaḍā for this fast but also pay expiation for it provided that the conditions are met. *(Rad-dul-Muḥtār, vol. 3, pp. 404)*

14. Offering Ṣalāĥ and fasting during menses or post natal bleeding are Ḥarām and will not be valid. Moreover, reciting or touching verses of the Holy Quran or their translations in this state is also Ḥarām. *(Baĥār-e-Sharī'at, part 2, pp. 88-89)*

15. A woman in her menses or post natal bleeding has the choice whether to eat in secret or openly. It is not necessary for her to give the impression as if she is fasting. *(Al-Jauĥara-tun-Nayyaraĥ, vol. 1, pp. 186)*

16. However it is better for her to eat secretly, especially for the one experiencing menses. *(Baĥār-e-Sharī'at, part 5, pp. 135)*

17. If there is a very old man who is growing weaker and weaker day by day and is quite unable to fast and there seems no chance of him being capable enough to fast in the future either, he is allowed not to keep his fasts. He has to give a Ṣadaqaĥ-e-Fiṭr (about 1.920 Kilograms of wheat or its flour or money equivalent to its value) as Fidyaĥ for each missed fast to a Miskīn[1]. *(Durr-e-Mukhtār, vol. 3, pp. 410)*

---

[1] A Miskīn is the one who does not possess anything and who has to beg others for food or clothes for covering the body. Begging is Ḥalāl (allowed) for him.

18. If such an old man cannot fast in summer but can in winter so he can miss his fasts in summer but it will be Farḍ for him to make up for them in winter. *(Rad-dul-Muḥtār, vol. 3, pp. 472)*

19. If he pays his Fidyaĥ (expiation) but later on regains his strength to fast, his given Fidyaĥ will turn into a Nafl Ṣadaqaĥ and he will have to make up for those missed fasts. *(Fatāwā 'Ālamgīrī, vol. 1, pp. 207)*

20. He can pay the Fidyaĥ for the whole month in one payment at the beginning or the end of Ramadan. *(Fatāwā 'Ālamgīrī, vol. 1, pp. 207)*

21. Paying each Fidyaĥ to a different person is not necessary. He can give the Fidyaĥ of several Fasts to the same person. *(Durr-e-Mukhtār, vol. 3, pp. 410)*

22. If somebody starts a Nafl fast deliberately, it will become Wājib for him to complete it. If he breaks it he will have to make up for it (it will be Wājib to do so). *(Rad-dul-Muḥtār, vol. 3, pp. 411)*

23. If somebody fasted assuming that he has to keep a missed fast as Qaḍā, but having started the fast, he realised that he does not have to, he can break this fast instantly in this case but if he didn't break it instantly, he can no longer break it and if he broke, it would become Wājib for him to make up for it. *(Durr-e-Mukhtār, vol. 3, pp. 411)*

24. If a Nafl fast becomes invalid unintentionally, for instance, if a woman's menses begin whilst she is in the state of fast, making up for it will still be Wājib. *(Durr-e-Mukhtār, vol. 3, pp. 412)*

25. If somebody fasts on Eid-ul-Fiṭr or any of the four days of Eid-ul-Aḍḥā, 10th 11th 12th and 13th of Żul-Ḥijja-til-Ḥarām, it is not Wājib for him to complete the fast because fasting on these days is Ḥarām. Further, in case of breaking such a fast, its Qaḍā is not Wājib either. Instead, it will be Wājib for him to break it. If he vowed to fast on any of these days it would be Wājib for him to fulfil his vow but not on these days (on other days). *(Rad-dul-Muḥtār, vol. 3, pp. 412)*

26. It is not permissible to break a Nafl fast without a valid exemption. If a guest feels resentment due to the host not eating with him or if a host feels resentment due to the guest not eating, it is a valid exemption for breaking a Nafl fast to eat with the

other, provided that he is certain to make its Qaḍā another day, and that he breaks it before Ḍaḥwā Kubrā, not after it. (سُبْحٰنَ اللّٰه عَزَّوَجَلَّ! This shows how profusely Sharī'aĥ values the honour of a Muslim). *(Fatāwā 'Ālamgīrī, vol. 1, pp. 208)*

27. A guest can only break his fast before Ḍaḥwā Kubrā if the host is not pleased with his mere presence and will resent if the guest doesn't eat, provided he (the guest) is sure to make up for the fast later. However, if the host is pleased with the mere presence of the guest and will not mind if he doesn't eat then he (the guest) will not be allowed to break his fast. *(Fatāwā 'Ālamgīrī, vol. 1, pp. 208)*

28. It is permissible to break a Nafl fast even after Ḍaḥwā Kubrā in case of parents' displeasure. One can break this fast any time before 'Aṣr but not after 'Aṣr. *(Durr-e-Mukhtār, Rad-dul-Muḥtār, vol. 3, pp. 414)*

29. A woman should not have a Nafl, vow or sworn fast without her husband's permission. If she does, her husband can make her break it, and if she breaks the fast it will become Wājib for her to make up for it, but she needs her husband's permission even for keeping this Qaḍā fast. However, she can fast of her own accord, if her husband has died or given her a 'Bāin' divorce (a divorce in which Nikāḥ becomes invalid and the husband cannot revert).

    If the woman's fasting does not cause her husband any problem she can keep a Qaḍā fast even without his permission. For instance, if he is on a journey or ill or in a state of Iḥrām (pilgrimage) she can keep Qaḍā fasts even if he asks her not to. However, she cannot keep a Nafl fast without her husband's permission even in these cases. *(Rad-dul-Muḥtār, vol. 3, pp. 415)*

30. She does not need her husband's permission to keep Ramadan fasts or fasts for Qaḍā of Ramadan. She must fast even if he prevents her from fasting. *(Durr-e-Mukhtār, Rad-dul-Muḥtār, vol. 3, pp. 415)*

31. If one is an employee or does a job on wages he cannot have a Nafl fast without his employer's permission because fasting will cause sluggishness at work. However, if he is strong enough to work normally and completely without sluggishness despite fasting, he does not need permission to keep a Nafl fast in this case. *(Rad-dul-Muḥtār, vol. 3, pp. 416)*

32. For Nafl fasts, a daughter does not need her father's, a mother does not need her son's, and a sister does not need her brother's permission. *(Rad-dul-Muḥtār, vol. 3, pp. 416)*

33. If parents prevent their son from having a Nafl fast for fear of illness, he must obey his parents. *(Rad-dul-Muḥtār, vol. 3, pp. 416)*

Here are twelve points about the acts that make only Qaḍā necessary. Doing Qaḍā means observing one fast after Ramadan for each missed fast.

Twelve points about Qaḍā

1. If somebody ate, drank or engaged in intercourse assuming that some part of night was still left but he came to know later on that it was the time of dawn (Ṣubḥ-e-Ṣādiq), so his fast would be invalid. It is necessary to keep this fast as Qaḍā later on. *(Rad-dul-Muḥtār, vol. 3, pp. 380)*

2. If somebody is forced to the extent of Ikrāĥ-e-Shar'ī to eat, as it is a valid exemption for eating, only making up for that fast will be mandatory for him, even if he eats with his own hands. *(Durr-e-Mukhtār, vol. 3, pp. 402)*

   The summary of this ruling is that if somebody forces the fasting person to break his fast by threatening him to kill, cut any body part or beat severely, and the fasting person knows that the threatening person would do what he threatens, so Ikrāĥ-e-Shar'ī is there, the fasting person can break his fast in this situation, but it is mandatory to make up for it later.

3. If somebody ate, drank or engaged in intercourse in the state of forgetfulness, or ejaculated due to a lustful look, or experienced a nocturnal emission, or vomited and thus assumed that his fast had broken and so he ate something deliberately, only making up for this fast would be necessary for him. *(Durr-e-Mukhtār, vol. 3, pp. 375)*

4. Inhaling medicine through the nose in the state of fast will invalidate the fast and it would be mandatory to make up for it. *(Durr-e-Mukhtār, vol. 3, pp. 376)*

5. Eating a stone, grit, soil, wool, grass, paper or anything else that people feel disgusted by, will invalidate the fast but one will only have to make up for it (expiation is not Wājib). *(Durr-e-Mukhtār, vol. 3, pp. 377)*

6. If rain-water or flake of snow goes down the throat, the fast will become invalid and it would be mandatory to make up for it. *(Durr-e-Mukhtār, vol. 3, pp. 378)*

7. Likewise, swallowing a large amount of sweat or tears will invalidate the fast. One will have to make up for it. *(ibid)*

8. If somebody continued to eat assuming that some part of night was still left but came to know later on that the time of Saḥarī had ended while he was eating, his fast would be invalid and he will have to make up for it. *(Rad-dul-Muḥtār, vol. 3, pp. 380)*

9. If somebody breaks the fast assuming that the sun had set, but came to know later that it hadn't set, his fast will become invalid and he will have to make up for it. *(Rad-dul-Muḥtār, vol. 3, pp. 380)*

10. If someone mistakenly does Ifṭār before the sunset as a result of premature utterance of Maghrib Ażān or siren-wailing, and comes to know later on that siren or Ażān started earlier than the sunset, even if it is not his fault his fast will still become invalid and he will have to make up for it. *(Derived from Rad-dul-Muḥtār, vol. 3, pp. 383)*

11. Unfortunately, people have been heedless about the matters of Sharī'aĥ these days. Every Muslim should be careful about his fasts himself. Rather than relying on sirens or radio and TV announcements or even the Ażān, every one should get the correct information of Saḥarī and Ifṭār timings.

12. During Wuḍū, if water reached the brain or went down the throat while sniffing water into nose the fast would become invalid and its Qaḍā would be mandatory provided one was aware that he was fasting. However, if one was unaware of the fast at that moment his fast will not become invalid. *(Fatāwā 'Ālamgīrī, vol. 1, pp. 202)*

Rulings regarding expiation

Dear Islamic brothers! In some cases, breaking a fast in Ramadan deliberately without a valid exemption will only make it Wājib to do Qaḍā but in some cases, it will make it necessary to pay expiation, in addition to making up for the broken fast.

Method of paying expiation for fasting

The expiation for breaking (invalidating) a fast is to free a male or female slave, if possible. If this isn't possible, for example, he does not have a slave or slave girl nor can he afford to buy them or though he has enough money, slaves and slave girls are not available (like in present age) then he will have to keep 60 fasts consecutively. If this isn't possible either, he will have to serve 60 Miskīn[1] people with lunch and dinner (such that they are full). It is necessary to serve both the meals to the same 60 people. If one wants, he can give one Ṣadaqaĥ-e-Fiṭr (i.e. about 1.920 Kilograms wheat or money equivalent to its value) to each of the 60 different Miskīn people, but he can't give 60 Ṣadaqaĥ-e-Fiṭr to the same person at once. However, he can give the same Miskīn a separate Ṣadaqaĥ-e-Fiṭr each day for 60 days.

In case of paying expiation in the form of fast, it is necessary to keep all the 60 fasts consecutively. If one misses even a single fast in between these 60 fasts, he will have to resume fasting from the very first fast. The previously observed fasts will not be counted, even if he had kept 59 fasts, and whether he missed (that one fast) due to illness or any other reason. However, if a woman experiences her menses whilst keeping fast for expiation her previously kept fasts will not lapse. In other words, she will not have to resume her fasting from the very first fast. After menses, she will keep the remaining fasts only to complete her sixty fasts. Her expiation will get paid. *(Derived from Rad-dul-Muḥtār, vol. 3, pp. 390)*

One who makes the intention of fasting during the night but then deliberately breaks his fast in the morning or any time during the day or even just a single moment before the time of Ifṭār, without a valid exemption, with something that human nature does not dislike (i.e. food, water, tea, fruits, biscuits, drinks, honey, sweets etc.) then he must keep one fast after Ramadan with the intention of making up for this fast. Further, he will also have to pay the expiation for it.

Eleven points about expiation

1. If a sane, adult and resident Muslim (who is not a traveller by Sharī'aĥ) deliberately engages in intercourse or eats or drinks something for pleasure in the state of the

[1] The definition of Miskīn is given on page 646 of the same book.

fast of Ramadan without a valid exemption his fast will become invalid. Both the expiation and the Qaḍā are mandatory for him. *(Rad-dul-Muḥtār, vol. 3, pp. 388)*

2. In all such cases in which expiation becomes mandatory for breaking the fast, it is a condition that the intention for the fast of Ramadan is made at night. If the intention of the fast was made during the day, and the fast was then broken, expiation is not mandatory, only Qaḍā is enough. *(Al-Jauĥara-tun-Nayyaraĥ, vol. 1, pp. 180)*

3. If somebody vomited or ate something or engaged in intercourse forgetfully, and he was aware that his fast hasn't become invalid because of these acts; even then, he ate something, expiation will not be mandatory for him. *(Rad-dul-Muḥtār, vol. 3, pp. 375)*

4. If somebody had a nocturnal emission and then ate something despite knowing that his fast hadn't become invalid, expiation will be mandatory for him. *(Rad-dul-Muḥtār, vol. 3, pp. 375)*

5. If somebody spits his own saliva and then swallows it or swallows someone else's saliva, expiation will not be mandatory for him. However, if he swallows the saliva of his lover with lust or that of a religious saint for blessings, expiation will be mandatory for him. *(Fatāwā 'Ālamgīrī, vol. 1, pp. 203)* If somebody eats such skin of a melon or water-melon that is dry or is such that people feel disgusted by eating it, there is no expiation in this case. If the skin is watery that people like to eat, expiation will be mandatory. *(Fatāwā 'Ālamgīrī, vol. 1, pp. 202)*

6. If somebody eats uncooked rice, maize or lentils, expiation will not be mandatory. The same ruling applies to eating uncooked barley. However, if they are baked expiation will be mandatory. *(Fatāwā 'Ālamgīrī, vol. 1, pp. 202)*

7. If there was a morsel of food in somebody's mouth at Saḥarī and the time ended (with the morsel still in his mouth) or if somebody was eating forgetfully and he recalled his fast whilst the morsel of food in mouth, but he swallowed it despite being aware that he was fasting, expiation will be Wājib in both the cases. However, if he took the morsel out of his mouth and then ate it, only Qaḍā of the fast will be Wājib, there will be no expiation. *(Fatāwā 'Ālamgīrī, vol. 1, pp. 203)*

8. If somebody suffers from fever on specific days and, it was one of the days when he usually gets fever; he broke fast deliberately assuming that he would get fever,

expiation will lapse (i.e. expiation is not necessary, just making up for it is enough). Similarly, if a woman experiences menses on a fixed date and, it was the day when she normally experiences menses; assuming that she would experience menses she broke fast deliberately but her menses didn't start, expiation will lapse (i.e. expiation will not be necessary, just making up for it is enough). *(Durr-e-Mukhtār, Rad-dul-Muḥtār, vol. 3, pp. 391)*

9. If somebody broke two fasts in two different months of Ramadan, he has to pay two expiations even if he had not yet paid expiation for the first fast. If he broke two fasts in the same month of Ramadan and he has not yet given expiation for the first fast, only one expiation will be enough for both the fasts. *(Al-Jauĥara-tun-Nayyaraĥ, vol. 1, pp. 182)*

10. After the fast has broken, for expiation to become mandatory, it is also necessary that any such act that is in contradiction to fast or any involuntary act that permits a person to break fast, should not take place.

    For example, if a woman experiences her menses or post-natal bleeding on the same day or if someone falls so severely ill, having broken fast, that allows him to miss his fast, expiation will lapse. This does not include travelling as travelling is an intentional act. *(Al-Jauĥara-tun-Nayyaraĥ, vol. 1, pp. 181)*

11. In all such cases in which expiation does not become mandatory despite breaking the fast, it is a precondition that the act of breaking the fast is done only once and without the intention of committing a sin, otherwise expiation will have to be paid. *(Durr-e-Mukhtār, Rad-dul-Muḥtār, vol. 3, pp. 440)*

Save fasts from being ruined!

Dear Islamic brothers! These days, most of the Muslims don't have even basic Islamic knowledge. They make such mistakes that invalidate worships. Regretfully, all our efforts are focussed on learning worldly education and skills. Unfortunately, we neither have the time nor interest in learning the Sunan or rules about the Islamic commandments. Even worse, we feel disgusted if a sincere Islamic brother draws our attention towards our mistakes. These days, many wrong practices seem to have become part and parcel of our worship including Saḥarī and Ifṭār. May Allah عَزَّوَجَلَّ protect us!

People talk unreasonably about such issues and then try to defend themselves stubbornly. For instance some people say: '*The time of Saḥarī does not end unless so much light of morning spreads that ants appear.*'

Similarly, some people wrongly believe that one can continue to eat till the Ażān of Fajr ends and if the sound of many Ażāns is coming they continue to eat and drink until the last Ażān finishes. How irrational and shocking it is! Just think! What will you do if you live at such a place where you can't hear the sound of Ażān?

Dear Islamic brothers! Do not ruin your worships due to carelessness of a few minutes. The following verse of Sūraĥ Al-Baqaraĥ has already been mentioned, here it is mentioned again, please read it and ponder:

وَ كُلُوْا وَاشْرَبُوْا حَتّٰى يَتَبَيَّنَ لَكُمُ الْخَيْطُ

الْاَبْيَضُ مِنَ الْخَيْطِ الْاَسْوَدِ مِنَ الْفَجْرِ ۪ ثُمَّ اَتِمُّوا الصِّيَامَ اِلَى الَّيْلِ ۚ

And eat and drink until the white thread becomes distinct to you from the black thread at dawn; then complete the fasts till the coming of night.

[Kanz-ul-Īmān (Translation of Quran)] (Part 2, Sūraĥ Al-Baqaraĥ, verse 187)

Obviously, the foregoing verse does not refer to ants or the Fajr Ażān, instead it refers to Ṣubḥ-e-Ṣādiq. So don't wait for the Ażān, use a reliable timetable to get to know the timings for Saḥarī and Ifṭār and act accordingly.

Yā Allah عَزَّوَجَلَّ! Make us honour Ramadan according to Sharī'aĥ and Sunnaĥ, make us fast, offer Tarāwīḥ, recite the Holy Quran and offer Nafl Ṣalāĥ in abundance, and accept our worships and forgive us with Your grace and mercy.

آمِين بِجَاهِ النَّبِيِّ الْاَمِين صَلَّى اللهُ تَعَالٰى عَلَيْهِ وَاٰلِهٖ وَسَلَّم

صَلُّوْا عَلَى الْحَبِيْب صَلَّى اللهُ تَعَالٰى عَلٰى مُحَمَّد

اَلْحَمْدُ لِلّٰه عَزَّوَجَلَّ I have changed!

How excellent the global & non-political religious movement of the Quran and Sunnaĥ, Dawat-e-Islami and its Madanī Qāfilaĥs are! An Islamic brother who lives at Shalimar Town (Markaz-ul-Auliyā, Lahore) gave the following account:

I was an extremely wicked person and had indulged in many evils such as watching films and dramas daily, teasing girls, friendship with loafers and wandering with them till late night. Even my relatives did not like to meet me; they would resent when I went their home and would prevent their children from meeting me.

Luckily, the dark night of my sins turned into a bright morning when a devotee of Rasūl of Dawat-e-Islami met me very politely and tried to persuade me to travel with a Madanī Qāfilaĥ. Impressed by his polite behaviour and his sincere invitation, I travelled with a Madanī Qāfilaĥ during which the company of the devotees of Rasūl caused a Madanī transformation in my life.

اَلْحَمْدُ لِلّٰه عَزَّوَجَلَّ! By the blessings of the company of Rasūl's devotees in the Madanī Qāfilaĥ I received the gift of repentance as well as the enthusiasm to wear dress and turban according to the blessed Sunnaĥ. The very same relatives that once used to avoid me now meet me affectionately. I was once the worst in my family but now I have become the dearest due to the blessings of Dawat-e-Islami's Madanī Qāfilaĥs, اَلْحَمْدُ لِلّٰه عَزَّوَجَلَّ.

صَلُّوْا عَلَى الْحَبِيْب   صَلَّى اللّٰهُ تَعَالٰى عَلٰى مُحَمَّد

Company of those not offering Ṣalāĥ

Dear Islamic brothers! Did you see the harm of sitting in bad company! Everyone despises the people who stay in bad company. There are great blessings of good and pious company because it prevents a person from committing sins and makes people like him. One should always adopt the company of those who augment keenness for worshipping and enthusiasm to practice blessed Sunnaĥ. A good companion is the one whose sight makes you remember Allah عَزَّوَجَلَّ; whose speech encourages you to perform good deeds and whose company makes you stay away from the love for the world and develop love for

Allah عَزَّوَجَلَّ, His Beloved Prophet صَلَّى اللهُ تَعَالٰى عَلَيْهِ وَاٰلِهٖ وَسَلَّم and the afterlife. One should avoid the company of those missing Ṣalāĥ, adopting fashion and doing funny activities.

In reply to a question about people who don't offer their Ṣalāĥ, A'lā Ḥaḍrat رَحْمَةُ اللهِ تَعَالٰى عَلَيْه has stated: Politely make them realise (the sin they are committing), talk to them repeatedly about the severe punishments mentioned in the Holy Quran and the blessed Aḥādīš for missing Ṣalāĥ and Jamā'at, and for not attending the Masjid. This will surely benefit the people who have faith in their hearts. Allah عَزَّوَجَلَّ says in verse 55 of Sūraĥ Aż-Żāriyāt, (part 27):

وَ ذَكِّرْ فَاِنَّ الذِّكْرٰى تَنْفَعُ الْمُؤْمِنِيْنَ ﴿۵۵﴾

And advise, for advice benefits the Muslims.

[Kanz-ul-Īmān (Translation of Quran)] (Part 27, Sūraĥ Aż-Żāriyāt, verse 55)

Remind them of Allah's speech and commandments because they will surely benefit the believers. If an individual doesn't listen, then pressurise him with the help of some influential person and if this doesn't work either, then instantly stop meeting him. Allah عَزَّوَجَلَّ says in verse 68 of Sūraĥ Al-An'ām:

وَ اِمَّا يُنْسِيَنَّكَ الشَّيْطٰنُ فَلَا تَقْعُدْ بَعْدَ الذِّكْرٰى مَعَ الْقَوْمِ الظّٰلِمِيْنَ ﴿۶۸﴾

And whenever the devil (Satan) makes you forget, then sit not you after recollection with the unjust people.

[Kanz-ul-Īmān (Translation of Quran)] (Part 7, Sūraĥ Al-An'ām, verse 68)

(Fatāwā Razawiyyaĥ referenced, vol. 6, pp. 191, 192)

صَلُّوْا عَلَى الْحَبِيْب صَلَّى اللهُ تَعَالٰى عَلٰى مُحَمَّد

اَلْحَمْدُ لِلّٰهِ رَبِّ الْعٰلَمِيْنَ وَ الصَّلٰوةُ وَ السَّلَامُ عَلٰى سَيِّدِ الْمُرْسَلِيْنَ

اَمَّا بَعْدُ فَاَعُوْذُ بِاللّٰهِ مِنَ الشَّيْطٰنِ الرَّجِيْمِ ؕ بِسْمِ اللّٰهِ الرَّحْمٰنِ الرَّحِيْمِ ؕ

Blessings of Tarawih

Excellence of Ṣalāt-'Alan-Nabī ﷺ

Amīr-ul-Mūminīn Sayyidunā 'Umar Fārūq A'ẓam رَضِیَ اللّٰہُ تَعَالٰی عَنْہُ has said, 'Du'ā (supplication) remains suspended between the earth and the sky and does not climb (i.e. it is not accepted) until you recite Ṣalāt upon your Beloved Rasūl صَلَّی اللّٰہُ تَعَالٰی عَلَیْہِ وَاٰلِہٖ وَسَلَّم.' *(Jāmi' Tirmiẓī, vol. 2, pp. 28, Ḥadīš 486)*

صَلُّوْا عَلَى الْحَبِيْب صَلَّى اللّٰهُ تَعَالٰى عَلٰى مُحَمَّد

Excellence of Sunnaĥ

اَلْحَمْدُ لِلّٰہ عَزَّوَجَلَّ! We are blessed with great bounties in Ramadan. Amongst these bounties is the Sunnaĥ of the Tarāwīḥ Ṣalāĥ. Words cannot express the greatness of the Sunnaĥ! The Prophet of mankind, the Peace of our heart and mind, the most Generous and Kind صَلَّی اللّٰہُ تَعَالٰی عَلَیْہِ وَاٰلِہٖ وَسَلَّم has said, 'The one who loved my Sunnaĥ, loved me, and the one who loved me, will be with me in the Heaven.' *(Jāmi' Tirmiẓī, vol. 4, pp. 310, Ḥadīš 2687)*

Finishing the Quran 61 times in Ramadan

The Tarāwīḥ Ṣalāĥ is a Sunnat-ul-Muakkadaĥ. Reciting the whole Quran in the Tarāwīḥ Ṣalāĥ is also Sunnat-ul-Muakkadaĥ. Our Imām A'ẓam Sayyidunā Imām Abū Ḥanīfaĥ رَضِیَ اللّٰہُ تَعَالٰی عَنْہُ used to recite the Holy Quran sixty one times in Ramadan, thirty during the day, thirty at night and one during the Tarāwīḥ Ṣalāĥ. For forty five years, he رَضِیَ اللّٰہُ تَعَالٰی عَنْہُ offered his Fajr Ṣalāĥ with the Wuḍū he would make for his 'Ishā Ṣalāĥ.

(Baĥār-e-Sharī'at, part 4, pp. 37)

According to a narration, Imām A'ẓam رَضِیَ اللّٰہُ تَعَالٰی عَنْہُ performed Hajj fifty five times in his life and recited the Holy Quran seven thousand times in the house in which he passed away. *('Uqūd-ul-Jamān, pp. 221)*

Recitation of Quran and Auliyā

A'lā Ḥaḍrat رَضِیَ اللّٰہُ تَعَالٰی عَنْہُ has stated, 'For thirty years Sayyidunā Imām A'ẓam (Abū Ḥanīfaĥ) رَضِیَ اللّٰہُ تَعَالٰی عَنْہُ recited the whole Quran in one Rak'at every night.' *(Fatāwā Razawiyyaĥ (Jadīd), vol. 7, pp. 476)* The respected scholars رَحِمَہُمُ اللّٰہُ تَعَالٰی have said that some of Auliyā رَحِمَہُمُ اللّٰہُ تَعَالٰی used to recite the whole Quran twice a day, some four times a day and some eight times a day. Imām 'Abdul Waĥĥāb Sha'rānī قُدِّسَ سِرُّہُ النُّوْرَانِی has stated in his '*Mīzān-ush-Sharī'aĥ*' that Sayyidī 'Alī Murṣafī عَلَیْہِ رَحْمَۃُ اللّٰہِ الْقَوِی used to recite the whole Quran three hundred and sixty thousand times in one day. *(Mīzān-ush-Sharī'at-ul-Kubrā, vol. 1, pp. 79)*

According to a narration mentioned in *Āšār*, Amīr-ul-Mūminīn Sayyidunā 'Alī رَضِیَ اللّٰہُ تَعَالٰی عَنْہُ used to start reciting the Holy Quran when placing his left foot in the stirrup (of his horse) and finish reciting it before placing his right foot in the other stirrup. *(Fatāwā Razawiyyaĥ (Jadīd), vol. 7, pp. 477)*

The Holy Prophet صَلَّی اللّٰہُ تَعَالٰی عَلَیْہِ وَاٰلِہٖ وَسَلَّم has said that Sayyidunā Dāwūd عَلٰی نَبِیِّنَا وَ عَلَیْہِ الصَّلٰوۃُ وَالسَّلَام would order his mount to be saddled and he would recite the whole of the Holy Zabūr before its saddle was tied. *(Ṣaḥīḥ Bukhārī, vol. 2, pp. 447, Ḥadīš 3417)*

Dear Islamic brothers! A question may arise as to how it is possible for a person to recite the whole Quran and the whole Holy Zabūr several times a day or within a few moments. The answer is quite simple and credible; it was a Prophetic miracle of Sayyidunā Dāwūd عَلٰی نَبِیِّنَا وَعَلَیْہِ الصَّلٰوۃُ وَالسَّلَام and saintly miracles of Islamic saints. Miracles are such types of action which are impossible to occur in usual circumstances.

Mispronouncing letters

Regretfully, most of the people don't pay ample attention to religious matters these days. The Holy Quran is not usually recited properly even a single time in the Tarāwīḥ Ṣalāĥ. The Holy Quran should be recited slowly, but these days, if an Imām recites it slowly people refuse to offer Tarāwīḥ with him. These days, people prefer such a Ḥāfiẓ who finishes the Tarāwīḥ Ṣalāĥ as quickly as possible.

Remember! Mispronouncing the Quranic letters is Ḥarām irrespective of whether it is Tarāwīḥ Ṣalāĥ or any other Ṣalāĥ. If a Ḥāfiẓ misses even a single letter of the Holy Quran the Sunnaĥ of reciting the entire Quran will remain unfulfilled. Therefore, if you miss even a single letter or fail to pronounce it from its correct origin, so recite it again properly without feeling shyness, and then proceed. It is also regrettable that these days there are many such Ḥuffāẓ who are unable to recite the Quran slowly! If they try to recite slowly they forget words!

It is my sincere Madanī suggestion for such Ḥuffāẓ not to feel ashamed at all in this matter. By Almighty! The wrath of Allah عَزَّوَجَلَّ will result in innumerable troubles, so rectify your recitation of the Holy Quran from beginning to end with the help of a Qārī who teaches according to the rules of Tajwīd. Reciting every 'Madd' and 'Līn' properly is necessary[1]. Be careful about the rules of 'Madd', 'Ghunnaĥ', 'Iẓĥār' and 'Ikhfā[2]' as well.

The author of *Bahār-e-Sharī'at* Ṣadr-ush-Sharī'aĥ, Badr-uṭ-Ṭarīqaĥ 'Allāmaĥ Maulānā Muftī Amjad 'Alī A'ẓamī رَحْمَةُ اللهِ تَعَالٰى عَلَيْه has stated, 'One should recite the Quran slowly in Farḍ Ṣalāĥ and, at a medium pace, in Tarāwīḥ. Fast recitation in Nawāfil of the night is permissible. However, words should be clearly understandable, i.e. the Maddat should be pronounced with at least the minimum degree of length set by Qurrā. Otherwise, it is Ḥarām, because we have been commanded to recite the Quran with Tartīl (slowly).' *(Durr-e-Mukhtār, Rad-dul-Muḥtār, vol. 2, pp. 262)* Allah عَزَّوَجَلَّ says in the 4th verse of Sūraĥ Al-Muzzammil (part 29):

وَ رَتِّلِ الْقُرْاٰنَ تَرْتِيْلًا ؕ﴿۴﴾

And recite the Quran slowly and thoughtfully.

[Kanz-ul-Īmān (Translation of Quran)] (Part 29, Sūraĥ Al-Muzzammil, verse 4)

---

[1] If a واؤ, ي or الف is Sākin (without a Zabar, Zayr or Paysh) and the letter before it carries a convenient Ḥarakāt (Paysh before a واؤ, Zayr before a ي, and a Zabar before الف) then it (the واؤ, ي or الف) is called a Madd. If a واؤ or ي is Sākin and the letter before it has a Zabar on it then it (the واؤ or ي) is called a Līn.

[2] See the details of these rules in *Madanī Qāidaĥ* (English) published by Maktaba-tul-Madīnaĥ.

Elaborating the word 'Tartīl' A'lā Ḥaḍrat رَحْمَةُ اللهِ تَعَالٰی عَلَيْه has stated with the reference of '*Kamālayn 'Ala Ḥāshiyah Jalālayn*:' 'Recite the Holy Quran so slowly that the listener can count even the number of verses and words.' *(Fatāwā Razawiyyah (Jadīd), vol. 6, pp. 276)* Further, in Farḍ Ṣalāĥ, recite the Holy Quran in such a way that each and every letter can separately be understood. As for Tarāwīḥ Ṣalāĥ recite it with medium pace and in Nafl Ṣalāĥ at night, one can recite it quickly provided that he could understand what he recites. *(Durr-e-Mukhtār, vol. 1, pp. 80)*

According to '*Madārik-ut-Tanzīl*', 'Reciting the Quran slowly refers to reciting it calmly by separating each and every letter, pausing wherever a pause is required and pronouncing each letter from its correct origin. The word 'Tartīlan' (in the verse) lays stress, which means that it is necessary for the reciter to do this (i.e. recite slowly).' *(Tafsīr Madārik-ut-Tanzīl, vol. 4, pp. 203 – Fatāwā Razawiyyaĥ referenced, vol. 6, pp. 278, 279)*

Lead Tarāwīḥ Ṣalāĥ without salary

Sincerity is necessary not only for the Imams leading the Tarāwīḥ Ṣalāĥs, and the committees that appoint them but also for the people that offer Tarāwīḥ. If a Ḥāfiẓ recites the Holy Quran for praise, applause, fame or for showing off his speed of recitation, he won't be rewarded at all, instead, he will fall into the abyss of ostentation and desire for fame. Salaries for reciting the Holy Quran should be avoided. A fixed amount of money is not the only form of salary, it can be in some other forms such as cloth or grain etc. as well. If a Ḥāfiẓ recites the Holy Quran in a particular Masjid because he knows that the people will give him something for it, then whatever they give him will be considered salary (even though a formal agreement was not made).

However, if a Ḥāfiẓ makes it clear in advance with a good intention that he will not receive any thing in exchange for the recitation of the Quran or the committee members of Masjid clearly state that they will not give him anything, but if they give him something later, so it does no harm because it is stated in a Ḥadīš اِنَّمَا الْاَعْمَالُ بِالنِّيَّات (*Acts are dependent upon intentions*). *(Ṣaḥīḥ Bukhārī, vol. 1, pp. 6, Ḥadīš 1)*

It is Ḥarām to take wage for Tilāwaĥ, Żikr and Na'at

Once, A'lā Ḥaḍrat Imām-e-Aĥl-e-Sunnat Maulānā Shāĥ Aḥmad Razā Khān عَلَيْهِ رَحْمَةُ الرَّحْمٰن was asked a question about paying money for reciting the Holy Quran and Żikr for the Īṣāl-e-Šawāb of a deceased person. Answering the question, he رَحْمَةُ اللهِ تَعَالٰى عَلَيْه said, 'Both paying and receiving money for reciting the Holy Quran and Żikr are Ḥarām. Both the giver and the taker are sinners, and how can they be able to send any reward (to the deceased) for committing a Ḥarām act? In fact, expecting a reward for committing a sin is a much more severe sin.

If somebody wants to send reward in a permissible way, he should hire the reciter (of the Quran) for an hour or two in exchange for a fixed payment, e.g. he should say 'I hire you from such and such time to such and such time, I will make you do whatever I want during this period, the (other should) say 'I accept.' In this way, he will become an employee for that duration of time and (the employer) can make him do whatever he wants. The employer should then say to his employee 'Recite the Holy Quran or the Kalimaĥ or Ṣalāt-'Alan-Nabī for so-and-so deceased person.' This is a permissible way.'
(Fatāwā Razawiyyaĥ (Jadīd), vol. 10, pp. 193-194)

A permissible way of salary for Tarāwīḥ

In the light of the blessed Fatwā issued by A'lā Ḥaḍrat رَحْمَةُ اللهِ تَعَالٰى عَلَيْه, a permissible way of paying money to the Ḥāfiẓ for leading the Tarāwīḥ Ṣalāĥ can also be obtained. Masjid committees can hire a Ḥāfiẓ with a fixed amount of salary to lead the 'Ishā Ṣalāĥ during Ramadan and then he can lead the Tarāwīḥ Ṣalāĥ as well because the Tarāwīḥ Ṣalāĥ is considered a part of 'Ishā in Ramadan. Another way is to appoint the Ḥāfiẓ for three hours every day (e.g. 8 p.m. to 11 p.m.) on the condition that he must carry out whatever he is asked. The amount to be paid to him must also be fixed in advance. If the Ḥāfiẓ agrees, he will become an employee. Now the employer (i.e. Masjid committee) can make him lead the Tarāwīḥ Ṣalāĥ during those three hours.

Remember! Whether it is Imāmat (leading Ṣalāĥs), Khiṭābat (delivering speeches), uttering the Ażān or any other type of job that entails a salary, it is Wājib to fix the amount in advance, otherwise both the (employer and employee) will be sinners. However, if the amount or price of some thing is already clear and definite, for example a bus fare or fixed amount for loading and unloading each sack (of grain etc.) in markets; it is not necessary to fix amount or price in such cases.

Remember! When a Ḥāfiẓ (or any one else) is going to be employed for any job it is not permissible to say 'We'll give you whatever is appropriate' or 'We'll please you.' Instead, it is mandatory to fix the salary. The employer should say, for example, 'We will give you 12000 rupees.' Further, the approval of the Ḥāfiẓ is also necessary for the appointment. If the appointment is made, the employer will have to give the Ḥāfiẓ 12000 rupees whether the weekly donations (of the Masjid) add up to that amount or not. The employer (committee) can also give the Ḥāfiẓ more than the agreed amount without the demand of Ḥāfiẓ Sahib.

The Ḥāfiẓ who cannot lead Tarāwīḥ or cannot recite the Quran without money or the Na'at reciter who cannot recite Na'at due to the same reason should not commit unlawful acts because of hesitation. Acting upon the method formulated by A'lā Ḥaḍrat رَحْمَةُ اللّٰهِ تَعَالٰی عَلَیْه they should earn lawful earnings. If they don't need the money, they should avoid earning it even through the Ḥīlaĥ (the method prescribed by A'lā Ḥaḍrat رَحْمَةُ اللّٰهِ تَعَالٰی عَلَیْه) because the actions performed selflessly have their own unique reward. A great trial is that when someone doesn't accept the money offered to him, people praise him (for his selflessness) a lot and it becomes extremely difficult for him to avoid ostentation. How good it would be, if such a person (Ḥāfiẓ, Na'at reciter etc.) takes the money according to the previously mentioned method and then secretly gives it as a donation without letting even his closest friend or even his family know about it, otherwise it will become very difficult for him to avoid showing off. The pleasure of worship lies in the fact that only the worshipper and his Rab عَزَّوَجَلَّ are aware of the worships.

Mayrā ĥar 'amal bas Tayray wāsiṭay ĥo
Kar ikhlāṣ aysā 'aṭā Yā Ilāĥī

My every deed be solely for You, Almighty
Bless me with such a treasure of sincerity

Finishing the Holy Quran with spiritual passion

Wherever the Holy Quran is recited once in the Tarāwīḥ Ṣalāĥ, it is preferable to finish it on the 27th night. There should be a feeling of sadness and grief at the time of finishing the Quran. The thoughts of carelessness and inattention during reciting or listening to the Quran, mistakes during recitation and lack of sincerity should sadden us and make us cry.

Unfortunately, the speech of worldly personalities is listened to attentively but the sacred words of the Creator of the universe عَزَّوَجَلَّ are listened to inattentively. The feeling that only a few moments of Ramadan are left, and '*I don't know if I'll be alive to attain its blessings next year or not*' should deeply sadden us. We all should feel ashamed of our carelessness and mistakes committed in Ramadan. If possible, we should weep or at least wear a weeping look as it is good to imitate the pious. If only a single drop of tear shed sincerely in the love of the Holy Quran or in the grief of the departure of Ramadan pleases Allah عَزَّوَجَلَّ, then all those present at the time of finishing the Quran are expected to be forgiven due to the blessing of only one that sincere tear.

Lāj rakĥ lay gunaĥgāraun kī
Nām Raḥmān ĥay Tayrā Yā Rab!
'Ayb mayray na kĥol Maḥshar mayn
Nām Sattār ĥay Tayrā Yā Rab!
Bay-sabab bakhsh day na pūcĥ 'amal
Nām Ghaffār ĥay Tayrā Yā Rab!

Have mercy on sinners
Your name is Raḥmān, Yā Rab
Do not expose my faults on Judgement Day
Your name is Sattār, Yā Rab
Forgive me without accountability of my deeds
Your name is Ghaffār, Yā Rab

Tarāwīḥ Jamā'at is a good innovation (Bid'at-e-Ḥasanaĥ)

The Prophet of mankind, the Peace of our heart and mind, the most Generous and Kind صَلَّى اللهُ تَعَالٰى عَلَيْهِ وَاٰلِهٖ وَسَلَّم performed the Tarāwīḥ Ṣalāĥ himself and liked it very much. Therefore, he صَلَّى اللهُ تَعَالٰى عَلَيْهِ وَاٰلِهٖ وَسَلَّم has said: 'Whoever offers Ṣalāĥ in Ramadan due to faith for earning reward his next and previous sins (the minor ones) will be forgiven.'

However, he صَلَّى اللهُ تَعَالٰى عَلَيْهِ وَاٰلِهٖ وَسَلَّم didn't offer it consistently lest it (the Tarāwīḥ Ṣalāĥ) becomes Farḍ for the Ummaĥ. During his reign, Amīr-ul-Mūminīn, Sayyidunā 'Umar Fārūq A'ẓam رَضِىَ اللهُ تَعَالٰى عَنْهُ saw people at a night of Ramadan offer the Tarāwīḥ Ṣalāĥ individually in the Masjid. Some of them were offering alone while some others were offering with an Imām. Observing this situation, he رَضِىَ اللهُ تَعَالٰى عَنْهُ said, 'I consider it appropriate to gather them all behind one Imām.' Therefore, he رَضِىَ اللهُ تَعَالٰى عَنْهُ appointed Sayyidunā Ubay Ibn Ka'b رَضِىَ اللهُ تَعَالٰى عَنْهُ as their Imām. The following night, he رَضِىَ اللهُ تَعَالٰى عَنْهُ saw people offer (Tarāwīḥ) together with Jamā'at (congregation). Pleased, he commented 'نِعْمَ الْبِدْعَةُ هٰذِهِ' (*This is a good innovation*). *(Ṣaḥīḥ Bukhārī, vol. 1, pp. 658, Ḥadīš 2010)*

Dear Islamic brothers! Did you realize how intensely the Beloved and Blessed Prophet صَلَّى اللهُ تَعَالٰى عَلَيْهِ وَاٰلِهٖ وَسَلَّم cares about us! He صَلَّى اللهُ تَعَالٰى عَلَيْهِ وَاٰلِهٖ وَسَلَّم did not offer Tarāwīḥ Ṣalāĥ consistently just for fear that it might become Farḍ for his Ummaĥ. This narration removes some doubts and misconceptions as well. For example, Beloved Rasūl صَلَّى اللهُ تَعَالٰى عَلَيْهِ وَاٰلِهٖ وَسَلَّم could have launched the Tarāwīḥ Jamā'at himself, but he didn't do so giving his Ummaĥ the opportunity to introduce good and useful innovations.

Sayyidunā 'Umar Fārūq A'ẓam رَضِىَ اللهُ تَعَالٰى عَنْهُ enforced such an act that the Holy Prophet صَلَّى اللهُ تَعَالٰى عَلَيْهِ وَاٰلِهٖ وَسَلَّم did not do (i.e. offering Tarāwīḥ with Jamā'at). He رَضِىَ اللهُ تَعَالٰى عَنْهُ did not do this on the basis of his personal opinion. In fact, our Beloved Rasūl صَلَّى اللهُ تَعَالٰى عَلَيْهِ وَاٰلِهٖ وَسَلَّم had already permitted his Ummaĥ in his visible life up to the Day of Judgement to introduce such new and useful innovations, as clearly stated in the following Ḥadīš.

The Beloved and Blessed Prophet صَلَّى اللهُ تَعَالٰى عَلَيْهِ وَاٰلِهٖ وَسَلَّم has said, 'The one enforcing a good innovation in Islam will get its reward as well as the reward of those acting upon it after him without any reduction in their reward. And the one enforcing an evil innovation in Islam will have its sin as well as the sin of those acting upon it after him, without any reduction in their sins.' *(Ṣaḥīḥ Muslim, pp. 1438, Ḥadīš 1017)*

Twelve good innovations

The foregoing blessed Ḥadīš has made it as clear as a bright day that the permission of introducing new and good innovations in Islam up to the Day of Judgement has already been granted. اَلْحَمْدُ لِلّٰه عَزَّوَجَلَّ! Many such useful innovations were introduced. Some are as follows:

1. Amīr-ul-Mūminīn Sayyidunā 'Umar Fārūq A'ẓam رَضِیَ اللّٰهُ تَعَالٰی عَنْهُ enforced the Tarāwīḥ Jamā'at, declaring it a good innovation. Therefore, it is obvious that if the blessed companions رَضِیَ اللّٰهُ تَعَالٰی عَنْهُم introduced a new innovation after the apparent demise of Beloved Rasūl صَلَّى اللّٰهُ تَعَالٰى عَلَيْهِ وَاٰلِهٖ وَسَلَّم it would be considered a Bid'at-e-Ḥasanaĥ.

2. In past, there used to be no arch (Miḥrāb) in the Masājid for Imams. It was Sayyidunā 'Umar Bin 'Abdul 'Azīz رَضِیَ اللّٰهُ تَعَالٰی عَنْهُ who first got an arch constructed in Masjid-un-Nabawī. This innovation (Bid'at-e-Ḥasanaĥ) has now become so popular that Masājid throughout world are identified by the arch (Miḥrāb).

3. Likewise, domes and minarets on Masājid throughout the world are an innovation. Even the minarets of Masjid-ul-Ḥarām did not exist in the time of the Holy Prophet صَلَّى اللّٰهُ تَعَالٰى عَلَيْهِ وَاٰلِهٖ وَسَلَّم or his blessed companions رَضِیَ اللّٰهُ تَعَالٰی عَنْهُم.

4. Īmān-e-Mufaṣṣal

5. Īmān-e-Mujmal

6. The six Kalimaĥs, their numbers, their sequence (the 1st Kalimaĥ, 2nd Kalimaĥ etc.), and their names.

7. Dividing the Holy Quran into 30 parts, diacritical marks, dividing it into sections (Rukū'), the punctuation marks, and even the dots (above and beneath the letters), publishing it with attractive covers etc.

8. Publishing Ḥadīš books, arguing the authenticity of narrations, dividing Aḥādīš into categories such as Ṣaḥīḥ, Ḥasan, Ḍa'īf, Mauḍū' etc.

9. Fiqĥ, Uṣūl-ul-Fiqĥ and 'Ilm-ul-Kalām.

10. Paying Zakāĥ and Ṣadaqaĥ-e-Fiṭr in the form of coins and printed notes.

11. Going on Hajj-pilgrimage by liners and aeroplanes instead of camels.

12. The four orders of Sharī'aĥ and Ṭarīqaĥ; Ḥanafī, Shāfi'ī, Mālikī, Ḥanbalī, Qādirī, Naqshbandī, Suĥarwardī and Chishtī.

Every Bid'aĥ isn't heterodoxy

A question may arise in someone's mind as to what the following two blessed Aḥādīš mean:

1. كُلُّ بِدْعَةٍ ضَلَالَةٌ وَّ كُلُّ ضَلَالَةٍ فِى النَّار [Every innovation is heterodoxy (i.e. deviation from Islamic teachings) and every heterodoxy leads to Hell]. *(Sunan Nasāī, vol. 2, pp. 189)*

2. شَرُّ الْاُمُوْرِ مُحْدَثَاتُهَا وَ كُلُّ بِدْعَةٍ ضَلَالَة [The worst of actions are innovations and every innovation is heterodoxy]. *(Ṣaḥīḥ Muslim, pp. 430, Ḥadīš 867)*

Without doubt, both the blessed Aḥādīš are true. In fact, the word Bid'aĥ mentioned in these two Aḥādīš refers to Bid'at-e-Sayyi'aĥ (بِدعَتِ سَيِّـئَه), (misleading innovation) and indeed every Bid'aĥ that contradicts or removes a Sunnaĥ is misleading.

The detailed description of this issue has been clearly mentioned in some other Aḥādīš. Therefore, the Noble Prophet صَلَّى اللهُ تَعَالٰى عَلَيْهِ وَاٰلِهٖ وَسَلَّم has said, 'The one who introduces such a misleading innovation that Allah عَزَّوَجَلَّ and His Beloved Rasūl صَلَّى اللهُ تَعَالٰى عَلَيْهِ وَاٰلِهٖ وَسَلَّم are not pleased with, will have the sin of all the followers of that Bid'aĥ, without any reduction in their sins.' *(Jāmi' Tirmiżī, vol. 4, pp. 309, Ḥadīš 2686)*

In another Ḥadīš the mother of the believers Sayyidatunā 'Āishaĥ Ṣiddīqaĥ رَضِىَ اللهُ تَعَالٰى عَنْهَا has narrated that the Holy Prophet صَلَّى اللهُ تَعَالٰى عَلَيْهِ وَاٰلِهٖ وَسَلَّم has said: مَنْ أَحْدَثَ فِىْ أَمْرِنَا هٰذَا مَا لَيْسَ فِيْهِ فَهُوَ رَدٌّ (*The innovation that is not based on our religion is rejected*). *(Ṣaḥīḥ Bukhārī, vol. 6, pp. 211, Ḥadīš 2697)*

These blessed Aḥādīš clarify that any innovation which contradicts the Sunnaĥ, misleads people and is not based on the principles of our religion is a Bid'at-e-Sayyi'aĥ, (misleading innovation) but any such innovation that helps people practice Sunnaĥ and is based on Sharī'aĥ is a Bid'at-e-Ḥasanaĥ (a good innovation).

Committing on the Ḥadīš 'وَّكُلُّ ضَلَالَةٍ فِى النَّار' Sayyidunā Shaykh 'Abdul Ḥaq Muḥaddiš Diĥlvī عَلَيْهِ رَحْمَةُ اللّٰهِ الْقَوِى has stated, 'Any Bid'aĥ that complies with the principles of Sunnaĥ and does not contradict Sharī'aĥ or Sunnaĥ is a Bid'at-e-Ḥasanaĥ. Otherwise it is a Bid'at-e-Ḍalālaĥ, i.e. a misleading innovation.' *(Ashi'at-ul-Lam'āt, vol. 1, pp. 135)*

We cannot do without good innovations

Anyway, it is necessary to categorize innovations into good and bad. At present era, there are many such good innovations which didn't exist in the first three ages, i.e. (i) the age of the Beloved and Blessed Rasūl صَلَّى اللّٰهُ تَعَالٰى عَلَيْهِ وَاٰلِهٖ وَسَلَّم and that of his companions رَضِىَ اللّٰهُ تَعَالٰى عَنْهُم (ii) the age of the honourable successors (Tabi'īn) and (iii) the age of followers of the honourable successors (Tab'-e-Tābi'īn). If such innovations are discarded, the existing religious system will not survive. For example, religious schools, Dars-e-Niẓāmī, publishing copies of the Holy Quran, and Ḥadīš books etc. are all such acts that were not done in the first three eras and were introduced later and are classed as Bid'at-e-Ḥasanaĥ.

Anyway, the Holy Prophet صَلَّى اللّٰهُ تَعَالٰى عَلَيْهِ وَاٰلِهٖ وَسَلَّم could have enforced all these acts during his apparent life, but Allah عَزَّوَجَلَّ has given many opportunities of earning perpetual reward (Šawāb-e-Jāriyaĥ) to the Ummaĥ of His Beloved Prophet صَلَّى اللّٰهُ تَعَالٰى عَلَيْهِ وَاٰلِهٖ وَسَلَّم. Therefore, in order to earn perpetual reward, pious people introduced a lot of innovations that do not contradict Sharī'aĥ. Such good innovations enforced by the pious include reciting Ṣalāt-'Alan-Nabī and Salām before the Aẓān, celebrating the Mīlād with illuminations, waving beautiful green flags and chanting slogans of Marḥabā in procession, Giyārĥwīn and the 'Urs of Auliyā رَحِمَهُمُ اللّٰهُ تَعَالٰى. This process still continues.

اَلْحَمْدُ لِلّٰه عَزَّوَجَلَّ! Dawat-e-Islami has also made its contribution to the introduction of good innovations in Islam by enforcing the slogans اُذْكُرُوا الله (i.e. Do the Żikr of Allah عَزَّوَجَلَّ) and صَلُّوْا عَلَى الْحَبِيْب (i.e. Send Ṣalāt upon the Beloved صَلَّى اللّٰهُ تَعَالٰى عَلَيْهِ وَاٰلِهٖ وَسَلَّم) in its Ijtimā'āt, making the atmosphere pleasant by the sound of the Żikr of Allah عَزَّوَجَلَّ and His Beloved Rasūl صَلَّى اللّٰهُ تَعَالٰى عَلَيْهِ وَاٰلِهٖ وَسَلَّم

History of green dome

The green dome that every devotee desires to behold with tear in eyes is also a Bid'at-e-Ḥasanaĥ because it was made hundreds of years after the apparent demise of the Holy Prophet صَلَّى اللّٰهُ تَعَالٰى عَلَيْهِ وَاٰلِهٖ وَسَلَّم.

Here is a brief history of the blessed dome: The first dome on the blessed tomb of our Beloved Rasūl صَلَّى اللّٰهُ تَعَالٰى عَلَيْهِ وَاٰلِهٖ وَسَلَّم was constructed in 678 AH (1269 AD). As it was yellow, it used to be referred to as the yellow dome. Then different changes took place in different eras. In 888 AH (1483 AD) a new dome was made from black stone and it was painted white. Devotees used to call it 'قُـبَّةُ البَيْضاء' or 'گنبدِ بَیضاء' meaning the white dome.

An extremely beautiful dome was made in 980 AH (1572 AD) and was adorned with different coloured stones, now it became multicoloured and didn't have just one colour. It was most probably referred to as the multicoloured dome due to its different attractive colours. It was reconstructed in 1233 AH (1818 AD) and painted green. It then began to be called the green dome, and has not been changed ever since. The green colour is blessed with the privilege of being used to paint the blessed dome.

The green dome, which is definitely and certainly a Bid'at-e-Ḥasanaĥ, is now the focal point of all Muslims throughout the world, the apple of our eyes, and the peace of our hearts. اِنْ شَــآءَاللّٰه عَزَّوَجَلَّ No power of the world can demolish it, and anyone who attempts to demolish it will be ruined himself, اِنْ شَــآءَاللّٰه عَزَّوَجَلَّ.

All these new innovations are based on the blessed Ḥadīš mentioned earlier with the reference of *Ṣaḥīḥ Muslim* that the one who introduces a good innovation in Islam will get its reward as well as the reward of all those acting upon it after him[1].

Beholding Holy Prophet صَلَّى اللّٰهُ عَلَيْهِ وَاٰلِهٖ وَسَلَّم

Dear Islamic brothers! For the rectification of beliefs and deeds and for acquisition of necessary religious knowledge, please travel with the Madanī Qāfilaĥs of Dawat-e-Islami, a global & non-political religious movement of the Quran and Sunnaĥ.

اَلْحَمْدُ لِلّٰه عَزَّوَجَلَّ! Dawat-e-Islami is the movement of the Muslims possessing correct Islamic beliefs. Listen to a faith-refreshing and heart-warming account.

Numerous Madanī Qāfilaĥs of Rasūl's devotees travel to various villages and cities at the end of the 3 day Sunnaĥ-Inspiring global Ijtimā' of Dawat-e-Islami. One of these Madanī Qāfilaĥs reached a Masjid in Agra Taj Colony (Bāb-ul-Madīnaĥ, Karachi). When the participants went to sleep at night, one of the Islamic brothers was blessed with beholding

[1] For further details of the types of Bid'aĥ/innovations please refer to the book '*Jā-al-Ḥaq-wa-Zaĥaq-al-Bāṭil*' by a renowned exegetist of the Quran, Muftī Aḥmad Yār Khān Na'īmī رَحْمَةُ اللّٰهِ تَعَالٰى عَلَيْه

the Holy Prophet صَلَّى اللهُ تَعَالٰى عَلَيْهِ وَاٰلِهٖ وَسَلَّم in his dream. He became very delighted and realized the truth and greatness of Dawat-e-Islami from the bottom of his heart and joined the Madanī environment.

صَلُّوْا عَلَى الْحَبِيْب صَلَّى اللهُ تَعَالٰى عَلٰى مُحَمَّد

Virtues of loving pious people

Dear Islamic brothers! Did you see! A fortunate Islamic brother was blessed with the vision of the Beloved and Blessed Prophet صَلَّى اللهُ تَعَالٰى عَلَيْهِ وَاٰلِهٖ وَسَلَّم due to the blessings of the company of Rasūl's devotees. Therefore, we should always adopt the company of good people and love them. The fortunate Islamic brothers who travel with Madanī Qāfilaĥs develop love for good people in their hearts. Here are seven virtues of loving good people.

1. On the Day of Judgement, Allah عَزَّوَجَلَّ shall say 'Where are those who loved one another for the sake of My honour, I shall keep them in shade today, there is no shade except My shade today.' *(Ṣaḥīḥ Muslim, pp. 1388, Ḥadīš 2566)*

2. Allah عَزَّوَجَلَّ says, 'My love becomes Wājib for those who love one another for My pleasure, sit together, meet each other and spend their wealth for My pleasure.' *(Muwaṭṭā Imām Mālik, vol. 2, pp. 439, Ḥadīš 1828)*

3. Allah عَزَّوَجَلَّ says, 'There shall be pulpits of Nūr for those who love one another for the sake of My honour. The Prophets and martyrs will be impressed by them.' *(Jāmi' Tirmiżī, vol. 4, pp. 174, Ḥadīš 2397)*

4. (When) two people love each other for the pleasure of Allah عَزَّوَجَلَّ, Allah عَزَّوَجَلَّ shall gather them on the Day of Judgement even if one of them is in the east and the other in the west. (Allah عَزَّوَجَلَّ will then) say, 'He is the one you loved for My pleasure.' *(Shu'ab-ul-Īmān, vol. 6, pp. 492, Ḥadīš 9022)*

5. In Heaven, there are pillars of rubies which have balconies of emeralds that shine like stars, the companions asked, 'Yā Rasūlallāĥ صَلَّى اللهُ تَعَالٰى عَلَيْهِ وَاٰلِهٖ وَسَلَّم who will live in them.' He صَلَّى اللهُ تَعَالٰى عَلَيْهِ وَاٰلِهٖ وَسَلَّم replied, 'Those who love one another, sit together and meet one another for the pleasure of Allah عَزَّوَجَلَّ.' *(Shu'ab-ul-Īmān, vol. 6, pp. 487, Ḥadīš 9002)*

6. Those who love one another for Allah عَزَّوَجَلَّ shall sit beside the divine 'Arsh on chairs made of rubies. *(Mu'jam Kabīr, vol. 4, pp. 150, Ḥadīš 3973)*

7. The one who loves someone for Allah عَزَّوَجَلَّ, hates (someone) for Allah عَزَّوَجَلَّ, gives for Allah عَزَّوَجَلَّ and forbids for Allah عَزَّوَجَلَّ has perfected his faith. *(Sunan Abī Dāwūd, vol. 4, pp. 290, Ḥadīš 4681)*

Thirty five Madanī pearls of Tarāwīḥ

1. Offering Tarāwīḥ Ṣalāĥ is a Sunnat-ul-Muakkadaĥ for every sane and adult Islamic brother and sister. *(Durr-e-Mukhtār, vol. 2, pp. 493)* Missing Tarāwīḥ is not permissible.

2. Tarāwīḥ consists of twenty Rak'āt. During the reign of Sayyidunā 'Umar Fārūq A'ẓam رَضِیَ اللّٰہُ تَعَالٰی عَنْہُ the Muslims would offer twenty Rak'āt of Tarāwīḥ. *(Sunan Kubrā, vol. 2, pp. 699, Ḥadīš 4617)*

3. The Jamā'at of Tarāwīḥ is a Sunnat-ul-Muakkadaĥ 'Alal Kifāyaĥ. If all the people miss it they all will be considered to have committed an undesirable act. If a few people offer it with Jamā'at then those offering individually will remain deprived of the reward of Jamā'at. *(Ĥidāyaĥ, vol. 1, pp. 70)*

4. The time for the Tarāwīḥ Ṣalāĥ begins after offering the Farḍ of 'Ishā and ends at dawn (Ṣubḥ-e-Ṣādiq). If it is offered before the Farḍ of 'Ishā it will not be valid. *(Fatāwā 'Ālamgīrī, vol. 1, pp. 115)*

5. Tarāwīḥ can be offered even after the Farḍ and Witr of 'Ishā as well. *(Durr-e-Mukhtār, vol. 2, pp. 494)* This sometimes happens when the witness of the appearance of the moon is obtained with delay on the 29th (of Sha'bān).

6. It is Mustaḥab to delay the Tarāwīḥ until one third (1/3) part of the night has passed. There is no harm in offering Tarāwīḥ even after the passing of the half part of the night. *(Durr-e-Mukhtār, vol. 2, pp. 495)*

7. If missed, there is no Qaḍā for the Tarāwīḥ Ṣalāĥ. *(Durr-e-Mukhtār, vol. 2, pp. 494)*

8. It is better to offer the twenty Rak'āt of Tarāwīḥ in sets of two Rak'āt with ten Salāms. *(Durr-e-Mukhtār, vol. 2, pp. 495)*

9. Though all twenty Rak'āt of Tarāwīḥ can be offered with a single Salām, it is Makrūĥ to do so. It is Farḍ to do Qa'daĥ (i.e. sitting for reciting Tashaĥĥud) after every two Rak'āt. One should recite Ṣalāt-'Alan-Nabī after Tashaĥĥud in every Qa'daĥ, and recite Šanā at the beginning of every odd Rak'at (i.e. 1st, 3rd, 5th etc). The Imām should also recite Ta'awwuż and Tasmiyyaĥ in every odd Rak'at. *(Durr-e-Mukhtār, vol. 2, pp. 496)*

10. When offering Tarāwīḥ in sets of two Rak'āt, separate intention should be made before every two Rak'āt. It is also permissible to make only one intention for all the twenty Rak'āt in the beginning. *(Durr-e-Mukhtār, vol. 2, pp. 494)*

11. Offering Tarāwīḥ Ṣalāĥ sitting without a valid exemption is Makrūĥ, and some respected Islamic jurists رَحِمَهُمُ اللّٰهُ تَعَالٰی have declared that Tarāwīḥ will be invalid in this case. *(Durr-e-Mukhtār, vol. 2, pp. 499)*

12. It is preferable to offer the Tarāwīḥ Ṣalāĥ with the Jamā'at in the Masjid. Though it is not a sin to offer it with a Jamā'at at home, one will not be able to get the reward of offering in the Masjid. *(Fatāwā 'Ālamgīrī, vol. 1, pp. 116)*

    In case of offering Tarāwīḥ at home or in a public hall, it is Wājib to offer the Farḍ of 'Ishā Ṣalāĥ with the Jamā'at in the Masjid first. Instead of Masjid, offering the Farḍ of 'Ishā Ṣalāĥ with Jamā'at at home or in the hall etc. without a valid Shar'ī exemption will amount to committing the sin of missing a Wājib. For more details on this issue, please go through the chapter of *Faīzān-e-Sunnat 'Excellence of Hunger* (page no. 490 & 491).'

13. A minor can lead the Jamā'at of minors only in Tarāwīḥ.

14. An adult cannot offer Tarāwīḥ Ṣalāĥ or any other Ṣalāĥ including even the Nafl Ṣalāĥ led by a minor. If an adult does so his Ṣalāĥ will not be valid.

15. Reciting and listening to the entire Quran in Tarāwīḥ is Sunnat-ul-Muakkadaĥ. *(Fatāwā Razawiyyaĥ (Jadīd), vol. 7, pp. 458)*

16. If a full-fledged Ḥāfiẓ is not available or the whole Quran could not be recited due to any other reason, one can recite any Sūraĥ in the Tarāwīḥ Ṣalāĥ. If he wants, he can recite from 'اَلَمْ تَـرَ' until 'وَالنَّاس' twice, this will make it easier to remember the twenty Rak'āt. *(Fatāwā 'Ālamgīrī, vol. 1, pp. 118)*

17. It is a Sunnaĥ to recite بِسۡمِ اللّٰهِ الرَّحۡـمٰنِ الرَّحِيۡمِ once loudly, whereas reciting it in low voice before each Sūraĥ is Mustaḥab. The Mutāakhkhirīn (succeeding scholars رَحِمَهُمُ اللّٰهُ تَعَالٰى have also declared) it Mustaḥab to recite قُلْ هُوَ اللّٰه three times in the completion of the whole Quran's recitation. Further, recitation from الٓمّ to مُفْلِحُوْنَ in the last Rak'at is also preferable on the day of the completion of the recitation. *(Baĥār-e-Sharī'at, part 4, pp. 37)*

18. If the Tarāwīḥ Ṣalāĥ becomes invalid due to some reason, the Sūraĥ or the part of the Quran recited during the invalid Rak'at should be repeated so that the recitation of the entire Quran would not remain incomplete. *(Fatāwā 'Ālamgīrī, vol. 1, pp. 118)*

19. If the Imām misses a verse or Sūraĥ by mistake and continues to recite, it is Mustaḥab to recite the missed part and then carry on. *(Fatāwā 'Ālamgīrī, vol. 1, pp. 118)*

20. If there's no harm in listening to the recitation of the complete Quran, one can offer Tarāwīḥ Ṣalāĥ in different Masājid. For example, if there are three such Masājid in which 1¼ parts of the Holy Quran is recited everyday, then one can go to each of them on different days.

21. If the one who has forgot to sit for Qa'daĥ after two Rak'āt has not yet performed the Sajdaĥ of the third Rak'at, he is to sit and complete his Ṣalāĥ with a Sajdaĥ Saĥw. In case of performing the Sajdaĥ of the third Rak'at, he is to complete the fourth Rak'at as well, but these four Rak'āt will be counted as two. However, if he had performed Qa'daĥ after two Rak'āt they will be regarded as four Rak'āt.

(Fatāwā 'Ālamgīrī, vol. 1, pp. 118)

22. If somebody did not sit after the second Rak'at and performed Salām (finished the Ṣalāĥ) after the third Rak'āt, then these Rak'āt will not be valid; he will have to offer a new set of two Rak'āt again. *(Fatāwā 'Ālamgīrī, vol. 1, pp. 118)*

23. After performing Salām, if there's a divergence of opinion over the number of Rak'āt (e.g. some say two Rak'āt were offered while some other opine three), so what Imām asserts on the basis of his memory will be accepted in this case. If the Imām is himself uncertain then he is to accept the opinion of the one he considers reliable. *(Fatāwā 'Ālamgīrī, vol. 1, pp. 117)*

24. If people are in doubt whether twenty Rak'āt were offered or eighteen they should all offer two Rak'āt individually. *(Fatāwā 'Ālamgīrī, vol. 1, pp. 117)*

25. The recitation of the equal amount of the Quran during each set of two Rak'at is preferable. If it is not done, there is still no harm. Likewise, the amount of the second Rak'at's recitation should be equal to that of the first Rak'at. The recitation of the second Rak'at should not exceed that of the first one. *(Fatāwā 'Ālamgīrī, vol. 1, pp. 117)*

26. Both the Imām and the Muqtadīs should recite the Šanā at the beginning of every first Rak'at (the Imām should recite Ta'awwuż and Tasmiyyaĥ as well). Both should also recite Durūd-e-Ibrāĥīm and Du'ā after Tashaĥĥud in Qa'daĥ. *(Durr-e-Mukhtār, vol. 2, pp. 498)*

27. If the Muqtadīs of Tarāwīḥ-Jamā'at feel discomfort, the Imām should only recite اَللّٰھُمَّ صَلِّ عَلٰی مُحَمَّدٍ وَّ اٰلِهٖ after Tashaĥĥud (and perform Salām). *(Durr-e-Mukhtār, vol. 2, pp. 499)*

28. Keep offering Tarāwīḥ up to the last night of Ramadan even if the recitation of the entire Holy Quran completes on the 27th night or earlier because it is Sunnat-ul-Muakkadaĥ. *(Fatāwā 'Ālamgīrī, vol. 1, pp. 118)*

29. After every set of four Rak'āt it is Mustaḥab to sit for rest for the amount of time in which four Rak'āt were offered. This pause is called a Tarwīḥaĥ. *(Fatāwā 'Ālamgīrī, vol. 1, pp. 115)*

30. During the Tarwīḥah̄, it is allowed whether to remain silent, recite Ṣalāt-'Alan-Nabī, do Żikr or offer Nafl Ṣalāh̄ individually. *(Durr-e-Mukhtār, vol. 2, pp. 497)* The following Tasbīḥ can also be recited.

سُبْحَانَ ذِی الْمُلْكِ وَالْمَلَكُوْتِ ۝ سُبْحَانَ ذِی الْعِزَّةِ وَالْعَظَمَةِ وَالْهَيْبَةِ وَالْقُدْرَةِ ط وَالْكِبْرِيَآءِ وَالْجَبَرُوْتِ ۝ سُبْحَانَ الْمَلِكِ الْحَيِّ الَّذِیْ لَا يَنَامُ وَلَا يَمُوْتُ ۝ سُبُّوْحٌ قُدُّوْسٌ رَّبُّنَا وَ رَبُّ الْمَلٰٓئِكَةِ وَالرُّوْحِ ۝ اَللّٰهُمَّ اَجِرْنَا مِنَ النَّارِ ۝ يَا مُجِيْرُ يَا مُجِيْرُ يَا مُجِيْرُ ۝ بِرَحْمَتِكَ يَا اَرْحَمَ الرَّاحِمِيْنَ ۝

31. After offering twenty Rak'āt, the fifth Tarwīḥah̄ is also Mustaḥab, but if it causes discomfort to people then don't recite it for the fifth time. *(Fatāwā 'Ālamgīrī, vol. 1, pp. 115)*

32. Some people keep sitting during the initial part of the first Rak'at and stand to join the Jamā'at when the Imām is about to perform Rukū', it is a trait of the hypocrites. The 142nd verse of Sūrah̄ An-Nisā says:

وَاِذَا قَامُوْۤا اِلَى الصَّلٰوةِ قَامُوْا كُسَالٰى ۙ

And when they stand up for Ṣalāh̄ they stand up lazily.

[Kanz-ul-Īmān (Translation of Quran)]

One should also join the Jamā'at of Farḍ Ṣalāh̄ immediately even if the Imām has stood after completing the Rukū'. Further, if the Imām is in the first sitting (Qa'dah̄), join in without waiting for him to stand. If you joined in during the Qa'dah̄ (sitting) but the Imām (has finished his Tashah̄h̄ud and) stood up, recite the whole Tashah̄h̄ud before standing. *(Bah̄ār-e-Sharī'at, part 4, pp. 36 – Ghunya-tul-Mustamlī, pp. 410)*

33. It is preferable to offer the Witr Ṣalāĥ with Jamā'at in Ramadan. However, if someone offered the Farḍ of 'Ishā without Jamā'at he is to offer his Witr individually as well. *(Baĥār-e-Sharī'at, part 4, pp. 36)*

34. There is no harm in offering the Farḍ of 'Ishā with one Imām, the Tarāwīḥ Ṣalāĥ with another Imām and the Witr with a third Imām.

35. Sayyidunā 'Umar Fārūq A'ẓam رَضِیَ اللّٰہُ تَعَالٰی عَنْہُ used to lead the Jamā'at of Farḍ and Witr of 'Isha while Sayyidunā Ubay Bin Ka'b رَضِیَ اللّٰہُ تَعَالٰی عَنْہُ used to lead the Tarāwīḥ Jamā'at. *(Fatāwā 'Ālamgīrī, vol. 1, pp. 116)*

O Allah عَزَّوَجَلَّ! Make us pious and sincere and bless us with the privilege of offering Tarāwīḥ with sincerity and concentration every year with a full-fledged Ḥāfiẓ, and accept our Ṣalāĥs!

اٰمِیْن بِجَاہِ النَّبِیِّ الْاَمِیْن صَلَّی اللّٰہُ تَعَالٰی عَلَیْہِ وَاٰلِہٖ وَسَلَّم

صَلُّوْا عَلَی الْحَبِیْب صَلَّی اللّٰہُ تَعَالٰی عَلٰی مُحَمَّد

Recovery from cancer

اَلْحَمْدُ لِلّٰہ عَزَّوَجَلَّ! Allah عَزَّوَجَلَّ and His Beloved Rasūl صَلَّی اللّٰہُ تَعَالٰی عَلَیْہِ وَاٰلِہٖ وَسَلَّم have greatly blessed Dawat-e-Islami. Many patients suffering from such deadly diseases declared incurable by doctors have found the cure for their lethal diseases in the Madanī Qāfilaĥs. Here is an account given by an Islamic brother of Maripur (Bāb-ul-Madīnaĥ, Karachi) 'An Islamic brother living at Hawk's bay (Bāb-ul-Madīnaĥ, Karachi) had cancer. He travelled with a Madanī Qāfilaĥ of Dawat-e-Islami, a global & non-political religious movement of the Quran and Sunnaĥ, in the company of Rasūl's devotees.

During the journey, he looked quite sad and disappointed. The participants of the Madanī Qāfilaĥ consoled him and made supplications for him. One morning, while he was sitting, all of a sudden, he vomited a piece of flesh, after which he felt greatly relieved.

Having returned from the Madanī Qāfilaĥ he went to see a doctor and had his tests done again. He was astonished to see results which indicated that he no longer had cancer. اَلْحَمْدُلِلّٰہ عَزَّوَجَلَّ He regained his health by the blessings of travelling with a Madanī Qāfilaĥ.

Ulcer-o-cancer yā ĥo dard-e-kamar
Day gā Maulā shifā, Qāfilay mayn chalo
Dūr bīmāriyān, aur parayshāniyān
Ĥaun bafaḍl-e-Khudā, Qāfilay mayn chalo

Even ulcer and cancer or backache severe
Will be cured by Almighty, travel with Madanī Qāfilaĥ
Illnesses and adversities will be removed
By divine bounty, travel with Madanī Qāfilaĥ

صَلُّوْا عَلَی الْحَبِیْب صَلَّی اللّٰهُ تَعَالٰی عَلٰی مُحَمَّد

Praise and privilege

Sayyidunā Imām 'Abdullāĥ Bin 'Umar Bayḍāwī عَلَیْهِ رَحْمَةُ اللّٰهِ الْقَوِی has stated, 'The one who obeys Allah عَزَّوَجَلَّ and His Beloved Prophet صَلَّی اللّٰهُ تَعَالٰی عَلَیْهِ وَاٰلِهٖ وَسَلَّم, is praised in the world and will be privileged in the Hereafter.'

(Tafsīr Al-Bayḍāwī, vol. 4, part 22, Al-Aḥzāb, pp. 388, Taĥt-al-Āyaĥ 71)

اَلۡحَمۡدُ لِلّٰهِ رَبِّ الۡعٰلَمِيۡنَ وَ الصَّلٰوةُ وَ السَّلَامُ عَلٰى سَيِّدِ الۡمُرۡسَلِيۡنَ

اَمَّا بَعۡدُ فَاَعُوۡذُ بِاللّٰهِ مِنَ الشَّيۡطٰنِ الرَّجِيۡمِ ؕ بِسۡمِ اللّٰهِ الرَّحۡمٰنِ الرَّحِيۡمِ ؕ

Blessings of Layla-tul-Qadr

Excellence of Ṣalāt-'Alan-Nabī ﷺ

The Prophet of mankind, the Peace of our heart and mind, the most Generous and Kind صَلَّى اللهُ تَعَالٰى عَلَيْهِ وَاٰلِهٖ وَسَلَّم has said, 'Whoever recites Ṣalāt upon me a thousand times daily shall not die until he sees his place in Heaven.' *(Attarghīb Wattarhīb, vol. 2, pp. 328, Ḥadīš 22)*

صَلُّوۡا عَلَى الۡحَبِيۡب   صَلَّى اللهُ تَعَالٰى عَلٰى مُحَمَّد

Dear Islamic brothers! Layla-tul-Qadr is an extremely blessed and sacred night. It is called Layla-tul-Qadr because the commandments of the whole year are enforced in this night. In other words, the angels make a record of whatever is going to happen the following year. It is stated in *Tafsīr Ṣāwī* on page 2398 volume 6:

اَیۡ اِظۡهَارُ هَا فِیۡ دَوَاوِیۡنِ الۡمَلَاءِ الۡاَعۡلٰی

Translation: It (destiny) appears in the registers of the angels.

There are several other reasons for the greatness of this night. A renowned exegetist of the Quran, Muftī Aḥmad Yār Khān عَلَيْهِ رَحْمَةُ الْحَنَّان has stated: This night is called Layla-tul-Qadr for several reasons:

1. In this night, the tasks of the following years are set and assigned to the angels. Qadr refers to either destiny or dignity.
2. The Holy Quran was revealed at this night.

3. The worship performed in this night has great Qadr (excellence).

4. Qadr also means 'narrowness.' Angels descend at this night in such a great number that the earth is crowded with them. For these reasons, this night is called Layla-tul-Qadr. *(Mawā'iẓ-e-Na'īmiyyaĥ, pp. 62)*

There is a Ḥadīš in *Bukhārī* Sharīf that says, 'Whoever offers Ṣalāĥ with faith and sincerity at this night shall be forgiven for all of his previous sins.' *(Ṣaḥīḥ Bukhārī, vol. 1, pp. 660, Ḥadīš 2014)*

More reward than worship of 83 years and 4 months

We must not spend this sacred night in heedlessness. Whoever worships in this night is rewarded more than the worship of 1000 months, (which implies) more than 83 years and 4 months. Only Allah عَزَّوَجَلَّ and His Beloved and Blessed Rasūl صَلَّى اللهُ تَعَالَى عَلَيْهِ وَاٰلِهٖ وَسَلَّم (who was informed by Allah عَزَّوَجَلَّ) know how much 'more.'

Sayyidunā Jibrāīl عَلَيْهِ السَّلَام and other angels descend at this night and shake hands with the worshippers. Each and every moment of this blessed night is full of peace that remains till dawn (Ṣubḥ-e-Ṣādiq). It is a huge grace of Allah عَزَّوَجَلَّ that He عَزَّوَجَلَّ has granted this glorious night only to His Beloved Prophet صَلَّى اللهُ تَعَالَى عَلَيْهِ وَاٰلِهٖ وَسَلَّم and his Ummaĥ for his sake. Allah عَزَّوَجَلَّ says in the Holy Quran:

$$ اِنَّاۤ اَنۡزَلۡنٰهُ فِیۡ لَیۡلَةِ الۡقَدۡرِ ۚ وَمَاۤ اَدۡرٰىکَ مَا لَیۡلَةُ الۡقَدۡرِ ؕ لَیۡلَةُ الۡقَدۡرِ ۙ خَیۡرٌ مِّنۡ اَلۡفِ شَهۡرٍ ؕ $$

$$ تَنَزَّلُ الۡمَلٰٓئِکَةُ وَالرُّوۡحُ فِیۡهَا بِاِذۡنِ رَبِّهِمۡ ۚ مِنۡ کُلِّ اَمۡرٍ ۙ سَلٰمٌ ۟ۛ هِیَ حَتّٰی مَطۡلَعِ الۡفَجۡرِ $$

Undoubtedly, We sent it down in the blessed night. And do you know what the blessed night is? The blessed night is better than a thousand months. Therein descend angels and Jibrāīl by the commandment of their Rab for every affair. That is all peace till the rising of the dawn. *[Kanz-ul-Īmān (Translation of Quran)] (Part 30, Sūraĥ Al-Qadr)*

Dear Islamic brothers! Did you see! Layla-tul-Qadr is so important that Allah عَزَّوَجَلَّ has revealed a whole Sūraĥ, describing its excellence. In this blessed Sūraĥ Allah عَزَّوَجَلَّ has mentioned several unique qualities of this sacred night.

Commenting on this Sūraĥ, the honourable exegetists of the Quran have said, 'In this night, Allah عَزَّوَجَلَّ sent down the Holy Quran from the Lauḥ-e-Maḥfūẓ to the first sky and then gradually revealed it to His Beloved Rasūl صَلَّى اللّٰهُ تَعَالٰى عَلَيْهِ وَاٰلِهٖ وَسَلَّم over a period of approximately 23 years.' *(Tafsīr Ṣāwī, vol. 6, pp. 2398)*

Our Holy Prophet ﷺ got dejected

It is stated in '*Tafsīr-e-'Azīzī*' that when the Beloved and Blessed Prophet صَلَّى اللّٰهُ تَعَالٰى عَلَيْهِ وَاٰلِهٖ وَسَلَّم considered the fact that the previous Ummaĥs were given long lives, whereas his Ummaĥ was given short lives as compared to them, he صَلَّى اللّٰهُ تَعَالٰى عَلَيْهِ وَاٰلِهٖ وَسَلَّم got dejected and concerned that his Ummaĥ would not be able to surpass previous Ummaĥs even if it worships abundantly. The mercy of Allah عَزَّوَجَلَّ intensified and He عَزَّوَجَلَّ granted His Beloved Rasūl صَلَّى اللّٰهُ تَعَالٰى عَلَيْهِ وَاٰلِهٖ وَسَلَّم Layla-tul-Qadr. *(Tafsīr-e-'Azīzī, vol. 4, pp. 434)*

A faith-refreshing parable

Explaining the background of the revelation of Sūraĥ Al-Qadr some honourable exegetists of the Quran have documented a very faith-refreshing parable that is as follows: Sham'ūn رَحْمَةُ اللّٰهِ تَعَالٰى عَلَيْه worshipped Allah عَزَّوَجَلَّ for a thousand years in such a way that he would offer Ṣalāĥ the whole night, fast during the day and fight unbelievers in the path of Allah عَزَّوَجَلَّ. He رَحْمَةُ اللّٰهِ تَعَالٰى عَلَيْه was so strong that he could break heavy iron chains with his hands. When the wicked unbelievers saw that they would not be able to defeat Sham'ūn رَحْمَةُ اللّٰهِ تَعَالٰى عَلَيْه they persuaded his wife, tempting her by a lot of wealth, to tie him with strong ropes while he was asleep and then hand him over to them.

The unfaithful wife tied him with ropes while he رَحْمَةُ اللّٰهِ تَعَالٰى عَلَيْه was asleep. When Sham'ūn رَحْمَةُ اللّٰهِ تَعَالٰى عَلَيْه awoke and found himself tied up, he رَحْمَةُ اللّٰهِ تَعَالٰى عَلَيْه broke the ropes with no difficulty, setting himself free. Then he رَحْمَةُ اللّٰهِ تَعَالٰى عَلَيْه asked his wife 'Who tied me?' Pretending to be loyal, the unfaithful wife lied, 'I was just testing as to how strong you are, and wanted to see how you would free yourself.' The incident was then ignored.

Despite failing the first time, his unfaithful wife constantly waited for another opportunity to tie her husband in the state of sleep. One night, she had another opportunity to do what she wanted. When he رَحْمَةُ اللّٰهِ تَعَالٰى عَلَيْه went to sleep, his cruel wife cunningly tied him with iron chains. As soon as he رَحْمَةُ اللهِ تَعَالٰی عَلَیْه woke up, he رَحْمَةُ اللهِ تَعَالٰی عَلَیْه broke the chains instantly and became free easily. Though shocked, his wife cunningly made the same excuse again, 'I was just testing your strength.' During the conversation, Sham'ūn رَحْمَةُ اللهِ تَعَالٰی عَلَیْه revealed his secret to his wife that Allah عَزَّوَجَلَّ has blessed him with the status of Wilāyat and nothing could harm him in the world except his own hair.'

The devious wife understood what he رَحْمَةُ اللهِ تَعَالٰی عَلَیْه meant. Worldly riches had blinded her. One day she found the opportunity to tie him with his own eight hair whose length was up to the ground. When he رَحْمَةُ اللهِ تَعَالٰی عَلَیْه awoke he tried hard to free himself but could not succeed.

The treacherous woman that was intoxicated by worldly riches handed over her pious and righteous husband to the enemies. The malicious unbelievers tied Sham'ūn رَحْمَةُ اللهِ تَعَالٰی عَلَیْه to a pillar and brutally mutilated his nose and ears and cut out his eyes. The wrath of Allah عَزَّوَجَلَّ was intensified by the helplessness of His Walī. The cruel unbelievers were sunk into the ground and a lightning of divine wrath struck the unfaithful, selfish, unfortunate wife, burning her to ashes. *(Extracted from Mukāshafa-tul-Qulūb, pp. 306)*

Our lives are very short

When the honourable companions رَضِیَ اللّٰهُ تَعَالٰی عَنْهُم heard about the worships, fights and struggles of Sayyidunā Sham'ūn رَحْمَةُ اللهِ تَعَالٰی عَلَیْه, they were impressed by him and said to the Noble Prophet صَلَّى اللهُ تَعَالٰی عَلَیْهِ وَاٰلِهٖ وَسَلَّم: 'Yā Rasūlallāĥ صَلَّى اللهُ تَعَالٰی عَلَیْهِ وَاٰلِهٖ وَسَلَّم! We have been given very short lives whose some part is spent in sleeping, working, preparing food and in other worldly affairs. We cannot worship like Sham'ūn رَحْمَةُ اللهِ تَعَالٰی عَلَیْه. Banī Isrāīl will surpass us in worship.'

Having listened to it, Beloved and Blessed Prophet صَلَّى اللهُ تَعَالٰی عَلَیْهِ وَاٰلِهٖ وَسَلَّم became sad. Instantly, Sayyidunā Jibrāīl عَلَیْهِ السَّلَام arrived and presented Sūraĥ Al-Qadr on behalf of Allah عَزَّوَجَلَّ. The Holy Prophet صَلَّى اللّٰهُ تَعَالٰی عَلَیْهِ وَاٰلِهٖ وَسَلَّم was comforted and reassured that 'Every year We have granted your Ummaĥ a sacred night; if they worship Me at this night they shall surpass the thousand months' worship of Sham'ūn رَحْمَةُ اللهِ تَعَالٰی عَلَیْه.' *(Derived from Tafsīr-e-'Azīzī, vol. 4, pp. 434)*

We are ungrateful

اَللهُ اَكْبَر! Dear Islamic brothers! How merciful and kind Allah عَزَّوَجَلَّ is to the Ummaĥ of His Beloved Rasūl صَلَّى اللهُ تَعَالٰى عَلَيْهِ وَاٰلِهٖ وَسَلَّم. He عَزَّوَجَلَّ has bestowed upon us this magnificent night for the sake of His Beloved Prophet صَلَّى اللهُ تَعَالٰى عَلَيْهِ وَاٰلِهٖ وَسَلَّم. If we worship in Layla-tul-Qadr we will earn more reward than the worship of a thousand months.

Unfortunately, we don't value this great night! There seems to be a great difference between the enthusiasm of the companions رَضِیَ اللّٰهُ تَعَالٰی عَنْهُم and that of ours. It was due to their grief that we have been given such an enormous blessing without asking for it. They treasured it but we are ungrateful, we don't have even time to worship. We waste this huge blessing in heedlessness every year.

Blessings of filling in Madanī In'āmāt booklets

Dear Islamic brothers! In order to develop the mindset of attaining the blessing of Layla-tul-Qadr, join the Madanī environment of Dawat-e-Islami, a global & non-political religious movement of the Quran and Sunnaĥ. اَلْحَمْدُ لِلّٰه عَزَّوَجَلَّ In order to spend life according to the Sunnaĥ, 72 Madanī In'āmāt (for Islamic brothers), 63 (for Islamic sisters), 92 (for male religious students), 83 (for female religious students) and 40 (for boys and girls) have been formulated. These are in the form of questions regarding worships and morals.

Everyone should fill in their Madanī In'āmāt booklets practicing Fikr-e-Madīnaĥ (pondering over deeds) every day and hand them in to their relevant responsible Islamic brother before[1] the 10th of every Madanī (Islamic) month. The Madanī In'āmāt have caused Madanī revolutions in the lives of many Islamic brothers and sisters.

Listen to a blessing of Madanī In'āmāt. An Islamic brother of Karachi gave the following account: The Imām of the Masjid of our area was associated with Dawat-e-Islami. Making individual effort, once he gave my elder brother a Madanī In'āmāt booklet as a gift. Having reached home, when he read the booklet, he was surprised to know that the small booklet contains a thorough guideline for the Muslims to spend their lives in conformity with Islamic teachings. Due to the blessings of the Madanī In'āmāt booklet, he started

[1] Islamic sisters will hand their booklets in to relevant responsible Islamic sister.

offering Ṣalāĥ with Jamā'at in the Masjid, اَلْحَمْدُ لِلّٰه عَزَّوَجَلَّ. Now he has also grown a beard and fills in his Madanī In'āmāt booklet.

Madanī In'āmāt kay 'āmil pay ĥar dam ĥar għaṙī
Yā Ilāĥī! Khūb barsā raḥmataun kī Tū jĥaṙī

One practicing Madanī In'āmāt be blessed every moment
With the rain of Divine mercy and bestowment

Glad tidings for those acting upon Madanī In'āmāt

Dear Islamic brothers! The following Madanī incident clearly shows how fortunate are those filling in the booklet of Madanī In'āmāt. An Islamic brother of Hyderabad (Bāb-ul-Islam, Sindh) gave the following statement under oath: One night in Rajab 1426 A.H., I was blessed with the huge privilege of beholding the Holy Prophet صَلَّى اللهُ تَعَالٰى عَلَيْهِ وَاٰلِهٖ وَسَلَّم in dream. His blessed lips began to move, and he صَلَّى اللهُ تَعَالٰى عَلَيْهِ وَاٰلِهٖ وَسَلَّم said, 'Whoever punctually does Fikr-e-Madīnaĥ about his Madanī In'āmāt every day in this month, Allah عَزَّوَجَلَّ shall forgive him.'

Madanī In'āmāt kī bĥī marḥabā kyā bāt ĥay
Qurb-e-Ḥaq kay ṭālibaun kay wāsiṭay sawghāt ĥay

How excellent are the Madanī In'āmāt, marḥabā!
A great gift for the seekers of the closeness of Allah عَزَّوَجَلَّ

صَلُّوْا عَلَى الْحَبِيْب   صَلَّى اللهُ تَعَالٰى عَلٰى مُحَمَّد

Who is deprived of all blessings?

Sayyidunā Anas Bin Mālik رَضِىَ اللهُ تَعَالٰى عَنْهُ has stated that once the month of Ramadan arrived, so the Prophet of mankind, the Peace of our heart and mind, the most Generous and Kind صَلَّى اللهُ تَعَالٰى عَلَيْهِ وَاٰلِهٖ وَسَلَّم said, 'A month has come to you in which there is one such night that is better than a thousand months. Whoever is deprived in that night is deprived of all goodness and only the one who is completely deprived is deprived of its goodness.'
(Sunan Ibn Mājaĥ, vol. 2, pp. 298, Ḥadīš 1644)

Thousand sons

Narrating another background regarding the revelation of Sūraĥ Al-Qadr, Sayyidunā Ka'b-ul-Aḥbār رضی اللہ تعالٰی عنہ, a Tābi'ī saint, has stated, 'There was a righteous king in the Banī Isrāīl. Allah عزّوجلّ commanded the then Prophet علیہ السّلام to ask the king to express his desire. When he heard the divine message, he said, 'Yā Allah عزّوجلّ! I want to sacrifice my wealth, children and life in Jihad.' Allah عزّوجلّ blessed him with a thousand sons. He used to groom each son for Jihad and send him along with an army to fight in the path of Allah عزّوجلّ. The son would fight for a month and then be martyred. The king would then groom another son and send him to fight along with the army, and in this way, every month he would sacrifice one of his sons. Further, the king used to offer Ṣalāĥ at night and fast during the day.

After a thousand months, all his thousand sons were martyred. Thereafter he fought himself and drank the beverage of martyrdom. Impressed by the sincere sacrifices made by the king, people said that no one can reach his status. So Allah عزّوجلّ revealed the verse:

لَيْلَةُ الْقَدْرِ ۙ خَيْرٌ مِّنْ اَلْفِ شَهْرٍ ۳ؕ

Layla-tul-Qadr is better than a thousand months.

[Kanz-ul-Īmān (Translation of Quran)]

In other words, Layla-tul-Qadr is better than the king's thousand months in which he offered Ṣalāĥ every night, fasted every day, and fought in the path of Allah عزّوجلّ with his wealth, life and children. *(Tafsīr Qurṭubī, vol. 20, part 30, pp. 122)*

Kingship of thousand cities

Sayyidunā Abū Bakr Warrāq رحمۃ اللہ تعالٰی علیہ has stated that Sayyidunā Sulaymān علیہ السّلام and Sayyidunā Żulqarnayn رضی اللہ تعالٰی عنہ both ruled 500 cities each. Thus both of them together ruled a thousand cities. Allah عزّوجلّ has made the worship of this night better than what these two great personalities ruled. *(Tafsīr Qurṭubī, vol. 20, part 30, pp. 122)*

Dear Islamic brothers! Layla-tul-Qadr is the night of goodness and peace. It is mercy from beginning to end. The honourable exegetists of the Quran have said: 'In this night there is protection from snakes, scorpions, calamities, problems and devils. It is also full of peace.'

Hoisting flags

According to a narration, in Layla-tul-Qadr, an army of angels under the command of Jibrāīl عَلَیْہِ السَّلَام descends from Sidra-tul-Muntaĥā with four flags. They hoist one flag on the blessed tomb of the Holy Prophet صَلَّی اللّٰہُ تَعَالٰی عَلَیْہِ وَاٰلِہٖ وَسَلَّم, one on the roof of Bayt-ul-Muqaddas, while the third on the top of the Ka'baĥ and the fourth on mount Sīnā. Then they enter the houses of all the believers and say Salām. They say, 'Salām (this is one of the names of Allah عَزَّوَجَلَّ) sends peace upon you.'

However, these angels do not enter the houses in which there are alcoholics, eaters of swine or the people who break ties without valid Shar'ī reasons. *(Tafsīr Ṣāwī, vol. 6, pp. 2401)* Another narration says that these angels outnumber even all grit of the earth, and they all come with peace and mercy. *(Ad-Dur-rul-Manšūr, vol. 8, pp. 579)*

Green flag

According to another detailed Ḥadīš reported by Sayyidunā 'Abdullāĥ Ibn 'Abbās رَضِیَ اللّٰہُ تَعَالٰی عَنْہُمَا, our Beloved and Blessed Prophet صَلَّی اللّٰہُ تَعَالٰی عَلَیْہِ وَاٰلِہٖ وَسَلَّم said, 'In Layla-tul-Qadr, Jibrāīl عَلَیْہِ السَّلَام, accompanied by a large number of angels, descends onto the earth with a green flag he hoists on the top of the Ka'baĥ. Jibrāīl عَلَیْہِ السَّلَام has 100 arms, two of which he opens only at this night. His arms spread across the east and the west. Then Jibrāīl عَلَیْہِ السَّلَام commands the angels to say Salām and shake hands with every Muslim who is offering Ṣalāĥ or making the Żikr of Allah عَزَّوَجَلَّ and to say Āmīn to their supplications. This process continues till dawn (Ṣubḥ-e-Ṣādiq).

In the morning, Jibrāīl عَلَیْہِ السَّلَام commands all the angels to return. The angels say 'O Jibrāīl عَلَیْہِ السَّلَام what about the needs of the Ummaĥ of Prophet Muhammad صَلَّی اللّٰہُ تَعَالٰی عَلَیْہِ وَاٰلِہٖ وَسَلَّم?' Jibrāīl عَلَیْہِ السَّلَام replies, 'Allah عَزَّوَجَلَّ has seen them with mercy and has forgiven all of them except four types of people.'

The honourable companions رَضِیَ اللّٰہُ تَعَالٰی عَنۡہُمۡ asked, 'Yā Rasūlallāĥ صَلَّی اللّٰہُ تَعَالٰی عَلَیۡہِ وَاٰلِہٖ وَسَلَّم! Who are those four types of people?' He صَلَّی اللّٰہُ تَعَالٰی عَلَیۡہِ وَاٰلِہٖ وَسَلَّم replied, '(1) Alcoholics (2) Disobedient to parents (3) Those who break ties with relatives (4) Those who bear malice and grudge against each other and break ties.' *(Shu'ab-ul-Īmān, vol. 3, pp. 336, Ḥadīš 3695)*

Unfortunate people

Dear Islamic brothers! Did you realize how blessed and sacred Layla-tul-Qadr is? Everyone is forgiven at this night, but the alcoholics, those who disobey their parents, break ties with relatives and have malice and grudge against fellow Muslim brothers without a valid reason of Sharī'aĥ are not forgiven.

Repent!

Dear Islamic brothers! Isn't it enough to make us fear the wrath of our Omnipotent Allah عَزَّوَجَلَّ? How extreme sinners would be the ones who are not being forgiven even at the sacred and blessed night of Layla-tul-Qadr! We must repent sincerely of our sins and settle all the matters concerning the rights of others. Indeed, the mercy and bounties of Allah عَزَّوَجَلَّ are immense.

Nuisance of quarrel

Sayyidunā 'Ubādaĥ Bin Ṣāmit رَضِیَ اللّٰہُ تَعَالٰی عَنۡہُ has narrated that our Noble Rasūl صَلَّی اللّٰہُ تَعَالٰی عَلَیۡہِ وَاٰلِہٖ وَسَلَّم came out to tell us about Layla-tul-Qadr (as to which night it is) but two Muslims were quarrelling with each other. He صَلَّی اللّٰہُ تَعَالٰی عَلَیۡہِ وَاٰلِہٖ وَسَلَّم said, 'I came to tell you about Layla-tul-Qadr but so and so persons were quarrelling, due to which its (exact) date has been concealed, it is possible that your betterment lies in it. Now look for it in the 9th, 7th and 5th night (of the last 10 nights).' *(Ṣaḥīḥ Bukhārī, vol. 1, pp. 663, Ḥadīš 2023)*

Our unmentionable state

Dear Islamic brothers! This blessed Ḥadīš contains a great lesson for us. Our Beloved and Blessed Prophet صَلَّی اللّٰہُ تَعَالٰی عَلَیۡہِ وَاٰلِہٖ وَسَلَّم was about to tell his companions the (exact) date of Layla-tul-Qadr but the quarrelling of two Muslims with each other proved to be a hurdle, causing the exact date of Layla-tul-Qadr to be concealed forever. This also indicates that

Muslims' quarrelling with each other can prove to be an obstacle in the attainment of mercy and blessing.

Alas! It seems no one is prepared to advise others. People argue with each other saying such sentences as: *These days, a naive person cannot live in this world; if someone is good to us we will also remain good to him but if anyone tries to harm us, we will teach him a lesson.* Even worse, people turn violent on trivial matters to the extent of quarrelling, fighting and even killing each others.

Regretfully, these days, some of the Muslims belonging to different races such as Pathans, Punjabis, Muhajir, Sindhis and Balouchis are killing each other and burning their fellow Muslims brothers' properties and other things just on the basis of racial and linguistic differences.

O Muslims! You were the protectors of each other, what has happened to you! Our Dear and Beloved Rasūl صَلَّى اللّٰهُ تَعَالٰى عَلَيْهِ وَاٰلِهٖ وَسَلَّم has said, 'All believers are like a (single) body; if one part is wounded the whole body feels the pain.' *(Ṣaḥīḥ Bukhārī, vol. 4, pp. 103, Ḥadīš 6011)*

A poet has rightly said:

Mubtalāye dard koī 'uzū ĥo rawtī ĥay ānkĥ
Kis qadar ĥamdard sāray jism kī ĥotī ĥay ānkĥ

When any part of the body has pain, weeps the eye
How sympathetic with the whole body, is the eye

Dear Islamic brothers! Instead of quarrelling and fighting, we must cooperate and assist each other sincerely. A Muslim does not fight, stab, rob and burn the shops and property of his other Muslim brother.

Definition of Muslim, Mūmin and Muĥājir

Sayyidunā Fuḍālaĥ Bin 'Ubayd رَضِىَ اللّٰهُ تَعَالٰى عَنْهُ has narrated that on the occasion of Ḥajja-tul-Wadā', the Prophet of Raḥmaĥ, the Intercessor of Ummaĥ صَلَّى اللّٰهُ تَعَالٰى عَلَيْهِ وَاٰلِهٖ وَسَلَّم said, 'Shall I not tell you who a Mūmin (believer) is?' Then he صَلَّى اللّٰهُ تَعَالٰى عَلَيْهِ وَاٰلِهٖ وَسَلَّم said, 'A Mūmin is the one whom people do not fear regarding their lives and wealth; a Muslim is the one who does not harm people with his tongue and hands; a Mujāĥid is the one who fights his Nafs in order to obey Allah عَزَّوَجَلَّ, and a Muĥājir is the one who gives up sins.' *(Al-Mustadrak, vol. 1, pp. 158)*

He صَلَّى اللهُ تَعَالٰى عَلَيْهِ وَاٰلِهٖ وَسَلَّم has also said, 'It is not permissible for a Muslim to hurt the feelings of another Muslim by (offensive) gestures. It is also unlawful to do anything that frightens or terrifies another Muslim.' *(Itḥāf-us-Sādat-il-Muttaqīn, vol. 7, pp. 177)*

Ṭarīq-e-Mustafa ko ĉhořnā ĥay wajĥ-e-barbādī
Isī say qawm dunyā mayn ĥūī bay-iqtidār apnī

Giving up the Sunnaĥ of Mustafa is the cause of destruction
And has deprived Muslims of their power, leading to subjection

Unbearable itch

Sayyidunā Mujāĥid رَحْمَةُ اللهِ تَعَالٰى عَلَيْه has said that Allah عَزَّوَجَلَّ would inflict a (severe) itch on some of the people of Hell. They will scratch so much that their skins will come off, exposing their bones. They will hear a voice, 'What do you think of this pain?' They will reply, 'It is severe and unbearable.' Then they will be told, 'This is your punishment for harming the Muslims.' *(Itḥāf-us-Sādat-il-Muttaqīn, vol. 7, pp. 175)*

Reward for removing difficulties

The Prophet of mankind, the Peace of our heart and mind, the most Generous and Kind صَلَّى اللهُ تَعَالٰى عَلَيْهِ وَاٰلِهٖ وَسَلَّم has said, 'I saw a man wander around in Heaven, do you know why? Simply because he had removed a tree in the world from a path in order to make it easier for Muslims to pass.' *(Ṣaḥīḥ Muslim, pp. 1410, Ḥadīš 1914)*

If you want to fight... fight your Nafs

Dear Islamic brothers! Learn a lesson from these Aḥādīš and avoid quarrelling and fighting with each other. If you really want to fight, then fight the rejected devil and your misleading Nafs (Nafs-e-Ammāraĥ). When Jihad becomes Farḍ, fight the unbelievers but treat each other like brothers. You may well have realized the great loss of quarrelling, which resulted in Layla-tul-Qadr being concealed forever. We are unaware that we may be deprived of other great blessings and bounties because of our (personal) conflicts and quarrels!

May Allah عَزَّوَجَلَّ have mercy on our miserable condition and make us realize whether we are Punjabi, Pathan, Sindhi, Balochi, Saraiki, Muhajir, Bengali, Bihari or anyone else we are all 'slaves' of our Noble Arab Rasūl صَلَّى اللّٰهُ تَعَالٰى عَلَيْهِ وَاٰلِهٖ وَسَلَّم.

The Holy Prophet صَلَّى اللّٰهُ تَعَالٰى عَلَيْهِ وَاٰلِهٖ وَسَلَّم is neither Pathan, Punjabi, Balochi, nor Sindhi; in fact, he صَلَّى اللّٰهُ تَعَالٰى عَلَيْهِ وَاٰلِهٖ وَسَلَّم is an Arab. If only we all would truly stick to the Sunnaĥ and teachings of our Beloved and Blessed Prophet صَلَّى اللّٰهُ تَعَالٰى عَلَيْهِ وَاٰلِهٖ وَسَلَّم ignoring all racial and linguistic differences so that we may become united and righteous once again!

The Holy Prophet صَلَّى اللّٰهُ تَعَالٰى عَلَيْهِ وَاٰلِهٖ وَسَلَّم smile while seeing Madanī In'āmāt booklet

اَلْحَمْدُ لِلّٰه عَزَّوَجَلَّ! There is no racial and linguistic difference in the Madanī environment of Dawat-e-Islami. People of all tribes and languages are under the shade of the mercy of our Holy Prophet صَلَّى اللّٰهُ تَعَالٰى عَلَيْهِ وَاٰلِهٖ وَسَلَّم.

Please join the Madanī environment of Dawat-e-Islami and practice the Madanī In'āmāt in order to live a righteous life. For your motivation and encouragement, here is a pleasant and fragrant Madanī incident about Madanī In'āmāt. Therefore, a Muballigh (preacher) from Rawalpindi gave the following account: He has stated, 'On the 5th of February 2005, in order to enroll in the Madanī Qāfilaĥ course, I came to Faīzān-e-Madīnaĥ, Bāb-ul-Madīnaĥ Karachi, the global Madanī Markaz of Dawat-e-Islami.

I was asleep in the global Madanī Markaz Faīzān-e-Madīnaĥ. My physical eyes closed but those of my heart opened, اَلْحَمْدُ لِلّٰه عَزَّوَجَلَّ. In my dream I saw our Beloved Rasūl صَلَّى اللّٰهُ تَعَالٰى عَلَيْهِ وَاٰلِهٖ وَسَلَّم on a high terrace. Next to him were some sacks of Madanī In'āmāt booklets. The Noble Prophet صَلَّى اللّٰهُ تَعَالٰى عَلَيْهِ وَاٰلِهٖ وَسَلَّم was smiling as he صَلَّى اللّٰهُ تَعَالٰى عَلَيْهِ وَاٰلِهٖ وَسَلَّم was looking at a booklet of Madanī In'āmāt. Then I woke up.

Madanī In'āmāt say 'Aṭṭār ĥam ko piyār ĥay
اِنْ شَآءَاللّٰه عَزَّوَجَلَّ, *Do jaĥān mayn apnā bayřā pār ĥay*

O 'Aṭṭār! We love Madanī In'āmāt indeed
اِنْ شَآءَاللّٰه عَزَّوَجَلَّ, *We will succeed*

صَلُّوْا عَلَى الْحَبِيْب صَلَّى اللّٰهُ تَعَالٰى عَلٰى مُحَمَّد

Magic fails

Sayyidunā Ismā'īl Ḥaqqī رَحْمَةُ اللّٰهِ تَعَالٰی عَلَيْه has stated, 'This is a night of peace; people are protected from many troubles such as illnesses, evil, calamities, storms, thunder, lightning and other things. In fact, everything that descends in this night contains peace, benefit and goodness. In this night, the devil cannot make people do evil and no magician's magic works; this night is full of peace.' *(Rūḥ-ul-Bayān, vol. 10, pp. 485)*

Signs of Layla-tul-Qadr

Sayyidunā 'Ubādaĥ Bin Ṣāmit رَضِیَ اللّٰهُ تَعَالٰی عَنْهُ asked the Noble Prophet صَلَّى اللّٰهُ تَعَالٰى عَلَيْهِ وَاٰلِهٖ وَسَلَّم about Layla-tul-Qadr. The Holy Prophet صَلَّى اللّٰهُ تَعَالٰى عَلَيْهِ وَاٰلِهٖ وَسَلَّم replied: 'Layla-tul-Qadr is in the odd nights of the last ten days of Ramadan, i.e. 21st, 23rd, 25th, 27th, 29th or the last night of Ramadan. Whoever worships in this night with faith in order to earn reward will be forgiven for all his previous sins. Some of its signs are as follows: The night will be open, bright and extremely clear. It is neither too hot nor too cold, the weather is quite normal at this night and the moon is clearly visible. The devils are not struck with stars the whole night.

There is another sign that is the rising of the sun without rays on the following morning, and the sun looks like the moon of the 14th night. Allah عَزَّوَجَلَّ has prevented the devil to come out with the sunrise of that morning (apart from that one day, whenever the sun rises in the morning the devil also comes out).' *(Musnad Imām Aḥmad, vol. 8, pp. 414, Ḥadīš 22829)*

Ocean water becomes sweet

Dear Islamic brothers! Layla-tul-Qadr falls on one of the odd nights of the last ten days of Ramadan. Sometimes it falls even on the 30th night. There may be thousands of reasons for keeping this night a secret, and most certainly one of the reasons is that Muslims will try to spend every night worshipping Allah عَزَّوَجَلَّ in search of Layla-tul-Qadr.

Many signs of Layla-tul-Qadr have been mentioned in Aḥādīš but it is not easy for everyone to see these signs. In fact, only men of insight can see them. Sometimes, Allah عَزَّوَجَلَّ shows these signs to His chosen people. One of the signs of Layla-tul-Qadr is that the salty ocean water turns sweet and (another sign is that) everything in the universe except humans and jinn submits to the Glory of Allah عَزَّوَجَلَّ by prostrating, but not everyone sees it.

Parable

Sayyidunā 'Ubayd Ibn 'Imrān رَضِىَ اللهُ تَعَالٰى عَنْهُ said, 'One night, while I was making Wuḍū at the Red Sea I tasted the water which was sweeter than even honey. I was extremely surprised. When I told Sayyidunā 'Uśmān Ghanī رَضِىَ اللهُ تَعَالٰى عَنْهُ about it, he رَضِىَ اللهُ تَعَالٰى عَنْهُ said, 'O 'Ubayd رَضِىَ اللهُ تَعَالٰى عَنْهُ it would be Layla-tul-Qadr.' He رَضِىَ اللهُ تَعَالٰى عَنْهُ further said, 'Whoever spends this night remembering Allah عَزَّوَجَلَّ it is as if he worshipped for more than a thousand months, and Allah عَزَّوَجَلَّ will forgive all of his sins.' *(Tażkira-tul-Wā'iẓīn, pp. 626)*

May Allah عَزَّوَجَلَّ have mercy on them and forgive us without accountability for their sake!

Parable

The slave of Sayyidunā 'Uśmān Ibn Abil 'Āṣ رَضِىَ اللهُ تَعَالٰى عَنْهُ once said to him, 'O master رَضِىَ اللهُ تَعَالٰى عَنْهُ! I've been a sailor for a long time. I've noticed a strange thing in the ocean water.' 'What is it?' He رَضِىَ اللهُ تَعَالٰى عَنْهُ asked. The slave replied, 'O master رَضِىَ اللهُ تَعَالٰى عَنْهُ! Every year, there is a night in which the ocean water turns sweet.' He رَضِىَ اللهُ تَعَالٰى عَنْهُ said to his slave, 'Be careful this year. Do tell me when the water turns sweet.' On the 27th night of Ramadan, the slave said to Sayyidunā 'Uśmān Ibn Abil 'Āṣ رَضِىَ اللهُ تَعَالٰى عَنْهُ, 'O master! The water has turned sweet tonight.' *(Rūḥ-ul-Bayān, vol. 10, pp. 481)*

May Allah عَزَّوَجَلَّ have mercy on them and forgive us without accountability for their sake!

Why don't signs appear to us?

Dear Islamic brothers! Several signs of Layla-tul-Qadr have been mentioned. A question may arise in one's mind as to why common people are unable to observe any of the signs of Layla-tul-Qadr despite the fact that it falls every year. To answer the question, the honourable scholars رَحِمَهُمُ اللهُ تَعَالٰى have said, 'Not everyone is able enough to discern these hidden things because they are related to Kashf (spiritual vision) and Karāmaĥ (saintly miracle). Only people with the gift of Baṣīrat (spiritual insight) can see them. How can the person who commits innumerable sins every day see these sacred signs?'

Look for it during odd nights

Dear Islamic brothers! Allah عَزَّوَجَلَّ has decided to keep Layla-tul-Qadr a secret, so we don't know for sure as to which night Layla-tul-Qadr is. Mother of the believers Sayyidatunā 'Āishaĥ Ṣiddīqaĥ رَضِیَ اللہُ تَعَالٰی عَنْہَا has narrated that the Beloved and Blessed Prophet صَلَّى اللّٰہُ تَعَالٰی عَلَیْہِ وَاٰلِہٖ وَسَلَّم has said, 'Look for Layla-tul-Qadr in the odd nights of the last ten days of Ramadan (i.e. the 21st, 23rd, 25th, 27th and the 29th).' *(Ṣaḥīḥ Bukhārī, vol. 1, pp. 662, Ḥadīš 2020)*

Look for it during last seven nights

Sayyidunā 'Abdullāĥ Ibn 'Umar رَضِیَ اللّٰہُ تَعَالٰی عَنْہُمَا said that Layla-tul-Qadr was revealed to some of the honourable companions رَضِیَ اللّٰہُ تَعَالٰی عَنْہُم of the Holy Prophet صَلَّى اللّٰہُ تَعَالٰی عَلَیْہِ وَاٰلِہٖ وَسَلَّم in dream in the last seven nights. The Noble Prophet صَلَّى اللّٰہُ تَعَالٰی عَلَیْہِ وَاٰلِہٖ وَسَلَّم said, 'I see your dreams have united in the last seven nights, so the one who desires it should look for it in the last seven nights.' *(Ṣaḥīḥ Bukhārī, vol. 1, pp. 660, Ḥadīš 2015)*

Why was Layla-tul-Qadr kept secret?

Dear Islamic brothers! It is a blessed Sunnaĥ of Allah عَزَّوَجَلَّ that He عَزَّوَجَلَّ has kept some very important things secret. Allah عَزَّوَجَلَّ has hidden His pleasure in pious deeds, His wrath in sins, and His Auliyā رَحِمَہُمُ اللّٰہُ تَعَالٰی among His servants.'

Therefore, we shouldn't miss any good deed even though it looks minor because we don't know which good deed would please Allah عَزَّوَجَلَّ. Many blessed Aḥādīš contain such incidents. For example, on the Day of Judgement, a fallen woman (a prostitute) will be forgiven simply for having given water to a thirsty dog to drink, in the world. Likewise, as His displeasure is hidden in sins, we should avoid each and every sin though it apparently looks minor because even a single sin can bring about the displeasure and wrath of Allah عَزَّوَجَلَّ.

Similarly, He عَزَّوَجَلَّ has hidden His Auliyā amongst His servants, so we should treat every pious Muslim with respect because we don't know as to who a Walī of Allah عَزَّوَجَلَّ is. If we treat pious people with respect, give up suspicion and consider every Muslim better than us, our society will get reformed, and we will succeed in the afterlife, اِنْ شَآءَ اللّٰہ عَزَّوَجَلَّ.

Madanī pearls

Imām Fakhruddīn Rāzī رَحْمَةُ اللهِ تَعَالٰى عَلَيْه has stated in his famous exegesis '*Tafsīr-e-Kabīr*', There are several reasons why Allah عَزَّوَجَلَّ has concealed the exact date of Layla-tul-Qadr:

1. He عَزَّوَجَلَّ has concealed many things such as His pleasure in obedience so that people would perform every form of worship, His wrath in sins so that people would avoid every single sin, His Auliyā amongst His servants so that people would respect every single person, the fulfilment of supplications in making supplications so that people would make supplications abundantly, the Ism-e-A'ẓam amongst His names so that people would respect every name and the Ṣalāt-e-Wusṭā amongst the Ṣalāĥ so that people would offer all the Ṣalāĥ.

   Likewise, the acceptance of repentance has been kept secret so that people always repent of their sins and the time of death has also been kept secret so that people always fear it. Similarly, Layla-tul-Qadr has been kept secret so that people respect all the nights of Ramadan.

2. It is as if Allah عَزَّوَجَلَّ says to His servants, 'I know your daring about sins; if I had declared a particular night as Layla-tul-Qadr, and if you had committed sins knowingly even at this sacred night due to your lust, it would be more severe than committing sins unknowingly.'

   According to a narration, once the Holy Prophet صَلَّى اللهُ تَعَالٰى عَلَيْهِ وَاٰلِهٖ وَسَلَّم entered the Masjid where he صَلَّى اللهُ تَعَالٰى عَلَيْهِ وَاٰلِهٖ وَسَلَّم saw a man sleep (inside). He صَلَّى اللهُ تَعَالٰى عَلَيْهِ وَاٰلِهٖ وَسَلَّم said, 'O 'Alī (كَرَّمَ اللهُ تَعَالٰى وَجْهَهُ الْكَرِيْم)! Wake him up so that he can perform Wuḍū.' Having awoken the man, Sayyidunā 'Alī كَرَّمَ اللهُ تَعَالٰى وَجْهَهُ الْكَرِيْم said, 'Yā Rasūlallāĥ صَلَّى اللهُ تَعَالٰى عَلَيْهِ وَاٰلِهٖ وَسَلَّم usually, you prefer to perform righteous deeds, why did you not wake him up yourself?' He صَلَّى اللهُ تَعَالٰى عَلَيْهِ وَاٰلِهٖ وَسَلَّم replied, 'I did not do so because his refusing you is not a Kufr; I did it to reduce his crime.'

   It is an example of the mercy of the Beloved Rasūl صَلَّى اللهُ تَعَالٰى عَلَيْهِ وَاٰلِهٖ وَسَلَّم. Considering this (Ḥadīš), imagine the mercy of Allah عَزَّوَجَلَّ. It is as if Allah عَزَّوَجَلَّ says, 'If you had worshipped in Layla-tul-Qadr after being aware of it, you would gain more reward than a thousand months' worship but if you had sinned in it you would have been punished for a thousand months, and protection from punishment is better than earning reward.'

3. It is as if Allah عَزَّوَجَلَّ says, 'I kept this night secret so that people would struggle hard to acquire it and earn reward for their struggles.'

4. Since people are unaware as to which night Layla-tul-Qadr is, they will try to worship Allah عَزَّوَجَلَّ every night of Ramadan in search of Layla-tul-Qadr. Referring to these people Allah عَزَّوَجَلَّ admonished the angels, 'You used to say that these humans will fight and shed blood, but (look) these are their efforts and struggles in a night that could be Layla-tul-Qadr (they are not even certain of it) so what would have they done if I had told them the exact night…? (In other words, they would worship even more abundantly).'

This is the secret to the answer Allah عَزَّوَجَلَّ gave to the angels when He عَزَّوَجَلَّ said to them:

إِنِّي جَاعِلٌ فِي الْأَرْضِ خَلِيفَةً ط

I am going to place a caliph in the earth.

[Kanz-ul-Īmān (Translation of Quran)] (Part 1, Sūrah Al-Baqarah, verse 30)

The angels said:

قَالُوٓا أَتَجْعَلُ فِيهَا مَن يُفْسِدُ فِيهَا وَيَسْفِكُ الدِّمَآءَ ج وَنَحْنُ نُسَبِّحُ بِحَمْدِكَ وَنُقَدِّسُ لَكَ ط

They said, 'Will You place such who will spread violence and shed blood in it? And we glorify You commending You and sanctify You.'

[Kanz-ul-Īmān (Translation of Quran)] (Part 1, Sūrah Al-Baqarah, verse 30)

Then He عَزَّوَجَلَّ said:

قَالَ إِنِّيٓ أَعْلَمُ مَا لَا تَعْلَمُونَ ﴿٣٠﴾

He عَزَّوَجَلَّ said, 'I know what you know not.'

[Kanz-ul-Īmān (Translation of Quran)] (Part 1, Baqarah, verse 30)

Thus, the secret behind this statement has been revealed. *(Tafsīr Kabīr, vol. 11, pp. 229)*

Any night of year may be 'Layla-tul-Qadr'

Layla-tul-Qadr has been kept secret for numerous reasons so that the pious people of Allah عَزَّوَجَلَّ spend the whole year looking for it and constantly striving to earn the reward of worships.

There is a wide divergence of opinion amongst the honourable scholars رَحِمَهُمُ اللّٰهُ تَعَالٰی regarding the exact date of Layla-tul-Qadr. Some scholars رَحِمَهُمُ اللّٰهُ تَعَالٰی say that Layla-tul-Qadr moves throughout the year. For example, Sayyidunā 'Abdullāĥ Ibn Mas'ūd رَضِیَ اللّٰہ تَعَالٰی عَنْهُ said, 'Only the man who searches carefully throughout the year for Layla-tul-Qadr will be able to find it.'

Favouring the foregoing saying, Imām-ul-'Ārifīn, Sayyidunā Shaykh Muḥiyyuddīn Ibn 'Arabī رَحْمَةُ اللّٰهِ تَعَالٰی عَلَيْه said, 'Once I found Layla-tul-Qadr on the 15th night of Sha'bān (Shab-e-Barā-at) and in another year, I found it on the 19th night of Sha'bān. I have also seen it on the 13th and the 18th nights of Ramadan. Further, in different years I have seen it on each of the odd nights of the last ten days of Ramadan. He رَحْمَةُ اللّٰهِ تَعَالٰی عَلَيْه further stated that though Layla-tul-Qadr mostly falls in Ramadan, in my experience, it falls on different nights of the year; so it isn't the same night every year.

The Noble Prophet ﷺ and the Shaykhayn رَضِیَ اللّٰہ عَنْهُمَا

اَلْحَمْدُ لِلّٰه عَزَّوَجَلَّ! In the Madanī environment of Dawat-e-Islami many blessings take place during Ramadan's I'tikāf. Islamic brothers and sisters gain the blessings of performing I'tikāf in Masājid and homes respectively around the world. Here is a faith-refreshing incident for persuasion:

A young Islamic brother who is responsible for Qāfilaĥs in the district Liyaqatpur, division Rahim Yar Khan (Punjab, Pakistan) gave the following account: I was a film-addict to such an extent that I had watched virtually half of the VCDs in the VCD shop of our village. اَلْحَمْدُ لِلّٰه عَزَّوَجَلَّ I was blessed with the opportunity to perform I'tikāf in the last ten days of Ramadan (1422 A.H. 2001) at Madanī Masjid in Talbani (a village). Words cannot express the blessings of the company of the Rasūl's devotees of Dawat-e-Islami! On the 27th of Ramadan, I cried the whole night asking the Holy Prophet صَلَّى اللّٰهُ تَعَالٰى عَلَيْهِ وَاٰلِهٖ وَسَلَّم to bless me with his vision.

اَلْحَمْدُلِلّٰه عَزَّوَجَلَّ! In the early morning, the door of mercy opened for me when I had a dream in which I found myself in a Masjid where an announcement was made: 'The Holy Prophet صَلَّى اللهُ تَعَالٰى عَلَيْهِ وَاٰلِهٖ وَسَلَّم is coming and will lead the Ṣalāĥ.' After a while, the Prophet of Raḥmaĥ, the Intercessor of Ummaĥ صَلَّى اللهُ تَعَالٰى عَلَيْهِ وَاٰلِهٖ وَسَلَّم came accompanied by the Shaykhayn رَضِىَ اللّٰهُ تَعَالٰى عَنْهُمَا and then I woke up. All I saw was just a glance and then his blessed face disappeared, filling my heart with grief and causing a flood of tears to flow from my eyes. I cried so much that I began to hiccup.

اَلْحَمْدُلِلّٰه عَزَّوَجَلَّ! Having had the blessed dream, my love for Dawat-e-Islami, a global & non-political religious movement of the Quran and Sunnaĥ intensified and I joined Dawat-e-Islami wholeheartedly. I headed for Bāb-ul-Madīnaĥ Karachi and joined Jāmi'a-tul-Madīnaĥ to enrol in the Dars-e-Niẓāmī course. Presently, I am in my first year and I am trying to serve Dawat-e-Islami as a Qāfilaĥ responsible in our area.

Jalwa-e-Yār kī ārzū ĥay agar,
Madanī Māḥaul mayn kar lo tum I'tikāf
Mīṫĥay Āqā صَلَّى اللهُ تَعَالٰى عَلَيْهِ وَاٰلِهٖ وَسَلَّم *karayn gey karam kī naẓar,*
Madanī Māḥaul mayn kar lo tum I'tikāf

If you desire holy vision
Do I'tikāf in the Madanī environment
Beloved Prophet صَلَّى اللهُ تَعَالٰى عَلَيْهِ وَاٰلِهٖ وَسَلَّم *will bless you*
Do I'tikāf in the Madanī environment

صَلُّوْا عَلَى الْحَبِيْب صَلَّى اللهُ تَعَالٰى عَلٰى مُحَمَّد

Two sayings of Imām A'ẓam رَحْمَةُ اللهِ عَلَيْه

Here are two sayings of Imām A'ẓam Abū Ḥanīfaĥ رَحْمَةُ اللهِ تَعَالٰى عَلَيْه in this regard:

1. Layla-tul-Qadr is in Ramadan but there is no specific night for it, whereas Sayyidunā Imām Abū Yūsuf and Sayyidunā Imām Muhammad رَحِمَهُمُ اللّٰهُ تَعَالٰى say that Layla-tul-Qadr is in the last 15 nights of Ramadan.

2. A famous saying of Sayyidunā Imām Abū Ḥanīfaĥ رَحْمَةُ اللهِ تَعَالٰی عَلَيْه is that Layla-tul-Qadr falls at different nights of the year, sometimes it is in Ramadan and sometimes in the other months. Sayyidunā 'Abdullāĥ Ibn 'Abbās, Sayyidunā 'Abdullāĥ Ibn Mas'ūd and Sayyidunā 'Ikramaĥ رَضِيَ اللّٰهُ تَعَالٰی عَنْهُم also favoured this opinion. *('Umda-tul-Qārī, vol. 8, pp. 253, Ḥadīš 2015)*

Sayyidunā Imām Shāfi'ī رَحْمَةُ اللهِ تَعَالٰی عَلَيْه has said that Layla-tul-Qadr is one of the last ten nights of Ramadan and it is the same night (every year), it will never change up to the Day of Judgement. *('Umda-tul-Qārī, vol. 8, pp. 253, Ḥadīš 2015)*

Layla-tul-Qadr changes

Sayyidunā Imām Mālik رَحْمَةُ اللهِ تَعَالٰی عَلَيْه has said that Layla-tul-Qadr falls in one of the odd nights of the last ten days in Ramadan but it is not the same night (every year), it changes every year within these odd nights. Sometimes it's the 21st night, sometimes it's the 23rd, 25th, 27th and sometimes the 29th night. *(Tafsīr Ṣāwī, vol. 6, pp. 2400)*

Abul Ḥasan Iraqi رَحْمَةُ اللهِ عَلَيْه and Layla-tul-Qadr

Some scholars have quoted Sayyidunā Shaykh Abul Ḥasan Iraqi رَحْمَةُ اللهِ تَعَالٰی عَلَيْه as saying: 'I have found Layla-tul-Qadr every year ever since I have reached puberty. Then, expressing his personal experience about Layla-tul-Qadr, he said, 'Whenever the first fast fell on Sunday or Wednesday, Layla-tul-Qadr was the 29th night. If the first fast was on a Monday it was the 21st night. If the first fast was on a Tuesday or Friday it was the 27th night. If the first fast was on a Thursday it was the 25th night and if the first fast was on a Saturday it was the 23rd night.' *(Nuzĥa-tul-Majālis, vol. 1, pp. 223)*

The 27th night, Layla-tul-Qadr

Despite the differences of opinion amongst the respected jurists, Quranic exegetists, Muḥaddišīn and the majority of scholars رَحِمَهُمُ اللّٰهُ تَعَالٰی اَجْمَعِيْن opine that Layla-tul-Qadr is the 27th night of Ramadan every year.

Sayyidunā Ubay Bin Ka'b رَضِيَ اللهُ تَعَالٰی عَنْه holds the opinion that the 27th night of Ramadan is Layla-tul-Qadr. *(Tafsīr Ṣāwī, vol. 6, pp. 2400)*

Ghauš-e-A'ẓam Sayyidunā Shaykh 'Abdul Qādir Jīlānī رَحْمَةُ اللهِ تَعَالٰی عَلَیْه and Sayyidunā 'Abdullāĥ Ibn 'Umar رَضِیَ اللّٰهُ تَعَالٰی عَنْهُمَا also had the same opinion.

Sayyidunā Shāĥ 'Abdul 'Azīz Muḥaddiš Diĥlvī رَحْمَةُ اللهِ تَعَالٰی عَلَیْه is also one of the scholars that favoured the opinion that Layla-tul-Qadr is the 27th night of Ramadan. He رَحْمَةُ اللهِ تَعَالٰی عَلَیْه has given two proofs in favour of his opinion. Firstly, there are 9 letters in the Arabic word 'لَیْلَةُ الْقَدْر' (Layla-tul-Qadr) and this word appeared 3 times in Sūraĥ Al-Qadr. If 9 is multiplied by 3 the total is 27, which hints that Layla-tul-Qadr is the 27th night. Secondly, there are 30 words in this Sūraĥ and the 27th word is 'هِيَ' (the Arabic pronoun for 'It') which refers to Layla-tul-Qadr. In other words, this is a hint from Allah عَزَّوَجَلَّ for the righteous that Layla-tul-Qadr is the 27th night. *(Tafsīr-e-'Azīzī, vol. 4, pp. 437)*

Dear Islamic brothers! By keeping Layla-tul-Qadr a secret Allah عَزَّوَجَلَّ has persuaded His servants to worship every single night. If He عَزَّوَجَلَّ had specified a particular night as Layla-tul-Qadr and revealed it to us, we would probably remain heedless in other nights of the year and carry out special worships only in this one night. As it has been kept secret, every wise man is supposed to search for this sacred night throughout the year and perform good deeds at every night of the year. If someone sincerely searches for it Allah عَزَّوَجَلَّ does not let his efforts go to waste. He عَزَّوَجَلَّ will definitely grant him the blessings of this night.

An easy way to spend every night in worship

The following narration has been mentioned on page 187 of *Gharāib-ul-Quran*, 'If anyone recites the following Du'ā three times at night it is as if he has found Layla-tul-Qadr.' We should recite it every night. Here is the Du'ā:

لَآ اِلٰهَ اِلَّا اللّٰهُ الْحَلِیْمُ الْكَرِیْمُ

سُبْحٰنَ اللّٰهِ رَبِّ السَّمٰوٰتِ السَّبْعِ وَ رَبِّ الْعَرْشِ الْعَظِیْم

Translation: There is no one worthy of worship except Allah عَزَّوَجَلَّ Who is Ḥalīm and Karīm. Allah عَزَّوَجَلَّ is Subḥān, Rab of the seven skies and the magnificent 'Arsh.

O seekers of the pleasure of Allah عَزَّوَجَلَّ! We should perform some good deeds at every night of the year. If we do so, we will be able to spend Layla-tul-Qadr in worship, اِنْ شَآءَاللّٰه عَزَّوَجَلَّ. Every night, there are two Farḍ Ṣalāĥ that are Maghrib and 'Ishā. Along with other Ṣalāĥ, we should try our best to offer these two Ṣalāĥ with complete Jamā'at every night. If we succeed in offering these Ṣalāĥ with Jamā'at at Layla-tul-Qadr, we will be successful not only in the world but also in the Hereafter. Make it your daily habit to offer all the five Ṣalāĥ including the Fajr and 'Ishā Ṣalāĥ with complete Jamā'at.

The Holy Prophet صَلَّى اللهُ تَعَالٰى عَلَيْهِ وَاٰلِهٖ وَسَلَّم has stated, 'If anyone offers 'Ishā Ṣalāĥ with Jamā'at, it is as if he has spent half night in Ṣalāĥ; and if he offers Fajr Ṣalāĥ with Jamā'at it is as if he has spent the entire night in Ṣalāĥ.' *(Ṣaḥīḥ Muslim, pp. 329, Ḥadīš 656)*

Imām Jalāluddīn Suyūṭī Shāfi'ī رَحْمَةُ اللهِ تَعَالٰى عَلَيْه has quoted the following saying of the Holy Prophet صَلَّى اللهُ تَعَالٰى عَلَيْهِ وَاٰلِهٖ وَسَلَّم, 'The one offering 'Ishā with the Jamā'at has definitely earned his share from Layla-tul-Qadr.' *(Al-Jāmi'-uṣ-Ṣaghīr, pp. 532, Ḥadīš 8796)*

Value the 27th night

O seekers of the mercy of Allah عَزَّوَجَلَّ! If we have the habit of offering Ṣalāĥ with Jamā'at throughout the year, اِنْ شَآءَاللّٰه عَزَّوَجَلَّ we will be blessed with offering these two Ṣalāĥ with Jamā'at in Layla-tul-Qadr as well, and in this way, we will attain the reward of the whole night's worship in Layla-tul-Qadr despite sleeping the entire night.

We should make special arrangements to worship in the nights that are more likely to be Layla-tul-Qadr. For example the last ten nights of Ramadan or at least the last five odd nights and especially the 27th night because there is a high probability that this night is Layla-tul-Qadr. We must not spend this night in heedlessness. We should spend the 27th night repenting of sins, reciting Istighfār, Ṣalāt-'Alan-Nabī, Salām and Żikr.

Recite this in Layla-tul-Qadr

Amīr-ul-Mūminīn, Sayyidunā 'Alī كَرَّمَ اللهُ تَعَالٰى وَجْهَهُ الْكَرِيْم has said: 'Whoever recites Sūraĥ Al-Qadr seven times in Layla-tul-Qadr, Allah عَزَّوَجَلَّ would protect him from every calamity, and seventy thousand angels would pray that he enter Heaven. Further, whoever recites it three times on Friday (any Friday of the year) before Ṣalāt-ul-Jumu'aĥ Allah عَزَّوَجَلَّ would write as many good deeds for him as the number of people offering Ṣalāĥ that day is.' *(Nuzĥa-tul-Majālis, vol. 1, pp. 223)*

Du'ā to be recited at Layla-tul-Qadr

Mother of the believers, Sayyidatunā 'Āishaĥ Ṣiddīqaĥ رَضِیَ اللّٰہُ تَعَالٰی عَنۡہَا narrated that she asked the Prophet of mankind, the Peace of our heart and mind, the most Generous and Kind صَلَّى اللهُ تَعَالٰى عَلَيْهِ وَاٰلِهٖ وَسَلَّم, 'Yā Rasūlallāĥ صَلَّى اللهُ تَعَالٰى عَلَيْهِ وَاٰلِهٖ وَسَلَّم! What should I recite if I find Layla-tul-Qadr?' The Beloved and Blessed Prophet صَلَّى اللهُ تَعَالٰى عَلَيْهِ وَاٰلِهٖ وَسَلَّم replied, 'Make this Du'ā:

اَللّٰھُمَّ اِنَّكَ عَفُوٌّ كَرِيْمٌ تُحِبُّ الْعَفْوَ فَاعْفُ عَنِّيْ

'Yā Allah عَزَّوَجَلَّ! You are indeed the Forgiver and the Benevolent, You also like forgiving, so forgive me.'

(Jāmi' Tirmiżī, vol. 5, pp. 306, Ḥadīš 3524)

Dear Islamic brothers! If only we all would recite this Du'ā at least once every night, we'll be blessed with Layla-tul-Qadr any night. If not every night, recite it repeatedly on at least the 27th night. In addition, if Allah عَزَّوَجَلَّ gives you the ability, stay awake the whole night and recite Ṣalāt-'Alan-Nabī and Salām abundantly, attend a Sunnaĥ-Inspiring Ijtimā' and try to spend your time offering Nafl Ṣalāĥ.

Nafl of Layla-tul-Qadr

Sayyidunā Ismā'īl Ḥaqqī رَحْمَةُ اللّٰهِ تَعَالٰی عَلَيْه has stated the following narration in his commentary '*Rūḥ-ul-Bayān*': All the previous sins of the one offering Nafl Ṣalāĥ sincerely in Layla-tul-Qadr will be forgiven. *(Rūḥ-ul-Bayān, vol. 10, pp. 480)*

The Prophet of Raḥmaĥ, the Intercessor of Ummaĥ صَلَّى اللهُ تَعَالٰى عَلَيْهِ وَاٰلِهٖ وَسَلَّم used to worship abundantly in the last days of Ramadan; he would remain awake the whole nights (for worship) and make his family stay awake. *(Sunan Ibn Mājaĥ, vol. 2, pp. 357, Ḥadīš 1768)*

Sayyidunā Ismā'īl Ḥaqqī رَحْمَةُ اللهِ تَعَالٰى عَلَيْه has narrated that our pious saints used to perform two Rak'at Nafl Ṣalāĥ in each of the last ten nights with the intention of attaining the blessings of Layla-tul-Qadr. Some of the saints have said that whoever recites ten verses every night with this intention shall not be deprived of its blessings and reward.

Faqīĥ Abul Layš Samarqandī رَحْمَةُ اللهِ تَعَالٰى عَلَيْه has stated: The Ṣalāĥ of Layla-tul-Qadr should contain at least 2 Rak'āt (Nafl), which can be up to 1000 Rak'āt at the most, and the average amount is 200 Rak'āt. The average recitation in each Rak'at is to recite Sūraĥ Al-Fātiḥaĥ, Sūraĥ Al-Qadr and then Sūraĥ Al-Ikhlāṣ three times and perform Salām after every set of two Rak'āt. Then send Ṣalāt on Rasūlullāĥ صَلَّى اللهُ تَعَالٰى عَلَيْهِ وَاٰلِهٖ وَسَلَّم and stand to offer Ṣalāĥ again. Continue to do this until you complete your 200 or less or more Rak'āt. This will be sufficient for attaining the blessings of this night that Allah عَزَّوَجَلَّ has mentioned and the Beloved and Blessed Prophet صَلَّى اللهُ تَعَالٰى عَلَيْهِ وَاٰلِهٖ وَسَلَّم has told us. *(Rūḥ-ul-Bayān, vol. 10, pp. 483)*

Dear Islamic brothers! This night is definitely a fountain of immense blessings. The Prophet of mankind, the Peace of our heart and mind, the most Generous and Kind صَلَّى اللهُ تَعَالٰى عَلَيْهِ وَاٰلِهٖ وَسَلَّم has said: Such a month has come to you in which there is a night that is better than a thousand months. Whoever is deprived in this night is deprived of all goodness; only a completely deprived person is left deprived of the goodness of Layla-tul-Qadr. *(Mishkāt-ul-Maṣābīḥ, vol. 1, pp. 372, Ḥadīš 1964)*

Wasting such a blessed and sacred night that has innumerable blessings and bounties indicates great deprivation. Therefore, everyone should search for Layla-tul-Qadr the whole Ramadan or at least spend the 27th night in worship.

Yā Allah عَزَّوَجَلَّ! For the sake of Your Beloved Prophet صَلَّى اللهُ تَعَالٰى عَلَيْهِ وَاٰلِهٖ وَسَلَّم grant us the blessings of Layla-tul-Qadr and the ability to worship You abundantly.

اٰمِيْن بِجَاهِ النَّبِيِّ الْاَمِيْن صَلَّى اللهُ تَعَالٰى عَلَيْهِ وَاٰلِهٖ وَسَلَّم

Beholding a great personage in wakefulness

Dear Islamic brothers! Make a habit of travelling with Rasūl's devotees in the Madanī Qāfilaĥs of Dawat-e-Islami, a global & non-political religious movement of the Quran and Sunnaĥ, اِنْ شَآءَاللّٰه عَزَّوَجَلَّ you will be motivated to search for Layla-tul-Qadr. Here is a faith-refreshing incident of a Madanī Qāfilaĥ for your persuasion. An Islamic brother of New Karachi has stated: It was the first time I travelled with a 12 day Madanī Qāfilaĥ; our Qāfilaĥ stayed in a Masjid in Nawabshah (Bāb-ul-Islam, Sindh). Due to the lack of inclination towards virtuous deeds, I felt quite bored. One day, according to the schedule, the participants were busy learning Sunnaĥ in the courtyard of the Masjid. As the sun was shining directly on us; one of the Islamic brothers moved inside the Masjid.

After a short while, we heard a voice from inside the Masjid. All of us saw the Islamic brother come out crying. He said, 'In a state of wakefulness I have just seen a bright-faced pious saint with a green turban on his blessed head; the saint said, 'Those learning the Sunnaĥ in the courtyard in the sun shine are earning more reward.' On hearing this, all the participants were moved to tears. Amazed, I made a firm intention never to leave the Madanī environment of Dawat-e-Islami.

اَلْحَمْدُ لِلّٰه عَزَّوَجَلَّ! Travelling regularly with Madanī Qāfilaĥs has now become a second nature to me. Once our Madanī Qāfilaĥ was in Mirpurkhas (Bāb-ul-Islam, Sindh), a devotee of Rasūl said that he saw the participants of the Qāfilaĥ being showered with light at the time of Taĥajjud. This incident further augmented my spirit and enthusiasm. اَلْحَمْدُ لِلّٰه عَزَّوَجَلَّ At present, I am serving Dawat-e-Islami as a responsible for Madanī In'āmāt in my area.

Don't sit with half your body in shade

Dear Islamic brothers! Did you see how those who travel with Madanī Qāfilaĥs are showered with blessings! It probably wasn't very hot and Rasūl's devotees may have sat in the cool sunlight of the morning to learn the Sunan; and they may have been encouraged in this way. However, it isn't appropriate to hold a learning session in extreme heat unnecessarily, as it will be hard to concentrate and the participants may misunderstand things. The environment for learning should be comfortable. If the sun is shining on parts of one's body it is Sunnaĥ to move; either sit completely in shade or completely in the sunshine.

Sayyidunā Abū Ĥurayraĥ رَضِیَ اللّٰہُ تَعَالٰی عَنْہُ has narrated that the Prophet of mankind, the Peace of our heart and mind, the most Generous and Kind صَلَّی اللّٰہُ تَعَالٰی عَلَیْہِ وَاٰلِہٖ وَسَلَّم has said, 'When someone is in shade and the shade then moves away, leaving him partially in the sunshine and partially in shade then he should move.' *(Sunan Abī Dāwūd, vol. 4, pp. 338, Ḥadīš 4821)*

Auliyā kā karam, khūb lutāyn gey ĥam
Āo mil kar chalayn, Qāfilay mayn chalo
Dĥūp mayn cĥāon mayn, jāūn mayn āūn mayn
Sab yeĥ niyyat karayn, Qāfilay mayn chalo
Ĥotī ĥayn sab sunayn Nūr kī bārishayn
Sab naĥānay chalayn Qāfilay mayn chalo

Blessings of saints we will hopefully gain
Let's travel together with Madanī Qāfilaĥ
In winter and summer, make intention firmer
Of travelling together with Madanī Qāfilaĥ
Everyone should hear, rain of Nūr showers
To bath in this rain, travel with Madanī Qāfilaĥ

صَلُّوْا عَلَی الْحَبِیْب　　صَلَّی اللّٰہُ تَعَالٰی عَلٰی مُحَمَّد

Control your anger

Sayyidunā Imām Ghazālī عَلَیْہِ رَحْمَۃُ اللّٰہِ الْوَالِی has narrated: 'A person talked harshly to Amīr-ul-Mūminīn Sayyidunā 'Umar Bin 'Abdul 'Azīz عَلَیْہِ رَحْمَۃُ اللّٰہِ الْعَزِیْز. Lowering his head, Sayyidunā 'Umar Bin 'Abdul 'Azīz عَلَیْہِ رَحْمَۃُ اللّٰہِ الْعَزِیْز said: 'Do you want me to get angry so that Satan would make me arrogant and cause me to oppress you because of my power, and so that you would take its revenge from me on the Day of Judgement? I will never do this.' After he said this, he became silent.

(Kīmiyā-e-Sa'ādat, vol. 2, pp. 597)

اَلْحَمْدُ لِلّٰهِ رَبِّ الْعٰلَمِیْنَ وَ الصَّلٰوۃُ وَ السَّلَامُ عَلٰی سَیِّدِ الْمُرْسَلِیْنَ

اَمَّا بَعْدُ فَاَعُوْذُ بِاللّٰهِ مِنَ الشَّیْطٰنِ الرَّجِیْمِ ؕ بِسْمِ اللّٰهِ الرَّحْمٰنِ الرَّحِیْمِ ؕ

Blessings of I'tikāf

Sayyidunā Abū Dardā رَضِیَ اللہُ تَعَالٰی عَنْهُ has narrated that the Prophet of mankind, the Peace of our heart and mind, the most Generous and Kind صَلَّى اللهُ تَعَالٰى عَلَيْهِ وَاٰلِهٖ وَسَلَّم has said:

مَنْ صَلّٰى عَلَيَّ حِيْنَ يُصْبِحُ عَشْرًا وَحِيْنَ يُمْسِيْ عَشْرًا أَدْرَكَتْهُ شَفَاعَتِيْ يَوْمَ الْقِيَامَةِ

Translation: Whoever recites Ṣalāt upon me 10 times in the morning and 10 times in the evening shall gain my intercession on the Day of Judgement.

(Majma'-uz-Zawāid, vol. 10, pp. 163, Ḥadīš 17022)

صَلُّوْا عَلَى الْحَبِيْب　　صَلَّى اللهُ تَعَالٰى عَلٰى مُحَمَّد

Dear Islamic brothers! What can we say about the blessings of Ramadan! No doubt, its every moment is full of bounties and blessings, but the most important thing in this blessed month is Layla-tul-Qadr. In order to find this night, the Prophet of mankind, the Peace of our heart and mind, the most Generous and Kind صَلَّى اللهُ تَعَالٰى عَلَيْهِ وَاٰلِهٖ وَسَلَّم performed I'tikāf even for the whole of Ramadan, and he صَلَّى اللهُ تَعَالٰى عَلَيْهِ وَاٰلِهٖ وَسَلَّم would not miss it especially in the last ten days.

Once he صَلَّى اللهُ تَعَالٰى عَلَيْهِ وَاٰلِهٖ وَسَلَّم could not do I'tikāf in Ramadan for some reason, so he did it in the last ten days of Shawwal. *(Ṣaḥīḥ Bukhārī, vol. 1, pp. 671, Ḥadīš 2031)* Similarly, once he صَلَّى اللهُ تَعَالٰى عَلَيْهِ وَاٰلِهٖ وَسَلَّم did not do I'tikāf due to travelling, so he صَلَّى اللهُ تَعَالٰى عَلَيْهِ وَاٰلِهٖ وَسَلَّم did I'tikāf for 20 days in the following Ramadan. *(Jāmi' Tirmižī, vol. 2, pp. 212, Ḥadīš 803)*

I'tikāf is an ancient form of worship

I'tikāf is an ancient form of worship which the earlier Ummaĥs would also perform, as stated in part 1 Sūraĥ Al-Baqaraĥ, verse 125 of the Holy Quran:

وَ عَهِدْنَاۤ اِلٰۤى اِبْرٰهٖمَ وَ اِسْمٰعِیْلَ اَنْ طَهِّرَا بَیْتِیَ لِلطَّآىٕفِیْنَ وَ الْعٰكِفِیْنَ وَ الرُّكَّعِ السُّجُوْدِ ﴿۱۲۵﴾

And We enjoined strictly upon Ibrāĥīm and Ismā'īl عَلَيْهِمُ السَّلَام to purify well My house for those who go around it and those who stay therein for I'tikāf and those who bow down (for Rukū') and prostrate. *[Kanz-ul-Īmān (Translation of Quran)] (Part 1, Sūraĥ Al-Baqaraĥ, verse 125)*

Keep Masājid clean

Dear Islamic brothers! Allah عَزَّوَجَلَّ has Himself commanded that the Holy Ka'baĥ be kept clean and pure for the performers of Ṣalāĥ and I'tikāf. Muftī Aḥmad Yār Khān عَلَيْهِ رَحْمَةُ الْمَنَّان, a renowned exegetist of the Quran has stated: 'So we must keep Masājid clean and pure. Dirty and smelly things must be kept away from them. This is a Sunnaĥ of the Prophets عَلَيْهِمُ السَّلَام. We have also learnt that I'tikāf, Rukū' and Sujūd were a part of the earlier Ummaĥs' worships. Further, we have also learnt that Masājid should have caretakers who should be pious.' He رَحْمَةُ اللهِ تَعَالٰى عَلَيْه has further stated: 'Ṭawāf, Ṣalāĥ, and I'tikāf are ancient forms of worship which existed in the time of Sayyidunā Ibrāĥīm عَلَيْهِ السَّلَام as well.' *(Nūr-ul-'Irfān, pp. 29)*

Ten days' I'tikāf

The Beloved and Blessed Rasūl صَلَّى اللهُ تَعَالٰى عَلَيْهِ وَاٰلِهٖ وَسَلَّم consistently did I'tikāf in the last ten days of Ramadan and his blessed wives, the mothers of the believers, also kept this Sunnaĥ alive by doing I'tikāf.

Mother of the believers, Sayyidatunā 'Āishaĥ Ṣiddīqaĥ رَضِیَ اللهُ تَعَالٰی عَنْهَا has said, 'The Holy Prophet صَلَّى اللهُ تَعَالٰى عَلَيْهِ وَاٰلِهٖ وَسَلَّم would do I'tikāf in the last ten days of Ramadan until he passed away (apparently). Thereafter, his chaste wives used to do I'tikāf.' *(Ṣaḥīḥ Bukhārī, vol. 1, pp. 664, Ḥadīš 2026)*

صَلُّوْا عَلَى الْحَبِيْب صَلَّى اللهُ تَعَالٰى عَلٰى مُحَمَّد

Eagerness of devotees

Dear Islamic brothers! Though there are innumerable blessings of I'tikāf, the mere fact that I'tikāf in the last ten days is a Sunnaĥ, is enough for the devotees. The mere thought of fulfilling a Sunnaĥ of the Prophet of Raḥmaĥ, the Intercessor of Ummaĥ صَلَّى اللّٰهُ تَعَالٰى عَلَيْهِ وَاٰلِهٖ وَسَلَّم makes our hearts sway in delight. A devotee tries his best enthusiastically to do whatever the Beloved and Blessed Prophet صَلَّى اللّٰهُ تَعَالٰى عَلَيْهِ وَاٰلِهٖ وَسَلَّم did. However, there should be no Shar'ī prohibition on the act we are willing to do. For example, the Beloved and Blessed Prophet صَلَّى اللّٰهُ تَعَالٰى عَلَيْهِ وَاٰلِهٖ وَسَلَّم used a bedstead during I'tikāf, but we cannot do so as it will reduce the space for the people who come to offer Ṣalāĥ in the Masjid and it will look strange as well.

Wisdom behind walking around with camel

Sayyidunā 'Abdullāĥ Ibn 'Umar رَضِىَ اللّٰهُ تَعَالٰى عَنْهُمَا was an ardent follower of Sunnaĥ. Whenever he رَضِىَ اللّٰهُ تَعَالٰى عَنْهُ came to know about a Sunnaĥ, he would do his level best to act upon it without delay. Once he رَضِىَ اللّٰهُ تَعَالٰى عَنْهُ was seen walking around a particular place with his camel. Astonished, the people asked as to why he رَضِىَ اللّٰهُ تَعَالٰى عَنْهُ did so, he رَضِىَ اللّٰهُ تَعَالٰى عَنْهُ answered, 'Once I saw the Noble Prophet صَلَّى اللّٰهُ تَعَالٰى عَلَيْهِ وَاٰلِهٖ وَسَلَّم do the same at this place, so I'm imitating the Holy Prophet صَلَّى اللّٰهُ تَعَالٰى عَلَيْهِ وَاٰلِهٖ وَسَلَّم.' *(Ash-Shifā, vol. 2, pp. 30)*

Do I'tikāf at least once

O devotees of the Sunnaĥs of the Holy Prophet! If possible, do I'tikāf every year. If not possible, do I'tikāf in the last ten days of Ramadan at least once in your life. Staying in the Masjid is a great blessing, a Mu'takif is so fortunate that he stays in the Masjid leaving all his activities in order to gain the pleasure of Allah عَزَّوَجَلَّ.

Fatāwā 'Ālamgīrī states, 'The benefits of I'tikāf are obvious, when a person does I'tikāf, he completely devotes himself to worship for the pleasure of Allah عَزَّوَجَلَّ, giving up all worldly affairs and activities that obstruct him in earning the pleasure of Allah عَزَّوَجَلَّ. All of his time is spent in Ṣalāĥ, either physically or spiritually, because the primary purpose of doing I'tikāf is to wait for Ṣalāĥ with Jamā'at and the reward of waiting for Ṣalāĥ is like that of offering Ṣalāĥ. A Mu'takif resembles the angels who do not disobey Allah عَزَّوَجَلَّ

and obey His every command, he resembles those who glorify Allah عَزَّوَجَلَّ day and night and never get tired of doing so.' *(Fatāwā 'Ālamgīrī, vol. 1, pp. 212)*

صَلُّوْا عَلَى الْحَبِيْب صَلَّى اللهُ تَعَالٰى عَلٰى مُحَمَّد

Benefit of one day's I'tikāf

There is a great reward for the one who does I'tikāf even for a single day with sincerity in any month of the year besides Ramadan. Persuading us to do I'tikāf, the Prophet of mankind, the Peace of our heart and mind, the most Generous and Kind صَلَّى اللهُ تَعَالٰى عَلَيْهِ وَاٰلِهٖ وَسَلَّم has said: 'Whoever does I'tikāf for the pleasure of Allah عَزَّوَجَلَّ for one day, Allah عَزَّوَجَلَّ shall place three trenches between him and Hell, and these trenches will be wider than even the distance between the east and the west.' *(Ad-Dur-rul-Manšūr, vol. 1, pp. 486)*

Forgiveness for all previous sins

Mother of the believers, Sayyidatunā 'Āishaĥ Ṣiddīqaĥ رَضِیَ اللهُ تَعَالٰى عَنْهَا has narrated the following fragrant saying of the Beloved and Blessed Prophet صَلَّى اللهُ تَعَالٰى عَلَيْهِ وَاٰلِهٖ وَسَلَّم:

مَنِ اعْتَكَفَ اِيْمَانًا وَّ اِحْتِسَابًا غُفِرَلَهُ مَا تَقَدَّمَ مِنْ ذَنْبِهٖ

Translation: Whoever did I'tikāf with faith in order to earn reward all of his previous sins will be forgiven.

(Al-Jāmi'-uṣ-Ṣaghīr, pp. 516, Ḥadīš 8480)

صَلُّوْا عَلَى الْحَبِيْب صَلَّى اللهُ تَعَالٰى عَلٰى مُحَمَّد

Place of I'tikāf of the Holy Prophet صَلَّى اللهُ تَعَالٰى عَلَيْهِ وَاٰلِهٖ وَسَلَّم

Sayyidunā Nāfi' رَضِیَ اللهُ تَعَالٰى عَنْهُ reports that Sayyidunā 'Abdullāĥ Ibn 'Umar رَضِیَ اللهُ تَعَالٰى عَنْهُمَا has said, 'The Beloved and Blessed Prophet صَلَّى اللهُ تَعَالٰى عَلَيْهِ وَاٰلِهٖ وَسَلَّم used to do I'tikāf in the last ten days of Ramadan.'

Sayyidunā Nāfi' رَضِیَ اللهُ تَعَالٰی عَنْهُ goes onto say, 'Sayyidunā 'Abdullāĥ Ibn 'Umar رَضِیَ اللّٰهُ تَعَالٰی عَنْهُمَا showed me the place of the Masjid where the Holy Prophet صَلَّی اللهُ تَعَالٰی عَلَیۡهِ وَاٰلِهٖ وَسَلَّم used to do I'tikāf.' *(Ṣaḥīḥ Muslim, pp. 597, Ḥadīš 1171)*

Dear Islamic brothers! Even today, in Masjid Nabawī زَادَهَا اللّٰهُ شَرَفًا وَّ تَعۡظِیۡمًا, there is a pillar called اُسْطُوَانَـةُ السَّرِیْر (Usṭuwāna-tus-Sarīr) which marks the place where the Prophet of Raḥmaĥ, the Intercessor of Ummaĥ صَلَّی اللّٰهُ تَعَالٰی عَلَیۡهِ وَاٰلِهٖ وَسَلَّم used to place his blessed bed made of date tree, bark etc. during I'tikāf. Fortunate devotees go to see it and offer Nafl Ṣalāĥ there for attaining blessings.

I'tikāf for entire month

The Beloved and Blessed Prophet صَلَّی اللهُ تَعَالٰی عَلَیۡهِ وَاٰلِهٖ وَسَلَّم would always try his best to gain the pleasure of Allah عَزَّوَجَلَّ. He صَلَّی اللهُ تَعَالٰی عَلَیۡهِ وَاٰلِهٖ وَسَلَّم would worship abundantly especially in Ramadan. As Layla-tul-Qadr is hidden in Ramadan, the Prophet of Raḥmaĥ, the Intercessor of Ummaĥ صَلَّی اللهُ تَعَالٰی عَلَیۡهِ وَاٰلِهٖ وَسَلَّم once did I'tikāf for the entire month in order to search this blessed night.

Sayyidunā Abū Sa'īd Khudrī رَضِیَ اللهُ تَعَالٰی عَنْهُ has narrated, 'Once the Noble Rasūl صَلَّی اللهُ تَعَالٰی عَلَیۡهِ وَاٰلِهٖ وَسَلَّم did I'tikāf from the 1st of Ramadan to the 20th and then said, 'In search of Layla-tul-Qadr, I spent the first ten days of Ramadan in I'tikāf, and then the middle ten days, then I was told that it is in the last ten days. Therefore, whoever amongst you wishes to do I'tikāf with me should do so.' *(Ṣaḥīḥ Muslim, pp. 594, Ḥadīš 1167)*

I'tikāf in Turkish tent

Sayyidunā Abū Sa'īd Khudrī رَضِیَ اللهُ تَعَالٰی عَنْهُ said, 'Beloved and Blessed Rasūl صَلَّی اللهُ تَعَالٰی عَلَیۡهِ وَاٰلِهٖ وَسَلَّم first did I'tikāf for the initial ten days of Ramadan in a Turkish tent, then he صَلَّی اللهُ تَعَالٰی عَلَیۡهِ وَاٰلِهٖ وَسَلَّم did I'tikāf for the middle ten days as well. Then he صَلَّی اللهُ تَعَالٰی عَلَیۡهِ وَاٰلِهٖ وَسَلَّم took his head out of the tent and said, 'I did I'tikāf for the first ten days in search of Layla-tul-Qadr and then did it in the middle ten days as well for the same purpose. Then I was informed by Allah عَزَّوَجَلَّ that it is in the last ten days. Therefore, whoever wishes to do I'tikāf with me should do so in the last ten days. First I was shown Layla-tul-Qadr but then I was made to forget it and now I have seen myself prostrating on the morning of Layla-tul-Qadr on wet soil. Therefore search for it in the odd nights of the last ten days.'

Sayyidunā Abū Sa'īd Khudrī رَضِیَ اللهُ تَعَالٰی عَنْهُ goes onto say that it rained that night and water began to drip from the roof of the blessed Masjid; so on the morning of the 21st Ramadan, my eyes saw that there was a mark of wet soil on the blessed forehead of the Beloved and Blessed Prophet صَلَّی اللهُ تَعَالٰی عَلَیْهِ وَاٰلِهٖ وَسَلَّم. *(Mishkāt-ul-Maṣābīḥ, vol. 1, pp. 392, Ḥadīš 2086)*

Most important purpose

Dear Islamic brothers! If not every year, we all should act upon the Sunnaĥ of doing I'tikāf for the whole of Ramadan at least once in our whole life. The most important purpose of doing I'tikāf in Ramadan is to search for Layla-tul-Qadr, and the strongest opinion is that Layla-tul-Qadr is in the odd nights of the last ten days. We have also learnt from this blessed Ḥadīš that Layla-tul-Qadr was on the 21st night that year but the Holy Prophet's صَلَّی اللهُ تَعَالٰی عَلَیْهِ وَاٰلِهٖ وَسَلَّم saying 'search for it in the odd nights of the last ten days' indicates that the date of Layla-tul-Qadr varies every year. Any of the odd nights of the last ten days from 21st to 29th Ramadan may be Layla-tul-Qadr.

Muslims have been persuaḍed to do I'tikāf in the last ten days in order to gain the blessings of Layla-tul-Qadr because a Mu takif remains in the Masjid for all 10 days, and one of these nights is Layla-tul-Qadr, so he succeeds in spending that night in the Masjid. Further, this Ḥadīš threw light on the humility of the Holy Prophet صَلَّی اللهُ تَعَالٰی عَلَیْهِ وَاٰلِهٖ وَسَلَّم as he صَلَّی اللهُ تَعَالٰی عَلَیْهِ وَاٰلِهٖ وَسَلَّم prostrated on soil, and the fortunate pieces of soil clung onto the blessed forehead of the Beloved and Blessed Prophet صَلَّی اللهُ تَعَالٰی عَلَیْهِ وَاٰلِهٖ وَسَلَّم

Prostrating directly on ground is preferable

اَللهُ اَکْبَر! Did you see the humility of the Holy Prophet صَلَّی اللهُ تَعَالٰی عَلَیْهِ وَاٰلِهٖ وَسَلَّم? His placing his blessed forehead for the sake of Allah عَزَّوَجَلَّ on the ground, and the soil particles' clinging onto his blessed forehead is the great humility of the Holy Prophet صَلَّی اللهُ تَعَالٰی عَلَیْهِ وَاٰلِهٖ وَسَلَّم. The respected scholars رَحِمَهُمُ اللهُ تَعَالٰی say: Prostrating directly on the ground (without anything in between the foreground and the ground) is preferable. *(Marāqil Falāḥ, pp. 85, part 3)* It is stated in *Mukāshafa-tul-Qulūb* that Sayyidunā 'Umar Bin 'Abdul 'Azīz رَضِیَ اللهُ تَعَالٰی عَنْهُ would always prostrate on the soil. *(Mukāshafa-tul-Qulūb, pp. 181)*

Reward of performing Hajj and 'Umraĥ twice

Sayyidunā 'Alī كَرَّمَ اللّٰهُ تَعَالٰى وَجْهَهُ الْكَرِيْم has narrated the following fragrant saying of the Prophet of Raḥmaĥ, the Intercessor of Ummaĥ صَلَّى اللّٰهُ تَعَالٰى عَلَيْهِ وَاٰلِهٖ وَسَلَّم:

مَنِ اعْتَكَفَ فِيْ رَمَضَانَ كَانَ كَحَجَّتَيْنِ وَ عُمْرَتَيْن

Translation: The one doing I'tikāf (for 10 days) in Ramadan is like the one who has performed Hajj and 'Umraĥ twice. *(Shu'ab-ul-Īmān, vol. 3, pp. 425, Ḥadīš 2966)*

Protection from sins

Sayyidunā 'Abdullāĥ Ibn 'Abbās رَضِىَ اللّٰهُ تَعَالٰى عَنْهُمَا has narrated the following saying of the Holy Prophet صَلَّى اللّٰهُ تَعَالٰى عَلَيْهِ وَاٰلِهٖ وَسَلَّم:

هُوَ يَعْكِفُ الذُّنُوْبَ يُجْرٰى لَهٗ مِنَ الْحَسَنَاتِ كَعَامِلِ الْحَسَنَاتِ كُلِّهَا

Translation: A Mu'takif remains safe from sins and the reward of righteous deeds is given to him as given to their doers. *(Sunan Ibn Mājaĥ, vol. 2, pp. 365, Ḥadīš 1781)*

Reward without performing deeds

Dear Islamic brothers! Another huge benefit of I'tikāf is protection from sins. As long as a Muslim is in the Masjid, he abstains from the sins including the ones he would commit outside the Masjid if he had not done I'tikāf. It is a special mercy of Allah عَزَّوَجَلَّ that the Mu'takif will gain the reward of even such righteous deeds he used to do outside the Masjid but can no longer perform them due to I'tikāf. It is as if he is still performing them, and their reward will be recorded for him. For example, if an Islamic brother used to visit sick people, but cannot do that due to I'tikāf he will still get its reward.

Reward for Hajj every day

Sayyidunā Ḥasan Başrī عَلَيْهِ رَحْمَةُ اللّٰهِ الْقَوِى has narrated, 'A Mu'takif is granted the reward of performing Hajj every day.' *(Shu'ab-ul-Īmān, vol. 3, pp. 425, Ḥadīš 3968)*

Definition of I'tikāf

I'tikāf implies staying in the Masjid with the intention of I'tikāf for the pleasure of Allah عَزَّوَجَلَّ. Sanity and purity from Janābat (major impurity) are conditions for a Muslim. Further, purity from menses and post natal bleeding is also a condition for women. Puberty is not a condition. If a sane child remains in a Masjid with the intention of I'tikāf his I'tikāf will also be valid. *(Fatāwā 'Ālamgīrī, vol. 1, pp. 211)*

Literal meaning of I'tikāf

The literal meaning of I'tikāf is 'To keep staying somewhere.' In other words, a Mu'takif persistently remains in the court of Allah عَزَّوَجَلَّ to worship Him fervently, his sole aim is to please his Allah عَزَّوَجَلَّ.

I've come to stay

Sayyidunā 'Aṭā Khurāsānī قُدِّسَ سِرُّهُ النُّوْرَانِي has said: A Mu'takif is like the person who comes to the court of Allah عَزَّوَجَلَّ and says, 'O Allah, my glorious Rab عَزَّوَجَلَّ! I won't leave until You forgive me.' *(Shu'ab-ul-Īmān, vol. 3, pp. 426, Ḥadīš 3970)*

Types of I'tikāf

There are 3 types of I'tikāf: (1) Wājib (2) Sunnaĥ (3) Nafl.

Wājib I'tikāf

If a vow is made to perform I'tikāf by saying the words (for example) *I will do I'tikāf on such-and-such day or so many days for Allah عَزَّوَجَلَّ*, it will become Wājib to do I'tikāf for the number of days mentioned in the vow.

It is particularly important that whenever any sort of vow is made, pronouncing it verbally is a condition; just making an intention for a vow in heart without pronouncing it verbally is insufficient, and fulfilling such a vow is not Wājib either.

(Rad-dul-Muḥtār, vol. 3, pp. 430)

Sunnaĥ I'tikāf

Men have to perform I'tikāf for vow in a Masjid, whereas women must perform it in the Masjid of their homes called 'Masjid-e-Bayt.' (The place a woman specifies for Ṣalāĥ in her home is called Masjid-e-Bayt) Fast is also a condition for such an I'tikāf.

I'tikāf in the last ten days of Ramadan is 'Sunnat-ul-Muakkadaĥ 'Alal Kifāyaĥ.' *(Durr-e-Mukhtār ma' Rad-dul-Muḥtār, vol. 3, pp. 430)* This implies that if any one person from the whole city does I'tikāf, it will be sufficient for everyone (in the city) but if no body did it then everyone is blameworthy. *(Baĥār-e-Sharī'at, part 5, pp. 152)*

In this I'tikāf, it is necessary to get to the Masjid with the intention of I'tikāf before the sun sets on the 20th of Ramadan, and stay there until the crescent of Shawwal appears on the 29th or the sun sets on the 30th. *(Baĥār-e-Sharī'at, part 5, pp. 151)*

If someone enters the Masjid after the sunset on 20th of Ramadan, the Sunnat-ul-Muakkadaĥ of I'tikāf will remain unfulfilled. Further, even if he entered the Masjid before the sunset but forgot to make the intention (e.g. there was no intention in heart at all) still the Sunnat-ul-Muakkadaĥ of I'tikāf will remain unfulfilled. If he makes the intention after the sunset it will be a Nafl I'tikāf. The intention of the heart is sufficient; pronouncing it verbally is not a condition. However it is better to pronounce it verbally provided the intention is present in heart.

Make intention for I'tikāf in these words

'I intend to do the Sunnaĥ I'tikāf in the last ten days of Ramadan for the pleasure of Allah عَزَّوَجَلَّ.'

Nafl I'tikāf

Apart from the I'tikāf of vow or Sunnat-ul-Muakkadaĥ, any other type of I'tikāf is Nafl and Sunnat-e-Ghayr Muakkadaĥ. *(Baĥār-e-Sharī'at, part 5, pp. 152)* Fasting is not a condition in this I'tikāf and there is no time limit for it either. Whenever you enter a Masjid, make the intention of I'tikāf, you will earn the reward for I'tikāf for as long as you remain in the Masjid, regardless of whether or not you perform any good deed such as reciting invocations or offering any Ṣalāĥ. As soon as you exit the Masjid this I'tikāf will end.

A'lā Ḥaḍrat رَحْمَةُ اللهِ تَعَالٰی عَلَيْه has stated: The Fatwā is that fasting is not a condition for (Nafl) I'tikāf. It can be done even for a single moment. You should make the intention of I'tikāf as soon as you enter (the Masjid), you will attain the reward of offering Ṣalāĥ as well as that of waiting for Ṣalāĥ in addition to the reward of I'tikāf for as long as you stay in the Masjid. *(Fatāwā Razawiyyaĥ (Jadīd), vol. 5, pp. 674)* He رَحْمَةُ اللهِ تَعَالٰی عَلَيْه has further stated: Whenever you enter a Masjid, make the intention of I'tikāf. You will get reward for I'tikāf as long as you are in the Masjid. *(ibid, vol. 8, pp. 98)*

Making the intention of I'tikāf isn't difficult. Intention refers to the intention of the heart (the willingness of heart to do something). It is sufficient to make an intention in heart like '*I intend to perform the Sunnaĥ of I'tikāf.*' To utter these words verbally along with the intention of the heart is better. One can also utter it in one's own language. Saying it in Arabic is better. If possible, learn the following Arabic intention as mentioned in part 2 of '*Al-Malfūẓ*' page 272:

نَوَيْتُ سُنَّةَ الْاِعْتِكَاف

Translation: I intend to fulfil the Sunnaĥ of I'tikāf.

If one enters the blessed Masjid Nabawī through its old and famous gate called 'Bāb-ur-Raḥmaĥ' he will find a pillar on the front with a clear inscription of the words نَوَيْتُ سُنَّةَ الْاِعْتِكَاف, from ancient time.

Dear Islamic brothers! While making an intention for any form of worship such as Ṣalāĥ, fasting, Iḥrām, Ṭawāf of the Holy Ka'baĥ etc., it is necessary to understand the meaning of the words of the intention as the intention of the heart is indeed a valid intention, and one can be able to make the intention in one's heart only when he understands its meaning. If he verbally utters the 'Arabic intention' or reads it from a book inattentively whilst thinking about something else without having the intention in heart, such a verbal intention will be invalid. So when a person enters a Masjid and says نَوَيْتُ سُنَّةَ الْاِعْتِكَاف he must also make intention in his heart that he is intending to do I'tikāf.

Remember that this isn't the I'tikāf of the last ten days of Ramadan, it is a Nafl I'tikāf and therefore can be done for even a single moment. This I'tikāf will end as soon as one exits the Masjid.

Eating and drinking in Masjid

Remember! By Sharī'aĥ, it is not allowed to eat, drink and sleep in the Masjid, but if one makes the intention of I'tikāf he will be allowed to do these acts in Masjid. In most of the Masājid here, people recite Ṣalāt-'Alan-Nabī etc. and then blow on water which Islamic brothers drink for blessings. No doubt, this is a good deed but if an Islamic brother hasn't made the intention of I'tikāf he cannot drink this water inside the Masjid. Similarly, only those who have made the intention of I'tikāf can do Ifṭār in the Masjid. Even in Masjid-ul-Ḥarām, one should make the intention of I'tikāf before drinking Zamzam water, doing Ifṭār or going to sleep. Likewise, one cannot drink water etc. without making the intention for I'tikāf in Masjid Nabawī.

It is also important that one shouldn't make the intention of I'tikāf just to eat, drink or sleep. It should be made to earn reward. It is stated in *Rad-dul-Muḥtār (Shāmī)*: 'If someone wants to eat, drink or sleep in a Masjid, he should make the intention of I'tikāf, make some Żikr and then do what he wants (i.e. eat, drink or sleep).' *(Rad-dul-Muḥtār, vol. 2, pp. 435)*

اَلْحَمْدُ لِلّٰه عَزَّوَجَلَّ! Dawat-e-Islami, a global & non-political religious movement of the Quran and Sunnaĥ, organises collective I'tikāf in numerous cities around the world. For these I'tikāf, there is a training schedule approved by the Markazī Majlis-e-Shūrā. Here is a list of intentions for those wishing to do I'tikāf. Those doing individual I'tikāf can also augment their reward by making as many intentions as possible for them.

Forty one intentions for collective I'tikāf

The Prophet of mankind, the Peace of our heart and mind, the most Generous and Kind صَلَّى اللّٰهُ تَعَالٰی عَلَيْهِ وَاٰلِهٖ وَسَلَّم has said:

نِيَّةُ الْمُؤْمِنِ خَيْرٌ مِّنْ عَمَلِهٖ

The intention of a Muslim is better than his deed.

(Mu'jam Kabīr, vol. 6, pp. 185, Ḥadīš 5942)

The great reward of I'tikāf can further be multiplied just by the addition of good and beneficial intentions. A'lā Ḥaḍrat ﷫ has described forty intentions. In addition to these forty intentions published by Maktaba-tul-Madīnaĥ in the form of a card, one can make many other good intentions while leaving for the Masjid. Good intentions can also be made according to the situation in the Masjid. Whenever one makes good intentions his aim should be to earn reward. The intentions are as follows:

1. I am going to do the Sunnaĥ I'tikāf for the last ten days (or entire month) of Ramadan.

2. I shall follow these Madanī principles of Taṣawwuf (mysticism):

    a. Less eating
    b. Less speaking
    c. Less sleeping

3. I shall perform all five daily Ṣalāĥ in the first row

4. With the first Takbīr

5. With Jamā'at.

6. I shall reply to every Aẕān and

7. Every Iqāmaĥ.

8. Each time I shall recite the Du'ā of Aẕān with Ṣalāt-'Alan-Nabī before and after it.

9. I shall perform the Nawāfil of Taĥajjud,

10. Ishrāq,

11. Chāsht and

12. Awwābīn every day.

13. I shall recite the Holy Quran and

14. Ṣalāt-'Alan-Nabī abundantly.

15. I shall recite or listen to the recitation of Sūraĥ Al-Mulk every night.

16. I shall perform Ṣalāt-ut-Tasbīḥ at least in the odd nights.

17. I shall participate in all the Sunnaĥ-Inspiring learning sessions and

18. Speeches from beginning to end.

19. Making individual effort, I will make my relatives and visitors attend the Sunnaĥ-Inspiring learning sessions.

20. I will apply the Madanī guard to my tongue. In other words, I shall refrain from idle speech and, if possible, I shall do even necessary conversations by writing and gestures in order to avoid useless and evil speech and noise.

21. I shall protect the Masjid from bad smells.

22. I shall keep a plastic bag in my pocket so that I would pick up any splinters or hair and put them into it. There is a saying of the Beloved Rasūl صَلَّى اللّٰهُ تَعَالٰى عَلَيْهِ وَاٰلِهٖ وَسَلَّم: Whoever removes a troublesome thing from the Masjid, Allah عَزَّوَجَلَّ will make a house for him in Paradise. *(Sunan Ibn Mājaĥ, vol. 1, pp. 419, Ḥadīš 757)*

23. I shall sleep only on my own shawl or mat so that Masjid floor is not stained from my sweat, saliva etc.

24. I shall be very careful about veil within veil[1] when sleeping. (At the time of sleeping it is appropriate to wrap a shawl around trousers and then cover it with blanket. This should be done in Madanī Qāfilaĥ, at home and everywhere else).

25. I shall apply oil and comb my hair in the Wuḍū area or 'Finā-e-Masjid' and pick up the fallen strands of hair. (If someone else is waiting to do Wuḍū, let him sit; comb your hair or apply oil elsewhere).

26. I shall not use other's things such as sandals etc. for the toilet.

27. I shall not ask others for things such as sandals, a shawl or pillow etc.

28. I shall eat in the Finā-e-Masjid on the eating mat. I will not eat on the mats used for Ṣalāĥ.

29. If the food is in less quantity, I shall eat slowly with the intention of making sacrifice for others so that other Islamic brothers may eat more. There is a great reward for sacrificing things for others. The Beloved and Blessed Prophet صَلَّى اللّٰهُ تَعَالٰى عَلَيْهِ وَاٰلِهٖ وَسَلَّم has

---

[1] Veil within veil is a term used in the Madanī environment of Dawat-e-Islami. It refers to the act of wrapping an extra shawl around dress from navel to knees.

said, 'Allah عَزَّوَجَلَّ forgives the person who gives someone else the thing he needs for himself.' *(Itḥāf-us-Sādat-il-Muttaqīn, vol. 9, pp. 779)*

30. I shall apply Madanī guard to my stomach. In other words, I shall eat less than appetite.
31. If someone hurts me I will have patience and
32. Forgive him for the pleasure of Allah عَزَّوَجَلَّ.
33. I shall be polite towards my neighbouring Mu'takifīn.
34. I shall obey my Ḥalqaĥ Nigrān.
35. I shall do Fikr-e-Madīnaĥ and fill in my Madanī In'āmāt booklet every day.
36. I shall earn the reward of Ṣadaqaĥ (charity) by looking at Islamic brothers with a smile.
37. If someone else smiles at me I shall recite اَضْحَكَ اللّٰهُ سِنَّكَ (*May Allah* عَزَّوَجَلَّ *keep you smiling*).
38. I shall make Du'ā for myself, my family, relatives and the entire Ummaĥ.
39. If a Mu'takif falls ill I shall console and serve him.
40. I shall behave extremely politely with old aged Mu'takifīn.
41. During the I'tikāf, I shall distribute as many booklets as possible. (I humbly request all Mu'takif Islamic brothers to distribute twenty five booklets, if possible, and Madanī pamphlets of Sunnaĥ-Inspiring Madanī Pearls published by Maktaba-tul-Madīnaĥ. Distribute audio cassettes of Sunnaĥ-Inspiring speech, booklet or at least a pamphlet of Madanī pearls to visitors. Your reward will multiply in Ramadan. It is important that there should be no disorder when distributing).

Which Masjid should one do I'tikāf in?

The best Masjid for I'tikāf is Masjid-ul-Ḥarām, then Masjid Nabawī عَلٰى صَاحِبِهَا الصَّلٰوةُ وَالسَّلَام, then Masjid-ul-Aqṣā (Bayt-ul-Muqaddas) and then any Jāmi' Masjid where the five daily Ṣalāĥ are offered with Jamā'at. If Ṣalāĥ is not offered with Jamā'at in the Jāmi' Masjid, it is then better to do I'tikāf in the Masjid of one's area. *(Fatḥ-ul-Qadīr, vol. 2, pp. 308)*

It is not a condition to do I'tikāf in the Jāmi' Masjid. Instead, I'tikāf can be done in any Masjid-e-Jamā'at. A Masjid-e-Jamā'at is such a Masjid in which there is an officially appointed Imām and a Műażżin, though the Jamā'at of five daily Ṣalāĥ is not held over there. It has also been said that I'tikāf is valid in any Masjid, even if it isn't a Masjid-e-Jamā'at. *(Rad-dul-Muḥtār, vol. 3, pp. 429)* Nowadays there are many such Masājid in which there is neither Imām nor Műażżin. *(Bahār-e-Sharī'at, part 5, pp. 151)*

صَلُّوْا عَلَى الْحَبِيْب　　صَلَّى اللّٰهُ تَعَالٰى عَلٰى مُحَمَّد

Mu'takifīn and Masjid's honour

Dear Mu'takif Islamic brothers! As you are to spend ten complete days in the Masjid, it is appropriate to learn a few etiquettes about Masjid's honour. During I'tikāf, it is permissible to engage in necessary worldly conversation keeping voice down and taking care about the honour of the Masjid. One should not shout while talking. The Masjid shouldn't echo with sounds of '*oi*', '*what*' and bursts of laughter; this is a sin. Remember, even a Mu'takif is not allowed to speak about worldly matters unnecessarily.

صَلُّوْا عَلَى الْحَبِيْب　　صَلَّى اللّٰهُ تَعَالٰى عَلٰى مُحَمَّد

Nothing to do with Allah عَزَّوَجَلَّ

Sayyidunā Ḥasan Baṣrī عَلَيْهِ رَحْمَةُ اللّٰهِ الْقَوِى has narrated that the Prophet of Raḥmaĥ, the Intercessor of Ummaĥ صَلَّى اللّٰهُ تَعَالٰى عَلَيْهِ وَاٰلِهٖ وَسَلَّم has said:

يَأْتِيْ عَلَى النَّاسِ زَمَانٌ يَكُوْنُ حَدِيْثُهُمْ فِيْ
مَسَاجِدِهِمْ فِيْ اَمْرِ دُنْيَاهُمْ فَلَا تُجَالِسُوْهُمْ فَلَيْسَ لِلّٰهِ فِيْهِمْ حَاجَةٌ

Translation: Upon people, a time will come when they will talk about worldly matters in Masājid. Do not sit with them for they have nothing to do with Allah عَزَّوَجَلَّ.

(Shu'ab-ul-Īmān, vol. 3, pp. 87, Ḥadīš 2962)

May you not find lost thing

Sayyidunā Abū Ĥurayraĥ رَضِىَ اللهُ تَعَالٰى عَنْهُ has narrated that the Prophet of mankind, the Peace of our heart and mind, the most Generous and Kind صَلَّى اللهُ تَعَالٰى عَلَيْهِ وَاٰلِهٖ وَسَلَّم has said:

مَنْ سَمِعَ رَجُلًا يَنْشُدُ ضَآلَّةً فِى الْمَسْجِدِ

فَقُوْلُوْا لَا رَدَّهَا اللهُ عَلَيْكَ فَاِنَّ الْمَسَاجِدَ لَمْ تُبْنَ لِهٰذَا

Translation: Whoever finds someone searching loudly for his lost thing in the Masjid, should say 'May Allah عَزَّوَجَلَّ not let you find what you have lost' because Masājid have not been made for this purpose.

(Ṣaḥīḥ Muslim, pp. 284, Ḥadīš 568)

Searching for shoes in Masjid

Dear Islamic brothers! The people who look for their lost shoes or other things in Masājid should learn a lesson from the foregoing blessed Ḥadīš. We must prevent every such activity that causes a noise and desecrates the Masājid's honour. Masājid are not made for worldly conversations, joking, laughing and other useless activities. Instead, they are made for divine worship. The blessed companions رَضِىَ اللهُ تَعَالٰى عَنْهُم would strongly dislike loud conversations in the Masjid, as mentioned in following narration:

Honour of Masjid

Sayyidunā Sāib Bin Yazīd رَضِىَ اللهُ تَعَالٰى عَنْهُ has said, 'I was standing in the Masjid when someone threw a tiny piece of stone at me. As I turned round I saw that it was Sayyidunā 'Umar Fārūq A'ẓam رَضِىَ اللهُ تَعَالٰى عَنْهُ. He asked me (with gestures) to bring those two men to him. I did as he رَضِىَ اللهُ تَعَالٰى عَنْهُ asked. Sayyidunā 'Umar رَضِىَ اللهُ تَعَالٰى عَنْهُ asked them, 'Where are you from?' They replied 'Ṭāif.' He رَضِىَ اللهُ تَعَالٰى عَنْهُ said, 'If you were the residents of Madīna-tul-Munawwaraĥ (who are well aware of Masjid's honour) I would definitely punish you because you raised your voices in the Masjid of the Beloved and Blessed Rasūl صَلَّى اللهُ تَعَالٰى عَلَيْهِ وَاٰلِهٖ وَسَلَّم!'

(Ṣaḥīḥ Bukhārī, vol. 1, pp. 178, Ḥadīš 470)

Mubāḥ speech ruins good deeds

Sayyidunā Mullā 'Alī Qārī عَلَيْهِ رَحْمَةُ اللهِ الْبَارِى has narrated with the reference of Muḥaqqiq-'alal-Iṭlāq Shaykh Ibn Ĥumām رَحْمَةُ اللهِ تَعَالٰى عَلَيْه:

اَلْكَلَامُ الْمُبَاحُ فِى الْمَسْجِدِ مَكْرُوْهٌ يَا كُلُ الْحَسَنَاتِ

Translation: Mubāḥ (permissible) speech in the Masjid is Makrūĥ (Taḥrīmī) and ruins virtuous deeds. *(Mirqāt-ul-Mafātīḥ, vol. 2, pp. 449)*

Sayyidunā Anas Bin Mālik رَضِىَ اللهُ تَعَالٰى عَنْهُ has narrated that the Prophet of mankind, the Peace of our heart and mind, the most Generous and Kind صَلَّى اللهُ تَعَالٰى عَلَيْهِ وَاٰلِهٖ وَسَلَّم has said:

اَلضَّحِكُ فِى الْمَسْجِدِ ظُلْمَةٌ فِى الْقَبْرِ

Translation: Laughing in the Masjid causes darkness in the grave.

(Al-Jāmi'-uṣ-Ṣaghīr, pp. 322, Ḥadīš 5231)

Darkness in grave

Dear Islamic brothers! Read the foregoing narrations repeatedly and tremble with fear of Allah عَزَّوَجَلَّ! A Mu'takif enters the Masjid to get reward, but (Allah عَزَّوَجَلَّ forbids) a lot of sins may be written in his book of deeds due to useless talking and laughing. Even speaking about permissible worldly matters in the Masjid ruins good deeds, so stay calm and quiet in the Masjid. Be serious even when delivering or listening to speech. Do not say any such thing that can make people laugh. Neither laugh yourself nor let others laugh because laughing in the Masjid causes darkness in the grave. However, there is no harm in smiling, if necessary. In order to develop the mindset of honouring the Masjid, please travel with the Madanī Qāfilaĥs of Dawat-e-Islami. Here is an encouraging Madanī blessing about I'tikāf:

I'tikāf of Muftī of Dawat-e-Islami

The following is the account given by a 52-year-old Islamic brother of Havelian Cantt (Sarhad, Pakistan): I was engulfed in sins; my children had grown older but I was still very fond of fashion. In the month of Ramadan, a 30-day Madanī Qāfilaĥ of Dawat-e-Islami, a global & non-political religious movement of the Quran and Sunnaĥ, came to Havelian from Bāb-ul-Madīnaĥ, Karachi. The particularity of this Madanī Qāfilaĥ was that one of the participants was a member of the Markazī Majlis-e-Shūrā, Muftī of Dawat-e-Islami, late Al-Ḥāj Muhammad Fārūq 'Aṭṭārī Madanī عَلَيْهِ رَحْمَةُ اللّٰهِ الْغَنِی.

My elder son took me to the Masjid where the participants of the Madanī Qāfilaĥ met me very politely. As a result of the individual effort of Muftī of Dawat-e-Islami قُدِّسَ سِرُّهُ السَّامِی I attended I'tikāf for the last ten days along with the Madanī Qāfilaĥ. The good manners of Muftī of Dawat-e-Islami قُدِّسَ سِرُّهُ السَّامِی won my heart. Other participants also made individual efforts on me and as a result, my hard heart turned soft and a Madanī transformation took place in my life, اَلْحَمْدُ لِلّٰه عَزَّوَجَلَّ. I gave up fashion, got rid of sins, adopted Sunnaĥ and sincerely joined the Madanī environment. I repented, grew a beard and began to wear a blessed turban. Now I try to follow every Sunnaĥ I learn. At present I am serving Dawat-e-Islami as the responsible of a Ḥalqaĥ in our area, اَلْحَمْدُ لِلّٰه عَزَّوَجَلَّ.

صَلُّوْا عَلَى الْحَبِيْب صَلَّى اللّٰهُ تَعَالٰى عَلٰى مُحَمَّد

Post-demise invitation of Qāfilaĥ from Muftī of Dawat-e-Islami

What a great man Muftī of Dawat-e-Islami قُدِّسَ سِرُّهُ السَّامِی was! He travelled with many Madanī Qāfilaĥs attaining perpetual reward for himself by rectifying the lives of numerous Islamic brothers.

He passed away after Jumu'aĥ Ṣalāĥ on 18th Muḥarram 1427 A.H. (17, February, 2006) and even after leaving this world, he persuaded an Islamic brother to travel with a Madanī Qāfilaĥ through the individual effort he made in a dream. He then appeared again in dream during the Madanī Qāfilaĥ and cured an Islamic brother from bladder problem with the power bestowed upon him by Allah عَزَّوَجَلَّ.

Therefore, an Islamic brother made the following statement: I had pain in my bladder for some time. In a dream, I beheld Muftī of Dawat-e-Islami Maulānā Muhammad Fārūq 'Aṭṭārī Madanī عَلَيْهِ رَحْمَةُ اللّٰهِ الْغَنِی who asked me to travel with a Madanī Qāfilaĥ. I made the intention but couldn't travel in Jumādal Aūlā (1427 AH.), However, I succeeded in travelling with a 3 day Madanī Qāfilah̄ with devotees of Rasūl on 24th Jumādal Ākhir (1427 A.H). When we reached the destination of the Qāfilah̄, I saw Muftī of Dawat-e-Islami قُدِّسَ سِرُّهُ السَّامِی again in a dream. He رَحْمَةُ اللهِ تَعَالٰی عَلَیْه was in the state of veil within veil. He رَحْمَةُ اللهِ تَعَالٰی عَلَیْه gave me some instructions which I couldn't understand. Almost a week has passed since I returned from the Madanī Qāfilah̄, I no longer feel the pain in my bladder, اَلْحَمْدُ لِلّٰه عَزَّوَجَلَّ

صَلُّوْا عَلَی الْحَبِیْب صَلَّی اللهُ تَعَالٰی عَلٰی مُحَمَّد

Nineteen Madanī pearls regarding Masjid

1. According to a narration, once a Masjid headed towards the court of Allah عَزَّوَجَلَّ to complain about the people engaging in worldly conversations inside it. Some angels met it on the way and said, 'We have been sent to ruin them (i.e. the people who engage in worldly conversations inside the Masjid).' *(Fatāwā Razawiyyah̄ (Jadīd), vol. 16, pp. 312)*

2. It is narrated that the people who backbite and talk in the Masjid, angels complain about them to Allah عَزَّوَجَلَّ due to the foul smell. (Backbiting is strictly Ḥarām and worse than even fornication).

   If these are the detrimental consequences of engaging in permissible worldly conversations unnecessarily in the Masjid, then how harmful the impermissible and Ḥarām acts in the Masjid would be! *(ibid)*

3. A tailor is not allowed to sew clothes in the Masjid; however, he can do so if the basic purpose of his stay is to prevent children (from entering the Masjid) and take care of the Masjid. Similarly a scribe (writer) cannot do paid work in the Masjid. *(Fatāwā 'Ālamgīrī, vol. 1, pp. 110)*

4. Do not throw any form of rubbish inside the Masjid. Sayyidunā Shaykh 'Abdul Ḥaq Muḥaddiš Diĥlvī رَحْمَةُ اللهِ تَعَالٰی عَلَیْه has reported in '*Jażb-ul-Qulūb*' that even a very small particle (e.g. splinter etc.) lying in the Masjid causes as much pain to the Masjid as a human feels pain when there is a small particle of something in his eye.

   (Jażb-ul-Qulūb, pp. 257)

5. Spitting, blowing nose, taking out dirt from nose or ear and staining the Masjid wall, floor, mat or carpet and breaking pieces off the Masjid's carpet or mat, are all prohibited.

6. There is no harm in blowing nose with a handkerchief, if necessary.

7. Do not throw the Masjid rubbish at such a place where it may be desecrated.

8. If you want to take your shoes with you in the Masjid, take them off and dust them off outside before you enter. If there is dust on the soles of your feet then wipe them off with something like a handkerchief before entering the Masjid.

9. After doing Wuḍū, dry your feet properly in the Wuḍū area; walking inside the Masjid with wet feet dirties the Masjid floor and mats etc.

Now, some of the Masjid's manners described by A'lā Ḥaḍrat, Imām-e-Aĥl-e-Sunnat Maulānā Shāĥ Aḥmad Razā Khān عَلَيْهِ رَحْمَةُ الرَّحْمٰن in his *Malfūẓāt* are being presented.

10. Running or stamping feet in the Masjid is not allowed.

11. After doing Wuḍū, do not let a single drop of water drip from your washed body parts onto the Masjid floor. (Remember! Letting drops of water drip on to the Masjid floor from washed body parts is prohibited).

12. Whenever you go from one part of the Masjid to the other (for instance, from the courtyard of the Masjid to the inner portion or vice versa) place your right foot first. If the prayer-mats are laid on the floor of the Masjid, step on them with your right foot first and also step off them onto the floor of the Masjid with your right foot (i.e. whilst walking, step onto every mat with your right foot first). Likewise, when the Khaṭīb (religious orator) steps onto the Mimbar (the pulpit) he should place his right foot on it first and he should also step off the Mimbar with his right foot first.

13. If you sneeze or cough in the Masjid, try to keep the voice as quiet as possible. The Beloved and Blessed Prophet صَلَّى اللّٰهُ تَعَالٰى عَلَيْهِ وَاٰلِهٖ وَسَلَّم disliked the loud voice of sneeze in the Masjid. One should also avoid belching. If it is not possible to stop belch, one should keep the voice of belch as quiet as possible whether or not he is in the Masjid. Care should also be taken in this regard whilst one is present in an Ijtimā' or before a

religious personality. A Ḥadīš states, 'A man belched in the presence of the Holy Prophet صَلَّى اللهُ تَعَالٰى عَلَيْهِ وَاٰلِهٖ وَسَلَّم. He صَلَّى اللهُ تَعَالٰى عَلَيْهِ وَاٰلِهٖ وَسَلَّم said, 'Keep your belch away from us as those who fill their stomachs in the world will remain hungry for a long time in the Hereafter.' *(Sharḥ-us-Sunnaĥ, vol. 7, pp. 294, Ḥadīš 2944)*

One should not make sound while yawning whether he is in the Masjid or anywhere else because yawning is the laughing of the devil. Try your best to keep your mouth closed (because) when a person yawns the devil spits into his mouth. If yawn does not stop, press your lower lip with your upper teeth. If it doesn't stop either, avoid opening your mouth too much and put the back of your left hand on the mouth. As yawning is from the devil and Prophets عَلَيْهِمُ السَّلَام are safe from it, so if you begin to yawn, recall that the Prophets عَلَيْهِمُ السَّلَام never yawned, this thought will instantly stifle the yawn, اِنْ شَآءَ اللّٰه عَزَّوَجَلَّ. *(Rad-dul-Muḥtār, vol. 2, pp. 413)*

14. Joking is already forbidden and is strictly impermissible in Masjid.

15. Laughing in Masjid is forbidden because it causes darkness in grave; however, there is no harm in smiling when appropriate.

16. Do not throw anything on the Masjid floor, but place it on the floor gently. In summer, people often use hand-operated fans and then throw them onto the floor of the Masjid, causing sound. (Do not throw cap, shawl etc. and also avoid creating sound whilst dusting the Masjid floor with shawl or handkerchief). Some people place sticks, umbrellas etc. onto the Masjid floor carelessly producing sounds. This is not allowed. Respecting the Masjid is Farḍ for every Muslim.

17. Breaking wind in the Masjid is prohibited. Those who are not in I'tikāf are to go out, if necessary. Therefore, a Mu'takif should eat less food during I'tikāf and keep his stomach rather empty so that he would not have to break wind except at the time of defecation. He will not be allowed to leave the Masjid for this (but he can go to the toilet area within the Masjid precincts).

18. Stretching legs towards Qiblaĥ is prohibited everywhere and one should avoid doing so towards any direction in a Masjid as it is quite inappropriate at such an honourable place.

Once Sayyidunā Ibrāĥīm Bin Adĥam رَحْمَةُ اللهِ تَعَالٰی عَلَيْه was sitting in the Masjid alone, he stretched his legs out. Suddenly he heard a voice from a corner of the Masjid 'Ibrāĥīm! Should you sit in this manner in the court of kings?' He رَحْمَةُ اللهِ تَعَالٰی عَلَيْه immediately pulled his legs back and did not stretch them out again till his death. (Take care even when rocking babies/children and putting them to sleep that their legs are not towards Qiblaĥ; it is also important to keep this in mind whilst making them relieve themselves).

19. Entering a Masjid with used shoes on is the desecration of the Masjid. *(Derived from Al-Malfūẓ, part 2, pp. 377)*

Keep Masājid fragrant

Mother of the believers Sayyidatunā 'Āishaĥ Ṣiddīqaĥ رَضِیَ اللهُ تَعَالٰی عَنْهَا has narrated that the Holy Prophet صَلَّی اللهُ تَعَالٰی عَلَيْهِ وَاٰلِهٖ وَسَلَّم ordered that Masājid be made at populous places and that they be kept clean and fragrant. *(Sunan Abī Dāwūd, vol. 1, pp. 197, Ḥadīš 455)*

Air fresheners could cause cancer

Dear Islamic brothers! We have learnt that building Masājid and keeping them fragrant with pure and pleasant fragrance and incense sticks etc. is an act of reward. Avoid lighting matchsticks in the Masjid because they smell of gunpowder and it is Wājib to refrain from spreading such unpleasant smells in the Masjid. Make it sure that the smell of smoke does not enter the Masjid, therefore, burn the frankincense or incense sticks outside the Masjid and then bring them inside. It is also important that the incense sticks be placed in a large tray or something similar so that its ashes do not fall onto the Masjid's floor.

If there is an image of a human or animal on the packet of incense sticks, scratch it away. Do not spray Masājid (your homes, cars etc.) with air fresheners as their chemical substances spread into the air and reach lungs by inhalation and can cause harm. According to a medical research, the use of air fresheners could cause skin cancer.

Entering Masjid with bad breath is Ḥarām

Dear Islamic brothers! One should make it a habit to eat less than one's appetite, i.e. stop eating while still hungry. If a person eats in excess and gobbles down different things such as burgers, pizzas, ice cream, cold drinks every now and then, damaging his stomach and consequently suffering from the disease of bad breath[1], he will get into an extremely difficult situation as entering the Masjid with bad breath is Ḥarām. Entering the Masjid even for offering Ṣalāĥ with Jamā'at is also a sin in this state. As most people are not so much concerned about their afterlife nowadays, they seem to have become greedy for food. Further, the 'food culture' has become popular everywhere and resulted in a number of people having bad breath.

Many times, I (i.e. the author) have personally experienced that when someone talks to me with his mouth closer to mine, I have to hold my breath due to his bad breath. Sometimes, even Imams and Mūażżins have the problem of bad breath. If it happens, they should instantly take leaves and have treatment for it as entering the Masjid with bad breath is Ḥarām.

Unfortunately, Allah عَزَّوَجَلَّ forbid, many people suffering from bad breath also do I'tikāf in the Masjid. In Ramadan, the number of people with bad breath increases due to stuffing themselves with fried and oily foods. The best cure for this problem is to eat simple foods less than appetite so that one does not have any digestive problem. It is Wājib to protect the Masjid from all foul odours including bad breath.

Having bad breath makes Ṣalāĥ Makrūĥ

It is stated in *Fatāwā Razawiyyaĥ* (vol. 7, pp. 384), '(For a person to offer Ṣalāĥ at home whilst) having bad breath makes the Ṣalāĥ Makrūĥ and to go to the Masjid in such a condition is Ḥarām. To cause distress to the people offering Ṣalāĥ is Ḥarām and even if there is no one in the Masjid, it distresses the angels. It is stated in a Ḥadīš, 'Things that cause discomfort to humans also cause discomfort to the angels.' *(Ṣaḥīḥ Muslim, pp. 282, Ḥadīš 564)*

Prohibition of entering Masjid after applying smelly ointment

A'lā Ḥaḍrat رَحْمَةُ اللهِ تَعَالٰى عَلَيْه has stated, 'The one from whose body such bad smell emanates that troubles others, for instance, bad breath, bad smell from the armpits or one who has applied sulphur to his body because of itching or has applied any other bad smelling ointment or lotion should not be allowed to enter the Masjid.' *(Fatāwā Razawiyyaĥ (Jadīd), vol. 8, pp. 72)*

[1] Bad breath or halitosis is a disease in which offensive smell emanates from mouth with breath.

Eating raw onions also causes bad breath

Radish, onion, garlic and every bad smelling thing should not be eaten before going to the Masjid as it is impermissible to enter the Masjid whilst having a bad smell from the hands and the mouth etc. because it troubles the angels. It is stated in a Ḥadīš that the Beloved and Blessed Rasūl صَلَّى اللهُ تَعَالٰى عَلَيْهِ وَاٰلِهٖ وَسَلَّم has said, 'Whoever has eaten onion, garlic or leek should not come near our Masjid.' He صَلَّى اللهُ تَعَالٰى عَلَيْهِ وَاٰلِهٖ وَسَلَّم has further said, 'If he wants to eat it, he should remove the smell by cooking it.' *(Ṣaḥīḥ Muslim, pp. 282, Ḥadīš 564)*

'Allāmaĥ Maulānā Muftī Muhammad Amjad 'Alī A'ẓamī رَحْمَةُ اللهِ تَعَالٰى عَلَيْه has stated, 'It is not permissible to eat uncooked garlic and onion in the Masjid or before going to the Masjid if the smell exists. This ruling applies to everything which has a bad smell e.g. leek, radish, uncooked meat, kerosene oil, the matchstick which produces a bad smell when struck, breaking wind etc. The one suffering from bad breath, bad smelling wound or uses medicine which has a bad smell is not permitted to enter the Masjid until the smell is removed.' *(Baĥār-e-Sharī'at, part 3, pp. 154)*

Avoid sliced onion & its paste

During the timing of Ṣalāĥ, avoid eating chickpeas with unripe onion-paste, sliced onion, pickle and sauce of unripe garlic. Sometimes, fried items also emit a smell of uncooked onion and garlic. These should also be avoided before Ṣalāĥ. It is not permissible to bring such bad smelling things into the Masjid.

Prohibition on attending Muslim gatherings with bad smell

Muftī Aḥmad Yār Khān عَلَيْهِ رَحْمَةُ الْمَنَّان has said, 'Do not join the gathering of the Muslims and Dars of the Quran in the state of bad breath. Further, do not go in front of Islamic scholars and saints (in this state).' *(Mirāĥ, vol. 6, pp. 25)* He رَحْمَةُ اللهِ تَعَالٰى عَلَيْه has further stated, 'As long as the bad smell remains, stay at home. Do not go in the procession or gathering of the Muslims. Those who smoke and eat 'Pān' (betel leaf) with tobacco and do not gargle afterwards should also learn a lesson. Respectable Jurists رَحِمَهُمُ اللّٰهُ تَعَالٰى have said that the one who suffers from bad breath is exempted from attending the Masjid.' *(Mirāĥ, vol. 6, pp. 26)*

How is it to eat onion during Ṣalāĥ time?

Question: The one suffering from bad breath is exempted from attending the Masjid, so can a person eat uncooked onion with fried items or the foods that contain raw onion and garlic which emit a bad smell just before the Jamā'at with the intention of having bad breath so that the Jamā'at will no longer remain Wājib for him?

Answer: It is not allowed to do so. One should not eat such salad or food which contains uncooked radish, onion or garlic after Ṣalāt-ul-Maghrib because the time of Ṣalāt-ul-'Ishā is close and cleaning the mouth before 'Ishā would be difficult. However, if cleaning the mouth before 'Ishā is possible or someone is exempted from attending the Masjid for any other reason, for example, women do not have to attend Masjid, or there is enough time in Ṣalāĥ and there will be no bad smell by that time, so eating such food is permissible in the aforementioned cases.

A'lā Ḥaḍrat Imām Aḥmad Razā Khān عَلَيْهِ رَحْمَةُ الرَّحْمٰن has stated, 'No doubt, eating uncooked garlic and onion is Ḥalāl, but going to the Masjid after eating it is prohibited unless the smell is removed. Similarly, near the time of Jamā'at, smoking the Ḥuqqaĥ (i.e. water pipe) that causes bad smell which cannot be removed even by gargling is also not allowed as it will lead to either missing the Jamā'at or entering the Masjid with bad breath, which is prohibited and impermissible. By Sharī'aĥ, every such permissible act that leads to unlawful act is prohibited and impermissible.' *(Fatāwā Razawiyyaĥ (Jadīd), vol. 25, pp. 94)*

Method of discovering bad breath

If there is a bad smell in the mouth, using a Miswāk and rinsing the mouth is necessary unless the smell is removed completely. There is no limit in doing this. It is necessary for cigarette and pipe smokers to be cautious about bad breath as they are prone to suffering from it.

Likewise, extreme care is to be taken by those who eat tobacco as it forms a layer in the mouth. All of them must use a Miswāk and rinse the mouth until the smell is removed completely. The smell of mouth can be tested by taking the palm closer to the mouth, breathing out three times onto the palm through mouth, and then smelling it immediately. The smell of the mouth is hardly felt. The person suffering from bad breath rarely feels his smell himself without this method. If there is bad breath, entering the Masjid is Ḥarām and joining Ṣalāĥ is not permissible either. *(Fatāwā Razawiyyaĥ (Jadīd), vol. 1, pp. 623)* وَاللهُ الْهَادِی

Cure for bad breath

If eating anything causes bad breath, eat coriander leaves by chewing them and clean the teeth using dry or fresh rose petals. اِنْ شَآءَاللّٰه عَزَّوَجَلَّ it will be beneficial. If the bad breath is due to any stomach problem, one should make a habit of having a light diet which will cure many diseases including bad breath, pain in different parts of the body, constipation, acidity, warts in the mouth, frequent cough and cold, pain in the throat, gums bleeding etc, اِنْ شَآءَاللّٰه عَزَّوَجَلَّ. To eat less than hunger prevents 80% of diseases. (For detailed information, study the chapter '*Excellence of Hunger*' from *Faīzān-e-Sunnat*). If the greed of bodily desires is cured, lots of spiritual and bodily diseases will automatically be cured.

Madanī cure for bad breath

اَللّٰهُمَّ صَلِّ وَسَلِّمْ عَلَى النَّبِيِّ الطَّاهِرِ

If this Ṣalāt-'Alan-Nabī is recited 11 times in a single breath from time to time, bad breath will be removed اِنْ شَآءَاللّٰه عَزَّوَجَلَّ. A better method of reciting it in a single breath is to first inhale breath from the nostrils slowly and store as much air in the lungs as possible. Now start reciting Ṣalāt-'Alan-Nabī. By practicing it for a few times, you will succeed in reciting it 11 times in one breath اِنْ شَآءَاللّٰه عَزَّوَجَلَّ. Inhaling air through the nose in the same method and holding a deep breath for as long as possible and exhaling it from the mouth is extremely beneficial to health.

It should be done whenever one gets the chance preferably in open air. To do this a few times daily is more beneficial. Once an old doctor told me (i.e. the author) that he can hold his breath for half an hour, or rather, for two hours and he can perform his religious invocations and Du'ās in this duration. According to that doctor, there are even such experts in the world that inhale breath in the morning and exhale in the evening!

How far should toilets be made from Masjid?

Imām Aḥmad Razā Khān عَلَيْهِ رَحْمَةُ الرَّحْمٰن was asked, 'How far should the toilets be from the Masjid?' He رَحْمَةُ اللهِ تَعَالٰى عَلَيْه replied, 'Protecting Masājid from bad smells is Wājib. Therefore, burning kerosene oil and lighting a matchstick in the Masjid is Ḥarām (as it causes bad smell). According to a Ḥadīš, it is not permissible to bring uncooked meat into the Masjid despite the fact that the smell of uncooked meat is very slight. *(Sunan Ibn Mājaĥ, vol. 1, pp. 413, Ḥadīš 748)* Therefore, making toilets at such a place from where smell could reach the Masjid will be prohibited. *(Fatāwā Razawiyyaĥ (Jadīd), vol. 16, pp. 232)*

When uncooked meat with slight bad smell is not permissible then uncooked fish will definitely be prohibited because of its strong smell. Occasionally, the hand and the mouth become smelly while eating it because of the carelessness of the cooks. In such a condition, do not go to the Masjid unless the smell is removed. When toilets are being cleaned, bad smells spread a lot. Therefore, it is necessary to keep an appropriate distance (between the Masjid and washrooms) to prevent bad smells from entering the Masjid. If the door of the washroom opens into the precincts of the Masjid, a wall may be made in the place of the door and another door may be made that opens outside the Masjid to protect it from bad smells.'

Develop habit of checking your clothing and so on

Bringing bad smells into the Masjid is Ḥarām. Furthermore, entrance of the person having a bad smell is also Ḥarām. Do not use a toothpick inside the Masjid as those who are not in the habit of picking their teeth after every meal have a bad smell in the mouth. A Mu'takif should pick his teeth at such a distance even in Finā-e-Masjid that the smell does not enter the Masjid. People who have smelly wounds or the patients with a stool-bag or a urine-bag should not enter the Masjid.

Similarly, the bottle of blood or urine taken for a laboratory test and clothes covered in blood gushing at the time of the slaughter of the animal cannot be brought in the Masjid even if they are wrapped. Jurists رَحِمَهُمُ اللهُ تَعَالٰى have said that bringing impurity in the Masjid is not allowed even if it does not make the Masjid's floor etc. dirty. Likewise, if there's impurity on a person's body, he is not allowed to enter the Masjid. *(Rad-dul-Muḥtār, vol. 1, pp. 614)* It is also not permissible to take urine or blood inside the Masjid. *(Durr-e-Mukhtār, vol. 1, pp. 614)*

If a person has pure unpleasant smell that does not spread (for example sweat) he is allowed to enter the Masjid because it is hidden underneath the clothing. Similarly, if a handkerchief smells bad, do not take it out from the pocket. If a bad smell spreads due to removing the turban or cap, do not remove them inside the Masjid. Similarly, if uncooked meat or fish is packed in such a manner that no bad smell spreads then it is permissible to bring it inside the Masjid. Giving an example of this, Muftī Aḥmad Yār Khān عَلَيْهِ رَحْمَةُ الْمَنَّان has stated, 'However, if the bad smell of kerosene oil is removed in any way, or the oil is filled in the lamp in such a manner that bad smell does not spread, then it is permissible to bring it inside the Masjid.' *(Fatāwā Na'īmiyyaĥ, pp. 65)*

Every Muslim should take care that his face, body, handkerchief, dress and footwear etc. are not smelly. Do not come to the Masjid in such a dirty dress that causes disgust to others. Regretfully, fine and expensive dresses are worn on the occasion of meetings with worldly officers but no care is taken about cleanliness while going to the court of our beloved Allah عَزَّوَجَلَّ. Before coming to the Masjid one should wear at least such decent dress which he wears on the occasion of ceremonies; but the dress should be according to Sharī'aĥ and Sunnaĥ.

Prohibition on bringing children into Masjid

The Beloved and Blessed Prophet صَلَّى اللهُ تَعَالٰى عَلَيْهِ وَاٰلِهٖ وَسَلَّم has said, 'Save Masājid from children, the insane, sale and purchase, quarrels, raising voices, enforcing penalties and drawing swords.' *(Sunan Ibn Mājaĥ, vol. 1, pp. 415, Ḥadīš 750)*

It is Ḥarām to bring such a child into the Masjid (that may make the Masjid's floor impure by urinating etc.). Bringing an insane person into the Masjid is also Ḥarām. If there is no fear of impurity then it is Makrūĥ. People who take their slippers into the Masjid should clean off any impurity beforehand. Walking into the Masjid wearing shoes is the disrespect of the Masjid. *(Rad-dul-Muḥtār, vol. 2, pp. 518)*

By Sharī'aĥ, it not allowed to bring small children, the insane (an unconscious person or the one captured by a jinn) into the Masjid even for spiritual remedies. A baby cannot be brought into the Masjid even if wrapped properly into a piece of clothing etc. If you have ever made the mistake of bringing such children into the Masjid, repent instantly and make a firm intention of not doing it again. However; it is permissible to bring children into Finā-e-Masjid (for example, the Imām's room) provided one does not have to pass through the actual part of the Masjid.

Butchers and fish mongers

As the clothes of butchers and fish mongers smell extremely bad, they should have a proper bath, put on a clean dress and apply fragrance before coming to the Masjid. Bathing and applying fragrance is not a condition, rather it's just a suggestion. The thing is, one has to remove the bad smell completely.

Bad smelling sweat due to some foods

Some foods cause bad smelling sweat. Those who have bad smelling sweat should avoid such food.

Method of cleaning mouth

Most of those who do not act upon the Sunnaĥ of using Miswāk and picking their teeth and do not clean their teeth properly due to laziness have the problem of bad breath. Just using a Miswāk or a toothpick carelessly as a formality is not enough, instead, each and every tiny bit of food is to be removed from teeth taking care not to hurt the gums. Otherwise, these food crumbs will rot causing bad smell.

There is another way of cleaning the teeth. After having any food and tea or when you are working while sitting, take a mouthful of water and keep moving it inside the mouth. This will clean the teeth. Normal water can also be used, but tepid and rather salty water will serve as an excellent mouthwash اِنْ شَآءَاللہ عَزَّوَجَلَّ

صَلُّوْا عَلَی الْحَبِیْب   صَلَّی اللّٰہُ تَعَالٰی عَلٰی مُحَمَّد

Save beard from bad smell

Tiny food crumbs often get stuck in the beard, and sometimes, bad smelling saliva also goes into the beard, causing smell in it. It's a Madanī suggestion that the beard be washed with soap on a daily basis.

An easy way to make fragrant oil

Sometimes, bad smell spreads in the air when someone using mustard oil in hair removes his cap or turban. Therefore, if possible, try to use good quality fragrant oil. An easy way of making fragrant oil is to put a few drops of your favourite fragrance in the coconut oil bottle, and shake it properly (particular essence for making the fragrant oil can also be bought from perfume shops). Wash your hair with soap on a regular basis.

Bath daily, if possible

If possible, take a bath on a daily basis because it will remove bad smell a great deal and this is also beneficial to health (but Mu'takifīn should avoid using the bathrooms of the Masjid unless it is necessary because there might be a water shortage for Wuḍū and the water motor may also run down, if used repeatedly).

Method of protecting turban from bad smell

Some Islamic brothers are very keen to wear a large sized turban but they do not keep it clean and, sometimes, unintentionally become a cause of spreading bad smell in the Masjid. Therefore, it's a Madanī request that the Islamic brothers using a turban, a head cloth (used underneath a turban) or a shawl should wash them once a week or more frequently depending upon the weather, otherwise these things smell bad due to dirt, sweat and oil. Although one does not notice the smell himself, others may feel disgusted. The reason why one does not notice the smell himself is that he has become used to it.

Which type of turban should be worn?

To use the turban which is already tied on a hard cap can also cause bad smell. If possible, use a thin, soft and light-fabric turban and wear the cap which adheres to the head, as wearing this type of cap is also Sunnaĥ. Instead of wearing and taking off the already tied turban, tie one fold after another according to Sunnaĥ and unfold it in the same manner.

By doing so, according to a Ḥadīš, one will be given the reward of one good deed and one Nūr for each fold and when unfolding (when there is an intention of tying it again) one sin will be forgiven. *(Kanz-ul-'Ummāl, vol. 15, pp. 132-133, Ḥadīš 41126, 41138)* اِنْ شَآءَاللّٰه عَزَّوَجَلَّ, The turban will have no bad smell in it because of being repeatedly tied and untied as the air will remove smell. Bad smell of sweat can also be removed by putting the turban, head cloth, shawl, dress etc. under sunlight. Using fragrance with good intentions can also remove bad smells.

Forty seven intentions of using fragrance

The Prophet of Raḥmaĥ, the Intercessor of Ummaĥ صَلَّى اللهُ تَعَالٰى عَلَيْهِ وَاٰلِهٖ وَسَلَّم has said: 'The intention of a Muslim is better than his deeds.' *(Mu'jam Kabīr, vol. 6, pp. 185, Ḥadīš 5942)* Some intentions of applying fragrance are being presented:

1. I will apply fragrance because it is a Sunnaĥ of the Holy Prophet صَلَّى اللهُ تَعَالٰى عَلَيْهِ وَاٰلِهٖ وَسَلَّم.
2. I will recite بِسْمِ اللّٰه before applying fragrance.
3. I will recite Ṣalāt-'Alan-Nabī while applying fragrance
4. and اَلْحَمْدُ لِلّٰهِ رَبِّ الْعٰلَمِيْنَ as a gratitude after applying fragrance.
5. I will please the angels and
6. Muslims (by fragrance)
7. If my intellect increases by using fragrance I will gain power to learn Islamic rulings and various Sunan (Imām Shāfi'ī رَحْمَةُ اللهِ تَعَالٰى عَلَيْه has stated: Intellect increases by using fine fragrance).
8. I will save the Muslims from the sin of backbiting by removing bad smell from my clothes etc. (without the permission of Sharī'aĥ, saying such a sentence as 'so and so person's clothes or hands or mouth smelt bad' in his absence is backbiting).
9. The following intentions can also be made in certain conditions.
10. I will gain elegance for Ṣalāĥ

    Fragrance can also be used with the intention of honouring the following places/worships/occasions etc.

11. Masjid,

12. Taĥajjud,
13. Friday,
14. Monday,
15. Ramadan,
16. Eid-ul-Fiṭr,
17. Eid-ul-Aḍḥā,
18. The night of Mīlād,
19. Eid-e-Mīlād-un-Nabī صَلَّى اللهُ تَعَالٰى عَلَيْهِ وَاٰلِهٖ وَسَلَّم
20. Mīlād procession,
21. Night of Mi'rāj,
22. Shab-e-Barā-at,
23. Giyārĥwīn,
24. Razā day,
25. Dars from the Quran,
26. Dars from Ḥadīš,
27. Recitation of the Quran.
28. Awrād and Waẓāif (invocations)
29. Ṣalāt-'Alan-Nabī
30. Study of an Islamic book,
31. Teaching of Islamic education,
32. Learning of Islamic education,
33. Writing of an Islamic ruling,
34. Writing and editing Islamic books,

35. Sunnaĥ-Inspiring Ijtimā',
36. Ijtimā' of Żikr and Na'at,
37. Recitation of Quran in congregation
38. Dars from *Faīzān-e-Sunnat*,
39. Call to righteousness,
40. At the time of delivering a Sunnaĥ-Inspiring speech,
41. When visiting a scholar,
42. Mother,
43. Father,
44. Pious Muslim,
45. Murshid
46. When looking at the blessed hair of the Beloved and Blessed Prophet صَلَّى اللهُ تَعَالٰى عَلَيْهِ وَاٰلِهٖ وَسَلَّم and
47. When visiting a shrine.

The more good intentions one makes, the more reward he will attain provided that the intention is permissible by Sharī'aĥ, and there is an appropriate occasion as well. If all the intentions cannot be made one should make at least two or three of them.

O Allah عَزَّوَجَلَّ! If we have ever brought odour into the Masjid, we repent of this sin and make a firm intention not to cause any type of odour in the Masjid in the future.

O Allah عَزَّوَجَلَّ! Give us the ability to keep the Masājid fragrant. O Allah عَزَّوَجَلَّ enable us to purify ourselves from every type of unpleasant smell before entering the Masjid.

O Allah عَزَّوَجَلَّ! For the sake of the fragrance of the Holy Prophet صَلَّى اللهُ تَعَالٰى عَلَيْهِ وَاٰلِهٖ وَسَلَّم, save us from sins and grant us a place in the fragrant neighbourhood of Your Beloved and Blessed Prophet صَلَّى اللهُ تَعَالٰى عَلَيْهِ وَاٰلِهٖ وَسَلَّم in Jannat-ul-Firdaus!

اٰمِيْن بِجَاهِ النَّبِيِّ الْاَمِيْن صَلَّى اللهُ تَعَالٰى عَلَيْهِ وَاٰلِهٖ وَسَلَّم

Mu'takifīn and Finā-e-Masjid

Dear Islamic brothers! If a Mu'takif enters Finā-e-Masjid, his I'tikāf will not become invalid. A Mu'takif can enter Finā-e-Masjid even unnecessarily. The Finā-e-Masjid includes the areas within the boundary[1] of the Masjid that are used for the needs of Masjid such as the minaret, Wuḍū area, toilets, bathrooms, any Madrasaĥ that is adjacent to the Masjid, rooms for the Imām and Mūażżin, place for shoes etc.

In some cases, rulings of the Masjid are applied in these areas, whereas they are regarded out of Masjid in some other cases. For example, a Junubī (the one who must take a ritual bath) can enter these areas. Similarly, a Mu'takif can also enter these areas even unnecessarily, it will be as if he has stepped into another part of the (actual) Masjid.

Mu'takif can enter Finā-e-Masjid

Ṣadr-ush-Sharī'aĥ Shaykh Maulānā Amjad 'Alī A'ẓamī عَلَيْهِ رَحْمَةُ اللّٰهِ الْقَوِى, the author of *Bahār-e-Sharī'at*, has stated: 'To go to Finā-e-Masjid (which is) the area outside the Masjid but is adjacent to it and is used for the need of the Masjid, such as the place where shoes are taken off, bathrooms etc., will not invalidate the I'tikāf.' He رَحْمَةُ اللّٰهِ تَعَالٰی عَلَيْه has further stated: 'In this case, Finā-e-Masjid is considered a part of the Masjid.' *(Fatāwā Amjadiyyaĥ, vol. 1, pp. 399)*

The minaret is also included in Finā-e-Masjid. If the path leading to the minaret is within the Masjid, a Mu'takif can enter it whenever he wishes, but if the path is outside the Masjid, then he can only use it for the Ażān because calling the Ażān is a Shar'ī necessity.

Fatwā of A'la Hadrat رَحْمَةُ اللّٰهِ عَلَيْه

A'lā Ḥaḍrat رَحْمَةُ اللّٰهِ تَعَالٰی عَلَيْه has stated, 'If the Madāris are within the Masjid boundaries and there isn't any path separating them from the Masjid, there is only a wall marking the division between them, walking into them will not amount to walking outside the Masjid in this case. A Mu'takif can enter these places; it is like any other part of the Masjid.'

[1] Nowadays Finā-e-Masjid is also referred to as the Masjid.

It is stated in *Rad-dul-Muḥtār* (vol. 3, pp. 436) with reference to '*Badāi'-uṣ-Ṣanāi*" 'If a Mu'takif climbs the minaret (of the Masjid) his I'tikāf will not become invalid. There is no difference of opinion in this matter because the minaret is (considered) inside the Masjid (for a Mu'takif). *(Fatāwā Razawiyyaĥ (Jadīd), vol. 7, pp. 453)*

Did you see! A'lā Ḥaḍrat Imām-e-Aĥl-e-Sunnat, reviver of Sunnaĥ, eradicator of Bid'aĥ, scholar of Sharī'aĥ, guide of Ṭarīqaĥ, 'Allāmaĥ Maulānā Al-Ḥāj Al-Ḥāfiẓ Al-Qārī Ash-Shāĥ Imām Aḥmad Razā Khān عَلَيْهِ رَحْمَةُ الرَّحْمٰن has declared that it is permissible for a Mu'takif to enter the Madāris next to the Masjid (even without necessity) and he has declared these Madāris as a part of the Masjid in this respect.

Walking on roof of Masjid

As the yard is a part of the Masjid and a Mu'takif is allowed to walk and sit around the yard, he can also walk on the roof of the Masjid provided that the way to the roof is inside the Masjid. However, if the steps to the roof are outside the Masjid then the Mu'takif isn't allowed to go to the roof. If he does, his I'tikāf will become invalid. It should also be remembered that it is Makrūĥ for everyone (whether Mu'takif or not) to go to the roof of the Masjid needlessly as this is a sign of desecration.

When can Mu'takif exit Masjid?

A Mu'takif can exit the Masjid (boundaries) during I'tikāf due to the following two reasons:

1. Shar'ī needs
2. Physical needs

1. Shar'ī needs

A Shar'ī need refers to the need of exiting the Masjid in order to fulfil such a commandment or act, declared obligatory by Sharī'aĥ, which cannot be fulfilled by the Mu'takif staying in the I'tikāf area. These include the Ṣalāt-ul-Jumu'aĥ and the Ażān etc.

Three points regarding Shar'ī needs

1. Even if the path leading to the minaret is outside the Masjid precincts, the Mu'takif can walk to the minaret in order to call the Ażān as this is a Shar'ī need. *(Rad-dul-Muḥtār, vol. 3, pp. 436)*

2. If the Ṣalāt-ul-Jumu'aĥ is not offered in the Masjid where one is performing I'tikāf, it is permissible for him to leave the Masjid to offer the Ṣalāt-ul-Jumu'aĥ in such a Masjid where Ṣalāt-ul-Jumu'aĥ is offered. The Mu'takif should leave his I'tikāf area at such an appropriate time that he could get to the Jāmi' Masjid and offer four Rak'āt Sunnaĥ before the sermon (Khuṭbaĥ) starts. He can stay after Ṣalāt-ul-Jumu'aĥ for as long as four or six Rak'āt are offered. If he stays later than this or completes the rest of the I'tikāf in that Masjid though his I'tikāf will not become invalid, remaining in that Masjid after the Ṣalāt-ul-Jumu'aĥ longer than the amount of time in which six Rak'āt are offered is Makrūĥ. *(Durr-e-Mukhtār, Rad-dul-Muḥtār, vol. 3, pp. 437)*

3. If one performs I'tikāf in such a local Masjid where the Jamā'at isn't held he cannot leave the Masjid for Jamā'at because it is better for him to offer Ṣalāĥ without Jamā'at in that Masjid. *(Jad-dul-Mumtār, vol. 2, pp. 222)*

2. Physical needs

Physical needs include the necessities which are unavoidable such as defecation, urination etc.

Six points about physical needs

1. If there is no particular place to relieve oneself within the Masjid precincts, the Mu'takif can exit the Masjid for this purpose. *(Durr-e-Mukhtār ma' Rad-dul-Muḥtār, vol. 3, pp. 435)*

2. If there is no Wuḍū area or pond inside the Masjid and it is also impossible to do Wuḍū using a tub etc. inside the Masjid without letting drops of water fall onto the (actual) Masjid floor, one can go outside to do Wuḍū. *(Rad-dul-Muḥtār, vol. 3, pp. 435)*

3. In case of nocturnal emission, if there is neither a bathroom in the Masjid precincts nor doing Ghusl is possible in Masjid in any other way, the Mu'takif can go out of the Masjid to do ritual Ghusl. *(Rad-dul-Muḥtār, vol. 3, pp. 435)*

4. If the Mu'takif goes home to relieve himself, he has to return immediately after defecation. He is not allowed to stay there. If his house is far from the Masjid and his friend's house is near, it is not necessary for him to go to his friend's house to relieve himself, he can go to his own house. If he has two houses one of which is near, he has to go to the near one. Some of the respected scholars رَحِمَهُمُ اللّٰهُ تَعَالٰی have said that going to the home that is further away will invalidate the I'tikāf. *(Fatāwā 'Ālamgīrī, vol. 1, pp. 212)*

5. There are usually toilets, bathrooms and Wuḍū areas within the Masjid precincts to facilitate the people who come to offer Ṣalāĥ, therefore the Mu'takif should use them.

6. In some Masājid the path leading to the toilet, bathroom etc. is outside the Masjid boundaries, so the Mu'takif cannot go to these toilets, bathrooms etc. without a physical need.

Acts that invalidate I'tikāf

Now, the acts which invalidate I'tikāf are being described. In the following account, the invalidation of I'tikāf as a result of going out of the Masjid refers to going out of the Masjid boundaries completely.

The mother of the believers Sayyidatunā 'Āishaĥ Ṣiddīqaĥ رَضِیَ اللّٰهُ تَعَالٰی عَنْهَا has narrated: 'A Mu'takif should neither visit a sick person, nor attend a funeral, nor touch a woman, nor have intercourse with her nor exit the Masjid for any need except for the ones that are unavoidable.' *(Sunan Abī Dāwūd, vol. 2, pp. 492, Ḥadīš 2473)*

Sixteen points about acts that invalidate I'tikāf

1. To go out of the Masjid precincts even for a single moment for any reason other than the foregoing necessities will invalidate I'tikāf. *(Marāqil Falāḥ, pp. 179)*

2. Remember! 'To go out of the Masjid' means stepping out in such a manner that is usually considered stepping out of the Masjid. Sticking only head out of the Masjid will not invalidate I'tikāf. *(Al-Baḥr-ur-Rāiq, vol. 2, pp. 530)*

3. To go out of the Masjid without a Shar'ī need will invalidate I'tikāf regardless of whether it was deliberate, unintentional or by mistake. However, if it was unintentional or by mistake it will not be a sin. *(Rad-dul-Muḥtār, vol. 3, pp. 438)*

4. If a Mu'takif goes out of the Masjid precincts for a Shar'ī need and stays out for even a single moment after the fulfilment of his need, I'tikāf will become invalid. *(Ḥāshiya-tuṭ-Ṭaḥṭawī 'Alal Marāqī, pp. 703)*

5. As fasting is a condition for I'tikāf, breaking of fast will automatically invalidate the I'tikāf regardless of whether or not there was a valid exemption for invalidating the fast and whether it was broken deliberately or mistakenly. In all these cases the I'tikāf will become invalid. Breaking the fast by mistake implies though one was aware that he was fasting, he happened to do such an unintentional act that negates the fast. For example, eating after dawn (Ṣubḥ-e-Ṣādiq) or breaking the fast before sunset due to the premature uttering of Ażān or wailing of siren, the fast will become invalid in both these cases. Similarly, if water goes down the throat unintentionally while rinsing the mouth despite being aware that one was fasting, both the fast and the I'tikāf will become invalid.

6. If the Mu'takif ate or drank something whilst he had forgotten the fast, neither his fast nor his I'tikāf will become invalid in this case.

7. Mu'takif Islamic brothers and sisters should remember the basic principle that all such acts that invalidate the fast invalidate the I'tikāf as well.

8. Copulation (intercourse) will also invalidate the I'tikāf, regardless of whether it was deliberate or in a state of forgetfulness, during the day or at night, in the Masjid or out of the Masjid, and whether or not ejaculation takes place. I'tikāf will become invalid in all these cases. *(Durr-e-Mukhtār ma' Rad-dul-Muḥtār, vol. 3, pp. 442)*

9. Kissing and caressing during I'tikāf is impermissible and if it leads to ejaculation the I'tikāf will become invalid. If ejaculation doesn't take place though the I'tikāf will not become invalid, it is still impermissible. *(Rad-dul-Muḥtār, vol. 3, pp. 442)*

10. If the Mu'takif exits (the Masjid boundaries) to relieve himself and his creditor stops him, his I'tikāf will become invalid. *(Fatāwā 'Ālamgīrī, vol. 1, pp. 212)*

11. If a Mu'takif becomes unconscious or insane and his unconsciousness or insanity prolongs to the extent that he is unable to carry out his fast, his I'tikāf will become invalid and it will be Wājib for him to make up for it, even if he regains his health several years later. *(Fatāwā 'Ālamgīrī, vol. 1, pp. 213)*

12. A Mu'takif can eat and drink inside the Masjid only. If he goes out of the Masjid for this purpose, his I'tikāf will become invalid. *(Tibyīn-ul-Ḥaqāiq, vol. 2, pp. 229)* While eating inside the Masjid, a Mu'takif should take care not to dirty the Masjid floor etc.

13. If there is no one to bring the Mu'takif food, he can exit the Masjid to bring food, but he still has to eat the food in the Masjid. *(Al-Baḥr-ur-Rāiq, vol. 2, pp. 530)*

14. To go out of the Masjid for the treatment of an illness will invalidate I'tikāf. *(Rad-dul-Muḥtār, vol. 3, pp. 438)*

15. If the Mu'takif suffering the disease of sleepwalking, sleepwalks outside the Masjid, his I'tikāf will become invalid.

16. (Allah عَزَّوَجَلَّ forbid) If an unfortunate person becomes a Murtad (apostate) during I'tikāf his I'tikāf will become invalid and then if Allah عَزَّوَجَلَّ blesses him with faith again, he does not have to make up for that invalid I'tikāf, because religious apostasy ruins all the good deeds performed in the state of Islam. *(Durr-e-Mukhtār ma' Rad-dul-Muḥtār, vol. 3, pp. 437)*

Relief from back pain

Dear Islamic brothers! Words cannot express the greatness of I'tikāf; and if one is blessed with the company of devotees of Rasūl during I'tikāf, the blessings and benefits multiply. An Islamic brother of 'Aṭṭārābād (Bāb-ul-Islam, Sindh) gave the following account: I was a loafer and had got a dirty mind. Talking about filthy things with my friends and then laughing was my favourite pastime. The nuisance of an indecent sin had caused constant back pain that was not cured despite different medical treatments.

Fortunately, some Islamic brothers, who were acquainted with me, insisted me that I join them in the collective I'tikāf in the Ramadan of 1426 A.H. (2005). At first, I refused but they insisted and so I had to agree. I became a Mu'takif for the last ten days of Ramadan (1426) with devotees of Rasūl in Memon Masjid ('Aṭṭārābād). It seemed to me as if I had entered a new world. The blessings of all five Ṣalāĥ, Sunnaĥ-Inspiring speeches, supplications, learning sessions, the compassion and politeness of Islamic brothers, all had impressed me beyond measure.

اَلْحَمْدُ لِلّٰه عَزَّوَجَلَّ! During the I'tikāf my back pain vanished without any medicines and a Madanī transformation took place in my heart. I repented of sins, adorned my face with the sign of the love of our Beloved Rasūl صَلَّى اللهُ تَعَالٰى عَلَيْهِ وَاٰلِهٖ وَسَلَّم, the beard, and began to wear a green turban as well. اَلْحَمْدُ لِلّٰه عَزَّوَجَلَّ! I had the privilege of participating in a 41 day Madanī Qāfilaĥ course and now I am trying to promote the Madanī working of Dawat-e-Islami in my area.

اِنْ شَآءَاللّٰه عَزَّوَجَلَّ, Ĥo ṫĥīk dard-e-kamar, Madanī Māḥaul mayn kar lo tum I'tikāf
Marz-e-'iṣyān say chuṫĥkārā chāĥo agar, Madanī Māḥaul mayn kar lo tum I'tikāf

Backache will get cured, Allah willing, do I'tikāf in the Madanī environment
Here is cure for disease of sins, do I'tikāf in the Madanī environment

صَلُّوْا عَلَى الْحَبِيْب صَلَّى اللّٰهُ تَعَالٰى عَلٰى مُحَمَّد

Fast of silence

The Prophet of mankind, the Peace of our heart and mind, the most Generous and Kind صَلَّى اللهُ تَعَالٰى عَلَيْهِ وَاٰلِهٖ وَسَلَّم prohibited 'Ṣaum-ul-Wiṣāl' and 'Ṣaum-us-Sukūt', which imply fasting constantly without doing Saḥarī and Ifṭār and constant silence during fast respectively. *(Musnad Imām A'ẓam, pp. 110)*

There is a general misconception amongst people that a Mu'takif should seclude himself inside a curtain in the Masjid and remain completely silent. In fact, this isn't correct. One should use curtains as it is a Sunnaĥ to perform I'tikāf in a tent, it increases concentration as well but there is no harm in doing I'tikāf without a curtain.

The respected scholars رَحِمَهُمُ اللّٰهُ تَعَالٰى have said: Remaining silent during I'tikāf and believing that it is a form of worship is Makrūĥ Taḥrīmī but if somebody stays silent not considering it as a good deed, it does no harm. Remaining silent to avoid indecent speech is excellent, because avoiding such speech is Wājib and indulging in it is a sin. Any speech that is Mubāḥ (i.e. neither good nor bad) is also Makrūĥ for a Mu'takif. However, if necessary, it is permissible. Unnecessary Mubāḥ speech inside a Masjid ruins good deeds as fire ruins wood. *(Durr-e-Mukhtār, vol. 3, pp. 441)*

Committing sins in I'tikāf

Misusing eyes, suspicion, insulting someone without a valid reason, lying, backbiting, telling-tale, jealousy, laying a false blame, mocking or hurting someone, impolite speech, listening to music, abusing, unfair quarrelling, shaving beard or trimming it less than a fist-length are all already sins, they will become even more severe sins in a Masjid in the state of I'tikāf. Repent of these sins sincerely and give up them for good. (Allah عَزَّوَجَلَّ forbid) Though taking an intoxicant at night during I'tikāf will not invalidate the I'tikāf, intoxication is Ḥarām and is a major sin in I'tikāf; repentance is Wājib.

Seven permissible cases for invalidating I'tikāf

In all the following cases, I'tikāf will become invalid and one will have to make up for it later, but invalidation will not be a sin.

1. During I'tikāf, if a Mu'takif suffers from such an illness that cannot be treated within the Masjid, he is allowed to break the I'tikāf. *(Rad-dul-Muḥtār, vol. 3, pp. 438)*

2. If a person is drowning or burning in the fire, the Mu'takif should go out of the Masjid invalidating I'tikāf to rescue him. *(Rad-dul-Muḥtār, vol. 3, pp. 438)*

3. If a general proclamation is made for Jihad (i.e. when it is Farḍ-e-'Ayn) break I'tikāf and take part in Jihad. *(Rad-dul-Muḥtār, vol. 3, pp. 438)*

4. If a funeral (a dead body) arrives and there is no one to offer the funeral Ṣalāĥ, the Mu'takif can break I'tikāf in this case in order to offer it (exiting the Masjid boundaries). *(Rad-dul-Muḥtār, vol. 3, pp. 438)*

5. If the Mu'takif is turned out of the Masjid under coercion, for example, there is an arrest warrant against him from the government, it is permissible to break the I'tikāf in this case provided it isn't possible to enter another Masjid instantly. *(Rad-dul-Muḥtār, vol. 3, pp. 438)*

6. The Mu'takif can break the I'tikāf to offer the funeral Ṣalāĥ of a Maḥram or his wife (but it will be Wājib for him to make up for it). *(Ḥāshiya-tuṭ-Ṭaḥṭawī 'Alal Marāqī, pp. 703)*

7. If the Mu'takif is a witness in a judicial case and the decision depends on his evidence, it is permissible for him to break I'tikāf in order to give evidence and prevent the rights of an individual from being violated. *(Rad-dul-Muḥtār, vol. 3, pp. 438)*

Helping needy person and a day's I'tikāf

The respected Muḥaddis̄īn (scholars of Ḥadīs̄) رَحِمَهُمُ اللّٰهُ تَعَالٰى have narrated the following faith-refreshing incident that took place shortly after the apparent demise of the Holy Prophet صَلَّى اللّٰهُ تَعَالٰى عَلَيْهِ وَاٰلِهٖ وَسَلَّم. Sayyidunā 'Abdullāĥ Ibn 'Abbās رَضِىَ اللّٰهُ تَعَالٰى عَنْهُمَا was Mu'takif in the luminous and merciful atmosphere of the Masjid of Beloved Rasūl صَلَّى اللّٰهُ تَعَالٰى عَلَيْهِ وَاٰلِهٖ وَسَلَّم. He رَضِىَ اللّٰهُ تَعَالٰى عَنْهُ was approached by an extremely sad man, he رَضِىَ اللّٰهُ تَعَالٰى عَنْهُ politely asked the reason for his sadness. The man replied, 'O son of the uncle of the Beloved and Blessed Rasūl صَلَّى اللّٰهُ تَعَالٰى عَلَيْهِ وَاٰلِهٖ وَسَلَّم! I owe money to so and so person.' Then pointing to the luminous tomb of the Noble Prophet صَلَّى اللّٰهُ تَعَالٰى عَلَيْهِ وَاٰلِهٖ وَسَلَّم he said, 'I swear by the sanctity of the merciful Rasūl صَلَّى اللّٰهُ تَعَالٰى عَلَيْهِ وَاٰلِهٖ وَسَلَّم who is resting in this blessed grave! I am not in a position to pay back.'

Sayyidunā 'Abdullāĥ Ibn 'Abbās رَضِىَ اللّٰهُ تَعَالٰى عَنْهُمَا said, 'Shall I intercede for you?' 'As you wish' he replied. So Ibn 'Abbās رَضِىَ اللّٰهُ تَعَالٰى عَنْهُ instantly came out of the blessed Masjid. The man asked surprisingly, 'Your honour! Have you forgotten your I'tikāf?' He replied, 'I haven't forgotten my I'tikāf.' Then, he looked at the luminous tomb of the Prophet of Raḥmaĥ, the Intercessor of Ummaĥ صَلَّى اللّٰهُ تَعَالٰى عَلَيْهِ وَاٰلِهٖ وَسَلَّم and was moved to tears because the apparent demise of Beloved Rasūl صَلَّى اللّٰهُ تَعَالٰى عَلَيْهِ وَاٰلِهٖ وَسَلَّم had recently taken place; memories of the Holy Prophet صَلَّى اللّٰهُ تَعَالٰى عَلَيْهِ وَاٰلِهٖ وَسَلَّم had made him anxious. Then, pointing to the luminous tomb of the Holy Prophet صَلَّى اللّٰهُ تَعَالٰى عَلَيْهِ وَاٰلِهٖ وَسَلَّم he said crying: 'It is not long ago since I heard the Beloved Prophet صَلَّى اللّٰهُ تَعَالٰى عَلَيْهِ وَاٰلِهٖ وَسَلَّم say, 'To satisfy your brother's need is better than ten years' I'tikāf, and whoever does a day's I'tikāf for the pleasure of Allah عَزَّوَجَلَّ, He عَزَّوَجَلَّ shall place three trenches between him and Hell and the distance between these trenches will be greater than that of even (the distance between) the east and west.' *(Shu'ab-ul-Īmān, vol. 3, pp. 424, Ḥadīs̄ 3965)*

May Allah عَزَّوَجَلَّ have mercy on them and forgive us without accountability for their sake!

صَلُّوْا عَلَى الْحَبِيْب صَلَّى اللّٰهُ تَعَالٰى عَلٰى مُحَمَّد

Dear Islamic brothers! سُبۡحٰنَ اللّٰه عَزَّوَجَلَّ! It is the blessings of a day's I'tikāf, then how can anyone estimate the blessings of the act that is 'better than 10 years' I'tikāf?' This parable throws ample light on the importance of helping our Islamic brothers. To comfort Muslims is extremely important. A blessed Ḥadīš says, 'After the obligatory acts, the act that is the most pleasing to Allah عَزَّوَجَلَّ is to please a Muslim's heart.' *(Mu'jam Kabīr, vol. 11, pp. 59, Ḥadīš 11079)*

Really, if we all sincerely try to comfort and sympathise with one another, hatred, enmity and jealousy will be replaced by love, peace and brotherhood, but unfortunately, these days the Muslims are disgracing, plundering and even killing each other! May Allah عَزَّوَجَلَّ enable us to remove hatred and adopt brotherhood!

اٰمِين بِجَاهِ النَّبِيِّ الْاَمِين صَلَّى اللهُ تَعَالٰى عَلَيْهِ وَاٰلِهٖ وَسَلَّم

Eight Madanī pearls regarding acts permissible during I'tikāf

The following acts are permissible during I'tikāf:

1. Eating, drinking and sleeping (eat and sleep on your own shawl or mat instead of the Masjid's mats).
2. Talking about worldly matters, if necessary (but do quietly, do not talk unnecessarily).
3. Changing clothes in the Masjid, applying 'Iṭr and oil to hair or beard.
4. Trimming beard or hair and combing hair, but make sure that no strands of hair fall inside the Masjid while doing these things. Further, be careful not to stain the Masjid mats and walls with oil or food. It will be easier to do these things in the Wuḍū area or the Finā-e-Masjid on one's own mat or shawl.
5. Examining a patient, suggesting medicines or writing prescriptions inside the Masjid without fee.
6. Learning or teaching the Holy Quran, Islamic knowledge, Sunan and supplications inside the Masjid without any fee.

7. If necessary, buying or selling things for oneself or family inside the Masjid is permissible for a Mu'takif, but he is not allowed to bring any merchandise inside the Masjid. However, if it is in small quantity that doesn't take up much space, it will be allowed to do so in this case. This buying and selling is allowed only in case of necessity. It will not be permitted if it is aimed at earning wealth, regardless of whether the goods are inside the Masjid or outside. *(Durr-e-Mukhtār, vol. 3, pp. 440)*

8. Washing clothes, pots etc. inside the Masjid is permissible provided that not even a single splash of water falls onto the Masjid mats or floor. It can be done properly using a large pot.

   In addition to the cases mentioned above, the acts that are basically permissible by Sharī'aĥ, and that are neither prohibited during I'tikāf nor invalidate it and that do not desecrate the Masjid either in any way; are all permissible for Mu'takif, but a Mu'takif should abstain from unnecessary things.

Two Aḥādīš are presented regarding permissible acts for a Mu'takif:

Mu'takif can take his head out of Masjid

1. Sayyidatunā 'Āishaĥ Ṣiddīqaĥ رَضِیَ اللّٰہُ تَعَالٰی عَنْہَا has narrated, 'When the Noble Prophet صَلَّی اللّٰہُ تَعَالٰی عَلَیْہِ وَاٰلِہٖ وَسَلَّم was in I'tikāf he used to take his blessed head out of the Masjid towards my room and I would comb his blessed hair and he صَلَّی اللّٰہُ تَعَالٰی عَلَیْہِ وَاٰلِہٖ وَسَلَّم would not enter the house except to relieve himself.' *(Ṣaḥīḥ Bukhārī, vol. 1, pp. 665, Ḥadīš 2029)*

If Mu'takif exits Masjid he can console a sick person whilst walking

2. Sayyidatunā 'Āishaĥ Ṣiddīqaĥ رَضِیَ اللّٰہُ تَعَالٰی عَنْہَا has narrated, 'Whenever the Beloved and Blessed Prophet صَلَّی اللّٰہُ تَعَالٰی عَلَیْہِ وَاٰلِہٖ وَسَلَّم walked past a sick person in the state of I'tikāf he صَلَّی اللّٰہُ تَعَالٰی عَلَیْہِ وَاٰلِہٖ وَسَلَّم would enquire about his health without stopping and without moving to one side of the path.' *(Sunan Abī Dāwūd, vol. 2, pp. 492, Ḥadīš 2472)*

Dear Islamic brothers! This blessed Ḥadīš clarifies that when the Prophet of mankind, the Peace of our heart and mind, the most Generous and Kind صَلَّی اللّٰہُ تَعَالٰی عَلَیْہِ وَاٰلِہٖ وَسَلَّم came out of the Masjid during his I'tikāf for a Shar'ī or physical need and walked past a sick person he صَلَّى اللهُ تَعَالٰى عَلَيْهِ وَاٰلِهٖ وَسَلَّم would neither move to the other path nor stop to console the sick person, but rather, he صَلَّى اللهُ تَعَالٰى عَلَيْهِ وَاٰلِهٖ وَسَلَّم would enquire about his health whilst walking. Whenever a Mu'takif Islamic brother exits the Masjid precincts due to any lawful reason he should not remain outside the Masjid unnecessarily even for a single moment. Doing Salām, talking or consoling someone whilst walking past him is permissible; but if Mu'takif stops or takes another path for any of these reasons, his I'tikāf will become invalid.

I'tikāf of Islamic sisters

Sayyidatunā 'Āishaĥ Ṣiddīqaĥ رَضِیَ اللّٰهُ تَعَالٰی عَنْهَا has narrated, 'The Prophet of Raḥmaĥ, the Intercessor of Ummaĥ صَلَّى اللهُ تَعَالٰى عَلَيْهِ وَاٰلِهٖ وَسَلَّم would do I'tikāf in the last ten days of Ramadan until his (apparent) demise took place, and then his chaste wives used to do I'tikāf.' *(Ṣaḥīḥ Bukhārī, vol. 1, pp. 664, Ḥadīš 2026)*

Islamic sisters should also do I'tikāf

Islamic sisters should also gain the privilege of doing I'tikāf. The modest Islamic sisters usually spend their time at homes because wandering around the streets and markets in the state of immodesty (without a veil) is a trait of the shameless women. So it is probably not so hard for modest Islamic sisters to do I'tikāf, and even if it seems slightly difficult, it does not matter. Ramadan doesn't come every day, and it's only a matter of ten days.

Islamic sisters do I'tikāf in their Masjid-e-Bayt (details will follow). 'Masjid-e-Bayt' is a very small space and therefore it reminds them of the grave. If sitting in one corner of the house despite the presence of daughters, sons and other relatives is hard, how will you be able to spend thousands of years alone in your grave, if Allah عَزَّوَجَلَّ and His Beloved Prophet صَلَّى اللهُ تَعَالٰى عَلَيْهِ وَاٰلِهٖ وَسَلَّم are displeased with you. If you do I'tikāf in your house for ten days and if Allah عَزَّوَجَلَّ gets pleased with you due to its blessings, all the veils between your grave and Madīna-tul-Munawwaraĥ may be lifted. Therefore, every Islamic sister should gain the privilege of doing I'tikāf at least once in their lives.

Twelve Madanī pearls for Islamic sisters

1. Islamic sisters can perform I'tikāf in Masjid-e-Bayt only, not in the Masjid. The Masjid-e-Bayt is the portion of the house a woman specifies for Ṣalāĥ. It is Mustaḥab for Islamic sisters to specify a particular area of their homes for offering Ṣalāĥ and to keep it clean and pure. It is better that this area be a little raised like a terrace. Islamic brothers should also specify a particular place in their homes for offering their Nawāfil as it is better to offer Nawāfil at home. *(Durr-e-Mukhtār, Rad-dul-Muḥtār, vol. 3, pp. 429)*

2. If an Islamic sister has not specified a particular place in her home for Ṣalāĥ, then she cannot perform I'tikāf. However, if she specifies a place for Ṣalāĥ at the time of intending to do I'tikāf she can do it within that specified area. *(Durr-e-Mukhtār, Rad-dul-Muḥtār, vol. 3, pp. 429)*

3. An Islamic sister cannot do I'tikāf in someone else's house.

4. It is not permissible for a wife to do I'tikāf without her husband's permission. *(Rad-dul-Muḥtār, vol. 3, pp. 429)*

5. If the wife has started I'tikāf with her husband's permission but the husband wants to prevent her later on (during the I'tikāf), he cannot do so. If he does, it is not Wājib for the wife to obey him. *(Fatāwā 'Ālamgīrī, vol. 1, pp. 211)*

6. It is also a prerequisite for Islamic sisters not to be experiencing menses or post natal bleeding because it is Ḥarām to offer Ṣalāĥ, fast and recite the Holy Quran in this state. *(Common books)*

   The maximum period of post natal bleeding is 40 days and 40 nights. If the bleeding continues even after 40 days and nights, it indicates an illness. Therefore, Islamic sister should take ritual bath and start offering Ṣalāĥ and fasting.

   A common misconception amongst Islamic sisters is that they assume that post natal bleeding period is (always) forty days, whereas this is not correct. The Shar'ī ruling is that even if the bleeding stops within a single day, or even if it stops immediately after the delivery, post natal bleeding will be considered to have ended in this case and thus the Islamic sister should perform Ghusl and start Ṣalāĥ and fast.

The minimum period for menses is three days and nights while its maximum period is ten days and nights. As soon as the bleeding stops after three days and nights Islamic sister should do Ghusl instantly and start offering Ṣalāĥ and fast[1]. If the bleeding continues even after ten days and nights, it is an illness. Therefore, as soon as ten days and nights pass, Islamic sister should do Ghusl and start offering Ṣalāĥ and fasting.

7. Before starting the Sunnaĥ I'tikāf Islamic sisters should consider whether their menses is going to start during the last ten days of Ramadan or not. If menses may start they shouldn't start the I'tikāf.

8. If a woman experiences her menses during I'tikāf her I'tikāf will become invalid. *(Badāi'-uṣ-Ṣanāi', vol. 2, pp. 287)* In this case, it is Wājib for her to make up for the only day her I'tikāf became invalid. *(Rad-dul-Muḥtār, vol. 3, pp. 500)*

   After attaining ritual purity from menses, she should do I'tikāf for one day with the intention of Qaḍā. If some days of Ramadan are still left, she can make up for it in Ramadan as well. In this case the fast of Ramadan will be sufficient. If she doesn't want to make up for it in Ramadan or Ramadan had ended when she attained purity, then she can do it any other day except on Eid-ul-Fiṭr and from the 10th to the 13th of Żul-Ḥijjaĥ because fasting in these five days is Makrūĥ Taḥrīmī. *(Durr-e-Mukhtār ma' Rad-dul-Muḥtār, vol. 3, pp. 391)*

   The method of Qaḍā is to enter the Masjid-e-Bayt at sunset (it is safer to enter a few minutes before sunset) with the intention of making up for the invalidated I'tikāf and remain there until the sunset of the next day. Fasting is a condition for this Qaḍā.

9. It is not permissible to leave the place of I'tikāf without Shar'ī needs. Islamic sisters cannot go to any other portion of the house either. I'tikāf will become invalid if they do so.

10. The rulings which apply to Islamic brothers regarding leaving the place of I'tikāf also apply to Islamic sisters. In other words, Islamic sisters can leave the place of I'tikāf for the same needs for which Islamic brothers are allowed to come out of the

[1] There are details here for married women, they should read part-2 of *Baĥār-e-Sharī'at*.

Masjid. Likewise, they are not allowed to leave their place of I'tikāf for the acts that men aren't allowed to leave the Masjid for.

11. During I'tikāf, Islamic sisters can sew and knit staying in their place of I'tikāf. They can also instruct others to do household chores but they cannot leave the place of I'tikāf.

12. During I'tikāf, it is better to focus completely on reciting the Holy Quran, Żikr, Ṣalāt-'Alan-Nabī, Tasbīḥāt, religious studies, listening to cassettes of Sunnaĥ-Inspiring speeches and other acts of worship. Avoid spending time in other activities unnecessarily.

Method of Qaḍā I'tikāf

Dear Islamic brothers! If you started I'tikāf for the last ten days of Ramadan but it became invalid (due to some reason) you do not have to make up for all ten days. Instead, you have to make up for the only day the I'tikāf became invalid.

If the days of Ramadan are still left, you can make up for it in the remaining days of Ramadan. If Ramadan has ended, you have to make up for it another day with fast except the day of Eid-ul-Fiṭr and from the 10th to 13th of Żul-Ḥijjaĥ because fasting in these days is Makrūĥ Taḥrīmī.

The method of Qaḍā is to enter the Masjid any day at sunset (it is safer to enter a few minutes before the sunset) with the intention of making up for the broken I'tikāf and remain there until the sunset of the next day. Fasting is a condition for this Qaḍā.

Fidyaĥ (expiation) for I'tikāf

If somebody did not make up for the broken I'tikāf despite having the opportunity to do, and now he is on his deathbed, it is Wājib for him to make a will to his heirs to pay a Fidyaĥ (expiation) in exchange for the I'tikāf. Even if he didn't make the will it is still permissible to pay Fidyaĥ provided his heirs give permission to pay it. *(Al-Fatāwā Al-Ĥindiyyaĥ, vol. 1, pp. 213)*

Paying Fidyaĥ is not difficult. What you have to do is to give one Ṣadaqaĥ-e-Fiṭr (i.e. 1.920 kilograms of wheat or money equivalent to its value) to someone who is entitled to receive Zakāĥ, with the intention of paying the Fidyaĥ of I'tikāf.

Repentance of breaking I'tikāf

If the I'tikāf was broken due to a valid exemption or by mistake, it is not a sin, but breaking it deliberately without a valid exemption is a sin. Therefore, one must repent in addition to making up for it.

It is Wājib to repent whenever a sin is committed. One should repent instantly without any delay because death can come anytime. Gently slapping one's cheeks a few times isn't repentance. Instead, one should mention the sin he has committed and humbly seek forgiveness from Allah عَزَّوَجَلَّ with remorse and make a firm intention never to commit that sin again. One of the conditions of repentance is to have resentment towards the sin in heart.

Boss of famous band repents

Many people who were previously wicked and impious are now leading their lives following the Sunnaĥ of Beloved and Blessed Rasūl صَلَّى اللهُ تَعَالٰى عَلَيْهِ وَاٰلِهٖ وَسَلَّم owing to the blessing of joining the Madanī environment of Dawat-e-Islami. Here is a faith-refreshing description of such an incident: In Mandsoor (M.P. India) there was a very famous band a young man used to run. As a result of the individual effort of an Islamic brother, that young man did I'tikāf in the last ten days of Ramadan in 1426 A.H. in the company of devotees of Rasūl. During I'tikāf he heard about the harms of sins, which softened his heart. The company of devotees of Rasūl affected him so much that he repented of his sins. He made the intention of growing a beard and travelling with a Madanī Qāfilaĥ for 30 days in the company of devotees of Rasūl. اَلْحَمْدُ لِلّٰه عَزَّوَجَلَّ! He has given up his sinful and Ḥarām profession of playing music.

صَلُّوْا عَلَى الْحَبِيْب صَلَّى اللهُ تَعَالٰى عَلٰى مُحَمَّد

Necessary things for Mu'takif

1. A curtain (green would be nice) with some strings and safety pins for concentration and protection of things,
2. Kanz-ul-Īmān
3. Needle and thread

4. Scissors
5. Tasbīḥ
6. Miswāk
7. Kohl
8. Bottle of oil
9. Comb
10. Mirror
11. 'Iṭr (perfume)
12. Two dresses
13. Taĥband (i.e. a piece of cloth used to cover the lower part of the body)
14. Turban with a cap and head cloth
15. Glass
16. Plate
17. Bowl (a clay bowl would be nice)
18. Cup and saucer
19. Thermos
20. Eating mat
21. Toothpicks
22. Towel
23. Bucket and mug (for doing Ghusl)
24. Handkerchief
25. Knife
26. Pen
27. A Qufl-e-Madīnaĥ pad for talking by writing so that the habit of unnecessary speaking is avoided.
28. *Faīzān-e-Sunnat* and other Islamic books (according to one's needs).
29. Madanī In'āmāt booklet

30. Notepad (diary)
31. If necessary, valueless pieces of cloth (which one can get from a tailor) or tissue paper for drying private parts after defecation or urination.
32. A sleeping mat. It is not permissible to bring such a mat from which splinters fall and spread into the Masjid.
33. A pillow, if necessary
34. A shawl or blanket to cover oneself
35. A shawl for observing veil within veil
36. Tablets for headache, cold, fever etc.

Madanī suggestion: Mark your things (with the picture of something like moon, star etc.) so that you can recognise them easily if they get mixed up with other peoples' things. Do not write your name or initials on your shawl because it will probably be disrespected. (There are some examples of symbols on the last page of this chapter '*Blessings of I'tikāf*).

Fifty Madanī pearls of I'tikāf

1. A Mu'takif must enter the Masjid with the intention of performing I'tikāf before the sunset on the 20th of Ramadan. If he enters the Masjid even a single moment after the sunset, the Sunnaĥ of performing the I'tikāf of the last ten days of Ramadan will remain unfulfilled.

2. If someone enters the Masjid before the sunset on 20th Ramadan with the intention of I'tikāf and then walks into the Finā-e-Masjid, for example, the Wuḍū area or toilets, situated within the Masjid precincts and then the sun sets whilst he was still in Wuḍū area or toilet, this will not invalidate I'tikāf, and there is no harm in doing so.

3. Though it is permissible for a Mu'takif to greet someone, to reply to his greeting or to talk to him whilst going to the toilet, if the Mu'takif stops even for a single moment, his I'tikāf will become invalid. However, there is no harm in stopping if the toilet is within the Masjid boundaries.

4. If the Mu'takif goes to the toilet but it is occupied beforehand, he does not have to come back into the Masjid to wait, he can wait outside the toilet.

5. After urination, a Mu'takif can do Istibrā outside the Masjid[1], if necessary. (After urinating, if one suspects that a drop of urine will be discharged, it is Wājib for him to do Istibrā, which implies doing such an act after urination that will cause the remaining drop of urine to be discharged. Istibrā can be done by ambling, stamping foot with force on the ground, pressing left foot onto the right one or vice versa, descending from a high place downwards, walking upwards, clearing throat or lying on left side. One should do Istibrā until one is satisfied. Some scholars have said that the one doing Istibrā should walk forty steps, but the correct verdict is that one should walk until he is satisfied. This ruling of Istibrā is for men only. If women [suspect that a drop of urine has remained which will be discharged] they should wait a short while after urinating and then have purity. *(Bahār-e-Sharī'at, part 2, pp. 115)* During Istibrā, keep the clod of earth at the tip of the penis, if necessary. Doing Istibrā is like urinating, so neither greet anyone nor talk. Facing or making the back face Qiblaĥ is Ḥarām during Istibrā just as it is Ḥarām whilst urination and defecation).

6. If the toilets outside the Masjid are extremely filthy and one feels disgusted by using them, there is no harm for the Mu'takif in going home to relieve himself in this case. *(Rad-dul-Muḥtār, vol. 3, pp. 435)*

7. If a Mu'takif exits the Masjid boundaries and the creditor stops him, his I'tikāf will become invalid.

8. The Mu'takif should lay his own dining mat when eating. Make sure the Masjid floor or mats are not stained.

9. Never touch the Masjid walls or mats with dirty or oily hands nor stain them with saliva. Similarly, do not stain them with dirt from ears or nose. Don't stain the walls or floor of the Finā-e-Masjid with Pān (betel) etc. Take part in cleaning the Masjid. If possible, each Mu'takif should keep a plastic bag in his pocket to pick up fallen

---

[1] Here, 'Outside the Masjid' implies outside the main Masjid but within the Finā-e-Masjid.

hair and splinters etc. and put them in the plastic bags. Here is a Ḥadīš in this regard:

The Holy Prophet صَلَّى اللهُ تَعَالٰى عَلَيْهِ وَاٰلِهٖ وَسَلَّم has said, 'If anyone removes something painful from the Masjid, Allah عَزَّوَجَلَّ will make a house for him in the Heaven.' *(Sunan Ibn Mājaĥ, vol. 1, pp. 419, Ḥadīš 757)*

10. Avoid pulling out threads or fluff from the mats and breaking off splinters from the mats of the Masjid (keep this in mind everywhere).

11. Don't give any money etc. to beggars in Masjid because begging in the Masjid is Ḥarām and it is prohibited to give them anything inside the Masjid. A'lā Ḥaḍrat رَحْمَةُ اللهِ تَعَالٰى عَلَيْه has said: If someone gives one penny to a beggar in the Masjid he should give seventy pence as charity (Ṣadaqaĥ) in expiation. (Don't give this Ṣadaqaĥ to a beggar in the Masjid). *(Fatāwā Razawiyyaĥ (Jadīd), vol. 16, pp. 418)*

12. There is no harm in taking only one foot out of the Masjid.

13. There is no harm in sticking both hands and head out of the Masjid either.

14. If a Mu'takif comes out of the Masjid by mistake, but then comes back into the Masjid instantly as soon as he recalls I'tikāf, his I'tikāf will become invalid.

15. If a Mu'takif suffers from such an illness that can only be treated outside the Masjid, though he can exit the Masjid for treatment in this case, his I'tikāf will become invalid. However, invalidating it will not be a sin. He must make up for that one day.

16. If there is no one to bring the Mu'takif food and water, he can exit the Masjid for this purpose, but he has to eat and drink inside the Masjid.

17. Allah عَزَّوَجَلَّ forbid, if any unfortunate person utters a statement of unbelief and becomes a Murtad (apostate) his I'tikāf will become invalid. He must renew his faith, i.e. to repent of the statement of unbelief and recite Kalimaĥ of Shaĥādaĥ. (He should) renew his Bay'at, and if he is married, he must renew his Nikāḥ. He is not required to make up for his I'tikāf because religious apostasy ruins all previous good deeds.

18. Allah عَزَّوَجَلَّ forbid, if a Mu'takif takes an intoxicant or shaves his beard, a blessed and holy Sunnaĥ, then despite the fact that both of these acts are already Ḥarām and even greater sins inside the Masjid, his I'tikāf will not become invalid.

19. It is quite permissible for a Mu'takif to trim his beard or hair (according to Sharī'aĥ and Sunnaĥ) or apply oil to his hair or beard, provided he carefully does it sitting on his own piece of cloth. He must neither stain the Masjid mats with oil nor let strands of hair fall on them.

20. A Mu'takif can study books of a religious Madrasaĥ.

21. At night, a Mu'takif can study religious books using the Masjid lights for as long as the lights are normally turned on. If he wants to use lights later than usual timings, he should approach the Masjid committee or administration and offer them an appropriate amount for consuming Masjid's electricity.

22. Avoid reading newspapers in the Masjid as they are usually full of images of living beings, and even films advertisements.

23. If someone steals the shoes of a Mu'takif or those of any other Islamic brother and runs away, the Mu'takif cannot exit the Masjid to catch him. If he does so, his I'tikāf will become invalid.

24. If there are several floors in the Masjid and the stairs to the upper floors are within the Masjid precincts, the Mu'takif can freely go to the upper floors as well as the roof. However, climbing onto the roof of the Masjid unnecessarily is Makrūĥ and disrespect of the Masjid.

25. If a Mu'takif wants to listen to the cassettes of Sunnaĥ-Inspiring speeches and Na'ats he should use his own batteries in his cassette player. If he wants to listen to cassettes using Masjid's electricity, it is better to estimate the total amount of electricity he has used and pay for it (at the end) with a bit extra to the committee. The Mu'takif should be careful not to disturb the worshipping or resting people while listening to cassettes.

26. If the Masjid ceiling etc. collapses or someone turns the Mu'takif out of the Masjid he should instantly go to any other Masjid and continue his I'tikāf over there. His I'tikāf will still be valid.

27. During I’tikāf, a Mu’takif should spend as much time as possible offering Nafl Ṣalāĥ, reciting the Holy Quran, Żikr, Ṣalāt-‘Alan-Nabī, studying, learning and teaching Sunan and supplications.

28. If a Mu’takif uses a curtain in the Masjid for I’tikāf he should not take up a large space of the Masjid so that the people offering Ṣalāĥ would not be inconvenienced. A’lā Ḥaḍrat رَحْمَةُ اللهِ تَعَالٰی عَلَیْه has said: It is strictly forbidden to keep things that reduce the space for Ṣalāĥ in the Masjid. *(Fatāwā Razawiyyaĥ (Jadīd), vol. 8, pp. 97)*

29. Keep the Masjid clean from all types of uncleanness, dirt, dust etc.

30. Strictly avoid making a noise, laughing, joking etc. in the Masjid as it is a sin to do so.

31. A Mu’takif leaves his house and heads to the Masjid in order to earn reward but it should not happen that he returns with a heap of sins. So beware, don’t utter even a single word in the Masjid unnecessarily. Strictly apply Madanī guard to your tongue.

32. Mu’takifīn Islamic brothers should make available all necessary items beforehand in the Masjid so that they don’t have to borrow anything from anyone, as asking someone for something isn’t nice. Some of the blessed companions رَضِیَ اللّٰہُ تَعَالٰی عَنْھُم used to avoid it so much that if even a whip of theirs would fall on the ground and they’d be on horse, they wouldn’t say, ‘Brother! Will you pass me that whip’ rather they would dismount the horse and retrieve it themselves.

33. In the presence of other people, recite the Holy Quran in low voice so that they would not be disturbed.

34. If other Islamic brothers are also doing I’tikāf in the Masjid where you are Mu’takif, then ensure that you fulfil the rights of companionship in every possible manner. Serve other Mu’takifīn wholeheartedly. Try your best to fulfil their requirements and demonstrate a polite, sincere and self-sacrificing attitude. There is great reward of self-sacrifice for others. The Beloved and Blessed Prophet صَلَّی اللّٰہُ تَعَالٰی عَلَیْہِ وَاٰلِہٖ وَسَلَّم has said, ‘Allah عَزَّوَجَلَّ forgives the person who gives someone else the thing he needs for himself.’ *(Itḥāf-us-Sādat-il-Muttaqīn, vol. 9, pp. 779)*

35. Try to teach other Mu’takifīn the supplications and Sunan you know, as it is not often that one gets such an easy opportunity of earning a treasure of reward.

36. During I'tikāf, try to practice as many Sunnaĥs as possible, for example use a mat, clay pots etc.

37. Act upon Madanī In'āmāt and fill in the Madanī In'āmāt booklet. Make a permanent habit of doing so.

38. Avoid sleeping on the Masjid floor and mats because there is a risk of them being stained by sweat, hair oil or being impure in case of nocturnal emission. Therefore, do bring your own mat with you. This will give you a chance to practice the Sunnaĥ of sleeping on a mat, and the mats of the Masjid will also not get stained.

39. If you don't have your own mat, lay down at least your own shawl.

40. Sleep in the state of veil within veil whether you are in the Masjid or at home or anywhere else. If possible, make a habit of wrapping one shawl around trousers and cover yourself with another one because sometimes there is extreme unveiling whilst sleeping despite wearing clothes.

41. Two Islamic brothers should never sleep using the same pillow or in the same blanket/shawl etc.

42. Similarly, avoid sleeping with your head on someone's thigh or lap, as it may invite objections.

43. When you hear about the appearance of the moon of Eid-ul-Fiṭr on the 29th of Ramadan or when the sun sets on the 30th, don't run out of the Masjid as if you've just been released from prison. As soon as you hear the news of the departure of Ramadan your heart should fill with grief. The Holy month has departed from us, bid farewell to Ramadan with tears in your eyes.

44. At the end of the I'tikāf shed tears and seek forgiveness from Allah عَزَّوَجَلَّ for your shortcomings, mistakes and all acts of desecrating the Masjid. Make Du'ā with extreme humility for the acceptance of your I'tikāf and the I'tikāf of every Islamic brother and sister of the entire world and for the forgiveness of the entire Ummaĥ.

45. Apologize to each other for the violation of rights.

46. If possible, offer gifts to the servants of the Masjid in order to please them.

47. Thank the administration of the Masjid for their cooperation.

48. If possible, spend the night of Eid-ul-Fiṭr in worship, or at least offer the 'Ishā and Fajr Ṣalāĥ with Jamā'at, اِنْ شَآءَاللّٰه عَزَّوَجَلَّ you will be rewarded for worshipping the entire night, as stated in a Ḥadīš.

49. Try to spend the night of Eid in Nafl I'tikāf in the same Masjid where you did the Sunnaĥ I'tikāf. Sayyidunā Imām Jalāluddīn Suyūṭī Shāfi'ī رَحْمَةُ اللّٰهِ تَعَالٰى عَلَيْه has narrated that Sayyidunā Ibrāĥīm Bin Adĥam رَحْمَةُ اللّٰهِ تَعَالٰى عَلَيْه has said: Our saints رَحِمَهُمُ اللّٰهُ تَعَالٰى would like to spend the night (of Eid-ul-Fiṭr) in the Masjid so that they would begin their day (of Eid-ul-Fiṭr) in the Masjid. Sayyidunā Imām Mālik رَحْمَةُ اللّٰهِ تَعَالٰى عَلَيْه mentions that our pious saints رَحِمَهُمُ اللّٰهُ تَعَالٰى didn't return to their homes until they had offered Eid Ṣalāĥ with people. *(Ad-Dur-rul-Manšūr, vol. 1, pp. 488)*

50. Avoid spending the blessed moments of Eid in markets. Allah عَزَّوَجَلَّ forbid, don't turn the day of Eid in to a day of Wa'īd (warning) by spending it in amusement parks, cinemas and theatres where there is the intermingling of men and women.

Devotees of Rasūl changed my life

The Mu'takifīn attending the collective I'tikāf held under the supervision of Dawat-e-Islami, a global & non-political religious movement of the Quran and Sunnaĥ, should travel with Madanī Qāfilaĥs in the company of devotees of Rasūl on the night of Eid or after spending the whole night in the Masjid. اِنْ شَآءَاللّٰه عَزَّوَجَلَّ They will see its blessings for themselves. If one spends Eid with modern friends in a sinful environment he may well lose the spirituality of the I'tikāf. Here is a faith-refreshing Madanī blessing about a Madanī Eid Qāfilaĥ. A young Islamic brother from Lines Area, Bāb-ul-Madīnaĥ Karachi has stated:

In my early life, I was a modern guy who did not offer even Ṣalāĥ. I was wasting the precious moments of my life in heedlessness and sins. In the month of Ramadan 1423 A.H., making individual effort, an Islamic brother persuaded me to take part in the Sunnaĥ-Inspiring collective I'tikāf being held in Faīzān-e-Razā Masjid (Lines Area). I agreed to take part in the I'tikāf and sought permission from my family and then I did I'tikāf for the last ten days of Ramadan. During the ten days of the I'tikāf I gained many blessings in the company of devotees of Rasūl and I made a firm intention to offer Ṣalāĥ steadfastly for the rest of my life. Apart from repenting of other sins, I repented of the sin of shaving my beard as well. I began to wear green turban and made the intention to wear clothing according to the Sunnaĥ.

On the second day of Eid, I travelled with a Sunnaĥ-Inspiring Madanī Qāfilaĥ of the devotees of Rasūl. My love for Dawat-e-Islami intensified due to the blessings of this journey. Now, I wish I remain associated with the Madanī environment of Dawat-e-Islami until death. I am no longer fond of fashion. اَلۡحَمۡدُ لِلّٰه عَزَّوَجَلَّ! The company of devotees of Rasūl during the I'tikāf and journey with the Madanī Qāfilaĥ completely changed my life. Moreover, by the grace of Allah عَزَّوَجَلَّ, at present I am serving the Sunnaĥ in my area as the responsible of Madanī In'āmāt.

صَلُّوۡا عَلَی الۡحَبِیۡب صَلَّی اللّٰهُ تَعَالٰی عَلٰی مُحَمَّد

Look after your belongings

اَلۡحَمۡدُ لِلّٰه عَزَّوَجَلَّ! Thousands of Islamic brothers who are associated with Dawat-e-Islami take part in collective I'tikāf every year at different Masājid of the world. I want to draw the attention of all such Islamic brothers towards an important matter. If your belongings accidentally mix with someone else's, so it is prohibited and a sin to use them even though they look like yours. Therefore, Mu'takifin (the students of Madrasaĥ and everyone else) should mark their belongings which can be mixed with others. I have provided some symbols as a guide (at the end of this chapter).

(Don't write your name or the letters of any language such as A and B on your sandals, shawl etc. If possible, remove the company label as well so that the alphabets would not be disrespected when you place foot on them. One should respect the letters of every language. For further details on this topic, please refer to the chapter of *Faīzān-e-Sunnat* entitled *Blessings of* بِسۡمِ اللّٰه).

Causes of illness during I'tikāf

اَلۡحَمۡدُ لِلّٰه عَزَّوَجَلَّ! Sag-e-Madīnaĥ عُفِیَ عَنۡهُ has had the privilege of spending ample time with Mu'takifin for many years. I have happened to see many ill Islamic brothers during I'tikāf. 'Carelessness in eating' has turned out to be the main cause of Mu'takifin's illness. Relatives and friends of the Mu'takifin bring them delicious meals, sweet dishes, fried items, pizzas, sour sauces and foods from marketplace for Saḥarī etc. and some Mu'takifīn gobble down the food without even chewing it properly yielding to greed without pondering over the consequences. Resultantly, this leads to constipation, wind problem, stomach-pain indigestion, diarrhoea, vomiting, fatigue, flu, fever, headaches and other body pains. These Islamic brothers leave their homes for I'tikāf enthusiastically to worship abundantly but they fall ill as a result of excessive eating. Sometimes, it is observed that the congregational Ṣalāĥ begins but these pitiable Islamic brothers remain lying in the Masjid due to headaches and fever.

Nā samajĥ bīmār ko amrat bĥī zaĥr āmayz ĥay
Sach yeĥī ĥay saw dawā kī aīk dawā parĥayz ĥay

For the unwise patient even elixir is toxin
The truth is that abstinence is best medicine

Benefits of food precautions

اَلْحَمْدُ لِلّٰه عَزَّوَجَلَّ! Thousands of Islamic brothers do I'tikāf in the last ten days of Ramadan in Faīzān-e-Madīnaĥ, Bāb-ul-Madīnaĥ Karachi, the global Madanī Markaz of Dawat-e-Islami. As a result of my constant requests to avoid the use of clarified butter, fried items and to reduce the amount of oil and spices, some useful changes have taken place, decreasing the number of patients during I'tikāf. I wish these precautions be implemented not only in every Masjid where I'tikāf is carried out but also in every home.

I hold Muslims' health dear

اَلْحَمْدُ لِلّٰه عَزَّوَجَلَّ! In addition to the spiritual reform of the Muslims, I desire their physical health as well. I wish all Mu'takifīn follow my suggestions by eating less than their hunger and by avoiding untimely meals and different things so that they could remain fit and healthy enough to worship Allah عَزَّوَجَلَّ, learn Islamic knowledge and travel with Sunnaĥ-Inspiring Madanī Qāfilaĥs of devotees of Rasūl at the end of the collective I'tikāf at the night of Eid. If you follow my suggested precautions about eating throughout your life, you will live a happy life and remain safe from doctors' fees and medicine expenses اِنْ شَآءَاللّٰه عَزَّوَجَلَّ. (Please read the meal timetable and health tips in the Maktūb-e-'Aṭṭār in the chapter of *Faīzān-e-Sunnat* entitled '*Islamic Manners of Eating*').

One of the reasons for being interested in your health is that it will increase your fervour for worshipping and the enthusiasm to travel with Sunnaĥ-Inspiring Madanī Qāfilaĥs اِنْ شَآءَاللّٰه عَزَّوَجَلَّ. If you are healthy you will easily be able to offer your Ṣalāĥ, practice the Sunnaĥ and serve your parents and family. If you carry out these good deeds following my suggestions, I will also earn great reward اِنْ شَآءَاللّٰه عَزَّوَجَلَّ.

Praying for long life of tyrant

May Allah عَزَّوَجَلَّ guide those Muslims who have drifted away from Ṣalāĥ and Farḍ worships, who oppress other Muslim brothers and commit different sins flagrantly. The good health of such people often results in the increase of sins. Ḥujjat-ul-Islam Sayyidunā Imām Muhammad Ghazālī عَلَیْهِ رَحْمَةُ اللّٰهِ الْوَالِی has stated, 'If someone makes Du'ā for the long life of sinners and oppressors it is as if he likes disobedience to Allah عَزَّوَجَلَّ on the earth.' (Ayyuĥal Waladu ma' Majmū'aĥ Rasāil, pp. 266)

However, it is permissible to make Du'ā for such oppressors and sinners' long lives and good health with the Du'ā that they give up cruelty and sins. For an excellent piece of advice about precautions of eating, please read the chapter of *Faīzān-e-Sunnat* entitled *'Excellence of Hunger.'*

Desiring well-being of Muslims is act of piety

Sayyidunā Jarīr Bin 'Abdullāĥ رَضِیَ اللّٰهُ تَعَالٰی عَنْهُ has said that I made a Bay'at (promise) with the Prophet of Raḥmaĥ, the Intercessor of Ummaĥ صَلَّی اللّٰهُ تَعَالٰی عَلَیْهِ وَاٰلِهٖ وَسَلَّم to offer my daily Ṣalāĥ, give my yearly charity (Zakāĥ) and benefit my fellow Muslims (i.e. I will desire their well-wishing).' (Ṣaḥīḥ Muslim, pp. 48, Ḥadīš 97)

اَلْحَمْدُ لِلّٰه عَزَّوَجَلَّ! I have presented some Madanī Pearls on how to remain healthy with the blessed intention of earning reward as suggesting something useful to Muslims is also a good deed. If you desire a healthy life just for the enjoyment of worldly pleasures, then stop reading this account. If, however, you intend to have good health so that you could carry out worship and preach Sunnaĥ, then read this letter completely making good intentions for earning reward in the Hereafter. Recite Ṣalāt-'Alan-Nabī and read on with good intentions:

صَلُّوْا عَلَی الْحَبِيْب   صَلَّی اللّٰهُ تَعَالٰی عَلٰی مُحَمَّد

May Allah عَزَّوَجَلَّ forgive me, you, our family and the entire Ummaĥ! May He عَزَّوَجَلَّ bless us with health and prosperity so that we may consistently serve Islam staying associated with Dawat-e-Islami! May Allah عَزَّوَجَلَّ remove all our diseases and make us a devotee of Madīnaĥ!

Attention kebab and samosa eaters!

Those who eat kebabs and samosas from the marketplace and in get-togethers should take note. Most of the people that sell kebabs and samosas often do not wash the mince they use. According to them, the taste of the kebabs and samosas reduces if the mince is washed. Further, listen to what is put into mince purchased from the markets. Some remove the skin from the guts of a cow and mix either spleen or, sometimes, Allah عَزَّوَجَلَّ forbid, congealed blood with guts that is minced so that the white flesh of the guts becomes pink in colour resembling meat. At times, the sellers have garlic, ginger etc. grinded with the mince which can no longer be washed. Spices are mixed and the same mince is used in the kebabs and samosas which are then sold. There is a risk of the same type of unclean mince in hotels and restaurants as well.

Therefore, don't buy even pakoras from these people that sell these impure kebabs and samosas as the pakoras are also fried in the same fryer in which the unclean mince is put in. However, Allah عَزَّوَجَلَّ forbid, I do not mean to say that all kebab and samosa sellers do such acts nor every kebab and samosa seller uses unclean mince. Definitely, mince of pure and clean meat is also available. My request is that mince, kebabs or samosas should be bought from a trustworthy Muslim, and the Muslims who do such fraudulent acts should repent and seek forgiveness.

Doctors' views about kebabs and samosas

We eat kebabs, Shāmī kebabs, samosas, pakoras, fish, fried chicken, pizzas, omelettes etc. with enjoyment but very few are aware of the damage and fatal diseases these harmful foods cause to the body. When the oil is heated for frying, according to medical research, many harmful substances are released, and when the food is put into the oil it starts to crackle, which indicates the breaking up of its chemical substances and the loss of vital vitamins and other useful nutrients.

Nineteen illnesses caused by eating fried foods

1. The body weight increases
2. It damages the walls of the intestines
3. It causes excretory problems
4. Severe stomach pain
5. Nausea
6. Vomiting
7. Diarrhoea
8. Compared to fat, the use of fried things quickly increases the amount of harmful cholesterol called LDL (Low-density lipoprotein cholesterol) in the body.
9. It decreases useful cholesterol called HDL (High-density lipoprotein cholesterol).
10. It causes blood clotting
11. indigestion
12. wind
13. Oil heated at very high temperatures makes a toxic chemical called 'Acrylon' which damages the walls of the intestines.
14. It can cause even cancer (may Allah عَزَّوَجَلَّ protect us!)
15. Heating the oil for a long time causes chemical reactions that release 'free radicals' that can cause heart diseases.
16. Cancer
17. Inflammation in the joints
18. Brain illnesses and
19. One gets old early.

Free radicals are also released from other things such as:

- Smoking tobacco
- Air-pollution (like we close windows and doors in the house not allowing fresh air or sunlight to enter).
- Car fumes,
- X-rays,

- Microwaves (i.e. microwave ovens etc.),
- Rays emitting from computer.
- Atmospheric radiation (the process of aeroplane's releasing rays).

Protection from dangerous poison

Allah عَزَّوَجَلَّ has also created the remedy for this dangerous poison called 'Free radicals.' The vegetables or fruits that are green, yellow or orange destroy this dangerous poison. The stronger the colour of these fruits and vegetables is, the more vitamins they contain and the stronger their reaction will be to this poison.

صَلُّوْا عَلَى الْحَبِيْب　　صَلَّى اللهُ تَعَالٰى عَلٰى مُحَمَّد

Reducing harm of fried foods

The harmful effects of fried things can be reduced to some extent by acting upon the following suggestions.

1. Make sure the frying pan or fryer being used to fry different items like omelettes, fish etc. is a 'non-stick' one.
2. After frying the food, wrap it up in an odourless tissue paper so that some amount of oil is absorbed.

Reusing oil

According to experts, the oil which has once been used for frying should not be heated again. If you do want to reuse it then sieve it and store it in a refrigerator, don't store it in the fridge without sieving it.

Medical science is not infallible

All that has been mentioned about fried food is not on the basis of my personal research; medical researchers and experts have provided this information. It is also noteworthy that the entire medical science is fallible.

Fashionable man becomes 'Muballigh of Sunnaĥ'

Dear Islamic brothers! In order to get rid of the greed for eating harmful foods, avoid non-Islamic fashion, adopt the Sunnaĥ and have love of the Beloved and Blessed Prophet صَلَّى اللهُ تَعَالٰى عَلَيْهِ وَاٰلِهٖ وَسَلَّم in your heart. Join the ever-blossoming Madanī environment of Dawat-e-Islami, a global & non-political movement of the Quran and Sunnaĥ. Here is a pleasant and faith-refreshing Madanī incident:

A modern young man of Indor city (M.P. India) was blessed with doing the collective I'tikāf organised by Dawat-e-Islami in the last ten days of the Ramadan in 1426 A.H. The Madanī atmosphere of Dawat-e-Islami and company of devotees of Rasūl caused a Madanī transformation in his heart. He grew his beard and adorned his head with a green turban. He also travelled for 12 days in a Madanī Qāfilaĥ in order to learn Sunnaĥ.

اَلْحَمْدُ لِلّٰه عَزَّوَجَلَّ! He became a Muballigh of Dawat-e-Islami. اَلْحَمْدُ لِلّٰه عَزَّوَجَلَّ! Till the time of writing this account, he is busy serving Dawat-e-Islami in his city as the Nigrān (responsible) of a Ḥalqaĥ Mushāwarat.

صَلُّوْا عَلَى الْحَبِيْب صَلَّى اللهُ تَعَالٰى عَلٰى مُحَمَّد

O Allah عَزَّوَجَلَّ! Accept the I'tikāf of every Islamic brother and Islamic sister, and grant them the blessings of I'tikāf. O Allah عَزَّوَجَلَّ! Bless us too with the privilege of doing I'tikāf.

اٰمِيْن بِجَاهِ النَّبِيِّ الْاَمِيْن صَلَّى اللهُ تَعَالٰى عَلَيْهِ وَاٰلِهٖ وَسَلَّم

صَلُّوْا عَلَى الْحَبِيْب صَلَّى اللهُ تَعَالٰى عَلٰى مُحَمَّد

Excellence of loving Masājid

Sayyidunā Abū Sa'īd Khudrī رَضِیَ اللهُ تَعَالٰی عَنْهُ has narrated the following saying of the Holy Prophet صَلَّی اللهُ تَعَالٰی عَلَیْهِ وَاٰلِهٖ وَسَلَّم: 'Whoever loves Masjid, Allah عَزَّوَجَلَّ loves him.' *(Mu'jam Awsaṭ, Ḥadīš 2379)*

Commenting on the foregoing Ḥadīš, 'Allāmaĥ 'Abdur Raūf Manāwī رَحْمَةُ اللهِ تَعَالٰی عَلَیْه has stated, 'To love the Masjid means doing I'tikāf for the pleasure of Allah عَزَّوَجَلَّ, Żikr and studying Islamic rulings. And love of Allah for the person means Allah عَزَّوَجَلَّ showers His mercy upon him and protects him.' *(Fayḍ-ul-Qadīr, vol. 6, pp. 107)*

Excellence of Looking at Masjid

Sayyidunā 'Abdullāĥ Bin Mas'ūd رَضِیَ اللهُ تَعَالٰی عَنْهُ has narrated that Rasūlullāĥ صَلَّی اللهُ تَعَالٰی عَلَیْهِ وَاٰلِهٖ وَسَلَّم has said, 'Verily, Masājid are the houses of Allah عَزَّوَجَلَّ and Allah عَزَّوَجَلَّ respects the one who looks at His house.' *(Mu'jam Kabīr, vol. 10, pp. 61, Ḥadīš 10324)*

Commenting on the foregoing Ḥadīš, 'Allāmaĥ Abdur Raūf Manāwī رَحْمَةُ اللهِ تَعَالٰی عَلَیْه has stated: It means that Masājid are the places Allah عَزَّوَجَلَّ has chosen for sending His mercy. *(Fayḍ-ul-Qadīr, vol. 2, pp. 552)*

Punishment for laughing in Masjid

Sayyidunā Anas رَضِیَ اللهُ تَعَالٰی عَنْهُ has narrated that the Noble Prophet صَلَّی اللهُ تَعَالٰی عَلَیْهِ وَاٰلِهٖ وَسَلَّم warned, 'To laugh in the Masjid causes darkness in the grave.' *(Firdaus - bimā Šaur-ul-Khaṭṭāb, vol. 2, pp. 431, Ḥadīš 3891)*

Name on gate of Hell

Sayyidunā Abū Sa'īd رَضِیَ اللهُ تَعَالٰی عَنْهُ has narrated that the Noble Prophet صَلَّی اللهُ تَعَالٰی عَلَیْهِ وَاٰلِهٖ وَسَلَّم warned, 'Whoever misses a single Ṣalāĥ deliberately, his name shall be written on the gate of Hell through which he shall enter Hell.' *(Ḥilyat-ul-Auliyā, vol. 7, pp. 299, Ḥadīš 10590)*

Deprived of Heaven

Sayyidunā Ḥużayfaĥ رَضِیَ اللہُ تَعَالٰی عَنْہُ has narrated that the Holy Prophet صَلَّی اللّٰہُ تَعَالٰی عَلَیْہِ وَاٰلِہٖ وَسَلَّم warned, 'The one telling tales will not enter Heaven.' *(Ṣaḥīḥ Bukhārī, pp. 512, Ḥadīš 6056)*

Excellence of repentance

Sayyidunā Ibn Mas'ūd رَضِیَ اللہُ تَعَالٰی عَنْہُ has narrated that the Prophet of mankind, the Peace of our heart and mind, the most Generous and Kind صَلَّی اللہُ تَعَالٰی عَلَیْہِ وَاٰلِہٖ وَسَلَّم has said, 'The one repenting of sin is like the one who has not committed the sin at all.' *(Sunan Ibn Mājaĥ, pp. 2735, Ḥadīš 425)*

Excellence of using Miswāk

Sayyidunā Abū Umāmaĥ رَضِیَ اللہُ تَعَالٰی عَنْہُ has narrated the following saying of the Holy Prophet صَلَّی اللہُ تَعَالٰی عَلَیْہِ وَاٰلِہٖ وَسَلَّم, 'Miswāk is a means of the purification of your mouths and the pleasure of your Rab عَزَّوَجَلَّ.' *(Sunan Ibn Mājaĥ, pp. 2495, Ḥadīš 289)*

صَلُّوْا عَلَی الْحَبِیْب　　صَلَّی اللّٰہُ تَعَالٰی عَلٰی مُحَمَّد

اَلْحَمْدُ لِلّٰهِ رَبِّ الْعٰلَمِيْنَ وَ الصَّلٰوةُ وَ السَّلَامُ عَلٰى سَيِّدِ الْمُرْسَلِيْنَ

اَمَّا بَعْدُ فَاَعُوْذُ بِاللّٰهِ مِنَ الشَّيْطٰنِ الرَّجِيْمِ ؕ بِسْمِ اللّٰهِ الرَّحْمٰنِ الرَّحِيْمِ ؕ

Blessings of Eid-ul-Fitr

Excellence of Ṣalāt-'Alan-Nabī ﷺ

A beggar once begged something from some unbelievers who sent him to Sayyidunā 'Alī كَرَّمَ اللّٰهُ تَعَالٰى وَجْهَهُ الْكَرِيْم that was standing there at a short distance away. The unbelievers did so with the intention of ridiculing Sayyidunā 'Alī كَرَّمَ اللّٰهُ تَعَالٰى وَجْهَهُ الْكَرِيْم. When the beggar asked Sayyidunā 'Alī كَرَّمَ اللّٰهُ تَعَالٰى وَجْهَهُ الْكَرِيْم to give him something, he رَضِیَ اللّٰهُ تَعَالٰی عَنْهُ recited Ṣalāt-'Alan-Nabī ten times and blew on the beggar's hand. Then, ordering the beggar to close his fist and open it in front of the unbelievers, he رَضِیَ اللّٰهُ تَعَالٰی عَنْهُ sent him to them.

The unbelievers were laughing expecting nothing to happen. When the beggar opened his fist, it was surprisingly full of gold dinars! Having seen this great saintly miracle (Karāmaĥ), many unbelievers embraced Islam. *(Rāḥat-ul-Qulūb, pp. 72)*

صَلُّوْا عَلَى الْحَبِيْب   صَلَّى اللّٰهُ تَعَالٰى عَلٰى مُحَمَّد

Dear Islamic brothers! Regarding the sanctity of Ramadan, the Prophet of mankind, the Peace of our heart and mind, the most Generous and Kind صَلَّى اللّٰهُ تَعَالٰى عَلَيْهِ وَاٰلِهٖ وَسَلَّم has said, 'Its first ten days are mercy, the middle ten days are forgiveness and the last ten days are freedom from Hell.' *(Ṣaḥīḥ Ibn Khuzaymaĥ, vol. 3, pp. 191, Ḥadīš 1887)*

We have learnt that Ramadan is the month of mercy, forgiveness and freedom from Hell. Therefore, we have been given the opportunity to celebrate Eid-ul-Fiṭr immediately after the departure of this blessed month. Celebrating Eid is a Mustaḥab act, so we should celebrate the bounties and mercy of Allah عَزَّوَجَلَّ. The Quran also persuades us to rejoice over the bounties and mercy of Allah عَزَّوَجَلَّ, the 58th verse of Sūraĥ Yūnus (part 11) says:

$$\text{قُلْ بِفَضْلِ اللهِ وَبِرَحْمَتِهٖ فَبِذٰلِكَ فَلْيَفْرَحُوْا}$$

Say you, only Allah's grace and only His mercy, on it therefore, let them rejoice.

[Kanz-ul-Īmān (Translation of Quran)] (Part 11, Sūraĥ Yūnus, verse 58)

Why shouldn't we celebrate Eid?

Ramadan is such a blessed and sacred month in which 'The Divine Law' was revealed in the form of the Holy Quran for the betterment, reform, well-being and the eternal salvation of humanity. It is the month in which every Muslim's faith is tested. Therefore, having found a perfect code of life in the form of the Quran and succeeded in the tough exam of a month, it is natural for a Muslim to feel and express happiness.

صَلُّوْا عَلَى الْحَبِيْب   صَلَّى اللهُ تَعَالٰى عَلٰى مُحَمَّد

Announcement of forgiveness for everyone

Dear Islamic brothers! Allah عَزَّوَجَلَّ has bestowed upon us a great bounty in the form of Eid-ul-Fiṭr immediately after Ramadan. This blessed Eid has many virtues. Sayyidunā 'Abdullāĥ Ibn 'Abbās رَضِىَ اللهُ تَعَالٰى عَنْهُمَا has narrated: The blessed night of Eid-ul-Fiṭr is referred to as the 'Layla-tul-Jāizaĥ', the 'Night of Reward.' On the morning of Eid, Allah عَزَّوَجَلَّ sends His angels to every city where they stand at the end of every street and call out, 'O Ummaĥ of Muhammad صَلَّى اللهُ تَعَالٰى عَلَيْهِ وَاٰلِهٖ وَسَلَّم! Come to the court of Beneficent Allah عَزَّوَجَلَّ who grants in abundance and forgives even the most severe sin.'

Allah عَزَّوَجَلَّ then says to His servants, 'O My servants! Ask for whatever you want! I swear by My Honour and Glory! I will grant whatever you ask for about your Hereafter in this gathering (of the Eid-Ṣalāĥ) today. And whatever you want regarding the world; I will see your betterment (i.e. I will do what is best for you). I swear by My honour! I will conceal your mistakes as long as you abide by my commandments. I swear by My Honour, I will not humiliate you with the sinners; so return to your homes, forgiven. You have pleased Me and I am pleased with you.' *(Attarghīb Wattarĥīb, vol. 2, pp. 60, Ḥadīš 23)*

Night of receiving Eid gift

سُبْحٰنَ اللہ عَزَّوَجَلَّ! Dear Islamic brothers! How kind our Merciful Allah عَزَّوَجَلَّ is to us! He showers His mercy upon us in the whole month of Ramadan and then, He عَزَّوَجَلَّ grants us the happiness of the Eid as soon as this blessed month ends.

According to the foregoing sacred Ḥadīš, the night of Eid-ul-Fiṭr is also called 'Layla-tul-Jāizaĥ', or the 'Night of Reward' in which the pious are given their reward. In other words, they are given their 'Eid Gift.'

Heart will remain alive

The Beloved and Blessed Prophet صَلَّى اللهُ تَعَالٰى عَلَيْهِ وَاٰلِهٖ وَسَلَّم has said, 'Whoever stood (to offer Ṣalāĥ) in the nights of Eid (Eid-ul-Fiṭr and Eid-ul-Aḍḥā) in order to earn reward, his heart will not die on the day when hearts (of people) will die.' *(Sunan Ibn Mājaĥ, vol. 2, pp. 365, Ḥadīš 1782)*

Entry into heaven becomes Wājib

Sayyidunā Mu'āż Bin Jabal رَضِیَ اللّٰہُ تَعَالٰی عَنْہُ has said, The one spending the following five nights worshipping Allah عَزَّوَجَلَّ, Heaven becomes Wājib for him: the nights of the 8th, 9th and 10th Żul-Ḥijjaĥ (3 nights), the night of Eid-ul-Fiṭr and the 15th night of Sha'bān (Shab-e-Barā-at). *(Attarghīb Wattarĥīb, vol. 2, pp. 98, Ḥadīš 2)*

According to the Ḥadīš narrated by Sayyidunā 'Abdullāĥ Ibn 'Abbās رَضِیَ اللّٰہُ تَعَالٰی عَنْہُمَا 'On the day of Eid, the angels make announcement of divine bounties. Allah عَزَّوَجَلَّ showers His mercy and blessing upon people. He عَزَّوَجَلَّ forgives the people that gather for the Eid Ṣalāĥ. Moreover, it is also announced that whoever desires goodness in worldly life and in the afterlife should ask for it, his desires will surely be satisfied.

If only we learn what to ask for on such sacred occasions when the prayers are likely to be answered! Usually, people ask for the worldly betterment, success, blessing in their sustenance and other worldly benefits only. Besides worldly betterment, we should do ask for the betterment and goodness of our Hereafter, steadfastness of our faith, death in the state of faith in Madīnah̄ at the feet of the Holy Prophet صَلَّى اللّٰهُ تَعَالٰى عَلَيْهِ وَاٰلِهٖ وَسَلَّم in the form of martyrdom, burial in Jannat-ul-Baqī' and neighbourhood of Beloved Rasūl صَلَّى اللّٰهُ تَعَالٰى عَلَيْهِ وَاٰلِهٖ وَسَلَّم in Jannat-ul-Firdaus without being held accountable.

No one is disappointed

Dear Islamic brothers! Ponder! How important the day of Eid-ul-Fiṭr is! It is the day of divine mercy; no one is disappointed. On one hand, the pious people of Allah عَزَّوَجَلَّ rejoice over mercy, forgiveness and blessing, while, on the other hand, the worst enemy of mankind, Satan burns in the fire of fury when he sees the believers being blessed with the huge bounties of Allah عَزَّوَجَلَّ.

Satan loses his senses

Sayyidunā Wah̄b Bin Munabbeh̄ رَضِیَ اللّٰهُ تَعَالٰى عَنْه has said, 'Satan screams and cries on the occasion of Eid every year. Seeing him cry, other Satans gather around him and ask, 'O Master! Why are you so furious and disappointed today?' He replies, 'Regretfully, Allah عَزَّوَجَلَّ has forgiven the Ummah̄ of Muhammad صَلَّى اللّٰهُ تَعَالٰى عَلَيْهِ وَاٰلِهٖ وَسَلَّم today, so make them indulge in satisfying their carnal desires.' *(Mukāshafa-tul-Qulūb, pp. 308)*

Has Satan succeeded?

Dear Islamic brothers! Did you see that the day of Eid is so tough for Satan that he orders his offspring to make the Muslims indulge in satisfying their carnal desires? Alas! These days, Satan seems to have succeeded in his mission. On the day of Eid, we should be thanking Allah عَزَّوَجَلَّ by worshipping Him in abundance, but unfortunately, it appears the Muslims have been unaware of the actual concept of Eid. Nowadays, Eid is celebrated by wearing attractive clothes of the latest fashion, and even the clothes bearing the images of living creatures are put on. [It is stated in *Bah̄ār-e-Sharī'at* that offering Ṣalāh̄ wearing such clothes that have images of animals or humans is Makrūh̄ Taḥrīmī (close to Ḥarām). It is Wājib to change such clothes or wear something over them and repeat the Ṣalāh̄. To wear clothes with images of living creatures is prohibited even when not offering Ṣalāh̄. *(Bah̄ār-e-Sharī'at, part 3, pp. 141-142)*

Further, dance-parties are held, different useless and time-wasting fairs and games are arranged in the name of enjoyment, films and dramas are watched at homes and cinemas, and a lot of time and wealth is wasted on such activities that are in contradiction to Sharī'aĥ and Sunnaĥ.

Dear Islamic brothers! These unlawful actions may turn this blessed Eid into a day of warning for the ungrateful. For the sake of Allah عَزَّوَجَلَّ! Have pity on you and give up fashion. Never waste money as Allah عَزَّوَجَلَّ has declared the spendthrift as the brothers of Satan. Therefore, the 26th and 27th verses of Sūraĥ Banī Isrāīl, part 15 say:

وَلَا تُبَذِّرۡ تَبۡذِيۡرًا ﴿۲۶﴾ اِنَّ الۡمُبَذِّرِيۡنَ كَانُوۡۤا اِخۡوَانَ الشَّيٰطِيۡنِ ؕ وَكَانَ الشَّيۡطٰنُ لِرَبِّهٖ كَفُوۡرًا ﴿۲۷﴾

And spend not extravagantly. No doubt, the spendthrifts are the brothers of the devils (Satan). And the devil is very ungrateful to his Rab عَزَّوَجَلَّ.

[Kanz-ul-Īmān (Translation of Quran)] (Part 15, Sūraĥ Banī Isrāīl, verse 26, 27)

Difference between human and animal

Dear Islamic brothers! The foregoing verse has made it clear that the Holy Quran strictly condemns the waste of money. Remember! No one can please Allah عَزَّوَجَلَّ by wasting money. The distinguishing factor between humans and animals is wisdom, strategy and far-sightedness. Unlike humans, animals aren't concerned about their 'future', and none of their actions is based on wisdom which has not naturally been granted to them. On the contrary, humans are concerned about their future, and Muslims are concerned about the Hereafter as well. Thus, the one making efforts for the betterment of the Hereafter with proper strategies is, in fact, a wise person, but unfortunately, no effort is made for the betterment of the Hereafter taking advantage of this mortal and transient world. Nowadays, earning wealth, eating excessively and then, sleeping deeply seem to have become people's aim of life.

What is aim of life?

Dear Islamic brothers! The aim of life isn't just to get high degrees, eat, drink and make merry. Instead, there is a very great and sacred aim of our life. Let's ask the Holy Quran,

O the True Book of Allah عَزَّوَجَلَّ! Please guide and tell us what the aim of our life and death is. The Holy Quran answers:

خَلَقَ الْمَوْتَ وَ الْحَيٰوةَ لِيَبْلُوَكُمْ اَيُّكُمْ اَحْسَنُ عَمَلًا ؕ

He عَزَّوَجَلَّ, Who has created death and life that He عَزَّوَجَلَّ might test you, as to whose work, is excellent among you.

[Kanz-ul-Īmān (Translation of Quran)] (Part 29, Sūraĥ Al-Mulk, verse 2)

Therefore, the creation of life and death is aimed at testing humans as to who the more obedient and sincere is.

Delivery at home

Dear Islamic brothers! In order to defend yourself against the attack of Satan, please spend the sacred moments of Eid in the company of the Rasūl's devotees with a Madanī Qāfilaĥ. A true account is presented for your persuasion: An Islamic brother from Jhelum (Punjab, Pakistan) has stated that his wife became pregnant nearly 6 months after the marriage. The doctor expressed serious concern over the case due to the lack of blood in her body, which might lead to a caesarean (an operation). The Islamic brother immediately made the intention of travelling with a Madanī Qāfilaĥ for 30 days. After a few days, he travelled with the Madanī Qāfilaĥ acting upon his intention. اَلْحَمْدُ لِلّٰه عَزَّوَجَلَّ! With the blessings of the Madanī Qāfilaĥ, a baby boy was safely born at his house without any operation.

صَلُّوْا عَلَی الْحَبِیْب   صَلَّی اللّٰهُ تَعَالٰی عَلٰی مُحَمَّد

Two spiritual cures for protection of pregnancy

1. Write لَآ اِلٰهَ اِلَّا اللّٰه 11 times on a bowl (or paper), pour water into it, shake the water and then make the woman drink it. اِنْ شَآءَاللّٰه عَزَّوَجَلَّ This will protect her pregnancy. This method is also beneficial to the woman who produces less milk or no milk at

all. It's allowed whether to act upon this method only one day or makes her drink water for many days acting upon the whole process everyday.

2. Write يَـا حَيُّ يَـا قَـيُّومُ 111 times on a piece of paper and tie it to the stomach of the pregnant woman. Let it remain tied to her stomach until she gives birth (there's no harm in taking it off for a short while, if necessary). اِنْ شَــآءَاللّٰه عَزَّوَجَلَّ Her pregnancy will remain safe and a healthy baby will be born.

Eid or Wa'īd (warning)

Dear Islamic brothers! Sins may well turn the day of Eid in to a day of 'Wa'īd' (warning), which may result in the sinner being punished.

Remember:

لَيْسَ الْعِيْدُ لِمَنْ لَّبِسَ الْجَدِيْد اِنَّمَا الْعِيْدُ لِمَنْ خَافَ الْوَعِيْد

Eid isn't for the one wearing new clothes;
Instead, Eid is for the one fearing the divine retribution.

The way in which Auliyā رَحِمَهُمُ اللّٰهُ تَعَالٰی would celebrate Eid

Dear Islamic brothers! There is a world of difference between today's Muslim's way of celebrating Eid and that of Auliyā. Allah عَزَّوَجَلَّ forbid, these days, people regard that wearing new clothes and eating delicious foods is all about Eid whereas our respected Auliyā رَحِمَهُمُ اللّٰهُ تَعَالٰی would avoid luxuries of the world and would always oppose their Nafs.

Special food on Eid

Sayyidunā Żunnūn Miṣrī رَحْمَةُ اللّٰهِ تَعَالٰی عَلَيْه had not eaten any delicious thing for ten years despite his Nafs' prolonged desire. He رَحْمَةُ اللّٰهِ تَعَالٰی عَلَيْه would often turn down his Nafs' demand. Once, on the sacred night of Eid, his heart suggested that he eat something delicious on the day of Eid. Putting his heart to the test, he رَحْمَةُ اللّٰهِ تَعَالٰی عَلَيْه replied, 'First I'll recite the entire Quran in two Rak'āt of Ṣalāĥ. O my heart! If you support me in doing so, then I'll eat something delicious tomorrow.'

Therefore, he رَحْمَةُ الله تَعَالٰى عَلَيْه succeeded in reciting the whole Quran in two Rak'āt with concentration on Eid and brought delicious food afterwards. As he picked up a morsel and was about to eat it, he suddenly became anxious and put it down without eating. When he was asked about it, he رَحْمَةُ الله تَعَالٰى عَلَيْه replied: 'As I was about to eat the food, my Nafs said to me triumphantly, 'At last, I've succeeded in satisfying my 10 year-long desire.' Listening to it, I became anxious and replied, 'If it's so, then I will never let you succeed and I will never eat the delicious food.'

Meanwhile, a man entered the house along with a tray of delicious food and said, 'I prepared this food last night for me. When I slept, my sleeping fate awoke. I was blessed with the vision of the Noble Rasūl صَلَّى اللهُ تَعَالٰى عَلَيْهِ وَاٰلِهٖ وَسَلَّم in my dream. The Holy Prophet صَلَّى اللهُ تَعَالٰى عَلَيْهِ وَاٰلِهٖ وَسَلَّم ordered, 'If you want to see me on the Day of Judgement as well, take this food to Żunnūn رَحْمَةُ الله تَعَالٰى عَلَيْه and say to him, 'Muhammad Bin 'Abdullāĥ Bin 'Abdul Muṭṭalib صَلَّى اللهُ تَعَالٰى عَلَيْهِ وَاٰلِهٖ وَسَلَّم has said, 'Have reconciliation with your Nafs for a moment and eat a few morsels of this delicious food.' Listening to the order of the Beloved Rasūl صَلَّى اللهُ تَعَالٰى عَلَيْهِ وَاٰلِهٖ وَسَلَّم, Sayyidunā Żunnūn Miṣrī رَحْمَةُ الله تَعَالٰى عَلَيْه immediately started eating the food saying emotionally, 'I am obedient, I am obedient.' *(Tażkira-tul-Auliyā, pp. 117)*

May Allah عَزَّوَجَلَّ have mercy on him and forgive us without accountability for his sake!

صَلُّوْا عَلَى الْحَبِيْب صَلَّى اللهُ تَعَالٰى عَلٰى مُحَمَّد

Our Beloved Rasūl صَلَّى اللهُ تَعَالٰى عَلَيْهِ وَاٰلِهٖ وَسَلَّم feeds us

Dear Islamic brothers! Did you see the pious people of Allah عَزَّوَجَلَّ did not follow their Nafs even on the day of Eid? They did not care about carnal desires and would always remain contented with the will of Allah عَزَّوَجَلَّ. They would avoid the luxuries of this worldly life for the pleasure of Allah عَزَّوَجَلَّ and His Beloved and Blessed Prophet صَلَّى اللهُ تَعَالٰى عَلَيْهِ وَاٰلِهٖ وَسَلَّم. These fortunate people are specially fed by Allah عَزَّوَجَلَّ and His Beloved and Blessed Prophet صَلَّى اللهُ تَعَالٰى عَلَيْهِ وَاٰلِهٖ وَسَلَّم

We have also learnt from this narration that the Prophet of mankind, the Peace of our heart and mind, the most Generous and Kind صَلَّى اللهُ تَعَالٰى عَلَيْهِ وَاٰلِهٖ وَسَلَّم is aware of the state of his

Ummaĥ even today. He صَلَّى اللهُ تَعَالٰى عَلَيْهِ وَاٰلِهٖ وَسَلَّم was watching his beloved servant Sayyidunā Żunnūn Miṣrī عَلَيْهِ رَحْمَةُ اللّٰهِ الْقَوِى, which is why he صَلَّى اللهُ تَعَالٰى عَلَيْهِ وَاٰلِهٖ وَسَلَّم sent one of his servants along with food and message for Sayyidunā Żunnūn Miṣrī عَلَيْهِ رَحْمَةُ اللّٰهِ الْقَوِى.

Sarkār kĥilātay ĥayn Sarkār pilātay ĥayn
Sultan-o-gadā sab ko Sarkār nibĥātay ĥayn

The Prophet provides for us
And is a great guide for us

Beautify your soul

Dear Islamic brothers! No doubt, having a bath, wearing new or washed clothes and applying 'Iṭr (pure perfume) on Eid all are sacred Sunnaĥs whereby we get the purification of our external body. In addition to this external purification and beauty, we should purify and beautify our souls as well with love and obedience to the Holy Prophet صَلَّى اللهُ تَعَالٰى عَلَيْهِ وَاٰلِهٖ وَسَلَّم and our Merciful Creator عَزَّوَجَلَّ who love us more than even our parents.

Cover of silver foil on filth!

Dear Islamic brothers! Please ponder! If somebody disobeyed Allah عَزَّوَجَلَّ in Ramadan instead of worshipping Him, missed all the fasts, spent the blessed nights partying, playing or watching games such as cricket, table football, video games, reading romantic novels instead of reciting the Holy Quran, listening to songs instead of Na'ats, and messing around the whole month, and then, he celebrates Eid by wearing English dress, it is just like covering impurity in silver paper and putting it on display.

Who deserves Eid celebration?

O devotees of Rasūl! In fact, the fortunate Muslims spending the sacred month of Ramadan fasting, offering Ṣalāĥ and doing other worships deserve the celebration of Eid which is a day of reward for them from Allah عَزَّوَجَلَّ. As for us, we should fear Allah عَزَّوَجَلَّ as we could not properly carry out worship even in this sacred month.

Eid of Sayyidunā 'Umar Fārūq A'ẓam رَضِىَ اللهُ عَنْهُ

On the day of Eid, some people came to the house of Sayyidunā 'Umar Fārūq A'ẓam رَضِىَ اللهُ تَعَالٰى عَنْهُ to meet and greet him, but the door was closed and the sound of crying was emanating from the house. When the door opened, they asked surprisingly, 'O Amīr-ul-Mūminīn رَضِىَ اللهُ تَعَالٰى عَنْهُ! Today is Eid and every one is delighted, why are you crying?' He رَضِىَ اللهُ تَعَالٰى عَنْهُ replied wiping his tears:

هٰذَا يَوْمُ الْعِيْدِ وَ هٰذَا يَوْمُ الْوَعِيْد

O People! This is the day of Eid (celebration) as well as the day of Wa'īd (warning).

Indeed, this is Eid for the one whose Ṣalāĥ and fasts have been accepted, but it is the day of Wa'īd (warning) for the one whose Ṣalāĥ and fasts have been rejected and thrown onto his face, and I am crying because:

اَنَا لَا اَدْرِیْ اَ مِنَ الْمَقْبُوْلِیْنَ اَمْ مِنَ الْمَطْرُوْدِیْنَ

I do not know whether my worship has been accepted or rejected.

Eid kay din 'Umar yeĥ raw raw kar
Baulay naykaun kī Eid ĥotī ĥay

'The righteous deserve celebrating Eid'
Was the saying of 'Umar, on the day of Eid

May Allah عَزَّوَجَلَّ have mercy on him and forgive us without accountability for his sake!

Our wishful thinking

اَللهُ اَكْبَر! Ponder! Fārūq A'ẓam رَضِىَ اللهُ تَعَالٰى عَنْهُ is one of the only ten fortunate companions who were blessed, during their life, with the glad tidings of entering the Heaven by the owner of Heaven صَلَّى اللهُ تَعَالٰى عَلَيْهِ وَاٰلِهٖ وَسَلَّم. He رَضِىَ اللهُ تَعَالٰى عَنْهُ was found crying on the day of Eid just for fear of his worships being rejected.

سُبْحٰنَ اللّٰه عَزَّوَجَلَّ! The one who absolutely deserved the celebration of Eid cried fearfully, on the other hand, we talkative, inactive and heedless people who are unable to carry out any worship properly, leave no stone unturned to boast about our so-called 'piety.' Those who unnecessarily reveal their worships such as Ṣalāĥ, fasts, Hajj, services to the Masjid and people etc. should particularly take some lesson from this heart-rending parable. Such people get the news of their social work published in the newspaper along with even their photograph. It seems extremely difficult to change their self-liking frame of mind and make them realize that unnecessarily revealing one's good deeds may, in some cases, result in the ruin of the good deeds, and in ostentation which may lead to damnation of Hell. Remember! Having photos willingly taken and published in the newspaper is Ḥarām.

May Allah عَزَّوَجَلَّ protect all the Muslims from ostentation, boasting and showing off!

آمِيْن بِجَاهِ النَّبِيِّ الْاَمِيْن صَلَّى اللهُ تَعَالٰى عَلَيْهِ وَاٰلِهٖ وَسَلَّم

صَلُّوْا عَلَى الْحَبِيْب صَلَّى اللهُ تَعَالٰى عَلٰى مُحَمَّد

Prince's Eid

Once on the day of Eid, Sayyidunā 'Umar Fārūq A'ẓam رَضِیَ اللهُ تَعَالٰی عَنْهُ saw his son in an old shirt. Saddened by his son's apparent poor condition, he رَضِیَ اللهُ تَعَالٰی عَنْهُ began to cry. Seeing his father crying, his son asked, 'Dear Father! Why are you crying?' He رَضِیَ اللهُ تَعَالٰی عَنْهُ replied, 'My son! I'm afraid, your heart will break when the other boys see you in old clothes today on the occasion of Eid.' His son replied, 'Dear father! The heart of the one who disobeys Allah عَزَّوَجَلَّ and one's parents should break; I am hopeful that Allah عَزَّوَجَلَّ will also be pleased with me because you are pleased with me.' When Sayyidunā 'Umar رَضِیَ اللهُ تَعَالٰی عَنْهُ listened to it, he رَضِیَ اللهُ تَعَالٰی عَنْهُ embraced his son and prayed for him. *(Mukāshafa-tul-Qulūb, pp. 308)*

May Allah عَزَّوَجَلَّ have mercy on them and forgive us without accountability for their sake!

Eid of princesses

The daughters of Sayyidunā 'Umar Bin 'Abdul 'Azīz رَضِیَ اللهُ تَعَالٰی عَنْهُ came to him a day before Eid and said, 'Father! Which clothes are we going to wear tomorrow on Eid?' He رَضِیَ اللهُ تَعَالٰی عَنْهُ

replied, 'The same clothes you are wearing right now, wash them and wear them tomorrow again.' 'No dear father! Buy new clothes for us' the girls insisted. He رضی اللہ تعالٰی عنہ said, 'My dear daughters! Eid is the day when we are supposed to worship and thank Allah عَزَّوَجَلَّ; wearing new clothes isn't necessary.' 'You're right father but our friends will taunt us saying that you are wearing the same old cloths even on Eid despite being the daughters of Amīr-ul-Mūminīn رضی اللہ تعالٰی عنہ!'

Saying so, the girls then began to cry. Compelled by his daughters' feelings, Sayyidunā 'Umar Bin 'Abdul 'Azīz رضی اللہ تعالٰی عنہ called and asked the treasurer to give him a month's salary in advance, but he refused to do so saying 'Sir! Are you sure that you will remain alive for another month?' He رضی اللہ تعالٰی عنہ thanked and prayed for the treasurer who then left without giving money. Then, he رضی اللہ تعالٰی عنہ said to his daughters, 'My dear daughters! Sacrifice your desires for the pleasure of Allah عَزَّوَجَلَّ and His Beloved Rasūl صَلَّى اللهُ تَعَالٰى عَلَيْهِ وَاٰلِهٖ وَسَلَّم.' *(Ma'dan-e-Akhlāq, part 1, pp. 257-258)*

May Allah عَزَّوَجَلَّ have mercy on him and forgive us without accountability for his sake!

Wearing new clothes on Eid isn't necessary

Dear Islamic brothers! It became obvious from the previous two parables that wearing fancy clothes on Eid is not necessary; Eid can be celebrated even without them.

اَللّٰہ اَکْبَر! How poor Sayyidunā 'Umar Bin 'Abdul 'Azīz رضی اللہ تعالٰی عنہ was! He didn't save money at all despite being the ruler of such an enormous empire. Further, his treasurer was also an honest and far-sighted person who wisely refused to pay him a month's salary in advance.

This parable contains a lesson for us as well. If we ever want to ask for our salary in advance, we should also consider as to whether or not we will remain alive till the particular period of time for which we are demanding our salary in advance. Even if we do remain alive, there is no guarantee that we will remain healthy and fit enough to work as it's often observed that a person suddenly suffers from a lethal disease or becomes injured as a result of an accident. If we have a Madanī frame of mind, we will get cautious about such matters.

In order to develop a Madanī mindset, please travel with Madanī Qāfilaĥs of Dawat-e-Islami. There are great blessings of Madanī Qāfilaĥs! A Madanī blessing which took place during a Madanī Qāfilaĥs is now presented:

Deceased father was blessed

An Islamic brother from Nishtar Basti (Bāb-ul-Madīnaĥ, Karachi) gave the following account: Once I had a dream in which I saw my deceased father in an extremely weak condition. He was wearing no clothes and walking with someone else's support. I got worried. Therefore, I intended to travel with Madanī Qāfilaĥs for three days every month with the intention of Īṣāl-e-Šawāb for my father. I began journeys regularly. Three months later, having returned from a Madanī Qāfilaĥ, when I went to sleep, I had a dream in which I saw my father again. This time, I found him smiling, dressed in a green garment. A light rain was also showering on him.

اَلْحَمْدُلِلّٰہ عَزَّوَجَلَّ! The importance of travelling with Madanī Qāfilaĥs became even more evident to me and now I am determined to continue travelling for three days every month with Rasūl's devotees – اِنْ شَآءَاللّٰہ عَزَّوَجَلَّ.

صَلُّوْا عَلَی الْحَبِیْب صَلَّی اللّٰهُ تَعَالٰی عَلٰی مُحَمَّد

Dear Islamic brothers! Did you see how the fortunate son made an excellent decision to travel with Madanī Qāfilaĥs in sympathy of his deceased father and what a brilliant blessing of the Madanī Qāfilaĥ took place? According to the scholars who interpret dreams (Mu'abbirīn), 'No one can tell a lie in Barzakh (the period from death to resurrection). A deceased person cannot give a false news in dream. They have further said that seeing a deceased person in dream in the state of sickness, weakness or anger indicates punishment, whereas seeing him in a white or green garment indicates that he is happy.'

صَلُّوْا عَلَی الْحَبِیْب صَلَّی اللّٰهُ تَعَالٰی عَلٰی مُحَمَّد

Are all dreams believable?

Dear Islamic brothers! Good dreams are certainly good. Remember! A Prophet's dream is based on revelation (Waḥī) but the dream of a non-Prophet does not have such credibility and his dream is not regarded as proof. For example, if somebody dreamt that the Holy Prophet صَلَّى اللهُ تَعَالٰى عَلَيْهِ وَاٰلِهٖ وَسَلَّم gave him the glad tidings of entering the Heaven, we cannot still declare that the dreaming person will surely enter the Heaven just on the basis of his dream. No doubt, whoever sees the Holy Prophet صَلَّى اللهُ تَعَالٰى عَلَيْهِ وَاٰلِهٖ وَسَلَّم in a dream has definitely seen him because the devil cannot appear in the form of Rasūlullāĥ صَلَّى اللهُ تَعَالٰى عَلَيْهِ وَاٰلِهٖ وَسَلَّم and whatever he صَلَّى اللهُ تَعَالٰى عَلَيْهِ وَاٰلِهٖ وَسَلَّم says in the dream is doubtlessly true. However, there is a possibility of mishearing and misunderstanding as a person's senses are weak in dream.

Therefore, one must refer to the ruling of Sharī'aĥ before carrying out the order given in the dream. If the command given in the dream does not contradict Sharī'aĥ, it can be fulfilled, still it is not Wājib to do so. On the other hand, if it contradicts Sharī'aĥ, then it will not be carried out at all. This issue can further be elaborated with the help of the following account:

Was he commanded to drink alcohol or abstain from it?

A'lā Ḥaḍrat Imām-e-Aĥl-e-Sunnat, reviver of Sunnaĥ, eradicator of Bid'aĥ, scholar of Sharī'aĥ, guide of Ṭarīqaĥ, 'Allāmaĥ Maulānā Al-Ḥāj Al-Ḥāfiẓ Al-Qārī Ash-Shāĥ Imām Aḥmad Razā Khān عَلَيْهِ رَحْمَةُ الرَّحْمٰن has stated, 'Once a man dreamt that the Prophet of Raḥmaĥ, the Intercessor of Ummaĥ صَلَّى اللهُ تَعَالٰى عَلَيْهِ وَاٰلِهٖ وَسَلَّم ordered him to drink alcohol (Allah عَزَّوَجَلَّ forbid). The dreaming person consulted Sayyidunā Imām Ja'far Ṣādiq عَلَيْهِ رَحْمَةُ اللهِ الرَّازِق about the interpretation of the dream. Imām Ja'far Ṣādiq عَلَيْهِ رَحْمَةُ اللهِ الرَّازِق said, 'The Noble Rasūl صَلَّى اللهُ تَعَالٰى عَلَيْهِ وَاٰلِهٖ وَسَلَّم prohibited you from drinking alcohol; you misheard.'

Remember! The sinners and the pious are equal in this matter. In other words, a pious person's dream will not necessarily be considered true just because of his piety. Similarly, a sinner's dream will not necessarily be considered unreliable because of his sins. The criterion for true and false dreams has already been explained. *(Derived from Fatāwā Razawiyyaĥ (Jadīd), vol. 5, pp. 100)*

Eid of Ghauš-e-A'ẓam رَحْمَةُ اللهِ عَلَيْه

There is a great lesson for us in each and every act of Auliyā of Allah. اَلْحَمْدُ لِلّٰه عَزَّوَجَلّ! Our Ghauš-e-A'ẓam رَحْمَةُ اللّٰهِ تَعَالٰى عَلَيْه is a great Walī of Allah عَزَّوَجَلّ, but still he expressed fear and humility on the occasion of Eid for our guidance. Therefore, he said in his Persian couplets:

Khalq gawīd keh fardā Rauz-e-Eid ast
Khūshī darrūḥ-e-ĥar Momin padīd ast
Darān rauzay keh bā-Īmān bamīram
Mirā dar mulk khud-ān Rauz-e-Eid ast

'People are saying 'Tomorrow is Eid! Tomorrow is Eid!' and everyone is happy, but the day when I leave this world with my faith will actually be the day of Eid for me.'

سُبْحٰنَ اللّٰه عَزَّوَجَلّ! Look at his piety and asceticism! He holds an extremely great status, and is the sovereign of all Auliyā رَحِمَهُمُ اللّٰهُ تَعَالٰى yet so humble! There is a warning here for us, and we are being taught, 'Beware! Don't be heedless regarding your faith; always remain concerned about its safety lest you lose your faith due to your heedlessness and sins.'

Razā kā khātimaĥ bil-khayr ĥogā
Agar raḥmat tayrī shāmil ĥay Yā Ghauš

Razā will have a good end
If the mercy of Ghauš, he gains

(Ḥadāiq-e-Bakhshish)

صَلُّوْا عَلَى الْحَبِيْب صَلَّى اللّٰهُ تَعَالٰى عَلٰى مُحَمَّد

Eid of a Walī

Sayyidunā Shaykh Najībuddīn رَحْمَةُ اللّٰهِ تَعَالٰى عَلَيْه Mutawakkil is the brother and caliph of Sayyidunā Shaykh Farīduddīn Ganj Shakar رَحْمَةُ اللّٰهِ تَعَالٰى عَلَيْه, his title is Mutawakkil (*the one trusting Allah* عَزَّوَجَلّ). He رَحْمَةُ اللّٰهِ تَعَالٰى عَلَيْه lived in the city for seventy years and his family led a very comfortable life despite having no apparent means of sustenance. He رَحْمَةُ اللّٰهِ تَعَالٰى عَلَيْه

remained so engrossed in the remembrance of Allah عَزَّوَجَلَّ that he رَحْمَةُ اللهِ تَعَالٰی عَلَيْه didn't even know what day or month was, and he didn't even know what the worth of a coin was.

Once many guests came to his house on the day of Eid. Coincidentally, there was no food at his home to serve the guests. He رَحْمَةُ اللهِ تَعَالٰی عَلَيْه went to the upstairs where he رَحْمَةُ اللهِ تَعَالٰی عَلَيْه remembered Allah عَزَّوَجَلَّ and prayed in his heart in this way, 'Yā Allah عَزَّوَجَلَّ! Today is Eid and guests have come to my house.' Suddenly a man appeared and presented a tray full of food and said, 'O Najībuddīn رَحْمَةُ اللهِ تَعَالٰی عَلَيْه! You are famous for your trust (Tawakkul) even among angels, and you are asking for food!' He رَحْمَةُ اللهِ تَعَالٰی عَلَيْه said, 'Allah عَزَّوَجَلَّ knows that I didn't do so for myself, but for my guests.'

Despite possessing saintly miracle, Sayyidunā Najībuddīn Mutawakkil رَحْمَةُ اللهِ تَعَالٰی عَلَيْه was extremely humble. Once a man came to meet him travelling a long distance and asked 'Are you Najībuddīn Mutawakkil?' He رَحْمَةُ اللهِ تَعَالٰی عَلَيْه humbly replied, 'I'm Najībuddīn Mutāakkil (*the one eating a lot*).' *(Akhbār-ul-Akhyār, pp. 60)*

May Allah عَزَّوَجَلَّ have mercy on him and forgive us without accountability for his sake!

A form of saintly miracle (Karāmaĥ)

Dear Islamic brothers! Did you see how simply and humbly righteous people would celebrate Eid? We have also learnt from this parable that Allah عَزَّوَجَلَّ satisfies the needs of His friends from Ghayb. These are all manifestations of His mercy. The sudden availability of food, drink and other necessities of life without any apparent means are a type of saintly miracle. This form of saintly miracle has also been mentioned in the book '*Sharḥ 'Aqāid-e-Nasafiyyaĥ*' which contains a thorough account about different types of saintly miracles. The Auliyā رَحِمَهُمُ اللهُ تَعَالٰی have divinely-given powers and saintly miracles. They are so great and pious people that Allah عَزَّوَجَلَّ fulfils whatever they say or desire.

Eid of generous man

Sayyidunā 'Abdur Raḥmān Bin 'Amr Al-Awzā'ī رَحْمَةُ اللهِ تَعَالٰی عَلَيْه has stated, 'On the night of Eid-ul-Fiṭr, one of my neighbours who was very poor came to my home and requested me to give him some money so that he may celebrate Eid happily with his family.

Consulting my wife, I asked her, 'Should I give him the only twenty five dirhams I have saved to meet the needs of our family on the occasion of Eid? Allah عَزَّوَجَلَّ will give us more.' My pious wife suggested that I help the destitute neighbour, so I gave him the twenty five dirhams. Extremely delighted he went making Du'ā for us.

Shortly after his departure, another person came and held my feet, and told me crying that he was my father's escaped slave. He further said that he had returned because his conscience pricked him. Offering me the twenty five dinars which he had earned, he requested me to accept them. Accepting the dinars, I freed him. I then said to my wife, 'Look (the Mercy of Allah عَزَّوَجَلَّ)! He has given us dinars in exchange for dirham.' (In the past, silver coins used to be called dirham while gold ones used to be called dinars).

May Allah عَزَّوَجَلَّ have mercy on them and forgive us without accountability for their sake!

صَلُّوْا عَلَى الْحَبِيْب صَلَّى اللّٰهُ تَعَالٰى عَلٰى مُحَمَّد

Salām upon one who helped the needy

Dear Islamic brothers! Did you see how Merciful and Beneficent Allah عَزَّوَجَلَّ is! Look! How He عَزَّوَجَلَّ instantly rewarded twenty five dinar to the one who gave twenty five dirham in His path. Further, we have also learnt that Auliyā رَحِمَهُمُ اللّٰهُ تَعَالٰى were extremely self-sacrificing, they would make sacrifice wholeheartedly for other Muslims. They had extreme love for Allah عَزَّوَجَلَّ and His Beloved and Blessed Prophet صَلَّى اللّٰهُ تَعَالٰى عَلَيْهِ وَاٰلِهٖ وَسَلَّم. They knew that Islam teaches us the message of mutual sympathy and cooperation. The Holy Prophet صَلَّى اللّٰهُ تَعَالٰى عَلَيْهِ وَاٰلِهٖ وَسَلَّم is mercy for the whole world, he صَلَّى اللّٰهُ تَعَالٰى عَلَيْهِ وَاٰلِهٖ وَسَلَّم blesses everyone. He صَلَّى اللّٰهُ تَعَالٰى عَلَيْهِ وَاٰلِهٖ وَسَلَّم would take special care of the poor, needy and orphans.

سُبْحٰنَ اللّٰه عَزَّوَجَلَّ! He صَلَّى اللّٰهُ تَعَالٰى عَلَيْهِ وَاٰلِهٖ وَسَلَّم is so great that he is the most respectable after Allah عَزَّوَجَلَّ and so humble that he صَلَّى اللّٰهُ تَعَالٰى عَلَيْهِ وَاٰلِهٖ وَسَلَّم would help even the one everyone had left alone.

صَلُّوْا عَلَى الْحَبِيْب صَلَّى اللّٰهُ تَعَالٰى عَلٰى مُحَمَّد

Power of hearing regained

Dear Islamic brothers! In order to light the candle of love and reverence for the Holy Prophet صَلَّى اللهُ تَعَالٰى عَلَيْهِ وَاٰلِهٖ وَسَلَّم in your heart and gain the true happiness of Eid, if possible, please travel with Sunnaĥ-Inspiring Madanī Qāfilaĥ of Dawat-e-Islami, a global & non-political religious movement of the Quran and Sunnaĥ, on the night of Eid in the company of Rasūl's devotees.

There are countless blessings of Madanī Qāfilaĥs. Therefore, an Islamic brother from Bāb-ul-Madīnaĥ Karachi gave the following account: A deaf Islamic brother attended the three day Sunnaĥ-Inspiring Ijtimā' of Dawat-e-Islami held in Quetta and travelled with a three day Madanī Qāfilaĥ afterwards in the company of the Rasūl's devotees to learn the Sunnaĥ. اَلْحَمْدُ لِلّٰه عَزَّوَجَلَّ! He regained his power of hearing during the blessed journey and he could now hear normally.

صَلُّوْا عَلَى الْحَبِيْب   صَلَّى اللهُ تَعَالٰى عَلٰى مُحَمَّد

Ṣadaqaĥ-e-Fiṭr is Wājib

The Prophet of Raḥmaĥ, the Intercessor of Ummaĥ صَلَّى اللّٰهُ تَعَالٰى عَلَيْهِ وَاٰلِهٖ وَسَلَّم ordered a person to make the announcement in the whole city of Makkaĥ that 'Ṣadaqaĥ-e-Fiṭr is Wājib.' *(Jāmi' Tirmižī, vol. 2, pp. 151, Ḥadīš 674)*

Ṣadaqaĥ-e-Fiṭr is Kaffāraĥ for useless speech

Sayyidunā Ibn 'Abbās رَضِىَ اللهُ تَعَالٰى عَنْهُ has stated, 'The Holy Prophet صَلَّى اللهُ تَعَالٰى عَلَيْهِ وَاٰلِهٖ وَسَلَّم declared Ṣadaqaĥ-e-Fiṭr Wājib so that it would cleanse (our) fasts from useless and immoral speech and that it would provide the poor with food.' *(Sunan Abī Dāwūd, vol. 2, pp. 158, Ḥadīš 1609)*

Fasts remain suspended

Sayyidunā Anas Bin Mālik رَضِىَ اللهُ تَعَالٰى عَنْهُ has stated that the Prophet of mankind, the Peace of our heart and mind, the most Generous and Kind صَلَّى اللهُ تَعَالٰى عَلَيْهِ وَاٰلِهٖ وَسَلَّم has said, 'Man's fast remains suspended (i.e. hanging) between the earth and sky unless Ṣadaqaĥ-e-Fiṭr is paid.' *(Kanz-ul-'Ummāl, vol. 8, pp. 253, Ḥadīš 24124)*

Sixteen Madanī pearls of Fiṭraĥ

1. Paying Ṣadaqaĥ-e-Fiṭr is Wājib for every such Muslim man and woman who is a Sahib-e-Niṣāb provided that the bare necessities of life (Ḥājāt-e-Aṣliyyaĥ) are excluded from their Niṣāb (wealth, possessions). *(Fatāwā 'Ālamgīrī, vol. 1, pp. 191)*

2. A Sahib-e-Niṣāb is the one who possesses 7.5 Tolas of gold or 52.5 Tolas of silver or the money or goods equivalent to 52.5 Tolas of silver (excluding bare necessities). Note that one Tola is equivalent to 11.664 grams.

3. Sanity and puberty are not the conditions for Ṣadaqaĥ-e-Fiṭr to become Wājib. If even a child or an insane person is Sahib-e-Niṣāb, their guardians should pay (the Ṣadaqaĥ-e-Fiṭr) from their wealth on their behalf. *(Rad-dul-Muḥtār, vol. 3, pp. 312)*

   Though there is the same amount of Niṣāb for Ṣadaqaĥ-e-Fiṭr as for Zakāĥ (as stated above), there is no such condition for Ṣadaqaĥ-e-Fiṭr as increase in wealth and the passing of a whole year. Likewise, if there are such things that are surplus to requirements (for example, such domestic things that are not used daily) and, if their value reaches the level of Niṣāb, Ṣadaqaĥ-e-Fiṭr will be Wājib on account of these things. *(Waqār-ul-Fatāwā, vol. 2, pp. 385)* This difference between the Niṣāb of Zakāĥ and that of Ṣadaqaĥ-e-Fitr depends upon the condition of a person.

4. In addition to paying his own Ṣadaqaĥ-e-Fiṭr, it is also Wājib for a Sahib-e-Niṣāb man to pay Ṣadaqaĥ-e-Fiṭr on behalf of his young children (who are minors). If he has any insane child, he has to pay on behalf of that child as well, even if the insane child has reached puberty. However, if the insane child or young children are Sahib-e-Niṣāb, the Ṣadaqaĥ may be paid from their own wealth. *(Fatāwā 'Ālamgīrī, vol. 1, pp. 192)*

5. It is not Wājib for a Sahib-e-Niṣāb man to pay the Fiṭraĥ for his wife, parents, younger brothers and sisters and other relatives. *(Fatāwā 'Ālamgīrī, vol. 1, pp. 193)*

6. In case of father's demise, it is Wājib for the grandfather to pay the Ṣadaqaĥ-e-Fiṭr for his poor and orphan grandsons and granddaughters. *(Durr-e-Mukhtār, Rad-dul-Muḥtār, vol. 2, pp. 315)*

7. It is not Wājib for a mother to pay Ṣadaqaĥ-e-Fiṭr on behalf of her young children. *(Rad-dul-Muḥtār, vol. 3, pp. 315)*

8. It is not Wājib for a father to pay the Ṣadaqaĥ-e-Fiṭr for his sane and adult offspring. *(Durr-e-Mukhtār, Rad-dul-Muḥtār, vol. 3, pp. 317)*

9. If somebody did not fast in Ramadan either due to any valid exemption or, Allah عَزَّوَجَلَّ forbid, without a valid reason, Ṣadaqaĥ-e-Fiṭr will still be Wājib for him provided he is a Sahib-e-Niṣāb. *(Rad-dul-Muḥtār, vol. 3, pp. 315)*

10. Ṣadaqaĥ-e-Fiṭr will be valid if a man pays it on behalf of his wife or adult offspring (whose necessities like food, clothing etc. he is responsible for) even without their permission. However, if he is not responsible for their necessities, for example, he has a married son who lives in his own home along with his family and affords his expenses himself (food, clothing etc.), then paying Fiṭraĥ on behalf of such offspring without his permission will not be valid.

11. If a wife pays her husband's Fiṭraĥ without his order, it will be invalid. *(Bahār-e-Sharī'at, pp. 69, part 5)*

12. Ṣadaqaĥ-e-Fiṭr is Wājib for every such Muslim who is Sahib-e-Niṣāb at the time of Ṣubḥ-e-Ṣādiq (dawn) on the day of Eid-ul-Fiṭr. If someone becomes Sahib-e-Niṣāb after Ṣubḥ-e-Ṣādiq it is not Wājib for him to pay the Fiṭraĥ. *(Fatāwā 'Ālamgīrī, vol. 1, pp. 192)*

13. Though the preferable time for paying Ṣadaqaĥ-e-Fiṭr is that it be paid on Eid after Ṣubḥ-e-Ṣādiq before offering Eid Ṣalāĥ, if it is paid on the night of Eid (before Ṣubḥ-e-Ṣādiq) or any day during Ramadan or even before Ramadan it will still be valid. All these cases are permissible. *(Fatāwā 'Ālamgīrī, vol. 1, pp. 192)*

14. If the day of Eid passed and somebody did not pay the Fiṭraĥ, the Fiṭraĥ will not lapse on this account. Fiṭraĥ will be considered valid whenever it is paid in the whole life. *(ibid)*

15. Ṣadaqaĥ-e-Fiṭr can be spent only where Zakāĥ can be spent. In other words, Fiṭraĥ can be given to only those whom Zakāĥ can be given to. *(Fatāwā 'Ālamgīrī, vol. 1, pp. 194)*

16. It is not permissible to give Ṣadaqaĥ-e-Fiṭr to the honourable descendants of the Holy Prophet صَلَّى اللّٰهُ تَعَالٰى عَلَيْهِ وَاٰلِهٖ وَسَلَّم.

Amount of Ṣadaqaĥ-e-Fiṭr

1.920 Kilograms of wheat or its flour or the money equivalent to the value of this much wheat is the amount of one Ṣadaqaĥ-e-Fiṭr.

Thousand Nūr enter grave

According to a narration, whoever recites 'سُبْحٰنَ اللّٰهِ وَبِحَمْدِهٖ' 300 times on the day of Eid and then sends its reward to the souls of all the deceased Muslims, thousand Nūr will enter the grave of every Muslim. Further, when the reciter dies, a thousand Nūr will enter his grave as well. (This can be recited on both Eids). *(Mukāshafa-tul-Qulūb, pp. 308)*

A Sunnaĥ before Eid Ṣalāĥ

Dear Islamic brothers! Now the acts that are Sunnaĥ on the occasion of both Eid (Eid-ul-Fiṭr and Eid-ul-Aḍḥā) are described.

Sayyidunā Buraydaĥ رَضِىَ اللّٰهُ تَعَالٰى عَنْه has stated, 'On the day of Eid-ul-Fiṭr, the Holy Prophet صَلَّى اللّٰهُ تَعَالٰى عَلَيْهِ وَاٰلِهٖ وَسَلَّم would go to offer Eid Ṣalāĥ after eating something, whereas on Eid-ul-Aḍḥā, he صَلَّى اللّٰهُ تَعَالٰى عَلَيْهِ وَاٰلِهٖ وَسَلَّم would not eat anything unless he صَلَّى اللّٰهُ تَعَالٰى عَلَيْهِ وَاٰلِهٖ وَسَلَّم had offered Eid-Ṣalāĥ.' *(Jāmi' Tirmiżī, vol. 2, pp. 70, Ḥadīš 542)*

Similarly, in *Bukhārī*, there is another Ḥadīš narrated by Sayyidunā Anas رَضِىَ اللّٰهُ تَعَالٰى عَنْه, 'On the day of Eid-ul-Fiṭr, the Beloved and Blessed Prophet صَلَّى اللّٰهُ تَعَالٰى عَلَيْهِ وَاٰلِهٖ وَسَلَّم would not go until he صَلَّى اللّٰهُ تَعَالٰى عَلَيْهِ وَاٰلِهٖ وَسَلَّم ate a few dates in odd numbers.' *(Ṣaḥīḥ Bukhārī, vol. 1, pp. 328, Ḥadīš 953)*

It is narrated by Sayyidunā Abū Ĥurayraĥ رَضِىَ اللّٰهُ تَعَالٰى عَنْه that the Holy Prophet صَلَّى اللّٰهُ تَعَالٰى عَلَيْهِ وَاٰلِهٖ وَسَلَّم would go to offer Eid Ṣalāĥ from one path and would return from the other one. *(Jāmi' Tirmiżī, vol. 2, pp. 69, Ḥadīš 541)*

Method of offering Eid Ṣalāĥ (Ḥanafī)

First make the following intention: 'I intend to offer two Rak'āt Ṣalāĥ of Eid-ul-Fiṭr (or Eid-ul-Aḍḥā) with six additional Takbīrāt, for the sake of Allah عَزَّوَجَلَّ following this Imām.'

Having made the intention, raise the hands up to the ears, utter اَللّٰهُ اَكۡبَر and then fold the hands below the navel and recite the Šanā. Then raise your hands to your ears, utter اَللّٰهُ اَكۡبَر and leave them at sides; then raise hands to ears again, utter اَللّٰهُ اَكۡبَر and leave them at sides; then raise hands to ears once again, utter اَللّٰهُ اَكۡبَر and fold them. In short, hands will be folded after first and fourth Takbīr while they will be left at sides after second and third Takbīr. In other words, hands will be folded when something is to be recited in Qiyām after Takbīr, while they will be left at sides when nothing is to be recited. *(Derived from Durr-e-Mukhtār, Rad-dul-Muḥtār, vol. 3, pp. 66)* Then, the Imām is to recite Ta'awwuż and Tasmiyyaĥ in low voice whereas Sūraĥ Al-Fātiḥaĥ and another Sūraĥ will be recited loudly. Thereafter, he will perform Rukū'. In the second Rak'at, the Imām is to first recite Sūraĥ Al-Fātiḥaĥ and another Sūraĥ aloud.

After the recitation, the Imām as well as all the Muqtadīs (followers) will utter three Takbīrāt (the Imām would utter loudly and the followers in low voice) raising their hands to the ears each time and leaving them at sides. Then Rukū' will be performed with the fourth Takbīr without raising hands and the rest of the Ṣalāĥ will be completed as per usual method. To stand silent between every two Takbīrāt for the amount of time in which سُبۡحٰنَ الله can be uttered thrice is necessary.' *(Fatāwā 'Ālamgīrī, vol. 1, pp. 150)*

What to do if somebody misses a part of Eid Jamā'at?

If someone joins the Jamā'at in the first Rak'at after the Imām had uttered the Takbīrāt, he should utter the three Takbīrāt (other than the Takbīr-e-Taḥrīmaĥ) instantly even if the Imām has commenced recitation. Utter only three Takbīrāt even though the Imām had uttered more than three Takbīrāt. If the Imām bent for Rukū' before you uttered Takbīrāt, then don't utter them in a standing posture. Instead, perform Rukū' with the Imām and utter the Takbīrāt in the Rukū'. However, if the Imām is in Rukū' and you think that you can utter the Takbīrāt and join the Imām in Rukū', then utter them whilst you are standing, otherwise, utter أَللّٰهُ أَكْبَر, perform Rukū' and then utter the Takbīrāt in Rukū'. If the Imām raises his head from Rukū' before you finish the Takbīrāt in Rukū' then do not utter the remaining Takbīrāt; they are no longer required.

If you joined the Jamā'at after the Imām had performed the Rukū' then do not utter the Takbīrāt, utter them when you offer the remaining part of your Ṣalāĥ (after the Imām has performed Salām). Do not raise your hands when uttering the missed Takbīrāt in Rukū.'

If you join the Jamā'at in the second Rak'at, then don't utter the missed Takbīrāt of the first Rak'at now, instead, utter them when you perform the remaining part of your Ṣalāĥ. Likewise, if you succeed in uttering the Takbīrāt of the second Rak'at with the Imām, its all right, otherwise, the same ruling as mentioned above with regard to the first Rak'at would apply. *(Derived from Durr-e-Mukhtār & Rad-dul-Muḥtār, vol. 3, pp. 55, 56, 57)*

What to do if someone misses whole Jamā'at?

If someone missed the whole Jamā'at of Eid-Ṣalāĥ, whether he couldn't join the Jamā'at at all or his Ṣalāĥ became invalid due to any reason after joining, then if possible, he should join Jamā'at elsewhere; otherwise he cannot offer it (without Jamā'at). However, it is preferable for him to offer four Rak'āt of Chāsht Ṣalāĥ. *(Durr-e-Mukhtār, vol. 3, pp. 58, 59)*

Rulings for Eid sermon

After the Eid Ṣalāĥ, the Imām should deliver two sermons. The acts that are Sunnaĥ for the Jumu'aĥ sermon are also Sunnaĥ for the Eid sermon. Likewise, the acts that are Makrūĥ for the Jumu'aĥ sermon are also Makrūĥ for the Eid sermon. There are only two differences between these two sermons. Firstly, it is a Sunnaĥ for the Imām not to sit before the first sermon of Eid Ṣalāĥ whereas Imām's sitting before first sermon of Jumu'aĥ is a Sunnaĥ. Secondly, in the Eid sermon, it is a Sunnaĥ for the Imām to recite أَللّٰهُ أَكْبَر nine times before the first sermon, seven times before the second sermon and fourteen times before coming down from the pulpit while uttering these Takbīrāt is not Sunnaĥ for Jumu'aĥ sermon. *(Durr-e-Mukhtār, vol. 3, pp. 57-58 - Baĥār-e-Sharī'at, part 4, pp. 109)*

Twenty one Mustaḥabbāt of Eid

Following acts are Mustaḥab on the Eid day:

1. To get hair cut (get your hair cut according to Sunnaĥ, not according to the English styles).
2. To cut nails.
3. To have a bath.
4. To use Miswāk (this is in addition to the one used during Wuḍū).
5. To wear nice clothes, either new or washed ones.
6. To apply perfume.
7. To wear a ring (Islamic brothers are allowed to wear only one silver ring which weighs less than 4.5 Masha. There must be only one gem in the ring; they shouldn't wear the ring without a gem either; there is no limit for the weight of the gem. They are not allowed to wear more than one ring. Men cannot wear the ring made of any other metal except silver with the afore-mentioned conditions).
8. To offer Ṣalāt-ul-Fajr in the Masjid of one's locality.
9. To eat some dates in odd numbers such as 3, 5, 7 etc. before going to offer Eid-ul-Fiṭr Ṣalāĥ. If dates are not available, then eat something sweet. If nothing is eaten before the Ṣalāĥ, there will be no sin, but if nothing is eaten till Ṣalāt-ul-'Ishā, he will be rebuked.
10. To offer the Eid Ṣalāĥ at a place that is designated for offering the Eid Ṣalāĥ.
11. To go to the designated place for Eid Ṣalāĥ on foot.
12. Although there is no harm in using conveyance, walking on foot is better for those who can do so; there is no harm at all in returning by conveyance.

13. To go to the designated place for Eid Ṣalāĥ from one path and returning from the other path.

14. To pay Ṣadaqaĥ-e-Fiṭr before the Eid Ṣalāĥ (this is better, but if you couldn't pay it before the Eid Ṣalāĥ, pay it after the Ṣalāĥ).

15. To express happiness.

16. To donate Ṣadaqaĥ in abundance.

17. To head towards the designated place for Eid Ṣalāĥ calmly, in a dignified manner, with lowered gaze.

18. To congratulate each other.

19. To embrace and to shake hands with one another after the Eid Ṣalāĥ as Muslims usually do. It is a good act because it expresses happiness. *(Bahār-e-Sharī'at, part 4, pp. 71)* However, embracing a young attractive boy may lead to allegation.

20. In most cases, there are the same rulings for Eid-ul-Aḍḥā as for Eid-ul-Fiṭr. However, there are a few differences; for example, it is Mustaḥab not to eat anything before the Eid Ṣalāĥ on Eid-ul-Aḍḥā regardless of whether or not one is performing the sacrifice (of cattle), but if one eats something, still there is no harm.

21. To utter the following Takbīr in low voice while on your way to the designated place for Eid Ṣalāĥ to offer Eid-ul-Fiṭr Ṣalāĥ, and to utter it loudly while heading for the designated place for Eid Ṣalāĥ to offer Eid-ul-Aḍḥā Ṣalāĥ.

اَللّٰهُ اَكْبَرُ ط اَللّٰهُ اَكْبَرُ ط

لَآ اِلٰهَ اِلَّا اللّٰهُ وَ اللّٰهُ اَكْبَرُ ط اَللّٰهُ اَكْبَرُ ط وَلِلّٰهِ الْحَمْدُ ط

Translation: Allah عَزَّوَجَلَّ is the greatest. Allah عَزَّوَجَلَّ is the greatest. There is none worthy to worthy of worship except Allah عَزَّوَجَلَّ and Allah عَزَّوَجَلَّ is the greatest. Allah عَزَّوَجَلَّ is the Greatest and all the praise is for Allah عَزَّوَجَلَّ.

I did not use to offer even Eid Ṣalāĥ

Dear Islamic brothers! Gain the privilege of performing I'tikāf every year, and attain the blessings of Ramadan. Travel with a Madanī Qāfilaĥ in the company of the devotees of Rasūl to multiply the happiness of Eid and avoid different types of sins openly committed on the occasion of Eid these days.

An extremely pleasant blessing of a Madanī Qāfilaĥ is presented for your persuasion and motivation. An Islamic brother (about 25 years old) living near the main Korangi Road in Bāb-ul-Madīnaĥ, Karachi gave the following account:

I used to work in a garage. Even though repairing vehicles is basically a permissible occupation, it's extremely difficult to avoid sins these days. Those who have worked in garages would be well aware that the environment of garages is extremely filthy and earning Ḥalāl money for mechanics is like getting blood out of a stone nowadays. As a result of the filthy environment and unlawful earning, I did not offer even Jumu'aĥ and Eid Ṣalāĥ. I'd spend the whole night watching films and dramas; I would commit every minor and major sin.

Fortunately, once I listened to an audio-cassette of a Sunnaĥ-Inspiring speech namely '*Allah* عَزَّوَجَلَّ *kī Khufyaĥ Tadbīr*' released by Maktaba-tul-Madīnaĥ, which proved to be a turning point in my life. Thereafter, I was blessed with the privilege of performing I'tikāf in Ramadan and travelling with a three day Madanī Qāfilaĥ in the company of the Rasūl's devotees. Due to the blessing of I'tikāf and Madanī Qāfilaĥ, اَلْحَمْدُلِلّٰه عَزَّوَجَلَّ! I have joined the Madanī environment of Dawat-e-Islami. I now offer all five Ṣalāĥ. Millions of thanks to Allah عَزَّوَجَلَّ who has enabled a sinner like me, who did not use to offer even Jumu'aĥ and Eid Ṣalāĥ, to call and persuade others to offer Ṣalāĥ.

اَلْحَمْدُلِلّٰه عَزَّوَجَلَّ! (At the time of giving this statement) I am making my contribution to the Madanī working of Dawat-e-Islami, a global & non-political religious movement of the Quran and Sunnaĥ as the head of the Żaylī Mushāwarat of a Masjid.

Bĥāī gar chāĥtay ĥo Namāzayn parĥūn,
Madanī Māḥaul mayn kar lo tum I'tikāf
Naykiyaun mayn tamannā ĥay āgay barĥūn
Madanī Māḥaul mayn kar lo tum I'tikāf

If you desire steadfastness in offering Ṣalāĥ
Do I'tikāf in the Madanī environment
If you aspire to perform good deeds
Do I'tikāf in the Madanī environment

صَلُّوْا عَلَى الْحَبِيْب صَلَّى اللهُ تَعَالٰى عَلٰى مُحَمَّد

Yā Allah عَزَّوَجَلَّ! Enable us to celebrate Eid according to the Sunnaĥ, and grant us the Madanī Eid of Hajj and seeing the city of Madīnaĥ as well as the Beloved and Blessed Prophet صَلَّى اللهُ تَعَالٰى عَلَيْهِ وَاٰلِهٖ وَسَلَّم again and again!

اٰمِيْن بِجَاهِ النَّبِيِّ الْاَمِيْن صَلَّى اللهُ تَعَالٰى عَلَيْهِ وَاٰلِهٖ وَسَلَّم

Drops of mercy showered on me

A 22-year-old Islamic brother of Korangi, Bāb-ul-Madīnaĥ, Karachi gave the following account: Unfortunately, I had indulged in many evils such as missing Ṣalāĥ, watching film and dramas, fashion and company of wicked friends. I was a spoilt youngster whose precious life was passing in sins.

The crescent of Ramadan (1426 A.H.) appeared and the rain of the mercy of Allah عَزَّوَجَلَّ began to shower. Some drops of mercy showered on me as well and I performed collective I'tikāf during the last ten days of Ramadan in the Karīmiyyaĥ Qādiriyyaĥ Masjid of Korangi, Bāb-ul-Madīnaĥ, Karachi.

The prolonged dark night of my life's autumn began to turn into the bright morning of the spring. اَلْحَمْدُ لِلّٰه عَزَّوَجَلَّ! Participation in the collective I'tikāf changed my life-style altogether. I not only repented of all the sins, began to offer Ṣalāĥ, grew beard, began to wear the turban but I also travelled with a 30-day Sunnaĥ-Inspiring Madanī Qāfilaĥ of

Dawat-e-Islami, a global & non-political religious movement of the Quran and Sunnaĥ in the company of Rasūl's devotees.

اَلْحَمْدُلِلّٰه عَزَّوَجَلَّ! At present, I am carrying out the Madanī work of Dawat-e-Islami as a Żaylī Qāfilaĥ responsible in a Masjid. May Allah عَزَّوَجَلَّ grant me steadfastness in my dear and beloved Dawat-e-Islami until my last breath!

Marz-e-'iṣyān say chuṫĥkārā gar chāĥiye,
Madanī Māḥaul mayn kar lo tum I'tikāf
Bandagī kī bĥī lażżat agar chāĥiye,
Madanī Māḥaul mayn kar lo tum I'tikāf

If you desire recovery from the disease of sins
Do I'tikāf in the Madanī environment
If you aspire to have pleasure in worship
Do I'tikāf in the Madanī environment

صَلُّوْا عَلَى الْحَبِيْب صَلَّى اللّٰهُ تَعَالٰى عَلٰى مُحَمَّد

Announcement of Day

Sayyidunā Imām Bayĥaqī عَلَيْهِ رَحْمَةُ اللّٰهِ الْقَوِى has stated in *Shu'ab-ul-Īmān*: The Prophet of Raḥmaĥ, the Intercessor of Ummaĥ صَلَّى اللّٰهُ تَعَالٰى عَلَيْهِ وَاٰلِهٖ وَسَلَّم has said: The day makes the announcement daily at the time of sunrise, 'If you want to perform any good deed today, then do it because I will never come back.'

(Shu'ab-ul-Īmān, vol. 3, pp. 386, Ḥadīš 3840)

اَلْحَمْدُ لِلّٰهِ رَبِّ الْعٰلَمِيْنَ وَ الصَّلٰوةُ وَ السَّلَامُ عَلٰى سَيِّدِ الْمُرْسَلِيْنَ

اَمَّا بَعْدُ فَاَعُوْذُ بِاللّٰهِ مِنَ الشَّيْطٰنِ الرَّجِيْمِ ؕ بِسْمِ اللّٰهِ الرَّحْمٰنِ الرَّحِيْمِ ؕ

Excellence of Nafl Fasts

Excellence of Ṣalāt-'Alan-Nabī ﷺ

The Prophet of mankind, the Peace of our heart and mind, the most Generous and Kind صَلَّى اللهُ تَعَالٰى عَلَيْهِ وَاٰلِهٖ وَسَلَّم has stated: On the Day of Judgement, there would be no shade other than the 'Arsh of Allah عَزَّوَجَلَّ. Three types of people would be under the shade of the 'Arsh. He صَلَّى اللهُ تَعَالٰى عَلَيْهِ وَاٰلِهٖ وَسَلَّم was asked, 'Yā Rasūlallāĥ صَلَّى اللهُ تَعَالٰى عَلَيْهِ وَاٰلِهٖ وَسَلَّم! Who are the people that would be under the shade?' He صَلَّى اللهُ تَعَالٰى عَلَيْهِ وَاٰلِهٖ وَسَلَّم replied: '(1) The person removing the difficulty of any of my followers (2) The one reviving my Sunnaĥ (3) The one reciting Ṣalāt upon me in abundance.' *(Al-budur-us-Sāfiraĥ fil-Umūr-il-Ākhiraĥ, pp. 131, Ḥadīš 366)*

صَلُّوْا عَلَى الْحَبِيْب   صَلَّى اللهُ تَعَالٰى عَلٰى مُحَمَّد

Religious and worldly benefits of Nafl fasts

Dear Islamic brothers! In addition to Farḍ fasts, we should also make a habit of having Nafl fasts as there are countless religious and worldly benefits for us in doing so.

There is so much reward in it that one feels like fasting abundantly. The religious benefits include protection of faith, protection from Hell and the attainment of Heaven. As for the worldly benefits, they include saving of time and money (the time and money spent on eating and drinking), a healthy digestive system, protection from many illnesses and, above all, the pleasure of Allah عَزَّوَجَلَّ.

Glad tidings of forgiveness for fasting people

Allah عَزَّوَجَلَّ says in the 35th verse of Sūraĥ Al-Aḥzāb:

وَ الصَّآىِٕمِیْنَ وَ الصّٰٓىِٕمٰتِ وَ الْحٰفِظِیْنَ فُرُوْجَهُمْ وَ الْحٰفِظٰتِ
وَ الذّٰكِرِیْنَ اللّٰهَ كَثِیْرًا وَّ الذّٰكِرٰتِۙ اَعَدَّ اللّٰهُ لَهُمْ مَّغْفِرَةً وَّ اَجْرًا عَظِیْمًا ﴿۳۵﴾

And fasting men and women, and men and women who guard their chastity and men and women who remember Allah عَزَّوَجَلَّ much, for all of them Allah عَزَّوَجَلَّ has prepared forgiveness and great reward.

[Kanz-ul-Īmān (Translation of Quran)] (Part 22, Sūraĥ Al-Aḥzāb, verse 35)

Allah عَزَّوَجَلَّ says in the 24th verse of Sūraĥ Al-Ḥāqqaĥ, part 29:

كُلُوْا وَ اشْرَبُوْا هَنِیْٓــٴًـۢا بِمَاۤ اَسْلَفْتُمْ فِی الْاَیَّامِ الْخَالِیَةِ ﴿۲۴﴾

Eat and drink with immense relish, recompense for that which you sent forth in the days gone by.

[Kanz-ul-Īmān (Translation of Quran)] (Part 29, Sūraĥ Al-Ḥāqqaĥ, verse 24)

Sayyidunā Wakī' رَحْمَةُ اللهِ تَعَالٰى عَلَيْه has stated, 'The words 'the days gone by' mentioned in this verse refer to the days of fasting in which people abstain from eating and drinking.' *(Al-Mutajir-ul-Rābi' fī Šawāb-il-'Amal-iṣ-Ṣāliḥ, pp. 335)*

EIGHTEEN BENEFITS OF NAFL FASTS

Unique tree in Paradise

1. Sayyidunā Qays Bin Zayd Juĥannī رَضِىَ اللهُ تَعَالٰى عَنْهُ has narrated the following statement of the Noble Prophet صَلَّى اللهُ تَعَالٰى عَلَيْهِ وَاٰلِهٖ وَسَلَّم: Whoever keeps a Nafl fast, Allah عَزَّوَجَلَّ will create a tree in Heaven for him, the fruit of the tree will be smaller than a pomegranate and larger than an apple. It will be as sweet as honey (that has not been separated from

its comb) and as delicious as (pure) honey (that has been separated from its comb). On the Day of Judgement, Allah عَزَّوَجَلَّ will feed the fruits of this tree to the fasting person. *(Mu'jam Kabīr, vol. 18, pp. 366, Ḥadīš 935)*

Forty years away from Hell

2. The Prophet of Raḥmaĥ, the Intercessor of Ummaĥ صَلَّى اللّٰهُ تَعَالٰى عَلَيْهِ وَاٰلِهٖ وَسَلَّم has stated, 'Whoever keeps a Nafl fast expecting reward, Allah عَزَّوَجَلَّ will move him as far away from Hell as is the distance of 40 years.' *(Kanz-ul-'Ummāl, vol. 8, pp. 255, Ḥadīš 24148)*

Fifty years distance away from Hell

3. The Beloved and Blessed Prophet صَلَّى اللّٰهُ تَعَالٰى عَلَيْهِ وَاٰلِهٖ وَسَلَّم has stated, 'Whoever keeps a Nafl fast for the pleasure of Allah عَزَّوَجَلَّ, Allah عَزَّوَجَلَّ will make the distance, between him and Hell, a fast (horse) rider covers in fifty years.' *(Kanz-ul-'Ummāl, vol. 8, pp. 255, Ḥadīš 24149)*

More reward than earth full of gold

4. The Prophet of Raḥmaĥ, the Intercessor of Ummaĥ صَلَّى اللّٰهُ تَعَالٰى عَلَيْهِ وَاٰلِهٖ وَسَلَّم has stated: If someone keeps a Nafl fast and (even if he) is given the whole earth full of gold (as a reward) his reward will still remain incomplete, he will be given his reward on the Day of Judgement only. *(Musnad Abī Ya'lā, vol. 5, pp. 353, Ḥadīš 6104)*

Far away from Hell

5. Sayyidunā 'Utbaĥ Bin 'Abd-e-Sulamī رَضِىَ اللّٰهُ تَعَالٰى عَنْهُ has narrated that the Beloved Rasūlullāĥ صَلَّى اللّٰهُ تَعَالٰى عَلَيْهِ وَاٰلِهٖ وَسَلَّم has stated: 'Whoever keeps one Farḍ fast in the path of Allah عَزَّوَجَلَّ, Allah عَزَّوَجَلَّ will put him as far away from Hell as is the distance between the seven earths and the seven skies. Whoever keeps a Nafl fast, Allah عَزَّوَجَلَّ shall put him as far away from Hell as is the distance between the earth and the sky.' *(Mu'jam Kabīr, vol. 17, pp. 120, Ḥadīš 295)*

Excellence of one fast

6. Sayyidunā Abū Ĥurayraĥ رَضِىَ اللّٰه تَعَالٰی عَنْه has narrated the following merciful statement of the Holy Prophet صَلَّی اللّٰه تَعَالٰی عَلَیْهِ وَاٰلِهٖ وَسَلَّم: Whoever fasts a day for the pleasure of Allah عَزَّوَجَلَّ, Allah عَزَّوَجَلَّ puts him as far away from Hell as is the distance covered by a baby crow flying continuously till it grows old and dies. *(Musnad Imām Aĥmad, vol. 3, pp. 619, Ĥadīš 10810)*

Best deed

7. Sayyidunā Abū Umāmaĥ رَضِىَ اللّٰه تَعَالٰی عَنْه has stated that he asked, 'Yā Rasūlallāĥ صَلَّی اللّٰه تَعَالٰی عَلَیْهِ وَاٰلِهٖ وَسَلَّم! Tell me any act (that will benefit me).' He صَلَّی اللّٰه تَعَالٰی عَلَیْهِ وَاٰلِهٖ وَسَلَّم replied, 'Keep fasts because no other deed is like it.' He asked again, 'Tell me any act.' He صَلَّی اللّٰه تَعَالٰی عَلَیْهِ وَاٰلِهٖ وَسَلَّم replied, 'Keep fasts because no other deed is like it.' He asked once again, 'Tell me any act.' He صَلَّی اللّٰه تَعَالٰی عَلَیْهِ وَاٰلِهٖ وَسَلَّم replied, 'Keep fasts because no other deed is like it.' *(Sunan Nasāī, vol. 4, pp. 166)*

8. It is stated in another narration that he رَضِىَ اللّٰه تَعَالٰی عَنْه asked the Noble Rasūl صَلَّی اللّٰه تَعَالٰی عَلَیْهِ وَاٰلِهٖ وَسَلَّم, 'Yā Rasūlallāĥ صَلَّی اللّٰه تَعَالٰی عَلَیْهِ وَاٰلِهٖ وَسَلَّم! Tell me such an act that benefits me.' He صَلَّی اللّٰه تَعَالٰی عَلَیْهِ وَاٰلِهٖ وَسَلَّم replied, 'Make fast obligatory for you because there is nothing like it.' *(ibid)*

9. It is stated in one more narration that he رَضِىَ اللّٰه تَعَالٰی عَنْه asked, 'Yā Rasūlallāĥ صَلَّی اللّٰه تَعَالٰی عَلَیْهِ وَاٰلِهٖ وَسَلَّم! Tell me such an act that leads me to the Heaven.' He صَلَّی اللّٰه تَعَالٰی عَلَیْهِ وَاٰلِهٖ وَسَلَّم replied, 'Make fast obligatory for you because there is no other deed like it.' *(Al-Iĥsān bittartīb Şaĥīĥ Ibn Ĥibbān, vol. 5, pp. 179, Ĥadīš 3416)*

The narrator has said, 'Smoke was never seen at the house of Sayyidunā Abū Umāmaĥ رَضِىَ اللّٰه تَعَالٰی عَنْه during the day except on the occasion of the arrival of guests. (In other words he didn't eat during the day because he would always fast). *(Al-Mutajir-ul-Rābi' fī Šawāb-il-'Amal-iş-Şāliĥ, pp. 338)*

Travel, you'll become rich

10. Sayyidunā Abū Ĥurayraĥ رَضِىَ اللّٰه تَعَالٰی عَنْه has reported that the Holy Prophet صَلَّی اللّٰه تَعَالٰی عَلَیْهِ وَاٰلِهٖ وَسَلَّم has said: 'Do Jihad, you will become self-sufficient. Keep fast, you will become healthy. Travel, you will become rich.' *(Mu'jam Awsaţ, vol. 6, pp. 1460, Ĥadīš 8312)*

Fasting people will be delighted on Judgement Day

11. Sayyidunā Anas رَضِیَ اللّٰہُ تَعَالٰی عَنْہُ has said, 'On the day of resurrection, fasting people will rise from their graves and be recognised by the fragrance of fasts. There shall be jugs of water on which there will be seals of musk, and the fasting people shall be told, 'Eat, you were hungry yesterday; drink, you were thirsty yesterday; rest, you were tired yesterday.' So they shall eat and rest, whereas other people shall be facing the difficulties of accountability in the state of thirst. *(Kanz-ul-'Ummāl, vol. 8, pp. 313, Ḥadīš 23639 / Al-Tadwīn fī Akhbāri Qazwīn, vol. 2, pp. 326)*

Dining cloth of gold

12. Sayyidunā Abū Dardā رَضِیَ اللّٰہُ تَعَالٰی عَنْہُ has said: 'Every hair of a fasting person makes Tasbīḥ for him. On the Day of Judgement, there shall be a mat of gold embroidered with pearls and gems and it will be as large as the earth. It will be full of Heavenly foods, drinks and fruits. The fasting people will eat and enjoy themselves whereas other people shall be facing the difficulties of accountability.' *(Firdaus - bimā Šaur-ul-Khaṭṭāb, vol. 5, pp. 490, Ḥadīš 8853)*

Fasting people will eat on Judgement Day

13. Sayyidunā 'Abdullāĥ Bin Rubāḥ رَضِیَ اللّٰہُ تَعَالٰی عَنْہُ has said, 'On the Day of Judgement, dining-mats shall be laid, and the fasting people will be eating from them before every one else.' *(Muṣannaf Ibn Abī Shaybaĥ, vol. 2, pp. 424, Ḥadīš 10)*

Fasting people shall enter Heaven

14. Sayyidunā Ḥużayfaĥ رَضِیَ اللّٰہُ تَعَالٰی عَنْہُ has narrated that the Holy Prophet صَلَّی اللّٰہُ تَعَالٰی عَلَیْہِ وَاٰلِہٖ وَسَلَّم has said, 'The one reciting the Kalimaĥ for the pleasure of Allah عَزَّوَجَلَّ will enter Heaven, and will die with Kalimaĥ (Īmān). The one fasting for the pleasure of Allah عَزَّوَجَلَّ will also die with it and will enter Heaven; and the one giving charity for the pleasure of Allah عَزَّوَجَلَّ will also die with it and will enter Heaven.' *(Musnad Imām Aḥmad, vol. 9, pp. 90, Ḥadīš 23384)*

Excellence of fasting on extremely hot day

15. Sayyidunā Ibn 'Abbās رَضِیَ اللّٰہُ تَعَالٰی عَنْهُمَا has stated that the Prophet of Raḥmaĥ, the Intercessor of Ummaĥ صَلَّى اللّٰهُ تَعَالٰى عَلَيْهِ وَاٰلِهٖ وَسَلَّم sent Sayyidunā Abū Mūsā رَضِیَ اللّٰہُ تَعَالٰی عَنْهُ for a sea-battle. One dark night, when the sails of the ship had been removed, a voice was heard from Ghayb, 'O people of the ship! Stop! Shall I tell you what Allah عَزَّوَجَلَّ has decided for Himself?' Sayyidunā Abū Mūsā رَضِیَ اللّٰہُ تَعَالٰی عَنْهُ said, 'If you can, do tell us?' The voice said, 'Allah عَزَّوَجَلَّ has decided that whoever bears thirst on an extremely hot day for His pleasure, Allah عَزَّوَجَلَّ will give him water to drink on the day of extreme thirst (Judgement Day).'

Imām Abū Bakr 'Abdullāĥ Al-Ma'rūf Ibn Abid-Dunyā has stated in *Kitāb-ul-Jū'* 'Ever since the day Sayyidunā Abū Mūsā رَضِیَ اللّٰہُ تَعَالٰی عَنْهُ heard the voice of Ghayb, he would fast even on such a hot day when other people would normally take off their extra clothes (due to extreme heat).' *(Attarghīb Wattarĥīb, vol. 2, pp. 51, Ḥadīš 18)*

Reward for patient fasting person seeing others eating

16. Sayyidatunā Umm-e-Anṣāriyyaĥ رَضِیَ اللّٰہُ تَعَالٰی عَنْهَا has stated, 'Once the Prophet of Raḥmaĥ, the Intercessor of Ummaĥ صَلَّى اللّٰهُ تَعَالٰى عَلَيْهِ وَاٰلِهٖ وَسَلَّم came to me, I presented some food to him. He صَلَّى اللّٰهُ تَعَالٰى عَلَيْهِ وَاٰلِهٖ وَسَلَّم said, 'You also eat.' I replied, 'I have kept fast.' Rasūlullāĥ صَلَّى اللّٰهُ تَعَالٰى عَلَيْهِ وَاٰلِهٖ وَسَلَّم said, 'Angels keep making Du'ā for the fasting person's forgiveness as long as someone eats before him.' The following words are also stated in another narration, 'Until the eater fills his stomach.' *(Al-Iḥsān bittartīb Ṣaḥīḥ Ibn Ḥibbān, vol. 5, pp. 181, Ḥadīš 3421)*

17. Sayyidunā Buraydaĥ رَضِیَ اللّٰہُ تَعَالٰی عَنْهُ has narrated that the Prophet of Raḥmaĥ, the Intercessor of Ummaĥ, the Owner of Jannaĥ صَلَّى اللّٰهُ تَعَالٰى عَلَيْهِ وَاٰلِهٖ وَسَلَّم said to (Sayyidunā) Bilāl رَضِیَ اللّٰہُ تَعَالٰی عَنْهُ, 'O Bilāl! Come and have breakfast.' Sayyidunā Bilāl رَضِیَ اللّٰہُ تَعَالٰی عَنْهُ replied, 'I have kept fast.' Rasūlullāĥ صَلَّى اللّٰهُ تَعَالٰى عَلَيْهِ وَاٰلِهٖ وَسَلَّم said, 'We are eating our sustenance while the sustenance of Bilāl (رَضِیَ اللّٰہُ تَعَالٰی عَنْهُ) is increasing in Paradise.' He صَلَّى اللّٰهُ تَعَالٰى عَلَيْهِ وَاٰلِهٖ وَسَلَّم then said, 'O Bilāl! Do you know that angels keep making Du'ā for the fasting person's forgiveness and his bones make Tasbīḥ as long as someone eats before him?' *(Sunan Ibn Mājaĥ, vol. 2, pp. 348, Ḥadīš 1749)*

Excellence of dying whilst fasting

18. Sayyidatunā 'Āishaĥ Ṣiddīqaĥ رَضِیَ اللهُ تَعَالٰی عَنۡهَا has narrated that the Beloved and Blessed Prophet صَلَّى اللّٰهُ تَعَالٰى عَلَيۡهِ وَاٰلِهٖ وَسَلَّم has said, 'Whoever dies in the state of fast, Allah عَزَّوَجَلَّ will record (the reward of) fasts till the Day of Judgement in his book of deeds.' *(Firdaus - bimā Šaur-ul-Khaṭṭāb, vol. 3, pp. 504, Ḥadīš 5557)*

Death during righteous deed

سُبۡحٰنَ اللّٰه عَزَّوَجَلَّ! Fortunate is the Muslim that meets his death in the state of fast. Death during any righteous deed is an extremely good omen. For instance, dying in the state of Wuḍū or whilst offering Ṣalāĥ, death during the journey to Madīnaĥ or demise in Madīna-tul-Munawwaraĥ, departing this life in Makka-tul-Mukarramaĥ, Minā, Muzdalifaĥ or 'Arafāt during Hajj or dying during a Sunnaĥ-Inspiring Madanī Qāfilaĥ of Dawat-e-Islami for learning the Sunnaĥ in the company of Rasūl's devotees. These are all blessed privileges that are only gifted to fortunate ones. Describing the pious desires of the honourable companions رَضِیَ اللّٰهُ تَعَالٰی عَنۡهُم Sayyidunā Khayšamaĥ رَضِیَ اللّٰهُ تَعَالٰی عَنۡهُ said: 'The companions would like to meet their death during a good deed such as Hajj, 'Umraĥ, fighting in the path of Allah عَزَّوَجَلَّ, fast in Ramadan etc.'

Faith-refreshing death of uncle Kālū

Death during a pious act is granted to the fortunate people only. In this respect, listen to one of the blessings of the collective I'tikāf organized by Dawat-e-Islami, a global & non-political religious movement of the Quran and Sunnaĥ, and make a firm intention to remain associated with the Madanī environment of Dawat-e-Islami throughout your life.

Sixty-year-old Uncle Kālū from Madīna-tul-Auliyā, Ahmadabad, India, attended the collective I'tikāf organized by Dawat-e-Islami during the last ten days of Ramadan (2004, 1425 A.H.) in Shāĥī Masjid, Ahmadabad. Even though he was already associated with the Madanī environment of Dawat-e-Islami, but this was the first time that he attended the collective I'tikāf with Rasūl's devotees. He learnt a lot during the I'tikāf and started offering Ṣalāĥ in the first row of the Masjid enthusiastically, which is the second Madanī In'ām out of 72 Madanī In'āmāt.

On the 2nd of Shawwāl, the second day of Eid-ul-Fiṭr, he travelled with a Sunnaĥ-Inspiring Madanī Qāfilaĥ for 3 days in the company of Rasūl's devotees. On the 11th of

Shawwāl 1425 A.H./2004, just five or six days after he had returned from the Qāfilaĥ, he went to the market to purchase something. As there was the possibility of missing the first row of the Jamā'at in the Masjid in case of staying in the market any longer, he reached the Masjid before the uttering of the Ażān leaving each and every sort of activity in the market. As soon as he stood up after performing his Wuḍū, he suddenly fell onto the ground, recited the Kalimaĥ and Ṣalāt-'Alan-Nabī and his soul left his body.

اِنَّا لِلّٰهِ وَ اِنَّاۤ اِلَيْهِ رٰجِعُوْنَ

اَلْحَمْدُ لِلّٰه عَزَّوَجَلَّ! Due to the blessings of the collective I'tikāf, the enthusiasm for acting upon the second Madanī In'ām of performing Ṣalāĥ in the first row took Uncle Kālū from the market's environment of heedlessness to the merciful atmosphere of the Masjid where he was blessed with the privilege of reciting the Kalimaĥ and Ṣalāt-'Alan-Nabī at the time of his death.

سُبْحٰنَ اللّٰه عَزَّوَجَلَّ! The one reciting Kalimaĥ at the time of death will succeed in the grave as well as on the day of resurrection as the Beloved and Blessed Prophet صَلَّى اللّٰهُ تَعَالٰى عَلَيْهِ وَاٰلِهٖ وَسَلَّم has said, 'The one whose last words are لَآ اِلٰهَ اِلَّا اللّٰهُ will enter Heaven.' *(Sunan Abī Dāwūd, vol. 3, pp. 132, Ḥadīš 3116)*

Listen to further blessings of the Madanī atmosphere of Dawat-e-Islami: A few days after the death of uncle Kālū, his son had a dream in which he saw uncle Kālū dressed in white clothes and a green turban, he said with a smile, 'Son! Keep doing the Madanī work of Dawat-e-Islami as I have been blessed due to the blessings of this Madanī movement.'

Maut fazl-e-Khudā say ĥo Īmān per,
Madanī Māḥaul mayn kar lo tum I'tikāf
Rab kī raḥmat say pāo gey Jannat mayn ghar,
Madanī Māḥaul mayn kar lo tum I'tikāf

You will meet death with Īmān by Divine grace
Do I'tikāf in the Madanī environment
By Divine mercy, you will find in heaven a place
Do I'tikāf in the Madanī environment

صَلُّوْا عَلَى الْحَبِيْب   صَلَّى اللّٰهُ تَعَالٰى عَلٰى مُحَمَّد

Virtues of Fast on ʻĀshūrā

Twenty five virtues of ʻĀshūrā

1. The repentance of Sayyidunā Ādam عَلٰى نَبِيِّنَا وَ عَلَيْهِ الصَّلٰوةُ وَالسَّلَام was accepted on the 10th of Muḥarram.
2. Ādam عَلَيْهِ السَّلَام was born on this day and
3. He عَلَيْهِ السَّلَام entered Heaven on this day.
4. On this day the ʻArsh
5. Kursī
6. sky
7. earth
8. sun
9. moon
10. stars and
11. Heaven were created.
12. Sayyidunā Ibrāĥīm عَلَيْهِ السَّلَام was born on the day of ʻĀshūrā.
13. He عَلَيْهِ السَّلَام was saved from the fire on this day.
14. Sayyidunā Mūsā عَلَيْهِ السَّلَام and his Ummaĥ were saved and pharaoh was drowned along with his people on this day.
15. Sayyidunā ʻĪsā عَلَيْهِ السَّلَام was born on this day.
16. He عَلَيْهِ السَّلَام was raised up to the skies on this day.
17. The ark of Sayyidunā Nūḥ عَلَيْهِ السَّلَام settled at Kauĥ-e-Jūdī (a hill) on this day.
18. A great kingdom was bestowed upon Sayyidunā Sulaymān عَلَيْهِ السَّلَام on this day.
19. Sayyidunā Yūnus عَلَيْهِ السَّلَام was brought out of the whale's stomach on this day.

20. Sayyidunā Ya'qūb عَلَيْهِ السَّلَام gained his eyesight back on this day.

21. Sayyidunā Yūsuf عَلَيْهِ السَّلَام was taken out from the deep well on this day.

22. Sayyidunā Ayyūb عَلَيْهِ السَّلَام was relieved of his affliction on this day.

23. Rain descended from the sky for the first time on this day.

24. The fast on this day was common even among previous Ummaĥs. It is even said that the fast on this day was Farḍ before the blessed month of Ramadan but it was revoked later. *(Mukāshafa-tul-Qulūb, pp. 311, Bistān-ul-Wā'iẓīn lil Jauzī, pp. 228)*

25. On the day of 'Āshūrā, Sayyidunā Imām Ḥusayn رَضِیَ اللّٰہ تَعَالٰی عَنْهُ, his family and companions were all brutally martyred on the plains of Karbalā after facing three consecutive days of thirst and starvation.

Six virtues of Muḥarram and fasts of 'Āshūrā

1. Sayyidunā Abū Ĥurayraĥ رَضِیَ اللّٰہ تَعَالٰی عَنْهُ has narrated that the Prophet of Raḥmaĥ, the Intercessor of Ummaĥ صَلَّى اللّٰهُ تَعَالٰى عَلَيْهِ وَاٰلِهٖ وَسَلَّم has said: 'After Ramadan, the fast of Muḥarram is the greatest, and after the obligatory [Ṣalāĥ] the night Ṣalāĥ (Ṣalāt-ul-Layl) is the greatest.' *(Ṣaḥīḥ Muslim, pp. 891, Ḥadīš 1163)*

2. The Prophet of mankind, the Peace of our heart and mind, the most Generous and Kind صَلَّى اللّٰهُ تَعَالٰى عَلَيْهِ وَاٰلِهٖ وَسَلَّم has said: Every fast of Muḥarram is equivalent to a whole month of fasts. *(Mu'jam Ṣaghīr, vol. 2, pp. 87, Ḥadīš 1580)*

Day of Mūsā

3. Sayyidunā 'Abdullāĥ Ibn 'Abbās رَضِیَ اللّٰہُ تَعَالٰی عَنْهُ stated that when Rasūlullāĥ صَلَّى اللّٰهُ تَعَالٰى عَلَيْهِ وَاٰلِهٖ وَسَلَّم arrived in Madīna-tul-Munawwaraĥ زَادَهَا اللّٰهُ شَرَفًا وَّتَعْظِيْمًا the Jews were in the state of fast on the day of 'Āshūrā, so he صَلَّى اللّٰهُ تَعَالٰى عَلَيْهِ وَاٰلِهٖ وَسَلَّم asked, 'Why have you kept fast this day?' They replied, 'This is a great day when Allah عَزَّوَجَلَّ saved Mūsā عَلَيْهِ السَّلَام and his Ummaĥ, and drowned pharaoh and his people. Mūsā عَلَيْهِ السَّلَام kept fast this day to thank Allah عَزَّوَجَلَّ, so we also keep fast.' He صَلَّى اللّٰهُ تَعَالٰى عَلَيْهِ وَاٰلِهٖ وَسَلَّم said, 'We are more worthy to follow Mūsā عَلَيْهِ السَّلَام than you.' So the Holy Prophet صَلَّى اللّٰهُ تَعَالٰى عَلَيْهِ وَاٰلِهٖ وَسَلَّم kept fast and ordered us to keep fast as well. *(Ṣaḥīḥ Bukhārī, vol. 1, pp. 656, Ḥadīš 2004)*

Dear Islamic brothers! We have learnt from this sacred Ḥadīš that marking the day on which Allah عَزَّوَجَلَّ has blessed us with a special favour is absolutely permissible because this will make us remember the favour. This would also be a way of expressing our gratitude for it. This has been commanded in the Holy Quran:

وَ ذَكِّرْهُمْ بِاَيّٰىمِ اللّٰهِ ؕ

And remind them of the days of Allah عَزَّوَجَلَّ.

[Kanz-ul-Īmān (Translation of Quran)] (Part 13, Sūraĥ Ibrāĥīm, verse 5)

Commenting on the verse, 'Allāmaĥ Maulānā Muhammad Na'īmuddīn Murādābādī رَحْمَةُ اللهِ تَعَالٰى عَلَيْه has stated that اَيّٰمِ اللّٰهِ (the days of Allah عَزَّوَجَلَّ) refer to the days when Allah عَزَّوَجَلَّ graced His servants. For example, the day when 'Mann-o-Salwā' descended for the Banī Isrāīl (is one of such days). Similarly, the day the ocean gave way to Sayyidunā Mūsā عَلَيْهِ السَّلَام and, above all, days of birth and Mi'rāj (ascension) of the Beloved and Blessed Prophet صَلَّى اللهُ تَعَالٰى عَلَيْهِ وَاٰلِهٖ وَسَلَّم. To remember these days is in compliance with this verse. *(Derived from Khazāin-ul-'Irfān, pp. 409)*

Eid of Mīlād-un-Nabī ﷺ and Dawat-e-Islami

Dear Islamic brothers! The birthday of the Prophet of Raḥmaĥ, the Intercessor of Ummaĥ, the Owner of Jannaĥ صَلَّى اللهُ تَعَالٰى عَلَيْهِ وَاٰلِهٖ وَسَلَّم is doubtlessly the greatest 'Day of Favour' for the Muslims as they have been given all the favours for his sake. This day is better than even Eid as even Eid was bestowed upon us by his blessings. Therefore, describing the reason of fasting on Monday, he صَلَّى اللهُ تَعَالٰى عَلَيْهِ وَاٰلِهٖ وَسَلَّم said: فِيْهِ وُلِدْتُّ, *this is the day I was born. (Ṣaḥīḥ Muslim, pp. 591, Ḥadīš 1162)*

اَلْحَمْدُلِلّٰه عَزَّوَجَلَّ! Under the supervision of Dawat-e-Islami, Eid-e-Mīlād-un-Nabī صَلَّى اللهُ تَعَالٰى عَلَيْهِ وَاٰلِهٖ وَسَلَّم is celebrated in a glorious way in numerous parts of the world every year. On the 12th night of Rabī'-un-Nūr huge Mīlād-congregations are held at countless places including Bāb-ul-Madīnaĥ Karachi, where probably the largest Mīlād gathering of the world is held. On the day of Eid (12th Rabī'-un-Nūr), innumerable processions are also held in which thousands of Rasūl's devotees enthusiastically take part chanting the slogans 'Marḥabā Yā Mustafa صَلَّى اللهُ تَعَالٰى عَلَيْهِ وَاٰلِهٖ وَسَلَّم.'

Eid-e-Mīlād-un-Nabī to Eid kī bĥī Eid ĥay
Bil-yaqīn ĥay Eid-e-Eidān Eid-e-Mīlād-un-Nabī

Eid-e-Mīlād-un-Nabī is the 'Eid' of Eid
It is the day of great rejoicing indeed

Fast of 'Āshūrā

4. Sayyidunā 'Abdullāĥ Ibn 'Abbās رَضِىَ اللّٰهُ تَعَالٰى عَنْهُمَا has stated, 'I never saw the Beloved and Blessed Prophet صَلَّى اللّٰهُ تَعَالٰى عَلَيْهِ وَاٰلِهٖ وَسَلَّم prefer the fast of a day to that of other days but it was the day of Āshūrā', and the month of Ramadan.' *(Ṣaḥīḥ Bukhārī, vol. 1, pp. 657, Ḥadīš 2006)*

Go against the Jews

5. The Holy Prophet صَلَّى اللهُ تَعَالٰى عَلَيْهِ وَاٰلِهٖ وَسَلَّم has said, 'Keep fast on the day of 'Āshūrā and go against the Jews; keep fast a day before or after it as well.' *(Musnad Imām Aḥmad, vol. 1, pp. 518, Ḥadīš 2154)* Whenever one keeps the fast of 'Āshūrā, it is better for him to keep fast on either the 9th or 11th of Muḥarram as well.

6. It is narrated by Sayyidunā Abū Qatādaĥ رَضِىَ اللهُ تَعَالٰى عَنْهُ that the Prophet of Raḥmaĥ, the Intercessor of Ummaĥ صَلَّى اللّٰهُ تَعَالٰى عَلَيْهِ وَاٰلِهٖ وَسَلَّم has said, 'I have presumption from Allah عَزَّوَجَلَّ that fast on 'Āshūrā removes the sins of the previous year.' *(Ṣaḥīḥ Muslim, pp. 590, Ḥadīš 1162)*

Protection from illness and eye pain for whole year

A renowned exegetist of the Quran, Muftī Aḥmad Yār Khān عَلَيْهِ رَحْمَةُ الْمَنَّان has stated, 'If a person keeps fast on the 9th and 10th of Muḥarram he/she will gain immense reward. If someone cooks delicious foods for his family on the 10th of Muḥarram, there will be blessings in his home for the whole year, اِنْ شَآءَ اللّٰه عَزَّوَجَلَّ. It is best to cook 'Kĥichřā' (a dish prepared by cooking grinded lentils, rice and meat together) and make Fātiḥaĥ for Sayyidunā Imām Ḥusayn رَضِىَ اللهُ تَعَالٰى عَنْهُ. This is extremely tried and trusted. If someone takes a bath on this date (the 10th of Muḥarram) اِنْ شَآءَاللہ عَزَّوَجَلَّ he will be protected from illnesses for the whole year because the water of Zamzam reaches all the waters on this day.' *(Tafsīr Rūḥ-ul-Bayān, vol. 4, pp. 142 - Islāmī Zindagī, pp. 93)*

The Holy Prophet صَلَّى اللّٰهُ تَعَالٰى عَلَيْهِ وَاٰلِهٖ وَسَلَّم has said, 'Whoever applies 'Išmad Surmaĥ' (kohl) to his eyes on the day of 'Āshūrā, his eyes shall never hurt.' *(Shu'ab-ul-Īmān, vol. 3, pp. 367, Ḥadīš 3797)*

صَلُّوْا عَلَى الْحَبِيْب صَلَّى اللّٰهُ تَعَالٰى عَلٰى مُحَمَّد

Fasts of Rajab

Dear Islamic brothers! There are four months that are especially sacred in the court of Allah عَزَّوَجَلَّ. It is stated in Sūraĥ At-Taubaĥ:

اِنَّ عِدَّةَ الشُّهُوْرِ عِنْدَ اللّٰهِ اثْنَا عَشَرَ شَهْرًا فِیْ كِتٰبِ اللّٰهِ یَوْمَ خَلَقَ السَّمٰوٰتِ وَ الْاَرْضَ مِنْهَاۤ اَرْبَعَةٌ حُرُمٌ ؕ ذٰلِكَ الدِّیْنُ الْقَیِّمُ ۙ۬ فَلَا تَظْلِمُوْا فِیْهِنَّ اَنْفُسَكُمْ وَ قَاتِلُوا الْمُشْرِكِیْنَ كَآفَّةً كَمَا یُقَاتِلُوْنَكُمْ كَآفَّةً ؕ وَ اعْلَمُوْۤا اَنَّ اللّٰهَ مَعَ الْمُتَّقِیْنَ ﴿۳۶﴾

Indeed the number of months before Allah عَزَّوَجَلَّ is twelve; in the book of Allah عَزَّوَجَلَّ; since the day He عَزَّوَجَلَّ created the heavens and the earth. Four of them are sacred; this is the straight religion; so do not wrong yourselves in those months; and constantly fight against the polytheists as they constantly fight against you; and know well that Allah عَزَّوَجَلَّ is with the pious.

[Kanz-ul-Īmān (Translation of Quran)] (Part 10, Sūraĥ At-Taubaĥ, verse 36)

Dear Islamic brothers! The foregoing blessed verse refers to lunar months which are based on the appearance of the moon. The rulings of Sharī'aĥ are also observed on the basis of the lunar months. For example, the fasts of Ramadan, Zakāĥ, Hajj-rites, Islamic festivals such as Eid-e-Mīlād-un-Nabī صَلَّى اللّٰهُ تَعَالٰى عَلَيْهِ وَاٰلِهٖ وَسَلَّم, Eid-ul-Fiṭr, Eid-ul-Aḍḥā, Shab-e-Mi'rāj, Shab-e-Barā-at, Giyārĥwīn, annual 'Urs of Auliyā رَحِمَهُمُ اللّٰهُ تَعَالٰی etc. are all observed according to lunar months.

Unfortunately, today's Muslims have drifted away from religious teachings to such an extent that they don't even know the exact Islamic dates. Probably, if a million Muslims are asked a question as to what the exact Islamic date (with month and year) today is; there will hardly be only a hundred Muslims who will reply correctly.

Commenting on the aforementioned verse, Maulānā Sayyid Na'īmuddīn Murādābādī عَلَيْهِ رَحْمَةُ اللّٰهِ الْهَادِى has stated in '*Khazāin-ul-'Irfān*', '(Out of the four sacred months) three are consecutive: Żul-Qa'daĥ, Żul-Ḥijjaĥ and Muḥarram and one is separate which is Rajab. Even in the era of ignorance, Arabs would consider killing each other Ḥarām in these months. Islam further enhanced the significance and sacredness of these months.' *(Khazāin-ul-'Irfān, pp. 309)*

A faith-refreshing parable

In the time of Sayyidunā 'Īsā عَلٰى نَبِيِّنَا وَعَلَيْهِ الصَّلٰوةُ وَالسَّلَام, there was a person who was in love with a woman. One day, he got the opportunity to satisfy his lust, but suddenly he heard a commotion and had the inkling that people were talking about the appearance of the moon. He asked the woman as to which month's moon the people were sighting. She replied, 'The month of Rajab.' Although this person was an unbeliever, as soon as he heard the word 'Rajab', he immediately left the woman refraining from adultery with the intention of honouring Rajab. Allah عَزَّوَجَلَّ commanded Sayyidunā 'Īsā عَلٰى نَبِيِّنَا وَعَلَيْهِ الصَّلٰوةُ وَالسَّلَام to go and meet that person, so Sayyidunā 'Īsā عَلٰى نَبِيِّنَا وَعَلَيْهِ الصَّلٰوةُ وَالسَّلَام went and informed him about the message of Allah عَزَّوَجَلَّ and the purpose of arrival. Upon hearing this, his heart shone with the Nūr of Islam and he immediately became a Muslim. *(Anīs-ul-Wā'iẓīn, pp. 177)*

Dear Islamic brothers! Did you see the 'blessings of Rajab?' An unbeliever was blessed with the treasure of Īmān due to respecting the sacred month of Rajab. So, if a Muslim respects 'Rajab', he will undoubtedly receive tremendous blessings and rewards. Muslims should do honour the month of Rajab. The Holy Quran also prohibits people from wronging themselves (committing sins) in the sacred months.

It is stated in '*Nūr-ul-'Irfān*' with regard to فَلَا تَظْلِمُوْا فِيْهِنَّ اَنْفُسَكُمْ (Translation from Kanz-ul-Īmān: *Do not wrong yourselves in those months*), 'Do not commit sins, especially in these four sacred months; committing sins is tantamount to wronging oneself (or) do not oppress and harm each other.' *(Nūr-ul-'Irfān, pp. 306)*

Reward of two years

Sayyidunā Anas رَضِیَ اللّٰهُ تَعَالٰی عَنْهُ has narrated that the Prophet of Raḥmaĥ, the Intercessor of Ummaĥ صَلَّی اللّٰهُ تَعَالٰی عَلَیْهِ وَاٰلِهٖ وَسَلَّم has said, 'The one keeping fast on three days (Thursday, Friday and Saturday) in the sacred months will get the reward of two years' worship.' *(Majma'-uz-Zawāid, vol. 3, pp. 438, Ḥadīš 5151)*

Blessings of Rajab

Ḥujjat-ul-Islam Sayyidunā Imām Muhammad Ghazālī عَلَیْهِ رَحْمَةُ اللّٰهِ الْوَالِی has stated in his book '*Mukāshafa-tul-Qulūb*', 'Rajab has actually been derived from the word 'تَرْجِیْب' (Tarjīb) which means 'to honour.' It is also known as 'اَلْاَصَبّ' (Al-Aṣab) (i.e. fastest flow), because the flow of mercy is increased for those who repent in this blessed month. Further, the light of acceptance descends upon the worshippers in this month. It is also called 'اَلْاَصَمّ' (Al-Aṣam) (i.e. the most deaf) because the sound of war and weapons isn't heard at all during this month. Its another name is 'رَجَب' which is the name of a Heavenly stream whose water is whiter than milk, sweeter than honey and cooler than snow. Only those who fast in the month of Rajab will drink from it.' *(Mukāshafa-tul-Qulūb, pp. 301)*

It is stated in *Ghunya-tuṭ-Ṭālibīn* that this month is also called 'شَهْرِ الرَّجَم' because Satans are stoned in this month so that they may not harm the Muslims. This blessed month is also known as 'اَلْاَصَمّ' (very deaf) because nobody heard about any Ummaĥ being punished by Allah عَزَّوَجَلَّ in this month, whereas previously divine retribution took place in all other months. *(Ghunya-tuṭ-Ṭālibīn, pp. 229)*

Three letters of Rajab

سُبْحٰنَ اللّٰه عَزَّوَجَلَّ! Dear Islamic brothers! Rajab is one of the blessed and sacred Islamic months. It is stated in '*Mukāshafa-tul-Qulūb*' that our pious saints رَحِمَهُمُ اللّٰهُ تَعَالٰی said, 'There are three letters in Rajab, ر, ج and ب. The ر stands for Raḥmat-e-Ilāĥī (mercy of Allah عَزَّوَجَلَّ), the ج stands for Jurm (crime) of the person and the ب stands for Birr (kindness). In other words, it is as if Allah عَزَّوَجَلَّ says, 'Place my servant's crime between My mercy and My kindness.' *(Mukāshafa-tul-Qulūb, pp. 301)*

Month of sowing seeds

Sayyidunā 'Allāmaĥ Ṣaffaurī رَحْمَةُ اللهِ تَعَالٰی عَلَيْه has stated, 'Rajab is the month of sowing seeds, Sha'bān is the month of watering them and Ramadan is the month of reaping the harvest. Therefore, if someone does not sow the seeds of worship in Rajab and does not water them with tears of remorse in Sha'bān, how will he be able to reap the harvest of mercy in Ramadan?' He رَحْمَةُ اللهِ تَعَالٰی عَلَيْه has further stated, 'Rajab purifies the body, Sha'bān purifies the heart and Ramadan purifies the soul.' *(Nuzĥa-tul-Majālis, vol. 1, pp. 155)*

I learnt in ten days what I couldn't learn in my whole life

Dear Islamic brothers! Join the Madanī environment of Dawat-e-Islami in order to enhance the spirit of worshipping and fasting in Rajab. Travel with the Madanī Qāfilaĥ and attend the collective I'tikāf organized by Dawat-e-Islami, a Madanī transformation will take place in your life اِنْ شَآءَاللّٰه عَزَّوَجَلَّ. A blessing of the sacred environment of Dawat-e-Islami is presented in the form of an incident for your persuasion. Therefore, an Islamic brother of Saeedabad Baldiyah Town, Bāb-ul-Madīnaĥ Karachi gave the following account:

I was a student of matriculation in those days. As a result of the individual effort of my landlord who was associated with Dawat-e-Islami, I took part in the collective I'tikāf organized by Dawat-e-Islami, in the last ten days of Ramadan in Ghausia Masjid, New Saeedabad Memon colony. I cannot express the blessings of the company of the Rasūl's devotees in words. In short, during those ten days, I learnt what I could not learn in my whole life.

Participation in I'tikāf proved to be a turning point in my life. I began to wear a turban regularly and travelled with a Sunnaĥ-Inspiring Madanī Qāfilaĥ in the company of Rasūl's devotees on the second day of Eid. اَلْحَمْدُ لِلّٰه عَزَّوَجَلَّ My participation in the Madanī activities of Dawat-e-Islami further increased and I am currently serving Dawat-e-Islami as a responsible for Madanī In'āmāt.

صَلُّوْا عَلَى الْحَبِيْب صَلَّى اللهُ تَعَالٰى عَلٰى مُحَمَّد

Five blessed nights

Sayyidunā Abū Umāmaĥ رضی اللہ تعالٰی عنہ has narrated that the Beloved and Blessed Prophet صَلَّی اللہُ تَعَالٰی عَلَیْہِ وَاٰلِہٖ وَسَلَّم has said, 'There are five nights in which Du'ā is not turned down:

1. The first night of Rajab
2. 15th Sha'bān
3. The night between Thursday and Friday
4. The night of Eid-ul-Fiṭr and
5. The night of Eid-ul-Aḍḥā.'

(Al-Jāmi'-uṣ-Ṣaghīr, pp. 241, Ḥadīš 3952)

Sayyidunā Khālid Bin Ma'dān رحمۃ اللہ تعالٰی علیہ has said, 'There are five particular nights in a year. The one spending them in worship testifying them with the intention of gaining reward will enter Heaven:

1. The first night of Rajab (one should worship at the night and fast during the day).
2. The night of Eid-ul-Fiṭr &
3. That of Eid-ul-Aḍḥā (one should worship at these nights but fast is impermissible on both Eid days).
4. The 15th night of Sha'bān (one should worship at the night and fast the following day) and
5. The night of 'Āshūrā (10th night of Muḥarram-ul-Ḥarām) (worship at the night and fast the following day).' *(Ghunya-tuṭ-Ṭālibīn, pp. 236)*

First fast is Kaffāraĥ for three years' sins

Sayyidunā 'Abdullāĥ Ibn 'Abbās رضی اللہ تعالٰی عنہما has narrated that the Beloved and Blessed Prophet صَلَّی اللہُ تَعَالٰی عَلَیْہِ وَاٰلِہٖ وَسَلَّم has said, 'The fast of the first day of Rajab is the expiation for three years, the fast of the second day is the expiation for two years and that of the third day is the expiation for one year and then the fast of each remaining day is the expiation for one month.' *(Al-Jāmi'-uṣ-Ṣaghīr, pp. 311, Ḥadīš 5051)*

Rajab is name of a heavenly river

Sayyidunā Anas Bin Mālik رَضِیَ اللّٰہُ تَعَالٰی عَنْہُ has narrated that the Prophet of Raḥmaĥ, the Intercessor of Ummaĥ, the Owner of Jannaĥ صَلَّی اللّٰہُ تَعَالٰی عَلَیْہِ وَاٰلِہٖ وَسَلَّم has said, 'In Heaven, there is a river called 'Rajab' whose water is whiter than milk and sweeter than honey. The one keeping a fast in the month of Rajab will be given its water to drink by Allah عَزَّوَجَلَّ.'
(Shu'ab-ul-Īmān, vol. 3, pp. 367, Ḥadīš 3800)

Shiny mountain

Once, Sayyidunā 'Īsā عَلٰی نَبِیِّنَا وَ عَلَیْہِ الصَّلٰوۃُ وَالسَّلَام passed by a luminous mountain that was sparkling with light. He عَلَیْہِ السَّلَام said to Almighty, 'Yā Allah عَزَّوَجَلَّ! Give this mountain the power of speaking.' The mountain spoke, 'O Rūḥullāĥ (عَلٰی نَبِیِّنَا وَعَلَیْہِ الصَّلٰوۃُ وَالسَّلَام)! What do you want to ask me?' He عَلٰی نَبِیِّنَا وَعَلَیْہِ الصَّلٰوۃُ وَالسَّلَام replied, 'Tell me about your state.' The mountain said, 'A person lives inside me.' Sayyidunā 'Īsā عَلَیْہِ السَّلَام humbly said to Allah عَزَّوَجَلَّ, 'Allow me to see him.'

The mountain split open and a very beautiful pious man emerged from it. The man said, 'I am a follower of Sayyidunā Mūsā عَلٰی نَبِیِّنَا وَ عَلَیْہِ الصَّلٰوۃُ وَالسَّلَام. I prayed Allah عَزَّوَجَلَّ to keep me alive until the era of His Last Rasūl صَلَّی اللّٰہُ تَعَالٰی عَلَیْہِ وَاٰلِہٖ وَسَلَّم so that I behold him and get the privilege of becoming his follower. اَلْحَمْدُ لِلّٰہِ عَزَّوَجَلَّ! I have been worshipping Allah عَزَّوَجَلَّ in this mountain for six hundred years.' Sayyidunā 'Īsā عَلَیْہِ السَّلَام asked, 'Yā Allah عَزَّوَجَلَّ! Is there anyone dearer to You on the earth than this person?' Allah عَزَّوَجَلَّ answered 'O 'Īsā (عَلَیْہِ السَّلَام)! Whoever from the Ummaĥ of Muhammad صَلَّی اللّٰہُ تَعَالٰی عَلَیْہِ وَاٰلِہٖ وَسَلَّم fasts a single day in the month of Rajab, is dearer to Me than this person.' *(Nuzĥa-tul-Majālis, vol. 1, pp. 155)*

May Allah عَزَّوَجَلَّ have mercy on them and forgive us without accountability for their sake!

Excellence of one fast

Sayyidunā Shaykh 'Abdul Ḥaq Muḥaddiš Diĥlvī رَحْمَۃُ اللّٰہِ تَعَالٰی عَلَیْہ has quoted a saying of our Holy Rasūl صَلَّی اللّٰہُ تَعَالٰی عَلَیْہِ وَاٰلِہٖ وَسَلَّم, 'Rajab is one of the sacred months and its days are inscribed on the portal of the sixth sky. If a person fasts a day in Rajab with piety, the portal and the day (he fasted) will seek repentance for that person in the court of Allah عَزَّوَجَلَّ and will say, 'Yā Allah عَزَّوَجَلَّ, forgive him.' If the person fasts without piety, the portal and day will not intercede for his forgiveness and they will say to him, 'Your Nafs has betrayed you.' *(Māšabata-bis-Sunnaĥ, pp. 342)*

Dear Islamic brothers! We have learnt that staying hungry and thirsty is not the sole aim of fast; avoiding every type of sin is also necessary. Committing sins despite having fast can lead to intense deprivation.

Blessing of Rajab's fast in ark of Prophet Nūḥ عَلَيْهِ السَّلَام

Sayyidunā Anas رَضِیَ اللّٰهُ تَعَالٰی عَنْهُ has narrated that Rasūlullāĥ صَلَّى اللّٰهُ تَعَالٰی عَلَيْهِ وَاٰلِهٖ وَسَلَّم has said: 'Whoever keeps one fast in Rajab it will be equivalent to one year's fasts. Whoever keeps seven fasts, the seven gates of Hell will be closed for him. Whoever keeps eight fasts, the eight portals of Heaven will be opened for him. Whoever keeps ten fasts, Allah عَزَّوَجَلَّ shall grant him whatever he asks for. If someone keeps fifteen fasts, an announcement is made for him from the sky, 'Your previous sins have been forgiven, so start your deeds again because your sins have been turned into virtues', and if anyone does more, Allah عَزَّوَجَلَّ shall give him more. Prophet Nūḥ عَلَيْهِ السَّلَام boarded the ark in Rajab. He عَلَيْهِ السَّلَام not only fasted himself but also ordered his companions to fast. His ark travelled continuously for six months until it stopped on 10th Muḥarram.' *(Shu'ab-ul-Īmān, vol. 3, pp. 368, Ḥadīš 3801)*

Heavenly palace

Tabi'ī Sayyidunā Abū Qilābaĥ رَضِیَ اللّٰهُ تَعَالٰی عَنْهُ has stated, 'There is a grand palace in Heaven for those who fast in Rajab.' *(Shu'ab-ul-Īmān, vol. 3, pp. 368, Ḥadīš 3802)*

Excellence of removing difficulty

Sayyidunā 'Abdullāĥ Ibn Zubayr رَضِیَ اللّٰهُ تَعَالٰی عَنْهُ has said, 'Whoever relieves someone of difficulty in the month of Rajab, Allah عَزَّوَجَلَّ will bestow upon him a Heavenly palace which will be as spacious as the limit of one's vision. Honour Rajab, Allah عَزَّوَجَلَّ will honour you a thousand times more.' *(Ghunya-tuṭ-Ṭālibīn, pp. 234)*

Reward for hundred years of fasting

The 27th of Rajab is such a sacred day when the Noble Prophet صَلَّى اللّٰهُ تَعَالٰی عَلَيْهِ وَاٰلِهٖ وَسَلَّم received his first revelation and his glorious miracle in the form of Mi'rāj (ascension) also took place on the same day.

There is great excellence of fasting on the 27th of Rajab. Sayyidunā Salmān Fārsī رَضِیَ اللهُ تَعَالٰی عَنْهُ has narrated that the Prophet of Raḥmaĥ, the Intercessor of Ummaĥ صَلَّى اللهُ تَعَالٰی عَلَيْهِ وَاٰلِهٖ وَسَلَّم has said, 'There is a day and a night in the month of Rajab; if a person fasts during the day and stands (for worship) in the night, it will be as if he has fasted for one hundred years. This is the 27th of Rajab. This is the day on which the Prophet of mankind, the Peace of our heart and mind, the most Generous and Kind صَلَّى اللهُ تَعَالٰی عَلَيْهِ وَاٰلِهٖ وَسَلَّم was given Prophethood.' *(Shu'ab-ul-Īmān, vol. 3, pp. 373, Ḥadīš 3811)*

One virtue is equivalent to hundred years of virtues

In Rajab, there is one such night at which the one performing good deed gets the reward of hundred years' worship, (and) it is the 27th night of Rajab. The one who offers twelve Rak'āt at this night reciting Sūraĥ Al-Fātiḥaĥ and another Sūraĥ in every Rak'at and Tashaĥĥud after every two Rak'āt and performs Salām after all twelve Rak'āt and then recites the following hundred times:

سُبْحٰنَ اللهِ وَالْحَمْدُ لِلّٰهِ وَ لَآ اِلٰهَ اِلَّا اللهُ وَ اللهُ اَكْبَرُ

Istighfār hundred times, Ṣalāt-'Alan-Nabī hundred times and then makes Du'ā for anything of the world and the hereafter and then fasts in the morning; all of his prayers (Du'ās) will be answered except the one made for any sin. *(Shu'ab-ul-Īmān, vol. 3, pp. 374, Ḥadīš 3812)*

صَلُّوْا عَلَى الْحَبِيْب صَلَّى اللهُ تَعَالٰی عَلٰی مُحَمَّد

Fast of the 27th compensates for ten years' sins

A'lā Ḥaḍrat Imām Aḥmad Razā Khān عَلَيْهِ رَحْمَةُ الرَّحْمٰن has stated with reference to '*Fawāid-e-Ĥanād*' that Sayyidunā Anas رَضِیَ اللهُ تَعَالٰی عَنْهُ has narrated that the Holy Prophet صَلَّى اللهُ تَعَالٰی عَلَيْهِ وَاٰلِهٖ وَسَلَّم has said, 'I was given Prophethood on the 27th of Rajab. Whoever fasts this day and makes Du'ā at the time of Ifṭār, it will be expiation for his ten years' sins.' *(Fatāwā Razawiyyaĥ (Jadīd), vol. 10, pp. 648)*

Reward for sixty months of fasting

Sayyidunā Abū Ĥurayraĥ رَضِیَ اللّٰہُ تَعَالٰی عَنْہُ has stated, 'If someone keeps fast on the 27th of Rajab, he will be given the reward of fasting for sixty months (five years) and this is the day when Jibrāīl عَلَیْہِ السَّلَام came down to give Prophethood to Beloved Rasūl Muhammad صَلَّی اللّٰہُ تَعَالٰی عَلَیْہِ وَاٰلِہٖ وَسَلَّم.' *(Tanzī-ush-Sharī'aĥ, vol. 2, pp. 161, Ḥadīš 41)*

Reward for hundred years of fasting

Sayyidunā Salmān Fārsī رَضِیَ اللّٰہُ تَعَالٰی عَنْہُ has narrated that the Holy Prophet صَلَّی اللّٰہُ تَعَالٰی عَلَیْہِ وَاٰلِہٖ وَسَلَّم has said, 'There is a day and a night in the month of Rajab. If a person fasts during the day and stands (for worship) in the night, it will be as if he fasted for one hundred years. This is the 27th of Rajab. This is the day on which the Noble Prophet صَلَّی اللّٰہُ تَعَالٰی عَلَیْہِ وَاٰلِہٖ وَسَلَّم was given Prophethood.' *(Shu'ab-ul-Īmān, vol. 3, pp. 374, Ḥadīš 3811)*

Dawat-e-Islami and Mi'rāj-un-Nabī صَلَّی اللّٰہُ تَعَالٰی عَلَیْہِ وَاٰلِہٖ وَسَلَّم

Dear Islamic brothers! Another speciality of Rajab lies in the miracle of Mi'rāj (ascension) which Allah عَزَّوَجَلَّ granted to His Beloved Rasūl صَلَّی اللّٰہُ تَعَالٰی عَلَیْہِ وَاٰلِہٖ وَسَلَّم on the 27th night of Rajab. At this sacred night, he صَلَّی اللّٰہُ تَعَالٰی عَلَیْہِ وَاٰلِہٖ وَسَلَّم travelled from Masjid-ul-Ḥarām to Masjid-ul-Aqṣā (Bayt-ul-Muqaddas) and then to the skies. He صَلَّی اللّٰہُ تَعَالٰی عَلَیْہِ وَاٰلِہٖ وَسَلَّم saw the wonders of Heaven and Hell as well. He صَلَّی اللّٰہُ تَعَالٰی عَلَیْہِ وَاٰلِہٖ وَسَلَّم blessed the 'Arsh with the privilege of kissing his blessed feet and saw his Creator عَزَّوَجَلَّ with his eyes in the state of complete wakefulness. He صَلَّی اللّٰہُ تَعَالٰی عَلَیْہِ وَاٰلِہٖ وَسَلَّم completed this journey and returned within a few moments. The 27th night of Rajab is a very sacred night.

اَلْحَمْدُلِلّٰہ عَزَّوَجَلَّ! Dawat-e-Islami, a global & non-political, religious movement of Quran and Sunnaĥ, organises Ijtimā'āt every year on the 27th night at numerous venues of different countries of the world in order to commemorate the Mi'rāj-un-Nabī صَلَّی اللّٰہُ تَعَالٰی عَلَیْہِ وَاٰلِہٖ وَسَلَّم. Hundreds of thousands of Rasūl's devotees gain spiritual blessings from these Ijtimā'āt. In my opinion, اَلْحَمْدُلِلّٰہ عَزَّوَجَلَّ, the biggest Ijtimā' in the commemoration of Mi'rāj is held in Bāb-ul-Madīnaĥ, Karachi every year. This Ijtimā' lasts almost the whole night.

صَلُّوْا عَلَی الْحَبِیْب صَلَّی اللّٰہُ تَعَالٰی عَلٰی مُحَمَّد

Return of shroud

A pious lady used to live in Basra. At the time of her death, she made the will to her son that he shroud her in the clothes she used to wear to perform worship in Rajab. When the lady passed away, her son forgetfully shrouded her in any other cloth. After the burial, when he returned home from the cemetery, he was astonished to discover that the cloth in which he mistakenly shrouded his mother was at home and the clothes she made her will about had disappeared! Suddenly, a voice was heard saying, 'Take back your shroud. We have shrouded her (in the cloth she willed). We do not leave the people who fast in Rajab unhappy in their graves.' *(Nuzĥa-tul-Majālis, vol. 1, pp. 208)*

May Allah عَزَّوَجَلَّ have mercy on her and forgive us without accountability for her sake!

صَلُّوْا عَلَى الْحَبِيْب صَلَّى اللّٰهُ تَعَالٰى عَلٰى مُحَمَّد

Too much love made me stubborn

Dear Islamic brothers! In order to break the habit of sins, to get the spiritual pleasure of worship, and to develop enthusiasm for keeping fasts in Rajab, please travel routinely with the Madanī Qāfilaĥs of Dawat-e-Islami along with Rasūl's devotees.

A blessing of Madanī Qāfilaĥ is presented for your encouragement and persuasion. An Islamic brother of Shahdarah (Markaz-ul-Auliyā, Lahore) gave the following account: I was the only child of my parents; their excessive love had spoilt me and made me a disobedient son. I used to stay up late and waste my time and sleep till late in the day.

If my parents tried to advise me, I'd shout at them and tell them off. Sometimes they'd even cry. My mother's eyes would fill with tears making Du'ā for my reform. May millions of salutations be to the moment when I was blessed with meeting an Islamic brother of Dawat-e-Islami. Making individual effort, he convinced me, a sinner and extremely wicked person, to travel in a Madanī Qāfilaĥ. I took part in a three day Madanī Qāfilaĥ with Rasūl's devotees. The blessed company of Rasūl's devotees transformed me so profoundly in those three days that my hard heart which did not get any effect even by my mother's tears became soft.

A Madanī revolution took place in my heart and I started offering Ṣalāĥ regularly during Madanī Qāfilaĥ. When I returned, I said Salām, kissed my father's hand and my mother's feet. Everyone was shocked to see such a great positive change in my behaviour!

اَلۡحَمۡدُلِلّٰہ عَزَّوَجَلَّ! The company of Rasūl's devotees during the Madanī Qāfilaĥ completely changed me and, at the time of making this statement, this sinner who did not use to offer Ṣalāĥ, has now got the responsibility of waking up Muslims for Fajr Ṣalāĥ by calling Ṣadā-e-Madīnaĥ. (In the Madanī atmosphere of Dawat-e-Islami the term 'Ṣadā-e-Madīnaĥ' refers to the act of waking Muslims up for Fajr Ṣalāĥ).

Garchay a'māl-e-bad, aur af'āl-e-bad
Nay ĥay ruswā kiyā, Qāfilay mayn chalo
Kar safar āo gey, tum sudĥar jāo gey
Māngo chal kar Du'ā, Qāfilay mayn chalo

Even if misdeeds have caused disgrace, travel with Madanī Qāfilaĥ
You will get reformed, come and make Du'ā in Madanī Qāfilaĥ

صَلُّوْا عَلَى الْحَبِيْب صَلَّى اللهُ تَعَالٰى عَلٰى مُحَمَّد

Three narrations about companionship

Dear Islamic brothers! Did you see! The one who did not use to offer any Ṣalāĥ, started not only offering Ṣalāĥ himself but also waking up others for Ṣalāĥ due to the blessing of the company of Rasūl's devotees. There is no doubt that company has its effects, good company makes you good and bad company makes you bad. Therefore, one must always adopt the company of the pious people. Here are three sacred Aḥādīš regarding company:

1. A good companion is the one that helps you (remember Allah عَزَّوَجَلَّ) when you remember Him, and reminds you (of remembering Him) when you forget. *(Al-Jāmi'-uṣ-Ṣaghīr, pp. 244, Ḥadīš 3999)*

2. A good companion is the one whose sight makes you remember Allah عَزَّوَجَلَّ and whose actions make you remember the afterlife. *(ibid, pp. 247, Ḥadīš 4063)*

3. Sayyidunā 'Umar Fārūq A'ẓam رَضِیَ اللہُ تَعَالٰی عَنۡہُ has said, 'Do not get involved in something that doesn't benefit you. Stay away from your enemy, and avoid your friend unless

he is trustworthy because no one is like a trustworthy man. A trustworthy man is the one who fears Allah عَزَّوَجَلَّ and stays away from sinners (who disobey Allah عَزَّوَجَلَّ and His Beloved Prophet صَلَّى اللهُ تَعَالٰى عَلَيْهِ وَاٰلِهٖ وَسَلَّم) because he will teach you sin. Don't tell him your secret and seek the advice of people who fear Allah عَزَّوَجَلَّ.' *(Kanz-ul-'Ummāl, vol. 9, pp. 75, Ḥadīš 25565)*

Refrain from bad company

By Sharī'aĥ, it is forbidden to adopt the company of those who don't offer Ṣalāĥ, abuse, watch films and dramas, listen to music, lie, backbite, tell tales, break promises, steal, bribe and drink alcohol. Similarly, one must stay away from sinners, apostates and unbelievers. Anyone who deliberately joins their company without a Shar'ī exemption is a sinner.

It is stated on page 237 of the 22nd volume of *Fatāwā Razawiyyaĥ* that A'lā Ḥaḍrat رَحْمَةُ اللّٰهِ تَعَالٰى عَلَيْه was asked: 'To what extent should we avoid a fornicator and Dayyūš (someone who doesn't care about the immodesty of his wife or other Maḥram women and does not make all possible attempts to stop them)?' He رَحْمَةُ اللّٰهِ تَعَالٰى عَلَيْه replied: 'The fornicator and the Dayyūš are sinners. One must stay away from them.' After saying this he رَحْمَةُ اللّٰهِ تَعَالٰى عَلَيْه mentions the 68th verse of Sūraĥ Al-An'ām (part 7):

وَ اِمَّا یُنۡسِیَنَّکَ الشَّیۡطٰنُ فَلَا تَقۡعُدۡ بَعۡدَ الذِّکۡرٰی مَعَ الۡقَوۡمِ الظّٰلِمِیۡنَ ﴿۶۸﴾

And when the devil (Satan) makes you forget then sit not you after recollection with the unjust people.

[Kanz-ul-Īmān (Translation of Quran)] (Part 7, Sūraĥ Al-An'ām, verse 68)

Commenting on the foregoing verse, a renowned exegetist of the Quran, Muftī Aḥmad Yār Khān عَلَيْهِ رَحْمَةُ الْحَنَّان has stated, 'This verse clearly states that avoiding bad company is extremely important. A bad companion is worse than even a snake because a snake will take your life but a bad companion may take your faith.' *(Nūr-ul-'Irfān, pp. 215)*

Rajab kā wāsiṭaĥ ĥam sab kī maghfirat farmā
Ilāĥī Jannat-e-Firdaus marḥamat farmā

Forgive all of us for the sake of Rajab
Bless us with Jannat-ul-Firdaus, Yā Rab

FASTS OF SHA'BĀN

Month of the Holy Prophet ﷺ

Describing the importance of Sha'bān, the Prophet of Raḥmaĥ, the Intercessor of Ummaĥ, the Owner of Jannaĥ صَلَّى اللهُ تَعَالٰى عَلَيْهِ وَاٰلِهٖ وَسَلَّم has said: 'Sha'bān is the month of mine and Ramadan is the month of Allah عَزَّوَجَلَّ.' *(Al-Jāmi'-uṣ-Ṣaghīr, pp. 301, Ḥadīš 4779)*

Blessings of Sha'bān

The Arabic word شَعْبَان (Sha'bān) contains five letters: ش, ع, ب, ا and ن. The ش stands for Sharaf (nobility), the ع for 'Ulūw (upliftment), the ب for Birr (piety), the ا for Ulfat (admiration) and the ن for Nūr (light). These are the gifts from Allah عَزَّوَجَلَّ to His servants in this month. It is the month in which the doors of good deeds are opened, blessings are sent down, faults are forgiven, sins are expiated and Ṣalāt is recited in huge numbers upon the Beloved and Blessed Prophet صَلَّى اللهُ تَعَالٰى عَلَيْهِ وَاٰلِهٖ وَسَلَّم. *(Ghunya-tuṭ-Ṭālibīn, vol. 1, pp. 246)*

Enthusiasm of companions رَضِیَ اللهُ عَنْهُم

Sayyidunā Anas Bin Mālik رَضِیَ اللهُ تَعَالٰی عَنْه has stated, 'When the blessed companions رَضِیَ اللهُ تَعَالٰی عَنْهُم saw the crescent of Sha'bān, they would busy themselves in reciting the Holy Quran and pay Zakāĥ so that the weak and the poor may also make preparation for the fasting of the month of Ramadan. The governors would summon the prisoners to enforce sentence to those who were to be sentenced (by Sharī'aĥ) and set the rest free. Businessmen would pay their debts and collect their dues. (In this way, they would become free for worship before the appearance of the moon of Ramadan), and as soon as the moon of Ramadan appeared, they would perform Ghusl and (some) would take part in I'tikāf for the whole month.' *(Ghunya-tuṭ-Ṭālibīn, vol. 1, pp. 246)*

Enthusiasm of today's Muslims

سُبْحٰنَ اللّٰه عَزَّوَجَلَّ! The Muslims of earlier times loved worshipping, but today's Muslims are generally interested in accumulating wealth. They possessed Madanī mindset and worshipped Allah عَزَّوَجَلَّ in abundance in the sacred months and strived to gain the nearness and closeness of Allah عَزَّوَجَلَّ, but unfortunately, today's Muslims often plan how to earn the despicable wealth of this world in the blessed months especially in Ramadan. Having mercy on the people, Allah عَزَّوَجَلَّ increases rewards but on the contrary, the unfortunate people increase the price on their items in the blessed month of Ramadan causing trouble for their own Muslim brothers.

Fasting in Sha'bān to respect Ramadan

The Prophet of mankind, the Peace of our heart and mind, the most Generous and Kind صَلَّى اللهُ تَعَالٰى عَلَيْهِ وَاٰلِهٖ وَسَلَّم has said: 'After Ramadan, the best fasts for honouring Ramadan are the fasts of Sha'bān.' *(Shu'ab-ul-Īmān, vol. 3, pp. 377, Ḥadīš 3819)*

Fasting in most days of Sha'bān is Sunnaĥ

Sayyidatunā 'Āishaĥ Ṣiddīqaĥ رَضِیَ اللهُ تَعَالٰى عَنْهَا has stated, 'I did not see the Beloved and Blessed Prophet صَلَّى اللهُ تَعَالٰى عَلَيْهِ وَاٰلِهٖ وَسَلَّم keep fasts more abundantly in any month than in Sha'bān. He صَلَّى اللهُ تَعَالٰى عَلَيْهِ وَاٰلِهٖ وَسَلَّم used to keep fasts the entire month except a few days.' *(Jāmi' Tirmižī, vol. 2, pp. 182, Ḥadīš 736)*

صَلُّوْا عَلَى الْحَبِيْب صَلَّى اللهُ تَعَالٰى عَلٰى مُحَمَّد

List of the dead is made

Sayyidatunā 'Āishaĥ Ṣiddīqaĥ رَضِیَ اللهُ تَعَالٰى عَنْهَا has narrated, 'The Beloved and Blessed Prophet صَلَّى اللهُ تَعَالٰى عَلَيْهِ وَاٰلِهٖ وَسَلَّم would keep fasts throughout Sha'ban.' She رَضِیَ اللهُ تَعَالٰى عَنْهَا once asked, 'Yā Rasūlallāĥ صَلَّى اللهُ تَعَالٰى عَلَيْهِ وَاٰلِهٖ وَسَلَّم! Do you like fasting in Sha'ban the most?' He صَلَّى اللهُ تَعَالٰى عَلَيْهِ وَاٰلِهٖ وَسَلَّم replied, 'Allah عَزَّوَجَلَّ records the name of every person who will die this year and I like to be in the state of fasting at the time of my demise.' *(Musnad Abī Ya'lā, vol. 4, pp. 277, Ḥadīš 4890)*

Favourite month

Sayyidunā 'Abdullāĥ Bin Abī Qays رَضِیَ اللهُ تَعَالٰى عَنْه has narrated that he heard Sayyidatunā 'Āishaĥ Ṣiddīqaĥ رَضِیَ اللهُ تَعَالٰى عَنْهَا say, 'Sha'ban was the favourite month of the Holy Prophet صَلَّى اللهُ تَعَالٰى عَلَيْهِ وَاٰلِهٖ وَسَلَّم. He صَلَّى اللهُ تَعَالٰى عَلَيْهِ وَاٰلِهٖ وَسَلَّم would fast during this month and join it with Ramadan.' *(Sunan Abī Dāwūd, vol. 2, pp. 476, Ḥadīš 2431)*

People are heedless of Sha'bān's significance

Sayyidunā Usāmaĥ Bin Zayd رَضِیَ اللّٰہُ تَعَالٰی عَنْہُ has stated, 'I asked the Beloved and Blessed Prophet صَلَّى اللهُ تَعَالٰى عَلَيْهِ وَاٰلِهٖ وَسَلَّم, 'Yā Rasūlallāĥ صَلَّى اللهُ تَعَالٰى عَلَيْهِ وَاٰلِهٖ وَسَلَّم, 'I have seen you keep fasts in the month of Sha'ban so abundantly that I have never seen you keep fasts so abundantly in any other month.' The Beloved and Blessed Prophet صَلَّى اللهُ تَعَالٰى عَلَيْهِ وَاٰلِهٖ وَسَلَّم replied, 'This month is between Rajab and Ramadan; people are heedless of it. It is the month in which people's deeds are presented before Allah عَزَّوَجَلَّ. I wish that my deeds be presented at a time when I am in the state of fast.' *(Sunan Nasāī, vol. 4, pp. 200)*

Act according to your strength

Sayyidatunā 'Āishaĥ Ṣiddīqaĥ رَضِیَ اللّٰہُ تَعَالٰی عَنْھَا has narrated, 'The Prophet of Raḥmaĥ, the Intercessor of Ummaĥ صَلَّى اللهُ تَعَالٰى عَلَيْهِ وَاٰلِهٖ وَسَلَّم would keep more fasts in Sha'ban than in any other month. He صَلَّى اللهُ تَعَالٰى عَلَيْهِ وَاٰلِهٖ وَسَلَّم would keep fasts throughout Sha'ban and say, 'Act according to your strength because Allah عَزَّوَجَلَّ does not prevent His bounties until you get tired.' Indeed the most pleasing (Nafl) Ṣalāĥ to Allah عَزَّوَجَلَّ is the one that is offered steadfastly, though in less amount, so whenever he صَلَّى اللهُ تَعَالٰى عَلَيْهِ وَاٰلِهٖ وَسَلَّم offered any (Nafl) Ṣalāĥ he used to offer steadfastly.' *(Ṣaḥīḥ Bukhārī, vol. 1, pp. 648, Ḥadīš 1970)*

Ḥujjat-ul-Islam Sayyidunā Imām Muhammad Ghazālī عَلَيْهِ رَحْمَةُ اللّٰهِ الْوَالِي has stated, 'In the previous sacred Ḥadīš, fasting for the whole of Sha'bān means fasting for the most days of the month. *(Mukāshafa-tul-Qulūb, pp. 303)* There is nothing wrong with fasting all the days of Sha'bān as well.'

اَلْحَمْدُ لِلّٰه عَزَّوَجَلَّ! Many Islamic brothers and sisters of Dawat-e-Islami fast continuously for three months (Rajab and Sha'bān and Ramadan). In order to develop a habit of fasting and acting upon the Sunnaĥ, please join the Madanī environment of Dawat-e-Islami. A Madanī blessing is presented to encourage you:

I was fond of flying kites

An Islamic brother of Bāb-ul-Madīnaĥ Karachi gave the following account: Unfortunately, I spent my past life in sins. I used to fly kites and play computer games. I would stick my nose into everyone's business, argue with people unnecessarily and start fights without any reason.

Luckily, I performed I'tikāf for the last ten days of Ramadan in my local Masjid as a result of the individual effort of an Islamic brother. I saw some extremely pleasant dreams and felt immense peace. I was blessed with performing I'tikāf for another two years. Making individual effort, once the Mūażżin of the Masjid convinced me to attend the weekly Sunnaĥ-Inspiring Ijtimā' of Dawat-e-Islami in its global Madanī Markaz, Faīzān-e-Madīnaĥ. When we reached Faīzān-e-Madīnaĥ, a Muballigh was delivering a speech. He was dressed in white clothes with a brown shawl over his shoulders and a green turban on his head. He also had a fist-length beard on his face. I'd never seen such a refulgent face before. The attraction and refulgence of the Muballigh's face captured my heart and hence I joined the Madanī environment of Dawat-e-Islami. For the past two years I have been performing I'tikāf in the global Madanī Markaz, Faīzān-e-Madīnaĥ (Bāb-ul-Madīnaĥ). اَلْحَمْدُلِلّٰه عَزَّوَجَلَّ! I have also grown my beard according to Sunnaĥ.

صَلُّوْا عَلَى الْحَبِيْب صَلَّى اللّٰهُ تَعَالٰى عَلٰى مُحَمَّد

Which month is best after Ramadan?

Sayyidunā Anas رَضِیَ اللّٰہ تَعَالٰی عَنْہ has stated, 'Someone asked the Beloved and Blessed Prophet صَلَّى اللهُ تَعَالٰى عَلَيْهِ وَاٰلِهٖ وَسَلَّم as to which fast is the best after Ramadan? He صَلَّى اللهُ تَعَالٰى عَلَيْهِ وَاٰلِهٖ وَسَلَّم replied, 'The fast of Sha'bān for honouring Ramadan.' He صَلَّى اللهُ تَعَالٰى عَلَيْهِ وَاٰلِهٖ وَسَلَّم was further asked what the best charity was, and he صَلَّى اللهُ تَعَالٰى عَلَيْهِ وَاٰلِهٖ وَسَلَّم replied, 'To give charity in the month of Ramadan.' *(Jāmi' Tirmiżī, vol. 2, pp. 145, Ḥadīš 663)*

Manifestation of specific attribute at 15th night

Sayyidatunā 'Āishaĥ Ṣiddīqaĥ رَضِیَ اللّٰہ تَعَالٰی عَنْہَا has reported that the Holy Prophet صَلَّى اللهُ تَعَالٰى عَلَيْهِ وَاٰلِهٖ وَسَلَّم has said: Allah عَزَّوَجَلَّ reveals His specific attribute on the 15th night. (He عَزَّوَجَلَّ) forgives those who ask for forgiveness and showers mercy upon those who ask for mercy but leaves those who hold malice (in their hearts for each other). *(Shu'ab-ul-Īmān, vol. 3, pp. 382, Ḥadīš 3835)*

صَلُّوْا عَلَى الْحَبِيْب صَلَّى اللّٰهُ تَعَالٰى عَلٰى مُحَمَّد

Nuisance of people who hold grudges

Sayyidunā Mu'āż Bin Jabal رَضِیَ اللّٰہُ تَعَالٰی عَنْهُ has reported that the Prophet of Raḥmaĥ, the Intercessor of Ummaĥ صَلَّى اللّٰهُ تَعَالٰى عَلَيْهِ وَاٰلِهٖ وَسَلَّم has said: 'On the 15th night, Allah عَزَّوَجَلَّ reveals His specific attribute to the whole of creation and forgives everyone except the unbeliever and the one who has malice (in his heart for another Muslim).' *(Al-Iḥsān bittartīb Ṣaḥīḥ Ibn Ḥibbān, vol. 7, pp. 470, Ḥadīš 5636)*

Dear Islamic brothers! Any two Muslims that have enmity against each other due to any worldly matter should apologize to each others before the arrival of Shab-e-Barā-at so that they aren't deprived of the mercy of Allah عَزَّوَجَلَّ.

اَلْحَمْدُ لِلّٰه عَزَّوَجَلَّ! Motivated by these Aḥādīš, my leader A'lā Ḥaḍrat رَحْمَةُ اللّٰهِ تَعَالٰی عَلَيْه had established a custom in Madīna-tul-Murshid Bareilly, inspiring the Muslims to apologize to each other prior to the arrival of Shab-e-Barā-at. It is my Madanī request that all Islamic brothers should do this, and Islamic sisters should also seek forgiveness from each other by phone etc.

صَلُّوْا عَلَى الْحَبِيْب صَلَّى اللّٰهُ تَعَالٰى عَلٰى مُحَمَّد

Message of Imām-e-Aĥl-e-Sunnat

Shab-e-Barā-at is approaching. At this night, the deeds of all the people are presented in the court of Allah عَزَّوَجَلَّ. For the sake of the Beloved Prophet صَلَّى اللّٰهُ تَعَالٰى عَلَيْهِ وَاٰلِهٖ وَسَلَّم, Allah عَزَّوَجَلَّ forgives the sins of the Muslims, however, He عَزَّوَجَلَّ says about those two Muslims who have malice due to worldly matter, 'Leave them as they are unless they reconcile.'

Everyone should fulfill others' rights or have them forgiven so that (by the grace of Allah عَزَّوَجَلَّ) the book of deeds is presented to Allah عَزَّوَجَلَّ in such a state that there is no violation of others' rights in it. For the forgiveness of the rights of Allah عَزَّوَجَلَّ, a sincere repentance is sufficient as a Ḥadīš says, 'اَلتَّائِبُ مِنَ الذَّنْبِ كَمَنْ لَّا ذَنْبَ لَهٗ' (*The one repenting of his sin is like the one who has not committed the sin at all*). By the blessing of repenting in the aforementioned way, (by the grace of Allah عَزَّوَجَلَّ) there is a strong hope of complete forgiveness provided the beliefs are correct. وَهُوَ الْغَفُوْرُ الرَّحِيْم

In Bareilly, this is a long-standing practice that the Muslims are reconciled with each others and forgive each others' rights. Hopefully, by starting this trend among the Muslims of your city, you would also get deserving of the reward described in the narration that says:

مَنْ سَنَّ فِی الْاِسْلَامِ سُنَّةً حَسَنَةً فَلَهٗ اَجْرُهَا
وَاَجْرُ مَنْ عَمِلَ بِهَا اِلٰی یَوْمِ الْقِیٰمَةِ لَا یَنْقُصُ مِنْ اُجُوْرِهِمْ شَیْءٌ

The one who promotes a good innovation in Islam will get its reward in addition to the reward of those practicing upon it till the Day of Judgement without any reduction in their reward.

Make supplication for this beggar's salvation and peace in the world as well as in the Hereafter. This beggar supplicates and will continue to supplicate for you (اِنْ شَآءَاللّٰه عَزَّوَجَلَّ). All the Muslims should be made to realize that reconciliation and forgiveness should be made sincerely and wholeheartedly as neither lip-service is acknowledged nor hypocrisy is liked in the court of Allah عَزَّوَجَلَّ.

وَالسَّلَام

Aḥmad Razā Qādirī
From: Bareilly

Those who are deprived on Shab-e-Barā-at

Sayyidatunā 'Āishaĥ Ṣiddīqaĥ رَضِیَ اللّٰهُ تَعَالٰی عَنْهَا has narrated that the Holy Prophet صَلَّى اللّٰهُ تَعَالٰی عَلَیْهِ وَاٰلِهٖ وَسَلَّم has stated, 'Jibrāīl عَلَیْهِ السَّلَام came to me and said, 'This is the 15th night of Sha'ban. At this night, Allah عَزَّوَجَلَّ frees as many people from fire as the number of the hair growing on the sheep of the tribe of Banī Kalb; but He عَزَّوَجَلَّ does not have mercy on those associating partners with Allah عَزَّوَجَلَّ, having malice in their heart (against someone), breaking ties with relatives, wearing clothes dangling down the ankles (as a sign of pride), disobeying parents, and habitual drinker.' *(Shu'ab-ul-Īmān, vol. 3, pp. 383, Ḥadīš 3837)*

The narration which Sayyidunā Imām Aḥmad رَضِیَ اللّٰهُ تَعَالٰی عَنْهُ has taken from Sayyidunā 'Abdullāĥ Ibn 'Umar Ibn Zayd رَضِیَ اللّٰهُ تَعَالٰی عَنْهُمَا mentions a murderer as well.

(Musnad Imām Aḥmad, vol. 2, pp. 589, Ḥadīš 6653)

Everyone is forgiven except...

Sayyidunā Kašīr Bin Murraĥ رَضِیَ اللهُ تَعَالٰی عَنْهُ has reported that the Beloved and Blessed Prophet صَلَّى اللهُ تَعَالٰی عَلَيْهِ وَاٰلِهٖ وَسَلَّم has said: 'On the 15th night of Sha'ban, Allah عَزَّوَجَلَّ forgives everyone dwelling on the earth except the unbeliever and the one who holds grudge.' *(Al-Mutḥa-rul-Rābi', pp. 376, Ḥadīš 769)*

Ask for whatever you want in Shab-e-Barā-at

Amīr-ul-Mūminīn Sayyidunā 'Alī كَرَّمَ اللّٰهُ تَعَالٰى وَجْهَهُ الْكَرِيْم has reported that the Prophet of Raḥmaĥ, the Intercessor of Ummaĥ, the Owner of Jannaĥ صَلَّى اللهُ تَعَالٰی عَلَيْهِ وَاٰلِهٖ وَسَلَّم has said: 'When the 15th night of Sha'bān comes, stand (to offer Ṣalāĥ) in it and fast on the day because Allah عَزَّوَجَلَّ reveals His specific attribute on the sky of the world from sunset and says, 'Is there anyone who seeks forgiveness from Me so that I forgive him! Is there anyone who seeks sustenance so that I provide him with sustenance! Is there any troubled person so that I relieve him from his trouble! Is there anyone like this! Is there anyone like this!' He عَزَّوَجَلَّ keeps saying this till Fajr.' *(Sunan Ibn Mājaĥ, vol. 2, pp. 160, Ḥadīš 1388)*

Supplication of Sayyidunā Dāwūd عَلَيْهِ السَّلَام

Amīr-ul-Mūminīn Sayyidunā 'Alī كَرَّمَ اللّٰهُ تَعَالٰى وَجْهَهُ الْكَرِيْم would often go outside on the 15th night of Sha'bān. Once, as usual, he رَضِیَ اللهُ تَعَالٰی عَنْهُ came out, raised his gaze towards the sky and said, 'Once, the Beloved Prophet of Allah, Sayyidunā Dāwūd عَلَيْهِ السَّلَام looked upwards on the 15th night of Sha'bān and said, 'This is the time of (acceptance), whoever made Du'ā to Allah عَزَّوَجَلَّ for anything, Allah عَزَّوَجَلَّ has accepted his Du'ā. Whoever asked for forgiveness, Allah عَزَّوَجَلَّ has forgiven him provided he is not an 'Ushshār (the person who unjustly demands tax money), a magician, fortune teller, cruel policeman, one who tells tales to a ruler, singer and a musical instruments player.' Then he عَلَيْهِ السَّلَام recited:

اَللّٰهُمَّ رَبَّ دَاوٗدَ اغْفِرْ لِمَنْ دَعَاكَ فِيْ هٰذِهِ اللَّيْلَةِ اَوِ اسْتَغْفَرَكَ فِيْهَا

Translation: 'Yā Allah عَزَّوَجَلَّ! O Rab of Dāwūd (عَلَيْهِ السَّلَام)! Whoever makes Du'ā to You or seeks forgiveness from You, forgive him.'

(Māšabata-bis-Sunnaĥ, pp. 354)

Revering Shab-e-Barā-at

The Syrian (Tabi'īn) saints رَضِیَ اللّٰہُ تَعَالٰی عَنْہُم would honour Shab-e-Barā-at a lot and worship abundantly in it. Other Muslims also learnt to honour this night from them. Some Syrian scholars رَحِمَہُمُ اللّٰہُ تَعَالٰی have said: To worship collectively on Shab-e-Barā-at in the Masjid is desirable (Mustaḥab). To honour this night, Sayyidunā Khālid and Luqmān رَضِیَ اللّٰہُ تَعَالٰی عَنْہُمَا and other honourable Tabi'īn رَضِیَ اللّٰہُ تَعَالٰی عَنْہُم used to wear nice clothes, apply kohl and perfume and offer (Nafl) Ṣalāĥ in the Masjid. *(Laṭāif-ul-Ma'ārif, pp. 263)*

Nights of goodness

Sayyidatunā 'Āishaĥ Ṣiddīqaĥ رَضِیَ اللّٰہُ تَعَالٰی عَنْہَا has stated that I heard the Beloved and Blessed Prophet صَلَّی اللّٰہُ تَعَالٰی عَلَیْہِ وَاٰلِہٖ وَسَلَّم say, 'Allah عَزَّوَجَلَّ opens the portals of goodness at four nights:

1. Night of Eid-ul-Aḍḥā
2. Night of Eid-ul-Fiṭr
3. Night of the 15th of Sha'ban as the names of those who would die and perform Hajj (this year) and sustenance are inscribed this night.
4. Night of Arafat (9th Żul-Ḥijjaĥ) till the Ażān of Fajr. *(Ad-Dur-rul-Manšūr, vol. 7, pp. 402)*

Groom's name amongst the dead

The Prophet of mankind, the Peace of our heart and mind, the most Generous and Kind صَلَّی اللّٰہُ تَعَالٰی عَلَیْہِ وَاٰلِہٖ وَسَلَّم has said: The lives (of people) come to an end from the period of one Sha'bān to the next Sha'bān. A man gets married and is blessed with offspring but his name is written amongst those who are going to die. *(Kanz-ul-'Ummāl, vol. 15, pp. 292, Ḥadīš 42773)*

Name of the one making house amongst the dead

Sayyidunā Imām Ibn Abid Dunyā رَحْمَۃُ اللّٰہِ تَعَالٰی عَلَیْہ has narrated from Sayyidunā 'Aṭā Bin Yasār رَحْمَۃُ اللّٰہِ تَعَالٰی عَلَیْہ when the 15th night of Sha'bān (Shab-e-Barā-at) comes, the angel of death is given a scripture and is told, 'Take this scripture. There would be a man lying on bed and would marry a woman and make a house, yet his name will have been written amongst the dead.' *(Ad-Dur-rul-Manšūr, vol. 7, pp. 402)*

Division of year's affairs

Sayyidunā Ibn 'Abbās رَضِیَ اللّٰہُ تَعَالٰی عَنْہُمَا has stated, '(Sometimes) A man is walking, yet his name is amongst the dead.' Then he رَضِیَ اللّٰہُ تَعَالٰی عَنْہُ recited the 3rd and 4th verses of Sūraĥ Ad-Dukhān (part 25):

إِنَّآ أَنزَلْنَٰهُ فِى لَيْلَةٍ مُّبَٰرَكَةٍ إِنَّا كُنَّا مُنذِرِينَ ۝٣ فِيهَا يُفْرَقُ كُلُّ أَمْرٍ حَكِيمٍ ۝٤

Undoubtedly, We sent it down in a blessed night; verily we are to warn.' Therein every affair of wisdom is divided.

[Kanz-ul-Īmān (Translation of Quran)]

He رَضِیَ اللّٰہُ تَعَالٰی عَنْہُ then said, 'At this night, the worldly affairs from one year to the other are divided.' *(Tafsīr Ṭabarī, vol. 11, pp. 223)* Commenting on this verse, a renowned exegetist of the Quran, Muftī Aḥmad Yār Khān عَلَیْہِ رَحْمَۃُ الْحَنَّان has stated, 'This night refers to either Layla-tul-Qadr (which is) the 27th night or Shab-e-Mi'rāj (the night of the Ascension) or the Shab-e-Barā-at (which is) the 15th night of Sha'bān. At this night, the entire Holy Quran descended from Lauḥ-e-Maḥfūẓ to the sky of the world and then from there was revealed to the Beloved and Blessed Prophet صَلَّى اللهُ تَعَالٰى عَلَيْهِ وَاٰلِهٖ وَسَلَّم gradually in the period of twenty three years.

This verse also clarifies that the night in which the Holy Quran was revealed is sacred, so likewise, the night in which the Sahib-e-Quran صَلَّى اللهُ تَعَالٰى عَلَيْهِ وَاٰلِهٖ وَسَلَّم (the one to whom the Quran was revealed) came into this world is also sacred. At this night, the year's sustenance, death, life, honour, disgrace, and all other affairs are transferred from the Lauḥ-e-Maḥfūẓ to the scriptures of the angels and each scripture is given to the angel appointed for that task. For example, the angel of death is given the list of all people who would die that year.' *(Nūr-ul-'Irfān, pp. 790)*

Crucial decisions

Dear Islamic brothers! How crucial the 15th night of Sha'bān-ul-Mu'aẓẓam is! Who knows what will be predestined for him. Sometimes, a person is heedless but he is unaware of what is in store for him. It is stated in *Ghunya-tuṭ-Ṭālibīn*, 'The shrouds of many people are washed and ready but the people who are going to wear those shrouds are wandering around in the marketplaces. There are many people whose graves have been dug and are ready but those who are going to be buried in them are lost in happiness. Some people are laughing but the time of their ruin is close. The construction of many houses is going to be completed but the time of the death of their owners has also approached.' *(Ghunya-tuṭ-Ṭālibīn, vol. 1, pp. 251)*

Attention!

In Shab-e-Barā-at the deeds of people are raised. Therefore, if possible, fast on the 14th of Sha'bān and stay in the Masjid with the intention of Nafl I'tikāf after offering 'Aṣr Ṣalāĥ so that the deeds of fasting, sitting in the Masjid and I'tikāf etc. would be written just before the arrival of the night in which books of deeds are raised, and Shab-e-Barā-at would begin in the merciful atmosphere of the Masjid.

صَلُّوۡا عَلَی الۡحَبِیۡب صَلَّی اللّٰہُ تَعَالٰی عَلٰی مُحَمَّد

Six Nawāfil after Maghrib Ṣalāĥ

To offer six Nafl after the Farḍ and Sunan of Maghrib is one of the practices of the pious saints رَحِمَهُمُ اللّٰهُ تَعَالٰی. After offering the Farḍ and Sunan etc., offer six Rak'āt of Nafl in sets of two. Before offering the first two Rak'āt, make the intention: '*Yā Allah* عَزَّوَجَلَّ*! By the blessing of these two Rak'āt, grant me a well long life.*' Similarly, before offering the second two Rak'āt, make the intention: '*Yā Allah* عَزَّوَجَلَّ*! By the blessing of these two Rak'āt, save me from afflictions.*' Before offering the last two Rak'āt, make the intention: '*Yā Allah* عَزَّوَجَلَّ*! By the blessing of these two Rak'āt, do not make me dependent on anyone except You.*'

After every two Rak'āt, recite Sūraĥ Al-Ikhlāṣ twenty one times or Sūraĥ Yāsīn once. If possible, recite them both. It is also possible that one Islamic brother recites Sūraĥ Yāsīn while the rest listen. Keep in mind that the other brothers do not have to recite Sūraĥ Yāsīn etc. individually while loud recitation is going on. اِنْ شَآءَاللّٰه عَزَّوَجَلَّ You will attain huge rewards at the very beginning of the night. After each Sūraĥ Yāsīn, recite the Du'ā of Sha'bān:

Du'ā for mid-Sha'bān

بِسْمِ اللّٰهِ الرَّحْمٰنِ الرَّحِيْمِ ؕ

With the name of Allah عَزَّوَجَلَّ the most Kind, the Most Merciful!

اَللّٰهُمَّ يَا ذَا الْمَنِّ وَلَا يُمَنُّ عَلَيْهِ ؕ يَا ذَا الْجَلَالِ وَالْاِكْرَامِ ؕ يَا ذَا الطَّوْلِ وَالْاِنْعَامِ ؕ لَآ اِلٰهَ
اِلَّا اَنْتَ ؕ ظَهْرُ اللَّاجِيْنَ ؕ وَجَارُ الْمُسْتَجِيْرِيْنَ ؕ وَاَمَانُ الْخَآئِفِيْنَ ؕ اَللّٰهُمَّ اِنْ كُنْتَ كَتَبْتَنِيْ
عِنْدَكَ فِيْٓ اُمِّ الْكِتٰبِ شَقِيًّا اَوْ مَحْرُوْمًا اَوْ مَطْرُوْدًا اَوْ مُقَتَّرًا عَلَيَّ فِي الرِّزْقِ فَامْحُ اللّٰهُمَّ
بِفَضْلِكَ شَقَاوَتِيْ وَحِرْمَانِيْ وَطَرْدِيْ وَاقْتِتَارَ رِزْقِيْ ؕ وَاَثْبِتْنِيْ عِنْدَكَ فِيْٓ اُمِّ الْكِتٰبِ سَعِيْدًا
مَّرْزُوْقًا مُّوَفَّقًا لِّلْخَيْرَاتِ ؕ فَاِنَّكَ قُلْتَ وَقَوْلُكَ الْحَقُّ فِيْ كِتَابِكَ الْمُنْزَلِ ؕ عَلٰى لِسَانِ نَبِيِّكَ
الْمُرْسَلِ ؕ ﴿يَمْحُوا اللّٰهُ مَا يَشَآءُ وَيُثْبِتُ ۚۖ وَعِنْدَهٗٓ اُمُّ الْكِتٰبِ ۝﴾ اِلٰهِيْ بِالتَّجَلِّي الْاَعْظَمِ ؕ
فِيْ لَيْلَةِ النِّصْفِ مِنْ شَهْرِ شَعْبَانَ الْمُكَرَّمِ ؕ الَّتِيْ يُفْرَقُ فِيْهَا كُلُّ اَمْرٍ حَكِيْمٍ وَّيُبْرَمُ ؕ اَنْ تَكْشِفَ
عَنَّا مِنَ الْبَلَآءِ وَالْبَلْوَآءِ مَا نَعْلَمُ وَمَا لَا نَعْلَمُ ؕ وَاَنْتَ بِهٖ اَعْلَمُ ؕ اِنَّكَ اَنْتَ الْاَعَزُّ الْاَكْرَمُ ؕ
وَصَلَّى اللّٰهُ تَعَالٰى عَلٰى سَيِّدِنَا مُحَمَّدٍ وَّعَلٰى اٰلِهٖ وَاَصْحَابِهٖ وَسَلَّمَ ؕ وَالْحَمْدُ لِلّٰهِ رَبِّ الْعٰلَمِيْنَ ۝

Translation: Yā Allah عَزَّوَجَلَّ! You shower favours on everyone and no one can do You any favour! O Possessor of majesty and honour! O Distributor of bounty and rewards! There is none worthy of worship except You. You help the troubled and provide refuge to the refuge-seekers and give peace to those who are in fear. Yā Allah عَزَّوَجَلَّ! In the mother of all books (i.e. Lauḥ-e-Maḥfūẓ) that is with You, if You have written my name among the unfortunate, the deprived, the rejected or those without enough sustenance, then Yā Allah عَزَّوَجَلَّ, with Your grace, remove this misfortune, deprivation and lack of sustenance in the mother of all books that is with You, write my name among those who are blessed with good fortune, increased sustenance and

ability to perform good deeds. Indeed, You have truly mentioned in Your book (i.e. the Quran) as described by Your Prophet صَلَّى اللهُ تَعَالٰى عَلَيْهِ وَاٰلِهٖ وَسَلَّم: Translation from Kanz-ul-Īmān: 'Allah عَزَّوَجَلَّ wipes out what He wills and establishes (what He wills) and with Him is the Actual writing..' *(Part 13, Sūraĥ Ar-Ra'd, verse 39)* **O my Rab عَزَّوَجَلَّ! For the sake of the specific attribute on this fifteenth night of the blessed month of Sha'bān in which wise and irrevocable decrees are issued, remove from us all calamities and hardships, those that we know about as well as those that we don't, while You know everything. Truly, You are the most powerful, most honourable. And may Allah Almighty عَزَّوَجَلَّ shower blessings and peace on Sayyidunā Muhammad, and on his family and his companions رَضِیَ اللّٰہُ تَعَالٰی عَنْهُم and all praise is for Allah عَزَّوَجَلَّ, Rab of the worlds.**

Request of Sag-e-Madīnaĥ

اَلْحَمْدُ لِلّٰه عَزَّوَجَلَّ! It is my (the author's) long standing practice to offer six Nafl and do Tilāwaĥ at Shab-e-Barā-at. This form of worship after Maghrib is Nafl. It is neither Farḍ nor Wājib, and there is no prohibition in Sharī'aĥ about Nafl and Tilāwaĥ after Maghrib. Therefore, if possible, each Islamic brother should make proper arrangement for this worship in their local Masjid and gain reward in abundance. Islamic sisters should offer these Nafl at home.

Protection from magic whole year

At the 15th night of Sha'bān, boil seven leaves of a berry tree in water and perform Ghusl with that water (unboiled water can also be added, if needed). اِنْ شَآءَالله عَزَّوَجَلَّ You will remain safe from magic for the whole year. *(Islāmī Zindagī, pp. 113)*

Shab-e-Barā-at and visiting graves

Sayyidatunā 'Āishaĥ Ṣiddīqaĥ رَضِیَ اللّٰہُ تَعَالٰی عَنْهَا has narrated, 'One night I did not find the Holy Prophet صَلَّى اللهُ تَعَالٰى عَلَيْهِ وَاٰلِهٖ وَسَلَّم but (then) I came across him in Baqī'. The Beloved and Blessed Prophet صَلَّى اللهُ تَعَالٰى عَلَيْهِ وَاٰلِهٖ وَسَلَّم said to me, 'Were you afraid that Allah عَزَّوَجَلَّ and His Prophet صَلَّى اللهُ تَعَالٰى عَلَيْهِ وَاٰلِهٖ وَسَلَّم would not fulfil your rights?' I politely replied 'Yā Rasūlallāh صَلَّى اللهُ تَعَالٰى عَلَيْهِ وَاٰلِهٖ وَسَلَّم, I thought that you had probably gone to one of your other chaste wives.'

The Prophet of Raḥmaĥ, the Intercessor of Ummaĥ صَلَّى اللهُ تَعَالٰى عَلَيْهِ وَاٰلِهٖ وَسَلَّم said, 'Without doubt, on the 15th night of Sha'ban, Allah عَزَّوَجَلَّ reveals His specific attribute on the sky of the world and forgives more people than even the number of hair growing on the goats of the tribe Banī Kalb.' *(Jāmi' Tirmiżī, vol. 2, pp. 183, Ḥadīš 739)*

Lighting candles on graves

It is Sunnaĥ for Islamic brothers to visit the graveyard on Shab-e-Barā-at (by Sharī'aĥ, Islamic sisters are not allowed). It is not allowed to burn candles on the graves. However, if there is darkness in the cemetery and one needs light for the recitation of the Quran etc., a candle may be lit in this case for light at some distance away from the grave.

Similarly, there is no harm in burning incenses at some distance away from the grave for spreading fragrance among the attendees. To lay shawl at the blessed graves of the Auliyā and burning lamps beside them is permissible as these acts would attract people and they would develop the respect and reverence of saints in their hearts, gaining spiritual and worldly benefits. If the graves of Auliyā and those of common people are kept in the same condition, many religious benefits would come to an end.

Green paper

Once, at the 15th night of Sha'bān, Amīr-ul-Mūminīn, Sayyidunā 'Umar Bin 'Abdul 'Azīz رَضِیَ اللّٰہُ تَعَالٰی عَنْہُ was busy worshipping. When he رَضِیَ اللّٰہُ تَعَالٰی عَنْہُ raised his head, he رَضِیَ اللّٰہُ تَعَالٰی عَنْہُ discovered a green slip. Its light was spreading out towards the sky and it read, 'هٰذِهٖ بَرَاءَةٌ مِّنَ النَّارِ مِنَ الْمَلِكِ الْعَزِيْزِ لِعَبْدِهٖ عُمَرَ بْنِ عَبْدِالْعَزِيْزِ' (Translation): '*This is a letter of forgiveness from Allah عَزَّوَجَلَّ to His servant 'Umar Bin 'Abdul 'Azīz رَضِیَ اللّٰہُ تَعَالٰی عَنْہُ.*' *(Tafsīr Rūḥ-ul-Bayān, vol. 8, pp. 402)*

Who invented fireworks?

Dear Islamic brothers! اَلْحَمْدُلِلّٰہ عَزَّوَجَلَّ, Shab-e-Barā-at is a night to gain freedom and salvation from the fire of Hell but unfortunately, today's Muslims are buying fire themselves wasting their hard-earned money in the form of fireworks instead of gaining freedom from the fire. In this manner, they violate the honour and sacredness of this night.

In the book entitled '*Islāmī Zindagī*', Muftī Aḥmad Yār Khān عَلَیْہِ رَحْمَۃُ الْمَنَّان has stated, 'The tyrant king Namrūd invented fireworks. When Sayyidunā Ibrāĥīm عَلٰی نَبِیِّنَا وَ عَلَیْہِ الصَّلٰوۃُ وَالسَّلَام

was placed into fire, the fire cooled and turned into a garden of flowers, so Namrūd's people prepared portable firework which they set on fire and threw towards Sayyidunā Ibrāĥīm عَلٰی نَبِیِّنَا وَعَلَیْہِ الصَّلٰوۃُ وَالسَّلَام.' *(Islāmī Zindagī, pp. 63)*

Fireworks are Ḥarām

Sadly, the futile tradition of fireworks is rapidly spreading amongst Muslims. Every year, Muslims waste millions of rupees buying fireworks. It's often reported that so many houses have been burnt and so many people have tragically lost their lives as a result of fireworks. It can result in the loss of life and property; it is a complete waste of money either. Above all, this act is disobedience to Allah عَزَّوَجَلَّ. Muftī Aḥmad Yār Khān عَلَیْہِ رَحْمَۃُ الْمَنَّان has stated, 'Making, purchasing, selling and setting off fireworks are all Ḥarām.' *(Islāmī Zindagī, pp. 63)*

Tujĥ ko Sha'bān-e-Mu'aẓẓam kā Khudāyā wāsiṭaĥ
Bakhsh day Rab-e-Muhammad Tū mayrī ĥar aīk khaṭā

Forgive every mistake of mine, O Rab of Mustafa
For the sake of Sha'bān-ul-Mu'aẓẓam, Yā Allah

صَلُّوْا عَلَی الْحَبِیْب   صَلَّی اللّٰہُ تَعَالٰی عَلٰی مُحَمَّد

The Holy Prophet صَلَّی اللّٰہُ تَعَالٰی عَلَیْہِ وَاٰلِہٖ وَسَلَّم and green turban

Dear Islamic brothers! In order to develop the mindset of worshipping, fasting and avoiding sins including fireworks in Sha'bān, please travel with the Sunnaĥ-Inspiring Madanī Qāfilaĥs of Dawat-e-Islami in the company of Rasūl's devotees, and gain the blessings of the collective I'tikāf of Dawat-e-Islami in Ramadan.

Now I am going to present such a heart-warming Madanī blessing that will delight you, making your heart leap with joy, اِنْ شَآءَاللّٰہ عَزَّوَجَلَّ. Therefore, an Islamic brother of Wah Cantt (Punjab, Pakistan) gave the following account: I was a college-student. Like my other fellows, I was also fond of fashion. I was crazy about watching and playing cricket, and I used to loaf about till late night. I did not use to offer any Ṣalāĥ except Eid ones.

In Ramadan (1422 A.H./2001) I went to a Masjid to offer Ṣalāĥ due to my parents' insistence. After 'Aṣr Ṣalāĥ a bearded Islamic brother dressed in white clothes with a green turban on his head gathered the people together and delivered Dars from *Faīzān-e-Sunnat*. I also listened sitting at a distance. I left immediately after the Dars; this happened for about two or three days.

One day, I stayed in the Masjid. An Islamic brother met me very warmly. He asked my name and address and told me some of the benefits of I'tikāf inviting me to take part in the collective I'tikāf going to be held in the Madanī environment of Dawat-e-Islami. At first, I refused, but he was an enthusiastic Islamic brother. He didn't give up hope, he even came to my home and insisted that I perform I'tikāf. As a result of his constant individual efforts, I made up my mind to take part in the collective I'tikāf and handed in my contribution to the Saḥarī and Ifṭār expenses. During the last ten days of Ramadan I performed I'tikāf with Rasūl's devotees in the Jāmi' Masjid Na'īmiyyaĥ (Lala Rukh, Wah Cantt).

The heart-warming atmosphere of the collective I'tikāf and the company of Rasūl's devotees completely changed my heart. During the I'tikāf, I offered Taĥajjud, Ishrāq, Chāsht and Awwābīn Ṣalāĥ. I felt extremely ashamed of missing my Ṣalāĥs in my previous life. My eyes shed tears of shame and hence I made a firm intention to offer my Ṣalāĥ punctually in the future.

During the supplication, on the 25th night, I was so sad that I burst into tears. Suddenly, I dozed and had a dream in which I saw an extremely honourable and bright-faced personality. There was a crowd of people around him. When I asked about him, I was told that he was the Holy Prophet صَلَّى اللهُ تَعَالٰى عَلَيْهِ وَاٰلِهٖ وَسَلَّم. The crown of green turban was shining on his blessed head. I got such spiritual peace for the first time in my life by beholding the Prophet of mankind, the Peace of our heart and mind, the most Generous and Kind صَلَّى اللهُ تَعَالٰى عَلَيْهِ وَاٰلِهٖ وَسَلَّم. When I awoke everyone was reciting Ṣalāt-o-Salām. I was in an extremely strange state and my body was trembling. I cried uncontrollably and couldn't hold back my tears.

After the Ṣalāt-o-Salām Islamic brothers were lined up to have turbans tied around their heads (these were brothers who had made the intention to practice the Sunnaĥ of wearing a turban). I could hardly manage to tell the following words to Islamic brothers standing near me, 'I also want to tie a turban.' After a short while, I also wore the crown of the blessed turban. During the I'tikāf, I had made the intention of travelling with a Madanī Qāfilaĥ for thirty days.

اَلْحَمْدُ لِلّٰه عَزَّوَجَلَّ! I travelled with the Madanī Qāfilaĥ during which I not only learnt a lot of things including the method of delivering Dars and Bayān but started delivering Dars and Bayān as well. At the time of giving this statement, I am offering Ṣalāĥ punctually and making efforts for the Madanī work of Dawat-e-Islami as the Nigrān of a Żaylī Mushāwarat.

صَلُّوْا عَلَى الْحَبِيْب صَلَّى اللّٰهُ تَعَالٰى عَلٰى مُحَمَّد

THREE VIRTUES OF SIX FASTS AFTER EID

Pure like a new born baby

1. Sayyidunā 'Abdullāĥ Bin 'Umar رَضِیَ اللّٰہُ تَعَالٰی عَنْہُمَا has narrated that the Noble Prophet صَلَّی اللّٰہُ تَعَالٰی عَلَیْہِ وَاٰلِہٖ وَسَلَّم has said: 'The one fasting in Ramadan and then fasting six days in Shawwal has been cleansed from sins as if he was born from his mother's womb today.' *(Majma'-uz-Zawāid, vol. 3, pp. 425, Ḥadīš 5102)*

Fast of whole life

2. Sayyidunā Abū Ayyūb رَضِیَ اللّٰہُ تَعَالٰی عَنْہُ has narrated the following statement of the Holy Prophet صَلَّی اللّٰہُ تَعَالٰی عَلَیْہِ وَاٰلِہٖ وَسَلَّم: 'Whoever keeps fasts in Ramadan and then keeps six fasts in Shawwal, it is as if he has kept fasts for his entire life.' *(Ṣaḥīḥ Muslim, pp. 592, Ḥadīš 1164)*

Fast throughout year

3. Sayyidunā Šaubān رَضِیَ اللّٰہُ تَعَالٰی عَنْہُ has narrated that the Prophet of mankind, the Peace of our heart and mind, the most Generous and Kind صَلَّی اللّٰہُ تَعَالٰی عَلَیْہِ وَاٰلِہٖ وَسَلَّم has said: 'The one fasting six days after Eid-ul-Fiṭr (in Shawwal) has fasted the entire year because whoever brings one good deed will get ten rewards (for it).' *(Sunan Ibn Mājaĥ, vol. 2, pp. 333, Ḥadīš 1715)*

Ten times more reward for a single virtue

Dear Islamic brothers! By the grace of Allah عَزَّوَجَلَّ and for the sake of His Beloved Prophet صَلَّى اللهُ تَعَالٰى عَلَيْهِ وَاٰلِهٖ وَسَلَّم how easy it is for us to earn the reward of the fast of the whole year. Every Muslim should seize this opportunity. The wisdom behind the reward of a year's fasts is that Allah عَزَّوَجَلَّ bestows ten time reward upon the Muslims for every single deed just because of His mercy. Thus, the Merciful Allah عَزَّوَجَلَّ has said:

مَنْ جَآءَ بِالْحَسَنَةِ فَلَهٗ عَشْرُ اَمْثَالِهَا

Whoever brings one good, then for him there are ten like thereof.

[Kanz-ul-Īmān (Translation of Quran)] (Part 8, Sūraĥ Al-An'ām, verse 160)

اَلْحَمْدُ لِلّٰه عَزَّوَجَلَّ! The foregoing verse makes it clear that the fasts of Ramadan are equivalent to those of ten months and then six more fasts are equivalent to sixty fasts (two months of fasting). In this way, one will earn the reward of the fast of the entire year. اَلْحَمْدُ لِلّٰهِ عَلٰى اِحْسَانِهٖ

When to keep six fasts after Eid?

Dear Islamic brothers! Ṣadr-ush-Sharī'aĥ Badr-uṭ-Ṭarīqaĥ Shaykh 'Allāmaĥ Maulānā Muftī Muhammad Amjad 'Alī A'ẓamī عَلَيْهِ رَحْمَةُ اللّٰهِ الْقَوِی has stated in a footnote to *Baĥār-e-Sharī'at*: 'It is better to have these six fasts separately (on alternate days or after every two/three days), but there is still no harm if somebody fasts consecutively after Eid-ul-Fiṭr.' *(Baĥār-e-Sharī'at, part 5, pp. 140)*

Khalīl-e-Millat Shaykh 'Allāmaĥ Maulānā Muhammad Khalīl Khān Qādirī Barakātī رَحْمَةُ اللّٰهِ تَعَالٰى عَلَيْه has stated, 'Though there is no harm if somebody keeps these fasts consecutively after Eid-ul-Fiṭr, it is better to keep them separately, i.e. one after Eid-ul-Fiṭr, then two in every week. If it takes the whole month to have these six fasts, it seems even more appropriate.' *(Sunnī Baĥashtī Zaywar, pp. 347)* In other words, one can keep six fasts whenever he wants in the whole month of Shawwāl except the day of Eid-ul-Fiṭr.

Virtues of first ten days of Żul-Ḥijjaĥ

According to some Aḥādīš, the first ten days of Żul-Ḥijjaĥ are the best days after (the days of) Ramadan.

FOUR NARRATIONS REGARDING ŻUL-ḤIJJAĤ

Best days for performing good deeds

1. The Prophet of Raḥmaĥ, the Intercessor of Ummaĥ صَلَّى اللّٰہ تَعَالٰی عَلَیۡہِ وَاٰلِہٖ وَسَلَّم has stated: 'No deed, performed any other day, is liked by Allah عَزَّوَجَلَّ more than the deed performed during these ten days.' The sacred companions رَضِیَ اللّٰہُ تَعَالٰی عَنۡہُم asked, 'Yā Rasūlallāĥ صَلَّى اللّٰہ تَعَالٰی عَلَیۡہِ وَاٰلِہٖ وَسَلَّم! Not even Jihad?' He صَلَّى اللّٰہ تَعَالٰی عَلَیۡہِ وَاٰلِہٖ وَسَلَّم replied, 'And not even Jihad, except the person who leaves his home with his life and wealth and does not bring any thing back.' (In other words, only the Mujāĥid who succeeds in sacrificing his life and wealth in the path of Allah عَزَّوَجَلَّ can be better than the one who performs good deeds in the first ten days of Żul-Ḥijjaĥ). *(Ṣaḥīḥ Bukhārī, vol. 1, pp. 333, Ḥadīš 969)*

As excellent as Layla-tul-Qadr

2. A blessed Ḥadīš says that Allah عَزَّوَجَلَّ likes to be worshipped during the (first) ten days of Żul-Ḥijjaĥ more than any other day. The fast of any one of these days is equivalent to a year's fasts and the night Ṣalāĥ during any one of these nights (is equivalent) to Layla-tul-Qadr. *(Jāmi' Tirmiżī, vol. 2, pp. 192, Ḥadīš 758)*

Fast of 'Arafaĥ

3. Sayyidunā Abū Qatādaĥ رَضِیَ اللّٰہُ تَعَالٰی عَنۡہُ has narrated the following fragrant statement of the Holy Prophet صَلَّى اللّٰہ تَعَالٰی عَلَیۡہِ وَاٰلِہٖ وَسَلَّم: 'I have presumption from Allah عَزَّوَجَلَّ that the fast of 'Arafāt (9th Żul-Ḥijjaĥ) removes the sins of the previous year and the next year.' *(Ṣaḥīḥ Muslim, pp. 590, Ḥadīš 196)*

One fast is equivalent to a thousand fasts

4. Sayyidatunā 'Āishaĥ Ṣiddīqaĥ رَضِیَ اللّٰہُ تَعَالٰی عَنۡہَا has narrated that Rasūlullāĥ صَلَّى اللّٰہ تَعَالٰی عَلَیۡہِ وَاٰلِہٖ وَسَلَّم has said: 'The fast on 'Arafāt (9th Żul-Ḥijjaĥ) is equivalent to a thousand fasts.' *(Shu'ab-ul-Īmān, vol. 3, pp. 357, Ḥadīš 3764)*

However, this fast is Makrūh for the one who is in the plains of 'Arafāt to perform Hajj as Sayyidunā Ibn Khuzaymah رَضِىَ اللهُ تَعَالىٰ عَنْهُ has narrated from Sayyidunā Abū Ḥurayrah رَضِىَ اللهُ تَعَالىٰ عَنْهُ that the Prophet of Raḥmah, the Intercessor of Ummah, the Owner of Jannah صَلَّى اللهُ تَعَالىٰ عَلَيْهِ وَاٰلِهٖ وَسَلَّم forbade Ḥujjāj (Hajj-pilgrims) to keep fast on the day of 'Arafāt (9th Żul-Ḥijjaĥ) in 'Arafāt (plains). *(Ṣaḥīḥ Ibn Khuzaymaĥ, vol. 3, pp. 292, Ḥadīš 2101)*

Fasts of 13th, 14th and 15th (Ayyām-ul-Bīḍ)

Every Islamic brother and sister should fast at least three days every Madanī (Islamic) month as there are many worldly and religious benefits and advantages of this righteous act. It is best to fast during the 'Ayyām-ul-Bīḍ', which are the 13th, 14th and 15th of (every) lunar month.

Eight narrations regarding fasts of 'Ayyām-ul-Bīḍ'

1. Sayyidatunā 'Āishaĥ Ṣiddīqaĥ رَضِىَ اللهُ تَعَالىٰ عَنْهَا has narrated that there were four things the Holy Prophet صَلَّى اللهُ تَعَالىٰ عَلَيْهِ وَاٰلِهٖ وَسَلَّم never missed: (1) The fast of 'Āshūrā (2) The fast of (first) ten days of Żul-Ḥijjaĥ (3) Three fasts in every month and (4) Two Rak'āt (Sunnaĥ) before (the Farḍ of) Fajr. *(Sunan Nasāī, vol. 4, pp. 220)*

2. Sayyidunā Ibn 'Abbās رَضِىَ اللهُ تَعَالىٰ عَنْهُمَا has narrated that the Beloved and Blessed Prophet صَلَّى اللهُ تَعَالىٰ عَلَيْهِ وَاٰلِهٖ وَسَلَّم would always keep fasts during 'Ayyām-ul-Bīḍ' whether he was in the state of journey or in residence. *(Sunan Nasāī, vol. 4, pp. 198)*

Three days of fasting

3. Sayyidatunā 'Āishaĥ Ṣiddīqaĥ رَضِىَ اللهُ تَعَالىٰ عَنْهَا has narrated: The Beloved and Blessed Prophet صَلَّى اللهُ تَعَالىٰ عَلَيْهِ وَاٰلِهٖ وَسَلَّم would keep fasts on Saturday, Sunday and Monday in one month, and he would keep fasts on Tuesday, Wednesday and Thursday in the next month. *(Jāmi' Tirmiżī, vol. 2, pp. 186, Ḥadīš 746)*

Shield for protection from Hell

4. Sayyidunā 'Ušmān Bin Abū 'Āṣ رَضِىَ اللهُ تَعَالىٰ عَنْهُ has said that he رَضِىَ اللهُ تَعَالىٰ عَنْهُ heard the Prophet of Raḥmaĥ, the Intercessor of Ummaĥ, the Owner of Jannah صَلَّى اللهُ تَعَالىٰ عَلَيْهِ وَاٰلِهٖ وَسَلَّم

say: 'As any one of you have a shield for protection during war, likewise, fast is also your shield from Hell and three fasts every month are the best fasts.' *(Ṣaḥīḥ Ibn Khuzaymaĥ, vol. 3, pp. 301, Ḥadīš 2125)*

5. Fasting three days every month is like fasting for the entire life. *(Ṣaḥīḥ Bukhārī, vol. 1, pp. 649, Ḥadīš 1975)*

6. The fasts of Ramadan and three fasts every month remove the evil of chest. *(Musnad Imām Aḥmad, vol. 9, pp. 36, Ḥadīš 23132)*

7. Whoever can fast three days every month should do so because every fast removes ten sins and cleanses (the sinner) from sins as water washes clothes. *(Mu'jam Kabīr, vol. 25, pp. 35, Ḥadīš 60)*

8. If you want to fasts three days in a month, so fast on the 13th, 14th and 15th. *(Sunan Nasāī, vol. 4, pp. 221)*

Prayer for death

Dear Islamic brothers! In order to make the habit of fasting in Ayyām-ul-Bīḍ, practicing Sunan and performing other good deeds, please join the Madanī environment of Dawat-e-Islami, a global & religious non-political movement of the Quran and Sunnaĥ. Just watching the Madanī activities from the sidelines will not prove to be so effective, please travel with Sunnaĥ-Inspiring Madanī Qāfilaĥ with the devotees of Rasūl, take part in the collective I'tikāf in Ramadan as well, you will experience so much spiritual peace that you will be amazed, إِنْ شَاءَ اللّٰه عَزَّوَجَلَّ.

Listen! How even extremely wicked people become pious due to the blessing of joining the Madanī environment of Dawat-e-Islami. An Islamic brother of Thul, (Bāb-ul-Islam, Sindh) has stated: I was an extremely wicked and evil person. I used to quarrel with people over trivial matters. All the neighbours were distressed due to my misdeeds and my family was so fed up with me that they used to pray for my death.

Luckily, making individual effort, some Islamic brothers invited me to take part in the collective I'tikāf in Ramadan, I agreed due to considerateness. I wasn't serious about it, but I performed I'tikāf with Rasūl's devotees in Ramadan (1420 A.H. 1999) in Memon

Masjid 'Aṭṭārābād with the intention of passing my time. During the I'tikāf, I learnt about the method of Wuḍū, Ghusl, Ṣalāĥ, the rights of Allah عَزَّوَجَلَّ, those of people and respect of Muslims. Sunnaĥ-Inspiring speeches and heart-rending Du'ās had a great effect on me! With remorse, I repented of my previous sins and developed a desire to do good deeds.

اَلْحَمْدُ لِلّٰه عَزَّوَجَلَّ! I grew my beard, which is a symbol of love for the Beloved and Blessed Rasūl صَلَّى اللهُ تَعَالٰى عَلَيْهِ وَاٰلِهٖ وَسَلَّم, started wearing a green turban and calling people towards the right path, giving up fighting and arguing.

Āo ā kar gunāĥaun say taubaĥ karo
Madanī Māḥaul mayn kar lo tum I'tikāf
Raḥmat-e-Ḥaq say dāman tum ā kar bĥaro
Madanī Māḥaul mayn kar lo tum I'tikāf

To repent of sins and immorality
Do I'tikāf in the Madanī environment
To be blessed by Divine bounty
Do I'tikāf in the Madanī environment

صَلُّوْا عَلَى الْحَبِيْب صَلَّى اللهُ تَعَالٰى عَلٰى مُحَمَّد

Five sacred Aḥādīš about fasting on Mondays and Thursdays

1. Sayyidunā Abū Ĥurayraĥ رَضِىَ اللّٰهُ تَعَالٰى عَنْهُ has reported that the Beloved and Blessed Prophet صَلَّى اللهُ تَعَالٰى عَلَيْهِ وَاٰلِهٖ وَسَلَّم has said: Deeds are presented every Monday and Thursday (in the court of Allah عَزَّوَجَلَّ) so I want that my deeds be presented whilst I am fasting. *(Jāmi' Tirmiżī, vol. 2, pp. 747)*

2. The Prophet of mankind, the Peace of our heart and mind, the most Generous and Kind صَلَّى اللهُ تَعَالٰى عَلَيْهِ وَاٰلِهٖ وَسَلَّم would keep fasts on Monday and Thursday. When asked about the reason for this, he صَلَّى اللهُ تَعَالٰى عَلَيْهِ وَاٰلِهٖ وَسَلَّم said, 'In these two days, Allah عَزَّوَجَلَّ forgives every Muslim except such two Muslims who have ended relations with each other. He عَزَّوَجَلَّ orders the angels to leave them until they reconcile.' *(Sunan Ibn Mājaĥ, vol. 2, pp. 344, Ḥadīš 1740)*

3. Sayyidatunā 'Āishaĥ Ṣiddīqaĥ رَضِیَ اللّٰہُ تَعَالٰی عَنۡهَا has stated: The Beloved and Blessed Prophet صَلَّی اللّٰہُ تَعَالٰی عَلَیۡهِ وَاٰلِهٖ وَسَلَّم would particularly keep fasts on Monday and Thursday. *(Jāmi' Tirmiżī, vol. 2, pp. 186, Ḥadīš 745)*

4. Sayyidunā Abū Qatādaĥ رَضِیَ اللّٰہُ تَعَالٰی عَنۡهُ has stated: The Prophet of Raḥmaĥ, the Intercessor of Ummaĥ, the Owner of Jannaĥ صَلَّی اللّٰہُ تَعَالٰی عَلَیۡهِ وَاٰلِهٖ وَسَلَّم was asked about the reason for keeping fast on Monday, he صَلَّی اللّٰہُ تَعَالٰی عَلَیۡهِ وَاٰلِهٖ وَسَلَّم replied: I was born on this day (i.e. Monday) and this is the day I received my first revelation. *(Ṣaḥīḥ Muslim, pp. 591, Ḥadīš 1162)*

Loving Sunnaĥ

5. The slave of Sayyidunā Usāmaĥ Bin Zayd رَضِیَ اللّٰہُ تَعَالٰی عَنۡهُمَا has stated: Sayyidunā Usāmaĥ Bin Zayd رَضِیَ اللّٰہُ تَعَالٰی عَنۡهُ would not miss the fasts of Monday and Thursday even in the state of journey. I asked him why he keeps fasts on Monday and Thursday despite his old age. He رَضِیَ اللّٰہُ تَعَالٰی عَنۡهُ replied: 'Rasūlullāĥ صَلَّی اللّٰہُ تَعَالٰی عَلَیۡهِ وَاٰلِهٖ وَسَلَّم would also keep fasts on Monday and Thursday, I (Usāmaĥ Bin Zayd رَضِیَ اللّٰہُ تَعَالٰی عَنۡهُ) asked, 'Yā Rasūlallāĥ صَلَّی اللّٰہُ تَعَالٰی عَلَیۡهِ وَاٰلِهٖ وَسَلَّم! Why do you keep fasts on Monday and Thursday?' He صَلَّی اللّٰہُ تَعَالٰی عَلَیۡهِ وَاٰلِهٖ وَسَلَّم replied, 'The deeds of people are presented (in the court of Allah عَزَّوَجَلَّ) on Monday and Thursday.' *(Shu'ab-ul-Īmān, vol. 3, pp. 392, Ḥadīš 3859)*

Dear Islamic brothers! We have learnt from these blessed Aḥādīš that the deeds of people are presented in the court of Allah عَزَّوَجَلَّ every Monday and Thursday, and Allah عَزَّوَجَلَّ forgives the Muslims out of His grace in both these days, but the people who have ended relations with each other are not forgiven. It is a matter of concern for all of us. These days, there would hardly be any person who does not have malice (in his heart for other Muslims).

Malice is the feeling of hatred and enmity in the heart. We should seriously ponder over this issue. If we have hatred for a Muslim we should remove that hatred from our heart. If we have any domestic quarrel, we should be the first to approach others and make attempts for reconciliation.

If all sincere efforts of reconciliation fail, then the person who made the first approach will be relieved of his responsibility, اِنۡ شَآءَ اللّٰہ عَزَّوَجَلَّ. Anyhow, the Noble Prophet صَلَّی اللّٰہُ تَعَالٰی عَلَیۡهِ وَاٰلِهٖ وَسَلَّم

used to fast on Mondays and Thursdays. One of the reasons for fasting on Mondays was his blessed birth, so it is as if the Holy Prophet صَلَّى اللهُ تَعَالٰى عَلَيْهِ وَاٰلِهٖ وَسَلَّم used to celebrate his birth by fasting every Monday.

صَلُّوْا عَلَى الْحَبِيْب صَلَّى اللهُ تَعَالٰى عَلٰى مُحَمَّد

Three virtues of fasting on Wednesday and Thursday

1. Sayyidunā 'Abdullāĥ Ibn 'Abbās رَضِىَ اللّٰهُ تَعَالٰى عَنْهُمَا has reported the following blessed saying of the Beloved and Blessed Prophet صَلَّى اللهُ تَعَالٰى عَلَيْهِ وَاٰلِهٖ وَسَلَّم: If anyone keeps fasts on Wednesday and Thursday, protection from Hell is written for him. *(Musnad Abī Ya'lā, vol. 5, pp. 115, Ḥadīš 5610)*

2. Sayyidunā Muslim Bin 'Ubaydullāĥ Qarashī رَضِىَ اللّٰهُ تَعَالٰى عَنْهُ has narrated from his honourable father رَضِىَ اللّٰهُ تَعَالٰى عَنْهُ that either he asked the Holy Prophet صَلَّى اللهُ تَعَالٰى عَلَيْهِ وَاٰلِهٖ وَسَلَّم himself or someone else asked, 'Yā Rasūlallāĥ صَلَّى اللهُ تَعَالٰى عَلَيْهِ وَاٰلِهٖ وَسَلَّم! Shall I fast every day?' He صَلَّى اللهُ تَعَالٰى عَلَيْهِ وَاٰلِهٖ وَسَلَّم remained silent. He asked again but the Beloved and Blessed Prophet صَلَّى اللهُ تَعَالٰى عَلَيْهِ وَاٰلِهٖ وَسَلَّم remained silent. When he asked for the third time, the Noble Prophet صَلَّى اللهُ تَعَالٰى عَلَيْهِ وَاٰلِهٖ وَسَلَّم asked, 'Who asked about fast?' He replied, 'Me, Yā Rasūlallāĥ صَلَّى اللهُ تَعَالٰى عَلَيْهِ وَاٰلِهٖ وَسَلَّم.' He صَلَّى اللهُ تَعَالٰى عَلَيْهِ وَاٰلِهٖ وَسَلَّم replied, 'Verily, your family has a right over you; keep fast in Ramadan and in the following month (i.e. Shawwal) and every Wednesday and Thursday. If you do this it will be as if you have fasted forever.' *(Shu'ab-ul-Īmān, vol. 3, pp. 395, Ḥadīš 3868)*

3. Whoever fasted in Ramadan, Shawwal, on Wednesday and Thursday shall enter Heaven. *(Sunan Kubrā, vol. 2, pp. 147, Ḥadīš 2778)*

Three benefits of fasting on Thursday and Friday

1. Sayyidunā 'Abdullāĥ Ibn 'Abbās رَضِىَ اللّٰهُ تَعَالٰى عَنْهُمَا has reported the following saying of the Holy Prophet صَلَّى اللهُ تَعَالٰى عَلَيْهِ وَاٰلِهٖ وَسَلَّم: 'Whoever fasted on Wednesday, Thursday and Friday; Allah عَزَّوَجَلَّ shall make (such) a house for him in Heaven that its exterior will be visible from the inside and its interior will be visible from the outside.' *(Majma'-uz-Zawāid, vol. 3, pp. 452, Ḥadīš 5204)*

2. Sayyidunā Anas رضی اللہ تعالٰی عنہ has reported that Allah عزّوجلّ will make a palace of pearls, rubies and emeralds for him (the person who keeps fasts on Wednesday, Thursday and Friday) and freedom from Hell shall be written for him. *(Shu'ab-ul-Īmān, vol. 3, pp. 397, Ḥadīš 3873)*

3. Sayyidunā 'Abdullāĥ Ibn 'Umar رضی اللّٰہ تعالٰی عنہما has stated that whoever keeps fasts in these three days and then gives charity on Friday (whether it be) a little or a lot, he shall be forgiven for his sins and become as pure as he was the day his mother gave birth to him. *(Mu'jam Kabīr, vol. 12, pp. 266, Ḥadīš 13308)*

صَلُّوْا عَلَى الْحَبِيْب صَلَّى اللهُ تَعَالٰى عَلٰى مُحَمَّد

Five virtues of fasting on Friday

1. The Prophet of Raḥmaĥ, the Intercessor of Ummaĥ صَلَّی اللہ تَعَالٰی عَلَیْہِ وَاٰلِہٖ وَسَلَّم has said: 'Whoever keeps fast on Friday, Allah عزّوجلّ shall grant him the reward of 10 days of the afterlife, and they are not like the days of this world.' *(Shu'ab-ul-Īmān, vol. 3, pp. 393, Ḥadīš 3862)*

   Dear Islamic brothers! One day in the afterlife is equivalent to a thousand years of this world. In other words, the one who fasts on Friday will be given the reward of fasting for ten thousand years, but one should not fast on Friday alone, instead, one should fast on Thursday or Saturday as well. (The narration that mentions the prohibition of fasting on Friday alone is stated on the next page).

2. Sayyidunā Abū Umāmaĥ رضی اللّٰہ تعالٰی عنہ has reported the following faith-refreshing saying of the Holy Prophet صَلَّی اللہ تَعَالٰی عَلَیْہِ وَاٰلِہٖ وَسَلَّم: 'Whoever offered Ṣalāt-ul-Jumu'aĥ, kept fast, consoled a sick person, walked with a funeral and witnessed a Nikāḥ on Friday, Heaven has become Wājib for him.' *(Mu'jam Kabīr, pp. 97, part 8, Ḥadīš 7484)*

3. Sayyidunā Abū Ĥurayraĥ رضی اللّٰہ تعالٰی عنہ has reported that the Beloved and Blessed Prophet صَلَّی اللہ تَعَالٰی عَلَیْہِ وَاٰلِہٖ وَسَلَّم has said: 'Whoever is in the state of fast on Friday morning, consoles a sick person, walks with a funeral and donates charity, he makes Heaven Wājib for himself.' *(Shu'ab-ul-Īmān, vol. 3, pp. 394, Ḥadīš 3864)*

4. Sayyidunā Jābir Bin 'Abdullāĥ رَضِیَ اللہُ تَعَالٰی عَنْہ has reported that Rasūlullāĥ صَلَّی اللہُ تَعَالٰی عَلَیْہِ وَاٰلِہٖ وَسَلَّم has said: 'Whoever kept fast, consoled a sick person, fed a beggar and walked with a funeral, would remain safe from sins for 40 years.' *(Shu'ab-ul-Īmān, vol. 3, pp. 394, Ḥadīš 3865)*

5. Sayyidunā 'Abdullāĥ Bin Mas'ūd رَضِیَ اللہُ تَعَالٰی عَنْہ has said that the Prophet of Raḥmaĥ, the Intercessor of Ummaĥ صَلَّی اللہُ تَعَالٰی عَلَیْہِ وَاٰلِہٖ وَسَلَّم very rarely missed the fast of Friday. *(Shu'ab-ul-Īmān, vol. 3, pp. 394, Ḥadīš 3865)*

Dear Islamic brothers! As one should fast a day before or after the fast of 'Āshūrā, one should do the same for Friday, because fasting on Friday or Saturday alone is Makrūĥ Tanzīĥī. However, if a particular date (such as 15th Sha'bān, 27th Rajab etc.) falls on a Friday or Saturday there is no harm in fasting on Friday or Saturday alone in this case.

صَلُّوْا عَلَی الْحَبِیْب   صَلَّی اللہُ تَعَالٰی عَلٰی مُحَمَّد

Prohibition on fasting on Friday alone

1. Sayyidunā Abū Ĥurayraĥ رَضِیَ اللہُ تَعَالٰی عَنْہ has reported that he رَضِیَ اللہُ تَعَالٰی عَنْہ heard the Beloved and Blessed Prophet صَلَّی اللہُ تَعَالٰی عَلَیْہِ وَاٰلِہٖ وَسَلَّم say, 'None of you should fast on Friday but when he joins a day before or after it.' *(Ṣaḥīḥ Bukhārī, vol. 1, pp. 653, Ḥadīš 1985)*

2. Sayyidunā Abū Ĥurayraĥ رَضِیَ اللہُ تَعَالٰی عَنْہ has reported that the Beloved and Blessed Prophet صَلَّی اللہُ تَعَالٰی عَلَیْہِ وَاٰلِہٖ وَسَلَّم has said: 'Do not specify Friday night amongst all nights for standing (in Ṣalāĥ), and do not specify Friday amongst all days for fasting, but when it is the fast you have to keep.' *(Ṣaḥīḥ Muslim, pp. 576, Ḥadīš 1144)*

3. Sayyidunā 'Āmir Bin Ludayn Ash'arī رَضِیَ اللہُ تَعَالٰی عَنْہ has said that he heard Rasūlullāĥ صَلَّی اللہُ تَعَالٰی عَلَیْہِ وَاٰلِہٖ وَسَلَّم say: 'The day of Friday is Eid for you, do not keep fast on it unless you keep fast before or after it as well.' *(Attarghīb Wattarĥīb, vol. 2, pp. 81, Ḥadīš 11)*

   It is obvious from the foregoing Aḥādīš that we should not keep fast on Friday alone. However, if there is any particular reason to do so, for example, if the 27th of Rajab falls on a Friday there is no harm in keeping fast on that Friday.

Fasting on Saturday and Sunday

Sayyidatunā Umm-e-Salamaĥ رَضِیَ اللهُ تَعَالٰی عَنۡهَا has said that the Holy Prophet صَلَّى اللهُ تَعَالٰى عَلَيْهِ وَاٰلِهٖ وَسَلَّم would fast on Saturday and Sunday and he would say, 'These two (Saturday and Sunday) are the days of Eid for the polytheists (Mushrikīn) and I want to oppose them.' *(Ṣaḥīḥ Ibn Khuzaymaĥ, vol. 3, pp. 318, Ḥadīš 2167)*

Fasting on Saturday alone is prohibited. Sayyidunā 'Abdullāĥ Bin Busr رَضِیَ اللّٰهُ تَعَالٰی عَنْهُ has narrated from his sister that Rasūlullāĥ صَلَّى اللهُ تَعَالٰى عَلَيْهِ وَاٰلِهٖ وَسَلَّم has said: 'Do not fast on Saturday unless it is an obligatory (Farḍ) fast.'

Sayyidunā Imām Abū 'Īsā Tirmižī رَضِیَ اللّٰهُ تَعَالٰی عَنْهُ has stated that this Ḥadīš is 'Ḥasan' and refers to the prohibition on fasting on Saturday alone because the Jews respect this day. *(Jāmi' Tirmižī, vol. 2, pp. 186, Ḥadīš 744)*

Twelve Madanī pearls about Nafl fasts

1. If parents prevent their son from Nafl fast for fear of illness, the son should obey them. *(Rad-dul-Muḥtār, vol. 3, pp. 416)*

2. A wife cannot keep a Nafl fast without her husband's permission. *(Durr-e-Mukhtār, Rad-dul-Muḥtār, vol. 3, pp. 415)*

3. In case of having a Nafl fast deliberately, it becomes Wājib to complete it. If it is broken it will be Wājib to make up for it. *(Durr-e-Mukhtār, vol. 3, pp. 411)*

4. If a Nafl fast became invalid unintentionally, not deliberately, for example, if a woman's menses begin during her fast, the fast will become invalid and it will be Wājib to make up for it. *(Durr-e-Mukhtār, vol. 3, pp. 412)*

5. It is not permissible to break a Nafl fast without a valid exemption. If a fasting host realizes that the guest will resent if the host does not eat with the guest, or if a fasting guest realizes that the host will resent in case of his not eating with the host, it is a valid exemption for breaking the fast provided the fast is broken before the Islamic

midday (Ḍaḥwā Kubrā), and the one breaking the fast is certain to make up for it later. *(Durr-e-Mukhtār, Rad-dul-Muḥtār, vol. 3, pp. 413)*

6. Due to the annoyance of parents, one can break a Nafl fast before 'Aṣr (not after 'Aṣr). *(Durr-e-Mukhtār, Rad-dul-Muḥtār, vol. 3, pp. 414)*

7. If a fasting person is invited to a meal by an Islamic brother, he can break Nafl fast before the Islamic midday, but it will be Wājib for him to make up for it later. *(Durr-e-Mukhtār, vol. 3, pp. 414)*

8. 'If I'm invited to a meal then I'll not fast but if I'm not then I will fast', this type of intention and fast are invalid regardless of whether or not one is invited to a meal. *(Fatāwā 'Ālamgīrī, vol. 1, pp. 195)*

9. If an employee or labourer will not be able to carry out his work properly and completely due to Nafl fast, it is necessary for him to seek the permission of his employer. However, if he can do work completely he does not require his employer's permission[1] in this case. *(Durr-e-Mukhtār, vol. 3, pp. 416)*

10. Sayyidunā Dāwūd عَلَيْهِ السَّلَام used to fast on alternate days. Fasting in this manner is called 'Fasting of Dāwūd.' This is a preferable manner of fasting for us, as Rasūlullāĥ صَلَّى اللّٰهُ تَعَالٰى عَلَيْهِ وَاٰلِهٖ وَسَلَّم has said: 'The preferable fast is the fast of my brother Dāwūd عَلَيْهِ السَّلَام. He عَلَيْهِ السَّلَام used to fast one day and not the next, and he never fled from the enemy.' *(Jāmi' Tirmiżī, vol. 2, pp. 197, Ḥadīš 770)*

11. Sayyidunā Sulaymān عَلَيْهِ السَّلَام used to fast the first three days, the middle three days, and the last three days of the month. Hence he used to be in the state of fasting in the beginning, middle and end of the month. *(Kanz-ul-'Ummāl, vol. 8, pp. 304, Ḥadīš 24624)*

12. Fasting the whole year is Makrūĥ Tanzīĥī. *(Durr-e-Mukhtār, vol. 3, pp. 337)*

[1] For detailed information about the rulings of employment please study the booklet '*21 Madanī Pearls for Employees*' published by Maktaba-tul-Madīnaĥ.

O Rab عَزَّوَجَلَّ of Mustafa صَلَّى اللهُ تَعَالٰى عَلَيْهِ وَاٰلِهٖ وَسَلَّم! Enable us to make the use of our lives, health and free time in worship by keeping Nafl fasts abundantly, accept them and forgive us!

اٰمِين بِجَاهِ النَّبِيِّ الْاَمِين صَلَّى اللهُ تَعَالٰى عَلَيْهِ وَاٰلِهٖ وَسَلَّم

صَلُّوْا عَلَى الْحَبِيْب صَلَّى اللهُ تَعَالٰى عَلٰى مُحَمَّد

A means of sustenance

During the visible life of the Holy Prophet صَلَّى اللهُ تَعَالٰى عَلَيْهِ وَاٰلِهٖ وَسَلَّم there were two brothers. One of them used to come to him (to acquire knowledge). (One day) the other brother complained to the Noble Prophet صَلَّى اللهُ تَعَالٰى عَلَيْهِ وَاٰلِهٖ وَسَلَّم about his brother (that he had left all the work to me and he should also take some responsibilities). The Beloved and Blessed Prophet صَلَّى اللهُ تَعَالٰى عَلَيْهِ وَاٰلِهٖ وَسَلَّم said: لَعَلَّكَ تُرْزَقُ بِهٖ, 'Maybe it is because of him that you are being given your sustenance.' *(Jāmi' Tirmiżī, pp. 1887, Ḥadīš 2345 - Ashi'at-ul-Lam'āt, vol. 4, pp. 262)*

صَلُّوْا عَلَى الْحَبِيْب صَلَّى اللهُ تَعَالٰى عَلٰى مُحَمَّد

Modesty is from Īmān

The Beloved Prophet صَلَّى اللهُ تَعَالٰى عَلَيْهِ وَاٰلِهٖ وَسَلَّم has said, 'Modesty is from Īmān (faith).' *(Musnad Abī Ya'lā, vol. 6, pp. 291, Ḥadīš 7463)* As Īmān prevents a Muslim from committing Kufr (unbelief), modesty prevents a modest person from disobedience. This is further explained in the narration of Sayyidunā Ibn 'Umar رَضِىَ اللّٰهُ تَعَالٰى عَنْهُمَا: 'Without doubt, modesty and Īmān are interlinked. When one (of them) ceases to exist, the other is also taken away.'

(Al-Mustadrak lil-Ḥākim, vol. 1, pp. 176, Ḥadīš 66)

اَلْحَمْدُ لِلّٰهِ رَبِّ الْعٰلَمِیْنَ وَ الصَّلٰوةُ وَ السَّلَامُ عَلٰی سَیِّدِ الْمُرْسَلِیْنَ

اَمَّا بَعْدُ فَاَعُوْذُ بِاللّٰهِ مِنَ الشَّیْطٰنِ الرَّجِیْمِ ؕ بِسْمِ اللّٰهِ الرَّحْمٰنِ الرَّحِیْمِ ؕ

Twelve Parables about Fasting People

Allah عَزَّوَجَلَّ says in the Holy Quran:

لَقَدْ كَانَ فِیْ قَصَصِهِمْ عِبْرَةٌ لِّاُولِی الْاَلْبَابِ ؕ

No doubt, the eyes of the wise men are opened by their tidings (stories).

[Kanz-ul-Īmān (Translation of Quran)] (Sūraĥ Yūsuf, verse 111)

The Prophet of mankind, the Peace of our heart and mind, the most Generous and Kind صَلَّى اللهُ تَعَالٰى عَلَيْهِ وَاٰلِهٖ وَسَلَّم has said: 'Whoever recites Ṣalāt upon me three times during the day and three times at night with love and devotion, Allah عَزَّوَجَلَّ will forgive the sins he committed during that day and that night.' *(Mu'jam Kabīr, vol. 18, pp. 361, Ḥadīš 928)*

صَلُّوْا عَلَى الْحَبِيْب   صَلَّى اللهُ تَعَالٰى عَلٰى مُحَمَّد

1. Fast in summer

Once, during the journey of Hajj, Ḥajjāj Bin Yūsuf stopped at a place between Makka-tul-Mukarramaĥ and Madīna-tul-Munawwaraĥ and had the lunch prepared. He then instructed his guard to bring a guest. The guard came out of the tent and saw a Bedouin lying on the ground. Wakening him up the guard said, 'Come, Ḥajjāj Bin Yūsuf is calling you.' When the Bedouin came, Ḥajjāj Bin Yūsuf said, 'Accept my invitation, wash your hands and sit down to eat with me.' The Bedouin replied, 'I am sorry, I have already accepted the invitation of someone else who is more generous and gracious than you.'

Ḥajjāj Bin Yūsuf asked, 'Whose invitation?' The Bedouin replied, 'The invitation of Allah عَزَّوَجَلَّ who has invited me to keep a fast and hence I have fasted today.' Ḥajjāj asked, 'You have fasted in such scorching heat!' The Bedouin replied, 'Yes, in order to save myself from the blazing heat of the Judgement Day.' Ḥajjāj said, 'Please eat now and make up for the fast tomorrow.' The Bedouin immediately replied, 'Can you guarantee me that I will remain alive till tomorrow?' Ḥajjāj replied, 'I'm afraid I can't.' The pious Bedouin said, 'I'm afraid I can't eat with you.' Saying this, he then left Ḥajjāj behind. *(Rauḍ-ur-Riyāḥīn, pp. 212)*

May Allah عَزَّوَجَلَّ have mercy on him and forgive us without accountability for his sake!

صَلُّوْا عَلَى الْحَبِيْب صَلَّى اللّٰهُ تَعَالٰى عَلٰى مُحَمَّد

Dear Islamic brothers! The pious servants of Allah عَزَّوَجَلَّ aren't afraid of even kings and rulers. We have also learnt that those who observe fasts bearing heat will be protected from the intense and scorching heat of the Judgement Day, اِنْ شَآءَاللّٰه عَزَّوَجَلَّ.

2. Satan's worry

A pious person رَحْمَةُ اللّٰهِ تَعَالٰى عَلَيْه saw Satan stand in worry by a Masjid door and asked, 'What's the matter with you?' Satan replied, 'Look inside.' When the pious person looked inside he saw a person offer Ṣalāĥ, and another person sleeping by the Masjid door. Satan said, 'I want to enter the Masjid to distract the person offering Ṣalāĥ by putting evil thoughts in his heart, but the man sleeping by the door is a fasting person. When he breathes out, his breath prevents me from entering like a flame of fire.' *(Rauḍ-ul-Fāiq, pp. 39)*

صَلُّوْا عَلَى الْحَبِيْب صَلَّى اللّٰهُ تَعَالٰى عَلٰى مُحَمَّد

Dear Islamic brothers! In order to be protected from the attacks of Satan 'fasting' is a strong protective shield. Even though the fasting person is asleep, his breath is a sword against Satan. We have learnt that Satan is extremely afraid of the fasting person. As Satan is captured, chained and imprisoned during Ramadan, he gets into trouble whenever he sees a fasting person.

3. A unique expiation

A blessed companion رَضِیَ اللهُ تَعَالٰی عَنْهُ presented himself before Beloved Rasūl صَلَّى اللهُ تَعَالٰى عَلَيْهِ وَاٰلِهٖ وَسَلَّم and said, 'Yā Rasūlallāĥ صَلَّى اللهُ تَعَالٰى عَلَيْهِ وَاٰلِهٖ وَسَلَّم! In the state of fast in Ramadan, I purposely had intercourse with my wife. I am ruined, what should I do?' The Prophet of Raḥmaĥ, the Intercessor of Ummaĥ صَلَّى اللهُ تَعَالٰى عَلَيْهِ وَاٰلِهٖ وَسَلَّم asked, 'Can you free a slave?' He رَضِیَ اللهُ تَعَالٰی عَنْهُ politely replied, 'I'm afraid I can't, O the Noble Prophet صَلَّى اللهُ تَعَالٰى عَلَيْهِ وَاٰلِهٖ وَسَلَّم.' He صَلَّى اللهُ تَعَالٰى عَلَيْهِ وَاٰلِهٖ وَسَلَّم asked, 'Can you fast consecutively for two months?' The blessed companion replied, 'O the Holy Prophet صَلَّى اللهُ تَعَالٰى عَلَيْهِ وَاٰلِهٖ وَسَلَّم I'm afraid I won't be able to do so.' He صَلَّى اللهُ تَعَالٰى عَلَيْهِ وَاٰلِهٖ وَسَلَّم asked, 'Can you feed sixty Miskīn people?' Again he politely replied in the negative.

Meanwhile, someone gifted some dates in the court of the Holy Prophet صَلَّى اللهُ تَعَالٰى عَلَيْهِ وَاٰلِهٖ وَسَلَّم. Giving all those dates to that companion the Beloved and Blessed Prophet صَلَّى اللهُ تَعَالٰى عَلَيْهِ وَاٰلِهٖ وَسَلَّم said, 'Give it as charity, your expiation [Kaffāraĥ] will be paid.' He رَضِیَ اللّٰهُ تَعَالٰی عَنْهُ replied, 'Yā Rasūlallāĥ صَلَّى اللهُ تَعَالٰى عَلَيْهِ وَاٰلِهٖ وَسَلَّم! I am the poorest person in Madīna-tul-Munawwaraĥ.' The Noble Prophet صَلَّى اللهُ تَعَالٰى عَلَيْهِ وَاٰلِهٖ وَسَلَّم smiled until his molars appeared and said: فَاَطْعِمْهُ اَهْلَكَ '*Feed it to your family.*' (Your expiation will be paid). *(Ṣaḥīḥ Bukhārī, vol. 4, pp. 341, Ḥadīš 6822)*

May Allah عَزَّوَجَلَّ have mercy on them and forgive us without accountability for their sake!

Dear Islamic brothers! If the blessed companions رَضِیَ اللّٰهُ تَعَالٰی عَنْهُم ever made any mistake due to human nature, they would immediately compensate for it. Moreover, they would also present themselves before the Holy Prophet صَلَّى اللهُ تَعَالٰى عَلَيْهِ وَاٰلِهٖ وَسَلَّم for its forgiveness and expiation. They truly believed that the pleasure of Allah عَزَّوَجَلَّ lies in the pleasure of His Beloved Prophet صَلَّى اللهُ تَعَالٰى عَلَيْهِ وَاٰلِهٖ وَسَلَّم.

This narration also makes it clear that the blessed companions رَضِیَ اللّٰهُ تَعَالٰی عَنْهُم firmly believed that the Holy Prophet صَلَّى اللّٰهُ تَعَالٰى عَلَيْهِ وَاٰلِهٖ وَسَلَّم possesses immense divinely-given authority, and that Sharī'aĥ is the other name of his sayings. This is why the Beloved and Blessed Rasūl صَلَّى اللهُ تَعَالٰى عَلَيْهِ وَاٰلِهٖ وَسَلَّم offered different forms of expiations to that companion by asking him 'If he could free a slave', or 'If he was able to fast consecutively for sixty days?' or 'If he was able to feed sixty Miskīn people?' and the companion kept on replying 'No, Yā Rasūlallāĥ صَلَّى اللهُ تَعَالٰى عَلَيْهِ وَاٰلِهٖ وَسَلَّم.'

In other words, that companion firmly believed that if the Beloved and Blessed Prophet صَلَّى اللهُ تَعَالٰى عَلَيْهِ وَاٰلِهٖ وَسَلَّم had wanted he could have told any forth method of expiation other than the first three ones. The Noble Prophet صَلَّى اللهُ تَعَالٰى عَلَيْهِ وَاٰلِهٖ وَسَلَّم also affirmed to his authority saying that the expiation that I'll impose upon you is to give these dates. When the companion expressed his personal need saying that no one in Madīna-tul-Munawwaraĥ was poorer than him, the Noble Prophet صَلَّى اللهُ تَعَالٰى عَلَيْهِ وَاٰلِهٖ وَسَلَّم ordered him to take the dates and feed them to his family; his expiation will get paid.

The general ruling of expiation for deliberately breaking a fast of Ramadan is to free a slave (provided the conditions of expiation are met). If this is not possible, then to fast successively for sixty days', if this isn't possible either, then to feed sixty poor people, but the expiation that was imposed upon the blessed companion was not to give [and do all of those things] but to take and spend upon his own family instead of spending upon anybody else! This is the supreme court of refuge for the helpless and destitute.

4. Generosity of Ṣiddīqaĥ رَضِیَ اللهُ عَنْهَا

Mother of the believers, Sayyidatunā 'Āishaĥ Ṣiddīqaĥ رَضِیَ اللهُ تَعَالٰی عَنْهَا was immensely generous and benevolent. Sayyidunā 'Urwaĥ Bin Zubayr رَضِیَ اللهُ تَعَالٰی عَنْهُ has stated he saw that the mother of the believers رَضِیَ اللهُ تَعَالٰی عَنْهَا donated and distributed seventy thousand dirhams for the pleasure of Allah عَزَّوَجَلَّ, whereas there were patches on her clothes. Sayyidunā 'Abdullāĥ Bin Zubayr رَضِیَ اللهُ تَعَالٰی عَنْهُ sent one hundred thousand dirhams to her but she distributed the entire money in the path of Allah عَزَّوَجَلَّ in a day. She had fast that day. At evening, her maid said, 'Wouldn't it be better if you had kept just one dirham for bread.' She replied, 'This thought didn't cross my mind, if it had come into my mind I would have saved.' *(Madārij-un-Nubūwwaĥ, vol. 2, pp. 473)*

May Allah عَزَّوَجَلَّ have mercy on her and forgive us without accountability for her sake!

صَلُّوْا عَلَى الْحَبِيْب صَلَّى اللهُ تَعَالٰى عَلٰى مُحَمَّد

Dear Islamic brothers! Despite possessing huge amount of wealth, the mother of believers Sayyidatunā 'Āishaĥ Ṣiddīqaĥ رَضِیَ اللهُ تَعَالٰی عَنْهَا led a very simple, pious and noble life. Whenever wealth or money was presented to her, she رَضِیَ اللهُ تَعَالٰی عَنْهَا donated and distributed all of it in the path of Allah عَزَّوَجَلَّ. Even when she received a hundred thousand dirhams she رَضِىَ اللهُ تَعَالٰى عَنْهَا donated the entire amount for virtuous causes. She رَضِىَ اللهُ تَعَالٰى عَنْهَا did not keep money to buy food even for Ifṭār. On the other hand, if we observe a single Nafl fast, we want various types of foods such as fried items, cold drinks etc.

We should also follow in the footsteps of the mother of all believers Sayyidatunā 'Āishaĥ Ṣiddīqaĥ رَضِىَ اللهُ تَعَالٰى عَنْهَا. We should not love wealth and monetary possessions to the extent that we begin to hesitate spending it in the path of Allah عَزَّوَجَلَّ and for righteous causes.

To remain associated with the Madanī environment of Dawat-e-Islami is extremely useful for getting rid of the love of the world and for having betterment in afterlife. Whenever any Madanī Qāfilaĥ of Dawat-e-Islami arrives in your area, do adopt their company because even just looking at the travellers of the path of Allah عَزَّوَجَلَّ with good intentions is a good deed and their companionship will lead you to Heaven. Let me tell you the story of a spoilt young man whose life was transformed just by looking at a devotee of Rasūl:

Blessings of meeting Rasūl's devotee

An Islamic brother from Qusoor city (Punjab, Pakistan) gave the following account: I was a matriculation student at that time. Due to evil company, I was wasting my life in sins, indecency and wrongdoings. I was temperamental, rude and ill-mannered to the extent that I misbehaved my parents and even my grandparents.

One day, a Madanī Qāfilaĥ of Dawat-e-Islami, a global & non-political movement for the propagation of Quran & Sunnaĥ, arrived at our local Masjid. I went to visit the devotees of Rasūl. Making individual effort, an Islamic brother dressed in white clothes with a green turban on his head politely invited me to attend the Dars. Hence, I sat down and began listening to the Dars. After the Dars, they told me that the three day Sunnaĥ-Inspiring global Ijtimā' of Dawat-e-Islami was going to be held in Madīna-tul-Auliyā Multan, after a couple of days. They invited me to attend the global Ijtimā'. Impressed by their Dars which had a great positive effect on me, I couldn't refuse. So I participated in the Ijtimā'.

I was surprised to see the blessings of the Ijtimā'. The last speech, '*The Perils of Music*' had an overwhelming effect on me, causing tears to fall from my eyes. I repented of my sins and joined the Madanī environment of Dawat-e-Islami. My family took a sigh of relief to see this positive change in me. With the blessings of Dawat-e-Islami, my elder brother also grew a beard and adorned his head with a turban because he was immensely impressed to see a sudden Madanī change in an extremely bad mannered person. I've a sister who has also started wearing a Madanī Burqa' (veil).

اَلْحَمْدُ لِلّٰه عَزَّوَجَلَّ! All of my family members have got the privilege of doing Bay'at in the Qādiriyyaĥ Razawiyyaĥ order, becoming the disciples of Ghauš-e-A'ẓam رَضِیَ اللہُ تَعَالٰی عَنْہُ. By the grace of Allah عَزَّوَجَلَّ I have learnt the Quran by heart and have enrolled on the Dars-e-Niẓāmī course. At the time of writing this account, I'm in the second year of my course. I'm also making efforts as the responsible of Dawat-e-Islami's Madanī Qāfilaĥ in our area. I have intended to travel with a Madanī Qāfilaĥ for twelve months in Sha'bān, اِنْ شَآءَاللہ عَزَّوَجَلَّ.

Dil pay gar zang ĥo, sārā g̱ĥar tang ĥo
Ĥogā sab kā bĥalā, Qāfilay mayn chalo

If the heart is rusty with sins, and the family is disturbed by evildoings
All will get good and blessings, travel with Madanī Qāfilaĥ

صَلُّوْا عَلَى الْحَبِيْب صَلَّى اللّٰهُ تَعَالٰى عَلٰى مُحَمَّد

5. Cold water

Once Sayyidunā Sarī Saqaṭī رَحْمَةُ اللهِ تَعَالٰی عَلَیْه had a fast. He placed a goblet of water inside the walls' recess so that the water would get cool. After the 'Aṣr Ṣalāĥ, while he رَحْمَةُ اللهِ تَعَالٰی عَلَیْه was engrossed in meditation, Heavenly maidens began to visit him. He رَحْمَةُ اللهِ تَعَالٰی عَلَیْه would ask each maiden as to who she was for and she would tell the name of a devoted servant of Allah عَزَّوَجَلَّ. Then another one came, he رَحْمَةُ اللهِ تَعَالٰی عَلَیْه asked the same, she replied, 'I am for the one who, whilst fasting, doesn't place water to cool.' Listening to this, he رَحْمَةُ اللهِ تَعَالٰی عَلَیْه said, 'If you're right then drop this goblet.' So she dropped the goblet whose sound awoke the meditating saint. When he رَحْمَةُ اللهِ تَعَالٰی عَلَیْه saw the goblet it was broken into pieces. *(Al-Malfūẓ, part 1, pp. 124)*

May Allah عَزَّوَجَلَّ have mercy on him and forgive us without accountability for his sake!

صَلُّوْا عَلَى الْحَبِيْب صَلَّى اللّٰهُ تَعَالٰى عَلٰى مُحَمَّد

Dear Islamic brothers! In order to attain the everlasting blessings & pleasures of the Hereafter, one has to subdue and control his Nafs staying away from worldly desires and pleasures. The Auliyā of Allah عَزَّوَجَلَّ battled against their carnal desires. Once, in an extremely hot day, a pious person saw someone carry ice. He desired, 'If only I had money to buy ice and enjoy a cold drink.' Instantly, he felt ashamed and said to himself, 'Why did I listen to the trick of my Nafs?' He then promised never to drink cold water. Hence, even in hot summer days, he always heated the water before drinking it.

Niĥang-o-axdaĥā-o-shayr-e-nar mārā to kyā mārā
Bařay mūżī ko mārā Nafs-e-Ammāraĥ ko gar mārā

Killing crocodile, serpent and lion is not a feat
Suppressing one's Nafs is a great action indeed

6. Reward from Beloved Rasūl صَلَّى اللّٰهُ عَلَيْهِ وَاٰلِهٖ وَسَلَّم

Ramadan was approaching. The prominent historian Sayyidunā Wāqidī رَحْمَةُ اللهِ تَعَالٰی عَلَيْه had nothing to meet his needs. He رَحْمَةُ اللهِ تَعَالٰی عَلَيْه wrote a letter to his 'Alawī friend stating, 'Ramadan is approaching, and I have nothing to spend. Please send 1000 dirhams to me as debt.' So the 'Alawī sent a bag containing 1000 dirhams to him.

After a short while Sayyidunā Wāqidī رَحْمَةُ اللهِ تَعَالٰی عَلَيْه received a letter from his another friend with the following message, 'I need 1000 dirhams to spend in the month of Ramadan.' Sayyidunā Wāqidī رَحْمَةُ اللهِ تَعَالٰی عَلَيْه sent the bag of dirhams to him.' The next day, the 'Alawī friend who gave Sayyidunā Wāqidī رَحْمَةُ اللهِ تَعَالٰی عَلَيْه the dirhams and the friend who received the dirhams from Sayyidunā Wāqidī رَحْمَةُ اللهِ تَعَالٰی عَلَيْه both came to the house of Sayyidunā Wāqidī رَحْمَةُ اللهِ تَعَالٰی عَلَيْه. 'Alawī friend said, 'Ramadan is arriving and I had nothing except for those 1000 dirhams. When I received your letter I gave all of my 1000 dirhams to you. For my own need, I wrote a letter to this friend of mine to lend me 1000 dirhams. He sent me the same bag of dirhams I sent to you. I sent you the bag of dirhams which you sent to him, and he sent it to me again.' With mutual consent they agreed to distribute the money equally among themselves.

The following night Sayyidunā Wāqidī رَحْمَةُ اللهِ تَعَالٰی عَلَيْه was privileged to see the Holy Prophet صَلَّى اللّٰهُ تَعَالٰی عَلَيْهِ وَاٰلِهٖ وَسَلَّم in his dream. He صَلَّى اللّٰهُ تَعَالٰی عَلَيْهِ وَاٰلِهٖ وَسَلَّم said, 'اِنْ شَآءَاللّٰه عَزَّوَجَلَّ You'll get a lot tomorrow.' Hence, the following day, the chief Yaḥyā Barmakī called Sayyidunā Wāqidī رَحْمَةُ اللهِ تَعَالٰى عَلَيْه and said, 'I saw you in trouble last night in my dream, what's the matter?' Sayyidunā Wāqidī رَحْمَةُ اللهِ تَعَالٰى عَلَيْه explained to him the entire story. Yaḥyā Barmakī responded, 'I am unable to decide as to which of you is more generous. You are all generous and deserve to be respected. The chief then gave 30,000 dirhams to Sayyidunā Wāqidī رَحْمَةُ اللهِ تَعَالٰى عَلَيْه and 20,000 dirhams each to the other two. Further, he appointed Sayyidunā Wāqidī رَحْمَةُ اللهِ تَعَالٰى عَلَيْه as a Judge as well. *(Ḥujjatullāĥi-'alal-'Ālamīn, pp. 577)*

May Allah عَزَّوَجَلَّ have mercy on them and forgive us without accountability for their sake!

صَلُّوْا عَلَى الْحَبِيْب صَلَّى اللهُ تَعَالٰى عَلٰى مُحَمَّد

Dear Islamic brothers! True Muslims are generous, courteous, self-sacrificing and considerate. In order to remove the difficulty and anguish of a Muslim brother, they would even tolerate their own difficulties and inconveniences. We also have learnt from this parable that generosity is a very beneficial deed which does not decrease but increases the wealth of a person.

Further, this parable also shows us that the Prophet of Raḥmaĥ, the Intercessor of Ummaĥ, the Owner of Jannaĥ صَلَّى اللهُ تَعَالٰى عَلَيْهِ وَاٰلِهٖ وَسَلَّم is aware of the state of his Ummaĥ and he صَلَّى اللهُ تَعَالٰى عَلَيْهِ وَاٰلِهٖ وَسَلَّم blesses those who demonstrate generosity. Verily, there are many virtues of making sacrifice for others. The Holy Prophet صَلَّى اللهُ تَعَالٰى عَلَيْهِ وَاٰلِهٖ وَسَلَّم has said, 'Allah عَزَّوَجَلَّ forgives the person who gives someone else the thing he needs for himself.' *(Itḥāf-us-Sādat-il-Muttaqīn, vol. 9, pp. 779)*

7. Fragrance of fast

Sayyidunā 'Abdullāĥ Bin Ghālib Ḥaddānī قُدِّسَ سِرُّهُ الرَّبَّانِي the Ḥadīš teacher of Sayyidunā Imām Qatādaĥ رَضِیَ اللهُ تَعَالٰی عَنْهُ was martyred. After the burial, the soil of the blessed grave smelt of musk. Someone saw him in a dream and asked, 'مَا صُنِعْتَ? How were you treated?' He رَحْمَةُ اللهِ تَعَالٰى عَلَيْه replied, 'Allah عَزَّوَجَلَّ forgave me.' The dreaming person further asked where he was taken to?' He رَحْمَةُ اللهِ تَعَالٰى عَلَيْه replied 'Heaven.' The dreaming person then enquired, 'Due to which deed?' He رَحْمَةُ اللهِ تَعَالٰى عَلَيْه replied, 'Perfect Īmān, Taĥajjud and summer fasts.' Finally he رَحْمَةُ اللهِ تَعَالٰى عَلَيْه was asked, 'Why does fragrance emanate from your grave?'

He رَحْمَةُ اللهِ تَعَالٰی عَلَیْه replied, 'This is the fragrance of my recitation and thirst I bore in fast.' *(Ḥilyat-ul-Auliyā, vol. 6, pp. 266, Ḥadīš 8553)*

May Allah عَزَّوَجَلَّ have mercy on him and forgive us without accountability for his sake!

Dear Islamic brothers! Similarly, the fragrance of musk used to emanate from the soil of the blessed grave of Sayyidunā Imām Bukhārī رَحْمَةُ اللّٰهِ تَعَالٰی عَلَیْه. Soil used to be added to his grave repeatedly but people would take it as relic due to fragrance. *(Muqaddamaĥ Ṣaḥīḥ Bukhārī, vol. 1, pp. 3)*

Likewise, the fragrance of musk used to emanate from the grave of the author of *Dalāil-ul-Khayrāt*, Shaykh Sayyid Muhammad Bin Sulaymān Jazūlī رَحْمَةُ اللهِ تَعَالٰی عَلَیْه who used to recite Ṣalāt upon the Holy Prophet صَلَّى اللهُ تَعَالٰی عَلَیْهِ وَاٰلِهٖ وَسَلَّم in abundance.

Seventy seven years after his demise, his body was transferred from 'Sous' to Morocco for some legitimate reason. When his blessed body was exhumed it was in an absolutely fine state, quite untouched. There was no sign of decay. Even his shroud did not get dirty at all. Prior to his demise, he had his beard lawfully trimmed. It looked as if the beard was trimmed just today. Someone put a finger onto his cheek and pressed; the cheeks became pale due to blood-circulation just like an alive person. *(Muṭāli'-ul-Masarrāt, pp. 4)*

8. Blessings of fasts of Ramadan and six fasts after Eid

Sayyidunā Sufyān Šaurī رَحْمَةُ اللهِ تَعَالٰی عَلَیْه has stated, 'Once I stayed in Makka-tul-Mukarramaĥ زَادَهَا اللّٰهُ شَرَفًا وَّتَعْظِيْمًا. At around midday, a person from Makkaĥ would perform Ṭawāf of the Holy Ka'baĥ and two Rak'āt Ṣalāĥ daily. He would say Salām to me and then return to his home. I had developed a liking for that pious person. One day, he fell seriously ill. I went to visit him; he was on his deathbed. Handing his will over to me, he said, 'When I die, give me Ghusl and lead my funeral Ṣalāĥ, and after burial, please don't leave me alone, stay at my graveside the whole night and perform Talqīn[1] at the time of the arrival of the angels Munkar and Nakīr.' I agreed to fulfil his will.

When he died, I acted upon his will. While I was sitting beside his grave I fell asleep. I heard a voice from Ghayb saying, 'O Sufyān رَحْمَةُ اللهِ تَعَالٰی عَلَیْه! He doesn't require your Talqīn

---

[1] See the details of Talqīn in the booklet '*40 Madanī Wills*' published by Maktaba-tul-Madīnaĥ.

and your closeness because we have ourselves comforted him and made Talqīn to him. I asked, 'Due to which deed has he been granted this status?' The voice spoke, 'Due to the blessings of the fasts of Ramadan and the six fasts of Shawwal.' Sayyidunā Sufyān Šaurī رَحْمَةُ اللهِ تَعَالٰی عَلَيْه stated, 'I saw this dream three times in that night alone.' I politely beseeched Allah عَزَّوَجَلَّ, 'Yā Allah عَزَّوَجَلَّ! With your grace and benevolence, give me also the ability to observe these fasts.' *(Qalyūbī, pp. 14)*

May Allah عَزَّوَجَلَّ have mercy on him and forgive us without accountability for his sake!

صَلُّوْا عَلَى الْحَبِيْب صَلَّى اللهُ تَعَالٰى عَلٰى مُحَمَّد

9. Moon of Ramadan

Once there was some controversy regarding the appearance of the moon of Ramadan. Some people said that the moon had appeared while some others denied. The respected and honourable mother of Sayyidunā Ghauš-e-A'ẓam رَضِیَ اللهُ تَعَالٰی عَنْهُ spoke, 'My son doesn't drink milk during the days of Ramadan. As he has not drunk milk today, the moon of Ramadan may well have appeared last night.' Hence, after further findings and observations it came out that the moon had appeared last night. *(Baĥjat-ul-Asrār, pp. 172)*

May Allah عَزَّوَجَلَّ have mercy on him and forgive us without accountability for his sake!

Ghauš-e-A'ẓam رَحْمَةُ اللهِ تَعَالٰی عَلَيْه muttaqī ĥar ān mayn
Ĉauřā mā kā dūdĥ bĥī Ramazān mayn

Ghauš-e-A'ẓam رَحْمَةُ اللهِ تَعَالٰی عَلَيْه is very pious and ascetic
In Ramadan he avoided even mother's milk

صَلُّوْا عَلَى الْحَبِيْب صَلَّى اللهُ تَعَالٰى عَلٰى مُحَمَّد

Liver cancer was cured

Dear Islamic brothers! In order to develop the love of Ghauš-e-A'ẓam رَضِیَ اللهُ تَعَالٰی عَنْهُ and other blessed saints رَحِمَهُمُ اللهُ تَعَالٰی in your heart, always remain associated and attached with the Madanī environment of Dawat-e-Islami and gain great blessings. Here is a faith-refreshing Madanī incident for your encouragement.

An Islamic brother from Gulistān-e-Mustafa (Bāb-ul-Madīnaĥ, Karachi) has stated: I invited a brother to attend the three day global Ijtimā' of Dawat-e-Islami being held in Multan. His daughter was a patient of liver cancer. With the intention of making Du'ā for his daughter, he participated in the Ijtimā'. He made Du'ā abundantly with intense humility in the Ijtimā'.

اَلْحَمْدُ لِلّٰه عَزَّوَجَلَّ! Having returned from the Ijtimā', he got his daughter's tests carried out. To the utter astonishment of doctors, the test results showed no cancer at all. The entire team of doctors was amazed as to how the cancer that is considered an incurable disease was cured. Prior to his participation in the Ijtimā', the condition of his daughter was so serious that pus used to be drawn from her body by a syringe on a daily basis, but by the blessings of participating in the Ijtimā', that girl has completely recovered from cancer, اَلْحَمْدُ لِلّٰه عَزَّوَجَلَّ. She has now been healthy and has got married as well.

Agar dard-e-sar ĥo, kay yā cancer ĥo,
Dilāye gā tum ko shifā Madanī Māḥaul
Shifā-ayn milayn gī, balā-ayn ṫalayn gī
Yaqīnan ĥay barakat bĥarā Madanī Māḥaul

Even if one has cancer and his life is in danger
He'll get cured by blessings of the Madanī environment
Cures will be granted and adversities will be averted
Very blessed is indeed the Madanī environment

صَلُّوْا عَلَى الْحَبِيْب صَلَّى اللّٰهُ تَعَالٰى عَلٰى مُحَمَّد

10. Three fasts of Aĥl-e-Bayt رَضِىَ اللّٰه عَنْهُم

Once in childhood, Sayyidunā Ḥasan and Sayyidunā Ḥusayn رَضِىَ اللّٰه تَعَالٰى عَنْهُمَا became ill. Sayyidunā 'Alī كَرَّمَ اللّٰه تَعَالٰى وَجْهَهُ الْكَرِيْم, Sayyidatunā Fāṭimaĥ and their slave-girl Sayyidatunā Fiḍḍaĥ رَضِىَ اللّٰه تَعَالٰى عَنْهُمَا vowed to fast for three days for the health of the two princes, Imām Ḥasan and Imām Ḥusayn رَضِىَ اللّٰه تَعَالٰى عَنْهُمَا. Allah عَزَّوَجَلَّ blessed both princes with health and hence three fasts were observed.

Sayyidunā 'Alī كَرَّمَ اللّٰه تَعَالٰى وَجْهَهُ الْكَرِيْم brought three Ṣā' [almost three hundred grams] of barley. They used a hundred grams each day. Breads were served to them at the time of

Ifṭār. On the first day, a destitute person came and begged for bread. On the second and third day, an orphan and a captive came respectively and they also begged for bread. Therefore, all the breads were given to them each day, and Sayyidunā 'Alī كَرَّمَ اللّٰهُ تَعَالٰى وَجۡهَهُ الۡكَرِيۡم, Sayyidatunā Fāṭimaĥ رَضِىَ اللّٰهُ تَعَالٰى عَنۡهَا and their slave girl did Ifṭār with mere water, and fasted the next day without eating any thing. *(Khazāin-ul-'Irfān, pp. 926)*

May Allah عَزَّوَجَلَّ have mercy on them and forgive us without accountability for their sake!

Bĥūkay reĥ kay khud auraun ko kĥilā daytay tĥay
Kaysay ṣābir tĥay Muhammad kay gĥarānay wālay

They fed others despite remaining hungry
How patient was Muhammad's family

صَلُّوۡا عَلَى الۡحَبِيۡب   صَلَّى اللّٰهُ تَعَالٰى عَلٰى مُحَمَّد

Allah عَزَّوَجَلَّ has mentioned the faith-refreshing sacrifice of His Beloved Rasūl's daughter and her family in Sūraĥ Ad-Daĥr, verse 8 and 9:

وَ يُطۡعِمُوۡنَ الطَّعَامَ عَلٰى حُبِّهٖ مِسۡكِيۡنًا وَّ يَتِيۡمًا وَّ اَسِيۡرًا ﴿۸﴾ اِنَّمَا نُطۡعِمُكُمۡ لِوَجۡهِ اللّٰهِ لَا نُرِيۡدُ مِنۡكُمۡ جَزَآءً وَّ لَا شُكُوۡرًا ﴿۹﴾

And they feed, for love of Him, the poor, the orphan and the prisoner. They say to them, 'We feed you only for the pleasure of Allah عَزَّوَجَلَّ. We desire no recompense or thanks from you.'

[Kanz-ul-Īmān (Translation of Quran)] (Sūraĥ Ad-Daĥr, verse 8, 9)

سُبۡحٰنَ اللّٰه عَزَّوَجَلَّ! This faith-refreshing parable clearly shows the enthusiasm of Aĥl-e-Bayt رَضِىَ اللّٰهُ تَعَالٰى عَنۡهُم to make sacrifice for others. To keep three fasts with mere water isn't easy. When we fast we are served with cold and sweet drinks, fried dishes, fresh fruits and other delicious foods at the time of Ifṭār. This type of great sacrifice in the state of poverty was indeed an extraordinarily righteous deed.

The excellence of sacrifice mentioned in the sixth parable is being presented again. The Holy Prophet صَلَّى اللهُ تَعَالٰى عَلَيْهِ وَاٰلِهٖ وَسَلَّم has said, 'Allah عَزَّوَجَلَّ forgives the person who gives someone else the thing he needs for himself.' *(Itḥāf-us-Sādat-il-Muttaqīn, vol. 9, pp. 779)*

Pay heed to the following part of the blessed Quranic verse which shows the greatness and grandeur of the Aĥl-e-Bayt. '*We only feed you for the pleasure of Allah عَزَّوَجَلَّ. We desire no recompense or thanks from you.*' These Quranic words express a high degree of sincerity. If only we too learn how to perform every deed merely for the pleasure of Allah عَزَّوَجَلَّ. If only we assist and benefit others expecting nothing from them, not even a word of appreciation and thank. When helping someone or giving food or money to a beggar, it is better not to even say to him, 'Remember me in Du'ā' as it also seems a type of reward in exchange for your good deed. Now, whether or not he makes Du'ā for us and whether or not his Du'ā is accepted in our favour, it is simply our fate!

Mayrā ĥar 'amal bas Tayray wāsiṭay ĥo
Kar ikhlāṣ aysā 'aṭā Yā Ilāĥī

My every deed be solely for You, Almighty
Bless me with such a treasure of sincerity

11. Fasting successively for forty years

Sayyidunā Dāwūd Ṭāī رَحْمَةُ اللهِ تَعَالٰى عَلَيْه observed fasts successively for forty years. He was so sincere in his worship that he would not let even his family know about his fasts. While going to work at noon, he would take along with him meal which he would give to someone on the way. After Maghrib, he would arrive home and eat food. *(Ma'dan-e-Akhlāq, part 1, pp. 182)*

صَلُّوْا عَلَى الْحَبِيْب صَلَّى اللهُ تَعَالٰى عَلٰى مُحَمَّد

Sayyidunā Dāwūd Ṭāī's subduing his Nafs and desires

سُبْحٰنَ اللّٰه عَزَّوَجَلَّ! This is the superb level of sincerity! Sayyidunā Dāwūd Ṭāī رَحْمَةُ اللهِ تَعَالٰى عَلَيْه had great control over his Nafs. It is mentioned in '*Tażkira-tul-Auliyā*' that once he was busy with worship on a hot summer day in the sunshine. His respected mother said, 'Son! It would be better if you came under a shade.' He رَحْمَةُ اللهِ تَعَالٰى عَلَيْه politely replied, 'Dear mother!

I feel ashamed of following and satisfying my Nafs and its desire.' Once, someone saw his water pot in the sunshine and said, 'Sayyidī! It would be better if you placed it in the shade. He رَحْمَةُ اللهِ تَعَالٰى عَلَيْه replied, 'When I had placed it there it was under the shade but now I feel ashamed of putting it in shade just to please my Nafs giving up the remembrance of Allah عَزَّوَجَلَّ.'

On another occasion, while he رَحْمَةُ اللهِ تَعَالٰى عَلَيْه was reciting the Holy Quran, somebody requested him to come under a shade. He رَحْمَةُ اللهِ تَعَالٰى عَلَيْه replied, 'I dislike obeying my Nafs' i.e. the Nafs is also insisting me that I come in a shade but I cannot obey it. The following night, he رَحْمَةُ اللهِ تَعَالٰى عَلَيْه passed away. After his demise, a voice from Ghayb was heard, 'Dāwūd Ṭāī has attained salvation because Allah عَزَّوَجَلَّ is pleased with him.'

(Tažkira-tul-Auliyā, pp. 201-202, part 1)

May Allah عَزَّوَجَلَّ have mercy on him and forgive us without accountability for his sake!

Revealing one's good deeds

Dear Islamic brothers! Those who mention their good deeds to others without a valid Shar'ī reason just to show off committing the sin of ostentation and insincerity should take lesson from the foregoing parable. For example, someone says, 'I observe the fasts of Rajab, Sha'bān and Ramadan every year' (despite the fact that the fasts of Ramadan are already Farḍ, that ostentatious and insincere person will say that he fasted for three successive months just to make it seem more impressive).

Some say, 'I have been fasting on Ayyām-ul-Bīḍ every month from many years.' 'I recite Ṣalāt-'Alan-Nabī in abundance and have been reading *Dalāil-ul-Khayrāt* for a long time.' 'I've recited many parts of the Quran.' 'Every month I donate a lot of money to a Madrasaĥ.' Some brag about the number of Hajj and 'Umraĥ they performed. In short, people reveal their Nafl Ṣalāĥ, Taĥajjud Ṣalāĥ, Nafl fasting and other forms of worships unnecessarily. Alas! Sincerity seems to have disappeared altogether. Remember! No one will be able to bear the punishment of ostentation.

The Holy Prophet صَلَّى اللهُ تَعَالٰى عَلَيْهِ وَاٰلِهٖ وَسَلَّم has said, 'Seek Allah's refuge from Jab-bul-Ḥuzn.' The blessed companions رَضِىَ اللّٰهُ تَعَالٰى عَنْهُم humbly asked, 'What is Jab-bul-Ḥuzn?' He صَلَّى اللهُ تَعَالٰى عَلَيْهِ وَاٰلِهٖ وَسَلَّم replied, 'In Hell, there is a well (called Jab-bul-Ḥuzn) from whose severity even Hell itself seeks refuge 400 times a day. This well is the abode for the ostentatious Qāris of (the Quran).' *(Sunan Ibn Mājaĥ, vol. 1, pp. 167, Ḥadīš 256)*

Ḥifẓ ceremony

Nowadays, when a child completes his/her Ḥifẓ a special ceremony is held. The child is congratulated and presented with bouquets of flowers, garlands and gifts. The family would perhaps be under the impression that they are encouraging the child by holding such ceremonies. Sorry to say, the child was already courageous; this is why he became the Ḥāfiẓ. No doubt, the child should be encouraged and appreciated when he starts the Ḥifẓ as it will develop passion in him but once he has completed the Ḥifẓ, he needs to be instructed to remember it throughout his life and act according to the Quranic teachings. Anyway, this type of ceremony can cause ostentation in the child instead of encouragement. Please do consider these issues before arranging this type of ceremony.

I searched very hard for sincerity

I have searched very hard for sincerity in such ceremonies but failed to find it. I only saw ostentation. Allah عَزَّوَجَلَّ forbid, sometimes even photographs are taken. Instead of gathering people for a ceremony, take the child to pious people and request them to make Du'ā for the child to remember the Quran throughout his life and spend his life following the teachings of the Holy Quran. اِنْ شَآءَاللّٰه عَزَّوَجَلَّ there will be more blessings.

وَاللّٰهُ وَرَسُوْلُهٗ اَعْلَم عَزَّوَجَلَّ وَصَلَّى اللّٰهُ تَعَالٰى عَلَيْهِ وَاٰلِهٖ وَسَلَّم

Consider all aspects

One should consider all aspects. Will the proposed ceremony be beneficial to your afterlife? If you are certain that the purpose of the Ḥifẓ-e-Quran ceremony is not to show off, and you are also sure that your child will remain safe from ostentation and insincerity, i.e. you have already given him excellent training of sincerity and humility, then hold the ceremony. May Allah عَزَّوَجَلَّ accept it!

اٰمِيْن بِجَاهِ النَّبِيِّ الْاَمِيْن صَلَّى اللّٰهُ تَعَالٰى عَلَيْهِ وَاٰلِهٖ وَسَلَّم

It's easy to become Ḥāfiẓ but difficult to remain Ḥāfiẓ!

It is a matter of great concern that a large number of Ḥāfiẓaĥ girls and Ḥāfiẓ boys whose parents hold ceremonies for learning the Holy Quran are made to forget the Quran later. In some families, it is customary to make children Ḥuffāẓ. This is indeed a very good act but remember that it is easy to become a Ḥāfiẓ but difficult to remain the Ḥāfiẓ. Therefore, it is a Madanī request to all those parents who want their child to become Ḥāfiẓ to keep an eye on the child and advise him repeatedly to recite at least one part a day so that he would not forget.

The Holy Prophet صَلَّى اللّٰهُ تَعَالٰى عَلَيْهِ وَاٰلِهٖ وَسَلَّم has said, 'Always recite the Quran. I swear by the One in Whose omnipotence my life is, the Quran tends to be released more quickly than the camel tied with ropes.' *(Ṣaḥīḥ Bukhārī, vol. 3, pp. 412, Ḥadīš 5033)*

In other words, as tied camels want to be released and they will run away if proper attention and care is not given, likewise, if one does not keep remembering and revising the Quran, he will be made to forget it. *(Fatāwā Razawiyyaĥ (Jadīd), vol. 23, pp. 745)*

Punishment for forgetting Ḥifẓ

The Ḥuffāẓ that revise the Quran just a few days before the arrival of Ramadan in order to be able to recite it in Tarāwīḥ Ṣalāĥ but, Allah عَزَّوَجَلَّ forbid, forget numerous verses for the whole year due to heedlessness should repeatedly read the following narration and tremble with fear of Allah عَزَّوَجَلَّ. Anyone who has forgot even one verse must memorise it again and repent sincerely of forgetting it. '*One who forgets the Holy Quran after memorising it will be resurrected blind on the Day of Judgement.*' *(Deduced from part 16, Sūraĥ Ṭāḥā, verses 125-126)*

Three blessed sayings of the Beloved Prophet ﷺ

1. The good deeds of my Ummaĥ were presented to me. I even saw a splinter which a person took out from the Masjid. The sins of my Ummaĥ were also presented to me and I did not see any sin greater than forgetting a chapter or a verse of the Quran after memorising it. *(Jāmi' Tirmiżī, vol. 4, pp. 420, Ḥadīš 2925)*

2. Whoever memorises the Quran and then forgets it will be raised as a leper on the Day of Judgement. *(Sunan Abī Dāwūd, vol. 2, pp. 107, Ḥadīš 1474)*

3. The sin for which my Ummaĥ will be given complete punishment on the Day of Judgement, is the forgetting of a memorized chapter of the Quran. *(Kanz-ul-'Ummāl, vol. 1, pp. 306, Ḥadīš 2843)*

Saying of Imām Aḥmad Razā رَحْمَةُ الله عَلَيْه

A'lā Ḥaḍrat Imām Aḥmad Razā Khān عَلَيْهِ رَحْمَةُ الرَّحْمٰن has stated, 'How unwise is the person whom Allah عَزَّوَجَلَّ blesses with memorising the Quran but he forgets and loses it. If this person were aware of the great virtue and excellence promised for memorising the Holy Quran, he would hold it dearer more than anything else.'

Imām Aḥmad Razā Khān عَلَيْهِ رَحْمَةُ الرَّحْمٰن has further stated, 'Such a person should make every possible effort to teach and help others memorise the Quran, and he himself must do constant revision of the memorised Quran so that he may gain the virtues and excellences that have been promised and so that he is not resurrected blind and leper on the Day of Judgement.' *(Fatāwā Razawiyyaĥ (Jadīd), vol. 23, pp. 645, 647)*

When is it permissible to reveal good deeds?

It is permissible to reveal good deeds if the intention is to express gratitude for a divine favour. Similarly, if a religious leader reveals his deeds intending that his followers and disciples will be encouraged by his deed, this will not be considered as ostentation.

However, every one should consider the condition of his heart before showing his good deeds and virtuous actions to others because Satan is very cunning. It is possible that he makes you indulge in ostentation by making you think that you are informing others of your good deeds to express gratitude but you would inwardly feel overjoyed and expect others to respect you due to showing your good deeds. This is, undoubtedly, ostentation. Then, telling others that it is just to express gratitude is an even bigger act of ostentation as well as a great lie. (For detailed information read the chapters 'Intention', 'Sincerity' and 'Show off' in either *Iḥyā-ul-'Ulūm* or *Kīmīyā-e-Sa'ādat* by Ḥujjat-ul-Islam Sayyidunā Imām Muhammad Ghazālī (عَلَيْهِ رَحْمَةُ اللّٰهِ الْوَالِى). If only we are not deprived by Satan of studying these books because he will never want a Muslim's deed to become sincere and thus be accepted.

O Allah عَزَّوَجَلَّ! Give us the ability and privilege to perform worship and observe Nafl fasts abundantly with sincerity. Enable us to recognise the tricks of Satan by which he ruins our deeds.

آمِيْن بِجَاهِ النَّبِيِّ الْاَمِيْن صَلَّى اللّٰهُ تَعَالٰى عَلَيْهِ وَاٰلِهٖ وَسَلَّم

Riyā kāriyaun say bachā Yā Ilāĥī
Mujĥay 'abd-e-mukhliṣ banā Yā Ilāĥī

Save me from ostentation, O Almighty
Make me a sincere servant, O Almighty

12. Neighbourhood of fasting people

Sayyidunā Mālik Bin Dīnār رَحْمَةُ اللّٰهِ تَعَالٰی عَلَیْه has not eaten even a single piece of date for forty years. His desire of eating dates had intensified. To subdue his Nafs, he رَحْمَةُ اللّٰهِ تَعَالٰی عَلَیْه fasted for eight successive days. Finally, he bought some dates and entered a Masjid situated in an area of Basra in day timing.

As he was about to eat the dates, all of a sudden, a child started to call out, 'O father! A Jew has entered our Masjid!' When his father heard this, he rushed towards the Masjid brandishing a stick. When he arrived, he recognised the eminent saint رَحْمَةُ اللّٰهِ تَعَالٰی عَلَیْه. Apologising he politely said, 'Your Eminence! The thing is, all the Muslims in this area keep fast. Other than the Jews no one eats during the day. This is the reason why my child assumed that you were a Jew; please forgive us for this misunderstanding.' He رَحْمَةُ اللّٰهِ تَعَالٰی عَلَیْه said, 'The children's tongue is a tongue from Ghayb.' He رَحْمَةُ اللّٰهِ تَعَالٰی عَلَیْه then swore never to eat dates. *(Tażkira-tul-Auliyā, part 1, pp. 52)*

Content with just aroma of meat

Dear Islamic brothers! Did you see how our pious saints رَحِمَهُمُ اللّٰهُ تَعَالٰی fought their Nafs? Sayyidunā Mālik Bin Dīnār رَحْمَةُاللّٰهِ تَعَالٰی عَلَیْه did not satisfy the desire of his Nafs! He رَحْمَةُاللّٰهِ تَعَالٰی عَلَیْه did not eat delicious food for many years. Often he fasted during the day and did Ifṭār with just a dry piece of bread. Once, he رَحْمَةُاللّٰهِ تَعَالٰی عَلَیْه had a desire for meat. So he bought some meat. On the way back, he smelt it and said to himself, 'O Nafs! You have attained pleasure by smelling the meat; this is the only benefit for you. Saying this, he gave the meat to a Faqīr (poor person) and then said, 'O Nafs! I'm not hurting you due to enmity. I'm trying to make you patient so that you may attain the precious treasure of divine pleasure!' *(Tażkira-tul-Auliyā, part 1, pp. 52)*

We have also learnt that the Muslims of earlier times would like to keep Nafl fasts as mentioned in the previous parable that all the Muslims of an area of Basra observed Nafl fast every day!

Call to righteousness from children

The saying of Sayyidunā Mālik Bin Dīnār رَحْمَةُ اللّٰهِ تَعَالٰی عَلَیْه that children's words are 'from Ghayb' is also very important. Without doubt, there are often Madanī pearls of admonition for us in the talking and practices of young children.

Sag-e-Madīnaĥ عُفِیَ عَنْهُ (i.e. the author) wrote the aforementioned 12th parable on the 9th Shawwal 1422 A.H. in an Islamic brother's house in Karachi. During the meal, two children of the Islamic brother also sat down to eat. Their greed, quarrelsome attitude, disrespecting and devaluing one another, impatience, intolerance, tale-telling, jealousy, self-pride, self-importance, showing-off, unnecessary talking and needless complaining provided me with a great lesson to ponder over! You may probably be thinking as to how two children can deliver Dars on so many topics? In fact, the person possessing a Madanī mindset can learn many things from their behaviour and attitude. For example, they filled their plates with too much food; they ate some food, dropped some and then left some in their plates.

The lesson I learnt is that filling the plate with too much food is a sign of greed and a manner of silly people. A wise and sensible person refrains from this. Further, not picking up the dropped food which will be thrown away is Isrāf (wasting). After eating, it is a Sunnaĥ to clean the plate (with finger). The wise are not supposed to waste food but act upon the Sunnaĥ. Unwise people waste food like children. The son of the Islamic brother filled his glass with cold drink, which annoyed his sister. She first placed the bottle beside me but still wasn't satisfied. Later she picked up the bottle and put it somewhere else outside the room. This fighṭing gave me the lesson of greed (shown by the son) and jealousy (shown by the daughter). As both were quarrelling and arguing, they began to show each others' faults.

In other words, they were saying, 'Look! We're naive and unwise, because of which we're talking unnecessarily, demonstrating impatience, disrespecting and quarrelling with one another and showing each others' faults & weaknesses. If a (so called) wise person does what we are doing, isn't he a fool? We are praising ourselves and bragging, we are revealing one another's mistakes, but as we are minors, we will not be held accountable for this in the afterlife but, if you disrespect and dishonour one another, show off, lie and commit sins such as jealousy etc. you may well be held accountable and then sentenced to Hell on the Day of Judgement. If this happens, it'll be the greatest tragedy for you.'

Madanī daughter shows her henna-coloured hands

Dear Islamic brothers! To be honest, I have mentioned just a few habits of those children. They were not aware that they were preaching and providing us unknowingly with a great lesson. If we carefully examine a child's habits and behaviour from morning till night, we can obtain many Madanī pearls of admonition and wisdom from his every action and comment.

Once, on the eve of Eid Mīlād-un-Nabī صَلَّى اللهُ تَعَالٰی عَلَیْهِ وَاٰلِهٖ وَسَلَّم, an Islamic brother brought his little Madanī daughter. She wanted to attract my attention by showing her henna-coloured hands. In other words, she gave the lesson that showing one's abilities without a religious necessity, either directly or indirectly, is indeed a sign of showing off. This desire for praise is the habit of unwise and naive people like us. Young girls show their henna-coloured hands and young boys show their attractive clothes etc. to other people expecting praise and admiration, it contains a lesson for the adults.

Nowadays, a large number of people seem to have indulged in the bad habit of showing off. The disease of desiring fame and praise is also common. Further, people desire and expect admiration by their virtuous activities like donating money for the construction of Masājid & Madāris etc. This is indeed a 'deadly disease' but people don't pay any attention towards it.

The Prophet of mankind, the Peace of our heart and mind, the most Generous and Kind صَلَّى اللهُ تَعَالٰى عَلَيْهِ وَاٰلِهٖ وَسَلَّم has warned, 'Two hungry wolves let loose at a herd of sheep don't cause as much harm as desire of respect and love of wealth cause harm to a person's religion.' *(Jāmi' Tirmiżī, vol. 4, pp. 166, Ḥadīš 2383)*

I did not offer even Ṣalāt-ul-Jumu'aĥ

Dear Islamic brothers! In order to develop the spirit to get rid of showing off and love of wealth, always remain associated with Dawat-e-Islami. Make it your habit to travel with the Madanī Qāfilaĥs of Dawat-e-Islami. There are great blessings of the Madanī environment of Dawat-e-Islami.

Therefore, an Islamic brother of Gujranwala (Punjab, Pakistan) sent me his letter in which he mentioned, 'I was living my life in fashion, sins and indecent deeds. Due to bad company, I had even become an alcoholic. I had been so wicked that I did not offer even Jumu'aĥ Ṣalāĥ. Despite being a Ḥāfiẓ of the Quran, I didn't even open the Quran for almost twelve years and, as a result, I had been made to forget almost all of it. I was living a life of ignorance. Luckily, the star of my fortune shone when I met an Islamic brother of Dawat-e-Islami. I was impressed by his good character and affectionate behaviour. He invited me to attend Dawat-e-Islami's three day Sunnaĥ-Inspiring global Ijtimā' being held in Madīna-tul-Auliyā, Multan. I politely excused telling him that I am jobless and cannot afford the expenses of journey. He encouraged me very politely and arranged my ticket.

اَلْحَمْدُ لِلّٰه عَزَّوَجَلَّ! I was privileged to participate in the Sunnaĥ-Inspiring Ijtimā'. The Sunnaĥ-Inspiring speeches and the heart-rending Du'ā changed my life altogether. When I returned from the Ijtimā', a Madanī transformation had taken place in my heart. Then, along with Rasūl's devotees, I was privileged to travel with a Madanī Qāfilaĥ in which I adopted many Sunnaĥ. اَلْحَمْدُ لِلّٰه عَزَّوَجَلَّ With the blessings of the Madanī environment I learnt the forgotten Quran by heart again. I also got the privilege of performing Imāmat for seven successive years. At present, I am serving Dawat-e-Islami as a responsible member of 'Punjab Makkī Majlis'.

Gunaĥgāraun āo, siyāĥ kāraun āo
Gunāĥaun ko day gā cĥuřā Madanī Māḥaul
Pilā kar ma-ay 'ishq day gā banā yeĥ
Tumĥayn 'āshiq-e-Mustafa Madanī Māḥaul

Come O sinners, you also O transgressors
You will give up sins in the Madanī environment
You will have a drink of devotion and become
A devotee of Mustafa in the Madanī environment

صَلُّوْا عَلَى الْحَبِيْب صَلَّى اللّٰهُ تَعَالٰى عَلٰى مُحَمَّد

O Allah عَزَّوَجَلَّ! Bestow steadfastness upon us in the Madanī environment of Dawat-e-Islami! Make us eager to travel with Madanī Qāfilaĥs. Bless us with the treasure of sincerity. Save us from showing off, ostentation and love of wealth. Give us the privilege and ability to observe Nafl fasts as well as the Farḍ fasts and also accept them from us. O Allah عَزَّوَجَلَّ! Forgive us and the entire Ummaĥ of Your Beloved Prophet صَلَّى اللّٰهُ تَعَالٰى عَلَيْهِ وَاٰلِهٖ وَسَلَّم!

اٰمِيْن بِجَاهِ النَّبِيِّ الْاَمِيْن صَلَّى اللّٰهُ تَعَالٰى عَلَيْهِ وَاٰلِهٖ وَسَلَّم

True servant

There are three signs of a true servant: (1) To abide by the commandments of Sharī'aĥ (2) To remain pleased with predestination, and distribution of favours as done by Allah عَزَّوَجَلَّ (3) To sacrifice the desire of Nafs for the pleasure of Allah عَزَّوَجَلَّ.

(Bayṫay ko Waṣiyyat, pp. 37)

اَلْحَمْدُ لِلّٰهِ رَبِّ الْعٰلَمِيْنَ وَ الصَّلٰوةُ وَ السَّلَامُ عَلٰى سَيِّدِ الْمُرْسَلِيْنَ

اَمَّا بَعْدُ فَاَعُوْذُ بِاللّٰهِ مِنَ الشَّيْطٰنِ الرَّجِيْمِ ؕ بِسْمِ اللّٰهِ الرَّحْمٰنِ الرَّحِيْمِ ؕ

41 Inspiring Parables of Mu'takifīn

Dawat-e-Islami, a global & non-political religious movement of the Quran and Sunnaĥ, holds collective I'tikāf every year in the blessed month of Ramadan in numerous parts of the world. As a result of the religious and moral training provided to the Mu'takifīn during the collective I'tikāf, thousands of sinners sincerely repent of their sins and turn over a new leaf according to the Madanī mission, '**I must strive to reform myself and the people of the entire world**' and get busy reforming other people.

The following pages contain an account of those fortunate people who repented of their sins by the blessing of collective I'tikāf. The Islamic brothers wrote the following statements in their own words but Sag-e-Madīnaĥ عُفِيَ عَنْهُ (the author of this book) has made a humble effort to make these statements more interesting by making some slight changes.

Excellence of Ṣalāt-'Alan-Nabī ﷺ

The Prophet of Raḥmaĥ, the Intercessor of Ummaĥ, the Owner of Jannaĥ صَلَّى اللّٰهُ تَعَالٰى عَلَيْهِ وَاٰلِهٖ وَسَلَّم has said, 'Whoever recites Ṣalāt upon me 100 times, Allah عَزَّوَجَلَّ will write between his eyes that this person is free from hypocrisy and hellfire and Allah عَزَّوَجَلَّ will keep him with the martyrs on Day of Judgement.' *(Majma'-uz-Zawāid, vol. 10, pp. 253, Ḥadīš 172998)*

صَلُّوْا عَلَى الْحَبِيْب   صَلَّى اللّٰهُ تَعَالٰى عَلٰى مُحَمَّد

1. Hunter becomes prey!

An Islamic brother has stated, 'Ignorance prevailed in our home. I was brought up in such an environment in which speaking ill of the blessed and honourable companions رَضِىَ اللّٰهُ تَعَالٰى عَنْهُم was considered an act of virtue. Unfortunately, I was also involved in this blasphemy, but something else was predestined for me.

In the last ten days of Ramadan, 1426 A.H., 2005 I'tikāf was held by Dawat-e-Islami in 'Aṭṭārābād. As some boys from my neighbourhood participated in the I'tikāf, I visited the Madanī Markaz Faīzān-e-Madīnaĥ with the intention of teasing them. As I arrived, I noticed that people were sitting in groups, learning and teaching the Sunan. I also sat waiting for an opportunity to irritate them and cause any mischief. Meanwhile, an Islamic brother politely invited me to join those learning sessions. I couldn't refuse as he invited me in a very polite, humble and gentle manner. I sat down and began listening to the speech of the Muballigh attentively. There was a strange attraction in his speech. Slowly, the beautiful Madanī Pearls of the speech held me spellbound.

Some devotees of Rasūl invited me to participate in the I'tikāf for the remaining days. I agreed and attained the blessings of the I'tikāf. Everything even the concept of I'tikāf was new and unusual to me. During the I'tikāf, I realised that I had deviated from the straight path.

اَلْحَمْدُلِلّٰه عَزَّوَجَلَّ! I repented of false and corrupt beliefs, recited the Kalimaĥ and boarded the beautiful ship of the Aĥl-e-Sunnat, spiritually sailing towards beautiful Madīnaĥ. I adorned my face with a beard and also my head with a beautiful green turban. I also completed a sixty three day Madanī Tarbiyyatī (training) course, and was given the responsibility of a Ḥalqaĥ in our area. Now اَلْحَمْدُلِلّٰه عَزَّوَجَلَّ, as a totally different person, I am trying to reform other people as well as myself.

May Allah عَزَّوَجَلَّ bless me with steadfastness in the Madanī environment of Dawat-e-Islami, and guide the people who have deviated from true Islamic teachings!'

2. Several attempts to commit suicide

An Islamic brother from Shujabad division Multan (who is currently living in Bāb-ul-Madīnaĥ, Karachi) has stated: I was extremely rude to my parents. I wasted my days playing cricket and my nights watching films.

Once, in the blessed month of Ramadan, I had a severe quarrel with my parents and broke even the house furniture. I was myself fed up with my sinful life. I was very temperamental and, Allah عَزَّوَجَلَّ forbid, had attempted to commit suicide many times but the attempt of suicide failed each time, اَلْحَمْدُ لِلّٰه عَزَّوَجَلَّ. By the grace of Allah عَزَّوَجَلَّ I became interested in attending I'tikāf in the last ten days of Ramadan. At first, I decided to perform I'tikāf in my local Masjid but then I luckily met an Islamic brother. As a result of the Islamic brother's individual effort, I joined the collective I'tikāf in the company of Rasūl's devotees in Faīzān-e-Madīnaĥ, the global Madanī Markaz of Dawat-e-Islami.

اَلْحَمْدُ لِلّٰه عَزَّوَجَلَّ! How great the blessings of the collective I'tikāf are! Before attending the I'tikāf, I was clean shaven, used to wear a shirt and trousers, but the learning sessions, the Sunnaĥ-Inspiring speeches and the company of Rasūl's devotees had all an immense Madanī impact upon me. I started to grow a beard, began wearing the blessed turban on my head and, on the eve of Eid, repented of my sins crying immensely. Instead of returning home, I travelled with a three day Sunnaĥ-Inspiring Madanī Qāfilaĥ with Rasūl's devotees. I spent all three days of Eid in the path of Allah عَزَّوَجَلَّ.

I swear by Allah عَزَّوَجَلَّ! This was my first ever Eid which I thoroughly enjoyed. When I came home, I clung onto my mother's feet and cried so much that I passed out. When I recovered about half an hour later, I saw that my family had surrounded me. They were amazed to see such a major positive change in my attitude. اَلْحَمْدُ لِلّٰه عَزَّوَجَلَّ The environment of our home has also been nice. At present, I am a responsible member of the local Majlis of Dawat-e-Islami. اَلْحَمْدُ لِلّٰه عَزَّوَجَلَّ After completing the Tarbiyyatī course in Faīzān-e-Madīnaĥ, the global Madanī Markaz, I have joined 126 days Imāmat Course. I request you to pray for my steadfastness.

Bigřay akhlāq sāray sanwar jāyaīn gey
Madanī Māḥaul mayn kar lo tum I'tikāf
Bas mazaĥ kyā mazaĥ ko mazay āyaīn gey
Madanī Māḥaul mayn kar lo tum I'tikāf

Ill manners will turn into good manners
Do I'tikāf in the Madanī environment
You will get great spiritual pleasure
Do I'tikāf in the Madanī environment

صَلُّوا عَلَى الْحَبِيْب صَلَّى اللّٰهُ تَعَالٰى عَلٰى مُحَمَّد

3. I never offered Ṣalāĥ except Eid Ṣalāĥ

An Islamic brother who lives in Mianwali colony, Manghupir Road Bāb-ul-Madīnaĥ, Karachi has stated: There would be only a few sinners like me. I had several girlfriends. I had such a filthy mind that I had the habit of watching obscene films every day. Believe me or not, I never offered any Ṣalāĥ in my entire life other than Eid Ṣalāĥ and I didn't even know how to offer Ṣalāĥ! Fortunately, the mercy of Allah عَزَّوَجَلَّ showered upon me, blessing with the privilege of taking part in the collective I'tikāf held in Faīzān-e-Madīnaĥ, the global Madanī Markaz of Dawat-e-Islami in the last ten days of Ramadan. How fantastic the Madanī atmosphere in Faīzān-e-Madīnaĥ is! My eyes opened; the veil of heedlessness was removed from my heart and a Madanī transformation took place.

اَلْحَمْدُ لِلّٰه عَزَّوَجَلَّ! I learnt how to offer Ṣalāĥ and became punctual in my five daily Ṣalāĥ with the Jamā'at. I started to deliver Dars from Faīzān-e-Sunnat in two Masjids. اَلْحَمْدُ لِلّٰه عَزَّوَجَلَّ! The Islamic brothers gave me the responsibility of Żaylī Nigrān of a Masjid Mushāwarat. To express my appreciation I would like to mention that by the blessings of the Madanī environment of Dawat-e-Islami I was honoured with the privilege of seeing the Beloved and Blessed Prophet صَلَّى اللّٰهُ تَعَالٰى عَلَيْهِ وَاٰلِهٖ وَسَلَّم in my dream.

صَلُّوْا عَلَى الْحَبِيْب صَلَّى اللّٰهُ تَعَالٰى عَلٰى مُحَمَّد

4. Whole family embraced Islam

An Islamic brother has stated: A new Muslim (who embraced Islam as a result of the efforts of a Muballigh of Dawat-e-Islami) was blessed with the opportunity to take part in the collective I'tikāf that was held in the Memon Masjid of Kalyan (Maharashtra, India) by Dawat-e-Islami in Ramadan (1426 A.H./2005). The Sunnaĥ-Inspiring speeches, cassette Ijtimā'āt and Sunnaĥ-Inspiring learning sessions all had a deep Madanī impact upon him. Due to the blessings of I'tikāf, he developed a passion to preach his blessed religion. His other family members were still wandering in the dark valley of unbelief. After attending the I'tikāf, he began making attempts for the reform of his family. He even called Muballighīn of Dawat-e-Islami to his house to invite his family to embrace Islam.

اَلْحَمْدُ لِلّٰه عَزَّوَجَلَّ! His parents, two sisters and a brother embraced Islam and were initiated in the spiritual Qādiriyyaĥ Razawiyyaĥ order and hence they became disciples of Ghauš-e-A'ẓam رَضِیَ اللّٰهُ تَعَالٰی عَنْهُ.

Walwalaĥ Dīn kī tablīgh kā pāo gey
Madanī Māḥaul mayn kar lo tum I'tikāf
Fazl-e-Rab say zamānay pay chā̂ jāo gey
Madanī Māḥaul mayn kar lo tum I'tikāf

You will get inspired to Islamic-preaching
Do I'tikāf in the Madanī environment
By Divine bounty you will be dominating
Do I'tikāf in the Madanī environment

صَلُّوْا عَلَى الْحَبِيْب صَلَّى اللّٰهُ تَعَالٰى عَلٰى مُحَمَّد

5. I was engulfed in a secular lifestyle

An Islamic brother of Sukkur city (Bāb-ul-Islam, Sindh) has stated: I was a hedonist and would lead my life enjoying worldly pleasures. The only aim of my life was to earn money. I had drifted away from religious teachings and was lost in the darkness of sins. اَلْحَمْدُ لِلّٰه عَزَّوَجَلَّ In Ramadan, some sympathetic devotees of Rasūl met and invited me to join the collective I'tikāf, but I refused. The Rasūl's devotees were experts and experienced and it seemed they didn't even know how to give up hope. They weren't prepared to leave me to my own devices. They kept getting reward by constantly inviting me to righteousness. Due to their constant individual effort, the heart of this sinner, criminal and lover of the world eventually softened and I performed I'tikāf with them in the last ten days of Ramadan (Probably in 1410 A.H. 1990). I couldn't imagine that the world of these preachers would be so different from mine. The company of Rasūl's devotees had an immense effect on me.

اَلْحَمْدُ لِلّٰه عَزَّوَجَلَّ! I began to offer my Ṣalāĥ punctually, grew a beard and adorned my head with the crown of the blessed turban. In addition to many other important things which I learnt during the I'tikāf, I also learnt that it is strictly prohibited to relieve oneself whilst having one's face or back towards Qiblaĥ. During the I'tikāf, it came to my attention that the toilets of the Masjid where we performed I'tikāf were facing the wrong direction. For the pleasure of Allah عَزَّوَجَلَّ I called in some labourers and got the direction of the toilets corrected. I paid them from my own pocket. اَلْحَمْدُلِلّٰه عَزَّوَجَلَّ! After the I'tikāf I travelled with many Sunnaĥ-Inspiring Madanī Qāfilaĥs with Rasūl's devotees.

صَلُّوْا عَلَى الْحَبِيْب صَلَّى اللّٰهُ تَعَالٰى عَلٰى مُحَمَّد

6. I want to be like you

An Islamic brother of Rawalpindi (Punjab, Pakistan) gave the following account: I was a student of matriculation at that time. In the last ten days of Ramadan (1421 A.H. 2000) I performed I'tikāf in the Bilāl Masjid of our area. There were about fourteen or fifteen Mu'takifīn including me. Probably, on the 28th of Ramadan, after Ẓuĥr Ṣalāĥ, one of my ex-class fellows (whom we used to tease because of his naivety) came to meet us. He was wearing a green turban. After greeting us with Salām, he made individual effort and politely said: 'Can I ask any one of you to tell me the method of Eid Ṣalāĥ!' None of us knew so we started staring at each other sheepishly. Then he said, 'Can you explain the method of the funeral Ṣalāĥ!' Sadly, none of us knew this either. Then he showed us a demonstration of Ṣalāĥ. His practical demonstration made us realise the mistakes we used to make in our Ṣalāĥ. After that he explained to us the method of offering the Eid Ṣalāĥ and the funeral Ṣalāĥ in an excellent and easily-understandable way. We were immensely pleased.

Truly speaking, the only thing we learnt during the I'tikāf was the method of Ṣalāĥ that Muballigh of Dawat-e-Islami taught us. On the day of Eid, I offered Eid Ṣalāĥ on the roof of the Masjid. When the Imām uttered the second Takbīr, almost everyone bent for Rukū' except me. This wasn't the time to do Rukū', everyone was supposed to raise their hands to their ears and then lower them to their sides. If I hadn't learnt the method of the Eid Ṣalāĥ I would also have bent for the Rukū' like others. I felt intensely grateful to the Muballigh of Dawat-e-Islami who taught me the method of Eid Ṣalāĥ during I'tikāf. At that moment, I also realised the importance of Dawat-e-Islami. When I met the Muballigh on Eid, I said to him, 'I also want to be like you.' He encouraged me very compassionately. Due to his individual effort, I joined the Madanī environment of

Dawat-e-Islami. At present, I am serving Sunnaĥ as a member of the education Majlis of Dawat-e-Islami.

صَلُّوْا عَلَى الْحَبِيْب صَلَّى اللّٰهُ تَعَالٰى عَلٰى مُحَمَّد

7. Tears came into my eyes

An Islamic brother from Jinnahabad (Bāb-ul-Madīnaĥ, Karachi) has stated: In Ramadan (1420 A.H. 2004) I was blessed with the privilege of taking part in the collective I'tikāf in Faīzān-e-Madīnaĥ, the global Madanī Markaz of Dawat-e-Islami. I had many evil habits which I gave up and repented of many other sins due to the blessing of collective I'tikāf. I was unaware of the Sunnaĥ method of eating, but in addition to many other Sunan, I learnt the Sunan of eating and drinking during the I'tikāf. I don't know why tears came to my eyes when I noticed an Islamic brother eating according to Sunnaĥ.

اَلْحَمْدُ لِلّٰه عَزَّوَجَلَّ! It has become my habit to eat according to Sunnaĥ ever since I have learnt the Sunnaĥ method of eating (almost three years back). By the grace of Allah عَزَّوَجَلَّ, I have joined the Madanī environment of Dawat-e-Islami.

Sunnatayn kĥānā kĥānay kī tum jān lo

Madanī Māḥaul mayn kar lo tum I'tikāf

You will be learning the Sunnaĥs of eating
Do I'tikāf in the Madanī environment

صَلُّوْا عَلَى الْحَبِيْب صَلَّى اللّٰهُ تَعَالٰى عَلٰى مُحَمَّد

8. Affection of Rasūl's devotees

A modern youngster of Indor Shehr (M.P. India) has stated that he was wasting his life in sins owing to the company of bad friends. In the last ten days of Ramadan (1425 A.H. 2004) he took part in the collective I'tikāf with some devotees of Rasūl. The company of the devotees of Rasūl changed him entirely and he was blessed with repentance. He grew his beard and began to wear a green turban on his head. He acquired a strong passion to serve the Sunnaĥ and so he eventually became a Muballigh. At present, he is spreading the blessings of Sunnaĥ as a member of a local Majlis.

Laynay khayrāt tum raḥmataun kī chalo
Madanī Māḥaul mayn kar lo tum I'tikāf
Lūṫnay barakatayn Sunnataun kī chalo
Madanī Māḥaul mayṇ kar lo tum I'tikāf

To gain mercies of Allah
Do I'tikāf in the Madanī environment
To attain blessings of Sunnaĥ
Do I'tikāf in the Madanī environment

صَلُّوْا عَلَى الْحَبِيْب صَلَّى اللّٰهُ تَعَالٰى عَلٰى مُحَمَّد

9. Repentance of communists

A responsible Islamic brother of Sukkur (Bāb-ul-Islam, Sindh) has stated: Although the message of Dawat-e-Islami had reached 'Aṭṭārābād (Jacobabad) which is situated near Sukkur, there was still a need to improve Madanī work. The Islamic brothers of 'Aṭṭārābād were very weak in organisational matters. They often used to demand that the Muballighīn from Sukkur be sent to 'Aṭṭārābād for the improvement of Madanī work. In view of their constant demand, we made a lot of individual effort in Ramadan (1410 A.H. 1990) and persuaded the Islamic brothers of 'Aṭṭārābād to take part in the collective I'tikāf that was going to be held in Sukkur. As a result of the concerted efforts, numerous Islamic brothers from 'Aṭṭārābād performed I'tikāf in Munawwaraĥ Masjid, Station Road, Sukkur.

Prior to the I'tikāf, not even a single Islamic brother knew how to deliver Dars from *Faīzān-e-Sunnat* but seventeen Islamic brothers became Mu'allims (those who give Dars) and Muballighs (preachers) in that collective I'tikāf by the blessings of the company of the devotees of Rasūl, اَلْحَمْدُ لِلّٰه عَزَّوَجَلَّ. They adorned their faces with blessed beards and their heads with crowns of green turbans. They were given organisational responsibilities for the Madanī work of Dawat-e-Islami. Somehow, some communists (non-Muslims) also came close to the Madanī environment. اَلْحَمْدُ لِلّٰه عَزَّوَجَلَّ All of them repented of their unbelief, read the Kalimaĥ and embraced Islam. Moreover, they made the intention to spend the rest of their lives in the Madanī environment of Dawat-e-Islami.

اَلْحَمْدُ لِلّٰه عَزَّوَجَلَّ! At present, the Islamic brothers of 'Aṭṭārābād who were blessed with the privilege of taking part in the collective I'tikāf of Ramadan (1410 A.H.) and the newly reverted Muslims who repented of communism are now excellent Muballighs, able enough to deliver Sunnaĥ-Inspiring speeches in large gatherings even in the global Ijtimā'. They also hold important responsibilities in various provincial Majālis and are striving to reform themselves and the people of whole the world. May Allah عَزَّوَجَلَّ bless us and them with steadfastness in the Madanī environment of Dawat-e-Islami!

آمِيْن بِجَاهِ النَّبِيِّ الْاَمِيْن صَلَّى اللّٰهُ تَعَالٰى عَلَيْهِ وَاٰلِهٖ وَسَلَّم

صَلُّوْا عَلَى الْحَبِيْب صَلَّى اللّٰهُ تَعَالٰى عَلٰى مُحَمَّد

10. My head can be cut off but...

An Islamic brother who lives in Korangi number 6, Bāb-ul-Madīnaĥ Karachi gave the following account: My younger brother was twenty six years old, he didn't offer his Ṣalāĥ, and was clean shaven. Making individual effort, I persuaded him to take part in the collective I'tikāf in the last ten days of Ramadan (1421 A.H. 2000) with Rasūl's devotees in Faīzān-e-Madīnaĥ, the global Madanī Markaz of Dawat-e-Islami. Due to the blessed company of Rasūl's devotees during the I'tikāf, my younger brother who neither offered any Ṣalāĥ nor acted upon any Sunnaĥ, had completely changed.

اَلْحَمْدُ لِلّٰه عَزَّوَجَلَّ! He began to offer his five daily Ṣalāĥ and grew beard. He developed such a strong passion that he was heard saying, 'Now my head can be cut off but my beard cannot be separated from my face.'

صَلُّوْا عَلَى الْحَبِيْب صَلَّى اللّٰهُ تَعَالٰى عَلٰى مُحَمَّد

11. I was cured from epilepsy

An Islamic brother has stated: An Islamic brother took part in the collective I'tikāf that was held in Ramadan (1426 A.H.) in the Kurla district of Mumbai (India) under the supervision of Dawat-e-Islami, a global & non-political movement of the Quran & Sunnaĥ. This Islamic brother used to have epileptic fits every other day. اَلْحَمْدُ لِلّٰه عَزَّوَجَلَّ, During the entire I'tikāf, he didn't suffer even a single epileptic fit. اَلْحَمْدُ لِلّٰه عَزَّوَجَلَّ Since that day he never suffered from epilepsy again.

Dear Islamic brothers! Did you see! Due to the blessings of I'tikāf in the company of Rasūl's devotees people are granted relief from problems and calamities. اَلْحَمْدُ لِلّٰه عَزَّوَجَلَّ! This Islamic brother was cured of epilepsy, and didn't suffer a single fit in the Masjid. Indeed this is due to the special grace of Allah عَزَّوَجَلَّ. However, keep it in mind that such a patient who gets unconscious due to epileptic fits or any other reason shouldn't perform I'tikāf in the Masjid because he could have a fit anytime even during the Ṣalāĥ, which will cause severe problems for other people. Especially the one captured by a Jinn should not be allowed to do I'tikāf because his erratic jumping around, screaming and shouting will cause problems for other worshippers.

12. I was clean shaven

An Islamic brother of Naseerabad (Bāb-ul-Islam, Sindh) gave the following account: I was clean shaven and was wasting my days in heedlessness. Due to the encouragement and individual effort of various Islamic brothers I took part in the collective I'tikāf in Ramadan (1425 A.H. 2004) in the company of Rasūl's devotees in the Madanī environment of Dawat-e-Islami. اَلْحَمْدُ لِلّٰه عَزَّوَجَلَّ, The I'tikāf changed my heart. I cried out of shame and made a firm intention to give up sins forever. I began to wear a green turban and adorned my face with beard. اَلْحَمْدُ لِلّٰه عَزَّوَجَلَّ! At present, I am the servant (i.e. responsible) of a Mushāwarat in the Naseerabad district of Dawat-e-Islami.

Sīkĥnay ko milayn gī tumĥayn Sunnatayn
Madanī Māḥaul mayn kar lo tum I'tikāf
Lūṭ lo ā kar Allah kī raḥmatayn
Madanī Māḥaul mayn kar lo tum I'tikāf

To gain mercies of Allah
Do I'tikāf in the Madanī environment
To attain blessings of Sunnaĥ
Do I'tikāf in the Madanī environment

صَلُّوْا عَلَى الْحَبِيْب　　صَلَّى اللّٰهُ تَعَالٰى عَلٰى مُحَمَّد

13. I had habit of singing songs

A 25-year-old Islamic brother from Drig Road (Bāb-ul-Madīnaĥ, Karachi) has stated: I performed I'tikāf in the last ten days of Ramadan in the company of Rasūl's devotees in Faīzān-e-Madīnaĥ, the global Madanī Markaz of Dawat-e-Islami, a global & non-political movement of the Quran and Sunnaĥ. I was blessed in that I'tikāf. One of the blessings was that I gave up my habit of singing songs walking in streets like loafers and I began to recite blessed Na'at instead, اَلْحَمْدُ لِلّٰه عَزَّوَجَلَّ. I also developed the mindset of observing the Madanī guard of the tongue (avoiding unnecessary and evil speech). Now, whenever I utter any useless and unimportant word, I instantly recite Ṣalāt-'Alan-Nabī to compensate for it.

Gīt gānay kī 'ādat nikal jāye gī
Madanī Māḥaul mayn kar lo tum I'tikāf
Bay-jā bak bak kī khaṣlat bĥī ṭal jāye gī
Madanī Māḥaul mayn kar lo tum I'tikāf

The habit of singing songs will go away
Do I'tikāf in the Madanī environment
The practice of useless talking will go away
Do I'tikāf in the Madanī environment

صَلُّوْا عَلَى الْحَبِيْب   صَلَّى اللّٰهُ تَعَالٰى عَلٰى مُحَمَّد

14. Fashionable young man became Muballigh...

In Baikala (Mumbai, India) a modern youngster who was an electrical engineer by profession participated in the collective I'tikāf organised by Dawat-e-Islami in the last ten days of Ramadan (1419 A.H. 1998). He remained in the company of Rasūl's devotees for ten days. The refulgence of beard, which is a symbol of love for the Beloved and Blessed Prophet صَلَّى اللّٰهُ تَعَالٰى عَلَيْهِ وَاٰلِهٖ وَسَلَّم began to shine on his face. He began to wear a green turban as well, and the blessings of I'tikāf transformed him into a great Muballigh of Sunnaĥ. اَلْحَمْدُ لِلّٰه عَزَّوَجَلَّ! He continued to take part in the Madanī activities of Dawat-e-Islami and is now busy spreading the blessings of the Sunnaĥ as a member of India's Makkī Kābīnaĥ.

صَلُّوْا عَلَى الْحَبِيْب   صَلَّى اللّٰهُ تَعَالٰى عَلٰى مُحَمَّد

15. How I gave up taking drugs

An Islamic brother who lives in Hyderabad (Bāb-ul-Islam, Sindh) has stated: I was a drug addict and did not use to offer Ṣalāĥ. My family was very worried and concerned about me. Luckily, I was blessed with the privilege of attending the three day Sunnaĥ-Inspiring global Ijtimā' of Dawat-e-Islami held in the plains of Ṣaḥrā-e-Madīnaĥ, Madīna-tul-Auliyā, Multan in 1426 A.H. 2005. During the Ijtimā', I made the intention to perform I'tikāf in Faīzān-e-Madīnaĥ. So I came to Bāb-ul-Madīnaĥ and gained the privilege of doing I'tikāf for the last 10 days of Ramadan (1426 A.H. 2005). No doubt, the three day Ijtimā' of Multan had its affect on me but the blessings of collective I'tikāf cannot be expressed in words!

Truly speaking, it completely changed my heart. I repented sincerely of my sins, grew my beard and instantly started to wear a green turban. When I returned to Hyderabad after the I'tikāf my family and neighbours were surprised to see me with a beard and a green turban.

اَلْحَمْدُ لِلّٰه عَزَّوَجَلَّ! I stopped taking drugs. Now I make efforts to spread the Madanī work of Dawat-e-Islami. My daughter has enrolled on a Sharī'aĥ course in one of the branches of Jāmi'a-tul-Madīnaĥ of Dawat-e-Islami and my two Madanī sons are memorising the Holy Quran in Madrasaĥ-tul-Madīnaĥ.

Gar Madīnay kā gham chashm-e-nam chāĥiye
Madanī Māḥaul mayn kar lo tum I'tikāf
Madanī Āqā صَلَّى اللّٰهُ عَلَيْهِ وَسَلَّم *kī naẓr-e-karam chāĥiye*
Madanī Māḥaul mayn kar lo tum I'tikāf

If you want devotion to Madīnaĥ with eyes shedding tears
Do I'tikāf in the Madanī environment
If you desire the merciful gaze of the Prophet Dear صَلَّى اللّٰهُ عَلَيْهِ وَسَلَّم
Do I'tikāf in the Madanī environment

صَلُّوْا عَلَى الْحَبِيْب صَلَّى اللّٰهُ تَعَالٰى عَلٰى مُحَمَّد

16. What is I'tikāf?

An Islamic brother who resides in Dera Allah Yar (Baluchistan, Pakistan) has stated: I had neither the fear of Allah عَزَّوَجَلَّ nor love of the Holy Prophet صَلَّى اللهُ تَعَالٰى عَلَيْهِ وَاٰلِهٖ وَسَلَّم. The precious moments of my life were being wasted in sins. By the grace of Allah عَزَّوَجَلَّ, the Madanī work of Dawat-e-Islami had started in our city. Dawat-e-Islami held a Sunnaĥ-Inspiring Ijtimā' on Shab-e-Barā-at (1416 A.H. 1995) for the first time in our city; I also attended the Ijtimā'. Even though I got immensely impressed by Dawat-e-Islami when I saw a huge number of bearded, turbaned and well-mannered devotees of Rasūl, but I stayed away from them. I did not even attend the Sunnaĥ-Inspiring weekly Ijtimā'.

However, when the 27th night of Ramadan (1416 A.H. 1995) arrived, I took part in the collective Du'ā in the Masjid where the Ijtimā' was held. At the end of the Ijtimā', I met some Islamic brothers one of whom told me that some Islamic brothers attended 'I'tikāf' in the Masjid. The word 'I'tikāf' was new to me. I curiously asked 'What does I'tikāf mean?' Explaining the meaning of 'I'tikāf', the Islamic brothers politely told me some of its blessings. After listening to some blessings of I'tikāf performed in the Madanī environment of Dawat-e-Islami, I made a firm intention in my heart that I would also perform I'tikāf the following year اِنْ شَآءَاللّٰه عَزَّوَجَلَّ.

Time passed gradually. When the next Ramadan arrived I performed I'tikāf with devotees of Rasūl in the last 10 days. Words cannot express what I learnt in just ten days in the company of devotees of Rasūl. During I'tikāf, someone suggested that I enrol on the Dars-e-Niẓāmī course. Responding positively to his sincere suggestion, I came to Bāb-ul-Madīnaĥ, Karachi where I joined Jāmi'a-tul-Madīnaĥ. After the completion of Daura-e-Ḥadīš, the degree of Dars-e-Niẓāmī was conferred on me during the traditional degree-conferring ceremony held in 1425 A.H. 2004 in the Faīzān-e-Madīnaĥ, Bāb-ul-Madīnaĥ, Karachi. At present, I am a teacher at a branch of Jāmi'a-tul-Madīnaĥ of Dawat-e-Islami in Hyderabad.

Dear Islamic brothers! Did you see! A boy who didn't even know what I'tikāf meant not only became a scholar due to the blessings of I'tikāf with Rasūl's devotees but also became a teacher of Dars-e-Niẓāmī students at a branch of Dawat-e-Islami's Jāmi'a-tul-Madīnaĥ and is making other Islamic brothers scholars.

Sunnatayn sīkĥ lo raḥmatayn lūṫ lo,
Madanī Māḥaul mayn kar lo tum I'tikāf
'Ilm ḥāṣil karo barakatayn lūṫ lo,
Madanī Māḥaul mayn kar lo tum I'tikāf

To gain mercy and learn Sunnaĥ, do I'tikāf in the Madanī environment
To acquire knowledge and gain blessings, do I'tikāf in the Madanī environment

صَلُّوْا عَلَى الْحَبِيْب صَلَّى اللّٰهُ تَعَالٰى عَلٰى مُحَمَّد

17. Which of my sins shall I mention!

An Islamic brother of Bāb-ul-Madīnaĥ, Karachi has stated: Which sins of mine should I mention! Allah عَزَّوَجَلَّ forbid, not offering Ṣalāĥ, playing computer games, watching obscene programmes on television every day, lying and even stealing were some of the sins I used to commit fearlessly.

Luckily, in the last ten days of Ramadan in 1421 A.H. 2000, I was blessed with the privilege of taking part in the collective I'tikāf with some Rasūl's devotees of Dawat-e-Islami in Jāmi' Masjid Āminaĥ, situated in Shakeel Garden, Aukhai complex, Bāb-ul-Madīnaĥ, Karachi. After the collective I'tikāf, I joined the Madrasa-tul-Madīnaĥ that was held on the second floor of Āminaĥ Masjid.

اَلْحَمْدُ لِلّٰه عَزَّوَجَلَّ! I began to attend the weekly Sunnaĥ-Inspiring Ijtimā' of Dawat-e-Islami which was held in Faīzān-e-Madīnaĥ. اَلْحَمْدُ لِلّٰه عَزَّوَجَلَّ! As a result of my efforts, a Madanī atmosphere has been created in my home. I play the cassettes of Sunnaĥ-Inspiring speeches released by Maktaba-tul-Madīnaĥ at home. اَلْحَمْدُ لِلّٰه عَزَّوَجَلَّ! I have memorised the entire Holy Quran and I'm currently doing Dars-e-Niẓāmī in Jāmi'a-tul-Madīnaĥ. I also teach in Madrasa-tul-Madīnaĥ and I am trying to spread the Madanī work of Dawat-e-Islami under the guidance of the Nigrān of my Żaylī Mushāwarat.

18. Markaz by blessings of I'tikāf

A responsible Islamic brother from India has stated: The trustees and some local Muslims of 'Masjid-e-A'ẓam' in Chitra Durga, Karnataka, India, had some misconceptions about

Dawat-e-Islami. Due to their misconceptions, we had to face many difficulties in obtaining permission to perform I'tikāf collectively in Ramadan. The sons of two trustees also joined the collective I'tikāf. When the trustees observed the Sunnaĥ-Inspiring learning sessions and speeches, Na'ats, heart-rending supplications, all according to the Madanī Markaz schedule, and the well organised behaviour of a large number of Mu'takifin, they became so impressed that they presented gifts and flowers to all the Mu'takifin on the last day of I'tikāf. All of their misconceptions were removed and they finally realized that Dawat-e-Islami is sincerely making religious efforts. They gave full authority to Dawat-e-Islami to carry out its Madanī work in the splendid 'Masjid-e-A'ẓam' under their trusteeship.

اَلْحَمْدُلِلّٰہ عَزَّوَجَلَّ! 'Masjid-e-A'ẓam' has now become the Madanī Markaz of that city. اَلْحَمْدُلِلّٰہ عَزَّوَجَلَّ! The sons of both trustees adorned their faces with blessed beards and joined the Madanī environment of Dawat-e-Islami.

Żikr karnā Khudā kā yaĥān subḥ-o-shām
Madanī Māḥaul mayn kar lo tum I'tikāf
Pāo gey Na'at-e-Maḥbūb kī dĥūm dĥām
Madanī Māḥaul mayn kar lo tum I'tikāf

You'll be making the Żikr of Allah all the while here
Do I'tikāf in the Madanī environment
You'll be hearing the Na'ats of the Prophet Dear
Do I'tikāf in the Madanī environment

صَلُّوْا عَلَى الْحَبِيْب صَلَّى اللهُ تَعَالٰى عَلٰى مُحَمَّد

19. Blessing of I'tikāf reaches England

An Islamic brother of Sukkur (Bāb-ul-Islam, Sindh) gave the following account: In Ramadan (1410 A.H. 1990) my brother-in-law arrived in Sukkur (Bāb-ul-Islam, Sindh, Pakistan) from England. Encouraged by the persuasion of some Islamic brothers, I made individual effort on him and invited him to join the blessings of collective I'tikāf with Rasūl's devotees. Accepting my invitation, اَلْحَمْدُلِلّٰہ عَزَّوَجَلَّ he attended the I'tikāf. When my brother-in-law who was accustomed to living in a completely non-Islamic environment performed I'tikāf, learnt the beautiful Sunan of the Holy Prophet صَلَّى اللهُ تَعَالٰى عَلَيْهِ وَاٰلِهٖ وَسَلَّم and other important religious rulings and heard about the affairs of the grave and afterlife, he felt intense impact on his heart.

اَلْحَمْدُلِلّٰه عَزَّوَجَلَّ! Due to the blessings of the collective I'tikāf he received the gift of repentance of his sins and joined the Madanī environment of Dawat-e-Islami. He adorned his face with a beard and began to wear a green turban. After learning the method of giving Dars and Sunnaĥ-Inspiring speech, he began to deliver speeches even during the I'tikāf. He made a firm intention to enthusiastically participate in the Madanī activities of Dawat-e-Islami on his return to England.

اَلْحَمْدُلِلّٰه عَزَّوَجَلَّ! At present, he is a Muballigh of Dawat-e-Islami in England and is responsible for the twelve Madanī activities. The mother of his children (my sister), also joined the Madanī environment and wears a Madanī Burqa' (veil) despite living in the immodest environment of England. After learning the correct method of reciting the Holy Quran, she is currently teaching other Islamic sisters in Madrasa-tul-Madīnaĥ for adult women. Further, she is currently a member of Dawat-e-Islami's Majlis for Madanī activities of Islamic sisters.

صَلُّوْا عَلَى الْحَبِيْب صَلَّى اللهُ تَعَالٰى عَلٰى مُحَمَّد

20. I'm not going to leave Faīzān-e-Madīnaĥ

An Islamic brother who lives in the division of Kamaliya, district Dār-us-Salām (Punjab) has stated: In those days, I was in grade 9. I had a group of friends in my class. We all used to play truant, roam around, play cricket till late night, waste lots of time in internet cafes and spend all day watching movies on cable. I loved listening to music so much that I would fall asleep whilst listening to songs and the very first thing I would do in the morning after waking up was listening to music. We all wore fashionable and trendy clothes and would go out to tease girls. I never obeyed my mother; whenever she tried to advise me, I would become furious and quarrel with her. My father also asked me to offer Ṣalāĥ, but I would turn a deaf ear. To be honest, there was no apparent hope of my reform.

May Allah عَزَّوَجَلَّ bless my elder brother who rescued me from drowning into the sea of sins. He asked me to perform I'tikāf in the last ten days of Ramadan. Believe me, I was so away from religion that I didn't even know what I'tikāf meant. As I was very rude, I blatantly refused but my brother did not give up hope. Somehow, he made up my mind and managed to persuade me to take part in the collective I'tikāf in Faīzān-e-Madīnaĥ in Sardarabad (Faisalabad, Pakistan). During the initial four or five days I didn't enjoy it at all and tried to run away but couldn't succeed. Then I slowly began to feel some peace. During the last days, I felt so much spiritual peace that on the eve of Eid I said, 'I don't want to go back home, I want to spend tonight in Faīzān-e-Madīnaĥ.'

Tum gĥar ko na khayncĥo naĥīn jātā naĥīn jātā

Mayn cĥaur kay Faīzān-e-Madīnaĥ naĥīn jātā

Don't drag me home, I won't go
Leaving Faīzān-e-Madīnaĥ, I won't go

صَلُّوْا عَلَى الْحَبِيْب   صَلَّى اللّٰهُ تَعَالٰى عَلٰى مُحَمَّد

21. Knee-pain disappeared due to blessing of I'tikāf

A student of Jāmi'a-tul-Madīnaĥ, Bāb-ul-Madīnaĥ, Karachi has stated: In the last 10 days of Ramadan in 1426 A.H. 2005 I was blessed with the privilege of participating in the collective I'tikāf in Faīzān-e-Madīnaĥ, Bāb-ul-Madīnaĥ, Karachi. During the I'tikāf, I met an elderly person who told me that he had been suffering from knee-pain for several years, but when he came to Faīzān-e-Madīnaĥ, Bāb-ul-Madīnaĥ, Karachi, the global Madanī Markaz to perform I'tikāf, his pain was relieved due to the blessings of I'tikāf, اَلْحَمْدُلِلّٰهِ عَزَّوَجَلَّ.

صَلُّوْا عَلَى الْحَبِيْب   صَلَّى اللّٰهُ تَعَالٰى عَلٰى مُحَمَّد

22. Face adorned with beard and head with green turban

An Islamic brother has stated: In the last ten days of Ramadan in 1423 A.H. 2002, a modern Islamic brother of Nosari Gujrat, India, attended the collective I'tikāf held by Dawat-e-Islami in Surat. He was deeply impressed by the Sunnaĥ-Inspiring learning sessions, heart-rending supplications and pleasant sounds of Żikr and Na'ats (all according to the training schedule of Madanī Markaz).

The blessings of the company of Rasūl's devotees were inexpressible. He not only grew his beard, began to wear a green turban but also kept serving his religion under the guidance of Dawat-e-Islami and, at present, he is spreading the Madanī work as the Nigrān of his city Mushāwarat.

Sunnataun kī tum ā kar kay sawghāt lo,
Madanī Māḥaul mayn kar lo tum I'tikāf
Āo baitī ĥay raḥmat kī khayrāt lo,
Madanī Māḥaul mayn kar lo tum I'tikāf

To attain blessings of Sunnaĥ, do I'tikāf in the Madanī environment
To gain mercies of Allah, do I'tikāf in the Madanī environment

صَلُّوا عَلَى الْحَبِيب صَلَّى اللّٰهُ تَعَالٰى عَلٰى مُحَمَّد

23. There's none like my Beloved ﷺ

'Abdur Razzāq 'Aṭṭārī, an Islamic brother of Hyderabad (Bāb-ul-Islam, Sindh Pakistan) was in charge of a laboratory in the Tando Adam Agricultural University. His two sons were associated with the Madanī environment of Dawat-e-Islami but he himself was far away from Ṣalāĥ and the Sunnaĥ. He had a complete secular mindset.

In Ramadan, when he was invited through individual effort to take part in the collective I'tikāf, he said: 'The mother of my children has fallen out with me and gone to her parental home; will she come back, if I do I'tikāf?' He was told that she would come back, اِنْ شَآءَاللّٰه عَزَّوَجَلَّ. Therefore, with Rasūl's devotees, he took part in the collective I'tikāf that was held in Faīzān-e-Madīnaĥ (Hyderabad) in the last ten days of Ramadan, in 1416 A.H., 1995. The learning sessions, Sunnaĥ-Inspiring speeches, heart-rending supplications and pleasant Na'ats caused a Madanī transformation in his heart. He repented of his sins, made a firm intention to offer his Ṣalāĥ, adorned his face with a beard and head with a green turban and began to recite Na'ats. During the I'tikāf, the mother of his children also returned home and their domestic differences were settled. Due to the blessings of I'tikāf, he joined the Madanī environment of Dawat-e-Islami, grew his hair, began to wear a green turban and clothes all according to the Sunnaĥ. He also travelled with Madanī Qāfilaĥs. Whilst remaining associated with the Madanī environment, he passed away the same year on Thursday the 27th of Rabī'-un-Nūr 1416 A.H. 1995. اِنَّا لِلّٰهِ وَ اِنَّاۤ اِلَيْهِ رٰجِعُوْنَ He was so fortunate. At the time of his death, he was reciting the following line of a Na'at's couplet: '*There's no one like my Beloved Rasūl* صَلَّى اللّٰهُ تَعَالٰى عَلَيْهِ وَاٰلِهٖ وَسَلَّم

May Allah عَزَّوَجَلَّ have mercy on him and forgive us without accountability for his sake!

اٰمِيْن بِجَاهِ النَّبِيِّ الْاَمِيْن صَلَّى اللّٰهُ تَعَالٰى عَلَيْهِ وَاٰلِهٖ وَسَلَّم

Gawr-e-tīraĥ ko tum jagmagānay chalo
Madanī Māḥaul mayn kar lo tum I'tikāf
Rāḥatayn rauz-e-maḥshar kī pānay chalo
Madanī Māḥaul mayn kar lo tum I'tikāf

To brighten the dark grave
Do I'tikāf in the Madanī environment
To gain comforts of the Judgement Day
Do I'tikāf in the Madanī environment

صَلُّوْا عَلَى الْحَبِيْب صَلَّى اللّٰهُ تَعَالٰى عَلٰى مُحَمَّد

Admonitory narration

Dear Islamic brothers! This parable teaches us several Madanī lessons. The late 'Abdur Razzāq 'Aṭṭārī رَحْمَةُ اللّٰهِ تَعَالٰى عَلَيْه was very lucky to have joined the Madanī environment just a few months before his death. Indeed the one who repents before his death and comes on the right track and begins to follow the Sunnaĥ is very fortunate. On the contrary, the one who performs good deeds and practices the Sunnaĥ but then, Allah عَزَّوَجَلَّ forbid, becomes heedless, falls into the abyss of sins and moves away from the Madanī environment a short while before his death, is very unfortunate.

Whenever Satan tries to make you drift away from the Madanī environment by making you fall out with a responsible Islamic brother or get lazy or busy with your worldly business, ponder over the following blessed Ḥadīš because it is often observed that when someone joins the Madanī environment whole-heartedly but then moves away, Allah عَزَّوَجَلَّ forbid, it becomes very difficult for him to carry on performing virtuous deeds.

Sayyidatunā 'Āishaĥ Ṣiddīqaĥ رَضِیَ اللهُ تَعَالٰی عَنْهَا has narrated: When Allah عَزَّوَجَلَّ intends somebody goodness, a year before his death, Allah عَزَّوَجَلَّ appoints an angel who persistently guides him to the straight path until he dies in a good state, and then people say: 'So and so person has died in a good state.' When such a person dies, his soul hastens to leave and, at that time, he likes to meet Allah عَزَّوَجَلَّ and Allah عَزَّوَجَلَّ likes to meet him. When Allah عَزَّوَجَلَّ intends anyone the harm (predestined for him), a year before his death, Allah عَزَّوَجَلَّ appoints a devil over him who misguides him until he dies in his worst state. When death comes to him, his soul hesitates to leave, and this person dislikes meeting Allah عَزَّوَجَلَّ and so does Allah عَزَّوَجَلَّ. *(Derived from Sharḥ-us-Ṣudūr, pp. 27)*

24. My family used to turn me out of home

An Islamic brother of Muzaffargarh (Punjab, Pakistan) has stated: I was extremely wicked. At night, I would listen to three or four music cassettes before going to sleep. I used to spend my entire nights loitering around and committing sins. I would quarrel with my family over trivial matters, my family used to turn me out of the house due to my misbehaviour. I would stay out of home for one or two days, then the situation settled down and I would come back. In short, the days of my life were being ruined.

My cousin was the Nigrān of the area Mushāwarat of Dawat-e-Islami. Making individual effort, he persuaded me to take part in the collective I'tikāf of Dawat-e-Islami in the last ten days of Ramadan (1425 A.H. 2004) in the 'Aḋḋay Walī' Masjid (Muzaffargarh). I got extremely impressed by the sincere and sound character of a Muballigh from Bāb-ul-Madīnaĥ, Karachi. I repented of my previous sins and adorned my head with a green turban.

On the 27th night, the Sunnaĥ-Inspiring speech and the heart-rending Du'ā had an immense effect on me, making me cry all night. On the second day of Eid, at the time of Fajr, whilst still asleep, I dreamt of a Holy person who called me by my name and said, 'It's time for Fajr, and you're still asleep!' Whilst asleep, I instantly folded my hands as though I was offering Ṣalāĥ and then I woke up. My hands were folded in the same state.

I received deep inspiration from this dream, and I went to the Masjid without delay and offered Fajr Ṣalāĥ with the Jamā'at. I consistently attended the weekly Ijtimā' in my city. By the grace of Allah عَزَّوَجَلَّ, I am now doing Dars-e-Niẓāmī in Jāmi'a-tul-Madīnaĥ (Bāb-ul-Madīnaĥ, Karachi). I am responsible of Madanī In'āmāt in my class. To express my gratitude, I would like to say that Allah عَزَّوَجَلَّ has especially blessed me because I practise all the 92 Madanī In'āmāt of students. It is my Madanī request that all Islamic brothers make Du'ā for my steadfastness.

25. I was made Khaṭīb of Masjid

An Islamic brother of Saeedabad, Baldiya Town, Bāb-ul-Madīnaĥ Karachi has stated: اَلْحَمْدُ لِلّٰه عَزَّوَجَلَّ I learnt to recite the Holy Quran in a branch of Madrasa-tul-Madīnaĥ of Dawat-e-Islami, but regretfully, I still didn't become punctual in my Ṣalāĥ. اَلْحَمْدُ لِلّٰه عَزَّوَجَلَّ I was blessed with the privilege of performing I'tikāf with Dawat-e-Islami's devotees of Rasūl in the last ten days of Ramadan. Participation in I'tikāf inflicted a Madanī wound on my heart. It woke me up from the sleep of heedlessness and opened my eyes. I became punctual in my Ṣalāĥ. The I'tikāf inspired me to travel with a Madanī Qāfilaĥ. I was unemployed. When I expressed my intention of travelling with the Madanī Qāfilaĥ to my Mushāwarat Nigrān, he said to me, 'اِنْ شَآءَاللّٰه عَزَّوَجَلَّ your problem will soon be solved.'

اَلْحَمْدُ لِلّٰه عَزَّوَجَلَّ! Due to the blessings of the Madanī Qāfilaĥ, the management of the Masjid where our Madanī Qāfilaĥ stayed liked the way of my speech and supplication, so they appointed me as the Khaṭīb of the Masjid and hence I got a means of livelihood. May Allah عَزَّوَجَلَّ grant me steadfastness in the Madanī environment of Dawat-e-Islami!

اٰمِیْن بِجَاہِ النَّبِیِّ الْاَمِیْن صَلَّی اللّٰہ تَعَالٰی عَلَیْهِ وَاٰلِهٖ وَسَلَّم

26. I was spending my life in heedlessness

A modern Islamic brother of Modasa (Gujrat, India) was wasting his life in heedlessness and sins. Luckily, in the last 10 days of Ramadan (1423 A.H. 2002) he was blessed with the privilege of taking part in the collective I'tikāf of Dawat-e-Islami in the company of Rasūl's devotees. Due to the blessings of the Sunnaĥ-Inspiring speeches, heart-rending Du'ās and pleasant Na'ats his life completely changed. He got such a passion that he gained the privilege to deliver Dars and Bayān during the I'tikāf. He intended to grow his beard and wear a green turban. He also travelled with a thirty day Madanī Qāfilaĥ with Rasūl's devotees. As he was a talented man, the Islamic brothers were so impressed with him that they appointed him as the Amir of the Qāfilaĥ.

'Āshiqān-e-Rasūl āo dayn gey bayān
Madanī Māḥaul mayn kar lo tum I'tikāf
Dūr ĥaun gī 'ibādāt kī khāmiyān
Madanī Māḥaul mayn kar lo tum I'tikāf

To listen to the speeches of devotees of Rasūl
Do I'tikāf in the Madanī environment
To rectify faults in performing worship
Do I'tikāf in the Madanī environment

صَلُّوْا عَلَى الْحَبِيْب   صَلَّى اللهُ تَعَالٰى عَلٰى مُحَمَّد

27. اَلْحَمْدُ لِلّٰه عَزَّوَجَلَّ I began to offer Taĥajjud

An elderly Islamic brother of Sukkur (Bāb-ul-Islam, Sindh) has stated: I was blessed with the privilege of taking part in the collective I'tikāf in the last ten days of Ramadan (1425 A.H. 2004) organised by Dawat-e-Islami, a global & non-political movement of the Quran & Sunnaĥ. There was a prearranged and organised schedule for the learning sessions. I learnt the rulings of Ṣalāĥ and many other Sunan relating to daily life. In those ten days, I learnt what I didn't learn in my entire life. The Sunnaĥ-Inspiring speeches and the company of Rasūl's devotees made me reflect about the afterlife, causing a Madanī revolution in my heart. I developed enthusiasm to practice the Madanī In'āmāt. اَلْحَمْدُلِلّٰه عَزَّوَجَلَّ! I especially practiced the 2nd Madanī In'ām, and with its blessings I have developed the habit of offering all five Ṣalāĥ in the first row of the Masjid, with Jamā'at and first Takbīr.

اَلْحَمْدُلِلّٰه عَزَّوَجَلَّ! I also became steadfast in offering Taĥajjud Ṣalāĥ. I hand in my Madanī In'āmāt booklet to the relevant responsible Islamic brother every month. I am also blessed with the privilege of participating in the weekly Ijtimā' punctually from start to end.

28. Yā Rasūlallāĥ ﷺ bless me with your vision

An Islamic brother who lives in Mittiyan (Khariyan, Punjab, Pakistan) has stated: Like other modern young guys, I would also watch films and dramas. Luckily, in the last ten days of Ramadan, I was blessed with the privilege of taking part in the collective I'tikāf with Rasūl's devotees. How blessed the company of Rasūl's devotees is! It was the first time in my life that I saw such a Madanī atmosphere. I developed an overwhelming liking for Dawat-e-Islami in my heart. I always wished to behold the Prophet of Raḥmaĥ, the Intercessor of Ummaĥ, the Owner of Jannaĥ صَلَّى اللهُ تَعَالٰى عَلَيْهِ وَاٰلِهٖ وَسَلَّم. During I'tikāf I used to make Du'ā every day to be blessed with the vision of the Beloved Rasūl صَلَّى اللهُ تَعَالٰى عَلَيْهِ وَاٰلِهٖ وَسَلَّم

On the 27th night, an Ijtimā'-e-Żikr-o-Na'at was held. During the Żikr of Allah عَزَّوَجَلَّ I was overcome with passion. Then it was time for the heart-rending Du'ā. I closed my eyes and wept as I repeated the same words over and over again: 'O Beloved and Blessed Rasūl صَلَّى اللهُ تَعَالٰى عَلَيْهِ وَاٰلِهٖ وَسَلَّم, bless me with your vision.' Suddenly, there was a bright flash of light in my eyes, and then I saw a bright face. I was sure that this was the blessed face of the Holy Prophet صَلَّى اللهُ تَعَالٰى عَلَيْهِ وَاٰلِهٖ وَسَلَّم. This beautiful and blessed face then disappeared.

اَلْحَمْدُ لِلّٰه عَزَّوَجَلَّ! A Madanī transformation took place in my heart. I repented of my sins, grew my beard and made the intention to adorn my head with a green turban. اَلْحَمْدُ لِلّٰه عَزَّوَجَلَّ, On Eid I travelled with a three day Madanī Qāfilaĥ with Rasūl's devotees. At present, I am doing Dars-e-Niẓāmī in Jāmi'a-tul-Madīnaĥ (Bāb-ul-Madīnaĥ, Karachi). I have also completed the Ta'wīżāt-e-'Aṭṭāriyyaĥ course and the Majlis-e-Maktūbāt-o-Ta'wīżāt-e-'Aṭṭāriyyaĥ has given me the duty to give Ta'wīżāt to people. Moreover, in Jāmi'a-tul-Madīnaĥ I'm responsible for Madanī Qāfilaĥs in my class.

صَلُّوْا عَلَى الْحَبِيْب   صَلَّى اللهُ تَعَالٰى عَلٰى مُحَمَّد

29. It's amazing how I gave up playing snooker!

An Islamic brother of Liaqatabad (Bāb-ul-Madīnaĥ, Karachi) has stated: I used to watch films and dramas, and was so fond of playing billiards and snooker that I wouldn't stop even if someone told me off or even beat me. I was so immersed in sins that (Allah عَزَّوَجَلَّ forbid) I used to fear offering Ṣalāĥ. With the mercy of Allah عَزَّوَجَلَّ, in the last 10 days of

Ramadan, (1425 A.H. 2004) I was privileged to join the collective I'tikāf with Rasūl's devotees in our local Furqaniya Masjid (Liaqatabad, Bāb-ul-Madīnaĥ, Karachi) under the supervision of Dawat-e-Islami, a global & non-political movement of the Quran and Sunnaĥ.

اَلْحَمْدُلِلّٰهِ عَزَّوَجَلَّ! Due to the blessings of the 'Madanī In'āmāt' I was encouraged to prepare for my afterlife and I refrained from sins to some extent. Then I became a disciple in the Qādiriyyaĥ Razawiyyaĥ spiritual order and became punctual in my Ṣalāĥ. I stopped playing snooker. I'm surprised as to how I managed to give up playing snooker.

Soon after, I was privileged to participate in the final day of Dawat-e-Islami's three day Sunnaĥ-Inspiring global Ijtimā' held in Ṣaḥrā-e-Madīnaĥ (Madīna-tul-Auliyā) Multan. The speech '*The Perils of Television*' was delivered in the Ijtimā'. When I heard the speech I trembled with fear of punishment in the grave and the Judgement Ḍay. I then vowed never to watch television again. I persuaded my mother to listen to the same speech on a cassette, she gave up watching television too. She also wanted to become a disciple of Ghauš-e-A'ẓam رَضِیَ اللّٰہُ تَعَالٰی عَنْہُ so I made her do Bay'at as well. Due to the blessings of Bay'at, my mother started to offer Taĥajjud, Ishrāq and Chāsht punctually in addition to Farḍ Ṣalāĥ. May I be sacrificed for the magnificence and glory of Allah عَزَّوَجَلَّ! After a few months, my mother was blessed to visit Madīnaĥ. My mother stated: 'All this is the blessing of doing Bay'at.' اَلْحَمْدُ لِلّٰهِ عَزَّوَجَلَّ At present, I am trying to serve my beloved movement 'Dawat-e-Islami' as a responsible for Madanī Qāfilaĥ at division level.

30. Comedian became Muballigh

There was a young comedian in Balan Sinor (Gujrat, India). To entertain people with jokes and amusing stories was his pastime. People used to call him to weddings to entertain the guests with his impersonations. Fortunately, he was blessed with the privilege of taking part in the collective I'tikāf with Rasūl's devotees in the last ten days of Ramadan. Prior to I'tikāf, he had a mania for earning money but in the Madanī atmosphere of the I'tikāf he gained a passion to earn reward for his afterlife. He repented of his sins and began to preach the Sunnaĥ. He devoted himself to Dawat-e-Islami and at present he is spreading the Madanī work of Dawat-e-Islami as the Nigrān of a divisional Mushāwarat.

He is so sincere, determined and self-sacrificing that he has devoted twenty five days every month to perform the Madanī work.

إن شاء الله عزوجل Bĥāī sudĥar jāo gey
Madanī Māḥaul mayn kar lo tum I'tikāf
Marz-e-'iṣyān say chuťĥkārā tum pāo gey
Madanī Māḥaul mayn kar lo tum I'tikāf

إن شاء الله عزوجل, You will get reformed
Do I'tikāf in the Madanī environment
Disease of sins will be cured
Do I'tikāf in the Madanī environment

صَلُّوْا عَلَى الْحَبِيْب صَلَّى اللهُ تَعَالٰى عَلٰى مُحَمَّد

31. I kissed Ḥajar-e-Aswad

An Islamic brother of Tando Allah Yar (Bāb-ul-Islam, Sindh) has stated: I used to commit sins fearlessly due to the company of wicked friends. Going to pubs had become my daily routine. Quarrelling and provoking people, fighting and arguing without any reason were my habits. Even my family members hated me due to my spiteful and troublesome behaviour. I was wandering in the valley of sins.

The star of my fortune shone when, as a result of the individual effort of an Islamic brother, I was blessed with the privilege of taking part in the collective I'tikāf in the last ten days of Ramadan (1426 A.H. 2005) in the company of Rasūl's devotees in my local Nūrānī Masjid (Tando Allah Yar) under the supervision of Dawat-e-Islami. During the I'tikāf, the beards and blessed turbans of the Islamic brothers, their love and compassion impressed me very much. I cannot describe what I learnt in those ten days in the company of Rasūl's devotees. On the 25th night while I was doing the Żikr of Allah عزوجل, I dozed off and saw myself standing before the Holy Ka'baĥ and I kissed Ḥajar-e-Aswad spontaneously. I was blessed on the 27th night as well. In a state of drowsiness, I saw myself in the blessed streets of Madīna-tul-Munawwaraĥ watching the beautiful green dome. These faith-refreshing dreams completely transformed the state of my heart. I made a firm intention never to leave this Madanī environment. الحمد لله عزوجل! Due to the generosity and benevolence of my Merciful Allah عَزَّوَجَلَّ, at present, I am doing Dars-e-Niẓāmī in a Jāmi'a-tul-Madīnaĥ of Dawat-e-Islami in Hyderabad.

32. I gave up sin of bad company

An Islamic brother of Orangi Town (Bāb-ul-Madīnaĥ, Karachi) has stated: Due to the company of modern and dishonest friends I had also become modern and wicked. Fortunately, I joined the Madanī environment of Dawat-e-Islami, a global & non-political movement of the Quran and Sunnaĥ by the blessings of taking part in the collective I'tikāf in the last ten days of Ramadan in my local Aqṣā Masjid, Orangi Town, Al-Fatḥ Colony (Bāb-ul-Madīnaĥ, Karachi). I started not only offering Ṣalāĥ but also following the Sunnaĥ. I developed a habit of attending the weekly Ijtimā'. I gave up my indecent habit of watching films and dramas. A great advantage was that I got rid of the bad company which was the root of many sins, اَلْحَمْدُلِلّٰه عَزَّوَجَلَّ.

Ṣuḥbat-e-bad mayn reĥnay kī 'ādat chuṭay
Madanī Māḥaul mayn kar lo tum I'tikāf
Khaṣlat-e-jurm-o-'iṣyān tumĥārī miṭay
Madanī Māḥaul mayn kar lo tum I'tikāf

Habit of remaining in bad company will go away
Do I'tikāf in the Madanī environment
Habit of committing sins and transgression will go away
Do I'tikāf in the Madanī environment

صَلُّوْا عَلَى الْحَبِيْب صَلَّى اللهُ تَعَالٰى عَلٰى مُحَمَّد

33. My passion got tremendous boost

An Islamic brother of Malaka (Ilahabad, U.P, India) gave the following account: He attended the Sunnaĥ-Inspiring Ijtimā held in Madīna-tul-Auliyā, Ahmadabad, India. By the blessing of attending the Ijtimā', he developed a passion to serve Islam. The same year, he took part in the collective I'tikāf held in the last ten days of Ramadan (1418 A.H., 1996) in the Nāgorī Ward Masjid (Ahmadabad) under the supervision of Dawat-e-Islami. He got extremely impressed by the company of Rasūl's devotees. His passion received a tremendous boost.

After the I'tikāf, when he returned to his ancestral village of Malaka (U.P.) he began to spread the Madanī work enthusiastically. The following year, as a representative of the Madanī Markaz, he visited many cities and inspired hundreds of Islamic brothers to perform I'tikāf. At the time of writing this account, he lives in Ahmadabad and is a responsible of Dawat-e-Islami's finance committee in his area.

صَلُّوْا عَلَى الْحَبِيْب صَلَّى اللّٰهُ تَعَالٰى عَلٰى مُحَمَّد

34. Comments of seventy years old Islamic brother

A 70-year old Islamic brother of Garden West (Bāb-ul-Madīnaĥ Karachi) has stated: Despite reaching old age, I didn't offer Ṣalāĥ. I used to enjoy watching films and dramas. I would shave my beard and wear latest fashionably-designed clothes. About ten years ago, when I was sixty years old, I experienced the blessings of I'tikāf for the first time in my life in the last 10 days of Ramadan in the company of Rasūl's devotees in Kausar Masjid, Musa lane, Liyari Bāb-ul-Madīnaĥ, Karachi. During the I'tikāf, an Islamic brother saw me recite the Holy Quran in Gujrati language. He informed me that it is necessary to recite the Quran in Arabic, otherwise it wouldn't be possible to recite the Arabic letters from their correct origin. I appreciated his advice. During the I'tikāf I received great blessings from Rasūl's devotees. I began to learn the Quran in Madrasa-tul-Madīnaĥ (for adults) held by Dawat-e-Islami. After one and a half year struggle, I managed to correct my pronunciation to some extent.

اَلْحَمْدُ لِلّٰه عَزَّوَجَلَّ! I can now recite the Holy Quran in Arabic. I spend the entire night in the Sunnaĥ-Inspiring weekly Ijtimā'. I am also blessed with the privilege of participating in the call towards righteousness once a week.

اَلْحَمْدُ لِلّٰه عَزَّوَجَلَّ! I adorned my face with a fist-length beard. Despite having no apparent means, I was granted the privilege to perform 'Umraĥ and visit the holy Madīnaĥ city. اَلْحَمْدُ لِلّٰه عَزَّوَجَلَّ, I travel with a three day Madanī Qāfilaĥ every month. Out of 72 Madanī In'āmāt, I am currently trying to practice more than 40 Madanī In'āmāt. I am working as an accountant in a private firm. For the previous four years I am being blessed with the opportunity to call people towards righteousness whilst commuting to and from work by bus in the morning and evening.

Once, I had a dream in which I saw myself calling the passengers towards righteousness; when I finished I saw a Muballigh, who I admire very much. He looked at me with a smile. When I saw this faith-refreshing scene, I began to cry and then I woke up. Inspired by this dream, I started calling people towards righteousness even more steadfastly.

Sīkĥ lo āo Quran pařĥnā sabĥī,
Madanī Māḥaul mayn kar lo tum I'tikāf

To learn recitation of Quran,
Do I'tikāf in the Madanī environment

صَلُّوْا عَلَى الْحَبِيْب   صَلَّى اللّٰهُ تَعَالٰى عَلٰى مُحَمَّد

Transliterating Quranic verses into any language other than Arabic is not permissible

Dear Islamic brothers! Did you see! Sometimes, the character of a person does not improve until he joins a good company. Nowadays, many old people are seen committing various sins. Even on deathbed they don't grow their beard. Even in that crucial state, they keep a TV beside their bed to watch and are interested in getting busy with worldly activities after recovery from their disease. That elderly Islamic brother was very lucky indeed. He joined the Madanī environment during I'tikāf and then his heedless life was transformed into a Madanī life.

Did you see he used to recite the Holy Quran in Gujrati because he did not know how to recite the Holy Quran in Arabic. When a devotee of Rasūl kindly persuaded him, so he began to attend the Madrasa-tul-Madīnaĥ (for adults) in the evening and eventually learnt reciting the Quran in Arabic to some degree.

Remember! Other than Arabic it is not permissible to transliterate (i.e. to write the words of) the Holy Quran into any language e.g. Gujrati, English or Hindi etc. The Quranic verses and supplications in monthly journals and other religious books/magazines should be written in their original Arabic form.

A renowned exegetist of the Quran, Muftī Aḥmad Yār Khān عَلَيْهِ رَحْمَةُ الرَّحْمٰن has stated in a detailed Fatwā: 'To transliterate the Holy Quran into Hindi or English is an obvious distortion (and the distortion of the Holy Quran is Ḥarām) because it contradicts the above mentioned restrictions. Furthermore, it will not be possible to differentiate between س, ص and ث, ق and ك, ز, ذ and ظ. For example, ظاهِر means apparent, whereas زاهِر means 'shiny' or 'fresh.' So if you write *Zahir* in English how will you know whether it implies ظاهِر or زاهِر. The same issue arises in many other words like تاهِر and طاهِر, قَدِير and قادِر, سامِع and سَمِيع, عالِم and عَلِيم. So let alone the distortion of attributes and words, even actual letters will change making the words meaningless.' *(Fatāwā Na'īmiyyaĥ, pp. 116)*

35. Madanī environment at home

An Islamic brother has stated: The days of I'tikāf were approaching in the month of Ramadan (1426 A.H. 2005). I met a 40-year-old Islamic brother from Rajuri (Jammu Kashmir, India). I tried to persuade him to attend the collective I'tikāf. Responding positively to my invitation, he took part in the collective I'tikāf in the last ten days of Ramadan in the railway station Masjid, under the supervision of Dawat-e-Islami. He was surprised to see the Madanī atmosphere that Rasūl's devotees had created. He decided to grow his beard and began to wear a green turban. He even started to deliver Dars and speech and created a Madanī atmosphere at home. He made the Islamic sisters of his house veil themselves and at present he is the Mushāwarat Nigrān of his city, Rajuri.

صَلُّوْا عَلَى الْحَبِيْب   صَلَّى اللّٰهُ تَعَالٰى عَلٰى مُحَمَّد

36. How I became pious

An Islamic brother of District Bhalwal region Gulzār-e-Ṭayyibaĥ (Sargodha, Punjab, Pakistan) has stated: I didn't offer Ṣalāĥ and was fond of fashion. I loved watching films and dramas and enjoyed listening to music. Allah عَزَّوَجَلَّ forbid, I used to keep only a few fasts in Ramadan. If someone advised me, I would turn a deaf ear.

One day, I was going somewhere, worried about something. I met a friend who was wearing a green turban. He was associated with the Madanī environment of Dawat-e-Islami. Making individual effort, he took me to Dawat-e-Islami's Sunnaĥ-Inspiring weekly Ijtimā' in the Jāmi' Masjid, but I left after a short while due to satanic thoughts. Two days later a friend of mine took me to watch a film but we had an argument, so I returned.

Luckily, in Ramadan, my elder brother took part in the collective I'tikāf organized by Dawat-e-Islami. The star of my fortune shone when I went to meet him. I got very impressed to see Rasūl's devotees wearing green turbans. On the eve of Eid, an Islamic brother gave my elder brother a Na'at cassette and a copy of *Faīzān-e-Sunnat*. I trembled with fear when I read the chapter '*Punishments of Missing Ṣalāĥ.*' When I heard the following Munājāt (supplications) in a cassette, I felt its profound impact on my heart.

Gunāĥaun kī 'ādat cĥuřā mayray Maulā
Mujĥay nayk insān banā mayray Maulā

Enable me to give up sins, O Almighty
Make me a pious person, O Almighty

اَلْحَمْدُلِلّٰہ عَزَّوَجَلَّ! I gave up listening to music but couldn't manage to offer my Ṣalāĥ punctually. On the invitation of a devotee of Rasūl, I attended the Sunnaĥ-Inspiring weekly Ijtimā' of Dawat-e-Islami once again, but this time I stayed till the end. After the Ijtimā', I became very impressed by the way in which the devotees of Rasūl met me, and eventually I joined Dawat-e-Islami. I adorned my face with beard and began to wear a green turban. I began to offer all five Ṣalāĥ with the Jamā'at. I also became a disciple in the honourable Qādiriyyaĥ Razawiyyaĥ spiritual order and became a follower of Ghauš-e-A'ẓam رَضِیَ اللہُ تَعَالٰی عَنْہُ.

At the time of writing this statement, I have a responsibility in a Żaylī Mushāwarat. In addition to delivering a Dars regularly I have also been blessed with the privilege of trying to memorise the Holy Quran in a Dawat-e-Islami Madrasa-tul-Madīnaĥ.

Āo Faīzān-e-Sunnat ko pāo gey tum
Madanī Māḥaul mayn kar lo tum I'tikāf
اِنْ شَآءَاللّٰہ عَزَّوَجَلَّ *Jannat mayn jāo gey tum*
Madanī Māḥaul mayn kar lo tum I'tikāf

Come and gain the blessings of Sunnaĥ
Do I'tikāf in the Madanī environment
اِنْ شَآءَاللّٰہ عَزَّوَجَلَّ, *You will go to Jannaĥ*
Do I'tikāf in the Madanī environment

صَلُّوْا عَلَی الْحَبِیْب صَلَّی اللّٰہُ تَعَالٰی عَلٰی مُحَمَّد

37. Relief from spinal pain

A Muballigh of Dawat-e-Islami gave the following account: By the blessings of individual effort, my cousin, a mill owner from Defence-View (Bāb-ul-Madīnaĥ, Karachi), made the intention of taking part in the collective I'tikāf in Ramadan going to be held under the supervision of Dawat-e-Islami. He has stated: I had been suffering from intense spinal pain for a long time. I visited numerous doctors and specialists and tried their prescribed medicines but there was no relief. I was worried as to how I would be able to perform I'tikāf for 10 days. Anyway, during I'tikāf I tried to sit against a wall. I was used to sleeping on a comfortable mattress but we were encouraged in I'tikāf to sleep on a mat on the floor, according to the blessed Sunnaĥ. This was extremely difficult for me but there was no other option. اَلْحَمْدُلِلّٰه عَزَّوَجَلَّ After just a few days of sleeping according to the Sunnaĥ, I felt my back pain reducing considerably. The pain was then relieved completely.

The pain of my back that was not relieved even by the use of the medicines prescribed by highly learned and experienced doctors was eventually relieved by the blessings of taking part in Dawat-e-Islami's Sunnaĥ-Inspiring I'tikāf اَلْحَمْدُلِلّٰه عَزَّوَجَلَّ.

Tum ko tařpā kay rakĥ day gaw dard-e-kamar
Madanī Māḥaul mayn kar lo tum I'tikāf
Pāo gey tum sukūn ĥogā ṫĥanḍā jigar
Madanī Māḥaul mayn kar lo tum I'tikāf

Even if you have backache severe
Do I'tikāf in the Madanī environment
You will have relief, my brother
Do I'tikāf in the Madanī environment

صَلُّوْا عَلَى الْحَبِيْب صَلَّى اللّٰهُ تَعَالٰى عَلٰى مُحَمَّد

38. New year celebrations

A Muballigh of Dawat-e-Islami has stated: In Jodhpur Rajasthan (India), there was a 28-year-old photographer who had a crazy passion for attending shameless new year parties on the 31st of December. He would travel as far as Mumbai to attend such parties.

Fortunately, اَلْحَمْدُلِلّٰه عَزَّوَجَلَّ, in the last 10 days of Ramadan (1426 A.H. 2005) he was blessed with the privilege of taking part in the collective I'tikāf with Rasūl's devotees in a Masjid in Udaipur (Rajasthan, India) under the supervision of Dawat-e-Islami, a global & non-political movement of the Quran and Sunnaĥ. The Sunnaĥ-Inspiring learning sessions, inspiring speeches and heart-rending supplications had an over-whelming effect on him. He repented of his previous sins, quit photography and began to perform Ṣadā-e-Madīnaĥ regularly, i.e. he began to wake up Muslims for Fajr Ṣalāĥ.

Rang raliyān manānay kā chaskā miṭay
Madanī Māḥaul mayn kar lo tum I'tikāf
Raqṣ kī maḥfilaun kī naḥūsat cĥuṭay
Madanī Māḥaul mayn kar lo tum I'tikāf

Habit of indecent deeds will go away
Do I'tikāf in the Madanī environment
Practice of attending dance parties will go away
Do I'tikāf in the Madanī environment

صَلُّوْا عَلَى الْحَبِيْب صَلَّى اللّٰهُ تَعَالٰى عَلٰى مُحَمَّد

Muslims' New Year

If only Muslims would enthusiastically welcome the new Madanī (Islamic) year instead of the non-Islamic new year. اَلْحَمْدُلِلّٰه عَزَّوَجَلَّ! The Muslims' New Year begins on 1st Muḥarram. If possible, promote the tradition of congratulating each other in Muḥarram upon the arrival of the new Madanī year.

39. Blessings of company of Rasūl's devotees

An Islamic brother of Bhalwal, district Gulzār-e-Ṭayyibaĥ (Sargodha, Punjab Pakistan) has stated: I was clean shaven, and was wandering in the dark valley of heedlessness. I had drifted away from the path of Sunnaĥ.

During the blessed month of Ramadan, one day, when I was sitting in my room, my father told my younger brother that collective I'tikāf is going to be held in 'Jāmi' Masjid

Khawājgān' in the last 10 days of Ramadan by Dawat-e-Islami, a global & non-political movement of the Quran and Sunnaĥ, so come quickly otherwise you won't get a place in the first row. Listening to what my father said, I also became eager to go and see Rasūl's devotees (in the I'tikāf). That day I offered the 'Ishā Ṣalāĥ along with the Tarāwīḥ Ṣalāĥ in that Masjid. After the Tarāwīḥ Ṣalāĥ the following Na'at of Ḥājī Mushtāq رَحْمَةُ اللهِ تَعَالٰی عَلَيْه was played on a cassette player:

Šānī na koī mayray sauĥnřay Nabī صَلَّى اللّٰهُ تَعَالٰى عَلَيْهِ وَاٰلِهٖ وَسَلَّم *Lajpāl dā*

No one is like my Holy Prophet صَلَّى اللّٰهُ تَعَالٰى عَلَيْهِ وَاٰلِهٖ وَسَلَّم

I liked it very much. The second day, I came again and as it was Thursday, the Sunnaĥ-Inspiring weekly Ijtimā' had begun. This was my first Ijtimā' I ever attended. I felt intense peace and tranquillity during the Ijtimā'. The next day when I came, the cassette of the speech entitled '*The Perils of Music*' was being played. The speech made me tremble with fear because it pointed out blasphemous songs that had become common. I had also committed the sin of singing blasphemous songs, so I repented and renewed my faith. As the activities of I'tikāf had won my heart, I decided to do I'tikāf for the remaining days.

During the I'tikāf, I read the Sunan and manners of wearing Islamic hair-style in *Faīzān-e-Sunnat*. I also intended to grow my hair according to Sunnaĥ. In the Ijtimā'-e-Żikr-o-Na'at on the 26th of Ramadan, I made the intention to grow my beard. I also became a disciple of Ghauš-e-A'ẓam رَضِىَ اللهُ تَعَالٰى عَنْهُ. I learnt the words of Ṣalāt-o-Salām during the I'tikāf. When I returned home I threw away TV from the house along with more than 100 song cassettes. Presently, اَلْحَمْدُ لِلّٰه عَزَّوَجَلَّ I have the responsibility of Madanī Qāfilaĥs at division level.

صَلُّوْا عَلَى الْحَبِيْب   صَلَّى اللهُ تَعَالٰى عَلٰى مُحَمَّد

40. Closure of business of adulterated spices

An Islamic brother of Ranchorpuri Road, Beempura (Madanī Pūraĥ) Bāb-ul-Madīnaĥ, Karachi has stated: I didn't offer even Ṣalāt-ul-Jumu'aĥ. Fortunately, in the last 10 days of Ramadan (1425 A.H. 2004) I was blessed with the privilege of joining the collective

I'tikāf with Rasūl's devotees in the Gulzār-e-Madīnaĥ Masjid Agra Taj under the supervision of Dawat-e-Islami, a global & non-political movement of the Quran & Sunnaĥ. The blessed company of Rasūl's devotees changed me altogether within ten days. اَلْحَمْدُ لِلّٰه عَزَّوَجَلَّ I learnt Ṣalāĥ to some extent and began to offer all five Ṣalāĥ with Jamā'at. I also became the disciple of Ghauš-e-A'ẓam رَحْمَةُ اللهِ تَعَالٰى عَلَيْه.

By the grace of Allah عَزَّوَجَلَّ I developed such a strong Madanī mindset that I am at present trying to practice over 63 Madanī In'āmāt. I have developed a habit of regularly reading the booklets published by Maktaba-tul-Madīnaĥ. Further, by the blessing of I'tikāf I left my sinful business of selling adulterated spices throughout Sindh. I had about 44 employees in my herbs and spices factory. I have closed the factory because it is a very crucial era. Running the business of pure herbs and spices honestly on a large scale is very difficult in today's competitive environment. Who cares about the health of Muslims these days! What people care about is money whether it comes from a Ḥalāl source or Allah عَزَّوَجَلَّ forbid, Ḥarām. Anyhow, by the blessings of the company of Rasūl's devotees I started a lawful business.

اَلْحَمْدُ لِلّٰه عَزَّوَجَلَّ! By the blessings of the Madanī environment of Dawat-e-Islami I have developed a habit of offering Ṣalāĥ in the first row of the Masjid as well as offering the Nafl Ṣalāĥ of Ishrāq, Chāsht, Awwābīn and Taĥajjud.

Chĥoř do chĥoř do bĥāī rizq-e-Ḥarām
Madanī Māḥaul mayn kar lo tum I'tikāf
Āo karnay lago gey baĥut nayk kām
Madanī Māḥaul mayn kar lo tum I'tikāf

Give up unlawful earning
Do I'tikāf in the Madanī environment
You will get its blessings
Do I'tikāf in the Madanī environment

صَلُّوْا عَلَى الْحَبِيْب صَلَّى اللهُ تَعَالٰى عَلٰى مُحَمَّد

41. I saw Jibrāīl عَلَيْهِ السَّلَام

An Islamic brother from an organisational district of Dawat-e-Islami called Jannat-ul-Baqī' (Bāb-ul-Madīnaĥ, New Karachi) gave the following account: Like other youngsters, I was also wandering in the dark valleys of fashion. I was spending my days and nights in sins. اَلْحَمْدُلِلّٰه عَزَّوَجَلَّ My star of fortune began to shine. In Ramadan (1426 A.H. 2005) I was blessed with the privilege of joining the collective I'tikāf in the Madanī environment of Dawat-e-Islami, a global & non-political movement of the Quran and Sunnaĥ, in the company of Rasūl's devotees. What I learnt in just ten days cannot be expressed in words. I made a firm intention to give up sins forever. I began to wear a blessed turban and grew my beard.

On the 29th of Ramadan, the Mu'takifin collectively cleaned the Masjid. After this, I continued to worship. While worshipping, I saw a pious person whose face was glowing. Approaching me he shook hands with me; I felt coolness in my heart. The thought occurred to me that he is Sayyidunā Jibrāīl عَلَيْهِ السَّلَام and this is probably Layla-tul-Qadr because a blessed Ḥadīš states: 'Jibrāīl comes to the earth on Layla-tul-Qadr and shakes hands with worshippers.'

صَلُّوْا عَلَى الْحَبِيْب صَلَّى اللهُ تَعَالٰى عَلٰى مُحَمَّد

O Rab عَزَّوَجَلَّ of Beloved Mustafa صَلَّى اللّٰهُ تَعَالٰى عَلَيْهِ وَاٰلِهٖ وَسَلَّم! Accept the I'tikāf of every Muslim! O Allah عَزَّوَجَلَّ! For the sake of the sincere Mu'takifin forgive us and grant us a place in Heaven without holding us accountable! O Allah عَزَّوَجَلَّ! Bestow upon us steadfastness in the Madanī environment of Dawat-e-Islami! O Allah عَزَّوَجَلَّ! Make us true devotees of Your Beloved Rasūl صَلَّى اللّٰهُ تَعَالٰى عَلَيْهِ وَاٰلِهٖ وَسَلَّم! O Allah عَزَّوَجَلَّ! Forgive the Ummaĥ of the Holy Prophet صَلَّى اللّٰهُ تَعَالٰى عَلَيْهِ وَاٰلِهٖ وَسَلَّم!

اٰمِيْن بِجَاهِ النَّبِيِّ الْاَمِيْن صَلَّى اللهُ تَعَالٰى عَلَيْهِ وَاٰلِهٖ وَسَلَّم

صَلُّوْا عَلَى الْحَبِيْب صَلَّى اللهُ تَعَالٰى عَلٰى مُحَمَّد

اَلْحَمْدُ لِلّٰهِ رَبِّ الْعٰلَمِيْنَ وَ الصَّلٰوةُ وَ السَّلَامُ عَلٰى سَيِّدِ الْمُرْسَلِيْنَ

اَمَّا بَعْدُ فَاَعُوْذُ بِاللّٰهِ مِنَ الشَّيْطٰنِ الرَّجِيْمِ ؕ بِسْمِ اللّٰهِ الرَّحْمٰنِ الرَّحِيْمِ ؕ

40 Ahadis about Excellence of Salat-'Alan-Nabi صَلَّى اللّٰهُ عَلَيْهِ وَاٰلِهٖ وَسَلَّم

1. The Noble Prophet صَلَّى اللّٰهُ تَعَالٰى عَلَيْهِ وَاٰلِهٖ وَسَلَّم has stated, 'The one who recites Ṣalāt one hundred times on me on Friday and the night of Friday, Allah عَزَّوَجَلَّ will fulfil one hundred of his needs.' *(Jāmi'-ul-Aḥādīš-lis-Suyūṭī, vol. 3, pp. 75, Ḥadīš 7377)*

صَلُّوْا عَلَى الْحَبِيْب صَلَّى اللّٰهُ تَعَالٰى عَلٰى مُحَمَّد

2. The Holy Prophet صَلَّى اللّٰهُ تَعَالٰى عَلَيْهِ وَاٰلِهٖ وَسَلَّم has stated, 'O people! Without doubt, the one to attain salvation quickly on the Day of Judgement from its horrors and accountability will be the one amongst you who will have recited Ṣalāt upon me in abundance in the world.' *(Firdaus-ul-Akhbār, vol. 5, pp. 375, Ḥadīš 8210)*

صَلُّوْا عَلَى الْحَبِيْب صَلَّى اللّٰهُ تَعَالٰى عَلٰى مُحَمَّد

3. The Noble Rasūl صَلَّى اللّٰهُ تَعَالٰى عَلَيْهِ وَاٰلِهٖ وَسَلَّم has stated, 'Anyone who recites Ṣalāt upon me three times in the day and three times in the night due to love and devotion to me, Allah عَزَّوَجَلَّ will forgive the sins he committed during that day and that night.' *(Ṣaḥīḥ Muslim, vol. 2, pp. 328, Ḥadīš 23)*

صَلُّوْا عَلَى الْحَبِيْب صَلَّى اللّٰهُ تَعَالٰى عَلٰى مُحَمَّد

4. The Beloved Prophet صَلَّى اللّٰهُ تَعَالٰى عَلَيْهِ وَاٰلِهٖ وَسَلَّم has stated, 'Recite Ṣalāt abundantly upon me; without doubt, it is purification for you.' *(Musnad Abī Ya'lā, vol. 5, pp. 458, Ḥadīš 6383)*

صَلُّوْا عَلَى الْحَبِيْب صَلَّى اللّٰهُ تَعَالٰى عَلٰى مُحَمَّد

5. The Noble Prophet صَلَّى اللّٰهُ تَعَالٰى عَلَيْهِ وَاٰلِهٖ وَسَلَّم has stated, 'Whoever recited the Holy Quran, praised Allah عَزَّوَجَلَّ, recited Ṣalāt upon the Prophet (صَلَّى اللّٰهُ تَعَالٰى عَلَيْهِ وَاٰلِهٖ وَسَلَّم) and then asked forgiveness from Allah عَزَّوَجَلَّ, he has sought goodness from its source.' *(Shu'ab-ul-Īmān, vol. 2, pp. 373, Ḥadīš 2084)*

صَلُّوْا عَلَى الْحَبِيْب　　صَلَّى اللّٰهُ تَعَالٰى عَلٰى مُحَمَّد

6. The Holy Prophet صَلَّى اللّٰهُ تَعَالٰى عَلَيْهِ وَاٰلِهٖ وَسَلَّم has stated, 'To recite Ṣalāt upon me is Nūr on the bridge of Ṣirāṭ. The one reciting Ṣalāt upon me eighty times on Friday, his eighty years' sins will be forgiven.' *(Al-Jāmi'-uṣ-Ṣaghīr, pp. 320, Ḥadīš 5191)*

صَلُّوْا عَلَى الْحَبِيْب　　صَلَّى اللّٰهُ تَعَالٰى عَلٰى مُحَمَّد

7. The Beloved Prophet صَلَّى اللّٰهُ تَعَالٰى عَلَيْهِ وَاٰلِهٖ وَسَلَّم has stated, 'The one who recites Ṣalāt 200 times upon me on Friday, his 200 years' sins will be forgiven.' *(Kanz-ul-'Ummāl, vol. 1, pp. 256, Ḥadīš 2238)*

صَلُّوْا عَلَى الْحَبِيْب　　صَلَّى اللّٰهُ تَعَالٰى عَلٰى مُحَمَّد

8. The Noble Rasūl صَلَّى اللّٰهُ تَعَالٰى عَلَيْهِ وَاٰلِهٖ وَسَلَّم has stated, 'Whoever recites Ṣalāt upon me hundred times on the day and night of Friday, Allah عَزَّوَجَلَّ will fulfil his hundred needs out of which seventy will be of the Hereafter and thirty will be of the world.' *(Kanz-ul-'Ummāl, vol. 1, pp. 256, Ḥadīš 2239)*

صَلُّوْا عَلَى الْحَبِيْب　　صَلَّى اللّٰهُ تَعَالٰى عَلٰى مُحَمَّد

9. The Holy Prophet صَلَّى اللّٰهُ تَعَالٰى عَلَيْهِ وَاٰلِهٖ وَسَلَّم has stated, 'When the day of Thursday comes, Allah عَزَّوَجَلَّ sends His angels who have papers made of silver and pens made of gold. They write the names of those who recite Ṣalāt on me in abundance on the day of Thursday and the night of Friday.' *(Kanz-ul-'Ummāl, vol. 1, pp. 250, Ḥadīš 2174)*

صَلُّوْا عَلَى الْحَبِيْب　　صَلَّى اللّٰهُ تَعَالٰى عَلٰى مُحَمَّد

10. The Beloved Rasūl صَلَّى اللهُ تَعَالٰى عَلَيْهِ وَاٰلِهٖ وَسَلَّم has stated, 'The one who writes Ṣalāt [with my name] in a book, angels will continue to seek forgiveness for him as long as my name remains in it.' *(Mu'jam Awsaṭ, vol. 1, pp. 497, Ḥadīš 1835)*

صَلُّوْا عَلَى الْحَبِيْب صَلَّى اللهُ تَعَالٰى عَلٰى مُحَمَّد

11. The Noble Rasūl صَلَّى اللهُ تَعَالٰى عَلَيْهِ وَاٰلِهٖ وَسَلَّم has stated, 'When the one who recites Ṣalāt upon me 100 times on Friday comes on the Judgement Day, he will be accompanied by such Nūr that will be sufficient for all the creation, if distributed.' *(Ḥilyat-ul-Auliyā, vol. 8, pp. 49, Ḥadīš 11341)*

صَلُّوْا عَلَى الْحَبِيْب صَلَّى اللهُ تَعَالٰى عَلٰى مُحَمَّد

12. The Holy Prophet صَلَّى اللهُ تَعَالٰى عَلَيْهِ وَاٰلِهٖ وَسَلَّم has stated, 'O people! Without doubt, the one to attain salvation quickly on the Day of Judgement from its horrors and accountability will be the one amongst you who will have recited Ṣalāt upon me in abundance in the world.' *(Firdaus-ul-Akhbār, vol. 5, pp. 375, Ḥadīš 8210)*

صَلُّوْا عَلَى الْحَبِيْب صَلَّى اللهُ تَعَالٰى عَلٰى مُحَمَّد

13. The Beloved Rasūl صَلَّى اللهُ تَعَالٰى عَلَيْهِ وَاٰلِهٖ وَسَلَّم has stated, 'Recite Ṣalāt upon me wherever you are, as it reaches me.' *(Mu'jam Kabīr, vol. 3, pp. 82, Ḥadīš 2829)*

صَلُّوْا عَلَى الْحَبِيْب صَلَّى اللهُ تَعَالٰى عَلٰى مُحَمَّد

14. The Beloved Prophet صَلَّى اللهُ تَعَالٰى عَلَيْهِ وَاٰلِهٖ وَسَلَّم has stated, 'The one who recites Ṣalāt upon me ten times in the morning and ten times in the evening will be granted my intercession on the Day of Judgement.' *(Majma'-uz-Zawāid lil-Ĥayshamī, vol. 10, pp. 163, Ḥadīš 17022)*

صَلُّوْا عَلَى الْحَبِيْب صَلَّى اللهُ تَعَالٰى عَلٰى مُحَمَّد

15. The Holy Prophet صَلَّى اللّٰهُ تَعَالٰى عَلَيْهِ وَاٰلِهٖ وَسَلَّم has stated, 'The one who forgot to recite Ṣalāt upon me, forgot the way to Jannaĥ.' *(Mu'jam Kabīr, vol. 12, pp. 139, Ḥadīš 12819)*

صَلُّوْا عَلَى الْحَبِيْب صَلَّى اللّٰهُ تَعَالٰى عَلٰى مُحَمَّد

16. The Noble Prophet صَلَّى اللّٰهُ تَعَالٰى عَلَيْهِ وَاٰلِهٖ وَسَلَّم has stated, 'Whoever recites Ṣalāt upon me on the day of Friday, I will intercede for him on the Day of Judgement.' *(Kanz-ul-'Ummāl, vol. 1, pp. 255, Ḥadīš 2236)*

صَلُّوْا عَلَى الْحَبِيْب صَلَّى اللّٰهُ تَعَالٰى عَلٰى مُحَمَّد

17. The Noble Rasūl صَلَّى اللّٰهُ تَعَالٰى عَلَيْهِ وَاٰلِهٖ وَسَلَّم has stated, 'Whoever recites Ṣalāt upon me three times during the day and three times at night with love and devotion, Allah عَزَّوَجَلَّ will forgive the sins the person committed during that day and that night.' *(Mu'jam Kabīr, vol. 18, pp. 361, Ḥadīš 928)*

صَلُّوْا عَلَى الْحَبِيْب صَلَّى اللّٰهُ تَعَالٰى عَلٰى مُحَمَّد

18. The Holy Prophet صَلَّى اللّٰهُ تَعَالٰى عَلَيْهِ وَاٰلِهٖ وَسَلَّم has stated, 'Whoever recites Ṣalāt upon me 100 times, Allah عَزَّوَجَلَّ will write between his eyes that this person is free from hypocrisy and hellfire and Allah عَزَّوَجَلَّ will keep him with the martyrs on the Day of Judgement.' *(Majma'-uz-Zawāid, vol. 10, pp. 253, Ḥadīš 172998)*

صَلُّوْا عَلَى الْحَبِيْب صَلَّى اللّٰهُ تَعَالٰى عَلٰى مُحَمَّد

19. The Noble Rasūl صَلَّى اللّٰهُ تَعَالٰى عَلَيْهِ وَاٰلِهٖ وَسَلَّم has stated, 'Whoever recites Ṣalāt upon me one time, Allah عَزَّوَجَلَّ sends ten mercies upon him.' *(Ṣaḥīḥ Muslim, vol. 1, pp. 166)*

صَلُّوْا عَلَى الْحَبِيْب صَلَّى اللّٰهُ تَعَالٰى عَلٰى مُحَمَّد

20. The Noble Prophet صَلَّى اللهُ تَعَالٰى عَلَيْهِ وَاٰلِهٖ وَسَلَّم has stated, 'The person closest to me on the Day of Judgement will be the one who would have recited Ṣalāt upon me the most in the world.' *(Jāmi' Tirmiżī, vol. 1, pp. 64)*

صَلُّوْا عَلَى الْحَبِيْب صَلَّى اللهُ تَعَالٰى عَلٰى مُحَمَّد

21. The Holy Prophet صَلَّى اللهُ تَعَالٰى عَلَيْهِ وَاٰلِهٖ وَسَلَّم has stated, 'Whoever recites one Ṣalāt upon me, Allah عَزَّوَجَلَّ sends ten mercies upon him and writes ten virtues in his book of deeds.' *(Jāmi' Tirmiżī, vol. 1, pp. 64)*

صَلُّوْا عَلَى الْحَبِيْب صَلَّى اللهُ تَعَالٰى عَلٰى مُحَمَّد

22. After Ṣalāĥ, a person glorified Allah عَزَّوَجَلَّ and then recited Ṣalāt-'Alan-Nabī. The Beloved Prophet صَلَّى اللهُ تَعَالٰى عَلَيْهِ وَاٰلِهٖ وَسَلَّم said to him, 'Make Du'ā! It will be accepted. Ask! [What you ask] will be granted.' *(Sunan Nasāī, vol. 1, pp. 189)*

صَلُّوْا عَلَى الْحَبِيْب صَلَّى اللهُ تَعَالٰى عَلٰى مُحَمَّد

23. The Holy Prophet صَلَّى اللهُ تَعَالٰى عَلَيْهِ وَاٰلِهٖ وَسَلَّم has stated, 'Whoever recites Ṣalāt upon me one time, Allah عَزَّوَجَلَّ sends ten mercies upon him, forgives his ten sins and raises his ten ranks.' *(Sunan Nasāī, vol. 1, pp. 191)*

صَلُّوْا عَلَى الْحَبِيْب صَلَّى اللهُ تَعَالٰى عَلٰى مُحَمَّد

24. The Noble Prophet صَلَّى اللهُ تَعَالٰى عَلَيْهِ وَاٰلِهٖ وَسَلَّم has stated, 'Whoever recites ten Ṣalāt upon me, Allah عَزَّوَجَلَّ sends one hundred mercies upon him.' *(Attarghīb Wattarĥīb, vol. 2, pp. 322)*

صَلُّوْا عَلَى الْحَبِيْب صَلَّى اللهُ تَعَالٰى عَلٰى مُحَمَّد

25. The Beloved Rasūl صَلَّى اللهُ تَعَالٰى عَلَيۡهِ وَاٰلِهٖ وَسَلَّم has stated, 'Recite Ṣalāt upon me wherever you are, as it reaches me.' *(Mu'jam Kabīr, vol. 3, pp. 82, Ḥadīš 2829)*

صَلُّوۡا عَلَى الۡحَبِيۡب صَلَّى اللهُ تَعَالٰى عَلٰى مُحَمَّد

26. The Holy Prophet صَلَّى اللهُ تَعَالٰى عَلَيۡهِ وَاٰلِهٖ وَسَلَّم has stated, 'Indeed your names are presented to me along with your identity; therefore, recite Ṣalāt upon me with eloquent words.' *(Muṣannaf 'Abdur Razzāq, vol. 2, pp. 214, Ḥadīš 3111)*

صَلُّوۡا عَلَى الۡحَبِيۡب صَلَّى اللهُ تَعَالٰى عَلٰى مُحَمَّد

27. The Beloved Rasūl صَلَّى اللهُ تَعَالٰى عَلَيۡهِ وَاٰلِهٖ وَسَلَّم has stated, 'Recite Ṣalāt upon me in abundance; without doubt, this is forgiveness for your sins.' *(Al-Jāmi'-uṣ-Ṣaghīr, pp. 87, Ḥadīš 1406)*

صَلُّوۡا عَلَى الۡحَبِيۡب صَلَّى اللهُ تَعَالٰى عَلٰى مُحَمَّد

28. The Noble Prophet صَلَّى اللهُ تَعَالٰى عَلَيۡهِ وَاٰلِهٖ وَسَلَّم has stated, 'Whoever recites Ṣalāt upon me on the day of Friday, I will intercede for him on the Day of Judgement.' *(Kanz-ul-'Ummāl, vol. 1, pp. 255, Ḥadīš 2236)*

صَلُّوۡا عَلَى الۡحَبِيۡب صَلَّى اللهُ تَعَالٰى عَلٰى مُحَمَّد

29. The Holy Prophet صَلَّى اللهُ تَعَالٰى عَلَيۡهِ وَاٰلِهٖ وَسَلَّم has stated, 'The one who forgot to recite Ṣalāt upon me, forgot the way to Jannaĥ.' *(Mu'jam Kabīr, vol. 12, pp. 139, Ḥadīš 12819)*

صَلُّوۡا عَلَى الۡحَبِيۡب صَلَّى اللهُ تَعَالٰى عَلٰى مُحَمَّد

30. The Beloved Rasūl صَلَّى اللهُ تَعَالٰى عَلَيۡهِ وَاٰلِهٖ وَسَلَّم has stated, 'The one who recites Ṣalāt upon me ten times in the morning and ten times in the evening will be granted my intercession on the Day of Judgement.' *(Majma'-uz-Zawāid lil-Ĥayshamī, vol. 10, pp. 163, Ḥadīš 17022)*

صَلُّوۡا عَلَى الۡحَبِيۡب صَلَّى اللهُ تَعَالٰى عَلٰى مُحَمَّد

31. The Noble Prophet صَلَّى الـلّٰهُ تَعَالـٰى عَلَيْهِ وَاٰلِهٖ وَسَلَّم has stated, 'Whoever recites Ṣalāt upon me ten times, Allah عَزَّوَجَلَّ sends one hundred mercies upon him.' *(Attarghīb Wattarhīb, vol. 2, pp. 322)*

صَلُّوْا عَلَى الْحَبِيْب   صَلَّى الـلّٰهُ تَعَالـٰى عَلٰى مُحَمَّد

32. The Holy Prophet صَلَّى الـلّٰهُ تَعَالـٰى عَلَيْهِ وَاٰلِهٖ وَسَلَّم has stated, 'Whoever recites Ṣalāt upon me 100 times, Allah عَزَّوَجَلَّ will write between his eyes that this person is free from hypocrisy and hellfire and Allah عَزَّوَجَلَّ will keep him with the martyrs on the Day of Judgement.' *(Majma'-uz-Zawāid, vol. 10, pp. 253, Ḥadīš 172998)*

صَلُّوْا عَلَى الْحَبِيْب   صَلَّى الـلّٰهُ تَعَالـٰى عَلٰى مُحَمَّد

33. The Noble Rasūl صَلَّى الـلّٰهُ تَعَالـٰى عَلَيْهِ وَاٰلِهٖ وَسَلَّم has stated, 'Whoever recites Ṣalāt upon me one time, Allah عَزَّوَجَلَّ sends ten mercies upon him.' *(Ṣaḥīḥ Muslim, vol. 1, pp. 166)*

صَلُّوْا عَلَى الْحَبِيْب   صَلَّى الـلّٰهُ تَعَالـٰى عَلٰى مُحَمَّد

34. The Holy Prophet صَلَّى الـلّٰهُ تَعَالـٰى عَلَيْهِ وَاٰلِهٖ وَسَلَّم has stated, 'To recite Ṣalāt upon me is Nūr on the bridge of Ṣirāṭ. The one reciting Ṣalāt upon me eighty times on Friday, his eighty years' sins will be forgiven.' *(Al-Jāmi'-uṣ-Ṣaghīr, pp. 320, Ḥadīš 5191)*

صَلُّوْا عَلَى الْحَبِيْب   صَلَّى الـلّٰهُ تَعَالـٰى عَلٰى مُحَمَّد

35. The Noble Prophet صَلَّى الـلّٰهُ تَعَالـٰى عَلَيْهِ وَاٰلِهٖ وَسَلَّم has stated, 'The one who recites Ṣalāt upon me one hundred times on Friday and the night of Friday, Allah عَزَّوَجَلَّ will fulfil one hundred of his needs.' *(Jāmi'-ul-Aḥādīš-lis-Suyūṭī, vol. 3, pp. 75, Ḥadīš 7377)*

صَلُّوْا عَلَى الْحَبِيْب   صَلَّى الـلّٰهُ تَعَالـٰى عَلٰى مُحَمَّد

36. The Holy Prophet صَلَّی اللّٰہ تَعَالٰی عَلَیْہِ وَاٰلِہٖ وَسَلَّم has stated, 'When the day of Thursday comes, Allah عَزَّوَجَلَّ sends His angels who have papers made of silver and pens made of gold. They write the names of those who recite Ṣalāt on me in abundance on the day of Thursday and the night of Friday.' *(Kanz-ul-'Ummāl, vol. 1, pp. 250, Ḥadīš 2174)*

صَلُّوْا عَلَی الْحَبِیْب صَلَّی اللّٰہُ تَعَالٰی عَلٰی مُحَمَّد

37. The Beloved Prophet صَلَّی اللّٰہ تَعَالٰی عَلَیْہِ وَاٰلِہٖ وَسَلَّم has stated, 'The one who recites Ṣalāt 200 times upon me on Friday, his 200 years' sins will be forgiven.' *(Kanz-ul-'Ummāl, vol. 1, pp. 256, Ḥadīš 2238)*

صَلُّوْا عَلَی الْحَبِیْب صَلَّی اللّٰہُ تَعَالٰی عَلٰی مُحَمَّد

38. The Holy Prophet صَلَّی اللّٰہ تَعَالٰی عَلَیْہِ وَاٰلِہٖ وَسَلَّم has stated, 'The one who forgot to recite Ṣalāt upon me, forgot the way to Jannaĥ.' *(Mu'jam Kabīr, vol. 12, pp. 139, Ḥadīš 12819)*

صَلُّوْا عَلَی الْحَبِیْب صَلَّی اللّٰہُ تَعَالٰی عَلٰی مُحَمَّد

39. The Noble Prophet صَلَّی اللّٰہ تَعَالٰی عَلَیْہِ وَاٰلِہٖ وَسَلَّم has stated, 'The person closest to me on the Day of Judgement will be the one who would have recited Ṣalāt upon me the most in the world.' *(Jāmi' Tirmižī, vol. 1, pp. 64)*

صَلُّوْا عَلَی الْحَبِیْب صَلَّی اللّٰہُ تَعَالٰی عَلٰی مُحَمَّد

40. After Ṣalāĥ, a person glorified Allah عَزَّوَجَلَّ and then recited Ṣalāt-'Alan-Nabī. The Beloved Prophet صَلَّی اللّٰہ تَعَالٰی عَلَیْہِ وَاٰلِہٖ وَسَلَّم said to him, 'Make Du'ā! It will be accepted. Ask! [What you ask] will be granted.' *(Sunan Nasāī, vol. 1, pp. 189)*

صَلُّوْا عَلَی الْحَبِیْب صَلَّی اللّٰہُ تَعَالٰی عَلٰی مُحَمَّد

اَلْحَمْدُ لِلّٰهِ رَبِّ الْعٰلَمِيْنَ وَ الصَّلٰوةُ وَ السَّلَامُ عَلٰى سَيِّدِ الْمُرْسَلِيْنَ

اَمَّا بَعْدُ فَاَعُوْذُ بِاللّٰهِ مِنَ الشَّيْطٰنِ الرَّجِيْمِ ؕ بِسْمِ اللّٰهِ الرَّحْمٰنِ الرَّحِيْمِ ؕ

22 Madanī Pearls of Giving Dars from Faīzān-e-Sunnat

1. The Holy Prophet صَلَّى اللهُ تَعَالٰى عَلَيْهِ وَاٰلِهٖ وَسَلَّم has stated, 'Whoever conveys an Islamic teaching to my Ummaĥ so that a Sunnaĥ would be established by it or corrupt beliefs would be removed by it, will enter Heaven.' *(Ḥilyat-ul-Auliyā, vol. 1, pp. 45, Ḥadīš 14466)*

2. The Noble Prophet صَلَّى اللهُ تَعَالٰى عَلَيْهِ وَاٰلِهٖ وَسَلَّم has stated, 'May Allah عَزَّوَجَلَّ keep the one fresh who listens to my Ḥadīš, memorises it and conveys it to others.' *(Jāmi' Tirmiżī, vol. 4, pp. 298, Ḥadīš 2665)*

3. One of the wisdoms of the sacred name of Sayyidunā Idrīs عَلٰى نَبِيِّنَا وَعَلَيْهِ الصَّلٰوةُ وَالسَّلَام is that he would abundantly teach divinely-bestowed scriptures to people. Therefore, he was known as Idrīs (i.e. the one who teaches lessons). *(Tafsīr Kabīr, vol. 7, pp. 550 – Tafsīr-ul-Ḥasanāt, vol. 4, pp. 148)*

4. Sayyidunā Ghauš-e-A'ẓam رَضِیَ اللهُ تَعَالٰى عَنْه has stated, دَرَسْتُ الْعِلْمَ حَتّٰى صِرْتُ قُطْبًا '*I kept disseminating knowledge until I became a Quṭb.*' *(Qaṣīdaĥ-e-Ghaušiyyaĥ)*

5. To give Dars from *Faīzān-e-Sunnat* is one of the Madanī activities of Dawat-e-Islami. Spread Sunnaĥs and earn a huge reward by giving Dars at house, Masjid, shop, school, college and other busy places at a predetermined time.

6. Everyone should try to get the privilege of either giving or listening to at least two Dars daily from *Faīzān-e-Sunnat.*

7. In Sūraĥ At-Taḥrīm, part 28, verse 6, Allah عَزَّوَجَلَّ has said:

يٰۤاَيُّهَا الَّذِيْنَ اٰمَنُوْا قُوْۤا اَنْفُسَكُمْ وَ اَهْلِيْكُمْ نَارًا وَّ قُوْدُهَا النَّاسُ وَ الْحِجَارَةُ

O those who believe, save yourselves and your family from the fire whose fuel are men and stones. *[Kanz-ul-Īmān (Translation of Quran)]*

One of the ways of saving yourself and your family from Hell-fire is Dars from *Faīzān-e-Sunnat*. Apart from giving Dars, persuade your family-members to listen to a Bayān or a Madanī Mużākaraĥ daily through the cassettes released by Maktaba-tul-Madīnaĥ.

8. The responsible Islamic brother should make arrangement for Dars at busy places at a predetermined time. For example, Dars should be given at 9:00 p.m. at a place, at 9:30 p.m. at another place and so on. Give more than one Dars at different places on holidays. (But make sure that public rights are not violated. For example, Muslims' way should not be blocked as it is a sin).
9. Give Dars after the Ṣalāĥ after which most people could attend Dars.
10. Offer the Ṣalāĥ, after which you have to give Dars, with Jamā'at with the first Takbīr in the first row of the Masjid where you will be giving Dars.
11. Give Dars at such a place (rather away from the arch) where others offering Ṣalāĥ or reciting the Quran should not be disturbed. Once a place has been chosen for Dars, there should be no unnecessary change of place.
12. The responsible Islamic brother of Żaylī Mushāwarat should assign two well-wishers (Islamic brothers) the responsibility of politely stopping those going out of the Masjid and requesting them to listen to Dars. The well-wishers should also make all the attendees of Dars (or Bayān) sit closer.
13. Give Dars whilst sitting in a folded-legs posture (as one sits in Qa'daĥ during Ṣalāĥ) observing veil within veil[1]. If there are a large number of listeners, there is no harm in giving the Dars standing and by using a mike, but others offering Ṣalāĥ or reciting the Quran should not be disturbed.
14. Your voice should not be very loud. Try to give Dars in moderate voice so that only the attendees listen, and other people offering their Ṣalāĥ are not disturbed.
15. Always give Dars slowly and calmly.

[1] Veil within veil is a term used in the Madanī environment of Dawat-e-Islami. It refers to the act of wrapping an extra shawl around dress from navel to knees.

16. Study in advance whatever you will be reading out. Do this at least once so that you would not make any mistake during Dars.

17. Ensure the correct pronunciation of the words of Faīzān-e-Sunnat so that it becomes your habit.

18. Get checked your pronunciation of Ḥamd, Ṣalāt, the Ṣalāt-'Alan-Nabī read out at the commencement of Dars, the verse of Ṣalāt-'Alan-Nabī and the concluding verse etc. by some Sunnī scholar or Qārī. Likewise, do not recite Arabic Du'ās etc. individually unless you have had your pronunciation corrected with the help of a Sunnī scholar.

19. Besides *Faīzān-e-Sunnat*, Dars may also be given from other Madanī booklets[1] published by Maktaba-tul-Madīnaĥ.

20. Finish Dars including the concluding Du'ā within seven minutes.

21. Every Muballigh should memorise the method of giving Dars, the post-Dars persuasion and the concluding Du'ā.

22. Islamic sisters should amend the method of giving Dars as per their requirements.

---

[1] It is not allowed to give Dars from any book other than the booklets of Amīr-e-Aĥl-e-Sunnat دَامَتْ بَرَكَاتُهُمُ الْعَالِيَه.

[Markazī Majlis-e-Shūrā]

اَلۡحَمۡدُ لِلّٰهِ رَبِّ الۡعٰلَمِیۡنَ وَ الصَّلٰوةُ وَ السَّلَامُ عَلٰی سَیِّدِ الۡمُرۡسَلِیۡنَ
اَمَّا بَعۡدُ فَاَعُوۡذُ بِاللّٰهِ مِنَ الشَّیۡطٰنِ الرَّجِیۡمِ ؕ بِسۡمِ اللّٰهِ الرَّحۡمٰنِ الرَّحِیۡمِ ؕ

Method of Delivering Dars from Faīzān-e-Sunnat

Say the following three times:

'Please come closer.'

Then, observing veil within veil, sit in the position you sit in for Ṣalāĥ (in Tashaĥĥud) and recite the following:

اَلۡحَمۡدُ لِلّٰهِ رَبِّ الۡعٰلَمِیۡنَ وَالصَّلٰوةُ وَالسَّلَامُ عَلٰی سَیِّدِ الۡمُرۡسَلِیۡنَ
اَمَّا بَعۡدُ فَاَعُوۡذُ بِاللّٰهِ مِنَ الشَّیۡطٰنِ الرَّجِیۡمِ ؕ بِسۡمِ اللّٰهِ الرَّحۡمٰنِ الرَّحِیۡمِ ؕ

Then recite the following Ṣalāt-'Alan-Nabī, making the participants of the Dars repeat after you:

اَلصَّلٰوةُ وَالسَّلَامُ عَلَيۡكَ يَا رَسُوۡلَ الله وَعَلٰى اٰلِكَ وَاَصۡحٰبِكَ يَا حَبِيۡبَ الله
اَلصَّلٰوةُ وَالسَّلَامُ عَلَيۡكَ يَا نَبِيَّ الله وَعَلٰى اٰلِكَ وَاَصۡحٰبِكَ يَا نُوۡرَ الله

If you are in a Masjid, say the following words, with the participants repeating after you, making the intention of I'tikāf:

نَوَيۡتُ سُنَّتَ الۡاِعۡتِكَافِ

Translation: I have made the intention of Sunnaĥ I'tikāf.

Then say the following:

'Dear Islamic brothers! Come closer and, if possible, in respect of Dars, sit in the position you sit in for Ṣalāĥ (in Tashaĥĥud). If you get tired, then sit in any comfortable position. Lower your gaze and listen to the Dars from Faīzān-e-Sunnat with full concentration for the pleasure of Allah with the intention of acquiring Islamic knowledge because listening to it inattentively, looking around, playing on the floor with your finger or messing around with your clothes, body or hair could result in its blessings being lost[1].'

After saying this, read out an excellence of reciting Ṣalāt-'Alan-Nabī from Faīzān-e-Sunnat. Then say the following so that the attendees would also recite Ṣalāt-'Alan-Nabī.

صَلُّوْا عَلَى الْحَبِيْب　　صَلَّى اللّٰهُ تَعَالٰى عَلٰى مُحَمَّد

Read out what is written in the book only. Read only the translation of Quranic verses and Arabic text. Do not explain any Quranic verse or Ḥadīš on the basis of your opinion.

Make persuasion in the following words at the end of the Dars.

(Each Muballigh should memorize the following paragraph by heart and make persuasion accordingly at the end of Dars and Bayān without any alteration).

By the grace of Allah عَزَّوَجَلَّ*, Sunnaĥs are abundantly learnt and taught in the Madanī environment of Dawat-e-Islami, a global and non-political movement for the preaching of Qurān and Sunnaĥ.*

It is a Madanī request that you spend the whole night in the weekly Sunnaĥ-Inspiring Ijtimā', taking place after Ṣalāt-ul-Maghrib every Thursday in your city, for the pleasure of Allah عَزَّوَجَلَّ *with good intentions. With the intention of gaining reward, make it a part of your routine to travel in Sunnaĥ-Inspiring Madanī Qāfilaĥs with the devotees of Rasūl, to fill out the Madanī In'āmāt booklet every day practicing Fikr-e-Madīnaĥ and to submit it to the relevant responsible Islamic brother of your locality within the first ten days of every*

[1] Also convey similar words of persuasion at the start of a Bayān, and have the participants make good intentions.

Islamic month. Through the blessings of this, you will develop a mindset and a yearning to adopt Sunnaĥs, to have hatred for sins and to protect your faith, اِنْ شَآءَاللّٰه عَزَّوَجَلَّ.

Every Islamic brother should develop the Madanī mindset that ***'I must strive to reform myself and people of the entire world,*** اِنْ شَآءَاللّٰه عَزَّوَجَلَّ.*' In order to reform ourselves, we must act upon Madanī In'āmāt and to strive to reform people of the entire world we must travel with Madanī Qāfilaĥs*[1], اِنْ شَآءَاللّٰه عَزَّوَجَلَّ.

Allah عَزَّوَجَلَّ *karam aysā karay tujĥ pay jaĥān mayn*
Ay Dawat-e-Islami tayrī dĥūm machī ĥo

May Allah عَزَّوَجَلَّ *bless Dawat-e-Islami with such a grace*
That it becomes glorious at each and every place!

Finally, with the humility of the body and the heart, and with absolute certainty of Du'ā being accepted, make the following Du'ā conforming to the manners of raising hands without adding and leaving out anything:

اَلْحَمْدُ لِلّٰهِ رَبِّ الْعٰلَمِيْنَ وَالصَّلٰوةُ وَالسَّلَامُ عَلٰى سَيِّدِ الْمُرْسَلِيْنَ

'Yā Allah عَزَّوَجَلَّ*! For the sake of Muṣṭafā* صَلَّى اللهُ تَعَالٰى عَلَيْهِ وَاٰلِهٖ وَسَلَّم *forgive us, our parents, and the entire Ummaĥ. Yā Allah* عَزَّوَجَلَّ*! Forgive the mistakes of Dars and all our sins, give us the passion to perform good deeds. Make us pious and obedient to our parents. Yā Allah* عَزَّوَجَلَّ*! Give us true love for You, and for Your Beloved Prophet* صَلَّى اللهُ تَعَالٰى عَلَيْهِ وَاٰلِهٖ وَسَلَّم*. Cure us from the disease of sins. Yā Allah* عَزَّوَجَلَّ*! Give us the ability to act upon the Madanī In'āmāt and travel with the Madanī Qāfilaĥs. Yā Allah* عَزَّوَجَلَّ*! Bless us with the enthusiasm of making individual effort to persuade others to carry out Madanī activities. Yā Allah* عَزَّوَجَلَّ*! Free Muslims from diseases, debt, unemployment, childlessness, wrongful court cases and all types of worries. Yā Allah* عَزَّوَجَلَّ*! May Islam dominate and the enemies of Islam be disgraced! Yā Allah* عَزَّوَجَلَّ*! Bless us with steadfastness in the Madanī environment of Dawat-e-Islami! Yā Allah* عَزَّوَجَلَّ*! Bless us with martyrdom under the green dome while*

[1] Here, Islamic sisters should say, 'We have to make our male (Maḥram) relatives travel with Madanī Qāfilaĥs.'

being blessed with the vision of the Beloved Prophet صَلَّى اللهُ تَعَالٰى عَلَيْهِ وَاٰلِهٖ وَسَلَّم, with burial in Jannat-ul-Baqī, and with closeness to Your Beloved Prophet صَلَّى اللهُ تَعَالٰى عَلَيْهِ وَاٰلِهٖ وَسَلَّم in Jannat-ul-Firdaus! Yā Allah عَزَّوَجَلَّ for the sake of the fragrant breeze of Madīnah, accept all our lawful Du'ās.'

Keĥtay reĥtay ĥayn Du'ā kay wāsiṭay banday Tayray
Kar day pūrī ārzū ĥar baykas-o-majbūr kī

Yā Allah عَزَّوَجَلَّ! Your servants ask me to make supplications
Fulfil their Du'ās and relieve them of all complications

اٰمِيْن بِجَاهِ النَّبِيِّ الْاَمِيْن صَلَّى اللهُ تَعَالٰى عَلَيْهِ وَاٰلِهٖ وَسَلَّم

Next, recite the following verse as part of the Du'ā:

اِنَّ اللّٰهَ وَمَلٰٓئِكَتَهٗ يُصَلُّوْنَ عَلَى النَّبِيِّ ؕ
يٰۤاَيُّهَا الَّذِيْنَ اٰمَنُوْا صَلُّوْا عَلَيْهِ وَسَلِّمُوْا تَسْلِيْمًا ﴿۵۶﴾

(Part 22, Sūraĥ Al-Aḥzāb, verse 56)

After all the attendees have recited Ṣalāt-'Alan-Nabī, read out the following verse to finish Du'ā.

سُبْحٰنَ رَبِّكَ رَبِّ الْعِزَّةِ عَمَّا يَصِفُوْنَ ﴿۱۸۰﴾
وَسَلٰمٌ عَلَى الْمُرْسَلِيْنَ ﴿۱۸۱﴾ وَالْحَمْدُ لِلّٰهِ رَبِّ الْعٰلَمِيْنَ ﴿۱۸۲﴾

(Part 23, Sūraĥ Aṣ-Ṣāfāt)

In order to achieve maximum benefit from Dars, sit down and warmly meet participants with the intention of gaining reward. Make some new Islamic brothers sit around you and, making individual effort with a smiling face, explain to them the blessings of acting upon Madanī In'āmāt and travelling with Madanī Qāfilaĥs. (The wisdom in meeting participants whilst you are sitting is that at least a few Islamic brothers may sit with you, otherwise, the participants greeting you whilst standing usually go, leaving you deprived of the privilege of making individual effort).

Tumĥayn ay Muballigh yeĥ mayrī Du'ā ĥay
Kiye jāo ṭay tum taraqqī kā zīnaĥ

O Muballigh! For you, it is my prayer
May you keep ascending success-stair!

Du'ā of 'Aṭṭār

Yā Allah عَزَّوَجَلَّ! Forgive me and all those regularly giving and listening to at least two Dars everyday from *Faīzān-e-Sunnat* (one at home and the other at school, Masjid or a busy place etc.) and make us an embodiment of good character.

آمِيْن بِجَاهِ النَّبِيِّ الْاَمِيْن صَلَّى اللّٰهُ تَعَالٰى عَلَيْهِ وَاٰلِهٖ وَسَلَّم

Mujĥay Dars-e-Faīzān-e-Sunnat kī taufīq
Milay din mayn dau martabaĥ Yā Ilāĥī عَزَّوَجَلَّ

Bless me with this ability
May I give two Dars daily, O Almighty عَزَّوَجَلَّ*!*

صَلُّوْا عَلَى الْحَبِيْب صَلَّى اللّٰهُ تَعَالٰى عَلٰى مُحَمَّد

Glossary

Note: This glossary consists of only an introductory explanation to Islamic terms. For thorough understanding, please consult some Sunnī scholar.

'Arafaĥ [عَرَفَه]: 9th day of Żul-Ḥijjaĥ (last Islamic month).

'Imāmaĥ [عِمَامَه]: Turban

Bid'at-e-Ḥasanaĥ [بِدْعَتِ حَسَنَه]: Good innovation

Collective I'tikāf [اِجتِمَاعِی اِعتِکاف]: The I'tikāf in which a group of Muslims take part in the same Masjid.

Ḍaḥwā Kubrā [ضَحْوٰی کُبْرٰی]: Islamic midday

Du'ā [دُعَا]: Supplication

Exegetist [مُفَسِّر]: An erudite scholar who gives a detailed explanation of scriptures.

Farḍ [فَرْض]: It is an obligation without performing which one cannot be freed from duty and if some act is Farḍ in worship, the worship will not be accomplished without performing that act. Not performing a Farḍ deliberately is a grave sin.

Fikr-e-Madīnaĥ [فِکْرِ مَدِیْنَة]: Fikr-e-Madīnaĥ is a term used in Dawat-e-Islami which refers to the act of holding oneself accountable for sins, pondering over grave and resurrection, and filling in Madanī In'āmāt booklet whilst reflecting upon virtuous and evil deeds.

Fiqĥ [فِقْه]: Islamic jurisprudence

Ghusl [غُسْل]: Ritual bath

Ḥāfiẓ [حَافِظ]: The one who has memorized the entire Quran by heart.

Ḥājī [حَاجِی]: One who has performed Hajj.

Ḥalāl [**حَلَال**]: Lawful (by Sharī'aĥ)

Ḥanafī [**حَنَفِی**]: One out of four schools of Islamic jurisprudence.

Ḥarām [**حَرَام**]: It is opposite of Farḍ; committing it deliberately even once is a grave sin.

Ḥifẓ [**حِفْظ**]: Memorizing the Quran by heart.

Ḥujjāj [**حُجَّاج**]: Plural of Ḥājī, i.e. pilgrims of Hajj.

I'tikāf [**اِعْتِکَاف**]: Staying in Masjid etc. with sole intention of seeking Allah's عَزَّوَجَلَّ pleasure by worshiping Him.

Ifṭār [**اِفْطَار**]: To eat/drink something to break the fast lawfully at sunset.

Ijtimā' [**اِجْتِمَاع**]: Religious congregation

Imām [**اِمَام**]: A Muslim who leads others in congregational Ṣalāĥ.

Iqāmaĥ [**اِقَامَة**]: A set of fixed words uttered rather loudly just before the commencement of congregational Ṣalāĥ.

Īṣāl-e-Šawāb [**اِیْصَالِ ثَوَاب**]: Īṣāl-e-Šawāb refers to the act of spiritually donating the reward of virtuous deeds to the Muslims. Īṣāl-e-Šawāb may be made to all deceased and living male and female Muslims including even Muslim jinns. See its detailed method in the booklet '*Method of Fātiḥaĥ*' published by Maktaba-tul-Madīnaĥ.

Jamā'at [**جَمَاعَت**]: Congregational Ṣalāĥ

Jāmi'a-tul-Madīnaĥ [**جَامِعَةُ الْمَدِيْنَة**]: An institution for learning Islamic sciences run by Dawat-e-Islami.

Kaffāraĥ [**کَفَّارَه**]: Expiation or atonement

Kanz-ul-Īmān [**کَنْزُالْاِیْمَان**]: Name of the Urdu translation of the Holy Quran by Imām-e-Aĥl-e-Sunnat, Al-Ḥāj, Al-Ḥāfiẓ, Al-Qārī Imām Aḥmad Razā Khan عَلَیْہِ رَحْمَةُ الرَّحْمٰن

Khilāl [خِلَال]: Passing fingers of both hands into each other or passing fingers of right hand through beard (during Wuḍū) or cleaning teeth by toothpicks.

Madanī Mashwaraĥ [مَدَنِی مَشْوَرَه]: Madanī Mashwaraĥ is a meeting to discuss and review the righteous activities of Dawat-e-Islami.

Madanī Qāfilaĥ [مَدَنِی قَافِلَہ]: Caravans of Dawat-e-Islami travelling near and far for the promotion of Islamic teachings.

Makrūĥ [مَکْرُوْه]: Disliked

Makrūĥ Taḥrīmī [مَکْرُوْه تَحْرِیْمِی]: It is in comparison with Wājib. If it occurs in worship, the worship gets defective and the committer of Makrūĥ Taḥrīmī is considered a sinner. Although its gravity is lesser than that of Ḥarām, committing it a few times is a grave sin.

Makrūĥ Tanzīĥī [مَکْرُوْه تَنْزِیْہِی]: It is in comparison with Sunan-e-Ghayr Muakkadaĥ. It is an act which Sharī'aĥ dislikes to be committed, although there is no punishment for the one who commits it.

Maktaba-tul-Madīnaĥ [مَکْتَبَةُ الْمَدِیْنَة]: The publishing department of Dawat-e-Islami.

Miskīn [مِسْکِیْن]: A Miskīn is the one who possesses nothing and has to beg others for food to satisfy hunger and clothes to cover the body. Begging is Ḥalāl (allowed) for him.

Miswāk [مِسْوَاک]: Natural tooth-stick made from a twig of a tree. Typically made from peelu, olive or walnut tree.

Mu'takif/Mu'takifīn [مُعْتَکِف/مُعْتَکِفِیْن]: The one/those taking part in I'tikāf.

Mūażżin [مُؤَذِّن]: One who has been appointed to utter Ażān for Ṣalāĥ.

Mubāḥ [مُبَاح]: An act doing or not doing which is neither an act of Šawāb nor a sin.

Muballigh [مُبَلِّغ]: A preacher

Muftī [مُفْتِی]: An authorized scholar who is expert in Islamic jurisprudence to answer religious queries.

Muḥaddiš [مُحَدِّث]: A scholar of Ḥadīš.

Murīd [مُرِيْد]: Disciple

Mustaḥab [مُسْتَحَب]: An act which Sharī'aĥ likes to be performed but its abandonment is not disliked.

Na'at [نَعْت]: Poetic eulogy in praise of the Prophet of Raḥmaĥ, the Intercessor of Ummaĥ, the Owner of Jannaĥ صَلَّى اللّٰهُ تَعَالٰى عَلَيْهِ وَاٰلِهٖ وَسَلَّم

Nafl [نَفْل]: Supererogatory act/worship

Nafs [نَفْس]: Centre of sensual desires in human body, psyche.

Nażr-e-Ghayr Mu'ayyan [نَذْرِ غَيْر مُعَيَّن]: Unspecified vow

Nażr-e-Mu'ayyan [نَذْرِ مُعَيَّن]: Specified vow

Qaḍā [قَضَا]: To make up or compensate for any missed worship.

Qiblaĥ [قِبْلَه]: The direction which Muslims face during Ṣalāĥ etc.

Rak'at [رَكْعَت]: Unit/cycle of Ṣalāĥ

Ṣadā-e-Madīnaĥ [صَدائے مَدِينَة]: Calling (waking up) Muslims for Ṣalāt-ul-Fajr (one of the several Madanī activities of Dawat-e-Islami).

Ṣadaqaĥ [صَدَقَه]: Charity or alms

Saḥarī [سَحَرِى]: Pre-dawn food taken for day-fast.

Ṣalāt/Ṣalāt-'Alan-Nabī ﷺ [صَلَاة عَلَى النَّبِى]: Supplication for asking blessings for the Beloved and Blessed Prophet صَلَّى اللّٰهُ تَعَالٰى عَلَيْهِ وَاٰلِهٖ وَسَلَّم.

Shar'ī [شَرْعِى]: According to Sharī'aĥ

Sharī'at/Sharī'aĥ [شَرِيْعَة]: Commandments of Allah عَزَّوَجَلَّ and His Noble Prophet صَلَّى اللّٰهُ تَعَالٰى عَلَيْهِ وَاٰلِهٖ وَسَلَّم.

Ṣubḥ-e-Ṣādiq [صُبْح صَادِق]: The true dawn

Sunan-e-Ghayr Muakkadaĥ [سُنَّتِ غَيْر مُؤكدَه]: An act which the Holy Prophet صَلَّى اللهُ تَعَالٰى عَلَيْهِ وَاٰلِهٖ وَسَلَّم neither practised continually nor emphasized to practice it but Sharī'aĥ disliked its outright abandonment.

Sunnat-ul-Muakkadaĥ [سُنَّةُ الْمُؤَكَّدَه]: An act which the Holy Prophet صَلَّى اللهُ تَعَالٰى عَلَيْهِ وَاٰلِهٖ وَسَلَّم practiced continually but at times, also forsook it to show permissibility of its abandonment.

Sūraĥ [سُوْرَة]: Chapter of the Holy Quran

Taĥajjud [تَهَجُّد]: A supererogatory Ṣalāĥ offered at night after awakening, having offered Ṣalāt-ul-'Ishā.

Takbīr-e-Aūlā [تَكْبِيْرِ اُولٰى]: The primary Takbīr (i.e. saying اَللّٰهُ اَكْبَرُ) for starting of Ṣalāĥ.

Tarāwīḥ [تَرَاوِيْح]: Tarāwīḥ Ṣalāĥ is offered in Ramadan after Ṣalāt-ul-'Ishā with Jamā'at. It is Sunnaĥ to complete the recitation of the whole Quran during this Ṣalāĥ.

Ṭarīqaĥ [طَرِيْقَة]: Methodology of Islamic mysticism.

Tasbīḥ [تَسْبِيْح]: Glorification of Allah عَزَّوَجَلَّ.

Ṭawāf [طَوَاف]: Moving around the Holy Ka'baĥ.

Ummaĥ [اُمَّة]: Believers of the Noble Prophet صَلَّى اللهُ تَعَالٰى عَلَيْهِ وَاٰلِهٖ وَسَلَّم as a whole.

Umm-ul-Mūminīn [اُمُّ الْمُؤْمِنِيْن]: Mother of believers

Veil within veil [پردے میں پردہ]: Veil within veil is the translation of the Urdu term 'Parday mayn Pardaĥ' used in the Madanī environment of Dawat-e-Islami. It refers to the act of wrapping an extra shawl around dress from navel to knees.

Wājib [وَاجِب]: It is an obligation without performing which one will not be freed from obligation and if a Wājib act is missed in worship, that worship will be considered defective; however the worship will be considered performed. Not performing a Wājib once deliberately is a minor sin and leaving it a few times is a grave sin.

Transliteration Chart

Arabic/Urdu Letter	Latin Equivalent	Example	Transliteration
ء	A/a	أمِیر	Amīr
ا	A/a	اَللّٰہ	Allāĥ
ب	B/b	بَیتُ اللّٰہ	Baytullāĥ
پ	P/p	پَنج تَن پاک	Panj Tan Pāk
ت	T/t	تَسبِیح	Tasbīḥ
ٹ	Ṫ/ṫ	ٹَماٹَر	Ṫamāṫar
ث	Š/š	ثَمَر	Šamar
ج	J/j	جَنَّت	Jannat
چ	Ch/ch	چادَر	Chādar
ح	Ḥ/ḥ	حَدِیث	Ḥadīš
خ	Kh/kh	خالِق	Khāliq
د	D/d	دَاتا	Dātā
ڈ	Ḋ/ḋ	ڈنکا	Ḋankā
ذ	Ż/ż	ذَخِیرَہ	Żakhīraĥ
ر	R/r	رَازِق	Rāziq
ڑ	Ř/ř	پَہاڑ	Paĥāř
ز	Z/z	زَمزَم	Zamzam
ژ	X/x	ژالَہ	Xālaĥ
س	S/s	سَبز	Sabz
ش	Sh/sh	شَعبان	Sha'bān

Arabic/Urdu Letter	Latin Equivalent	Example	Transliteration
ص	Ṣ/ṣ	صَلٰوۃ	Ṣalāĥ
ض	Ḍ/ḍ	رَمَضان	Ramaḍān
ط	Ṭ/ṭ	طاهِر	Ṭāĥir
ظ	Ẓ/ẓ	ظُلْمَت	Ẓulmat
ع	ʻ	عادِل	ʻĀdil
غ	Gh/gh	غَریب	Gharīb
ف	F/f	فَیضان	Faīzān
ق	Q/q	قافِلَه	Qāfilaĥ
ك	K/k	كَعبَه	Ka'baĥ
گ	G/g	گُنبَد	Gumbad
ل	L/l	مُسَلمان	Musalmān
م	M/m	مَدِینَة	Madīnaĥ
ن	N/n	نَصِیحَت	Naṣīḥat
و	V/v, W/w	وُضُو	Wuḍū
ه / ه / ة	Ĥ/ĥ	بَهائِی	Bĥāī
ی	Y/y	یٰسین	Yāsīn
َ◌	A/a	اَذکار	Ażkār
ِ◌	I/i	اِمام	Imām
ُ◌	U/u	قُرآن	Qurān
ا مدّه	Ā/ā	سَیِّدُنا	Sayyidunā
و مدّه	Ū/ū	سُورَة	Sūraĥ
ی مدّه	Ī/ī	اِسلَامِی	Islāmī

Bibliography

Blessings of بِسۡمِ اللّٰہ & Excellence of Hunger

Ad-Dur-rul-Manšūr, Imām Jalāluddīn Suyūṭī, Dār-ul-Fikr, Beirut.

Aḥsan-ul-Wi'ā, Maulānā Naqī 'Alī Khān, Maktaba-tul-Madīnaĥ, Karachi.

Al-Uṣābaĥ fī Tamīz-iṣ-Ṣaḥābaĥ, Aḥmad Bin Ḥajar 'Asqalānī, Dār-ul-Kutub 'Ilmiyyaĥ, Beirut.

Al-Akhbār-ul-Akhyār Ma' Maktūbāt, 'Abdul Ḥaq Muḥaddiš Diĥlvī, Maktaba Nūriyāĥ Razawiyyaĥ.

Al-Baḥr-ur-Rāiq, 'Allāmaĥ Zaīnuddīn Ibn Nujaym, Quetta.

Al-budur-us-Sāfirah fil-Umūr-il-Ākhirah, Imām Jalāluddīn Suyūṭī.

Al-Iḥsān bittartīb Ṣaḥīḥ Ibn Ḥibbān, 'Allāmaĥ Amīr 'Alāuddīn 'Alī Bin Balbān, Dār-ul-Kutub 'Ilmiyyaĥ, Beirut.

Al-Jāmi'-uṣ-Ṣaghīr, Imām Jalāluddīn Suyūṭī, Dār-ul-Kutub 'Ilmiyyaĥ, Beirut.

Al-Khayrāt-ul-Ḥisān, 'Allāmaĥ Shaĥābuddīn Aḥmad Bin Ḥajar Makkī, Karachi.

Al-Majālis-us-Saniyyaĥ, Aḥmad Bin Ḥijāzī, Maktabaĥ Tajāriyaĥ.

Al-Mawāĥib-ul-Ladunniyyaĥ, Shaĥābuddīn Aḥmad Qasṭalānī, Dār-ul-Kutub 'Ilmiyyaĥ, Beirut.

Al-Munabbiĥāt, Aḥmad Bin 'Alī Muhammad 'Asqalānī, Al-Jābir Islamic Publisher.

Al-Mustadrak, Muhammad Bin 'Abdullāĥ Ḥākim, Dār-ul-Ma'rifaĥ, Beirut.

Anīs-ul-Wā'iẓīn, Maulānā Abū Bakr Al-Qarshī.

Asrār-ul-Fātiḥah, 'Allāmaĥ Mu'īn Marwī, Naulakshaw, Lucknow.

Attarghīb Wattarĥīb, Zakīuddīn 'Abdul 'Aẓīm Manżarī, Dār-ul-Kutub 'Ilmiyyaĥ, Beirut.

Baĥār-e-Sharī'at, Muftī Muhammad Amjad 'Alī A'ẓamī, Maktabaĥ Razawiyyaĥ, Karachi.

Baĥjat-ul-Asrār, 'Allāmaĥ Abul Ḥasan Shat'nufī, Dār-ul-Kutub 'Ilmiyyaĥ, Beirut.

Baḥr-ud-Dumū', 'Allāmaĥ 'Abdur Raḥmān Ibn Jawzī, Dār-ul-Fajr lit Turāš-ul-Qāĥiraĥ.

Durr-e-Mukhtār, 'Alāuddīn Ḥaṣkafī, Dār-ul-Kutub 'Ilmiyyaĥ, Beirut.

Fatāwā 'Ālamgīrī, Shaykh Niẓāmuddīn and 'Ulamā of Hind, Quetta.

Fatāwā Razawiyyaĥ (Jadīd), Razā Foundation, Lahore.

Firdaus-ul-Akhbār, Shaĥardār Daylmī, Dār-ul-Kutub-ul-'Arabī.

Ḥalbī Kabīr, 'Allāmaĥ Muhammad Ibrāĥīm Bin Ḥalbī, Suĥaīl Academy.

Ḥayāt-e-A'lā Ḥaḍrat, 'Allāmaĥ Ẓafaruddīn Muḥaddiš Biĥārī.

Ḥayāt-ul-Ḥaywān-ul-Kubrā, 'Allāmaĥ Kamāluddīn Muhammad Bin Mūsā Damayrī, Dār-ul-Kutub 'Ilmiyyaĥ, Beirut.

Ḥilyat-ul-Auliyā, Abū Na'īm Aḥmad Bin 'Abdullāĥ Aṣfaĥānī, Dār-ul-Kutub 'Ilmiyyaĥ, Beirut.

Ḥujjatullāĥi-'alal-'Ālamīn, Yūsuf Bin Ismā'īl Nabĥānī, Markaz Aĥl-e-Sunnat Barakat-e-Raza.

Iḥyā-ul-'Ulūm, Imām Muhammad Bin Muhammad Ghazālī, Dār-uṣ-Ṣādir.

Itḥāf-us-Sādat-il-Muttaqīn, Muhammad Murtaḍā Ḥusaynī, Dār-ul-Kutub 'Ilmiyyaĥ, Beirut.

Jāmi' Tirmiżī, Imām Muhammad Bin 'Īsā Tirmiżī, Dār-ul-Fikr, Beirut.

Kanz-ul-'Ummāl, 'Allāmaĥ 'Alī Muttaqī Ĥindī, Dār-ul-Kutub 'Ilmiyyaĥ, Beirut.

Kanz-ul-Īmān (Translation of Quran), A'lā Ḥaḍrat Imām Aḥmad Razā Khān.

Kashf-ul-Khifā, Imām Ismā'īl Bin Muhammad 'Ajlūnī, Dār-ul-Kutub 'Ilmiyyaĥ, Beirut.

Kashf-ul-Maḥjūb, Dātā Ganj Bakhsh 'Alī Ĥajwayrī, Farīd Book Stall, Lahore.

Khazāin-ul-'Irfān, Sayyid Muhammad Na'īmuddīn Murādābādī, Razā Academy, Mumbai.

Kīmiyā-e-Sa'ādat, Imām Muhammad Bin Muhammad Ghazālī, Intishārāt-e-Ganjīnaĥ.

Luqṭ-ul-Marjān, Imām Jalāluddīn Suyūṭī, Dār-ul-Kutub 'Ilmiyyaĥ, Beirut.

Majma'-uz-Zawāid, Imām Nūruddīn Ĥayshamī, Dār-ul-Fikr, Beirut.

Manāqib-e-Abī Ḥanīfaĥ, Muhammad Al-Kardarī, Maktaba-tul-Islāmiyyaĥ, Quetta.

Minĥāj-ul-'Ābidīn, Imām Muhammad Ghazālī, Dār-ul-Kutub 'Ilmiyyaĥ, Beirut.

Mirāt-ul-Manājīḥ, Muftī Aḥmad Yār Khān Na'īmī, Ziā-ul-Qurān Publishers.

Mishkāt-ul-Maṣābīḥ, Imām Muhammad Bin 'Abdullāĥ Khaṭīb, Karachi.

Mu'jam Kabīr, Sulaymān Bin Aḥmad Ṭabarānī, Dār Iḥyā-ut-Turāš-ul-'Arabī, Beirut.

Mukāshafa-tul-Qulūb, Imām Muhammad Ghazālī, Dār-ul-Kutub 'Ilmiyyaĥ, Beirut.

Muṣannaf 'Abdur Razzāq, Abū Bakr Bin Humām Ṣan'ānī, Dār-ul-Kutub 'Ilmiyyaĥ, Beirut.

Musnad Abī Ya'lā, Aḥmad Bin 'Alī Mauṣilī, Dār-ul-Kutub 'Ilmiyyaĥ, Beirut.

Musnad Ìmām Aḥmad, Imām Aḥmad Bin Ḥanbal, Dār-ul-Fikr, Beirut.

Nūr-ul-'Irfān, Muftī Aḥmad Yār Khān Na'īmī, Ziā-ul-Quran Publishers, Lahore.

Nuzĥa-tul-Majālis, 'Abdur Raḥmān Bin 'Abdus Salām Ṣaffūrī.

Qalyūbī Ḥikāyat, 'Allāmaĥ Aḥmad Shaĥābuddīn Qalyūbī, Karachi.

Qūt-ul-Qulūb, Abū Ṭālib Muhammad Bin 'Alī Makkī, Markaz Aĥl-e-Sunnat Barakāt Razā.

Rad-dul-Muḥtār, 'Allāmaĥ Ibn 'Ābidīn Amīn Shāmī, Dār-ul-Kutub 'Ilmiyyaĥ, Beirut.

Rauḍ-ur-Riyāḥīn, 'Abdullāĥ Bin As'ad Yāfi'ī, Al-Maṭbū'a-tul-Maīmniyaĥ.

Risāla-tul-Qushayriyyaĥ, Abul Qāsim 'Abdul Karīm Qushayrī, Dār-ul-Kutub 'Ilmiyyaĥ, Beirut.

Riyāḍ-uṣ-Ṣāliḥīn, 'Allāmaĥ Yaḥyā Bin Sharaf Nawavī, Shabbīr Brothers, Lahore.

Rūḥ-ul-Bayān, 'Allāmaĥ Ismā'īl Ḥaqqī Barūsawī, Dār Iḥyā-ut-Turāš-ul-'Arabī, Beirut.

Ṣaḥīḥ Bukhārī, Imām Muhammad Bin Ismā'īl Bukhārī, Dār-ul-Fikr, Beirut.

Ṣaḥīḥ Muslim, Imām Muslim Bin Ḥajjāj Nayshāpūrī, Dār Ibn Ḥazm, Beirut.

Shamāil-e-Rasūl, Shaykh Yūsuf Bin Ismā'īl Nabĥānī, Nūrī Kutub Kĥānā, Lahore.

Shamāil-e-Tirmiżī, Muhammad Bin 'Īsā Tirmiżī, Dār-ul-Kutub 'Ilmiyyaĥ, Beirut.

Shams-ul-Ma'ārif, Imām Aḥmad Bin 'Alī Al-Būnī.

Sharḥ-uṣ-Ṣudūr, Imām Jalāluddīn Suyūṭī, Dār-ul-Kutub 'Ilmiyyaĥ, Beirut.

Sharḥ-us-Sunnaĥ, Abū Muhammad Ḥusayn Bin Mas'ūd Baghwī, Dār-ul-Kutub 'Ilmiyyaĥ, Beirut.

Shu'ab-ul-Īmān, Abū Bakr Aḥmad Bin Ḥusayn Bayĥaqī, Dār-ul-Kutub 'Ilmiyyaĥ, Beirut.

Sunan Abī Dāwūd, Imām Sulaymān Bin Ash'aš, Dār Iḥyā-ut-Turāš-ul-'Arabī, Beirut.

Sunan Ibn Mājaĥ, Imām Muhammad Bin Yazīd Ibn Mājaĥ, Dār-ul-Ma'rifaĥ, Beirut.

Sunan Kubrā, Imām Abū Bakr Aḥmad Bin Ḥusayn Bayĥaqī, Dār-ul-Kutub 'Ilmiyyaĥ, Beirut.

Ṭabqāt-e-Ḥanābilaĥ, Abun-Nūr Muhammad Bashīr, Dār-ul-Kutub 'Ilmiyyaĥ, Beirut.

Tafĥīm-ul-Bukhārī, Shaykh-ul-Ḥadīš 'Allāmaĥ Ghulām Rasūl Razavī.

Tafsīr Kabīr, Imām Fakhruddīn Rāzī, Dār Iḥyā-ut-Turāš-ul-'Arabī, Beirut.

Tafsīr Ṣāwī, 'Allāmaĥ Aḥmad Bin Muhammad Ṣāwī Mālikī, Dār-ul-Fikr, Beirut.

Tafsīr-e-Na'īmī, Muftī Aḥmad Yār Khān Na'īmī, Ziā-ul-Qurān Publishers.

Tanbīĥ-ul-Mughtarīn, 'Allāmaĥ 'Abdul Waĥĥāb Sha'rānī, Al-Maṭbū'a-tul-Maīmniyaĥ.

Tażkira-tul-Auliyā, Shaykh Farīduddīn 'Aṭṭār.

Tażkira-tul-Wā'iẓīn, 'Allāmaĥ Muhammad Bin Ja'far Qurayshī, Quetta.

Islamic Manners of Eating & Blessings of Ramadan

'Umda-tul-Qārī, Badruddīn Abū Muhammad Maḥmūd Bin Aḥmad 'Aynī, Dār-ul-Fikr, Beirut.

Ad-Dur-rul-Manšūr, Imām Jalāluddīn Suyūṭī, Dār-ul-Fikr, Beirut.

Aḥsan-ul-Wi'ā, Maulānā Naqī 'Alī Khān, Maktaba-tul-Madīnaĥ, Karachi.

Akhbār-ul-Akhyār, Shaykh 'Abdul Ḥaq Muḥaddiš Diĥlvī, Maktaba Nūriyaĥ Razawiyyaĥ.

Akhlāq-uṣ-Ṣāliḥīn, Muhammad Sharīf Muḥaddiš Kotlawī, Maktaba-tul-Madīnaĥ, Karachi.

Al-Ashbāĥ wan-Naẓāir, 'Allāmaĥ Zaīnuddīn Bin Ibrāĥīm Miṣrī, Karachi.

Al-budur-us-Sāfiraĥ Fil-Umūr-il-Ākhiraĥ, Imām Jalāluddīn Suyūṭī.

Al-Iḥsān bittartīb Ṣaḥīḥ Ibn Ḥibbān, 'Allāmaĥ Amīr 'Alāuddīn 'Alī Bin Balbān, Dār-ul-Kutub 'Ilmiyyaĥ, Beirut.

Al-Jāmi'-uṣ-Ṣaghīr, Imām Jalāluddīn Suyūṭī, Dār-ul-Kutub 'Ilmiyyaĥ, Beirut.

Al-Jauĥara-tun-Nayyaraĥ, 'Allāmaĥ Abū Bakr Bin 'Alī Ḥadād, Multan.

Al-Kāmil fi Ḍu'fā-ir-Rijāl, Abū Aḥmad 'Abdullāĥ Bin 'Adī, Dār-ul-Kutub 'Ilmiyyaĥ, Beirut.

Al-Kāmil fit-Tārīkh, Abul Ḥasan 'Alī Bin Abī Karam Shaybānī, Dār-ul-Kutub 'Ilmiyyaĥ, Beirut.

Al-Khaṣāiṣ-ul-Kubrā, Imām Jalāluddīn Suyūṭī, Markaz Aĥl-e-Sunnat Barkāt Razā, Hind.

Al-Mustadrak, Imām Muhammad Bin 'Abdullāĥ Ḥākim, Dār-ul-Kutub 'Ilmiyyaĥ, Beirut.

Al-Qaul-ul-Badī', Imām Ḥāfiẓ Muhammad Bin Sakhāwī, Dār-ul-Kutub 'Ilmiyyaĥ, Beirut.

Anfās-ul-'Ārifīn, Shāĥ Walīyullāĥ Muḥaddiš Diĥlvī, Fazl Nūr Academy, Gujrat.

Ar-Risāla-tul-Qushayriyyah, Imām Abū Qāsim 'Abdul Karīm, Dār-ul-Khayr, Beirut.

Ashi'at-ul-Lam'āt, Shaykh 'Abdul Ḥaq Muḥaddiš Diĥlvī, Quetta.

Attarghīb Wattarĥīb, Imām Zakīuddīn 'Abdul 'Aẓīm Manżarī, Dār-ul-Kutub 'Ilmiyyaĥ, Beirut.

Baĥār-e-Sharī'at, Muftī Muhammad Amjad 'Alī A'ẓamī, Bareilly.

Baĥjat-ul-Asrār, Abul Ḥassan Nūruddīn 'Alī Bin Jarīr Shaṭnūfī.

Bināyaĥ Sharḥ-ul-Ĥidāyaĥ, 'Allāmaĥ Maḥmūd Bin Aḥmad 'Aynī, Quetta.

Durr-e-Mukhtār, 'Allāmaĥ 'Alāuddīn Ḥaṣkafī, Dār-ul-Kutub 'Ilmiyyaĥ, Beirut.

Faīḍ-ul-Qadīr, 'Allāmaĥ Muhammad 'Abdur Raūf Manāwī, Dār-ul-Kutub 'Ilmiyyaĥ.

Fatāwā 'Ālamgīrī, Shaykh Niẓāmuddīn and 'Ulamā of Hind, Quetta.

Fatāwā Razawiyyaĥ (Jadīd), A'lā Ḥaḍrat Imām Aḥmad Razā Khān, Razā Foundation, Lahore.

Fatḥ-ul-Qadīr, 'Allāmaĥ Kamāluddīn Ibn Ĥumām Muhammad, Quetta.

Fawāid-ul-Fuwād, Khuwājaĥ Amīr Ḥasan Sajzī Diĥlvī.

Firdaus - bimā Šaur-ul-Khaṭṭāb, Shaĥarwiya Bin Shaĥardār Bin Shaĥarwiya Daylmī.

Ghunya-tuṭ-Ṭālibīn, Shaykh 'Abdul Qādir Jīlānī, Dār Iḥyā-ut-Turāš-ul-'Arabī, Beirut.

Ḥayāt-e-Muḥaddiš-e-A'ẓam, Razā Foundation, Lahore.

Ḥayāt-ul-Ḥaywān-ul-Kubrā, 'Allāmaĥ Kamāluddīn Muhammad Bin Mūsā Damayrī, Dār-ul-Kutub 'Ilmiyyaĥ, Beirut.

Ĥidāyaĥ, 'Allāmaĥ 'Alī Bin Abī Bakr.

Ḥilyat-ul-Auliyā, Imām Abū Nu'aym Aḥmad Aṣfaĥānī, Dār-ul-Kutub 'Ilmiyyaĥ, Beirut.

Ḥujjatullāhi-'alal-'Ālamīn, 'Allāmaĥ Yūsuf Bin Ismā'īl Nabĥānī, Markaz Aĥl-e-Sunnat Barkāt Razā, Hind.

Iḥyā-ul-'Ulūm, Imām Muhammad Bin Muhammad Ghazālī, Dār-ul-Kutub 'Ilmiyyaĥ, Beirut.

Itḥāf-us-Sādat-il-Muttaqīn, Muhammad Murtaḍā Ḥusaynī, Dār-ul-Kutub 'Ilmiyyaĥ, Beirut.

Jāmi' Karāmāt-e-Auliyā, Yūsuf Bin Ismā'īl Nabĥānī, Markaz Aĥl-e-Sunnat Barkāt Razā, Hind.

Jāmi' Tirmiżī, Imām Muhammad Bin 'Īsā Tirmiżī, Dār-ul-Fikr, Beirut.

Jāmi'-ul-Bayān, Imām Abū Ja'far Muhammad Bin Jarīr Ṭabarī, Dār-ul-Kutub 'Ilmiyyaĥ, Beirut.

Kanz-ul-'Ummāl, 'Allāmaĥ 'Alī Muttaqī Ĥindī, Dār-ul-Kutub 'Ilmiyyaĥ, Beirut.

Kashf-ul-Khifā, Imām Ismā'īl Bin Muhammad 'Ajlūnī, Dār-ul-Kutub 'Ilmiyyaĥ, Beirut.

Kashf-ul-Maḥjūb, Dātā Ganj Bakhsh 'Alī Ḥajwayrī, Farīd Book Stall, Lahore.

Khazāin-ul-'Irfān, Sayyid Muhammad Na'īmuddīn Murādābādī, Razā Academy, Mumbai.

Kīmiyā-e-Sa'ādat, Imām Muhammad Bin Muhammad Ghazālī, Intishārāt-e-Ganjīnaĥ.

Kitāb-ul-Qalyūbī, 'Allāmaĥ Aḥmad Shaĥābuddīn Qalyūbī, Karachi.

Luqṭ-ul-Marjān, Imām Jalāluddīn Suyūṭī, Dār-ul-Kutub 'Ilmiyyaĥ, Beirut.

Ma'dan-e-Akhlāq, Muhammad Ramzān 'Alī Qadirī, Dār-ul-Kutub Ḥanafiyyaĥ, Karachi.

Madārij-un-Nubūwwaĥ, 'Abdul Ḥaq Muḥaddiš Diĥlvī, Maktaba Nūriyāĥ Razawiyyaĥ, Sukkur.

Majma'-uz-Zawāid, Imām Nūruddīn Ĥayshamī, Dār-ul-Fikr, Beirut.

Makārim-ul-Akhlāq, Imām Sulaymān Bin Aḥmad Ṭabarānī, Dār-ul-Kutub 'Ilmiyyaĥ, Beirut.

Maktūbāt, Imām Rabbānī Mujaddid Alf Šānī, Quetta.

Mawāĥib-ul-Laduniyyaĥ, 'Allāmaĥ Ibrāĥīm Bājūrī, Multan.

Mirāt-ul-Manājīḥ, Muftī Aḥmad Yār Khān Na'īmī, Lahore.

Mirqāt-ul Mafātīḥ, Mullā 'Alī Qārī.

Mishkāt-ul-Maṣābīḥ, Imām Muhammad Bin 'Abdullāĥ Khaṭīb.

Mīzān-ush-Sharī'at-ul-Kubrā, 'Allāmaĥ 'Abdul Waĥĥāb Sha'rānī, Egypt.

Mu'jam Awsaṭ, Imām Sulaymān Bin Aḥmad Ṭabarānī, Dār-ul-Kutub 'Ilmiyyaĥ, Beirut.

Mu'jam Kabīr, Imām Sulaymān Bin Aḥmad Ṭabarānī, Dār Iḥyā-ut-Turāš-ul-'Arabī, Beirut.

Mu'jam Ṣaghīr, Imām Sulaymān Bin Aḥmad Ṭabarānī, Dār-ul-Kutub 'Ilmiyyaĥ, Beirut.

Mukāshafa-tul-Qulūb, Imām Muhammad Ghazālī, Dār-ul-Kutub 'Ilmiyyaĥ, Beirut.

Muṣannaf Ibn Abī Shaybaĥ, Imām Abū Bakr 'Abdullāĥ Bin Abī Shaybaĥ, Dār-ul-Fikr, Beirut.

Musnad Abī Ya'lā, Imām Abū Ya'lā Aḥmad Mauṣilī, Dār-ul-Kutub 'Ilmiyyaĥ, Beirut.

Musnad Imām Aḥmad, Imām Aḥmad Bin Ḥanbal, Dār-ul-Fikr, Beirut.

Muwaṭṭā Imām Mālik, Imām Mālik Bin Anas, Dār-ul-Ma'rifaĥ, Beirut.

Nawādir-ul-Uṣūl, Imām Abū 'Abdullāĥ Muhammad Bin 'Alī Ḥakīm Tirmiżī, Damascus.

Nūr-ul-'Irfān, Muftī Aḥmad Yār Khān Na'īmī, Ziā-ul-Quran Publishers, Lahore.

Nuzĥa-tul-Majālis, 'Allāmaĥ 'Abdur Raḥmān Ṣaffūrī, Dār-ul-Kutub 'Ilmiyyaĥ, Beirut.

Qūt-ul-Qulūb, Abū Ṭālib Muhammad Bin 'Alī Makkī, Markaz Aĥl-e-Sunnat Barkāt Razā, Hind.

Rad-dul-Muḥtār, Ibn 'Ābidīn Muhammad Amīn Shāmī, Dār-ul-Kutub 'Ilmiyyaĥ, Beirut.

Rauḍ-ul-Fāiq, Shu'ayb Bin 'Abdul Kāfī, Dār Iḥyā-ut-Turāš-ul-'Arabī, Beirut.

Rauḍ-ur-Riyāḥīn, 'Abdullāĥ Bin As'ad Yāfa'ī, Al-Maṭbu'a-tul-Maīmniyaĥ.

Rūḥānī Ḥikāyāt, 'Allāmaĥ 'Abdul Mustafa A'ẓamī, Lahore.

Rūḥ-ul-Bayān, 'Allāmaĥ Ismā'īl Ḥaqqī Barūsawī.

Rūḥ-ul-Ma'ānī, 'Allāmaĥ Abul Fazal Sayyid Maḥmūd Ālūsī, Dār Iḥyā-ut-Turāš-ul-'Arabī, Beirut.

Sachchī Ḥikāyāt, Abun-Nūr Muhammad Bashīr, Maktabaĥ Jām-e-Nūr, Delhi.

Safīna-e-Nūḥ, Muhammad Shafī' Okāřvī, Ziā-ul-Quran Publishers, Lahore.

Ṣaḥīḥ Bukhārī, Imām Muhammad Bin Ismā'īl Bukhārī, Dār-ul-Kutub 'Ilmiyyaĥ, Beirut.

Ṣaḥīḥ Ibn Khuzaymaĥ, Muhammad Bin Isḥāq Bin Khuzaymaĥ, Al-Maktab-ul-Islāmī, Beirut.

Ṣaḥīḥ Muslim, Imām Muslim Bin Ḥajjāj Nayshāpūrī, Dār Ibn Ḥazm, Beirut.

Šamarāt-ul-Awrāq, Taqīuddīn Abī Bakr Bin 'Alī.

Shamāil-ut-Tirmiżī, Imām Muhammad Bin 'Īsā Tirmiżī, Dār-ul-Kutub 'Ilmiyyaĥ, Beirut.

Sharḥ-uz-Zurqānī 'Alal Muwaṭṭā, 'Allāmaĥ Muhammad Bin 'Abdul Bāqī Zurqānī, Dār Iḥyā-ut-Turāš-ul-'Arabī, Beirut.

Sharḥ-uṣ-Ṣudūr, Imām 'Abdur Raḥmān Jalāluddīn Suyūṭī, Dār-ul-Kutub 'Ilmiyyaĥ, Beirut.

Sharḥ-us-Sunnaĥ, Ḥusayn Bin Mas'ūd Baghwī, Dār-ul-Kutub 'Ilmiyyaĥ, Beirut.

Shawāĥid-un-Nubūwwaĥ, 'Allāmaĥ 'Abdur Raḥmān Jāmī, Maktaba-tul-Ḥaqīqaĥ, Turkey.

Shu'ab-ul-Īmān, Imām Abū Bakr Aḥmad Bin Ḥusayn Bayĥaqī, Dār-ul-Kutub 'Ilmiyyaĥ, Beirut.

Siyar-ul-Auliyā, Sayyid Muhammad Bin Mubārak Kirmānī.

Sunan Abī Dāwūd, Abū Dāwūd Sulaymān Bin Ash'aš, Dār Iḥyā-ut-Turāš-ul-'Arabī, Beirut.

Sunan Dārimī, Imām 'Abdullāĥ Bin 'Abdur Raḥmān Dārimī, Karachi.

Sunan Ibn Mājaĥ, Imām Muhammad Bin Yazīd Ibn Mājaĥ, Dār-ul-Ma'rifaĥ, Beirut.

Sunan Kubrā, Imām Abū Bakr Aḥmad Bin Ḥusayn Bayĥaqī, Dār-ul-Kutub 'Ilmiyyaĥ, Beirut.

Sunan Nasāī, Aḥmad Bin Shu'ayb Nasāī, Dār-ul-Jīl, Beirut.

Sunnī Baĥashtī Zaywar, Khalīl Khān Barakātī.

Ta'līm-ul-Muta'allim, Imām Burĥān-ul-Islam Zarnūjī, Karachi.

Ṭabqāt-ul-Kubrā, 'Allāmaĥ 'Abdul Waĥĥāb Sha'rānī, Dār-ul-Kutub 'Ilmiyyaĥ, Beirut.

Tafsīr Kabīr, Imām Fakhruddīn Rāzī, Dār Iḥyā-ut-Ṭurāš-ul-'Arabī, Beirut.

Tafsīr Khāzin, 'Allāmaĥ 'Alāuddīn 'Alī Bin Muhammad Bin Ibrāĥīm Baghdādī.

Tafsīr Na'īmī, Ziā-ul-Quran, Lahore.

Tafsīr Qurṭubī, Imām Abū 'Abdullāĥ Muhammad Bin Qurṭubī Aḥmad Anṣārī, Dār-ul-Fikr.

Tafsīr Ṣāwī, Aḥmad Bin Muhammad Anṣārī, Rauza-tul-Quran, Peshawar.

Tafsīr-e-Na'īmī, Muftī Aḥmad Yār Khān Na'īmī, Ziā-ul-Quran Publishers, Lahore.

Tanbīĥ-ul-Ghāfilīn, 'Allāmaĥ Abul Layš Naṣr Samarqandī, Dār Ibn Kašīr, Beirut.

Tanbīĥ-ul-Mughtarīn, 'Allāmaĥ 'Abdul Waĥĥāb Sha'rānī, Al-Maṭbū'a-tul-Maīmniyaĥ.

Tārīkh Baghdad, Abū Bakr Aḥmad Bin 'Alī Khaṭīb Baghdādī, Dār-ul-Kutub 'Ilmiyyaĥ, Beirut.

Tārīkh-ul-Khulafā, Imām Jalāluddīn Suyūṭī, Karachi.

Tażkira-tul-Auliyā, Shaykh Farīduddīn 'Aṭṭār.

Tażkira-tul-Ḥuffāẓ, Shamsuddīn Muhammad Bin Aḥmad Żaĥbī, Dār-ul-Kutub 'Ilmiyyaĥ, Beirut.

Tażkira-tul-Wā'iẓīn, Muhammad Bin Ja'far Al-Quraysh, Al-Maktaba-tul-Quetta.

Żayl-ul-Mudda'ā lī Aḥsan-il-Wi'ā, Maktaba-tul-Madīnaĥ, Karachi.

Index

B

C

D

G

H

I

J

K

N

O

P

Q

R

S

T

U

V

W

Y

Z

Table of Contents

Faizan-e-Sunnat

Islamic Manners of Eating

Haji Mushtaq Attari 407

Excellence of Hunger 415

52 Parables 481

Blessings of Ramadan

Blessings of I'tikāf 703

Blessings of Eid-ul-Fitr 769

Excellence of Nafl Fasts 797

41 Inspiring Parables of Mu'takifin 871

◈

After you have read this book, you would certainly like to know who has authored it. It was authored by the Great Spiritual and Scholarly Luminary of the 21st century, 'Allāmaĥ Maulānā Abu Bilal Muhammad Ilyas Attar Qadiri Razavi دَامَتْ بَرَكَاتُهُمُ الْعَالِيَه. He has founded **Dawat-e-Islami** (the global and non-political movement for the preaching of Quran and Sunnaĥ) which is spreading Islamic teachings in more than 93 walks of life. If you want to know about the Founder of Dawat-e-Islami, his books, booklets, and various departments of Dawat-e-Islami, then visit this website: www.dawateislami.net

Moreover, Dawat-e-Islami is also spreading the message of Islam all over the world through **Madani Channel**, a 100% purely Islamic channel. No matter wherever you are in the world, if you are interested in watching Madani Channel, then follow the given frequencies. If you want to contact us, then email us: overseas@dawateislami.net

MADANI CHANNEL

Satellite Frequencies

Satellite	Coverage	Downlink Frequency	Symbol Rate	Modulation	Polarization	FEC
Asia sat 3S	Asia	3739 MHz	2815 Msps	QPSK	Vertical	3/4
Astra 2F	UK	12640 MHz	22000 Msps	QPSK	Vertical	5/6
Intelsat 20	Africa Region	12562 MHz	26657 Msps	QPSK	Horizontal	2/3
Eutelsat 7 West A	Middle East Region	10815 MHz	27500 Msps	QPSK	Horizontal	5/6
Galaxy 19	USA Region	11960 MHz	22000 Msps	QPSK	Vertical	3/4

مکتبۃ المدینہ
MAKTABA TUL MADINA